55TH EDITION

KOVELS'®
ANTIQUES & COLLECTIBLES
PRICE GUIDE 2023

BLACK DOG
& LEVENTHAL
PUBLISHERS
NEW YORK

Copyright © 2022 Terry Kovel and Kim Kovel
The Kovels® is a registered trademark of Kovels Antiques, Inc.

Cover design by Katie Benezra

Front cover photographs, from left to right:
Toy, Car, Citroen, Red, Black, Spare Tire, License Plate, Clockwork
Clock, Figural, Girl, Seated, Dog, Bronze, Ormolu, Balthazard A Paris
Furniture, Desk, Chippendale, Tiger Maple, Slant Front, Carved, Pigeonholes

Back cover photographs, top to bottom:
Cranberry Glass, Sugar Shaker, Windows Swirl, Lid, Hobbs, Brockunier & Co.
Advertising, Figure, RCA, Nipper, Seated, Black & White, Chalkware
Spatterware, Plate, Bull's-Eye, Green & Blue, White Ground
Silver-English, Jug, Dome Lid, Flame Finial, Pear Shape, Gadroon Border, Ivory Handle

Spine:
Jewelry, Pin, Bee, 14K Gold, Openwork Body, Diamond, Sapphire & Ruby Wings

Authors' photographs © Kim Ponsky (top) and Alex Montes de Oca (bottom)

Cover copyright © 2022 by Hachette Book Group, Inc.

Hachette Book Group supports the right to free expression and the value of copyright.
The purpose of copyright is to encourage writers and artists to produce the creative works that enrich our culture.

The scanning, uploading, and distribution of this book without permission is a theft of the author's intellectual property.
If you would like permission to use material from the book (other than for review purposes), please contact
permissions@hbgusa.com. Thank you for your support of the author's rights.

Black Dog & Leventhal Publishers
Hachette Book Group
1290 Avenue of the Americas
New York, NY 10104

www.hachettebookgroup.com
www.blackdogandleventhal.com

First Edition: September 2022

Black Dog & Leventhal Publishers is an imprint of Perseus Books, LLC, a subsidiary of Hachette Book Group, Inc.
The Black Dog & Leventhal Publishers name and logo are trademarks of Hachette Book Group, Inc.

The publisher is not responsible for websites (or their content) that are not owned by the publisher.
The Hachette Speakers Bureau provides a wide range of authors for speaking events.
To find out more, go to www.HachetteSpeakersBureau.com or call (866) 376-6591.

Print book interior design by Sheila Hart Design/Hartsart

ISBN: 978-0-7624-8174-3

Printed in the United States of America

CCJC
10 9 8 7 6 5 4 3 2 1

BOOKS BY RALPH AND TERRY KOVEL

American Country Furniture, 1780–1875

A Directory of American Silver, Pewter, and Silver Plate

Kovels' Advertising Collectibles Price List

Kovels' American Antiques 1750–1900

Kovels' American Art Pottery

Kovels' American Collectibles 1900–2000

Kovels' American Silver Marks, 1650 to the Present

Kovels' Antiques & Collectibles Fix-It Source Book

Kovels' Antiques & Collectibles Price Guide (1968–2009)

Kovels' Bid, Buy, and Sell Online

Kovels' Book of Antique Labels

Kovels' Bottles Price List (1971–2006)

Kovels' Collector's Guide to American Art Pottery

Kovels' Collector's Guide to Limited Editions

Kovels' Collectors' Source Book

Kovels' Depression Glass & Dinnerware Price List (1980–2004)

Kovels' Dictionary of Marks— Pottery and Porcelain, 1650 to 1850

Kovels' Guide to Selling, Buying, and Fixing Your Antiques and Collectibles

Kovels' Guide to Selling Your Antiques & Collectibles

Kovels' Illustrated Price Guide to Royal Doulton (1980, 1984)

Kovels' Know Your Antiques

Kovels' Know Your Collectibles

Kovels' New Dictionary of Marks— Pottery and Porcelain, 1850 to the Present

Kovels' Organizer for Collectors

Kovels' Price Guide for Collector Plates, Figurines, Paperweights, and Other Limited Edition Items

Kovels' Quick Tips: 799 Helpful Hints on How to Care for Your Collectibles

Kovels' Yellow Pages: A Resource Guide for Collectors

The Label Made Me Buy It: From Aunt Jemima to Zonkers— The Best-Dressed Boxes, Bottles, and Cans from the Past

BOOKS BY TERRY KOVEL AND KIM KOVEL

Kovels' Antiques & Collectibles Price Guide (2010–2023)

INTRODUCTION

Kovels' Antiques & Collectibles Price Guide 2023 has current, reliable price information and makers' marks. The book has 12,500 prices, 3,150 new color photographs, more than 720 categories, hundreds of dated marks, plus an all-new center section on "Collecting Trends: Twentieth-Century Studio Ceramics."

There is important information in the introduction. Read it first.

We are frequently asked questions like "How old is my grandmother's dish?" Each of the 720 categories includes an introductory paragraph with history, locations, explanations, and other important information to help identify unknown pieces, and some include information about reproductions. We update these introductory paragraphs every year to indicate new owners, new distributors, or new information about production dates. This year we had updates to over 17 paragraphs, many that tell of the sale or closing of a company. This guide includes more than 500 marks. Even more dated marks can be found online at Kovels.com. You will also find more than 200 added facts of interest and tips about care and repair. Each collectible's photograph is shown with a caption that includes the item's description, price, and source. Information about the seller of the item, including address, is listed at the end of the book. The book has color tabs and color-coded categories that make it easy to find listings, and it uses a modern, readable typestyle. All antiques and collectibles priced here were offered for sale during the past year, most of them in the United States, from June 2021 to June 2022. Prices also came from online sales that accepted bids from all over the world. Almost all auction prices given include the buyer's premium since that is part of what the buyer paid. Very few include local sales tax or extra charges for things such as phone bids, online bids, credit card usage, storage, or shipping.

Most items in our original 1968 price book were made before 1860, so they were more than a century old. Today in *Kovels' Antiques & Collectibles Price Guide*, we list pieces made as recently as 2020s. There is great interest in furniture, glass, ceramics, and design made since 1950 in the midcentury modern style and pieces made after the 1980s. The word "design" has taken on a more contemporary meaning. Design isn't only about the way things look or function, but about incorporating new elements in new ways to make things better.

The 2023 edition is 640 pages long and crammed full of prices and photographs. We try to include a balance of prices and do not include too many items that sell for more than $5,000. By listing only a few very expensive pieces, you can realize that a great paperweight may cost $10,000, but an average one is only $25. Nearly all prices are from the American market for the American market. Only a few European sales are reported. These are for items that may be of interest to American collectors. We don't include prices we think result from "auction fever," but we do list verified bargains or amazingly high prices.

There is an index with cross-references. Use it often. It includes categories and much more. For example, there is a category for Celluloid. Most celluloid will be there, but a toy made of celluloid may be listed under Toy as well as indexed under Celluloid. There are also cross-references in the listings and in the category introductions. But some searching must be done. For example, Barbie dolls are in the Doll category; there is no Barbie category. And when you look at "doll, Barbie," you find a note that "Barbie" is under "doll, Mattel, Barbie" because Mattel makes Barbie dolls and most dolls are listed by maker.

Wherever we had extra space on a page, we filled it with tips about the care of collections and other useful information. Don't discard this book. Old Kovels' price guides can be used in the coming years as a reference source for identifying pictures and price changes and for tax, estate, and appraisal information.

The prices in this book are reports of the general antiques market. As we said, every price in the book is new. We do not estimate or "update" prices. Prices are either realized prices from auctions or completed sales in stores or at shows. We have also included a few that are asking prices, knowing that a buyer may have negotiated a lower price. We do not pay dealers, collectors, or experts to estimate prices. If a price range is given, at least two identical items were offered for sale at different prices. Price ranges are found only in categories such as Pressed Glass, where identical items can be identified. Some prices in *Kovels' Antiques & Collectibles Price Guide* may seem high and some low because of regional variations, but each price is what you could have paid for the object somewhere in the United States. Internet prices from individual sellers' ads or listings are avoided. Because so many non-collectors sell online but know little about the objects they are describing, there can be inaccuracies in descriptions. Sales from well-known Internet sites, shops, and sales, carefully edited, are included.

If you are selling your collection, do not expect to get retail value unless you are a dealer. Wholesale prices for antiques are 30 to 40 percent of retail prices. The antiques dealer must make a profit or go out of business. Internet auction prices are less predictable; because of an international audience or "auction fever," prices can be higher or lower than retail. The estimated price listed in an auction shows the expected retail price range.

Time has changed what people collect, the prices we pay, what is "best," and what has dropped in price. There are also laws about endangered species, not a concern when we started, and many changes in tax laws, estate problems, and even more and better reproductions and fakes that make buying more difficult. But there are many more ways to buy and sell. When we started, it was house sales, flea markets, and a few formal antiques shows and auctions. Now, computers and the Internet have made it possible for anyone to buy and sell any day of the week, in every price range. This year many shows came back and some were canceled because of the coronavirus, a number of auction houses merged, and many more people bid at online only auctions. Almost every auction is online as well as available by phone to buyers around the world. And there are frequently live bidders at the more expensive sales. But many auctions end up with unsold pieces, some offered for sale at a set price after the auction. Even eBay is selling only part of the offered antiques. There are thousands of places for us to look for prices!

READ THIS FIRST

This is a book for the buyer and the seller. It is an organized, illustrated list of average pieces, not million-dollar paintings and rare Chinese porcelains. Everything listed in this book was sold between June 2021 and June 2022. We check prices, visit shops, shows, and flea markets, read hundreds of publications and catalogs, check Internet sales, auctions, and other online services, and decide which antiques and collectibles are of most interest to most collectors in the United States. We concentrate on average pieces in any category. Prices of some items were very high because a major collection of top-quality pieces owned by a well-known collector, expert, or celebrity was auctioned. Fame adds to the value. Many catalogs now feature the name, picture, and biography of the collector and advertise the auction with the collector's name in all the ads.

The largest thing listed this year is an iron Garden Gate in the Napoleon III style with gilt lions and an acanthus scroll. It is 108 inches by 156 inches and sold for $2,440. The smallest is a brass button from the 1800s, domed with flowers on it. It is only one inch across and sold for $38. The most expensive item is a 1700s Meissen shelf clock with a gilt-bronze mount and a signed Barrey à Paris movement that

sold for $1,593,000. There was an amazing sale this year of rare and valuable pre-WWII Meissen owned by the Oppenheimers in Germany. This shelf or mantel clock was one of the important Meissen pieces in the sale. The least expensive entries were bottle caps. The "My Pop's Root Beer" crown cap from the 1960s and the bottle cap with "Pasteurized Milk" by "N.F. & J. C. Schoppee," Machias, Maine, picturing a cow's head each sold for $2. There was also a saucer by Taylor, Smith & Taylor that sold for $2.

There are always some strange and even weird things listed in our price books. We have listed artificial legs several times, usually the plain wooden stump that is pictured in stories of pirates of earlier days. This year the weirdest item was a taxidermy jackrabbit head with antlers.

RECORD-SETTING PRICES

COMICS, COMIC BOOKS & ORIGINAL COMIC ART

Original Peanuts artwork (image 1): $360,000 for a Peanuts comic strip by Charles Schulz, for December 18, 1966, Christmas, signed "Sparky." Sold September 10, 2021, by Heritage Auctions, Dallas.

Superman #1 comic (image 2): $2.6 million for a 1939 Superman #1 comic book. Sold December 17, 2021, by ComicConnect.com.

Comic book (image 3): $3.6 million for a copy of a 1962 Amazing Fantasy No. 15, first appearance of Spider-Man. Sold September 9, 2021, at Heritage Auctions, Dallas.

Marvel Comics #1 (image 4): $2.4 million for

1.

a copy of the November 1939 Marvel Comics #1, introduces Sub-Mariner and the Human Torch, "pay copy" with publisher's handwritten notes on writers' and artists' pay. Sold March 17, 2022, in an online auction by ComicConnect.com.

2.   *3.*   *4.*

FURNITURE

Original Eames storage unit (image 5): $48,000 for an Eames Storage Unit 1st Edition cabinet. Sold August 22, 2021, by Le Shoppe Auction House in Keego Harbor, Michigan.

5.

IKEA furniture (image 6): $16,725 for a Cavelli armchair, launched in 1958, designed by Bengt Ruda. Sold November 14, 2021, at Stadsauktion Sundsvall in Sweden.

6.

Enfield Shaker sisters' sewing desk (image 7): $330,400 for a rare, possibly one-of-a-kind Shaker sewing desk made in the Enfield community, with a red stain and retractable writing surface, designed for two to work at once. Sold November 20, 2021, by William Smith Auctions of Plainfield, New Hampshire.

7.

Charles Rohlfs oak hall chair (image 8): $306,000 for an Arts and Crafts oak hall chair by Charles Rohlfs, carved feet, artist's monogram, dated 1901, 58 in. tall. Sold March 19, 2022, by Cottone Auctions in Geneseo, New York.

GLASS

Single sand bottle (image 9): $956,000 for a sand bottle by Andrew Clemens, 8 ¾ in. tall, featuring a photorealistic black and white portrait of Orrin T. Fuller as a child, the only known Clemens bottle with a portrait. Sold September 30, 2021, at Hindman auctions in Chicago.

8.

9.

Dr. Renz's Herb Bitters bottle (image 10): $24,150 for a lime green Dr. Renz's Herb Bitters bottle with a tapered top, one of four known examples, 9 ¾ in. tall, San Francisco, 1868-81. Sold December 19, 2021, at American Bottle Auctions, Sacramento, California.

Dr. Miller's Ratafia Bitters bottle (image 11): $29,900 for a Dr. Miller's Ratafia Bitters bottle, Damania. Siebe Bros. & Plagemann, S.F., Sole Agent Pacific Coast, amber, winged sphinx, cylindrical, sloping collar, made c.1878-79. Sold March 14, 2022, by American Bottle Auctions, Sacramento, California.

10.   11.

MISCELLANEOUS

Mandt Homme decoy (image 12): $156,000 for a hollow-carved Canada goose decoy by Mandt Homme of Stoughton, Wisconsin, branded "A.T. Shearer" and inscribed "Carved by Mandt Homme." Sold November 10, 2021, by Guyette & Deeter, Inc. in St. Michaels, Maryland.

George Skerry decoy (image 13): $52,000 for a Canada goose field decoy carved by George Skerry of Prince Edward Island, Canada, in preening position, wing raised, mounted on an iron base, 25 in. tall. Sold November 10-11, 2021, by Guyette & Deeter, Inc. in St. Michaels, Maryland.

12.

Marvel movie prop (image 14): $259,540 for a Captain America shield prop used onscreen by actor Chris Evans in Avengers: Endgame. Sold November 3, 2021, by Hake's Auctions, York, Pennsylvania.

13.

14.

15.

Elizabeth Catlett artwork (image 15): $485,000 for "Head," a carved limestone sculpture by Elizabeth Catlett, 1943. Sold October 7, 2021, at Swann Auction Galleries in New York.

Sorcerer's mirror (image 16): £3,400 ($6,011) ("probably set a world record") for a Victorian sorcerer's mirror with 8 convex circles in the center, inset brushed steel garland, beveled edge, and a stepped mahogany frame, 19th century, 17 in. diameter. Sold February 15, 2022, at Sworders, U.K.

1907 Saint-Gaudens Ultra High Relief U.S. Gold Coin (image 17): $4.75 million for a 1907 Saint-Gaudens U.S. gold coin, Ultra High Relief, fewer than 20 minted, 13 to 15 in existence, sold in a private transaction between Great Collections Coin Auctions, Irvine, California and Heritage Auctions, Dallas.

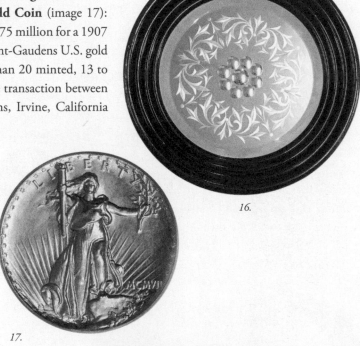

16.

17.

Jean Dunand room (image 18): £3,289,500 ($4,550,036 USD) for "Les Palmiers" Art Deco smoking room, lacquered wood, lacquered metal, gilded wood, from the residence of Mademoiselle Colette Aboucaya, Paris, one wall incised "Jean Dunand," 1930-1936, 135 x 155 x 233 in. Sold June 30, 2021, at Phillips in London.

18.

PAINTINGS & PRINTS

Paul Revere print "The Bloody Massacre" (image 19): $429,000 for Paul Revere's 1770 hand-colored engraving "The Bloody Massacre" of the Boston Massacre. Sold November 2, 2021, by Doyle, New York.

American folk art cat portrait (image 20): $152,000 for a folk art portrait of a black and white cat with an orange ball, oil on board, American school, late 19th/early 20th century. Sold November 18, 2021, by Jeffrey S. Evans & Associates, Mt. Crawford, Virginia.

19.

21.

20.

Hale Woodruff abstract artwork (image 21): $664,000 for "Carnival" by Hale Woodruff, oil on canvas, c.1958. Sold October 7, 2021, at Swann Auction Galleries in New York.

Gertrude Abercrombie artwork (image 22): $387,500 for "The Dinosaur," a late-career piece by American Surrealist artist Gertrude Abercrombie, oil on panel, depicting a small dinosaur facing a large egg in a landscape, 7 ½ x 9 ½ in. Sold February 17, 2022, at Hindman, Chicago.

22.

T.J. Walton artwork sold at auction (image 23): $5,313 for "Sunflowers" by T.J. Walton, oil on canvas, early 21st century. Sold March 12, 2022, in an online auction by Bakker Auctions, Provincetown, Massachusetts.

Alphonse Mucha study (image 24): $965,000 for "Young Couple from Rusadla," Alphonse Mucha, oil on canvas, 1920, 30 ¼ x 25 in., study for the large composition "Rusadla" illustrating a procession from a Slavic Midsummer Feast. Sold December 2, 2021, at Toomey & Co. Auctioneers, Oak Park, Illinois.

23.

24.

25.

Lonnie Holley artwork (image 25): $10,625 for an abstract ink and watercolor picture on paper by Lonnie Holley, framed, signed, dated 1991, 30 x 26 in. Sold March 19, 2022, by Ledbetter Folk Art Auction, Gibsonville, North Carolina.

Benny Carter painting (image 26): $8,610 for an early folk art painting by Benny Carter on framed artist board depicting a colorful, detailed New York City scene with the Statue of Liberty in the center and borders of taxis, buildings, and cars, c.1995. Sold July 10, 2021, by Ledbetter Folk Art Auction, Gibsonville, North Carolina.

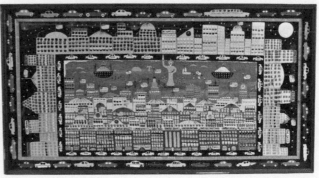

26.

27.

PAPER

Concert poster (image 27): $275,000 for an original concert poster for The Beatles at Shea Stadium, New York, August 23, 1966, final tour, sold as is. Sold April 16, 2022, at Heritage Auctions, Dallas.

Book, single modern novel (image 28): $471,000 for a first edition of Harry Potter and the Philosopher's Stone. Sold December 9, 2021, by Heritage Auctions, Dallas.

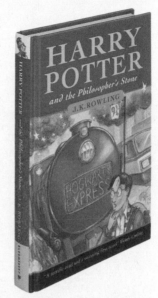

28.

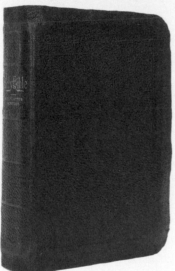

29.

Book signed by Harry Houdini (image 29): $102,000 for Harry Houdini's Bible used in a mind-reading act, signed and dated, the only known example with Houdini's signature. Sold December 11, 2021, by Potter & Potter Auctions, Chicago.

Sojourner Truth carte de visite (image 30): $13,750 for an uncredited carte de visite of abolitionist and activist Sojourner Truth, seated at a small table with flowers, knitting, caption "I Sell the Shadow to Support the Substance," imprinted "Entered according to act of Congress in the year 1864, by Sojourner Truth, in the Clerk's Office, of the US District Court, for the Eastern District of Mich." on reverse, sold with a group of 40 cartes-de-visite, an unmounted album, 3 tintypes, and 4 mounted gem-sized tintypes. Sold February 23, 2022, at Hindman in Cincinnati.

30.

Document or book: $43.2 million for a first printing of the U.S. Constitution. Sold November 18, 2021, by Sotheby's in New York.

31.

John Wilkes Booth broadside (image 31): $275,000 for a $100,000 reward broadside for John Wilkes Booth after Abraham Lincoln's assassination, issued by the U.S. War Department, April 20, 1865. Sold September 25, 2021, by Heritage Auctions in Dallas.

Abraham Lincoln-era presidential china (image 32): $93,750 for a celery dish from Abraham Lincoln's White House china. Sold September 25, 2021, by Heritage Auctions, Dallas.

32.

33.

Any pinback button (image 33): $185,850 for a James M. Cox/Franklin D. Roosevelt jugate political pinback button from the 1920 presidential election, 1 ¼ in., one of 6 known examples, one of 3 known examples with this particular design. Sold March 15, 2022, by Hake's Auctions, York, Pennsylvania.

Political cartoon (image 34): "Believed was a record." $81,250 for a Currier & Ives cartoon for the 1860 presidential election, "The National Game. Three 'Outs' and One 'Run'," baseball theme, depicts the 4 candidates with balloon captions, Abraham Lincoln on home base, 17 x 13 ½ in. Sold March 19, 2022, by Heritage Auctions, Dallas.

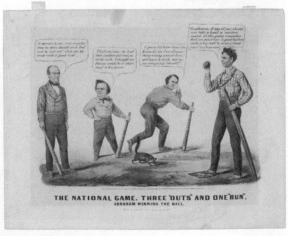

34.

Political ribbon (image 35): "Believed was a record." $118,750 for a silk jugate ribbon with photograph portraits of Stephen A. Douglas and Herschel Vespasian Johnson by Mathew Brady, 1860 presidential election, 7 x 2 in., few known to exist. Sold March 19, 2022, by Heritage Auctions, Dallas.

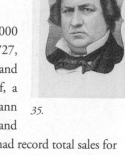

POTTERY & PORCELAIN

Italian majolica dish (image 36): £1,263,000 (about 1.7 million USD) for a 16th-century Italian majolica dish, istoriato style, telling the story of Samson and Delilah, attributed to Nicola di Gabriele Sbraghe c.1520-23. Sold October 6, 2021, by Lyon & Turnbull, Edinburgh, Scotland.

36.

Meissen mantel clock (image 37): $1,593,000 for a Meissen mantel clock case dated 1727, modeled by George Fritzsche with molded and painted scrollwork, a gilt simulated tile roof, a mythological group on top attributed to Johann Gottlieb Kirchner, gilt bronze mount, and movement signed Barrey à Paris. The auction had record total sales for European ceramics. Sold September 14, 2021, by Sotheby's, New York.

35.

American ceramics (image 38): $1.56 million for a 25-gallon poem jar with poured glaze creating olive-green striping, dated April 12, 1858, signed Dave, reading "A very Large Jar which has 4 handles / pack it full of fresh meats—then light candles." Made by David Drake, an enslaved potter at Lewis Miles' stoneware manufactory in Stony Bluff, South Carolina. There are fewer than 35 documented David Drake poem jars. Sold from July 23 to August 6, 2021, by Crocker Farm, Inc., Sparks, Maryland, in its absentee- and online-only auction.

Hans Coper ceramics (image 39): £651,700 ($890,168 USD) for a large oval pot, stoneware, deep vertical indent on each face, textured surface, layered porcelain slips and engobes, manganese glaze interior, 1968, 18 ¼ x 15 x 15 in. Sold November 10, 2021, at Phillips in association with Maak Contemporary Ceramics in London.

37.

38.

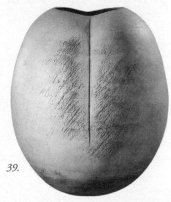

39.

SPORTS

Earliest known Michael Jordan regular season game worn Nike sneakers: $1.472 million for a pair of red and white 1984 size 13 Nike Air Ships with "Air" printed on heels, signed by Michael Jordan, worn in one of his first NBA games. Sold October 24, 2021, by Sotheby's in Las Vegas.

High school basketball jersey (image 40): $512,000 for LeBron James' St. Vincent – St. Mary's jersey, game worn and on the cover photograph of "Sports Illustrated" in February 2002. Sold July 17, 2021, at Julien's Auctions in Beverly Hills, California.

Mickey Mantle jersey (image 41): $2.19 million for a jersey worn by Mickey Mantle on September 28, 1968, for his last game with the New York Yankees and his 535th home run, signed in blue Sharpie at the upper right chest. Sold February 26-27, 2022, in the Winter Platinum Night Sports Auction, at Heritage Auctions, Dallas.

40.   41.

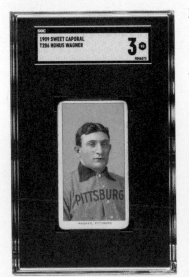

Most valuable baseball card (image 42): $6.6 million for a T206 Honus Wagner baseball card issued by the American Tobacco Co. between 1909 and 1911. Sold August 15, 2021, at Robert Edward Auctions, Chester, New Jersey.

Sporting-event ticket (image 43): $480,000 for a ticket stub from Jackie Robinson's big league debut game, Brooklyn Dodgers Opening Day, 1947, one of 7 known existing, section 11, row 7, seat 1. Sold February 26, 2022, at Heritage Auctions, Dallas.

42.

43.

TOYS, DOLLS & GAMES

J. & E. Stevens Girl Skipping Rope bank (image 44): $156,000 for a cast-iron mechanical bank in the Girl Skipping Rope form by J. & E. Stevens. Sold November 18, 2021, by Bertoia Auctions, Vineland, New Jersey.

Pokey the Turtle bank (image 45): $111,000 for a "Pokey the Turtle" bank by Kilgore Mfg. Company in Westerville, Ohio in the late 1920s, few produced because a design flaw caused the company to stop production. Sold March 5, 2022, at RSL Auction, Whitehouse Station, New Jersey.

44.

Video game (image 46): $1.56 million for a sealed copy of Super Mario 64 from 1996 for the Nintendo 64 game system. Sold July 11, 2021, by Heritage Auctions, Dallas.

45.

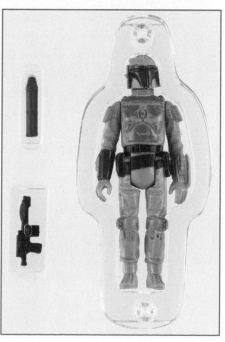

46.

Star Wars action figure (image 47): $204,435 for a Star Wars Boba Fett "J-slot" rocket-firing action figure, prototype, pre-production, designed by Kenner in 1979 but never produced commercially because of safety concerns. Sold March 16, 2022, at Hake's Auctions, York, Pennsylvania.

47.

There are a few rules for using this book. Each listing is arranged in the following manner: CATEGORY (such as silver), OBJECT (such as vase), DESCRIPTION (as much information as possible about size, age, color, and pattern). Some types of glass, pottery, and silver are exceptions to this rule. These are listed CATEGORY, PATTERN, OBJECT, DESCRIPTION, PRICE. All items are presumed to be in good condition and undamaged, unless otherwise noted. In most sections, if a maker's name is easily recognized, such as Gustav Stickley, we include it near the beginning of the entry. If the maker is obscure, the name may be near the end.

- To save space, dollar amounts do not include dollar signs, commas, or cents at the end so $1,234.00 is written 1234.

- You will find silver flatware in either Silver Flatware Plated or Silver Flatware Sterling. There is also a section for Silver Plate, which includes coffeepots, trays, and other plated hollowware. Most solid or sterling silver is listed by country, so look for Silver-American, Silver-Danish, Silver-English, etc. Silver jewelry is listed under Jewelry. Most pottery and porcelain is listed by factory name, such as Weller or Wedgwood; by item, such as Calendar Plate; in sections like Dinnerware or Kitchen; or in a special section, such as Pottery-Art, Pottery-Contemporary, Pottery-Midcentury, etc.

- Sometimes we make arbitrary decisions. "Fishing" has its own category, but "Hunting" is part of the larger category called "Sports." We have listed historic guns in "Weapons" and toy guns in the toy category. It is not legal to sell weapons without a special license, so guns are not part of the general antiques market. Air guns, BB guns, rocket guns, and others are listed in the Toy section. Everything is listed alphabetically.

- We made several editorial decisions. A butter dish is listed as a "butter." A salt dish is called a "salt" to differentiate it from a saltshaker. It is always "sugar and creamer," never "creamer and sugar." Where one dimension is given, it is the height; if the object is round, it's the diameter. The height of a picture is listed before width. Glass is clear unless a color is indicated. We never call glass "crystal." A crystal is a natural shape of a mineral.

- Some antiques terms, such as "Sheffield" or "Pratt," have two meanings. Read the paragraph headings to know the definition being used. All category headings are based on the vocabulary of the average person, and we use terms like "mud figures" even if not technically correct. Some categories are known by several names. Pressed glass is also called pattern glass or EAPG (Early American Pattern Glass). We use the name "pressed glass" because much of the information found in old books and articles uses that name.

- This book does not include price listings for fine art paintings, antiquities, stamps, coins, or most types of books. Comic books are listed only in special categories like Batman, but original comic art is listed in Comic Art, and cels are listed in Animation Art.

- Prices for items pictured can be found in the appropriate categories. Look for the matching entry with the abbreviation "illus." The color photograph will be nearby.

- Prices are reported from all parts of the United States, Canada, Europe, and Asia, and converted to U.S. dollars at the time of the sale. The average rate of exchange on June 1, 2022, was $1.00 to about $1.21 Canadian, €0.82 (euro), and £0.71 (British pound). Meltdown price for silver was $27.89 per ounce in June. Prices are from auctions, shops, Internet sales, shows, and even some flea markets. Every price is checked for accuracy, but we are not responsible for errors.

We cannot always answer your letters asking for price information, or where to sell, but please write if you have any requests for categories to be included or any corrections to the paragraphs or prices. You may find the answers to your other questions online at Kovels.com or in our newsletter, *Kovels On Antiques & Collectibles*.

- When you see us at shows, auctions, house sales, flea markets, or even the grocery store, please stop and say hello. Don't be surprised if we ask for your suggestions. You can write to us at P.O. Box 22192, Beachwood, OH 44122, or visit us at our website, Kovels.com.

TERRY KOVEL AND KIM KOVEL
July 2022

ACKNOWLEDGMENTS

The world of antiques and collectibles is filled with people who share knowledge and help, tell stories of record prices, amazing sales, online activities, and news, and make books like this possible. Dealers, auction galleries, antiques shops, serious collectors, clubs, publications, and even museum experts have given advice and opinions, sent pictures and prices, and made suggestions for changes. Thank you to all of them! Each picture is labeled with the name of the source. We list a phone number, postal address, and Web address at the end of the book, so you can learn more about any pictured piece. We also include the names of many of the people or places that reported some prices. Anyone who sells collectibles and antiques must buy them, so you may want to contact a source listed here.

And we want to give special thanks to the staff at Kovels'. They deserve the most credit. They helped gather the 12,500 prices, 3,150 pictures, marks, tips on care of collections, and hotlines (bits of information too important to ignore), put it all together, and made it work. This year it was completed during the days we were still following some pandemic rules and we had to invent new ways to share responsibilities.

Special thanks to Hachette Book Group, our publisher. Our thanks to the Hachette staff:

- Lisa Tenaglia, our editor, who has worked with us for over ten years to make sure the book gets finished on time. She is our advocate, our problem solver, and we couldn't do it without her. We couldn't be happier for her welcoming the newest member of her family.

- Joe Davidson, who stepped in seamlessly while Lisa was on maternity leave. He somehow filled the big shoes that Lisa left and kept us consistently on track and was always helpful resolving any issues that arose.

- Lillian Sun, senior production manager; Melanie Gold, senior production editor; and the others at Hachette who do all the things behind the scenes that are essential to creating the quality of the finished product. They may work outside the spotlight, but we always know how important it is.

- Kara Thornton, publicity manager, who gets stories in newspapers, magazines, book reviews, social media, TV talk shows, and the many online sites that are interested in collecting. We are grateful for what she does to keep us on the radar.

- Betsy Hulsebosch, director of marketing, who makes sure we get promoted in social media and online sources. Thanks for keeping folks tuned in to what we are doing.

- Katie Benezra, associate art director, who knows how to be sure the art is at its finest. We appreciate her unique abilities to elevate the beauty in visuals.

- Mary Flower, Robin Perlow, and Cynthia Schuster Eakin, copyeditors, who can find every typo, mislabeled picture, and misspelled name. From royal families to periods of furniture and from historic events to Chinese dynasties, their attention to detail is unparalleled. They are even experts at ensuring the most misspelled name of them all—Wedgwood—is correct.

- Sheila Hart, who has worked on many editions of the book—redesigning the pages to look great and adapting the layout each time we change the content. In addition, she also does the layout and design of the special features such as the record prices and this year's insert "Collecting Trends: Twentieth-Century Studio Ceramics." Somehow, she has solved the problem of getting all 12,500 prices and all 3,150 pictures in alphabetical order so readers can see them near each other.

And to those on the Kovels' staff who work on both the digital and print versions of this book:

- Janet Dodrill, our art director, who somehow can keep track of all the pictures and permissions for the items shown in this book as well as extra pictures used for our columns and other publications. She uses her superior photo-editing skills to improve the look and the quality of the pictures by outlining the objects, checking the color, and even working magic with close-ups of details. This year our deadlines were tight, and Janet still managed to get everything done on time — without sacrificing an ounce of her excellence.

- Elizabeth Burroughs-Heineman gets everything done. Prices, organizing data, making corrections and copyediting — you name it, and she does it. Her eye for details, grammar expertise, and flawless typing are invaluable.

- Renee McRitchie, who knows the vocabulary needed to get prices from all parts of the country and turn them into the proper form to sort into the book. She is essential in making content clear.

- Mary Beth Kohl, the office troubleshooter and researcher, who pilots our customer service and solves our tech issues. If we have a puzzle, we go to her, and she always knows just how to solve it to keep the office running smoothly.

- Jacquie Boisson, our accountant, who keeps all our finances up to date. Her patience is appreciated. She is always ready and eager to help with her invaluable feedback and solutions-oriented approach.

- Cherrie Smrckar, who helped us get the furniture section of the book in tip-top shape. She is literally irreplaceable as evidenced by the fact that, when we were in need, she came out of retirement to help with this year's book.

- Liz Lillis, the Kovels' staff copyeditor, writer, and researcher, who not only knows all the dates and names but tells us where the commas and periods go and solves other grammar problems. Her research and writing skills are only rivalled by her willingness to take on any project, which she demonstrates through writing online publicity for the book.

- Hamsy Mirre, our marketing director, who handles our book promotions as well as numerous other marketing responsibilities. She makes sure our readers stay informed of any and all Kovels good news. We appreciate her ability to keep us connected to all of you.

- Gay Hunter, who is the official boss of the price book production, tracks the prices and pictures in and out, suggests sources for prices at sales and shows, records where and when it was sold, and what the seller said about it. She keeps us meeting the book deadlines and keeps us always moving forward. She is truly a master of her craft.

- Maureen Bole, Eric Broder, and Susan Love who offer support and help whenever needed. Their kindness and thoughtful listening as we angst over approaching deadlines is invaluable.

- And Alberto Eiber, the expert who makes sure we are accurate with articles and reports of the recent things we include that are part of the "Design" genre. He also writes about the 20th-century and contemporary designers and wrote this year's insert "Collecting Trends: Twentieth-Century Studio Ceramics." We appreciate all he does to keep us up to date in this growing field.

- Special thanks to Bill and Jill Meier of billandjillinsulators.com, who gave their expert opinion for our Insulator category.

CONTRIBUTORS

The world of antiques and collectibles is filled with people who have answered our every request for help. Dealers, auction houses, and shops have given advice and opinions, supplied photographs and prices, and made suggestions for changes. Many thanks to all of them.

Photographs and information were furnished by: Abington Auction Gallery, Ahlers & Ogletree Auction Gallery, Alderfer Auction Company, Alex Cooper Auctioneers, American Bottle Auctions, Andrew Jones Auctions, Apple Tree Auction Center, Auctions at Showplace, NYC, Bakker Auctions, Bertoia Auctions, Bill and Jill Insulators, Blackwell Auctions, Blanchard's Auction Service LLC, Bonhams, Bruneau & Co. Auctioneers, Brunk Auctions, Bunch Auctions, California Historical Design, Carey Auctions, Carlsen Gallery, Charleston Estate Auctions, Charlton Hall Auctions, Chupp Auctions & Real Estate, LLC, Clars Auction Gallery, ComicConnect.com, Conestoga Auction Company, Copake Auction, Cordier Auctions, Cottone Auctions, Cowan's Auctions, Crescent City Auction Gallery, CRN Auctions, Crocker Farm, Inc., Donley Auctions, Doyle, DuMouchelles, Early American History Auctions, eBay, Eldred's, Etsy, Fairfield Auction, Fontaine's Auction Gallery, Freeman's, Garth's Auctioneers & Appraisers, Girard Auction & Land Brokers, Inc., Glass Works Auctions, Goldin Auctions, Greenwich Auction, Guyette & Deeter, Inc., Hake's Auctions, Hannam's Auctioneers, Hartzell's Auction Gallery Inc., Heritage Auctions, Hess Auction Group, Hindman, Hudson Valley Auctions, Hunt & Peck Auctions, LLC, I.M. Chait Gallery/Auctioneers, Jaremos, Jeffrey S. Evans & Associates, John McInnis Auctioneers, John Moran Auctioneers, Julien's Auctions, Kaminski Auctions, Kodner Galleries, Inc., Le Shoppe Auction House, Le Shoppe Too, Ledbetter Folk Art Auction, Leland Little Auctions, Lion and Unicorn, Lyon & Turnbull, Main Auction Galleries, Inc., Martin Auction Co., Matthew Bullock Auctioneers, Matthews Auctions, LLC, McMurray Antiques & Auctions, Merrill's Auctions, Michaan's Auctions, Mid-Hudson Auction Galleries, Milestone Auctions, Morphy Auctions, Nadeau's Auction Gallery, Nation's Attic, Neal Auction Company, Neue Auctions, New Haven Auctions, Norman C. Heckler & Company, North American Auction Co., Nye & Company, Palm Beach Modern Auctions, Pasarel Auctions, Phillips, Pook & Pook, Potter & Potter Auctions, Quittenbaum Kunstauktionen GmbH, Rachel Davis Fine Arts, Rafael Osona Nantucket Auctions, Rago Arts and Auction Center, Rich Penn Auctions, Richard D. Hatch & Associates, Richard Opfer Auctioneering, Inc., Ripley Auctions, Robert Edward Auctions, Roland NY Auctioneers & Appraisers, Ron Rhoads Auctioneers, Route 32 Auctions, RR Auction, RSL Auction, Ruby Lane, Sabertooth Auctions, Seeck Auctions, Selkirk Auctioneers & Appraisers, Sotheby's, Soulis Auctions, Stadsauktion Sundsvall, Stevens Auction Co., Stony Ridge Auction, Strawser Auction Group, Susanin's Auctioneers & Appraisers, Swann Auction Galleries, Sworders, Taranova Auctions Inc., TavernTrove Auctions, Thomaston Place Auction Galleries, Toomey & Co. Auctioneers, Treadway, Treasureseeker Auctions, Tremont Auctions, Turner Auctions + Appraisals, Ukiyo-e Gallery: Japanese Woodblock Prints, Weiss Auctions, White's Auctions, Wiederseim Associates, William Smith Auctions, Woody Auction, World Auction Gallery, and Wright.

To the others who knowingly or unknowingly contributed to this book, we say thank you: 1957 Estate Bargains, A & A Auction Gallery, A.H. Wilkens Auctions & Appraisals, Abbingdon Auctions Australia, Americana Auctions, Antique Factory, Antiques & Modern Auction Gallery, Artelisted, Atlanta Auction Gallery, Atlee Raber Auctions, Auctioneers Inc., Auctions by Adkins, LLC, Auctions By B. Langston, LLC, Auctions Neapolitan, BachOne Auctions, Basel Auction House, Belhorn Auctions, LLC, Blue Box Auction Gallery, Brookline Auction Gallery, Butterscotch Auction, Capsule Auctions, Cedarburg Auction & Estate Sales LLC, Central Mass Auctions, Christie's, Clarke Auction Gallery, COLLECTive

Hudson, Concept Art Gallery, Costea's Auction Service, Dane Fine Art, Dargate Auction Galleries, David Killen Gallery, Davies Auctions, Direct Auction Galleries, Donny Malone Auctions, Empire House, Inc., Epic Auctions and Estate Sales, Flannery's Estate Services, Fortune Auction Gallery, Gallery Auctions Inc., Helmuth Stone Gallery, Hidden Treasures Antiques & Fine Art, Hill House Wares, Hilliard & Co., Homestead Auctions, Homestead Auctions of Tennessee, Houston Auction Company, Ishtar Auctions LTD., JMW Auction Service, Judd's Auction Gallery, Inc., Kavanagh Auctions, Keene Auctions, Kensington Estate Auction, King Galleries, Lakeland Antiques Bazaar, Leonard's Auction Service, Link Auction Galleries, Locati, LLC, Lot 14 Auctions, Luther Auctions, M&M Auctions, M.J. Stasak Auctions, Macon Brothers Auctioneers, Material Culture, MBA Seattle, McCreary Auctions LLC, MiddleManBrokers Inc., Millea Bros., Mynt Auctions, Neely Auction, Nest Egg Auctions, Paul Arsenault Auctioneers, Potteries Auctions Ltd., Public Sale Auction House, Regency Auction House, Rentzel's Auction Service, Inc., Replacements, Ltd., Robbins Nest Collectibles, Searchlight Auction, Skinner, Inc., Sofe Design, Steven's Art & Antiques, Summit Auction Galleries, Taylor & Harris, Terri Peters & Associates, The Benefit Shop Foundation, The Cleveland Auction Co., Town & Country Estate Sales, Turkey Creek Auctions, Valley Auctions, W. Yoder Auction LLC, Westmount Auctions, Williston Auctions, Willow Auction House, Willow Creek Coin & Collectibles, and Withington Auctions Inc.

A. WALTER

A. Walter made pate-de-verre glass under contract at the Daum glassworks from 1908 to 1914. He decorated pottery during his early years in his studio in Sevres, where he also developed his formula for pale, translucent pate-de-verre. He started his own firm in Nancy, France, in 1919. Pieces made before 1914 are signed *Daum, Nancy* with a cross. After 1919 the signature is *A. Walter Nancy*.

Dish, Leaf Shape, Yellow, Green & Orange, Black Lizard, Fly, Marked, Early 1900s, 2¾ x 8½ x 4 In.	938
Paperweight, Beetle, Dark Green, Yellow & Brown Base, Signed, AW, N, HB, 1¼ x 2 x 1¾ In..	1664
Paperweight, Crab, Red Brown, Green Base, Signed, A. Walter Nancy & Berge, c.1920, 2 x 3 In.	1792
Paperweight, Snail, Signed, A. Walter Nancy, H. Berge, c.1920, 2½ In. .... *illus*	2178
Pendant, Chameleon, Yellow Orange Ground, Triangular, c.1920, 2½ x 2⅜ In.	1694
Pendant, Scarabee, Brown Beetle, Yellow Ground, 2 Holes, Oval, Signed, AW, N, HB, 2 x 1¼ In... *illus*	896
Vide Poche, Boat, Chameleon, Green, Signed, A. Walter Nancy, H. Berge, c.1920, 3 x 10 x 3 In... *illus*	8438
Vide Poche, Duck, Signed, A. Walter Nancy, H. Berge, c.1920, 2 x 5 x 2 In. .... *illus*	3146

ABC PLATE

ABC plates, or children's alphabet plates, were most popular from 1780 to 1860 but are still being made. The letters on the plate were meant as teaching aids for children learning to read. The plates were made of pottery, porcelain, metal, or glass. Mugs and other items were also made with alphabet decorations. Many companies made ABC plates. Shown here are marks used by three English makers.

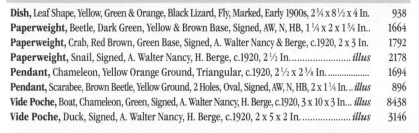

Charles Allerton & Sons
c.1890–1912

Enoch Wood & Sons
1818–1846

William E. Oulsnam & Sons
c.1880–1892

Plate, A Timely Rescue, Tiger Attacking Man, Grasses, Brown Transfer, Staffordshire, 7½ In.	18
Plate, Clock Face, Vaseline Glass, Notched Rim, 7 In.	25
Plate, Eliza Crosses The Ohio, Uncle Tom's Cabin, Multicolor Transfer, Staffordshire, 8½ In..	35
Plate, Farmer Plowing, Proverb, He That By The Plow Would Thrive, Meakin, 5¼ In...........	52
Plate, Oriental Hotel, Coney Island, Multicolor Transfer, Staffordshire, 7½ In.	59
Plate, Oriental Hotel, Coney Island, White Ground, Embossed, 1800s, 7½ In. .... *illus*	59
Plate, Robinson Crusoe, Multicolor Transfer, Brown Letters, Marked, B.P. Co., 7¼ In., Pair	53

ADAMS

Adams china was made by William Adams and Sons of Staffordshire, England. The firm was founded in 1769 and became part of the Wedgwood Group in 1966. The name *Adams* appeared on various items through 1998. All types of tablewares and useful wares were made. Other pieces of Adams may be found listed under Flow Blue and Tea Leaf Ironstone.

William Adams & Co.
1905–1917

William Adams & Sons
1917–1965

Adams under Wedgwood
1966–1975

Jardiniere, Jasperware, Blue Ground, White Hunt Scene, 8 x 9 In. .... *illus*	63
Plate, Blue Transfer, 2 Cherubs In Center, Flower Rim, Scalloped Edge, 10¼ In.	87
Plate, Dessert, Blue Transfer, Landscape, 2 People, Church, Marked, Delphi, 1829-61, 7 In., Pair..	13
Plate, Red, Catskill Mountain House, Scalloped Beaded Rim, Late 1800s, 10½ In., Pair	375

A. Walter, Paperweight, Snail, Signed, A. Walter Nancy, H. Berge, c.1920, 2½ In.
$2,178

Fontaine's Auction Gallery

A. Walter, Pendant, Scarabee, Brown Beetle, Yellow Ground, 2 Holes, Oval, Signed, AW, N, HB, 2 x 1¼ In.
$896

Treasureseeker Auctions

A. Walter, Vide Poche, Boat, Chameleon, Green, Signed, A. Walter Nancy, H. Berge, c.1920, 3 x 10 x 3 In.
$8,438

Fontaine's Auction Gallery

A. Walter, Vide Poche, Duck, Signed, A. Walter Nancy, H. Berge, c.1920, 2 x 5 x 2 In.
$3,146

Fontaine's Auction Gallery

This is an edited listing of current prices. Visit **Kovels.com** to check thousands of prices from previous years and sign up for free information on trends, tips, reproductions, marks, and more.

ABC, Plate, Oriental Hotel, Coney Island, White Ground, Embossed, 1800s, 7½ In. $59

Stony Ridge Auction

Adams, Jardiniere, Jasperware, Blue Ground, White Hunt Scene, 8 x 9 In. $63

Greenwich Auction

TIP
Looking for inexpensive collectibles or decorations? Advertising ashtrays can sell for $2 to $10 at flea markets and house sales.

Adams, Vase, Jasperware, Blue & White, Classical Greek Figures, 1900s, 5 x 8 In. $63

Lion and Unicorn

Plate, Spatter, Concentric Circles, Green, Blue, Red Rim, Scalloped, 9½ In.	123
Plate, Square, Canted Corners, Handles, Blue, White, 2 Vignettes, 3 Men, Bird, Flowers, 9¾ In.	19
Tureen, Lid, Pagoda Finial & Handles, Ladle, Blue, White, Tunstall, c.1900, 7 x 12 x 9½ In.	70
Vase, Jasperware, Blue & White, Classical Greek Figures, 1900s, 5 x 8 In. ....*illus*	63

ADVERTISING

Advertising containers and products sold in the old country store are now all collectibles. These stores, with crackers in a barrel and a potbellied stove, are a symbol of an earlier, less hectic time. Listed here are many advertising items. Other similar pieces may be found under the product name, such as Planters Peanuts. We have tried to list items in logical places, so enameled tin dishes will be found under Graniteware, auto-related items in the Auto category, paper items in the Paper category, etc. Store fixtures, cases, signs, and other items that have no advertising as part of the decoration are listed in the Store category. The early Dr Pepper logo included a period after "Dr," but it was dropped in 1950. We list all Dr Pepper items without a period so they alphabetize together. Some collectors call enameled iron or steel signs "porcelain signs." For more prices, go to kovels.com.

Banner, Argo Cornstarch, Native American Girl, Cardboard, Lithograph, Frame, 16 x 24 In. ..	240
Barrel, Quickarrow Soap Chips, Round, Wood, 5 Bands, Swift & Co., 34 In.	209
Bin & Sifter, Superior Flour, Lid, Tole, Red, Lower Door, Crank Handle, 1870s, 23 x 10 In.....*illus*	288
Bin, Celebrated Boston Roasted Coffee, Dwinell-Wright Co., 19 x 19 x 13 In.	344
Bin, Coffee, Woolson Spice Cos., Stenciled, Wood, Early 1900s, 22 x 15 In.....................*illus*	344
Bin, Hinged Lid, Yale Coffee, Painted, Tin, Black Ground, Yellow Text, 20 x 19½ x 13 In...*illus*	720
Bin, Roasted Coffee, Peaberry, Woolson Spice Co.s, Tin, Sliding Door, c.1900, 22 x 20 In......	435
Books may be included in the Paper category.	
Bottles are listed in the Bottle category.	
Bottle Openers are listed in the Bottle Opener category.	
Bowl, Briar Rose Vankai Waving Fluid, Hair Salon, Depression Glass, 1930s, 6 x 10 In.........	45
Box, see also Box category.	
Box, Eureka Japan Green Tea, Hinged Lid, Lithograph, Metal Interior, Harvest Scene, 10 x 12 In. .	65
Box, Golden Sun Coffee, Woolson Spice Cos., Toledo, Oh., F.G. Simmons Marietta, 18 x 23 In.	246
Box, Lydia E. Pinkham's Vegetable Compound, Lynn, Mass., U.S.A., Wood, 9 x 13 x 9¾ In....	124
Box, St. Louis Alpen Brau Beer, Cloth Hinged Lid, Red Text, c.1947, 10½ x 17½ In................	48
Broadside, Bennington Stoneware Pottery, Gilt Frame, Julius Norton, c.1860, 13½ x 9½ In..	179
Broadside, Grand Talking Machine Entertainment, Letterpress, c.1885, 16 x 12 In.	500
Broadside, Norbeck & Miley, Practical Carriage Builders, Lancaster, 7½ x 11¼ In.............	39
Broadside, Sun Cured Red Coon Chewing Tobacco, Cardboard, Frame, 23 x 19 In................	76
Brochure Holder, Pacific Folder Distributing Co., Oak, 8 Tiers, 80 Pockets, 48 x 66 In.	1200
Cabinet, Carborundum, Corner, Triangular, Glass Panels, Wood, 41 x 23 x 23 In.................	406
Cabinet, Corliss-Coon Brand, Oak, Glass, 14 Shirt Collars, Specialty Case Co., 25 x 14 In..*illus*	584
Cabinet, Crowley's Needles, 12 Drawers, Porcelain Knobs, Wood, Late 1800s, 9 x 18 x 10 In...*illus*	156
Cabinet, Davol, Anti-Colic Brand Nipples & Bottle Caps, Wood, Slant Front, 9 x 11 x 8 In..*illus*	92
Cabinet, Magic Dyes, Wood, J.W. Brant Co., Late 1800s, 37 x 29½ x 10 In. ....*illus*	3509
Cabinet, Spool, Brainerd & Armstrong, Hinged Door, Drawer, Glass, Oak, 16 x 16 x 28 In. .....*illus*	1680
Cabinet, Spool, Clark's, Oak, 4 Drawers, Pressed Brass Pulls, 17 x 21 x 14 In.	254
Cabinet, Spool, George A. Clark, Pine, 6 Drawers, Different Plaque, 22¼ x 24½ x 20 In.....	313
Cabinet, Spool, J. & P. Coats', Cylindrical, 4 Drawers, Wood, Brass Handles, 17 x 17 x 22 In. ..*illus*	750
Cabinet, Spool, John J. Clark's, Oak, 2 Drawers, Metal Knobs, Early 1900s, 9 x 21 x 16 In....	156
Cabinet, Spool, Merrick's, Six Cord Standard Spool Cotton, 6 Drawers, Walnut, 18 x 30 x 17 In. .	415
Cabinet, Spool, Richardson Perfect Silk, 36 Drawers, Metal Pulls, Plinth Base, 48 x 29 x 19 In...	633
Cabinet, Spool, Willimantic Linen Co., Best Thread, Walnut, 6 Drawers, 1850s, 21 x 25¾ In..	908
Cabinet, Spool, Willimantic Spool Cotton, 2 Drawers, Porcelain Knobs, Late 1800s, 6 x 24 x 14 In.	125
Calendars are listed in the Calendar category.	
Canisters, see introductory paragraph to Tins in this category.	
Cards are listed in the Card category.	
Case, Display, Brighton Garter, 8 Drawers, Oak, Countertop, 14 x 19 x 10 In...........................	1020
Case, Display, Disston, Professional Handsaws, Wood, Black, Yellow, 29 x 7½ x 25 In.	102

Advertising, Bin & Sifter, Superior Flour, Lid, Tole, Red, Lower Door, Crank Handle, 1870s, 23 x 10 In.
$288

Rachel Davis Fine Arts

Advertising, Bin, Coffee, Woolson Spice Cos., Stenciled, Wood, Early 1900s, 22 x 15 In.
$344

Hindman

Advertising, Bin, Hinged Lid, Yale Coffee, Painted, Tin, Black Ground, Yellow Text, 20 x 19 ½ x 13 In.
$720

Morphy Auctions

Advertising, Cabinet, Corliss-Coon Brand, Oak, Glass, 14 Shirt Collars, Specialty Case Co., 25 x 14 In.
$584

Route 32 Auctions

Advertising, Cabinet, Crowley's Needles, 12 Drawers, Porcelain Knobs, Wood, Late 1800s, 9 x 18 x 10 In.
$156

Hindman

Advertising, Cabinet, Davol, Anti-Colic Brand Nipples & Bottle Caps, Wood, Slant Front, 9 x 11 x 8 In.
$92

Route 32 Auctions

Advertising, Cabinet, Magic Dyes, Wood, J.W. Brant Co., Late 1800s, 37 x 29 ½ x 10 In.
$3,509

Fontaine's Auction Gallery

Advertising, Cabinet, Spool, Brainerd & Armstrong, Hinged Door, Drawer, Glass, Oak, 16 x 16 x 28 In.
$1,680

Chupp Auctions & Real Estate, LLC

Advertising, Cabinet, Spool, J. & P. Coats', Cylindrical, 4 Drawers, Wood, Brass Handles, 17 x 17 x 22 In.
$750

Hindman

A

Advertising, Chair, Piedmont, The Virginia Cigarette, Folding, Stenciled Sides, 30 x 16 x 15 In.
$339

Hartzell's Auction Gallery Inc.

Advertising, Chair, RCA Victor, Chrome, Bakelite Armrests, Upholstered, 33 x 21 In.
$625

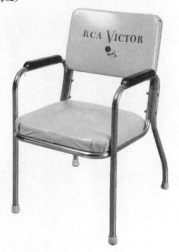

New Haven Auctions

Advertising, Cigar Box, Gen'l. Forrest, Lithographed Paper, Wood, Colorado Maduro, c.1903, 6 x 3 x 5 In.
$150

Cowan's Auctions

Advertising, Coaster, Crockery City Beer, Fox Hunt Scene, Octagonal, East Liverpool, O., 1937, 4 In.
$40

TavernTrove Auctions

Advertising, Coaster, F & S Beer, Fuhrmann & Schmidt, Red, Black, Round, Shamokin, Pa., 1933, 4 In.
$138

TavernTrove Auctions

Advertising, Coaster, Forest Rose Beer, Lancaster Brewing Co., Red Letters, Lancaster, Ohio, 1934, 4¼ In.
$115

TavernTrove Auctions

Advertising, Coaster, Old Reading Beer, The Old Reading Brewery, Covered Wagon Shape, 1945, 4¼ In.
$18

TavernTrove Auctions

Advertising, Coaster, Star Beer, Penn Star Brewing Co., Red & Blue, Lancaster, Pa., 1933, 4¼ In.
$81

TavernTrove Auctions

Advertising, Coaster, Stroh's Imperial Wurzburger Beer, Crest, Lion, Blue, Detroit, 1910, 4¼ In.
$40

TavernTrove Auctions

Advertising, Dispenser, Fowler's Cherry Smash Syrup, Cluster Of Cherries, White Ground, Early 1900s, 15 In.
$1,815

Fontaine's Auction Gallery

Advertising, Dispenser, Grape Kola, Lid, 5 Cents, Grapes, Counter
$630

Chupp Auctions & Real Estate, LLC

Advertising, Dispenser, Hires Root Beer, Metal Lid & Spigot, White Ground, Black & Red Text
$633

Donley Auctions

Advertising, Dispenser, Syrup, Ward's Orange Crush, Ceramic, Figural Pump, Painted Base, 15 x 10 x 10 In.
$1,560

Morphy Auctions

Advertising, Display, Kotex, Stand, Tin, Square Top, Arch Shape Base, c.1920, 25 x 20 x 17 In.
$303

Fontaine's Auction Gallery

Advertising, Display, Pabst Blue Ribbon Beer, Popular Prices, Bartender, Cast Metal, 14 ½ x 13 x 4 In.
$450

Morphy Auctions

Advertising, Display, Philip Morris Cigarettes, Bellboy, Plate, Standing, Cardboard, 19 x 44 In.
$330

Chupp Auctions & Real Estate, LLC

Advertising, Display, Steiff, Brown Bear, Stuffed, Standing, Red Collar, 50 In.
$438

Hindman

Advertising, Display, Winchester, Junior Rifle Corps, Window, Wood Frame, 42 x 24 In.
$492

Morphy Auctions

Advertising, Figure, Kool-Aid Man, Red, Standing, Interior Tray, Plastic, 35 In.
$120

Selkirk Auctioneers & Appraisers

Advertising, Figure, RCA, Nipper, Seated, Black & White, Chalkware, 1900s, 14½ In.
$594

Hindman

Advertising, Jug, M.E. Johnson, Wholesale Liquor Dealer, Derby, Conn., Stoneware, 1800s, 15½ In.
$531

New Haven Auctions

Case, Display, Sanipac Handkerchiefs, Reverse Painted Glass, Wood Base, 6 x 17 x 8 In.	280
Chair, Piedmont, The Virginia Cigarette, Folding, Stenciled Sides, 30 x 16 x 15 In. ....*illus*	339
Chair, RCA Victor, Chrome, Bakelite Armrests, Upholstered, 33 x 21 In. ....*illus*	625
Change Receiver, see also Tip Tray in this category.	
Charger, Bull Durham Smoking Tobacco, Woman, Tin, Frame, 1900s, 24 In.	2813
Cigar Box, Gen'l. Forrest, Lithographed Paper, Wood, Colorado Maduro, c.1903, 6 x 3 x 5 In.. *illus*	150
Cigar Cutter, Betsy Ross Cigar, A.S. Valentine & Son, Iron, Shield Shape, Portrait, Stand, 7 x 6 x 8 In.	885
Cigar Cutter, General Hartranft, 5 Cent, C.E. Bair & Sons, Electroplated Iron, Brunhoff, 9 In. ...	720
Cigar Cutter, Yankee, Union Shield, Dispenses Matches, Cast Iron, Early 1900s, 7 x 6 x 8 In.	787
Clocks are listed in the Clock category.	
Coaster, Crockery City Beer, Fox Hunt Scene, Octagonal, East Liverpool, O., 1937, 4 In.*illus*	40
Coaster, F & S Beer, Fuhrmann & Schmidt, Red, Black, Round, Shamokin, Pa., 1933, 4 In...*illus*	138
Coaster, Forest Rose Beer, Lancaster Brewing Co., Red Letters, Lancaster, Ohio, 1934, 4¼ In.*illus*	115
Coaster, Old Reading Beer, The Old Reading Brewery, Covered Wagon Shape, 1945, 4¼ In. *illus*	18
Coaster, Star Beer, Penn Star Brewing Co., Red & Blue, Lancaster, Pa., 1933, 4¼ In...*illus*	81
Coaster, Stroh's Imperial Wurzburger Beer, Crest, Lion, Blue, Detroit, 1910, 4¼ In......*illus*	40
Crate, After A Shave Use Ma-Le-Na, Cures Cuts, Chafes, Sores, Wood, 9 x 10 In.	60
Dispenser, Croome Hunt Whiskey, Pointed Lid, Round Body, Faucet, Circle Base, 27 In.......	265
Dispenser, Fowler's Cherry Smash Syrup, Cluster Of Cherries, White Ground, Early 1900s, 15 In.*illus*	1815
Dispenser, Grape Kola, Lid, 5 Cents, Grapes, Counter.....................................*illus*	630
Dispenser, Hires Root Beer, Metal Lid & Spigot, White Ground, Black & Red Text........*illus*	633
Dispenser, Syrup, Ward's Orange Crush, Ceramic, Figural Pump, Painted Base, 15 x 10 x 10 In.*illus*	1560
Dispenser, Zipp's, Fountain Drink, Barrel Shape, Glass Container, 16 In.....................	585
Display, Beeman's Pepsin Gum, 20 Sealed Packs, Box, American Chicle Co., 1936, 3½ x 3 x 4 In.	1025
Display, Bobby Lee Hats For Boys, Papier-Mache, Painted, c.1930, 11 x 10 In................	649
Display, Gainsborough Hair Net, Wood, Counter, Early 1900s, 17¼ x 17¾ In.	156
Display, Keen Kutter, Shears & Scissors, Wood, Glass, Vertical, 16 x 16 x 31 In.	2400
Display, Kleenex Tissues, Light-Up Wood Case, Rotates, 12¼ x 12⅝ x 5¼ In.	281
Display, Kotex, Stand, Tin, Square Top, Arch Shape Base, c.1920, 25 x 20 x 17 In.........*illus*	303
Display, Pabst Blue Ribbon Beer, Popular Prices, Bartender, Cast Metal, 14½ x 13 x 4 In......*illus*	450
Display, Philip Morris Cigarettes, Bellboy, Plate, Standing, Cardboard, 19 x 44 In. ......*illus*	330
Display, Stanley Works, Hinged Back Door, Wood, Heart Trademark, 16 x 12 x 19½ In.	240
Display, Steiff, Brown Bear, Stuffed, Standing, Red Collar, 50 In. ....*illus*	438
Display, Steiff, Mountain, Cabin, 14 Animals, Automaton, 49 x 42 x 27 In.................	1375
Display, Winchester, Junior Rifle Corps, Window, Wood Frame, 42 x 24 In..................*illus*	492
Dolls are listed in the Doll category.	
Door Push, Red Rose Tea, Is Good Tea, Porcelain, Red Ground, White Letters, 9¼ x 3 In...	425
Fans are listed in the Fan category.	
Figure, Kool-Aid Man, Red, Standing, Interior Tray, Plastic, 35 In............................*illus*	120
Figure, RCA, Nipper, Seated, Black & White, Chalkware, 1900s, 14½ In....................*illus*	594
Firkin, Mayflower, Cheddar Cheese, Bentwood, Lid, Mammoths, Red Paint, 17 x 20 In........	201
Glass, Moxie, Soda Fountain, Orange Band, Boston, Box, 4⅜ x 2⅝ In., 6 Piece	495
Jar, Zatek Chocolate Billets, Country Store Display, Dome Lid, Pittsburgh, Pa., 17 x 7 x 7 In.	360
Jug, M.E. Johnson, Wholesale Liquor Dealer, Derby, Conn., Stoneware, 1800s, 15½ In. *illus*	531
Lamps are listed in the Lamp category.	
Lunch Boxes are listed in the Lunch Box category.	
Mannequin, Lee, Child, Wearing Overalls, White Shirt, Plastic, c.1960, 32 In.............*illus*	531

Advertising mirrors of all sizes are listed here. Pocket mirrors range in size from 1½ to 5 inches in diameter. Most of these mirrors were given away as advertising promotions and include the name of the company in the design.

Mirror, DuBelle Grape Juice, Woman In Green Dress, Oval, 2¾ In..............................	276
Mirror, Kist Soda Pop, Did You Get Kist Today! Orange Lips, Reverse Painted, 11¾ In.........	192
Mirror, Van Houten's Cocoa, Silver Plate Frame, Handle, Art Nouveau, 10½ In..............	56
Mug, Drink Hires It Is Pure, Root Beer, Handle, Stoneware, 6¼ In., 9 Piece	71
Panel, Spencer & Calvert, Dealers, Marble Monuments, Carved, Maysville, Ky., 30 x 25 In...	344
Platter, Sparks' Perfect Health, Portrait, Ironstone, Frame, Late 1800s, 16 x 11 In.	938
Print, Chase & Sanborn, Old Fashioned New England Grocery, Abbott Graves, 1897, 28 x 40 In.	125
Rack, Plumb Axes, Metal, Counter, 7½ x 12 x 13 In.	150
Rack, Wrigley's Gum, 5 Compartments, c. 1920s, 5 x 17 x 4 In.	216

Advertising, Mannequin, Lee, Child, Wearing Overalls, White Shirt, Plastic, c.1960, 32 In.
$531

New Haven Auctions

Advertising, Scrubber, Salesman's Sample, Byberg Walnut Scrubber, Wood, Iron, 12 x 11 x 12 In.
$1,680

Chupp Auctions & Real Estate, LLC

Advertising, Shade, Ceiling Light, Kentucky Fried Chicken, Brown & White, Glass, 10 In., Pair
$523

Apple Tree Auction Center

Advertising, Sign, Adams Laundry, Curved Top, Hanging Sadiron, 12 x 14½ In.
$509

Hartzell's Auction Gallery Inc.

The First Cereal Premium
Kellogg's offered the first cereal premium in 1909, the Funny Jungleland Moving Pictures Booklet, available with the purchase of two boxes of Kellogg's Corn Flakes.

Advertising, Sign, Bar, Jim Beam, Light-Up, Black Ground, White & Gold Text, Metal Legs, 25 x 18½ In.
$69

Donley Auctions

Advertising, Sign, Borden, Ice Cream, Elsie The Cow, Yellow Daisy, White Ground, 24 x 36 In.
$230

Donley Auctions

Advertising, Sign, Buzz Buzz Electric, Cartoon, Bumblebee, Tin, P.D. Eller, 1900s, 24¼ x 29 In. $666

Fontaine's Auction Gallery

Advertising, Sign, Columbia Grafonola, Yellow, Tin, Chas. W. Norton, Farmington, Maine, 17⅝ x 23⅝ In. $978

Donley Auctions

Advertising, Sign, Disston, Stay Sharp Longer, Hand Saws, Cardboard, Frame, 12 x 16 In. $90

Chupp Auctions & Real Estate, LLC

Advertising, Sign, H.P. Hood & Son, Milk & Cream, Delivery Truck Shape, Die Cut Steel, 14 x 26¾ In. $338

Rich Penn Auctions

Advertising, Sign, Rocking Horse Inn, Wood, Painted, Blue & Red, White Ground, 38 x 14 In. $216

White's Auctions

Advertising, Sign, Sunbeam Bread, Stays Fresher Longer, Tin, Embossed, Red, Yellow Border, 1957, 29 x 11 In. $476

White's Auctions

Advertising, Sign, The Saw That Made Henry Disston Famous, Tin, Frame, 13¼ x 9½ In. $1,860

Chupp Auctions & Real Estate, LLC

Advertising, Tin, Biscuit, Huntley & Palmers, Gilt, Javanese, c.1900, 6¼ x 6¼ x 6¾ In. $840

Morphy Auctions

Advertising, Tin, Biscuit, Huntley & Palmers, Toby Mug, Embossed, Multicolor, 7 In. $180

Bertoia Auctions

Salt & Pepper Shakers are listed in the Salt & Pepper category.

Scales are listed in the Scale category.

Scrubber, Salesman's Sample, Byberg Walnut Scrubber, Wood, Iron, 12 x 11 x 12 In... *illus*	1680
Seed Counter, Sherer, Oak, Tag, Salesman's Sample, 18 x 5 x 7 In..........................	7800
Shade, Ceiling Light, Kentucky Fried Chicken, Brown & White, Glass, 10 In., Pair .... *illus*	523
Sign, Adams Laundry, Curved Top, Hanging Sadiron, 12 x 14 ½ In............................. *illus*	509
Sign, Anisetta Evangelisti Liquore, Monkey, Litho, C. Biscaretti Di Ruffia, Frame, 1925, 31 x 23 In..	688
Sign, Autys Royal Chocolatier, Wrought Iron, 1800s, 26 x 11 In., Pair............................	1188
Sign, Banner, North Shore RR Destinations, Lake Bluff, Highwood, Mundelein, Coated Canvas..	590
Sign, Bar, Jim Beam, Light-Up, Black Ground, White & Gold Text, Metal Legs, 25 x 18½ In...... *illus*	69
Sign, Bastine's Pure Flavoring Extracts, Black, Silver Text, Frame, 35 x 28 In.	813
Sign, Blue Ribbon Saw, Cardboard, Simonds, Frame, 10 ½ x 13 ¾ In.	228
Sign, Borden, Ice Cream, Elsie The Cow, Yellow Daisy, White Ground, 24 x 36 In. .... *illus*	230
Sign, Budweiser, Draft Beer, Red Ground, Light-Up, Gilt Base, 17 x 10¾ x 3 ½ In.	780
Sign, Bull Durham Smoking Tobacco, Cabin Scene, Figures, 19¾ x 24 ½ In..........................	51
Sign, Buy The Yellow Book, Howard Ainslee & Co., 1897, 13 ½ x 18 In.	188
Sign, Buzz Buzz Electric, Cartoon, Bumblebee, Tin, P.D. Eller, 1900s, 24 ¼ x 29 In. ...... *illus*	666
Sign, Camel Lights, Cigarettes Sold Here, White Ground, Wall Mount, 36 x 18 x 6 In.	316
Sign, Cavanaugh's Wonder Colic Remedy, Embossed, Tin Litho, Baltimore Sign Co., 13 x 20 In.....	349
Sign, Columbia Grafonola, Yellow, Tin, Chas. W. Norton, Farmington, Maine, 17⅝ x 23⅝ In. ..... *illus*	978
Sign, Disston, Stay Sharp Longer, Hand Saws, Cardboard, Frame, 12 x 16 In. .... *illus*	90
Sign, Dr Pepper, Good For Life!, Tin Over Wood, Yellow, Red, Black, 2-Sided, 12 x 27 In.......	1535
Sign, Drink Red Rock Cola, Bottle, Yellow & White Text, 22 x 14 In., 2-Sided	316
Sign, Dubonnet, The Perfect Cigar, Man & Woman, c.1928, 44 x 40 In.	469
Sign, E.H. Ervin Livery & Feed Stable, Reverse Painted, Foil, Frame, 16 x 21 In.	3438
Sign, Garfield & Rosen Inc., Wholesale Shoes, Metal, Black, Early 1900s, 32 x 27 In............	286
Sign, Gehe Im Bally Schuh, Go In Bally Shoes, Red Stripe, Yellow Text, Morach, Frame, 55 x 41 In.....	100
Sign, General Electric, Kitchen Appliances, Blue Ground, Neon, 57 ½ x 30 x 9 ¼ In.	3840
Sign, George Nelson & Associates, Bubbles Lamp, Howard Miller, Fiberglass, Metal Frame, 30 In..	563
Sign, H.P. Hood & Son, Milk & Cream, Delivery Truck Shape, Die Cut Steel, 14 x 26¾ In..... *illus*	338
Sign, Havana Cigars, Importer, Hotel Keepers & Trade Supplied, Est. 1853, 3 Parts, 18 x 77 In.....	615
Sign, Hoffman House Pure Rye, Glass, Painted, H.F. Corbin Co., Cincinnati, Gilt Frame, 14 x 12 In.	900
Sign, Indiana Hoosier Grain Drill, Board, Red Paint, c.1880, 8 x 66 In..........................	1200
Sign, Kodak, Verichrome Pan, Yellow, Red, Black, Light-Up, 1950s, 10 x 3 ¾ x 3 ¾ In..........	316
Sign, Luther Quality Vises, Cardboard, Display Frame, 6 ½ x 10 ½ In............................	150
Sign, Neapolitan Deluxe Ice Cream, Menu, Painted, Parcel Gilt, Rodwell Sign Co., 22 x 10 In. ...	500
Sign, Pennsylvania Fire Insurance Co., Chromolitho, Tin, Wells & Hope Co., Late 1800s, 19 x 27 In. ...	5938
Sign, Perrier Mineral Water, Green, Purple, Litho, Andy Warhol, Frame, c.1983, 17 x 23 In.	450
Sign, Pilgrim Fathers, 10 Cent Cigar That Merits The Name It Bears, Tin, 19 x 27 In.	900
Sign, Pingree Composite Shoe, Calvert Litho Co., Late 1800s, 54 x 42 In.	316
Sign, PKZ, Burger-Kehl, Man In Black, Charles Loupot, c.1921, 49 x 24 In....................	8125
Sign, R.G. Sullivan's Cigar, 7-20-4, Red Ground, Porcelain, Early 1900s, 10 x 23 In............	563
Sign, Rocking Horse Inn, Wood, Painted, Blue & Red, White Ground, 38 x 14 In.......... *illus*	216
Sign, Roland T. Allen, Real Estate, Licensed Broker, Black Ground, 1930s, 17 x 51 In.	84
Sign, Saw It With A Simonds Saw, Hand Saw, Cardboard, Frame, 10 x 12 In.	102
Sign, Schlitz Beer, Globe Logo, Trade Pure Mark, Gilt, Cardboard Back, 28 x 35 x 2 In........	150
Sign, Sioux Tools, Standard The World Over, Albertson & Co. Inc., 13 In...................	210
Sign, Squibb Drug Co., Milk Of Magnesia Dental Cream, Cardboard, 1920s, 11 x 21 In.	285
Sign, Stanley, Green End Rules, Cardboard, Hand Tools, Display Case, 27 x 37 In................	600
Sign, Sunbeam Bread, Stays Fresher Longer, Tin, Embossed, Red, Yellow Border, 1957, 29 x 11 In.*illus*	476
Sign, Sweet Sixteen Cigarettes, Stecher Litho Co., Frame, c.1910, 22 x 18 In......................	484
Sign, The Berkeley Shop, Hanging, Mahogany Interior, Painted Steel Logo, c.2000s, 26 x 33 In...	349
Sign, The Saw That Made Henry Disston Famous, Tin, Frame, 13 ¼ x 9 ½ In...............*illus*	1860
Sign, Toni Kola, 2 Parrots Holding Bottle, Robert Wolff, 1935, 78 x 50 In.	1690
Sign, Vermouth Martini, Man Holding 2 Bottles, Leonetto Cappiello, c.1905, 38 x 26 In.	1690
Sign, Wayne Feeds, Metal, Painted, Red Ground, 14 x 16 In.	413
Sign, Winchester, Junior Rifle Corps, 2 Boys Kneeling, Red Text, Wood Frame, 1923, 42 x 24 In.	492
Sign, Wings Cigarette, Die Cut, Display, Zoe Mozert, Multicolor Hat, c.1930, 36 x 36 In.........	826

Thermometers are listed in the Thermometer category.

Advertising, Tobacco Cutter, Dodge City Wholesale Grocer Co., Cast, Guillotine Type, Embossed, 9 x 15 In.
$295

Soulis Auctions

Advertising, Tobacco Cutter, P. Lorillard's Tomahawk, Black Paint, Red & Gold Pinstripes, 19 x 6 x 4 In.
$185

Morphy Auctions

Advertising, Tray, Jersey Creme, The Perfect Drink, Portrait Facing Left, Hanging Holes, Tin, 12 In.
$300

Chupp Auctions & Real Estate, LLC

Watch Out for Flour Dust
Cadwallader C. Washburn started the Minneapolis Milling Company in 1856. In 1880 his mills and five others were destroyed when flour dust caused an explosion. He immediately built a new, modern mill and won awards for his Gold Medal flour.

A

Agata, Creamer, Pink To White, Cream
Reeded Handle, Flared, Square Mouth,
4½ In.
$282

Jaremos

Alabaster, Bust, Dante's Beatrice,
Gold Paint, Shaped & Paneled Base,
10 x 10 x 5 In.
$585

Thomaston Place Auction Galleries

Alabaster, Bust, Woman, Smiling,
Head, Shoulder, Prof. G. Besje, 1800s,
19 In.
$600

Cottone Auctions

Advertising tin cans or canisters were first used commercially in the
United States in 1819 and were called tins. Today the word *tin* is used by
most collectors to describe many types of containers, including food tins,
biscuit boxes, roly poly tobacco containers, gunpowder cans, talcum
powder sprinkle-top cans, cigarette flat-fifty tins, and more. Beer Cans are listed in
their own category. Things made of undecorated tin are listed under Tinware.

Tin, Biscuit, Huntley & Palmers, Gilt, Javanese, c.1900, 6¼ x 6¼ x 6¾ In.............*illus*	840
Tin, Biscuit, Huntley & Palmers, Toby Mug, Embossed, Multicolor, 7 In.............*illus*	180
Tin, Carr's Biscuits, Bus Shape, Double-Decker, Chad Valley, 8 In.	300
Tin, Parnall & Sons, Red & Yellow, Curved Top, 1800s, 9 In.	63
Tin, Popper's Ace Cigar, 10 Cents, Biplane, Cube Shape, Lithograph............................	420
Tin, Westminster Whiskey, Lithograph, Chas. W. Shonk Co., Chicago, Ill., c.1890, 37 x 25½ In.....	2250

Advertising tip trays are decorated metal trays less than 5 inches in
diameter. They were placed on the table or counter to hold either the bill or
the coins that were left as a tip. Change receivers could be made of glass,
plastic, or metal. They were kept on the counter near the cash register and
held the money passed back and forth by the cashier. Related items may be listed in
the Advertising category under Change Receiver.

Tip Tray, I Just Love Moxie, Don't You?, Woman, Tin Lithograph, 6 in.	330
Tip Tray, Sparrow's Chocolates, Girl On Chair, Tin, Fluted Corners, 8 in.	600
Tobacco Cutter, Chew Flat Iron Plug, Scotten Dillon Co., 8 x 15¾ In.	360
Tobacco Cutter, Dodge City Wholesale Grocer Co., Cast, Guillotine Type, Embossed, 9 x 15 In.. *illus*	295
Tobacco Cutter, P. Lorillard's Tomahawk, Black Paint, Red & Gold Pinstripes, 19 x 6 x 4 In....... *illus*	185
Tray, Jersey Creme, The Perfect Drink, Portrait Facing Left, Hanging Holes, Tin, 12 In.*illus*	300
Tray, Loux Ice Cream, Children, Cat, Dog, Tin, Carl Hirschberg, American Art Works, 13 x 13 In..	840
Tray, Zipp's Cherri-O, Bird, On Branch, Glass, White & Red Text, 12 In.	615
Tumbler, 7Up, Green Glass, Cylindrical, Pinched Sides, White Logo, Bubbles, c.1950, 5 In. .	35

AGATA

Agata glass was made by Joseph Locke of the New England Glass Company
of Cambridge, Massachusetts, after 1885. A metallic stain was applied to
New England Peachblow, which the company called Wild Rose, and the mottled design
characteristic of agata appeared. There are a few known items made of opaque green
with the mottled finish.

Creamer, Pink To White, Cream Reeded Handle, Flared, Square Mouth, 4½ In. ....*illus*	282
Finger Bowl, Pink To White, Ruffled Rim, Purple Spots, 2½ x 5¼ In.	270
Toothpick Holder, Peachblow, Crimped Rim, 4½ x 2½ In.	179

AKRO AGATE

Akro Agate glass was founded in Akron, Ohio, in 1911 and moved to
Clarksburg, West Virginia, in 1914. The company made marbles and toys.
In the 1930s it began making other products, including vases, lamps, flowerpots, candlesticks, and children's dishes. Most of the glass is marked with a crow flying through the
letter *A.* The company was sold to Clarksburg Glass Co. in 1951. Akro Agate marbles
are listed in this book in the Marble category.

Flowerpot, Orange, Marbleized, 2 In..	16
Vase, Raised Lily Pattern, Blue & White, Slag Glass, 4½ In...	15

ALABASTER

Alabaster is a very soft form of gypsum, a stone that resembles marble. It
was often carved into vases or statues in Victorian times. There are alabaster
carvings being made even today.

Bust, Dante Alighieri, Wreath Crown, Cream Ground, Italy, Late 1800s, 9¾ In.....................	344

Alabaster, Figure, Crouching Lion, Pigment & Gilding, Peruvian Huamanga, 3 ½ x 5 In., Pair
$561

Neue Auctions

TIP
To clean alabaster first dust with a soft brush. Then wipe with turpentine or dry-cleaning fluid. Do not use water. Alabaster dissolves in water. Some people like to polish it with paste furniture wax, but the wax will eventually yellow slightly.

Alabaster, Figure, Woman, Nude, Reclining, Grapes, Alessandro Michelotti, Italy, Early 1900s, 7 x 20 x 6 In.
$1,815

Fontaine's Auction Gallery

Alabaster, Fountain, 3 Tiers, Carved, Bowl, Flowers, Centerpiece, Neoclassical, Italy, 17 ¾ x 8 ½ In.
$281

Auctions at Showplace, NYC

Alabaster, Lamp, Resting Boy, Globe Shape, White Shade, Column Post, Marble Base, 33 In.
$633

Stevens Auction Co.

TIP
Do not put an alabaster figure or vase outside. It is softer than marble and will eventually fall apart if exposed to rain.

Alabaster, Planter, Carved, Maiden, Flowers, Cream Ground, Italy, c.1900s, 8 ¼ x 14 In., Pair
$1,536

Neal Auction Company

A

Aluminum, Cocktail Shaker, Bullet Shape, Copper Plated, c.1930, 14 x 3 In. $910

Wright

Aluminum, Desk Organizer, 2 Tiers, West Engineering Co., Virginia, c.1950, 8½ x 10½ x 14½ In. $688

Wright

Aluminum, Platter, Serving, Fish Shape, Base Signed, Bruce Cox, 2 x 22½ x 9 In. $94

Auctions at Showplace, NYC

Aluminum, Sculpture, Bars XXVI, Bolts, Nuts, Signed, Larry Mohr, 1983, 21 x 32 x 13 In. $563

Wright

Bust, Dante's Beatrice, Gold Paint, Shaped & Paneled Base, 10 x 10 x 5 In. .... *illus*	585
Bust, Woman, Bonnet, Green Marble Pedestal Base, Early 1900s, 15 x 12 x 8½ In.	352
Bust, Woman, Side View, Curly Hair, Rectangular Base, Late 1800s, 11 x 10 x 4 In.	250
Bust, Woman, Smiling, Head, Shoulder, Prof. G. Besje, 1800s, 19 In. .... *illus*	600
Bust, Woman, Wearing Hat, Carved, Socle Base, Signed, C. Cipriani, 1900s, 21 In.	281
Figure, Crouching Lion, Pigment & Gilding, Peruvian Huamanga, 3½ x 5 In., Pair.... *illus*	561
Figure, Woman, Nude, Reclining, Grapes, Alessandro Michelotti, Italy, Early 1900s, 7 x 20 x 6 In.*illus*	1815
Figure, Woman, Seated On Rock, Mounted Light Post, Incised Flowers, 24½ In.	320
Figure, Woman, Seminude, Standing, Classical Greek, Plinth Base, 12¾ In.	219
Fountain, 3 Tiers, Carved, Bowl, Flowers, Centerpiece, Neoclassical, Italy, 17¾ x 8½ In. ..... *illus*	281
Group, 2 Children, Sitting, Reading Book, Signed, Auguste Moreau, 24½ In.	4538
Lamp, Domed Shade, Tall, Slender, Circular Base, Standard, Continental, 1900s, 27 x 13 In. Diam.	480
Lamp, Fluted, White, Bell Shape, Contrasting Base, 26 x 11 In.	488
Lamp, Resting Boy, Globe Shape, White Shade, Column Post, Marble Base, 33 In. .... *illus*	633
Planter, Carved, Maiden, Flowers, Cream Ground, Italy, c.1900s, 8¼ x 14 In., Pair ..... *illus*	1536
Plaque, Mother & Child, Curved Top, Brown & Black Frame, Italy, 1800s, 18 x 17 In..........	281
Seal, Dragon, Pierced, Carved, Chinese, 6 x 3 x 3 In., Pair.......................................	61
Tazza, Greek Key, 3 Ram's Heads, Tripod Legs, Claw Feet, Circular Base, Late 1800s, 10 x 9 In.	531
Tray, Carved, Cream Ground, Rectangular, 19 x 12 In...	688
Urn, Neoclassical Style, Lobed, Mask Handles, Pedestal Base, Egg & Dart Trim, 15 x 17 In. .	985

ALUMINUM

Aluminum was more expensive than gold or silver until the 1850s. Chemists learned how to refine bauxite to get aluminum. Jewelry and other small objects were made of the valuable metal until 1914, when an inexpensive smelting process was invented. The aluminum collected today dates from the 1930s through the 1950s. Hand-hammered pieces are the most popular.

Ashtray, Circletron, Robert J. Gargiule, Jenfred-Ware, c.1950, 1¾ x 6¼ In.	625
Bowl, Hammered, Wavy Triangular Shape, Tripod Triangle Feet, Marked, 4 x 11¾ In.........	75
Cocktail Shaker, Bullet Shape, Copper Plated, c.1930, 14 x 3 In. .... *illus*	910
Desk Organizer, 2 Tiers, West Engineering Co., Virginia, c.1950, 8½ x 10½ x 14½ In.......*illus*	688
Lamp, Bakelite, Frosted Glass, Brass, Pattyn Products, c.1935, 20 x 8 In................................	4160
Pitcher, Round Lobed Body, Leafy Handle, Argental Handwrought, Cellini-Craft, 8½ x 7 In.........	40
Planter, Hanging, Cast Bowl, Ornament, Woven Cords, 2-Wheel Shape, Don Drumm, 11½ x 16 In..	130
Platter, Serving, Fish Shape, Base Signed, Bruce Cox, 2 x 22½ x 9 In........................... *illus*	94
Sculpture, Bars XXVI, Bolts, Nuts, Signed, Larry Mohr, 1983, 21 x 32 x 13 In. .... *illus*	563
Tray, Serving, Gilt, Brass, 2 Crab Handles, Herco, S.A., Mexico, 1950s, 24½ x 16 In. ..... *illus*	469
Urn, Greek Key Border, Black Paint, Square Base, 26 x 21 In., Pair.......................................	173
Vase, Flower, Acrylic, Shiro Kuramata, Ishimaru Co., Japan, 1989, 8 x 3 x 3 In.	1875
Wastebasket, Enamel, Black & Yellow, Plastic Cording, Dutch, c.1930, 14 x 10 x 9 In...........	938

AMBER, *see Jewelry category.*

AMBER GLASS

Amber glass is the name of any glassware with the proper yellow-brown shading. It was a popular color just after the Civil War and many pressed glass pieces were made of amber glass. Depression glass of the 1930s–1950s was also made in shades of amber glass. Other pieces may be found in the Depression Glass, Pressed Glass, and other glass categories. All types are being reproduced.

Bowl, Moser Style, Centerpiece, Pastoral Landscape, Courting Couple, 1900s, 13 In......*illus*   344

AMBERINA

Amberina, a two-toned glassware, was originally made from 1883 to about 1900. It was patented by Joseph Locke of the New England Glass Company but was also made by other companies and is still being made. The glass shades from red to amber. Similar pieces of glass may be found in the

Baccarat, Libbey, Plated Amberina, and other categories. Glass shaded from blue to amber is called *Blue Amberina* or *Bluerina*.

Bowl, Swirl, Gold Flowers, Gilt Crane, 11 x 10 In.	230
Pickle Castor, Barrel Shape, Panel Optic, Quadruple Plate Stand, c.1880, 7 In.	508

AMERICAN DINNERWARE, *see Dinnerware.*

AMETHYST GLASS

Amethyst glass is any of the many glasswares made in the dark purple color of the gemstone amethyst. Included in this category are many pieces made in the nineteenth and twentieth centuries. Very dark pieces are called *black amethyst.*

Bobeche, Scalloped, 8 Hanging Prisms, 4 In., Pair	99
Compote, Molded, Ribbed, Flared Lip, Knop Stem, Ohio, Late 19th Century, 8¾ x 10 In.	157
Dresser Box, Hinged Lid, Round, White & Gold Enamel, 6-Point Star, Flowers, 4½ x 6¾ In.. *illus*	96
Tantalus, Hinged Lid, Black Exterior, Decanter, 6 Shot Glasses, 12½ x 10½ x 8 In.	157
Wine Rinser, Double Lip, Ground Pontil, Early 19th Century, 3½ x 4¾ In., Pair	64

AMPHORA *pieces are listed in the Teplitz category.*

ANDIRONS *and related fireplace items are included in the Fireplace category.*

ANIMAL TROPHY

Animal trophies, such as stuffed animals (taxidermy), rugs made of animal skins, and other similar collectibles made from animal, fish, or bird parts, are listed in this category. Collectors should be aware of the endangered species laws that make it illegal to buy and sell some of these items. Any eagle feathers, many types of pelts or rugs (such as leopard), ivory, rhinoceros horn, and many forms of tortoiseshell can be confiscated by the government. Related trophies may be found in the Fishing category. Ivory items may be found in the Scrimshaw or Ivory categories.

Bird, Taxidermy, Vitrine, Glass Dome, Black Paint, Wood Base, Victorian, 1800s, 23½ In.	2794
Buffalo Horn, On Plaque, 5¾ x 17¾ x 5½ In.	63
Fish, Blue Marlin, Full Body, Fiberglass, Iron Strap Hanger, 90 x 28 In.	468
Jackrabbit, Head, Taxidermy, 2-Prong Antlers, On Display Board, Wall Mount	136
Moose Antlers, Mounted On Wood, Shield Shape, 50 x 35 In. *illus*	197
Owl, Side Face, Perched, Full Body Mount, Taxidermy, 1900s, 18¼ In. *illus*	563
Rug, Zebra Skin, Brown & White, Backside, Black Nose, Tail, 122 x 64 In.	1375
Sailfish, Blue Fin, Taxidermy, 1900s, 41 x 72 In. *illus*	132
Sawfish Bill, Teeth, Taxidermy, Teeth, Stand, Base, 27¾ In.	594
Sea Turtle, Figured Shell, Head & Appendages, Taxidermy, c.1900s, 28 x 24 In. *illus*	1715
Texas Longhorn, Mounted, Tooled Leather Center, Brass Tacks, 61 In.	156
Tortoise, Polished Blond Carapace, Taxidermy Figure, 19 x 16½ In.	2304
Wild Boar Head, Brown Hair, Teeth, Eyes & Ears, Taxidermy, 22 In. *illus*	254
Wild Boar Head, Hair, Eyes, Teeth, Tongue, Wood Board, Bracket, 21 x 16 x 15 In.	115

ANIMATION ART

Animation art collectibles include cels that are painted drawings on celluloid needed to make animated cartoons shown in movie theaters or on TV. Hundreds of cels were made, then photographed in sequence to make a cartoon showing moving figures. Early examples made by the Walt Disney Studios are popular with collectors today. Original sketches used by the artists are also listed here. Modern animated cartoons are made using computer-generated pictures. Some of these are being produced as cels to be sold to collectors. Other cartoon art is listed in Comic Art and Disneyana.

Cel, Disney, Jiminy Cricket, Top Hat, Umbrella, Butterfly, California, c.1950, 13¼ x 12 In.	2151
Cel, Mickey Mouse, Armadillo, Courvoisier Background, Frame, 1943, 7 x 7 In. *illus*	3120

Aluminum, Tray, Serving, Gilt, Brass, 2 Crab Handles, Herco, S.A., Mexico, 1950s, 24½ x 16 In.
$469

Hindman

Amber Glass, Bowl, Moser Style, Centerpiece, Pastoral Landscape, Courting Couple, 1900s, 13 In.
$344

Lion and Unicorn

Amethyst Glass, Dresser Box, Hinged Lid, Round, White & Gold Enamel, 6-Point Star, Flowers, 4½ x 6¾ In.
$96

Woody Auction

Animal Trophy, Moose Antlers, Mounted On Wood, Shield Shape, 50 x 35 In.
$197

Apple Tree Auction Center

A

Animal Trophy, Owl, Side Face, Perched, Full Body Mount, Taxidermy, 1900s, 18¼ In.
$563

Hindman

Animal Trophy, Sailfish, Blue Fin, Taxidermy, 1900s, 41 x 72 In.
$132

Garth's Auctioneers & Appraisers

Animal Trophy, Sea Turtle, Figured Shell, Head & Appendages, Taxidermy, c.1900s, 28 x 24 In.
$1,715

White's Auctions

Animal Trophy, Wild Boar Head, Brown Hair, Teeth, Eyes & Ears, Taxidermy, 22 In.
$254

White's Auctions

Cel, Mushroom Dancers, Fantasia, Courvoisier Setup, Walt Disney, Frame, 1940, 7 x 6 In....... *illus*	2160
Cel, Pinocchio, Ink, Painted, Courvoisier Ground, Jiminy Cricket, Walt Disney, 1940, 12 x 13 In....	1440
Cel, Snow White, Watercolor, Woodgrain Ground, Disney, 14 x 12 In............... *illus*	2500
Storyboard, 12 Faces, Jack Skellington, Ornate Black Shadowbox, c.1990, 16 x 13 x 3 In....	1200

Anna Pottery **ANNA POTTERY**

Anna Pottery was started in Anna, Illinois, in 1859 by Cornwall and Wallace Kirkpatrick. They made many types of utilitarian wares, bricks, drain tiles, and giftware. The most collectible pieces made by the pottery are the pig-shaped bottles and jugs with special inscriptions, applied animals, and figures. The pottery closed in 1894.

Flask, Pig Shape, Railroad Map, Black Hills, Chestnut Brown, c.1880, 6 In............... *illus*	6600
Inkwell, Frog, Wheel Thrown, Stoneware, 1879, 3½ x 2½ In...............	6000

APPLE PEELERS *are listed in the Kitchen category under Peeler, Apple.*

ARCHITECTURAL

Architectural antiques include a variety of collectibles, usually very large, that have been removed from buildings. Hardware, backbars, doors, paneling, and even old bathtubs are now wanted by collectors. Pieces of the Victorian, Art Nouveau, and Art Deco styles are in greatest demand.

Box Block, Post Office, 4 Compartments, Buzzer, United Metal Box Co., Brooklyn, 18 x 20 In.	115
Bracket, Earthenware, Neoclassical Style, Wall Mount, Multicolor, 12 x 13 x 8½ In., 4 Piece	1020
Bracket, Wall, Giltwood, Eagle, Spread Wings, Early 1800s, 10 x 8 In.	3936
Column, Terra-Cotta, 3 Piece, Multicolor, Flat Base, Early 1900s, 35 x 14 In............... *illus*	118
Column, Wood, Carved, Capital, Sculptural Base, Flower, 11 x 11 x 11 In.	219
Corbel, Plaster, Face, Figural, Carved & Painted, c.1880s............... *illus*	127
Corbel, White Marble, Carved, 10½ x 7 x 5½ In., Pair	156
Door Handle, Brass, Squid Shape, 6 Tentacles, Ceramic Inlay, Mexico, c.1960, 11 x 8 x 1 In...... *illus*	1040
Door, Oak, Iron, Grate, Horse Stable, Brown Paint, Early 1900s, 17½ x 37 In.	958
Door, Parcel Gilt, Painted, Cherub, Flower Urn, Green Ground, 1800s, 84 x 22 In., Pair......	3125
Door, Wood, Painted Pine, Swinging, Saloon, Shutter, Philadelphia, 1800s, 58¾ x 23 In....	48
Doorknocker, Brass, Figural, Sperm Whale, Brown, 8 x 7 In...............	549
Doorknocker, Bronze, Dragonfly Shape, Textured Detail, c.1970s, 7 x 7½ In.	370
Doorknocker, Bronze, Woman's Hand, Holding Ball, Raised Ring & Cuff, Victorian, 5 x 2 In.....	190
Doorknocker, Iron, Right Hand, Holding Ball, Ornate Background, 8¼ x 5½ In....... *illus*	181
Element, Cast Bronze, Neoclassical, Doorway Pediment, Grecian Urn, 1800s, 20 x 67 x 4 In........	878
Element, Cast Iron, Wall, Horse Head Shape, 15 x 7 In., Pair..............	704
Element, Wood, Griffins, Scrollwork, 1800s, 14 In., Pair...............	1280
Fan Light, Transom, Leaded, Semi-Elliptical, Central Floret, Glass Pane, 18 x 75 In...........	410
Faucet, Brass, Bathroom, Swan Shape, Gilt, Brass, Antarctica, 14 x 10 In.	63
Figure, Eagle, Cast Metal, Mount, Open Wings, Federal Shield, 42 x 13 In.	207
Finial, Cast Zinc, Eagle, Spread Wings, M.J. Frand Co., Camden, N.J., Late 1800s, 19½ In. ..	750
Fragment, Bronze, Cast Iron, Blue Glaze, George Mann Niedecken, Illinois, 13 x 8 x 2⅝ In.	1375
Fragment, Cast Cement, Art Deco, Coca-Cola Bottle, Leaf Surround, c.1920, 27 x 23 x 6 In.	1404
Fragment, Giltwood, Carved, Lion's Head, Plaque, Paws Overhanging Edge, 1700s, 12 x 8 x 4 In.	1755
Fragment, Wood, Bird, Hanging Hook, Circular, 9¼ x 10⅞ x ¾ In.	594
Gate, Wrought Iron, Urn Finials, Scrolled Arch, Black, Late 1800s, 44½ x 46½ In...... *illus*	2541
Mantel, Bird's-Eye Maple, Gilt, Bronze, Mounted, Beveled Glass, Late 1800s, 84 x 92 x 20 In........	1063
Mantel, Cypress, Painted, White, Shaped Shelf, Brackets, Blocked Pilasters, 47½ In.	475
Mantel, Marble, Louis XV Style, Creamy White, Leafy Crest, Late 1800s, 43 x 52 In. ...... *illus*	5748
Mantel, Pine, Federal, Carved, Painted, Heart Design, 53½ x 64 In.	677
Mantel, White Marble, Baroque, Symmetrical Scrollwork, 32 x 11 x 3 In., Pair...............	234
Model, Es Propiedad, Alhambra, No. 58, Enrique Linares, Frame, 1800s, 13⅝ x 9 In.	1550
Model, Facade, Gilt, Railed Balcony, 2 Staircases, Multicolor, 43 x 107 In...............	1220
Model, House, Wood, Revolving Figures, Painted, c.1900s, 11 x 11 x 11 In...............	984

Animation Art, Cel, Mickey Mouse, Armadillo, Courvoisier Background, Frame, 1943, 7 x 7 In.
$3,120

Weiss Auctions

Animation Art, Cel, Mushroom Dancers, Fantasia, Courvoisier Setup, Walt Disney, Frame, 1940, 7 x 6 In.
$2,160

Weiss Auctions

Animation Art, Cel, Snow White, Watercolor, Woodgrain Ground, Disney, 14 x 12 In.
$2,500

Turner Auctions + Appraisals

Anna Pottery, Flask, Pig Shape, Railroad Map, Black Hills, Chestnut Brown, c.1880, 6 In.
$6,600

Crocker Farm, Inc.

Architectural, Column, Terra-Cotta, 3 Piece, Multicolor, Flat Base, Early 1900s, 35 x 14 In.
$118

Soulis Auctions

Architectural, Corbel, Plaster, Face, Figural, Carved & Painted, c.1880s
$127

White's Auctions

Architectural, Door Handle, Brass, Squid Shape, 6 Tentacles, Ceramic Inlay, Mexico, c.1960, 11 x 8 x 1 In.
$1,040

Wright

Architectural, Doorknocker, Iron, Right Hand, Holding Ball, Ornate Background, 8 1/4 x 5 1/2 In.
$181

Hartzell's Auction Gallery Inc.

Architectural, Gate, Wrought Iron, Urn Finials, Scrolled Arch, Black, Late 1800s, 44 1/2 x 46 1/2 In.
$2,541

Fontaine's Auction Gallery

Architectural, Mantel, Marble, Louis XV Style, Creamy White, Leafy Crest, Late 1800s, 43 x 52 In.
$5,748

Ahlers & Ogletree Auction Gallery

Architectural, Overmantel Mirror, Federal, Gilt, Neoclassical, Corinthian Columns, c.1800, 39 x 65 In.
$410

Thomaston Place Auction Galleries

Architectural, Pedestal, Oak, Gothic Style, Square Top, Tripod Legs, 13 x 13 x 44½ In.
$649

Copake Auction

Model, Well, Roof, Pulley, Crank, Bucket, Salesman's Sample, Wood Box, 13 x 12 x 10½ In.	320
Ornament, Carved Wood, Ribbon Crest, Fruit, Leaves, Vertical, Spain, 1900s, 48 In.	95
Overmantel Mirror, Brass, Sconce, Victorian, Bacchus, Embossed B & H, c.1890, 16 In.	131
Overmantel Mirror, Federal, Gilt, Neoclassical, Corinthian Columns, c.1800, 39 x 65 In. *illus*	410
Overmantel Mirror, Giltwood, Acanthus Wrapped Columns, Flower Heads, c.1825, 71 x 70 x 7 In.	4725
Overmantel Mirror, Reverse Panel, 2 Ships Battling, Pilasters, 1800s, 33 x 16 In.	270
Overmantel Mirror, Venetian, Etched, Applied Black Designs, Gilt Frame, 41½ x 60 In.	288
Panel, Glass, Fox, Standing, Art Deco, Etched, c.1935, 33 x 38 In.	469
Pedestal, Copper, Hammered, Cylindrical, Arts & Crafts, Religious Relief, 49¼ In.	540
Pedestal, Oak, Gothic Style, Square Top, Tripod Legs, 13 x 13 x 44½ In. *illus*	649
Remnant, Wood, Boiserie, Carved, Corn, Grape, Leaf, Naturalistic Motifs, 1800s, 22 In.	295
Screens are also listed in the Fireplace and Furniture categories.	
Shrine, Marble, White & Black, Gilt, Columns, Painted, Green Base, 1800s, 27 x 18 x 9 In.	1250
Tile, Roof, Dragon, Earthenware, Multicolor Glaze, Hand Modeled, 13 x 4 x 8 In., Pair	610
Tile, Wall Mount, Plaque, Female Figure, Late 1800s, 24½ x 48 In.	96
Valance, Metal, Scenic, Embossed, Over Door, 37 x 78 In. *illus*	512

AREQUIPA POTTERY

Arequipa Pottery was produced from 1911 to 1918 by the patients of the Arequipa Sanatorium in Marin County, north of San Francisco. The patients were trained by Frederick Hurten Rhead, who had worked at Roseville Pottery.

Vase, Light Blue Matte, Raised Brown Vine, Earthenware, 1911-18, 3½ x 4 In.	1430
Vase, Mottled Olive Green, Raised Scroll Band, Tapered Neck, Curved Base, 5 In.	960
Vase, Squat, Chocolate Brown Glaze, Curved Base, 5 In.	406
Vase, Squat, Green Matte Glaze, Eucalyptus, c.1915, 6¼ x 1½ In. *illus*	1046

ARGY-ROUSSEAU, *see G. Argy-Rousseau category.*

右田 ARITA

Arita is a port in Japan. Porcelain was made there from about 1616. Many types of decorations were used, including the popular Imari designs, which are listed under Imari in this book.

Bottle, Double Gourd, Blue & White, Crazing, 6 In.	42
Charger, Multicolor, Foo Dogs, Orange Ground, Blue & Iron Red Flowers On Exterior, 23 In.	875
Dish, Saucer, Multicolor Flower Ground, Scattered Medallions, 6-Character Mark, 8⅜ In.	384
Ewer, Blue & White, Flowers, Oval Body, Cup Shape Mouth, Footed, 17th Century, 10¼ In. *illus*	1764
Hibachi, Blue & White, Flowers, Butterflies, Flower Shape Vignettes, Gilt, Late 1800s, 13 x 16 In. *illus*	256
Hibachi, Blue & White, Landscape, Trees, Mountains, Late 19th Century, 8 x 8 In.	192
Hibachi, Blue & White, River Scene Vignettes, Sepia Accents, Late 1800s, 14½ x 20½ In.	1920
Plate, Blue & White, Landscape, Island, Tree, House, Cloud, Flying Birds, 6¼ In., 5 Piece	96
Plate, Blue & White, Phoenixes, Flowers, Ruyi Border, 6-Character Mark, 8½ In., 5 Piece	25
Plate, Blue Flower, Red Foo Dog, Scalloped Rim, Gilt, 6-Character Mark, 8 In., 4 Piece *illus*	210
Vase, Blue Flowers, White Ground, 2 Handles, 9⅜ In.	63
Vase, Bottle Shape, Blue & White, Deer, Trees, Bamboo, Mounted As Lamp, c.1800, 11¾ In.	677
Vase, Bottle, Faux Bois, Multicolor Medallions, Mounted As Lamp, Early 1900s, 26 x 12 In., Pair.	5500

ART DECO

Art Deco, or Art Moderne, a style started at the Paris Exposition of 1925, is characterized by linear, geometric designs. All types of furniture and decorative arts, jewelry, book bindings, and even games were designed in this style. Additional items may be found in the Furniture category or in various glass and pottery categories, etc.

Ashtray Stand, Belmont Rollodor, Chrome Rollers, Floor, Round Base, c.1930, 24 x 7 x 8 In.	156
Figurine, Gerdago Girl, Sitting, Holding Ball, Cast Metal, Painted, Marble Base, 8 In.	177
Group, Figural, White Metal, Girl, Hound, 1930s, 12 x 15¾ x 4½ In.	175
Lamp, Alabaster, Glass, Seated, Female Figure, Brass Ball Feet, J.B. Hirsch Gerdago, c.1950, 8 In. *illus*	360

Architectural, Valance, Metal, Scenic, Embossed, Over Door, 37 x 78 In.
$512

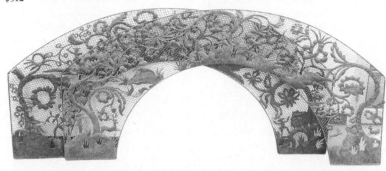

Nadeau's Auction Gallery

TIP
Screens for doors and windows were patented in 1882. The electric fan was invented in 1886.

Art Deco, Lamp, Alabaster, Glass, Seated, Female Figure, Brass Ball Feet, J.B. Hirsch Gerdago, c.1950, 8 In.
$360

Selkirk Auctioneers & Appraisers

TIP
A stained glass window is probably more stable than it looks. Small cracks in the glass, even a bowed window, are usually not a problem. Cracked solder joints between pieces of glass should be repaired.

Arequipa, Vase, Squat, Green Matte Glaze, Eucalyptus, c.1915, 6¼ x 1½ In.
$1,046

California Historical Design

Arita, Ewer, Blue & White, Flowers, Oval Body, Cup Shape Mouth, Footed, 17th Century, 10¼ In.
$1,764

Doyle

Arita, Hibachi, Blue & White, Flowers, Butterflies, Flower Shape Vignettes, Gilt, Late 1800s, 13 x 16 In.
$256

Alex Cooper Auctioneers

Arita, Plate, Blue Flower, Red Foo Dog, Scalloped Rim, Gilt, 6-Character Mark, 8 In., 4 Piece
$210

Leland Little Auctions

Art Deco, Tray, Reverse Painted Glass, Nickel Plated Steel, Lacquered Wood, c.1935, 2 x 18 x 12 In.
$1,063

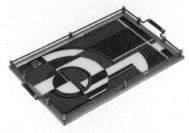

Wright

Arts & Crafts, Box, Pyrography, Carved, Painted, Flowers, c.1910, 14¾ x 7½ x 4 In.
$185

California Historical Design

A

Auto, Cabinet, Edison Mazda Super, Lamps, Porcelain, Hanging, 7 x 7 x 16 In.
$960

Chupp Auctions & Real Estate, LLC

Road Maps
The first automobile road maps were printed in 1914.

Auto, Gas Pump, Wayne, Visible, Texaco, Ethyl, Globe, Red, Green, White & Black Paint
$2,415

Donley Auctions

Lamp, Brass, Zigzag, Bird Shape Arm, Standard, 1900s, 59 ½ In.	270
Tray, Reverse Painted Glass, Nickel Plated Steel, Lacquered Wood, c.1935, 2 x 18 x 12 In.*illus*	1063

ART GLASS, *see Glass-Art category.*

ART NOUVEAU

Art Nouveau is a style of design that was at its most popular from 1895 to 1905. Famous designers, including Rene Lalique and Emile Galle, produced furniture, glass, silver, metalwork, and buildings in the new style. Ladies with long flowing hair and elongated bodies were among the more easily recognized design elements. Copies of this style are being made today. Many modern pieces of jewelry can be found. Additional Art Nouveau pieces may be found in Furniture or in various glass and porcelain categories.

Decanter, Red Violet Glass, Stopper, Silver Overlay, Squat, c.1900, 8 x 6 ½ In.	1188
Ewer, Bacchus Top, Female Body Handle, Circular Base, Jean Massier, 24 In., Pair	1440
Plaque, Plaster, Woman Sitting, Moon, Flowers, 13 x 19 In.	59
Vase, Silver Overlay, Green Glass, Scalloped Rim, Circular Foot, c.1900, 12 x 5 ½ In.	975

ART POTTERY, *see Pottery-Art category.*

ARTS & CRAFTS

Arts & Crafts was a design style popular in American decorative arts from 1894 to 1923. In the 1970s collectors began to rediscover Mission furniture, art pottery, metalwork, linens, and light fixtures from this period. The interest has continued. Today everything from this era is collectible, including jewelry, graphics, and silverware. Additional items may be found in the Furniture category and other categories.

Box, Dome Lid, Silver, Enamel Decoration, Round, 1 ½ x 3 ¾ In.	500
Box, Pyrography, Carved, Painted, Flowers, c.1910, 14 ¾ x 7 ½ x 4 In.*illus*	185
Frame, Picture, Mahogany, Brass & Abalone, G. Ghedina, Verra-Cortina Tirol, Italy, 5 x 4 ¼ In.	308
Vase, Carved, Black, Signed, Frater, Rochester Mechanics Institute, c.1905, 8 x 3 ¾ In.	461
Vase, Glazed Porcelain, Ribbed & Bulbous Design, 14 x 10 In.	96

AURENE *pieces are listed in the Steuben category.*

AUSTRIA *is a collecting term that covers pieces made by a wide variety of factories in Austria. They are listed in this book in categories like Royal Dux or Porcelain.*

AUTO

Auto parts and accessories are collectors' items today. Gas pump globes and license plates are part of this specialty. Prices are determined by age, rarity, and condition. Collectors say "porcelain sign" for enameled iron or steel signs. Packaging related to automobiles may also be found in the Advertising category. Lalique hood ornaments are listed in the Lalique category.

Ashtray, Michelin Man, Bakelite, Black Base, England, c.1940	92
Cabinet, Edison Mazda Super, Lamps, Porcelain, Hanging, 7 x 7 x 16 In.*illus*	960
Display, Dealer, Mercury, Remote Control, Rear View Mirror, 12 x 17 In.	266
Gas Pump Globe, Tydol, Ethyl Gasoline, Frosted Lenses, Metal Frame, 19 x 6 x 15 In.	1155
Gas Pump, Wayne, Visible, Texaco, Ethyl, Globe, Red, Green, White & Black Paint *illus*	2415
Hood Ornament, Plymouth, Sails, Reticulated, Bow, Protruding, c.1950, 13 ¼ In.	74
License Plate, Illinois 1946, Red Ground, White Numbers, 5 ½ x 11 ½ In., Pair	36
License Plate, Truck, Wyoming 2137, Embossed, Red Text & Border, White Ground, 1941 .. *illus*	92
Light Box, Sinclair, Duck Winter Trouble, Cardboard, Flashing Light, Box, 42 x 34 In.	1845

Auto, License Plate, Truck, Wyoming 2137, Embossed, Red Text & Border, White Ground, 1941
$92

Donley Auctions

Auto, Mannequin, Texaco, Man, Standing, Old Texaco Uniform, 6 In.
$1,440

Chupp Auctions & Real Estate, LLC

Auto, Oil Can, Bingham's Cardinal Brand, Red, Cylindrical, Spout Top, Utility Can, 5 Gal., 16 In.
$295

Route 32 Auctions

Auto, Oil Can, Lincoln, Blue, White, Red, Cylindrical, Spout Top, Boston, Mass., 5 Gal., 16 In.
$861

Route 32 Auctions

Auto, Oil Can, Pennzoil, The Tough Film, Yellow, Red & Black Graphics, Flat Top, 5 Qt., 9 ½ In.
$135

Route 32 Auctions

Auto, Oil Can, Red Giant, Yellow Ground, Red & Black Graphics, Council Bluffs, Iowa, Composite, Qt.
$98

Route 32 Auctions

Auto, Oil Can, Zeppelin, Blue & White Graphic, Red Letters, Rectangular, Spigot, 2 Gal., 11 ½ In.
$492

Route 32 Auctions

Auto, Poster, Gyro Ride, Nitrogen Powered, Black Light, Paper, Fluorescent Ink, c.1950, 24 x 19 In.
$84

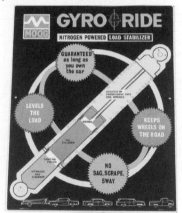

Selkirk Auctioneers & Appraisers

Auto, Radiator Ornament, Pontiac, Figural, Face, Nickel Plate, Oak Stand, 1926, 4 x 2 ½ In.
$837

Jeffrey S. Evans & Associates

A

Auto, Sign, Goodrich Tires, White Text, Dark Blue Ground, Porcelain, Early 1900s, 78 x 18 In.
$908

Fontaine's Auction Gallery

Auto, Sign, Mobiloil, Flying Pegasus, Red, Plastic, Screwed Into Board, 48 x 36 In.
$390

Chupp Auctions & Real Estate, LLC

Autumn Leaf, Cookie Jar, Lid, Pretzel Handles
$85

Strawser Auction Group

Mannequin, Texaco, Man, Standing, Old Texaco Uniform, 6 In. .... *illus*	1440
Model, 1962 Chrysler 300, Light Blue, Friction, Dealer Promo, Jo-Han Models, 2¼ x 8¼ In.	19
Oil Can, Bingham's Cardinal Brand, Red, Cylindrical, Spout Top, Utility Can, 5 Gal., 16 In...*illus*	295
Oil Can, Blue Seal, Red, White, Blue, Cylindrical, Illinois Farm Supply Co., Chicago, Qt., 5½ In...	369
Oil Can, Hold 'Em, Wire Jacket, Spout Top, Clear Glass, Black, 12 In.	72
Oil Can, Hudson Motor Oil, Red & Black Graphics, Cylindrical, Kansas City, Qt., 5½ In......	338
Oil Can, Lincoln, Blue, White, Red, Cylindrical, Spout Top, Boston, Mass., 5 Gal., 16 In......*illus*	861
Oil Can, McCormick-Deering Farm Machine & Implements, Tin, Stenciled, Penn., 8½ In..	150
Oil Can, Ocean Liner, Airplane, Red, White, Blue, Rectangular, Traymore Lubricants, 2 Gal......	271
Oil Can, Pennzoil, The Tough Film, Yellow, Red & Black Graphics, Flat Top, 5 Qt., 9½ In... *illus*	135
Oil Can, Red Giant, Yellow Ground, Red & Black Graphics, Council Bluffs, Iowa, Composite, Qt.. *illus*	98
Oil Can, Sinclair, Opaline, Green & Red Lettering, Rocker, 5 Gal., 16½ In.	338
Oil Can, Wearwell, Black & White, Western Auto Stores, Rectangular, 2 Gal., 11½ In.	738
Oil Can, Your Friend, Outstretched Hand, Cylindrical, Top Spout, Billups Petroleum, 5 Gal., 16 In.	185
Oil Can, Zeppelin, Blue & White Graphic, Red Letters, Rectangular, Spigot, 2 Gal., 11½ In...*illus*	492
Oil Dispenser, Self Measuring, Wood, Brass Tag, S.F. Bowser, Countertop, 13 x 11 x 29 In..	960
Oil Jar, Glass, Lid, Neck Stopper, E.C. Simmons, Keen Kutter, 14 In.	60
Poster, Grand Prix D'Europe, Reims, Jean Des Gachons, 1959, 25 x 18 In.	910
Poster, Gyro Ride, Nitrogen Powered, Black Light, Paper, Fluorescent Ink, c.1950, 24 x 19 In. *illus*	84
Poster, Packards For 1953, Dealership, Cars Pictured, 5 Models, 18½ x 32 In.	74
Radiator Ornament, Pontiac, Figural, Face, Nickel Plate, Oak Stand, 1926, 4 x 2½ In. *illus*	837
Radio, Control Head, Automatic, Motorola, Hudson, 1946, 4 x 11 In.	123
Sign, Gas Station, Pegasus Mobil, Red & White, Light-Up, 60 In.	1265
Sign, Globe Battery Automobile Service, Swing Handle, Red & Yellow Paint, c.1920s, 17 x 9 In......	254
Sign, Goodrich Tires, White Text, Dark Blue Ground, Porcelain, Early 1900s, 78 x 18 In.....*illus*	908
Sign, Goodyear Tires, Diamond Shape, Horizontal, Blue Ground, 60 x 32 In.	2040
Sign, Mobiloil, Flying Pegasus, Red, Plastic, Screwed Into Board, 48 x 36 In. .... *illus*	390
Sign, Pennzoil, Supreme Quality, Raised Text, Yellow, Plastic, Oval, 18 x 31 In.	60
Sign, Sinclair, Motor Oil, Dinosaur, Pennsylvania, Round, 11 In.	960
Sign, Texaco, Fire-Chief Gasoline, Porcelain, Pump Plate, Red Fire Helmet, 12 x 18 In........	216
Spark Plug Cleaner, Steel, Painted, A-C, Air Operated, Compressed, Compound Bag, 23 x 11 In.	677
Steering Wheel, Buick, 3 Banjo Spokes, Horn Button, c.1936, 18 In.	492
Uniform, Texaco, Gas Station Attendant, Green Wool & Polyester Blend, Lion Uniform, 1970s	475

AUTUMN LEAF

Autumn Leaf pattern china was made for the Jewel Tea Company beginning in 1933. Hall China Company of East Liverpool, Ohio, Crooksville China Company of Crooksville, Ohio, Harker Potteries of Chester, West Virginia, and Paden City Pottery, Paden City, West Virginia, made dishes with this design. Autumn Leaf has remained popular and was made by Hall China Company until 1978. Some other pieces in the Autumn Leaf pattern are still being made. For more prices, go to kovels.com.

Coffeepot, Finial, 8 Cup, 9 In.	45
Cookie Jar, Lid, Pretzel Handles..*illus*	85
Custard Cup, Gold Trim, 2⅛ In., Pair..	20
Mixing Bowl, Ribbed, Qt., 6 In.	10
Mug, Loop Handle, Footed, 4¾ In.	14
Punch Bowl, 13 In...*illus*	107
Sugar & Creamer, Gold Trim, Footed..	32
Warmer Stand, Oval, Dunbar Stamp, 5 x 4 x 3¼ In.......................................	95

AVON *bottles are listed in the Bottle category under Avon.*

AZALEA

Azalea dinnerware was made for Larkin Company customers from about 1915 to 1941. Larkin, the soap company, was in Buffalo, New York. The

dishes were made by Noritake China Company of Japan. Each piece of the white china was decorated with pink azaleas.

Celery Tray, Closed Handle, 4½ x 10 In.	199
Gravy, 2 Spouts, 7½ x 3 In., Underplate, 9 In.	35
Platter, 8¾ x 11¾ In.	55
Platter, Oval, Red Wreath Mark, 16 In. ....*illus*	49
Sugar & Creamer, Green Stamp	47
Tobacco Jar, Lid, Stepped, Gilt Ball Finial, Octagonal, Red Wreath Mark, 5 In.	64
Tray, Applied Handle, 5½ In.	15
Vase, Bulbous Body, Neck, Flared Lip, Red Flower Mark, 6 In.	450

BACCARAT

Baccarat glass was made in France by La Compagnie des Cristalleries de Baccarat, located 150 miles from Paris. The factory was started in 1765. The firm went bankrupt and began operating again about 1822. Cane and millefiori paperweights were made during the 1845 to 1880 period. The firm is still working near Paris making paperweights and glasswares.

Ashtray, Faceted, Asymmetrical, Clear, Marked, France, 1900s, 3 x 7 In.	125
Bowl, Cut Glass, Gilt Bronze, Footed, Artichoke Finial, France, c.1900, 8¾ In.	424
Candelabrum, 3-Light, Dauphin, Scalloped Rim, Drip Pan, Hanging Prisms, 1900s, 28 In...... *illus*	1125
Candelabrum, 3-Light, Drip Pan, Knop Stem, Octagonal Base, 1900s, 10 x 11 x 6 In., Pair	625
Candlestick, Aladdin, Molded Socle, Twirl Stem, 1900s, 6½ In., Pair	313
Candlestick, Clear, Swirls, Round Base, Marked, 6½ In., Pair	180
Champagne Bucket, Round, Marked, St. Louis, 13½ x 9¼ In.	216
Cologne Bottle, Rose Teinte, Swirl, 5½ x 3¾ In. ....*illus*	70
Figurine, Cat, Seated, Black, Marked, 6¼ In. ....*illus*	160
Figurine, Glass Block, Persian Winged Bull, Acid Stamp, 1969, 5 x 6 In.	600
Paperweight, Millefiori, Ouranos, Concentric, Garlands, Multicolor Canes, 1996, 3⅜ In...	761
Paperweight, Stylized Giraffe, Clear, Acid Etched Mark, 7½ In.	50
Plate, Clear, Signed, 7½ In., 8 Piece	240
Sculpture, Clear, Frosted Faces, Robert Rigot, France, 10 x 7 x 5 In.	325
Urn, Dome Lid, Acorn Finial, Clear, Mounted, Gilt Metal, Square Base, 1900s, 13 In., Pair.....*illus*	938
Urn, Gilt Bronze Mounts, Handle, Late 1900s, 25 x 15¼ In..........................*illus*	3188
Urn, Lid, Acorn Finial, Neoclassical Style, Gilt Bronze, Mounts, Late 1800s, 28 In.	1694
Vase, Clear, Cranberry & White Cutback Overlay, Gold Enamel, 8¼ x 4¼ In. ....*illus*	125
Vase, Faceted, Cylindrical, Ormolu, Mounted, Lobed Rim, 1900s, 14¾ In., Pair	1280
Vase, Flared Rim, Etched, Pedestal, Disc Foot, 6½ x 4 In.	75
Vase, Sculpted, Angular Pattern, Stamped, 9 x 7 In.	192
Vase, Tornado, Swirling, Openwork, Acid Etched Marks, 8⅞ x 5⅛ In., Pair	1476

BADGE

Badges have been used since before the Civil War. Collectors search for examples of all types, including law enforcement and company identification badges. Well-known prison or law enforcement badges are most desirable. Most are made of nickel or brass. Many recent reproductions have been made.

Conductor, Silver, Blue Lettering, Border Detail, Disneyland, Hat, c.1950, 4 In. ....*illus*	688
Deputy Sheriff, Star Shape, Circle Ends, 2 x 2 In.	250
Fire Department, Assistant Chief, Goldtone, Silvertone Ring, Eagle Crest, Cleveland, 2¾ In....	120
Fire Department, Battalion Chief, Goldtone, Eagle Crest, Cleveland, Ohio, 2¾ In......*illus*	120
Fire Department, Captain, Cleveland, O., No. 1, Goldtone, Shield Shape, Scrolled Trim, 2½ In.	132
Marshal, Virginia City, Nevada, Eagle, Mixed Metal, c.1915-40, 1¾ x 2⅞ In. ....*illus*	375
Rank, Embroidered, Cranes, Clouds, Waves, Blue Ground, Korea, Frame, 13 x 22 x 2½ In., Pair..	1722
Superintendent, Suburban Patrol, Goldtone, Shield Shape, Eagle Crest, 3 x 2¼ In.	36
U.S. Marine Corps, Silver, Goldtone Anchor, Striped Ribbon On Bar, Cap, Meyer of New York	30

Autumn Leaf, Punch Bowl, 13 In.
$107

Strawser Auction Group

Azalea, Platter, Oval, Red Wreath Mark, 16 In.
$49

redfranklin on eBay

TIP

Be careful when burning candles in glass candlesticks. If the candle burns too low, the hot wax and flame may break the glass.

Baccarat, Candelabrum, 3-Light, Dauphin, Scalloped Rim, Drip Pan, Hanging Prisms, 1900s, 28 In.
$1,125

Hindman

Baccarat, Cologne Bottle, Rose Teinte, Swirl, 5 ½ x 3 ¾ In.
$70

Woody Auction

Baccarat, Figurine, Cat, Seated, Black, Marked, 6 ¼ In.
$160

Apple Tree Auction Center

Baccarat, Urn, Dome Lid, Acorn Finial, Clear, Mounted, Gilt Metal, Square Base, 1900s, 13 In., Pair
$938

Hindman

Baccarat, Urn, Gilt Bronze Mounts, Handle, Late 1900s, 25 x 15 ¼ In.
$3,188

Bonhams

> ### TIP
> *To remove stains from a glass vase, fill it with warm water and drop in a denture-cleaning tablet.*

Baccarat, Vase, Clear, Cranberry & White Cutback Overlay, Gold Enamel, 8 ¼ x 4 ¼ In.
$125

Woody Auction

Badge, Conductor, Silver, Blue Lettering, Border Detail, Disneyland, Hat, c.1950, 4 In.
$688

Potter & Potter Auctions

Badge, Fire Department, Battalion Chief, Goldtone, Eagle Crest, Cleveland, Ohio, 2 ¾ In.
$120

Milestone Auctions

Badge, Marshal, Virginia City, Nevada, Eagle, Mixed Metal, c.1915-40, 1 ¾ x 2 ⅞ In.
$375

Cowan's Auctions

BANK

Banks of metal have been made since 1868. There are still banks, mechanical banks, and registering banks (those that show the total money deposited on the face of the bank). Many old iron or tin banks have been reproduced since the 1950s in iron or plastic. Some old reproductions marked *Book of Knowledge*, *John Wright*, or *Capron* may be listed. Pottery, glass, and plastic banks are also listed here. Mickey Mouse and other Disneyana banks are listed in Disneyana.

Baseball On 3 Bats, Silver, Red, Cast Iron, Hubley, 1914, 5 x 3 In.	720
Battleship, Iowa, Cream Paint, Green Base, Cast Iron, J. & E. Stevens, 10 x 4¾ x 5¾ In.	1080
Beehive, Cast Iron, Painted Yellow, Square Base, Combination Drawer, 8 x 10 In.	1088
Building, Bank, Flatiron, 3-Sided, Cast Iron, Gray Paint, Kenton, 5½ In.	79
Building, Bank, Home Bank, Cast Iron, Man On Porch, H.L. Judd, Late 1800s, 4 x 3 x 4 In.	168
Building, Bank, Home Savings, 2 Story, Cast Iron, Painted, Multicolor, Late 1800s, 5 x 4 x 3 In. *illus*	7200
Building, Bungalow, Green, Red Roof, Grey Iron Casting, 3¾ In.	3300
Building, Cottage, Red Riding Hood, Green, Red, Tin, 2 In. *illus*	1440
Building, Independence Hall, Gilt, Cast Iron, Enterprise, 10 x 9¼ In. *illus*	192
Bunny, Porcelain, Pink & White, Tiffany & Co., Italy, 4½ x 4 x 8 In.	94
Cat, Spelter, Gray, Green Eyes, Trick Lock, Germany, 3¼ In.	549
Clown, Red Hair, White Ground, Aluminum, Mingo Mfg. Co., Roversford, Pa., 5 x 6 x 6 In. *illus*	2280
Coconut, Grisly Native American Scene, Carved, Veracruz, Mexico, 1850s, 4½ In.	1000
Dolphin Boy In Boat, Sailor Hat, Cast Iron, Grey Iron Casting, 1900s, 4½ In.	236
Donation, Cat Shape, RSPCA, Please Help, Blue Glaze, Doulton Lambeth, c.1900, 7¼ In.	9375
Gas Pump, Cast Iron, Red, Gilt Trim, Arcade, 5¾ In.	300
George Washington, Standing, Cast Iron, Patinated Bronze Finish, 7 In.	48
Hall Clock, Pendulum, Black, Gilt, Arcade, 6 In.	900
House, 2 Story, Steel, Gambrel Roof, B.T. Corp., Chicago, 3¾ x 2¼ x 2½ In.	18

Mechanical banks were first made about 1870. Any bank with moving parts is considered mechanical. The metal banks made before World War I are the most desirable. Copies and new designs of mechanical banks have been made in metal or plastic since the 1920s. The condition of the paint on the old banks is important. Worn paint can lower a price by 90 percent.

Mechanical, Artillery, Soldier, Cannon, Cast Iron, J. & E. Stevens, 6 x 8 x 4 In. *illus*	10200
Mechanical, Bird On Roof Of House, Gold Highlights, J. & E. Stevens, 5 x 7 In.	2006
Mechanical, Creedmoor, Cast Iron, Painted, Red Pants, J. & E. Stevens, 6 x 10 In.	325
Mechanical, Dentist, Black Bag, Cast Iron, Footed Base, J. & E. Stevens, 9½ x 7 In. *illus*	3250
Mechanical, Eagle & Eaglets, Nest, Glass Eyes, J. & E. Stevens, 1883, 6 In.	1000
Mechanical, Elephant Howdah, Man Pops Out, Enterprise, Late 1800s, 5⅝ x 6¾ In. *illus*	726
Mechanical, I Always Did 'Spise A Mule, Cast Iron, 1800s, 8 x 10½ In.	313
Mechanical, Kicking Horse, Man Sitting, Painted, Cast Iron, 6 x 10 In.	240
Mechanical, Leap Frog, Cast Iron, Shepard Hardware, Buffalo, N.Y., c.1891, 5 x 7½ In.	2510
Mechanical, Mammy & Child, Cast Iron, Kyser & Rex, 4½ x 8 x 4 In.	1320
Mechanical, Organ Bank, Donkey, Cat & Dog, Musical, Kyser & Rex, Late 1800s, 7⅝ x 5¼ In.	1573
Mechanical, Panorama, Cast Iron, Yellow, Brown Roof, J. & E. Stevens, 7 x 5 In.	30000
Mechanical, Penny Pineapple, Cast Iron, Hawaii Statehood, July 4, 1960, 8 In. *illus*	74
Mechanical, Pistol, Cast Iron, Silver Finish, Richard Elliot Co., 5½ x 4½ In.	250
Mechanical, Red Riding Hood, Seated On Grandma's Bed, Cast Iron, W.S. Reed Co., 8 In. *illus*	33600
Mechanical, Satellite Bank, Rocket Ship, Michigan National Bank, Duro Mold Mfg., 10½ In.	104
Mechanical, Scotsman, Tin Lithograph, Saalheimer & Strauss, Germany, 3½ x 7 x 2 In. *illus*	270
Mechanical, Sonny Boy Clown, Aluminum, Thomas Ashworth Mfg., England, c.1945, 6 In. *illus*	4500
Mechanical, Tammany, Man Wearing Suit, Seated, Cast Iron, Painted, 5½ In.	160
Mechanical, Teddy & The Bear, Cast Iron, J. & E. Stevens, Cromwell, Conn., c.1900, 10 In. *illus*	1188
Mechanical, Trick Dog, Jumps Through Hoop, Barrel, Cast Iron, Shepard Hardware, Box, 10 x 8 In.	2880
Mechanical, Uncle Sam, Standing, Box Base, Shepard Hardware, 11½ In. *illus*	5100
Mechanical, William Tell, Cast Iron, J. & E. Stevens, Late 1800s, 6 x 10 x 3 In. *illus*	484
Mourner's Purse, Lead, Brass Handle, Lock, 1880, 4 In.	207
Pagoda, 9 Tiers, 6-Sided, Dragon Spouts, Cast Iron, 6-Footed, Chinese, 1700s, 22½ In.	878

Bank, Building, Bank, Home Savings, 2 Story, Cast Iron, Painted, Multicolor, Late 1800s, 5 x 4 x 3 In. $7,200

Garth's Auctioneers & Appraisers

TIP
Never repaint an old bank. It lowers the resale value.

Bank, Building, Cottage, Red Riding Hood, Green, Red, Tin, 2 In. $1,440

Bertoia Auctions

Bank, Building, Independence Hall, Gilt, Cast Iron, Enterprise, 10 x 9¼ In. $192

Morphy Auctions

This is an edited listing of current prices. Visit **Kovels.com** to check thousands of prices from previous years and sign up for free information on trends, tips, reproductions, marks, and more.

B

Bank, Clown, Red Hair, White Ground, Aluminum, Mingo Mfg. Co., Royersford, Pa., 5 x 6 x 6 In.
$2,280

Bank, Mechanical, Elephant Howdah, Man Pops Out, Enterprise, Late 1800s, 5 ⅝ x 6 ¾ In.
$726

Morphy Auctions

Fontaine's Auction Gallery

Bank, Mechanical, Artillery, Soldier, Cannon, Cast Iron, J. & E. Stevens, 6 x 8 x 4 In.
$10,200

Bank, Mechanical, Penny Pineapple, Cast Iron, Hawaii Statehood, July 4, 1960, 8 In.
$74

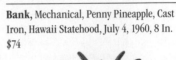

Morphy Auctions

Bank, Mechanical, Dentist, Black Bag, Cast Iron, Footed Base, J. & E. Stevens, 9 ½ x 7 In.
$3,250

Apple Tree Auction Center

Bank, Mechanical, Red Riding Hood, Seated On Grandma's Bed, Cast Iron, W.S. Reed Co., 8 In.
$33,600

Morphy Auctions

Bertoia Auctions

Bank, Mechanical, Scotsman, Tin Lithograph, Saalheimer & Strauss, Germany, 3 ½ x 7 x 2 In.
$270

Morphy Auctions

Bank, Mechanical, Sonny Boy Clown, Aluminum, Thomas Ashworth Mfg., England, c.1945, 6 In.
$4,500

Bertoia Auctions

Bank, Mechanical, Teddy & The Bear, Cast Iron, J. & E. Stevens, Cromwell, Conn., c.1900, 10 In.
$1,188

Potter & Potter Auctions

Bank, Mechanical, Uncle Sam, Standing, Box Base, Shepard Hardware, 11 ½ In.
$5,100

Bertoia Auctions

Bank, Mechanical, William Tell, Cast Iron, J. & E. Stevens, Late 1800s, 6 x 10 x 3 In.
$484

Fontaine's Auction Gallery

Bank, Puzzle, Stoneware, Cobalt Decoration, William & Daisy Parkinson, 1886, 10 ¾ In., Pair
$3,125

Hindman

B

Barber, Cabinet, Mug,
21 Compartments, Wood, Wall Mount,
39 x 31 In.
$1,560

Chupp Auctions & Real Estate, LLC

TIP
*Look at your home
from the viewpoint
of a trespasser. Do
bushes hide the
windows or doors?
Are ladders lying
around? Can a window
be reached by
standing on a table
or air conditioning
compressor? Does
your fence hide the
burglar from view
while he or she
breaks in?*

Barber, Chair, Child's, Upholstered Seat
Cushion, Backrest, Koken
$2,400

Chupp Auctions & Real Estate, LLC

Pay Phone, Crank, Receiver & Trap, Cast Iron, J. & E. Stevens, 5 x 3 x 7 In.	510
Pig, Standing, Pottery, Multicolor Glaze, 1940s, 6 ¼ In., Pair	113
Puzzle, Stoneware, Cobalt Decoration, William & Daisy Parkinson, 1886, 10 ¾ In., Pair *illus*	3125
Safe, Coin Deposit, Cast Iron, Gilt, Silver & Black, 5 ½ x 4 In.	37
Safe, Jewel, Gothic Revival, Bronze & Enamel Case, Fitted Interior, 8 ½ In.	281
Safe, Security Safe Deposit, Cast Iron, Embossed Scrolls, Lion's Head Handles, 1800s, 8 In.	500
Statue Of Liberty, Cast Iron, Gold Paint, Kenton, 10 In.	330
Young Black Man, Cast Iron, Smiling Face, Red Shirt, Coin Slot, England, 5 In.	148

BARBER

Barber collectibles range from the popular red and white striped pole that used to be found in front of every shop to the small scissors and tools of the trade. Barber chairs are wanted, especially the older models with elaborate iron trim.

Cabinet, Mug, 21 Compartments, Wood, Wall Mount, 39 x 31 In. *illus*	1560
Chair, Black Upholstery, Porcelain Base, Emil J. Paidar, 48 x 40 x 30 In.	1035
Chair, Child's, Upholstered Seat Cushion, Backrest, Koken *illus*	2400
Chair, Wood, Cast Iron, Stool, Crushed Velvet Upholstery, Victorian, Archer Mfg. Co., 45 In.	677
Pole, Flat Post, Tapered End, Red & White Striped, Modern Base, Late 1800s, 91 x 18 x 9 In.	132
Pole, Painted, Red & White Stripes, Square Box Base, Wood, 54 In.	480
Pole, Red, White, Leaded Glass, Porcelain Top & Base, 33 ½ x 10 x 13 In.	2160
Pole, Turned Wood, Painted, Red, White, Blue, Cannonball Finial, c.1900, 84 x 6 x 6 In.	484
Pole, Turned Wood, Red, White, Blue, Metal Base, Cannonball Finial, Late 1800s, 84 In. *illus*	600
Rack, Shaving Mug, Walnut, Hanging, Gallery, 42 Mugs, Victorian, c.1880, 53 ¾ x 38 ¾ x 7 ¾ In.	568
Shaving Mirror, Revolving, Stand, Lather Brush, Nickel Plate, Hexagonal Base, 17 x 7 x 6 In.	640
Sign, 3 Master Barbers, Neon, Reverse Painted, Jefferson Electric Co., 1932, 24 x 12 x 6 In.	730
Sign, Barber Shop, Multicolor Stripe, Chrome, Electric, 18 ½ x 6 In. *illus*	250
Sign, Barber Shop, Neon, Domed Glass, Octagonal, Scrollwork Bracket, 2-Sided, 22 x 24 ½ In.	3840
Sign, Barber Shop, Wood, Painted, Red Stripes, White Ground, Folk Art, c.1890, 24 x 8 x 4 In.	219
Steamer, Hot Towel, Ball Top, Copper, Cast Iron Base, Signed, S. Blickman, 60 x 22 x 16 In.	1016

BAROMETER

Barometers are used to forecast the weather. Antique barometers with elaborate wooden cases and brass trim are the most desirable. Mercury column barometers are also popular with collectors. It is difficult to find someone to repair a broken one, so be sure your barometer is in working condition..

Aneroid, Brass, Canvas, Portrait Of Cardinal On Back, Oval, France, 1800s, 3 ¾ x 2 ½ In.	156
Banjo, Hygrometer, Thermometer, Weather Dial, Bubble Level, Mahogany, c.1900, 36 In.	448
Banjo, Mahogany, Peter Bergonzi, Hereford Warranted, England, Georgian, 39 x 10 ½ In.	219
Black Forest, Bear, Paw Raised, Carved, Rectangular Base, Late 1800s, 8 ¾ In. *illus*	151
Giltwood, Neoclassical, Marked, Bourgeois Opticien, France, Late 1800s, 6 ¾ x 5 ½ x 2 In.	151
Marine, Brass & Silver, Wood Case, Painted, Rectangular, 46 In.	228
Marine, Stick, Rosewood Case, Brass Inlay, Silvered Dial, Arched Top, 1800s, 36 x 3 x 1 In.	1170
Nautical, Clock, Ship's Wheel, Brass, Walnut, Glass, Hermes, France, c. 1935, 18 In.	5250
Stick, C. Taber & Co., Walnut, Mounted, Gimbal, New Bedford, Mass., 36 x 2 ½ x 2 In.	2340
Stick, Cemco Mercury, Central Scientific Company, c.1930s, 37 x 3 x 2 In.	105
Stick, Crichton Bros., Rosewood Case, Ivory Scales, Marked, 39 ½ In.	1875
Stick, G.H. Wadsworth, Inlaid Mahogany, Mercury, Halifax, England, 1800s, 35 ¼ In.	441
Stick, Neoclassical, Giltwood, Beaded Body, Florentia, Italy, Mid 1900s, 37 ½ x 13 ¼ x 2 In.	484
Stick, S. Pike & Sons, Mahogany, Rococo Style Flowers, Profile Head, c.1845, 45 In. *illus*	3250
Thermometer, Benetfink & Co., Vertical Over Circular Dial, Oak Plaque, England, c.1950, 35 In.	180
Thermometer, Louis XV Style, Gilt, Bronze Mounted, Boulle Marquetry, 1800s, 28 x 11 ½ In. *illus*	2000
Thermometer, Neoclassical, Garlands, Eagle Crest, Giltwood, France, 19th Century, 34 x 21 In.	1540
Thermometer, Woolsey, Fiberglass, Wood, Aluminum, Steel, 27 In.	86
Wheel, Dominic Gugeri, Mahogany, Veneer Case, Fruitwood Inlay, Boston, c.1810, 38 In. *illus*	625
Wheel, Fagioli & Son, Mahogany, Pressure, Humidity, Temperature Gauges, 41 In.	120
Wheel, Inlaid Mahogany, Steel Dial, Estilo Fecit, George III, c.1790, 39 x 10 In.	366

Barber, Pole, Turned Wood, Red, White, Blue, Metal Base, Cannonball Finial, Late 1800s, 84 In.
$600

Barometer, Black Forest, Bear, Paw Raised, Carved, Rectangular Base, Late 1800s, 8¾ In.
$151

Barometer, Thermometer, Louis XV Style, Gilt, Bronze Mounted, Boulle Marquetry, 1800s, 28 x 11½ In.
$2,000

Fontaine's Auction Gallery

Barometer, Stick, S. Pike & Sons, Mahogany, Rococo Style Flowers, Profile Head, c.1845, 45 In.
$3,250

Hindman

Barometer, Wheel, Dominic Gugeri, Mahogany, Veneer Case, Fruitwood Inlay, Boston, c.1810, 38 In.
$625

Garth's Auctioneers & Appraisers

Barber, Sign, Barber Shop, Multicolor Stripe, Chrome, Electric, 18½ x 6 In.
$250

New Haven Auctions

Eldred's

Eldred's

Basket, Bee Skep, Rye Straw, Bentwood Base, Pennsylvania, 1800s, 13 x 14 In. $1,353

Pook & Pook

Basket, Buttocks, Ribbed, Arched, Wood Handle, 1900s, 10¾ x 11½ In. $128

Brunk Auctions

Basket, Coiled, Rye Straw, Lid, Drum Shape, Pennsylvania, 1800s, 14 x 13½ In. $502

Conestoga Auction Company

Collectors Are Difficult to Please

Don't buy collectors something for their collection. Buy a book with information or something related to the collection, like a T-shirt picturing a bank for a bank collector.

Wheel, Pensotti, Mahogany, Slender Neck, Thermometer, Gravesend, England, 1800s, 38 In..	210
Wheel, Schalfino, Mahogany, Inlaid, Shell, White Lion Court, England, 1800s, 38 In.	313

BASEBALL *collectibles are in the Sports category. Baseball cards are listed under Baseball in the Card category.*

BASKET

Baskets of all types are popular with collectors. American Indian, Japanese, African, Nantucket, Shaker, and many other kinds of baskets may be found in other sections. Of course, baskets are still being made, so a collector must learn to judge the age and style of a basket to determine its value. Also see Purse.

Bee Skep, Hole At Center, Brown, Signed, Paul Tyson, 6 In.	466
Bee Skep, Rye Straw, Bentwood Base, Pennsylvania, 1800s, 13 x 14 In. ....*illus*	1353
Buttocks, Open, Oval Shape, Fabric Liner, Leather Handles, Lisa Ahern, 1900s, 10 x 13 x 7 In.	1586
Buttocks, Ribbed, Arched, Wood Handle, 1900s, 10¾ x 11½ In. ....*illus*	128
Buttocks, Woven, Rectangular, Handle, Miniature, 3 x 6½ x 5½ In.	113
Coiled, Rye Straw, Lid, Drum Shape, Pennsylvania, 1800s, 14 x 13½ In......*illus*	502
Gathering, Woven, Cylindrical, 2 Cutout Handles, 28 x 21 In. ....*illus*	113
Nantucket, Bentwood Handle, Brass Tabs, Wood Disc Base, Early 1900s, 10 x 9 In.	300
Nantucket, Bentwood Swing Handles, Signed, Rogerson, 5¼ x 10 x 7⅝ In.	500
Nantucket, Carved Swing Handle, Brass Ears, Wood Base, William & Jeanne Reis, 13 x 10 In.	819
Nantucket, Lid, Plaque, Love, 2 Swing Handles, G.L. Brown, 1992, 14 x 19 x 14 In. ....*illus*	2500
Nantucket, Round, Open, 2 Swing Handles, Painted, Paul Willer, 6 x 12 In.	976
Nantucket, Round, Swing Handle, Open, Wrapped Rim, Wood Base, Late 1800s, 8 x 6¾ In..*illus*	527
Nantucket, Round, Swing Handle, Sherwin Boyer, 1910s, 3¼ x 5¼ In.	1000
Pack, Adirondack, Tight Weave, Rattan, Handle, Dark, 13 x 12 x 20 In.	106
Picnic, Double Hinged Lid, 2 Swing Handles, Painted, Manny Dias, 8 x 16 x 14 In. ......*illus*	671
Picnic, Oval, Pine, Top Carved Ebony Whale, Signed, Jose Formoso Reyes, c.1950, 6 x 7 x 5 In.	4270
Raffia, Cylindrical, Red & Orange Design, 1930s, 4 x 8 In.	63
Rye, Bentwood Handles, Woven, Cleats On Bottom, 23 In.	124
Splint, Berry, Woven, Oak, Squat Shape, Curved Handle, Pennsylvania, 5 x 6¼ In.	30
Splint, Swing Handle, Round, Deep, 1800s, 8 x 13 In.	416
Splint, White Oak, Woven, Arched Handle, Green Painted Weavers, Virginia, c.1915, 8¾ In.	478
Splint, Woven, Double Walled, Red, White & Blue Exterior Paint, Early 1900s, 5 x 20 In.	600
Splint, Woven, Oak, Circular Field, Green Paint, Bentwood Rim & Handles, 16 x 20 In.	472
Splint, Woven, Rectangular, Removable Lid, Red & Black Painted Bands, Late 1800s, 2 x 4 In.	2280
Wedding, 3 Tiers, Woven Rattan, Intricate Design, Chinese, 16 x 14 x 25 In.	53
Wedding, Openwork, Applied Rim, 2 Handles, Circular Base, 1880s, 5 In.	156
Wicker, Oval, 2 Hinged Lids, Green, Painted, Fixed Handle, 16 x 17 x 14 In.	105
Woven, Centerpiece, Painted Spun Cotton Fruit, Multicolor, c.1900, 11 In.	101
Woven, Lid, Center Handle, Dark Brown, 23 x 10 In.	74
Woven, Rattan Body, Bentwood Handle, Metal Braces, Chinese, 1800s, 15 x 23 x 12 In.	94

BATCHELDER
LOS ANGELES
BATCHELDER

Batchelder products are made from California clay. Ernest Batchelder established a tile studio in Pasadena, California, in 1909. He went into partnership with Frederick Brown in 1912 and the company became Batchelder and Brown. In 1920 he built a larger factory with a new partner. The Batchelder-Wilson Company made all types of architectural tiles, garden pots, and bookends. The plant closed in 1932. In 1936 Batchelder opened Batchelder Ceramics, also in Pasadena, and made bowls, vases, and earthenware pots. He retired in 1951 and died in 1957. Pieces are marked *Batchelder Pasadena* or *Batchelder Los Angeles.*

Bookends, Children Reading, Boy & Girl, Book On Knees, White, c.1920, 4½ x 4 x 5 In...*illus*	313
Catalog, Designs For Fountains, 2nd Edition, Batchelder-Wilson Co., 1924, 11½ x 8½ In...	188
Cornice, Cherub, Standing On Head, c.1920, 9 x 3¾ x 3¼ In.	282

Basket, Gathering, Woven, Cylindrical,
2 Cutout Handles, 28 x 21 In.
$113

Hartzell's Auction Gallery Inc.

Basket, Nantucket, Lid, Plaque, Love,
2 Swing Handles, G.L. Brown, 1992,
14 x 19 x 14 In.
$2,500

Eldred's

Basket, Nantucket, Round, Swing Handle,
Open, Wrapped Rim, Wood Base, Late 1800s,
8 x 6 ¾ In.
$527

Thomaston Place Auction Galleries

TIP
*Never oil a basket.
It will attract dirt.*

Basket, Picnic, Double Hinged Lid, 2 Swing
Handles, Painted, Manny Dias, 8 x 16 x 14 In.
$671

Rafael Osona Nantucket Auctions

Batchelder, Bookends, Children Reading,
Boy & Girl, Book On Knees, White, c.1920,
4 ½ x 4 x 5 In.
$313

California Historical Design

Batchelder, Tile, Hexagonal, Turquoise Blue, Dirk Van Erp Frame, c.1920, 4 ¾ x 4 ¼ In.
$2,125

California Historical Design

Batchelder, Tile, Owl On Branch, Leaves,
Berries, Red Clay, Worn Light Blue Glaze,
c.1920, 4 x 4 In.
$94

California Historical Design

Batchelder, Tile, Viking Ship, On Water,
Blue Sky, Oak Frame, c.1920, 25 x 25 In.
$7,500

California Historical Design

29

B

Batman, Action Figure, World's Greatest Super Heroes, Mego, Box, Unopened, 1976, 12 In.
$408

Weiss Auctions

Batman, Toy, Batman, Walking, Mechanical, Tin Lithograph, Mego, Box, 8 In.
$132

Weiss Auctions

Bauer, Ring, Bowl, Fruit, Turquoise, Tripod Feet, c.1920s, 3 ½ x 10 In.
$215

California Historical Design

TIP

If you are using glue to fix an antique, work in a room that is about 70°F. Glue will not work well if it's too hot or too cold.

Fireplace, Yellow & Brown Tiles, Flowers, Grapevines, Salesman's Sample, 20 x 31 x 11 In.	4375
Tile, Castle, Trees In Foreground, Blue Sky, 13 x 8 ⅓ In.	469
Tile, Hexagonal, Turquoise Blue, Dirk Van Erp Frame, c.1920, 4 ¾ x 4 ¼ In. ....*illus*	2125
Tile, Owl On Branch, Leaves, Berries, Red Clay, Worn Light Blue Glaze, c.1920, 4 x 4 In.*illus*	94
Tile, Reindeer, In Profile, Facing Left, Green Matte Ground, 3 ¾ x 3 ¾ In.	125
Tile, Viking Ship, On Water, Blue Sky, Oak Frame, c.1920, 25 x 25 In.............*illus*	7500

BATMAN

Batman and Robin are characters from a comic book created by Bob Kane. Batman first appeared in a 1939 issue of *Detective Comics.* The first Batman comic book was published in 1940. In 1966, the characters became part of a popular television series. There have been radio and movie serials that featured the pair. The first full-length movie was made in 1989.

Action Figure, World's Greatest Super Heroes, Mego, Box, Unopened, 1976, 12 In........*illus*	408
Batmobile, Remote Control, Black, Light-Up Features, 1997	11
Book, Son Of The Demon, Hardcover, First Edition, 1987	48
Book, Untold Legend Of The Bat Man, DC Comics, Soft Cover, August 1982	12
Lithograph, Artist Proof, Batman & Robin, Bob Kane, c.1978, 20 x 27 In.	1950
Mug, Glass, Batman, Robin, c.1995, 4 ⅛ In.	15
Toy, Batman, Walking, Mechanical, Tin Lithograph, Mego, Box, 8 In.........*illus*	132
Toy, Batmobile, Die Cast, Rocket Tubes, Suspension, Figures, Box, Corgi Toys, c.1966	771

BAUER

Bauer pottery is a California-made ware. J.A. Bauer bought Paducah Pottery in Paducah, Kentucky, in 1885. He moved the pottery to Los Angeles, California, in 1910. The company made art pottery after 1912 and introduced dinnerware marked *Bauer* in 1930. The factory went out of business in 1962 and the molds were destroyed. Since 1998, a new company, Bauer Pottery Company of Los Angeles, has been making Bauer pottery using molds made from original Bauer pieces. The pottery is now made in Highland, California. Pieces are marked *Bauer Pottery Company of Los Angeles.* Original pieces of Bauer pottery are listed here. See also the Russel Wright category. Ring is one of the most popular Bauer patterns.

Ashtray, Square, Copper Holder, Black, Light Blue, Yellow, Cobalt Blue, 3 In., 4 Piece	144
Cal-Art, Planter, Figural, Swan, Chartreuse, c.1950, 3 ½ x 6 In.	12
Cal-Art, Vase, Swirl, Footed, White, 1940s, 8 ¼ x 5 In.	12
Candleholder, Hand Thrown, Finger Loop, Saucer Base, Cobalt Blue, Matt Carlton, Pair....	114
Gloss Pastel Kitchenware, Teapot, Aladdin, Pink, 2 Cup	54
Mixing Bowl, Yellow, 16 In.	72
Monterey, Coffee Server, Lid, Orange Red, Wood Handle, 8 In.	29
Monterey, Salt & Pepper, Burgundy, 2 ¾ In.	15
Plain, Coffee Server, Lid, Black Glaze, Wood & Copper Handle, 8 ½ In.	27
Ring, Bowl, Fruit, Turquoise, Tripod Feet, c.1920s, 3 ½ x 10 In...............*illus*	215
Ring, Bowl, Salad, Burgundy, 1930s, 12 In.	36
Ring, Coffee Server, Lid, Chinese Yellow, Wood & Copper Handle, 1930s, 9 In.	48
Ring, Coffee Server, Lid, Delph Blue, Copper Mount, Raffia Wrapped Handle, 1930s, 8 ¼ In.	60
Ring, Coffee Server, Lid, Jade Green, Wood & Copper Handle, 1930s, 4-6 Cups, 7 ½ In.	21
Ring, Coffeepot, Lid, Drip, Chinese Yellow, 1930s, 8 In.	90
Ring, Cookie Jar, Lid, Jade Green, 7 ½ In.	78
Ring, Creamer, Jade Green, Large, 1930s, 4 In.	24
Ring, Flowerpot, Chinese Yellow, 1930s, 3 In.	17
Ring, Flowerpot, Jade Green, 8 In.	17
Ring, Gravy Boat, Attached Underplate, Burgundy, 6 ½ In.	22
Ring, Jardiniere, Light Green, c.1930s, 17 x 13 ¾ In., Pair	615
Ring, Pitcher, Orange Red, 1 ½ Pint, 4 ¼ In.	17

Ring, Planter, Turquoise, Bottom Hole, 10 x 12 In.	188
Ring, Spice Jar, Lid, Orange Red, 5½ x 7½ In.	102
Ring, Sugar & Creamer, Lid, Royal Blue, Mid 1930s, 2½ In.	42
Ring, Teapot, Lid, Snub Nose, Copper Handle, Royal Blue, Mid 1930s, 7¼ In.	180
Vase, Globular, Closed Handles, Standup Rim, Custard Yellow, 1940s, 5¼ In.	17

BAVARIA

Bavaria is a region in Europe where many types of porcelain were made. In the nineteenth century, the mark often included the word *Bavaria*. After 1871, the words *Bavaria, Germany*, were used. Listed here are pieces that include the name *Bavaria* in some form, but major porcelain makers, such as Rosenthal, are listed in their own categories.

Cake Plate, Square, Center Flowers, Maroon Inner Rim, Gilt Trim, Tirschenreuth, 7¾ In., 14 Piece	125
Chocolate Set, Pink Flowers, Long Stems, Gold Trim, Angled Handle, Pot, Cup & Saucer, 11 Piece	45
Coffee Set, Marie Luise, Black, Flower, Silver Overlay, Spahr, Seltmann Weiden, c.1950, 3 Piece..*illus*	300
Cup & Saucer, Echt Cobalt, Gilt Vine, Flowers, Lindner Kueps, 20th Century, 1¾ x 4½ In.	25
Jug, Echt Cobalt, Chrysanthemum, Gilt Flowers, Lindner Kueps, 1900s, 8¾ In.............*illus*	32
Mug, Art Nouveau, Gold Luster, Peacocks, Turned In Rim, Angled Handle, 7¼ In.	50
Plate, Art Deco, Blue & Gray Rim, Geometric, Signed, Blanche Lazzell, Kromach, 1916, 9¾ In.	567
Plate, Dinner, Gold Encrusted, Wide Rim, Floral Sprays, H&C Selb, Heinrich & Co., 11 In., 12 Piece	216
Plate, Echt Cobalt, Carla, Center Flower Spray, Gilt, Lindner Kueps, 20th Century, 11 In.	38
Plate, Echt Cobalt, Brussel, Gilt Lacy Rosette & Rim, Lindner Kueps, 20th Century, 11 In.	50
Plate, Multicolor Flower Rim, Urn Center, Black Knight, Hohenberg, 1900s, 10½ In., 12 Piece	150
Plate, Service, Green, White, Flowers, 22K Gold Rim, Heinrich, c.1940, 11 In., 8 Piece..*illus*	217
Tea & Coffee Set, Pot, Sugar & Creamer, Tray, Gilt Trim, Monogram, Bareuther, 4 Piece	60
Tea Set, White Luster, Gilt Trim, Flowers, Teapot, Sugar, Creamer, 6 Cups & Saucers, Mittertiech.	750
Vase, Tapered, White, Scaly Textured Panels, Green Shield Mark, Schumann Arzberg, 20½ In., Pair.	100

BEADED BAGS *are included in the Purse category.*

BEATLES

Beatles collectors search for any items picturing the four members of the famous music group or any of their recordings. The condition is very important and top prices are paid for items in mint condition. The Beatles first appeared on American network television in 1964. The group disbanded in 1971. Ringo Starr and Paul McCartney are still performing. John Lennon died in 1980. George Harrison died in 2001.

Album, Let It Be, Vinyl, Capitol Records, c.1979, 12 In.	50
Button, Pinback, Sgt. Pepper's Lonely Hearts Club Band, 1960s, 3 In.	18
Button, We Want The Beatles Back, Beatles, Yellow, Red, Tin, c.1973, 3½ In.	39
Poster, Beatles In Doorway, Lithograph, Louis Dow, c.1964, 13 x 16 In.	265
Ring, John, George, Paul, Ringo, Brass Tone, Adjustable, 4 Piece	259
Tile, Portraits, Signatures, Ceramic, Black Wire Frame, c.1964, 5 x 5 In.	47

BEEHIVE

Beehive, Austria, or Beehive, Vienna, are terms used in English-speaking countries to refer to the many types of decorated porcelain bearing a mark that looks like a beehive. The mark is actually a shield, viewed upside down. It was first used in 1744 by the Royal Porcelain Manufactory of Vienna. The firm made what collectors call Royal Vienna porcelains until it closed in 1864. Many other German, Austrian, and Japanese factories have reproduced Royal Vienna wares, complete with the original shield or beehive mark. This listing includes the expensive, original Royal Vienna porcelains and many other types of beehive porcelain. The Royal Vienna pieces include that name in the description.

Bavaria, Coffee Set, Marie Luise, Black, Flower, Silver Overlay, Spahr, Seltmann Weiden, c.1950, 3 Piece
$300

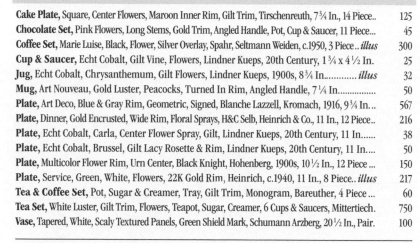

Heritage Auctions

Stolen Art & Antiques
It is said that art and antiques worth a total of $6 billion are stolen each year.

Bavaria, Jug, Echt Cobalt, Chrysanthemum, Gilt Flowers, Lindner Kueps, 1900s, 8¾ In.
$32

Lion and Unicorn

Bavaria, Plate, Service, Green, White, Flowers, 22K Gold Rim, Heinrich, c.1940, 11 In., 8 Piece
$217

DuMouchelles

B

Beehive, Cup & Saucer, Woman, Seated, Cherub, Brown Border, Gold Trim, Germany, 4 x 5 In. $400

Woody Auction

Beehive, Loving Cup, Cobalt Blue Ground, Classical Medallion Design, 3 Handles, 7 x 7 In. $150

Woody Auction

Beehive, Plate, 2 Figures, Donkeys Carrying Fruits & Fabrics, Royal Vienna, 1800s, 9 In. $275

Bruneau & Co. Auctioneers

Billy Beer Is a Bust
The Billy Beer can, made when Jimmy Carter, Billy's brother, was president, is now worth about a dollar.

Imperial and Royal Porcelain Manufactory
Vienna, Austria
1749–1827

Bourdois & Bloch
Paris, France
c.1900

Waechtersbach Earthenware Factory
Schlierbach, Hesse, Germany
1921–1928

Item	Price
Cup & Saucer, Woman, Seated, Cherub, Brown Border, Gold Trim, Germany, 4 x 5 In. ..*illus*	400
Cup, Woman, Sitting, Angel On Shoulder, Titled Liebesstimme, Signed, Hauser, 2 x 2¼ In.	50
Figurine, Horse & Rider, Oval Wood Base, Royal Vienna, 11 x 8 In.	135
Lamp, Banquet, Cobalt Blue, Courting Scene, Angel, Flowers, Royal Vienna, 32 In.	690
Loving Cup, Cobalt Blue Ground, Classical Medallion Design, 3 Handles, 7 x 7 In.....*illus*	150
Plaque, Amicita Portrait, Hand Painted, Grapes & Vine Borders, Royal Vienna, c.1915, 11⅝ In.	24
Plate, 2 Figures, Donkeys Carrying Fruits & Fabrics, Royal Vienna, 1800s, 9 In. ....*illus*	275
Plate, Cherub, Bow & Arrow, Woman, Seated, Maroon & Pink Border, Gold Stencil, 9½ In.	100
Plate, Cupid, Maiden, Hand Painted, Bronze Holder, Signed, Royal Vienna, 8 x 10½ In.	406
Plate, Portrait, Blue Dress, Reticulated Rim, Austria, c.1900s, 8 In.	270
Plate, Portrait, Female Figure, Red Border, Giltwood Frame, Royal Vienna, 17 x 16 In.	480
Tea Caddy, Rinaldo, Armetha & Horatio, Gilt, Gold Finial, Vienna, 1800s, 6 x 3 x 1 In.	188
Tray, 3 Figures, Beauty Crowning Virtue, Signed, Hauser, Royal Vienna, Late 1800s, 13 x 10 In..*illus*	644
Urn, Lid, Gracien, Greek Couples, Royal Vienna, Late 1800s, 11¾ In.	351
Urn, Lid, Greek Mythological Scenes, Black Ground, Royal Vienna, Late 1800s, 14 In..*illus*	726
Urn, Painted, Blue Ground, Ornate Design, Gilt Acorn Finial, Royal Vienna, 23 In., Pair	1955
Vase, Iridescent Tiffany Ground, Pink Roses, Royal Vienna, 7 x 4 In.	225
Vase, Medallion Portrait, Woman, 2 Handles, Iridescent Bronze Ground, Signed, Wagner, 7 x 3 In.	750
Vase, Titled Winter, Signed, Wagner, Royal Vienna, Austria, Late 1800s, 6 In..*illus*	164
Vase, Urn Shape, Deep Blue, Gilt, Classical Scene, C. Herr, Royal Vienna, 1900s, 16 In. *illus*	1125

BEER BOTTLES *are listed in the Bottle category under Beer.*

BEER CAN

Beer cans are a twentieth-century idea. Beer was sold in kegs or returnable bottles until 1934. The first patent for a can was issued to the American Can Company in September of that year, and Gotfried Kruger Brewing Company, Newark, New Jersey, was the first to use the can. The cone-top can was first made in 1935, the aluminum pop-top in 1962. Collectors should look for cans in good condition, with no dents or rust. Serious collectors prefer cans that have been opened from the bottom.

Item	Price
Burger, Flat Top, Light, Sparkle Brewed, Red On White, Aluminum, Cincinnati, c.1960, 12 Oz.	19
Burgermeister, Fan Tab, King Size, White, Blue, Gold, Jos. Schlitz, Calif., c.1960, 15 Oz.	98
Du Bois Budweiser, Pull Tab, Gold Ground, Script Lettering, Du Bois, Penn., c.1960, 12 Oz.	135
Esslinger's, Bottle Cap Lid, Canister Shape, Red & Yellow, 5¾ x 3 x 3 In. ..*illus*	240
Foodtown, Pull Tab, Premium Beer, Gold, Red Stripe, Old Dutch Brewing Co., Penn., c.1960, 12 Oz.	171
Gambrinus Gold Label, Pull Tab, Ohio State Golden Highlights, Pittsburgh Brewing Co., 12 Oz.	23
Goebel, Copper Ground, Red & Black Germanic Eagle, Prewar, Detroit, Mich., 1930s, 12 Oz.	2318
Goebel, Flat Top, Real Draft Beer, Blue Border, Gold Ground, Detroit, Mich., c.1960, 12 Oz.	244
Heileman's Old Style Lager, Cone Top, Outdoor Scene, 3 Figures At Table, 12 Oz., Pair..*illus*	261
James Bond's 007 Special Blend, Pull Tab, Woman, Guards, National Brewing, 1960s, 12 Oz.	3294
Leinenkugel's, Pull Tab, Red & White, Chippewa Falls, Wis., c.1970, 12 Oz.	122
Malt Duck, Pull Tab, Foil Label, Blue, Pink Letters, National Brewing Co., c.1960, 16 Oz.	9610
Mountain Brew, Pull Tab, Ring Top, Red, Gold, Mountains, Queen City Brewing, Md., 1968, 12 Oz.	58
North Star, Pull Tab, Ring Top, Red Letters, Blue Ground, White Stars, Cold Spring, Minn., 12 Oz.	6
Orbit, Pull Tab, Premium Beer, Rocky Landscape, Earth, Miami, c.1960, 12 Oz.	69 to 171
Pabst, Pull Tab, Contoured, Embossed, Blue Panels, Red Stripe, White Ground, c.1970, 12 Oz.	5856
Pickwick Ale, Pull Tab, Red Ground, Coat Of Arms, Haffenreffer, Rhode Island, c.1960, 12 Oz.	147

Beehive, Tray, 3 Figures, Beauty Crowning Virtue, Signed, Hauser, Royal Vienna, Late 1800s, 13 x 10 In.
$644

Jeffrey S. Evans & Associates

TIP
Gummed tags can be removed by heating the tag with a hair dryer, then loosening it with a flat knife.

Beehive, Urn, Lid, Greek Mythological Scenes, Black Ground, Royal Vienna, Late 1800s, 14 In.
$726

Fontaine's Auction Gallery

Beehive, Vase, Titled Winter, Signed, Wagner, Royal Vienna, Austria, Late 1800s, 6 In.
$164

Jeffrey S. Evans & Associates

TIP
If there is crossover interest between two different collector groups, prices go up, often over auction estimates.

Beehive, Vase, Urn Shape, Deep Blue, Gilt, Classical Scene, C. Herr, Royal Vienna, 1900s, 16 In.
$1,125

Lion and Unicorn

Beer Can, Esslinger's, Bottle Cap Lid, Canister Shape, Red & Yellow, 5¾ x 3 x 3 In.
$240

Morphy Auctions

Beer Can, Heileman's Old Style Lager, Cone Top, Outdoor Scene, 3 Figures At Table, 12 Oz., Pair
$261

Matthew Bullock Auctioneers

Bell, Bronze, Snail Shape, Gilt, Mixed Metal Shell Body, Antenna, Toledo, Spain, 2 ½ x 6 ¾ In.
$390

Treasureseeker Auctions

Bell, Chimes, Dinner, Xylophone, Heart Cutout, Stickley Brothers, c.1902, 9 x 10 x 7 ½ In.
$2,952

California Historical Design

Bell, Dinner, Arts & Crafts, Oak, Hanging, Copper Trim, Hammered, c.1910s, 7 ¾ x 4 x 11 ¾ In.
$800

California Historical Design

Bell, Door, Hand Crank, Brass & Cast Iron, Embossed, Taylor's, c.1860, 6 ⅜ x 5 In.
$500

Hindman

Pikes Peak Ale, Pull Tab, Red Banner, Gold Trim, Walter Brewing Co., Colorado, c.1960, 12 Oz. ..	74
Richbrau Bock, U-Tab, Banner, Shield, Ram's Head, Home Brewing Co., Virginia, c.1960, 12 Oz.	2013
Schmidt Beer, Fan Tab, Logging Scene, Moose, Jacob Schmidt Brewing Co., Minn., 1965, 12 Oz.	58
Schmidt Select, Pull Tab, Near Beer, Blue & White, Gold Ring, Associated Brewing, 1969, 12 Oz.	6
Skol, Fan Tab, Red Lettering, Blue, Red & Yellow Steins, Drewrys Ltd., Indiana, 1965, 12 Oz.	81
Soul, Fan Tab, Stout Malt Liquor, Red, Gold Grain Stalks, Maier Brewing, Calif., 1967, 16 Oz.	661

BELL

Bell collectors collect all types of bells. Favorites include glass bells, figural bells, school bells, and cowbells. Bells have been made of porcelain, china, or metal through the centuries.

Brass, Cup Shape, Circular Top, Tibet, 21 In.	61
Brass, Rousseau, Wrought Iron, New Bedford, Frame Mounted, 1800s, 18 x 19 In.	5000
Bronze, Native Woman, Sitting Cross-Legged, Patina, Marble Base, 8 In.	780
Bronze, Newport News Shipbuilding & Drydock Co., Virginia, 1923, 65 In.	10000
Bronze, Snail Shape, Gilt, Mixed Metal Shell Body, Antenna, Toledo, Spain, 2 ½ x 6 ¾ In.... *illus*	390
Call, Wrought Iron, Ornate, Wall Mount Frame, Flowers, Leaves, 1800s, 23 x 18 x 6 ¼ In. ...	227
Chimes, Dinner, Xylophone, Heart Cutout, Stickley Brothers, c.1902, 9 x 10 x 7 ½ In.. *illus*	2952
Dinner, Arts & Crafts, Oak, Hanging, Copper Trim, Hammered, c.1910s, 7 ¾ x 4 x 11 ¾ In.. *illus*	800
Door, Hand Crank, Brass & Cast Iron, Embossed, Taylor's, c.1860, 6 ⅜ x 5 In. ....*illus*	500
Door, Lever, Cut Glass, Gilt Bronze, Switchette, 1800s, 6 ½ In.	90
Gong, Brass, Bow & Arrow Mark, Wood Handle, Leather Mallet, Rope String, Germany, 19 In.	59
Locomotive, Iron Yoke, Circular Base, Brass, 19 x 10 x 13 In.	649
Silver, Ball Shape Finial, Turned Wood Handle, William Spratling, Mexico, 1940, 4 In....*illus*	556
Sleigh, 4 Shaft Bells, Leather Strap, Securing Belts, c.1900, 2 ¾ x 3 x 13 In.	568
Sleigh, 20 Brass Bells, Leather Strap, Buckle, Boge Harness Shop, Earlville, 1900s, 81 In. ...	180
Sleigh, 30 Brass Bells, Leather Strap, 74 In. ....*illus*	99
U.S. Army Camel Corps, Eagles, Shield On Breast, Starbursts, 1860s	213
Wind, Bronze, Copper, Paolo Soleri, Arcosanti, Paradise Valley, Arizona, 26 x 6 ½ x 4 ½ In.	845

BELLEEK

Belleek china was made in Ireland, other European countries, and the United States. The glaze is creamy yellow and appears wet. The first Belleek was made in 1857 in the village of Belleek, County Fermanagh, in what is now Northern Ireland. In 1884 the name of the company became the Belleek Pottery Works Company Ltd. The mark changed through the years. The first mark, black, dates from 1863 to 1891. The second mark, black, dates from 1891 to 1926 and includes the words *Co. Fermanagh, Ireland.* The third mark, black, dates from 1926 to 1946 and has the words *Deanta in Eireann.* The fourth mark, same as the third mark but green, dates from 1946 to 1955. The fifth mark (second green mark) dates from 1955 to 1965 and has an *R* in a circle added in the upper right. The sixth mark (third green mark) dates from 1965 to 1981 and the words *Co. Fermanagh* have been omitted. The seventh mark, gold, was used from 1981 to 1992 and omits the words *Deanta in Eireann.* The eighth mark, used from 1993 to 1996, is similar to the second mark but is printed in blue. The ninth mark, blue, includes the words *Est. 1857,* and the words *Co. Fermanagh Ireland* are omitted. The tenth mark, black, is similar to the ninth mark but includes the words *Millennium 2000* and *Ireland.* It was used only in 2000. The eleventh mark, similar to the millennium mark but green, was introduced in 2001. The twelfth mark, black, is similar to the eleventh mark but has a banner above the mark with the words *Celebrating 150 Years.* It was used in 2007. The thirteenth trademark, used from 2008 to 2010, is similar to the twelfth but is brown and has no banner. The fourteenth mark, the Classic Belleek trademark, is similar to the twelfth but includes Belleek's website address. The Belleek Living trademark was introduced in 2010 and is used on items

from that giftware line. All pieces listed here are Irish Belleek. The word *Belleek* is now used only on pieces made in Ireland even though earlier pieces from other countries were sometimes marked *Belleek*. These early pieces are listed in this book by manufacturer, such as Ceramic Art Co., Lenox, Ott & Brewer, and Willets.

Belleek Pottery Co.
1863–1891

Ceramic Art Co.
1894–1906

Willets Manufacturing Co.
1879–1912+

Bowl, Swan Shape, Off-White, Yellow Iridescent Wings & Head, Ireland, c.1965, 4¼ In.	24
Candleholder, Snowflake Design, Cream Ground, Scalloped Rim, 1990s, 4½ In.	42
Centerpiece, Shamrock Sleigh, Flared Edges, Flowers, 6 In., Pair	86
Figurine, Leprechaun, Ivory Cream, Seated, Toadstool Base, 6th Mark, Ireland, 1965, 5 In.	52
Mug, Curved Handle, Wolfhound, Round Tower, Irish Harp, White Ground, 3⅝ In.	16
Vase, 2 Dolphin Handles, Scalloped Rim, Shell Shape Base, 6th Mark, Ireland, 1965, 6 In.	93

BENNINGTON

Bennington ware was the product of two factories working in Bennington, Vermont. Both the Norton Company and Lyman Fenton & Company were out of business by 1896. The wares include brown and yellow mottled pottery, Parian, scroddled ware, stoneware, graniteware, yellowware, and Staffordshire-type vases. The name is also a generic term for mottled brownware of the type made in Bennington.

Bowl, Brown Sponge, Yellow Ground, 6 x 11½ In.	64
Chamber Pot, Lid, Flint Enamel, Brown, Handle, Lyman, Fenton & Co., 1850s, 8¾ x 9 In.	688
Churn, Lid, Stoneware, Cobalt Blue Flowers, Stick, E. & L.P. Norton, 1800s, 20 In.	213
Crock, Cobalt Blue Bird On Branch, Stoneware, Incised Band, E. & L.P. Norton, 11 In.	325
Crock, Cobalt Blue Bird, Tooled Shoulder, Lug Handles, Stoneware, J. & E. Norton, c.1855, 7⅜ In.	600
Cuspidor, Rockingham Glaze, Paneled Sides, Copper Green Flecks, 1800s, 5½ x 12 In.	185
Figurine, Cat, Seated, Brown Glaze, Rectangular Base, 1900s, 13½ In.	189
Paperweight, Figural, Eagle, White, Gilt Shield, Rectangular Base, 1850s, 2¾ x 4 In.	531
Pitcher, Swans, Brown Glaze, 9½ In.	19
Pitcher, Tulip & Heart, Flint Enamel, Brown, Blue, Lyman, Fenton & Co. 1849, 10½ In.	406

BERLIN

Berlin, a German porcelain factory, was started in 1751 by Wilhelm Kaspar Wegely. In 1763, the factory was taken over by Frederick the Great and became the Royal Berlin Porcelain Manufactory. It is still in operation today. Pieces have been marked in a variety of ways.

Cup & Saucer, Blanc De Chine, Flowers, Branched Handle, W Mark, Wegley, 1750s.....*illus*	598
Cup & Saucer, Flowers, Gilt, Square Handle, Monogram, Blue Scepter Mark, 2⅜ x 5 In.	576
Plaque, Whispering Secrets, 2 Young Women, Holding Rose & Fan, Paper Label, c.1880, 7 x 5 In.*illus*	240
Plaque, Young Woman, Long Hair, Head Tilted, Gilt Gesso Frame, Carved, Leafy, 8 x 6½ In.	192
Teapot, Lid, Blue Flowers, Cream Ground, Reeded, Blue Scepter Mark, 18th Century, 4¾ In.	88
Tureen, Lid, Putto Finial, Raised Pink Flowers, Blue & Gilt Trim, Blue Scepter Mark, 12 x 14 x 9 In.	640
Urn, Campana Shape, 2 Handles, Square Base, 18¾ x 15¾ In., Pair	1913

BESWICK

Beswick started making pottery in Staffordshire, England, in 1894. The pottery became John Beswick Ltd. in 1936. The company became part of Royal Doulton Tableware, Ltd.in 1969. Production ceased in 2002 and the John Beswick brand

---

Bell, Silver, Ball Shape Finial, Turned Wood Handle, William Spratling, Mexico, 1940, 4 In.
$556

Thomaston Place Auction Galleries

Bell, Sleigh, 30 Brass Bells, Leather Strap, 74 In.
$99

Apple Tree Auction Center

Berlin, Cup & Saucer, Blanc De Chine, Flowers, Branched Handle, W Mark, Wegley, 1750s
$598

Doyle

Berlin, Plaque, Whispering Secrets, 2 Young Women, Holding Rose & Fan, Paper Label, c.1880, 7 x 5 In.
$240

Michaan's Auctions

Beswick, Beatrix Potter, Figurine, Flopsy Bunny, Blue Dress, Pink Bag, Arthur Gredington, 1968, 4 In.
$44

Lion and Unicorn

Beswick, Beatrix Potter, Figurine, Old Mr. Brown, Owl & Squirrel, Kissing, A. Hallam, 1973, 3¼ In.
$38

Lion and Unicorn

was bought by Dartington Crystal in 2004. Figurines, vases, and other items are being made and use the name Beswick. Beatrix Potter figures were made from 1948 until 2002. They shouldn't be confused with Bunnykins, which were made by Royal Doulton.

Beatrix Potter, Character Jug, Mrs. Tiggy-Winkle, Ted Chawner, Royal Albert, c.1990, 3 In.	25
Beatrix Potter, Figurine, Duchess, Black Dog, Blue Bow, With Pie, Graham Tongue, 1979-82, 3 In..	88
Beatrix Potter, Figurine, Flopsy Bunny, Blue Dress, Pink Bag, Arthur Gredington, 1968, 4 In.*illus*	44
Beatrix Potter, Figurine, Foxy, Reading Newspaper, Amanda Hughes-Lubeck, England, 1990, 4 In...	125
Beatrix Potter, Figurine, Mr. Jackson, Sitting, Green Coat, Toad, Albert Hallam, 1974, 3 In..	16
Beatrix Potter, Figurine, Mrs. Tiggy-Winkle, Hedgehog, Washing, David Lyttleton, 1998, 2½ In.	19
Beatrix Potter, Figurine, Old Mr. Brown, Owl & Squirrel, Kissing, A. Hallam, 1973, 3¼ In...*illus*	38
Beatrix Potter, Figurine, Samuel Whiskers, Rat, Arthur Gredington, Royal Albert, 1948, 3¼ In..	48
Beatrix Potter, Figurine, Susan, Basket, David Lyttleton, Royal Albert, c.1989, 4 In. ....*illus*	625
Beatrix Potter, Figurine, Tom Kitten, Blue Jacket, Trousers, Arthur Gredington, 1948, 3½ In. ..	24
Beatrix Potter, Music Box, Mrs. Rabbit, Rocking Chair, 2 Baby Rabbits, Schmid, 1981, 7½ In.....	43
Decanter, Figural, Monk, Dark Brown Robe, Removable Head, c.1950, 8½ In.	50
Figurine, Bulldog, Standing, Champion Basford, British Mascot, Marked, 6 In.	63
Figurine, Dog, Collie, Brown & White, Lochinvar of Lady Park, 6¼ x 7 In.	39
Figurine, Dog, Pug, Standing, Champion Cutmil Cupie, Marked, 5 x 4½ In.	39
Figurine, Fox, Sitting, White & Brown Glaze, No. 2348, Fireside, 12½ In.	228

BETTY BOOP

Betty Boop, the cartoon figure, first appeared on the screen in 1930. Her face was modeled after the famous singer Helen Kane and her body after Mae West. In 1935, a comic strip was started. Her dog was named Pudgy. Although the Betty Boop cartoons ended by 1938, there was a revival of interest in the Betty Boop image in the 1980s and new pieces are being made.

Doll, Red Dress, Gloves, Vale, Plastic, Marty Toys, Box, 1986, 12 In.	45
Figurine, Betty Boop, Bisque, Red Dress, High Heels, Syd Hap, King Features, 1997, 14 x 1 In..... *illus*	113
Paper Dolls, Betty Goes To Hollywood, Uncut, 8 Pages, 1984	15
Pen & Pencil Holder, Die-Cut Figures, Red Squirrel, Celluloid, c.1930, 3⅜ In. ....*illus*	559
Pendant, Pewter, Enamel, Betty, Crescent Moon, Red Dress, 1 x 1 In.	25
Purse, Betty, Winking, On Motorcycle, Black Outfit, Fishnets, Cloth, 12 x 10 In..............	110
Toy, Acrobat, Red Dress, Celluloid, Swing, Windup, Box, C.K. Japan, Prewar, 9 x 6 In....*illus*	600

BICYCLE

Bicycles were invented in 1839. The first manufactured bicycle was made in 1861. Special ladies' bicycles were made after 1874. The modern safety bicycle was not produced until 1885. Collectors search for all types of bicycles and tricycles. Bicycle-related items are also listed here. Many posters have been reproduced.

Boneshaker, Child's, Carved, Red Paint, Turned Handles, Wood, 1800s, 35 x 21 x 52 In..*illus*	813
Columbia, Expert, High Wheel, Curved Body, Bulb Shape Handles, c.1885, 57 In.	5658
Columbia, Five Star, Cruiser, Leaf Spring, Leather Seat, 42½ x 70 In.	840
Lantern, Solar, Handle, Wood Grip, Badger Brass Co., c.1898, 6½ x 9½ In............	108
Poster, 6 Day Bike Race, Blue & Orange, Bicyclist, Frame, c.1920, 19 x 17½ In.	325
Poster, Motorettes, Francisco Tamagno, Terrot & Co., 1909, 54 x 38 In.	5500
Poster, Peugeot, Tiger Carrying Bike, Georges Favre, 1928, 45 x 30 In.	750
Raleigh, Super Tourer, Road Bike, Leather Saddle, Campagnolo Pedals, 27 In.	675
Schwinn, Black Phantom, Men's, Black, Red, Streamlined, Front Light, Back Carrier, 1950s	1800
Sears, Spaceliner, Schwinn Seat, Red, Yellow, c.1965, 40 x 68 In. ....*illus*	431
Tricycle, Aluminum, Enameled Steel, Rubber Wheels, American, c.1935, 30 x 20 x 36 In.	625
Tricycle, American National, Silver Bell, Metal, Toledo, Ohio, 29 x 36 In. ....*illus*	154
Tricycle, Fast & Reliable Deliveries, Painted, Wood, Iron, Child's, Late 1800s, 21 x 13 x 30 In......	313
Tricycle, Rollfast, Black & White Highlights, Horseshoe Shape, Saddlebag, 1952, 29 x 22 In......	270

Beswick, Beatrix Potter, Figurine, Susan, Basket, David Lyttleton, Royal Albert, c.1989, 4 In.
$625

Lion and Unicorn

Betty Boop, Figurine, Betty Boop, Bisque, Red Dress, High Heels, Syd Hap, King Features, 1997, 14 x 1 In.
$113

Lion and Unicorn

Betty Boop, Pen & Pencil Holder, Die-Cut Figures, Red Squirrel, Celluloid, c.1930, 3⅜ In.
$559

Hake's Auctions

Betty Boop, Toy, Acrobat, Red Dress, Celluloid, Swing, Windup, Box, C.K. Japan, Prewar, 9 x 6 In.
$600

Morphy Auctions

Bicycle, Boneshaker, Child's, Carved, Red Paint, Turned Handles, Wood, 1800s, 35 x 21 x 52 In.
$813

Hindman

Bicycle, Sears, Spaceliner, Schwinn Seat, Red, Yellow, c.1965, 40 x 68 In.
$431

Rich Penn Auctions

Bicycle, Tricycle, American National, Silver Bell, Metal, Toledo, Ohio, 29 x 36 In.
$154

Conestoga Auction Company

Bing & Grondahl, Tureen, Lid, Undertray, Saxon Flower, Round, Dragon Finial, 11 x 12 In.
$123

Pook & Pook

Bing & Grondahl

When Bing & Grondahl became part of Royal Copenhagen in 1987, some Bing & Grondahl dinnerware, figurines, and vases were discontinued; some remained in production but were marked with the Royal Copenhagen mark. The Bing & Grondahl name was used only on commemorative and annual pieces and a few overglaze-decorated figurines.

Binoculars, Naval Officer's, Burnished Brass, Adjustable, Magnifications, Diopter, Continental, 1900s
$60

Selkirk Auctioneers & Appraisers

TIP
A good way to clean bisque, according to several readers, is with a toothbrush and white toothpaste. Brush gently, then rinse completely in warm water.

BING & GRONDAHL

Bing & Grondahl is a famous Danish factory making fine porcelains from 1853 to the present. Underglaze blue decoration was started in 1886. The annual Christmas plate series was introduced in 1895. Dinnerware, stoneware, and other ceramics are still being made today. The figurines remain popular. The firm has used the initials *B & G* and a stylized castle as part of the mark since 1898. The company became part of Royal Copenhagen in 1987.

B. & G.	B & G	
Bing & Grondahl 1895+	Bing & Grondahl 1915+	Bing & Grondahl 1983+

Figurine, Girl & Dog, Sitting, White Dress, Brown Dog, 3 In.	256
Figurine, Girl With Milk Can, Pouring Milk, Axel Locher, Marked, B & G, 8¼ In.	52
Figurine, Rooster, Standing, Brown & White, No. 2192 On Base, 4 In.	50
Plate, Christmas, 1916, Christmas Prayer Of The Sparrows, 7 In.	20
Plate, Christmas, 1918, Fishing Boat Returning Home For Christmas, 7 In.	31
Plate, Christmas, 1944, Sorgenfri Castle, 7 In.	32
Plate, Christmas, 1953, Royal Boat In Greenland Waters, 7 In.	8
Plate, Christmas, 1956, Christmas In Copenhagen, 7 In.	22
Plate, Christmas, 1981, Christmas Peace, 7 In.	12
Plate, Napoleon, Josephine, Multicolor, Laurel Wreath, Gilt Rim, c.1950, 10¾ In., Pair	88
Tureen, Lid, Undertray, Saxon Flower, Round, Dragon Finial, 11 x 12 In. *illus*	123
Vase, Landscape, Church, Trees, Hills, Green Mark, 1962-70, 10 x 5 In.	50
Vase, Sea Gull, Oval, Shoulders, Danbury Mint, 5 In.	18

BINOCULARS
Binoculars of all types are wanted by collectors. Those made in the eighteenth and nineteenth centuries are favored by serious collectors. The small, attractive binoculars called opera glasses are listed in their own category.

Leica, Trinovid, 12x50, Nylon Sling, Black, Box	984
LeMair, Brass, Leather Covered Barrels, Leather Case, Paris, 1800s, 2½ x 4 x 1¼ In.	62
Naval Officer's, Burnished Brass, Adjustable, Magnifications, Diopter, Continental, 1900s *illus*	60
R & J Beck Ltd., Lookout Glasses, Folding, Brass, Brown Leather Case, 1857	108
Multiple Lens Settings, Tripod Base, Japan, 1900s, 24 x 38 In. *illus*	1250

BIRDCAGE
Birdcages are collected for use as homes for pet birds and as decorative objects of folk art. Elaborate wooden cages of the past centuries can still be found. The brass or wicker cages of the 1930s are popular with bird owners.

Bamboo, Carved, Cylindrical, Cuttlebone Holder, Sliding Gate, 3 Triangular Legs, 29 x 14 In. *illus*	610
Brass, On Stand, Tripod Feet, Art Deco, France, c.1930, 57 In.	188
Ceramic, Glazed, White, Domed Roof, France, 21 x 10½ x 10½ In.	125
Wire, Victorian Style, Mahogany, Doors, Stretcher Base, Late 1900s, 73 x 27 x 27 In.	540
Wood, Hinged Lid, Painted, Swing Handle, Victorian, 15½ x 13½ In. *illus*	154
Wood, House Shape, 2 Story, Painted, Multicolor, Folk Art, American, 1800s, 20 x 14 In.	875

BISQUE
Bisque is an unglazed baked porcelain. Finished bisque has a slightly sandy texture with a dull finish. Some of it may be decorated with various colors. Bisque gained favor during the late Victorian era when thousands of bisque figurines were made. It is still being made. Additional bisque items may be listed under the factory name.

Brushpot, 2 Panels, Relief Flowers, Geometric Ground, Chinese, 20th Century, 14½ In.	160

TIP
Binoculars should be checked by looking into the big end to be sure there are no cracks, chips, or even fungus. These problems may not change the view, but they will lower the price.

Binoculars, Multiple Lens Settings, Tripod Base, Japan, 1900s, 24 x 38 In.
$1,250

Eldred's

TIP
Thought of the day: "The things people discard tell more about them than the things they keep." Really? We saw this saying in a magazine and aren't sure we agree.

Birdcage, Bamboo, Carved, Cylindrical, Cuttlebone Holder, Sliding Gate, 3 Triangular Legs, 29 x 14 In.
$610

Rafael Osona Nantucket Auctions

Bisque, Figurine, Girl, Standing, Holding Puppy In Skirt, Yellow Dress, Germany, 11 ½ x 5 In.
$65

Woody Auction

Birdcage, Wood, Hinged Lid, Painted, Swing Handle, Victorian, 15 ½ x 13 ½ In.
$154

Pook & Pook

BISQUE

Black Americana, Broadside, Anti-Slavery Meetings, With Date & Time, Salem, Ohio, 1845, 15 x 20 In. $2,646

Pook & Pook

Blenko, Vase, Art Glass, Jonquil, No. 1580, Etched, West Virginia, c.1959, 11 ⅞ In. $120

Jeffrey S. Evans & Associates

Boch Freres, Vase, Yellow Roses, Mustard Ground, 1960s, 10 ¾ In. $120

Garth's Auctioneers & Appraisers

Brushpot, Cylindrical, High Relief Flowers, Marked, Chinese, Late 20th Century, 14 x 5 In.	160
Bust, Apollo, Round Pedestal, 11 ½ x 8 x 3 ½ In.	250
Figure, Cherub, Sevres Style, Blue Base, Martial Redon & Co., 1800s, 13 ¼ In., Pair	1125
Figure, Eagle, Spread Wings, Perched On Rock, Round Base, Green Marble, 10 ¾ x 14 ¾ In.	192
Figurine, Cat, Seated, Orange Bow, Fur, Eyes & Ears, Triade, 1900s, 2 ½ x 2 In.	188
Figurine, Colonial Man, Standing, Holding Nest, Basket, Multicolor, Shreve, Crump & Low, 16 In.	75
Figurine, Girl, Standing, Holding Puppy In Skirt, Yellow Dress, Germany, 11 ½ x 5 In. *illus*	65
Figurine, Man With Nest & Basket, Painted, Multicolor, Shreve, Crump & Low, 15 ¾ In.	75
Figurine, Portrait, Bust, Vladimir Lenin, Lomonosov, 1930s, 9 ¾ x 7 x 5 ½ In.	50
Vase, Cupid, Pierced Rim, Flowers, Leaves, Shaded Blue, Gilt, Footed, Japan, 9 ¾ In., Pair	50

BLACK AMERICANA

Black Americana has become an important area of collecting since the 1970s. The best material dates from past centuries, but many recent items are also of interest. F & F is the mark used on plastic made by Fiedler & Fiedler Mold & Die Works, Inc. in the 1930s and 1940s. Objects that picture a black person may also be listed in this book under Advertising, Sign; Bank; Bottle Opener; Cookie Jar; Doll; Salt & Pepper; Sheet Music; Toy; etc.

Ashtray, Butler, Holding Tray, Yellow Coat, Square Base, 1800s, 35 ½ x 9 ½ x 7 ½ In.	363
Broadside, Anti-Slavery Meetings, With Date & Time, Salem, Ohio, 1845, 15 x 20 In. *illus*	2646
Card Holder, Bellboy, Side View, Carved, Blue, White & Red, 38 ½ In.	300
Cookie Jars are listed in the Cookie Jar category.	
Doll, Girl, 1358, Bisque Socket Head, Mohair Wig, Glass Sleep Eyes, Simon & Halbig, 16 ½ In.	1169
Figurine, Uncle Tom, Little Eva On Knee, Staffordshire, 10 ½ x 5 x 4 In.	144
Lithograph, 4 Boys, Sitting On Fence, Eating, Watermelon, Paper, Folk Art, 1900s, 24 x 18 In.	2271
Puzzle, Game, Patriotic, Couple Dancing, Multicolor, Tin Frame, Mirrored Back, 2 In.	118
Puzzle, Who Stole The Goose, Policeman Chasing Robber, Metal Frame, Mirrored Back, 2 In.	146
Toys are listed in the Toy category.	

BLENKO GLASS COMPANY

Blenko Glass Company is the 1930s successor to several glassworks founded by William John Blenko in Milton, West Virginia. In 1933, his son, William H. Blenko Sr., took charge. The company made tablewares and vases in classical shapes. In the late 1940s it hired talented designers and made innovative pieces. The company made a line of reproductions for Colonial Williamsburg. It is still in business and is best known today for its decorative wares and stained glass.

Bottle, Clear, Blown, Pear Form, Flattened Rim, Faceted Teardrop Stopper, 34 In.	250
Vase, Art Glass, Jonquil, No. 1580, Etched, West Virginia, c.1959, 11 ⅞ In. *illus*	120

BLOWN GLASS, *see Glass-Blown category.*

BLUE GLASS, *see Cobalt Blue category.*

BLUE ONION, *see Onion category.*

BLUE WILLOW, *see Willow category.*

BOCH FRERES

Boch Freres factory was founded in 1841 in La Louviere in eastern Belgium. The pottery wares resemble the work of Villeroy & Boch. The factory closed in 1985. M.R.L. Boch took over the production of tableware but went bankrupt in 1988. Le Hodey took over Boch Freres in 1989, using the name Royal Boch Manufacture S.A. It went bankrupt in 2009.

Vase, Oval, Art Deco Flowers, Blue, Turquoise, Yellow, White Ground, Crazed, c.1920, 10 ¾ In.	625
Vase, Oval, Tapered Neck, Yellow Ground, Rose Panels, Dark Brown Trim, Mid 1900s, 11 In.	125

Vase, Oval, White Ground, Art Deco Flowers & Leaves, Brown, Orange, Green, Crazed, 11 ½ In.	440
Vase, Yellow Roses, Mustard Ground, 1960s, 10 ¾ In. .... *illus*	120

BOEHM

Boehm is the collector's name for the porcelains of Edward Marshall Boehm. In 1953 the Osso China Company was reorganized as Edward Marshall Boehm Inc. In the early days of the factory, dishes were made, but the elaborate and lifelike bird figurines are the best-known ware. Edward Marshall Boehm, the founder, died in 1969, but the firm continued to design and produce porcelain. The Museum of American Porcelain Art bought the assets, including the molds and trademarks, in 2015. The museum is located in South Euclid, Ohio, a suburb of Cleveland. The Boehm Showroom in Trenton, New Jersey, has exclusive use of the molds and trademarks. It also does restoration work and has some retired figures for sale.

Boehm Porcelain, LLC 1952–1954	Boehm Porcelain, LLC 1959–1970	Boehm Porcelain, LLC 1971+

American Goldfinch, Tail Raised, Perched On Leafy Stem, Violets, No. 400-39, 7 x 6 In.....	132
Baby Lovebird, 2 Birds, Heads Turned, Perched On Branch, No. 400-58, 6 In.	71
Duck, Mallard, Flying, Reeds, Marked, Mallards 406, 1900s, 11 ½ In., Pair	677
Flower, Iris Silver Showers, 16 In.. *illus*	448
Flying Goose, Black Marble Pedestal, Hattakitkosol Somchai, Thailand, 22 x 11 In.	275
Great Horned Owl, Raised Wings, Landing On Stump, Limited Edition, Signed, 12 ½ x 11 In....	250
Hooded Merganser, Male, Perched On Log, Fish In Beak, Limited Edition, No. 496, 11 x 12 In. .	469
Nuthatch, Head Lowered, Perched On Branch, Leaves, Yellow Flowers, No. 469W, 10 In.......	72
Parakeet, Open Wings, Orange, Orchids, 1900s, 11 ½ In.	1875
Rufous Hummingbird, Male, Raised Wings, Female, Perched, Yellow Flower & Bud, 487W, 15 In.	384
Tiger, Brown Orange, White, Black Strip, Golf Ball, 1998, 5 In.	63

BOHEMIAN GLASS, *see Glass-Bohemian*

BONE

Bone includes those articles made of bone not listed elsewhere in this book.

Boar Tusk, Mounted, Silver, Marked, 925, Donatus Solingen, Western Germany, 10 ½ In...	242
Figurine, Female, Holding Flower Sprig, Pierced, Footed Wood Base, c.1950, 11 ½ In... *illus*	330
Pie Crimper, Unicorn, Carved, Walnut, Central Band, Contemporary, 7 ½ In......................	313

BONE DISH

Bone dishes were considered a necessary part of a table setting for the Victorian table. The crescent-shaped dish was kept at the edge of the dinner plate so the bones removed from the fish could be stored away from the uneaten food. Some bone dishes were made in more fanciful shapes and many resemble fish.

4 Seasons, Flowers & Leaves, Gilt Trim, Scalloped Rim, Japan, 6 ¼ In., 4 Piece....................	4
Flower Spray, Multicolor, White Ground, Gilt Trim, Fluted Edge, Japan, 6 In., 6 Piece.........	10
Gilt Scrolls, Small Yellow Flowers, Cream Ground, Hand Painted, Lenwile Ardalt, Japan, 9 In....	18
Glass, Diamond Cut Border, Gilt U.S. Seal, 8 In.	120

BOOKENDS

Bookends have probably been used since books became inexpensive. Early libraries kept books in cupboards, not on open shelves. By the 1870s bookends

Boehm, Flower, Iris Silver Showers, 16 In.
$448

Nadeau's Auction Gallery

Bone, Figurine, Female, Holding Flower Sprig, Pierced, Footed Wood Base, c.1950, 11 ½ In.
$330

Selkirk Auctioneers & Appraisers

Bookends, Copper, Hammered, Handwrought, Signed, Craftsman Studios, c.1920s, 4 x 2 ¾ In.
$154

California Historical Design

This is an edited listing of current prices. Visit **Kovels.com** to check thousands of prices from previous years and sign up for free information on trends, tips, reproductions, marks, and more.

Bookends, End Of Trail, Bronze, Black, Horse, Signed, Armor Bronze Co., Buffalo, N.Y., c.1920, 6 x 4 x 2 In. $277

California Historical Design

Bookends, Panther, Green Patinated Bronze, Art Deco, c.1930, 8 x 14 x 5 In. $1,098

Rafael Osona Nantucket Auctions

Bookends, Ship, Clipper, Brass, 7 Sails, Figural, Painted, Stamped, Roycroft, 5 In. $122

Rafael Osona Nantucket Auctions

Bookends, Skull On Books, Bronze Clad, Felted Base, Armor Bronze Corp., Early 1900s, 5 x 4 x 5 In., One Of A Pair $556

Thomaston Place Auction Galleries

appeared, especially homemade fret-carved wooden examples. Most bookends listed in this book date from the twentieth century. Bookends are also listed in other categories by manufacturer or material. All bookends listed here are pairs.

Bison Head, Bronze, Bowing, Joza Krupka, Czech, Austria, c.1914, 8 x 9 x 4 In.	854
Cask, Dome Lid, Wood, Arched L-Shaped Pad, Ostrich, Gilt, Paw Feet, Maitland Smith, 9 x 10 In..	315
Copper, Arts & Crafts, Hammered, Loop Handle, c.1915, 5 x 4 x 3 In...........................	277
Copper, Hammered, Handwrought, Signed, Craftsman Studios, c.1920s, 4 x 2¾ In..... *illus*	154
Dante & Beatrice Busts, Copper Patina, Jennings Brothers, 1935, 6 In.	71
Dog, Scottie, Cast Iron, Flowered Fence, Hand Painted, Hubley, c.1930, 5 x 3 In............	115
Elephant, Cast Iron, Standing, Painted Green, Stamped 33, 4 In.....................	122
Elephant, Mixed Metal, Sitting Down, Trunk Up, 5¼ x 4 x 4¼ In......................	63
End Of Trail, Bronze, Black, Horse, Signed, Armor Bronze Co., Buffalo, N.Y., c.1920, 6 x 4 x 2 In. *illus*	277
Golfers, Brass, Man & Woman, Rubbed, Patina, Square Base, 6¼ x 4¾ x 3¼ In..............	88
Griffon, Sitting, Black Paint, Square Base, Jim Crouch, 10 In.	750
Horse Head, Cast Iron, Patina, Glass Eyes, Rope Base, 1900s, 9½ In.	704
Panther, Green Patinated Bronze, Art Deco, c.1930, 8 x 14 x 5 In. .... *illus*	1098
Pointer, Setter, Tree, Gilt, Bronze Base, England, 1800s, 9½ In.	554
Ship, Clipper, Brass, 7 Sails, Figural, Painted, Stamped, Roycroft, 5 In. .... *illus*	122
Ship, Copper, Hammered, Signed, Roycroft, c.1920s, 5 x 5½ In.	277
Skull On Books, Bronze Clad, Felted Base, Armor Bronze Corp., Early 1900s, 5 x 4 x 5 In.....*illus*	556
Spiral Shape, Copper, Walter Von Nessen, Chase Brass & Copper Co., c.1930, 4 x 4 x 2 In......*illus*	2000
Thinker, Rodin, White Metal, Bronze Wash, West Point Crest, Jennings Brothers, 1929, 7¾ In. ..	192

BOOKMARK

Bookmarks were originally made of parchment, cloth, or leather. Soon woven silk ribbon, thin cardboard, celluloid, wood, silver, tortoiseshell, and metals were used. Examples made before 1850 are scarce, but there are many to be found dating before 1920.

14K Gold, Magnifying Glass, Clip, Engraved Flowers, Monogram, Marked, c.1918, 5⅛ In. ..	480
18K Gold, Stylized Figure, Tourmaline Face, Elbows & Knees Bent, Marguerite Stix, 3½ In........	813
Aetna Insurance, Die Cut Metal, White Lettering, 2-Sided, Hartford, Conn., 12½ In.	60
Carmencita, Light Pink Tassel, Leather, Silvertone Chain With Clasp, Hermes, 6¾ In........	300
Cracker Jack, Dog, Scottie, In Profile, Clip, Marked, 1930s, Pair	36
Cracker Jack, Puppy, Tin Lithograph, Clip, Marked, 1930s, Pair	60
Elephant, Silver, Trunk Lowered, Oval Clip, 3 In.	36
Gold Plate, Clip, Double G On End, Tan Leather Sleeve, Gucci, Italy, 5¾ x ¾ In.	260
Taxco, Face In Profile, Engraved, Bird Headdress, Large Earring, Clip, Silver, 3½ In..........	31

BOSSONS

Bossons character wall masks (heads), plaques, figurines, and other decorative pieces of chalkware were made by W.H. Bossons, Limited, of Congleton, England. The company was founded in 1946 and closed in 1996. Dates shown are the date the item was introduced.

Wall Mask, Eskimo, Fur Hood, 1968, 6 x 7 In..	40
Wall Mask, Poodle, White, Red Collar, 1968, 5 In.	38
Wall Mask, Samuel Pickwick, Red Shirt, Glasses, 1964, 5½ x 3½ In.	22

BOSTON & SANDWICH CO. *pieces may be found in the Sandwich Glass category.*

BOTTLE

Bottle collecting has become a major American hobby. There are several general categories of bottles, including historic flasks, bitters, household, ink, snuff, soda, and figural. Perfume bottles are listed in their own category in this book. ABM means the bottle was made by an automatic bottle machine after 1903. Pyro is the shortened form of the word *pyroglaze*, an enameled lettering used on bottles after the mid-1930s.

This form of decoration is also called ACL or applied color label. Shapes of bottles often indicate the age of the bottle. For more prices, go to kovels.com.

Case gin bottle
1650–1920

Teakettle ink
1830–1885

Calabash flask
1840–1870

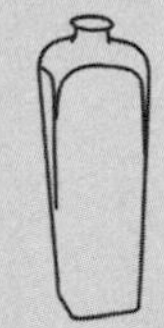

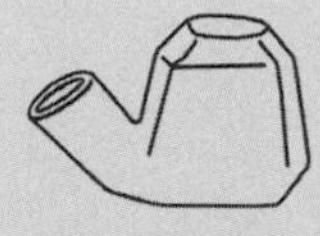

Ale, Abner & Drury Brewers, Washington, D.C., Pure Malt & Hops, Banner, Amber, 9 In.	72
Ale, Anheuser Busch Br'g Assn., Eagle In A, Baltimore Branch, Amber, c.1890, 9 In.	60
Ale, Bunker Hill Lager, Banner, Amber, Vertical Ribs, Lightning Closure, 1875-90, 9¾ In.	168
Ale, Hartmann & Fehrenbach Brewing Co., Winged Horse, Wilmington, Del., Orange Amber, 9¾ In.	120
Ale, John Schusler Brewing Co., The Finest, Glass On Beer Keg, Buffalo, N.Y., Yellow Amber, 10 In.	144
Ale, Joseph Schlitz's Milwaukee Lager, J. Gahm, J.G. In Beer Mug, Yellow Olive, 9⅝ In.	355
Ale, Milwaukee Lager, Adams Ale House, Concord, N.H., Yellow Amber, Lightning Closure, 9½ In.	204
Ale, Milwaukee Lager, J. Gahm, 83 State St., Boston, Mass., J.G. In Beer Mug, Olive, 10 In.	390
Ale, Milwaukee Lager, J. Gahm, J.G. In Beer Mug, Boston, Yellow Amber, 9½ In.	192
Atlanta Brewing & Ice Co., Stoneware, Crackle Ground, Brown Top, c.1892, 8¾ In.	625

Avon started in 1886 as the California Perfume Company. It was not until 1929 that the name Avon was used. In 1939, it became Avon Products, Inc. Avon has made many figural bottles filled with cosmetic products. Ceramic, plastic, and glass bottles were made in limited editions from 1965 to 1980. There was a limited-edition bottle collecting frenzy and prices rose. By 2018 the bottle prices were back to a very low level.

Avon, Bell, Sweet Honesty, Emerald Green Glass, Handle With Faceted Bead, 1978, 5¾ In.	24
Avon, Dapper Snowman, Figural, Moonwind Cologne, 1970s, Box, 3¼ In.	14
Avon, Deer, Blue Glass, White Deer In Forest, Plastic Deer Finial, 1981-82, 7½ In.	16
Avon, Dog, Baby Basset Hound, Topaz Cologne, Brown Glass, 1960s, 3¼ In.	30
Avon, Duck, Mallard, Aftershave, Green Glass, Silver Plastic Head, 1967, 3½ x 6 In.	13
Avon, Faucet, Chrome Tone, White Porcelain Tap, Just A Twist, Aftershave, 1970s, 4 In.	18
Avon, Field Flowers Cologne Mist, Green Glass, Tapered, Fluted, Brass Collar, 6 In.	25
Avon, Horse, Standing, Wild Country Cologne, Brown Glass, 1970s, 6 In.	11
Avon, Skunk, Sweet Honesty, Black & White Glass & Plastic, 3⅛ In.	9

Beam bottles were made to hold Kentucky Straight Bourbon, made by the James B. Beam Distilling Company. The Beam series of figural ceramic bottles began in 1953.

Beam, Barney's Slot Machine, Red, 1978, 5 x 8½ x 9 In.	66
Beam, Bird, Ducks Unlimited, 2 American Widgeons, In Flight, 1983	30
Beam, Car, 1904 Oldsmobile, 75th Anniversary	37
Beam, Car, 1953 Corvette Convertible, Teal, Tan Roof, Gray Trim, Box, 1989, 11 In.	63
Beam, Car, 1956 Ford Thunderbird, Blue, Original Box, 1964	100
Beam, Car, 1957 Corvette Convertible, Red, White Trim, Tan Inside, Box, 1990, 11 In.	75
Beam, Car, 1964 Ford Mustang, Black, Original Box	100
Beam, Car, 1968 Corvette Convertible, Red, Porcelain Undercarriage, Box, 1992, 14 In.	50
Beam, Car, 1978 Corvette Convertible, Hard Top, Red, Box, 1984, 14 In.	25
Beam, Car, 1978 Corvette Convertible, Hard Top, Yellow, Box, 1984, 14 In.	31
Beam, Car, Fire Chief, C.F.D., Red, Box, 15 x 7 In.	105
Beam, Car, Stutz Bearcat, Yellow, Original Box, 16¼ x 6¾ In.	80
Beam, Chicago Cubs, Bear Dressed As Player, Original Box	168
Beam, Elks Centennial, 1868-1968 On Star On Canteen Decanter, Shaded Brown, 11 In.	25
Beam, Key West 150th Anniversary, Dolphin On Waves, Beach Scene, 1972	25
Beam, London Bridge, Horseshoe Shape, 1971 .... *illus*	16
Beam, Pilgrim Woman, Holding Basket On Arm	60
Beam, Republican Elephant, Democrat Donkey, Standing, Wearing Suits, 1960, 12 In., Pair	36
Beam, Straw Hats, Republican Elephant, Democrat Donkey, 1968, 12 In., Pair	38

Bookends, Spiral Shape, Copper, Walter Von Nessen, Chase Brass & Copper Co., c.1930, 4 x 4 x 2 In.
$2,000

Wright

Bottle, Beam, London Bridge, Horseshoe Shape, 1971
$16

pca9219 on eBay

Bottle, Bitters, Digestine, P.J. Bowlin Liquor Co., St. Paul, Minn., Amber, 8½ In.
$344

Glass Works Auctions

B

Bottle, Bitters, Fish, W.H. Ware, Patented 1866, Citron, Applied Lip, 11 1/8 In.
$4,200

Glass Works Auctions

Bottle, Bitters, Hall's, E.E. Hall, New Haven, Barrel, Red Amber, Puce Tone, Square Lip, 9 1/2 In.
$3,300

Glass Works Auctions

Bottle, Cologne, Toilet Water, 20 Ribs, Swirled To Left, Cobalt Blue, Tam Stopper, 6 In.
$252

Glass Works Auctions

Bottle, Bitters, Great Universal Compound Stomach, Patented 1870, Amber, Sloping Collar, 10 1/2 In.
$1,140

Glass Works Auctions

Bottle, Bitters, National, Ear Of Corn, Patent 1867, Golden Yellow, Applied Double Collar, 12 5/8 In.
$2,040

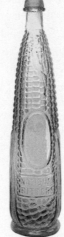

Glass Works Auctions

Bottle, Cosmetic, Mrs. S.A. Allen's World's Hair Restorer, Olive Green, Double Collar, 7 1/4 In.
$2,400

Glass Works Auctions

Bottle, Bitters, H.P. Herb Wild Cherry, Reading, Pa., Cabin, Grass Green, 1885-95, 8 7/8 In.
$6,600

Glass Works Auctions

Bottle, Blown, Amber, Thin Neck, Rolled Rim, Late 1800s, 9 x 6 x 5 In.
$531

Bruneau & Co. Auctioneers

Bottle, Demijohn, Amber Shaded To Yellow, Loaf Of Bread Shape, Sloping Collar, 1855-70, 10 In.
$660

Glass Works Auctions

B

Beam, Train, Baggage Car, Central Railroad Of New Jersey, Green, Box	54
Beam, Train, Passenger Car, Central Railroad Of New Jersey, Green & Tan, Box	96
Beam, Train, Red Caboose, New Jersey Central, Original Box	96
Beam, Trolley, San Francisco Cable Car, 1983	48
Beam, Truck, 1928-29 Ford Model A Pickup, Green, Porcelain, Regal China, Original Box	125
Beam, Truck, Police Tow Truck, Blue, 3 In Star On Side, Original Box, 14 In.	271
Bininger, A.M. & Co., 19 Broad St., N.Y., Old London Dock, Amber, 1855-70, 8 In.	403
Bininger, A.M. & Co., 19 Broad St., N.Y., Old London Dock, Green, 1855-70, 8 In.	805
Bitters, Aromatic Orange, Berry, Nashville, Semi-Cabin, Orange Amber, c.1870, 10 In.	1680
Bitters, Bennet's Celebrated Stomach, Amber, Square, Case, Sloping Collar, 1871-79, 9 In.	633
Bitters, Bourbon Whiskey, Barrel, Pink Puce, Squared Lip, Label, 1860-70, 9⅜ In.	720
Bitters, Brown's Celebrated Indian Herb, Patented Feb. 11, 1868, Light Amber, 12¼ In.	1955
Bitters, Catawba Wine, Green, Embossed Grapes, Arched Sides, Sloping Collar, 9½ In.	6900
Bitters, Celebrated Crown, F. Chevalier & Co., Pale Amber, Sloping Collar, 1880-86, 8¾ In.	575
Bitters, Digestine, P.J. Bowlin Liquor Co., St. Paul, Minn., Amber, 8½ In. ....illus	344
Bitters, Dr. Carson's Victoria Wine, Whitby, C.W., Blue, 8-Sided, Canada, c.1860, 12⅝ In.	6600
Bitters, Dr. Manly Hardy's Genuine Jaundice, Bangor, Me., Aqua, Tombstone Sides, 7¼ In.	390
Bitters, Drake's Plantation, 6 Log, Amber, Sloping Collar, 10 In.	288
Bitters, Drake's Plantation, 6 Log, Old Amber, Yellow Tone, Sloping Collar, 10 In.	978
Bitters, Drake's Plantation, 6 Log, X, 1860, Cabin, Deep Cherry Puce, Sloping Collar, 10 In.	450
Bitters, Drake's Plantation, 6 Log, Yellow, Sloping Collar, 10 In.	2530
Bitters, Fish, W.H. Ware, Patented 1866, Citron, Applied Lip, 11⅛ In. ....illus	4200
Bitters, Grand Prize, Amber, Square, Arched Sides, Indented Panels, Early 1880s, 9¼ In.	575
Bitters, Great Universal Compound Stomach, Patented 1870, Amber, Sloping Collar, 10½ In.illus	1140
Bitters, Greeley's Bourbon Whiskey, Barrel, Blue Aqua, Applied Lip, 1865-75, 9½ In.	7200
Bitters, Greeley's Bourbon Whiskey, Barrel, Puce, Applied Lip, 1865-75, 9¼ In.	720
Bitters, Greeley's Bourbon, Barrel, Smoky Olive Green, Squared Lip, 1860-70, 9⅜ In.	1320
Bitters, H.P. Herb Wild Cherry, Reading, Pa., Cabin, Grass Green, 1885-95, 8⅞ In. ....illus	6600
Bitters, Hall's, E.E. Hall, New Haven, Barrel, Red Amber, Puce Tone, Square Lip, 9½ In. ....illus	3300
Bitters, Hibernia, Yellow Amber, Square, Case, Sloping Collar, 1880s, 10 In.	403
Bitters, Horse Shoe Medicine Co., Collinsville, Ills., Running Horse, Red Amber, 8⅞ In.	9600
Bitters, Keystone, Barrel, Red Amber, Sloping Collar, 1865-75, 10 In.	600
Bitters, Lacours, Amber, Column Form, Applied Lip, 1866-75, 9 In.	2530
Bitters, National, Ear Of Corn, Deep Red Puce, Double Collar, 1867-75, 12½ In.	1560
Bitters, National, Ear Of Corn, Patent 1867, Golden Yellow, Applied Double Collar, 12⅝ In....illus	2040
Bitters, Old Sachem & Wigwam Tonic, Barrel, Yellow Amber, Applied Lip, 1860-70, 9⅜ In.	660
Bitters, Pineapple, W & Co., N.Y., Amber, Applied Double Collar, 8⅝ In.	1610
Bitters, Reed's, Yellow, Amber Tint, Lady's Leg Neck, Double Collar, 1865-75, 12⅜ In.	780
Bitters, Wormser Bros., San Francisco, Barrel, Light To Medium Amber, Sloping Collar, 9¾ In.	2530
Black Glass, Wine, Dark Yellow Olive, Cylindrical, Squat, String Lip, England, 1700-80, 9 In.	556
Blown, Amber, Thin Neck, Rolled Rim, Late 1800s, 9 x 6 x 5 In. ....illus	531
Car, Model T Ford, Black, Original Box, 13½ In.	135
Coca-Cola Bottles are listed in the Coca-Cola category.	
Cologne, 14 Vertical Ribs, Light Blue, Cobalt Blue Striations, Melon Shape, Flared Lip, c.1830, 4 In.	300
Cologne, 16 Ribs, Swirled To Left, Amethyst, Flared Lip, Pontil, Pittsburgh, 5¾ In.	3000
Cologne, Barrel, Flattened, Swan & Fountain, Amethyst Tint, Flared Lip, Pontil, 6½ In.	252
Cologne, Toilet Water, 20 Ribs, Swirled To Left, Cobalt Blue, Tam Stopper, 6 In. ....illus	252
Cosmetic, Cuticine Lotion For Face & Hands, Geo. P. Rogers Druggist, Canton, N.Y., Teal, 5 In.	480
Cosmetic, Dr. Tebbitts' Physiological Hair Regenerator, Dark Pink Amethyst, 7½ In.	216
Cosmetic, Dr. Jayne's Hair Tonic, Philada., Aqua, Oval, Rolled Lip, 4⅝ In.	276
Cosmetic, Mrs. S.A. Allen's World's Hair Restorer, Olive Green, Double Collar, 7¼ In...illus	2400
Cure, Craig's Kidney & Liver, Amber, Oval, Double Collar, 1870-75, 9½ In.	192
Cure, Dr. Zeublin's Safe & Quick, For The Sick Headache, Aqua, Cylindrical, Rolled Lip, 3½ In.	480
Cure, Warner's Safe Kidney & Liver Cure, Rochester, N.Y., Amber, 9⅝ In.	288
Decanter, Pillar Molded, 8 Pillars, Sun Colored Amethyst, Double Collar, 10¼ In.	108
Demijohn, Amber Shaded To Yellow, Loaf Of Bread Shape, Sloping Collar, 1855-70, 10 In... illus	660
Demijohn, Cobalt Blue, Tapered Collar, 1870-85, 17 In.	3900
Figural, Night, Robed Man With Lantern, Flask, Brown Glaze, Pottery, England, 1800s, 10 In.	113
Figural, Pig, Good Old Bourbon In A Hog's, Amber, 1880-95, 6½ In.	480
Fire Grenade, Babcock, Non-Freezing, Cobalt Blue, Horizontal Ribs, 1880-1900, 7½ In..... illus	1560

Bottle, Fire Grenade, Babcock, Non-Freezing, Cobalt Blue, Horizontal Ribs, 1880-1900, 7½ In.
$1,560

Glass Works Auctions

Bottle, Fire Grenade, Harden's Hand, Star, Amber, Vertical Ribs, 1875-95, Qt.
$900

Glass Works Auctions

Bottle, Fire Grenade, Hayward's Hand, Pat Aug 8 1871, Lime Green, Contents, 6 In.
$360

Glass Works Auctions

Bottle, Flask, Corn For The World, Yellow Olive, Applied Double Collar, 1860-70, Qt.
$9,600

Glass Works Auctions

Bottle, Flask, Flag & New Granite Glass Works, Stoddard, Golden Amber, Pt.
$19,890

Norman C. Heckler & Company

Bottle, Flask, Lafayette & Liberty, Old Amber, Sheared Mouth, Pontil, ½ Pt.
$1,020

Glass Works Auctions

Fire Grenade, Harden's Hand, Star, Amber, Vertical Ribs, 1875-95, Qt. .... *illus*	900
Fire Grenade, Hayward's Hand, Pat Aug 8 1871, Lime Green, Contents, 6 In. .... *illus*	360
Flask, 20 Ribs, Swirled To Right, Cobalt Blue, Flared Out Lip, Pocket, 1815-35, 3¾ In.	330
Flask, Chestnut, 12 Vertical Ribs, Deep Cobalt Blue, Outward Rolled Lip, Pittsburgh, 4⅝ In.......	1080
Flask, Chestnut, 24 Ribs, Swirled To Left, Amber, Sheared Mouth, Zanesville, 1820-35, 5 In.	300
Flask, Chestnut, 24 Ribs, Swirled To Right, Green Aqua, Sheared Mouth, 1815-35, 6½ In. ..	450
Flask, Columbia & Eagle, Aqua, Sheared Mouth, Pontil, 1825-35, Pt.	1440
Flask, Corn For The World, Ear Of Corn, Monument, Aqua, Sheared Mouth, Qt...................	1920
Flask, Corn For The World, Yellow Olive, Applied Double Collar, 1860-70, Qt. .... *illus*	9600
Flask, Cornucopia & Urn, Blue Green, Sheared Mouth, 1840-50, Pt.	660
Flask, Double Eagle, Deep Olive Green, Double Collar, 1860-70, Qt.	720
Flask, Double Eagle, Olive Yellow, Sheared Mouth, 1825-35, ½ Pt.	330
Flask, Eagle & Masonic Arch, Blue Aqua, Green Tint, Sheared Mouth, 1835-45, Pt.............	1020
Flask, Eagle & Masonic Arch, Red Amber, Sheared Mouth, 1835-45, Pt.	1920
Flask, Flag & New Granite Glass Works, Stoddard, Golden Amber, Pt......................... *illus*	19890
Flask, Flora Temple & Horse, Apricot Puce, Double Collar, Handle, 1859-65, Qt.	1320
Flask, Flora Temple & Horse, Copper Puce, Applied Ring Lip, Handle, 1859-60, Pt.	510
Flask, History Of Holland, Book Shape, Pottery, Dark Blue Glaze, 1860-80, 5¾ In.	240
Flask, Hunter & Hounds, Emerald Green, Double Collar, 1850-60, Pt.	1320
Flask, Jenny Lind, Calabash, Emerald Green, Double Collar, 1855-65..........................	1680
Flask, Lafayette & Liberty Cap, Yellow Amber, 1825-30, ½ Pt.	900
Flask, Lafayette & Liberty, Old Amber, Sheared Mouth, Pontil, ½ Pt. .... *illus*	1020
Flask, Masonic & Eagle, Blue Green, Pontil, Keene Glassworks, Pt..............................	2106
Flask, Masonic & Eagle, Medium To Dark Purple Amethyst, Sheared Mouth, Keene, 1820-30, Pt.*illus*	36270
Flask, Milk Glass, Enameled Flowers & Peafowl, Half Post, Pewter Ring, Germany, c.1785, 6 In. .	276
Flask, Nailsea, Clear, Milk Glass Herringbone, Sheared Mouth, Pontil, 7⅛ In.	132
Flask, Pattern Molded, Diamond Daisy, Pink Amethyst, Sheared Mouth, Pontil, 5¾ In.	420
Flask, Pitkin Type, 16 Broken Ribs, Grass Green, Half Post, 5⅞ In. .... *illus*	480
Flask, Pitkin Type, 16 Broken Ribs, Shaded Grass Green, Half Post, Sheared Mouth, 1815-30, 6 In.	480
Flask, Scroll, Blue Green, Applied Ring, 1845-55, Pt..	1080
Flask, Scroll, Cobalt Blue, Sheared Mouth, Tooled Lip, Iron Pontil, 1840-50, Qt. .... *illus*	3600
Flask, Scroll, Golden Yellow, Olive Tone, Sheared Mouth, 1845-50, Qt.	4800
Flask, Scroll, Medium Sapphire Blue, Sheared Mouth, Pontil Scar, ½ Pt.	8190
Flask, Scroll, Shaded Green, Sheared Mouth, 1840-50, Pt..	1020
Flask, Sheaf Of Grain & Tree, Calabash, Dark Claret, Double Collar, 1855-65.................	900
Flask, Summer & Winter, Deep Emerald Green, Sheared Mouth, 1840-60, Qt.	25740
Flask, Sunburst, Apple Green, Sheared Mouth, Pontil, 1815-35, Pt. .... *illus*	720
Flask, Tankard, Acid Etched, Engraved, Bird, Silver Handle, Acorn Wreaths, c.1880, 11 In....	47
Flask, Taylor & Eagle, Blue Aqua, Sheared Mouth, 1830-40, Qt.	1920
Flask, Taylor & Masterson, Rough & Ready, Blue Aqua, Sheared Mouth, Qt. .... *illus*	1920
Flask, Traveler's Companion & Ravenna Glass Co., Amber, Double Collar, 1850-60, Pt.	1200
Flask, Union, Clasped Hands & Cannon, Light Blue, Pittsburgh, 1800s, 7¾ In.	195
Flask, Washington & Eagle, Shaded Citron, Sheared Lip, Pontil, 1825-35, Qt...................	1800
Flask, Washington & Frigate, Golden Amber, Applied Double Collar, Iron Pontil, Pt.	1112
Flask, Washington & Taylor Never Surrenders, Emerald Green, 1848-55, Qt......................	660
Flask, Washington & Taylor, Teal, 1848-55, Qt.	1320
Flask, Washington & Taylor, Yellow Amber, Puce Tint, Applied Lip, Pontil, Pt. .... *illus*	5850
Flask, Waterford, Clasped Hands & Eagle, Light Apple Green, Square Collar, Qt. .... *illus*	510
Flask, Whiskey, Canteen, Admiral Dewey, Our Hero, Rope Handle, U.S., Red Text, 1900s, 5 In. ..	349
Food, Maple Sap & Boiled Cider Vinegar, C.I. Co., East Rindge, N.H., Cobalt Blue, 11⅝ In.....	1560
Food, Spice, G. Venard, San Francisco, Light Blue Aqua, Indented Sides, Rolled Lip	138
Food, Spice, J.W. Hunnewell, Boston, Aqua, 8-Sided, Concave Panels, Applied Lip, 7¼ In.	23
Fruit Jar, Beaver, Facing Right, Chewing On Log, Apple Green, Zinc Lid, Qt................. *illus*	192
Fruit Jar, Blue Aqua, Bell Shape, Dip Mold, Wax Seal Ring, 1850-60, 10¼ In.......................	1560
Fruit Jar, Clarke, Cleveland, O., Aqua, Metal Clamp, 24 Oz.	204
Fruit Jar, Gilberds Improved, Star, Aqua, Glass Lid, Wrap Around Wire Closure, Qt.............	330
Fruit Jar, King, Blue Aqua, Iron Yoke Clamp, Glass Insert, 1870-80, Qt........................ *illus*	540
Fruit Jar, Magic, Wm. McCully & Co., Pittsburgh, Blue Aqua, ½ Gal.............................	1680
Fruit Jar, Petal, Emerald Green, 10 Shoulder & Neck Panels, Wax Seal Mouth, Qt...............	3000
Fruit Jar, Safety, Yellow Amber, Deep Amber Glass Lid, Metal Closure, Pt.	288

Bottle, Flask, Masonic & Eagle, Medium To Dark Purple Amethyst, Sheared Mouth, Keene, 1820-30, Pt.
$36,270

Norman C. Heckler & Company

Bottle, Flask, Sunburst, Apple Green, Sheared Mouth, Pontil, 1815-35, Pt.
$720

Glass Works Auctions

Bottle, Flask, Waterford, Clasped Hands & Eagle, Light Apple Green, Square Collar, Qt.
$510

Glass Works Auctions

Bottle, Flask, Pitkin Type, 16 Broken Ribs, Grass Green, Half Post, 5⅞ In.
$480

Glass Works Auctions

Bottle, Flask, Taylor & Masterson, Rough & Ready, Blue Aqua, Sheared Mouth, Qt.
$1,920

Glass Works Auctions

Bottle, Fruit Jar, Beaver, Facing Right, Chewing On Log, Apple Green, Zinc Lid, Qt.
$192

Glass Works Auctions

Bottle, Flask, Scroll, Cobalt Blue, Sheared Mouth, Tooled Lip, Iron Pontil, 1840-50, Qt.
$3,600

Glass Works Auctions

Bottle, Flask, Washington & Taylor, Yellow Amber, Puce Tint, Applied Lip, Pontil, Pt.
$5,850

Norman C. Heckler & Company

Bottle, Fruit Jar, King, Blue Aqua, Iron Yoke Clamp, Glass Insert, 1870-80, Qt.
$540

Glass Works Auctions

Bottle, Gin, Case, Grass Green, Outward Rolled Mouth, 1760-90, 11 ⅝ in.

$300

Glass Works Auctions

Bottle, Household, C.M. Lina & Co., Oil, Blacking, Blue Aqua, Inward Rolled Lip, 5 In.

$252

Glass Works Auctions

Bottle, Household, Clough's Liquid Stove Polish, Aqua, Applied Double Collar, 6 ½ In.

$420

Glass Works Auctions

Gin, Case, Amber, Apricot Tone, Unembossed, Rounded Lip, Fifth	345
Gin, Case, Grass Green, Outward Rolled Mouth, 1760-90, 11 ⅝ in. ....*illus*	300
Gin, Charles Cordial Gin, London, Case, Olive Amber, Sloping Collar, Fifth............	489
Gin, Fairchild's Excelsior, Case, Aqua, Sloping Collar...............................	265
Gin, Hendrick Walter Aromatic Schnapps, Schiedam, Light Blue, 7 ¼ In.	242
Gin, Hoboken's Aromatic Schnapps, Case, Light Green, Sloping Collar, 8 In.	196
Gin, Holland Schnapps, Jan Van Walter, Citron, Applied Collar, 8 In.	92
Gin, J.T. Daly Club House, Case, Olive Green, Flared & Rounded Lip, Fifth	1380
Gin, Royal Imperial, Case, Medium Blue, Sloping Collar, Fifth	1495
Gin, Royal Palm, L.G. & Co., Case, Aqua, Sloping Collar, Fifth	1725
Gin, T.J. Dunbar & Co. Cordial Schnapps, Green, Sloping Collar, Fifth................	748
Gin, Udolpho Wolfe's Aromatic Schnapps, Case, Apricot, Sloping Collar, 8 In.........	431
Gin, Udolpho Wolfe's Aromatic Schnapps, Case, Blue Green, Sloping Collar, 8 In. ...	978
Gin, Udolpho Wolfe's Aromatic Schnapps, Case, Green, Fifth	1150
Gin, Vanderveer's Medicated, Case, Olive Green, Tapered, Sloping Collar, 7 In.......	633
Gin, Voldner's Aromatic Schnapps, Green, Yellow Tint, Bubbles, Square, Arched Sides, Fifth	1380
Gin, Vonthofen's Aromatic Schnapps, Schiedam, Case, Green, Fifth...................	2070
Globular, 20 Vertical Ribs, Yellow Amber, Applied Lip, Pittsburgh, 1815-35, 8 ¼ In............	480
Household, C.M. Lina & Co., Oil, Blacking, Blue Aqua, Inward Rolled Lip, 5 In...........*illus*	252
Household, Clough's Liquid Stove Polish, Aqua, Applied Double Collar, 6 ½ In...........*illus*	420
Household, Dr. J. Kendall's Transparent Water Proof & Leather Preservative, Aqua, 4 In. ...	1560
Household, Golden Lustral, Aqua, Long Neck, Sloping Collar, 7 ¼ In......................	120
Household, W.M. Child & Co. Oil Polish, Aqua, 12-Sided, Thin Flared Out Lip, c.1865, 5 In.	192
Ink, Geometric, Old Amber, Hobnail, Fluted Base, Keene Glass Works, 1815-35, 1 ⅝ In.........	480
Ink, Harrison's Columbian, Green, Cylindrical, Applied Double Collar, Master, 7 ¼ In. *illus*	960
Ink, J. & I.E.M., Igloo, Yellow Amber, Sheared Mouth, 1875-90, 1 ⅝ In.	390
Ink, J. & I.E.M., Igloo, Deep Cobalt Blue, Sheared Mouth, 1875-90, 1 ¾ In...................*illus*	1320
Ink, Opdyke Bros., Barrel, Aqua, Tooled Lip, 2 ½ In.	216
Ink, Pitkin Type, 36 Ribs, Swirled To Right, Olive Green, 1790-1825, 1 ⅝ In. ....*illus*	2280
Ink, S. Fine Blk. Ink, Cylinder, Emerald Green, Rolled Lip, 3 In.	570
Ink, S.I. Comp., Cottage, Aqua, Tooled Lip, 1870-80, 2 ⅝ In.....................*illus*	420
Ink, Teakettle, 8-Sided, Concave Panels, Cobalt Blue, Brass Cap, 2 In.................	633
Ink, Teakettle, 8-Sided, Concave Panels, Purple, Brass Cap, 2 In.....................	920
Ink, Teakettle, 8-Sided, Concave Panels, Ribs, Amethyst, Metal Ring, 1875-90, In........*illus*	510
Ink, Teakettle, 8-Sided, Flat Panels, Light Blue, Brass Cap, 2 In.....................	855
Ink, Teakettle, 8-Sided, Milk Glass, Painted Flowers, Brass Cap, 2 In.................	690
Ink, Teakettle, 8-Sided, Rounded Panels, Green, Brass Cap, 2 In.....................	1093
Ink, Teakettle, Barrel, Amethyst, Made For W.H. Harrison Presidential Campaign, 1840, 2 In......	5060
Ink, Teakettle, Barrel, Shaded Sapphire Blue, Brass Cap, 2 ⅛ In....................	2300
Ink, Teakettle, Barrel, Teal, Sheared Mouth, Original Metal Cap, 1875-90, 2 ¼ In............	5100
Ink, Teakettle, Humpback Snail Shell, Clear, Sheared Mouth, 1 ⅝ In.	480
Ink, Teakettle, Porcelain, 8-Sided, White, Enameled Green Coral Panels, Gold Trim, 2 In...	1800
Ink, Teakettle, Turtle, Embossed Scrolls, Pale Aqua, 1875-90, 2 In.	720
Ink, Umbrella, 6-Sided, Yellow Amber, Rolled Lip, Pontil, Stoddard Type, 2 ½ In..........	855
Ink, Umbrella, 8-Sided, Amber, Rolled Lip, 2 ½ In.	276
Ink, Umbrella, 8-Sided, Citron, Rolled Lip, 2 ½ In.	978
Ink, Umbrella, 8-Sided, Cobalt Blue, Inward Rolled Lip, 1840-60, 2 ½ In..............	3000
Ink, Umbrella, 8-Sided, Electric Blue, Rolled Lip, Smooth Base, 2 ½ In................	1093
Ink, Umbrella, 8-Sided, Green, Rolled Lip, Open Pontil, 2 ½ In.......................	242
Ink, Umbrella, 8-Sided, Light Citron, Rolled Lip, 2 ½ In.............................	575
Ink, Umbrella, 8-Sided, Olive Yellow, Inward Rolled Lip, 2 ¼ In.................*illus*	660
Ink, Umbrella, 8-Sided, Plum Color, Rolled Lip, 2 ½ In..............................	3450
Ink, Ward's, Green, Cylindrical, Sloping Collar, Master, 5 In........................	489
Jar, Apothecary, Applied Finial, Round Base, Pittsburgh, Mid 1800s, 10 In.............	108
Jar, Globe Tobacco Co., Detroit & Windsor, Yellow Amber, Barrel, Screw Lid, 7 In.......	450
Mallet, Wine, Dark Yellow Amber, Deep Kickup, Sheared Mouth, String Lip, England, 8 In.	330
Medicine, A. McEckron's R.B Liniment, N.Y., Aqua, Oval, Sloping Collar, Label, 6 In.	276
Medicine, Apothecary, Cannabis, Cobalt Blue, Rolled Rim, 1800s, 15 ½ x 9 ¾ In. ....*illus*	726
Medicine, Apothecary, Cocaine, Broad Mouth, Flared Rim, Cobalt Blue, Gilt Band, 7 ¾ x 8 ¼ In.	1872
Medicine, Apothecary, Earthenware, Glazed, White Ground, 1700s, 6 ½ In. ....*illus*	125

B

Medicine, Apothecary, Lid, White Crackle Ground, Leaves, Earthenware, 1800s, 9¼ In., Pair .... *illus*	63
Medicine, Arthur's Renovating Syrup, Blue Green, Sloping Collar, 7⅞ In.................... *illus*	3900
Medicine, Bonfland's Fever & Ague Remedy, Aqua, Tapered Collar, Label, 5¼ In.	96
Medicine, Bush & Co., Botanic Druggists, Worcester, Mass., Aqua, Indented Panels, 6¾ In.	570
Medicine, Celliniana Balm, Aqua, Cylindrical, Inward Rolled Lip, 6¾ In.	805
Medicine, Chinese Liniment, Price 20 Cts., Clear, Rounded Shoulder, Rolled Lip, 4 In........	360
Medicine, Davis & Miller, Baltimore, Druggist, Blue Aqua, Rounded Shoulder, 6½ In.	450
Medicine, Doct. Curtis' Inhaling Hygean Vapor, Smoky Clear, Double Collar, 7¼ In.	132
Medicine, Doct. Fowler's Anti Epicholic, Canton, N.Y., Blue Aqua, Sloping Collar, 5⅞ In.	216
Medicine, Dr. E. McCoy's Magic Liniment, Wheeling, Aqua, Rolled Lip, 1840-60, 4½ In.	540
Medicine, Dr. Foord's Pectoral Syrup, New York, Aqua, Tapered Collar, 1840-60, 5⅝ In....	132
Medicine, Dr. G.W. Phillips Cough Syrup, Cincinnati, O, Blue Aqua, Collar, c.1850, 7⅝ In..	252
Medicine, Dr. Hamilton's Syrup Of Blackberry & Sassafras, Aqua, Oval, Rolled Lip, 4¾ In.	510
Medicine, Dr. Henley's Celery, Beef & Iron, Amber, Cylinder, Ring Mouth, 11½ In..............	84
Medicine, Dr. J.S. Wood's Elixir, Albany, N.Y., Tombstone, Emerald Green, 8⅞ In........ *illus*	1800
Medicine, Dr. Jas. McClintock's Family Medicines, Clear, Indented Panels, 8 In....................	156
Medicine, Dr. M. Ireland's Eclectic Liniment, Aqua, 8-Sided, Rolled Lip, c.1850, 4¼ In.	600
Medicine, Dr. M.G. Kerr, Asiatic Balsam, Norristown, Pa., Aqua, Flared Lip, 4¾ In.	204
Medicine, Dr. Mann's Celebrated Ague, Balsam, Galion, Ohio, Blue Aqua, Double Collar, 7 In. ...	330
Medicine, Dr. Steph. Jewett's Celebrated Pulmonary Elixir, Rindge, N.H., Aqua, 5¾ In.	420
Medicine, Dr. Van Vleck's Family Medicine, Pittsburgh, Aqua, Arched Shoulder, 6½ In.	720
Medicine, Dr. W.J. Haas's Expectorant, Schuylkill Haven, Pa., Aqua, Flared Lip, c.1850, 5¼ In.	300
Medicine, E. Byam's Liquid Opodeldoc, Clear, Cylindrical, Flared Lip, 1820-25, 4¾ In.	1200
Medicine, E. Warner Indian Physician Syrup, Aqua, Rounded Shoulder, 7¼ In.	840
Medicine, Genessee Liniment, Blue Aqua, Inward Rolled Lip, Pontil, 5½ In.	120
Medicine, George W. Carpenter, Philadelphia, Genuine Preparations, Pale Aqua, 6 In.	156
Medicine, Gibb's Bone Liniment, Yellow Olive, 6-Sided, Sloping Collar, Pontil, 6⅜ In.	2160
Medicine, Holman's Nature's Grand Restorative, Boston, Blue Aqua, Applied Lip, 7 In........	330
Medicine, Howard's Vegetable Cancer & Canker Syrup, Yellow Old Amber, Square Lip, 7⅜ In..... *illus*	3300
Medicine, Keller's Catarrh Remedy & Blood Purifier, Aqua, Indented Panels, 7⅝ In.	385
Medicine, Kimball's Anodyne Toothache Drops, Amber, Cylindrical, Label, c.1850, 7¼ In..	720
Medicine, Lewis & Fletcher's New Vegetable Compound, Blue Aqua, Double Collar, 8 In.....*illus*	2040
Medicine, McLean's Strengthening Cordial, Cornflower Blue, Oval, 9¼ In......................	360
Medicine, Mede's Mexican Fluid, Yellow Topaz, 6-Sided, Double Panel, 5½ In.	540
Medicine, Orrick's Vermifuge Or Worm Destroyer, Baltimore, Aqua, Cylindrical, 4⅝ In.	390
Medicine, Owl Drug Co., Owl On Mortar & Pestle, Amber, Beer Bottle Shape, 8 In. .... *illus*	96
Medicine, Queru's Cod Liver Oil Jelly, Aqua, Jar, Wide Mouth, Rolled Lip, 5½ In.	330
Medicine, Snow & Mason, Providence, R.I., Croup & Cough Syrup, Aqua, Cylinder, 5 In.	204
Medicine, Sparks Perfect Health, Bust Of Man, For Kidney & Liver Diseases, Amber, 9⅜ In.........	420
Medicine, Spooners Hygeian Tonic, Price $1.00, Yellow Olive, 8-Sided, Sloping Collar, 6 In.	10530
Medicine, Swaim's Panacea, Philada., Olive Amber, Oval, Ribbed, Double Collar, c.1860, 8 In....	510
Medicine, Swift's Syphilitic Specific, Cobalt Blue, Applied Lip, 1870-80, 9 In........................	1560
Medicine, Telfer's Bronchial Tincture, Deep Olive, Flared Lip, 1810-40, 12¼ In....................	1205
Medicine, Thomson's Compound Of Tar, For Consumption, Green Aqua, Arched Panels, 5⅝ In..	108
Medicine, U.S.A. Hosp. Dept., Yellow Olive, Amber Tone, 4-Part Mold, Double Collar, 9½ In....	2040
Medicine, U.S.A. Hosp. Dept., Yellow Peach, 4-Part Mold, Double Collar, c.1865, 9¼ In.	3600
Milk, Bordens, Elsie The Cow, If It's Bordens It's Got To Be Good, Cream, 4 Oz................	10
Milk, Gates Homestead Farm, Chittenango, N.Y., Embossed Letters In Circle, ½ Pt.	25
Milk, Goodenough's Dairy, Red Pyroglaze Letters, Wide Mouth Cream, 2¼ In..................	20
Milk, Hevner's Pasturized Milk & Cream, Red Letters, Wide Mouth Cream, 2¼ In.	23
Milk, Lykens Dairy Inc., Lykens, Pa., Red Letters & Rays, Qt.	11
Milk, Southern Dairies, Knoxville, Tenn., Embossed Letters, ½ Pt.	17
Milk, Valley Farms, Quality Milk From Nearby Farms, Red Pyro, Farm At Sunrise, Qt.	18
Milk, Varney's Dairy, Nashville, Michigan, Embossed Letters, 1930s, Pt.	6
Milk, Wabuda's, Shelton, Conn., Red Pyroglaze Letters, Qt...	10
Milk, Wheeler's Dairy, Stonington, Conn., Green Pyro Letters, 1944, Qt.	25
Milk, Wilson Dairy Co., Atlantic City, N.J., Red Letters, Cream...	18
Mineral Water, Adirondack Spring, Whitehall, N.Y., Emerald Green, Pt...............................	84
Mineral Water, Artesian Water, Louisville, Ky., Black Glass, Pontil, Sloping Collar, Pt.........	840
Mineral Water, Brand's, Toledo, O., Cobalt Blue, Blob Top, Iron Pontil, 7⅜ In............ *illus*	450

Bottle, Ink, Harrison's Columbian, Green, Cylindrical, Applied Double Collar, Master, 7¼ In.
$960

Glass Works Auctions

Bottle, Ink, J. & I.E.M., Igloo, Deep Cobalt Blue, Sheared Mouth, 1875-90, 1¾ In.
$1,320

Glass Works Auctions

Bottle, Ink, Pitkin Type, 36 Ribs, Swirled To Right, Olive Green, 1790-1825, 1⅝ In.
$2,280

Glass Works Auctions

B

Bottle, Ink, S.I. Comp., Cottage, Aqua, Tooled Lip, 1870-80, 2 5/8 In.
$420

Glass Works Auctions

Bottle, Ink, Teakettle, 8-Sided, Concave Panels, Ribs, Amethyst, Metal Ring, 1875-90, In.
$510

Glass Works Auctions

Whittle Marks

Whittle marks are caused by iron molds that have not been preheated properly. If the glass and the mold are at different temperatures, cooling causes the whittled appearance.

Bottle, Ink, Umbrella, 8-Sided, Olive Yellow, Inward Rolled Lip, 2 1/4 In.
$660

Glass Works Auctions

Mineral Water, Clarke & Co., New York, Deep Blue Green, High Shoulder, Double Collar, Qt.	390
Mineral Water, Clarke & Co., New York, Deep Olive Green, Double Collar, Qt.	120
Mineral Water, Congress & Empire Spring Co., C, Saratoga, N.Y., Olive Green, Qt.	120
Mineral Water, Congress & Empire Spring Co., Hotchkiss Sons, C, New York, Grass Green, Pt.	330
Mineral Water, D.A. Knowlton, Saratoga, N.Y., Olive Green, High Shoulder, Qt.	72
Mineral Water, F. Gleason, Rochester, N.Y., Cobalt Blue, Sloping Collar, 7 1/2 In.	450
Mineral Water, G.W. Weston & Co., Saratoga, N.Y., Deep Olive, Double Collar, Qt.	345
Mineral Water, Gettysburg Water, Deep Olive Green, Double Collar, 1865-75, Magnum	2880
Mineral Water, Gleason & Cole, Pittsbg., Cobalt Blue, 10-Sided, Sloping Collar, 7 1/2 In.	720
Mineral Water, High Rock Congress Spring, Rock, C&W, Saratoga, N.Y., Olive Amber, Qt.	720
Mineral Water, High Rock Congress Spring, Rock, C&W, Saratoga, N.Y., Yellow Amber, Pt.	345
Mineral Water, Hopkins' Chalybeate, Baltimore, Deep Grass Green, Sloping Double Collar, Pt.	660
Mineral Water, J.H.V. Premium, Troy, Cobalt Blue, Blob Top, 1840-60, 7 In.	780
Mineral Water, John H. Gardner & Son, Sharon Springs, N.Y., Teal, 1865-75, Pt.	252
Mineral Water, M.T. Crawford, Hartford, Ct., Teal, Blob Top, 1840-60, 7 1/8 In.	390
Mineral Water, M.T. Crawford, Springfield, Union Glass Works, Blue, Mug Base, Blob Top, 7 1/2 In.	840
Mineral Water, Massena Spring Water, Monogram, Emerald Green, Qt.	1440
Mineral Water, Middletown Healing Springs, Deep Emerald Green, Wire Closure, Qt.	570
Mineral Water, Oak Orchard, Acid Springs, Yellow Amber, Double Sloping Collar, Qt.	345
Mineral Water, Oak Orchard, Acid Springs, Yellow Green, Double Sloping Collar, Qt.	4200
Mineral Water, Owell & Dr. Burr's, Burlington, N.J., Cobalt Blue, 8-Sided, 7 1/4 In.	1560
Mineral Water, Pavilion & United States Spring Co., Saratoga, N.Y., Emerald Green, Pt.	264
Mineral Water, S. Meyer, Trenton, N.J., Slug Plate, Blue Green, Union Glass Works, 7 1/2 In.	1920
Mineral Water, St. Leon Spring, J In Diamond, Blue Green, Double Collar, Qt.	720
Mineral Water, St. Regis Water, Massena Springs, Teal, Double Collar, 1865-80, Qt.	288
Mineral Water, St. Regis Water, Massena Springs, Yellow Olive Amber, Double Collar, Pt.	1320
Mineral Water, Syracuse Springs, D, Excelsior, New York, Golden Yellow, Olive Tint, 1/2 Pt.	1920
Mineral Water, T. & R. Morton, Newark, N.J., Cobalt Blue, Blob Top, 7 1/4 In.	1560
Onion, Blue Green, Sheared Mouth, Applied String Lip, Pontil, 1720-50, 7 1/8 In.	420
Onion, Horse's Hoof, Deep Olive Amber, Applied String Lip, Dutch, 8 In.	330
Pepper Sauce, Aqua, 6 Fluted Sides, Applied Sloping Collar, 8 1/4 In.	115
Pepper Sauce, Cathedral, 4-Sided, Aqua, Tapered, Double Collar, 9 3/4 In.	288
Pepper Sauce, Cathedral, 6-Sided, Aqua, Double Collar, 9 In.	92
Pepper Sauce, Cathedral, 6-Sided, Aqua, Double Collar, Pontil, 10 1/2 In.	184
Perfume Bottles are listed in the Perfume Bottle category.	
Pickle, Cathedral, 4-Sided, Aqua, Applied Rolled Lip, 7 3/4 In.	150
Pickle, Cathedral, 4-Sided, Blue Green, Arched Panels, Rolled Lip, 11 In. _illus_	374
Pickle, Cathedral, 4-Sided, Teal Blue, Rolled Lip, Iron Pontil, 11 1/2 In.	1150
Pickle, Green Aqua, Indented Panels, Ferns, 13 1/2 In.	288
Pickle, Skilton Foote & Co.'s, Bunker Hill, Lighthouse, Yellow, Sloping Collar, 11 In.	3510
Poison, Embossed Poison, Cobalt Blue, Vertical Ribs, Sawtooth Stopper, E.R.S. & S., 5 1/2 In.	180
Poison, Flask, Green, Raised Hobnail, Inward Rolled Lip, c.1860, 5 1/4 In.	390
Poison, Giftflasche, Skull & Crossbones, Lime Green, 3-Sided, Germany, 9 3/4 In. _illus_	344
Poison, Owl Drug Co., Script, Owl, Embossed Poison, Cobalt Blue, 3-Sided, Label, 5 In.	264
Poison, Poison On Shoulder, Red Amber, Cylindrical, Wide Vertical Ribs, England, c.1920, 8 In.	84
Sarsaparilla, Dr. Guysott's Compound Extract Of Yellow Dock, Yellow Olive Amber, 9 1/4 In.	4500
Sarsaparilla, Dr. Townsend's, Albany, Shaded Olive, Sticky Ball Pontil, 9 1/4 In.	518
Sarsaparilla, Dr. Townsend's, New York, Green, Sloping Collar, Iron Pontil, 9 3/4 In.	460
Sarsaparilla, Wynkoop's Katharismic Honduras, Blue, Sloping Collar, 1840-60, 10 1/4 In.	6600
Seal, Star Whiskey, New York, Bell Shape, Amber, Vertical Ribs, Double Collar, 8 1/4 In. _illus_	1920
Seal, Thomas Gerrard, Gibbstown, Black Glass, High Shoulder, Sloping Collar, 11 In.	120
Snuff, 14K Gold Finish, Tapered, Lapis Lazuli Stopper, Oval Foot, Chinese, Late 1700s, 2 1/2 In._illus_	3240
Snuff, Agate, Butterscotch, Black Flecks, Oval, Gilt Bronze Stopper, 2 3/4 In.	378
Snuff, Agate, Carved, Brown, Fish Shape, Incised Fins, Red Stone Stopper, 2 3/4 In.	1680
Snuff, Agate, Shadow, Phoenix & Hawk, Peach Branch, 1780, 2 1/4 In.	4080
Snuff, Amber, Textured Basket Weave, Jade & Red Coral Stopper, Chinese, 2 In.	160
Snuff, Black Lacquer, Mother-Of-Pearl Inlay, Quatrefoils In Diamonds, Oval, Japan, 2 In.	438
Snuff, Cinnabar, Carved Roses & Flowering Trees, Bulbous, Tapered, Qianlong Mark, 3 In.	540
Snuff, Cinnabar, Carved, Landscape, Pagoda, Spade Shape, Metal Cap, 1870, 3 In.	829
Snuff, Cinnabar, Lacquered, Carved Landscape With Scholars, Orange Cabochon Cap, 3 In.	1260

Bottle, Medicine, Apothecary, Cannabis, Cobalt Blue, Rolled Rim, 1800s, 15 ½ x 9 ¾ In.
$726

Fontaine's Auction Gallery

Bottle, Medicine, Apothecary, Earthenware, Glazed, White Ground, 1700s, 6 ½ In.
$125

Hindman

Bottle, Medicine, Apothecary, Lid, White Crackle Ground, Leaves, Earthenware, 1800s, 9 ¼ In., Pair
$63

Hindman

Bottle, Medicine, Arthur's Renovating Syrup, Blue Green, Sloping Collar, 7 ⅞ In.
$3,900

Glass Works Auctions

Bottle, Medicine, Dr. J.S. Wood's Elixir, Albany, N.Y., Tombstone, Emerald Green, 8 ⅞ In.
$1,800

Glass Works Auctions

Bottle, Medicine, Howard's Vegetable Cancer & Canker Syrup, Yellow Old Amber, Square Lip, 7 ⅜ In.
$3,300

Glass Works Auctions

Bottle, Medicine, Lewis & Fletcher's New Vegetable Compound, Blue Aqua, Double Collar, 8 In.
$2,040

Glass Works Auctions

Bottle, Medicine, Owl Drug Co., Owl On Mortar & Pestle, Amber, Beer Bottle Shape, 8 In.
$96

Glass Works Auctions

Bottle, Mineral Water, Brand's, Toledo, O., Cobalt Blue, Blob Top, Iron Pontil, 7 ⅜ In.
$450

Glass Works Auctions

Bottle, Pickle, Cathedral, 4-Sided, Blue Green, Arched Panels, Rolled Lip, 11 In.
$374

American Bottle Auctions

Bottle, Poison, Giftflasche, Skull & Crossbones, Lime Green, 3-Sided, Germany, 9¾ In.
$344

Glass Works Auctions

Bottle, Seal, Star Whiskey, New York, Bell Shape, Amber, Vertical Ribs, Double Collar, 8¼ In.
$1,920

Glass Works Auctions

Bottle, Snuff, 14K Gold Finish, Tapered, Lapis Lazuli Stopper, Oval Foot, Chinese, Late 1700s, 2½ In.
$3,240

Selkirk Auctioneers & Appraisers

Bottle, Snuff, Glass, Medium Forest Green, Tooled Mouth, Pontil, Keene, 1815-30, 7 x 3½ In.
$30,420

Norman C. Heckler & Company

Bottle, Snuff, Glass, Snowstorm Ground, Red Overlay, Horse, Standing, Rocky Terrain, 1760, 3 In.
$1,530

Bonhams

Snuff, Enamel, Cloisonne, Teardrop Shape, Dark Blue, Lilies, Ginbari, Japan, 1868, 2 5/16 In.	701	
Snuff, Glass, 8 Horses, Lakeside, Reverse Painted, Ye Zhongsan, 1898, 2 1/2 In.	3570	
Snuff, Glass, Clear With Milky Accents, Flattened Oval, White Stone Stopper, 2 1/4 In.	750	
Snuff, Glass, Daoist Immortal, Deer, White, Red, Rectangular, Wang Su, 1821, 2 5/8 In.	3825	
Snuff, Glass, E. Roome, Troy, New York, Deep Old Amber, Flared Out Lip, 1835-55, 4 In.	540	
Snuff, Glass, Ink Calligraphy, Reverse Painted, Rectangular, Zhou Leyuan, 1889, 2 3/16 In. .	1275	
Snuff, Glass, Medium Forest Green, Tooled Mouth, Pontil, Keene, 1815-30, 7 x 3 1/2 In. .... *illus*	30420	
Snuff, Glass, Night Scene, Candlelight, Reverse Painted, Rectangular, Ma Shaoxuan, 1897, 2 1/2 In. ...	2168	
Snuff, Glass, Painted, Black Flying Cranes, Mountains, Orange Setting Sun, Characters, 4 In.....	125	
Snuff, Glass, Realgar, Mottled Red, Orange & Brown, Jadeite Stopper, Ivory Spoon, c.1790, 2 3/4 In..	1020	
Snuff, Glass, Reverse Painted, Coral Stopper, Signed, Ye Zhongshan, Beijing, Early 1900s, 2 3/4 In. .	570	
Snuff, Glass, Ruby Red, Octagonal, Imperial Glassworks, Beijing, 1730, 1 1/2 In.	9563	
Snuff, Glass, Sapphire, Round, Rose Quartz Stopper, Chinese, Early 1800s, 2 1/2 In.	360	
Snuff, Glass, Semi Transparent, White, Green, Jadeite, Spade Shape, 1780, 2 1/8 In.	1084	
Snuff, Glass, Snowflake, Blue Overlay, Chi Dragon, Carved, Chinese, Mid 1800s, 2 3/4 In.	660	
Snuff, Glass, Snowstorm Ground, Red Overlay, Horse, Standing, Rocky Terrain, 1760, 3 In...*illus*	1530	
Snuff, Glass, White, Blue Overlay, Chained Hound & Hawk, Round, 1750, 2 3/8 In.	2168	
Snuff, Glass, White, Green Overlay, Spade Shape, Swirls, 1730, 2 In.	4463	
Snuff, Hardstone, Carved Flowers, Chilong, Double Gourd, Coral Stone Stopper, 2 1/4 In.	3528	
Snuff, Hardstone, Creamy White, Green Striations, 5 Carved Bats, Shou Symbol, 2 3/8 In.	1197	
Snuff, Hardstone, Olive Green, Relief Carved Bamboo, Mask Handles, Coral Cap, 2 3/4 In.	945	
Snuff, Jade, Pebble Shape, Carved, Pale Green & Russet, With Spoon, 2 5/8 In.	1521	
Snuff, Jade, Spinach Nephrite, Dark Green, Circular Panels, 1820, 2 1/8 In...................*illus*	2295	
Snuff, Jade, Spinach, Carved Grapes, Oval, Jade Stopper, Chinese, 2 1/2 In.....................	219	
Snuff, Jade, White Nephrite, Oval, Cylindrical Neck, Flattened Lip, 1770, 1 1/2 In.	3188	
Snuff, Jade, White, Relief Carved, Woman, Man With Banner, Mask Handles, Footed, Coral Cap, 2 In.	5040	
Snuff, Jadeite, Lavender & Green Tint, Relief Branches, Chinese, 2 1/2 In....................	531	
Snuff, Milk Glass, Multicolor, Flattened Spade Shape, Chinese, 1800s, 2 1/2 In.............*illus*	500	
Snuff, Peking Glass, Green, 8-Sided, Tapered, Coral Stone Stopper, 2 3/4 In.	256	
Snuff, Porcelain, Moth Shape, Open Wings, Multicolor, 1820, 1 3/4 In.	1020	
Snuff, Porcelain, Painted, 2 Asian Women In Garden, Canteen Form, Red Stone Stopper, 4 In....	625	
Snuff, Porcelain, White, Painted Iron Red Bats & Clouds, Coral Cabochon Cap, 2 1/2 In.	5040	
Snuff, Porcelain, White, Painted, Blue Carp, Seaweed, Clouds, Cylindrical, Jade Stopper, 2 1/4 In.	1408	
Snuff, Rock Crystal, Rectangular, River Landscape, Gan Xuanwen, Lingnan, 1810, 2 In.	1913	
Snuff, Rock Crystal, Rounded Rectangular Shape, Oval Foot, 1750, 2 5/8 In.	2550	
Snuff, Shadow Agate, Relief Carved Phoenix Bird & Flowers, Blue Glass Stopper, 2 1/2 In......	375	
Soda, Bay City Soda Water, S.F., Star, Sapphire Blue, Blob Top, 7 1/4 In. ....*illus*	570	
Soda, C. Abel & Co., St. Louis, Shaded Blue Green, 12-Sided, Blob Top, 7 3/8 In........................	300	
Soda, Coburn Lang & Co., Boston, American Ginger Ale, Aqua, Wire Closure, 9 In................	192	
Soda, Coughlan, Balto., Torpedo, Grass Green, Sloping Collar, 1855-65, 8 1/2 In.	720	
Soda, Crystal Palace Premium, W. Eagle, New York, Blue Green, Blob Top, 7 1/4 In.	960	
Soda, E.N. Ladley, German Town, Deep Sapphire Blue, Shouldered, Double Collar, 7 In.	4800	
Soda, Genuine, D.P. Cotton & Co., Barbados, Torpedo, Green, Sloping Collar, c.1885, 8 1/4 In. ..	360	
Soda, Hollister & Co., Honolulu, Torpedo, Aqua, Tooled Lip, Metal Stand, 1885-95, 8 In.	204	
Soda, J. & A. Dearborn, N.Y., Albany Glass Works, Deep Sapphire Blue, Blob Top, 7 In.	600	
Soda, J. Lake, Schenectady, N.Y., Deep Sapphire Blue, Sloping Collar, 1840-60, 7 1/2 In.	900	
Soda, J.R. Donaldson, 5-Point Star, Newark, N.J., Cobalt Blue, 10-Sided, 7 1/2 In.	1680	
Soda, J.R. Donaldson, Newark, N.J., Cobalt Blue, Mug Base, Blob Top, 7 1/4 In....................	330	
Soda, J.T. Brown, Chemist, Boston, Double, Emerald Green, Blob Top, 8 3/4 In.....................	192	
Soda, J.T. Brown, Chemist, Boston, Double, Teal, Blob Top, Metal Stand, 8 3/4 In...................	960	
Soda, Keach, Balto., Shaded Green, Torpedo Shape, Sloping Collar, 1855-65, 9 In.........*illus*	720	
Soda, Knicker Bocker, Deep Sapphire Blue, 10-Sided, Sloping Collar, 7 3/4 In.	510	
Soda, Luke Beard, Blue Green, Tenpin, Blob Top, Lightning Closure, 7 1/8 In.	252	
Soda, Luke Beard, Deep Emerald Green, Tenpin, Sloping Collar, 1840-60, 7 1/8 In.	1020	
Soda, M.B. Patten, Charlestown, Bunker Hill, Ginger Ale, Aqua, Wire Closure, 8 1/2 In.........	168	
Soda, M.J. Seibert, Pottsville, Pa., Aqua, Union Glass Works, Blob Top, 7 3/8 In...............	1800	
Soda, Smith & Fotheringham, St. Louis, Cobalt Blue, 10-Sided, Sloping Collar, 7 1/2 In.	2760	
Soda, Southwick & Tupper, New York, Cobalt Blue, 10-Sided, 1840-60, 7 1/2 In.	840	
Soda, Usse Freres Nogent Sur Seine, Light Green, Etched, Hunt & Cie, Paris, 13 In., Pair	250	
Soda, Virgin Forest Water Co., St. Lawrence Co., N.Y., Red Amber, c.1903, 11 5/8 In.	2520	

Bottle, Snuff, Jade, Spinach Nephrite, Dark Green, Circular Panels, 1820, 2 1/8 In.
$2,295

Bonhams

Bottle, Snuff, Milk Glass, Multicolor, Flattened Spade Shape, Chinese, 1800s, 2 1/2 In.
$500

Eldred's

Bottle, Soda, Bay City Soda Water, S.F., Star, Sapphire Blue, Blob Top, 7 1/4 In.
$570

Glass Works Auctions

Bottle, Soda, Keach, Balto., Shaded Green, Torpedo Shape, Sloping Collar, 1855-65, 9 In.
$720

Glass Works Auctions

Bottle, Target Ball, Amethyst, 3-Piece Mold, Hand Blown, Sheared Mouth, 2 ⅝ In.
$510

Glass Works Auctions

Bottle, Target Ball, Bogardus, Pat'd Apr 10 1877, Diamond, Cobalt Blue, Sheared Mouth, 2 ⅜ In.
$780

Glass Works Auctions

Bottle, Target Ball, Charlottenburg Glashutten, Dr. A. Frank, Diamond, Yellow Amber, 2 ⅝ In.
$216

Glass Works Auctions

Bottle, Tonic, Rohrer's Expectoral Wild Cherry, Lancaster, Pa., Amber, Roped Corners, 10 ⅝ In.
$540

Glass Works Auctions

Bottle, Whiskey, Casper's, Made By Honest North Carolina People, Cobalt Blue, Lady's Leg Neck, 12 In.
$510

Glass Works Auctions

Bottle, Whiskey, Jameson's Old Irish, Pottery, Cream Glaze, Harp, Shamrocks, Jug, 1890-1910, ¼ Gal.
$252

Glass Works Auctions

Bottle, Whiskey, Mist Of The Morning, S.N. Barnett & Co., Barrel, Yellow Amber, Sloping Collar, 10 In.
$450

Glass Works Auctions

Bottle, Whiskey, Phoenix Old Bourbon, Amber, Coffin Flask, Neck Ring, 1870-88, 7 ¼ In.
$390

Glass Works Auctions

Soda, Willis & Ripley, Portsmouth, W & R, Ohio, Sapphire Blue, Sloping Collar, 7 ½ In.	510
Target Ball, Amethyst, 3-Piece Mold, Hand Blown, Sheared Mouth, 2 ⅝ In. ...... *illus*	510
Target Ball, Bogardus, Pat'd Apr 10 1877, Diamond, Cobalt Blue, Sheared Mouth, 2 ⅜ In. *illus*	780
Target Ball, Charlottenburg Glashutten, Dr. A. Frank, Diamond, Yellow Amber, 2 ⅝ In. ..... *illus*	216
Tonic, Rohrer's Expectoral Wild Cherry, Lancaster, Pa., Amber, Roped Corners, 10 ⅝ In. *illus*	540
Whiskey, Bulkley, Fiske & Co., Brandy, Chestnut, Yellow Green, Aqua Handle, 8 ⅜ In.	10800
Whiskey, Casper's, Made By Honest North Carolina People, Cobalt Blue, Lady's Leg Neck, 12 In. *illus*	510
Whiskey, Choice Old Bourbon, John Gibson Sons, Yellow, Topaz Tint, Double Collar, 9 ¾ In. ..	1140
Whiskey, Cognac, W. & Co., Seal, Amber, Applied Ring, Handle, Pontil, 1855-65, 6 ⅛ In.	840
Whiskey, Dunbar & Co. Wormwood Cordial, Boston, Aqua, Case, Sloping Collar, Qt.	1150
Whiskey, Henry Chapman & Co., Montreal, Teardrop Flask, Olive Yellow, 1860s, 5 ¾ In.	960
Whiskey, Jameson's Old Irish, Pottery, Cream Glaze, Harp, Shamrocks, Jug, 1890-1910, ¼ Gal. *illus*	252
Whiskey, Mist Of The Morning, S.N. Barnett & Co., Barrel, Yellow Amber, Sloping Collar, 10 In. *illus*	450
Whiskey, Parker's Rochelle Schnapps, Aqua, Case, Sloping Collar, Iron Pontil, Fifth	1610
Whiskey, Phoenix Old Bourbon, Amber, Coffin Flask, Neck Ring, 1870-88, 7 ¼ In. *illus*	390
Whiskey, Sackett, Belcher & Co., Old Amber, Chestnut, Applied Seal, Handle, c.1860, 8 ¼ In.	1440
Whiskey, Star, New York, Amber, Tapered, Vertical Ribs, Applied Seal, Handle, c.1860, 8 ¼ In.	1920
Whiskey, Tippecanoe, North Bend, Cabin, Yellow Olive, Sloping Collar, c.1840, Pt	15210
Whiskey, Voldner's Aromatic Schnapps, Schiedam, Yellow, Case, Sloping Collar, 9 ½ In. *illus*	1150
Whiskey, William H. Daly, New York, Green, Cylindrical, Long Neck, Squared Collar, Fifth.	403

BOTTLE CAP

Bottle caps for milk bottles are the printed cardboard caps used since the 1920s. Crown caps, used after 1892 on soda bottles, are also popular collectibles. Unusual mottoes, graphics, and caps from bottlers that are out of business bring the highest prices.

Crown, Gem Orange Drink, Wellston, Oh., Cork Lined, Orange, Black, 1950s	6
Crown, My Pop's Root Beer, Balloons, Fireworks, Yellow, 1960s	2
Crown, Punch, Artificially Colored & Flavored, Red, White	3
Hancock County Creamery, Heavy Cream, Ellsworth, Maine, 4 Piece	5
N.F. & J.C. Schoppee, Pasteurized Milk, Cow's Head, Red, White	2
Oaklands Milk, Gardiner, Maine, From Federally Accredited Herd, c.1930	16
Racine Pure Milk Company, Pasteurized Milk, 2 Piece	12

BOTTLE OPENER

Bottle openers are needed to open many bottles. As soon as the commercial bottle was invented, the opener to be used with the new types of closures became a necessity. Many types of bottle openers can be found, most dating from the twentieth century. Collectors prize advertising and comic openers.

Cowboy, Playing Guitar, Cast Iron, c.1925, 5 In.	75
Football Player, Cast Iron, Painted, Green Shirt, Homecoming '54, 4 ¼ In. *illus*	120
Giraffe's Head, Wood, Carved, 5 ¾ In.	15
Hawaiian Hula Girl, Cast Iron, Enameled, 7 ½ x 3 ½ In.	113
Jenner Brewing Co., Brass, Embossed, Pre Prohibition, Boswell, Pa., 2 ½ In. *illus*	192
McKenchie Brewing Co., Canandaigua High Hopped Ale, Metal, 2-Sided, Multicolor, 3 x 2 In.	590
Mermaid, Brass, Germany, 5 ¼ In.	65
Stainless Steel, Bakelite, Butterscotch Swirl, 1950s	19

BOTTLE STOPPER

Bottle stoppers are made of glass, metal, plastic, and wood. Decorative and figural stoppers are used to replace the original cork stoppers and are collected today.

Cork, Mother-Of-Pearl Plaque, Rum, c.1950	135
Lead Crystal, Grape Cluster, Mikasa, 6 In.	15
Teak, Cat's Head, Leather Ears, Painted Eyes, Pourer, c.1960, 3 ¼ In.	40
Wood, Anri Dog, Floppy Ears, 3 In.	63
Wood, Train Conductor, Black Forest, 5 In.	45

Bottle, Whiskey, Voldner's Aromatic Schnapps, Schiedam, Yellow, Case, Sloping Collar, 9 ½ In.
$1,150

American Bottle Auctions

Bottle Opener, Football Player, Cast Iron, Painted, Green Shirt, Homecoming '54, 4 ¼ In.
$120

Milestone Auctions

Bottle Opener, Jenner Brewing Co., Brass, Embossed, Pre Prohibition, Boswell, Pa., 2 ½ In.
$192

Carey Auctions

Box, Bandbox, Lid, Canister, Painted, Street Scene, Eagle, Lew Hudnall, Ohio, Dated '67, 10 In.
$176

Pook & Pook

Box, Bible, Lift Lid, Oak, Carved, Iron Lock & Hasp, Rectangular, 1700s, 6 x 17 x 11 In.
$819

Thomaston Place Auction Galleries

Box, Bride's, Bentwood, Band, Oval, Flowers, Blue Paint, Umber Trim, 1800s, 6 x 16 x 9 In.
$266

Soulis Auctions

TIP

Be sure copies of lists of valuables, photographs, and other information can be found in case of an insurance loss. Give copies and tell a trusted friend how to find them. Do not keep them in the house.

BOX

Boxes of all kinds are collected. They were made of wood, metal, tortoiseshell, embroidery, or other material. Additional boxes may be listed in other sections, such as Advertising, Battersea, Ivory, Shaker, Tinware, and various Porcelain categories. Tea Caddies are listed in their own category.

Artist's, Rosewood, Folding Top, Sam S. Folken, Royal Colonnade, Brighton, 1825, 4 x 15 x 11 In. 1989
Ballot, 2 Sliding Lids, Walnut, Dovetailed, 1800s, 3¾ x 9 x 4 In. 84
Ballot, Wood, Federal, Grain Paint, Drawer, Shaped Handle, 1800s, 15 x 5 x 4 In. 406
Bandbox, Bentwood, Wallpaper, Oval, 1842 Newspaper Lining, Hannah Davis, N.H., 6 x 10 In. .. 240
Bandbox, Lid, Canister, Painted, Street Scene, Eagle, Lew Hudnall, Ohio, Dated '67, 10 In. *illus* 176
Bandbox, Lid, Sunflowers, Painted, Black Ground, 7⅝ x 20 x 8⅝ In. 250
Bandbox, Oval, Lithograph, Nantucket Map, Tony Sarg, 6 x 18 x 10 In. 122
Bentwood, Lift Lid, Pine, Green Paint, Brass, Lettered, Coffee, c.1880, 5 In. 108
Bible, Lift Lid, Oak, Carved, Flowers & Leaves, 2 Drawers, 1700s, 12 x 25 x 16 In. 1404
Bible, Lift Lid, Oak, Carved, Iron Lock & Hasp, Rectangular, 1700s, 6 x 17 x 11 In. ...... *illus* 819
Bible, Lift Lid, Oak, Carved, Lunette Carving, Massachusetts, Late 1600s, 7 x 24 x 16 In. 17500
Bible, Slanted Hinged Lid, Pine, Drawer, Bracket Base, Queen Anne, 12 x 14 x 12 In. 878
Bonbonniere, Porcelain, Silver Hinged Lid, White Ground, 1¼ x 2½ In. 352
Book Shape, Drawer, Titled, The Impatient Virgins, Wood, Inlay, Late 1800s, 10 x 7¾ In. .. 100
Bride's, Bentwood, Band, Oval, Flowers, Blue Paint, Umber Trim, 1800s, 6 x 16 x 9 In..... *illus* 266
Bride's, Bentwood, Pivot Lid, Carved, Wood Devices, Wrought Iron Handle, 1800s, 8 x 16 x 9 In. .. 266
Bride's, Hinged Dome Lid, Wallpaper, Light Blue Ground, 1700s, 8 x 15 x 9 In. .... *illus* 4063
Bride's, Lid, Bentwood, Painted, Flowers, Heart, Figures, 1800s, 7 x 19 x 11 In. 554
Bride's, Oval, Removable Lid, Painted, Multicolor, Flowers, Brown Ground, 7 x 18 x 11 In. . 1063
Bronze, Gilt, Favrile, Gold Iridescent Panel Lid, 4-Footed, Douglas Nash, 2 x 6 x 3 In. . *illus* 330
Candle, Oak, Tapered Sides & Front, Raised Panels, Mid 1800s, 20 x 5 x 5 In. 108
Candle, Slide Lid, Thistle, Carved, Oak, Rectangular, c.1820, 3¾ x 12 x 6 In. .... *illus* 1500
Candle, Slide Lid, Tiger Maple, Dovetailed, Key Lock, 5¾ x 15 x 8 In. 396
Candle, Slide Lid, Walnut, Dovetailed, 1800s, 17 x 5 x 4 In. 315
Candle, Slide Lid, Wood, Tapered, Arched Hanger, New England, 1800s, 18 In. 213
Candle, Wall, Cherry, Tacks, Curved Crest, Dovetailed, 1910s, 8 x 18 x 7 In. 216
Candle, Wall, Embossed Brass, Armorial, Coat Of Arms, 8 x 3⅝ x 6¾ In. 22
Captain's, Quarter, Hinged Lid, Mahogany, Brass, 2 Doors, Square Legs, c.1840, 35 x 19 x 12 In... 3050
Casket, Table, Hinged Lid, Wood, Carved, 2 Birds, Reptiles, Black Forest, Late 1800s, 11 x 13 x 9 In..... 563
Cave A Liqueur, Hinged Lid & Sides, Brass, Ebonized, 4 Decanters, 16 Cordials, 10½ In..... 1708
Cigar, Walnut Inlaid, 8-Point Star, Keyhole, c.1950, 4½ x 12 x 8 In. 125
Cigarette, Bacchus, Rockwell Kent, Chase Brass & Copper Co., 1935, 1¾ x 6 x 5 In. .... *illus* 875
Cigarette, Embossed, 2 Dragons On Lid, Sides, Corners, Ornate Feet, Japan, 7 x 4 x 2½ In. 259
Cigarette, Lift Lid, Bird, Insect, Scalloped, Gilt Rim, 2 x 5 x 4 In. 120
Copper, Lid, Hammered, Repousse Flower, Arts & Crafts, c.1905, 3½ x 4 In. 492
Cutlery, Whalebone Embellishments, Voluted Handle, Mid 1800s, 8½ x 6¾ In. 10000
Decanter Case, Slant Lid, Mahogany, Brass, Bail Handles, Paw Feet, Georgian, 13¾ In. 640
Desk, Bronze, Slag Glass, Green, Copper Bottom, Colonial Manufacturing Co., 1 x 8 x 2 In. 84
Desk, Hinged Lid, Wood, Brass Band, Side Handles, 7 x 18 x 9¾ In. 63
Desk, Slant Lid, Oak, Chip Carved, Fans, Snipe Hinges, Iron Lock & Hasp, 1672, 7 x 13 x 9 In. ... *illus* 1872
Desk, Travel, Hinged Lid, Walnut, Diamond Shape Plaque, 1800s, 5 x 13 In. 156
Ditty, Whalebone & Wood, Oval, Diamond Trellis Laps, Pine Base, c.1850, 4 x 5 x 6 In. 3050
Document, Dome Lid, Flowers, Blue Ground, Iron Handle, Continental, 1800s, 7 x 12 x 7 In. 960
Document, Dome Lid, Folk Art, Iron Handles, Rosemaling, Norway, 1872, 12 x 26 x 13 In. *illus* 354
Document, Hinged Lid, Camphorwood, Brassbound, 1800s, 8½ x 19½ In. 281
Document, Hinged Lid, Curly Maple, Cribbage Board Style, 1900s, 5 x 13 In. 344
Document, Hinged Lid, Heavy Cardboard, Book Form, 7 Leather Bound Books, 8¼ x 12½ x 7 In. 288
Document, Hinged Lid, Wood, Chippendale, Double Eagle, Scrolls, Talon On Ball Feet, 7 x 13 In. 1440
Dome Lid, Hinged Lid, Basswood, Dovetailed Case, Painted, 1800s, 11 x 22 x 11 In. 131
Dome Lid, Pine, Tin Hinges, Partial Lock, Brown & White Block, Mid 1800s, 5 x 10 In. 216
Donation, Club, Wood, Carved, Trumpeter, Flowers, 6 x 9 x 4 In. 84
Dowry, Nettur Petti, Peaked Temple Shape Lid, Brass Fittings, India, 9 x 13 x 10 In. 192
Dresser, Burlwood, Mother-Of Pearl, Brass Claw, Ball Feet, England, 1800s, 6½ x 12 x 9 In. . 219

Box, Bride's, Hinged Dome Lid, Wallpaper, Light Blue Ground, 1700s, 8 x 15 x 9 In.
$4,063

Hindman

Box, Bronze, Gilt, Favrile, Gold Iridescent Panel Lid, 4-Footed, Douglas Nash, 2 x 6 x 3 In.
$330

Treasureseeker Auctions

Box, Candle, Slide Lid, Thistle, Carved, Oak, Rectangular, c.1820, 3¾ x 12 x 6 In.
$1,500

Hindman

Box, Cigarette, Bacchus, Rockwell Kent, Chase Brass & Copper Co., 1935, 1¾ x 6 x 5 In.
$875

Wright

Box, Desk, Slant Lid, Oak, Chip Carved, Fans, Snipe Hinges, Iron Lock & Hasp, 1672, 7 x 13 x 9 In.
$1,872

Thomaston Place Auction Galleries

Box, Document, Dome Lid, Folk Art, Iron Handles, Rosemaling, Norway, 1872, 12 x 26 x 13 In.
$354

Soulis Auctions

Box, Dresser, Hinged Lid, Courting Scene, Gilt, Round, Signed, Watteau, 3¾ x 8 In.
$240

Richard Opfer Auctioneering, Inc.

Box, Dresser, Lid, Pine, Painted, Scandinavia, 1800s, 4½ x 9¼ In.
$378

Pook & Pook

Box, Humidor, Cigar, Campaign, Mahogany, Brassbound, Benson & Hedges, 1900s, 10 x 25 x 12 In.

$500

Eldred's

Box, Knife, Dome Slide Lid, Inlaid Mahogany, Carved Paw Feet, Regency, c.1815, 24 x 12 x 12 In.

$438

Charlton Hall Auctions

Box, Knife, Slant Lid, Georgian, Mahogany, Flame Grain, String Inlay, Late 1700s, 14 x 9 x 11 In.

$180

Garth's Auctioneers & Appraisers

Dresser, Dome Lid, Hinged, Faux Tortoiseshell, Brass, Gilt Handles, Ogee Feet, 8 x 9 x 6 In.	125
Dresser, Flowers & Fruit, Ormolu Trim, Latch, Le Tellec Co., France, 5 x 3½ x 2 In.	125
Dresser, Hinged Clock Lid, Enamel, Silver, Fleur-De-Lis, Figures, Garden, Early 1900s, 2 x 4 In.	3267
Dresser, Hinged Lid, Courting Scene, Gilt, Round, Signed, Watteau, 3¾ x 8 In. ....*illus*	240
Dresser, Hinged Lid, Inlaid Burl, Brown, 1800s, 5 x 10 In.	76
Dresser, Hinged Lid, Oval, Opaline Glass, Brass Band, Blue, France, 1800s, 4 x 6 x 4½ In.	813
Dresser, Lid, Pine, Painted, Scandinavia, 1800s, 4½ x 9¼ In. ....*illus*	378
Dresser, Lid, Porcelain, Sevres Style, Bronze, Courting Couples, Flowers, Griffin's Feet, 8½ In.	275
Dresser, Lid, Porcelain, Sevres Style, Gilt, Cobalt Blue Ground, Flowers, E. Froger, 1800s, 6 In.	244
Dresser, Lift Lid, Bass Wood, Grain Paint, Hinged Frame On Lid, 1850s, 11 x 12 x 8 In.	84
Dresser, Pine, Painted, Green Sponge Decor, Initials On Lid, 1800s, 5 x 8 x 7 In.	492
Dresser, Pine, Painted, Reeded Design, Blue Surface, New England, 1800s, 8 x 15 x 10 In.	3690
Enamel, Egg Shape, Cobalt Blue Ground, Fruit & Flowers, Battersea Bilston, 3 In.	246
Frog Shape, Bronze, Patinated, Hardwood Stand, Japan, 4¼ x 7½ In.	1375
Hat, Bentwood, Multicolor, Painted, Flowers, Light Brown Ground, Pennsylvania, 8 x 18 x 12 In.	469
Hinged Lid, Inlaid, Satinwood, Dove, Black & White Squares, Folk Art, c.1850, 6 x 12 x 8 In.	344
Horn, Tessellated, Brass, Painted, Maitland Smith, 8 x 5 x 12 In.	106
Humidor, Botanical Marquetry, Brass Urn & Ring Handles, Switzerland, 1900s, 5 x 15 In.	350
Humidor, Cigar, Campaign, Mahogany, Brassbound, Benson & Hedges, 1900s, 10 x 25 x 12 In. *illus*	500
Iron, Hinged Lid, Arts & Crafts, Strap, c.1910, 10¼ x 6¾ x 3½ In.	431
Jewelry, Black Forest, Carved, Hinged Door, 4 Drawers, Fox Finial, Late 1800s, 10 x 7 x 4 In.	484
Jewelry, Casket, Hinged Lid, Gilt Bronze, Marble, France, 1800s, 4¼ x 7½ x 5½ In.	1080
Jewelry, Commode Style, Bronze Dore, Quatre Faces, Rocaille, 3 Drawers, Bracket Feet, 7 x 9 In.	960
Jewelry, Copper, Hidden Locking Mechanism, Applied Initials, Arts & Crafts, 2 x 5 x 3⅝ In.	97
Jewelry, Dome Lid, Edwardian, Mahogany, Stand, Tapered Legs, 1800s, 34 x 14¾ In.	832
Jewelry, Enamel Lid, Couple, Cherub, Trees & Lakes, Gilt, Bronze Frame, c.1900, 6½ x 4 x 3¼ In.	660
Jewelry, Flower Panels, Carved, Bands, Geometric Inlay, Folk Art, Early 1900s, 7 x 11⅝ x 8½ In.	313
Jewelry, Frosted Clear, Enamel Violets, Gilt Metal Feet, 5 x 5 In.	90
Jewelry, Hinged Lid, Burlwood, 3 Drawers, Jere, 1900s, 8¾ x 13½ In.	180
Jewelry, Hinged Lid, Oak, Red Velvet Lining, 7 x 17½ x 7 In.	51
Jewelry, Hinged Lid, Porcelain, Painted, Gilt Brass, Flowers, Multicolor, 8 x 6 x 4 In.	55
Jewelry, Hinged Lift Lid, Pyramid Shape, Brown, 4 Layers, 10 x 10 In.	366
Jewelry, Leather, Wood Insert, Gold Metal Accents, Gucci, Italy, 2 x 8½ x 8¼ In.	63
Jewelry, Marbleized Paper Lid, Arch & Column Design, Wood, Alabaster, Drawers, 6 x 12 x 8 In.	1320
Jewelry, Rosewood, Shagreen, Shells, Mirror, Ria & Youri Augousti, UK, c.1995, 12 x 8 x 10 In.	975
Jewelry, Silver Bound, Floral Etching, Blue Velvet, Jack Storck, Vienna, 1800s, 7 x 14 x 10 In.	1098
Jewelry, Victorian, Portrait Plaque, Velvet, Gilt Ormolu Trim, 1800s, 4½ x 8 x 6 In.	50
Knife, Dome Slide Lid, Inlaid Mahogany, Carved Paw Feet, Regency, c.1815, 24 x 12 x 12 In. *illus*	438
Knife, George III, Mahogany, Inlaid, Silver Hardware, Late 1700s, 14½ x 8½ x 10 In., Pair	945
Knife, George III, Mahogany, Marquetry Shell Inlay, Late 1700s, 14 x 8 x 11 In., Pair	1220
Knife, Georgian, Mahogany, Nautical Shell Inlaid, England, c.1880, 13¾ x 9 x 11 In., Pair	1020
Knife, Hepplewhite, Mahogany, Inlaid, Old Color, Fitted Cutlery, 1795, 14 x 8 In., Pair	1037
Knife, Mahogany, Carved, Star, Heart Cutout, 1800s, 5 x 14½ x 6½ In.	88
Knife, Satinwood, Mahogany, Hepplewhite, Serpentine Front, England, 1800s, 15 In.	210
Knife, Slant Lid, Georgian, Mahogany, Flame Grain, String Inlay, Late 1700s, 14 x 9 x 11 In. *illus*	180
Knife, Sloped Hinged Lid, George III, Mahogany, Shell Inlay, Late 1700s, 16 x 9 In., Pair	4514
Letter, Hinged Lid, Oak, Gilt Hardware, Victorian, c.1870, 7 x 15 x 10 In.	156
Letter, Hinged Lid, Slant Front, Drawer, Burlwood, 1800s, 13 x 13 x 10 In.	500
Letter, Mahogany, Lattice Sides, 2 Slots, Answered, Unanswered, Handle, England, 1800s, 11 In.	250
Lid, Nose, Mouth, Stars, Hinged, Walnut, Maple, Inlay, Bob Trotman, c.1979, 5 x 7 In.	1950
Lock, Cast Iron, W.F. & Co. St. Louis, Wells Fargo, 8½ x 13½ x 9½ In.	3143
Lock, Hinged Lid, Pine, Painted, Rosewood Grain, New England, 1800s, 12 x 25 In.	338
Lock, Pine, Wrought Iron Strapping, Swing Handle, Scandinavia, 1800s, 9 x 18 In. ......*illus*	554
Mahogany, Hinged Lid, Pagoda Shape, Buried Cross Banding, Brass Paw Feet, c.1840, 6 x 9 x 7 In.	305
Mail, Hinged Lid, Walnut, Locked, Painted Gilt, Ball Feet, Counter, c.1915, 8 x 11¼ x 8 In.	478
Maple, Slide Lid, 6 Interior Compartments, 1800s, 2⅜ x 8 x 5 In.	406
Money, Zelkovia, Carved Bosses Border, Drawer, Japan, c.1825, 12 x 12 In.	281
Necessaire, De Toilette, Burlwood, Brassbound, Fitted Interior, 1800s, 7¼ x 12¾ In.	650
Onyx, Removable Lid, Gray & Black, Gilt, Dolphin Finial & Feet, 1800s, 3 x 6 x 4 In.	250
Peacock, Feathers, Art Nouveau, Round, Japan, c.1910, 2 x 5¼ In.	400

Box, Lock, Pine, Wrought Iron Strapping, Swing Handle, Scandinavia, 1800s, 9 x 18 In.
$554

Pook & Pook

Box, Pipe, Pine, Painted, Heart & Circle Finial, Old Red Weathered Surface, 1800s, 24 x 6 In.
$5,166

Pook & Pook

Box, Ruby Glass, Egg Shape, Palais Royale Style, Hinged Lid, Bronze Bands, Footed, c.1900, 6 In.
$273

Ahlers & Ogletree Auction Gallery

Box, Strong, Iron, Bail Handle, Top Key, 8-Lever Locking Mechanism, Continental, 1700s, 6 In.
$2,250

Neal Auction Company

Box, Tantalus, Hinged Lid, Baccarat Style, Gilt Bronze, Glass, Footed, c.1900, 15 x 17 ½ In.
$5,490

Neal Auction Company

Box, Trinket, Dome Lid, Reeded Design, Painted, Blue & Red, Early 1800s, 10 x 25 In.
$1,169

Pook & Pook

Box, Wall, Pine, Heart Cutouts, Dovetailed, Pennsylvania, 1800s, 6 x 13 ¾ In.
$492

Pook & Pook

Box, Wood, Dome Lid, Shell & Banded Inlay, Brass Ball, Claw Feet, Federal, c.1825, 6 x 10 x 6 In.
$406

New Haven Auctions

Box, Writing, Hinged Lid, Rosewood, Side Drawer, On Stand, Regency, c.1830, 38 x 24 x 13 In.
$2,196

Rafael Osona Nantucket Auctions

Boy Scout, Figure, Scout Standing, In Uniform, Hat In Hand, Deer Tracks, Round Base, Plaster, 17 x 7 In.
$210

Donley Auctions

Pen, Hinged Lid, Gold Color Leaf, Wood, c.1890s, 9 1/2 x 4 3/4 x 6 In.	185
Pill, Round, Cranberry Case, Tapestry Decoration, 1 1/4 x 2 In.	80
Pine, Dome Lid, Brass Tack Decoration, Curved Side Handles, 1800s, 9 x 21 In.	76
Pine, Dome Lid, Stenciled, Sun, Moon, Stars, Black Ground, New England, 1800s, 13 x 30 In.	338
Pine, Rectangular, Horizontally Fluted Sides, New England, 1800s, 5 x 10 x 5 In.	188
Pine, Red Painted, Iron Handle, Locking Mechanism, 6 1/2 x 13 1/4 x 7 1/4 In.	63
Pipe, Carved Eagle, Drawer, Tiger Maple, Curly Sides & Back, 12 1/2 x 6 In.	3068
Pipe, Pine, Painted, Heart & Circle Finial, Old Red Weathered Surface, 1800s, 24 x 6 In. ..... *illus*	5166
Pipe, Slant Lid, Oak, Canted Sides, Crest, Hanging Hole, Iron Tacks, 1800s, 18 In.	132
Puzzle, Folk Art, Painted, Pin Stripes, Woman's Portrait, T Handle, 1800s, 4 x 8 x 5 In.	767
Quill, Inlaid, Burlwood, Tangerine Ground, 1800s, 6 1/2 x 12 x 9 In.	236
Removable Lid, Painted, Wraparound Tigers, Black Ground, Tibet, 18 x 27 x 14 In., Pair...	2223
Ring, Copper, Hammered, Flower, Red, Yellow, Green, Arts & Crafts, Boston, c.1905, 4 x 3 1/4 x 1 In.	738
Ruby Glass, Egg Shape, Palais Royale Style, Hinged Lid, Bronze Bands, Footed, c.1900, 6 In. *illus*	273
Sailor's, Hinged Lid, Wood, Ropework Decor, Rectangular, 1800s, 6 x 11 x 6 In.	610
Sarcophagus, Egyptian Revival, Casket, Metal Inlays, Chariots, Bronze Feet, 17 x 21 x 13 In.	1560
Sarcophagus, Fighting Scene, Wood, Inlaid Bronze, Egyptian Revival, Late 1800s, 17 x 21 x 13 In.	8168
Stationery, Hinged Dome Lid, Leatherette, Silver Floral Filigree, 8 x 12 In.	240
Storage, Cannabis, Hinged Lid, Tin, Black Paint, Gilt Text, 2-Sided Handle, 8 x 13 x 9 In.	1063
Strong, Art Nouveau, Brass, Plated Metal, Hand Hammered, Japan, 2 1/2 x 7 1/2 x 4 1/2 In.	72
Strong, Iron, Bail Handle, Top Key, 8-Lever Locking Mechanism, Continental, 1700s, 6 In. *illus*	2250
Strong, Wood, Painted, Black, Metal Hinge, Wells Fargo & Co., c.1879, 10 x 20 x 12 In.	10200
Table, Dome Lid, Walnut, Malachite, Mounted, Brassbound, 1850s, 3 1/2 x 11 x 5 In.	100
Tantalus, Hinged Lid, Baccarat Style, Gilt Bronze, Glass, Footed, c.1900, 15 x 17 1/2 In. *illus*	5490
Tantalus, Oak, 3 Leaded Glass Decanters, Mirrored Back, Brass Fittings, 13 x 14 x 10 1/2 In.	192
Tobacco, Iron, Silver, Inlaid, Brass Handle, Etched Details, Joseon, Korea, 2 1/4 x 4 x 2 1/2 In.	800
Tobacco, Lid, Cast Iron, Abolitionist, Shackled Slave, Humanity, England, c.1840, 3 x 5 x 3 In.	995
Tobacco, Lift-Off Lid, Circular Shape, Cherubs, Devil Face, Ornate Metal, 6 In.	136
Travel, Hinged Lid, Mahogany, Ivory Monogrammed Plaque, Drawer, 1800s, 6 x 11 In.	140
Travel, Hinged Lid, Marquetry, Divided Interior, Mirror, 1800s, 4 1/4 x 9 x 6 3/4 In.	312
Travel, Wood Case, Bronze Pulls, Carved Handle, Japan, Late 1800s, 9 x 15 x 9 In.	438
Trinket, Dome Lid, Reeded Design, Painted, Blue & Red, Early 1800s, 10 x 25 In. .... *illus*	1169
Trinket, Famille Rose, Flowers, Multicolor, Chinese, Late 1800s, 2 1/2 x 7 x 3 3/4 In.	360
Trinket, Gilt Metal, Bow & Arrow, Ribbed Base, France, 1900s, 3/8 x 3 7/8 In.	121
Valuables, Panel Exterior Opens, 6 Drawers, Flowers, England, Early 1700s, 10 x 13 x 8 In.	1500
Vanity, Silver Plate, Classical Design, Continental, Late 1800s, 4 x 13 x 4 In.	375
Wall, Carved Pine, Decorated Front Panel, Potted Flowers, Drawer, 1800s, 15 1/2 x 7 In.	492
Wall, Pine, Heart Cutouts, Dovetailed, Pennsylvania, 1800s, 6 x 13 3/4 In. *illus*	492
Wood, 4 Drawers, Brass, Hardware & Accents, Swing Handle, 10 x 6 In.	99
Wood, Dome Lid, Shell & Banded Inlay, Brass Ball, Claw Feet, Federal, c.1825, 6 x 10 x 6 In. *illus*	406
Wood, Hinged Dome Lid, Painted, Black Decoration, c.1850, 12 x 28 x 13 In.	281
Wood, Hinged Lid, Rectangular, Dark Brown, With Key, 14 x 9 x 4 In.	62
Wood, Locking Lid, Putty Painted, Circles & Fans, Dovetailed, New England, c.1815, 11 x 28 In.	1750
Wood, Slide Lid, Yellow Paint, Leaves, New England, c.1830, 3 x 8 x 4 In.	313
Writing, Hinged Lid, Rosewood, Side Drawer, On Stand, Regency, c.1830, 38 x 24 x 13 In. *illus*	2196
Writing, Tambour Lid, Mahogany, Brass Handles & Lock, Drawer, c.1850, 7 x 15 x 11 In.	351

🛡️ BOY SCOUT

Boy Scout collectibles include any material related to scouting, including patches, manuals, and uniforms. The Boy Scout movement in the United States started in 1910. The first Jamboree was held in 1937. Girl Scout items are listed under their own heading.

Crate, Wood, Hinged Lid, Boy Scouts Of America, Red Letters, Black Graphics, 10 x 22 x 13 In.	62
Figure, Scout Standing, In Uniform, Hat In Hand, Deer Tracks, Round Base, Plaster, 17 x 7 In. *illus*	210
Postcard, Photograph, Scouts, Wagon, St. Paul To San Francisco, Black & White, Divided Back.	39
Sign, Eagle, Shield, Yellow & Blue, White Ground, Boy Scouts Of America, 18 In.	92
Sign, Safety First, Boy Scout Profile, Join Your Local Troop, Blue, Porcelain, 59 x 33 In. ....*illus*	2043
Toy, Boy Scout Holding Flagstaff, Swings, Rings Bell, 4 Wheels, Pull String, 7 In.	563

BRADLEY & HUBBARD

Bradley & Hubbard is a name found on many metal objects. Walter Hubbard and his brother-in-law, Nathaniel Lyman Bradley, started making cast iron clocks, tables, frames, andirons, bookends, doorstops, lamps, chandeliers, sconces, and sewing birds in 1854 in Meriden, Connecticut. The company became Bradley & Hubbard Manufacturing Company in 1875. Charles Parker Company bought the firm in 1940. There is no mention of Bradley & Hubbard after the 1950s. Bradley & Hubbard items may be found in other sections that include metal.

Lamp, Arts & Crafts, Bronze, Palm Frond, Table, Slag Glass Shade, 30 x 21 x 21 In.	*illus*	2560
Lamp, Banquet, Swirl, Cranberry Shade, Ruffled Rim, Nickel, Brass, Alabaster Stem, c.1890, 33 In.		480
Lamp, Leaded Glass, Yellow, Green, Squares, Round Base, c.1920, 21½ x 16¾ In.		1845
Lamp, Oil, Gilt Dragons, Red Globe, Double Burner, Brass, Victorian, 24 x 11 In.		2530
Lamp, Organ, Brass, Clear Chimney, Etched Shade, Ornate Frame, Late 1800s, 57 In.		300
Lamp, Victorian, Banquet, Cherubs, Gold Dragons, Fighting, Red Shade, Alabaster Base, 35 In.		1265

BRASS

Brass has been used for decorative pieces and useful tablewares since ancient times. It is an alloy of copper, zinc, and other metals. Additional brass items may be found under Bell, Candlestick, Tool, or Trivet.

Alms Dish, Raised Central Boss, Rolled Rim, Cherub Faces, Dutch, 1700s, 3 x 14¾ In.		293
Bed Warmer, Engraved Decoration, Rooster, Flowers, Wood Handle, 1800s, 44¼ In.		72
Bed Warmer, Turned Handle, Leafy & Flowers, Hanging Hook, Early 1800s, 42 x 12 In.		250
Bowl, Hexagonal, 2 Handles, Engraved, Pen Case, Chinese, 1800s, 7 x 9½ In.		125
Bucket, Bail Handle, Hiram Hayden, Waterbury, 1851, 5¾ x 8½ In.	*illus*	28
Bucket, Peat, Mahogany, Swing Handle, Oval, Ireland, 1700s, 14½ x 13¾ x 10 In.	*illus*	936
Cigar Cutter, Hinged Lid Box, Engraved Flowers & Leaves, India, 2 x 10 x 2¼ In.		108
Coaster, Wine, Nickel Plate, Reticulated, Josef Hoffmann, Neue Galerie, Austria, c.1905, 5 In.		375
Compote, Dished Top, Scalloped Rim, Round Stepped Base, 1700s, 6 x 9⅜ In.		468
Cooler, Wine, Art Deco, 2 Bottles, Ice Chamber, Round Base, 11 x 9 x 9 In.	*illus*	395
Curtain Ring, Pressed, Gilt, Beaded, 3¼ In., 30 Piece.	*illus*	1250
Dish, Nuremburg, Gold, Circular, Pressed Leafy Design, Germany, 1700s, 15 In.		344
Figure, Mask, Crown, Mohra, Pahari, Shiva, 1600s, 7 x 5 In.		156
Figure, Pharaoh, Standing, Silvered Exterior, Egyptian, 45 In., Pair		320
Finial, Bulbous Middle, Maitland Smith, 6 x 6 x 13 In., Pair		248
Hot Pot, Miniature, Etched Top, Butterfly Handles, Round Pedestal Base, 5 x 6 x 5½ In., Pair		60
Jardiniere, Baroque, Oval, Repousse Scrolled Flowers, France, 1800s, 8¾ x 18 x 6¾ In.		484
Jardiniere, Round, Ring Handles, Continental, Late 1900s, 19½ x 26 x 21 In.		303
Jug, Lid, Loop Handle, Hammered, Lion Shape Spout, Late 1800s, 27 In.		192
Planter, Jardiniere, Dragon Design, Liner, 2 Handles, Chinese, 13 x 22½ x 18 In.		384
Plate Warmer, Cabriole Legs, Bail Handle, Trivet, 3 Oval Feet, 1800s, 23 x 17 In.	*illus*	956
Pot, Hammered, Lion's Head Bail Handles, 3 Ball Feet, 11 x 14½ In.		192
Samovar, Porcelain Handles, Hinged Wood Handles, Spigot, Russia, Late 1800s, 17¼ In.	*illus*	150
Stand, Music, Adjustable, Loop Designs, England, 9 x 9 In.	*illus*	118
Teapot, Teardrop Shape, 2 Dragon Shape Scrolled Handles, Leaf & Vine Design, 10 x 12 x 5 In.		468
Tray, Micro Mosaic, 9 Inset Floral Vignettes, Beaded Rim, Italy, 8⅝ In.		313
Tray, Oval, Applied Tulip Handles, Rosemar, 2¾ x 12 x 6¼ In.		31
Tray, Serving, Handles, Cutouts, Elongated Octagonal Shape, WMF, c.1910, 21 x 8 In.	*illus*	492
Tray, Serving, Flowers, Engraved, Flared Handle, 23 x 13 In.		71
Urn, Lid, Melon Shape, Maitland Smith, Label, Late 1900s, 6¾ x 6¼ In., Pair		182
Urn, Neoclassical Style, Flared Rim, Black Marble Base, Late 1800s, 13¼ In., Pair		150

BRASTOFF, *see Sascha Brastoff category.*

BREAD PLATE, *see various silver categories, porcelain factories, and pressed glass patterns.*

Boy Scout, Sign, Safety First, Boy Scout Profile, Join Your Local Troop, Blue, Porcelain, 59 x 33 In.
$2,043

Heritage Auctions

Bradley & Hubbard, Lamp, Arts & Crafts, Bronze, Palm Frond, Table, Slag Glass Shade, 30 x 21 x 21 In.
$2,560

Roland NY Auctioneers & Appraisers

Brass, Bucket, Bail Handle, Hiram Hayden, Waterbury, 1851, 5¾ x 8½ In.
$28

Hartzell's Auction Gallery Inc.

This is an edited listing of current prices. Visit Kovels.com to check thousands of prices from previous years and sign up for free information on trends, tips, reproductions, marks, and more.

BRIDE'S BOWL OR BASKET

Brass, Bucket, Peat, Mahogany, Swing Handle, Oval, Ireland, 1700s, 14 ½ x 13 ¾ x 10 In.
$936

Thomaston Place Auction Galleries

Brass, Cooler, Wine, Art Deco, 2 Bottles, Ice Chamber, Round Base, 11 x 9 x 9 In.
$395

Charleston Estate Auctions

Brass, Curtain Ring, Pressed, Gilt, Beaded, 3 ¼ In., 30 Piece
$1,250

Neal Auction Company

Brass, Plate Warmer, Cabriole Legs, Bail Handle, Trivet, 3 Oval Feet, 1800s, 23 x 17 In.
$956

Jeffrey S. Evans & Associates

Brass, Samovar, Porcelain Handles, Hinged Wood Handles, Spigot, Russia, Late 1800s, 17 ¼ In.
$150

Selkirk Auctioneers & Appraisers

Brass, Stand, Music, Adjustable, Loop Designs, England, 9 x 9 In.
$118

Charleston Estate Auctions

Brass, Tray, Serving, Handles, Cutouts, Elongated Octagonal Shape, WMF, c.1910, 21 x 8 In.
$492

California Historical Design

Bride's Basket, Mother-Of-Pearl Glass, Pink Satin, Herringbone, Green, Gold Enamel, Victorian, 12 x 10 In.
$300

Woody Auction

Bride's Basket, Peach Bowl, Shaped Handle, Silver Plate Frame, Footed, Victorian, 11 x 10 In.
$230

Stevens Auction Co.

BRIDE'S BOWL OR BASKET

Bride's bowls or baskets were usually one-of-a-kind novelties made in American and European glass factories. They were especially popular about 1880 when the decorated basket was often given as a wedding gift. Cut glass baskets were popular after 1890. All bride's bowls lost favor about 1905. Bride's bowls and baskets may also be found in other glass sections. Check the index at the back of the book.

Cranberry Opalescent Glass, Lattice, Scalloped Rim, Silver Plate Frame, Footed, 14 x 14 In.	150
Diamond Quilted, Mother-Of-Pearl, Satin Glass, Fleur-De-Lis, Square Shape, 2¾ x 5½ In...	125
Mother-Of-Pearl Glass, Pink Satin, Herringbone, Green, Gold Enamel, Victorian, 12 x 10 In.. *illus*	300
Peach Bowl, Shaped Handle, Silver Plate Frame, Footed, Victorian, 11 x 10 In. .... *illus*	230
Peachblow, Ruffled Rim, Gold Enamel, Fern & Blossom, Silver Plate Frame, Victorian, 10 x 10 In.	200
Pink Cased, Ruffled, Enamel, Flowers, Silver Plate Frame, Victorian, 12 x 13 In.	70
Satin Glass, Ruffled Rim, Green & White, Silver Plate Frame, Victorian, 10¾ x 10 In.	125
White Art Glass, Orange Cased, Square Shape, Scalloped Edge, Tripod, Victorian, 14 x 12 In.....	175

BRISTOL

Bristol glass was made in Bristol, England, after the 1700s. The Bristol glass most often seen today is a Victorian, lightweight opaque glass that is often blue. Some of the glass was decorated with enamels.

Lamp, Multicolor Flowers, Pink Borders, Frosted Chimney, Finger Loop, 4¾ In.	36
Lamp, Wall, Pink Base, Vine On Font, Roses, Blue Ribbons, Round Mirror, Victorian, 12½ In......	36
Tea Bowl, Saucer, Enamel Wreaths & Swags, Rose Garlands, Gilt, Marked, c.1775, 5 In.	945
Urn, Courting Scene, Painted, Gilt Design, Pink Ground, Victorian, 20 In.	115
Vase, Hand Painted, Flowers, Metal Base, Victorian, 27 x 13 In...	230
Vase, Hawk, Perched, On Branch, Blue Band Top, Painted, 17½ In.	132
Vase, Indian, Portrait, Spotted Horse, High Hawk, Mint Green Ground, Early 1900s, 12 In., Pair.. *illus*	303

BRITANNIA, *see Pewter category.*

BRONZE

Bronze is an alloy of copper, tin, and other metals. It is used to make figurines, lamps, and other decorative objects. Bronze lamps are listed in the Lamp category. Pieces listed here date from the eighteenth, nineteenth, and twentieth centuries. Shown here are marks used by three well-known makers of bronzes.

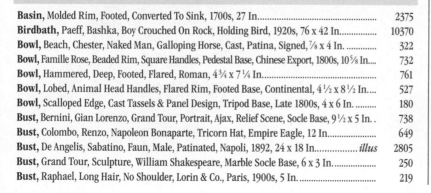

Armor Bronze Corp.	Bradley and Hubbard Mfg. Co.	Pompeian Bronze Co.
c.1919–c.1926, 1934–1948	1875–c.1940	1920s

POMPEIAN BRONZE COMPANY

Basin, Molded Rim, Footed, Converted To Sink, 1700s, 27 In...	2375
Birdbath, Paeff, Bashka, Boy Crouched On Rock, Holding Bird, 1920s, 76 x 42 In...............	10370
Bowl, Beach, Chester, Naked Man, Galloping Horse, Cast, Patina, Signed, ⅞ x 4 In.	322
Bowl, Famille Rose, Beaded Rim, Square Handles, Pedestal Base, Chinese Export, 1800s, 10⅝ In...	732
Bowl, Hammered, Deep, Footed, Flared, Roman, 4¾ x 7¼ In...	761
Bowl, Lobed, Animal Head Handles, Flared Rim, Footed Base, Continental, 4½ x 8½ In....	527
Bowl, Scalloped Edge, Cast Tassels & Panel Design, Tripod Base, Late 1800s, 4 x 6 In.	180
Bust, Bernini, Gian Lorenzo, Grand Tour, Portrait, Ajax, Relief Scene, Socle Base, 9½ x 5 In. .	738
Bust, Colombo, Renzo, Napoleon Bonaparte, Tricorn Hat, Empire Eagle, 12 In.....................	649
Bust, De Angelis, Sabatino, Faun, Male, Patinated, Napoli, 1892, 24 x 18 In................. *illus*	2805
Bust, Grand Tour, Sculpture, William Shakespeare, Marble Socle Base, 6 x 3 In.	250
Bust, Raphael, Long Hair, No Shoulder, Lorin & Co., Paris, 1900s, 5 In.	219

B

Bristol, Vase, Indian, Portrait, Spotted Horse, High Hawk, Mint Green Ground, Early 1900s, 12 In., Pair
$303

Fontaine's Auction Gallery

Bronze, Bust, De Angelis, Sabatino, Faun, Male, Patinated, Napoli, 1892, 24 x 18 In.
$2,805

Bonhams

Bronze, Canister, Dog's Head, Pineapple Shape Finial, Late 1900s, 8½ x 7 In.
$563

Eldred's

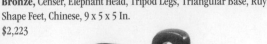
B

Bronze, Censer, Elephant Head, Tripod Legs, Triangular Base, Ruyi Shape Feet, Chinese, 9 x 5 x 5 In.
$2,223

Thomaston Place Auction Galleries

Bronze, Cooler, Wine, Gilt, Champleve, Stand, Elkington & Co., Victorian, 1850s, 41 ½ In.
$2,500

Hindman

Bronze, Clip, Holds Paper, Acrobat, Child, Push Down, Gilt, Black Marble Base, c.1860, 8 x 4 x 6 In.
$450

Treasureseeker Auctions

Bronze, Jardiniere, Figural Cartouches, Lion's Mask Handle, Japan, Late 1800s, 10 x 13 In.
$125

Charlton Hall Auctions

Bronze, Compote, Diamond, Glass Bowl, Gilt, Square Base, Paw Feet, 6 ½ x 7 ¼ In., Pair
$469

New Haven Auctions

Bronze, Sculpture, Barye, Antoine-Louis, Eagle, Spread Wings, Patina, Signed, 9 x 13 x 10 In.
$3,050

Rafael Osona Nantucket Auctions

Bronze, Sculpture, Barye, Antoine-Louis, Tiger, Eating Gazelle, Barbedienne, France, 1875, 5 x 13 x 5 In.
$1,845

Brunk Auctions

Bronze, Sculpture, Bergman, Franz, 2 Foxes, Playing Chess, Sitting, Austria, 2¾ x 4½ x 2 In.
$1,063

Wiederseim Auctions

Bronze, Sculpture, Bhumisparsha Buddha, Seated, Lotus Throne, Gilt, Chinese, 23 x 16 x 11 In.
$1,989

Thomaston Place Auction Galleries

Bronze, Sculpture, Evers, Dale Joseph, Whale, Turtle, Light, Blue, Circular Base, Late 1900s, 17 In.
$504

Pook & Pook

Bronze, Sculpture, Fisherman, Crab, After Giovanni De Martino, Italy, 1870, 42 x 22 x 14 In.
$2,125

Charlton Hall Auctions

Bronze, Sculpture, Foo Dog, Male & Female, Custom Wood Base, Asian, 1800s, 11 x 13 In., Pair
$1,220

CRN Auctions

Bronze, Sculpture, Halahmy, Oded, Moon Tide, Patina, Iraq, 1976, 25½ x 22 x 8 In.
$1,830

CRN Auctions

Bronze, Sculpture, Hirst, Damien, Skull, Patinated Metal, Polished, 11 x 16 x 9 In.
$875

Palm Beach Modern Auctions

Bronze, Sculpture, Ispanky, Laszlo, Zeus, Let There Be Light, Signature, New York, 1976, 20 x 20 x 12 In.
$1,260

Main Auction Galleries, Inc.

BRONZE

B

Bronze, Sculpture, Jason, Mario, Ballerina, Cabriole, Marble Base, Signed, 1990s, 31 x 11 x 15 In.
$1,140

Alderfer Auction Company

Bronze, Sculpture, Kauba, Carl, Indian Chief, Running, Feathered Baton, Agate Base, 11 In.
$635

White's Auctions

Bronze, Sculpture, Lion, Mid Roar, Seal Marks, Bronze Base, Japan, Late 1800s, 8½ x 13 In.
$300

Selkirk Auctioneers & Appraisers

Bust, Young, Mahonri Mackintosh, Rembrandt, Head, Chest, Base, 1931, 9½ In.	1380
Candlestand, Napoleon III Style, Gilt, Cherubs, Holding Torch, Footed, 9 In., Pair	305
Canister, Dog's Head, Pineapple Shape Finial, Late 1900s, 8½ x 7 In. *illus*	563
Cannon, Dolphin Shape Handles, Wood Carriage, Wheels, Mediterranean, 1700s, 32 In.	300
Cassolette, Acorn Finial, Gilt, Patina, Tripod Legs, Plinth, Empire Style, 1800s, 9 x 4 In., Pair	375
Censer, Elephant Head, Tripod Legs, Triangular Base, Ruyi Shape Feet, Chinese, 9 x 5 x 5 In. *illus*	2223
Censer, Stand, Rectangular, 2 Scrolled Upswept Handles, Japan, 1910s, 14 x 11 In.	469
Censer, Xuande, 6-Character Mark, 2 Handles, 3½ x 9¼ In.	875
Centerpiece, Chinoiserie, Figural, Basket, Black, Stone Base, Contemporary, 15¾ x 12 In.	424
Centerpiece, Debut, Marcel, Neoclassical, Gilt, Patinated, Tazza, France, 6 x 21 x 15 In.	1216
Centerpiece, Gilt, Ram's Head Handles, Stepped Base, France, Late 1800s, 7 x 16 x 11 In.	625
Charger, Bird, Leaves, Scalloped Rim, Patina, Continental, 1900s, 23 In.	448
Charger, Gilt, Embossed, Devil's Head, Patina Ground, Hallmark, c.1930, 11¾ In.	125
Clip, Holds Paper, Acrobat, Child, Push Down, Gilt, Black Marble Base, c.1860, 8 x 4 x 6 In. *illus*	450
Compote, Diamond, Glass Bowl, Gilt, Square Base, Paw Feet, 6½ x 7¼ In., Pair *illus*	469
Compote, Gilt, Shallow Bowl, Slender Tapering, Circular Foot, Enameled Glass, Signed, 6 x 7 In.	590
Cooler, Wine, Gilt, Champleve, Stand, Elkington & Co., Victorian, 1850s, 41½ In. *illus*	2500
Coupe, Neoclassical, Gilt, 3 Ram's Heads & Legs, Cut Glass Ornament, Late 1800s, 6 x 4 In.	94
Decanter, Empire, Gilt, Mounted, Rectangular Shape, Sphinxes, Stars, Late 1800s, 10 x 4 x 4 In.	535
Ewer, Classical, Floor, Grapevine, Cherubs, Ram's Head Handle, 1800s, 38 In.	480
Ewer, Cupid On Handles, Victorian, 25 x 12 In., Pair	575
Ewer, Napoleon III, Dore, Round Marble Base, 1800s, 12½ In., Pair	250
Ewer, Ribbed Body, Bust, Pan, Gilt, Mercury, Base, 24¾ In.	384
Font, Holy Water, Cross, Byzantine, Champleve, Agate Mount, 14 x 8 In.	60
Frame, Calendar, Green, Red, Art Crafts Shop, Buffalo, N.Y., c.1905, 5¾ x 5¾ In.	431
Garniture, 3-Light, Dore, Square Base, Marble, Louis XV Style, Electrified, 30 x 13 x 6½ In., Pair	2500
Garniture, Green Onyx, Flower Top, Leafy Handles, 5 x 4 x 12 In., Pair	94
Garniture, Urn, Giltwood Base, Rose, Lion Head, Paw Feet, France, c.1850, 10 x 5 In., Pair	281
Humidor, Multicolor, Cedar, Louis C. Tiffany Furnaces, Inc., N.Y., c.1925, 2 x 6 x 4 In.	687
Incense Burner, Foo Dog, 3-Legged, Asian, 1900s, 8½ x 4¾ In.	594
Incense Burner, Regency, Urn Shape, Pineapple Finial, Triparte Base, 1800s, 3½ In., Pair.	121
Incense Burner, Tang Style, Foo Dog Finial, Figural Handles, Chinese, 1910s, 8 In.	96
Jardiniere, Archaic Design, Bulbous Body, Tapered Foot, Wood Stand, 1900s, 15 x 16 In.	313
Jardiniere, Dragons & Turtles Relief, 3 Figural Feet, 20 x 20 In.	390
Jardiniere, Figural Cartouches, Lion's Mask Handle, Japan, Late 1800s, 10 x 13 In. *illus*	125
Medallion, Circular, Indian, Marked, Shawmut Lodge, A.F. & A.M., c.1911, 7 In.	121
Model, Roman Emperor, Seated, Rectangular Base, Continental, Late 1800s, 11½ x 5 x 9 In.	500
Page Turner, Upright Robed Monkey, Toad, Pierced & Incised Blade, Japan, Late 1800s, 13 In.	108
Pedestal, Circular Top, Reeded Column, Winged Panther, Leafy Base, 52 x 7 x 12 In.	720
Planter, Elephant Handles, Birds, Phoenixes, Flowers, Japan, 16½ In.	605
Planter, Van Der Straeten, Herve, Patinated, Root Shape Feet, France, 2006, 11 x 9 In., Pair	4000
Plaque, Bird, Sun Shining, Standing, Open Wings, Art Deco, 11¼ x 8 In.	344
Plaque, Commemorating The Great Flood, Massachusetts & Connecticut, 1936, 3 x 16 In.	313
Plaque, D'Angers, David, Napoleon, Patina, Continental, 1835, 8 In.	305
Plaque, Gilt, Crab, Dragonfly, Frog, Bird, Encircling Fish, Aesthetic Movement, c.1890s, 10⅝ In.	492
Plaque, Neoclassical, Mythological, Luna Dimming Lamp Of Life, Continental, 1800s, 8½ In.	242
Plaque, Proctor, Alexander Phimister, Cowboy, Running Horse, Round, 16 In.	950
Plaque, Sword, Velvet Frame, After Etienne-Alexandre Stella, Late 1800s, 17 x 21 In.	409
Plaque, Yensesse, Ovide, Primeveres, Brown Patina, Marked, France, 7 In.	98
Sculpture, Ahlberg, Olof, Diana, Bow, Bended Knee, Gold Patina, Sweden, 1920s, 21½ In.	5400
Sculpture, Aizelin, Eugene Antoine, Woman, Jar, La Perrette, France, 32 x 11 x 13 In.	2400
Sculpture, Alvarez, Henry, Jessica Rabbit, Standing, Marble Base, Plaque, 9 x 19 x 10 In.	2125
Sculpture, Arson, Alphonse Alexandre, Sea Bird, Head Lowered, France, 1800s, 15 In.	288
Sculpture, Augustine, Rick, Pillar Of Antiquity, Horse Head, Wood & Marble Socle, 1900s, 21 In.	600
Sculpture, Avalokitesvara, 4 Arms, Seated, Lotus Position, Gilt, Chinese, 1900s, 20 x 14 x 9 In.	556
Sculpture, Barye, 2 Rabbits, Lying Down, Cabbage Head, France, 2 x 3½ In.	660
Sculpture, Barye, Alfred, Camel, Dromedary, Standing, Brown Patina, 6 x 7½ x 2¼ In.	2500
Sculpture, Barye, Antoine-Louis, African Elephant, Head & Trunk Up, France, 1900s, 15 x 13 In.	319
Sculpture, Barye, Antoine-Louis, Arab On Horseback, Oval Marble Base, 30 x 23 x 13 In.	960

Sculpture, Barye, Antoine-Louis, Cow, Scratching Neck, Cast, France, 1800s, 5 x 7 ½ In. ...	438
Sculpture, Barye, Antoine-Louis, Eagle, Spread Wings, Patina, Signed, 9 x 13 x 10 In. *illus*	3050
Sculpture, Barye, Antoine-Louis, Tiger, Eating Gazelle, Barbedienne, France, 1875, 5 x 13 x 5 In.*illus*	1845
Sculpture, Bearded Man, Draped Fabric, Standing, Italy, Early 1900s, 18 x 8 In..................	300
Sculpture, Bennett, Tom, Dancing Nude, Black Marble Base, Signed, 10 In.	156
Sculpture, Bergman, Franz, 2 Foxes, Playing Chess, Sitting, Austria, 2 ¾ x 4 ½ x 2 In. *illus*	1063
Sculpture, Bhumisparsha Buddha, Seated, Lotus Throne, Gilt, Chinese, 23 x 16 x 11 In....*illus*	1989
Sculpture, Biblical, Angel & Child, Reading, Octagonal Slate Base, 12 In.	180
Sculpture, Blackamoor, Holding Staff, Standing, Gilt, Shaped Base, 16 In., Pair..................	313
Sculpture, Blondat, Max, Fontaine Jeunesse Ou Fontaine, Children, Sitting, 14 x 12 x 15 In........	638
Sculpture, Bonheur, Isidore-Jules, Equestrian, Steeplechase, Patina, 1900s, 18 x 26 x 6 In.	1275
Sculpture, Brueggemann, Winni, Sonambient, Sound, Metal Strands, Tabletop, 25 x 7 x 7 In.	1625
Sculpture, Buddha Shakyamuni, Seated, Downcast Eyes, Closed Mouth, Prominent Ribs, 7 In.	2700
Sculpture, Buddha, Sitting, Old Surface, Chinese, 14 ½ x 11 x 7 In...	1375
Sculpture, Buddha, Tibetan, Seated, Gilt, Bhumisparsha Mudra, Southeast Asia, 17 ¾ In..	605
Sculpture, Butzke, Bernhard, Rehkitz Fawn, Cast, Art Deco, Integral Base, 22 x 13 x 7 In..	4388
Sculpture, Castleberry, Metz, Bison, Standing, Bull, Brown, Wood Base, 8 In.	765
Sculpture, Colinet, C.J., Andalusian Dancer, Nude Woman, Gilt, Marble Base, France, 20 In......	3630
Sculpture, De Saint Marceaux, Rene, Harlequin, Standing, Signed, 34 x 12 x 11 In.............	1770
Sculpture, De Tirtoff, Romain, Arabian Nights, Woman, Cold Paint, Gilt, Erte, 1990, 22 x 10 x 6 In. ..	1750
Sculpture, Devries, Andrew, Rebecca, Ballet Dancer, Wood Stand, Massachusetts, 1993, 11 x 32 In....	375
Sculpture, Egyptian Style, Cat, Seated, Green Patina, Brown Base, 1900s, 9 In.	94
Sculpture, Elephant, White Tusks, Trunk Down, Marked, Chinese, 8 x 7 In.	320
Sculpture, Elk, Walking Position, Open Mouth, Rocky Base, 1900s, 96 In.............................	2813
Sculpture, Evers, Dale Joseph, Whale, Turtle, Light, Blue, Circular Base, Late 1900s, 17 In. *illus*	504
Sculpture, Evers, Dale, 2 Tortoises, Mounted, Black Marble, Signed, Hawaii, 12 x 6 In........	380
Sculpture, Fisherman, Crab, After Giovanni De Martino, Italy, 1870, 42 x 22 x 14 In...*illus*	2125
Sculpture, Foo Dog, Male & Female, Custom Wood Base, Asian, 1800s, 11 x 13 In., Pair....*illus*	1220
Sculpture, Foo Dog, Miniature, Male & Female, Applied Enamel, Chinese, 1900s, 2 ¾ x 4 In., Pair	510
Sculpture, Foo Dog, Patinated, Seated, Fierce Expression, Chinese, 7 ½ In., Pair.................	325
Sculpture, Gach, G., Cowboy, Rectangular Walnut Base, Signed, 8 ½ x 9 ¼ x 4 In.	130
Sculpture, Gach, George, Sea Nymph, Man, Upside Down, Square Base, 1971, 20 In.	1063
Sculpture, Geissbuhler, Arnold, Woman's Head, Brown Patina, Wood Base, Signed, 6 x 9 In.....	767
Sculpture, Goddess, Votive, Standing, Splayed Legs, Lotus Base, Calligraphy, 1900s, 16 In.	125
Sculpture, Grand Tour, Nude, Male, Narcissus, Italy, 1800s, 11 In.	787
Sculpture, Great Spirit, Indian, After Cyrus Edwin Dallin, 20 x 15 ½ x 5 ½ In.	1280
Sculpture, Gross, Chaim, Human Figure, 1-Hand Stand, Austria, 1962, 13 ½ x 6 ½ x 6 ½ In.	1875
Sculpture, Hagenauer, Karl, Female Figure, Dancing, Mounted On Brass Dish, Marked, 5 x 4 In.	384
Sculpture, Halahmy, Oded, Moon Tide, Patina, Iraq, 1976, 25 ½ x 22 x 8 In. .... *illus*	1830
Sculpture, Henckel, Carl, Dying Bison, Head Down, Slightly Red, Germany, 1900s, 11 In. ..	1403
Sculpture, Hirst, Damien, Skull, Patinated Metal, Polished, 11 x 16 x 9 In.................. *illus*	875
Sculpture, Hound Master, Dogs, Man On Horseback, Oval Base, After P.J. Mene, 28 x 30 x 23 In.	896
Sculpture, Houser, Allan, Woman, Seated, Abstract, Base, 3 ½ In.	875
Sculpture, Ispanky, Laszlo, Zeus, Let There Be Light, Signature, New York, 1976, 20 x 20 x 12 In.*illus*	1260
Sculpture, Jason, Mario, Ballerina, Cabriole, Marble Base, Signed, 1990s, 31 x 11 x 15 In.....*illus*	1140
Sculpture, Javelin Thrower, Nude Man, Red Hardstone Base, France, Late 1800s, 7 x 10 In..........	200
Sculpture, Kaesbach, Rudolf, Blacksmith, Anvil, Sledgehammer, Germany, 10 x 4 ½ In.....	406
Sculpture, Kauba, Carl, Chief White Cloud, Indian, Standing, Multicolor, Marble Base, 21 In.....	2178
Sculpture, Kauba, Carl, Indian Chief, Running, Feathered Baton, Agate Base, 11 In...*illus*	635
Sculpture, Keck, Hans, Nude Woman, Standing, Parrot, Circular Base, Austria, 10 ½ In. ...	500
Sculpture, Kowalczewski, P., Woman, Water Carrier, Mounted, Marble Base, 13 ½ In..........	288
Sculpture, Kratzmann, Peter, Hopi Man, Standing, Blanket, Spear, Staff, 1985, 13 In........	118
Sculpture, Le Fagways, Pierre, Olympic Female, Javelin Thrower, France, 1935, 11 ½ x 7 In.	125
Sculpture, Lion, Mid Roar, Seal Marks, Bronze Base, Japan, Late 1800s, 8 ½ x 13 In...*illus*	300
Sculpture, Luristan, Figural, Facing Animals, Mahogany Stand, Felted Base, 8 ½ x 3 ½ In........	585
Sculpture, MacDonald, Richard, Dove, Man & Woman, Dancing, Marble Base, 17 x 11 In..	4375
Sculpture, Marioton, Eugene, La Danse, Man & Woman, Marble Base, Signed, 11 x 6 In.....	270
Sculpture, Marly Horse, Rearing, Groom, After Guillaume Coustou, 1800s, 24 x 22 x 8 In., Pair	6300
Sculpture, McGary, Dave, In Victory I Stand, Indian Warrior, Walnut Base, 2001, 30 x 15 x 11 In.	10200
Sculpture, Medieval Warrior, Standing, Holding Ax, Full Armor, Gilt, 1800s, 4 In...............	156

B

Bronze, Sculpture, Newton, Garry, Dachshund, 2 Dogs, Looking In Mirror, Texas, 1993, 14 ½ In.

$1,150

Merrill's Auctions

Bronze, Sculpture, Pyramid Style, Dancing Camel, Frolicking Monkeys, W.B. Geschutzt, 14 In.

$210

Treasureseeker Auctions

Bronze, Sculpture, Steiner, Clement Leopold, Tentation, Seminude Maiden, Cupid, 25 x 12 x 14 In.
$3,360

Abington Auction Gallery

Bronze, Sculpture, Tourgueneff, Pierre Nicolas, German Shepherd, Lying Down, Patina, 7 x 15 In.
$1,200

Selkirk Auctioneers & Appraisers

Bronze, Sculpture, Vishnu, Seated, 4 Hands, Hindu Deity, 1800s, 12½ x 6½ x 6 In.
$1,638

Thomaston Place Auction Galleries

Sculpture, Mercie, Marius-Jean-Antonin, David Vainqueur De Goliath, Travertine Base, 1845, 25 In.	2000
Sculpture, Mercury, Hermes, Running Position, Marble Base, 15½ In.	295
Sculpture, Mermaid, Painted, 8 Dolphins, 1900s, 12 x 14 x 29 In.	307
Sculpture, Mirval, C., Dancer, Art Deco, Bronze, Silvered, Onyx Base, Signed, 1900s, 26¾ In.	2500
Sculpture, Moigniez, Jules, Eagle, Spread Wings, Green Marble Base, Signed, 29 x 24 x 16 In.	1610
Sculpture, Moigniez, Jules, Eagle, Spread Wings, Marble Base, 30 x 17 x 20 In.	1063
Sculpture, Nebeker, Bill, Feathers, Furs & Fiddlin, Wood Base, 1987, 10 In.	375
Sculpture, Nelson, Paul Joseph, Male Nude, Standing, Red, Signed, 27 x 6½ In.	625
Sculpture, Newton, Garry, Dachshund, 2 Dogs, Looking In Mirror, Texas, 1993, 14½ In.....*illus*	1150
Sculpture, Plunkett, Bill, Sunning His Heels, Cowboy, Horse, Mid Jump, Wood Base, 23 In.	450
Sculpture, Polutanovich, Greg, Billy The Kid, Half Body, Dark Brown, Marble Base, 10 In.. *illus*	765
Sculpture, Prat, Woman, Nude, Seated, Cupid, Bow & Arrows, Signed, c.1980, 40 In.	660
Sculpture, Pyramid Style, Dancing Camel, Frolicking Monkeys, W.B. Geschutzt, 14 In.*illus*	210
Sculpture, Quaintance, Louis Thiele, Man Standing, Holding Head, 1900s, 27 x 12 x 7 In..	250
Sculpture, Rooster, Standing, Crowing, Black Patina, Chinese, 25 In.	863
Sculpture, Rumsey, Charles Cary, Horse, Standing, Nancy Hanks, Signed, 1911, 15¾ In. ...	2625
Sculpture, Russell, Charles Marion, Stagecoach, 6 Horses, Coachman, 1900s, 14 x 42 x 12 In....	1148
Sculpture, Saalmann, Erich, Moose, Standing, Marble Base, Germany, 1900s, 8¼ x 10 In.	780
Sculpture, Saleeby, Cherie, Abstract, Female Torso, Stone Base, 28 x 12 x 10 In.	300
Sculpture, Sammis, Anne Mimi, Couple, Child, Playing, Rotating Base, 17 In.	460
Sculpture, Steiner, Clement Leopold, Tentation, Seminude Maiden, Cupid, 25 x 12 x 14 In...*illus*	3360
Sculpture, Stuckenberg, Jim, To The Paddock, Horse, Trainer, Patinated, 1992, 8½ x 10½ In....	383
Sculpture, Tiot, A., Cat Goddess, Sitting On Hind Legs, Hollywood Regency, 1970s, 24 x 9 In.	1095
Sculpture, Tofanari, Sirio, Baboon, Mandrill, Walking, Italy, c.1930, 13¼ x 15½ In.	1658
Sculpture, Tourgueneff, Pierre Nicolas, German Shepherd, Lying Down, Patina, 7 x 15 In...*illus*	1200
Sculpture, Turner, William, Barn Owl, Spread Wings, Standing On Top Of Books, 10 In.	2337
Sculpture, Vishnu, Seated, 4 Hands, Hindu Deity, 1800s, 12½ x 6½ x 6 In..............*illus*	1638
Sculpture, Voulkos, Peter, Ribar, Signed Base, 1970, 7 x 12¾ x 11 In..........*illus*	9600
Sculpture, Weigl, Robert, Hunter With Wild Boar, Brown Patina, Austria, 1912, 14 x 7 In. ..	570
Sculpture, Winfield, Rodney, 2-Sided, Bear, Rainstorm, Bull, Clover Field, 5½ x 3 In.	330
Sculpture, Woman, Seated, Holding Flower Tray, 7 x 4 In.	94
Sculpture, Woman, Sitting, Nude, Inspecting Foot, Marble Base, Myrom, 8 x 5½ x 11 In. ..	413
Sculpture, Woman, Standing, Round Stone Base, Plaque, Late 1900s, 20 In.	270
Sculpture, Wrathful Deity, Seated, Holding Rosary, Rectangular Base, Sino-Tibetan, 11 In.	390
Signal Cannon, Brass Barrel, Mounted, Tripod, New York, c.1895, 65 In.	750
Tazza, Flared Base, Grand Tour, Renaissance Style, Late 1800s, 5¾ In..............*illus*	438
Tazza, Garniture, Black Marble Base, Victorian, 11¾ x 8 x 5⅜ In., Pair	128
Tazza, Grath, Anton, Figural, Jugendstil, Lauchhammer Foundry, c.1930, 10 x 12 x 8 In.	500
Tazza, Nordic Style, Circular Base, Gustavsberg, Sweden, 1900s, 8½ x 11 In.	125
Teapot, Lid, Repousse, Swing Handle, Spout, Japan, 1900s, 9 In.	188
Tray, Don Quixote, Fighting Scene, Gilt, Flowers, Black Ground, Signed, Young, 4¾ x 4¾ In. ...	48
Tray, Hurley, E.T., Patina, Black Widow Spider & Moths, Web, Ohio, c.1915, 5⅜ In.	552
Trinket Box, Hinged Lid, Decorated Body, Ball Feet, Art Deco, France, 1900s, 4 x 3 In.	96
Urn, Arts & Crafts, 4 Handles, Vase, Narrow Foot, 10¾ x 11½ In.	322
Urn, Classical Figures, Egg & Dart Rim, Marble Base, Late 1800s, 14 x 10 In...........*illus*	545
Urn, Egret, Worms, Frogs, Deer, Silvered, Bird Feet Base, c.1880, 14 In., Pair..........*illus*	450
Urn, Grotesque Faces, Putti, Domed Base, Late 1800s, 12½ In., Pair	840
Urn, Louis XVI Style, Gilt, Panther Handles, Grapevines, 9½ In., Pair	350
Urn, Neoclassical, Verde Antico, Black Marble, Continental, Late 1800s, 7 x 5 x 4 In., Pair...	175
Vase, Apollo Studios, Green, Metal Overlay, Square, Butterfly, c.1910, 3 x 3 x 3 In.	246
Vase, Archaic Lappet, Dragon Handles, Japan, Late 1800s, 18 x 7 In., Pair	410
Vase, Barbedienne, Trumpet Shape Top, Raised Birds, Leaves & Twigs, H. Cahieux, 19 In. ..	240
Vase, Ceremonial, 2 Handles, Mounted, Applied Design, Continental, 19 In.	704
Vase, Collar, Over Sloping Design, Gilt, Late 1900s, 13 In.	1416
Vase, De Tirtoff, Romain, Fantasy, Woman, Aqua Robe, Marked, Erte, 1985, 14 x 7 In.. *illus*	1500
Vase, Ferville-Suan, Winged Fairy, Circular, c.1900, 8½ In., Pair	330
Vase, Flared Rim, Cavorting Monkeys, Continental, 1900s, 25 In.	976
Vase, Flowers, Bird, Thorns, Japan, c.1900, 8 x 6¼ In.	738
Vase, Leaves, Ring Handles, Shaped Top, Japan, 8 In.	54
Vase, Levasseur, Napoleon III, Nude Female Figure, Cylindrical, Sloping Shoulder, France, 9 In....	720

Bronze, Sculpture, Voulkos, Peter, Ribar, Signed Base, 1970, 7 x 12¾ x 11 In.
$9,600

Michaan's Auctions

Bronze, Vase, De Tirtoff, Romain, Fantasy, Woman, Aqua Robe, Marked, Erte, 1985, 14 x 7 In.
$1,500

John Moran Auctioneers

Bronze, Tazza, Flared Base, Grand Tour, Renaissance Style, Late 1800s, 5¾ In.
$438

Eldred's

Bronze, Urn, Egret, Worms, Frogs, Deer, Silvered, Bird Feet Base, c.1880, 14 In., Pair
$450

TIP
Dust your bronze, then try the Chinese method of polishing. Rub the bronze with the palm of your hand. This puts a little oil on the metal.

Bronze, Urn, Classical Figures, Egg & Dart Rim, Marble Base, Late 1800s, 14 x 10 In.
$545

Fontaine's Auction Gallery

Treasureseeker Auctions

Bronze, Vase, Mixed Metal, Flower Branches, Signed, Gilt Stamp, Japan, 1800s, 11 x 7 In.
$960

Main Auction Galleries, Inc.

B

Bronze, Vase, Moreau, Auguste, Figural Cupid, Blood Red Marble Base, Signed, 10 In., Pair
$439

Thomaston Place Auction Galleries

Bronze, Vase, Round Body, Squat, Long Neck, Dragon Grasping, Pearl, Japan, Late 1800s, 9 In.
$270

Selkirk Auctioneers & Appraisers

Brownies, Candy Container, Christmas, Brownie On Log, Sitting, Red Hat, Blue Coat, 4 In.
$660

Milestone Auctions

Vase, Levillain & Barbedienne, Neoclassical, Paw-Footed Base, 15 x 7 ½ x 7 ½ In.	1408
Vase, Mixed Metal, Flower Branches, Signed, Gilt Stamp, Japan, 1800s, 11 x 7 In. .... *illus*	960
Vase, Moreau, Auguste, Figural Cupid, Blood Red Marble Base, Signed, 10 In., Pair ..... *illus*	439
Vase, Round Body, Squat, Long Neck, Dragon Grasping, Pearl, Japan, Late 1800s, 9 In.*illus*	270
Vase, Tapered, Triangular, Mother & Daughter In Bonnets, Long Dresses, 7 In.	60

BROWNIES

Brownies, the cartoon figures, were first drawn in 1883 by Palmer Cox (1840–1924). They are characterized by large round eyes, downturned mouths, and skinny legs. Toys, books, dinnerware, and other objects were made with the Brownies as part of the design.

Candy Container, Christmas, Brownie On Log, Sitting, Red Hat, Blue Coat, 4 In. .... *illus*	660
Doll, Cloth, 6 Brownies, Uncut, Frame, 22 ¼ x 27 ½ In.	60
Match Holder, Cigar, Uncle Sam, Standing, 3 Wells, Multicolor, Green Base, 8 ½ In.... *illus*	180
Sign, If You Like Chocolate Soda, Drink Brownie, Cardboard, Wood Frame, 21 x 60 In.	2520
Toy, Brownie On Horse, White, Red & Green Paint, Rectangular Base, 4 Wheels, Hubley, 6 In.	532

BRUSH-MCCOY, *see Brush category and related pieces in McCoy category.*

BRUSH POTTERY

Brush Pottery was started in 1925. George Brush first worked in 1901 in Zanesville, Ohio. He started his own pottery in 1907, but it burned to the ground soon after. In 1909 he became manager of the J.W. McCoy Pottery. In 1911, Brush and J.W. McCoy formed the Brush-McCoy Pottery Co. After a series of name changes, the company became The Brush Pottery in 1925. It closed in 1982. Old Brush was marked with impressed letters or a palette-shaped mark. Reproduction pieces are being made. They are marked in raised letters or with a raised mark. Collectors favor the figural cookie jars made by this company. Because there was a company named Brush-McCoy, there is great confusion between Brush and Nelson McCoy pieces. Most collectors today refer to Brush pottery as Brush-McCoy. See McCoy category for more information.

Cookie Jar, Panda, Sitting, Black Spots, Green Bow, Pink Paws, 9 ¾ x 10 ½ In.	24
Cookie Jar, Squirrel, On Gray Log, Holding Mallet, Acorn, 11 ¼ x 11 In.	60
Flower Frog, Flower Shape, Blue Green, Scalloped Rim, Marked, Brush USA, 3 ¾ x 14 In.	57
Radio, Beetle, Blue Green, Mystic Crystal, Headphones, Brush-McCoy, 1920s, 9 ½ x 5 ½ In.	1332

BUCK ROGERS

Buck Rogers was the first American science fiction comic strip. It started in 1929 and continued until 1967. Buck has also appeared in comic books, movies, and, in the 1980s, a television series. Any memorabilia connected with the character Buck Rogers is collectible.

Comic Book, No. 2, Dick Galkins Cover Art, Eastern Color Printing, July 1941, 13 x 8 In.	407
Toy, Figure, Dr. Huer, Blue Suit, Purple Sash, Mego, Box, 1979	101
Toy, Figure, Draconian Guard, Red & White Uniform, Mego, Box, 1979	113
Toy, Rocket Ship, Tin Lithograph, Orange, Fins, Wilma & Buck, Windup, Marx, Box, 4 ½ x 12 In.	2040
Toy, Twiki, Windup, Walks, Moves Arms, Multicolor Decal On Chest, 7 In. .... *illus*	131

BUFFALO POTTERY

Buffalo Pottery was made in Buffalo, New York, beginning in 1901. The company was established by the Larkin Company, famous manufacturers of soap. The wares are marked with a picture of a buffalo and the date of manufacture. Deldare ware is the most famous pottery made at the factory. It has either a khaki-colored or green background with hand-painted transfer designs. The company reorganized in 1956 and was renamed Buffalo China before being bought by Oneida Silver Company in 1983.

Oneida sold the company to Niagara Ceramics in 2004 but Oneida still sells a few lines of Buffalo China dinnerware.

Buffalo Pottery
1907

Deldare Ware
1909

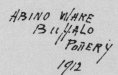
Emerald Deldare
1912

BUFFALO POTTERY

Pitcher, Roosevelt Bears, Multicolor Transfer, Square, Handle, Marked, c.1905, 8 In....	431 to 815
Pitcher, Whaling Scene, Brown Transfer, 1907, 6 ½ In..........	594
Tray, Dr. Syntax, Advertisement For A Wife, Blue & White, Flower Border, 11 ¼ x 14 ¼ In.....	108

BUFFALO POTTERY DELDARE

Humidor, Dome Lid, Ye Lion Inn, 8-Sided, Tapered, Signed, N. Sheenan, 7 ¼ x 6 In.	191
Plate Set, Ye Olden Days, Largest 10 In., Smallest 6 ¼ In., 5 Piece	125
Plate, Ye Village Gossips, 3 Men Standing, Marked, 10 In......	44
Tray, Heirlooms, 3 Women At Table, Rectangular, W. Fazter, c.1907, 10 ¼ x 14 In..........	49

BUNNYKINS, *see Royal Doulton category.*

BURMESE GLASS

Burmese glass was developed by Frederick Shirley at the Mt. Washington Glass Works in New Bedford, Massachusetts, in 1885. It is a two-toned glass, shading from peach to yellow. Some pieces have a pattern mold design. A few Burmese pieces were decorated with pictures or applied glass flowers of colored Burmese glass. Other factories made similar glass also called Burmese. Burmese glass was made by Mt. Washington until about 1895, by Gundersen until the 1950s, and by Webb until about 1900. Fenton made Burmese glass after 1970. Related items may be listed in the Fenton category and under Webb Burmese.

Biscuit Jar, Silver Plate Lid, White & Pink Flowers, Leafy Overlay, Bail Handle, 9 x 6 In.	150
Bride's Bowl, Glossy Finish, Flared, Ruffled, 8 Petals, 4 x 11 ¼ x 3 ½ In................	48
Ewer, Pale Yellow To Rose, Queen's, Pontillist Flowers, Mt. Washington, 12 ½ In.	4200
Ginger Jar, Verse, Should Auld Acquaintance Be Forgot, Mt. Washington, 8 x 6 In........	1500
Jam Jar, Butterfly, Blossoms, Branch, Brass Lid & Bail, Queen's, Thomas Webb, 5 x 3 In. .... *illus*	550
Mustard Pot, Squat, Lobed, Purple & Yellow Flowers, Quadruple Plate Lid & Handle, 3 ½ In......	162
Sconce, Pink Foldover Rim, Enameled Flowers & Branches, 2 Side Leaves, Mirrored Back, 13 x 9 In.	1107
Vase, Acorns, Star Crimped Top, Queen's, Thomas Webb & Sons, 3 x 3 In.	150
Vase, Bag Shape, Pink Flared Rim, Applied Rigaree Around Neck, 4 ½ x 5 In................	480
Vase, Bottle Shape, Striped Flowers, Applied Cabochons, 9 ¾ x 5 ½ In.	952

BUSTER BROWN

Buster Brown, the comic strip, first appeared in color in 1902. Buster and his dog, Tige, remained a popular comic and soon became even more famous as the emblem for a shoe company, a textile firm, and other companies. The strip was discontinued in 1920. Buster Brown sponsored a radio show from 1943 to 1955 and a TV show from 1950 to 1956. The Buster Brown characters are still used by Brown Shoe Company, Buster Brown Apparel, Inc., and Gateway Hosiery.

Bank, Good Luck, Black Horse, Gilt Horseshoe, Buster & Tige, Iron, Arcade, 4 ½ In. ...	63 to 120
Doll, Schoenhut, Roly Poly, Composition, Orange Outfit, Weighted, c.1908, 10 In.........	300
Pin, Buster Brown Bread, Davy Jones, Buster & Tige, Pennant, Morton's, Yellow Ground, 1910, 1 ¼ In.	404
Pin, Buster Brown Bread, Ty Cobb, Buster & Tige, Flag, Morton's, Yellow Ground, 1 ¼ In.....	3328
Toy, Horse, Rocking, Springs, Red, Buster & Tige On Side, Shoe Store Display, 28 x 35 In.	279
Toy, Rocker, Buster Brown, Tige, Ball Rolls, Tin, Germany, 8 In.	780

Brownies, Match Holder, Cigar, Uncle Sam, Standing, 3 Wells, Multicolor, Green Base, 8 ½ In.
$180

Milestone Auctions

Buck Rogers, Toy, Twiki, Windup, Walks, Moves Arms, Multicolor Decal On Chest, 7 In.
$131

Matthew Bullock Auctioneers

Burmese, Jam Jar, Butterfly, Blossoms, Branch, Brass Lid & Bail, Queens, Thomas Webb, 5 x 3 In.
$550

Woody Auction

B

TIP

Check wall-hung and glass shelves regularly to be sure they have not loosened or bent.

Button, Bakelite, Black, Carved & Engraved Fans, Ribbed Back, 3-Way Box Shank, Large
$375

Lion and Unicorn

Button, Bakelite, Cat On Fence, Black, Butterscotch Ground, Martha Sleeper, Large
$563

Lion and Unicorn

Button, Brass, Pierced Scrolls, Faceted Yellow Glass Jewels, 1890s, Large
$281

Lion and Unicorn

BUTTER CHIP

Butter chips, or butter pats, were small individual dishes for butter. They were the height of fashion from 1880 to 1910. Earlier as well as later examples are known. Many sell for under $15.

Famille Rose, Center Butterflies, Green & Pink Rim, 3 In., 5 Piece	42
Painted, Pink Flowers, Butterflies, Birds, Turquoise Rim, Gilt Trim, Chinese, 2¾ In., 12 Piece ..	282

BUTTON

Button collecting has been popular since the nineteenth century. Buttons have been used on clothing throughout the centuries, and there are millions of styles. Gold, silver, or precious stones were used for the best buttons, but most were made of natural materials, like bone or shell, or from inexpensive metals. Only a few types favored by collectors are listed for comparison. Political buttons may also be listed in Political.

Bakelite, Black, Carved & Engraved Fans, Ribbed Back, 3-Way Box Shank, Large	*illus*	375
Bakelite, Black, Gold Metal Trim, Octagonal, Raised Center, 1½ In.		25
Bakelite, Cat On Fence, Black, Butterscotch Ground, Martha Sleeper, Large	*illus*	563
Brass, Flowers, Domed, 1800s, 1 In.		38
Brass, Pierced Scrolls, Faceted Yellow Glass Jewels, 1890s, Large	*illus*	281
Celluloid, Domed, Pinwheel Design, Brown		10
Enamel, 2 Koi Fish, Cloisonne, Multicolor, Cream Ground, Pre 1918, Extra Large	*illus*	406
Metal, Picture, 2 Children, Multicolor Lithograph, Paste Jewel Border, Faith Strobel, Large	*illus*	88
Mica, White Plaster Figures, Under Glass, Reverse Painted Border, Copper Rim, 1700s.	*illus*	4000
Moonglow, Green, Gold Luster, Art Deco Design		7
Pearl, Carved, Scalloped Edge, Lacy, Center Paste Pinshank, Rhinestone Ring, 1700s, Large.	*illus*	375

CALENDAR

Calendars made to hang on the wall or to be displayed on a desk top have been popular since the last quarter of the nineteenth century. Many were printed with advertising as part of the artwork and were given away as premiums. Calendars illustrated by famous artists or with guns, gunpowder, or Coca-Cola advertising are most prized.

1899, A.G. Van Nostrand, Bunker Hill Breweries, Frame, 39½ x 30 In.	*illus*	3600
1905, Woman's Portrait, Rose Bouquet, All Months, American Lithograph Co., 27 x 11½ In.	*illus*	119
1908, Adam Deck, Jeweler, Girl Behind Curtains, Flowers, Irregular Shape, Hennepin, 17 x 13 In.		78
1913, Cat's Paw Heels, Couples, Picnic In Countryside, January, Frame, 29½ x 25 In.		266
1925, G.W. Herrington's Drug Store, Woman At Vanity, Multicolor Aquatint, 14 x 8½ In.		12
1933, Pennsylvania Railroad, Spirit of America, Grif Teller, Frame, 34 x 33 In.		107
1934, Winchester, Painted, Boy, Fence, Dog, Eugene Iverd, Wood Frame, 14 x 27 In.	*illus*	813
1942, Fremont Bottling Co., Woman, Sitting, Orange Drape, Billy DeVorss, Frame, 24 x 12 In..		118
1947, Eastman's Tin Shop, Campsite, 2 Hunters In Canoe, Bear, 2 Cubs, Saginaw, Mich., 13 x 12 In....		98
1948, Antonides Pharmacy, Woman, Sitting, Orange Lingerie, Billy DeVorss, Frame, 24 x 12 In..		83
1978, Punk Magazine, Ramones Caricature, Black & White, Bobby London, 12 Pages, 17 x 11 In.		875
1989, Cars, Multicolor, Spiral Binding, Andy Warhol, 22¼ x 14½ In.		51
Perpetual, Desk, J.H. Thomas, Gilt Base, W.T. & J. Mersereau, N.Y., 1800s, 7 x 5 In.		156

CALENDAR PLATE

Calendar plates were popular in the United States as advertising giveaways from 1906 to 1929. Since then, a few plates have been made every year. A calendar and the name of a store, a picture of flowers, a girl, or a scene were featured on the plate.

1909, Center Flowers, Months Around Rim, Marked, John E. Hoffman, Tower City, Pa., 9½ In....		39
1964, Green & White, Home Of Abraham Lincoln, Months Around Rim, Royal Staffordshire, 9 In.		14
1975, Currier & Ives, Blue & White, Royal China, 10 In.		6
1986, Garden Birds, Around Rim, Months Around Center, Box, Wedgwood, 10 In.		100
2001, Beatrix Potter, Peter Rabbit, Rabbits Gardening, Multicolor, Wedgwood, 8 In.		13

Button, Enamel, 2 Koi Fish, Cloisonne, Multicolor, Cream Ground, Pre 1918, Extra Large
$406

Lion and Unicorn

Button, Metal, Picture, 2 Children, Multicolor Lithograph, Paste Jewel Border, Faith Strobel, Large
$88

Lion and Unicorn

Button, Mica, White Plaster Figures, Under Glass, Reverse Painted Border, Copper Rim, 1700s
$4,000

Lion and Unicorn

Button, Pearl, Carved, Scalloped Edge, Lacy, Center Paste Pinshank, Rhinestone Ring, 1700s, Large
$375

Lion and Unicorn

Calendar, 1899, A.G. Van Nostrand, Bunker Hill Breweries, Frame, 39 ½ x 30 In.
$3,600

Morphy Auctions

Calendar, 1905, Woman's Portrait, Rose Bouquet, All Months, American Lithograph Co., 27 x 11 ½ In.
$119

Matthew Bullock Auctioneers

Calendar, 1934, Winchester, Painted, Boy, Fence, Dog, Eugene Iverd, Wood Frame, 14 x 27 In.
$813

Morphy Auctions

Cambridge, Crown Tuscan, Compote, Nude, Holding Shell Aloft, Ruffled Rim, Pink Opaque, 7 In.
$49

Apple Tree Auction Center

Cameo Glass, Vase, Cobalt Blue, 2 Parrots, Valerie Surjan, 11 x 4½ In.
$313

Greenwich Auction

Cameo Glass, Vase, Flower, Canary, Wheel, Carved, Signed, Burgun & Schverer, France, 5½ In.
$5,625

Treadway

CAMBRIDGE GLASS COMPANY

Cambridge Glass Company was founded in 1901 in Cambridge, Ohio. The company closed in 1954, reopened briefly, and closed again in 1958. The firm made all types of glass. Its early wares included heavy pressed glass with the mark *Near Cut*. Later wares included Crown Tuscan, etched stemware, and clear and colored glass. The firm used a *C* in a triangle mark after 1920.

NEAR – CUT

TUSCAN

Cambridge Glass Co. c.1906–c.1920	Cambridge Glass Co. c.1937	Cambridge Glass Co. 1936–1954

Bashful Charlotte, Flower Frog, Round Base, Vaseline, 8½ In.		108
Caprice, Bowl, Ruffled Rim, Silver Overlay Flowers, 4-Footed, 12½ In.		18
Crown Tuscan, Compote, Nude, Carrying Shell, Round Base, 8½ In.		148
Crown Tuscan, Compote, Nude, Holding Shell Aloft, Ruffled Rim, Pink Opaque, 7 In.	*illus*	49
Crown Tuscan, Goblet, Nude Stem, Yellow Bowl		83
Fernland, Pitcher, Water, Ruby Stain		166
Honeycomb Optic, Compote, Rubina Verde, Baluster Stem, Unmarked, 8 In.		60
Rose Point, Bowl, Divided, 3 Sections, Silver Base, 8 In.		40
Rose Point, Cake Plate, Scalloped Edge, 3-Footed, 13 In.		30
Rose Point, Pitcher, Flowers, Loop Handle, Silver Base, 6 In.		115

CAMEO GLASS

Cameo glass was made in much the same manner as a cameo in jewelry. Parts of the top layer of glass were cut away to reveal a different colored glass beneath. The most famous cameo glass was made during the nineteenth century. Signed cameo glass pieces by famous makers are listed under the glasswork's name, such as Daum, Galle, Legras, Mt. Joye, Webb, and more. Others, signed or unsigned, are listed here. These marks were used by three lesser-known cameo glass manufacturers.

Albert Dammouse 1892+	Ernest–Baptiste Lèveillé c.1869–c.1900	François–Eugène Rousseau 1855–1885

Lamp, Electric, Junior, Flowers, Butterfly, Signed, Webb & Sons, Late 1800s, 12½ x 5½ In.		2340
Liqueur, Pedestal, White Translucent Ground, Green Cameo, Leafy Vines, France, 2 x 1 In.		100
Vase, Cobalt Blue, 2 Parrots, Valerie Surjan, 11 x 4½ In.	*illus*	313
Vase, Flower, Canary, Wheel, Carved, Signed, Burgun & Schverer, France, 5½ In.	*illus*	5625
Vase, Green Leaves & Stems, Yellow Ground, Handle, Le Gras, France, 8 In.		330
Vase, Iridescent Green, Dragon Design, Wavy Rim, Custard Ground, Signed, T. Gibson, 8 x 4 In.		80
Vase, Scenic, Ruined Castle, Slender Baluster Shape, Red, Signed, Edmond Rigot, 11½ In.		590
Vase, White Ground, Carved, Flowers & Leaf Overlay, Signed, G. Raspiller, 4¼ x 6 In.	*illus*	125

CAMPAIGN *memorabilia are listed in the Political category.*

CAMPBELL KIDS

Campbell Kids were first used as part of an advertisement for the Campbell Soup Company in 1904. The kids were created by Grace Drayton, a popular illustrator of the day. The kids were used in magazine and newspaper ads

until about 1951. They were presented again in 1966; and in 1983, they were redesigned with a slimmer, more contemporary appearance.

Cookie Jar, Soup Can Shape, 2 Kids On Lid, 1 Holds Spoon, Benjamin & Medwin, 1998, 12 In.	25
Lunch Box, Kids Playing Sports, Blue Trim, White Handle, Tin, 8¾ x 3½ x 6½ In.	24
Thermometer, Kid Holding Soup Can At Top, Tomato Half At Bottom, Wood, 18 In.	24

CANDELABRUM

Candelabrum refers to a candleholder with more than one arm to hold many candles; a candlestick is designed to hold one candle. The eccentricity of the English language makes the plural of *candelabrum* into *candelabra*.

2-Light, Brass, Iron, Pointed Top, Twisted Stem, Adjustable, Curved Legs, 1700s, 57 x 14 In..	497
2-Light, Bronze, Figural, Grecian Female, Standing, Horizontal Arms, 13½ In.	130
2-Light, Bronze, Figural Woman, Pedestal, Plinth Base, Marked, Luneville, 20 x 8 In., Pair	200
2-Light, Gilt Bronze, Candle Arms, Swan Heads, Lyre Mount, Black Square Base, 1800s, 17 In., Pair	738
2-Light, Gilt Bronze, Figural, Cherub, Empire, Statuary Bronze, Patina, Base, 1800s, 15½ In., Pair.	765
2-Light, Gilt Bronze, French Empire, Patina Cherub, Engine Turned Base, 1800s, 21 In., Pair.	1408
2-Light, Gilt Bronze, Neoclassical, Drip Pan, Baltic, c.1780, 7 x 8 x 4 In., Pair. *illus*	813
2-Light, Porcelain, Painted, Gilt, Mounted, Footed, France, 12¼ In., Pair	125
2-Light, Silver Plate, Bow Shape, Glass, Christofle, Paris, 9 x 8¾ In., Pair. *illus*	325
2-Light, Silver Plate, Urn Shape Candlecups, Removable, Sheffield, 15½ In., Pair	704
2-Light, Silver, Art Deco, Weighted Base, Gorham, 7¼ In., Pair.	793
2-Light, Silver, Drip Pan, Weighted, Fisher Silversmiths, N.J., 1900s, 5 x 11 In., Pair.	313
3-Light, Aluminum, Flower Shape, Bobeches, Scrolls, Rectangular Base, 1900s, 13 x 15 In., Pair *illus*	84
3-Light, Bronze, Green Patina, Round Base, E.T. Hurley, c.1920s, 14½ x 10 In., Pair... *illus*	2214
3-Light, Copper, 2 Rings, Dome Base, Arts & Crafts, 10 x 6½ In.	100
3-Light, Gilt Bronze, Continental, Baluster, Malachite, Square Base, 12½ x 9 In., Pair	1320
3-Light, Gilt Metal, Figural, Candle Arms, Bracket Base, France, Early 1900s, 15½ x 9 x 5 In., Pair	1071
3-Light, Gilt Metal, Onyx, Scrolling Vines, Candle Sockets, Column Support, 1800s, 28 In., Pair.	188
3-Light, Giltwood, Scrolls & Leaves, Rectangular Base, 22¾ In., Pair. *illus*	704
3-Light, Porcelain, Applied Oranges & Pink Flowers, 2 Putti, Germany, 21 In., Pair	240
3-Light, Porcelain, Cherubs, Greek Key Base, Continental, 12 x 9 In., Pair	63
3-Light, Porcelain, Rosebud On Top, Matching Flower, Matching Stem, Continental, 1900s, 22¼ In.	150
3-Light, Silver Plate, Curved Arm, Tripod Stepped Base, WMF, Early 1900s, 7 x 9 In.	250
3-Light, Silver Plate, Removable Arm & Bobeches, Leaves, Cement Base, 24 x 16 In., Pair... *illus*	600
3-Light, Silver, Candleholders, Tapering, Round Base, 11 In., Pair	230
3-Light, Silver, Scroll, Flowers, Weighted Base, Gorham, 1905, 14½ In., Pair. *illus*	448
3-Light, Wood, Tree Shape, Clear Finial, Hanging Grapes, Painted, Late 1800s, 37 In.	1063
3-Light, Wrought Iron, Craftsman, Tripod Legs, Circular Base, 22 x 10½ In., Pair	281
4-Light, Bronze, Man & Woman, Holding Sconces, Gilt, Late 1800s, 34 x 14 x 13 In., Pair... *illus*	5445
4-Light, Enameled Steel, Rattan, U-Shape Candleholders, Arthur Umanoff, c.1950, 47 x 17 x 16 In.	313
4-Light, Gilt Bronze, Cherub Supports, 25 x 11 x 6½ In., Pair.	352
4-Light, Gilt Bronze, Empire Style, Angel, Standing, Patina, Late 1800s, 25½ In., Pair	4063
4-Light, Gilt Bronze, Leaf, Rosebud Holder, 12 x 11 In., Pair.	156
4-Light, Gilt Bronze, Seated Putto Shape, Flowers, Late 1800s, 17 x 9 x 7 In., Pair	563
4-Light, Gilt Metal, Clear & Purple Glass, Hanging Prisms, 1900s, 24 x 12 In., Pair.	188
4-Light, Gilt Metal, Neoclassical Style, Glass Columns, Base, 36 In., Pair. *illus*	829
4-Light, Gilt Metal, Stag Shape, Mounted, Wood Base, 1900s, 19¼ In.	219
4-Light, Porcelain, Meissen Style, Flowers, Multicolor, Paw Feet, 1900s, 20¼ In., Pair. *illus*	488
4-Light, Silver Plate, Beaded Edge, Hawksworth, Eyre & Co., Sheffield, Late 1800s, 20 In., Pair.	1170
5-Light, Bronze, Louis XV Style, Seated Putti, Marble Base, France, Late 1800s, 24 In., Pair ..*illus*	363
5-Light, Forged Iron Pricket, Curved Design, Trailing Flower, 3 Ball Feet, c.1930, 15 x 24 In.	117
5-Light, Gilt Metal Stand, Clear Cover On Shaft, Electric, 27 x 16 In., Pair.	500
5-Light, Glass, Hanging Prisms, Brass, Circular, Stepped Base, Late 1800s, 28 In., Pair.	344
5-Light, Metal, Long Stem, Round Nozzle, Imperial Zinn, Germany, 15½ x 8 In.	813
5-Light, Silver Plate, Rococo Style, Urn Shape Candlecups, Royal Castle, Sheffield, 27½ In., Pair	2432
5-Light, Silver Plate, Rococo, Rocaille, Flambeau Finial, Gorham, Late 1800s, 16½ x 13¾ In..	438

Cameo Glass, Vase, White Ground, Carved, Flowers & Leaf Overlay, Signed, G. Raspiller, 4¼ x 6 In.
$125

Woody Auction

Candelabrum, 2-Light, Gilt Bronze, Neoclassical, Drip Pan, Baltic, c.1780, 7 x 8 x 4 In., Pair
$813

Hindman

TIP
Watch out when burning candles. If the wick gets too short and the flame hits the metal holder used in some candlesticks, lead fumes are released.

Candelabrum, 2-Light, Silver Plate, Bow Shape, Glass, Christofle, Paris, 9 x 8¾ In., Pair
$325

Treadway

Candelabrum, 3-Light, Aluminum, Flower Shape, Bobeches, Scrolls, Rectangular Base, 1900s, 13 x 15 In., Pair
$84

Selkirk Auctioneers & Appraisers

Candelabrum, 3-Light, Bronze, Green Patina, Round Base, E.T. Hurley, c.1920s, 14 ½ x 10 In., Pair
$2,214

California Historical Design

Candelabrum, 3-Light, Giltwood, Scrolls & Leaves, Rectangular Base, 22 ¾ In., Pair
$704

Neal Auction Company

Candelabrum, 3-Light, Silver Plate, Removable Arm & Bobeches, Leaves, Cement Base, 24 x 16 In., Pair
$600

Richard Opfer Auctioneering, Inc.

Candelabrum, 3-Light, Silver, Scroll, Flowers, Weighted Base, Gorham, 1905, 14 ½ In., Pair
$448

Brunk Auctions

Candelabrum, 4-Light, Bronze, Man & Woman, Holding Sconces, Gilt, Late 1800s, 34 x 14 x 13 In., Pair
$5,445

Fontaine's Auction Gallery

Candelabrum, 4-Light, Gilt Metal, Neoclassical Style, Glass Columns, Base, 36 In., Pair
$829

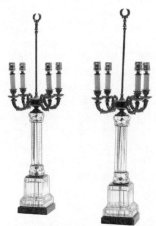

Bonhams

Candelabrum, 4-Light, Porcelain, Meissen Style, Flowers, Multicolor, Paw Feet, 1900s, 20¼ In., Pair
$488

Neal Auction Company

Candelabrum, 5-Light, Bronze, Louis XV Style, Seated Putti, Marble Base, France, Late 1800s, 24 In., Pair
$363

Fontaine's Auction Gallery

Candelabrum, 7-Light, Brass, Candleholders, Porcelain Flowers, 31 x 13½ In., Pair
$576

Nadeau's Auction Gallery

Candelabrum, 17-Light, Wrought Iron, Standing, Pricket Shape, 2 Tiers, Scroll Base, c.1900, 73 x 28 In.
$819

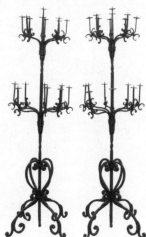

Thomaston Place Auction Galleries

Candelabrum, Girandole, 5-Light, Glass, Pendalogue Drops, Scroll Arms, Tripod Base, c.1915, 35 x 16 In., Pair
$875

John Moran Auctioneers

Candelabrum, Sconce, Wrought Iron, 9 Prickets, Flowers, Pointed Leaves, Gold Paint, 1800s, 35 x 19 In., Pair
$1,250

New Haven Auctions

Candlestick, Brass, Gilt, Rococo Pattern, Removable Bobeches, France, 1900s, 10¼ In., Pair
$259

Merrill's Auctions

Candlestick, Brass, Tavern Stick, Fine Chisel, Faux Timber Bell, Pan Base, 1800s, 11 x 6 In., Pair
$5,490

Rafael Osona Nantucket Auctions

5-Light, Silver, Drip Pan, Flared Rim, Column Stem, P.A. Ljunglof, Stockholm, 1845, 24 In. ...	1875
5-Light, Silver, Drip Pan, Weighted Base, Vander & Hedges, London, c.1920, 23 In., Pair	6875
5-Light, Silver, Gadroon, Domed Base, Marked, Ventrella Roma, 800, 1900s, 18¼ In. Pair.	4235
5-Light, Silver, Repousse, Paw Feet, Weighted, Bailey Banks & Biddle, Whiting, 20 In., Pair	2520
6-Light, Bronze, Charles X, Gilt, Patina, Stone Base, c.1830, 31½ In., Pair............	1084
6-Light, Bronze, Figural, Winged Victory, Arms Support, Lamp Extenders, France, 1800s, 44 In., Pair	915
6-Light, Bronze, Tree Trunk Shape, Woman's Figure, 4 Scrolled Feet, 1800s, 32 x 17 In., Pair.......	1750
6-Light, Candlecups, Drip Pan, White Marble Columns, France, 1800s, 27 x 12 In., Pair.....	805
6-Light, Gilt Bronze, Grand Tour, Lion, Etruscan Element, Tripod, Footed, France, c.1880, 32 x 11 In.	688
6-Light, Red & Clear Glass, Enameled Steel, Sonata, Hans-Agne Jakobsson, Sweden, 1960, 65 In.	3500
6-Light, Silver Plate, Shaped Base, D. Vollgold & Sohne, Berlin, Late 1800s, 21 In., Pair......	1968
7-Light, Brass, Candleholders, Porcelain Flowers, 31 x 13½ In., Pair ....*illus*	576
7-Light, Candleholder, Enameled Steel, Brass, Piet Hein, Denmark, 1953, 29 x 22 x 5 In. ...	6000
7-Light, Gilt Bronze, Leaves, Insects, Claw Paw Feet, France, c.1900, 28 x 12 In., Pair	1599
7-Light, Silver, Acanthus Leaves, Beaded Trim, Continental, 1900s, 29 In.............	4840
9-Light, Enameled Steel, Black, Mounted, Square Base, c.1965, 47 x 11 In.............	625
9-Light, Wrought Iron, Urn Shape Candlecups, Spiral Feet, c.1920, 72 In., Pair.............	344
10-Light, Louis XV Style, Gilt Bronze, Cherub, Leaves, Ornate Base, Late 1800s, 34 In., Pair	5313
12-Light, Banquet, 3 Layers Of Glass Prisms, Clear & Amethyst, 35 x 24 In., Pair	2070
17-Light, Wrought Iron, Standing, Pricket Shape, 2 Tiers, Scroll Base, c.1900, 73 x 28 In. ... *illus*	819
Girandole, 2-Light, Giltwood, Mirror, Flowers, Urn Finial, Italy, 33 x 11 In., Pair................	640
Girandole, 4-Light, Glass, Gilt Bronze Dore, Louis XV Style, Triparte Stem, 1900s, 28 In., Pair......	787
Girandole, 4-Light, Silver Bronze, Louis XV Style, Rock Crystal, Brown Pendants, 27½ In., Pair..	1125
Girandole, 5-Light, Glass, Pendalogue Drops, Scroll Arms, Tripod Base, c.1915, 35 x 16 In., Pair.*illus*	875
Girandole, 6-Light, Bronze, Neoclassical, Opaline Glass, Cut Glass, Late 1700s, 23 In., Pair	732
Sconce, Wrought Iron, 9 Prickets, Flowers, Pointed Leaves, Gold Paint, 1800s, 35 x 19 In., Pair...*illus*	1250
Silver Plate, On Copper, Braided Arm, Mathew Boulton, Birmingham, c.1810, 22 x 17 x 6 In., Pair....	750

🕯 CANDLESTICK

Candlesticks were made of brass, pewter, glass, sterling silver, plated silver, and all types of pottery and porcelain. The earliest candlesticks, dating from the sixteenth century, held the candle on a pricket (sharp pointed spike). These lost favor because in times of strife the large church candlesticks with prickets became formidable weapons, so the socket was mandated. Candlesticks changed in style through the centuries, and designs range from Classical to Rococo to Art Nouveau to Art Deco.

Altar, Renaissance Style, Laurel, Leaves Repousse, Cherub, Paw & Ball Feet, Gilt, 38 In.......	156
Brass, Ejector Socket Holes, Turned Stem, Drip Pan, Domed Base, Heemskirk, 1700s, 7 x 4 In..	380
Brass, Flared Rim, Knopped Stem, Gilt, Shaped Base, 1700s, 8⅞ In., Pair............	125
Brass, Flat, Pierced Knops, Spread Base, Shell Shape Feet, Dutch, 1800s, 13 In., Pair..........	344
Brass, Georgian, Flared Rim, Gilt, Shell Shape Base, 1700s, 7 x 5 In., Pair	644
Brass, Gilt, Cylindrical Candlecups, Knopped Stem, Scalloped Foot, England, 1700s, 7 In., Pair .	188
Brass, Gilt, Flared Top, Long Base, Jens Quistgaard, Dansk, Denmark, c.1955, 9 x 2 In., 3 Piece..	1000
Brass, Gilt, Griffins, Dish Base, Footed, 8 In., Pair	125
Brass, Gilt, Rococo Pattern, Removable Bobeches, France, 1900s, 10¼ In., Pair..........*illus*	259
Brass, Holder, Elongated Shape, Trumpet Base, Dutch, 1700s, 8⅜ In., Pair	210
Brass, Pricket, Knopped Stem, Triangular Base, Footed, 1700s, 24½ In., Pair	188
Brass, Pricket, Mid Drip Pan, Domed Base, Dutch, 1700s, 12 x 7 In.	531
Brass, Queen Anne, Shell Base, Gilt, Mid 1700s, 9 In., Pair........................	2460
Brass, Ringed, Faceted Stems, Plinth Base, Square, Dutch, 1700s, 11 x 4 In., Pair	375
Brass, Tavern Stick, Fine Chisel, Faux Timber Bell, Pan Base, 1800s, 11 x 6 In., Pair...*illus*	5490
Brass, Triangles, Oval Handles, Round Base, WMF, Germany, c.1910, 9 x 5 In.....................	492
Brass, Victorian, Figural Woman, Man, Dog On Base, 16 In., Pair	62
Bronze, Art Nouveau, Curved Support, Leaf Shape Base, Early 1900s, 8½ In., Pair .....*illus*	968
Bronze, Foo Dog, Bared Teeth, Rectangular Pedestal, Tibet, 13 x 6¼ x 4¾ In., Pair............	500
Bronze, Heron, Standing, Tortoise Base, Snake Beak, Cup, Bobeche, 1800s, 11½ In., Pair..	140
Bronze, Louis XV Style, Dore, Rocaille Style, Flowers, France, 12 x 6½ In., Pair..................	995
Bronze, Pricket, 5-Toed Dragons, Verdigris Surface, Chinese, 19 x 27 x 7 In., Pair...............	468

TIP
Rub the base of a candlestick with a little olive oil before lighting a candle. Any wax that drips can easily be peeled off.

Candlestick, Bronze, Art Nouveau, Curved Support, Leaf Shape Base, Early 1900s, 8½ In., Pair
$968

Fontaine's Auction Gallery

Candlestick, Bronze, Seahorse, Green Patina, Signed, E.T. Hurley, 13 x 5¼ In., Pair
$1,820

Treadway

Candlestick, Chamber, Silver, Candlecup, Basket Weave, Paul Storr, London, George III, 1815, 7 In.
$2,813

Hindman

Candlestick, Copper, Hammered, Brown Patina, G. Stickley, c.1905, 9¼ x 7 In.
$492

California Historical Design

Candlestick, Cut Glass, Photophore, Diamond Diaper, Removable Shade, Holder, 13¾ In., Pair
$100

Neal Auction Company

Candlestick, Earthenware, Figural, Woman, Standing, Orange Glaze, Germany, c.1930, 10 x 4 In.
$32

Wright

Candlestick, Giltwood, Grapevines, Repousse, Circular Base, Continental, 1900s, 39¾ In., Pair
$644

Hindman

Candlestick, Giltwood, Wall, Pricket, Carved, Cherub, Scroll Design, 1800s, 18 In., Pair
$768

Neal Auction Company

Candlestick, Metal, Dragon, Seated, Wings, Leafy Bobeches, Black, Early 1900s, 6½ x 6 In., Pair
$156

Eldred's

Candlestick, Pewter, Globe Shape Chimney, Marked, Sherwoods, Birmingham, Victorian, 14 In., Pair
$63

Turner Auctions + Appraisals

Candlestick, Silver Plate, Anthropomorphic Monkey, Metal, Figural, Candlecup On Tray, 6 x 5 x 6 In., Pair
$644

Thomaston Place Auction Galleries

Candlestick, Silver, Hexagonal, Flared Rim, Circular Drip Pan, Conical Base, Heemskirk, 1700s, 4 x 5 In.
$1,125

Hindman

Bronze, Round Stepped Base, Signed, Art Crafts Shop, Buffalo, N.Y., c.1905, 6¾ x 4 In., Pair	584
Bronze, Seahorse, Green Patina, Signed, E.T. Hurley, 13 x 5¼ In., Pair...................*illus*	1820
Bronze, Seahorse, Patinated, Signed, E.T Hurley, Ohio, c.1905, 7 x 4⅝ In., Pair..................	1820
Cast Iron, Drip Pan, Black Column, Tubular Steel, Embossed Label, 1950s, 41 In................	30
Chamber, Brass, Handle, Plain Base, England, 3 x 8 x 7 In.	61
Chamber, Silver, Candlecup, Basket Weave, Paul Storr, London, George III, 1815, 7 In. ......*illus*	2813
Chamber, Silver, George III, Crested, Bobeche, Conical Snuffer, John Robins, 3 In., Pair.....	384
Chamber, Silver, Urn Shape Candlecup, Removable Bobeche, Henry Chawner, London, 1791, 6¼ In.	320
Copper, Hammered, Brown Patina, G. Stickley, c.1905, 9¼ x 7 In. ....*illus*	492
Cut Glass, Photophore, Diamond Diaper, Removable Shade, Holder, 13¾ In., Pair......*illus*	100
Earthenware, Figural, Woman, Standing, Orange Glaze, Germany, c.1930, 10 x 4 In......*illus*	32
Gilt Bronze, Flared Rim, Column Stem, Dome Base, Louis XVI Style, Late 1800s, 10 In., Pair.....	688
Gilt Bronze, Lamp, Reverse Fluted, Faux Bamboo Shape, 22 x 7 In., Pair......................	256
Gilt, Trophy Shape, Flared Rim, Beaded, Domed Base, 1850, 10 In., Pair	688
Giltwood, Grapevines, Repousse, Circular Base, Continental, 1900s, 39¾ In., Pair.....*illus*	644
Giltwood, Wall, Pricket, Carved, Cherub, Scroll Design, 1800s, 18 In., Pair ....*illus*	768
Glass, Etched, Leaves, Knopped Stem, Footed, Hurricane, c.1870, 22 x 7½ In., Pair	625
Glass, Pink, Gold Etching, Stepped Base, c.1920s, 6 x 4⅜ In., Pair.............................	31
Glass, Verre De Soie Style, White, Frederick Carder, c.1920, 15 In., Pair	1020
Marble, Napoleon III, Man Holding Cage, Woman Holding Bird, 10¾ In., Pair....................	2688
Metal, Dragon, Seated, Wings, Leafy Bobeches, Black, Early 1900s, 6½ x 6 In., Pair....*illus*	156
Metal, Gilt, Mounted, Rootwood, Serpent Shape, India, Post 1950, 9 x 4½ x 3¾ In., Pair ...	750
Ormolu, Louis XVI, Neoclassical, Gilt Bronze, Domed Base, France, 1800s, 10¼ x 5 In., Pair......	726
Pewter, Globe Shape Chimney, Marked, Sherwoods, Birmingham, Victorian, 14 In., Pair... *illus*	63
Porcelain, Figural, Flower Sprigs, White Ground, 4 Scrolled Feet, 13 x 6 x 6 In.	270
Pressed Glass, Hurricane Shade, Dolphin Stem, Square Base, 17½ x 4½ In., Pair.............	63
Pressed Glass, White Enamel, Gilt, Urn Shape Socket, Bobeche, Prisms, c.1880, 14 In., Pair.......	359
Pricket, Knopped Column, Flared Base, 3 Scrolled Feet, 1800s, 29 x 8 In., Pair	688
Pricket, Pine, Baroque Style, Carved Leaves, Turned Columns, Footed, 1900s, 35 In., Pair..	156
Pricket, Stand, Giltwood, 3-Footed Base, 1700s, 34½ In., Pair	431
Silver & Bone, Square Base, Redlich & Company, New York, 1800s, 9 In., Pair....................	1020
Silver Plate, Anthropomorphic Monkey, Metal, Figural, Candlecup On Tray, 6 x 5 x 6 In., Pair...*illus*	644
Silver Plate, Column Stem, Stepped Base, Ellis Barker Co., Birmingham, Early 1900s, 12 In., 4 Piece	281
Silver Plate, Plate, Ornate Grapevine Decoration, Signed, W.N. Galw, 1800s, 12 In., Pair....	71
Silver Plate, Urn Shape Candlecup, Fluted Shaft, Stepped Base, Neoclassical Style, 8 In., 4 Piece.	704
Silver, Baroque, Ornate Repousse, Fruit, Leaves, Weighted Base, Germany, 14 x 5 In., Pair.	439
Silver, Bobeches, Square Base, Carved Flowers, Hallmark, John Cafe, 1761, 10 In., Pair.......	1830
Silver, Circular Base, Marked, Stieff, 5 x 4 In., Pair...	549
Silver, Circular, Half Round Base, Leaf Feet, Marked, W. Doran, 6 In.	126
Silver, Cone Shape, Spiral Stem, Ball Feet, Rectangular Base, Mexico, c.1950, 5⅞ In., Pair	375
Silver, Copper, Hammered, Derby International, c.1910, 12 x 5½ In.	123
Silver, Corinthian Column, Weighted, Hawksworth, Eyre & Co., Sheffield, 1888, 11 x 4 In., Pair ...	819
Silver, Drip Pan, Repousse, Flowers, Openwork, Wood Base, 1800s, 9¼ In., Pair	875
Silver, Etched, Tapered Stem, Square Base, Victor Seidman, 10 In., Pair........................	266
Silver, Flower Shape Top, Domed Base, Howard & Co., Late 1800s, 10¾ In., Pair..............	1331
Silver, Flowers, Scrolls, Monogram, Cartouche, Gorham, Weighted, 1898, 9¾ x 5 In., Pair.	344
Silver, George IV, Knopped Stem, Mark Obscured, Sheffield, 1821, 10¾ In., Pair	1750
Silver, George IV, Removable Bobeches, Weighted Base, Creswick & Co., 9 x 5 In., 3 Piece....	761
Silver, Hexagonal, Flared Rim, Circular Drip Pan, Conical Base, Heemskirk, 1700s, 4 x 5 In.. *illus*	1125
Silver, Knopped Stem, Weighted, Black, Starr & Frost, N.Y., Early 1900s, 10½ In., Pair........	125
Silver, Octagonal, Flared Rim, Urn Shape, Domed Base, Crichton Bros., 7½ In., Pair	313
Silver, Petal Shape Sockets, Ribbed Baluster Stems, Austro-Hungary, 11 In., Pair..............	300
Silver, Repousse, Flower Shape, Square Base, Weighted, 10 x 3½ In., Pair	767
Silver, Rose Point, Flowers, Trumpet Base, Wallace, 10¼ x 4 In., Pair............................	406
Silver, Scroll, Flowers, Shells, Weighted Base, Sheffield, 1821, 11 In., Pair......................	1536
Silver, Trophy Shape Candlecups, Weighted, Cartier, Early 1900s, 12¾ In., 4 Piece.............	4063
Silver, Urn Shape Holder, Round Base, 3 In., Pair...*illus*	120
Silver, Urn Shape, John Winter & Co., Sheffield, George III, 1777, 11½ x 4⅞ In., Pair	1638

| Silver, Wedgwood Pattern, Weighted, International Silver Co., Meriden, 1910s, 10 In., Pair. | 281 |
| Wood, Pricket, Carved, 3 Putti Heads, Tripod Feet, Continental, 1800s, 22 x 7 In., Pair........ | 375 |

CANDLEWICK GLASS *items may be listed in the Imperial Glass and Pressed Glass categories.*

CANDY CONTAINER

Candy containers have been popular since the late Victorian era. Collectors have long favored the glass containers, but now all types, including tin and papier-mache, are collected. Probably the earliest glass container sold commercially was the Liberty Bell made in 1876 for sale at the Centennial Exposition. Thousands of designs were made until the cost became too high in the 1960s. By the late 1970s, reproductions were being made and sold without the candy. Containers listed here are glass unless otherwise described. A Belsnickle is a nineteenth-century figure of Father Christmas. Some candy containers may be listed in Toy or in other categories.

Airplane, Liberty Motor, Clear, Stamped, Tin Wings, Propeller, American Flag, c.1920, 3 x 5 In...*illus*	508
Firecracker, Red & White, Dressed Up, Glasses, Lighting Fuse Top, Paper & Composition, 7½ In.	210
Halloween, Goblin Head, Glass, Bell Shape, Orange & Green Paint, Hanging Loop, 1910s, 4 x 3 In.....	598
Halloween, Witch, Black Hat, Apron, Broom, Plaster, Bottom Detaches, Germany, 11 x 4 In. *illus*	6600
Halloween, Witch, Holding Broom, Plaster Head, Arms & Legs, Germany, Early 1900s, 12 In. .	6600
Santa Claus, Composition, Rabbit Fur Beard, Feather Tree, Cardboard Tube, Germany, 7 In.	1300
Santa Claus, Feather Tree Branch, Red Coat, Composition, Fur Beard, c.1910, 8 In.	1415
Santa Claus, Log Sleigh, Papier-Mache, Early 1900s, 10 x 17¼ In..............................*illus*	6250
Santa Claus, Next To Chimney, Glass, Clear, Interior Canister, Slit Lid, 1910s, 4 x 3⅝ In. ..	2271
Santa Claus, Red Robe, Hood, Feather, Tree Branch, Rope Belt, 8 In...........................*illus*	1416
Tree Trunk, Narrow, Curvy, Brown, England, 1800s, 23 x 9 In.................................	375
Turkey, Papier-Mache, Paint, Metal Feet, Head Removes, Germany, 5 x 3 In........................	200
Vegetable Man, Holding Vegetable, Carrot Arms, Apple Buttons, Wood Base, 1920s, 11 x 7 In....*illus*	31200
Vegetable Man, Jack-O'-Lantern, Candleholder, Yellow, Green Arms & Legs, 1920s, 8 x 5½ In....*illus*	2706

CANE

Canes and walking sticks were used by every well-dressed man in the nineteenth century, but by World War I the style had changed. Today canes are used by few but the infirm. Collectors prize old canes and walking sticks made with special features, like hidden swords, whiskey flasks, or risqué pictures seen through peepholes. Examples with solid gold heads or made from exotic materials are among the higher-priced canes. See also Scrimshaw.

Bone Handle, Carved, Monkeys, Brass, Mounted, Rectangular, Plinth Base, Japan, 4½ In.	281
Presentation, Bone Handle, Walnut Shaft, Carved, Dr. C.C Williams, Philadelphia, 1800s, 36 In.*illus*	750
Silver Handle, Dog's Head, Elongated Mouth, Collar, 1900s, 5 In..	219
Walking Stick, 14K Gold Handle, Black Shaft, Gilt Tip, 1800s, 36 In...................................	625
Walking Stick, American, Carved, Birds, Lizard, Spiraling Snakes, Late 1800s, 36 In.	167
Walking Stick, Baleen, Coiled Grip, 28 Brass Rivets, 4 Woven Rings, c.1840, 33 In.	1342
Walking Stick, Bird Shape, Bone Handle, Wood Shaft, Gilt Tip, 37½ In.......................	219
Walking Stick, Blackwood, Carved, Bone Top, Hidden Compass, Silver, Guilloche Cover, 36 In...*illus*	556
Walking Stick, Carved Lion, Ivory, Open Mouth, Oak Shaft, Brass Ferrule Tip, Handle, 1800s, 34 In.	625
Walking Stick, Carved, Nude Woman On Top, 4 Faces, Shaft, Africa, 34½ In.	40
Walking Stick, Carved, Spread Winged Eagle, Military Medal, Late 1800s, 34 In.	491
Walking Stick, Crocodile, Wood & Ivory, Hidden Dagger, Folk Art, Late 1800s, 36 In..........	878
Walking Stick, Erotic, Phallus Handle, Folk Art Style, Silver Tip, c.1900, 40 In.....................	210
Walking Stick, Gambler's, Dice, Segmented, Maple Shaft, Circular, Container, Early 1900s, 34 In.	502
Walking Stick, Gold Handle, Tip, Ring, Black, Ebonized, Samuel Colt, 1861, 36¾ In.........	10200
Walking Stick, Horn Handle, Burrwood, Silver Mounted, Early 1900s, 34¼ In...................	438
Walking Stick, Native, Head Knob Handle, Silver Ferrule, 1900s, 34 In.	66
Walking Stick, Painted, Multicolor, Figure On Crook, Signed, Sam The Dot Man McMillan, 37 In.....	220
Walking Stick, Polar Bear Handle, Carved Walrus Ivory, Inset Wood Eyes, 1800s, 36¼ In.	531

Candlestick, Silver, Urn Shape Holder, Round Base, 3 In., Pair
$120

Chupp Auctions & Real Estate, LLC

Candy Container, Airplane, Liberty Motor, Clear, Stamped, Tin Wings, Propeller, American Flag, c.1920, 3 x 5 In.
$508

Jeffrey S. Evans & Associates

Candy Container, Halloween, Witch, Black Hat, Apron, Broom, Plaster, Bottom Detaches, Germany, 11 x 4 In.
$6,600

Morphy Auctions

This is an edited listing of current prices. Visit **Kovels.com** to check thousands of prices from previous years and sign up for free information on trends, tips, reproductions, marks, and more.

Candy Container, Santa Claus, Log Sleigh, Papier-Mache, Early 1900s, 10 x 17 ¼ In.
$6,250

Hindman

Candy Container, Santa Claus, Red Robe, Hood, Feather, Tree Branch, Rope Belt, 8 In.
$1,416

Stony Ridge Auction

Candy Container, Vegetable Man, Holding Vegetable, Carrot Arms, Apple Buttons, Wood Base, 1920s, 11 x 7 In.
$31,200

Morphy Auctions

Candy Container, Vegetable Man, Jack-O'-Lantern, Candleholder, Yellow, Green Arms & Legs, 1920s, 8 x 5 ½ In.
$2,706

Morphy Auctions

Cane, Presentation, Bone Handle, Walnut Shaft, Carved, Dr. C.C Williams, Philadelphia, 1800s, 36 In.
$750

Potter & Potter Auctions

Cane, Walking Stick, Blackwood, Carved, Bone Top, Hidden Compass, Silver, Guilloche Cover, 36 In.
$556

Thomaston Place Auction Galleries

Cane, Walking Stick, Watch, Hinged Bezel, Malacca Type Shaft, A. Duncan, London, 1795, 35 In.
$708

Soulis Auctions

TIP
Brass collars on old canes are usually nickel-plated.

Canton, Bowl, Curry, Oval, Quatrefoil, c.1840, 2 x 12 x 9 In.
$610

Rafael Osona Nantucket Auctions

Canton, Pitcher, Cider, Foo Dog Finial, River Scene, Twisted Handle, c.1820, 10 x 9 x 6 In.
$1,342

Rafael Osona Nantucket Auctions

Walking Stick, Union Veteran's, Mother-Of-Pearl Inlay, Corps Insignia, Wood, 31⅝ In......	469
Walking Stick, Watch, Hinged Bezel, Malacca Type Shaft, A. Duncan, London, 1795, 35 In... *illus*	708
Walking Stick, Wood, Carved, Flowers & Leaves Design, c.1900, 34 In..................................	1046
Walking Stick, Wood, Snake, Clenched Fist, 36 In.	207
Whalebone, Tooth Handle, Octagonal Shaft, Port Scenes, Pacific, Indian Oceans, 38½ In........	188
Wood, Figure, Female, Pleated Skirt, Carved, Metal Ferrule, 36½ In..............................	281

CANTON CHINA

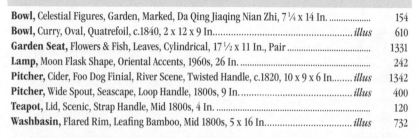

Canton china is blue-and-white ware made near the city of Canton, in China, from about 1795 to the early 1900s. It is hand decorated with a landscape, pagoda, bridge, boats, trees, and a special border. There is never a person on the bridge. The "rain and cloud" border was used. It is similar to Nanking ware, which is listed in this book in its own category.

Bowl, Celestial Figures, Garden, Marked, Da Qing Jiaqing Nian Zhi, 7¼ x 14 In.	154
Bowl, Curry, Oval, Quatrefoil, c.1840, 2 x 12 x 9 In......................................*illus*	610
Garden Seat, Flowers & Fish, Leaves, Cylindrical, 17½ x 11 In., Pair	1331
Lamp, Moon Flask Shape, Oriental Accents, 1960s, 26 In.	242
Pitcher, Cider, Foo Dog Finial, River Scene, Twisted Handle, c.1820, 10 x 9 x 6 In........*illus*	1342
Pitcher, Wide Spout, Seascape, Loop Handle, 1800s, 9 In..*illus*	400
Teapot, Lid, Scenic, Strap Handle, Mid 1800s, 4 In.	120
Washbasin, Flared Rim, Leafing Bamboo, Mid 1800s, 5 x 16 In................................*illus*	732

CAPO-DI-MONTE

Capo-di-Monte porcelain was first made in Naples, Italy, from 1743 to 1759. The factory was started by Charles VII, King of Naples, who lived in the Palace of Capodimonte. He became King Charles III of Spain in 1759 and the factory moved near Madrid, Spain. Charles' son, Ferdinand, reopened the factory in Italy in 1771 and it operated until 1821. The Ginori factory of Doccia, Italy, acquired the molds and began using the crown and *N* mark. In 1896 the Doccia factory combined with Societa Ceramica Richard of Milan. It eventually became the modern-day firm known as Richard Ginori, often referred to as Ginori or Capo-di-Monte. This company also used the crown and *N* mark. Richard Ginori was purchased by Gucci in 2013. The Capo-di-Monte mark is still being used. "Capodimonte-style" porcelain is being made today by several manufacturers in Italy, sometimes with a factory name or mark. The Capo-di-Monte mark and name are also used on cheaper porcelain made in the style of Capo-di-Monte.

Candlestick, Centerpiece, 8 Apples, Leaves, Circular, 3 x 9½ In., Pair..................................	63
Centerpiece, Multicolor, Flowers, Mounted, Brown, Domed Base, Italy, 1900s, 8 x 15 In...........	344
Cigarette Box, Lid, Glazed, Blue, Gio Ponti, Richard Ginori, Italy, c.1930, 4 x 3 x 3 In.........	813
Coffer, Multicolor, Gilt, Classical Figures, Ornate Lock, Key, 1800s, 13 x 14 x 8 In........*illus*	896
Figurine, Woman, Snakeskin & Gilt Dress, White Hat, Marble Base, Edoardo Tasca, Italy, 18 In..*illus*	2750
Figurine, Woman, Holding Flowers, Flower Basket At Feet, Wood Base, B. Merli, 1900s, 10 In.	163
Figurine, Woman, Seated In Chair, Lacy Dress, Feathered Fan, Chair, Giuseppe Cappe, 1900s, 8 In.	189
Figurine, Woman, Standing, Peach Dress, Flower Design, 1900s, 9½ In. ....*illus*	125
Group, Children Playing, 4 Kids, Toddler, Tree Trunk, Bruno Merli, 1800s, 8½ In.	375
Group, Elderly Couple, Seated, Cat, Glazed, Marked, 1900s, 11½ In.................................	121
Ornament, Shell, Corals, Shaped Base, Blanc De Chine, Ginori, 1900s, 7 In.	125
Teapot, Glazed, Loop Handle, Red, Black, Gio Ponti, Richard Ginori, Italy, c. 1930, 5 x 8 x 4 In...	1375
Urn, 2-Light, Multicolor, Gilt, Mounted As Lamp, 1900s, 27 In., Pair.............................	125
Urn, Dome Lid, Face Handles, Multicolor Flowers, Gilt, Shaped Base, 1800s, 17 In...............	125
Urn, Pedestal, Cobalt Blue Ground, Classic Design, Figural Mythological Handles, Marked, 13 x 7 In.	150
Vase, Glazed, Gilt, Bulbous, Giovanni Gariboldi, Richard Ginori, Italy, c. 1937, 7 x 6 In.	2000

Canton, Pitcher, Wide Spout, Seascape, Loop Handle, 1800s, 9 In.
$400

Pook & Pook

Canton, Washbasin, Flared Rim, Leafing Bamboo, Mid 1800s, 5 x 16 In.
$732

Rafael Osona Nantucket Auctions

TIP
August is the peak month for residential burglaries. April has the fewest home break-ins. Most home burglaries occur in the daytime and the average break-in lasts 17 minutes.

Capo-Di-Monte, Coffer, Multicolor, Gilt, Classical Figures, Ornate Lock, Key, 1800s, 13 x 14 x 8 In.
$896

Neal Auction Company

CAPTAIN MARVEL

Capo-Di-Monte, Figurine, Woman, Snakeskin & Gilt Dress, White Hat, Marble Base, Edoardo Tasca, Italy, 18 In.
$2,750

Lion and Unicorn

CAPTAIN MARVEL

Captain Marvel was introduced in February 1940 in Whiz comic books. An orphan named Billy Batson met the wizard, Shazam, and whenever he said the magic word he was transformed into a superhero. A movie serial was released in 1940. The comic was discontinued in 1954. A second Captain Marvel appeared in 1966, a third in 1967. Only the original was transformed by shouting "Shazam."

Comic Book, Shazam No. 1, DC Comics, February 1973	178
Pin, Captain Marvel Club, Shazam, Red, White, Blue, Pinback, 1940s, ⅞ In.	26
Toy, Car, Shazam, Yellow, Lighting, Driver, Die Cast Metal, On Card, Corgi, 1979, 8 Piece	119
Toy, Figure, Jointed, Comic Action Heroes, On Card, Mego, 1970s, 3¾ In.	235
Toy, Figure, Shazam, Mego, 1973	143
Toy, Figure, Shazam, Poseable, World's Greatest Super-Heroes, Box, Mego, 1970s, 8 In.	207 to 520

CAPTAIN MIDNIGHT

Captain Midnight began as a network radio show in September 1940. The first comic book appeared in July 1941. Captain Midnight was really the aviator Captain Albright, who was to defeat the Nazis. A movie serial was made in 1942 and a comic strip was published for a short time. The comic book version of Captain Midnight ended his career in 1948. Radio premiums are the prized collector memorabilia today.

Badge, Photomatic, Code-O-Graph, Pinback, 1942, 2 x 2¾ In.	149
Mug, Handle, Plastic, Red, Decal, Hot Ovaltine, Heart Of A Healthy Breakfast, Radio Premium	6

CARAMEL SLAG, *see Imperial Glass category.*

T I P
Don't use rubber gloves when washing figurines with protruding arms and legs. The gloves may snag and cause damage.

Capo-Di-Monte, Figurine, Woman, Standing, Peach Dress, Flower Design, 1900s, 9½ In.
$125

Lion and Unicorn

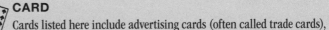

CARD

Cards listed here include advertising cards (often called trade cards), baseball cards, playing cards, and others. Color photographs were rare in the nineteenth century, so companies gave away colorful cards with pictures of children, flowers, products, or related scenes that promoted the company name. These were often collected and stored in albums. Baseball cards also date from the nineteenth century, when they were used by tobacco companies as giveaways. Gum cards were started in 1933, but it was not until after World War II that the bubble gum cards favored today were produced. Today over 1,000 cards are issued each year by the gum companies. Related items may be found in the Christmas, Halloween, Movie, Paper, and Postcard categories.

Baseball, Babe Ruth, World Wide Gum, No. 80, 1933	*illus*	11520
Baseball, Don Mattingly, O-Pee-Chee, No. 8, 1984		1328
Baseball, Ed Walsh, Cabinet, Turkey Red Cigarettes, 1911		406
Baseball, Jackie Robinson, Third Base, Brooklyn Dodgers, Topps, No. 30, 1956	*illus*	4500
Baseball, Lou Gehrig, Goudey, Big League Chewing Gum, No. 92, 1933, 5 x 3 In.		3780
Baseball, Mickey Mantle, Outfield, New York Yankees, Topps, No. 135, 1956		4200
Baseball, Mickey Mantle, Swing Follow-Through, Outfield, N.Y. Yankees, Topps, No. 95, 1957		1624
Baseball, Roberto Clemente, Outfield, Pittsburgh Pirates, Topps, No. 33, 1956		1800
Baseball, Sandy Koufax, Pitcher, Brooklyn Dodgers, Topps, No. 123, 1955		8400
Baseball, Ted Williams, Outfield, Boston Red Sox, Topps, No. 5, 1956		2040
Basketball, Michael Jordan, Bulls, Guard, Rookie, Fleer, No. 57, 1986		2125 to 4600
Basketball, Michael Jordan, Dunking, Rookie, Air Jordan, Nike Promo, 1985		3168
Basketball, Pete Maravich, Ball, Forward, Atlanta, Topps, No. 123, 1970-71		555
Boxing, Mike Tyson, Topps, Allen & Ginter's, Topps, No. 301, 2006		313
Football, Bob Waterfield, Quarterback, LA Rams, Bowman, No. 40, 1951		84
Football, Joe Namath, Quarterback, Topps, No. 98, 1967		2448

Football, OJ Simpson, Bills, Running Back, Rookie, Topps, No. 90, 1970	173
Football, Otto Graham, Quarterback, Cleveland Browns, Bowman, No. 2, 1951	72
Football, Paul Brown, Coach, Cleveland Browns, Bowman, No. 14, 1952	72
Football, R. Yale Lary, Running Back, Rookie, Detroit Lions, Bowman, No. 140, 1952	54
Football, Tom Landry, Quarterback, New York Giants, Bowman, No. 20, 1951	300
Golf, Jack Nicklaus, Goldflake, Famous Sportsmen, No. 6, Barratt & Co. Ltd., 1971	1624
Greeting, Valentine, Red Flower, Gold Border, To One I Love, Shadowbox, Victorian, 20 x 14 In.	13
Soccer, Pele, Brazil, International Footballers, Rookie Year, Green Back, Monty Gum, 1958	2875

CARDER, see Steuben category.

CARLSBAD

Carlsbad is a mark found on china made by several factories in Germany, Austria, and Bavaria. Many pieces were exported to the United States. Most of the pieces available today were made after 1891.

Vase, Flowers, Circular, Cylindrical Neck, Flared Rim, Footed, Victorian, 1900s, 15 In., Pair	138

CARLTON WARE

Carlton ware was made at the Carlton Works of Stoke-on-Trent, England, beginning about 1890. The firm traded as Wiltshaw & Robinson until 1957. It was renamed Carlton Ware Ltd. in 1958. The company was bought and sold several times. Production stopped in 1992. Frank Salmon bought the trademark, molds, and pattern books in 1997. Production was outsourced to other potteries. Carlton Ware production ceased by 2016.

Plate, Mephistopheles, Red Devil Pattern, Freehand Painted, Marie Graves, 1900s, 12½ In...illus	625

CARNIVAL GLASS

Carnival glass was an inexpensive, iridescent pressed glass made from about 1907 to about 1925. More than 1,000 different patterns are known. Carnival glass is currently being reproduced. Here are three marks used by companies that have made 20th-century carnival glass.

Cambridge Glass Co.
1901–1954, 1955–1958

Imperial
1910–1924

Northwood Glass Co.
1910–1918

Basket, Rose, Clear, Aqua Feet, Handle, Raised Flower, 9 In.	55
Blackberry, Bowl, Open Edge, Basketweave, Ruffled Edge, Scalloped, Green, 3 x 5½ In.	32
Butterfly & Berry, Berry Set, Ruffled Edge, 3-Footed, Cobalt Blue, Master 9½ In., 7 Piece	142
Cherries, Bowl, Ice Cream, Marigold, 7 In., 4 Piece	18
Cherries, Sauce Bowl, Ruffled Edge, Marigold, Signed, Robert Hansen, 4½ In.	40
Coin Dot, Cake Stand, Solid Green, 7 x 10 In.	70
Crackle, Vase, Epergne, Marigold, Metal Holder, Leafy, 9½ In.	48
Good Luck, Plate, Stippled, Ribbed Back, Flowers, Leaves, Blue, 9 In.	130
Grape & Cable, Bowl, Fruit, Persian Medallion Interior, Amethyst, Fenton, 5 x 10 In...illus	60
Grape & Cable, Plate, Stippled, Ribbed Back, Black, Purple, 9 In.	225
Grape & Cable, Plate, Variation, Old Rose Distilling Co., Serrated Edge, Green, 9 In.	225
Holly, Compote, Ruffled Edge, Blue, 4 In.	54
Iris, Water Set, Pitcher, Squat Base, Ruffled Edge, Tumblers, 5 Piece	130
Mary Ann, Vase, 2 Scrolled Handles, Footed, Scalloped, Marigold, 6¼ In.	60
Mary Ann, Vase, Marigold, Flowers, Scalloped Base, 6 In.	50
Nippon, Bowl, Ruffled Edge, Ice Blue, 8¼ In.	60

Card, Baseball, Babe Ruth, World Wide Gum, No. 80, 1933
$11,520

Goldin Auctions

Card, Baseball, Jackie Robinson, Third Base, Brooklyn Dodgers, Topps, No. 30, 1956
$4,500

Alderfer Auction Company

Carlton Ware, Plate, Mephistopheles, Red Devil Pattern, Freehand Painted, Marie Graves, 1900s, 12½ In.
$625

Lion and Unicorn

TIP
Never leave the key under the doormat.

Carnival Glass, Grape & Cable, Bowl, Fruit, Persian Medallion Interior, Amethyst, Fenton, 5 x 10 In.
$60

Woody Auction

Carriage, Sleigh, Push, Red, Black & Gold Trim, Side Handles, Victorian, Child's, 31 x 17 x 52 In.
$128

Rachel Davis Fine Arts

Cash Register, Morford Register Co., Wood, Brass Back Fence, Hinged Lid, Square, 15 x 20 x 20 In.
$113

Hartzell's Auction Gallery Inc.

Cash Register, National, Model 39, Porcelain, Glass Key Checks, Top Sign, Metal Base, 1902, 22 x 17 x 16 In.
$480

Morphy Auctions

Orange Tree, Loving Cup, Flowers, Green, 5 ¾ In.	60
Peacock & Grape, Bowl, Amberina, Ruffled Edge, Tripod Feet, Fenton, c.1915, 8 In.	180
Peacock & Urn, Bowl, Scalloped Edge, Flared Rim, Amethyst, 9 ½ In.	89
Peacock, Plate, Ribbed Back, Flowers, Leaves, Marigold, 9 In.	80
Peacocks On The Fence, Plate, Ribbed Exterior, Ruffled Edge, Blue, Northwood, 9 In.	175
Ripple, Vase, Ruffled Edge, Blue, 14 In.	77
Singing Birds, Tumbler, Blue, 4 In., Pair	12
Strawberry, Bowl, Ruffled, Serrated Edge, Basketweave Exterior, Green, 9 ½ In.	42
Three Fruits, Bonbon, Basketweave, 2 Handles, Pedestal Foot, Amethyst, 4 x 7 ¾ In.	30
Three Fruits, Plate, Stippled, Ribbed Back, Leaves, Sapphire, 9 In.	375

CAROUSEL

Carousel or merry-go-round figures were first carved in the United States in 1867 by Gustav Dentzel. Collectors discovered the charm of the hand-carved figures in the 1970s, and they were soon classed as folk art. Most desirable are the figures other than horses, such as pigs, camels, lions, or dogs. A stander has all four feet on the carousel platform; a prancer has both front feet in the air and both back feet on the platform; a jumper has all four feet in the air and usually moves up and down. Both old and new animals are collected.

Bear, Stander, Wood, Carved Details, Saddle, Multicolor, 1900s, 26 ¾ x 51 In.	2160
Giraffe, Stander, Multicolor, Wood, Brass Pole, Gustav Dentzel Style, 1900s, 68 ½ x 55 In.	2178
Horse, Jumper, American Flag, Carved, Tucked Head, Jeweled, C.W. Parker Co., 61 x 60 x 11 In.	590
Horse, Jumper, Inner Row, Carved, Painted, Jeweled, Saddle, C.W. Parker Co., c.1920, 61 x 43 x 12 In.	384
Horse, Jumper, Outer Row, Indian Pony, Carved, Star Gazer, Head Up, Parker Co., 60 x 62 x 11 In.	472
Horse, Jumper, Painted, Stirrup Holders, Black Saddle, Parker, 45 x 48 x 13 In.	615
Horse, Jumper, Rectangular Base, Wood, Herschell-Spillman, 48 x 44 In.	978
Horse, Miniature, Cast Metal, Painted, Pastel Colors, Stand, 33 x 31 In.	125
Horse, Prancer, Wood, Carved, Painted, Contemporary, 49 ½ x 45 ½ In.	517
Ostrich, Stander, Hinged Neck, 2-Seater, Brass Pole, Frederick Savage, c.1900, 70 x 16 x 65 In.	1180
Panel, Boat, Ocean Scene, Flowers, Herschell-Spillman, c.1915, 58 x 38 x 1 ½ In.	250
Rooster, Stander, Wood, Carved, Saddle, Half Round, Painted, 45 ½ x 43 In.	706

CARRIAGE

Carriage means several things, so this category lists baby carriages, buggies for adults, horse-drawn sleighs, and even strollers. Doll-sized carriages are listed in the Toy category.

Pull Cart, Wood, White Paint, 4 Wheels, Child's, 1800s, 28 x 47 x 31 In.	363
Sleigh, Painted, Brown & Black, Green Upholstery, Wood Handle, Iron Base, 33 x 43 In.	340
Sleigh, Push, Red, Black & Gold Trim, Side Handles, Victorian, Child's, 31 x 17 x 52 In. *illus*	128
Wagon, Goat, Wood, Bench Seat, Bell, Brown Paint, 2 Wheels, 52 x 22 In.	173

CASH REGISTER

Cash registers were invented in 1883 because an eye on the cash was a necessity in stores of the nineteenth century, too. John and James Ritty invented a large model that resembled a clock and kept a record of the dollars and cents exchanged in the store. John Patterson improved the cash register with a paper roll to record the money. By the early 1900s, elaborate brass registers were made. More modern types were made after 1920. Cash registers made by National Cash Register Company are the most popular with collectors.

Morford Register Co., Wood, Brass Back Fence, Hinged Lid, Square, 15 x 20 x 20 In. *illus*	113
National, Model 3, Embossed, Gilt, 1892, 18 x 16 In.	219
National, Model 39, Porcelain, Glass Key Checks, Top Sign, Metal Base, 1902, 22 x 17 x 16 In. *illus*	480
National, Model 312, Candy Store, 15-Key, Embossed Flowers, Gilt, 21 x 11 x 17 In.	857

National, Model 313, Brass, White Marble, 14-Key, Wood Base, 17 x 10 x 16 In......................	708
National, Model 317, Brass, Patina, 15-Key, 17 x 11 x 16 In..	240
National, Model 317, Bronze, Relief Patterns, Wood Base, Early 1900s, 17 x 10 x 16 In........	363
National, Model 442X, Brass, Plaque To Front & Base, 1911, 24 x 21 x 16 In......................	300
National, Model 532, Mounted, Cabinet, 3 Drawers, 1914, 35 x 28 x 21 In..........................	406
National, Peck's, Brass Marquee Stamped, Mild Color, Syracuse, N.Y., c.1900, 14 x 20 In.	227

CASTOR JAR

Castor jars for pickles are glass jars about six inches in height, held in special metal holders. They became a popular dinner table accessory about 1890. Each jar had a top that was usually silver or silver plate. The frame, also of a silver metal, had a handle that arched above the jar and a hook that held a pair of tongs. The glass jar was often painted. By 1900, the pickle castor was out of fashion. Many examples found today have reproduced glass jars in old holders. Additional pickle castors may be found in the various Glass categories.

Pickle, Cranberry, Stenciled, Flowers, Gilt, Silver Plate Frame & Lid, 9 x 4 In.............. *illus*	80
Pickle, Dome Lid, Cut Glass, Floral, Silver Plate, Pierced Frame, Hook, 13 ½ In....................	60
Pickle, Double, Clear Block Pattern Glass, Silver Plate Frame, 10 x 6 In................................	50

CASTOR SET

Castor sets holding just salt and pepper castors were used in the seventeenth century. The sugar castor, mustard pot, spice dredger (shaker), bottles for vinegar and oil, and other spice holders became popular by the eighteenth century. These sets were usually made of sterling silver with glass bottles. The American Victorian castor set, the type most collected today, was made of silver plated Britannia metal. Colored glass bottles were introduced after the Civil War. The sets were out of fashion by World War I. Be careful when buying sets with colored bottles; many are reproductions. Other castor sets may be listed in various porcelain and glass categories in this book.

5 Bottles, Blue Opaque, Swirl, Mt. Washington, Silver Plate Frame, Simpson Hall Miller, 13 In...	38
5 Bottles, Cranberry Glass, Brass Plate Frame, Scrolls, Pedestal Base, Victorian, 15 x 8 In.	88
6 Bottles, Cut Glass, Silver Plate Frame, 4 Ball Feet, Sheffield, 1895, 9 ¼ In.	225
6 Bottles, Etched Glass, Silver Plate Frame, Center Vase, 3 Cherub Supports, Revolving, 18 In.....	83
6 Bottles, Etched Glass, Silver Plate Frame, Stirrup Handle, Mask, Middletown, Conn., 13 x 8 In..	63
7 Bottles, Cut Glass, Cane, Silver Plate Frame, Bead Rim, Leaf Shape Feet, England, 10 ½ In....	210

CATALOGS *are listed in the Paper category.*

CAUGHLEY

Caughley porcelain was made in England from 1772 to 1814. Caughley porcelains are very similar in appearance to those made at the Worcester factory. See the Salopian category for related items.

Eyecup, Blue & White, Fisherman, Baluster Stem, Round Foot, c.1785, 2 In........................	551
Jar, Blue & White, 4 Flower Vignettes, Marked, 4 ½ In..	50
Jug, Blue & White, 5 Landscape Vignettes, Molded, Mask Spout, 18th Century, 7 ¾ In..........	190
Jug, Blue & White, Fisherman & Cormorant, Molded, Mask Spout, 9 ½ In..............................	243
Jug, Blue & White, Parrots, Butterflies, Fruit, Flowers, Molded Spout, 1700s, 7 ½ In.............	300

CAULDON

Cauldon Limited worked in Staffordshire, Great Britain, and went through many name changes. John Ridgway made porcelain at Cauldon Place, Hanley, until 1855. The firm of John Ridgway, Bates and Co. of Cauldon

Castor Jar, Pickle, Cranberry, Stenciled, Flowers, Gilt, Silver Plate Frame & Lid, 9 x 4 In.
$80

Woody Auction

Cauldon, Pitcher, Abraham Lincoln, With Malice Toward None, Blue Transfer, c.1870, 6 x 5 In.
$600

Early American History Auctions

Cauldon, Plate, Pale Green Rim, Gilt Leaves & Birds, Marked, C.A. Seltzer, 9 In., 14 Piece
$570

Turner Auctions + Appraisals

Celadon, Bowl, Carved Interior, Phoenix, Dragon, Cloud, 2⅜ x 8 In. $1,230

Brunk Auctions

Celadon, Bowl, Phoenix, Flared Rim, Daoguang Mark, Chinese, 2¾ x 5¾ In. $9,600

Michaan's Auctions

Celadon, Dish, Tobacco Leaf Shape, Hand Painted, Flowers & Grasshopper, Late 1800s, 2 x 11 In. $192

Garth's Auctioneers & Appraisers

Celadon, Vase, Belmont, Flared Rim, Strap Handle, Crackle Glaze, Simon Pearce, 12 x 9 In. $88

Greenwich Auction

Place worked from 1856 to 1859. It became Bates, Brown-Westhead, Moore and Co. from 1859 to 1862. Brown-Westhead, Moore and Co. worked from 1862 to 1904. About 1890, this firm started using the words *Cauldon* or *Cauldon Ware* as part of the mark. Cauldon Ltd. worked from 1905 to 1920, Cauldon Potteries from 1920 to 1962. Related items may be found in the Indian Tree category.

Bullion Service, Blue Green Rim, Flowers, Gilt, 2-Handled Cup, Saucer, Crown Mark, 22 Piece.	272
Pitcher, Abraham Lincoln, With Malice Toward None, Blue Transfer, c.1870, 6 x 5 In.. *illus*	600
Plate, Pale Green Rim, Gilt Leaves & Birds, Marked, C.A. Seltzer, 9 In., 14 Piece........... *illus*	570
Tea Set, Gilt Rim, Multicolor Flower Reserves, Cup & Saucer, Luncheon Plate, 35 Piece.......	154

CELADON

Celadon is the name of a velvet-textured green-gray glaze used by Chinese, Japanese, Korean, and other factories. This section includes pieces covered with celadon glaze with or without added decoration.

Bowl, Carved Interior, Phoenix, Dragon, Cloud, 2⅜ x 8 In..*illus*	1230
Bowl, Curved Rim, Crackle Ground, 1910s, 4 x 16 In.	750
Bowl, Interior Leaves, Flowers, Exterior Medallions, Crackle Glaze, Korea, 3 x 7¾ In.	1125
Bowl, Phoenix, Flared Rim, Daoguang Mark, Chinese, 2¾ x 5¾ In............................*illus*	9600
Centerpiece, Diamond Shape, Birds, Flowers, Leaves, Base, Chinese, 1700s, 4 x 15 In.	540
Dish, Octagonal, Dore Bronze Base, Paw Feet, Nicholas Haydon, New York, 3½ x 7 In.	545
Dish, Tobacco Leaf Shape, Hand Painted, Flowers & Grasshopper, Late 1800s, 2 x 11 In. ...... *illus*	192
Jar, Crackled, Banded Rim, Bisque Foot Ring, Iron Red, Chinese, 1900s, 8 x 4⅞ In.	313
Jar, Dome Lid, Gray White Glaze, Drippy Celadon Splashes, 10 x 7 In.	576
Jar, White, Flowers, Leaf Pattern, Wood Stand, Ball Feet, 4 In..	1599
Lamp, Electric, Silk Shades, Ring Handles, Chinese, 1800s, 11 x 8 x 11 In., Pair	439
Plate, Paneled Floral, Butterflies, Gilt Rim, Famille Rose, Chinese, 8 In., 8 Piece..................	322
Vase, Belmont, Flared Rim, Strap Handle, Crackle Glaze, Simon Pearce, 12 x 9 In....... *illus*	88
Vase, Longquan, Kinuta, Pear Shape, Ring Handles, Flared Rim, Raised Bands, 10½ In. ...	480
Vase, Mold Cast, Flower, Porcelain, Cylinder, Lotus Decoration, 9½ In.	640
Vase, Mounted As Lamp, Hardwood Base, Late 1800s, 25 In., Pair...	875

CELLULOID

Celluloid is a trademark for a plastic developed in 1868 by John W. Hyatt. Celluloid Manufacturing Company, the Celluloid Novelty Company, Celluloid Fancy Goods Company, and American Xylonite Company all used celluloid to make jewelry, games, sewing equipment, false teeth, and piano keys. The name *celluloid* was often used to identify any similar plastic. Celluloid toys are listed under Toy.

Box, Collar, Hinged Lid, Molded Flowers, Leaf Borders, Silk Lined, Victorian, 5½ In.	36
Comb, Tortoiseshell, Curved, Cameo Center, Pierced Leafy Scrolls, 7 x 6½ In.	30
Dresser Box, Hinged Lid, Multicolor Necktie, 2 Bicyclists, c.1890, 13 x 4 In...........................	36
Dresser Set, Green, Marbled, Pearlized, 12½ In. Mirror, 20 Piece	18
Dresser Set, Ivory, Butterscotch Trim, 2 Round Boxes, Tray, 7 x 11 In., 3 Piece....................	12
Jewelry Box, Chinoiserie, Ivory Color, Molded Scenes, 3 Drawers, 7½ x 6½ In.	13
Mold, Doll, Production, Front Half, Hollow, Nesting, France, 1920s, 6½ In., 10 Piece...........	96
Painting, Marie Antoinette, After Elizabeth Vigee Le Brun Portrait, Brass Frame, 5 x 4 In. .	30
Painting, Winston Churchill, Acrylic, Joan Patricia Carter, Frame, 2½ x 2¼ In.	112
Photo Album, Woman's Portrait, Flowery Ground, Stand, Drawer, Mirror, Victorian, 18 x 15 In.	500
Skirt Hoop, Belle O' The Ball, Ivorene, Collapsible, Clayton Mfg. Co., Round Box, 4 x 8½ In.....	167
Tile, Musician, Stringed Instrument, Dancer, Anatolian Style, Frame, c.1950, 12 x 9 In.	71

CELS are listed in this book in the Animation Art category.

CERAMIC ART COMPANY

Ceramic Art Company of Trenton, New Jersey, was established in 1889 by Jonathan Coxon and Walter Scott. It was an early producer of American belleek porcelain. It became Lenox, Inc. in 1906. Do not confuse this ware with the pottery made by the Ceramic Arts Studio of Madison, Wisconsin.

Urn, Lion, Cherub, Leafy, White Ground, Gien, 18 x 21 In.................................*illus*	295
Vase, Cylindrical, Concentric Rings, Multicolor Glaze, Signed, 14 ¼ x 5 In.	1534
Vase, Elongated Oval Shape, Geometric Decor, Raoul Lachenal, 19 x 6 In....................*illus*	2560
Vase, Pink Roses, Green Shaded Ground, Signed, L. Bartholomew, CAC Belleek, 1800s, 12 In.	438

CERAMIC ARTS STUDIO

Ceramic Arts Studio was founded about 1940 in Madison, Wisconsin, by Lawrence Rabbitt and Ruben Sand. Their most popular products were molded figurines. The pottery closed in 1955. Do not confuse these products with those of the Ceramic Art Co. of Trenton, New Jersey.

Figurine, Balinese Dancers, Green Costume, Bent Arms, Man & Woman, 1942-55, 9 ½ In., Pair ..	77
Figurine, Cinderella's Castle, Pointed, Blue & Gold, Heather Goldminc, 14 In......................	100
Figurine, Comedy & Tragedy, Women In Black, Theatrical Masks, 1950s, 10 In., Pair.. *illus*	381

CHALKWARE

Chalkware is really plaster of Paris decorated with watercolors. One type was molded from Staffordshire and other porcelain models and painted and sold as inexpensive decorations in the nineteenth century. This type is collected today. Figures of plaster, made from about 1910 to 1940 for use as prizes at carnivals, are also known as chalkware. Kewpie dolls made of chalkware will be found in the Kewpie category.

Figurine, Deer, Lying Down, Painted, Sponge Spots, Coin Slot, Plaster Of Paris, 1800s, 9 x 6 In....	177
Figurine, Dog, White Paint, Standing, Rectangular Base, Pennsylvania, 1800s, 7 x 5 x 3 In. . *illus*	188
Figurine, Persian Cat, Sitting, Round Face, Painted, 1800s, 13 In.............................*illus*	443
Garniture, Ruffled Edge, Carved, Fruits & Leaves, Yellow & White, 14 In..............................	63
Lamp, Seated Figures, Glass Globe, Pierrot & Columbine, 1900s, 15 ¾ In..............................	72

CHARLIE CHAPLIN

Charlie Chaplin, the famous comedian, actor, and filmmaker, lived from 1889 to 1977. He made his first movie in 1913. He did the movie *The Tramp* in 1915. The character of the Tramp has remained famous, and in the 1980s appeared in a series of television commercials for computers. Dolls, candy containers, and all sorts of memorabilia with the image of Charlie's Tramp are collected. Pieces are being made even today.

Dexterity Puzzle, Glass Top, Mirrored Back, Get Hat On Charlie's Head, Germany, 2 In.	295
Doll, Papier-Mache, Composition, Hands In Pockets, 1920s, 4 ¾ In.	95
Mask, Paper Lithograph, 7 ¾ In.	45
Toy, Dancer, Celluloid Body, Wood Legs, Powered By Phonograph, Box, 8 x 4 x 3 In......*illus*	1093

CHARLIE McCARTHY

Charlie McCarthy was the ventriloquist's dummy used by Edgar Bergen from the 1930s. He was famous for his work in radio, movies, and television. The act was retired in the 1970s. Mortimer Snerd, another Bergen dummy, is also listed here.

Button, Portrait, Celluloid, Black & White, Pinback, 1930s, ¾ In....................................	75
Dummy, Ventriloquist, Black Tuxedo, Monocle, Cloth Body, Vinyl Head, 30 In....................	125
Spoon Ring, Duchess Silverplate, Size 8	30
Toy, Celluloid, Windup, Swinging Arms, Hat, Cane, Black, Japan, 7 In.	150
Toy, Drummer, Strike Up The Band, White, Blue & Red, Tin, Windup, Marx, 8 In.	450

Ceramic Art Co., Urn, Lion, Cherub, Leafy, White Ground, Gien, 18 x 21 In. $295

Copake Auction

Ceramic Art Co., Vase, Elongated Oval Shape, Geometric Decor, Raoul Lachenal, 19 x 6 In. $2,560

Nadeau's Auction Gallery

Ceramic Arts Studio, Figurine, Comedy & Tragedy, Women In Black, Theatrical Masks, 1950s, 10 In., Pair $381

Clars Auction Gallery

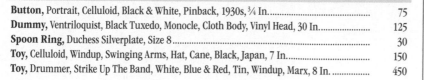

C

Chalkware, Figurine, Dog, White Paint, Standing, Rectangular Base, Pennsylvania, 1800s, 7 x 5 x 3 In. $188

New Haven Auctions

Chalkware, Figurine, Persian Cat, Sitting, Round Face, Painted, 1800s, 13 In. $443

Stony Ridge Auction

Charlie Chaplin, Toy, Dancer, Celluloid Body, Wood Legs, Powered By Phonograph, Box, 8 x 4 x 3 In. $1,093

Donley Auctions

⚓ CHELSEA

Chelsea porcelain was made in the Chelsea area of London from about 1745 to 1769. Some pieces made from 1770 to 1784 are called Chelsea Derby and may include the letter *D* for *Derby* in the mark. Ceramic designs were borrowed from the Meissen models of the day. Pieces were made of soft paste porcelain. The gold anchor was used as the mark, but it has been copied by many other factories. Recent copies of Chelsea have been made from the original molds. Do not confuse Chelsea porcelain with Chelsea Grape, a white pottery with luster grape decoration. Chelsea Keramic is listed in the Dedham category.

Figurine, Woman, Holding Basket Of Flowers, Dead Hare, Green Dress, Gilt, 7 ½ In. ....*illus*   313

🍇 CHELSEA GRAPE

Chelsea grape pattern was made before 1840. A small bunch of grapes in a raised design, colored with purple or blue luster, is on the border of the white plate. Most of the pieces are unmarked. The pattern is sometimes called Aynsley or Grandmother. Chelsea Sprig is similar but has a sprig of flowers instead of the bunch of grapes. Chelsea Thistle has a raised thistle pattern. Do not confuse these Chelsea patterns with Chelsea Keramic Art Works, which can be found in the Dedham category, or with Chelsea porcelain, the preceding category.

Dinnerware Set, Plates, Cups & Saucers, Bowls, Sugar, Lid, Adderley, 62 Piece   48

⊙ CHINESE EXPORT

Chinese export porcelain comprises the many kinds of porcelain made in China for export to America and Europe in the eighteenth, nineteenth, and twentieth centuries. Other pieces may be listed in this book in Canton, Celadon, Nanking, Rose Canton, Rose Mandarin, Rose Medallion and other categories.

Basin, Famille Rose, Double Happiness, Deep Round Sides, Fluttering Butterflies, 13 ⅝ In.	840
Bough Pot, Lid, Famille Rose, Flowers, Dragons, Multicolor, 1800s, 9 ½ x 7 ½ x 8 In., Pair	2520
Bowl, Bronze Mounted, Famille Rose, French Market, 1900s, 8 x 12 x 9 In...................*illus*	250
Bowl, Dark Mahogany, Tortoiseshell Glaze, Chinese, 2 ½ In.	120
Bowl, Famille Rose, Gilt Metal Mounted, Brass Bands, Flowers, 3 ½ x 4 In..................*illus*	121
Bowl, Famille Rose, Lotus & Shou Symbol, Flared Gilt Rim, 5 Red Bats, Xianfeng Mark, 6 In....	1140
Bowl, Famille Rose, Phoenix, Lotus, Red, Gilt Border, Guangxu Mark, 3 ½ x 8 ¼ In.	2280
Bowl, Mughal Style, Dragonhead Shape, 2 Handles, Footed, White, 1800s, 6 ¼ In.	1403
Bowl, Underplate, Reticulated, Painted, Landscape Scene, 4 ½ x 10 In.................................	168
Bowl, Vegetable, Oval, Clobbered, Mandarin, Early 1800s, 11 x 8 In.................................	366
Brush Box, Famille Rose, Gilt, Fitzhugh, Overglazed, 1800s, 29 x 48 In.	468
Brush Rest, Bat Shape, Washer, Water Dropper, Sancai Glaze, Late 1800s, 3 In...................	173
Brush Washer, Famille Rose, Dragon, Yellow Ground, Globular, 10 ¼ In.	660
Cachepot, Flowers, Green Trim, White Ground, Square Base, 1900s, 12 x 6 In., Pair............	188
Candlestick, Famille Rose, Foo Dog, Clobbered, Painted, Socket On Back, c.1840, 3 x 5 x 2 In... *illus*	488
Censer, Blue & White Phoenix, Globular Shape, Painted, Lotus Scrolls, 6 ⅜ In.	1080
Censer, Famille Jaune, Peaches, Bats, Coins, Fish, 1800s, 3 x 4 In.	50
Chamberstick, Famille Rose, Figural, Bat Shape, Multicolor, 2 ½ x 4 ¼ x 4 In.....................	1573
Charger, Famille Rose, Flower, Spearhead Border, Riverscape Scene, c.1770, 14 In......*illus*	1750
Charger, Famille Rose, Green Ground, Flowers Trim, Carved Wood Stand, 3 x 18 In............	1440
Charger, Round, Painted, Flowers, Geometric Design, Early 1900s, 14 x 14 x 1 In.	94
Compote, Famille Rose, Shaped, Painted, Butterflies, Footed, 11 In.	1132
Dish, Famille Rose, Bat & Peach, Shallow Round Sides, Lotus Band, 1851-61, 8 In.......*illus*	720
Dish, Famille Rose, Dragon, Phoenix, Shallow Flared Sides, Copper Red, 1862-75, 4 In.	300
Dish, Shell Shape, Flowers, Blue Rim, White Ground, 1800s, 7 x 6 In., Pair.........................	305
Ewer, Tall Neck, Tobacco Leaves, River Scene, c.1840, 11 x 5 In.	610
Figurine, Famille Rose, Phoenix Bird, Multicolor, Enameled, 1800s, 18 x 6 x 5 In., Pair	2440
Figurine, Foo Dog, Male, Green, Brown, White Glaze, 8 x 10 x 5 ½ In............................*illus*	63

Chelsea, Figurine, Woman, Holding Basket Of Flowers, Dead Hare, Green Dress, Gilt, 7 ½ In.
$313

Lion and Unicorn

Chinese Export, Bowl, Bronze Mounted, Famille Rose, French Market, 1900s, 8 x 12 x 9 In.
$250

Charlton Hall Auctions

Chinese Export, Bowl, Famille Rose, Gilt Metal Mounted, Brass Bands, Flowers, 3 ½ x 4 In.
$121

Ahlers & Ogletree Auction Gallery

TIP
Re-key all locks when you move to a new house or apartment or if you lose a key.

Chinese Export, Candlestick, Famille Rose, Foo Dog, Clobbered, Painted, Socket On Back, c.1840, 3 x 5 x 2 In.
$488

Rafael Osona Nantucket Auctions

Chinese Export, Charger, Famille Rose, Flower, Spearhead Border, Riverscape Scene, c.1770, 14 In.
$1,750

Charlton Hall Auctions

Chinese Export, Dish, Famille Rose, Bat & Peach, Shallow Round Sides, Lotus Band, 1851-61, 8 In.
$720

Michaan's Auctions

Chinese Export, Figurine, Foo Dog, Male, Green, Brown, White Glaze, 8 x 10 x 5 ½ In.
$63

Auctions at Showplace, NYC

Chinese Export, Planter, Famille Rose, Fishbowl Shape, Court Scene, Flowers, 16 x 19 In.
$144

Alderfer Auction Company

Chinese Export, Plate, Elephant, Man Riding, Flowers, Scalloped Rim, 1700s, 9 In.
$938

Wiederseim Auctions

TIP
Glue broken china with an invisible mending cement that is waterproof.

Chinese Export, Plate, Gilt, Painted, Diamond Trelliswork, Rococo, Scroll Border, c.1745, 9 In.
$2,706

Brunk Auctions

Chinese Export, Tureen, Famille Rose, Lid, Fenced Garden Landscapes, White Ground, 9 x 14 In., Pair
$640

Neal Auction Company

Chinese Export, Vase, Famille Jaune, Yellow Ground, Deities, Scrolling Clouds, Bats, Wood Stand, 11¼ x 5 In.
$1,169

Auctions at Showplace, NYC

Foot Bath, Lobed, Landscape Panels, Blue Crackle Ground, 7 x 18 In.	768
Ginger Jar, Famille Rose, Landscape, Signed With Characters, 1800s, 10¼ x 8 In.	120
Ginger Jar, Fitzhugh Style, Bird, Open Wing, 1900s, 13 x 10 In.	125
Incense Burner, Parrot, Green Glaze, Standing, Rock Form Bases, 1800s, 9¾ x 3 x 4 In., Pair	600
Jar, Bird, Flowers, Rocks, 6¾ x 5½ In.	108
Jar, Globular Shape, Wood Lid, Painted, Various Figures, Garden, 1800s, 8½ x 10¼ In.	461
Jar, Lid, Blue & White, 2 Happiness Symbols, 9½ In., Pair	175
Jardiniere, Famille Rose, Cartouches, Women, Garden Scene, Black Ground, 15½ In.	200
Lamp, Ginger Jar, Lid, Lotus Blossom, Palm Leaf Border, 21 In.	484
Planter, Blue & White, Pagoda River Scene, Hardwood Stand, 13 x 17¾ In.	480
Planter, Dragon, Molded, Tiger Shape Handles, Jiaqing Mark, 3¼ x 5¾ In.	1845
Planter, Famille Rose, Fishbowl Shape, Court Scene, Flowers, 16 x 19 In. .... *illus*	144
Plate, Blue, White, Dragon, Central Medallion, Flaming Pearl, 18th Century, 8½ In.	330
Plate, Butterflies, Peach Branches, c.1800s, 7¼ In., Pair	330
Plate, Elephant, Man Riding, Flowers, Scalloped Rim, 1700s, 9 In. *illus*	938
Plate, Famille Rose, Silver Mounted, Spring Flowers, Peonies, Late 1700s, 9 In., Pair	610
Plate, Gilt Rim, 2 Birds, Central Decoration, Floral Border, Late 1700s, 8¾ In.	406
Plate, Gilt, Painted, Diamond Trelliswork, Rococo, Scroll Border, c.1745, 9 In. .... *illus*	2706
Plate, Mandarin, Spring Landscape Border, Fairy Tale Scenes, c.1830, 8 In., Pair	2750
Platter, Blue & White, Flower, Butterfly, 1800s, 8¾ x 12¼ In., Pair	338
Platter, Famille Rose, Hand Painted, Flowers, Octagonal, 1700s, 14 x 11 x 2 In.	201
Punch Bowl, Famille Rose, Gilt Accents, Guilloche Patterned Rim, 1700s, 4¾ x 11 In.	363
Saucer, Deep, Wavy Rim, Blue & White, 1800s, 1 x 5 In., Pair	122
Serving Dish, Square, Round Corners, Black Enamel, Gilt Crest, c.1805, 8½ x 8½ In.	2000
Temple Jar, Dome Lid, Blue & White Glaze, Figures, Foo Dog Handles, 19¼ x 9 In., Pair	270
Tureen, Famille Rose, Lid, Fenced Garden Landscapes, White Ground, 9 x 14 In., Pair .... *illus*	640
Tureen, Famille Verte, Rooster Shape, Sitting, Crowing, Wood Stand, 1900s, 10 x 10½ In.	281
Tureen, Sauce, Lid, Blue Fitzhugh, Bulbous, 2 Strap Handles, 1800s, 6 x 7½ In.	190
Urn, French Ormolu, Bronze Mounted Handles & Base, 20 x 19 In., Pair	360
Urn, Gilt Metal, Armorial, Carved, Griffins Design, Flowers, 13 x 4¼ In., Pair	96
Vase, Blue, Round Body, Thin Neck, Applied Chilong, 6-Character Mark, 1800s, 9 In.	2560
Vase, Blue, White, Garlic Mouth, Pear Shape, Slender Neck, Flowers, Gilt Bronze Stand, 11¾ In.	1080
Vase, Blue & White, Oriental Figures, 16 In., Pair	1037
Vase, Champleve, Engraved Bottom, 12-Character Mark, 1800s, 9 In., Pair	240
Vase, Copper Red Glaze, Oval, Long Neck, Flared Rim, 20th Century, 23 In., Pair	1250
Vase, Famille Jaune, Yellow Ground, Deities, Scrolling Clouds, Bats, Wood Stand, 11¼ x 5 In. .... *illus*	1169
Vase, Famille Rose, Interior Scenes, Flowers, Gilt Handles, 13 x 6 In., Pair	330
Vase, Famille Rose, People, Bird, Gilt Grounds, Floral Vines, Butterflies, 1800s, 14 In., Pair	732
Vase, Famille Rose, Tobacco Leaf, Covered Tureen, Molded Ram's Head Handles, 9½ In. .... *illus*	320
Vase, Famille Rose & Blue Tongzhi, Birds, Blossoming Branches, Dragon & Peony Band, 11 x 4 In.	366
Vase, Flowers, Birds, Cylindrical, 11 x 5 In., Pair	300
Vase, Qing Style, Multicolor, Bulbous, Cylindrical Neck, 22¼ x 16 In.	236
Vase, White Glaze, Pear Shape, Deer Head Handles, 1900s, 12¼ x 8½ In.	330
Wall Pocket, Vase Shape, Landscape Vignettes, c.1800s, 8 x 4 x 1 In.	1159
Washbasin, Famille Rose, Flower, Fruit, Daily Life Scene, 1900s, 6¾ In.	120

CHINTZ

Chintz is the name of a group of china patterns featuring an overall design of flowers and leaves, similar to the design on chintz fabric. The design became popular with English makers about 1928. A few pieces are still being made. The best known are designs by Royal Winton, James Kent Ltd., Crown Ducal, and Shelley. Crown Ducal and Shelley are listed in their own sections.

Atlas China Co.
c.1934–1939

Old Foley/James Kent
c.1955

Royal Winton
c.1951+

Hydrangea, Sugar Shaker, Metal Top, 100th Anniversary, James Kent, Box, 1998, 7 In.. *illus*	188
May Medley, Creamer, Pink & White Flowers, Gilt Trim, Bone China, Royal Standard.........	35
Old Cottage, Dinnerware Set, Multicolor Flowers, Gilt, Royal Winton, 19th Century, 43 Piece	313
Rosina, Saucer, Multicolor Flowers, Gilt Trim, Bone China, 5 ½ In.	20
Sophie, Plate, Salad, Yellow Ground, Purple Flowers, Scalloped Rim, Sadler, 8 ¼ In............	100

CHOCOLATE GLASS

Chocolate glass, sometimes mistakenly called caramel slag, was made by the Indiana Tumbler and Goblet Company of Greentown, Indiana, from 1900 to 1903. It was also made at other National Glass Company factories. Fenton Art Glass Co. made chocolate glass from about 1907 to 1915. More recent pieces have been made by Imperial and others.

Cat In Hamper, Dish, Cat Head Lid, Basketweave, Indiana Tumbler & Goblet Co., c.1900, 5 x 3 In. .	104
Dish, Lid, Cow On Nest, McKee, 4 x 5 ½ In...	2380
Leaf Bracket, Cruet, Molded Stopper, Greentown, Pair .... *illus*	36

CHRISTMAS, *Plates that are limited edition are listed in the Collector Plate category or in the correct factory listing.*

CHRISTMAS

Christmas collectibles include not only Christmas trees and ornaments listed below, but also Santa Claus figures, special dishes, and even games and wrapping paper. A Belsnickle is a nineteenth-century figure of Father Christmas. A kugel is an early, heavy ornament made of thick blown glass, lined with zinc or lead, and often covered with colored wax. Christmas cards are listed in this section under Greeting Card. Christmas collectibles may also be listed in the Candy Container category. Christmas trees are listed in the section that follows.

Calendar, 1905, Wreath Shape, Center Image, 2 Children In Bed, Bells With Months, 9 ½ In..	40
Candy Containers are listed in the Candy Container category.	
Chocolate Mold, Santa Claus, Butt Plug, Tube Case, Ribbon, Dark, France, c.2007, 10 x 5 x 2 In.......	250
Figure, Gift From Santa, Bag Of Toys, Glossy, No. 6575, Juan Huerta, Lladro, 1999, 6 ¾ In. .	138
Figure, Santa Claus, Mask Face, Cloth, Red Felt Suit, Black Boots, 26 In.	148
Figure, Santa Claus, Red Satin, Outfit, Black Highlight, Glossy, Papier-Mache Boots, 1950s, 25 In.....	150
Figure, Santa Claus, Seated, Sled, Black Boots, Red, Blue, Germany, 1900s, 6 In.	219
Figure, Santa Claus, Standing, Light Brown & Yellow, Fenton, 8 ½ In.	86
Figure, Santa Claus, Standing, With Child, Multicolor, Celluloid, Japan, Prewar, 9 In.. *illus*	1200
Figure, Santa Claus, Standing, Wood, Carved, Gemany, 1920s-30s, 48 In.	968
Lamp, Electric, Figural, Santa Claus, Painted, White & Red, Miniature, 9 x 3 In. .... *illus*	1700
Lamp, Santa Claus, Kerosene, Standing, Arms Crossed, Domed Base, c.1894, 9 ¼ In.	1554
Picture, Embossed Santa Claus, Sleigh, Reindeer, Green Ground, Frame, c.1900, 12 x 16 ¼ In. ..	320
Picture, Mechanical, Family With Tree, Wood, Litho, Clockwork, Schoenhut, 15 ½ x 21 ½ In.	5100
Picture, Mechanical, Santa Claus Surprises Child, Paper Litho, Clockwork, Schoenhut, 14 In.. *illus*	2700
Postcard, Santa Claus At Window, Green Coat, Undivided Back, Postmarked 1905 ...... *illus*	90
Postcard, Santa Claus In Biplane, Children Catching Toys, Divided Back, John Winsch, 1913 *illus*	57
Postcard, Santa Claus In Zeppelin Basket, A Merry Christmas, Germany, Postmarked 1910	68
Postcard, Santa Claus, 2 Children, Tree, Frohliche Weihnachten, Undivided Back, Germany.	113
Postcard, Santa Claus, Blue Coat, Carrying Lantern, Divided Back, Germany, 1911..... *illus*	158
Postcard, Santa Claus, Brown Coat, Child, Tree, Snow, Holly Border, Divided Back, Germany	136
Postcard, Santa Claus, Carrying Tree & Toys, A Merry Christmas, Divided Back, Germany.	73
Postcard, Santa Claus, Green Coat, Child, German Text & Postmark, Undivided Back....... *illus*	124
Postcard, Woodland Scene, Santa Claus, Tan Cloak, Cherub, Divided Back, Germany, 1915	181
Santa Claus Head, Painted, Beard, Carved, Wood, Wall Hanging, c.1910, 15 ¾ x 9 ¾ x 4 In.. *illus*	303
Toy, Santa Claus & Sleigh, Carved, Painted, Pam Schifferl, 14 x 13 ½ In.	403
Toy, Santa Claus Chiming Bell, Painted, Windup, Issmayer, 6 In. .... *illus*	2040

Chinese Export, Vase, Famille Rose, Tobacco Leaf, Covered Tureen, Molded Ram's Head Handles, 9 ½ In.
$320

Nadeau's Auction Gallery

Chintz, Hydrangea, Sugar Shaker, Metal Top, 100th Anniversary, James Kent, Box, 1998, 7 In.
$188

Lion and Unicorn

Chocolate Glass, Leaf Bracket, Cruet, Molded Stopper, Greentown, Pair
$36

Strawser Auction Group

Christmas, Figure, Santa Claus, Standing, With Child, Multicolor, Celluloid, Japan, Prewar, 9 In.
$1,200

Morphy Auctions

Christmas, Lamp, Electric, Figural, Santa Claus, Painted, White & Red, Miniature, 9 x 3 In.
$1,700

Woody Auction

Christmas, Picture, Mechanical, Santa Claus Surprises Child, Paper Litho, Clockwork, Schoenhut, 14 In.
$2,700

Bertoia Auctions

Christmas, Postcard, Santa Claus At Window, Green Coat, Undivided Back, Postmarked 1905
$90

Matthew Bullock Auctioneers

Christmas, Postcard, Santa Claus In Biplane, Children Catching Toys, Divided Back, John Winsch, 1913
$57

Matthew Bullock Auctioneers

Christmas, Postcard, Santa Claus, Blue Coat, Carrying Lantern, Divided Back, Germany, 1911
$158

Matthew Bullock Auctioneers

Christmas, Postcard, Santa Claus, Green Coat, Child, German Text & Postmark, Undivided Back
$124

Matthew Bullock Auctioneers

Christmas, Santa Claus Head, Painted, Beard, Carved, Wood, Wall Hanging, c.1910, 15¾ x 9¾ x 4 In.
$303

Fontaine's Auction Gallery

Christmas, Toy, Santa Claus Chiming Bell, Painted, Windup, Issmayer, 6 In.
$2,040

Bertoia Auctions

CHRISTMAS TREE

Christmas trees made of feathers and Christmas tree decorations of all types are popular with collectors. The first decorated Christmas tree in America is claimed by many states, including Pennsylvania (1747), Massachusetts (1832), Illinois (1833), Ohio (1838), and Iowa (1845). The first glass ornaments were imported from Germany about 1860. Paper and tinsel ornaments were made in Dresden, Germany, from about 1880 to 1940. Manufacturers in the United States were making ornaments in the early 1870s. Electric lights were first used on a Christmas tree in 1882. Character light bulbs became popular in the 1920s, bubble lights in the 1940s, twinkle bulbs in the 1950s, plastic bulbs by 1955. In this book a Christmas light is a holder for a candle used on the tree. Other forms of lighting include light bulbs. Other Christmas collectibles are listed in the preceding section.

Feather, Green, Cylindrical Wood Base, Germany, 71 In.................................*illus*	960
Feather, Paper Wrapped Rod, Branches, Turned Wood Base, Germany, Late 1800s, 32 In. ..	228
Feather, Wire Branches, Paper Wrapped Trunks, Red & Gold Paint, 1950s, 34 In., Pair.......	168
Fence, Surround, Wood Stand, 4-Part, Red, Green End Posts, Arched Gate, Wirework, 6 x 17 x 17 In.	210
Goose Feather, Red Berries, Wood Block Base, Garlands, Bows, Germany, c.1900, 22 In.	590
Ornament, Bishop's Bounty, Basket Of Fruits, Glitter Accents, Christopher Radko, 2001, 8 In.	88
Ornament, Christmas Ball, Nativity Scenes, No. 6009, Lladro, 1993, 3 In............................	75
Ornament, Dorothy & Toto, Multicolor, Christopher Radko, Package, 1997, 3 x 5 In.......... *illus*	125
Ornament, Glass, Pink Iridescent, Blue Feather Threading, Daniel Lotton, 4 ½ In.............	72
Ornament, Hanging Cage, Parrot, Tin Bird, 1800s, 5 ½ In.	207
Ornament, Hot Air Balloon, Clear Glass, Wirework, Top Hook, 5 ½ In................................	150
Ornament, Kugel, Mercury, Glass Ball, Orange, Cane Star, Brass Cap, Germany, 1900s, 6 In..	120
Ornament, Parrot, Perched On Ring, Black Forest, 1800s, 33 x 18 In......................... *illus*	2813
Ornament, Pressed Paper, Fish, Birds, Alligator, Dog, House Fly, Elephants, Dresden, 7 In., 22 Piece..	390
Ornament, Santa Claus In Sleigh, Lying Down, Red & White, Gilt, 2 ¼ In............................	38
Ornament, Snowman, Raven On Shoulder, Plush, Metal Saucepan Hat, Ear Button, Steiff, 8 In..	110
Ornament, Woman, Seated, Cotton Body, Paper Face, Glass Sled, Sebnitz, Germany, 1950s, 5 In.	210
Skirt, Metallic Thread, Gold, Red Velvet, Polyester, Bloomingdale's, Late 1900s, 6 x 20 In...*illus*	406
Stand, Cast Iron, Old Green Paint, Stylized Flowers, Scrolls, Turn Screws, 8 x 10 In.............	125
Stand, Music, Plays 3 Songs, Rotating, Antique, Eckhardt, 10 x 14 In................................	540
Stand, Musical, Revolves, Silver Paint Base, J.C. Eckhardt, Germany, c.1900, 29 ½ x 14 In. .	182

CHROME

Chrome items in the Art Deco style became popular in the 1930s. Collectors are most interested in high-style pieces made by the Connecticut firms of Chase Brass & Copper Co., Manning-Bowman & Co., and others.

Ashtray, Smoke Stand, Jars & Lighter, Center Glass Ball, Domed Base, 1920 .... *illus*	58
Box, Lid, Rectangular, Cedar Interior, 3 Sections, Art Deco, Chase USA, 1930s, 3 x 7 In........	60
Champagne Bucket, Lid, Ball Finial, Brass Rings, Side Handles, 1950s, 10 ¼ x 10 ½ In.	38
Cocktail Shaker, Black Enamel Bands, Flared Finial, Gaiety, Chase Brass & Copper, 1930s, 11 In.	50
Cocktail Shaker, Empire, Butterscotch Bakelite Trim, D Handle, Revere, 1938, 12 x 6 In...	1060
Figure, Dog, Bulldog, Standing, Head Turned, Midcentury, 11 x 19 x 8 In.	277
Food Warmer, Lid, Oval, Side Handles, Platter Insert, Early 20th Century, 19 In.................	12
Lamp, Desk, Disc Base, C Support, Domed Shade, Apollo Electric Co., Chicago, c.1930, 22 In....	935
Lamp, Desk, Spherical Shade, Modern Style, Square Base, c.1970s, 20 In. .... *illus*	118
Lamp, Electric, 3-Light, 3-Lamp Stand, White Glass Shades, Bulb Shape, 12 x 56 In.	936
Lamp, Electric, 4-Light, Gooseneck, Glass Shades, Multicolor, 20 x 18 x 18 In......................	63
Pedestal, Square, 2-Panel Sides, Lighted, Neal Smal, 42 x 14 In.	344
Pitcher, Normandie, Revere Copper, Brass, Peter Muller-Munk, 1935, 12 x 9 x 3 In.............	1820
Rack, Magazine, Bullet, Coiled Divider, J.W. Carpenter, McKay Craft, 1933, 13 x 20 x 9 In....	720
Sculpture, Wall, Hollywood Horse, Fiberglass, Silver Leaf, Gilt, MCM, Steel, 36 x 38 x 4 In.. *illus*	500
Tea & Coffee Set, Teapot, Percolator, Urn, Sugar, Creamer, Deco, Manning Bowman, 1930, 5 Piece	195

C

Christmas Tree, Feather, Green, Cylindrical Wood Base, Germany, 71 In. $960

Rachel Davis Fine Arts

Christmas Tree, Ornament, Dorothy & Toto, Multicolor, Christopher Radko, Package, 1997, 3 x 5 In. $125

Lion and Unicorn

Christmas Tree, Ornament, Parrot, Perched On Ring, Black Forest, 1800s, 33 x 18 In. $2,813

Hindman

CIGAR STORE FIGURE

Christmas Tree, Skirt, Metallic Thread, Gold, Red Velvet, Polyester, Bloomingdale's, Late 1900s, 6 x 20 In. $406

Eldred's

Chrome, Ashtray, Smoke Stand, Jars & Lighter, Center Glass Ball, Domed Base, 1920
$58

Donley Auctions

Chrome, Lamp, Desk, Spherical Shade, Modern Style, Square Base, c.1970s, 20 In.
$118

Neue Auctions

CIGAR STORE FIGURE

Cigar store figures of carved wood or cast iron were used as advertisements in front of the Victorian cigar store. The carved figures are now collected as folk art. They range in size from counter type, about three feet, to over eight feet tall.

Indian, Wood, Multicolor, Feathered Headdress, Knife & War Club, Fish, Base, c.1900, 84 In.. *illus* 5120

CINNABAR

Cinnabar is a vermilion or red lacquer. Pieces are made with tens to hundreds of thicknesses of the lacquer that is later carved. Most cinnabar was made in the Orient.

Box, Lid, Square, Lacquer, Relief Dragons, Clouds, Tapered Top, Sunburst, Chinese, 3 In., Pair... 945
Censer, Skull Shape, Faux, Carved, 4-Claw Dragon, Chinese, 3¾ x 4¼ In. 63
Snuff Bottle, Carved, Rose & Flowering Tree, Dome Stopper, 1800s, 3 x 2 x 1 In. .... *illus* 527
Tray, Carved Relief, Men, Servants, Flower Scrolls, Qianlong Mark, 2½ x 18 x 18 In. 480
Vase, Figural, Landscape & Scrolls, Flared Rim & Foot, Chinese, 1900s, 10 x 5 In., Pair....... *illus* 380
Vase, Gooseneck, Mountain Landscape, Qianlong Mark, Chinese, 23½ In., Pair 900

CIVIL WAR

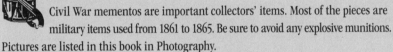

Civil War mementos are important collectors' items. Most of the pieces are military items used from 1861 to 1865. Be sure to avoid any explosive munitions. Pictures are listed in this book in Photography.

Backpack, Union, Leather & Wood, Leather Straps, Marked 21 Mass., 15 x 13 In. .... *illus* 1397
Badge, 9th Illinois Cavalry, Company C, Sharps Carbine Bullet Attached, 4⅛ In. 688
Badge, IX Corps Officer's, Gold Plated Brass, Shield Shape, 3-Color Ribbon, 3¼ In.............. 500
Badge, Society Of The Army Of The Potomac, Enamel, Gilt, Late 1800s, 1⅝ In. 188
Badge, Star Shape, 3rd Division, XII Corps, H.G. Clagston, Philadelphia, 1863, 1¼ In. 1875
Badge, Volunteer, Star, No. 5, Company K, Private Daniel Hudson, 1862, 1⅞ In........... *illus* 8125
Bayonet, Confederate, Saber, Scabbard, Yataghan Blade, Cast Hilt, Boyle Gamble & McFee, 25 In.. 2640
Belt, Officer's Sword, Leather, Folded, Seam, Eagle Plate, 1¾ x 38 In..................... 469
Billy Club, Andersonville Prison Pen, Blue & Gold Star, Braided Rope, Wood, 10⅜ In. 1548
Box, Pistol Cartridge, Officer's, Leather, Brass Eagle, c.1850, 5 x 3 x 1 In. 313
Broadside, Union Forever!, Lockwood Legion!, Recruiting, c.1861, 37 x 23 In.............. *illus* 12500
Bugle, U.S. Regulation, Copper, Artillery Cord, Horstmann, 19 x 7½ x 5½ In............. *illus* 15000
Cannonball, Naval, Cast Iron, Exploding Shell, Hole Gauge, 9 In........................ 293
Canteen, Hand Painted, Country Lane, Boats On Water On Reverse, 8½ x 7½ In................ 320
Cape, Shoulder, Wool, Eagle Buttons, Red Lining, Dark Blue Ground 445
Caricature, Soldier Eating Hardtack, Cardstock, 1861, 2 x 4 In. 531
Cartridge Box, Leather, Federal, Tins, Watertown Arsenal, 1864, 7 x 5¼ x 1⅝ In.............. 688
Chair, Camp, Folding, Canvas Seat, Wood, Iron Rivets & Hardware, 18 x 29 x 16¾ In.......... 594
Cutlass, Model 1860, Ames U.S. Navy, Black Leather Grip, Scabbard & Frog, 1861, 32 In...... 882
Desk, Field, Capt. John A. Caldwell, 4th Massachusetts Cavalry, 1865, Wood, 17 x 16 x 13 In...... 4800
Desk, Field, Drawer, Wood, Brass Hardware, 23½ x 24⅜ x 12 In........................ 375
Ditty Bag, Confederate, Embroidered, Dress Material, Drawstring, Woman's, 4¾ x 7 In.. *illus* 1500
Drum, Snare, Painted, 4 Drummers, Officer, Rope, W.G. Metzerott & Co., 14½ x 17 In.*illus* 12500
Flag Pole, Eagle Topper, Spread Wings, Brass Bottom & Top, 1800s, 70 x 6 x 7 In. 508
Flag Pole, Hardwood, Bronze, Eagle Finial, 2 Parts, 69 In. & 44 In. 344
Footlocker, Lieut. A.W. Kredel, Union Soldier, Contents, Painted, Red Ground 5842
Hat, GAR Dress Cap, Gold Lace Trim, Ribbon, Buttons, Quatrefoiling, Private Jacob H. Perine... 1188
Hat, Slouch, Tan Gray, Silver Wire Cord, Confederate Veteran's, 5 In............................ *illus* 688
Hat, Union Artillery Insignia, Reg. No. 4, Crossed Cannons, Embroidered, 3½ x 2⅜ In. 688
Jacket, Cavalry, Sergeant, Union, Dark Blue Wool, Yellow Piping, Shell, Cuffs, 1855 6250
Jacket, Shell, Cavalry Style, Blue Gray Wool, Gilt Buttons, South Carolina, 23 In. 1250
Knife, Union Army, Folding Spoon, Fork, Keyhole Slots, A. Hills, 6⅞ In. 281
Knuckle Duster, Wood, Carved, New Market Battlefield, Virginia, 1864, 4⅜ x 2½ In. illus 1875
Pharmacology Case, Doctor's, Mahogany, Brass Bound, Lower Drawer, 8¾ x 10 x 7 In..... *illus* 936
Pipe, Folk Art, Carved, Laurel Root, Silver, Hinged Lid, Fredericksburg, C.F. Morse, 1862, 5 In. 1408

Chrome, Sculpture, Wall, Hollywood Horse, Fiberglass, Silver Leaf, Gilt, MCM, Steel, 36 x 38 x 4 In.
$500

New Haven Auctions

Cigar Store Figure, Indian, Wood, Multicolor, Feathered Headdress, Knife & War Club, Fish, Base, c.1900, 84 In.
$5,120

Neal Auction Company

Cinnabar, Snuff Bottle, Carved, Rose & Flowering Tree, Dome Stopper, 1800s, 3 x 2 x 1 In.
$527

Thomaston Place Auction Galleries

Cinnabar, Vase, Figural, Landscape & Scrolls, Flared Rim & Foot, Chinese, 1900s, 10 x 5 In., Pair
$380

Thomaston Place Auction Galleries

Civil War, Backpack, Union, Leather & Wood, Leather Straps, Marked 21 Mass., 15 x 13 In.
$1,397

White's Auctions

Civil War, Badge, Volunteer, Star, No. 5, Company K, Private Daniel Hudson, 1862, 1 7/8 In.
$8,125

Hindman

Civil War, Broadside, Union Forever!, Lockwood Legion!, Recruiting, c.1861, 37 x 23 In.
$12,500

Cowan's Auctions

Civil War, Bugle, U.S. Regulation, Copper, Artillery Cord, Horstmann, 19 x 7 1/2 x 5 1/2 In.
$15,000

Hindman

Civil War, Ditty Bag, Confederate, Embroidered, Dress Material, Drawstring, Woman's, 4 3/4 x 7 In.
$1,500

Hindman

Civil War, Drum, Snare, Painted, 4 Drummers, Officer, Rope, W.G. Metzerott & Co., 14½ x 17 In.
$12,500

Hindman

Civil War, Hat, Slouch, Tan Gray, Silver Wire Cord, Confederate Veteran's, 5 In.
$688

Cowan's Auctions

Civil War, Knuckle Duster, Wood, Carved, New Market Battlefield, Virginia, 1864, 4⅜ x 2½ In.
$1,875

Hindman

Civil War, Pharmacology Case, Doctor's, Mahogany, Brass Bound, Lower Drawer, 8¾ x 10 x 7 In.
$936

Thomaston Place Auction Galleries

TIP
Never bid at an auction if you have not previewed the items.

Civil War, Shackles, Leg, Iron, Worn, Union Soldier, Escaped Libby Prison, 1861, 28 In.
$875

Hindman

Clarice Cliff, Crocus, Multicolor, Diamond Shape, Handle, Hand Painted, 9½ x 8 x 7 In.
$1,375

Palm Beach Modern Auctions

Clewell, Vase, Copper Clad, Chalice Shape, Blue Green, Charles Walter, Ohio, c.1930, 6¾ x 3½ In.
$250

Toomey & Co. Auctioneers

Clock, Advertising, Harp's Standard, Neon, Metal, Glass, Octagonal, 25 x 25 In.
$1,920

Chupp Auctions & Real Estate, LLC

Clock, Advertising, Winchester Repeating Arms, Wall, Wood, Black, Glass, Sessions, 36 x 18 In.
$633

Donley Auctions

Clock, Animated, Cat, Blinking Eye, Wall, Tin Lithograph, Yellow Ground, 8 In.
$480

Rachel Davis Fine Arts

Pitcher, Union Soldier's Face, Clover Corps Badge, c.1900, 9 x 9 In.	281
Portrait, Watercolor, Sergeant Thomas H. Sheehan, Frame, 1878, 16 x 18 In.	344
Print, Lithograph, Battle Of Champion Hills, Gold Frame, Kurz & Allison, 1887, 25 x 31 In.	256
Recruiting, 7th Regt., Crack Regt. Of N.H., 10 Dollar Bounty!, Gen. J.C. Abbot, Frame, 36 x 28 In.	720
Shackles, Leg, Iron, Worn, Union Soldier, Escaped Libby Prison, 1861, 28 In. *illus*	875
Spurs, Brass, Eagle, Red Garnet Eyes, Engraved, 4⅞ x 3⅝ In.	3750
Strap, Shoulder, Cavalry Captain, Black, Orange, John A. Caldwell, 1865, 4⅜ x 1¾ In., Pair	1875
Strap, Shoulder, Cavalry Colonel, Stamped Brass Eagle & Borders, 4 x 1½ In., Pair	1375
Sword, Confederate, Brass, Crossguard Hilt, Fish Scale Grip, Fuller Blade, c.1860, 24 x 18 In.	570
Sword, Officer's, Regulation, U.S. Navy, Gilt Brass Hilt, Leather Scabbard, 36 In.	693
Sword, Shagreen Grip, Scabbard, Hilt Engraved, Col. Francis E. Heath, 38½ In.	6435
Walking Stick, United Confederate Veterans, Ebony, South Carolina Button On Top, 36⅜ In.	344

CKAW, *see Dedham category.*

CLARICE CLIFF

Clarice Cliff was a designer who worked in several English factories, including A.J. Wilkinson Ltd., Wilkinson's Royal Staffordshire Pottery, Newport Pottery, and Foley Pottery after the 1920s. She is best known for her brightly colored Art Deco designs, including the Bizarre line. She died in 1972. Pieces of some of her early work have been made again by Wedgwood.

Aura, Demitasse Set, Orange, Coffeepot, Lid, Sugar, Creamer, Cups & Saucer, 15 Piece	660
Caprice, Isis, Vase, Orange, 2 Handles, Signed, c.1930, 10 x 9 In.	1063
Crocus, Bowl, Straight-Sided, Orange Tapered Base, Yellow Interior, c.1930, 3 x 5 In.	375
Crocus, Multicolor, Diamond Shape, Handle, Hand Painted, 9½ x 8 x 7 In. *illus*	1375
Inspiration, Vase, Aqua, Stepped, Square, Blue Lion Mark, Newport Pottery, 7½ x 4 In.	1280
Toby Jug, Seated Man, Drinking, Red Coat, Green Mark, Newport Pottery, 8½ In.	50
Tulip, Bizarre, Lotus, Jug, Cafe-Au-Lait, Green, Orange, Marked, 11¾ In.	1375

CLEWELL

Clewell was made in limited quantities by Charles Walter Clewell of Canton, Ohio, from 1902 to 1955. Pottery was covered with a thin coating of bronze, then treated to make the bronze turn different colors. Pieces covered with copper, brass, or silver were also made. Mr. Clewell's secret formula for blue patinated bronze was burned when he died in 1965.

Bowl, Copper Clad, Rivets, Panels, Tapered Sides, Signed, c.1910, 2¾ x 6¾ In.	375
Vase, Chalice Shape, Blue Green Patina, Signed, c.1930, 6¾ x 3½ In.	250
Vase, Copper Clad, Avon Cutout, Signed, Vance F Co., c.1910, 7½ x 5½ In.	461
Vase, Copper Clad, Chalice Shape, Blue Green, Charles Walter, Ohio, c.1930, 6¾ x 3½ In. *illus*	250
Vase, Vase, Mottled Patina, Brown To Blue To Green, Shoulders, 10½ In.	1240

CLIFTON POTTERY

Clifton Pottery was founded by William Long in Newark, New Jersey, in 1905. He worked there until 1909 making lines that included Crystal Patina and Clifton Indian Ware. Clifton Pottery made art pottery until 1911 and then concentrated on wall and floor tile. By 1914, the name had been changed to Clifton Porcelain and Tile Company. Another firm, Chesapeake Pottery, sold majolica marked *Clifton Ware.*

Candlestick, Indian Ware, Red Clay, Pueblo Viejo, Arizona, c.1906, 9½ x 5 In.	185

CLOCK

Clocks of all types have always been popular with collectors. The eighteenth-century tall case, or grandfather's, clock was designed to house a works with a long pendulum. The name on the clock is usually the maker but sometimes it is a merchant or other craftsman. In 1816, Eli Terry patented a new, smaller works

Clock, Ansonia, Regulator, Brass, Beveled Glass Panels, Porcelain Dial, c.1900, 11 x 6 x 5 In.
$360

Garth's Auctioneers & Appraisers

Clock, Ansonia, Shelf, Figural, Shakespeare, Black Marble Base, 1800s, 15 x 17 x 7½ In.
$330

Selkirk Auctioneers & Appraisers

Clock, Black Forest, Cuckoo, Carved Wood, Owl, Pendulum, Acorn Weights, c.1950, 20 x 14 x 8 In.
$1,140

Selkirk Auctioneers & Appraisers

Clock, Bonnet & Pottier, Egyptian Revival, Cleopatra, Bronze, Marble Base, 1800s, 22 x 24 In.
$1,320

Treasureseeker Auctions

TIP

Clean a clock face as seldom as possible. The brass trim may be coated with colored lacquer, and brass polish will remove the color.

Clock, Caldwell, J.E., Desk, Blue Guilloche, Ormolu, Ribbons, 8-Day, Easel, France, 4¾ x 3½ In.
$480

Alderfer Auction Company

Clock, Cartier, Travel, Santos, 2-Tone, Rivet Detail, Black Roman Numerals, Late 1900s, 3 In.
$484

Ahlers & Ogletree Auction Gallery

for a clock, and the case became smaller. The clock could be kept on a shelf instead of on the floor. By 1840, coiled springs were used and even smaller clocks were made. Battery-powered electric clocks were first made in the late 1800s but the average household in the United States did not use a battery-operated clock until the 1930s. A garniture set can include a clock and other objects displayed on a mantel.

Advertising, Bartender, Animated, Woman Holding Beer, Relief Bar Scene, Repeal Co., 13 x 9 In.	330
Advertising, Calumet Baking Powder, Wall, Wood, Roman Numerals, c.1900, 38 x 19 In. ...	250
Advertising, Harp's Standard, Neon, Metal, Glass, Octagonal, 25 x 25 In.................*illus*	1920
Advertising, Pepsi-Cola, Wall, Electric, Thomas A. Schutz Co., 1989, 24 x 11 x 5 In.............	92
Advertising, Rival Dog Food, Metal, Square, Yellow, White, Black, Red, 1940s, 14 x 14 In....	286
Advertising, Stanley, Helps You Do Things Right, White Ground, Light-Up, 26½ x 12 In. ...	120
Advertising, Use Kodak Film, Box of Film, Wall, Metal, Plastic, Light-Up, 16 In............	230
Advertising, Winchester Repeating Arms, Wall, Wood, Black, Glass, Sessions, 36 x 18 In.. *illus*	633
Alarm, Flashlight, Electric, Deposit Box Sides, Darche Mfg. Co., c.1907, 8 x 13 x 6 In............	246
Alarm, Westclox, Big Ben, Chime, Round, White, Original Box	30
Animated, Cat, Blinking Eye, Wall, Tin Lithograph, Yellow Ground, 8 In. ....*illus*	480
Annular Dial, Cupid, Seated, White Marble, Gilt Bronze Ormolu, Blue Urn, France, 1800s, 22½ In. .	3250
Ansonia, Bobbing Doll, Child On Swing, Bisque, Spring, Nickel Case, 30-Hour, 1886, 15 In.	218
Ansonia, Metal, Figural, Cherub Holding Wreath, Roman Numerals, Shaped Feet, 12 In. ...	201
Ansonia, Regulator, Brass, Beveled Glass Panels, Porcelain Dial, c.1900, 11 x 6 x 5 In. *illus*	360
Ansonia, Shelf, Figural, Shakespeare, Black Marble Base, 1800s, 15 x 17 x 7½ In........ *illus*	330
Ansonia, Shelf, Gilt Bronze, Painted Columns, Roman Numerals, 10½ x 11 x 5 In.	250
Ansonia, Shelf, Man, Seated, Bronze, Porcelain Dial, Claw Feet, 1800s, 13 x 17 x 7 In........	63
Ansonia, Shelf, Wood, Glass Dome, Zinc Dial, Brass Bezel, Roman Numerals, 17½ In.	213
Ansonia, Shelf, Wood, Hinged Glass Door, Painted Eagle, 15½ In................................	125
Art Deco, Desk, Gilt Metal, Starburst Shape, Spread Foot, Spaulding & Co., 1900s, 7¾ In....	968
Automaton, Birdcage, Hanging, Bird Pendulum, Key Wind, 3-Footed, 6 In.....................	102
Banjo, Brass, Eagle Finial, Reverse Painted Glass, George Washington, White House, 35 In.	98
Banjo, Mahogany, Reverse Painted Tablets, Iron Dial, Roman Numerals, New England, 29 In..	406
Banjo, Waltham, Mahogany, Brass, Eagle Finial, Reverse Painted Panel, Naval Scene, 1900s, 21 In.	188
Banjo, Willard, Aaron, Federal, Giltwood, Eglomise, Boston, Early 1800s, 40 x 10 In.	5040
Banjo, Willard, Mahogany, Eagle Finial, Painted Panel, Boston, Early 1800s, 34 x 10 In.	556
Black Forest, Cuckoo, Carved Wood, Owl, Pendulum, Acorn Weights, c.1950, 20 x 14 x 8 In. .....*illus*	1140
Black Forest, Wood, Carved, Stag, Dogs, c.1890, 23½ x 19 x 7 In..............................	1750
Bonnet & Pottier, Egyptian Revival, Cleopatra, Bronze, Marble Base, 1800s, 22 x 24 In....... *illus*	1320
Boulle, Figural Top, Classical Woman, Birds, Signed, J.G. Duchesnete, Paris, 31 x 14 x 6 In.	2415
Boulle, Louis XV Style, Gilt Urn Finial, Roman Numerals, Z & Co., 1800s, 20 In.	908
Boulle, Louis XVI, Tortoiseshell, Ormolu Mount, Brass Inlay, Maison Wurtel, Paris, 1800s, 15 x 8 In..	1890
Bracket, Bronze, Ebonized Wood, Chinoiserie, Figures, Landscape, Marked, V.A.P. Brevete, 7 x 5 In.	330
Bracket, George III, Ebonized Mahogany, Gilt Bronze, Musical, 3-Fusee, 8 Bells, 26 x 15 x 11 In.	2530
Bracket, Louis XV, Bronze, Urn Finial, Painted Red Flowers, Roman Numerals, c.1760, 38 x 17 In.	750
Bracket, Louis XVI Style, Gilt Bronze, Cherub Finial, Porcelain Numerals, Striking Bell, 41 In. ...	1586
Bradley & Hubbard, Blinking Eye, Topsy, Black Woman, Tambourine, Cast Iron, 16½ In.	1625
Brass Case, Glass Panel Windows, Front Plaque, Swiss, Tiffany & Co., 9 In.	1792
Bruel, Auguste, Shelf, Cathedral, Gilt Bronze, Pierced Rose Window Dial, Paris, 1800s, 18 In......	3025
Bulgari, Shelf, Sterling Silver, Half Column Shape, Swiss, 4 In.....................................	1152
Bundy Time Recorder, Oak, Brass, Roman Numerals, Binghamton, N.Y., Late 1800s, 50 x 17 In..	349
Caldwell, E.F., Desk, Bronze, Alabaster, Rope Twist, Ribbon, Jasperware Cameo, c.1900, 10 In....	610
Caldwell, J.E., Desk, Blue Guilloche, Ormolu, Ribbons, 8-Day, Easel, France, 4¾ x 3½ In.. *illus*	480
Carriage, Brass, Glass, Blue Enamel, Flowers, Halcyon Days Enamels, England, 4 x 2 In....	439
Carriage, Brass, Glass, Lionel Peck, London, 5 x 3 x 2 In.................................	63
Carriage, Gilt Brass, Beveled Glass, Double Dial, Alarm, France, 5 x 3 In.	400
Carriage, Gilt Bronze, Glass Panels, Wreath Handle, France, Late 1800s, 6 x 3 In.	375
Carriage, Gothic Style, Gilt & Silvered Ormolu, Square Feet, French, c.1850, 10 x 5 x 4 In.	1188
Carriage, Grand Sonnerie, Gilt, Beveled Glass, Columns, Putti, France, 8½ In.	2125
Carriage, Officers, Neoclassical, Gilt Bronze, Trophies, Serpent Handle, Swiss, c.1800, 8 x 5 x 4 In.	726
Cartel, Gilt Metal, Ribbon & Bows, Roman Numerals, Boston, 22 x 9 x 4 In.	128
Cartel, Louis XVI, Gilt Bronze Ormolu, Lyre Shape, Laurel Swags, 33 x 14 In.	1599
Cartier, Travel, Santos, 2-Tone, Rivet Detail, Black Roman Numerals, Late 1900s, 3 In....... *illus*	484

Chelsea, Shelf, 2 Kneeling Men, Bronze, Gilt Leaves & Roman Numerals, Wood Base, 1900s, 11 In.....	960
Cincinnati Time Recorder Co., No. 4, Oak, Glass, Roman Numerals, Early 1900s, 35 x 17 In.	281
Cuckoo, Wood, Carved, Eagles, Leaves, Folk Art Style, Morton Riddle, Kentucky, 1970, 34 x 29 In.*illus*	761
Desk, Glass, Pate-De-Verre, Mineral Form, Roman Numerals, Signed, Daum, France, 3 x 3 1/2 In.	369
Desk, Gump's, Brass, Pocket Watch Shape, Quartz, Roman Numerals, Marked, Germany, 4 In...	125
Desk, Jade Bracelet Frame, Carved Ball Feet, Easel Back, Swiss, 4 x 2 1/2 In.	225
Desk, Silver Plate, Glass, Round, Ring Stand, Signed, Hermes, Paris, 3 In....*illus*	875
Figural, 2 Putti, Seated, Black Marble, Gilt Bronze Doves, Tiffany & Co., France, 16 x 20 1/2 In... *illus*	1920
Figural, Bust, Charles X, Bronze, Yellow Marble Pedestal, Silk Suspension Works, 1800s, 22 x 8 In.	875
Figural, Calliope, Flute, Bronze, Blue Turquin Marble Base, France, 1900s, 41 x 32 In.	2550
Figural, Ceres, Seated Boy, Coffer, Bronze, Etched Slate, 1864, 24 x 17 In.	720
Figural, Classical Woman, Chariot, Empire, Gilt Bronze, Horses, Rectangular Base, 1900s, 17 x 14 In.	1625
Figural, Dog, St. Bernard, Dial On Back, Cast Iron, 1900s, 11 x 8 1/2 In......*illus*	148
Figural, Elephant, Trunk Up, Bronze, With Key, France, 24 x 16 In. ......*illus*	2880
Figural, Empire, Classical God, Bronze, Orange Marble Base, Brass Trim, 16 1/2 x 14 In.	246
Figural, Flute Player, Seated, Charles X Style, Troy Gadour, c.1820, 13 x 9 1/2 In......*illus*	480
Figural, Girl, Seated, Dog, Bronze, Ormolu, Balthazard A Paris, Early 1800s, 16 x 12 In....*illus*	1320
Figural, Lion Prowling, Hanging Icicles, Electrified, 1920s, 19 x 16 In......*illus*	150
Figural, Louis XVI, Man Sitting, Gilt, White Marble, 12 1/4 x 14 In.	406
Figural, Man Tied To Galloping Horse, Gilt Bronze, Damascene Dial, Ivy Bezel, 1800s, 24 x 19 In..	2813
Figural, Monkey Man, Dog, Bird, Terra-Cotta, Roman Numerals, Continental, 1900s, 7 x 6 In.	156
Figural, Shelf, Classical Woman, Putti, Brass, Pendulum, Signed, Narbonne, 21 x 17 x 6 In.	690
French, Art Deco, Onyx, 4 Faceted Columns, Brass Dial, Rectangular Base, 9 x 15 In........	968
French, Classical Woman, Cherub, Bronze, Black Slate, 1800s, 22 x 10 1/2 x 8 3/4 In.	5400
French, Figural, 2 Winged Lovers, Brass, Patina, Wood Base, Silk Suspension, 1800s, 19 x 16 In...	546
Friedeberg, Pedro, Astroclock, Mahogany, Steel, Blue Lacquer, Gilt, Mexico, 1979, 21 x 17 In....*illus*	8125
Gilbert, Shelf, Delft Case, Architectural, Blue & White, Brass Bezel, Signed, Early 1900s, 13 x 13 In. .	500
Gilbert, Wm. L., Shelf, Oak, Flat Top, Slant Sides, Brass Bezel, Arts & Crafts, 7 x 9 In..........	65
Gilbert, Wm. L., Shelf, Oak, Metal, Green Slag Glass, Arts & Crafts, Dated 1913, 12 x 12 In..	780
Gilt Metal, Rosewood Case, Roman Numerals, Chinese Floral Design, Mid 1800s, 19 In......	4375
Herman Miller, Maidou Burl, Aluminum, Gilbert Rohde, c.1933, 7 x 13 x 2 In.	1250
Herman Miller, Shelf, Chrome Plated Steel, Glass, Aluminum, Gilbert Rohde, c.1933, 6 x 6 In. *illus*	1040
Herman Miller, Walnut, Enameled Aluminum, Chrome, Model 6366, G. Rohde, c.1932, 6 x 17 In.	2500
Hermle, Franz, Boulle, Brass, Faux Tortoiseshell, Balance Wheel, Germany, c.1900s, 29 3/4 In.....	540
Hermle, Franz, Bracket, Louis XIV, Faux Wood Inlay, Pedestal Base, Gilt Metal Mounts, 84 In. .	2700
Hermle, Franz, Shelf, Louis XVI Style, Brass, Marble, 2 Cherubs, 2 Bell Movement, 1900s, 24 In.	500
Herschede, Shelf, Brass, Beveled Glass, Painted Dial, Cupids, 12 x 7 x 5 In.	201
Howard Miller, Enameled Steel, Black, Glass, Plastic, Wall, G. Nelson, 1970s, 14 1/2 In.	162
Howard Miller, Omar the Owl, Wall, Masonite, Steel, Blue, G. Nelson, 10 x 10 1/2 In. ...*illus*	688
Howard Miller, Pine, Lacquer, Enameled Aluminum, Orange Hands, Wall, c.1955, 2 x 8 In.	375
Howard Miller, Swallow, Wall, Masonite, Steel, Orange, G. Nelson & Assoc., c.1965, 10 x 11 In...	813
Howard, E. & Co., Figure 8 Shape, Walnut, Painted Metal Dial, Pendulum Bob, 1800s, 34 In. *illus*	3600
Ingraham, Corrugated Gallery, Mahogany, Scalloped Bezel, Roman Numerals, 1880, 22 In.....	1500
Ingraham, E., Shelf, Regent, Wood, Marble, Black, 8-Day, Gong, Gilt Paw Feet, c.1885, 10 x 16 In..	250
Ingraham, Rooster, Painted Dial, Square, White, Black, Wood Grain, Black Numbers, 10 In..	17
Ithaca Calendar Clock Co., Walnut Case, 2 Paper Dials, H.B. Horton's Patents, c.1866	286
Jerome, Regulator, Tole, Papier-Mache, Flowers, Dog, 8-Day, c.1880, 30 x 19 In..........*illus*	244
Junghans, Regulator, Mahogany, Enamel, Pendulum, Roman Numerals, Mahogany, 32 x 13 In.	188
LeCoultre, Atmos, Brass & Glass, Skeleton Movement, Bracket Feet, 1900s, 9 x 8 x 6 In.	406
LeCoultre, Atmos, Brass Frame, Glass Panels, Swiss, 9 1/2 x 6 1/2 In.	413
LeCoultre, Atmos, Brass, Glass, Arabic Numerals, Perpetual, 8 3/4 x 7 x 5 1/4 In.	469
LeCoultre, Atmos, Brass, Glass, Perpetual Motion, 15 Jewel, Swiss, 1900s, 8 3/4 x 7 In. ..*illus*	688
LeCoultre, Atmos, Brass, Lapis Lazuli Dial, Swiss, 1900s, 9 x 8 1/4 x 6 1/2 In.	1920
LeCoultre, Shelf, Acrylic, Brass, Chinoiserie, Woman, Flower, 1960, 6 x 8 3/4 x 2 In.	1785
Lenzkirch, Black Forest Style, Bronze, Enameled Dial, Gothic Revival, Marked, c.1875, 33 x 11 In.	250
Lenzkirch, Shelf, Burl Walnut, Gilt Bronze Mounts, c.1877, 16 x 11 1/2 x 8 In..........	1080
Lenzkirch, Shelf, Jugendstil, Brass, Art Nouveau Flowers, Pendulum, 18 x 10 x 5 In.	500
LeRoy, Gilt, Acanthus Frame, Plinth Base, Cornucopia & Urn, 15 In.	438
Lyre, Mahogany, Glass Door, Turned Bezel, Engraved Brass Dial, Roman Numerals, Alarm, 39 In.	2625
Manross, Elisha, Steeple, Rosewood, Glass, Zinc Dial, Eagle, Brass Numerals, 24 In..........	3250

Clock, Cuckoo, Wood, Carved, Eagles, Leaves, Folk Art Style, Morton Riddle, Kentucky, 1970, 34 x 29 In.
$761

Thomaston Place Auction Galleries

Clock, Desk, Silver Plate, Glass, Round, Ring Stand, Signed, Hermes, Paris, 3 In.
$875

Hindman

Clock, Figural, 2 Putti, Seated, Black Marble, Gilt Bronze Doves, Tiffany & Co., France, 16 x 20 1/2 In.
$1,920

Kaminski Auctions

This is an edited listing of current prices. Visit Kovels.com to check thousands of prices from previous years and sign up for free information on trends, tips, reproductions, marks, and more.

Clock, Figural, Dog, St. Bernard, Dial On Back, Cast Iron, 1900s, 11 x 8 ½ In. $148

Copake Auction

Clock, Figural, Elephant, Trunk Up, Bronze, With Key, France, 24 x 16 In. $2,880

Kaminski Auctions

Clock, Figural, Flute Player, Seated, Charles X Style, Troy Gadour, c.1820, 13 x 9 ½ In. $480

Kaminski Auctions

Clock, Figural, Girl, Seated, Dog, Bronze, Ormolu, Balthazard A Paris, Early 1800s, 16 x 12 In. $1,320

Kaminski Auctions

Clock, Figural, Lion Prowling, Hanging Icicles, Electrified, 1920s, 19 x 16 In. $150

Kaminski Auctions

Clock, Herman Miller, Shelf, Chrome Plated Steel, Glass, Aluminum, Gilbert Rohde, c.1933, 6 x 6 In. $1,040

Wright

Clock, Howard Miller, Omar the Owl, Wall, Masonite, Steel, Blue, G. Nelson, 10 x 10 ½ In. $688

Wright

Clock, Friedeberg, Pedro, Astroclock, Mahogany, Steel, Blue Lacquer, Gilt, Mexico, 1979, 21 x 17 In. $8,125

Wright

Clock, Howard, E. & Co., Figure 8 Shape, Walnut, Painted Metal Dial, Pendulum Bob, 1800s, 34 In.
$3,600

Clock, LeCoultre, Atmos, Brass, Glass, Perpetual Motion, 15 Jewel, Swiss, 1900s, 8¾ x 7 In.
$688

Eldred's

Clock, New Haven, Alarm, Double Bell, Nickel, Round, Goldtone, Egg & Dart Rim, c.1890, 8 In.
$128

Rachel Davis Fine Arts

Cottone Auctions

Clock, Jerome, Regulator, Tole, Papier-Mache, Flowers, Dog, 8-Day, c.1880, 30 x 19 In.
$244

Rachel Davis Fine Arts

Clock, Parker, Desk, Nickel, Goldtone, Suspended Dial, Chains, Leafy Crest, 3-Footed Base, c.1890, 9 In.
$205

Rachel Davis Fine Arts

TIP
Don't put an old clock that is wound near a heat or air-conditioning duct. The air will dry out the oil used in the clock. Fireplaces and wood-burning stoves can also dry the works, and the clock may not keep correct time— or could stop.

Clock, Regulator, Vienna, Walnut, Black Lacquer, Ogee Crown, Enameled Dial, 50 x 18 In.
$468

Thomaston Place Auction Galleries

Clock, Seth Thomas, Bracket, Mahogany, Glass, Arched, Sonora Chime, J.B. Van Sciver & Co., 16 x 12 In. $2,750

Wiederseim Auctions

Clock, Shelf, Deer Antlers, Wood, Bark, Westminster Chime, Big Sky Carvers, Montana, 12 x 18 In. $53

Charleston Estate Auctions

Clock, Shelf, Gilt Bronze, Broken Arch, Woman's Head, Porcelain Plaques, c.1890, 21 x 14 In. $3,267

Fontaine's Auction Gallery

TIP
Clocks should be cleaned and lubricated every five years.

Marshall Field & Co., Bronze & Glass Case, Flower Form Face, France, c.1950, 10 x 9 x 4 In.	424
Marti, S., Shelf, Boy In Boat, Praying, Gilt Metal, Scrolling Base, France, Late 1800s	115
Mourey, Philippe, Figural, Woman, Gilt Bronze, Giltwood, c.1900, 14 x 13 x 5 In.	375
Mystery, Figural, Beveled Glass, Roman Numerals, Pendulum, Robert Houdin, Paris, c.1890, 25 In.	8125
New Haven, Alarm, Double Bell, Nickel, Round, Goldtone, Egg & Dart Rim, c.1890, 8 In. *illus*	128
New Haven, Desk, Winged Putti, Standing & Seated, Dial In Cartouche, c.1900, 9¾ In.	96
New Haven, Shelf, Art Nouveau, Gilt, Cast Flowers, Enamel Dial, c.1900, 11 In.	108
New Haven, Shelf, Stick & Ball, Oak, Rounded Top, 16 x 10 x 4 In.	563
New Haven, Shelf, Wood, Black Columns, Metal Scrolls, Bowed Front, 11 x 13 x 5 In.	63
Night, Kerosene, Milk Glass Dome, Rotates, Nickel Base, Finger Loop, 30-Hour, c.1900, 6 In.	416
Parker, Alarm, Double Bell, Nickel, Goldtone, Embossed Flowers & Scrolls, c.1880, 5 In.	288
Parker, Desk, Nickel, Goldtone, Suspended Dial, Chains, Leafy Crest, 3-Footed Base, c.1890, 9 In. *illus*	205
Patek Philippe, Grand Sovereign II, Glass Dome, Skeleton, F. Hermle, 13 In.	4688
Pendulette, Heartbeat, Flower, Brass, Mother Of Pearl Petals, Travel Case, Swiss, 3 x 2 In.	125
Regency, Mahogany, Stepped Roof, Brass Fretwork, Handles, Adams, London, 1800s, 16 x 11 In.	500
Regulator, Brass Case, Roman Numerals, Pendulum, Tiffany & Co., Late 1800s, 13 x 7½ x 6 In.	594
Regulator, Ebony Case, Rectangular, Finials, Glass Door, Pendulum, 39 x 12 In.	275
Regulator, Mahogany, Arched, Turned Columns, Brass Pendulum, Roman Numerals, 33 In.	246
Regulator, Vienna, Walnut, Black Lacquer, Ogee Crown, Enameled Dial, 50 x 18 In. *illus*	468
Regulator, Vienna, Walnut, Oak, Peaked Gable, Ebonized Trim, Brass Bezel, c.1890, 69 x 19 In.	2808
Sessions, Shelf, Mahogany, Painted, Folk Art Style, Vine, Flower, Bird, 1800s, 20 x 14 In.	127
Seth Thomas, Bracket, Mahogany, Glass, Arched, Sonora Chime, J.B. Van Sciver & Co., 16 x 12 In. *illus*	2750
Seth Thomas, Shelf, Art Nouveau, Woman Leaning, Undulating Spread Base, c.1905, 9 x 5½ In.	615
Seth Thomas, Shelf, Mahogany, Pillar & Scroll, Brass Finials, 1800s, 31 x 17 x 5 In.	508
Seth Thomas, Wall, Oak, Broken Arch, Glass Door, Tin Face, Pendulum, c.1900, 42 x 15 In.	360
Seth Thomas, Wall, Octagonal, Short Drop, Painted Glass Panel, Flowers, 24 In.	74
Seth Thomas, Wall, Walnut, Round Top, Rectangular Drop, Pendulum, 1900s, 36 x 16 In.	688
Shelf, Arts & Crafts Style, Oak, Eucalyptus Tile, 1999, 15 x 12 x 4¾ In.	492
Shelf, Boudoir, Ormolu, Turquoise, Cameo Decorated, Etched Dial, Cherubs, France, 8 In.	1250
Shelf, Brass, Female Goddess, Flames, Medusa Head Urn, Enameled Sunset, Art Nouveau, 4 In.	390
Shelf, Brass, Lion Head & Urn Finial, Roman Numerals, White Marble Base, Late 1700s, 16 x 9 In.	1320
Shelf, Bronze, Porcelain Plaque, Painted, Courting Scene, 8-Day, Pendulum, France, 12 x 8 In.	400
Shelf, Corchia & De Harak, Aurora, Chrome Plated Aluminum & Steel, Acrylic, 1970, 8 In.	286
Shelf, Deer Antlers, Wood, Bark, Westminster Chime, Big Sky Carvers, Montana, 12 x 18 In. *illus*	53
Shelf, Directoire, Marble Columns, Gilt Bronze, Sun Face Drop, La Follie Jeune, 1800s, 15 x 10 In.	1125
Shelf, Empire, Ebony Finish, 4 Columns, Gilt Ormolu, Lyre Pendulum, Phoenix, 24 x 11 In.	293
Shelf, French, Brass, Enamel, Woman, Mountain Landscape, Cloisonne Urn Finial, 12 In.	480
Shelf, French, Figural, Chariot, Apollo, 2 Lions, Ormolu, Footed Base, 1800s, 12 x 12 x 4 In.	1188
Shelf, Gilt Bronze, Broken Arch, Woman's Head, Porcelain Plaques, c.1890, 21 x 14 In. *illus*	3267
Shelf, Gilt Bronze, Porcelain, Champleve Enamel, Jeweled, France, 1900s, 17 In.	6375
Shelf, Gilt Bronze, Urn Top, Floral Spray, Black Roman Numerals, 1800s, 19 x 8 In.	1188
Shelf, Gilt Metal, Blue Hardstone, Enamel, Inset Pearls, Leaf Feet, Continental, c.1900, 7 x 4 In.	750
Shelf, Gilt Metal, Urn Top, Columns, Dolphins, Paw Foot, Continental, c.1910, 20 x 11 x 4 In.	450
Shelf, Louis XV, Bronze Dore, Patinated Cherub, Satyr Heads, Ornate Footed Base, 10 In.	510
Shelf, Louis XV, Figural, Woman Lounging, Gilt Bronze, Porcelain Panels, c.1890, 16 x 20 In.	840
Shelf, Louis XVI Style, Gilt Bronze, Urn Finial, Scrolls, Leaves, Striking Bell, Mougin, c.1900, 28 In.	1375
Shelf, Louis XVI Style, Porphyry, Gilt Bronze Mount, Lapis Dial, Paillard, c.1890, 26 In.	8960
Shelf, Louis XVI, Brass, Flame Finials, Alabaster Columns, Arabic Numerals, 19 x 11½ In.	281
Shelf, Louis XVI, Gilt Bronze, Enamel Face, LeMerle-Charpentier & Cie, Paris, 1800s, 22 x 16 In. *illus*	2268
Shelf, Metal, Engraved, Dolphin, Dome Top, Open Scrollwork, France, 1700s, 11 x 4 x 4 In.	549
Shelf, Napoleon III, Brass, Urn, Dolphin Mounts, Marked, 1800s, 14 x 12 x 8 In.	313
Shelf, Neoclassical Style, Gilt Metal, 2 Putti, Lapis Lazuli Inset, Footed, 1900s, 8 In.	1000
Shelf, Neuchatel Style, Wood, Painted Flowers, 2 Lovers, Gilt, Pendulum, L. Boname, 15 x 10 In.	690
Shelf, Onyx, Black Marble Sides, Brass Movement, Pendulum, Continental, c.1885, 15 x 12 x 6 In.	108
Shelf, Porcelain, Cobalt Blue, Gilt, Glass, Arabic Numerals, Limoges, 17¼ In.	531
Shelf, Portico, Hour Lavigne, Bronze, White Columns, Ball Feet, 10 In.	125
Shelf, Portico, Louis XVI, Gilt Bronze, Marble, Urns, Dial Signed, Thiery, Paris, c.1810, 23 x 12 In.	800
Shelf, Victorian, Rosewood, Architectural Case, Metal Dial, Pendulum, 1800s, 18¾ x 12 In.	390
Shelf, Wood, Arched, Inlaid Leaves, Glass Door, Flowers, Roman Numerals, Stepped Base, 15 x 21 In.	86
Swinging Arm, Figural, Boy, Bronze, White Metal, Holding Gilt Clock Frame, 18 x 8 In. *illus*	330

Clock, Shelf, Louis XVI, Gilt Bronze, Enamel Face, LeMerle-Charpentier & Cie, Paris, 1800s, 22 x 16 In.
$2,268

Freeman's

TIP

A damaged porcelain clockface is difficult to repair. It will lower the price of a clock by 20 to 30 percent.

Clock, Swinging Arm, Figural, Boy, Bronze, White Metal, Holding Gilt Clock Frame, 18 x 8 In.
$330

Kaminski Auctions

Clock, Tall Case, Elliott, Mahogany, Chimes, R.J. Horner Case, London, 1900s, 100 x 27 In.
$1,440

Michaan's Auctions

Clock, Tall Case, Nathaniel Seddon, George I, Figured Walnut, Gilt, c.1720, 85 x 20 In.
$7,500

Hindman

Clock, Terry, Eli & Samuel, Shelf, Mahogany, Eglomise Panel, Mt. Vernon, c.1825, 29 x 16 In.
$585

Thomaston Place Auction Galleries

Clock, Tiffany & Co., Alarm, Easel Back, 8-Day, 15 Jewel, Swiss Works, Concord Watch Co., 3 x 3 In.
$150

Woody Auction

Clock, Tiffany & Co., Carriage, Brass, Glass, Porcelain Dial, Quarter Repeater, 1800s, 7 x 5 x 3 In.
$2,318

Rafael Osona Nantucket Auctions

Clock, Vincenti, Shelf, Figural, Scholar, Gilt Bronze, Glass Dome, France, 1800s, 17 x 13 In.
$556

Thomaston Place Auction Galleries

Clock, Wall, Chrome, Thank You, Call Again, Neon, Black Numbers, Art Deco Style, c.1940, 15½ In.
$469

New Haven Auctions

Clock, Wall, Dutch Mannerist, Wood, Gilt Metal, Crown, Badge Reads Salve, 39 x 17½ In.
$570

Michaan's Auctions

Tall Case Style, Wood, Carved, Steeple, Western Clock Mfg. Co., Early 1900s, 25 x 8 x 5¼ In.	188
Tall Case, Benj. Shuckforth, Oak, Molded Cornice, Inlaid, Brass Dial, c.1750, 76 x 17 In.	480
Tall Case, Breguet, Mahogany, Arched, Brass Regulator, Roman Numeral, Month Gong, 1931, 68 In.	40625
Tall Case, Chippendale, Mahogany, Brass Finials, Iron Dial, 1700s, 87 x 21 In.	1521
Tall Case, Comtoise, Painted Grapes, Brass & Enamel Dial, France, 1800s, 93 x 21 In.	406
Tall Case, D.J. Wendling, Cherry, Inlaid, Eagle, Stars, Older Dial, Dutch Theme, 1998, 92 x 20 In.	4200
Tall Case, Edward Gibson, Mahogany, Brass Filigree, Date Window, London, c.1840, 86 x 20 In.	3355
Tall Case, Elliott, Mahogany, Chimes, R.J. Horner Case, London, 1900s, 100 x 27 In....*illus*	1440
Tall Case, Empire, Mahogany, 9-Tube, Pendulum, 90 x 24 x 17 In.	920
Tall Case, Federal, Cherry, White Pine, Flowers, Second & Date Dials, Mass., c.1800, 91 x 21 In.	2125
Tall Case, Federal, Mahogany, Arched Bonnet, Brass Fretwork, Eagle, Iron Dial, School, 90 x 21 In.	936
Tall Case, Gustav Becker, Oak, Flat Overhanging Top, Paneled, Arts & Crafts, c.1900, 80 x 21 In.	625
Tall Case, J.E. Caldwell & Co., Mahogany, Brass Filigree Face, Claw Feet, 99 x 23 In.	660
Tall Case, Levi Hutchins, Cherry, Birch, Inlaid, Fretwork, Bird, Iron Dial, N.H., c.1800, 91 In.	4065
Tall Case, Mahogany, Centennial, Painted Dial, Rocking Ship, Pendulum, Key, c.1880, 59 x 12 In.	610
Tall Case, Mahogany, Inlaid, Iron Dial, Bracket Feet, Signed, G. Savage, Huddersfield, 90 In.	375
Tall Case, Mahogany, Steeple, Arched Glass Door, Brass Dial, 2 Chimes, Bun Feet, 83 x 28 In.	570
Tall Case, Nathaniel Seddon, George I, Figured Walnut, Gilt, c.1720, 85 x 20 In.............*illus*	7500
Tall Case, Oak, Arched Bonnet & Door, Brass Dial, Ball Feet, Continental, 1900s, 86 x 22 In.	125
Tall Case, Oak, Carved, Aesop's Fables, Urn Finials, England, 1800s, 88 x 18 In.	875
Tall Case, Paul Rogers & Son, Red Walnut, Tombstone Door, Iron Dial, Flowers, c.1800, 89 In.	1521
Tall Case, Pine, Painted, Folk Art Style, Multicolor, Green Face, 2 Shelves, 2 Drawers, 80 x 16 In.	1170
Tall Case, Thomas Hally, George III, Japanned, Chinoiserie, London, c.1790, 97 x 18 x 9 In.	1638
Tall Case, Thomas Pace, Mahogany, Pagoda Top, Rocking Ship, Columns, 91 In.	1875
Tall Case, Thos. Pearsall, Chippendale, Mahogany, Chime, Brass Face, N.Y., c.1760, 94 x 19 In.	5040
Tall Case, Wood, Heavily Carved, Brass Trim, Weights, Pendulum, Continental, 1800s, 79 x 21 In.	640
Terry, Eli & Samuel, Shelf, Mahogany, Eglomise Panel, Mt. Vernon, c.1825, 29 x 16 In...*illus*	585
Terry, Eli Jr., Shelf, Tiger Maple, Painted Glass Panel, Georgian House, 1900s, 33 x 17 In.	563

Tiffany clocks that are part of desk sets made by Louis Comfort Tiffany are listed in the Tiffany category. Clocks sold by the store Tiffany & Co. are listed here.

Tiffany & Co., Alarm, Easel Back, 8-Day, 15 Jewel, Swiss Works, Concord Watch Co., 3 x 3 In. *illus*	150
Tiffany & Co., Boudoir, Sterling Silver, Guilloche Enamel, Chalcedony Base, 8-Day, 1900s, 5½ In.	550
Tiffany & Co., Carriage, Brass, Glass, Porcelain Dial, Quarter Repeater, 1800s, 7 x 5 x 3 In.*illus*	2318
Tiffany & Co., Desk, Brushed Metal, Round, Embossed Roman Numerals, Slant Base, Swiss, 4 In.	59
Tiffany & Co., Desk, Sterling Silver, Blue Enamel, Hexagonal Dial, 1900s, 3½ In.	613
Tiffany & Co., Shelf, 2 Classical Women, Ormolu, Gray Marble, Late 1800s, 24 In.	780
Tiffany & Co., Shelf, Balloon Shape, Inlaid Brass Vines, Painted Dial, Rose Swags, France, 11 In.	375
Tiffany & Co., Wall, Brass, Acanthus Leaf, Filigree Hands, Roman Numerals, France, c.1900, 21 In.	600
Timby, T.R., Solar, Mahogany, Blue, Inset Joslin Terrestrial Globe, L.E. Whiting, c.1865, 26 In.	4880
Train Station, Neoclassical, Bronze, Column, 4 Windows, Warren Telechron Co., c.1930, 51 x 19 In.	5000
Travel, Art Deco, Enamel, Painted Venetian Scene, Dragonfly Corners, c.1920s, 4 x 4 In.	123
Travel, Movado, Ermeto, Sliding Case, Leather, Moon Phase, 3 Calendars, 1930s, 2 In.	875
Vincenti, Shelf, Figural, Scholar, Gilt Bronze, Glass Dome, France, 1800s, 17 x 13 In...*illus*	556
Wall, Bank, Oak, Molded Cornice, Bull's Eye, 30-Day, Brass Pendulum, c.1910, 56 x 20 In.	702
Wall, Chrome, Thank You, Call Again, Neon, Black Numbers, Art Deco Style, c.1940, 15½ In. *illus*	469
Wall, Dutch Mannerist, Wood, Gilt Metal, Crown, Badge Reads Salve, 39 x 17½ In......*illus*	570
Wall, Eastlake, Walnut, Carved Face, Pilasters & Finials, Brass Pendulum, 41 x 14 In.	63
Wall, Elliott, J.J., Bracket, Baroque Style, Oak, 3-Fusee, 1800s, 55 x 26 x 16 In.	5748
Wall, Empire Style, Figural, 2 Gilt Winged Females, Oak Leaves, Dark Wood, 1900s, 33 In.	425
Wall, Japy Freres, Majolica, 2 Cherubs, Lion's Mask, Scrolls, 8-Day, 1800s, 17 x 12 In.	440
Wall, Japy Freres, Sunburst, Giltwood, Hinged Brass & Convex Glass Bezel, 8-Day, 16 In.	702
Wall, Pine, 8-Day, Half Columns, Black, Gilt, Mirror, Warranted By Bucklin T, N.H., 30 In.	1125
Wall, Wood, Turned Columns, Urns, Horse Finial, Enamel & Brass Dial, Pendulum, 42 x 16 In.	313
Waltham, Regulator, Precision, Mahogany, 3-Tube Mercury Pendulum, 1913, 68 x 18 In.	7200
Waterbury, Shelf, Sartoris, Gilt, Porcelain Panel & Urn, Splayed Legs, 14 In. ....*illus*	400
Willard, Simon, Figural, Lighthouse, Mahogany, Glass, Brass, Bone Feet, 1900s, 31 In.	9840
Zenith, Desk, Green Marble, Removable Orb, Seconds Dial, 8-Day, c.1910, 6 x 8 In.	531

CLOISONNE

Cloisonne enamel was developed during the tenth century. A glass enamel was applied between small ribbons of metal on a metal base. Most cloisonne is Chinese or Japanese. Pieces marked *China* were made after 1900.

Bowl, Bronze, Metal, Flower Head, Leaf, Dragon, Clouds, Wood Stand, 1700s, 5 In.......*illus*	256
Bowl, Footed, Phoenix Birds, Dragons, Flower Band, Flared Rim, Chinese, 1800s, 4 1/4 x 10 1/4 In. .	410
Bowl, Gilt, Metal, Hardstone, Mounted, Multicolor, Chinese, 6 1/2 x 16 1/2 In.	688
Bowl, Lotus Shape, Flowers, Scaled Banding, Chinese, 1800s, 4 1/2 In.	344
Box, Hinged Lid, Scene Of Flowers, Cobalt Blue Ground, Bracket Feet, Japan, 2 x 6 x 3 In. ...	293
Box, Lid, Dragon, Flower, Gilt, Metal, Brass, Japan, 6 1/2 x 2 1/2 x 7 1/4 In......................	108
Box, Lift Lid, Multicolor Blossoms, Oval, Copper, 1800s, 3 x 5 In.	122
Censer, Bull Shape, Standing, Head Turned, Leafy Scroll, Brown, Chinese, 1900s, 7 1/2 x 8 In., Pair....	1000
Censer, Horse, Green Ground, Multicolor Accent, Hollow Interior, 1911, 5 1/2 In., Pair...*illus*	431
Censer, Horse, Multicolor Accent, Saddle, Gilt Bronze, Dark Red Ground, 10 3/4 In., Pair...........	896
Censer, Partridge Shape, Lid, Gilt, White Ground, Mirrored, Chinese, 1700s, 5 3/4 In., Pair ..	1063
Cigarette Case, Hinged Lid, Ivan Petrovich Khlebnikov, Late 1800s, 44 x 2 x 7/8 In. ...... *illus*	1521
Egg, Cobalt Blue Ground, Flowers, Bird, Stand, Chinese, 15 1/2 In.	47
Figure, Bronze, Buddha, Seated, Double Lotus Base, Chinese, 10 7/8 In...............................	480
Figure, Seated, Multicolor, Flower Robe, Gilt Stepped Base, 17 1/2 x 12 1/4 x 8 In. .... *illus*	303
Ginger Jar, Blue Flowers, Turquoise Interior, Chinese, 6 x 6 x 10 In.	59
Ginger Jar, Foo Dog Finial, Flowers, Blue Interior, Wood Base, 9 1/2 x 7 1/2 In., Pair ...... *illus*	540
Ginger Jar, Lid, Black Ground, Prunus & Bat Design, Chinese, 9 1/2 In.	121
Goat, Standing, Gilt Horns, Ears & Hooves, Black Ground, 23 x 26 In., Pair........................	732
Jar, Lid, Dark Green Ground, Foo Dog, Brocade Roundels, Mythical Felines, 25 In., Pair......	960
Jar, Lid, Oval, Flat Top, Champleve Ground, Red Roundels, Flowers, Chinese, 1900s, 6 3/8 In.........	113
Jar, Lid, Squared, Phoenix, Moth Cartouches, Dark Blue Ground, Japan, 1900s, 11 3/4 In.*illus*	896
Jarlet, Guan, Gold, Brown, Black, Double Crackle, 2 3/4 In...	1230
Kovsh, Silver Gilt, Cyrillic, Handle, Segmented Body, Russia, 1908, 4 3/4 x 9 1/2 In.	20000
Panel, Multicolor, Chickens, Flowers, Iron, Continental, Early 1900s, 31 x 28 In.......... *illus*	2925
Plate, Bird, Flowers, Blue, Green, Pink, Yellow, White, Japan, 11 7/8 In.	63
Sculpture, Ram, Standing, Stylized Animals, Multicolor, Chinese, Late 1800s, 12 x 12 x 5 In.... *illus*	300
Teapot, Blue Ground, Abstract, Dragons, High Handle, Tripod Base, Chinese, Late 1800s, 9 1/2 In.	210
Vase, Blue Chrysanthemums, Flowers, Butterflies, Chinese, Early 1900s, 15 x 9 In., Pair...*illus*	550
Vase, Blue Ground, Gilt, Flared Rim, Flowers, Birds, Chinese, c.1900, 8 In.	99
Vase, Champleve, Waisted Neck, Lotus Scroll, Splayed Foot, Chinese, Late 1900s, 20 In........	375
Vase, Dark Ground, Birds Flying, Flowers, Wood Stand, Chinese, c.1950, 20 1/2 In..................	180
Vase, Flowers, Multicolor, Chinese, 1900s, 27 x 14 1/2 In.	250
Vase, Garlic Head Shape, Multicolor, Scrolled, Lotus, Gilt Base, Chinese, 8 In., Pair	151
Vase, Gilt Bronze, Quatrefoil, 2 Handles, Wood Stand, Chien Lung, 1700s, 6 1/2 In. .... *illus*	4800
Vase, Hexagonal, Flowers, Flared Rim, Porcelain, Chinese, 19 In....................................	671
Vase, Multicolor, Flowers, Leaves, Domed Base, Chinese, c.1980, 10 In................................	60
Vase, Pink Flower, Light Blue Ground, Silver Metal Rim & Base, 1800s, 7 In., Pair	303
Vase, Urn Shape, Floral Sprays, Elephant Handle, 38 x 16 In.	600
Water Pipe, Paktong, Opium, Flowers, Stylized Character, Chinese, 1900s, 14 3/4 x 3 x 1 3/8 In. ..	375

CLOTHING

Clothing of all types is listed in this category. Dresses, hats, shoes, underwear, and more are found here. Other textiles are to be found in the Coverlet, Movie, Quilt, Textile, and World War I and II categories.

Christian Dior	Norman Norell	Arnold Scaasi
Christian Dior 1947–present	Norman Norell 1958–1972	Arnold Scaasi 1956–2015

Belt, Black Leather, Silver Buckle, Horseshoe Shape, Elsa Peretti, Tiffany & Co., 48 In. 1063

Clock, Waterbury, Shelf, Sartoris, Gilt, Porcelain Panel & Urn, Splayed Legs, 14 In. $400

Apple Tree Auction Center

Cloisonne, Bowl, Bronze, Metal, Flower Head, Leaf, Dragon, Clouds, Wood Stand, 1700s, 5 In. $256

Brunk Auctions

Cloisonne, Censer, Horse, Green Ground, Multicolor Accent, Hollow Interior, 1911, 5 1/2 In., Pair $431

Brunk Auctions

Cloisonne, Cigarette Case, Hinged Lid, Ivan Petrovich Khlebnikov, Late 1800s, 44 x 2 x ⅞ In.
$1,521

Thomaston Place Auction Galleries

Cloisonne, Figure, Seated, Multicolor, Flower Robe, Gilt Stepped Base, 17½ x 12¼ x 8 In.
$303

Ahlers & Ogletree Auction Gallery

Cloisonne, Ginger Jar, Foo Dog Finial, Flowers, Blue Interior, Wood Base, 9½ x 7½ In., Pair
$540

Abington Auction Gallery

Cloisonne, Jar, Lid, Squared, Phoenix, Moth Cartouches, Dark Blue Ground, Japan, 1900s, 11¾ In.
$896

Neal Auction Company

Cloisonne, Panel, Multicolor, Chickens, Flowers, Iron, Continental, Early 1900s, 31 x 28 In.
$2,925

Thomaston Place Auction Galleries

Cloisonne, Sculpture, Ram, Standing, Stylized Animals, Multicolor, Chinese, Late 1800s, 12 x 12 x 5 In.
$300

Bruneau & Co. Auctioneers

Cloisonne, Vase, Blue Chrysanthemums, Flowers, Butterflies, Chinese, Early 1900s, 15 x 9 In., Pair
$550

Bruneau & Co. Auctioneers

Cloisonne, Vase, Gilt Bronze, Quatrefoil, 2 Handles, Wood Stand, Chien Lung, 1700s, 6½ In.
$4,800

Alex Cooper Auctioneers

Clothing, Belt, Goldtone Link, Medusa, Black Enamel, Medallions, Gianni Versace, Italy, 34 In.
$688

Auctions at Showplace, NYC

Belt, Black Patent Leather, Trompe L'Oeil Chain Buckle, Stamped, Chanel, France, 1990s, 34 In.	490
Belt, Goldtone Link, Medusa, Black Enamel, Medallions, Gianni Versace, Italy, 34 In. . *illus*	688
Belt, Leather, White, Goldtone Hardware, Stamped, Loro Piana, Italy, 39 In.	63
Blazer, Denim, White, Hook Closure, Lace Details, Ralph Lauren, 27 ½ In.	31
Blouse, Poncho, Silk, Paisley, Yellow, Waist Tie, Ralph Lauren, 26 In.	63
Boots, Leather, Brown, Pebbled, Goldtone Medallion, Knight Figure, Gucci, Size 8 ½ B *illus*	281
Boots, Leather, Pull On, Lace Up, Brown, Wood Stretchers, Men's, 1800s, 17 ½ In.	188
Cap, Embroidered, 6 Linen Panels, Memorial Design, England, Late 1800s, 9 In.	750
Chaps, Western, Tooled Leather, Dirty White & Brown, Fringes, Mounted, 40 In. .... *illus*	625
Chaps, White, Black Pockets, Studded Heart, Diamond, Spade, Leather Belt, Frame, 42 x 49 In.	1664
Coat, Brown, Satin, Embroidery, Hook, Eye, Belt, Velvet, Pocket, Label, 1800, 49 In.	800
Coat, Duffle, Chocolate Brown, Silvertone Toggles, Nienhaus Sherpa, Faux Shearling, Full Length	63
Coat, Mink, Silk Lining, Monogram, Full Length, 35 x 37 In.	281
Coat, Ranch Mink, Fur, Shawl Collar, Silk Lining, Hook Closure, Full Length........................	125
Coat, Silk, Brown, Double Breasted, Notched Collar, Buttons, Chanel, France, 1990s, Size 36.......	1800
Coat, Wolf Fur, Dark Brown, Canada, Full Length..	172
Dress, 3-Layer Panels, Black, Long Sleeves, Beaded Collars, 24 x 42 x 52 In.	123
Dress, Black Silk Shirt, Short Sleeves, Tropical Motif, Belt, Valentino, Italy, Size 10...... *illus*	594
Dress, Brocade, Linen, Cotton, Satin Band, Woven, Gathered Skirt, 1890s.................... *illus*	180
Dress, Cocktail, Asymmetrical, Black, Label, Jacques Fath, Joseph Halpert, c.1957	360
Dress, Cocktail, Wool Knit, Printed, Red, James Galanos, Amelia Gray, Beverly Hills, c.1970	450
Dress, Coffee Beans, Cotton, Vinyl Belt, Valentino Clemente Ludovico Garavini, Italy, c.1968...	180
Dress, Equestrian, Silk, Blue, Boat Neck, Polo Mallet, Bridle Belt, Ralph Lauren, 34 In....*illus*	94
Dress, Evening, Black Velvet, White Silk Lining, Sleeveless, Claire Comte, Paris, c.1964	192
Dress, Evening, Satin, Black Silk, Sweetheart Cut, Mesh Net Skirting, Luis Estevez, c.1962 ..	204
Dress, Sleeveless, Burgundy, Form Fitting, Low Cowl Neck, Folded Detail, Label, Vera Wang, 63 In.	65
Dress, Tunic, Knit, Black, Gray Shawl Collar, Tie Detail, Label, Balenciaga, Paris, Size 40..	125
Dress, Victorian, 2 Piece, Lace, Silk, High Collar, Green & Cream, 1870s	318
Dress, Victorian, 2 Piece, Purple, Crocheted Bodice, Pleated Bottom & Satin Waistband, 1870s.....	413
Hat, Bycocked, Green Felt, Pointed Front, Folded Edge, 8 x 17 In.	50
Hat, Fur, Guard's Uniform, White Plume, Leather Back Scale, Chin Strap, England, c.1950, 17 In.	450
Hat, White Mohair, Black Velvet, Squared, Christian Dior, 1960s.....................................	192
Headdress, Horsehair Cap, Wire Frames, Black Silk, Manchu, Woman's, Late 1800s, 19 In. *illus*	1200
Helmet, Oxfordshire Light Infantry, Blue Cloth, Nickel Spike, England, Late 1800s, 10 ¼ In.	270
Jacket, Denim, Flower Embellished, Rosebuds, Valentino, 24 ½ In.	125
Jacket, Hood, Beige Fur, Gray Leather, Car Length .... *illus*	148
Jacket, Metal Thread, Silk, Embroidered, Brown, Blue, Chinese, 43 x 58 In...........................	813
Jacket, Mink, Brown, Embroidery Lining, Lunaraine, 32 In.	125
Kimono, Dragon, Brocade Silk, Multicolor, Asian, 52 ½ x 84 In. .... *illus*	10000
Raincoat, Coir, Farmer's Garment, Woven Coconut, Palm Fiber, Traditional, Chinese, 47 x 41 In.....	240
Robe, Ceremonial, Silk, Embroidered, Black & White, Flowers, Chinese, 64 x 39 In......*illus*	1888
Robe, Floral, Dark Blue, Silk, Cream Sleeves, Chinese, 43 ½ x 47 ¾ In.	750
Robe, Qipao, Purple, Embroidered, Gilt Sphere Buttons, Informal, Manchu, Woman's, 56 ½ In.. *illus*	3900
Robe, Silk, Embroidered, Blue Field, Floral & Fauna Vignettes, Chinese, Frame, 1800s, 57 In.	1375
Robe, Silk, Embroidered, Peking Stitch, Landscape, Chinese, Mid 1900s, 41 x 21 In.	188
Robe, Silk, Multicolor Brocade Balls, Forbidden Stitch, Chinese, 1910s, 18 ½ In.	188
Robe, Silk, Pink, Multicolor, Flowers, ¾ Sleeves, 1930s, 58 In. .... *illus*	2813
Robe, Winter, Silk, Embroidered, Multicolor, Gold & Silver Metallic, Chinese, Men's, 55 ½ In.	1521
Scarf, Beloved India Pattern, Silk, Philippe Dumas, Hermes, 55 In.	1063
Scarf, Cashmere, Silk, Gucci, Repeating Logo, Blue With Gold Interlocking Gs, 72 x 28 In. .	245
Scarf, Hermes, Couvertures Et Tenues De Jour, 10 Horses, Equestrian Accents, 38 x 38 In. ..	570
Scarf, Mousseline, Silk, Brides, Swarovski, Hermes, Hugo Grygkar, Paris, 1900s, 55 x 55 In.. *illus*	320
Scarf, Silk, Champignons, Mushrooms, Olive Ground, A. Gavarni & F. De La Pierre, Hermes, 35 In....	315
Scarf, Silk, Marching Animals, Sabino Ship, Black Background, Elizabeth Mumford, 34 x 34 In.*illus*	188
Scarf, Silk, Stylized Sun, Multicolor, Hand Rolled & Stitched Edge, Vera, 1970s, 27 x 27 In..	25
Scarf, Turkey, Flower, Faune Et Flore Du Texas, Hermes, Kermit Oliver, Box, 1992, 35 x 35 In.....	781
Shako, West Point Cadet Dress, Parade, Feather Plume, 1900s, 6 x 18 In.	150
Shawl, Black, Multicolor Flowers, Embroidered, Crocheted Fringe, 1950s, 60 x 40 In.	84
Shoes, Dress, Brown, Leather, Lace, Brooks Brothers, Peal & Co., 11 ½ In.	59
Shoes, Gray Leather, Black, Strappy Sling Back, Interlocking CC Logo, Chanel, Italy, 15 ½ In. *illus*	156

Clothing, Boots, Leather, Brown, Pebbled, Goldtone Medallion, Knight Figure, Gucci, Size 8 ½ B
$281

Ripley Auctions

Clothing, Chaps, Western, Tooled Leather, Dirty White & Brown, Fringes, Mounted, 40 In.
$625

New Haven Auctions

Clothing, Dress, Black Silk Shirt, Short Sleeves, Tropical Motif, Belt, Valentino, Italy, Size 10
$594

Hindman

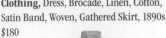

Clothing, Dress, Brocade, Linen, Cotton, Satin Band, Woven, Gathered Skirt, 1890s
$180

Michaan's Auctions

Clothing, Dress, Equestrian, Silk, Blue, Boat Neck, Polo Mallet, Bridle Belt, Ralph Lauren, 34 In.
$94

Auctions at Showplace, NYC

Clothing, Headdress, Horsehair Cap, Wire Frames, Black Silk, Manchu, Woman's, Late 1800s, 19 In.
$1,200

Michaan's Auctions

Clothing, Jacket, Hood, Beige Fur, Gray Leather, Car Length
$148

Apple Tree Auction Center

Clothing, Kimono, Dragon, Brocade Silk, Multicolor, Asian, 52 ½ x 84 In.
$10,000

New Haven Auctions

Clothing, Robe, Ceremonial, Silk, Embroidered, Black & White, Flowers, Chinese, 64 x 39 In.
$1,888

Charleston Estate Auctions

Clothing, Robe, Qipao, Purple, Embroidered, Gilt Sphere Buttons, Informal, Manchu, Woman's, 56 ½ In.
$3,900

Michaan's Auctions

Clothing, Robe, Silk, Pink, Multicolor, Flowers, ¾ Sleeves, 1930s, 58 In.
$2,813

John Moran Auctioneers

Clothing, Scarf, Mousseline, Silk, Brides, Swarovski, Hermes, Hugo Grygkar, Paris, 1900s, 55 x 55 In.
$320

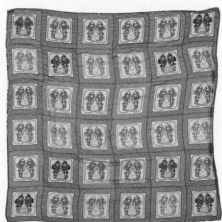

Brunk Auctions

Clothing, Scarf, Silk, Marching Animals, Sabino Ship, Black Background, Elizabeth Mumford, 34 x 34 In.
$188

Eldred's

Clothing, Shoes, Gray Leather, Black, Strappy Sling Back, Interlocking CC Logo, Chanel, Italy, 15 ½ In.
$156

Auctions at Showplace, NYC

Clothing, Shoes, Sneakers, Air Jordan VI, Rust Pink, Crimson, Aleali May, Nike, Box, 2019, Women's 11
$1,230

Morphy Auctions

Clothing, Shoes, Sneakers, Israfil, Yeezy Boost 350 V2, Knit, Gray, Light Blue, Adidas, Box, 2020, Size 10
$256

Morphy Auctions

Clothing, Shoes, Sneakers, Orange Bear, SB Dunk Low, Faux Fur, Grateful Dead, Nike, 2020
$5,412

Morphy Auctions

Clothing, Shoes, Sneakers, Tiffany, SB Dunk Low, Aqua, Black, Diamond Supply Co., Nike, 2005
$4,920

Morphy Auctions

Clothing, Wedding Dress, Nylon Net, Organza, Long Sleeves, Marc Bohan, Christian Dior, 1979
$3,750

Hindman

Cluthra, Vase, White To Pink, Bubbling, Flared Rim & Base, Steuben, 8½ x 4 In.
$520

Treadway

Coalport, Cachepot, Fruiting Holly Branches, Lion's Head Ring Handles, 1800s, 8 x 10 x 11 In., Pair
$1,830

Rafael Osona Nantucket Auctions

Shoes, Leather, Camellia Flower, Black & Tan, Slingback, Storage Bag, Chanel, Size EU 38½.....	430
Shoes, Sneakers, Air Jordan VI, Rust Pink, Crimson, Aleali May, Nike, Box, 2019, Women's 11 ... *illus*	1230
Shoes, Sneakers, Green Lobster, SB Dunk Low, Nubuck, Concepts, Nike, Box, 2018, Size 9...	3444
Shoes, Sneakers, Israfil, Yeezy Boost 350 V2, Knit, Gray, Light Blue, Adidas, Box, 2020, Size 10... *illus*	256
Shoes, Sneakers, Orange Bear, SB Dunk Low, Faux Fur, Grateful Dead, Nike, 2020...... *illus*	5412
Shoes, Sneakers, Tiffany, SB Dunk Low, Aqua, Black, Diamond Supply Co., Nike, 2005.. *illus*	4920
Skirt, Silk, Black, Lace, Embroidered, Ralph Lauren, 34 x 29½ In......................................	94
Wedding Dress, Nylon Net, Organza, Long Sleeves, Marc Bohan, Christian Dior, 1979 *illus*	3750

CLUTHRA

Cluthra glass is a two-layered glass with small bubbles and powdered glass trapped between the layers. The Steuben Glass Works of Corning, New York, first made it in 1920. Victor Durand of Kimball Glass Company in Vineland, New Jersey, made a similar glass from about 1925. Durand's pieces are listed in the Durand category. Related items are listed in the Steuben category.

Compote, White, Black Speckled Rim, Cone Shape Foot, Shape 6885, Steuben, c.1930, 5 x 8 In.	390
Vase, 3 Tiers, Pink To Orange, Ruby Overlay, Godfrey Pattern, Steuben, c.1927, 14 x 7 In.	3660
Vase, Black To White, Flared Neck, Shoulders, Shape 6883, Steuben, c.1927, 8 x 6¼ In........	512
Vase, Double, Pink To White, Clear Oval Base, Shape 6874, Acid Mark, Steuben, 10¼ In.	438
Vase, Red, Round Shoulders, Flared Neck, Tapered Base, Shape 8494, Steuben, 13 x 9 In. ...	4575
Vase, White To Pink, Bubbling, Flared Rim & Base, Steuben, 8½ x 4 In. .... *illus*	520
Vase, White, Oval, Flared Rim, Shoulders, Marked, Durand, c.1925, 6½ x 5½ In.	60

COALBROOKDALE

Coalbrookdale was made by the Coalport porcelain factory of England during the Victorian period. Pieces are decorated with floral encrustations.

Flower Pot, Conforming Handles, Blue & Gilt Leaves, Country Scene, 4⅜ x 9¾ In., Pair ...	390
Urn, Lid, 3 Cherubs, Gilt, Pink, Cylindrical, Pedestal Foot, 1800s, 12 In...............................	375

COALPORT

Coalport ware was made by the Coalport Porcelain Works of England beginning about 1795. Early pieces were unmarked. About 1810–1825 the pieces were marked with the name *Coalport* in various forms. Later pieces also had the name *John Rose* in the mark. The crown mark was used with variations beginning in 1881. The date 1750 is printed in some marks, but it is not the date the factory started. Coalport was bought by Wedgwood in 1967. Coalport porcelain is no longer being produced. Some pieces are listed in this book under Indian Tree.

Coalport Porcelain Manufactory 1820	 Coalport Porcelain Manufactory c.1881	Coalport Porcelain Manufactory 1960

Cachepot, Fruiting Holly Branches, Lion's Head Ring Handles, 1800s, 8 x 10 x 11 In., Pair ... *illus*	1830
Cup & Saucer, Bouillon, 2 Handles, Gilt, Scalloped Edge, Tillman Collamore, 16 Piece	400
Cup & Saucer, Demitasse, Hazelton, Blue, Gold Grapes, Bone China, 2 x 4½ In., 10 Piece .	63
Cup & Saucer, Demitasse, Jeweled, Cobalt Blue, Enamel, Gilt, Late 1800s, 3½ In.	438
Figurine, Katheryn Howard, Gilt Accents, Robert Worthington, 1900s, 8¼ In.	175
Figurine, Rosalinda, Blond Woman, 18th Century Dress, Brown & Tan, Bone China, 6¼ In. .	19
Loving Cup, 2 Handles, Pink Ground, Cupid & Psyche, Gilt, Pedestal Base, c.1900, 11 In.....	1530
Plate, Panel Green, Multicolor Flowers, Gilt Trim, Early 1900s, 9¾ In., 6 Piece	875
Urn, Lake View, Bridge, Painted, Gilt, Ram's Head Handles, 16½ In. .... *illus*	500

COBALT BLUE

Cobalt blue glass was made using oxide of cobalt. The characteristic bright dark blue identifies it for the collector. Most cobalt glass found today was made after the Civil War. There was renewed interest in the dark blue glass in the late 1930s and glass dinnerware was made.

Biscuit Jar, Silver Plate Lid & Bail, White Enamel Flowers, Gold Stencil, 8 In.	96
Candy Dish, Boat Shape, Silver Wirework Body, Grapes, Side Handles, Footed, 8 In.	166
Creamer, Beehive, Clear Lower Body, Handle, Footed, New England Glass Co., c.1840, 6 In.	938
Cuspidor, Woman's, Bulbous, Pinched Neck, Flared Rolled Lip, C Handle, 1865-85, 4 In.	70
Garniture, Gilt Greek Key & Leaves, Urn & 2 Vases, France, Early 1900s, 14 3/8 In. Urn	281
Goblet, Sandwich Style, Clear Stem & Foot, Faceted Knop, 6 3/4 In., 6 Piece	250
Jar, Lid, Baluster Shape, Pedestal Base, Round Foot, 16 In.	128
Urn, Lid, French Style, Gilt Mounts, Scrolled Handles, Leafy Foot, Square Base, 20 In., Pair	369
Vase, Gilt Chinoiserie Scene, Round Foot, Continental, 20th Century, 10 In., Pair	125
Vase, Wood Lid & Base, Openwork Scrolls & Flowers, Chinese, c.1800, 15 1/4 In.	406

COCA-COLA

Coca-Cola was first served in 1886 in Atlanta, Georgia. It was advertised through signs, newspaper ads, coupons, bottles, trays, calendars, and even lamps and clocks. Collectors want anything with the word *Coca-Cola,* including a few rare products, like gum wrappers and cigar bands. The famous trademark was patented in 1893, the *Coke* mark in 1945. Many modern items and reproductions are being made.

Calendar, 1925, Flapper Girl, February Pad, Tan Mat, Wood Frame, 29 x 15 In. .... *illus*	468
Cooler, Lift Top, Cap Catcher, Carrying Case, Red & White, Salesman's Sample, 10 x 12 x 7 In. ..... *illus*	6150
Cooler, Metal, Red Paint, White Lettering, Westinghouse, c.1950, 36 1/2 In.	359
Cooler, Picnic, Embossed Panels, Handle Latches, Sandwich Tray, 19 x 20 In.	554
Dispenser, Soda Fountain, Richardson Root Beer, 2 Spouts, Oak Barrel, 27 x 16 In.	185
Display, Window Sign, Coca-Cola Club Meets Here, 3-D, Cardboard, 20 1/2 x 12 x 2 1/2 In. .. *illus*	900
Rack Stand, Enjoy Coca-Cola At Home, Bottle, 3 Tiers, Painted, Tin, 15 1/2 x 15 1/2 x 51 3/4 In.	677
Sign, Bottle Shape, Die Cut, Painted, Metal, 1950s, 109 x 31 1/2 In. .... *illus*	3600
Sign, Coca-Cola, White Script Letters, Red Border, Neon, Wall Mount, 10 1/2 x 23 1/4 In.	84
Sign, Drink Coca-Cola In Bottles, Cap, Metal, c.1950, 16 In.	418
Sign, Ice Cold, Red, White Letters, Bottle, Wall Flange, 17 x 22 In.	1560
Sign, Refreshing New Feeling, Fishtail Logo, Bottle, Rhyne & Son, Tin, Embossed, 53 x 17 In.	215
Sign, Window Display, Cardboard, Die Cut, Elizabeth Thorpe, Wide Hat, 1933, 31 x 31 In. ...... *illus*	1461
Thermometer, Coke, 5 Cents, Bottle, Yellow Text, Green, 38 1/2 x 8 1/4 In. .... *illus*	6600
Tip Tray, Exhibition Girl, Blue Dress, Tin, Oval, 1904, 4 1/2 x 6 In.	420
Trolley Sign, Tired?, Coca-Cola Relieves Fatigue, Wood Frame, 1907, 15 1/2 x 24 7/8 In...*illus*	420

COFFEE MILL

Coffee mills are also called coffee grinders, although there is a difference in the way each grinds the coffee. Large floor-standing or counter-model coffee mills were used in the nineteenth-century country store. Small home mills were first made about 1894. They lost favor by the 1930s. The renewed interest in fresh-ground coffee has produced many modern electric mills, hand mills, and grinders. Reproductions of the old styles are being made.

Arcade, Wood Handle, Crank, Orange Paint	29
Bell, Red-Orange, Black, Wall Mount, Crank Handle, Tin Cup	330
Elgin National, 2 Side Wheels, Red Paint, Cast Iron, C.H. Woodruff & Co., 28 x 23 x 63 In.....*illus*	575
Enterprise Mfg. Co., Iron, Eagle Finial, Red Paint, Wood Base, Late 1800s, 23 x 18 x 17 In....... *illus*	787
Enterprise No. 7, Cast Iron, Eagle Finial, Wood Base, Philadelphia, c.1873, 24 x 17 x 17 In....... *illus*	625
Enterprise, 2 Wheels, Painted, Cast Iron, Wood Handle & Base, Pay, 1800s, 12 x 11 x 9 In..	281
Enterprise, Countertop, Rust Red Paint, Cast Iron, Black Shade, Mounted As Lamp, c.1880, 27 In.	270
Enterprise, Red Paint, Standard Shape, Cast Iron, 1900s, 12 1/2 In.............................. *illus*	84
Landers, Frary & Clark, 2 Wheels, Wood Handle, Black Ground, Wood Base, 12 x 10 x 11 In... *illus*	704

Susanin's Auctioneers & Appraisers

Coca-Cola, Calendar, 1925, Flapper Girl, February Pad, Tan Mat, Wood Frame, 29 x 15 In.
$468

Thomaston Place Auction Galleries

Coca-Cola, Cooler, Lift Top, Cap Catcher, Carrying Case, Red & White, Salesman's Sample, 10 x 12 x 7 In.
$6,150

Morphy Auctions

C

Coca-Cola, Display, Window Sign, Coca-Cola Club Meets Here, 3-D, Cardboard, 20 ½ x 12 x 2 ½ In.
$900

Coca-Cola, Sign, Window Display, Cardboard, Die Cut, Elizabeth Thorpe, Wide Hat, 1933, 31 x 31 In.
$1,461

Coffee Mill, Elgin National, 2 Side Wheels, Red Paint, Cast Iron, C.H. Woodruff & Co., 28 x 23 x 63 In.
$575

White's Auctions

Coca-Cola, Thermometer, Coke, 5 Cents, Bottle, Yellow Text, Green, 38 ½ x 8 ¼ In.
$6,600

Morphy Auctions

Coca-Cola, Sign, Bottle Shape, Die Cut, Painted, Metal, 1950s, 109 x 31 ½ In.
$3,600

Donley Auctions

Coca-Cola Slogans
Date original Coca-Cola items from slogans used in the advertising campaigns: *Drink Coca-Cola* (1886), *Deliciously Refreshing* (1904), *The Pause That Refreshes* (1929), *It's the Real Thing* (1942), *Things Go Better with Coke* (1954), *Coke Is It* (1982), and *Coca-Cola. Enjoy* (2000).

Morphy Auctions

Morphy Auctions

Coca-Cola, Trolley Sign, Tired?, Coca-Cola Relieves Fatigue, Wood Frame, 1907, 15 ½ x 24 ⅞ In.
$420

TIP
Most Coca-Cola trays had green or brown borders in the 1920s, red borders in the 1930s.

Morphy Auctions

Tax Donations

If you plan to give your collection to a museum and get a tax deduction, you must find the proper museum. Your gift must fit into the museum's collection and be displayed most of the time. Museums want pieces that fill gaps in their collections and are given without too many restrictions. But you might want to set rules for any future sale of the items. Perhaps ask that the money from a sale be used to purchase another item for the same collection.

Coffee Mill, Enterprise Mfg. Co., Iron, Eagle Finial, Red Paint, Wood Base, Late 1800s, 23 x 18 x 17 In.
$787

Fontaine's Auction Gallery

Coffee Mill, Enterprise No. 7, Cast Iron, Eagle Finial, Wood Base, Philadelphia, c.1873, 24 x 17 x 17 In.
$625

Fontaine's Auction Gallery

Coffee Mill, Enterprise, Red Paint, Standard Shape, Cast Iron, 1900s, 12 ½ In.
$84

Selkirk Auctioneers & Appraisers

Coffee Mill, Landers, Frary & Clark, 2 Wheels, Wood Handle, Black Ground, Wood Base, 12 x 10 x 11 In.
$704

Morphy Auctions

Coffee Mill, Walnut & Yellow Pine, Dovetailed Case, Turned Wood Knob, Virginia, c.1815, 9 ¼ x 8 x 8 In.
$329

Jeffrey S. Evans & Associates

Coin-Operated, Arcade, Ms. Pac-Man, Glass Top, Wood Case, Midway-Bally Co., 29 x 22 In.
$1,342

Neal Auction Company

Coin-Operated, Gumball, Baker Boy, Metal, Name Plate, Manikin Vendor Co., Portland, Ore., c.1920-30
$2,500

Hindman

Coin-Operated, Gumball, Rectangular, Vertical, Vendor, Wood, Metal, Glass, Key
$390

Chupp Auctions & Real Estate, LLC

Coin-Operated, Piano, Leaded Glass Front, Mandolin Rail, Oak, Electra Piano Co., 1920, 56 x 63 x 29 In.
$1,725

Donley Auctions

Coin-Operated, Slot, 1-Arm Bandit, 25 Cent, Wood, Painted, Metal, Mills Novelty Co., Early 1900s, 76 In.
$3,025

Fontaine's Auction Gallery

Coin-Operated, Slot, Watling, 5 Cent, Twin Jackpot, Wood Side & Base, Early 1900s, 20 x 15 x 15 In.
$605

Fontaine's Auction Gallery

Landers, Frary & Clark, Red Paint, Wood Handle & Base, Cast Iron, Conn., 1800s, 14 x 12 x 10 In....	250
National Specialty, 2 Wheels, Grinder, Cast Iron, Wood Handle & Base, Pay, 1800s, 12 x 10 x 8 In...	1063
National, No. 40, 2 Wheels, Grinder, Eagle Finial, Red Paint, 31 x 17 x 19 In.	313
Regal, Black Paint, Mounted, Crank, Cast Iron, 17 x 5 x 6 In..	29
Walnut & Yellow Pine, Dovetailed Case, Turned Wood Knob, Virginia, c.1815, 9¼ x 8 x 8 In. .. *illus*	329

COIN-OPERATED MACHINE

Coin-operated machines of all types are collected. The vending machine is an ancient invention dating back to 200 BC, when holy water was dispensed from a coin-operated vase. Smokers in seventeenth-century England could buy tobacco from a coin-operated box. It was not until after the Civil War that the technology made modern coin-operated games and vending machines plentiful. Slot machines, arcade games, and dispensers are all collected.

Arcade, Chicago, 2 Joysticks, Blue & Black, Atari Games, c.2004, 67 x 33 x 25 In.	660
Arcade, Ms. Pac-Man, Glass Top, Wood Case, Midway-Bally Co., 29 x 22 In................. *illus*	1342
Arcade, Pistol Shot Game, Wood Case, Cast Aluminum Marquee, 1930, 18 x 22 x 8 In.	1180
Arcade, Space Invaders Part II, Cocktail Table, Midway Deluxe, Bally Co., 29 x 22 x 32 In...	295
Arcade, Time Cross, Digital Screen, With Tokens, Yamasa, Japan, Late 1900s, 32 x 18½ x 15 In.	180
Cabinet, Slot, Liberty, 3-Reel, Countertop, Groetchen Mfg., Chicago, c.1939, 10 x 9 x 10 In..	230
Dartboard, English Mark Darts, Multicolor, 80 In.	136
Gumball, Baker Boy, Metal, Name Plate, Manikin Vendor Co., Portland, Ore., c.1920-30..... *illus*	2500
Gumball, Rectangular, Vertical, Vendor, Wood, Metal, Glass, Key.............................. *illus*	390
Gumball, Spring Loaded Marquee, Glass Globe, Pedestal Base, Ford	104
Music Box, Cylinder, Tiger Oak Case, Brass T Bar Handle, 17 x 25 x 13 In.	1416
Music Box, Regina, Oak, Metal Plate, 52 Discs, Wood Case, c.1900, 10 x 21 x 21 In..............	2500
Peanut, Gumball, Columbus Model A, Cast Iron, Red Paint, 1 Cent, Pull Lever, Keys, 1920s, 5 In.	385
Piano, Leaded Glass Front, Mandolin Rail, Oak, Electra Piano Co., 1920, 56 x 63 x 29 In. ..... *illus*	1725
Pinball, 25 Cent, High Speed, Top Light, c.1985, 79 x 53 x 30 In....................................	2242
Pinball, Poplar Board, Multicolor, White Ground, Red Pinstripes, c.1900, 28 x 12 x 2 In.	125
Pinball, William Pitch & Bat, Baseball, Green, Glass, 4 Legs, c.1966, 70 x 25 x 66 In............	900
Slot, 1 Cent, Silver Moon Club, Wood Base, 1941, 27 x 15 x 15 In....................................	1500
Slot, 1-Arm Bandit, 25 Cent, Wood, Painted, Metal, Mills Novelty Co., Early 1900s, 76 In........ *illus*	3025
Slot, Bally, Western Belle, 25 Cent, Oak, Reverse Painted Glass, Footed, 1900s, 53 x 21 x 20 In.	1815
Slot, Mills, Castle Front, 5 Cent, Blue Paint, Back Door, Decal, Wood Base	1495
Slot, Mills, Ten Cent, Orange Case, Fruit, Bars, Devil On Reels, Wood Base, 26 x 15 x 16 In..	1243
Slot, Watling, 5 Cent, Twin Jackpot, Wood Side & Base, Early 1900s, 20 x 15 x 15 In..... *illus*	605
Trade Stimulator, 20th Century Novelty Co., Copper Spiral, 5 Cents, c.1903, 17 x 10½ In..	2160
Trade Stimulator, Roulette, Aluminum Case, Pebbled Ground, Midget, Dome Glass, 9 x 10 x 8 In.	1416
Train Ride, Santa Fe, Train On Track, Southland Engineering, 40 x 82 In.	1920
Vending, Matchbook, 1 Cent, McKinley Home For Boys, Countertop, 1930, 8 x 5 x 16 In.*illus*	345
Vending, Stamp, 10 Cents, 5 Cents, Metal, Blue, Enamel, Porcelain............................ *illus*	240
Weight & Fortune, Chicago Penny, Watling Scale Co., 49 In..	308

COLLECTOR PLATE

Collector plates are modern plates produced in limited editions. Some may be found listed under the factory name, like Bing & Grondahl, Royal Copenhagen, Royal Doulton, and Wedgwood.

American Greetings, Lasting Memories, Holly Hobbie, Grandmother, Child, Verse, 1983, 6 In...	9
Armstrong's, Anyone For Tennis?, Red Skelton, Clown, Racquet, Verse, 1986, 8½ In...........	75
Avon, Cardinal, North American Songbird, Don Eckelberry, 1974, 10 In...................................	19
Erte, Le Soleil Ebony, Stylized Woman, Red & Gold Dress, Black Rim, Japan, 12 In.	50
Franklin Mint, Mother & Child, Mother's Day, 1972, Irene Spencer, Silver, Frame, 8 In......	120
Gorham, Triple Self Portrait, Saturday Evening Post Cover, Norman Rockwell, 1985, 9 In..	9
Lynell, Spring, Eyes Of The Seasons, Steven Klein, Cat & Kitten On Table, 1981, 9½ In.	7
Norman Rockwell, Under The Mistletoe, Sterling Silver, Wood Frame, 1971, 8 In........ *illus*	108

Coin-Operated, Vending, Matchbook, 1 Cent, McKinley Home For Boys, Countertop, 1930, 8 x 5 x 16 In.
$345

Donley Auctions

Coin-Operated, Vending, Stamp, 10-Cents, 5-Cents, Metal, Blue, Enamel, Porcelain
$240

Chupp Auctions & Real Estate, LLC

Collector Plate, Norman Rockwell, Under The Mistletoe, Sterling Silver, Wood Frame, 1971, 8 In.
$108

Alderfer Auction Company

Comic Art, Cover Art, DC Comics, Just Imagine, Stan Lee, Batman, Joe Kubert, March 2001
$5,100

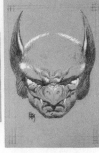

Weiss Auctions

Comic Art, Strip, Peanuts, 1 Page, 4 Panels, Signed, Schulz, 6 x 28 In.
$23,750

Swann Auction Galleries

Comic Art, Strip, Terry & The Pirates, Dragon Lady Appears, Milton Caniff, April 30, 1946, 7 x 24 In.
$2,520

Weiss Auctions

Commemorative, Plate, Bicentennial, Voice Of My People, 12K Gold Figures, Frame, 12 x 12 In.
$150

Nadeau's Auction Gallery

COMIC ART

Comic art, or cartoon art, includes original art for comic strips, magazine covers, book pages, and even printed strips. The first daily comic strip was printed in 1907. The paintings on celluloid used for movie cartoons are listed in this book under Animation Art.

Cartoon, Rejected By The School Of Hard Knocks, The New Yorker, Signed, R. Chast, 12 x 9 In.	1375
Cartoon, You've Been Eating Again, The New Yorker, Signed, Lorenz, 14 x 11 In.	688
Cover Art, DC Comics, Just Imagine, Stan Lee, Batman, Joe Kubert, March 2001.........*illus*	5100
Illustration, Men Fighting, Kings Tavern, Blank Ink, Signed, Tom Yeates, 1977, 10 x 14 In.	300
Strip, Bib & Tucker, 12 Panels, Gilt Frame, Romer, Joe Kubert, 1930s, 19 x 29 In.	216
Strip, Daily, Dan Dunn, Secret Operative 48, 4 Panels, Paul Pinson, July 11, 1940s, 16 x 5 In.	66
Strip, Peanuts, 1 Page, 4 Panels, Signed, Schulz, 6 x 28 In.........*illus*	23750
Strip, Peanuts, Daily, 4 Panels, Snoopy & Charlie Brown, Charles Schulz, 1973, 30 x 7 In.	28800
Strip, Peanuts, Daily, 4 Panels, Snoopy & Lucy, Charles Schulz, July 10, 1972, 30 x 7 In.	24600
Strip, Pogo, 2 Pages, Sunday, Signed, Walt Kelly, Dated 1958, 17 x 24 In.	2125
Strip, Terry & The Pirates, Dragon Lady Appears, Milton Caniff, April 30, 1946, 7 x 24 In.....*illus*	2520
Sunday, Billy Debeck, Bunky, July 27, 1941, 12 x 18 In.	240

COMMEMORATIVE

Commemorative items have been made to honor members of royalty and those of great national fame. World's Fairs and important historical events are also remembered with commemorative pieces. Related collectibles are listed in the Coronation and World's Fair categories.

Medallion, George IV, Engraved, Bull, Fruit, Flowers, Silver Gilt, Edw. Barton, London, 1825, 3½ In..	344
Plate, Bicentennial, Voice Of My People, 12K Gold Figures, Frame, 12 x 12 In. ....*illus*	150
Wreath, Cleveland Opera Co., Premiere, Gold Leaves, Ribbon, Shadowbox, 1924, 30 x 28 x 5 In..*illus*	128

COMPACT

Compacts hold face powder. A woman did not powder her face in public until after World War I. By 1920, the beauty parlor, permanent waves, and cosmetics had become acceptable. A few companies sold cake face powder in a box with a mirror and a pad or puff. Soon the compact was designed by jewelers and made of gold, silver, and precious materials. Cosmetic companies began to sell powder in attractive compacts of less valuable metal or plastic. Collectors today search for Art Deco designs, famous brands, compacts from World's Fairs or political events, and unusual examples. Many were made with companion lipsticks and other fittings.

Beaded, Rhinestone Cover, Silver Frame, Black Fabric, Victorian, 4 In.	24
Gilt Metal, Faux Malachite, Woman, Goldtone Frame, Continental, 1910s, 3 x 3⅛ In..*illus*	188
Silver, Enamel, 3 Women, Man, Near Ponte Vecchio, Multicolor, Germany, 1900s, 3¾ In....	188
Silver, Enamel, Courting Scene, Multicolor, Germany, 1900s, 2¾ In.	219
Silver, Enamel, Scalloped, Amorous Scene, Beveled Mirror, Italy, Late 1800s, 3 x 2 In. ....*illus*	270
Volupte, Gazelle Shape, Head Down, Horn, Brass, Frederic Weinberg, c.1955, 6 x 1½ x 6 In........	438

CONSOLIDATED LAMP AND GLASS COMPANY

Consolidated Lamp and Glass Company of Coraopolis, Pennsylvania, was founded in 1894. The company made lamps, tablewares, and art glass. Collectors are particularly interested in the wares made after 1925, including black satin glass, Cosmos (listed in its own category in this book), Martele (which resembled Lalique), Ruba Rombic (1928–1932 Art Deco line), and colored glasswares. Some Consolidated pieces are very similar to those made by the Phoenix Glass Company.

C

The colors are sometimes different. Consolidated made Martele glass in blue, crystal, green, pink, white, or custard glass with added fired-on color or a satin finish. The company closed for the final time in 1967.

Dessert Set, Pressed Glass, Bird Of Paradise, Amethyst, c.1930, 12-In. Dish, 8 Plates, 9 Piece	410
Lamp, Junior, Satin Glass, Scroll & Fleur-De-Lis, c.1899, 12 x 5 In.	497
Lampshade, Domed, Figural, Molded Fruits, Painted, 4½ x 9 In.	55
Pitcher, Water, Guttate, Satin Pink, Applied Handle, Pressed Feather Design, c.1894, 9¼ In.	48
Sugar Shaker, Bulging Loops, Pigeon Blood, Period Lid, c.1894, 5½ In. .... *illus*	215

CONTEMPORARY GLASS, *see Glass-Contemporary.*

COOKBOOK

Cookbooks are collected for various reasons. Some are wanted for the recipes, some for investment, and some as examples of advertising. Cookbooks and recipe pamphlets are included in this category.

Betty Crocker, Ring Binder, Tabs, Pie Cover, 480 Pages, 1972..	75
General Foods Kitchens, Hardcover, 436 Pages, 1959	60
Julia Child & Co., Hardcover, 1979...	49
Pillsbury, Softcover, 126 Pages, c.1914, 9½ x 6½ In...	20
Saturday Evening Post Family Cookbook, 175 Recipes, 1984	20
The French Chef Cookbook, Child, Julia, Hardcover, Signed, Knopf, 1968............. *illus*	180
The Mary Frances Cook Book, Fryer, Jane, Hardcover, Philadelphia, 1912.............. *illus*	36
White House Cook Book, Ziemann, Hugo, Hardcover, Illustrated, Werner, 1899, 10 x 8 In....... *illus*	154

COOKIE JAR

Cookie jars with brightly painted designs or amusing figural shapes became popular in the mid-1930s. They became very popular again when Andy Warhol's collection was auctioned after his death in 1987. Prices have gone down since then and are very low. Many companies made them and collectors search for cookie jars either by design or by maker's name. Listed here are exa mples by the less common makers. Major factories are listed under their own names in other categories of the book, such as Abingdon, Brush, Hull, McCoy, Metlox, Red Wing, and Shawnee. See also the Disneyana category. These are marks of three cookie jar manufacturers.

Brush Pottery Co. 1925–1982	Fitz and Floyd Enterprises LLC 1960–1980	Twin Winton Ceramics 1946–1977

Apple, Lid, Leaf Handle, White, Porcelain, Tiffany by Haeger, 1980s, 11 x 7 In. .... *illus*	90
Apple, Red, Ceramic, USA, 11 x 9 In.	55
Basket, Cookies On Lid, Ceramic, Bail Handle, 1950s, 10 x 7 In.	25
Bear, With Cookie, Rompers, American Bisque Co., c.1958, 10 In.	110
Christmas Tree, White, Gold Balls, Holly & Star On Top, Marked, Lenox, 12 x 7 In.	20
Glass, Farmhouse Design, Daisies, Anchor Hocking, 9½ In..	45
Liberty Bell, Lid, Carnival Glass, Marigold Yellow .... *illus*	12
Old Gray Haired Woman, Wrinkles, Side Knob Handles, 6½ x 6½ In..............................	30
Pillsbury, Flour Sack Shape, Lemon Kiss Recipe, Benjamin & Medwin Inc., 1988, 11 x 5 x 6 In.	55
Purse Shape, Blue, Red Tulips, WCL Collectables, Chinese, 10 x 9 In................................	100
Sgrafitto, Dome Lid, Bird, Floral & Leaves, Breininger, 1990, 13 In.	325
Stoneware, Lid, Brown Glaze, Molded, Painted Apples, 9 x 7½ In............................... *illus*	12

Commemorative, Wreath, Cleveland Opera Co., Premiere, Gold Leaves, Ribbon, Shadowbox, 1924, 30 x 28 x 5 In.
$128

Rachel Davis Fine Arts

Compact, Gilt Metal, Faux Malachite, Woman, Goldtone Frame, Continental, 1910s, 3 x 3⅛ In.
$188

Hindman

Compact, Silver, Enamel, Scalloped, Amorous Scene, Beveled Mirror, Italy, Late 1800s, 3 x 2 In.
$270

Garth's Auctioneers & Appraisers

"Flapjacks"
Flapjacks are oversized compacts about 4 to 6 inches in diameter. They were popular in the 1930s and made of plastic as well as metal, often with modern designs.

Consolidated, Sugar Shaker, Bulging Loops, Pigeon Blood, Period Lid, c.1894, 5 ½ In.
$215

Jeffrey S. Evans & Associates

Cookbook, The French Chef Cookbook, Child, Julia, Hardcover, Signed, Knopf, 1968
$180

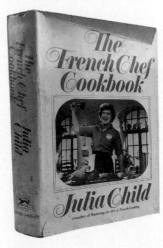

Alderfer Auction Company

Cookbook, The Mary Frances Cook Book, Fryer, Jane, Hardcover, Philadelphia, 1912
$36

Bunch Auctions

Cookie Jars
Figural cookie jars were first made in the mid-1930s. Many reproductions have been made since then.

Cookbook, White House Cook Book, Ziemann, Hugo, Hardcover, Illustrated, Werner, 1899, 10 x 8 In.
$154

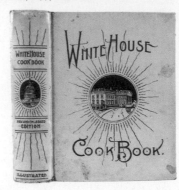

North American Auction Co.

Cooking Stars
Cooking has become a way of life. Successful restaurant chefs are now stars. Out-of-print cookbooks by memorable personalities like Julia Child sell quickly online. There is even a market for the pamphlets given away by food companies over the past century, even if the instructions don't take into account microwaves or frozen food.

Cookie Jar, Apple, Lid, Leaf Handle, White, Porcelain, Tiffany by Haeger, 1980s, 11 x 7 In.
$90

Leland Little Auctions

Cookie Jar, Liberty Bell, Lid, Carnival Glass, Marigold Yellow
$12

Strawser Auction Group

COORS

Coors dinnerware was made by the Coors Porcelain Company of Golden, Colorado, a company founded with the help of the Coors Brewing Company. Its founder, John Herold, started the Herold China and Pottery Company in 1910 on the site of a glassworks owned by Adolph Coors, the founder of the Coors brewery. The company began making art pottery using clay from nearby mines. Adolph Coors Company bought Herold China and Pottery Company in early 1915. Chemical porcelains were made beginning in 1915. The company name was changed to Coors Porcelain Company in 1920, when Herold left. Several lines of dinnerware were made in the 1920s and 1930s. Marks on dinnerware and cookware made by Coors include Rosebud, Glencoe Thermo-Porcelain, Colorado, and other names. Coors stopped making nonessential wares at the start of World War II. After the war, the pottery made ovenware, teapots, vases, and a general line of pottery, but no dinnerware—except for special orders. In 1986 Coors Porcelain became Coors Ceramics. In 2000, Coors Ceramics changed its name to CoorsTek. The company is still in business making industrial porcelain. For more prices, go to kovels.com.

Coors Porcelain Co.
1920s

Coors Porcelain Co.
1934–1942

Coors Porcelain Co.
1934–1942

Custard Cup, Rosebud, Yellow, 1930s, 2 1/2 x 4 In. 22
Dish, White, Thermo, 1930s, 3 In. 10
Mortar & Pestle, White, Spout, Numbered, Nesting, Largest 4 3/4 x 8 1/2 In., 3 Piece 108
Pie Plate, Open Window, Thermo, 10 In. 7
Planter, Coorsite, Burgundy, Swirl, 5 1/2 x 5 1/2 In. 20
Salt & Pepper, Rosebud, Blue, Straight Sides 26
Teapot, Lid, Coorsite, Round, Light Blue Swirl, 1950s 40

COPELAND

Copeland pieces listed here are those that have a mark including the word *Copeland* used between 1847 and 1976. Marks include *Copeland Spode* and *Copeland & Garrett.* See also Copeland Spode, Royal Worcester, and Spode.

Cup & Saucer, Pink Roses, Gilt, Hand Painted, Marked, 6 In. Saucer, 7 Piece 308
Dish, Spaniel, Partridge In Mouth, Scrollwork Rim, Copeland & Garrett, 1837, 11 In... *illus* 1111
Pedestal, Classical, Acanthus Leaves, Octagonal Base, Greece, 1900s, 37 x 12 1/4 In. 72
Plate, Cabinet, Octagonal, Crimped Rim, Canary, Open Cage, Bouquet, C.F. Hurten, c.1880, 9 In... 5467
Plate, Interlocking Petals, Rose, Peony, Smaller Flowers, C.F. Hurten, c.1885, 9 1/4 In. 5126
Puzzle Teapot, Brown Rockingham Glaze, Raised Flowers & Leaves, Footed, 5 3/4 In. 38
Vase, Aloe Vera, Begonia, Fern, Rock, Bamboo, Vine, Palm Handle, C.F. Hurten, c.1880, 23 In. 9397

COPELAND SPODE

Copeland Spode appears on some pieces of nineteenth-century English porcelain. Josiah Spode established a pottery at Stoke-on-Trent, England, in 1770. In 1833, the firm was purchased by William Copeland and Thomas Garrett and the mark was changed. In 1847, Copeland became the sole owner and the mark changed again. W.T. Copeland & Sons continued until a 1976 merger when it became Royal Worcester Spode. The company was bought by the Portmeirion Group in 2009. Pieces are listed in this book under the name that appears in the mark. Copeland, Royal Worcester, and Spode have separate listings.

Cookie Jar, Stoneware, Lid, Brown Glaze, Molded, Painted Apples, 9 x 7 1/2 In.
$12

Matthew Bullock Auctioneers

Andy Warhol's Cookie Jars
The 1987 auction of more than 125 cookie jars from pop artist Andy Warhol's collection of ceramic cookie jars brought $250,000! Cookie jar prices went up immediately after the sale, but collectors were disappointed that prices for most jars soon went down to more reasonable levels, $50 to $300 each.

Copeland, Dish, Spaniel, Partridge In Mouth, Scrollwork Rim, Copeland & Garrett, 1837, 11 In.
$1,111

Bonhams

This is an edited listing of current prices. Visit **Kovels.com** to check thousands of prices from previous years and sign up for free information on trends, tips, reproductions, marks, and more.

Copper, Charger, Hammered, Galleon Ship, Fish, Big Waves, Newlyn, c.1900s, 16 In.
$800

California Historical Design

Copper, Chocolate Pot, Dovetailed, Lid, Wood Handle, Spout, 1800s, 10 In.
$554

Pook & Pook

Copper, Coal Scuttle, Lid, Black, Orange Cat, Gilt Bronze, Creamware Handle, Shovel, 1800s, 16 In.
$819

Brunk Auctions

Copper, Fish Poacher, Iron Bail Handle, Oval, Continental, 1800s, 24¾ x 8½ x 5½ In.
$150

Selkirk Auctioneers & Appraisers

Plate, Dinner, Transferware, Horse Chariot, Grecian Urn, Greek, 10½ In., 8 Piece	2530
Tureen, Soup, Oak Leaves, Acorns, Gilt, Foot, Marked, Late Spode, Copeland & Garrett, 10½ x 12 In.	156

COPPER

Copper has been used to make utilitarian items, like teakettles and cooking pans, since the days of the early American colonists. Copper became a popular metal with the Arts & Crafts makers of the early 1900s, and decorative pieces, like desk sets, were made. Copper pieces may also be found in Arts & Crafts, Bradley & Hubbard, Kitchen, Roycroft, and other categories.

Chase Brass and Copper Co., Inc.
1930s

Craftsman Workshop
Mark of Gustav Stickley
c.1900–1915

POTTER STUDIO

Potter Studio
c.1900–1929

Ash Box, Dome Lift-Off Lid, Finial, Cast Brass Legs, 18 x 12 x 12 In.	322
Bedpan, Brass Lid, Pierced, Rolled Rim, Repousse Lion & Leaves, Iron Stem, 1700s, 24 x 9 x 4 In.	527
Bowl, Hammered, Lakeland Rural Industries, Borrowdale, 1940s, 1½ x 7¼ In.	185
Bowl, Hammered, Sybil Foster, Boston, Arts & Crafts, c.1914, 5½ x 1½ In.	185
Cauldron, Cooking, Wrought Iron Handle, 16¼ x 23 In.	213
Charger, Hammered, Galleon Ship, Fish, Big Waves, Newlyn, c.1900s, 16 In. .... *illus*	800
Charger, Handwrought, Signed, 20 In.	502
Chocolate Pot, Dovetailed, Lid, Wood Handle, Spout, 1800s, 10 In. .... *illus*	554
Coal Scuttle, Footed, Bin, Ring Handles, 2 Adjacent Sides, Arts & Crafts, England, 18 x 14 In.	1250
Coal Scuttle, Lid, Black, Orange Cat, Gilt Bronze, Creamware Handle, Shovel, 1800s, 16 In. ...... *illus*	819
Eagle, Wings Outstretched, Standing On Rocks, Gilt, 32 x 64 In.	488
Fish Poacher, Iron Bail Handle, Oval, Continental, 1800s, 24¾ x 8½ x 5½ In. .... *illus*	150
Horn, Hunting, Thin, Brown, Circle Shape At Top & Bottom, 38 In.	164
Kettle, Apple Butter, Swing Handle, Dovetailed, Hand Churn, 20 x 26 In.	330
Kettle, Apple Butter, Thimble Shape, With Handle, 14 x 21 In.	66
Kettle, Apple Butter, Wrought Iron Handles, 12 x 26 x 33 In.	144
Kettle, Dome Lid, Swing Handle, Philadelphia, 1800s, 10 In.	677
Kettle, Hammered, Handle, Signed, Avon Coppersmith, Arthur Cole, N.Y., c.1930s, 5 x 9½ In..... *illus*	461
Kettle, Wrought Loop Iron Handle, Urn Shape Finial, Spout, 30 In.	156
Lamp, Manhattan Skyline, Cast Iron, Edward Miller & Co., c.1920, 24¾ x 20½ In.	975
Molds are listed in the Kitchen category.	
Picture Frame, Hammered, Acid Etched, Arts & Crafts, c.1910, 4½ x 5¾ In.	215
Pitcher, Hammered, Mounted Lid, Ball Finial, Russia, Arts & Crafts, c.1910, 8 x 6 x 4 In. ..... *illus*	123
Pitcher, Hammered, Silver Bull's Head On Rim, Joseph Heinrichs, c.1905, 11½ x 7½ In.	6150
Plaque, Father, Mother, Children, Relief, Continental School, Frame, 18¼ x 21 x 1¾ In. ...	63
Plaque, Wall, Egyptian, Silver Decoration, Circular, 10 In.	56
Pot, Hand Hammered, Dovetailed, Brown, Hope North, Geneseo, 1840, 8¼ x 13¾ In.	960
Pot, Lid, Side Handles, Spigot Near Base, France, 19th Century, 15 x 18 In.	590
Sculpture, Plowman, Horse, Patina, Ebonized Wood Base, 5 x 13½ x 4 In.	125
Sculpture, Sonambient, 2 Columns, Beryllium, Brass Base, Val Bertoia, 59 x 7 In.	4688
Stand, Plant, Glass Top, Cattails & Dragonfly Sculpture, Ron Bertocchi, 29 x 10 x 9 In.	117
Teapot, Metal, Pumpkin Shape, Burner Stand, Japan, 1900s, 6 x 6 x 5 In.	94
Tray, Hammered, 2 Handles, Signed, Falick Novick, Chicago, c.1910, 12¾ In............. *illus*	246
Tray, Hammered, Rectangular, Als Ik Kan Mark, G. Stickley, New York, 18 x 11⅞ In. .. *illus*	2250
Tray, Hammered, Silver Rim, Signed, Joseph Heinrichs, c.1910, 7¾ In.	400
Tray, Oval, Shaped Ends, Frost Arts & Crafts Workshop, Dayton, Ohio, c.1910, 20½ x 11½ In.	325
Umbrella Stand, Brass, Handles, N Monogram, Benedict Art Studios, New York, 25⅜ x 12⅜ In.....	875
Umbrella Stand, Hammered, Flared Rim, Tack Joints, 2-Handled Sides, Arts & Crafts, 28 In.....	443
Washtub, Lid, Boiler, Oval, Mounted, 2 Handles, 13 x 24 In.	74

COPPER LUSTER *items are listed in the Luster category.*

CORALENE

Coralene glass was made by firing many small colored beads on the outside of glassware. It was made in many patterns in the United States and Europe in the 1880s. Reproductions are made today. Coralene-decorated Japanese pottery is listed in the Japanese Coralene category.

Bride's Basket, Ruffled Edge, Silver Plate Stand, Flower, 13¼ In.	213
Bride's Bowl, Apricot, Mother-Of-Pearl Satin, Diamond Quilted, Fleur-De-Lis, 3 x 5 In.	150
Cup, Vaseline, Cased, Cut Velvet, Red Coral, Applied Clear Handle, 3½ In., 4 Piece	179
Ewer, Yellow Satin, Pedestal, Round Foot, Applied Thorn Handle, Amber Glass, 12 In.	48
Rose Bowl, Yellow Satin, Coralene Bubbles, Scalloped Rim, Victorian, 3 x 6 In.	156
Vase, Green, White Enamel Flower Panel, Coralene, Greek Key, 3-Footed, 7 In., Pair	72
Vase, Shaded Blue, Mother-Of-Pearl, Diamond Quilted, Orange Coral, Ruffled Rim, 5½ In.	84
Vase, Shaded Pink, Bulbous, Mother-Of-Pearl, Diamond Quilted, Coralene Floral Vine, 7 In.	270
Vase, Shaded Pink, Cased, Yellow Coral, Shaped Rim, 6½ In.	130
Vase, Shaded Pink, Satin, Quilted, Coralene Quatrefoils, c.1900, 7¾ In.	138

CORDEY

Cordey China Company was founded by Boleslaw Cybis in 1942 in Trenton, New Jersey. The firm produced gift shop items. In 1969 it was acquired by the Lightron Corp. and operated as the Schiller Cordey Co., manufacturers of lamps. About 1950 Boleslaw Cybis began making Cybis porcelains, which are listed in the Cybis category in this book.

Bust, Woman, Curly Hair, Lace Veil, Blue Sleeves, Clasped Hands, Scrolled Base, 12½ In.	25
Figurine, Man & Woman, Fruit Pickers, Green Shaded Clothes, Nos. 304 & 305, 16½ In., Pair	63
Figurine, Woman, Purple Shaded Coat, Green Dress, Flowered Hat, Arms Out, Scrolled Base, 12 In.	13
Group, Man & Woman, Curly Hair, Pink & Blue Clothes, Scrolled Base, 13¼ In.	13

CORKSCREW

Corkscrews have been needed since the first bottle was sealed with a cork, probably in the seventeenth century. Today collectors search for the early, unusual patented examples or the figural corkscrews of recent years.

Bacchus, Figural, Grapevine Wreath, Mechanical, Silver Plate, Italy, Godinger, 8 x 3 In.	102
Champagne Tap, Corkscrew End, Dolphin Finial, France, 13 In.	544
Champagne Tap, Silver Plate, Leather Case, Continental, 3½ In.	190
Helix, Wrought Iron, Rosewood Handle, Brush End, 19th Century, 5 x 3½ In.	50
Tusk, Boar's, Carved, Silver End Cap, Bell, 1900s, 6½ In.	216
Tusk, Walrus, Cigar Cutter End, Silver Mount, Applied Elephant's Head, 9 x 6 In.	360
Wing Shape, Open Hinge, Silver, Chrome Plate, Cerniera, Bulgari, 3½ x 3¾ In.	500
Yankee, No. 7, Cast Iron, Hand Operated, Table Clamp, Early 1900s, 7½ In. *illus*	156

CORONATION

Coronation souvenirs have been made since the 1800s. Pottery, glass, tin, silver, and paper objects with a picture of the monarchs and date have been sold at many coronations. The pieces that mention King Edward VIII, the king who was never crowned, are not rare; collectors should be sure to check values before buying. Related pieces are found in the Commemorative category.

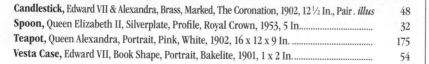

Candlestick, Edward VII & Alexandra, Brass, Marked, The Coronation, 1902, 12½ In., Pair. *illus*	48
Spoon, Queen Elizabeth II, Silverplate, Profile, Royal Crown, 1953, 5 In.	32
Teapot, Queen Alexandra, Portrait, Pink, White, 1902, 16 x 12 x 9 In.	175
Vesta Case, Edward VII, Book Shape, Portrait, Bakelite, 1901, 1 x 2 In.	54

Copper, Kettle, Hammered, Handle, Signed, Avon Coppersmith, Arthur Cole, N.Y., c.1930s, 5 x 9½ In.
$461

California Historical Design

Copper, Pitcher, Hammered, Mounted Lid, Ball Finial, Russia, Arts & Crafts, c.1910, 8 x 6 x 4 In.
$123

California Historical Design

Copper, Tray, Hammered, 2 Handles, Signed, Falick Novick, Chicago, c.1910, 12¾ In.
$246

California Historical Design

Copper, Tray, Hammered, Rectangular, Als Ik Kan Mark, G. Stickley, New York, 18 x 11⅞ In.
$2,250

Toomey & Co. Auctioneers

COSMOS

Corkscrew, Yankee, No. 7, Cast Iron, Hand Operated, Table Clamp, Early 1900s, 7½ In.
$156

Hindman

TIP

If your front entrance has glass windows or doors that give a view of your front hall, be sure the control pad for your alarm is out of sight. A burglar can look in to see if it is off.

Coronation, Candlestick, Edward VII & Alexandra, Brass, Marked, The Coronation, 1902, 12½ In., Pair
$48

Bunch Auctions

Cosmos, Butter, Dome Cover, Milk Glass, Pink Stripe, Pastel Flowers, 5¾ x 8 In.
$48

Woody Auction

COSMOS

Cosmos is a pressed milk glass pattern with colored flowers made from 1894 to 1915 by the Consolidated Lamp and Glass Company. Tablewares and lamps were made in this pattern. A few pieces were also made of clear glass with painted decorations. Other glass patterns are listed under Consolidated Lamp and also in various glass categories. In later years, Cosmos was also made by the Westmoreland Glass Company.

Butter, Dome Cover, Milk Glass, Pink Stripe, Pastel Flowers, 5¾ x 8 In. ....*illus*	48
Lamp, Oil, Opaque White Ground, Yellow Trim, 8 In.	42

COVERLET

Coverlets were made of linen or wool during the nineteenth century. Most of the coverlets date from 1800 to the 1880s. There was a revival of hand weaving in the 1920s and new coverlets, especially geometric patterns, were made. The earliest coverlets were made on narrow looms, so two woven strips were joined together and a seam can be found. The weave structures of coverlets can include summer and winter, double weave, overshot, and others. Jacquard coverlets have elaborate pictorial patterns that are made on a special loom or with the use of a special attachment. Makers often wove a personal message in the corner. Quilts are listed in this book in their own category.

John Henry Meily (1817–1884)
1842–1850s

Matthew Rattray (1796–1872)
1822–1872

Samuel Stinger (c.1801–1879)
1838–1879

Double Weave, Blue, Red, Snowball & Pine Tree, Wool, Cotton, 2 Panel, 1800s, 86 x 71 In.	810
Double Weave, Blue, White, Flowers, Willow & Eagle Border, 2 Panel, 1838, 88 x 80 In.......	282
Double Weave, Red, White, Blue, Peacock & Eagle Blocks, Washington Corners, 1800s, 75 x 75 In....	813
Jacquard, Black, Red, Flowers, Chambersburg, Pennsylvania, 1844, 93 x 84 In.	328
Overshot, Blue, Green, Pink, Natural, Catalpa Flower, Wool, Cotton, 2 Panel, Late 1800s, 67 x 90 In..	200
Overshot, Blue, Natural, Geometric, Medallions In Squares, 2 Panel, Mid 1800s, 87 x 80 In.	123
Overshot, Blue, White, Snowflake, Pine Tree Border, Wool, Linen, 2 Panel, 80 x 71 In.........	101
Overshot, Blue, White, Vine, Leaf, Floral Border, Side Fringe, 1872, 93 x 79 In.....................	226
Overshot, Wool, Blue, Rust Red, Natural Cotton, Block Pattern, Mid-Atlantic, 1850s, 72 x 86 In.. *illus*	155
Summer & Winter, Blue & White, Grid, Geometric, 2 Panel, 87 x 80 In.	63
Summer & Winter, Red, Blue, White, Checked, Bound Top, Lower Fringe, Wool, 1800s, 81 x 71 In. ...	572
Summer & Winter, Red, Green, Blue, White, Jacquard, Knox County, Oh., 2 Panel, 1847, 80 x 76 In.	313
Summer & Winter, Red, White, Blue, Medallion, Leaf Borders, Umbros Miller, 1869, 82 x 76 In..	123
Summer & Winter, Red, White, Leaves Border, Eagles, Medallion, 1861, 86 x 96 In. ....*illus*	390
Summer & Winter, Red, White, Medallion, Eagles, Animals, Temple & Leaf, 1861, 96 x 86 In.	407
Woven, Twill, Dark Blue, Rust Red Wool, Diamond, Pennsylvania, 1800s, 74 x 90 In.	167

COWAN POTTERY

Cowan Pottery made art pottery and wares for florists. Guy Cowan made pottery in Rocky River, Ohio, a suburb of Cleveland, from 1913 to 1931. A stylized mark with the word *Cowan* was used on most pieces. A commercial, mass-produced line was marked *Lakeware.* Collectors today search for the Art Deco pieces by Guy Cowan, Viktor Schreckengost, Waylande Gregory, Thelma Frazier Winter, and other artists.

Bookends, Pelican Head, Black Glaze, Albert Drexler Jacobson, c.1931, 5 x 4 x 2 In..............	6000
Bookends, Ram, Black, Glazed, Waylande Gregory, c.1930, 7 x 7 x 4 In.	3750
Figurine, Burlesque Dancer, Earthenware, Waylande Gregory, Ohio, c.1929, 18 x 6 x 4 In. .....*illus*	8125

Figurine, Introspection, Bird Shape, Black, Albert Drexler Jacobson, c.1928, 8 x 4 x 3 In. ...	813
Lamp, Flowers, Gilt, Glass Shades, Waylande Gregory, 32 ¼ In., Pair	213
Vase, Blue Luster, Flared Rim & Base, Signed, c.1920s, 9 ⅜ x 3 ¼ In.	123

CRACKER JACK

Cracker Jack, the molasses-flavored popcorn mixture, was first made in 1896 in Chicago, Illinois. A prize was added to each box in 1912. Collectors search for the old boxes, toys, and advertising materials. Many of the toys are unmarked. New toys are usually paper, older toys are tin, paper, or plastic.

Charm, Rat, Plastic, Orange, 1960s, ⅝ In.	10
Doll, Rubber Head, Cloth Body, Sailor Suit, Vogue Dolls, c.1980, 12 In.	40
Shirt Stud, Cannon, Pot Metal	10
Tin, Advertising Scenes, Red, White, Blue, c.1990, 8 x 6 In.	15

CRANBERRY GLASS

Cranberry glass is an almost transparent yellow-red glass. It resembles the color of cranberry juice. The glass has been made in Europe and America since the Civil War. It is still being made, and reproductions can fool the unwary. Related glass items may be listed in other categories, such as Rubina Verde.

Compote, Swirled Optic, Clear Lyre Shape Stem, Late 1900s, 8 ¼ In.	121
Fountain, Perpetual, Perfume, Ruffled Bowl Top, 1870-85, 21 ½ In.	3328
Lamp, Electric, Gilt Floral Panel, Mounted Base, Vase Converted To Lamp, 1900s, 21 In., Pair	62
Pitcher, Buttons & Braids, Hexagonal Crimped Rim, Clear Handle, 1902-10, 10 In.	478
Sugar Shaker, Windows Swirl, Lid, Hobbs, Brockunier & Co., c.1888, 5 ⅛ In. .... *illus*	269
Syrup, Ribbed, Quadruple Plate Lid, James W. Tufts, Late 1800s, 6 ¾ In. .... *illus*	156
Tumbler, Swirling Maze, Polished Rim, Jefferson Glass Co., c.1905, 4 In.	359
Vase, Bubble Design, High Shouldered, Polished Pontil Base, 10 x 8 In. .... *illus*	585
Vase, Silver Overlay, Leaves, Flowers & Vines, Early 1900s, 18 In.	605
Water Set, Inverted Thumbprint, Pitcher, Ruffled Rim, Tumblers, Pitcher 9 ¾ In., 7 Piece.	90

CREAMWARE

Creamware, or queensware, was developed by Josiah Wedgwood about 1765. It is a cream-colored earthenware that has been copied by many factories. Similar wares may be listed under Pearlware and Wedgwood.

Bowl, Molded Vine, Fruit, Lattice & Basketweave Base, Staffordshire, 1750s, 4 ½ In.	88
Jug, Molded Lattice & Vine, Extruded Handle, Staffordshire, 1760s, 4 ½ In.	188
Jug, Salt Glaze, Multicolor, Bird, Flowers, Loop Handle, Footed, Late 1700s, 4 In.	219
Jug, Success To America, Black Transfer, Map, American Flag, England, Early 1800s, 8 In. ....*illus*	2106
Pitcher, Marbled & Blue Slip Bands, Reeded Neck, Strap Handle, England, c.1825, 9 In.	1250
Pitcher, Sprig Molded, Vine, Brown Slip Bands, Green Glaze, England, c.1780, 6 In.	188
Plate, Dinner, Wavy Rim, Molded Diamond, Tortoiseshell Glaze, Staffordshire, 1760s, 9 ½ In.	469
Teapot, Lid, Globular, Tortoiseshell, Molded Figures, Staffordshire, 1760s, 4 ½ x 7 ⅛ In. ....*illus*	599
Teapot, Molded Vine, Fruit, Lattice & Basketweave Base, Staffordshire, 1750s, 4 ⅜ In.	281

CREIL

Creil, France, had a faience factory as early as 1794. The company merged with a factory in Montereau in 1819. It made stoneware, mocha ware, and soft paste porcelain. The name *Creil* appears as part of the mark on many pieces. The Creil factory closed in 1895.

Flowerpot, Flared, Brown Seaweed, Round Foot, Underplate, 6 ⅜ x 7 In.	217
Pitcher, Blue Marbling, White Ground, Et Montereau, Late 1800s, 10 ½ In.	246
Tureen, Lid, Underplate, Faience, White Glaze, 9 ½ x 13 ½ In.	313

CROWN DERBY, *see Royal Crown Derby category.*

Coverlet, Overshot, Wool, Blue, Rust Red, Natural Cotton, Block Pattern, Mid-Atlantic, 1850s, 72 x 86 In.
$155

Jeffrey S. Evans & Associates

Coverlet, Summer & Winter, Red, White, Leaves Border, Eagles, Medallion, 1861, 86 x 96 In.
$390

Garth's Auctioneers & Appraisers

Cowan, Figurine, Burlesque Dancer, Earthenware, Waylande Gregory, Ohio, c.1929, 18 x 6 x 4 In.
$8,125

Toomey & Co. Auctioneers

Cranberry Glass, Sugar Shaker, Windows Swirl, Lid, Hobbs, Brockunier & Co., c.1888, 5⅛ In.
$269

Jeffrey S. Evans & Associates

Cranberry Glass, Syrup, Ribbed, Quadruple Plate Lid, James W. Tufts, Late 1800s, 6¾ In.
$156

Jeffrey S. Evans & Associates

Cranberry Glass, Vase, Bubble Design, High Shouldered, Polished Pontil Base, 10 x 8 In.
$585

Thomaston Place Auction Galleries

Creamware, Jug, Success To America, Black Transfer, Map, American Flag, England, Early 1800s, 8 In.
$2,106

Jeffrey S. Evans & Associates

Creamware, Teapot, Lid, Globular, Tortoiseshell, Molded Figures, Staffordshire, 1760s, 4½ x 7⅛ In.
$599

Doyle

TIP
The best defense against a burglary is a nosy neighbor.

Crown Milano, Biscuit Jar, Melon Ribbed Shape, Silver Plate Lid, Applied Jewels, Leaf, Cream Tones, 5 x 6 In.
$300

Woody Auction

Crown Milano, Biscuit Jar, Square, Yellow, Flowers, Enamel Scrolls, Beads, Metal Lid, Bail Handle, 8 In.
$431

Neue Auctions

Crown Milano, Ewer, Bulbous, Lily Pads, Gilt, Shaped Rim, Applied Snake Handle, Curled Tail, 8 x 8 In.
$2,040

Woody Auction

Crown Milano, Ewer, Oval Body, Multicolor Flowers, Dotted Outlines, Amber Ground, Twisted Handle, 12 In.
$500

Jaremos

CROWN DUCAL

Crown Ducal is the name used on some pieces of porcelain made by A.G. Richardson and Co., Ltd., of Tunstall and Cobridge, England. The name has been used since 1916. Crown Ducal is a well-known maker of chintz pattern dishes. The company was bought by Wedgwood in 1974.

Dinnerware Set, Florentine, Multicolor Fruit, Square Plates, Demitasse Cups & Saucers, 36 Piece	62
Pail, Hummingbirds, Flying Insects, Pine Branches, Shaded Cream Ground, 10¼ x 13¼ In. ...	500
Plate, Colonial Times, Purple Transfer, 10½ In., 8 Piece...	30
Plate, Hunting Scene, Marked, For Ovington's New York, 8 In., 7 Piece........................	100
Plate, Salad, Florentine, Creamware, 8 In., 10 Piece..	63

CROWN MILANO

Crown Milano glass was made by the Mt. Washington Glass Works about 1890. It was a plain biscuit color with a satin finish decorated with flowers and often had large gold scrolls. Not all pieces are marked.

Biscuit Jar, Melon Ribbed Shape, Silver Plate Lid, Applied Jewels, Leaf, Cream Tones, 5 x 6 In..... *illus*	300
Biscuit Jar, Square, Yellow, Flowers, Enamel Scrolls, Beads, Metal Lid, Bail Handle, 8 In. ...... *illus*	431
Bowl, Lid, Ring, Yellow, Pink Flowers, Metal Collar, Swirled Body, 2¾ x 3 In.	210
Ewer, Bulbous, Lily Pads, Gilt, Shaped Rim, Applied Snake Handle, Curled Tail, 8 x 8 In. ..... *illus*	2040
Ewer, Bulbous, Thistles, White, Yellow, Mottled Ground, Rope Handle, 10 x 6 In.	550
Ewer, Oval Body, Multicolor Flowers, Dotted Outlines, Amber Ground, Twisted Handle, 12 In.... *illus*	500
Jar, Gold, Enamel, Blossom, Silver Plate Lid, Mustard, Cream Tones, Coral Mold, 3 x 3 In. ..	100
Jar, Temple, Lid, Teardrop Shape, Cherubs, Dotted Ground, Gold Scrolled Frame, 12 x 7 In.	2261
Jardiniere, Autumn Leaves, Gold Enamel Branches & Berries, Cream Ground, 6¼ x 7½ In.	298
Potpourri, Burmese, Melon Ribbed, Flowering Branch, Pierced Silver Lid, 4¾ x 3½ In.	480
Sweetmeat, Silver Plate Lid, Melon Ribbed, Water Lily, Burmese, 4 x 5 In. .... *illus*	125
Vase, Blue & Red Pointilist Flowers, Cream Ground, Gold Scrolls, Fluted Rim, 4½ In.	50
Vase, Bulbous, Pansies, Gold Enamel, Leaf Shape Handles, Short Flared Neck, 4¾ In..........	563
Vase, Bulbous, Wavy Rim, Pink Scroll, Gold & Silver, Blossom, Cream Tones, 13 x 6 In.*illus*	550
Vase, Cherubs & Scrollwork, 2 Handles, White, Gold Design, 8 x 6 In........................... *illus*	1500
Vase, Squat, Blue Scrolling Leaves, Gold Enamel Flowers & Trim, Unmarked, 5 x 6½ In.....	150
Vase, Squat, Bulbous, White, Pink Rim, Roses, Gold Enamel Scrolls, Handles, 4½ x 5¾ In.	780
Vase, Stick, Colonial Ware, Flowering Branches, Wreath At Top, Gold Enamel, 11¾ In., Pair....*illus*	1920
Vase, Trumpet, Colonial Ware, Yellow & Pink Flowers, 2 Applied Rigaree Rings, 8 In.	210
Vase, Yellow, Autumn Leaves, Blue Berries, Swirled, Shaped Rim With 4 Petals, 3¼ In.	594

CROWN TUSCAN *pattern is included in the Cambridge glass category.*

CRUET

Cruets of glass or porcelain were made to hold vinegar, oil, and other condiments. They were especially popular during Victorian times and have been made in a variety of styles since the eighteenth century. Additional cruets may be found in the Castor Set category and also in various glass categories.

Blue Opaline Glass, Octagonal Stopper, Handle, Enamel Scrolls & Trefoils, Pedestal Base, 7 In.*illus*	60
Cut Glass, Stopper, Amethyst To Clear, Pinwheel, Star & Fan, Triple Notched Handle, 7 In..	330
Etched Glass, Hinged Lid, Blue & White, Nature Scenes, Animals, 20th Century, 7½ In., Pair..	150
Etched Glass, Silver Stopper & Mounts, Figural Finial, Child With Cymbals, Hanau, 12¼ In. .	305
Satin Glass, Stopper, White, Cylindrical, Multicolor Flowers, Hand Painted, Handleless, 10 In..	12

CURRIER & IVES

Currier & Ives made the famous American lithographs marked with their name from 1857 to 1907. The mark used on the print included the street address in New York City, and it is possible to date the year of the original issue from this information. Earlier prints were made by N. Currier and use that name from 1835 to 1847. Many reprints of the Currier or Currier & Ives prints have been made.

Crown Milano, Sweetmeat, Silver Plate Lid, Melon Ribbed, Water Lily, Burmese, 4 x 5 In.
$125

Woody Auction

Crown Milano, Vase, Bulbous, Wavy Rim, Pink Scroll, Gold & Silver, Blossom, Cream Tones, 13 x 6 In.
$550

Woody Auction

Crown Milano, Vase, Cherubs & Scrollwork, 2 Handles, White, Gold Design, 8 x 6 In.
$1,500

Woody Auction

Crown Milano, Vase, Stick, Colonial Ware, Flowering Branches, Wreath At Top, Gold Enamel, 11¾ In., Pair
$1,920

Woody Auction

Cruet, Blue Opaline Glass, Octagonal Stopper, Handle, Enamel Scrolls & Trefoils, Pedestal Base, 7 In.
$60

Woody Auction

Currier & Ives, Gold Mining In California, Frame, c.1871, 10 x 13¼ In.
$688

Hindman

Some collectors buy the insurance calendars that were based on the old prints. The words *large, small,* or *medium folio* refer to size. The original print sizes were very small (up to about 7 x 9 in.), small (8⅘ x 12⅘ in.), medium (9 x 14 in. to 14 x 20 in.), and large (larger than 14 x 20 in.). Other sizes are probably later copies. Copies of prints by Currier & Ives may be listed in Card, Advertising and in the Sheet Music category. Currier & Ives dinnerware patterns may be found in the Adams or Dinnerware categories.

Buffalo Bull, Chasing Back, Turn About Is Fair Play, Geo. Catlin, Frame, 21½ x 26½ In.	1344
Clipper Ship Three Brothers, 2972 Tons, Largest Sailing Ship In The World, Frame, 29 x 37 In.	375
Gold Mining In California, Frame, c.1871, 10 x 13¼ In. .... *illus*	688
John L. Sullivan, Champion Pugilist Of The World, Copy, 11¾ x 9 In.	50
Leaving The Junction, Lightning Express Trains, Frame, 1900s, 25 x 33½ In.	299
Mr. Bonner's Horse Joe Elliott, Driven By J. Bowen, 1873, 17 x 26¼ In.	625
Outward Bound, Dublin, Man Carrying Bindle, 15¾ x 11¼ In.	188
Pride Of America, Lady Liberty, Holding American Flag, Frame, 12¾ x 17 In.	1008
The American National Game Of Base Ball, Hoboken, N.J., Frame, Copy, 1886, 8½ x 11 In.	188
The Great East River Suspension Bridge, 1892, 23¾ x 33¾ In.	360
The Iron Steamship Great Eastern, 22,500 Tons, Frame, c.1858, 27¼ x 36¼ In.	1188
The Port Of New York, Frame, 29½ x 42¾ In.	4688
Two Little Fraid Cats, Frame, Copy, 14 x 18 In.	84
Village Blacksmith, Trees, 1864, 16 x 23¼ In.	781
Volunteer, Yacht On Water, America's Cup Defender, Frame, 1887, 31 x 37 In.	938
Yacht Puritan Of Boston, Frame, C.R. Parsons, 1885, 24½ x 29½ In.	688

CUSTARD GLASS

Custard glass is a slightly yellow opaque glass. It was made in England in the 1880s and was first made in the United States in the 1890s. It has been reproduced. Additional pieces may be found in the Cambridge, Fenton, and Heisey categories. Custard glass is called *Ivorina Verde* by Heisey and other companies.

Chrysanthemum Sprig, Table Set, Blue, Gilt, Northwood, 5 Piece	156
Diamond Fan, Table Set, Gilt, Butter, Cover, 2 Bowls, Sugar & Creamer, Waste Bowl, Dugan, 6 Piece	270
Hobstars, Punch Bowl, Stand, Scalloped Rim, c.1900, 11½ x 14½ In.	93
Intaglio, Shaker, Bulbous, Metal Cap, Northwood, 3¼ In., Pair	30
Inverted Fan & Feather, Bowl Set, 4-Footed, Northwood, Master 5½ x 9½ In., 5 Piece	125
Poinsettia & Lattice, Bowl, Nutmeg Stained Interior, 3-Footed, Northwood, c.1900, 8¾ In., Pair	63

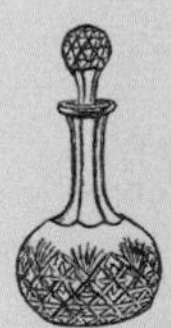

CUT GLASS

Cut glass has been made since ancient times, but the large majority of the pieces now for sale date from the American Brilliant period of glass design, 1875 to 1915. These pieces have elaborate geometric designs with a deep miter cut. Modern cut glass with a similar appearance is being made in England, Ireland, Poland, the Czech Republic, and Slovakia. Chips and scratches are often difficult to notice but lower the value dramatically. A signature on the glass, usually on the smooth inside of a bowl, adds significantly to the value. Other cut glass pieces are listed under factory names, like Hawkes, Libbey, Pairpoint, Sinclaire, and Stevens & Williams.

Bowl, Centerpiece, Fruit, Crosshatch, Cartier, 3¼ x 7¾ In. .... *illus*	188
Bowl, Flared, Gadroon Rim, Flowers, Etched, Disc Foot, 1950s, 4 x 12½ In.	94
Bowl, Grapes, Silver Rim, c.1900, 5 In.	150
Bowl, Intaglio, Berries & Flowers, Scalloped Rim, 3½ x 8 In.	188
Bowl, Silver Rim, Flowers, J.F. Fradley & Co., New York, 1866, 4 x 8 In.	188
Bowl, Star, Silver Banding & Grapes, 4½ x 10½ In.	633
Butter Chip, Star Block, Fan Edge, 3½ In., 9 Piece .... *illus*	36
Butter, Dome Cover, Strawberry Diamond & Fan Design, Hobstar, Arch, Cane, 5 x 8 In.	125
Candlestick, St. Louis Diamond Stem, Scalloped Hobstar Foot, 7 x 4 In.	150
Celery Dish, 3 Circular Hobstar Clusters, Nailhead Diamond, 13 x 6 In.	175

Cut Glass, Bowl, Centerpiece, Fruit, Crosshatch, Cartier, 3 ¼ x 7 ¾ In.
$188

Auctions at Showplace, NYC

TIP
*A signature adds
25 percent to the value
of cut glass.*

Cut Glass, Butter Chip, Star Block, Fan Edge, 3 ½ In., 9 Piece
$36

Woody Auction

Cut Glass, Claret Jug, Reeded Glass, Silver Mounts, Berries, Vines, Acanthus Handle, France, 1800s, 11 In.
$1,250

Charlton Hall Auctions

Cut Glass, Decanter, Cranberry To Clear, Diamonds & Fans Band, Stopper, Continental, c.1880, 16 In.
$269

Jeffrey S. Evans & Associates

Cut Glass, Decanter, Pattern Cut Stopper, 3 Notched Handles, Blue Paint, Hobstar Base, c.1908, 7 x 5 In.
$850

Woody Auction

Cut Glass, Dresser Box, Hinged Lid, Baccarat Style, France, 1900s, 4 x 7 In.
$125

Neal Auction Company

Cut Glass, Dresser Box, Square, Odolet Pattern, Beveled Mirror, C.F. Monroe, 5 x 7 In.
$650

Woody Auction

Cut Glass, Ice Bucket, Iskender, Marked Cristal Hermes, Paris, 5 ⅜ In.
$625

Hindman

Cut Glass, Pitcher, Cranberry, Silver Rim, Zipper & Column, Ribbed Handle, Ray Cut Base, 10 x 5 In.
$3,250

Woody Auction

C

SELECTED CUT GLASS MARKS WITH DATES USED

c

J.D. Bergen & Co.
1885–1922
Meriden, Conn.

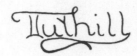

Tuthill Cut Glass Co.
1902–1923
Middletown, N.Y.

Pairpoint Corporation
1880–1938
New Bedford, Mass.

Libbey Glass Co.
1888–1925
Toledo, Ohio

C. Dorflinger & Sons
1852–1921
White Mills, Pa.

T.B. Clark and Co.
1884–1930
Honesdale, Pa.

Majestic Cut Glass Co.
1900–1916
Elmira, N.Y.

Wright Rich Cut Glass Co.
1904–1915
Anderson, Ind.

T.G. Hawkes & Co.
1880–1962
Corning, N.Y.

H.C. Fry Glass Co.
1901–1934
Rochester, Pa.

H.P. Sinclaire & Co.
1905–1929
Corning, N.Y.

House of Birks
c.1894–1907+
Montreal, Quebec, Canada

Laurel Cut Glass Co.
1903–1920
Jarmyn, Pa.

J. Hoare & Co.
1868–1921
Corning, N.Y.

L. Straus & Sons
c.1894–1917
New York, N.Y.

Cheese Dome, Underplate, Fan & Star, Seesaw Rim, Ball Shape Finial, 7 In.		250
Claret Jug, Reeded Glass, Silver Mounts, Berries, Vines, Acanthus Handle, France, 1800s, 11 In. . *illus*		1250
Claret Jug, Silver Plate Mounts, Lion, Holding Shield Lid, England, c.1900, 11 In.		344
Compote, Hobstars, Feathers, Frosted Leaves, Millersburg, 5 ½ In.		45
Compote, Pedestal Dish, Hobstar, Hexagon Base, 14 x 6 ½ In.		130
Decanter, Cranberry To Clear, Diamonds & Fans Band, Stopper, Continental, c.1880, 16 In. *illus*		269
Decanter, Pattern Cut Stopper, 3 Notched Handles, Blue Paint, Hobstar Base, c.1908, 7 x 5 In. *illus*		850
Dresser Box, Hinged Lid, Baccarat Style, France, 1900s, 4 x 7 In. *illus*		125
Dresser Box, Monroe, Octagonal, Engraved Floral Lid, Miter Cut Base, 4 x 6 In.		125
Dresser Box, Square, Odolet Pattern, Beveled Mirror, C.F. Monroe, 5 x 7 In. *illus*		650
Ferner, 3-Footed, Engraved Roses, Kohinoor & Diamonds, 4 x 7 In.		60
Humidor, Arch, Fan & Nailhead Diamond Design, Hobstar Cut Lid, Ray Cut Base, 8 x 4 In.		225
Ice Bucket, Iskender, Marked Cristal Hermes, Paris, 5 ⅜ In. *illus*		625
Jar, Apothecary, Clear, Applied Finial, Polished Pontil, Mid 1800s, 18 In.		84
Jar, Horseradish, Horse Head Lid, Heinz Noble, 5 In.		30
Jar, Vanity, Diamond Cutting, Gold Ormolu Bands, Round, Hinged Lid, 1800s, 2 ½ In.		90
Knife Rest, Diamond, Cylindrical, Flat Side, Colored Ends, Faberge, Box, 2 ½ In.		315
Pitcher, Cranberry, Silver Rim, Zipper & Column, Ribbed Handle, Ray Cut Base, 10 x 5 In. *illus*		3250
Pitcher, Flowers, Diamond, Wide Spout, Late 1800s, 11 ⅛ In.		80
Pitcher, Water, Prism Cut Body, Alternate Hobstar, Crosscut Diamond, Ray Cut Base, 8 ¾ In.		70
Punch Bowl, Diamond, Starburst, Scalloped Edge, Wafer Stem, Bakewell, 1850s, 9 x 10 In. *illus*		360
Punch Bowl, Footed, Deep, Paneled Post, Squared Base, Late 1800s, 11 ½ x 10 ¾ In.		344
Punch Bowl, Harvard, Clear, Late 1800s, 7 x 13 In. *illus*		563
Punch Bowl, Star, Fan, Diamond, Seesaw Rim, 10 ½ x 12 In., 2 Piece		345
Relish, Canoe Shape, Strawberry Diamond & Prism, Hobstar, 3 x 8 In.		150
Scent Bottle, Silver Overlay, Stopper, Diamonds, Buttons, 5 In.		201
Sugar Shaker, Strawberry Diamond, Star & Fan, 5 x 2 In. *illus*		200
Syllabub, Lid, Star Whirl, Shaped Finial, Glass Ladle, 13 x 9 In.		69
Tankard, Cylindrical, Handle, Silver Banding & Grapes, 12 In.		374
Tantalus, Globe Shape, Gilt Bronze Stand, Baluster Legs, Late 1800s, 14 In. *illus*		960
Tumbler, Green To Clear, Diamonds & Fans, Polished Rim, Late 1800s, 3 ⅝ In. *illus*		132
Urn, Diamond Body, Octagonal Base, Anglo-Irish, 1800s, 15 x 5 ¾ In.		484
Urn, Diamond, Clear, Bronze Lid, Square Base, Penny Feet, Anglo-Irish, 15 x 8 In.		380
Urn, Dome Lid, Empire Style, Red, Bronze Mounts, Cross, Round Base, 32 x 8 In., Pair		819
Urn, Empire Style, Bronze Mounts, Malachite Base, Loop Handles, Paw Feet, 1900s, 20 ½ In., Pair		1408
Vase, Clear To Light Emerald, Carved, Horses & Riders, Domed Base, 20 In. *illus*		688
Vase, Concave Diamonds, Stretch, Gold Rim, Celeste Blue, 6 In.		50
Vase, Cranberry, Flared Top, Tapered Waist, c.1900s, 8 In.		191
Vase, Hobstar, Strawberry, Diamond, Cane, Tusks, Star & Fan, 12 x 5 In.		90
Vase, Pedestal, Fan Shape, Prism, Cane, Diamond & Fan, Ray Cut Foot, Pitkin & Brooks, 7 x 8 In.		300
Vase, Seesaw Rim, Stylized Design, Dorflinger, 16 In.		250
Vase, Trumpet, Pedestal, Prism Pattern, Ball Cut Stem, Scalloped Hobstar Foot, 14 x 5 In.		250

CYBIS

Cybis porcelain is a twentieth-century product. Boleslaw Cybis came to the United States from Poland in 1939. He started making porcelains in Long Island, New York, in 1940. He moved to Trenton, New Jersey, in 1942 as one of the founders of Cordey China Co. and started his own company, Cybis Porcelains, about 1950. Boleslaw died in 1957. It appears Cybis made porcelains until the 1990s and old ones are still selling. See also Cordey.

CYBIS

Bust, Clown, Peaked Cap, Ruffled Collar, Red & Green Trim, Holly Leaves, Square Base, 10 In.		96
Bust, Clown, Pompom Cap, Ruffled Collar, Pink Girl, Blue Boy, Square Base, 10 In., Pair		120
Bust, Eros & Psyche, Boy & Girl, Short Curly Hair, Blue Eyes, Square Base, 9 ½ In., Pair		60
Bust, Guinevere, Long Braid, Light Cream Dress, Wood Base, 1900s, 11 In. *illus*		750
Bust, Madonna, Draped Veil, Flower Crown, Wood Base, 10 ½ In. *illus*		59
Figurine, Desiree, White Deer, Lying Down, Flowers, Susan Eaton, 1980s, 4 ½ In.		48
Figurine, Fleurette, Young Woman, Blond Hair, Pink Lined Cape, Pink & Blue Flowers, 8 ½ In.		83
Figurine, Icarus, Winged Man, Falling, Looking Up, 18 x 10 In.		469

Cut Glass, Punch Bowl, Diamond, Starburst, Scalloped Edge, Wafer Stem, Bakewell, 1850s, 9 x 10 In.
$360

Garth's Auctioneers & Appraisers

TIP
Repairs to cut glass can be seen with a black light. It will also show most added plastic repairs. Look at where the foot, knob, or handles might have been reattached. Many auctions have a black light available at the preview.

Cut Glass, Punch Bowl, Harvard, Clear, Late 1800s, 7 x 13 In.
$563

Fontaine's Auction Gallery

Cut Glass, Sugar Shaker, Strawberry Diamond, Star & Fan, 5 x 2 In.
$200

Woody Auction

C

Cut Glass, Tantalus, Globe Shape, Gilt Bronze Stand, Baluster Legs, Late 1800s, 14 In.
$960

Abington Auction Gallery

Cut Glass, Tumbler, Green To Clear, Diamonds & Fans, Polished Rim, Late 1800s, 3 5/8 In.
$132

Jeffrey S. Evans & Associates

Cut Glass, Vase, Clear To Light Emerald, Carved, Horses & Riders, Domed Base, 20 In.
$688

Lion and Unicorn

Cybis, Bust, Guinevere, Long Braid, Light Cream Dress, Wood Base, 1900s, 11 In.
$750

Lion and Unicorn

Cybis, Bust, Madonna, Draped Veil, Flower Crown, Wood Base, 10 1/2 In.
$59

Apple Tree Auction Center

Cybis, Figurine, Melody, Fairy, Flowers, Land of Chimeric, Lynn Klockner Brown, 1981, 6 3/4 In.
$163

Lion and Unicorn

Czechoslovakia Glass, Vase, Cobalt Blue Ground, Gold Splotches, Flared, Rolled Rim, Molded Base, 6 1/2 In
$260

Treadway

Czechoslovakia Glass, Vase, Trumpet, Gold Iridescent, Rolled Rim, Circular Base, Loetz Style, 12 x 6 In.
$225

Woody Auction

D'Argental, Vase, Grapes, Leaves & Vines, Red, Yellow Ground, Signed, 3 x 3 1/2 In.
$240

Treasureseeker Auctions

Figurine, Melody, Fairy, Flowers, Land of Chimeric, Lynn Klockner Brown, 1981, 6¾ In..... *illus* 163
Figurine, Pip The Elfin Player, Sitting On Log, Fox, Multicolor Matte, Phoenix Mark, 8 In.. 75
Figurine, Small Bird, Brown & Gray, In Nest, On Branch, Dogwood Flowers, Signed, 5½ In..... 42

CZECHOSLOVAKIA GLASS

Czechoslovakia is a popular term with collectors. The name, first used as a mark after the country was formed in 1918, appears on glass and porcelain and other decorative items. Although Czechoslovakia split into Slovakia and the Czech Republic on January 1, 1993, the name continues to be used in some trademarks.

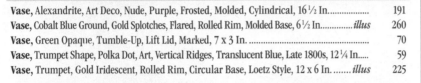

Vase, Alexandrite, Art Deco, Nude, Purple, Frosted, Molded, Cylindrical, 16½ In.................. 191
Vase, Cobalt Blue Ground, Gold Splotches, Flared, Rolled Rim, Molded Base, 6½ In..............*illus* 260
Vase, Green Opaque, Tumble-Up, Lift Lid, Marked, 7 x 3 In. 70
Vase, Trumpet Shape, Polka Dot, Art, Vertical Ridges, Translucent Blue, Late 1800s, 12¼ In..... 59
Vase, Trumpet, Gold Iridescent, Rolled Rim, Circular Base, Loetz Style, 12 x 6 In. ....*illus* 225

DANIEL BOONE

Daniel Boone, a pre–Revolutionary War folk hero, was a surveyor, trapper, and frontiersman. A television series, which ran from 1964 to 1970, was based on his life and starred Fess Parker. All types of Daniel Boone memorabilia are collected.

Book, Wilderness Scout, Hardcover, Green Spine, Orange Lettering, 1957, 254 Pages, 8 x 5 In.... 12
Box, Dome Lid, Hinged, Daniel Leading Pioneers Across Country, 7 x 4 x 2 In. 85
Spoon, Bust, Kentucky State Seal, Sterling Silver, Gorham, 5½ In. 31

D'ARGENTAL

D'Argental is a mark used in France by the Compagnie des Cristalleries de St. Louis. The firm made multilayered, acid-cut cameo glass in the late nineteenth and twentieth centuries. Cameo glass was made with the D'Argental mark from 1919 to 1925. D'Argental is the French name for the city of Munzthal, home of the glassworks. Later the company made enameled etched glass.

Vase, Flowers & Leaves, Cranberry, Shaded Ground, 6 x 3 In. 358
Vase, Grapes, Leaves & Vines, Red, Yellow Ground, Signed, 3 x 3½ In.........................*illus* 240
Vase, Lilies, Shaded Yellow Ground, Etched, Signed, 10 x 4 In. 625
Vase, Maple Branch, Leaves, Seeds, Cranberry, Vaseline Ground, Signed, 10 x 4½ In. .*illus* 960
Vase, Squat, Flowers, Cranberry, Yellow Ground, Round Foot, 3¾ x 5 In.............................. 420

DAUM

Daum, a glassworks in Nancy, France, was started by Jean Daum in 1878. The company, now called *Cristalleries de Nancy,* is still working. The *Daum Nancy* mark has been used in many variations. The name of the city and the artist are usually both included. The term *martele* is used to describe applied decorations that are carved or etched in the cameo process.

Daum 1890	Daum 1960–1971	Daum 1960–1971

Ashtray, Iris, Frosted White, Acid Cut Ground, Gold Highlights, 1 x 4¼ In. 350
Bowl, Dome Lid, Grape & Butterfly Finial, Pedestal, Etched, Pate-De-Verre, 5½ x 5 In. *illus* 540
Bowl, Etched, Bell Flowers, Shaped Rim, Signed, 2½ x 4½ In.. 406
Bowl, Orange Blossom, Cameo, Footed Base, Marked, Nancy, 6½ x 11½ In......................... 768
Bowl, Pink, Iron Frame, Louis Majorelle, 3½ x 6 In... 960
Compote, 2 Running Horses, Marley Gray, Pate-De-Verre, Orange, 4 x 6 In........................... 476

D'Argental, Vase, Maple Branch, Leaves, Seeds, Cranberry, Vaseline Ground, Signed, 10 x 4½ In.
$960

Woody Auction

TIP
A hair dryer set for cool can be used to blow the dust off very ornate pieces of porcelain.

Daum, Bowl, Dome Lid, Grape & Butterfly Finial, Pedestal, Etched, Pate-De-Verre, 5½ x 5 In.
$540

Treasureseeker Auctions

Daum, Dish, Lizard, Gazing At Butterfly, Green & Purple, Pate-De-Verre, Signed, 8 x 4½ x 2 In.
$240

Treasureseeker Auctions

Daum, Perfume Bottle, Etched, Cameo, Silver Lid & Base, 6¾ x 1¼ In.
$455

Treadway

Daum, Salt, Forest Scene, Cameo, Nancy, Lorraine, 1 x 2 In., Pair
$1,320

Treasureseeker Auctions

Daum, Toothpick Holder, Frosted, Acid Cut Ground, Blossoms & Branches, 1¾ x 1½ In.
$200

Woody Auction

Daum, Vase, Flower, Martele & Etched Glass, Signed, 7½ x 3½ In.
$3,125

Treadway

Daum, Vase, Red & Purple Fuchsias, White & Blue Ground, Cameo, Signed, 3¼ In.
$1,020

Treasureseeker Auctions

Daum, Vase, Winter Scene, Mottled, Amber Ground, Oval, c.1900, 4 x 4¾ In.
$1,664

Brunk Auctions

Dish, Lizard, Gazing At Butterfly, Green & Purple, Pate-De-Verre, Signed, 8 x 4 1/2 x 2 In. .... *illus*		240
Figurine, Elephant, Trunk Up, Amber, Clear Glass, Leroy, Pate-De-Verre, 5 x 6 x 2 1/2 In......		469
Inkwell, Red Roses, Leaves, Frosted Cracked Ice, Brass Lid, Etched Mark, c.1920, 5 x 3 1/2 In......		400
Lamp Base, Gilt Socket, Shaped Base, c.1965, 19 1/2 In........		188
Light, Ceiling, Dome Shape, White & Caramel Glass, Metal Acanthus Leaf, 1900s, 13 x 16 In. .		300
Perfume Bottle, Etched, Cameo, Silver Lid & Base, 6 3/4 x 1 1/4 In................*illus*		455
Plate, Ludwig Van Beethoven Portrait, Center, Signed, Numbered, 1970, 9 3/4 In.		63
Rose Bowl, Spherical Shape, River Scene, Cameo, Signed, Nancy, 3 x 3 1/2 In.........		649
Salt, Forest Scene, Cameo, Nancy, Lorraine, 1 x 2 In., Pair ......*illus*		1320
Sculpture, Chariot, Acanthus Leaves, 2 Horses, Arnaldo Giannelli, Italy, 1900s, 12 x 16 In.		350
Sculpture, Crescent, Free Shape Block Base, 20 x 6 In.		80
Toothpick Holder, Frosted, Acid Cut Ground, Blossoms & Branches, 1 3/4 x 1 1/2 In.......*illus*		200
Tray, Lizard On Palm Leaf, Insect, Figural, Pate-De-Verre, 2 x 8 In.		500
Vase, Art Deco, Mottled Glass, Orange Ground, White Flowers, Blue Base, 10 1/2 In.		390
Vase, Art Deco, Wrought Iron, Signed, 1900s, 8 1/2 In.		2193
Vase, Beetle, Cornet, Clear, Pink, Green Base, Pate-De-Verre, Signed, 13 1/2 In.		300
Vase, Bud, Notched Rim, Oxblood Leaf & Branch, Cameo, Early 1900s, 8 x 5 In.		375
Vase, Chardon, 4-Sided, Gilt Relief, Thistles, Green, 4 3/4 In.		281
Vase, Flower, Martele & Etched Glass, Signed, 7 1/2 x 3 1/2 In......................*illus*		3125
Vase, Flowers & Vine, Emerald Green, Silver Rim, Cameo, Signed, 10 x 6 In.		900
Vase, Grapevine, Green, Orange, Pate-De-Verre, c.1900s, 8 x 6 In.		508
Vase, Red & Purple Fuchsias, White & Blue Ground, Cameo, Signed, 3 1/4 In................*illus*		1020
Vase, Tall, Tapered, Acid, Landscape, Pale, Blue Sky, Cameo, Signed, 1900s, 14 In.		6400
Vase, White Flowers, Leaves, Cameo, Signed, Early 1900s, 5 3/8 In..........		1815
Vase, Winter Scene, Mottled, Amber Ground, Oval, c.1900, 4 x 4 3/4 In. ....*illus*		1664
Vase, Yellow & Orange Ground, Lake, Trees, Brown, Cylindrical, Oval Mouth & Base, Cameo, 13 In....		384

DAVENPORT

Davenport pottery and porcelain were made at the Davenport factory in Longport, Staffordshire, England, from 1793 to 1887. Earthenwares, creamwares, porcelains, ironstone, and other ceramics were made. Most of the pieces are marked with a form of the word *Davenport.*

DAVENPORT
LONGPORT
STAFFORDSHRE.

Coffee Set, Imari, Gold Accents, Coffeepot, Cups & Saucers, Sugar & Creamer, Tray, 12 Piece.....		425
Plate, Center Scene, Flower Garland & Mythical Animal Border, Scalloped Rim, 9 In., 3 Piece..		240
Plate, Cobalt Blue, Gold Flowers, Scalloped Rim, c.1880, 9 1/4 In., Pair....................		313
Tea Service, Imari, Teapot, Cup & Saucer, Sugar & Creamer, Tray, Crown Mark, c.1860, 12 Piece...		425
Tea Service, Imari, Teapot, Cup & Saucer, Sugar & Creamer, Tray, Crown Mark, c.1870, 8 Piece *illus*		600
Urn, Flower Spray, Gilt Trim, Pedestal & Handles, Leafy Scrolls, Square Base, 15 1/2 In., Pair...		558

DAVY CROCKETT

Davy Crockett, the American frontiersman, was born in 1786 and died in 1836. The historical character gained new fame in 1954 when the Walt Disney television show ran a series of episodes featuring Fess Parker as Davy Crockett. Coonskin caps and buckskins became popular and hundreds of different Davy Crockett items were made.

Belt Buckle, Name, Cross Flint Rifles, Coonskin Hat, Metal, c.1955		39
Cookie Jar, Young Davy, Brown, Tan, Name On Gun Stock, Brush Pottery, 1956..........		245
Glass, Davy, Fighting Bear With Knife, c.1950, 4 3/4 In.		13
Neck Piece, Blue, Davy, Bear, Indian, Satin, 1950s, 34 x 5 In.		44
Suspenders, Brown Elastic, Indians, Cowboys, Guns, Wagon, 22 In.........		62

DE VEZ

De Vez was a signature used on cameo glass after 1910. E. S. Monot founded the glass company near Paris in 1851. The company changed names many times. Mt. Joye, another glass by this factory, is listed in its own category.

Save the Label
Save all labels and written information found on antiques to help determine the history of the object. Do not remove labels. To copy a bottle label, you can try rolling the bottle on a scanner bed at the scan speed. It is easier than it sounds. Put a wide rubber band on the bottle if it has embossed lettering. It helps make a smoother roll.

Davenport, Tea Service, Imari, Teapot, Cup & Saucer, Sugar & Creamer, Tray, Crown Mark, c.1870, 8 Piece
$600

Heritage Auctions

De Vez, Vase, Gourd Shape, Carved Overlay, Water, Jungle, Cockatoo, Blue Cameo, 8 x 3 3/4 In.
$350

Woody Auction

Decoy, Canada Goose, Black & White Paint, Wood, 1910s, 28 In.
$90

Garth's Auctioneers & Appraisers

Decoy, Duck, Carved, Painted Black, Flat Base, c.1900, 19 In.
$923

Pook & Pook

Decoy, Merganser Drake, Glass Eyes, Mounted Oval Base, Brian
Mitchell, 1900s, 10¾ In.
$344

Eldred's

Decoy, Merganser Duck, Carved, Painted, Brad Schifferl, 13 x 20 In.
$617

Pook & Pook

Decoy, Owl, Stuffed Cloth, Flying Position, Open Wings, Early 1900s,
18 x 24 In.
$594

Hindman

Decoy, Shorebird, Carved, Red Knot, Painted, Jim & Pat Slack, 7½ In.
$265

Pook & Pook

Decoy, Swan, Resin Sculpture, Composition, White, 26 x 20 In.
$384

Copake Auction

Bowl, Lake Scene, Trees, Birds, Pink Mountains, Yellow Ground, Cameo, 3 x 4½ In.	188 to 256
Vase, Cockatoo Bird, Blue Cameo, Pink & White Ground, Double Gourd, 8 In.	420
Vase, Deer & Hunting Dogs, Green Cameo, Orange & Yellow, Swollen Neck, Flat Sides, 9¾ In.....	125
Vase, Fishing Boats, Pink Cameo, Pink & Blue Ground, Cylindrical, 12¼ In.	861
Vase, Flowers & Butterflies, Red & Brown Cameo, Yellow Ground, Globular, c.1910, 9½ In..	1250
Vase, Fuchsia, Cranberry Cameo, Shouldered, 3¾ In., Pair..	750
Vase, Gourd Shape, Carved Overlay, Water, Jungle, Cockatoo, Blue Cameo, 8 x 3¾ In.. *illus*	350
Vase, Landscape, Tower, Steamship, Green Cameo, Pink & Light Blue, Pinched Mouth, 5¾ In..	246

DECOY

Decoys are carved or turned wooden copies of birds, fish, or animals. The decoy was placed in the water or propped on the shore to lure flying birds to the pond for hunters. Some decoys are handmade; some are commercial products. Today there is a group of artists making modern decoys for display, not for use in a pond. Many sell for high prices.

Bluebill Drake, White & Black, Susquehanna River, 14½ In.	118
Bluebill Hen, Mason Challenge Grade, Hollow, 7 x 14½ x 5¾ In.	438
Canada Goose, Black & White Paint, Wood, 1910s, 28 In.............................*illus*	90
Canada Goose, Canvas Covered, Signed, Jamie Snow, Powell Point, N.C., 22 In....................	113
Canvasback Drake, Gilmore B. Wagoner, Havre De Grace, Md., 1987, 16½ In.	165
Curlew, Wood Carving, Standing, Gray, White, Driftwood, Dorothy Anna Blackman, 16½ x 18 In. .	203
Duck, Carved, Painted Black, Brown Head, Mid 1900s, 15½ In.	63
Duck, Carved, Painted Black, Flat Base, c.1900, 19 In..............................*illus*	923
Duck, Carved, Painted, Metal Rings, Ardell Allen Waterfield, 5 x 10 x 4½ In........................	180
Duck, Loon, Carved, Painted, Black & White, Lou Schifferl, 16¾ In.	378
Fish, Ice Fishing, Lead Weights, Wood, Tin Fins, Red Paint, 1950s, 10 In...........................	240
Fish, Sucker, Tin Fins, Lead Weight, Green Paint, Carved, Wood, 1950s, 5 In.	120
Goose, Slat, Wood, Black & White Paint, Early 1900s, 26 x 14 In.	75
Green-Winged Teal Drake, Capt. Harry Jobes, 13½ In.	142
Green-Winged Teal Drake, Miniature, Cedar Base, Peter Peltz, Sandwich, Mass., 1915, 4 In..	469
Mallard Hen, Carved, Painted, Wood, Signed, Late 1900s, 6 x 16 In.................................	590
Merganser Drake, Glass Eyes, Mounted Oval Base, Brian Mitchell, 1900s, 10¾ In......*illus*	344
Merganser Duck, Carved, Painted, Brad Schifferl, 13 x 20 In.......................*illus*	617
Owl, Papier-Mache, Yellow Glass Eyes, Brown, White, Swisher & Soules, Decatur, Ill., 12½ In.....	180
Owl, Stuffed Cloth, Flying Position, Open Wings, Early 1900s, 18 x 24 In. ....*illus*	594
Pigeon, Carved, Painted, Wood, Metal Counter-Balance Base, 12 x 14 x 4 In.........................	549
Shorebird, Carved, Painted, Signed, Herb Daisey Jr., Chincoteague, 5½ In.	118
Shorebird, Carved, Red Knot, Painted, Jim & Pat Slack, 7½ In. ....*illus*	265
Shorebird, Yellowlegs, Carved, Painted, Driftwood Base, 1800s, 9 x 9 x 5 In.	293
Swan, Hollow Carved, Signed, J Hand, New Jersey, 12 x 49 x 14 In.	750
Swan, Resin Sculpture, Composition, White, 26 x 20 In.............................*illus*	384

DEDHAM POTTERY

Dedham Pottery was started in 1895. Chelsea Keramic Art Works was established in 1872 in Chelsea, Massachusetts, by members of the Robertson family. The factory closed in 1889 and was reorganized as the Chelsea Pottery U.S. in 1891. The firm used the marks *CKAW* and *CPUS*. It became the Dedham Pottery of Dedham, Massachusetts, in 1896. The factory closed in 1943. It was famous for its crackleware dishes, which picture blue outlines of animals, flowers, and other natural motifs. Pottery by Chelsea Keramic Art Works and Dedham Pottery is listed here.

Azalea, Bowl, Cereal, Flowers, Blue Rim, c.1910s, 2 x 5½ In......................................	123
Grapevine, Plate, Blue Rim, Rectangular, c.1910, 9⅞ x 6⅛ In.	369
Paperweight, Rabbit, Blue Rabbit Mark, 1910s, 3¼ In..............................*illus*	250
Poppy, Plate, Flower, Seed Pod Border, Blue Ground, Impressed Rabbit, 1896-1929, 8½ In.	595
Rabbit, Creamer, Blue Band, c.1910s, 3¼ x 4 x 2¾ In..............................*illus*	185
Vase, Blue, High Glaze, Impressed Mark, BE, 4⅞ x 4 In.	218

Dedham, Paperweight, Rabbit, Blue Rabbit Mark, 1910s, 3¼ In.
$250

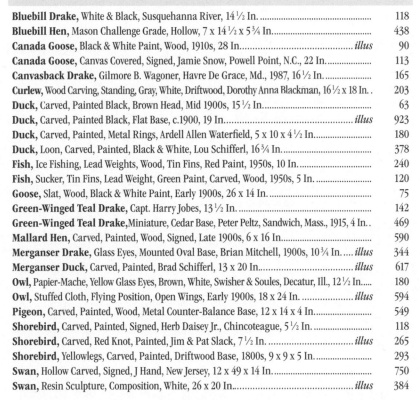

Eldred's

Dedham, Rabbit, Creamer, Blue Band, c.1910s, 3¼ x 4 x 2¾ In.
$185

California Historical Design

Collecting Is Green
Collectors are environmentally friendly. They rescue old pieces that would end up in a landfill. They reuse materials if they're packing and shipping, and they save energy because they often buy at shows, shops, and flea markets where no shipping is necessary. Their homes have better air quality, because old wooden pieces do not emit fumes from new paint or waxes. Next time someone asks why you collect old things, tell them you are saving the environment. Don't mention the gas you used getting to the flea market.

Degue, Lamp, Blown-Out Glass, Blue, Wrought Iron Frame, Art Deco, c.1930, 14¾ x 7¾ In.
$1,071

Doyle

TIP

Don't keep a house key in an obvious spot in the garage.

Degue, Vase, Yellow Orange Ground, Black, Acid Cut Squiggle Design, Cameo, Art Deco, 15 In.
$720

Treasureseeker Auctions

138

DEGENHART

Degenhart is the name used by collectors for the products of the Crystal Art Glass Company of Cambridge, Ohio. John and Elizabeth Degenhart started the glassworks in 1947. Quality paperweights and other glass objects were made. John died in 1964 and his wife took over management. Over 145 colors of glass were made. In 1978, after the death of Mrs. Degenhart, the molds were sold. The D in a heart trademark was removed, so collectors can easily recognize the true Degenhart pieces.

Mug, Peacock & Stork, Amethyst, Blue, Yellow, Red, Signed, Robert Hansen 160

DEGUE

Degue is a signature acid etched on pieces of French glass made by the Cristalleries de Compiegne beginning about 1925. Cameo, mold blown, and smooth glass with contrasting colored rims are the types most often found. The factory closed in 1939.

Chandelier, 3-Light, Domed Shade, Frosted, Molded Flowers & Leaves, Art Deco, 16 x 13¾ In....	325
Chandelier, 4-Light, Frosted Glass, Nickel Over Brass, Art Deco, 1900s, 24½ In.	1625
Lamp, Blown-Out Glass, Blue, Wrought Iron Frame, Art Deco, c.1930, 14¾ x 7¾ In....*illus*	1071
Vase, Mottled Green, Dark Red Drip & Foot, Signed, Art Deco, c.1920, 9½ In.	224
Vase, Purple, Low Relief Flowers, Leaves, Inverted Cone Neck, Round Foot, Marked, 20 x 9 In. ..	308
Vase, Yellow Orange Ground, Black, Acid Cut Squiggle Design, Cameo, Art Deco, 15 In... *illus*	720

DELATTE

Delatte glass is a French cameo glass made by Andre Delatte. It was first made in Nancy, France, in 1921. Lighting fixtures and opaque glassware in imitation of Bohemian opaline were made.

Vanity Set, Mottled Pink & Blue, Cased, 3 Bottles, Atomizer, Jar, Cup, 2 Trays, c.1920, 8 Piece ...	768
Vase, Etched Horses, Front Hooves Raised, Green, Ball Shape, c.1930, 6½ x 5¾ In., Pair	3750
Vase, Lime Green & Orange, Ball Shape, Short Neck, Flared Lip, Ring Foot, Signed, 6 x 5 In.	64
Vase, Mottled Pink, Ball Shape, Iron Collar & 3 Flowered Handles, Signed, Art Deco, 9 In.... *illus*	416
Vase, Standing Horse, Etched, Jarvil, France, c.1930, 6 x 5 In., Pair	3750
Vase, White, Red Morning Glory Flowers & Leaves, Cameo, Bulbous, 7 In.	500
Vase, Yellow Ground, Dark Red Flowers & Leaves, Cameo, Oval, Signed, c.1920, 5¾ In.	224

DELDARE, *see Buffalo Pottery Deldare.*

DELFT

Delft is a special type of tin-glazed pottery. Early delft was made in Holland and England during the seventeenth century. It was usually decorated with blue on a white surface, but some was multicolor, decorated with green, yellow, and other colors. Most delftware pieces were dishes needed for everyday living. Figures were made from about 1750 to 1800 and are rare. Although the soft tin-glazed pottery was well-known, it was not named delft until after 1840, when it was named for the city in Holland where much of it was made. Porcelain became more popular because it was more durable, and Holland gradually stopped making the old delft. In 1876 De Porceleyne Fles factory in Delft introduced a porcelain ware that was decorated with blue and white scenes of Holland that reminded many of old delft. It became popular with the Dutch and tourists. By 1990 all of the blue and white porcelain with Dutch scenes was made in Asia, although it was marked *Delft*. Only one Dutch company remains that makes the traditional old-style delft with blue on white or with colored decorations. Most of the pieces sold today were made after 1891, and the name *Holland* usually appears with the Delft factory marks. The word *Delft* appears alone on some inexpensive twentieth- and twenty-first-century pottery from Asia and Germany that is also listed here.

Charger, Blue Flowers, Starburst Design, White Ground, 1700s, 13½ In.......... *illus*	240
Charger, Flower Medallions, Central Flower Head, Blue, White, Green, Yellow, England, 1700s, 13 In.	690
Charger, Tulip Design, Blue Dash, Round, c.1690, 14 In.	5166
Dish, Squirrel, Leaves, Blue & White Glazed, Dutch, 1700s, 8¾ In........................	1000
Lamp, Banquet, Brass, Faience, Blue & White, Oil To Electric, Footed, France, 1800s, 24 x 8 In...	819
Mug, Floral Sprigs, Multicolor, Blue & Gold Band, Applied Handle, 1700s, 6 In.	210
Mug, Mermaid, Earthenware, Round Handle, Michelle Erickson, Dated 1997, 3¾ In.	388
Plaque, Dutch Scene, Earthenware, Oval, Makkum, c.1900, 22 x 18⅝ In..................	380
Plate, Flowers, Manganese Ground, Round, Mid 1700s, 8 In., Pair...........................	431
Punch Bowl, Chinoiserie, Hand Painted, Flowers, White Ground, Late 1700s, 5 x 12 In.	300
Tea Strainer, Blue, White, Drip Catcher, Silver Plate Strainer, Holland, 1½ x 2¾ In.	12
Tobacco Jar, Brass Lid, Tabac De Virginie, Smoking Figures, Lion Heads, 1700s, 16 x 12 In..	1250
Tobacco Jar, Havana, Flowers, Blue & White, Flared Rim, 1700s, 11¾ In.......... *illus*	2000
Vase, Dome Lid, Bud Finial, Flowers & Leaves, Blue & White, 1700s, 21 x 7 In., Pair..... *illus*	1625
Vase, Long Neck, Blue & White Glaze, Chinese Design, Dutch, 1700s, 14½ In.............	750
Watering Can, Sea Scape, Blue & White, C-Shape Handle, 1800s, 6½ x 3½ In............	500

DENTAL

Dental cabinets, chairs, equipment, and other related items are listed here. Other objects may be found in the Medical category.

Cabinet, 8 Drawers, Bracket Feet, Harvard Co., Canton, Ohio, Early 1900s, 67 x 29 x 15 In... *illus*	2125
Cabinet, Figural, House, Green, White Trim, Brown Roof, 8 Drawers, Door, Child's, 54 x 33 x 15 In.	861
Cabinet, Mahogany, Brass Trim, 6 Drawers, 4 Doors, 4 Shelves, 1900, 16 x 67 x 31 In.	1270
Cabinet, Oak, Black Marble Top, Glass Door, Metal Pulls, Turned Feet, 50 x 16 In...............	546
Cabinet, Painted Black, Drawers, Upper Shelf, Art Deco, 58 x 29½ x 12½ In.	169
Cabinet, Walnut, Carved, Brass Plate, Graduated Drawers, Late 1800s, 65 x 32 x 16 In.	875
Cabinet, Wood, Painted, Beige, Black Trim, 10 Drawers, Metal Top, Rolling, 52 x 29¾ x 15 In.	96
Cabinet, Wood, Painted, Light Green, 3 Top Cabinets, Lower Cabinet, Drawers, 62 x 39 x 13 In.... *illus*	240
Chair, Cream Frame, Brown Seat & Back, Footrest, Child's, 40 In.	62
Drill, Floor, Foot Pedal, S.S. White Dental Mfg. Co., 57 In................................. *illus*	219
Pliers, Tooth Pulling, Pointed Tips, Diamond Pattern Handles, Iron, 7½ x 1¼ In...............	20

DENVER

Denver is part of the mark on an American art pottery. William Long of Steubenville, Ohio, founded the Lonhuda Pottery Company in 1892. In 1900 he moved to Denver, Colorado, and organized the Denver China and Pottery Company. This pottery, which used the mark Denver, worked until 1905, when Long moved to New Jersey and founded the Clifton Pottery. Long also worked for Weller Pottery, Roseville Pottery, and American Encaustic Tiling Company. Do not confuse this pottery with the Denver White Pottery, which worked from 1894 to 1955 in Denver.

Vase, Denaura, Matte Green, Incised Tulips, Oval, 1903, 8½ In...	2375
Vase, Denaura, Matte Green, Leafy Handles, Waisted, 8¼ In..	240
Vase, Denaura, Raised Leaves, Green Glaze, Handles, Cylindrical, Flared Base, 8¼ In.........	240

DEPRESSION GLASS

Depression glass is an inexpensive glass that was manufactured in large quantities during the 1920s and early 1930s. It was made in many colors and patterns by dozens of factories in the United States. Most patterns were also made in clear glass, which the factories called *crystal*. If no color is listed here, it is clear. The name *Depression glass* is a modern one and also refers to machine-made glass of the 1940s through 1970s. Sets missing a few pieces can be completed through the help of a matching service.

Adam, Sugar, Lid, Pink, Jeannette...	16
Adam's Rib, Tray, Amber, Center Handle, Indiana Glass, 11½ In..................................	35
American Sweetheart, Plate, Bread & Butter, Pink, Macbeth-Evans, 6 In.	6

Treasureseeker Auctions

Delatte, Vase, Mottled Pink, Ball Shape, Iron Collar & 3 Flowered Handles, Signed, Art Deco, 9 In.
$416

Garth's Auctioneers & Appraisers

Delft, Charger, Blue Flowers, Starburst Design, White Ground, 1700s, 13½ In.
$240

Hindman

Delft, Tobacco Jar, Havana, Flowers, Blue & White, Flared Rim, 1700s, 11¾ In.
$2,000

Delft, Vase, Dome Lid, Bud Finial, Flowers & Leaves, Blue & White, 1700s, 21 x 7 In., Pair
$1,625

Hindman

Dental, Cabinet, 8 Drawers, Bracket Feet, Harvard Co., Canton, Ohio, Early 1900s, 67 x 29 x 15 In.
$2,125

Hindman

American Sweetheart, Plate, Salad, Pink, Macbeth-Evans, 8 In.	20
American, Bonbon, 3-Toed, 6 In.	10
American, Vase, Footed, Bulbous, 6 In.	17
Baltimore Pear, Sugar, Footed, Jeannette, 4 1/2 In.	10
Berwick, Juice, Anchor Hocking, 4 1/2 In.	6
Berwick, Sherbet, Amber, Anchor Hocking, 3 1/2 In.	6
Block Optic, Bowl, Cereal, Green, Hocking, 5 1/4 In.	15
Block Optic, Plate, Bread & Butter, Green, Hocking, 6 In.	4
Bowknot, Cup, Green	11
Cabaret, Wine, Persimmon	15
Cabaret, Wine, Pink, 5 1/2 In.	8
Cabbage Rose, Serving Bowl, Sharon Pink, Federal Glass, 10 In.	35
Cameo, Mayonnaise, Green, 5 In.	34
Celestial, Bowl, Federal Glass, 11 In.	21
Columbia, Bowl, Ruffled, Federal Glass, 11 In.	35
Columbia, Chop Plate, Federal Glass, 11 In.	20
Coronation, Berry Bowl, Ruby, 5 In.	7
Cube, Plate, Bread & Butter, Green, Jeannette, 5 In.	9
Cube, Sugar & Creamer, Pink, Jeannette	20
Daisy, Cake Plate, Amber, 11 1/4 In.	20
Dewdrop, Snack Set, Jeannette	8
Diamond Point, Butter, Cover, 8 3/4 In.	15
Diamond Point, Fairy Lamp, Blue, Indiana Glass, 5 1/2 In.	13
Diamond Quilted, Creamer, Pink, 3 1/4 In.	10
Dogwood, Tumbler, Pink, Macbeth-Evans, 11 Oz.	5
Fairfax, Plate, Bread & Butter, Amber, 6 In.	5
Floral, Salt & Pepper, Pink, Jeannette	27
Florentine, Water, Hazel Atlas, 7 In.	27
Georgian, Tumbler, Ruby, Anchor Hocking, 3 1/4 In.	9
Heritage, Mayonnaise, Federal Glass, 5 1/2 In.	5
Holiday, Water Set, Pitcher, Tumblers, Pink, 7 Piece........*illus*	42
Louisa, Bowl, Amber, Ruffled, 9 1/2 In.	15
Madrid, Bowl, Vegetable, Oval, 10 In.	15
Madrid, Sugar, Amber	17
Madrid, Sugar, Handles, Footed, Amber	12
Manhattan, Candy Dish, 3-Toed, Pink, Anchor Hocking, 6 1/2 In.	8
Mayfair, Tumbler, Amber, Hocking, 4 In.	16
Milano, Juice, Blue, 6 Oz.	4
Miss America, Berry Bowl, Hocking, 6 1/4 In.	5
Miss America, Plate, Bread & Butter, Hocking, 5 3/4 In.	20
Miss America, Relish, 5 Sections, Hocking, 11 3/4 In.	13
Monarch, Water Goblet, Ruby, 5 In.	12
Old Cafe, Ashtray, Hocking, 4 1/4 In.	6
Old Cafe, Relish, 3 Sections, Hocking, 12 In.	15
Pagoda, Juice, Blue, 3 In.	4
Pagoda, Tumbler, Olive Green, 5 In.	5
Park Avenue, Ashtray, Anchor Hocking	10
Patrician, Cookie Jar, Lid, Amber, Federal, 8 In.........*illus*	75
Pebble Leaf, Relish, Amber, 15 In.	28
Pretty Polly Party Dishes, Dish Set, Sugar, Creamer, 4 Cups & Saucers, Jeannette Junior, Box..*illus*	43
Princess, Candy Dish, Lid, Amber, 6 In.	18
Rainbow, Vase, Pink, Flared, Hocking, 5 In.	25
Sandwich, Bowl, Fruit, Gold	4
Sandwich, Sherbet, Indiana Glass, 3 In.	7
Sandwich, Sugar & Creamer	8
Sandwich, Tumbler, Forest Green, 9 Oz.	8
Sharon, Butter, Pink, 7 3/4 In.	30
Soreno, Butter, Cover, Green	10
Sunflower, Cake Stand, Green, 3-Footed, Jeannette, 1930s, 10 In.	29
Wexford, Butter, Cover, Anchor Hocking	12

Wexford, Plate, Dinner, Anchor Hocking, 9 ½ In.	20
Whitehall, Iced Tea, Amber, Indiana Glass, 6 In.	5
Whitehall, Iced Tea, Indiana Glass, 6 In.	7
Windsor, Cake Plate, Pedestal, 4 ½ x 11 In.	32
Windsor, Candy Dish, Lid, Pink, Indiana Glass	17
Windsor, Creamer, Pink, Jeannette, c.1940, 3 In.	10
Windsor, Plate, Dinner, Blue, Indiana Glass, 11 In.	23
Windsor, Tumbler, Green, 4 In.	8

DERBY, *see Royal Crown Derby category.*

DICK TRACY

Dick Tracy, the comic strip, started in 1931. Tracy was also the hero of movies from 1937 to 1947 and again in 1990, and starred in a radio series in the 1940s and a television series in the 1950s. Memorabilia from all these activities are collected.

Toy, Car, Police, Tin Lithograph, Audible Siren, Green Ground, Marx, 3 x 11 x 4 In. ...... *illus*	144
Toy, Foxhole Tommy Gun, Tin Lithograph, Battery Operated, TN, Japan, Box, 17 In.	186

DICKENS WARE *pieces are listed in the Royal Doulton and Weller categories.*

DINNERWARE

Dinnerware used in the United States from the 1930s through the 1950s is listed here. Most was made in potteries in southern Ohio, West Virginia, and California. A few patterns were made in Japan, England, and other countries. Dishes were sold in gift shops and department stores, or were given away as premiums. Many of these patterns are listed in this book in their own categories, such as Autumn Leaf, Azalea, Coors, Fiesta, Franciscan, Hall, Harker, Harlequin, Red Wing, Riviera, Russel Wright, Vernon Kilns, Watt, and Willow. For more prices, go to kovels.com. Sets missing a few pieces can be completed through the help of a matching service. Three examples of dated dinnerware marks are shown here.

W.S. George Pottery Co. Late 1930s–1940	Royal China Co. 1950s+	Salem China Co. 1940s–1960

Amberstone, Ashtray, Round Shape, 3 Slots, Homer Laughlin	73
Atomic Star, Platter, Paden City Pottery, 1950s, 11 x 14 In.	46
Autumn Leaves, Plate, Dinner, Salem China, 10 In.	7
Ballerina, Bowl, Fruit, Forest Green, Universal Potteries, 5 In.	7
Ballerina, Cup & Saucer, Forest Green, Universal Potteries	3
Bamboo, Plate, Bread & Butter, Harmony House, 6 In.	8
Blossom Time, Cup & Saucer, Royal Albert	32
Blossom Time, Plate, Dessert, Royal Albert, 7 In.	17
Blue Garland, Plate, Salad, Johann Haviland, 7 ¾ In.	9
Blue Vineyard, Cup & Saucer, Iroquois	5
Boutonniere, Creamer, Taylor, Smith & Taylor	10
Boutonniere, Cup & Saucer, Taylor, Smith & Taylor	5
Briarcliff, Bowl, Cereal, Salem, 6 In.	11
Briarcliff, Plate, Dinner, Salem, 10 In.	14
Bristol, Cup & Saucer, Castleton	32
Bristol, Plate, Bread & Butter, Castleton, 6 In.	10
Clarence, Bowl, Vegetable, Oval, Royal Albert, 10 In.	62
Classique Gold, Bowl, Soup, Harmony House, 7 ½ In.	9
Country Charm, Cake Plate, Tab Handles, Salem China, c.1955, 10 ¾ In.	35

Dental, Cabinet, Wood, Painted, Light Green, 3 Top Cabinets, Lower Cabinet, Drawers, 62 x 39 x 13 In.
$240

Cordier Auctions

Dental, Drill, Floor, Foot Pedal, S.S. White Dental Mfg. Co., 57 In.
$219

Fairfield Auction

Depression Glass, Holiday, Water Set, Pitcher, Tumblers, Pink, 7 Piece
$42

Strawser Auction Group

This is an edited listing of current prices. Visit **Kovels.com** to check thousands of prices from previous years and sign up for free information on trends, tips, reproductions, marks, and more.

Depression Glass, Patrician, Cookie
Jar, Lid, Amber, Federal, 8 In.
$75

Ruby Lane

Depression Glass, Pretty Polly Party
Dishes, Dish Set, Sugar, Creamer, 4 Cups
& Saucers, Jeannette Junior, Box
$43

Hartzell's Auction Gallery Inc.

Dick Tracy, Toy, Car, Police, Tin
Lithograph, Audible Siren, Green
Ground, Marx, 3 x 11 x 4 In.
$144

Garth's Auctioneers & Appraisers

Dinnerware, Golden Cabin, Plate,
Artist Signed, Alleene Miller, Blue Ridge
Pottery, 10 In.
$60

Richard D. Hatch & Associates

Country Charm, Cup, Royal China	5
Country Charm, Plate, Dinner, Royal China, 10½ In.	10
Dairy Maid, Bowl, Fruit, Crooksville, 5 In.	11
Dairy Maid, Cup & Saucer, Crooksville	21
Delphine, Vase, Ruffled Top, Pinched Neck, Blue Ridge, 9 In.	70
English Village, Plate, Dinner, Salem China, 10 In.	25
Falling Leaves, Platter, Royal China, 13 In.	20
Flair, Cup & Saucer, Castleton	25
Flower Fest, Plate, Dinner, Mikasa, 10¾ In.	13
Friendly Village, Plate, Dinner, Johnson Brothers	10
Friendly Village, Platter, Johnson Brothers, 15 In.	72
Friendly Village, Sugar, Lid, Footed, Handles, Johnson Brothers	33
Gloria, Plate, Dinner, Castleton, 7 In.	28
Golden Cabin, Plate, Artist Signed, Alleene Miller, Blue Ridge Pottery, 10 In. ....*illus*	60
Golden Scepter, Platter, Paden City Pottery, 8 x 11 In.	32
Golden Wheat, Creamer, Edwin Knowles	21
Golden Wheat, Cup & Saucer, Edwin Knowles	13
Golden Wheat, Plate, Salad, Homer Laughlin, 7 In.	5
Golden Willow, Cup & Saucer, Crooksville	9
Greenbrier, Casserole, Lid, Paden City	55
Greenbrier, Chop Plate, Dell Green, Paden City, 12¾ In.	62
Gretchen Green, Cup & Saucer, Johnson Brothers	5
Harvest Time, Gravy, Iroquois	20
Harvest Time, Plate, Bread & Butter, Iroquois, 6½ In.	8
Harvest Time, Salt & Pepper, Flared, Iroquois	15
His Majesty, Platter, Johnson Brothers, 20 x 16 In.	195
His Majesty, Platter, Turkey, Field, Fruit & Nut Border, Oval, Johnson Bros., 20 x 16 In.	235
Holland, Bowl, Vegetable, Oval, Johnson Brothers, c.1910, 9 x 7 In.	174
Hostess, Plate, Bread & Butter, Edwin Knowles, 6 In.	10
Ivory, Platter, Edwin Knowles, 14¾ In.	25
Ivy Lea, Cup & Saucer, Royal Albert	25
Jubilee, Sugar & Creamer, Footed, 1950s, Castleton	149
Laura, Serving Bowl, Blue Ridge, 9 In.	25
Lavender Rose, Creamer, Royal Albert	40
Lavender Rose, Cup & Saucer, Royal Albert	30
Lazy Daisy, Casserole, Lid, Taylor, Smith & Taylor, 2 Qt.	45
Lazy Daisy, Sugar & Creamer, Taylor, Smith & Taylor	32
Main Street, Plate, Dinner, Peach, Harmony House, 10 In.	12
Manor, Cup & Saucer, Footed, Castleton	10
Maple Leaf, Custard, Royal Albert, 1⅞ In.	12
Marble, Plate, Dinner, Taylor, Smith & Taylor, 10 In.	12
Marble, Platter, Taylor, Smith & Taylor, 13½ In.	21
Margaret Rose, Platter, Johnson Brothers, 12 In.	35
Maryland, Plate, Octagonal, Blue Border, Edwin Knowles, 8 Piece..............*illus*	50
Mayflower, Plate, Dinner, Scalloped Edge, Edwin Knowles, 10 In.	8
Melody, Bowl, Cereal, Square, Johnson Brothers, 6 In.	6
Minion, Bowl, Fruit, Paden City, 5½ In.	8
Mocha Pinecone, Cup & Saucer, Harmony House	9
Mongolia, Bowl, Vegetable, Round, Johnson Brothers, 8½ In.	153
Mongolia, Plate, Salad, Johnson Brothers, c.1925, 8 In.	63
Montana, Tureen, Lid, Footed, Oval, Johnson Brothers, c.1913, 12 x 7 x 6 In.	205
Morning Glory, Relish, Alfred Meakin, c.1890, 8 x 4 In.	42
Morning Glory, Tray, Serving, Tab Handles, Alfred Meakin, 10 x 8 In.	53
Mount Vernon, Platter, Oval, Harmony House, 13 In.	19
Nove Rose, Dish, Shell Shape, Ridged, Blue Ridge, 9 x 9 In.	39
Old Mill, Charger, Johnson Brothers, 11 In.	24
Old Mill, Creamer, Johnson Brothers	18
Old Mill, Mug, Johnson Brothers, 3⅜ In.	20
Palace, Bonbon, Ribbed, Blue Ridge, 9¼ In.	58
Palm Leaf, Grill Plate, Wallace	45

Paris, Bowl, Johnson Brothers, c.1910, 8 ¼ In.	79
Paris, Tray, Johnson Brothers, 8 x 4 In.	47
Petunias, Bowl, Soup, Mikasa, 8 ½ In.	8
Poinsettia, Plate, Salad, Blue Ridge, 7 ¼ In.	12
Poppy, Coffee Set, Percolator, Sugar & Creamer, Royal Rochester, 1930s, Coffeepot 12 x 9 In.	50
Potpourri, Serving Bowl, Johnson Brothers, 9 In.	32
Rodeo, Westward Ho, Plate, Dinner, Wallace, 10 ¾ In.	140
Rosalee, Plate, Dinner, Paden City, 9 In.	15
Rose Marie, Chocolate Pot, Blue Ridge, 8 In.	185
Rustic Plaid, Platter, Blue Ridge, 13 In.	18
Savoy, Platter, Crimped Ribbon Handles, Johnson Brothers, 1900s, 14 x 10 In.	268
Shell Pink, Cup & Saucer, Castleton	12
Silhouette, Butter, Cover	92
Silhouette, Coaster	7
Silhouette, Custard Cup, Flared, 2 ⅜ In.	23
Skytone, Cup & Saucer, Homer Laughlin	13
Splatter Blue, Bowl, Vegetable, Homer Laughlin, 9 ¼ In.	35
Splatter Blue, Cup & Saucer, Homer Laughlin	12
Streamline, Cup & Saucer, Coffee, Red, Tricorne Saucer, Salem, 4 Piece .... *illus*	59
Sweet Pea, Bowl, Cereal, Lug Handle, Blue Ridge, 7 In.	11
Symphony, Plate, Dinner, Chartreuse, Harmony House, 10 In.	12
Tropical, Plate, Dinner, Blue Ridge, 9 ¼ In.	15
Trousseau, Cup, Castleton	30
Verna, Cake Tray, Leaf Shape, Blue Ridge, 10 In.	63
Village, Butter, Cover, Pfaltzgraff	15
Village, Dish, Au Gratin, Pfaltzgraff, 8 ¼ In.	7
Weathervane, Plate, Dinner, Blue Ridge, 10 ¼ In.	24
Wheat, Bowl, Vegetable, Oval, Taylor, Smith & Taylor, 8 ½ In.	18
Wheat, Saucer, Taylor, Smith & Taylor	2
Wheat, Sugar & Creamer, Taylor, Smith & Taylor	27
White Dogwood, Cup & Saucer, Royal Albert	28
Whole Wheat, Gravy Boat, Underplate, Mikasa	40
Whole Wheat, Plate, Dinner, Mikasa, 10 ¾ In.	17
Wild Strawberry, Saucer, Blue Ridge	3
Winchester, Plate, Dinner, Johnson Brothers, 10 In.	31
Winchester, Sugar & Creamer, Johnson Brothers	89
Yellow Hibiscus, Cup & Saucer, Salem	8
Yellow Hibiscus, Plate, Bread & Butter, Salem, 6 In.	5
Yorktown, Bowl, Vegetable, Maroon, Edwin Knowles, 8 ½ In.	15
Yorktown, Plate, Bread & Butter, Blue, Edwin Knowles, 6 In.	6
Yorktowne, Butter, Cover, Pfaltzgraff	21
Yorktowne, Custard, Pfaltzgraff, 2 ¾ In.	3

DIONNE QUINTUPLETS

Dionne quintuplets were born in Canada on May 28, 1934. The publicity about their birth and their special status as wards of the Canadian government made them famous throughout the world. Visitors could watch the girls play; reporters interviewed the girls and the staff. Thousands of special dolls and souvenirs were made picturing the quints at different ages. Emilie died in 1954, Marie in 1970, Yvonne in 2001. Annette and Cecile still live in Canada.

Bowl, Cereal, Faces, Names, Stainless Steel, 1930s, 6 In.	55
Doll, Annette, Composition, Yellow Dress & Bonnet, Name Tag, Madame Alexander, 11 In. .	54
Doll, Bisque, Baby, 5-Section Pouch, Color Coded Ribbon & Bear, 4 ½ In., 5 Piece	101
Doll, Toddler, Composition, Coded Clothes, Name Pins, Madame Alexander, 7 ½ In., 5 Piece *illus*	249
Doll, Toddler, Composition, Dress, Bonnet, Socks, Shoes, Madame Alexander, 12 In., 5 Piece ..... *illus*	1185
Hankie, Quints Wearing Bonnets & Bows, Names, Black Script, Tom Lamb, 8 In.	38
Postcard, Quints, Dr. Dafoe, Sitting On Sidewalk, 1936, 5 x 3 In.	24
Sign, Advertising, Quaker Oats, 5 Panels, Red Ground, Black & White Pictures, 30 x 60 In. .	143

D

Dinnerware, Maryland, Plate, Octagonal, Blue Border, Edwin Knowles, 8 Piece
$50

Strawser Auction Group

Dinnerware, Streamline, Cup & Saucer, Coffee, Red, Tricorne Saucer, Salem, 4 Piece
$59

Apple Tree Auction Center

Dionne Quintuplets, Doll, Toddler, Composition, Coded Clothes, Name Pins, Madame Alexander, 7 ½ In., 5 Piece
$249

Matthew Bullock Auctioneers

Dionne Quintuplets, Doll, Toddler, Composition, Dress, Bonnet, Socks, Shoes, Madame Alexander, 12 In., 5 Piece
$1,185

Matthew Bullock Auctioneers

D

Dirk Van Erp, Bookends, Galleon Ship Tiles, Copper, Multicolor Glaze Ceramic, 4 x 3⅞ x 4¾ In., Pair
$4,687

Toomey & Co. Auctioneers

Dirk Van Erp, Bowl, Warty, Copper, Hammered, Squat, Signed, D'Arcy Gaw, c.1910, 2⅞ x 9¼ In.
$6,765

California Historical Design

Dirk Van Erp, Humidor, Brass, Hammered, Shell Casing, c.1907, 9 x 7½ In.
$984

California Historical Design

Mickey Is a Wagging Head Clock

An Ingersoll Mickey Mouse alarm clock was made with arms that were the hands that moved around the face of the clock and a head that bobs. The 1933 clock is called the "wagging head" clock.

DIRK VAN ERP

Dirk Van Erp was born in 1860 and died in 1933. He opened his own studio in 1908 in Oakland, California. He moved his studio to San Francisco in 1909 and the studio remained under the direction of his son until 1977. Van Erp made hammered copper accessories, including vases, desk sets, bookends, candlesticks, jardinieres, and trays, but he is best known for his lamps. The hammered copper lamps often had shades with mica panels.

Basket, Copper, Hammered, Canoe Shape, Handle, Windmill Stamp, 6½ x 11 In.		570
Basket, Flower, Copper, Hand Hammered, Marked, 6½ x 7 In.		704
Basket, Japanese, Copper Trim, Hammered, Conical, c.1917, 13 x 6 In.		1476
Bookends, Copper, Hammered, Cutout, Signed, D'Arcy Gaw, c.1910, 4 x 4½ In.............		1230
Bookends, Galleon Ship Tiles, Copper, Multicolor Glaze Ceramic, 4 x 3⅞ x 4¾ In., Pair .... *illus*		4687
Bookends, Thinker, Copper, Hammered Cutout, Oak Tree, 4⅝ x 4⅝ x 3⅝ In.		720
Bowl, Warty, Copper, Hammered, Squat, Signed, D'Arcy Gaw, c.1910, 2⅞ x 9¼ In....... *illus*		6765
Humidor, Brass, Hammered, Shell Casing, c.1907, 9 x 7½ In.................................. *illus*		984
Lamp, Electric, 4-Light, 4-Panel Mica Shade, Oil Canister, Copper Base, 19 In.....................		2400
Lamp, Electric, Copper & Mica, Vase Shape, Conical Shade, c.1920, 13 x 11⅝ In. .... *illus*		5400
Tile, Dutch Girl, Frame, c.1915, 5½ x 5½ In.		1845
Tray, Copper, Hammered, Silver Plate, Octagonal, c.1920s, 14½ In......................		215
Tray, Copper, Hammered, Woven, Warty Handle, c.1917, 20 x 15½ In......................		523
Vase, Copper, Hammered, Brown Glaze, Signed, c.1913, 8¼ x 5½ In.................. *illus*		1722
Vase, Copper, Hammered, Rolled Rim, Middle Bulge, Windmill Mark, 21 x 11 In..............		7200
Vase, Rolled Rim, Copper, Patina, 10 x 9 In.. *illus*		1500

DISNEYANA

Disneyana is a collectors' term. Walt Disney and his company introduced many comic characters to the world. Mickey Mouse first appeared in the short film *Steamboat Willie* in 1928. Collectors search for examples of the work of the Disney Studios and the many commercial products modeled after his characters, including Mickey Mouse and Donald Duck, and well-known films, like *Beauty and the Beast, The Little Mermaid*, the *Toy Story* series, and *Frozen*.

Cel, see Animation Art category.	
Clock, Cuckoo, Wood, Mickey & Minnie Mouse, Oak Leaves, Bird, Disney Time, Box, 20 In..	540
Doll, Donald Duck, Sheriff, Felt, Gun, White Hat, Checkered Shirt, Lars, Italy, c.1940, 21 In...*illus*	406
Doll, Mickey Mouse, Stuffed Cloth, 4 Stitched Fingers, Tag, Gund N.Y., 29 In.	95
Doll, Mickey Mouse, Yellow Gloves, Tag In Ear, No. 1416, Steiff, 1930s, 7 In........................	680
Doll, Snow White, Oilcloth Head, Wool Hair, Ideal Toy Co., c.1937-38, 16 In. .... *illus*	234
Egg, Mickey, Minnie, Goofy, Donald Duck, Cinderella's Castle, Stand, R. Vandergrift, 5 In....	180
Egg, Si & Am, Lady & The Tramp, Hand Painted, Glass Dome, Jutta Levasseur, 8 In.	688
Figurine, Alice In Wonderland, Porcelain, Wood Base, Capo-Di-Monte, 11 x 8 x 8 In.	630
Figurine, Captain Hook, I've Got You This Time, Scabbard, Classics Collection, 2000, 7½ x 7 In.	100
Figurine, Cruella De Vil, Standing, Fur Coat, Porcelain, Guiseppe Armani, 13 In.................	375
Figurine, Donald Duck, Bellboy, Wood, Handcrafted, ANRI, Italy, 4 In.	113
Figurine, Dumbo, Simply Adorable, Taking Bath, Wood Barrel, Thailand, 1995, 3¾ In...... *illus*	100
Figurine, Dutch Boy, It's A Small World, Sitting In Tulip, Traditional Attire, Thailand, 1900s, 6¾ In.	88
Figurine, Hola, Dancer, Brazil, It's A Small World, Fruit Basket On Head, Thailand, 1900s, 7 In...	125
Figurine, Mickey Mouse, Plane Crazy, Reading Manual, How To Fly, Thailand, 1998, 4½ In.... *illus*	63
Figurine, Multi Cats, Hand Crafted, Harmony Kingdom, Patrick Romandy Simmons, 2002, 5 In. .	88
Figurine, Scrooge McDuck, Hands Off My Playthings, Bronze, Carl Barks, 1997, 15 In. *illus*	5500
Figurine, Slue Foot Sue, Melody Time, American Folk Heroes, Walt Disney, Box, 10½ In. ...	62
Game, Dexterity, Donald Duck, Carrying Book, Mirrored Back, Metal Case, Germany, 2 In.	47
Game, Dexterity, Mickey Mouse, Metal Frame, Embossed Back, Marked, B.V. Paris, 2 In......	71
Lamp, Mickey Mouse, Toontown Fair, Resin, Yellow, White Shade, Walt Disney World, 1990s, 56 In...	344
Model, King Arthur Carousel, White Horse, Gilt Pole, Wood Base, 50th Anniversary, 2005, 7 In.....	250
Pin, Cast Member, Oval Design, No. 6194, Disneyland, c.1950, 2 In. .... *illus*	2000
Pin, Coffin, Haunted Mansion 30th Anniversary, Black, Silver Letters, Disneyland, 4 x 2 In.	210
Prop, Trophy, Finalist, Donald Duck Toontown Classic, Walt Disney World, 1988, 18¾ In...	1750
Prop, Vehicle, Atom Mobile, Adventure Thru Inner Space, 2 Passengers, Miniature, 11 In...	1800
Radio, Mickey Mouse, Syroco Wood Case, Emerson, 7½ In................................... *illus*	1216

Dirk Van Erp, Lamp, Electric, Copper & Mica, Vase Shape, Conical Shade, c.1920, 13 x 11 5/8 In.
$5,400

Michaan's Auctions

Dirk Van Erp, Vase, Copper, Hammered, Brown Glaze, Signed, c.1913, 8 1/4 x 5 1/2 In.
$1,722

California Historical Design

Dirk Van Erp, Vase, Rolled Rim, Copper, Patina, 10 x 9 In.
$1,500

Treadway

Disneyana, Doll, Donald Duck, Sheriff, Felt, Gun, White Hat, Checkered Shirt, Lars, Italy, c.1940, 21 In.
$406

Hindman

Disneyana, Doll, Snow White, Oilcloth Head, Wool Hair, Ideal Toy Co., c.1937-38, 16 In.
$234

Apple Tree Auction Center

Disneyana, Figurine, Dumbo, Simply Adorable, Taking Bath, Wood Barrel, Thailand, 1995, 3 3/4 In.
$100

Lion and Unicorn

Disneyana, Figurine, Mickey Mouse, Plane Crazy, Reading Manual, How To Fly, Thailand, 1998, 4 1/2 In.
$63

Lion and Unicorn

Disneyana, Figurine, Scrooge McDuck, Hands Off My Playthings, Bronze, Carl Barks, 1997, 15 In.
$5,500

Potter & Potter Auctions

Disneyana, Pin, Cast Member, Oval Design, No. 6194, Disneyland, c.1950, 2 In.
$2,000

Potter & Potter Auctions

145

Disneyana, Radio, Mickey Mouse, Syroco Wood Case, Emerson, 7 ½ In. $1,216

Morphy Auctions

Disneyana, Toy, Boat, Captain Hook's Fearsome Vessel, Pirate, Flag, The Jolly Roger, 11 In. $406

Potter & Potter Auctions

Disneyana, Toy, Donald Duck, Bak-Up, Pulling Mickey & Minnie In Cart, Windup, Fisher-Price, 8 In. $1,750

Bertoia Auctions

TIP
Don't let anyone smoke near your antique dolls. The nicotine residue is harmful and the odor of the smoke is objectionable.

Rocking Chair, Mickey Mouse, Wood, Painted, Kroehler, Prewar, 26 ¾ In.	1230
Silhouette, Walt Disney & Mickey, Disneyland, White Ground, Oval, Harry Brice, Frame, 9 x 7 In.	330
Tombstone, Happy Haunts, Grave, Raven, Hand Pokes Out, Disneyland, R. Noble, 2003, 8 x 9 x 6 In.	450
Toy, Boat, Captain Hook's Fearsome Vessel, Pirate, Flag, The Jolly Roger, 11 In. ....*illus*	406
Toy, Car, Cruella's, 101 Dalmatians, Black & Red, Box, 9 ½ In.	74
Toy, Donald Duck, Bak-Up, Pulling Mickey & Minnie In Cart, Windup, Fisher-Price, 8 In.......*illus*	1750
Toy, Dragon, Frightful Fountain, Nightmare Before Christmas, Box, 2007, 13 In.	420
Toy, Mickey & Donald Duck On Trapeze, Celluloid, Tin, Box, 8 ¼ In.	3444
Toy, Piglet, Disc Joints, Head, Arms & Legs, Green, Stockinette Body Suit, R. John Wright, 8 In.	185
Train, Mickey Mouse Express, Tin Lithograph, Windup, Walt Disney, Marx, Box, 9 ½ In.	510
Trinket Box, Glass Dome Lid, Pirates Of The Caribbean, Disneyland, 50th Anniv., 7 x 6 x 4 In.. *illus*	330

DOCTOR, *see Dental and Medical categories.*

DOLL

Doll entries are listed by marks printed or incised on the doll, if possible. If there are no marks, the doll is listed by the name of the subject or country or maker. Notice that Barbie is listed under Mattel, the manufacturer. G.I. Joe figures are listed in the Toy section. Eskimo dolls are listed in the Eskimo section and Indian dolls are listed in the Indian section. Doll clothes and accessories are listed at the end of this section. The twentieth-century clothes listed here are in mint condition.

A.M., Girl, Bisque Socket Head, Human Hair Wig, Glass Eyes, 1894, 13 In. ....*illus*	277
Advertising, Nauga, Uniroyal, White Naugahyde, Open Mouth, Sharp Teeth, 1957, 15 x 23 In.....*illus*	438
Alexander Dolls are listed in this category under Madame Alexander.	
Alice Leverett, Fashion, Porcelain Head, Painted, Mohair Wig, Resin Body, 12 In.	1538
Annette Himstedt, Madina, Russian Girl, Hard Vinyl, Human Hair, Glass Eyes, Box, 29 In.	185
Armand Marseille dolls are listed in this category under A.M.	
Automaton, Acrobat Clown, Clothes, Music Box Base, Germany, c.1900, 15 In.	720
Automaton, Fox Hunter, Standing, Carved, Top Hat, Coat, Boots, Germany, 14 ½ x 5 In.	469
Automaton, Organ Grinder, Musical, Bear, Red Jacket, Basket, Wood, Dome Base, c.1900, 8 ¼ In.*illus*	908
Barbie Dolls are listed in this category under Mattel, Barbie.	
Bergmann dolls are also in this category under S & H and Simon & Halbig.	
Bergmann, Bisque Head, Jointed Body, Brown, Sleep Eyes, Open Mouth, Hat, Lace, Germany, 18 In..	114
Bild Lilli, Plastic, Blond Ponytail, Pants & Shirt, Germany, 1955, 12 In.	1275
Black Dolls are also included in the Black Americana category.	
Bo Bergemann, Malia, Resin, Changeable Wig & Eyes, Ball-Jointed, 18 ½ In.............*illus*	221
Bru Jne, 2, Kissing Bru, Bisque Socket Head, Mohair Wig, Glass Eyes, Composition Body, 11 In. .	3690
Bucherer, Happy Hooligan, Green Jacket, Red Vest, Blue Pants, 8 ½ In.	720
Chad Valley, Bambina, Cloth, Swivel Head, Mohair Wig, Inset Eyes, 5-Piece Velvet Body, 15 In.	1290
Cloth, Oil Painted, Brown Hair, Blue Eyes, Plaid Dress, c.1880, 25 In. ....*illus*	1080
Door Of Hope, Woman, Wood Head & Arms, Cloth Body, Purple Coat, Yellow Pants, Chinese, 10 In.	95
Edgar Tolson, Boy, Wood, Carved, Articulated Limbs, 10 In.	2500
Effanbee, Patsy, Vinyl, Swivel Head, Synthetic Braids, Big Eyes, Jointed, R. Tonner, 10 ½ In..*illus*	135
French, Bride, Bisque Shoulder Head, Brown Hair, Teeth, Kid Body, Silk Dress, c.1900, 13 In.......	60
G.I. Joe figures are listed in the Toy category.	
Gaultier, Fashion, Composition, Brown Eyes, Blond Hair, Kid Body, Dress, Hat, 17 In.	3150
Gaultier, Fashion, Lady, Bisque Shoulder Head, Human Hair Wig, Kid Body, 18 In.	1169
Gebruder Heubach dolls may also be listed in this category under Heubach.	
Gebruder Heubach, 7925, Lady, Bisque Shoulder Head, Mohair, Oilcloth Body, 20 In. *illus*	1661
Gebruder Heubach, Baby Stuart, Bisque Socket Head, Bonnet, Intaglio Eyes, Bent Limb Body, 8 In.	277
Gebruder Heubach, Bisque Socket Head, Googly Side Glancing Eyes, Composition, Toddler, 8 In....	461
German, Dollhouse Soldier, Bisque, Cloth, Molded & Painted, Silk Uniform, Epaulettes, 6 In.	308
German, Queen Louise, Bisque Head, Blue Glass Sleep Eyes, Brown Hair, Ball-Jointed, 21 In.	83
German, Scottish Boy, Bisque Head, Composition Body, Sleep Eyes, Plaid Kilt, 9 In.	75
Half-Dolls are listed in the Pincushion Doll category.	
Hamburger & Co., Viola, Bisque Socket Head, Glass Sleep Eyes, Fur Eyelashes, 29 In.	62
Hertel Schwab, 136, Girl, Bisque Socket Head, Human Hair Wig, Glass Sleep Eyes, 28 In....	86
Heubach, see also Gebruder Heubach.	

Disneyana, Trinket Box, Glass Dome Lid, Pirates Of The Caribbean, Disneyland, 50th Anniv., 7 x 6 x 4 In.
$330

Potter & Potter Auctions

Doll, A.M., Girl, Bisque Socket Head, Human Hair Wig, Glass Eyes, 1894, 13 In.
$277

Apple Tree Auction Center

Doll, Advertising, Nauga, Uniroyal, White Naugahyde, Open Mouth, Sharp Teeth, 1957, 15 x 23 In.
$438

Wright

Doll, Automaton, Organ Grinder, Musical, Bear, Red Jacket, Basket, Wood, Dome Base, c.1900, 8 ¼ In.
$908

Fontaine's Auction Gallery

Doll, Bo Bergemann, Malia, Resin, Changeable Wig & Eyes, Ball-Jointed, 18 ½ In.
$221

Apple Tree Auction Center

Doll, Cloth, Oil Painted, Brown Hair, Blue Eyes, Plaid Dress, c.1880, 25 In.
$1,080

Garth's Auctioneers & Appraisers

Bisque Doll Heads
Bisque is unglazed porcelain that may be tinted or painted and used for dolls' heads and necks and perhaps hands and bodies. It is also used for figurines and dishes.

Doll, Effanbee, Patsy, Vinyl, Swivel Head, Synthetic Braids, Big Eyes, Jointed, R. Tonner, 10 ½ In.
$135

Apple Tree Auction Center

D

Doll, Gebruder Heubach, 7925, Lady, Bisque Shoulder Head, Mohair, Oilcloth Body, 20 In.
$1,661

Apple Tree Auction Center

Doll, Ives, Baby, Creeping, Composition, Wax Face, Dress, Bonnet, Clockwork, 12 In.
$390

Bertoia Auctions

Doll, Jumeau, Girl, Bisque Head, Mohair Wig, Big Blue Glass Eyes, Jointed Composition, 22 In.
$1,968

Apple Tree Auction Center

Heubach, Bisque Head, Painted, Blond Hair, Blue Eyes, Open Mouth, 1800s, 15 In.	64
Indian dolls are listed in the Indian category.	
Ives, Baby, Creeping, Composition, Wax Face, Dress, Bonnet, Clockwork, 12 In. .... *illus*	390
J.D.K. dolls are also listed in this category under Kestner.	
Jan McLean, Amy, Vinyl, Swivel Head, Shoulderplate, Human Hair, Glass Eyes, 20 In.	123
Jumeau, 6, Bisque Head, Paperweight Eyes, Pierced Ears, France, 1900s, 15 In.	1800
Jumeau, Girl, Bisque Head, Mohair Wig, Big Blue Glass Eyes, Jointed Composition, 22 In. .... *illus*	1968
Jumeau, Girl, Cork Pate, Mohair Wig, Neck Screw, Jointed, France, 20 In.	1440
Jumeau, Triste, Bisque Head, Blue Eyes, Closed Mouth, Pierced Ears, Bebe, 1800s, 28 In. ...... *illus*	2375
K * R, 101, Marie, Bisque Socket Head, Mohair Wig, Black Dress, 12¼ In.	461
K * R, Bisque Head, Brown Eyes, Open Mouth, Blue & Green Plaid Sailor Dress, 1909, 27 In.	152
Kathe Kruse, Girl, Plastic Swivel Head, Painted, Human Hair, Cloth Body, Tab-Jointed, 19 In.	190
Kathy Redmond, Lady In Pink, Molded & Painted, Flowers, Signed, 14½ In. .... *illus*	584
Kestner dolls are also in this category under J.D.K.	
Kestner, 143, Child, Bisque Socket Head, Mohair Wig, Glass Sleep Eyes, 12½ In.	523
Kestner, 162, Lady, Bisque Socket Head, Sleep Eyes, Human Hair, Jointed, Black Dress, 17 In. *illus*	615
Kewpie dolls are listed in the Kewpie category.	
Kley & Hahn, 525, Boy, Bisque Socket Head, Molded & Painted, Intaglio Eyes, 12 In.	308
Lenci, Girl In Regional Costume, Wool Felt, Mohair Wig, Disk Jointed Arms & Legs, 17 In. ..	615
Lenci, Girl, Felt, Pressed & Painted, Swivel Head, Mohair Wig, Side Glancing Eyes, 35 In.	1292
Madame Alexander, Cissy, Plastic, Synthetic Wig, Barrette, Sleep Eyes, Yellow Dress, 19½ In. .... *illus*	523
Madame Alexander, Jane Withers, Plastic, Mohair Wig, Sleep Eyes, Dress Tag, 15½ In. .... *illus*	369
Madame Alexander, Sonja Henie, Composition, Original Outfit, Ice Skates, 15 In.	25
Mattel, Barbie, 35th Anniversary, Blond, Ponytail, Striped Swimsuit, Box, 1994, 12 In.	26
Mattel, Barbie, American Girl, Blond, Fashion Luncheon Ensemble, Pink & White ...... *illus*	531
Mattel, Barbie, American Girl, Blond, Pretty As A Picture Ensemble, Black & White, Transitional.	325
Mattel, Barbie, American Girl, Blond, Vacation Time Ensemble, Pink	189
Mattel, Barbie, Autumn In Paris Ensemble, Jacket, Scarf, Boots, Walking Stick, Box, 1998, 13 In.	56
Mattel, Barbie, Blond Curly Hair, Sweet Dreams Pajamas, Box, Japan, c.1959, 12 In.	284
Mattel, Barbie, Bubble Cut, Titian Hair, Flowered Dress, On The Go Fashion Pak, Red Shoes	118
Mattel, Barbie, Bubble Cut, Titian Hair, Striped Swimsuit, Black Case, Outfits, 1962	310
Mattel, Barbie, Egyptian Queen, Royal Gown & Headdress, Turquoise Cape, Box, 1994, 13 In.	44
Mattel, Barbie, Evening Illusion, Charmeuse Dress, Fur Stole, Nolan Miller, Box, 1999, 15 In. .	94
Mattel, Barbie, George Washington, Coat, Vest, Ruffle, Plumed Hat, Powder Wig, 1997, 12 In.	16
Mattel, Barbie, German, Oktoberfest Costume, Dirndl Skirt, White Apron, Red Jacket, 1987, 11 In.	31
Mattel, Barbie, Glinda The Witch, Sparkly Pink Dress, Silver Stars, Crown, Wand, Box, 1999, 12 In. .	16
Mattel, Barbie, No. 3, Brunette, Ponytail, Striped Swimsuit, Black Mules, White Sunglasses.. *illus*	1239
Mattel, Barbie, No. 4, Blond, Ponytail, Blush Cheeks, Red Dress, Tag	418
Mattel, Barbie, Rapunzel, Long Blond Hair, Teal & Pink Dress, Hat, 1994, 11 In.	24
Mattel, Barbie, Talking, Brunette, Pink Swimsuit, Pink Ribbons, Not Speaking .... *illus*	201
Mattel, Barbie, Twist 'N Turn, Titian Hair, Silver Intrigue Ensemble .... *illus*	295
Mattel, Ken, Scarecrow, Wizard Of Oz, Floppy Straw Hat, Box, 2007, 12 In.	19
Mattel, Peter Pan, Green Tunic, Walt Disney, 1997, 13 In. .... *illus*	17
Mattel, Samurai, Traditional Attire, Black, Red, White, Sword, 2010, Box, 13 In.	88
Mattel, Todd, Young Boy, Black Shorts, White T-Shirt, Happy Meal, Malaysia, Box, 1993, 8 In..	19
Moravian, Polly Heckewelder, Cloth, Stitched Arms & Legs, Pink Gingham Dress, 18 In.	74
Nicole Marschollek-Menzner, Girl, Vinyl, Socket Head, Human Hair, Glass Eyes, Cloth Body, 19 In.	123
Paper Dolls are listed in their own category.	
Pincushion Dolls are listed in their own category.	
Precious Moments, Cory, Girl, Filipina, Floral Dress, Philippines, 1990, 9 In.	6
Precious Moments, Girl, Mazie, African American, Floral Dress, Philippines, 1990s, 9 In.. *illus*	6
R. John Wright, Joel, Mohair Wig, Provincial Costume, Leather Boots, 12½ In. .... *illus*	246
R. Tonner, Chicago Sophisticate, Tyler Wentworth, Sleek White Silk Gown, Box, 15½ In....	185
R. Tonner, Tarrant The Mad Hatter, Alice In Wonderland, Plastic, Jointed Limbs, 17 In.	148
Rag, Woman, Stuffed, Tropical Dress, Head Wrap, U.S. Virgin Islands, 1900s, 12 In.	5
Raggedy Ann, Button Eyes, Sunflower Apron, Anna Mae Enck, Enck's Country Crafts, 1993, 19 In. ...	7
S & H Dolls are also listed here as Bergmann and Simon & Halbig.	
S.F.B.J., 60, Girl, Bisque Head, Painted, Blue Glass Eyes, Composition Body, 1910s, 17 In..... *illus*	167
S.F.B.J., 227, Boy, Bisque Socket Head, Glass Eyes, Blue Suit, 15½ In. .... *illus*	400
S.F.B.J., 236, Laughing Baby, Bisque Head, Glass Sleep Eyes, Open-Close Mouth, 21 In.	450
S.F.B.J., 301, Girl, Bisque, Composition, Blue Glass Sleep Eyes, Human Hair, 24 In.	570

SELECTED DOLL MARKS WITH DATES USED

Effanbee Doll Co.
1922+
New York, N.Y.

Lenci
1922+
Turin, Italy

Hertwig & Co.
1864–c.1940
Katzhütte, Thuringia, Germany

K☆R
–39–

Kämmer & Rheinhardt
1886–1932
Waltershausen, Thüringia, Germany

J.D. Kestner Jr.
1805–1938
Waltershausen, Thuringia, Germany

Ideal Novelty & Toy Co.
1961
New York, N.Y.

L.A. & S.

Louis Amberg & Son
1909–1930
Cincinnati, Ohio; New York, N.Y.

BRU. J^{NE} R
11

Bru Jne. & Cie
c.1879–1899
Paris, France

Armand Marseille
c.1920
Köppelsdorf, Thüringia, Germany

DÉPOSE
TÊTE JUMEAU
◡

Maison Jumeau
1886–1899
Paris, France

Bähr & Pröschild
1871–1930s
Ohrdruf, Thüringia, Germany

DÉPOSE
S.F.B.J.

S.F.B.J. (Société Française de Fabrication de
Bébés & Jouets)
1905–1950+
Paris and Montreuil-sous-Bois, France

ALBEGO
10
Made in Germany

Alt. Beck & Gottschalck
1930–1940
Nauendorf, Thuringia, Germany

Schoenau & Hoffmeister
1901–c.1953
Sonneberg, Thuringia, Germany

Gebruder Heubach
1840–1938
Lichte, Thuringia, Germany

Doll, Jumeau, Triste, Bisque Head, Blue Eyes, Closed Mouth, Pierced Ears, Bebe, 1800s, 28 In.
$2,375

Greenwich Auction

Doll, Kathy Redmond, Lady In Pink, Molded & Painted, Flowers, Signed, 14 ½ In.
$584

Doll, Kestner, 162, Lady, Bisque Socket Head, Sleep Eyes, Human Hair, Jointed, Black Dress, 17 In.
$615

Apple Tree Auction Center

Doll, Madame Alexander, Cissy, Plastic, Synthetic Wig, Barrette, Sleep Eyes, Yellow Dress, 19 ½ In.
$523

Doll, Madame Alexander, Jane Withers, Plastic, Mohair Wig, Sleep Eyes, Dress Tag, 15 ½ In.
$369

Apple Tree Auction Center

> **TIP**
> Madame Alexander dolls are usually marked on the doll's back or at the back of the neck.

Doll, Mattel, Barbie, American Girl, Blond, Fashion Luncheon Ensemble, Pink & White
$531

Apple Tree Auction Center

Apple Tree Auction Center

Apple Tree Auction Center

Doll, Mattel, Barbie, No. 3, Brunette, Ponytail, Striped Swimsuit, Black Mules, White Sunglasses
$1,239

Doll, Mattel, Barbie, Twist 'N Turn, Titian Hair, Silver Intrigue Ensemble
$295

Doll, Precious Moments, Girl, Mazie, African American, Floral Dress, Philippines, 1990s, 9 In.
$6

Apple Tree Auction Center

Apple Tree Auction Center

Lion and Unicorn

Doll, R. John Wright, Joel, Mohair Wig, Provincial Costume, Leather Boots, 12 ½ In.
$246

Doll, Mattel, Barbie, Talking, Brunette, Pink Swimsuit, Pink Ribbons, Not Speaking
$201

Doll, Mattel, Peter Pan, Green Tunic, Walt Disney, 1997, 13 In.
$17

Apple Tree Auction Center

Apple Tree Auction Center

Lion and Unicorn

Apple Tree Auction Center

Doll, S.F.B.J., 60, Girl, Bisque Head, Painted, Blue Glass Eyes, Composition Body, 1910s, 17 In. $167

Jeffrey S. Evans & Associates

Doll, S.F.B.J., 227, Boy, Bisque Socket Head, Glass Eyes, Blue Suit, 15 ½ In. $400

Apple Tree Auction Center

Doll, S.F.B.J., Bebe, Bisque, Blue Glass Eyes, Open Mouth, Mohair Wig, France, 20 In. $330

Treasureseeker Auctions

Doll, Samurai, Composition, Painted, Brass Armor, Plexiglas Case, Mid 1900s, 18 x 9 In. $108

Garth's Auctioneers & Appraisers

Composition—A Mixture
The word *composition*, when used to describe dolls, refers to a combination of materials that is used to make molded bodies and heads. It is usually sawdust or wood pulp mixed with glue.

Doll, Simon & Halbig, Bisque Head, Sleep Eyes, Open Mouth, Pierced Ears, Dress, 28 In. $139

Pook & Pook

Doll, Terri Lee, Plastic, Molded & Painted Face, Brunette, Velvet Coat, Mitten, Boots, 16 In. $148

Apple Tree Auction Center

Doll, Viola H & Co., Bisque Head, Blue Sleep Eyes, Human Hair, Germany, 24 In. $120

Treasureseeker Auctions

Doll Clothes, Tammy, Ballet, Pink Leotard, Tights & Tutu, Flowers, Shoes, Ideal, Box, 1962 $78

Matthew Bullock Auctioneers

S.F.B.J., Bebe, Bisque, Blue Glass Eyes, Open Mouth, Mohair Wig, France, 20 In...........*illus*	330
Samurai, Composition, Painted, Brass Armor, Plexiglas Case, Mid 1900s, 18 x 9 In.....*illus*	108
Shirley Temple dolls are included in the Shirley Temple category.	
Simon & Halbig dolls are also listed here under Bergmann and S & H.	
Simon & Halbig, 1078, Girl, Bisque Socket Head, Flirty Glass Eyes, Mohair Wig, Dress, 24 In....	277
Simon & Halbig, Bisque Head, Brown Eyes, Human Hair Curls, Jointed Body, Chemise, 19½ In..	125
Simon & Halbig, Bisque Head, Sleep Eyes, Open Mouth, Pierced Ears, Dress, 28 In.....*illus*	139
Simon & Halbig, Girl, Bisque, Blond Hair, Sleep Eyes, Pierced Ears, Wood & Composition, 30 In.	94
Terri Lee, Plastic, Molded & Painted Face, Brunette, Velvet Coat, Mitten, Boots, 16 In..*illus*	148
Ventriloquist, Composite, Wood, Painted, Printed Cap, Necktie, 20 In.	150
Viola H & Co., Bisque Head, Blue Sleep Eyes, Human Hair, Germany, 24 In.................*illus*	120
Wislizenus, Girl, Bisque, Painted, Open Mouth, Peach & Cream Dress, Hat, Feather, 28 In.	127

DOLL CLOTHES

Dress, Cotton, Lace, Blue Blouse, White Dots & Trim, Mother-Of-Pearl Buttons, 1800s, 14 In.	63
Dress, Sailor Style, Navy Blue, White Stripes, Chapeau, Stockings, 15½ In............................	88
Tammy, Archery, Red Sweater With T, Jeans, Shoes, Bow, Arrows, Target, Ideal, Box, 1962..	78
Tammy, Ballet, Pink Leotard, Tights & Tutu, Flowers, Shoes, Ideal, Box, 1962............*illus*	78
Tammy, Ice Skating, White Jacket, Red Pants, Skates, Hat, Mittens, Scarf, Ideal, Japan, Box, 1962	89

DONALD DUCK *items are included in the Disneyana category.*

DOORSTOP

Doorstops have been made in all types of designs. The vast majority of the doorstops sold today are cast iron and were made from about 1890 to 1930. Most of them are shaped like people, animals, flowers, or ships. Reproductions and newly designed examples are sold in gift shops. These are three marks used by vintage doorstop makers.

Bradley & Hubbard Manufacturing Co. 1854–1940	Hubley Manufacturing Co. 1894–1965	Wilton Products, Inc. c.1935–1989

Basket, Nantucket, Oak & Ivory, Mermaid Finial, Cast Iron, 7 x 6 x 1 In...............................	397
Brass, Natural Trust, Historic Preservation, Reed & Barton, 1900s, 14 x 5½ x 3 In., Pair....	303
Cat, Black, Standing, Arched Back, Cast Iron, 10 x 6 x 2 In.	1121
Cat, Persian, Seated, White Paint, Cast Iron, Litco Product No. 21, c.1920, 8 In.	329
Cat, Seated, Green Eyes, Black Glaze, Full Figure, Hubley, c.1910s, 7 x 3½ x 3½ In.............	400
Cat, Siamese, Painted, Art Deco, Cast Iron, Nuydea, England, 13 x 4⅛ x 5 In.............*illus*	422
Cat, Standing, Tail Down, Glass Eyes, Collar Bell, Patina, Metal, 17 x 4 x 9 In.	246
Dog & Duck, Painted, No. 11, Cast Iron, A.M.Greenblatt Studios, Boston, 1924, 10 x 8 x 3 In.......*illus*	1053
Dog, Boston Terrier, Seated, White & Black Paint, Cast Iron, Early 1900s, 7 In.............*illus*	156
Dog, Doberman Pinscher, Standing, Hubley, Cast Iron, 1920, 8 In.	443
Dog, Fox Terrier, Wire Hair, Standing, Painted, Cast Iron, 9 In.	96
Dog, Mastiff, Lying Down, Rectangular Base, Cast Iron, 1900s, 14 x 12 x 21 In............*illus*	813
Dog, Pointer, Black & White, Standing, Cast Iron, Mid 1900s, 15½ In.	84
Dog, Scottie, Standing, Cast Iron, Black Paint, 8½ x 10 In.	30
Dog, Spaniel, Standing, Black & White, Cast Iron, 16 In.	160
Drum Major, Mace, Hat, Cast Iron, The Creations Company, Lancaster, 1930, 13 In...........	180
Duck, Wings Spread, Head Up, Preparing To Take Off, Cast Iron, Mid 1900s, 7 In., Pair.......	84
Elephant, Standing, Gilt Trunk, Patina, No. 7766, Rectangular Base, Bradley & Hubbard, 10 x 11 In.	826
Elephant, Under The Palm Tree, Gold, Raising Trunk, Cast Iron, 13 In. ....*illus*	488
Flower Urn, Painted, Cast Iron, Faux Marble Base, Bradley & Hubbard, 10 x 4 x 3 In.........	165
Flower, Fruit, Yellow Basket, Blue Ribbon, Painted, Cast Iron, 16 x 8 In............................	183
Footmen, Attention Position, Red & Black, Iron, Anne Fish, Hubley, c.1930, 12 x 8 x 2 In. ...	761
Girl, Kicking Flower, Red Dress, Cast Iron, c.1920, 9¾ In. ....*illus*	478

DOORSTOP

Doorstop, Cat, Siamese, Painted, Art Deco, Cast Iron, Nuydea, England, 13 x 4⅛ x 5 In.
$422

Toomey & Co. Auctioneers

Doorstop, Dog & Duck, Painted, No. 11, Cast Iron, A.M. Greenblatt Studios, Boston, 1924, 10 x 8 x 3 In.
$1,053

Thomaston Place Auction Galleries

Doorstop, Dog, Boston Terrier, Seated, White & Black Paint, Cast Iron, Early 1900s, 7 In.
$156

Garth's Auctioneers & Appraisers

Doorstop, Dog, Mastiff, Lying Down, Rectangular Base, Cast Iron, 1900s, 14 x 12 x 21 In.
$813

Hindman

Doorstop, Elephant, Under The Palm Tree, Gold, Raising Trunk, Cast Iron, 13 In.
$488

Rafael Osona Nantucket Auctions

Doorstop, Girl, Kicking Flower, Red Dress, Cast Iron, c.1920, 9¾ In.
$478

Jeffrey S. Evans & Associates

Doorstop, Golfer, Brown Coat & Pants, Green Base, Cast Iron, Hubley, c.1920, 8 x 7 x 2 In.
$330

Morphy Auctions

Doorstop, Mallard Duck, Swimming, Painted, Aquatic Plant, Cast Iron, C.J.O. Judd Mfg., 6 x 11 x 3 In.
$995

Thomaston Place Auction Galleries

Doorstop, Mary Quite Contrary, Black Dress, Painted, Cast Iron, c.1915, 15 In.
$418

Jeffrey S. Evans & Associates

Doorstop, Old Man, Black Hat, White Beard, Sweater & Pants, Iron, Painted, 6 In.
$427

Rafael Osona Nantucket Auctions

Doorstop, Punch, Seated, Dog Toby, Painted, Stepped Base, Cast Iron, c.1900, 12 x 9 x 4 In.
$1,404

Thomaston Place Auction Galleries

Doorstop, Sailor, Standing, Painted, Half Round, Integral Stepped Base, Cast Iron, Pa., c.1920, 11 x 5 In.
$857

White's Auctions

Golfer, Brown Coat & Pants, Green Base, Cast Iron, Hubley, c.1920, 8 x 7 x 2 In. .... *illus*	330
Horse, Stamping Foot, Victorian, England, 1800s, 9 ½ x 12 x 2 ¾ In., Pair	375
Horse, Standing, White Socks, Cast Iron, Hubley, 10 ¼ x 11 ½ In.	102
Indian Chief, Feathered Headdress, Weighted, Bronze, c.1920, 7 ⅜ In.	406
Lighthouse, Miniature, Cape Hatteras Light, White, Black, Stripe, Cast Iron, Buxton, 21 ¾ In.	354
Lion, Reclining, Sideward Glancing, Cast Iron, Late 1800s, 14 x 28 x 5 In.	363
Little Heiskell Soldier, Gun, Bronze & Brown Paint, Cast Iron, c.1915, 10 x 5 ¾ In.	96
Mallard Duck, Swimming, Painted, Aquatic Plant, Cast Iron, C.J.O. Judd Mfg., 6 x 11 x 3 In. ...... *illus*	995
Man, Old Salt, Smoking Pipe, Holding Lantern, Yellow Coat, Phillip Keenan, c.2004, 58 x 19 x 9 In.	305
Manor, Hilltop, Rectangular Base, Cast Iron, 9 x 8 x 3 In.	561
Mariner, Wrangling Porpoise, Bronze, Signed, Gift House, New York, 6 x 4 x 3 In.	244
Mary Quite Contrary, Black Dress, Painted, Cast Iron, c.1915, 15 In. .... *illus*	418
Mermaid, Lying Down, Patina, Cast Iron, 16 x 3 In.	63
Mr. Pickwick, Standing, Cast Iron, National Foundry, c.1920, 15 In.	180
Old Man, Black Hat, White Beard, Sweater & Pants, Iron, Painted, 6 In. .... *illus*	427
Peacock, Spread Feathers, Standing, Painted, Cast Iron, Early 1900s, 14 ½ In.	391
Punch, Seated, Dog Toby, Painted, Stepped Base, Cast Iron, c.1900, 12 x 9 x 4 In. .... *illus*	1404
Rabbit, Sitting, Painted, White, Cast Iron, 11 x 11 In.	98
Rabbit, Standing, Hands Down, Glass Eye, Bradley & Hubbard, 15 ½ In.	1830
Rooster, Painted, Red, Yellow, Black, Crowing, Cast Iron, c.1910, 7 x 5 ½ In.	461
Sailor, Standing, Painted, Half Round, Integral Stepped Base, Cast Iron, Pa., c.1920, 11 x 5 In.... *illus*	857
Ship, Clipper, Sailing, Cast Iron, Mfg. National Foundry, 9 ½ x 12 In. .... *illus*	885
Ship, Sailing, 3-Masted, Painted, Brown & Black, Cast Iron, Dated 1927, 7 In.	250
Ship, Sailing, Painted Surface, Wave Shape Base, Cast Iron, 9 In.	90
Woman, Bust, Curly Hair, Necklace, Patina, Circular Base, Cast Iron, 11 In.	94
Woman, Nude, Standing, Outdoor, Pedestal, Cast Iron, 56 In.	600
Woodsman, Pipe, Ax, Dog, Leaning On Tree, Cast Iron, c.1890, 13 ½ x 9 ½ x 3 In. .... *illus*	363

DORCHESTER POTTERY

DORCHESTER POTTERY WORKS BOSTON, MASS.

Dorchester Pottery was founded by George Henderson in 1895 in Dorchester, Massachusetts. At first, the firm made utilitarian stoneware, but collectors are most interested in the line of decorated blue and white pottery that Dorchester made from 1940 until it went out of business in 1979. Even in the 1970s, automated machines were not used; pieces were hand-formed and hand-dipped, and handles were applied individually.

Foot Warmer, Pig Shape, White Glaze, Cork, Stoneware, Marked, 11 x 5 In.	56
Mug, Blueberries, Signed, CaH, 2 ⅞ x 3 ¼ In.	25

DOULTON

Doulton was founded about 1858 in Lambeth, England. A second factory was opened in Burslem, England, by 1871. The name *Royal Doulton* appeared on the company's wares after 1902 and is listed in the Royal Doulton category in this book. Other Doulton ware is listed here. Doulton's Lambeth factory closed about 1956.

Doulton and Co. 1869–1877	Doulton and Co. 1880–1912, 1923	Doulton and Co. 1885–1902

Bibelot, Stoneware, Seated Pixie, Multicolor, Lambeth, 1900s, 4 In.	250
Biscuit Jar, 12-Sided, Cream, Pink Flowers, Gilt, Silver Plate Lid & Bail, Burslem, 8 x 6 ½ In. ...	48
Chamber Pot, Watteau, Serenade Scene, Gilt Accent, Burslem, 1900s, 11 ¼ x 6 In.	31
Dispenser, Water, Lid, Finial, Brown & Blue, Geometric Relief, Footed, Lambeth, 1883, 14 In.	512
Figurine, Jester, Sitting, Holding Puppet, Terra-Cotta, G. Tinworth, Lambeth, 1900s, 12 In...*illus*	10313
Figurine, Mouse On Currant Bun, Stoneware, G. Tinworth, Lambeth, c.1885, 2 ¾ In., Pair...*illus*	946

D

Doorstop, Ship, Clipper, Sailing, Cast Iron, Mfg. National Foundry, 9 ½ x 12 In.
$885

Copake Auction

Doorstop, Woodsman, Pipe, Ax, Dog, Leaning On Tree, Cast Iron, c.1890, 13 ½ x 9 ½ x 3 In.
$363

Fontaine's Auction Gallery

Doulton, Figurine, Jester, Sitting, Holding Puppet, Terra-Cotta, G. Tinworth, Lambeth, 1900s, 12 In.
$10,313

Lion and Unicorn

Doulton, Figurine, Mouse On Currant Bun, Stoneware, G. Tinworth, Lambeth, c.1885, 2¾ In., Pair
$946

Bonhams

Doulton, Group, Mouse Musicians, Trumpet Vase, Stoneware, G. Tinworth, Lambeth, c.1885, 5 In.
$2,581

Bonhams

Doulton, Group, Play Goers, Mice At Punch & Judy Show, G. Tinworth, Lambeth, c.1885, 5 In.
$2,581

Bonhams

Doulton, Group, Tea-Time Scandal, 3 Mice At Table, 1 Underneath, G. Tinworth, Lambeth, c.1885, 3¾ In.
$5,506

Bonhams

Doulton, Plaque, Greene King Ales, Stoneware, Lambeth, 1900s, 14 x 22 In.
$750

Lion and Unicorn

Doulton, Vase, Bulbous, Anne Hathaway's Cottage, Flared Rim, Flow Blue, Burslem, 11 x 11 In.
$225

Woody Auction

Doulton, Vase, Dog Portraits, Brown, Blue, Carved, Edward Dawson, Lambeth, Late 1800s, 9 In.
$1,088

Alex Cooper Auctioneers

> **TIP**
> *Mayonnaise can be used to remove old masking tape, stickers, or labels from glass or china.*

Doulton, Vase, Handle, Brown, Cobalt Blue, Relief Flowers, Stoneware, HW Mark, Lambeth, 1878, 5 In.
$313

Lion and Unicorn

Figurine, Oh! Law, 2-Sided, Ivory Color, Gilt Accents, Charles Noke, 1893, 9 In.	2375
Group, Mouse Musicians, Trumpet Vase, Stoneware, G. Tinworth, Lambeth, c.1885, 5 In.......*illus*	2581
Group, Play Goers, Mice At Punch & Judy Show, G. Tinworth, Lambeth, c.1885, 5 In....*illus*	2581
Group, Tea-Time Scandal, 3 Mice At Table, 1 Underneath, G. Tinworth, Lambeth, c.1885, 3¾ In.*illus*	5506
Loving Cup, Flowers, Silver Rim, 2 Handles, Florence Barlow, Lambeth, 1879, 6 In..............	688
Plaque, Greene King Ales, Stoneware, Lambeth, 1900s, 14 x 22 In................................*illus*	750
Vase, Bulbous, Anne Hathaway's Cottage, Flared Rim, Flow Blue, Burslem, 11 x 11 In..*illus*	225
Vase, Dog Portraits, Brown, Blue, Carved, Edward Dawson, Lambeth, Late 1800s, 9 In..*illus*	1088
Vase, Handle, Brown, Cobalt Blue, Relief Flowers, Stoneware, HW Mark, Lambeth, 1878, 5 In..*illus*	313
Vase, Handle, Stoneware, Tan Ground, Encircling Blue, Lambeth, c.1880, 3¼ In.........*illus*	175
Vase, Rusty Brown Ground, Gilded Flowers, Scalloped Rim, Stylized Base, c.1879, 5¾ In....	63
Vase, Umbrella, Scrolling, Flower, Transferware, Flared Top, Burslem, 23 x 13 In.	96

DRESDEN

Dresden and Meissen porcelain are often confused. Porcelains were made in the town of Meissen, Germany, beginning about 1706. The town of Dresden, Germany, has been home to many decorating studios since the early 1700s. Blanks were obtained from Meissen and other porcelain factories. Some say porcelain was also made in Dresden in the early years. Decorations on Dresden are often similar to Meissen, and marks were copied. Some of the earliest books on marks confused Dresden and Meissen, and that has remained a problem ever since. The Meissen "AR" mark and crossed swords mark are among the most forged marks on porcelain. Meissen pieces are listed in this book under Meissen. German porcelain marked "Dresden" is listed here. Irish Dresden and Dresden made in East Liverpool, Ohio, are not included in this section. These three marks say "Dresden" although none were used by a factory called Dresden.

Karl Richard Klemm
c.1891–1914

Ambrosius Lamm
c.1887+

Carl Thieme / Saxon Porcelain
Manufactory
c.1903

Cachepot, Figures, Chinoiserie, Richard Klemm, 1800s, 4½ x 5 In., Pair..............	968
Candelabrum, 5-Light, Multicolor, Flowers, 2 Putti, Bracket Feet, 13 In., Pair	375
Compote, Cherub, Flowers, Pierced Bowl, Continental, Late 1800s, 17 In., Pair	303
Compote, Flowers, Figural Base, Children Picking Apples, Ladder, 12½ x 9 In.	201
Compote, Putti, Flowers, Blue Ground, Gilt, Footed Base, 1800s, 19¾ In., Pair....................	1220
Dish, Oval, 2 Handles, Flowers, Gilt, 1900s, 11 x 2 In.	63
Figurine, Ballerina, Seated, Lace Dress, Red Shoes, Painted, 8½ x 8 x 5 In................*illus*	75
Figurine, Dog, Marked, Carl Thieme, 1900s, 8¾ In., Pair..*illus*	840
Group, 3 Women, Seated, Singing, Ruffled Lace Dresses, 6½ x 8 x 5 In.	88
Group, Figural, Woman, 2 Men, Sedan Chair, Marked, Unter Weiss Bach, 10 x 11⅝ x 8 In..	375
Lamp, Painted, Courting Scene, Flowers, White Ground, 33 x 8 In..	748
Plaque, Sistine Madonna, Multicolor Enamel, Raphael, Germany, Frame, 1800s, 15 x 21 In.	4063
Tureen, Figural Lid, Woman In Chariot, Mermaids, RK Mark, 1900s, 17 x 13 x 11½ In., Pair.......	1148
Urn, Flowers, Applied & Painted, Figures On Handles, 13 x 9 In.	144
Urn, Flowers, Painted, Gilt Accents, White Ground, 9 In., Pair...	106
Urn, Lift Lid, Hand Painted, Flowers, Goat Handle, Square Base, 15 In., Pair........................	720

DUNCAN & MILLER

Duncan & Miller is a term used by collectors when referring to glass made by the George A. Duncan and Sons Company or the Duncan and Miller Glass Company. These companies worked from 1893 to 1955, when the use of the name *Duncan* was discontinued and the firm became part of the United States Glass Company. Early patterns may be listed under Pressed Glass.

Doulton, Vase, Handle, Stoneware, Tan Ground, Encircling Blue, Lambeth, c.1880, 3¼ In.

$175

Lion and Unicorn

Dresden, Figurine, Ballerina, Seated, Lace Dress, Red Shoes, Painted, 8½ x 8 x 5 In.

$75

Greenwich Auction

Dresden, Figurine, Dog, Marked, Carl Thieme, 1900s, 8¾ In., Pair

$840

Nadeau's Auction Gallery

Durand, Vase, Threaded Designs, Iridescent Blue, Marked, 1995-96, 6 x 6 In.
$216

Alderfer Auction Company

Durand, Water Sprinkler, King Tut, Gooseneck Lip, Blue, Charles Lotton, 1986, 14 In.
$450

Garth's Auctioneers & Appraisers

Enamel, Candlestick, Champleve, Flared Rim, Gilt Bronze, Onyx Base, Footed, France, c.1900, 7 In., Pair
$360

Treasureseeker Auctions

Block, Ice Bucket, Tab Handles, 5 x 7 In.	12
Button Panel, Pitcher, Tankard, Ruby Flashed Rim, No. 44, 9¾ In.	48
Georgian, Bowl, Flared, Etched Rim, Gilt Bronze Base, 4 Cherubs, 6½ x 13 In.	125
Hobnail, Punch Set, Pink Opalescent, Bowl, Ladle, 12 Cups, 5½ x 10 In. Bowl, 14 Piece	99
Hobnail, Vase, Blue Opalescent, Ruffled Rim, 8½ x 8½ x 7½ In.	30

DURAND

Durand art glass was made from 1924 to 1931. The Vineland Flint Glass Works was established by Victor Durand and Victor Durand Jr. in 1897. In 1924 Martin Bach Jr. and other artisans from the Quezal glassworks joined them at the Vineland, New Jersey, plant to make Durand art glass. They called their gold iridescent glass Gold Luster.

Lamp, 3-Light, Tulip Shades, Patinated Metal, Iridescent Glass, 1900s, 13½ In.	893
Lamp, Electric, Gold King Tut, Pink Ground, Bronze, Round Base, 23 x 4 In.	300
Lamp, Gold, Threading & White Metal Fittings, c.1915, 12 x 27 In.	84
Torchiere, Wrought Iron, Eagle Cutout, Tripod Base, 1920, 60½ x 17 In., Pair	531
Torchiere, Wrought Iron, Scrolled Feet, 71½ x 22 In., Pair	313
Vase, Dome Lid, Gold Iridescent, Threading, 7 x 6 In.	563
Vase, Gold Iridescent, Acid Cut Bands, Roses, Cameo, Oval, Tapered Neck, 7½ x 7 In.	1765
Vase, Gold Iridescent, Cylindrical, White, King Tut, Round Rim & Base, 5 x 2 In.	450
Vase, Swirled Zigzag Design, Multicolor, Signed, 6 x 5 In.	100
Vase, Threaded Designs, Iridescent Blue, Marked, 1995-96, 6 x 6 In. ....*illus*	216
Water Sprinkler, King Tut, Gooseneck Lip, Blue, Charles Lotton, 1986, 14 In. ....*illus*	450

DURANT KILNS

DuranT

Durant Kilns was founded by Jean Durant Rice in 1910 in Bedford Village, New York. He hired Leon Volkmar to oversee production. The pottery made both tableware and artware. Rice died in 1919, leaving Leon Volkmar to run the business. After 1930 the name *Durant Kilns* was changed and only the *Volkmar* mark was used. See the Volkmar category.

Vase, Blue Drip Glaze, Shoulders, Tapered Base, Signed, Leon Volkmar, 1920, 15 x 9½ In.	813
Vase, Turquoise Glaze, Amorpha Shape, Curved Base, Bronze Tripod Stand, 1914, 16 In., Pair	256

ELVIS PRESLEY

Elvis Presley, the well-known singer, lived from 1935 to 1977. He became famous by 1956. Elvis appeared on television, starred in 27 movies, and performed in Las Vegas. Memorabilia from any of the Presley shows, his records, and even memorials made after his death are collected.

Necktie, Return To Sender, Stamped Envelopes, Red, Silk, 1993	19
Photograph, Elvis, Riding Bull, Black & White, 1968, 8 x 10 In.	75
Pocket Knife, Portrait, King Of Rock & Roll, 2 Blades, 3½ In.	18
Toy, Guitar, Stars & Notes Design, Box, 28 In.	62

ENAMEL

Enamels listed here are made of glass particles and other materials heated and fused to metal. In the eighteenth and nineteenth centuries, workmen from Russia, France, England, and other countries made small boxes and table pieces of enamel on metal. One form of English enamel is called *Battersea* and is listed under that name. There was a revival of interest in artist-made enameling in the 1930s and a new style evolved. There is a recently renewed interest in the artistic enameled plaques, vases, ashtrays, and jewelry. Enamels made since the 1930s are usually on copper or steel, although silver was often used for jewelry. Graniteware, the factory-made household pieces

made of tin or iron, is a separate category in this book. Enameled metal kitchen pieces may be included in the Kitchen category. Cloisonne is a special type of enamel using wire dividers and is listed in its own category. Descriptions of antique glass and ceramics often use the term *enamel* to describe paint, not the glass-based enamels listed here. Marks used by three important enamelists are shown here.

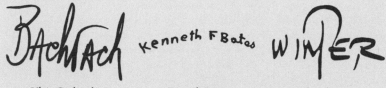

| Lilyan Bachrach 1955–2015 | Kenneth Bates 1920s–1994 | Edward Winter 1932–1976 |

Bowl, Raised Scroll Border, Copper, Duban Christel, Limoges, c.1950, 1 x 4 ½ In. 65
Candlestick, Champleve, Flared Rim, Gilt Bronze, Onyx Base, Footed, France, c.1900, 7 In., Pair*illus* 360
Cigarette Case, Flowers, Multicolor, Silver, Marked, 6th Artel, Moscow, c.1915, 4 In. 3125
Plaque, Battle Scene, Soldiers, Horses, Motto, Vini Vidi Vici, Frame, Limoges, 1700s, 17 x 15 In. .. 5513
Plaque, St. Andrew, Red Border, Frame, Sancte Andrea, Continental, 1700s, 4 x 4 In. 344
Tazza, Champleve, Gilt Bronze Border, Circular, 2 Rocaille Handles, c.1880s, 1 x 13 x 9 In. 875
Triptych, Classical Figures, Stepped Base, Giltwood Frame, Late 1800s, 11 x 18 In. 1188
Urn, Champleve, Gilt Finial, Bronze, Yellow Green Onyx, c.1900, 16 In., Pair .... *illus* 720
Vase, Bud, Dore Bronze, Dolphin Feet, Triangular Base, 5 ½ In. 150
Vase, Teal Ground, Interior Objects, Flower Band, Foot, Japan, 1910s, 13 In., Pair........ *illus* 36

ERPHILA

Erphila is a mark found on Czechoslovakian and other pottery and porcelain made after 1920. This mark was used on items imported by Ebeling & Reuss, Philadelphia, a giftware firm that was founded in 1866 and out of business sometime after 2002. The mark is a combination of the letters *E* and *R* (Ebeling & Reuss) and the first letters of the city, Phila(delphia). Many whimsical figural pitchers and creamers, figurines, platters, and other giftwares carry this mark.

Figurine, Cat, Crouched, Head Lowered, Tail Raised, Gilt Ball In Front Paw, Germany, 10 ¾ In.... 25
Figurine, Man, Standing, Red Coat, Hat, Tall Boots, Powdered Wig, Holding Staff, Germany, 8 In.*illus* 38
Figurine, Woman, Standing, Red Dress, Hat, Holding Parasol, Germany, 8 ½ In................. 32

ES GERMANY

ES Germany porcelain was made at the factory of Erdmann Schlegelmilch from 1861 to 1937 in Suhl, Germany. The porcelain, marked *ES Germany* or *ES Suhl,* was sold decorated or undecorated. Other pieces were made at a factory in Saxony, Prussia, and are marked *ES Prussia.* Reinhold Schlegelmilch also made porcelain. There is no connection between the two factories. Porcelain made by Reinhold Schlegelmilch is listed in this book under RS Germany, RS Poland, RS Prussia, RS Silesia, RS Suhl, and RS Tillowitz.

Box, Hinged Lid, Classical Scene, Flower Borders, Rectangular, Prov Saxe, 2 x 5 ¾ x 3 ¾ In. 38
Pitcher, Molded, Multicolor Ground, Pink Flowers, Gilt, 7 In... 32
Vase, Gilt Handles, Portrait, Woman & Peacock, Green Luster Ground, Pink Flowers, 12 In. 210

ESKIMO

Eskimo artifacts of all types are collected. Carvings of whale or walrus teeth are listed under Scrimshaw. Baskets are in the Basket category.
All other types of Eskimo art are listed here. In Canada and some other areas, the term *Inuit* is used instead of Eskimo. It is illegal to sell some whale parts that are used to

Enamel, Urn, Champleve, Gilt Finial, Bronze, Yellow Green Onyx, c.1900, 16 In., Pair
$720

Treasureseeker Auctions

Enamel, Vase, Teal Ground, Interior Objects, Flower Band, Foot, Japan, 1910s, 13 In., Pair
$36

Selkirk Auctioneers & Appraisers

Erphila, Figurine, Man, Standing, Red Coat, Hat, Tall Boots, Powdered Wig, Holding Staff, Germany, 8 In.
$38

Lion and Unicorn

Eskimo, Carving, Human Head, Bear, Seal, Ptarmigan Bird, Greenstone, Inuit, c.1980, 14 x 8 x 5 In.
$293

Thomaston Place Auction Galleries

Eskimo, Figure, Man, Paddling Kayak, Carved, Rectangular Base, 3 x 15 x 6 In.
$469

New Haven Auctions

Eskimo, Figure, Songbird, On Rock, Carved, Soapstone, Inuit, c.1950, 4¼ In.
$90

Garth's Auctioneers & Appraisers

Eskimo, Sculpture, Hunter On Whale, Spear, Rope, Stone, Carved, Judas Ullulaq, Inuit, 11 x 16 x 8 In.
$3,375

Palm Beach Modern Auctions

made decorative items. The law has changed several times, so check the legality before you buy or sell.

Bookends, Argillite, Polar Bear, Resting, Black, Mid 1900s, 6 x 14 x 3½ In.	113
Carving, Human Head, Bear, Seal, Ptarmigan Bird, Greenstone, Inuit, c.1980, 14 x 8 x 5 In..*illus*	293
Carving, Walrus, Bear, Fighting, Carved, Stone, Inuit, 1974, 11 In.	180
Figure, Bear, Walking, Eating, Fish, Stone, Carved, Jon Puot, Inuit, 6½ x 7 In.	165
Figure, Dancing Bear, Carved Serpentine, Pauta Saila, Cape Dorset, Nunavut, Canada, 10 In.	9450
Figure, Man, Paddling Kayak, Carved, Rectangular Base, 3 x 15 x 6 In. *illus*	469
Figure, Songbird, On Rock, Carved, Soapstone, Inuit, c.1950, 4¼ In. *illus*	90
Sculpture, Halda Bear, Twin Cubs, Eagle Blanket, Argillite, Gary Minaker Russ, 1987, 3 In..	594
Sculpture, Head, Frown Face, Black Paint, Gray Hair, Carved, Stone, 10 x 8½ In.	250
Sculpture, Hunter, On Whale, Spear, Rope, Stone, Carved, Judas Ullulaq, Inuit, 11 x 16 x 8 In.....*illus*	3375
Sculpture, Seal, Eating Fish, Hardstone, Carved, Inuit, Canada Eskimo Art, 7 x 8 In.	281
Sculpture, Soapstone, Mother, Child, Black, Canada, Contemporary, Inuit, 18 In.	250

ETLING

Etling glass pieces are very similar in design to those made by Lalique and Phoenix Glass Company. They were made in France for Etling, a retail shop. They date from the 1920s and 1930s.

Bowl, Opalescent, Hexagonal, Molded Tortoise Stem, Square Base, 1930s, 7 x 12 In.	330
Figurine, Madonna Standing, Satin, Opalescent, Circular Plinth Base, 8 In.	150
Figurine, Madonna, Opalescent Glass, Domed Base, 7½ In. *illus*	240
Vase, Globular, 2 Zigzag Bands, c.1940, 9 In.	120

ФАБЕРЖЕ КΦ FABERGE

Faberge was a firm of jewelers and goldsmiths founded in St. Petersburg, Russia, in 1842, by Gustav Faberge. Peter Carl Faberge, his son, was jeweler to the Russian Imperial Court from about 1870 to 1917. The rare Imperial Easter eggs, jewelry, and decorative items he made are very expensive today. The name *Faberge* is also used for art made of precious metals and jewels by Peter Carl Faberge's grandson, Theo Faberge. He launched a collection of artistic things made of expensive materials in 1985. He made jeweled eggs in several sizes. The collection is sold in several museums.

Box, Lid, Round, Silver, Diamonds, Kokoshnik Mark, Henrik Wigstrom, 2 x 3⅛ In.	4305
Cigarette Case, Silver, Repousse, 3 Bird Heads, Ruby Eyes, Gold Wash Interior, 3¾ In..*illus*	4375
Letter Opener, Silver, Nephrite, 2-Headed Eagle, Handle Finial, Laurel Wreath, 11 x 1 x 1 In.	3510

FAIENCE

Faience refers to tin-glazed earthenware, especially the wares made in France, Germany, and Scandinavia. It is also correct to say that faience is the same as majolica or Delft, although usually the term refers only to the tin-glazed pottery of the three regions mentioned.

Bowl, Blue Matte Glaze, Squat, Kirby Brown, California, c.1915, 2 x 5¾ In.	338
Cachepot, Delftware, Flowers, Multicolor, Hubert Bequet, 1900s, 8 x 9¾ In., Pair	212
Charger, Cobalt Blue Rim, Putti Playing, Laurel Leaves, Italy, 1800s, 16 In.	125
Dish, Palissy, Octopus, Shellfish, Snakes, Trompe L'Oeil, Jose Francisco De Sousa, 13 In. ...*illus*	2048
Jar, White & Blue, Signed, Talavera, Marked, London, England, 9 In.	125
Pitcher, Duck Shape, Standing, Multicolor, St. Clement, Early 1900s, 13½ In.	125
Terrine, Rabbit, Lid, Cream Ground, Grape Leaves, Molded Base, 5 x 12 In.	350
Tureen, Lid, Underplate, White Glaze, Shaped Handles, 9½ x 13½ In.	313
Vase, Brown Matte Glaze, Bulbous, Signed, California, c.1915, 3 x 3½ In.	369
Vase, Face, Wearing Turban, Square Rim, Multicolor, Italy, c.1950, 14 In. *illus*	250
Vase, Turquoise, Blue, Ribbed, Signed, California, c.1920s, 5⅛ x 3¾ In.	554

FAIRING

Fairings are small souvenir boxes and figurines that were sold at country fairs during the nineteenth century. Most were made in Germany. Reproductions of fairings are being made, especially of the famous *Twelve Months after Marriage* series.

Figurine, Returning At One O'Clock In The Morning, Wife & Husband, Chamber Pot, 3 x 4 In.	42
Figurine, The Orphans, 3 Dogs On & Next To Chair, Studded Collars, c.1887	98
Pin Box, Fireplace, Mirror, Fruit Bowl, Conta & Boehme, Germany, Victorian, 4 x 2¾ In...*illus*	25
Trinket Box, Baby, Bassinet, Blond Hair, Pink, 4 In.	128

FAIRYLAND LUSTER *pieces are included in the Wedgwood category.*

FAMILLE ROSE, *see Chinese Export category.*

FAN

Fans have been used for cooling since the days of the ancients. By the eighteenth century, the fan was an accessory for the lady of fashion and very elaborate and expensive fans were made. Sticks were made of ivory or wood, set with jewels or carved. The fans were made of painted silk or paper. Inexpensive paper fans printed with advertising were giveaways in the late nineteenth and early twentieth centuries. Electric fans were introduced in 1882. There are collectors of electric fans who like to buy damaged ones to repair.

Advertising, Straus Gunst & Co., Woman's Portrait, Blue, Calendar, Framed, 1910, 26 x 20 In. ...	840
Electric, 4 Brass Blades, Black Base, General Electric, 12 In....*illus*	180
Electric, Emerson, 4 Blades, Steel Cage, 3-Speed, Tilt, No. 77648-AK, 1950s	84
Electric, Funeral Parlor, Copper Flash, Scroll Feet, Luminaire, 59 x 20 x 20 In....*illus*	2400
Electric, Multi Speed Lever, Purple, 4 Blades, Circular Base, Emerson, 1900s, 21½ In.	240
Electric, Westinghouse, Art Deco, Cast Iron Propeller, Adjustable Height & Speed, 63 x 18 In.	115
Electric, Zephyr, Aluminum, Steel, Edgar T. Ward's Sons Co., c.1929, 70 x 18 In.	2750
Ivory, French Silk, Pastoral Scene, Men & Women, Gold Filigree, Shadowbox Frame, 1800s	318
Lace, Black & Gold, White Border, Shadowbox Frame, Victorian, 15 x 28 In.	58
Mechanical, Shoo-Fly, 2 Fabric Fins, Fringe, 48 In. ...*illus*	608
Mother-Of-Pearl, Courting Scene, Landscapes, Sequins, Lace, Flowers, Frame, 12¾ x 16½ In. ...	32
Paper, Group, Painted, Gilt Rocaille, Folding, Horn Sticks, France, 1800s, 10½ In.	240
Paper, Hand Painted, Bamboo Ribs, Flowers, Central Lake Scene, c.1915, 11 x 18 In. ....*illus*	72
Paper, Outdoor Group, Flowers, Gilt, Folding, Mother-Of-Pearl Inlay, France, 1800s, 10¾ In.	300
Paper, Silvered, Landscape, Flowers On Reverse, Folding, Chinese, 19th Century, 12 In.	544
Silk, Embroidered, Courtyard Scene, Woman & Scholars, Round, Chinese, 17 x 10 In.	200

FAST FOOD *collectibles may be included in many categories, including Advertising, Coca-Cola, Glass, Toy, etc.*

FENTON

Fenton Art Glass Company was founded in 1905 in Martins Ferry, Ohio, by Frank L. Fenton and his brother, John W. Fenton. They painted decorations on glass blanks made by other manufacturers. In 1907 they opened a factory in Williamstown, West Virginia, and began making glass. The company stopped making art glass in 2011 and assets were sold. A new division of the company makes handcrafted glass beads and other jewelry. Copies are being made from leased original Fenton molds by an unrelated company, Fenton's Collectibles. The copies are marked with the Fenton mark and Fenton's Collectibles mark. Fenton is noted for early carnival glass produced between 1907 and 1920. Some of these pieces are listed in the Carnival Glass category. Many other types of glass were also made. Spanish Lace in this section refers to the pattern made by Fenton.

Etling, Figurine, Madonna, Opalescent Glass, Dome Base, 7½ In.
$240

Treasureseeker Auctions

Faberge, Cigarette Case, Silver, Repousse, 3 Bird Heads, Ruby Eyes, Gold Wash Interior, 3¾ In.
$4,375

Eldred's

Faience, Dish, Palissy, Octopus, Shellfish, Snakes, Trompe L'Oeil, Jose Francisco De Sousa, 13 In.
$2,048

Neal Auction Company

This is an edited listing of current prices. Visit **Kovels.com** to check thousands of prices from previous years and sign up for free information on trends, tips, reproductions, marks, and more.

Faience, Vase, Face, Wearing Turban, Square Rim, Multicolor, Italy, c.1950, 14 In.
$250

Hindman

Fairing, Pin Box, Fireplace, Mirror, Fruit Bowl, Conta & Boehme, Germany, Victorian, 4 x 2¾ In.
$25

VintageYardMarket on Etsy

Fan, Electric, 4 Brass Blades, Black Base, General Electric, 12 In.
$180

Chupp Auctions & Real Estate, LLC

Fan, Electric, Funeral Parlor, Copper Flash, Scroll Feet, Luminaire, 59 x 20 x 20 In.
$2,400

Morphy Auctions

Fan, Mechanical, Shoo-Fly, 2 Fabric Fins, Fringe, 48 In.
$608

Rachel Davis Fine Arts

Fan, Paper, Hand Painted, Bamboo Ribs, Flowers, Central Lake Scene, c.1915, 11 x 18 In.
$72

Garth's Auctioneers & Appraisers

Fenton, Bride's Basket, Cranberry Glass, Ruffled Rim, Cased Pink, Silver Plate Frame, 12 x 11 In.
$350

Woody Auction

Fenton, Daisy & Fern, Apothecary Jar, Lift Lid, Cranberry, Footed, 8 In.
$248

Charleston Estate Auctions

Fenton, Mosaic, Vase, 2 Handles, Centennial, Multicolor, Signed, George W. Fenton, 6 In.
$160

Seeck Auctions

| Fenton Art Glass Co. 1970–1975 | Fenton Art Glass Co. 1980s | Fenton Art Glass Co. 1983+ |

Atlantis, Vase, Hand Painted, Fish, Bubbles, Aqua, Signed, Michelle Kibbe, 6 ½ In. 170
Bicentennial, Paperweight, Eagle, Stars, Blue, Signed, Robert Hansen, 1976. 110
Bride's Basket, Cranberry Glass, Ruffled Rim, Cased Pink, Silver Plate Frame, 12 x 11 In. .... *illus* 350
Daisy & Fern, Apothecary Jar, Lift Lid, Cranberry, Footed, 8 In. .... *illus* 248
Grape & Cable, Bowl, Fruit, Persian Medallion, Scrolled Feet, Blue. 95
Grapes & Leaves, Cookie Jar, Dome Lid, Cream Ground, 7 In. 99
Hobnail, Vase, Cranberry, Flared & Scalloped Rim, Footed, 7 ½ In. 111
Lemonade Set, Green, Dark Blue Handles, Ribbed, Pitcher, 6 Cups, 10 In., 7 Piece 375
Mosaic, Vase, 2 Handles, Centennial, Multicolor, Signed, George W. Fenton, 6 In. .... *illus* 160
Peach Blow, Bowl, Square, Pink Satin, Hand Blown, White Interior, Gilt Rim 23
Stag & Holly, Bowl, Deep, Deer, Leaves, Scrolled Feet, Blue, Green, Yellow, 11 In. 80

FIESTA

Fiesta, the colorful dinnerware, was introduced in 1936 by the Homer Laughlin China Co., redesigned in 1969, and withdrawn in 1973. It was reissued again in 1986 in different colors. New colors, including some that are similar to old colors, have been introduced. One new color is introduced in March every year. The simple design was characterized by a band of concentric circles beginning at the rim. Cups had full-circle handles until 1969, when partial-circle handles were made. Harlequin and Riviera were related wares. The Fiesta® Tableware Company was formed in 2020 after Homer Laughlin China was bought by Steelite International, a British company. Fiesta is still being made at the plant in Newell, West Virginia, and is sold at the retail outlet store in Newell. Steelite sells Fiesta to the hospitality industry. For more prices, go to kovels.com.

| Fiesta 1936–1970 | Fiesta Kitchen Kraft 1939–c.1943 | Fiesta Casual 1962–c.1968 |

Cobalt Blue, Carafe, Lid, Handle, Sphere Body Shape, Spout, Footed, 9 ¼ In. .... *illus* 254
Cobalt Blue, Compote, Sweets, Round, Stand Base. 158
Dark Green, Eggcup, Footed 136
Dark Green, Pitcher, Water, Disc, Handle. .... *illus* 124
Ivory, Syrup, Lid, Handle. 254
Medium Green, Bowl, Dessert, 6 In. 254
Red, Candleholder, Tripod, Art Deco, Pyramid, Pair. .... *illus* 452
Turquoise, Candleholder, Bulb Shape, Plinth Base, Pair 73
Yellow, Salad Bowl, Half Sphere Shape, Footed. .... *illus* 215

FINCH, *see Kay Finch category.*

FINDLAY ONYX AND FLORADINE

Findlay onyx and Floradine are two similar types of glass made by Dalzell, Gilmore and Leighton Co. of Findlay, Ohio, about 1889. Onyx is a patented yellowish white opaque glass with raised silver daisy decorations. A few rare

Fiesta, Cobalt Blue, Carafe, Lid, Handle, Sphere Body Shape, Spout, Footed, 9 ¼ In.
$254

Strawser Auction Group

Fiesta, Dark Green, Pitcher, Water, Disc, Handle
$124

Strawser Auction Group

Fiesta, Red, Candleholder, Tripod, Art Deco, Pyramid, Pair
$452

Strawser Auction Group

Fiesta, Yellow, Salad Bowl, Half Sphere Shape, Footed
$215

Strawser Auction Group

Findlay, Spooner, Floradine, Ruby, Flowers, Polished Rim, c.1889, 4 In. $192

Jeffrey S. Evans & Associates

Findlay, Syrup, Onyx, Flowers, Applied Handle, c.1889, 7 In. $144

Jeffrey S. Evans & Associates

Firefighting, Bucket, Leather, Eagle Decor, Swing Handle, 1800s, 10 In. $281

Hindman

pieces were made of rose, amber, orange, or purple glass. Floradine is made of cranberry-colored glass with an opalescent white raised floral pattern and a satin finish. The same molds were used for both types of glass.

Celery Vase, Onyx, Opaline Glass, Silver Inclusions, 6 In.	75 to 240
Pitcher, Water, Onyx, Opaline Handle, Round Body, 8 In.	780
Saltshaker, Onyx, Metal Lid, Ivory Glass, Platinum Flowers, Round, c.1889, 3 In.	215
Spooner, Floradine, Ruby, Flowers, Polished Rim, c.1889, 4 In. .... *illus*	192
Sugar, Onyx, Flowers, Platinum Stain, Opal White Ground, Clambroth Lid, Finial, 1800s, 3 x 4 In.	517
Sugar Shaker, Onyx, Metal Lid, Ivory Glass, Platinum Flowers, c.1889, 5½ In.	215 to 316
Sugar Shaker, Onyx, Opaline Glass, Metal Lid, Daisies, 1888, 5½ In.	395
Syrup, Onyx, Flowers, Applied Handle, c.1889, 7 In. .... *illus*	144
Syrup, Onyx, Metal Lid & Handle, Opaline Glass, Silver Inclusions, 7 In.	282
Toothpick Holder, Onyx, Opaline, Silver Inclusions, Round, Scalloped Square Collar, 2⅜ In.	38
Tumbler, Onyx, Ivory Glass, Platinum Flowers, Barrel Shape, c.1889, 3¾ In., Pair	203
Vase, Onyx, Metallic, Flowers, Scalloped Rim, Hand Blown, Victorian, 5¼ In.	475

FIREFIGHTING

Firefighting equipment of all types is collected, from fire marks to uniforms to toy fire trucks. It is said that every little boy wanted to be a fireman or a train engineer 75 years ago and the collectors today reflect this interest.

Bell, Faraday, Electric, Wall Mount, Alarm, Sconce, 10 In.	90
Bell, Fire Engine, Brass Locomotive, Wax Apple Shape, 12 In.	390
Bucket, Leather, Eagle Decor, Swing Handle, 1800s, 10 In. .... *illus*	281
Bucket, Leather, Lady Liberty, Seated, Flower Border, Painted, Oval, 1700s, 12 In. .... *illus*	2223
Bucket, Leather, Painted, No. 1, George Payson, 1769, 11½ In.	1524
Bucket, Powder, Canvas, Painted Decor, Dieu Et Don Droit Banner, Late 1700, 19 In.	563
Bucket, W. Bedford, Painted, White Text, Swing Handle, 1846, 13 In. .... *illus*	375
Fire Grenade, Babcock, M.F.G. Co., Des Plaines St., Chicago, Cobalt Blue, Sheared, 7½ In.	1560
Fire Grenade, Barnum's Hand, Fire Ext., Diamond, Pat'd June 26th 1869, Yellow Olive, 6 In.	1020
Fire Grenade, Emerald Green, Vertical Ribs All Around, ABM Lip, Contents, 5½ In.	600
Fire Grenade, Extinctrice, Clear, Embossed Squares, Textured Band, France, 5½ In.	420
Fire Grenade, Harden's Hand Fire Extinguisher, Diamonds, Apple Green, Sheared, 6¼ In.	660
Fire Grenade, Harden's Hand, Embossed Star, Amber, Ribbed, Sheared, Qt., 1875-95, 8 In.	900
Fire Grenade, Harden's Hand, Embossed Star, Lime Green, Ribbed, Sheared, 1875-95, 6½ In.	900
Fire Grenade, Hayward's Hand, Patented Aug 8 1871, Diamond Panels, Light Amethyst, 6 In.	840
Fire Grenade, Hayward's Hand, Patented Aug 8 1871, Diamond Panels, Lime Green, 6 In.	360
Fire Grenade, Hayward's Hand, Patented Aug 8 1871, Diamond Panels, Smoky Sapphire Blue, 6 In.	570
Fire Grenade, L.B., Turquoise, Vertical Ribs, Shaped Neck, Sheared, France, 1880-1900, 5 In.	390
Fire Grenade, PSN, Monogram, Flattened Diamonds, Amber, Diamond, Label, 1870-15, 7½ In.	840
Fire Grenade, Santa Fe Route, Clear, Sheared, Contents, 1880-95, 7⅜ In.	3300
Fire Grenade, W.D. Allen, Chicago, Crescent Moon, Clear, Melon Form, Sheared Mouth, 8 In.	1140
Fire Grenade, Yellow Amber, Embossed Squares, Round Indented Label Panel, 5¾ In.	4200
Fire Mark, Bronze, American Eagle 1792, Insurance Co. Of North America, 1900s, 36 x 30 In. .. *illus*	469
Fire Mark, Cast Iron, Oval, Wheels, Chimney, Letters, 1800s, 8½ x 11 In.	517
Hose Reel, Hand Drawn, Wooden Wheels, Steel Tires, Red Paint, 60½ x 56 x 62 In.	360
Nozzle, 2 Handles, Arrow Brass Co., Brass, 30 In.	210
Sign, Hat Shape, New York Firemen's Association, Wood, Early 1900s, 17 x 20 x 32 In.	1815
Trumpet, Parade, Fireman's, Silver Plate, Presentation, Capt. E. Milford Bard, Phila, 1857, 24 In.	3803

FIREPLACE

Fireplaces were used to cook food and to heat the American home in past centuries. Many types of tools and equipment were used. A pair of andirons held the logs in place, firebacks reflected the heat into the room, and tongs were used to move either fuel or food. Chenets are a type of andirons. Many types of spits and roasting jacks were made and may be listed in the Kitchen category.

Firefighting, Bucket, Leather, Lady Liberty, Seated, Flower Border, Painted, Oval, 1700s, 12 In.
$2,223

White's Auctions

Firefighting, Bucket, W. Bedford, Painted, White Text, Swing Handle, 1846, 13 In.
$375

New Haven Auctions

Firefighting, Fire Mark, Bronze, American Eagle 1792, Insurance Co. Of North America, 1900s, 36 x 30 In.
$469

Eldred's

TIP

If you want to install an antique fireplace surround in an apartment or house that you might want to sell as a valuable antique when you move, try this: Make a wooden backing for the marble or wooden parts. Attach the antique parts to the backing and hang it in place at the opening for the fire. Check with experts to be sure it is not a fire hazard. Often the fireplace is decorative and never used.

Fireplace, Andirons, Brass, 2 Acorns, Chamfered Finial, Spurred Legs, Phila., Late 1700s, 20 x 11 In.
$671

Rafael Osona Nantucket Auctions

Fireplace, Andirons, Brass, Lemon Top, Plinth Pedestal, Slipper Feet, 19 x 18¾ x 12 In.
$234

Thomaston Place Auction Galleries

Fireplace, Andirons, Cast Iron, Architectural Elements, Mythological Creature, c.1915, 36 x 12 x 25 In.
$500

New Haven Auctions

Fireplace, Andirons, Cast Iron, Caribou, Pad Feet, Late 1800s, 27 x 29 x 14 In.
$438

Hindman

Fireplace, Andirons, Cast Iron, Owl, Yellow & Black Glass Eyes, Howes, 21 x 20 In.
$840

Michaan's Auctions

Fireplace, Andirons, Iron, Arts & Crafts, Hand Forged, Serpent, c.1910, 22¼ x 14 x 22¼ In.
$554

California Historical Design

Fireplace, Andirons, Wrought Iron, Arts & Crafts, Curled, Twisted Elements, 27 x 13 x 22 In.
$455

Toomey & Co. Auctioneers

TIP

Some disciplined collectors have a rule: Add a new piece to the collection only if you can get rid of a less desirable old one. Most of us just keep adding.

Fireplace, Bench, Fireside, Brass, Baluster Rail & Foot, Faux Leather Seat, 19 x 74 x 28 In.
$300

Garth's Auctioneers & Appraisers

Fireplace, Chenets, Bronze, Louis XVI Style, Putti, Floral Garland, Hoofed Feet, Late 1800s, 20 x 16 x 6 In.
$2,420

Fontaine's Auction Gallery

Fireplace, Chenets, Gilt Bronze, Lion, Rampant, Shells, 1800s, 11 ½ In.
$1,216

Brunk Auctions

Andirons, Brass & Cast Iron, Sunburst, Contemporary, 25 x 19 In.	427
Andirons, Brass, 2 Acorns, Chamfered Finial, Spurred Legs, Phila., Late 1700s, 20 x 11 In. *illus*	671
Andirons, Brass, Column Shape, Flame Finials, Paw Feet, Front Hooks, Late 1700s, 29 x 13 x 21 In.	702
Andirons, Brass, Federal, Curved Legs, Tripod Feet, c.1820, 15 ¼ In.	227
Andirons, Brass, Federal, Steeple Top, Gilt, c.1805, 21 In.	185
Andirons, Brass, Lemon Top, Plinth Pedestal, Slipper Feet, 19 x 18 ¾ x 12 In. *illus*	234
Andirons, Brass, Urn Finial, Ball & Claw Feet, 26 In.	325
Andirons, Brass, Urn, 3 Spurred Arched Legs, Ball Feet, 1800s, 19 x 18 In.	122
Andirons, Brass, Wrought Iron Supports, c.1800, 14 ¾ x 9 ¾ In.	152
Andirons, Bronze, Owl, Perched, Patina, Branches Shape Base, Early 1900s, 15 x 9 x 19 In.	726
Andirons, Cast Bronze, Lion Figure, Grotesque Masks, Iron Log Rests, 34 x 21 x 22 In.	1170
Andirons, Cast Iron, Architectural Elements, Mythological Creature, c.1915, 36 x 12 x 25 In. *illus*	500
Andirons, Cast Iron, Caribou, Pad Feet, Late 1800s, 27 x 29 x 14 In. *illus*	438
Andirons, Cast Iron, Cherub Girl Figures, Seated, 16 x 24 x 9 In.	345
Andirons, Cast Iron, Figural, Caduceus, Medicine Symbol, c.1915, 17 x 14 In.	329
Andirons, Cast Iron, Figural, Owl, Yellow Glass Eyes, Rostand, 14 ¼ In.	250
Andirons, Cast Iron, Owl, Yellow & Black Glass Eyes, Howes, 21 x 20 In. *illus*	840
Andirons, Cast Metal, Openwork, 2 Lions, Hoof Feet, Continental, Late 1800s, 24 In.	2000
Andirons, Copper Ring Mounted, Central Glass Balls, Steel Plinth Base, 11 x 8 In.	244
Andirons, Figural, Geo. Washington, Virginia Metal Crafters, Waynesboro Stove Co., 15 x 7 In.	90
Andirons, Forged Iron, Mushroom Shape Tops, Penny Feet, 1700s, 23 x 11 x 18 In.	497
Andirons, Iron, Arts & Crafts, Hand Forged, Serpent, c.1910, 22 ¼ x 14 x 22 ¼ In. *illus*	554
Andirons, Iron, Brass, Columnar, Urn Top, Square Plinths, Ball & Claw Feet, Early 1800s, 29 In.	3000
Andirons, Silvered Brass, Neoclassical, Openwork, Lion Masks, Late 1800s, 21 x 9 x 19 In.	125
Andirons, Wrought Iron, Arts & Crafts, 22 x 9 ½ x 22 In.	125
Andirons, Wrought Iron, Arts & Crafts, Curled, Twisted Elements, 27 x 13 x 22 In. *illus*	455
Andirons, Wrought Iron, Black, Twisted Loop Design, Scroll Shape Feet, 24 x 13 x 22 In.	702
Andirons, Wrought Iron, Punched Design, Faceted Finials, Miniature, 1800s, 5 In.	400
Andirons, Wrought Iron, Scrollwork, S-Shape Feet, 1700s, 28 x 12 x 31 In.	50
Bench, Fireside, Brass, Baluster Rail & Foot, Faux Leather Seat, 19 x 74 x 28 In. *illus*	300
Bucket, Brass, Hammered, Crest, Mask & Ring Handles, Paw Feet, England, 1800s, 29 x 27 In.	820
Chenets, Andirons, Bronze, Cherub Busts, Paw Feet, Renaissance Style, France, Late 1800s, 43 In.	1280
Chenets, Brass, Torch Shape, Gilt, Ball Feet, France, 1800s, 22 x 11 In.	656
Chenets, Bronze, Louis XVI Style, Putti, Floral Garland, Hoofed Feet, Late 1800s, 20 x 16 x 6 In. *illus*	2420
Chenets, Bronze, Renaissance Revival, Lion, Rampant, Stamped, 1800s, 21 In.	750
Chenets, Figural, Putti & Flame, 10 x 12 ½ In.	156
Chenets, Gilt Bronze, Flowers, France, 1800s, 19 x 13 x 6 In.	702
Chenets, Gilt Bronze, Lion, Lying Down, Plinth Base, Continental, 1800s, 10 x 9 x 3 In.	615
Chenets, Gilt Bronze, Lion, Rampant, Shells, 1800s, 11 ½ In. *illus*	1216
Chenets, Gilt Bronze, Louis XVI Style, Cherubs, France, Late 1800s, 21 x 13 x 5 In. *illus*	545
Chenets, Spelter, Opposing Rottweiler Dogs, 11 ½ x 5 ½ x 6 ½ In. *illus*	160
Coal Bucket, Brass, Gilt, Swing Handle, Pierced, Rosettes, 3 Paw Feet, 1800s, 19 x 10 In. *illus*	439
Coal Scuttle, Hinged Lid, Tole, Ornate Gilt Handle, Flowers, Lion's Head Feet, 24 x 14 x 12 In. *illus*	293
Coal Scuttle, Tole, Painted, Flowers, Gilt, Claw Feet, Victorian, Late 1800s, 18 x 22 x 14 In.	125
Fender, Brass & Iron, Stylized Wirework, Vertical Bars, c.1815, 43 ¾ x 12 ½ In. *illus*	329
Fender, Brass, Acanthus Scrolls, 1800s, 9 x 66 x 17 In.	293
Fender, Brass, Edwardian, Gilt, Pierced, Lion's Paw Feet, England, 12 x 55 x 16 In.	351
Fender, Brass, Neoclassical Style, Torches, Leaves Garlands, Paw Feet, 1900s, 9 ¼ x 56 In.	363
Fender, Cast Brass & Steel, Chippendale, Pierced, Cutout Top, 1800s, 7 x 44 x 11 In.	120
Fender, Gilt Bronze, Neoclassical, Acorn Finial, Openwork, Late 1800s, 19 x 38 In.	344
Fender, Wire, Brass Finials & Feet, c.1780s, 16 x 50 ½ In. *illus*	469
Fireback, Cast Iron, Deer Figures, Hillside, Arched Top, 23 x 23 ½ In.	156
Fireback, Cast Iron, Tombstone Top, Crown, Wing Pendant, Olive Branches, Early 1700s, 32 In.	527
Fireback, Silvered Cast Iron, Allegorical Scene, 32 x 35 In. *illus*	375
Fireplace, Steel, Enameled, Black & Red, Hoff & Windinge, Tasso, Denmark, 1942, 35 x 18 x 31 In.	2125
Flue Cover, Metal, Stamped, Painted, Red, Eagle, Shield, Victorian, 16 In. *illus*	167
Footman, Brass, Georgian Style, Rectangular Top, 2 Faux Drawers, England, c.1800s, 14 x 20 ½ In.	240
Footman, Brass, Pierced & Shaped Apron, Cabriole Legs, Paw Feet, 1700s, 12 x 19 x 13 In. *illus*	234

Fireplace, Chenets, Gilt Bronze, Louis XVI Style, Cherubs, France, Late 1800s, 21 x 13 x 5 In.
$545

Fontaine's Auction Gallery

Fireplace, Chenets, Spelter, Opposing Rottweiler Dogs, 11 ½ x 5 ½ x 6 ½ In.
$160

Roland NY Auctioneers & Appraisers

Fireplace, Coal Bucket, Brass, Gilt, Swing Handle, Pierced, Rosettes, 3 Paw Feet, 1800s, 19 x 10 In.
$439

Thomaston Place Auction Galleries

Fireplace, Coal Scuttle, Hinged Lid, Tole, Ornate Gilt Handle, Flowers, Lion's Head Feet, 24 x 14 x 12 In.
$293

Thomaston Place Auction Galleries

Fireplace, Fender, Brass & Iron, Stylized Wirework, Vertical Bars, c.1815, 43 ¾ x 12 ½ In.
$329

Jeffrey S. Evans & Associates

Fireplace, Fender, Wire, Brass Finials & Feet, c.1780s, 16 x 50 ½ In.
$469

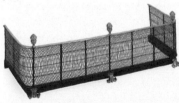

Eldred's

Fireplace, Fireback, Silvered Cast Iron, Allegorical Scene, 32 x 35 In.
$375

Susanin's Auctioneers & Appraisers

Fireplace, Flue Cover, Metal, Stamped, Painted, Red, Eagle, Shield, Victorian, 16 In.
$167

Rachel Davis Fine Arts

Fireplace, Footman, Brass, Pierced & Shaped Apron, Cabriole Legs, Paw Feet, 1700s, 12 x 19 x 13 In.
$234

Thomaston Place Auction Galleries

TIP

Fire screens were used in the 19th century, when the open hearth was the main source of heat and light. People wore makeup made of wax, and an adjustable screen shielded the face and kept the makeup from melting off.

FIREPLACE

Fireplace, Footman, Stool, Iron, Brass, Engraved, Pine Trees, England, c.1790, 14 In.
$270

Cottone Auctions

Fireplace, Screen, Brass, Collapsible, 9 Fan Shape Panels, Music Lyre Design, 26 x 40 In.
$90

Woody Auction

Fireplace, Screen, Leaded Glass, Phoenix, Geometric Panels, Urns & Flowers, Early 1900s, 59 x 32 x 17 In.
$6,958

Fontaine's Auction Gallery

Fireplace, Screen, Needlework, Tripod, Spider Legs, 1800s, 48 In.
$100

New Haven Auctions

Fireplace, Screen, Wrought Iron, Arts & Crafts, Painted, Peacock Set, Landscape, 31 x 37 ½ In.
$360

Michaan's Auctions

Fireplace, Tool Set, Cast Iron & Brass, Poker, Shovel, Tongs, Stand, 28 x 9 ½ x 6 In.
$63

Greenwich Auction

Footman, Brass, Rectangular, 2 Slanted Feet, 2 Side Handles, 1900s, 11 x 19 In.	76
Footman, Stool, Iron, Brass, Engraved, Pine Trees, England, c.1790, 14 In. *illus*	270
Grate, Cast Iron, Arts & Crafts, Early 1900s, 17 x 27 x 23 In.	563
Log Holder, Copper, Hand Hammered Rivets, Oak, Charles Rohlfs, 12 x 25 x 21 In.	3360
Mantel is listed in the Architectural category.	
Screen, Arts & Crafts, Galleon Ship, England, c.1910, 28 x 20¾ x 7 In.	154
Screen, Bamboo, Needlepoint Inset, Cat, Fishbowl, Framed, 36 x 27½ x 10½ In.	224
Screen, Brass, Arts & Crafts, Leaded Glass, Multicolor, Claw Feet, 36 x 29 x 14 In.	380
Screen, Brass, Collapsible, 9 Fan Shape Panels, Music Lyre Design, 26 x 40 In. *illus*	90
Screen, Brass, Leaded, Stained Glass, Flowers, 28 x 18 x 8 In.	375
Screen, Bronze, Foo Dog, Prunus, Pierced Frame, Sinuous Dragon Feet, 32 x 33 In	1159
Screen, Gilded, Bouquet, Painting, Leafy Stand, c.1920, 40½ x 37 In.	100
Screen, Iron, Arts & Crafts, Handwrought, c.1920s, 25¼ x 29 x 9 In.	677
Screen, Iron, Hand Forged, Willis Polk, Belvedere, Calif., 1893, 51 x 31½ x 12½ In.	984
Screen, Kirihame, Rosewood, Silk & Patchwork, Paw Feet, Glass Ball Casters, c.1880, 61 x 30 In.	384
Screen, Leaded Glass, Phoenix, Geometric Panels, Urns & Flowers, Early 1900s, 59 x 32 x 17 In.. *illus*	6958
Screen, Leather, 4 Panels, Foldable, Brown, France, c. 1940, 67 x 94 x 1 In.	4160
Screen, Mahogany, Centennial, Shield Shape Frame, Embroidered Panel, c.1880, 52 In.	60
Screen, Needlework, Mahogany, Couple With Dog, Barley Twist, England, 1800s, 48 x 26 In.	115
Screen, Needlework, Tripod, Spider Legs, 1800s, 48 In. *illus*	100
Screen, Pole, Mahogany, Silk Embroidered Panel, Candle Shelf, c.1770, 52 In.	984
Screen, Pole, Needlepoint, Queen Anne, Woman, Mahogany, Oval, Tripod Base, 56 x 15 In.	468
Screen, Pole, Needlework, George III, Adam & Eve, Sampler, c.1813, 17 x 13 In.	500
Screen, Needlework, Woman Standing, Tripod, 1700s, 11 x 14 x 54 In.	201
Screen, Pole, Queen Anne Style, Needlework, Tripod, 1900s, 56 In.	219
Screen, Rosewood, Beadwork, Caster Feet, Victorian, 42 x 22 In.	460
Screen, Tin, Embossed, Family Figure, Handle, Stand, 27x 18 In.	24
Screen, Walnut, Carved Crest, Tapestry, Flowers, Ribbons, Victorian, 40 x 26 In.	288
Screen, Wirework, Brass, Iron, Ornamented, Swags, Central Scrolls, Early 1800s, 20 x 42 In.	3250
Screen, Wrought Iron, Arts & Crafts, Painted, Peacock Set, Landscape, 31 x 37½ In.. *illus*	360
Screen, Wrought Iron, Chicken, Duck, Elephant, Arts & Crafts, Cincinnati, 32 x 31½ In.	625
Screens are also listed in the Architectural and Furniture categories.	
Stand, Wrought Iron, Forged, Trammel, Chain, Hook, Tripod Legs, c.1820, 54¾ x 14½ In.	819
Tool Set, Brass, Gilt Metal Ship, 5 Tools, Twist Post, 3-Legged, 48½ In.	83
Tool Set, Cast Iron & Brass, Poker, Shovel, Tongs, Stand, 28 x 9½ x 6 In. *illus*	63
Tool Set, Spanish Galleon, Hooks, Hanging Metal Fire Tools, Spiraling Tripod, 1900s, 48½ In. .	180
Tools, Arts & Crafts, Broom, Shovel, Tongs, Cahill, c.1910, 35 x 10½ In.	615
Tools, Iron, Arts & Crafts, Hand Forged, c.1910, 42½ x 16 In.	615
Trammel, Iron, Fish Hanger, Hook Shape Bottom, 1800s, 42½ In.	1845

FISCHER, *see Herend category.*

FISHING

Fishing reels of brass or nickel were made in the United States by 1810. Bamboo fly rods were sold by 1860, often marked with the maker's name. Lures made of metal, or metal and wood, were made in the nineteenth century. Plastic lures were made by the 1930s. All fishing material is collected today and even equipment of the past 30 years is of interest if in good condition with original box.

Float, Blue Glass, Hand Blown, Rope Net, 41 In. *illus*	141
Harpoon, Trident, Iron & Copper, Wood Shaft, 1800s, 89 In.	155
Ice Sled, Pine, Hinged Lid With Hole, Red, Blue Gray Interior, Metal Runners, 14½ x 26 In. .	250
Lure, Paw Paw Perch Style, Wood, 2 Hooks, 3¾ In. *illus*	25
Reel, B.F. Meek & Sons, Silver, Ivorine Handle, No. 44, 2 x 2 x 2 In. *illus*	3776
Spear, Iron, Wood, Shaft, Turned, New England, 1800s, 59 In.	156
Tackle Box, Paris Angling Co., Dome Top, Leather Covered, Fly Fishing, c.1850, 3½ x 6 In.	329

FLAGS *are included in the Textile category.*

Fishing, Float, Blue Glass, Hand Blown, Rope Net, 41 In.
$141

Rachel Davis Fine Arts

Fishing Lures
Lures are popular with collectors. Names to look for in fishing lures: Heddon, South Bend, Creek Chub, Paw Paw, Shakespeare, and Pflueger.

Fishing, Lure, Paw Paw Perch Style, Wood, 2 Hooks, 3¾ In.
$25

Hartzell's Auction Gallery Inc.

Fishing, Reel, B.F. Meek & Sons, Silver, Ivorine Handle, No. 44, 2 x 2 x 2 In.
$3,776

Soulis Auctions

Florence Ceramics, Figurine, Lady Harlequin, Crescent Moon, No. 680, Giuseppe Armani, c.1990, 15 ½ In. $2,000

Lion and Unicorn

Florence Ceramics, Figurine, Madame Pompadour, Standing, Dress, Flower, 1950, 12 ½ In. $138

Lion and Unicorn

Flow Blue, Footbath, Basin, Scenic Landscape, Double Handle, Unglazed Underside, England, 1900s $210

Selkirk Auctioneers & Appraisers

FLASH GORDON

Flash Gordon appeared in the Sunday comics in 1934. The daily strip started in 1940. The hero was also in comic books from 1930 to 1970, in books from 1936, in movies from 1938, on the radio in the 1930s and 1940s, and on television from 1953 to 1954. All sorts of memorabilia are collected, but the ray guns and rocket ships are the most popular.

Prop, Movie, Blaster, Dwarf Sword, Universal Pictures, 1980, 25 ½ In., Pair	1250
Toy, Sparkling Rocket, Red, Yellow, Black, Windup, Marx, Box, 12 In.	345

FLORENCE CERAMICS

Florence Ceramics were made in Pasadena, California, from the 1940s to 1977. Florence Ward created many colorful figurines, boxes, candleholders, and other items for the gift shop trade. Each piece was marked with an ink stamp that included the name *Florence Ceramics Co.* The company was sold in 1964 and although the name remained the same, the products were very different. Mugs, cups, and trays were made.

Figurine, Blue Boy & Pinkie, Neoclassical Style Dress, Boy In Blue, Girl In Pink, 12 In., Pair	69
Figurine, Lady Harlequin, Crescent Moon, No. 680, Giuseppe Armani, c.1990, 15 ½ In.*illus*	2000
Figurine, Madame Pompadour, Standing, Dress, Flower, 1950, 12 ½ In. *illus*	138

FLOW BLUE

Flow blue ceramics were made in England and other countries about 1830 to 1900. The dishes were printed with designs using a cobalt blue coloring. The color flowed from the design to the white body so that the finished piece has a smeared blue design. The dishes were usually made of ironstone china. More Flow Blue may be found under the name of the manufacturer. These three marks are used on flow blue dishes.

W.H. Grindley & Co. (Ltd.) c.1880–1891	Johnson Brothers c.1913+	Wood & Son(s) (Ltd.) 1891–1907

Bowl, Vegetable, Dome Lid, Octagonal Base, Scinde, J. & G. Alcock, China, 7¾ x 10 In.	331
Compote, Bentick, Fruit, Shaped Rim, Cauldon, England, 5¾ x 9½ In.	189
Footbath, Basin, Cobalt Blue, Floral Pattern, Marked, England, 1900s	180
Footbath, Basin, Scenic Landscape, Double Handle, Unglazed Underside, England, 1900s....*illus*	210
Platter, Flower Basket, Stone Plinth, Lysaght Service, Swansea, Rectangular, c.1817, 12 In.	4271
Platter, Octagonal, Dark Blue Decoration, White Ground, 18 x 13¾ In. *illus*	38
Platter, Scinde, Octagonal, Shaped Edge, J. & G. Alcock, 16 x 20⅜ In.	289
Platter, Sobraon, Shaped Edges, Jacob & Thomas Furnival, 14⅝ x 18¼ In.	148
Tureen, Dome Lid, Touraine, Underplate & Ladle, Stanley Pottery Co., England, 8 x 13 In.	295

FLYING PHOENIX, *see Phoenix Bird category.*

FOLK ART

Folk art is also listed in many categories of this book under the actual name of the object. See categories such as Box, Cigar Store Figure, Paper, Weather Vane, Wooden, etc.

Abe Lincoln, Slender, Carved, Wood, Kent Gutzmer, 37¼ In.	250
American Eagle, Full Body, Spread Wing, Oak, Gold Paint, Plaque Base, c.1900, 12 x 22 x 9 In.	644
American Indian, Standing, Arm Raised, Wood, Carved, c.1900, 15 In.	188

F

Flow Blue, Platter, Octagonal, Dark Blue Decoration, White Ground, 18 x 13¾ In.
$38

New Haven Auctions

Folk Art, Basket, Bottle Cap, Mounted As Lamp, 1900s, 19 x 15 x 8 In., Pair
$1,220

Rafael Osona Nantucket Auctions

Folk Art, Birdhouse, Outsider, Cardinal, Figure & Text, Multicolor, Wood, Willie Jinks, 9 x 8 x 9 In.
$120

Garth's Auctioneers & Appraisers

Folk Art, Cage, Squirrel, Painted Tin, Green, Yellow, Red, Wood Base, 1800s, 11½ In.
$338

Pook & Pook

Folk Art, Dancing Man, Butternut, Carved, Hinged Joints, Late 1800s, 14 In.
$360

Garth's Auctioneers & Appraisers

Folk Art, Eagle, Standing, Spread Wings, White, Carved, Pine, 1800s, 25½ x 18 In.
$1,000

Wiederseim Auctions

Folk Art, Frame, 2 Hinged Doors, Flowers, Vines, Purple Velvet Lining, Late 1800s, 10 x 7½ In.
$576

Rachel Davis Fine Arts

Folk Art, Frame, Walnut, Pine Board, Old Surface, Rich Color, Pennsylvania, Mid 1800s, 22 x 25 In.
$72

Jeffrey S. Evans & Associates

Folk Art is Younger

Folk art is still a hot collectible, but folk art can be "younger," items made into the early 1900s.

Folk Art, Horse, Standing, White Ground, Black Spots, Painted, Carved, 1800s, 11 7/8 x 3 x 12 In.
$1,250

New Haven Auctions

Folk Art, Plaque, Dog, Fido, Brown Spots, Wood, Carved, Painted, Ida Byron, Frame, 1800s, 7 x 9 3/4 In.
$1,792

Rachel Davis Fine Arts

Folk Art, Sailing Ship, Continental, Carved, Mast, Pole, Flags, Posts, Rails, Spain, c.1860, 38 x 46 x 11 In.
$330

Main Auction Galleries, Inc.

Arrow, Pine, Gray Paint, Carved, Pierced, Scrolls, 1900s, 12 x 60 In.	480
Basket, Bottle Cap, Mounted As Lamp, 1900s, 19 x 15 x 8 In., Pair...........*illus*	1220
Bird, Canada Geese, Carved, Driftwood Base, Miniature, Signed, 1900s, 7 In.	156
Bird, On Perch, Wood, Carved, Painted, Red Breast, Yellow Beak & Feet, 6 In.	704
Birdhouse, Outsider, Cardinal, Figure & Text, Multicolor, Wood, Willie Jinks, 9 x 8 x 9 In...*illus*	120
Bootjack, Wood, Carved, Painted, White Heron, Gold, Black Ground, 1857, 12 x 4 In.	590
Cage, Squirrel, Painted Tin, Green, Yellow, Red, Wood Base, 1800s, 11 1/2 In. ....*illus*	338
Cane, Brown Paint, Carved Animals, Steam Locomotive, Sailing Ship & Anchor, Late 1800s, 35 In.	132
Cat, Sitting, Tail Out, Orange & Black Spots, Carved, Painted, 19th Century, 3 In.	2816
Chest, Jewelry, Standing, Pine, Painted, Wavy Legs, Shoestring Creations, 54 x 16 x 13 In.	761
Dancing Man, Butternut, Carved, Hinged Joints, Late 1800s, 14 In...........*illus*	360
Diorama, Dollhouse, Triangular, Acrylic Top, Glass Front, Painted Frame, 1900s, 26 x 13 In.	418
Dog, Humanoid, Carved, Wood, Cow Print Suit, 2 Crows, Markus Pierson, 25 x 13 x 6 In.	550
Eagle, Spread Wings, Pedestal Base, Carved, Wm. Zwikl, 1976, 12 1/2 In.	79
Eagle, Standing, Spread Wings, White, Carved, Pine, 1800s, 25 1/2 x 18 In...........*illus*	1000
Eagle, Striking Shape, Black Paint, Mounted, Steel Stand, Iron Base, 1900s, 16 x 34 x 11 In.	2457
Fish, Blue Gill, Glass Eyes, Carved, Oval Wooden Plaque, Dated 1971, 9 x 15 In.	216
Fist, Holding Rod, Pine, Carved, Laminated Wood, Late 1800s, 7 x 8 In.	240
Frame, 2 Hinged Doors, Flowers, Vines, Purple Velvet Lining, Late 1800s, 10 x 7 1/2 In.. *illus*	576
Frame, Walnut, Cross, Cutout, Treen Butter Churn, Virginia, c.1880, 22 x 18 In., 2 Piece	96
Frame, Walnut, Pine Board, Old Surface, Rich Color, Pennsylvania, Mid 1800s, 22 x 25 In. ...*illus*	72
Horse, Standing, White Ground, Black Spots, Painted, Carved, 1800s, 11 7/8 x 3 x 12 In.*illus*	1250
Lampshade, Carved, 6 Panels, Biblical Scenes, 9 x 11 x 6 In.	156
Owl, Pine, Carved, Painted, Glass Eyes, Stamped, F & S, 1950s, 19 In.	150
Plaque, Dog, Fido, Brown Spots, Wood, Carved, Painted, Ida Byron, Frame, 1800s, 7 x 9 3/4 In...*illus*	1792
Plaque, Wood, Carved, Pine, Spread Wing Eagle, Fish, Dark Walnut Stain, c.1900, 16 x 18 In.	527
Robot, Red Necktie, Wood, Nuts & Bolts, Adjustable, Don Ellefson, 1900s.	36
Sailing Ship, Continental, Carved, Mast, Pole, Flags, Posts, Rails, Spain, c.1860, 38 x 46 x 11 In. *illus*	330
Sculpture, Bee Skep, Sandstone, Carved On Rough Block Base, Early 1900s, 21 x 14 x 11 In.	2880
Sculpture, Wood, Painted, Wire, Beaded Face, Glaring Sun, Bird, White Pedestal, 76 x 18 x 12 In.	439
Seashell Arrangement, Multicolor Flowers, Under Glass Dome, Victorian, 16 In........*illus*	576
Shelf, Butterfly Shape, Carved Wood, Multicolor, c.1930, 13 x 10 x 8 In.	281
Stand, Twig, Opera Theme, 3 Scenes, Verdi, Ballerina, Radames, Birch Legs, 25 In.	349
Stand, Vase, Flowers, Multicolor, Hinged Door, 2 Shelves, Pedestal, 30 x 11 x 11 In.	644
Wall Hanging, Stag, Cast Iron, Head, Horn, 7 1/2 x 12 In.	590
Whirligig, American Indian, Riding, Canoe, Glass Eyes, Multicolor, 1900s, 18 x 16 In. *illus*	1625
Whirligig, Man, Wearing Hat, Standing, Carved, Painted, Lou Schifferl, 31 1/4 In.	554
Whirligig, Sailor, Wearing Tin Hat, Standing, Painted, Early 1900s, 41 In...........*illus*	1599

FOOT WARMER

Foot warmers solved the problem of cold feet in past generations. Some warmers held charcoal, others held hot water. Pottery, tin, and soapstone were the favored materials to conduct the heat. The warmer was kept under the feet, then the legs and feet were tucked into a blanket, providing welcome warmth in a cold carriage or church.

Brass, Dome Lid, 6-Sided, Pierced, Twisted Swing Handle, Dutch, 1700s, 6 In.	438
Soapstone, Iron, Arrow Shape, Hand Carved, Sloped Handle, 5 3/4 x 8 In.	622
Stoneware, Crock, Handle, Timothy Whites, Reliable Cash Chemists, Round, Flat, 7 x 6 x 3 In.	270

FOOTBALL *collectibles may be found in the Card and the Sports categories.*

FOSTORIA

Fostoria glass was made in Fostoria, Ohio, from 1887 to 1891. The factory was moved to Moundsville, West Virginia, and most of the glass seen in shops today is a twentieth-century product. The company was sold to Lancaster Colony Corporation in 1983 and closed in 1986. Additional Fostoria items may be listed in the Milk Glass category. Original Fostoria Coin pattern was made in amber, blue,

crystal, green, olive green, and red. Reproduction colors include crystal, dark green, pale blue, and red. All coins on original Fostoria are frosted or gold decorated. The coins on new Lancaster Colony pieces are not frosted. Some of these unfrosted coins are being frosted—with either acid or sandblasting—after they are purchased.

American, Bowl, Blue, Serrated Rim, 3-Footed, 10 In.		24
American, Sandwich Tray, Footed, 4½ x 15 In.		270
Apple & Grape, Toothpick Holder, Green, Cylindrical, 2⅜ In.		125
Argus, Goblet, Water, Ruby, 6½ In.		17
Artichoke, Syrup, Metal Lid, Frosted, Clear Handle, c.1891, 7¾ In.		203
Artichoke, Vase, Frosted, Scalloped Rim, Flared Base, c.1891, 10½ In.		131
Cabaret, Iced Tea, Green, 6⅞ In.		12
Colony, Relish, 9½ In.		12
Fairfax, Grill Plate, Topaz, 10¼ In.		30
Seascape, Bowl, Sapphire Blue, Turned In Rim, 8 In.		48
Sun Ray, Nappy, 5 In.		21
Sylvan, Punch Set, Bowl, Pedestal, 17 Cups, c.1902, 15 In. Bowl, 19 Piece		84
Tut, Vase, Black, Wavy Handles, 8¼ In.		24
Victoria, Toothpick Holder, Satin Finish, 2⅜ In.		38

FOVAL, *see Fry category.*

FRAMES *are included in the Furniture category under Frame.*

FRANCISCAN

Franciscan is a trademark that appears on pottery. Gladding, McBean and Company started in 1875. The company grew and acquired other potteries. It made sewer pipes, floor tiles, dinnerware, and art pottery with a variety of trademarks. It began using the trade name *Franciscan* in 1934. In 1936, dinnerware and art pottery were sold under the name *Franciscan Ware.* The company made china and cream-colored, decorated earthenware. Desert Rose, Apple, El Patio, and Coronado were best sellers. The company became Interpace Corporation and in 1979 was purchased by Josiah Wedgwood & Sons. The plant closed in 1984, but production of a few patterns shifted to China and Thailand. For more prices, go to kovels.com.

Gladding, McBean & Co.
1934–1963

Gladding, McBean & Co.
c.1940

International Pipe and
Ceramics
1963+

Apple, Cup & Saucer		12
Apple, Pitcher, Shouldered, 8 In.		57
Blanc, Bowl, Vegetable, Divided, 10¾ In.		21
Cantata, Teapot, 4⅞ In.		25
Concord, Plate, Dinner, 10 In.		9
Coronado, Gravy Boat, Underplate, Aqua, Swirled Edge		19
Desert Rose, Chop Plate, 14 In.		38
El Patio, Cup & Saucer, Yellow, Footed		10
El Patio, Plate, Bread & Butter, Turquoise, 6 In.		6
Emerald Isle, Bowl, Soup, 6 In.		18
Happy Talk, Salt & Pepper		26
Indian Summer, Casserole, Lid, Qt.		25
Ivy, Bowl, Vegetable, Divided, 12 In.		28
Meadow Rose, Plate, 8 In.		20
Tulip Time, Salt & Pepper		16
Woodlore, Cup & Saucer, Footed		12

Folk Art, Seashell Arrangement, Multicolor Flowers, Under Glass Dome, Victorian, 16 In.
$576

Rachel Davis Fine Arts

Folk Art, Whirligig, American Indian, Riding, Canoe, Glass Eyes, Multicolor, 1900s, 18 x 16 In.
$1,625

Hindman

Folk Art, Whirligig, Sailor, Wearing Tin Hat, Standing, Painted, Early 1900s, 41 In.
$1,599

Pook & Pook

Fraternal, Masonic, Pin, Arch, Triangular Dangle, Etched, Red Ribbon, 14K Rose Gold, 1898, 3⅜ x 2 In.
$750

Alderfer Auction Company

Fraternal, Odd Fellows, Ceremonial Staff, Red Heart In Hand, Carved, Painted, Gilt, c.1875, 63 In.
$2,691

Jeffrey S. Evans & Associates

Fulper, Candlestick, Purple Matte Glaze, Blue Tones, Handle, c.1910s, 4½ x 3½ In.
$154

California Historical Design

FRANKART

Frankart Inc., New York, New York, mass-produced nude "dancing lady" lamps, ashtrays, and other decorative Art Deco items in the 1920s and 1930s. They were made of white lead composition and spray painted. *Frankart Inc.* and the patent number and year were stamped on the base.

Lamp, Aluminum Base, Figure, Skyscrapers, Black Enamel, Paper Shade, 1928, 20¾ In. ...	2080
Lamp, Figural Shade, Standing, Spread Wings, Aluminum Base, Black Enamel, c.1930, 11½ In. .	1820
Lamp, Glass Shade, Skyscraper, Green, 2 Figures On Base, Arms Raised, 20 In.	780
Lamp, Globe Shade, Amber, Crackle Glass, Black Base, 2 Figures, Kneeling, 9½ x 11 x 8 In.	720
Lamp, Green Base, 2 Figures, Seated, Skyscraper Shade, Custard Glass, 12½ x 10 x 4½ In.	2400
Stand, Smoking, Outstretched Hand, Ashtray & Cigarette Box, 7 x 8 x 4 In.	660
Tray, Desk, Smoker's, Nude Figures, Ashtray, Cigarette Box, Angular Base, 10 x 7 x 5 In.	720

FRANKOMA POTTERY

Frankoma Pottery was originally known as The Frank Potteries when John F. Frank opened shop in 1933. The name "Frankoma," a combination of his last name and the last three letters of Oklahoma, was used beginning in 1934. The factory moved to Sapulpa, Oklahoma, in 1938. Early wares were made from a light cream-colored clay from Ada, Oklahoma, but in 1956 the company switched to a red clay from Sapulpa. The firm made dinnerware, utilitarian and decorative kitchenwares, figurines, flowerpots, and limited edition and commemorative pieces. John Frank died in 1973 and his daughter, Joniece, inherited the business. Frankoma went bankrupt in 1990. The pottery operated under various owners for a few years and was bought by Joe Ragosta in 2008. It closed in 2010. The buildings, assets, name, and molds were sold at an auction in 2011.

Dish, Plainsman, Prairie Green, 4-Leaf Clover, 6½ x 6 In.	6
Figurine, Buffalo, White Glaze, Artist Signed, 7 In.	84
Figurine, Woman, Sitting, Inclined Ridged Base, White Glaze, Smith, PDC, 10¾ In.	115
Pitcher & Bowl, Plainsman, Prairie Green, Tab Handles On Bowl, 5½ In. Pitcher..............	21
Serving Dish, Plainsman, Prairie Green, Rectangular, Downturned Handles, 15 x 7 In......	19
Tile, Contemporary, Motawi, Green, Cross Shape, Frank Lloyd Wright, c.2000, 6 x 6 In........	154
Vase, Plainsman, Prairie Green, Molded Handles, 15½ In.	38
Vase, Plainsman, Prairie Green, Octagonal, Scalloped Rim, Footed, 9¼ In.	30

FRATERNAL

Fraternal objects that are related to the many different fraternal organizations in the United States are listed in this category. The Elks, Masons, Odd Fellows, and others are included. Also included are service organizations, like the American Legion, Kiwanis, and Lions Club. Furniture is listed in the Furniture category. Shaving mugs decorated with fraternal crests are included in the Shaving Mug category.

Fraternal Order Of Eagles, Ax, Eagle, Spread Wings, Aluminum, Wood Handle, 1910, 13¾ In.	148
Knights Templar, Poster, Triennial Conclave, San Francisco, HW Hansen, 1914, 36¾ x 24 In. ..	240
Knights Templar, Sword, Scabbard, Chain, Ceremonial, Ames Mfg. Co., 36¼ In.	250
Masonic, Ceremonial Sword, Presented To Glenn Skelton, Henderson Ames Co., 1900s, 36 In.....	150
Masonic, Globe, Terrestrial, Celestial, Painted Wood, Cube Stands, 1800s, 13 In., Pair........	1063
Masonic, Pendant, Knights Templar Symbols, Cross, Crown, 14K Gold, Enamel, 1 In.	490
Masonic, Pin, Arch, Triangular Dangle, Etched, Red Ribbon, 14K Rose Gold, 1898, 3⅜ x 2 In....*illus*	750
Masonic, Ring, 10K White Gold, Star, Aquamarine, Sapphire, Ruby, Citrine, Diamond, Size 5½..	219
Modern Woodmen Of The World, Ax, Hammerhead, Tote, Turned Wood Handle, c.1910, 13¾ In. .	148
Odd Fellows, Badge, Silver Frame, Feathered Prince Of Wales, Cresting, 1800s, 4½ In.	281
Odd Fellows, Ceremonial Ax, Painted, Heart In Hand, Wood, Folk Art, Late 1800s, 30½ In.........	263
Odd Fellows, Ceremonial Staff, Red Heart In Hand, Carved, Painted, Gilt, c.1875, 63 In.*illus*	2691
Odd Fellows, Lectern, Painted, Blue, Applied Letters & Symbols, c.1890, 29 x 19 x 15½ In..	192
Odd Fellows, Staff, Heart In Hand, Carved & Painted, Late 1800s, 58 In.	875

FRY GLASS

Fry glass was made by the H.C. Fry Glass Company of Rochester, Pennsylvania. The company, founded in 1901, first made cut glass and other types of glasswares. In 1922 it patented a heat-resistant glass called Pearl Ovenglass. For two years, 1926–1927, the company made Fry Foval, an opal ware decorated with colored trim. Reproductions of this glass have been made. Depression glass patterns made by Fry may be listed in the Depression Glass category. Some pieces of cut glass may also be included in the Cut Glass category.

FRY

Hair Receiver, Lid, Engraved Flowers & Pinstripes, Cut Glass, Signed, 3 ¼ x 4 ½ In.	84
Sandwich Tray, Pershing, Cut Glass, Center Handle, 10 In.	108
Vase, Amber Threaded Rim, Controlled Bubbles, Fan Shape, Footed, 9 ½ In........................	50

FRY FOVAL

Candlestick, Blue Opalescent, Sapphire Blue Threading & Wafers, 10 ½ In., Pair.......	156 to 204
Candlestick, Opalescent, Blue Threaded, Delft Blue Wafers, 10 ¾ In.....................................	60
Candlestick, Opalescent, Threaded, Delft Blue Wafers, c.1922, 12 In., Pair	108
Compote, Pearl Bowl & Foot, Delft Blue Stem, Mid 20th Century, 5 x 9 In.	88
Vase, Applied Jade Foot, Pulled, Radio Wave Pattern, 9 In.......................................	540

FULPER

Fulper Pottery Company was incorporated in 1899 in Flemington, New Jersey. It made art pottery from 1909 to 1929. The firm had been making bottles, jugs, and housewares since 1805. Vasekraft is a line of art pottery with glazes similar to Chinese art pottery that was introduced in 1909. Doll heads were made about 1928. The firm became Stangl Pottery in 1929. Stangl Pottery is listed in its own category in this book.

Bowl, Centerpiece, Scalloped Rim, Green Glaze, Footed, 13 In.	132
Bowl, Fruit, Square, Flower, Light Green, Squat, Signed, c.1910s, 3 ⅜ x 8 In.	677
Candlestick, Purple Matte Glaze, Blue Tones, Handle, c.1910s, 4 ½ x 3 ½ In. .... *illus*	154
Doorstop, Earthenware, Chinese Sleeping Cat, Flambe Glaze, New Jersey, c.1915, 5 x 9 x 5 In......	715
Flower Frog, Scarab, Blue, Black, Oval Base, c.1910s, 1 x 3 ½ x 2 ¼ In.	215
Lamp, Perfume, Egyptian Design, Woman Holding Jar, Bisque, 1917, 9 x 7 In. .... *illus*	2210
Pitcher, Twisted Handle, Flambe Glaze, Signed, c.1910s, 10 ¼ x 6 ¾ x 5 ½ In......................	246
Vase, Earthenware, Ivory & Cucumber Green Flambe Glaze, New Jersey, 1916, 15 ⅞ x 5 ¾ In.. *illus*	875
Vase, Earthenware, Urn Shape, 2 Handles, Blue Crystals, High Glaze, 1916, 12 x 12 x 8 In...	500
Vase, Flambe Glaze, 2 Handles, Signed, c.1910s, 11 ¼ x 5 In.....................................	738
Vase, Ivory Over Brown, Blue Flambe Glaze, Flared Rim, Incised Mark, c.1920, 10 x 6 In.....	260
Vase, Pinched Waist, Butterscotch Flambe, Signed, c.1910s, 7 ⅜ x 4 In.................................	523
Wall Pocket, Mahogany, Painted, Pierced Design, 1800s, 6 ¾ x 5 In.	308

FURNITURE

Furniture of all types is listed in this category. Examples dating from the seventeenth century to 2010 are included. Prices for furniture vary in different parts of the country. Oak furniture is most expensive in the West; large pieces over eight feet high are sold for the most money in the South, where high ceilings are found in the old homes. Modern is popular in New York, California, and Chicago. Condition is very important when determining prices. These are NOT average prices but rather reports of unique sales. If the description includes the word *style,* the piece resembles the old furniture style but was made at a later time. It is not a period piece. Small chests that sat on a table or dresser are also included here. Garden furniture is listed in the Garden Furnishings category. Related items may be found in the Architectural, Brass, and Store categories.

Fulper, Lamp, Perfume, Egyptian Design, Woman Holding Jar, Bisque, 1917, 9 x 7 In.
$2,210

Toomey & Co. Auctioneers

Fulper, Vase, Earthenware, Ivory & Cucumber Green Flambe Glaze, New Jersey, 1916, 15 ⅞ x 5 ¾ In.
$875

Toomey & Co. Auctioneers

Furniture, Bar Cart, Brass, 3 Tiers, Glass, Handle, Roller Wheels, 32 x 25 ¾ x 14 In.
$765

Bonhams

This is an edited listing of current prices. Visit **Kovels.com** to check thousands of prices from previous years and sign up for free information on trends, tips, reproductions, marks, and more.

TIP

Scratches on plastic furniture can be hidden with regular applications of automobile wax.

Furniture, Bar, Cabinets In H-Form, Shelves, Upholstery, Brass Tacks, Chrome, c.1950, 45 x 45 In.
$1,688

New Haven Auctions

TIP

Treat your furniture the same way you treat your face. Wash it to remove the dirt. You do not want to remove the skin. Don't sand too much.

Furniture, Barstool, Cone Shape, Upholstered, Chrome Plated Steel, Verner Panton, 1958, 36 x 18 In., Pair
$750

Clars Auction Gallery

Armchairs are listed under Chair in this category.

Armoire, French Provincial, Arched Paneled Doors, Interior Drawers, Shelves, 72 x 40 In. .	69
Armoire, French Provincial, Inlaid, 2 Doors, Molded Crown, Electrified, France, 78 x 61 In.	240
Armoire, Fruitwood, Scalloped Doors, Pegged Construction, France, 1800s, 73 x 49 In.	366
Armoire, Louis XVI Style, Inlaid, Bronze, 3 Doors, Mirror, Shelf, 1800s, 95 x 67 In.	938
Armoire, Louis XVI Style, Mahogany, Bronze, Beveled Mirror, Plaques, c.1890, 90 x 72 In. .	666
Armoire, Provincial, Painted, 4 Doors, 2 Central Drawers, Interior Shelf, 79 x 53 In.	384
Baby Tender, Molded Ring, Hinged Opening, Splayed Spindles, 1700s, 16 x 24 In.	1500
Bar Cart, Brass, 3 Tiers, Glass, Handle, Roller Wheels, 32 x 25 ¾ x 14 In. *illus*	765
Bar Cart, Mahogany, Oval, 3 Tiers, Brass, Casters, England, 1900s, 30 x 27 x 17 In.	1089
Bar, Cabinets In H-Form, Shelves, Upholstery, Brass Tacks, Chrome, c.1950, 45 x 45 In.*illus*	1688
Bar, Cocktail, Lift Top, Carved, 2 Doors, Wine Rack, Drawers, Chinese, c.1990, 39 x 38 In.	480
Barstool, Cone Shape, Upholstered, Chrome Plated Steel, Verner Panton, 1958, 36 x 18 In., Pair.*illus*	750
Barstool, Welded Steel Bar, Leatherette Upholstered Seats, 1950s, 29 x 18 In., Pair	320
Bed, Baby's, Walnut, Folding, Jennie Lynn Spindles, Caster Feet, 52 x 26 In.	144
Bed, Baroque Style, Rosewood, Bronze, Gilt, Mother-Of-Pearl Inlay, 87 x 72 x 57 In.	960
Bed, Brass, Iron, Painted, Black, Scrollwork, Claw Feet, American, c.1890, 65 x 59 x 80 In. *illus*	563
Bed, Canopy, Heart Pine, Cherry, Turned Reeded Posts, South Carolina, 1800s, 89 x 60 x 83 In.	1625
Bed, Directoire Style, Baldachin, Painted, Sideboards, 1800s, 88 x 46 x 31 In.	2250
Bed, Four-Poster, Cannonball, Walnut, Rope, Shenandoah Valley, c.1840, 61 x 53 In. *illus*	388
Bed, Four-Poster, D.R. Dimes, Tiger Maple, Painted, Stamped, King Size, 84 In.	7320
Bed, Four-Poster, Stephen Swift, Mushroom, Black Stain, King Size, 47 x 82 x 87 In.	5490
Bed, Four-Poster, Thos. Moser, Canopy, Cherry, 65 x 83 x 85 In.	2280
Bed, Four-Poster, Tiger Maple, Finials, Disc Feet, Rope, 1800s, 52 x 76 In.	450
Bed, Getama, Wegner, Oak, Attached Stands, GE 705, c.1960, 29 x 100 x 82 In. *illus*	5313
Bed, Louis XVI Style, Carved Frame, Gilt Trim, Upholstered Headboard, 1900s, 48 x 85 In.	384
Bed, Maple, Turned Posts, Headboard, Footboard, Rails, David T. Smith, 1800s, 50 x 67 x 87 In. .*illus*	4800
Bed, Mario Bellini, Breakfast, Black Leather, Steel, B & B Italia, 2002, 37 x 84 x 89 In.	4550
Bed, Oak, Mortis & Tenon, Paper Label, Hall & Lyon Furniture Co., 56 x 49 x 81 In. *illus*	120
Bed, R.J. Horner, Faux Bamboo, Casters, c.1890, Twin, 49 x 43 x 84 In., Pair *illus*	6400
Bed, Rococo Revival, Mahogany, Carved, Scrolled Acanthus, Flowers, Shells, 69 x 75 In.	344
Bed, Rococo Revival, Walnut, Carved, Floral, Splayed Legs, 1900s, 60 x 79 In.	938
Bed, Victorian, Walnut, High Back, Carved, Burl Trim, Shaped Legs, 59 x 73 x 97 In.	748
Bench, Arthus Umanoff, Ash, Painted, Leather, Washington Wood Products, 1960s, 16 x 60 In. .	625
Bench, Baroque Style, Silver Gilt, Carved Wood, Cushion, Scroll Legs, 19 In., Pair	976
Bench, Cast Iron, Spiral Stretcher, Blue Pad Seat, American, 1900s, 49 x 12 x 20 In.	210
Bench, Chippendale, Mahogany, Carved, Upholstered, Cabriole Legs, c.1900, 19 x 26 x 20 In. *illus*	313
Bench, Chippendale, Mahogany, Carved, Upholstered, Paw Feet, Ireland, 20 x 16 x 20 In., Pair	2691
Bench, Crock, Pine, Shaped Supports, Lower Shelf, Cutout Ends, c.1890, 29 x 42 x 12 In.	228
Bench, George III, Walnut, Carved, Needlepoint Cushion, 10 x 29 x 13 In.	128
Bench, Hall, Oak, Carved, S-Shape Sides, England, 1700s, Child's, 36 x 24 x 16 In. *illus*	938
Bench, Hall, Renaissance Revival Style, R.J. Horner, Carved, Hinged Seat, c.1900, 59 x 62 In.*illus*	2057
Bench, Jay Spectre, Eclipse, Ash, Leather, Nickel Plated Brass, c.1985, 28 x 64 x 18 In.	2860
Bench, Louis XIV Style, Painted, Green Upholstery, Stretcher Base, c.1900, 23 x 68 x 25 In..	1375
Bench, Louis XV Style, Carved Frame, Custom Upholstered Top, 21 x 60 x 19 In.	1024
Bench, Mammy's, Rocker, Mahogany, Spindles, Cradle Fence, 1800s, 27 x 47 x 27 In. *illus*	205
Bench, Mammy's, Rocker, Rectangular Seat, Grain Painted, c.1830, 48 In.	191
Bench, Neoclassical, Gilt Metal, Scroll Arms, Cushion, Palladio, Italy, c.1950, 26 x 45 In.	1089
Bench, Pine, Half Round Board, Splayed Legs, Sweden, Early 1900s, 15 x 58 x 16 In.	3000
Bench, Pine, Lift Lid, Old Red Paint, Rectangular, 1768, 18 x 54 In.	214
Bench, Regency, Mahogany, X-Base, Bronze Mounts, Brown Leather, c.1980, 18 x 21 x 17 In.	256
Bench, Scalloped Back Crest, Scroll Arms, Lift Seat, Applied Carving, c.1850, 32 x 74 x 19 In.	1440
Bench, Scandinavian, Pullout Bed, Carved Shaped Back, Turnings, 1876, 39 x 70 In.*illus*	958
Bench, Spindle Ends, Quartersawn Oak, Painted, 30 x 24 x 17 In.	480
Bench, Turned & Joined, Molded Rails, Splayed Legs, Square Stretchers, 1800s, 18 x 48 In.	2125
Bench, Victorian, Upholstered Seat, Silver Painted Metal Legs, Paw Feet, 19 x 24 x 13 In.	24
Bench, Watchmaker's, Bird's-Eye Maple, 14 Drawers, Catch Tray, Steel, 1900s, 49 x 60 In. .	2000
Bench, Window, Regency, Scrolled Back, Cane Seat, Cushion, England, 1800s, 27 x 60 x 16 In. .	492
Bench, Window, Venetian, Carved, Face & Claw Feet, 28 x 36 In. *illus*	640
Bench, Wood, Carved, 2 Lion Columns, Paw Up, Rectangular Feet, 22 x 24 x 12 In.	438
Bench, Yokeback, Folding, Hardwood, Pierced Splats, Rope Seat, X-Base, Chinese, 1800s	427

F

Furniture, Bed, Brass, Iron, Painted, Black, Scrollwork, Claw Feet, American, c.1890, 65 x 59 x 80 In.
$563

Fontaine's Auction Gallery

The Bed Is a Status Symbol

In the seventeenth and eighteenth centuries the bed was a status symbol. The head of the house and his wife used the bed, which had curtains that gave privacy. Others often slept in one room on small mats on the floor. The more people in the room, the warmer it was.

Furniture, Bed, Four-Poster, Cannonball, Walnut, Rope, Shenandoah Valley, c.1840, 61 x 53 In.
$388

Jeffrey S. Evans & Associates

Furniture, Bed, Getama, Wegner, Oak, Attached Stands, GE 705, c.1960, 29 x 100 x 82 In.
$5,313

Wright

Furniture, Bed, Maple, Turned Posts, Headboard, Footboard, Rails, David T. Smith, 1800s, 50 x 67 x 87 In.
$4,800

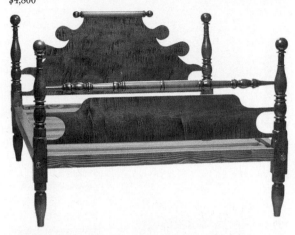

Garth's Auctioneers & Appraisers

Furniture, Bed, Oak, Mortis & Tenon, Paper Label, Hall & Lyon Furniture Co., 56 x 49 x 81 In.
$120

Alderfer Auction Company

Furniture, Bed, R.J. Horner, Faux Bamboo, Casters, c.1890, Twin, 49 x 43 x 84 In., Pair
$6,400

Cowan's Auctions

Furniture, Bench, Chippendale, Mahogany, Carved, Upholstered, Cabriole Legs, c.1900, 19 x 26 x 20 In. **$313**

Charlton Hall Auctions

Furniture, Bench, Hall, Oak, Carved, S-Shape Sides, England, 1700s, Child's, 36 x 24 x 16 In. **$938**

Hindman

Furniture, Bench, Hall, Renaissance Revival Style, R.J. Horner, Carved, Hinged Seat, c.1900, 59 x 62 In. **$2,057**

Ahlers & Ogletree Auction Gallery

TIP
Try not to put wooden furniture in direct sunlight. It will fade.

Bookcase, American Eastlake, Walnut, 3 Doors, Removable Cornice, c.1880, 84 x 74 In. *illus*	778
Bookcase, Art Deco, 3 Open Cases, Curved, Black Edge, Wood, Varnish, c.1935, 25 x 31 In. .	344
Bookcase, Arts & Crafts, Douglas Fir, G. Stickley Hardware, 3 Doors, c.1910, 64 x 71 In.	5228
Bookcase, Boullework, Rosewood, Glazed Doors, Lower Doors, Ebonized, Bronze, 90 x 53 In.	4160
Bookcase, Cherry, Open Shelves, Turned Supports, 4 Cabinet Doors, 1900s, 39 x 41 x 12 In.	288
Bookcase, Chestnut, Carved Benjamin Franklin Bust, Glazed Doors, Drawers, c.1876, 90 x 56 In.	840
Bookcase, Chippendale, Mahogany, Breakfront, Carved, Stand, Chinese, Late 1700s, 105 x 71 In.	4063
Bookcase, Corner, Renaissance Revival, L-Shape, Sliding Glass Door, c.1950, 61 x 58 In.	660
Bookcase, Federal, Mahogany, Glazed Desk, Inlay, Reeded Legs, 73 x 35 x 18 In.	375
Bookcase, G. Stickley, Arts & Crafts, Quartersawn Oak, 2 Glazed Doors, Shelves, 57 x 42 In. *illus*	4800
Bookcase, Globe-Wernicke, Oak, 4 Stacked Sections, Glass Fronts, c.1925, 58 x 34 In.	625
Bookcase, Globe-Wernicke, Quartersawn Oak, Glass Doors, 4 Sections, c.1915, 62 x 34 In. *illus*	720
Bookcase, Globe-Wernicke, Quartersawn Oak, Painted, 4 Sections, c.1915, 57 x 34 x 12 In.	600
Bookcase, Harvey Ellis, Oak, Doors, Glass Panes, Decal, Als Ik Kan, 1903, 58 x 54 In.	5625
Bookcase, Harvey Ellis, Open, 2 Shelves, Adjustable, G. Stickley, c.1903, 54 x 26 In.	3690
Bookcase, Limbert, Oak, No. 357, Glass Door, Shelves, Splayed Legs, c.1910, 57 x 29 In.	3500
Bookcase, Louis XVI Style, Cream Paint, Molded Cornice, Plinth Base, 118 x 54 In.	3416
Bookcase, Louis XVI, Bellanger, Mahogany, 3 Glass Doors, France, 1800s, 77 x 75 In.	320
Bookcase, Mahogany, 2 Glass Doors, Inlay, Bellflowers, Laurel Leaf, 1900s, 50 x 60 In.	690
Bookcase, Mahogany, Carved, 3 Doors, 12 Shelves, R.J. Horner & Co., c.1890, 67 x 83 In.	5313
Bookcase, Neoclassical, 4 Leaded Glass Doors, Shelf Interior, Fluted Stiles, 1800s, 60 x 101 In. *illus*	576
Bookcase, Oak, Beech Plywood, 2 Shelves, Giuseppe Pagano, Italy, c.1940, 29 x 19 In.	1000
Bookcase, Revolving, Slat Side Panels, Iron Supports, Danner, Late 1800s, 42 In. *illus*	540
Bookcase, Tiger Maple, 5 Narrow Open Shelves, 49 x 32 x 8 In.	1220
Bookcase, Victorian, Mahogany, Carved, Adjustable Shelves, Drawer, c.1880, 65 x 36 In.	318
Bookcase, Victorian, Walnut, Carved, Burl Accents, 2 Doors, Shelves, 2 Drawers, 64 x 47 In.	633
Bookcase, Wabash, 2 Drawers, 3 Shelves, Serpentine, Trifid Footing, c.1950, 44 x 39 x 11 In.	120
Bookcase, Walnut, 2 Doors, Half Glass, 3 Interior Shelves, 49 x 42 x 15 In.	59
Bookcase, Walnut, 2 Glass Doors, Drawers, Caster Feet, American, c.1870, 74 x 49 In.	545
Bookstand, Folding, Block-Turned, Spindles, Hinged Adjustable Braces, 14 x 16 In.	2250
Bookstand, Revolving, Mahogany, 3 Tiers, Slat Sides, Tripod Base, c.1915, 44 x 17 In.	280
Bracket, Wall, Gnome, Carved, Multicolor, Italy, 1900s, 22 x 14 x 10 In., Pair	563
Breakfront, Chippendale Style, Mahogany, Fretwork, 4 Glazed Doors, 4 Drawers, 85 x 72 In.	2520
Breakfront, George III Style, Chinoiserie Panels, 3 Sections, 1900s, 95 x 130 In.	5985
Breakfront, Georgian, Mahogany, Shelf Interior, 5 Drawers, Blocked Base, 1800s, 83 x 77 In.	3712
Breakfront, Regency, Rosewood, Brass Inlay, England, 1800s, 96 x 86 x 21 In.	4800
Buffet, Art Deco, Amboyna, Chrome, 4 Drawers, France, 1930s, 35 x 62 In. *illus*	1161
Buffet, Louis XV, Provincial, Walnut, 2 Tiers, Deux Corps, 1700s, 115 x 64 In.	9375
Buffet, Oak, Mirror Back, Carved, 2 Doors, 3 Drawers, Germany, c.1880, 81 x 73 In. *illus*	660
Buffet, Rectangular Top, Mirrored Door, Shelf, 4 Columns, 1830s, 37 x 57 x 22 In.	625
Buffet, Renaissance Revival, Oak, Carved, Doors, Drawers, Bun Feet, c.1890, 39 x 78 x 21 In.	688
Buffet, Renaissance Revival, Walnut, Carved, 4 Drawers, Doors, Italy, c.1790, 48 x 89 In.	2196
Bureau, George I, Walnut, Slant Front, Fitted Interior, 5 Drawers, 1700s, 36 x 28 In.	813
Bureau, Louis XV Style, Roll Top, Inlay, Gilt Metal Cherubs, 1900s, 57 x 63 In. *illus*	4688
Cabinet, 2 Doors, Painted Panels, Domed Top, Bun Feet, Continental, 1700s, 17 x 13 In. *illus*	2457
Cabinet, Aesthetic Revival, Ebonized, Painted Panels, Man, Woman, Flowers, c.1890, 39 x 60 In. *illus*	3125
Cabinet, Arne Vodder, Teak, Lacquered, Stainless Steel, Sibast Mobler, c.1960, 27 x 35 In.	6250
Cabinet, Art Deco, Hardwood, Gilt Bronze, Grain Painted, 1930s, 65 x 81 x 16 In.	250
Cabinet, Art Deco, Walnut Burl, Primavera, Cocobolo, Aluminum, Brass, Italy, 1934, 47 x 75 In. *illus*	2322
Cabinet, Bar, P. Evans, Welded, Patinated Copper, Brass, Aluminum, c.1970, 35 x 36 In. *illus*	11250
Cabinet, Barney Bellinger, Adirondack, 2 Tiers, Inlaid Twigs, Penn., 73 x 73 ½ In. *illus*	49800
Cabinet, Bedside, Neoclassical, Inlaid, Marble Top, 2 Drawers, Italy, c.1800, 34 x 23 In.	1169
Cabinet, Borge Mogensen, 5 Drawers, Stained Teak, Brass Handles, c.1958, 35 x 27 In.	1500
Cabinet, Burlwood, Inlay, 3 Drawers, Plinth Base, Tabletop, Continental, 1800s, 14 x 11 x 6 In.	250
Cabinet, Card Catalog, Oak, 32 Drawers, Metal Handles, c.1910, 27 x 25 ½ x 15 In. *illus*	563
Cabinet, Card Catalog, Oak, Multiple Drawers, Brass Pulls, 86 x 48 x 18 In.	1000
Cabinet, Charles X Style, Burlwood, Round Pedestal Shape, Single Door, 58 x 25 x 15 In., Pair .	1088
Cabinet, Chilton, Cherry, 2 Doors, Shelves, Apron, Late 1900s, 32 x 43 x 17 In.	875
Cabinet, China, Oak, Crest, Scrollwork, 3 Leaded Glass Panels, Claw Feet, c.1890, 77 x 52 In. *illus*	1573
Cabinet, China, Reverend Ben Davis, Adirondack, Oak, Chip Carved, Glass Door, 62 x 40 In. *illus*	31200
Cabinet, Chippendale, Cherry, Bifold Doors, D.R. Dimes, Late 1900s, 76 x 58 x 22 In.	660

F

Furniture, Bench, Mammy's, Rocker, Mahogany, Spindles, Cradle Fence, 1800s, 27 x 47 x 27 In.
$205

Thomaston Place Auction Galleries

Furniture, Bench, Scandinavian, Pullout Bed, Carved Shaped Back, Turnings, 1876, 39 x 70 In.
$958

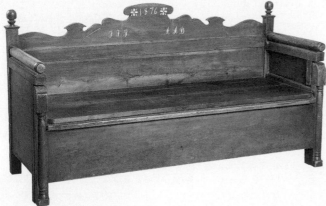

Pook & Pook

TIP
Liquid household
cleaner on a paper
towel is a good way to
clean gilding.

Furniture, Bench, Window, Venetian, Carved, Face & Claw Feet, 28 x 36 In.
$640

Nadeau's Auction Gallery

Furniture, Bookcase, American Eastlake, Walnut, 3 Doors, Removable Cornice, c.1880, 84 x 74 In.
$778

Jeffrey S. Evans & Associates

Furniture, Bookcase, G. Stickley, Arts & Crafts, Quartersawn Oak, 2 Glazed Doors, Shelves, 57 x 42 In.
$4,800

Alderfer Auction Company

TIP
When moving a chest of
drawers or a cabinet
with doors a long dis-
tance, tape the drawers
and doors shut with
masking tape or tie
them shut with rope.

Furniture, Bookcase, Globe-Wernicke, Quartersawn Oak, Glass Doors, 4 Sections, c.1915, 62 x 34 In.
$720

Garth's Auctioneers & Appraisers

Furniture, Bookcase, Neoclassical, 4 Leaded Glass Doors, Shelf Interior, Fluted Stiles, 1800s, 60 x 101 In.
$576

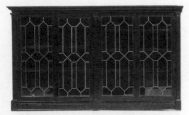

Neal Auction Company

Furniture, Bookcase, Revolving, Slat Side Panels, Iron Supports, Danner, Late 1800s, 42 In.
$540

Selkirk Auctioneers & Appraisers

TIP
Bring a price guide book to an auction. It isn't possible to remember everything, but it is possible to look up most items. We think Kovels' Antiques & Collectibles Price Guide *is the best resource.*

Furniture, Buffet, Art Deco, Amboyna, Chrome, 4 Drawers, France, 1930s, 35 x 62 In.
$1,161

Cowan's Auctions

Furniture, Buffet, Oak, Mirror Back, Carved, 2 Doors, 3 Drawers, Germany, c.1880, 81 x 73 In.
$660

Michaan's Auctions

Furniture, Bureau, Louis XV Style, Roll Top, Inlay, Gilt Metal Cherubs, 1900s, 57 x 63 In.
$4,688

Hindman

Furniture, Cabinet, 2 Doors, Painted Panels, Domed Top, Bun Feet, Continental, 1700s, 17 x 13 In.
$2,457

Thomaston Place Auction Galleries

Furniture, Cabinet, Aesthetic Revival, Ebonized, Painted Panels, Man, Woman, Flowers, c.1890, 39 x 60 In.
$3,125

Hindman

Furniture, Cabinet, Art Deco, Walnut Burl, Primavera, Cocobolo, Aluminum, Brass, Italy, 1934, 47 x 75 In.
$2,322

Cowan's Auctions

Furniture, Cabinet, Bar, P. Evans, Welded, Patinated Copper, Brass, Aluminum, c.1970, 35 x 36 In.
$11,250

Wright

Furniture, Cabinet, Barney Bellinger, Adirondack, 2 Tiers, Inlaid Twigs, Penn., 73 x 73½ In.
$49,800

Blanchard's Auction Service LLC

F

Furniture, Cabinet, Card Catalog, Oak,
32 Drawers, Metal Handles, c.1910,
27 x 25 ½ x 15 In.
$563

New Haven Auctions

Furniture, Cabinet, China, Oak, Crest,
Scrollwork, 3 Leaded Glass Panels, Claw Feet,
c.1890, 77 x 52 In.
$1,573

Fontaine's Auction Gallery

Furniture, Cabinet, China, Reverend Ben
Davis, Adirondack, Oak, Chip Carved, Glass
Door, 62 x 40 In.
$31,200

Blanchard's Auction Service LLC

Furniture, Cabinet, Corner, Chippendale,
Walnut, Bubbled Glass, 2 Drawers, Late
1700s, 89 x 43 In.
$878

Thomaston Place Auction Galleries

Furniture, Cabinet, Corner, Swan Neck
Pediment, Glass Door, Mahogany, Federal,
c.1930, 88 x 30 x 15 In.
$761

Thomaston Place Auction Galleries

Furniture, Cabinet, Display, Arts & Crafts,
Pine, 2 Doors, Glazed Panels, 1900s,
67 x 44 In.
$360

Selkirk Auctioneers & Appraisers

Furniture, Cabinet, Display, Biedermeier,
Oak, Star & String Inlay, Glass Panel Door,
c.1860, 64 x 27 In.
$360

Alex Cooper Auctioneers

Furniture, Cabinet, Display, Inlay, 2 Doors,
3 Drawers, Claw Feet, Dutch, 1700s,
80 x 52 x 15 In.
$1,063

Fontaine's Auction Gallery

Furniture, Cabinet, Display, Neoclassical,
Satinwood, Inlaid, Architectural, England,
1800s, 72 x 36 x 8 In.
$1,800

Selkirk Auctioneers & Appraisers

Furniture, Cabinet, Display, Queen Anne Style, Maple, Slant Front, Mirror, Glass Shelves, 1930s, 42 x 20 In. $360

Garth's Auctioneers & Appraisers

Furniture, Cabinet, Filing, Oak, Roll Top, Tambour Front, Carved, 15 Drawers, Gilt, c.1910, 80 x 14 x 18 In. $1,936

Fontaine's Auction Gallery

Furniture, Cabinet, G. Nakashima, Walnut, 3 Sliding Doors, Pandanus Cloth, 26 x 72 x 20 In. $43,750

Wright

Cabinet, Corner, Cherry, Painted Interior, 3 Doors, Drawer, Shelves, 1800s, 82 x 40 In.	366
Cabinet, Corner, Chippendale, Walnut, Bubbled Glass, 2 Drawers, Late 1700s, 89 x 43 In. .....*illus*	878
Cabinet, Corner, Pine, Paneled Door, Platform Base, Brass Hardware, 1700s, 74 x 39 x 20 In. ...	585
Cabinet, Corner, Swan Neck Pediment, Glass Door, Mahogany, Federal, c.1930, 88 x 30 x 15 In...*illus*	761
Cabinet, Corner, Venetian Style, Wood, 2 Paneled Doors, Gilt, Green Paint, 95 x 50 x 39 In.	1211
Cabinet, Dinette, Gilbert Rohde, 3 Doors, Steel, Wood, Herman Miller, c.1939, 30 x 48 In.	3380
Cabinet, Display, Arts & Crafts, Pine, 2 Doors, Glazed Panels, 1900s, 67 x 44 In.............*illus*	360
Cabinet, Display, Biedermeier, Oak, Star & String Inlay, Glass Panel Door, c.1860, 64 x 27 In.....*illus*	360
Cabinet, Display, Contemporary, Mahogany, Curved Glass, 77 x 36 x 15 In..........................	58
Cabinet, Display, French Style, Mahogany, Ormolu, Plexiglas Door & Panels, 52 In.	209
Cabinet, Display, Inlay, 2 Doors, 3 Drawers, Claw Feet, Dutch, 1700s, 80 x 52 x 15 In...*illus*	1063
Cabinet, Display, Neoclassical, Satinwood, Inlaid, Architectural, England, 1800s, 72 x 36 x 8 In. *illus*	1800
Cabinet, Display, Oak, 4 Panels, 3 Shelves, Carved Feet, American, 1900s, 58 x 22 In...........	60
Cabinet, Display, Oak, Round Glass Front, Rear Panel Opens, Countertop, c.1900, 7 x 14 x 9 In..	1008
Cabinet, Display, Parzinger, Walnut, Etched Glass Sides, 3 Shelves, Lower Doors, 89 x 44 In........	2990
Cabinet, Display, Pine, Painted, Glass Panel Doors, Bronze Trim, 60 x 24 x 14 In., Pair	690
Cabinet, Display, Queen Anne Style, Maple, Slant Front, Mirror, Glass Shelves, 1930s, 42 x 20 In. *illus*	360
Cabinet, Display, Rosewood, 3 Parts, Mirror Back, Carved, c.1890, 83 x 40 x 16 In.	3218
Cabinet, Display, Snuff Bottle, Hardwood, Multiple Shelves, Yellow Paint, Chinese, 35 x 24 In.	250
Cabinet, Display, Storage, Oak, 6 Doors, 17 Drawers, Caster Feet, 1800s, 65 x 44 In.............	625
Cabinet, Display, Walnut, Hanging, Inlay, 12 Glass Panes, Dutch, 1800s, 31 x 41 x 11 In.	995
Cabinet, Drawers, Doors, Turned Up Top, Brass Hardware, Openwork, Asia, 40 x 60 In.	60
Cabinet, Edwardian, Mahogany, Painted, Glazed, Flared Legs, Glass Shelves, 71 x 41 x 15 In.	1250
Cabinet, Federal, Blind Door, Inlay, Arch Pediment, Potthast Brothers, 1950s, 81 x 41 In....	420
Cabinet, Filing, Oak, Paneled Sides, 4 Drawers, Library Bureau Sole Makers, 52 x 17 x 26 In.	300
Cabinet, Filing, Oak, Roll Top, Tambour Front, Carved, 15 Drawers, Gilt, c.1910, 80 x 14 x 18 In..*illus*	1936
Cabinet, Filing, Oak, Tambour Front, 2 Rows, 16 Drawers, c.1900, 45 x 24 In.	540
Cabinet, Florence Knoll, Rosewood, Chrome Base, Knoll International, c.1968, 28 x 109 In.	6875
Cabinet, Fruitwood, Drawer, 2 Doors, Molded Feet, France, 36 x 38 x 20 In.........................	750
Cabinet, G. Nakashima, Walnut, 3 Sliding Doors, Pandanus Cloth, 26 x 72 x 20 In. .....*illus*	43750
Cabinet, Gansu Movement, Plank Top, 3 Doors, Shaped Sides, Chinese, 1800s, 17 x 65 x 12 In. ..	270
Cabinet, George II, Elm, Star Inlaid Door, 7 Drawers, Footed, 1700s, 18 x 13 ½ In.	1107
Cabinet, Georgian, Mahogany, 2 Paneled Doors, Shelf Interior, England, 1800s, 36 x 36 x 16 In.	246
Cabinet, Hanging, Maritime, Carved, 2 Bas-Relief, Doors, Drawer, c.1880, 20 x 19 x 10 In. .	549
Cabinet, Hanging, Red Painted, Glazed, New England, Early 1800s, 30 x 27 x 11 In.............	2125
Cabinet, Italian Rococo, Marble Top, Metal Mounts, Landscape, France, 31 x 28 x 14 In.	720
Cabinet, Jewelry, Asian Style, Hardwood, 5 Lined Drawers, Shou Design, 1900s, 13 x 10 x 8 In.*illus*	156
Cabinet, Jewelry, Mahogany, 4 Drawers, Edwards & Jones, England, c.1910, 15 x 14 x 10 In. ...*illus*	363
Cabinet, Kindt-Larsen, Teak, Painted, 6 Drawers, Doors, Sweden, c.1965, 40 x 59 In....*illus*	9375
Cabinet, Kitchen, 2 Upper Doors, Drawer, 2 Lower Doors, Grain Painted, c.1890 71 x 41 In.	381
Cabinet, L. & J.G. Stickley, Arts & Crafts, Quartersawn Oak, Door, Drawer, 29 x 20 x 16 In...*illus*	360
Cabinet, L. & J.G. Stickley, Glass & Leaded Glass Doors & Sides, c.1910, 67 x 44 x 15 In.*illus*	6150
Cabinet, Lingerie, Fruitwood, 7 Drawers, Demilune, Ormolu, Cabriole Legs, 47 x 30 x 17 In. ..	354
Cabinet, Louis XIII, Walnut, 2 Drawers, Doors, Diamond Shape Panels, 39 x 52 In.	1625
Cabinet, Louis XV, Marble Top, 2 Doors, Painted Faux Wood, France, c.1790, 28 x 55 In.	1920
Cabinet, Louis XVI Style, Dore Bronze, Ormolu, Inlay, Porcelain Plaque, 40 x 56 x 20 In.	3172
Cabinet, Mahogany, Demilune, Painted Flowers, Drawer, 2 Doors, 32 x 35 x 17 In.	130
Cabinet, Music, Harvey Ellis For G. Stickley, Oak, Pewter, Fruitwood, Inlay, c.1903, 58 x 23 In. ...	2875
Cabinet, Music, Neo-Grec, Inlaid Panel, Bronze Trim, Musical Trophies, 1885, 51 x 42 In........	1920
Cabinet, Music, Victorian, Walnut, Gallery Top, Beveled Mirror, Shelves, 55 x 20 x 16 In.	144
Cabinet, Neoclassical Revival, Pediment, Swing Doors, Fluted Columns, 107 x 41 In.	594
Cabinet, Oak, Art Nouveau, 2 Doors, 2 Shelves, 2 Drawers, France, c.1900, 34 x 42 x 20 In. ....*illus*	5000
Cabinet, Parzinger, Burl Ash, 4 Doors, Inside Drawers, Shelves, Chrome Metal, 32 x 69 In. ....*illus*	6175
Cabinet, Petticoat, Marble Top, Mirror Doors, American, 1800s, 37 x 49 x 18 In.	108
Cabinet, Phonograph Cylinder, Oak, Serpentine Top, 6 Drawers, Internal Spindles, 35 x 22 In.	510
Cabinet, Pine, 2 Glazed Doors, Shelf Interior, Iron Hardware, Block Feet, 1800s, 38 x 34 In....	384
Cabinet, Provincial Style, 2 Doors, Glazed Panes, Parenteau Studios, France, 84 x 48 x 18 In.	344
Cabinet, Regency, Faux Bois, Marble Top, Door, Fluted Columns, Wirework, 38 x 60 In.......	1121
Cabinet, Renaissance Revival, Ebonized, Gilt, Painted, Pottier & Stymus, c.1875, 59 x 47 In. .....*illus*	1375
Cabinet, Renaissance Revival, Horner Type, Oak, Carved, 4 Shelves, c.1875, 82 x 49 In.	900
Cabinet, Rocaille Design, 2-Pane Door Top, Drawer, 4 Legs, X-Stretcher, 1800s, 88 x 50 In.	5313

Furniture, Cabinet, Jewelry, Asian Style, Hardwood, 5 Lined Drawers, Shou Design, 1900s, 13 x 10 x 8 In.
$156

Eldred's

Furniture, Cabinet, Jewelry, Mahogany, 4 Drawers, Edwards & Jones, England, c.1910, 15 x 14 x 10 In.
$363

Fontaine's Auction Gallery

Furniture, Cabinet, Kindt-Larsen, Teak, Painted, 6 Drawers, Doors, Sweden, c.1965, 40 x 59 In.
$9,375

Wright

Furniture, Cabinet, L. & J.G. Stickley, Arts & Crafts, Quartersawn Oak, Door, Drawer, 29 x 20 x 16 In.
$360

Alderfer Auction Company

Furniture, Cabinet, L. & J.G. Stickley, Glass & Leaded Glass Doors & Sides, c.1910, 67 x 44 x 15 In.
$6,150

California Historical Design

Furniture, Cabinet, Oak, Art Nouveau, 2 Doors, 2 Shelves, 2 Drawers, France, c.1900, 34 x 42 x 20 In.
$5,000

Wright

Furniture, Cabinet, Parzinger, Burl Ash, 4 Doors, Inside Drawers, Shelves, Chrome Metal, 32 x 69 In.
$6,175

Palm Beach Modern Auctions

Furniture, Cabinet, Renaissance Revival, Ebonized, Gilt, Painted, Pottier & Stymus, c.1875, 59 x 47 In.
$1,375

Fontaine's Auction Gallery

Furniture, Cabinet, Sewing, Mahogany, Martha Washington, Roycroft, c.1910, 29 x 30 x 16½ In.
$2,460

California Historical Design

TIP

Don't store antique furniture in the attic, near a fireplace, or near a heat duct. Basements can be damp or hot and are not a good place for furniture.

F

Furniture, Cabinet, Spice, Pine, Hanging, Labels, 9 Drawers, Early 1900s, 10 ¼ x 6 ¼ In.
$277

Pook & Pook

Furniture, Cabinet, Vanity, Mahogany, Brass, Mirror Doors, Drawers, Miroir Brot, Paris, c.1900, 74 x 33 In.
$875

Hindman

Furniture, Cabinet, Wegner, RY 24, Teak, 2 Upper Sliding Doors, 6 Drawers, RY Mobler, 1958, 71 x 71 In.
$2,969

Wright

Furniture, Cabinet, Western, Maple, Natural Edge Top, 5 Drawers, Free-Form, Contemporary, 38 x 39 In.
$3,480

Blanchard's Auction Service LLC

Furniture, Cabinet, Wormley, Mahogany, Cane, Glass, Dunbar, Indiana, 1940s, 36 x 40 x 13 In.
$2,125

Toomey & Co. Auctioneers

Furniture, Candlestand, Hepplewhite, Tilt Top, Octagonal, Maple, Tapered Legs, c.1920, 28 x 17 In.
$330

Thomaston Place Auction Galleries

Furniture, Candlestand, Tilt Top, Mahogany, Turned Standard, Diamond Bone Inlay, 24 x 18 In.
$366

Rafael Osona Nantucket Auctions

Furniture, Candlestand, Tilt Top, Pine, Round Top, Tripod, 1800s, 24 ½ x 22 In.
$88

Pook & Pook

Cabinet, Rococo Revival, Rosewood, Carved, Mirror, 2 Shelves, 1800s, 80 x 35 x 19 In........	450
Cabinet, Sewing, Mahogany, Martha Washington, Roycroft, c.1910, 29 x 30 x 16½ In. *illus*	2460
Cabinet, Shipyard Office, 2 Paneled Doors, Marked, Amberg's Patent, Conn., c.1890, 30 x 31 In.	813
Cabinet, Spice, 11 Drawers, Porcelain Knobs, 25 In.	136
Cabinet, Spice, Oak, 8 Drawers, Wood Pulls, Board Shape Back, 17 x 11 x 5 In.	144
Cabinet, Spice, Pine, Hanging, Labels, 9 Drawers, Early 1900s, 10¼ x 6¼ In. .... *illus*	277
Cabinet, Vanity, Mahogany, Brass, Mirror Doors, Drawers, Miroir Brot, Paris, c.1900, 74 x 33 In. *illus*	875
Cabinet, Wegner, RY 24, Teak, 2 Upper Sliding Doors, 6 Drawers, RY Mobler, 1958, 71 x 71 In. .*illus*	2969
Cabinet, Western, Maple, Natural Edge Top, 5 Drawers, Free-Form, Contemporary, 38 x 39 In. ....*illus*	3480
Cabinet, Wormley, Mahogany, Cane, Glass, Dunbar, Indiana, 1940s, 36 x 40 x 13 In. ...*illus*	2125
Candle Screen, Ivory, Carved, 2 Parts, Baroque Decor, Huntsman Standing, 15 x 5 In........	1872
Candlestand, Ebonized, Brass, Mother-Of-Pearl Inlay, Ormolu, 3 Shaped Legs, 28 x 24 In.	240
Candlestand, Federal, Cherry, Turned Tripod, Cabriole Leg, 1800s, 26 x 16½ x 16 In........	138
Candlestand, Hepplewhite, Tilt Top, Mahogany, String Inlay, Massachusetts, c.1800, 30 In.	312
Candlestand, Hepplewhite, Tilt Top, Octagonal, Maple, Tapered Legs, c.1920, 28 x 17 In...... *illus*	330
Candlestand, Maple, Painted, Turned Pedestal, Square Top, Tripod, Early 1800s, 27 x 14 In......	800
Candlestand, Maple, Turned Pedestal, Cabriole Legs, Tripod, New England, 1800s, 26 x 14 In.....	861
Candlestand, Maple, Varnished Surface, Tripod Base, New England, c.1800, 26 x 13 In......	584
Candlestand, Queen Anne, Cherry, Circular Top, Tripod, New England, 1700s, 27 x 13 In..	406
Candlestand, Queen Anne, Cherry, Turned Shaft, Cabriole Legs, 26 x 16½ In.	150
Candlestand, Queen Anne, Cherry, Vase Turned Shaft, Cabriole Legs, c.1780, 27 x 16 In. ...	250
Candlestand, Queen Anne, Tilt Top, Mahogany, Carved, Thos. Burling, N.Y., c.1770, 28 x 24 In....	5355
Candlestand, Rectangular, Black Paint, Calla Lilies, Nantucket, c.1820, 29 x 20 x 13 In.....	976
Candlestand, Tilt Top, Mahogany Veneer, Turned Pedestal, 1800s, 30 x 22 x 17 In.	88
Candlestand, Tilt Top, Mahogany, Turned Standard, Diamond Bone Inlay, 24 x 18 In.*illus*	366
Candlestand, Tilt Top, Pine, Round Top, Tripod, 1800s, 24½ x 22 In......................... *illus*	88
Candlestand, Walnut, Tilt Top, Shaped Top, Tripod, Mid Atlantic, 1800s, 29 x 17 x 20 In....	299
Canterbury, Karpen Style, Wood, Carved, Lions, Turned Stretcher, Victorian, 26 x 17 x In.	375
Canterbury, Mahogany, Maple Drawer, Turned Legs, Casters, England, 1800s, 20 x 19 In. .	375
Canterbury, Mahogany, Turned Spindles, Drawer, Brass Casters, 1800s, 20 x 21 In..... *illus*	142
Canterbury, Regency, Rosewood, Lyre Shape, Carved, Top Shape Feet, Casters, 20 x 21 In. ..*illus*	350
Canterbury, Rococo Revival, Rosewood, Carved, Scroll Feet, Drawer, 1800s, 26 x 22 In.	375
Canterbury, Rococo Revival, Rosewood, Shaped Dividers, Casters, American, 1800s, 26 x 22 In.	605
Canterbury, Victorian, Stick & Ball, Collapsible, Slant Legs, Late 1800s, 23 x 19 x 14 In......	125
Cart, Bar, Drop Leaf, 2 Large Wheels, Casters, Inlay, Compartments, 31 x 16 x 27 In............	201
Cart, Modern, Chrome, 2 Tiers, Glass, Handles, Casters, c.1950, 25 x 17 x 27 In............*illus*	153
Cart, Rolling, Joe Colombo, Bobby, Plastic, Drawers, Shelves, Kartell, Italy, 1980s, 29 x 17 In.	390
Case, Collector's, Walnut, Tortoiseshell, 12 Drawers, Stepped Shape, 1800s, 30 x 47 x 14 In.	2304
Cassone, Hinged Lid, Walnut, Carved, Splayed Feet, Continental, 1800s, 20 x 53 x 19 In.....	531
Cellarette, Federal, Mahogany, Dome Lid, String Inlay, Hopper McGaw & Co., c.1820, 27 x 15 In..	960
Cellarette, Federal, Mahogany, Inlay, Drawer, Tapered Legs, Drawer, 37 x 21 x 17 In...........	4973
Cellarette, George III, Mahogany, Hinged Lid, 8-Sided, Gilt Bands, Handles, c.1780, 23 x 19 In.	438
Cellarette, Hinged Lid, Mahogany, Octagonal, Reed Frame, Scrolled Legs, c.1800, 27 x 19 x 19 In.....	1220
Cellarette, Inlaid Top, Fitted Interior, Dividers, 6 Bottle, 1800s, 22¼ In...................... *illus*	1046
Cellarette, Mahogany, Domed Case, Inlay, Divided Interior, Dutch, c.1800, 10 x 8 In... *illus*	461
Cellarette, Regency, Mahogany, Sarcophagus, Inlay, Benjamin Banks, London, c.1820, 20 x 34 In...	2925
Cellarette, William IV, Walnut, Sarcophagus, Carved, Paw Feet, 1810s, 21 x 27 In.	1280
Chair Set, Aida, Calligaris, Leather Over Steel, Studio 28, Italy, c.2000, 35 In., 4.................	157
Chair Set, Bentwood, Rattan, Safari Pattern, Upholstered, Arms, c.1950, 30 x 18 In., 6.......	1625
Chair Set, Bistro, Spindle Back, Red Paint, Yellow Cushion, Wavy Crest Rail, 34 In., 4	400
Chair Set, Chippendale Style, Mahogany, Pierced Back Splats, Square Legs, c.1915, 38 In., 4 ..	84
Chair Set, Eames, DCW, Molded Ash Plywood, Herman Miller, 1945, 29 In., 6......................	2860
Chair Set, Federal, Mahogany, Double Lyre & Panel Splat, Maple Inlay, 32 x 17 In., 6..........	4440
Chair Set, Milo Baughman, Brass Coated Steel, Upholstered, Thayer Coggin, c.1975, 43 In., 4....	282
Chair Set, Queen Anne Style, Walnut, Yoke Crest, Cabriole Legs, Pad Feet, 41 In., 4	384
Chair Set, Windsor, Mixed Wood, 11 Spindles, H-Stretcher, David Smith, 1900s, 38 In., 4 ...	940
Chair, Aalto, Cantilevered, Upholstery, Arms, Artek, Finland, 1933, 37 In., Pair ....*illus*	3120
Chair, Arched Back, Reeded Legs, Casters, Upholstered, Closed Arm, 1800s 40 In.	189
Chair, Art Nouveau, Carved, Nude Woman, Flowers, Upholstered Seat, c.1900, 46 In....*illus*	2375
Chair, Art Nouveau, Louis Majorelle, Walnut, Carved, Pierced Splat, Upholstered, 36 In. .*illus*	1440
Chair, Arts & Crafts, Oak, Leather Upholstery, Carved Apron, Child's, 27 x 15 In.	281

F

Furniture, Canterbury, Mahogany, Turned Spindles, Drawer, Brass Casters, 1800s, 20 x 21 In.
$142

Soulis Auctions

Furniture, Canterbury, Regency, Rosewood, Lyre Shape, Carved, Top Shape Feet, Casters, 20 x 21 In.
$350

Neal Auction Company

Furniture, Cart, Modern, Chrome, 2 Tiers, Glass, Handles, Casters, c.1950, 25 x 17 x 27 In.
$153

Charleston Estate Auctions

Furniture, Cellarette, Inlaid Top, Fitted Interior, Dividers, 6 Bottle, 1800s, 22 ¼ In. **$1,046**

Brunk Auctions

Furniture, Cellarette, Mahogany, Domed Case, Inlay, Divided Interior, Dutch, c.1800, 10 x 8 In. **$461**

Pook & Pook

Furniture, Chair, Aalto, Cantilevered, Upholstery, Arms, Artek, Finland, 1933, 37 In., Pair **$3,120**

Wright

TIP
Never pick up a chair by the arms. Pick it up under the seat. The arms could loosen or crack.

Chair, Banister Back, Concave Arched Crest, Rush Seat, Arms, c.1730, 43 x 24 x 19 In.	344
Chair, Bellflower, Eagle's Head, Carved Arms, Fretwork Skirt, Claw Feet, Arms, 1800s, 40 In.	800
Chair, Bergere, Art Moderne, Black Leather Upholstery, Closed Arms, 1950, 35 x 28 x 22 In. *illus*	625
Chair, Bergere, Louis Philippe, Mahogany, Ormolu, Closed Arms, 1830s, 35 x 21 x 17 In., Pair	1071
Chair, Bergere, Louis XV Style, Gilt Frame, Upholstered, Closed Arms, 39 In., Pair	1024
Chair, Bergere, Louis XV Style, Walnut, Carved, Scrolled Feet, Closed Arms, 1900s, 31 In.	62
Chair, Bergere, Louis XVI, Painted, Carved, Upholstered, Closed Arms, 1700s, 36 x 24 x 26 In.	1107
Chair, Bergere, Regency, Gilt, Carved, Brocade Silk Upholstery, Closed Arms, 46 x 29 In.	240
Chair, Bergere, Regency, Mahogany, Bamboo Turnings, Cane, Leather, Closed Arms, 34 In.	177
Chair, Carved, Padded Back & Seat, Head Shape Finial, Continental, 1800s, 47 x 24 In., Pair	200
Chair, Carved, Yellow Pine, Oak, 2-Slat Back, Finials, Plank Seat, Miniature, 1800s, 9 In.	200
Chair, Chinese Chippendale, Faux Bamboo, Cane Seat, Cushion, 36 In., Pair *illus*	640
Chair, Chippendale, Bamboo & Rattan, Openwork Back, Chinese, 35 In.	63
Chair, Chippendale, Colonial, Mahogany, Rush Seat, Box Stretchers, American, 37 In., Pair	351
Chair, Chippendale, Mahogany, Carved, Serpentine Crest, Square Legs, Late 1700s, 37 x 17 ½ In.	625
Chair, Chippendale, Mahogany, Pierced Splat, Scroll Crest, Slip Seat, Philadelphia, 38 In. *illus*	330
Chair, Chippendale, Mahogany, Shell Carved Crest, New England, c.1770, 38 x 17 In.	123
Chair, Chippendale, Walnut, Carved, Benjamin Randolph, Phila., c.1770, 38 x 23 x 18 In., Pair	3780
Chair, Chippendale, Walnut, Carved, Pierced Splat, Block Legs, Arms, 1700s, 39 In. *illus*	156
Chair, Club, Art Deco Style, Brown Leather, Square Feet, 34 x 29 x 36 In., Pair	480
Chair, Club, Art Deco, Upholstered, S-Shape Wood Arms & Legs, 31 In., Pair	1500
Chair, Club, John Gallis, Studebaker Route 66, Ottoman, Norseman Designs West. *illus*	9000
Chair, Club, Ottoman, Leather, Tuften, Brass Tacks, Casters, Hancock & Moore, 35 x 31 In.	2335
Chair, Club, Rolled Back & Arms, Slipcover, Richard Keith Langham, 33 x 32 In., Pair	5440
Chair, Corner, Aesthetic Revival, Spindles, Cane Seat, Spherule Feet, 1800s, 30 In. *illus*	640
Chair, Corner, Carved, Figural Head, Pierced Splat, Continuous Arm, Continental, c.1890, 32 In. *illus*	225
Chair, Dan Johnson, Lounge, Selig, Steel, Upholstered, Lacquered Wood, 1951, 27 In. *illus*	1690
Chair, Desk, Birch, Barrel Shape, Leather, Rivet Trim, Howard & Sons, c.1890, 29 In. *illus*	2880
Chair, Eames, LCW, Ash Plywood, Rubber, Herman Miller, 1945, 27 In.	1500
Chair, Eames, Lounge, Ottoman, Rosewood, Black Leather, 32 x 33 In. *illus*	3900
Chair, Eames, Ottoman, Black Leather, X-Shape Base, 34 x 33 In.	5400
Chair, Eastlake, Carved & Molded, Tapestry Upholstery, Victorian, Arms, 58 In.	224
Chair, Easy, Queen Anne, Walnut, Upholstered, Stretcher Base, Pad Feet, c.1760, 46 In. *illus*	2000
Chair, Emmanuelle Style, Peacock, Wicker, Cushion Seat, 59 In., Pair	600
Chair, Empire Style, Parcel Gilt, Ebonized, Velvet Upholstery, Ball Feet, Arms, 1900s, 40 In.	469
Chair, Fauteuil, Louis XV Style, Carved, Upholstered, Open Arms, American, c.1985, 37 In., Pair *illus*	510
Chair, Fauteuil, Louis XV Style, Upholstered, Open Padded Arms, 34 In., Pair	1159
Chair, Fauteuil, Louis XV, Walnut, Upholstered, Cabriole Legs, Open Arms, 1700s, 35 In.	250
Chair, Fauteuil, Mahogany, Sphinxes, Upholstered, Flat Back, Arms, 1800s, 33 In., Pair	732
Chair, Fireside, Mahogany, Pierced, Carved, Needlepoint Upholstery, Arms, 56 In.	374
Chair, Frank Lloyd Wright, Upholstered, Enameled Aluminum, Pedestal Base, 1956, 34 In.	10000
Chair, French Style, Carved, Padded Back, Needlepoint, Splayed Feet, Arms, 33 x 23 In., Pair	176
Chair, G. Rietveld, Red Blue, Wood, Aluminum, G.A. Van De Groenekan, 1918-51, 34 x 26 In. *illus*	27500
Chair, G. Stickley, Morris, Oak, Upholstered, Marked, Red Decal, New York, 41 In. *illus*	4225
Chair, George II Style, Carved, Upholstered Back, Cushion, Arms, Ireland, 1900s, 41 In., Pair	504
Chair, George III Style, Leather Upholstery, Brass Tacks, Arms, 1900s, 42 x 28 In.	563
Chair, George III, Mahogany, Carved, Cushion, Square Legs, Arms, c.1790, 36 x 21 In.	250
Chair, George III, Mahogany, Tan Leather, Open Arms, 1700s, 39 x 27 In.	1664
Chair, Gothic Revival, Mahogany, Upholstered Seat, Pierced Back, Open Arms, 1810s, 58 In. *illus*	1088
Chair, Gothic Revival, Oak, Throne, Fleur-De-Lis Finials, Hinged Seat, 1800s, 84 x 28 In.	2710
Chair, Gothic Revival, Upholstered, Figural Carved Arms, c.1890, 28 In.	288
Chair, Henri II Style, Walnut, Carved, Leather, Mohair Upholstery, Arms, 1700s, 45 In.	375
Chair, Henry P. Glass, Lounge, Swivel, Upholstered, Brass, c.1955, 29 In., Pair	4750
Chair, Horn, Victorian Upholstery, Arms, 41 x 23 In. *illus*	1024
Chair, Industrial, Wrought Iron, Welded, Abacus, Barrel Back, 26 In., Pair	480
Chair, Ironing, Shaker, Cherry, Single Slat, Sloped & Tapered Seat, Footrest, 1920s, 35 In.	370
Chair, Italian, Carved, Parcel Gilt, Crest Rail, Quatrefoil, Padded Arms, 1930s, 38 x 34 In., Pair	750
Chair, J. Hoffmann, U-Shape Top Rail, Beech, Upholstered, Austria, 1906, 30 x 21 In. *illus*	1170
Chair, Jean Prouve, Metropole, No. 306, Enameled Steel, Vinyl, c.1952, 31 x 16 x 19 In. *illus*	22500
Chair, Joe DiMaggio, De Pas, D'Urbino & Lomazzi, Mitt Shape, Leather, Poltronova, 37 x 71 In.	3250
Chair, Ladder Back, 5 Arched Slats, Rush Seat, Delaware River Valley, c.1800, 43 In. *illus*	125

F

Furniture, Chair, Art Nouveau, Carved, Nude Woman, Flowers, Upholstered Seat, c.1900, 46 In.
$2,375

Potter & Potter Auctions

Furniture, Chair, Art Nouveau, Louis Majorelle, Walnut, Carved, Pierced Splat, Upholstered, 36 In.
$1,440

Alderfer Auction Company

Furniture, Chair, Bergere, Art Moderne, Black Leather Upholstery, Closed Arms, 1950, 35 x 28 x 22 In.
$625

Andrew Jones Auctions

Furniture, Chair, Chinese Chippendale, Faux Bamboo, Cane Seat, Cushion, 36 In., Pair
$640

Nadeau's Auction Gallery

Furniture, Chair, Chippendale, Mahogany, Pierced Splat, Scroll Crest, Slip Seat, Philadelphia, 38 In.
$330

Alderfer Auction Company

Furniture, Chair, Chippendale, Walnut, Carved, Pierced Splat, Block Legs, Arms, 1700s, 39 In.
$156

Eldred's

Furniture, Chair, Club, John Gallis, Studebaker Route 66, Ottoman, Norseman Designs West
$9,000

Blanchard's Auction Service LLC

Furniture, Chair, Corner, Aesthetic Revival, Spindles, Cane Seat, Spherule Feet, 1800s, 30 In.
$640

Neal Auction Company

Furniture, Chair, Corner, Carved, Figural Head, Pierced Splat, Continuous Arm, Continental, c.1890, 32 In.
$225

Bruneau & Co. Auctioneers

Furniture, Chair, Dan Johnson, Lounge, Selig, Steel, Upholstered, Lacquered Wood, 1951, 27 In.
$1,690

Wright

Furniture, Chair, Desk, Birch, Barrel Shape, Leather, Rivet Trim, Howard & Sons, c.1890, 29 In.
$2,880

Roland NY Auctioneers & Appraisers

Furniture, Chair, Eames, Lounge, Ottoman, Rosewood, Black Leather, 32 x 33 In.
$3,900

Alderfer Auction Company

Furniture, Chair, Easy, Queen Anne, Walnut, Upholstered, Stretcher Base, Pad Feet, c.1760, 46 In.
$2,000

Hindman

> **TIP**
> If someone spills something on your upholstered furniture wipe with a damp cloth to avoid staining. Then let it dry before sitting on it to avoid creasing.

Furniture, Chair, Fauteuil, Louis XV Style, Carved, Upholstered, Open Arms, American, c.1985, 37 In., Pair
$510

Selkirk Auctioneers & Appraisers

Furniture, Chair, G. Rietveld, Red Blue, Wood, Aluminum, G.A. Van De Groenekan, 1918-51, 34 x 26 In.
$27,500

Wright

Furniture, Chair, G. Stickley, Morris, Oak, Upholstered, Marked, Red Decal, New York, 41 In.
$4,225

Toomey & Co. Auctioneers

Chair, Louis XIV, Walnut, Leafy Crest, Vine Back, Upholstered Seat, Square Legs, 43 In.	234
Chair, Louis XV Style, Carved, Walnut, Upholstered, Open Arms, France, 1800s, 40 In., Pair	431
Chair, Lounge, Chippendale Style, Leather, Claw Feet, Barcalounger, 45 In., Pair	153
Chair, Lounge, Multicolor Velvet Upholstery, Cabriole Legs, Paw Feet, Closed Arms, 39 In.	209
Chair, Lounge, Nick Weddell, Gorgon, Ceramic, Hand-Hooked Rug *illus*	44444
Chair, Lounge, Reclining, Felted Polyester Upholstery, Brass Tacks, c.1985, 36 x 34 In.	240
Chair, Lounge, Wheel Leg, Maple, Upholstered, David Edward, France, c.1966, 35 x 22 In., Pair *illus*	1170
Chair, Mahogany, Carved, Scrolled Back, Upholstered, Open Arms, 1800s, 43 In., Pair	2304
Chair, Mahogany, Parcel Gilt, Shaped Back, Outswept Arms, Carved, Paw Feet, Irish, 42 In., Pair	3965
Chair, Maison Jansen, Aluminum, Vinyl, Brass, Curved Slat Back, France, c.1975, 43 In., Pair	563
Chair, Marcel Breuer, Wassily, Chrome, Leather Strap Upholstery, Knoll, 1900s, 29 In., Pair *illus*	1125
Chair, Martin Eisler & Carlo Hauner, Lounge, Reversivel, Movable Seat, Backrest, 1955, 34 In.	10000
Chair, Mies Van Der Rohe, Lounge, Barcelona, Black Leather, Steel Base, Knoll, 29 In.	708
Chair, Morris, L. & J.G. Stickley, Quartersawn Oak, Slant Arms, c.1910, 40 In.	2000
Chair, Morris, Stickley, Oak, Recliner, Black Leather, Bow Arms, Slats, Label, 40 In.	1125
Chair, Needlepoint Upholstery, Carved Arms & Stretcher, Continental, c.1890, 48 In.	108
Chair, Oak, 3 Corner, U-Shape Back, Triangular Seat, England, 1700s, 31 x 17 In.	1188
Chair, Ole Wanscher, Mahogany, Leather, Snedkermester A.J. Iversen, c.1960, 37 In.	428
Chair, Peacock, Wicker, 2-Tone, Woven, Arms, Footstool, 1970s, 58 x 41 ½ x 24 In.	1065
Chair, Pesce, Up5, Red Stretch Fabric, B&B Italia, Italy, 43 x 45 In. *illus*	1875
Chair, Pierre Jeanneret, Lounge, Teak, Rush, France, India, 1955, 32 x 19 ½ x 24 In., Pair *illus*	81250
Chair, Plantation Style, Barrel Back, Cane Seat, Turned Legs, Bentwood, 31 In., Pair	63
Chair, Potty, Walnut, Cylindrical, Ring Turned Design, Hinged Padded Top, c.1890, 17 x 16 In. *illus*	108
Chair, Queen Anne Style, Mahogany, Loose Cushions, Fairfield, Open Arms, 41 In., Pair	472
Chair, Queen Anne, Corner, Mahogany, Pierced Splats, X-Stretchers, Salem, 1700s, 32 In.	7320
Chair, R.J. Horner, Ebonized, Carved Crest, Turned Stretchers, Claw Feet, 39 In.	125
Chair, Reclining, Walnut, Leather Upholstery, Turned Legs, Open Arms, c.1680, 47 x 26 In. *illus*	2574
Chair, Regency Style, Silvered Wood, Upholstered, Lion, Stripes, Open Arms, 42 In.	1403
Chair, Rococo Revival, Rosewood, Carved, Upholstered, Gold Silk, 34 x 19 x 12 In., Pair	403
Chair, Rococo Style, Mahogany, Parcel Gilt, Upholstered, Portugal, 46 In., Pair	383
Chair, Rohde, Beech, Vinyl Upholstery, Kroehler, Arms, c.1933, 31 In.	3000
Chair, Rosso, Derossi, Ceretti, Pratone, Polyurethane, Gufram, Italy, '86 Ed., 37 x 54 In. *illus*	10000
Chair, Samson Folding, Russel Wright, Shwayder Bros. Inc., 1950, 30 x 24 In., Pair *illus*	1250
Chair, Savonarola, Folding Seat, Wood Slats, 1800s, 38 x 27 In., Pair	1530
Chair, Savonarola, Walnut, X-Shape, Carved, Scroll Legs, Arms, Italy, c.1890, 35 x 26 In.	438
Chair, Shaped Splat, Yellow Paint, Box Stretcher, 1800s, Child's, 20 In.	113
Chair, Sheraton Style, Upholstered, Closed Arms, Open Grip Ends, Southwood, c.1985, 37 In.	270
Chair, Slipper, Henredon, Walnut Finish, Upholstered, 17 In., Pair	600
Chair, Slipper, Herter Bros. Style, Round Needlepoint Seat, Casters, Victorian, 20 x 19 In., Pair	293
Chair, Steer Horns, Faux Spotted Cowhide Upholstery, Arms, Texas, 37 x 21 In. *illus*	549
Chair, Stickley & Brandt Co., Oak, Griffin, Carved, Pierced, Curved, Claw Feet, 45 In.	1150
Chair, Stickley Bros., Morris, Oak, Leather, Grand Rapids, 39 In.	938
Chair, Tufted Leather, Buttons, Upholstered, Rolled Arms, Hancock & Moore, 37 In. *illus*	840
Chair, V. Panton, MCM, Plastic, Orange, Molded, Herman Miller 1974, 33 x 19 In.	403
Chair, V. Panton, Model K2, Cone Shape, Wire, Upholstery, Denmark, c.1959, 29 x 25 In. *illus*	750
Chair, Venetian Style, Grotto, Shell Shape Seat & Back, Dragon Arms, 1900s, 36 In., Pair	2813
Chair, Vermelha, Black, Cotton Rope, Steel Feet, Fernando & Humberto Campana, 31 x 34 In.	3000
Chair, Victorian, Flame Stitch Upholstery, Carved Crest, Open Arms, 44 In.	136
Chair, Victorian, Spoon Back, Button Back Upholstery, Cabriole Legs, Open Arms, 1890s, 41 In.	115
Chair, Victorian, Walnut, Arched Top, Upholstered, c.1890, Child's, 28 ½ x 15 In.	108
Chair, Victorian, Walnut, Carved, Scrollwork, Inlay, Brocade Upholstery, Arms, 41 In.	978
Chair, Walnut, Carved, Winged Maidens, Cherubs, Upholstered Seat, Arms, Italy, 1800s, 34 In. *illus*	1320
Chair, Wegner, Flag Halyard, Steel, Leather, Plastic, Getama, c.1960, 32 x 41 In.	25000
Chair, Wegner, Lounge, AP 27/18, Oak, Upholstery, A.P. Stolen, c.1954, 41 x 29 In. *illus*	6641
Chair, Wegner, Lounge, CH 25, Oak, Cord, Arms, Carl Hansen & Son, c.1957, 28 x 27 In.	8594
Chair, Wegner, Papa Bear, Black Leather, Teak, Beech, Ottoman, A.P. Stolen, 1950, 39 x 32 In. *illus*	17188
Chair, Wegner, Peacock, Slanted Back, Johannes Hansen, Denmark, Arms, 1947, 42 In., Pair *illus*	8750
Chair, Wegner, Shell, Curved Back, Elliptical Seat, Leather Pads, Carl Hansen, 29 In.	1500
Chair, Wegner, Shell, Teak, Beech, Leather, Fritz Hansen, Denmark, 1948, 27 In.	4375
Chair, William & Mary Style, Walnut, Wing, Upholstered Carved Stretchers, 1700s, 52 In.	281
Chair, William IV, Walnut, Carved, Turned Legs, Upholstered, Open Arms, c.1850, 40 In.	406

Furniture, Chair, Gothic Revival, Mahogany, Upholstered Seat, Pierced Back, Open Arms, 1810s, 58 In. $1,088

Neal Auction Company

Furniture, Chair, Horn, Victorian Upholstery, Arms, 41 x 23 In. $1,024

Nadeau's Auction Gallery

Rustic Furniture

Furniture made with antlers was in style in the last half of the 1800s for use in hunting lodges and rustic retreats. Out of favor by the 1930s, it came back into fashion in the 1990s and prices went up.

FURNITURE

Furniture, Chair, J. Hoffmann, U-Shape Top Rail, Beech, Upholstered, Austria, 1906, 30 x 21 In.
$1,170

Treadway

Furniture, Chair, Jean Prouve, Metropole, No. 306, Enameled Steel, Vinyl, c.1952, 31 x 16 x 19 In.
$22,500

Wright

Furniture, Chair, Ladder Back, 5 Arched Slats, Rush Seat, Delaware River Valley, c.1800, 43 In.
$125

New Haven Auctions

Furniture, Chair, Lounge, Nick Weddell, Gorgon, Ceramic, Hand Hooked Rug
$44,444

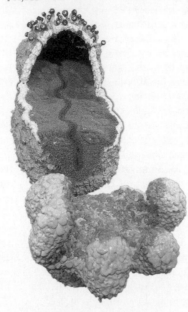

Furniture, Chair, Lounge, Wheel Leg, Maple, Upholstered, David Edward, France, c.1966, 35 x 22 In., Pair
$1,170

Wright

Furniture, Chair, Marcel Breuer, Wassily, Chrome, Leather Strap Upholstery, Knoll, 1900s, 29 In., Pair
$1,125

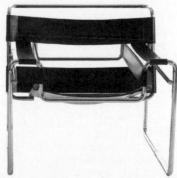

Charlton Hall Auctions

Furniture, Chair, Pesce, Up5, Red Stretch Fabric, B&B Italia, Italy, 43 x 45 In.
$1,875

Clars Auction Gallery

Furniture, Chair, Pierre Jeanneret, Lounge, Teak, Rush, France, India, 1955, 32 x 19 1/2 x 24 In., Pair
$81,250

Wright

Furniture, Chair, Potty, Walnut, Cylindrical, Ring Turned Design, Hinged Padded Top, c.1890, 17 x 16 In.
$108

Selkirk Auctioneers & Appraisers

Chair, Windsor Style, Mixed Woods, Scrolled Ears, Turned Legs, Late 1900s, 37 In.	780
Chair, Windsor, Arrow Back, Bamboo Turnings, Painted, New England, c.1825, Pair...........	861
Chair, Windsor, Birdcage, Old Black Surface, Arms, Pennsylvania, c.1825 .... *illus*	176
Chair, Windsor, Bow Back, 9 Spindles, Continuous Arm, Black Paint, Penn., c.1820, 35 In. .	550
Chair, Windsor, Fanback, Bamboo Turnings, Flowers, Grain Painted, c.1815, 34 In. ..... *illus*	120
Chair, Windsor, Fanback, Scrolled Out Ears, Knuckle Arms, Connecticut, c.1790, 43 In.	1125
Chair, Windsor, Fanback, Shaped Crest, Ears, Saddle Seat, Arms, D.R. Dimes, c.1980, 17 x 47 In..	600
Chair, Windsor, Fanback, Spindle Back, Turned Stiles & Legs, Pa., c.1800, Child's, 27 In.	5412
Chair, Windsor, Hoop Back, Steel, Silvered, Arms, Canton Art Metal Co., c.1926, 36 In., Pair	1935
Chair, Windsor, Sack Back, Painted, Arms, Early 1800s, 36 x 22 In.	488
Chair, Windsor, Sack Back, Painted, Continuous Arm, c.1790, 25 x 20 In.................... *illus*	584
Chair, Windsor, Slat Back, Grain Painted, Writing Arm, Turned Front Legs, 44 In.	2250
Chair, Wing, Chippendale Style, Leather, Brass Tacks, 1900s, 41 In., Pair................	3072
Chair, Wing, Chippendale Style, Mahogany, Upholstered, Outswept Arms, 49 In.	497
Chair, Wing, Louis XV Style, Ottoman, Carved Crest, Upholstered, 47 In., 2 Piece..................	313
Chair, Wing, Modern, Upholstered, Wood Feet, Closed Arms, 27 In., Pair..............	702
Chair, Wing, Queen Anne Style, Velvet Upholstery, Pad Feet, 1900s, 50 In.	125
Chair, Womb, Eero Saarinen, Upholstery, Steel Base, Knoll, c.1946, 37 x 41 In.	3900
Chair, Writing, Mixed Woods, Half-Arrow Back, Pillow Crest, Painted, Arms, c.1850, 40 In..	240
Chair, Rocker, is listed under Rocker in this category.	
Chair-Table, Bench, Pine, Flip Top, Painted, Blue Green Surface, 1800s, 27 x 60 x 41 In. ...	800
Chaise Longue, Curved Shape, Walnut Base, Upholstered, c.1985, 36 x 62 In. .... *illus*	2375
Chaise Longue, Distressed Leather, Single Arm, Headrest, Wood Feet, 28 x 59 In................	344
Chaise Longue, Empire Style, Mounted, Ebonized, Blue Upholstery, c.1890, 36 x 77 In.	688
Chaise Longue, Parzinger, Chrome Metal, Leather, Multicolor Upholstery, 29 x 64 In. *illus*	4550
Chaise Longue, Shito, Woven, Green Cord, Steel Frame, Paola Lenti, 31 x 51 x 35 In... *illus*	2700
Chest, Anglo-Indian, Hardwood, Carved, Brass Inlay, Removable Tray, 20 x 30 In....... *illus*	63
Chest, Blanket, 3 Drawers, Grain Painted, Hinged Lid, Ebonized, 26 x 49 In.	1250
Chest, Blanket, Cherry, Paneled, 2 Drawers, Brass Pulls, Hinged Lid, Kentucky, c.1860, 26 x 33 In..	940
Chest, Blanket, Chippendale Style, Lift Top, 5 Drawers, Bracket Feet, 40 x 45 x 18 In.	88
Chest, Blanket, Chippendale, Pine, 3 Lower Drawers, Snipe Hinges, 42 x 39 x 17 In........	585
Chest, Blanket, Chippendale, Pine, Painted, 3 Drawers, Initials ML & FR, 1786, 29 x 48 In.	2760
Chest, Blanket, Contemporary, Tiger Maple, Dovetailed, Miniature, 6 x 10 x 5 ½ In.	69
Chest, Blanket, Dovetailed, Till, Grain Painted, Hinged Lid, Bracket Feet, 1800s, 25 x 43 In.	590
Chest, Blanket, Federal, Poplar, Pine, Flowers, Compass, Elisabet Conradin, 1806, 23 x 51 In.....*illus*	10000
Chest, Blanket, Oak, Poplar & Pine, Pilgrim Style, Wallace Nutting, c.1910, 31 x 46 In.	2000
Chest, Blanket, Painted, Flowers, Orange, Bracket Feet, Scandinavia, 1864, 24 x 84 x 23 In.... *illus*	375
Chest, Blanket, Pine, 4 Drawers, Painted, Rattail Hinges, Bootjack Ends, c.1790, 31 x 40 In. ...	1250
Chest, Blanket, Pine, 6-Board Top, Chip Carved Edge, Cutouts, Mass., c.1820, 23 x 43 In. ...	4065
Chest, Blanket, Pine, Hinged Lid, 2 Handles, 1800s, 17 x 34 x 19 In.	366
Chest, Blanket, Poplar, Painted, Bracket Feet, Pennsylvania, 1800s, 24 x 40 In...................	176
Chest, Blanket, Red Paint, Hinged Lid, Arched Feet, New England, Late 1700s, 23 x 42 x 17 In.....	813
Chest, Bombe, Burl, 2 Drawers, Carved Apron, Tendril Pulls, France, 1900s, 29 x 33 In.	275
Chest, Bombe, Chinoiserie, Bronze Trim, Marble Top, Black Ground, Continental, 33 In. *illus*	725
Chest, Bow Front, Tiger Maple, 4 Graduated Drawers, Brass Pulls, 1800s, 37 x 39 In.	2160
Chest, Breakfront Top, Cupboard, Drawers, Turned Feet, Scotland, 1800s, 57 x 50 In.	1200
Chest, Campaign, Dovetailed Drawers, Brass Corners, Bracket Feet, Chinese, 1700s, 37 In. .	4920
Chest, Campaign, Mahogany, Brass Bound, 5 Drawers, Turned Feet, 1800s, 42 x 19 In.	3750
Chest, Campaign, Mahogany, Brass Bound, Fitted Desk Drawer, England, 1800s, 40 x 41 x 17 In.*illus*	3803
Chest, Campaign, Mahogany, Brass Side Handles, Ball Feet, 5 Drawers, 1800s, 43 x 39 In. ...	2340
Chest, Campaign, Maitland Smith, Georgian Style, Mahogany, 6 Tiered Drawers, 43 In.	968
Chest, Campaign, Wood, 2 Drawers, Brass Mounted, Side Handles, 21 x 32 x 18 In.	438
Chest, Camphorwood, Brass Bound, Side Handles, Hinged Lid, c.1850, 24 x 42 In.................	1125
Chest, Camphorwood, Lift Lid, Carved Panels, Drawers, Bracket Feet, Chinese, 40 x 37 In. .	293
Chest, Cedar, Dovetailed, Red Paint, Bracket Feet, Iron Handles, c.1875, 26 x 48 x 26 In......	65
Chest, Cedar, Hinged Lid, Lock, Brown & Gold, Footed, 17 x 9 x 8 In...............................	62
Chest, Charles II, Oak, Carved, 8 Various Drawer Sizes, Brass Handles, c.1700, 42 x 44 In......*illus*	1875
Chest, Charles II, Paneled Sides & Back, Turned Feet, 2 Parts, 1600s, 36 x 37 In.................	3198
Chest, Cherry, Soap Hollow Style, Red Paint, Flowers, 7 Drawers, Initials S.H., 55 x 39 In. ...	4182
Chest, Cherry, Transitional, Half Pilasters, Turned Legs, 6 Drawers, Ohio, 1830s, 45 x 42 x 21 In..	480

Furniture, Chair, Reclining, Walnut, Leather Upholstery, Turned Legs, Open Arms, c.1680, 47 x 26 In.
$2,574

Thomaston Place Auction Galleries

TIP
Watch out for arm-chairs that have been made by adding arms to side chairs.

Furniture, Chair, Rosso, Derossi, Ceretti, Pratone, Polyurethane, Gufram, Italy, '86 Ed., 37 x 54 In.
$10,000

Wright

Furniture, Chair, Samson Folding, Russel Wright, Shwayder Bros. Inc., 1950, 30 × 24 In., Pair
$1,250

Wright

FURNITURE

Furniture, Chair, Steer Horns, Faux Spotted Cowhide Upholstery, Arms, Texas, 37 x 21 In.
$549

CRN Auctions

Furniture, Chair, Tufted Leather, Buttons, Upholstered, Rolled Arms, Hancock & Moore, 37 In.
$840

Alex Cooper Auctioneers

Furniture, Chair, V. Panton, Model K2, Cone Shape, Wire, Upholstery, Denmark, c.1959, 29 x 25 In.
$750

Clars Auction Gallery

Furniture, Chair, Walnut, Carved, Winged Maidens, Cherubs, Upholstered Seat, Arms, Italy, 1800s, 34 In.
$1,320

Cottone Auctions

Furniture, Chair, Wegner, Lounge, AP 27/18, Oak, Upholstery, A.P. Stolen, c.1954, 41 x 29 In.
$6,641

Wright

Furniture, Chair, Wegner, Papa Bear, Black Leather, Teak, Beech, Ottoman, A.P. Stolen, 1950, 39 x 32 In.
$17,188

Wright

Furniture, Chair, Wegner, Peacock, Slanted Back, Johannes Hansen, Denmark, Arms, 1947, 42 In., Pair
$8,750

Wright

Furniture, Chair, Windsor, Birdcage, Old Black Surface, Arms, Pennsylvania, c.1825
$176

Pook & Pook

Furniture, Chair, Windsor, Fanback, Bamboo Turnings, Flowers, Grain Painted, c.1815, 34 In.
$120

Garth's Auctioneers & Appraisers

Furniture, Chair, Windsor, Sack Back, Painted, Continuous Arm, c.1790, 25 x 20 In.
$584

Pook & Pook

Furniture, Chaise Longue, Curved Shape, Walnut Base, Upholstered, c.1985, 36 x 62 In.
$2,375

Wright

Furniture, Chaise Longue, Parzinger, Chrome Metal, Leather, Multicolor Upholstery, 29 x 64 In.
$4,550

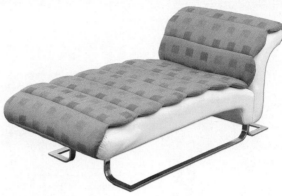

Palm Beach Modern Auctions

Furniture, Chaise Longue, Shito, Woven, Green Cord, Steel Frame, Paola Lenti, 31 x 51 x 35 In.
$2,700

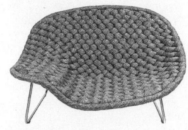

Michaan's Auctions

TIP
Touching up gilding does not change value if it is done by an expert.

Furniture, Chest, Anglo-Indian, Hardwood, Carved, Brass Inlay, Removable Tray, 20 x 30 In.
$63

Auctions at Showplace, NYC

Furniture, Chest, Blanket, Federal, Poplar, Pine, Flowers, Compass, Elisabet Conradin, 1806, 23 x 51 In.
$10,000

Hindman

Furniture, Chest, Blanket, Painted, Flowers, Orange, Bracket Feet, Scandinavia, 1864, 24 x 84 x 23 In.
$375

Hindman

Furniture, Chest, Bombe, Chinoiserie, Bronze Trim, Marble Top, Black Ground, Continental, 33 In.
$725

Neal Auction Company

Furniture, Chest, Campaign, Mahogany, Brass Bound, Fitted Desk Drawer, England, 1800s, 40 x 41 x 17 In.
$3,803

Thomaston Place Auction Galleries

Furniture, Chest, Charles II, Oak, Carved, 8 Various Drawer Sizes, Brass Handles, c.1700, 42 x 44 In.
$1,875

Hindman

Furniture, Chest, Document, Dome Lid, Painted Landscape Vignette, 13 x 19 x 12 In.
$144

Alderfer Auction Company

Furniture, Chest, Drexel, Declaration, Walnut, Divided Front, 8 Drawers, Tapered Legs, 31 x 60 In.
$531

Neue Auctions

Furniture, Chest, Federal, Bird's-Eye Maple, Tiger Maple Veneer, 4 Drawers, c.1810, 39 x 40 In.
$2,135

Rafael Osona Nantucket Auctions

Furniture, Chest, George III Style, Mahogany, 5 Drawers, Ogee Bracket Feet, 37 x 43 x 20½ In.
$1,107

Auctions at Showplace, NYC

Furniture, Chest, Louis XVI Style, Kingwood, Burl Walnut, Mother-Of-Pearl Inlay, c.1890, 21 x 23 In.
$545

Fontaine's Auction Gallery

Furniture, Chest, Mule, Camphorwood, Hinged Lid, Brass, Drawers, Chinese, 1800s, 22 x 46 In.
$878

Thomaston Place Auction Galleries

Furniture, Chest, Queen Anne, Maple, Carved, 5 Drawers, 2 Sections, New England, 1700s, 75 x 40 In.
$1,386

Freeman's

Furniture, Chest, R.J. Horner, Faux
Bamboo, 5 Drawers, Square Mirror, 1800s,
79 x 29 x 19 In.
$7,740

Cowan's Auctions

Furniture, Chest, Rustic, Twig Mosaic,
Applied Wood To Oilcloth, c.1900,
7 x 16 x 9 In.
$125

New Haven Auctions

Furniture, Chest, Tansu, Elm, Black Paint,
Drop Front, Engraved, Silvered Metal, Korea,
33 x 35 In.
$1,404

Thomaston Place Auction Galleries

Furniture, Chest, Victorian, Tartanware,
4 Drawers, Bail Handles, Scotland, 1880,
30 x 33 In.
$1,792

Neal Auction Company

> **TIP**
> *Watch out for side-
> boards or sofas that
> have been altered to a
> smaller, more easily
> sold size.*

Furniture, Chest-On-Chest, Chippendale
Style, Cherry, Oak, 13 Drawers, Ogee Feet,
c.1985, 89 x 41 In.
$1,200

Garth's Auctioneers & Appraisers

Furniture, Coat Rack, Industrial, Steel,
Circular Hook Top, Umbrella Holder, Enamel
Paint, 1920s, 68 In.
$250

New Haven Auctions

Furniture, Commode, Louis XV, Walnut,
Tulipwood, Bronze, Marble, Drawers, 1760s,
34 x 45 In.
$1,230

Auctions at Showplace, NYC

Furniture, Cradle, Plantation, Cherry,
Hooded, Dovetailed, Curved Legs, Rocker
Base, 45 x 44 x 27 In.
$288

Stevens Auction Co.

Furniture, Cupboard, Corner, Federal, Softwood, 2 Sections, 9-Pane Glass Door, Pa., 83 x 52 In.
$502

Conestoga Auction Company

Furniture, Cupboard, Corner, Federal, Walnut, Shaped Skirt, 12-Pane Door, 2 Sections, 85 x 43 In.
$900

Alderfer Auction Company

Furniture, Cupboard, Court, Jacobean Style, Oak, 6 Drawers Interior, Square Feet, 1700s, 69 x 52 In.
$688

Hindman

Chest, Chinoiserie, Relief Bird, Flowers, Scenic Decor, 1900s, 49 ½ x 38 x 21 In.	224
Chest, Chippendale, 2 Short & 2 Long Drawers, Reeded Columns, New Eng., 1700s, 32 x 39 In.	180
Chest, Chippendale, Birch, Flame, 4 Drawers, Massachusetts, Late 1700s, 33 x 42 x 18¾ In.	1500
Chest, Chippendale, Butternut, 2 Sections, 11 Drawers, Cabriole Legs, c.1760, 74 x 41 In.	1830
Chest, Chippendale, Mahogany, Serpentine, Dovetailed, Ball & Claw Feet, c.1790, 33 x 40 In.	8610
Chest, Chippendale, Maple, Tiger Grained Top, 4 Drawers, Late 1700s, 38 x 38 In.	1008
Chest, Chippendale, Walnut, 2 Over 4 Graduated Drawers, Brass Pulls, 48 x 41 x 22 In.	780
Chest, Chippendale, Walnut, Poplar, Quarter Fluted Pilasters, Ogee Feet, Pa., c.1790, 68 x 44 In.	1875
Chest, Document, Dome Lid, Painted Landscape Vignette, 13 x 19 x 12 In. *illus*	144
Chest, Dower, Painted, 3 Front Panels, Bracket Feet, Continental, c.1767, 35 x 62 x 23 In.	813
Chest, Drexel, Declaration, Walnut, Divided Front, 8 Drawers, Tapered Legs, 31 x 60 In. *illus*	531
Chest, Federal, Bird's-Eye Maple, Tiger Maple Veneer, 4 Drawers, c.1810, 39 x 40 In. *illus*	2135
Chest, George I Style, Oak, Oyster Veneer, 5 Drawers, Chamfered Corners, 1900s, 32 x 41 In.	945
Chest, George II, Mahogany, Dovetailed, 5 Drawers, Oak Linings, 1700s, 35 x 38 x 20 In.	677
Chest, George III Style, Mahogany, 5 Drawers, Ogee Bracket Feet, 37 x 43 x 20½ In. *illus*	1107
Chest, George III, Walnut, Oak, Mold Edge Top, 6 Drawers, Bracket Feet, c.1770, 35 x 39 In.	2125
Chest, Georgian, 5 Drawers, Brass Handles, Bracket Feet, Miniature, 1800s, 17 x 15 x 8 In.	360
Chest, Gothic Revival, Oak, Hinged Lid, Carved, Square Feet, Late 1800s, 26 x 54 x 21 In.	875
Chest, Hardwood, Brass Mounted, Padlock, Handle, India, 1800s, 27 x 57 x 27 In.	1530
Chest, Hepplewhite, Mahogany, Inlay, 4 Drawers, Post & Bale Hardware, c.1800, 38 x 36 In.	1340
Chest, Inlay, Scrolled Leaf Design, 3 Drawers, Bun Feet, Dutch, 31 x 36 x 20 In.	125
Chest, Kindel, Mahogany, 4 Drawers, Fluted Front, Turned Legs, Metal Pulls, 48 x 35 x 22 In.	360
Chest, Lingerie, Louis XVI Style, Fruitwood, Black Marble, 6 Drawers, Brass Pulls, 48 x 19 In.	375
Chest, Lingerie, Rosewood, Marble Top, 6 Drawers, Wood Pulls, 37 x 16 x 14 In.	633
Chest, Louis XVI Style, Kingwood, Burl Walnut, Mother-Of-Pearl Inlay, c.1890, 21 x 23 In. *illus*	545
Chest, Mahogany Veneer, 5 Drawers, Carved, Reeded, Bracket Base, England, 42 x 49 In.	438
Chest, Mahogany, Pine, 4 Graduated Drawers, Dovetailed, Miniature, 1850s, 10½ x 9¾ x 7¼ In.	227
Chest, Mule, Camphorwood, Hinged Lid, Brass, Drawers, Chinese, 1800s, 22 x 46 In. *illus*	878
Chest, Mule, Grain Painted, Pine, 3 Glove Drawers, 2 Lower Drawers, c.1875, 47 x 39 In.	96
Chest, Neoclassical, Cherry, Maple, 4 Drawers, Turned Legs, c.1835, Child's, 28 x 23 In.	1500
Chest, Neoclassical, Fruitwood, Inlay, 3 Drawers, Dutch, c.1790, 33 x 47 In.	2560
Chest, Oak, Fruitwood, Geometrics, Drawers Behind Doors, Fitted Interior, c.1670, 48 x 48 In.	1521
Chest, Oak, Lift Top, Geometric Design, 2 Drawers, Footed, Massachusetts, c.1690, 33 x 51 x 21 In.	21250
Chest, Parzinger, Wood, White, Metal Studs & Handle, Drop Front Door, 17 x 20 x 16 In.	3120
Chest, Pine, 4 Drawers, Wooden Knobs, Ogee Bracket Feet, New England, 1700s, 36 x 41 x 19 In.	469
Chest, Queen Anne, Maple, Carved, 5 Drawers, 2 Sections, New England, 1700s, 75 x 40 In. *illus*	1386
Chest, Queen Anne, Walnut, Inlay, 3 Short Drawers, 4 Graduated Drawers, c.1720, 44 In.	4800
Chest, R.J. Horner, Faux Bamboo, 5 Drawers, Square Mirror, 1800s, 79 x 29 x 19 In. *illus*	7740
Chest, Renaissance Revival, Burl Walnut, Marble Top, McCracken, 1800s, 26 x 37 In., Pair	1280
Chest, Robsjohn-Gibbings, Bachelor, Walnut, 3 Drawers, Platform, Signed, 30 x 34 In., Pair	826
Chest, Rustic, Twig Mosaic, Applied Wood To Oilcloth, c.1900, 7 x 16 x 9 In. *illus*	125
Chest, Serpentine, Painted, Bracket Feet, 3 Over 2 Long Drawers, Continental, c.1810, 30 x 17 In.	563
Chest, Stickley, Cherry, Drawers, Shaped Apron, Brass, Cabriole Legs, 1974, 64 x 40 In.	360
Chest, Storage, Geometric Design, Carved Front, Lift Top, Continental, 1800s, 30 x 49 x 26 In.	937
Chest, Tansu, Elm, Black Paint, Drop Front, Engraved, Silvered Metal, Korea, 33 x 35 In. *illus*	1404
Chest, Tansu, Elm, Carved Doors, 9 Drawers, Korea, c.1910, 23 x 52 x 70 In.	307
Chest, Tansu, Elm, Zelkovia, Iron Mounts, Sliding Doors, Wheels, Japan, 1910s, 38 x 46 In.	2875
Chest, Tansu, Wood, Safe, 4 Drawers, Iron Base, Asia, 16 x 13 In.	224
Chest, Tansu, Yonezawa, Drawers, Various Sizes, Door, Japan, 1910s, 36 x 41 In.	1500
Chest, Transitional, Poplar, 2 Over 3 Drawers, Scrolled Crest, Turned Feet, c.1835, 53 x 44 In.	300
Chest, Victorian, Butternut, Pine, Scalloped Back Splash, 6 Drawers, 1860s, 50 x 42 x 20 In.	96
Chest, Victorian, Pine, Cottage Style Design, 3 Drawers, Miniature, c.1890, 10 x 10 x 6 In.	84
Chest, Victorian, Tartanware, 4 Drawers, Bail Handles, Scotland, 1880, 30 x 33 In. *illus*	1792
Chest, Walnut, 2 Half Drawers Over 2 Graduated Drawers, England, c.1790, 35 x 35 In.	594
Chest, Wedding, Pine, Hinged Top, Chip Carved, Mixteca, Oaxaca, Mexico, 21 x 33 x 17 In.	761
Chest, Wedding, Wood, Ebonized, Relief Carved, Brass Escutcheon, Asian, 12 x 23 x 11 In.	35
Chest-On-Chest, Chippendale Style, Cherry, Oak, 13 Drawers, Ogee Feet, c.1985, 89 x 41 In. *illus*	1200
Chest-On-Chest, Chippendale, Cherry, 8 Drawers, Bracket Feet, c.1780, 76 x 45 x 20 In.	938
Chest-On-Chest, George III, Mahogany, 9 Drawers, Carved, c.1780, 66 x 47 In.	875
Chest-On-Chest, George III, Mahogany, Bracket Feet, Miniature, 1700s, 17 x 9 In.	1599

Chest-On-Chest, George III, Mahogany, Greek Key Molding, Block Feet, 71 x 44 x 21 ½ In.	750
Chest-On-Chest, George III, Mahogany, Molded Cornice, Bracket Feet, 1700s, 71 x 42 In. ..	2816
Chest-On-Chest, Mahogany, 7 Drawers, Gilt Pulls, Ogee Feet, England, c.1780, 63 x 44 x 24 In....	1495
Chest-On-Frame, Brassbound, Camphorwood, Leather, Painted, Chinese, 1800s, 16 x 36 x 18 In.	175
Chest-On-Frame, George II Style, Walnut, Scalloped Apron, Ball & Claw Feet, c.1910, 51 x 20 In.	726
Chest-On-Frame, Georgian Style, Mahogany, Inlay, Brass Handles, 22 x 20 x 11 In.	240
Chest-On-Frame, Hinged Top, 2 Doors, Floral Design, Leather, Chinese, 1900s, 21 x 14 In.	48
Chest-On-Frame, Queen Anne, Burl Walnut, Oak, Inlay, Drawers, Bun Feet, 1700s, 40 x 38 In..	1280
Chest-On-Frame, Queen Anne, Maple, Drawers, Carved, Drop Skirt, Frame, c.1790, 66 x 38 In.	1125
Chest-On-Frame, William & Mary, Burl, 7 Drawers, Scroll Panel Inlay, 48 x 43 x 23 In. ...	1770
Chest-On-Frame, William & Mary, Oak, 11 Drawers, Metal Pulls, Ball Feet, 1700s, 49 x 42 x 24 In..	688
Coat Rack, Industrial, Steel, Circular Hook Top, Umbrella Holder, Enamel Paint, 1920s, 68 In... *illus*	250
Coat Rack, Maple, Urn Finial, Turned Standard & Rods, Tripod Base, c.1850, 77 x 26 In. ..	793
Coat Rack, Wood, Scalloped, Wall Mount, 4 Whale Teeth, Whaler Made, 1800s, 24 In........	854
Coffer, Louis XIV Style, Walnut, Brass Mounted, Stand, 1900s, 31 x 27 x 17 In......................	875
Commode listed here is a chest. A commode that is a toilet is listed as Chair, Potty.	
Commode, Demilune, Marble Top, 3 Inlaid Veneered Drawers, 1900s, 36 x 47 In.	819
Commode, George III, Mahogany, Oak, Tambour Door, c.1870, 31 x 19 In.	330
Commode, Louis Philippe, Mahogany, Inlay, Molding, Frieze Drawer, 1800s, 36 x 46 In.	512
Commode, Louis XV Style, Bombe, Marble Top, 3 Drawers, Gilt Pulls, 1900s, 31 x 42 x 18 In.	406
Commode, Louis XV Style, Bombe, Shaped Top, 2 Drawers, 29 x 28 x 14 In.	189
Commode, Louis XV Style, Bronze, Inlay, Bombe, Marble, Figural Shoulders, Sabots, 45 x 42 In..	1464
Commode, Louis XV Style, Inlaid Top & Shelf, Drawer, Brass, R. Soraino Espana, 1900s, 27 In....	441
Commode, Louis XV Style, Marble Top, Demilune, Bronze Mounted, Italy, 29 x 28 x 14 In. .	256
Commode, Louis XV Style, Marble Top, Verni Martin Style Panels, Drawers, Doors, 37 x 53 In.	256
Commode, Louis XV, Provincial, Marble Top, Drawers, Painted, Brass, 29 x 37 x 17 In., Pair ...	1920
Commode, Louis XV, Walnut, Tulipwood, Bronze, Marble, Drawers, 1760s, 34 x 45 In... *illus*	1230
Commode, Louis XVI Style, Gilt Bronze Mounts, Parquetry, France, c.1890, 34 x 39 x 19 In. .	882
Commode, Mahogany, 3 Doors, Carved Legs, Claw Feet, Signed, Gillows, c.1890, 36 x 59 In.......	575
Commode, Mahogany, Marble Top, Gilt Bronze, 6 Drawers, Continental, 1700s, 37 x 50 In.	3750
Commode, Rococo Revival, Rosewood, Marble Top, Carved, Drawer, c.1890, 28 x 20 x 18 In.	3250
Commode, Serpentine Front, 2 Drawers, Painted, Hoof Feet, 1800s, 33 x 36 x 15 In.	438
Commode, Victorian, Rosewood, Marble Top, Pierced Carving, 30 x 38 x 19 In......................	1380
Commode, Walnut, Carved, Marble Top & Backsplash, Shelves, Drawer, c.1890, 44 x 33 In.	281
Commode, Wood, Marble Top, Ornate Brass, 3 Drawers, France, c.1810, 34 x 32 In.	563
Cradle, Pine, Arched Hooded Opening, Canted Sides, Rockers, 1700s, 26 x 32 In.	469
Cradle, Plantation, Cherry, Hooded, Dovetailed, Curved Legs, Rocker Base, 45 x 44 x 27 In...*illus*	288
Cradle, Rocking, Mahogany, Head Cover, Brown, Sleigh Foot, 24 x 17 x 36 In.	72
Credenza, Art Deco, Mahogany, Veneer, 3 Doors, Shelves, U.S., c.1935, 32 x 74 x 24 In.	344
Credenza, Burlwood, Ormolu Mounted, Marble Top, Mirror, 4 Drawers, 2 Doors, 64 x 67 In.	150
Credenza, Danish Modern, Rosewood, Tambour Door, Inside Shelves, Drawers, c.1950, 78 In. ...	3218
Credenza, Jacobean, Oak, Molded Top, 5 Drawers, Cabinets, c.1790, 35 x 70 In.	5185
Credenza, Teak, 4 Doors, 5 Drawers, Skovby Mobelfabrik, Denmark, 1900s, 32 x 80 In.......	650
Cupboard, Chippendale Style, Maple, Poplar, 12 Drawers, 2 Sections, c.1985, 83 x 49 In.	2040
Cupboard, Contemporary, Folk Art Decorated, 2 Sections, Panel Doors, Drawers, 76 x 42 In.......	585
Cupboard, Corner, Bench Made, 12 Panes Over Lower Doors, Shelf, Inlay, 40 x 25 x 84 In..	267
Cupboard, Corner, Chippendale, Pine, Poplar, Grain Painted, Glass Panes, c.1825, 97 x 56 In.	1875
Cupboard, Corner, Dutch Style, Painted, Reverse Painted Glass, Continental, c.1900, 71 In..	390
Cupboard, Corner, Federal, Softwood, 2 Sections, 9-Pane Glass Door, Pa., 83 x 52 In.. *illus*	502
Cupboard, Corner, Federal, Walnut, Shaped Skirt, 12-Pane Door, 2 Sections, 85 x 43 In.......*illus*	900
Cupboard, Corner, Hanging, Chippendale, Tiger Maple, Geo. Beshore, Pa., c.2000, 45 x 24 In. ...	1554
Cupboard, Corner, Hanging, Queen Anne, Walnut, Paneled Door, Pa., c.1750, 44 x 33 In.....	5670
Cupboard, Corner, Hanging, Softwood, Painted, Flowers, Continental, Late 1700s, 21 x 26 In.....	236
Cupboard, Corner, Walnut, Canted Corners, 4 Doors, Shelves, Bracket Base, 1800s, 86 x 47 In. ..	585
Cupboard, Corner, Walnut, Pine, 4 Paneled Doors, Inlay, Shelves, Pa., c.1825, 95 x 49 In.....	900
Cupboard, Country Empire, Cherry, Poplar, 2 Sections, 4 Doors, 2 Drawers, 80 x 50 In........	995
Cupboard, Court, Jacobean Style, Oak, 6 Drawers Interior, Square Feet, 1700s, 69 x 52 In. ...*illus*	688
Cupboard, Dutch, Chippendale, Walnut, Panel Doors, 2 Sections, Drawers, Pa., 89 x 66 In...*illus*	5900
Cupboard, Dutch, Painted, Swirl Design, Drawers, Doors, Pa., 1800s, 84 x 61 In..................	1968
Cupboard, Hanging, Cherry, Red Stain, Door, Drawer, Carved, 1800s, 41 x 23 x 12 In.	2500

Furniture, Cupboard, Dutch, Chippendale, Walnut, Panel Doors, 2 Sections, Drawers, Pa., 89 x 66 In.
$5,900

Conestoga Auction Company

Furniture, Cupboard, Hanging, Pine, Paint Decorated, Scandinavia, 1799, 23 x 15 In.
$706

Pook & Pook

Furniture, Cupboard, Jelly, Maple, 2 Doors, Punched Tin Panels, Drawer, Shelves, 1800s, 61 x 44 In.
$438

Eldred's

Furniture, Cupboard, Pine, Step Back, Glass Pane Doors Over 2 Doors, Bracket Feet, 80 x 45 In.
$1,140

Alderfer Auction Company

Furniture, Cupboard, Poplar, Stained, Old Red Surface, Bucket Bench Base, Pa., 1700s, 74 x 48 In.
$4,674

Pook & Pook

Furniture, Cupboard, Step Back, French Provincial, 3-Shelf Top, 2 Doors, Drawers, 1700s, 87 x 50 In.
$1,750

John Moran Auctioneers

Cupboard, Hanging, Pine, Chicken Wire Door, Yellow Paint, 1900s, 23 x 16 In.	164
Cupboard, Hanging, Pine, Paint Decorated, Scandinavia, 1799, 23 x 15 In. ....*illus*	706
Cupboard, Hanging, Spindle Turnings, 2 Sections, Door, England, 1800s, 27 x 26 x 10 In..	6875
Cupboard, Jelly, Maple, 2 Doors, Punched Tin Panels, Drawer, Shelves, 1800s, 61 x 44 In.*illus*	438
Cupboard, Jelly, Overhanging Top, Drawers, Paneled Doors, Louisiana, 1800s, 54 x 39 In..	345
Cupboard, Jelly, Softwood, Comb Grain & Sponge Painted, 2 Drawers, Pa., 1800s, 55 x 44 In. ..	590
Cupboard, Milk, Softwood, Red Grain Painted, Paneled Door, Pa., 1800s, 44 x 28 In.	738
Cupboard, Pewter, Pine, 2 Tiers, 3 Shelves, 4 Panel Doors, Late 1900s, 80 x 74 x 14 In.	600
Cupboard, Pine, Raised Panels Doors, Interior Shelves, Painted, 1800s, 77 x 36 In.	1169
Cupboard, Pine, Step Back, Glass Pane Doors Over 2 Doors, Bracket Feet, 80 x 45 In...*illus*	1140
Cupboard, Poplar, Stained, Old Red Surface, Bucket Bench Base, Pa., 1700s, 74 x 48 In..*illus*	4674
Cupboard, Side, Las Palmas, Sawtelle, Paint Decoration, Travertine Top, 33 x 72 x 22 In. ...	375
Cupboard, Softwood, Red Paint, Paneled Door, 4 Shelves, Pa., 1800s, 66 x 36 In.	974
Cupboard, Step Back, French Provincial, 3-Shelf Top, 2 Doors, Drawers, 1700s, 87 x 50 In. *illus*	1750
Cupboard, Step Back, Mahogany, Inlaid Doors, Open Shelves, 1800s, Child's, 45 x 24 x 12 In.	556
Cupboard, Step Back, Pine, 4 Paneled Doors, Shelves, 2 Drawers, c.1850, 80 x 52 In...........	1320
Cupboard, Step Back, Pine, Overhanging Top, Raised Panel Doors, Shelves, 1800s, 81 x 46 In...	527
Cupboard, Step Back, Walnut, Glass Doors, Fretwork, Drawers, Lower Doors, 1860s, 47 x 47 In....	330
Cupboard, Wall, Softwood, Gray Blue Paint, 3-Pane Door, Penn., c.1800, 84½ x 31 In. ..*illus*	224
Cupboard, Walnut, 2 Doors, Divided Shelves, Turned Feet, Pa., 1800s, 66 x 48 In.	1512
Daybed, Charles Webb, Cherry, Banister Side Rails & Backboard, 23 x 83 x 31½ In...........	1500
Daybed, Directoire, Painted, Parcel Ebonized, Acorn Finial, c.1810, 45 x 72 In., Pair	750
Daybed, Federal, Faux Bois, Mahogany, Scroll Ends, X-Supports, Cane Seat, c.1810, 30 x 78 In..	2048
Daybed, Limbert, No. 850, Oak, Leather, Michigan, Branded Mark, 25 x 30 x 79 In.............	1250
Daybed, Louis XV Style, Walnut, Back Drape Rail, Carved, Arms, c.1910, 75 x 49 x 80 In.	527
Daybed, Martin Visser, Spectrum, Enameled Steel, Upholstered, c.1960, 27 x 75 x 27 In.	1125
Daybed, Mies Van Der Rohe, Barcelona, Walnut, Leather, Stainless Steel, Knoll, c.1990, 77 In... *illus*	5000
Daybed, Wegner, GE 6, Teak, Caning, White Upholstery, Getama, c.1965, 29 x 78 In. ...*illus*	6250
Daybed, William & Mary, Reclining, Walnut, Upholstered, X-Stretcher, 40 x 60 In.......*illus*	1404
Desk, Aesthetic Movement, Walnut, Shakespearean, Minton Tiles, Spindles, c.1875, 62 x 27 In....	3510
Desk, Architect's, Georgian, Mahogany, Slant Front, Pullout, c.1810, 31 x 42 In.	510
Desk, Art Nouveau, Mahogany, Carved, Pierced, Dovetailed Drawers, c.1900, 38 In.	1792
Desk, Borge Mogensen, Teak, Brass, Kneehole, 8 Drawers, 2 Pullouts, 1958, 27 x 65 In.*illus*	1430
Desk, Butler's, Sheraton, Drop Front, Cherry, Tiger Maple, Drawers, c.1840, 48 x 45 In.	770
Desk, Chippendale Style, Executive, Leather Top, 5 Drawers, Henredon, 31 x 59 In.............	189
Desk, Chippendale Style, Mahogany, Demilune, Kneehole, 17 Drawers, 1930s, 29 x 51 In. ...	1029
Desk, Chippendale Style, Mahogany, Slant Front, Inlaid Fitted Interior, 1800s, 42 x 42 In. ...	375
Desk, Chippendale, Mahogany, Kneehole, Long Drawer Over 6 Drawers, 1700s, 30 x 33 In.	6958
Desk, Chippendale, Maple, Slant Front, Fitted Interior, Drawers, Brass, c.1780, 43 x 36 In.... *illus*	1353
Desk, Chippendale, Tiger Maple, Slant Front, Carved, Pigeonholes, New Eng., c.1790, 41 In...*illus*	1512
Desk, Chippendale, Tiger Maple, Slant Front, Pigeonholes, Drawers, c.1780, 41 x 37 In........	1875
Desk, Clerk's, Poplar, Slant Front, Gallery, Fitted Interior, Dovetailed Drawers, c.1850, 51 x 35 In..	168
Desk, Clerk's, Sheraton, Drop Front, Cherry, Dovetailed Drawer, 1830s, 36 x 40 In.	228
Desk, Danish Modern, Teak, Kneehole, 6 Drawers, Kai Kristiansen, 1950, 29 x 51 In.............	688
Desk, Davenport, Mahogany, 4 Drawers, Carved, Victorian, c.1870, 35 x 20 x 20 In. ......*illus*	156
Desk, Drop Front, Maple, Walnut, Pigeonholes, Drawers, Fold-Down Surface, 53 x 33 In.	96
Desk, Edwardian, Mahogany, Roll Top, 8 Drawers, Pull Out Side Panels, c.1915, 38 x 30 In....*illus*	188
Desk, Edwardian, Satinwood, Compartments, Drawers, Letter Holders, 1890, 38 x 36 In.	406
Desk, Federal, Mahogany, Tambour, Inlay, 2 Drawers, Tapered Legs, 46 x 36 In.	344
Desk, G. Stickley, Chalet, No. 505, Drop Front, Oak, Trestle Feet, 46 x 24 x 16 In.	1062
Desk, George III, Mahogany, Kneehole, 7 Drawers, Gilt, Bracket Feet, c.1790, 23 x 33 In.	875
Desk, Georgian, Oak, 9 Drawers, Kneehole, Embossed, Leather Top, 1800s, 31 x 54 In.........	256
Desk, Georgian, Walnut, Oak, Slant Front, 5 Drawers, Pigeonholes, Bracket Feet, 45 x 38 In........	1140
Desk, Gio Ponti, Walnut, 9 Drawers, Splayed Legs, Giordano Chiesa, Italy, c.1950, 31 x 62 In. ...	5000
Desk, Hepplewhite Style, Maple, Pine, Slant Front, Drawers, French Feet, c.1985, 29 x 21 In. ...	720
Desk, Hollywood Regency, Allover Mirror, 3 Drawers, Square Legs, 30 x 43 x 25 In..............	156
Desk, Kneehole, Leather, Painted, 9 Drawers, Molded Base, Continental, 1800s, 30 x 57 In.	438
Desk, Lady's, Inlay, 3 Drawers, Brass Borders, Splayed Legs, France, 1800s, 49 x 28 In........	188
Desk, Library, Mahogany, Leather, Flip Up Leaves, Drawers, Trestle Base, 1900s, 29 x 60 In. .... *illus*	200
Desk, Louis XV Style, Veneer, Leather, Inlay, Gilt Bronze, Drawers, c.1880, 31 x 65 In.	1250

F

Furniture, Cupboard, Wall, Softwood, Gray Blue Paint, 3-Pane Door, Penn., c.1800, 84½ x 31 In.
$224

TIP
Rub soap on noisy door hinges.

Furniture, Desk, Borge Mogensen, Teak, Brass, Kneehole, 8 Drawers, 2 Pullouts, 1958, 27 x 65 In.
$1,430

Wright

Furniture, Daybed, Mies Van Der Rohe, Barcelona, Walnut, Leather, Stainless Steel, Knoll, c.1990, 77 In.
$5,000

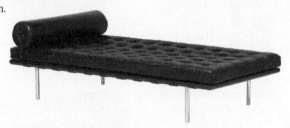

Wright

Furniture, Daybed, Wegner, GE 6, Teak, Caning, White Upholstery, Getama, c.1965, 29 x 78 In.
$6,250

Wright

Furniture, Daybed, William & Mary, Reclining, Walnut, Upholstered, X-Stretcher, 40 x 60 In.
$1,404

Thomaston Place Auction Galleries

Furniture, Desk, Chippendale, Maple, Slant Front, Fitted Interior, Drawers, Brass, c.1780, 43 x 36 In.
$1,353

Pook & Pook

Furniture, Desk, Chippendale, Tiger Maple, Slant Front, Carved, Pigeonholes, New Eng., c.1790, 41 In.
$1,512

Freeman's

Furniture, Desk, Davenport, Mahogany, 4 Drawers, Carved, Victorian, c.1870, 35 x 20 x 20 In.
$156

Hindman

F

Furniture, Desk, Edwardian, Mahogany, Roll Top, 8 Drawers, Pull Out Side Panels, c.1915, 38 x 30 In.
$188

John Moran Auctioneers

Furniture, Desk, Traveling, Victorian, Rosewood, Hinge Lid, Brass, Stand, 1840, 7 x 20 x 10 In.
$360

Alex Cooper Auctioneers

Furniture, Desk, Wooton, Walnut, Doors, Drawers, Casters, Standard Grade, c.1874, 69 x 42 x 31 In.
$6,050

Fontaine's Auction Gallery

Furniture, Desk, Library, Mahogany, Leather, Flip Up Leaves, Drawers, Trestle Base, 1900s, 29 x 60 In.
$200

Bruneau & Co. Auctioneers

Furniture, Desk, Mid-Century Modern, Wood, Iron Legs & Frame, Drawers, Side Shelves, 54 x 24 In.
$688

New Haven Auctions

Furniture, Desk, Risom, Executive, Walnut, 2 Stacks Of Drawers, Denmark, c.1950, 30 x 78 x 36 In.
$510

Selkirk Auctioneers & Appraisers

> **TIP**
> *Try to rearrange your furniture once a year to avoid noticeable sun fading.*

Furniture, Dresser, Drexel Declaration, Walnut, Doors, 4 Drawers, Tapered Legs, 47 x 42 In.
$502

Neue Auctions

Furniture, Dresser, Parzinger, Faux Parchment Over Wood, Chrome Metal, 6 Drawers, 31 x 96 In.
$9,750

Palm Beach Modern Auctions

Desk, Louis XVI, Walnut, Purpleheart, Banded, Inlay, c.1790, 28 x 30 x 17 In.........................	1845
Desk, Mid-Century Modern, Wood, Iron Legs & Frame, Drawers, Side Shelves, 54 x 24 In.... *illus*	688
Desk, Modern, White Oak Veneer, Curved Edges, Drawer, 29 ½ x 60 x 29 In.	1000
Desk, Neoclassical, Fruitwood, Drawers, Inlaid Garland, Tapered legs, Italy, 39 x 21 ½ In...	280
Desk, Partners, R.J. Horner, Mahogany, Carved, Winged Griffins, Claw Feet, c.1890, 56 In...	4375
Desk, Partners, Sheraton Style, Mahogany, Compartment Gallery, Drawer, 35 x 34 In.	325
Desk, Queen Anne Style, Maple, Carved Heart, Pa., G. Beshore, c.1990, 40 x 30 In.	2151
Desk, Queen Anne, Slant Front, Tiger Maple, Drawers, Fitted, New Eng., c.1790, 42 x 36 In..	440
Desk, R.J. Horner, Slant Front, Mahogany, 5 Drawers, Inlay, Cabriole Legs, 41 x 34 In..........	575
Desk, Regency, Mahogany, Gallery of Drawers, Carlton House, Casters, 1810s, 32 x 55 In. ...	3328
Desk, Risom, Executive, Walnut, 2 Stacks Of Drawers, Denmark, c.1950, 30 x 78 x 36 In....*illus*	510
Desk, Roll Top, Mahogany, Kneehole, 8 Drawers, Raised Panels, c.1910, 61 x 51 In..............	469
Desk, Schoolmaster's, Pine, Dovetailed Box, Slant Top, Gallery, 1800s, 41 x 31 In.	65
Desk, Shaped Gallery, Drawers, Red Paint, New Eng., c.1810, 45 x 23 x 22¾ In......................	3625
Desk, Slant Front, Maple, Drawers, Fitted Interior, Brass Chippendale Pulls, 1700s, 43 x 41 In. .	915
Desk, Traveling, Burl, Hinged Top, Pen & Ink Slots, Fitted Interior, Painted, 9 x 14 x 12 In.	120
Desk, Traveling, Victorian, Rosewood, Hinge Lid, Brass, Stand, 1840, 7 x 20 x 10 In.....*illus*	360
Desk, William IV Style, Mahogany, Carved, 3 Drawers On Either Side, Leather, 1900s, 66 In....	375
Desk, Wooton, Walnut, Doors, Drawers, Casters, Standard Grade, c.1874, 69 x 42 x 31 In.*illus*	6050
Desk, Writing, Anglo Colonial, Mahogany, Carved, Kneehole, 5 Drawers, 30 x 50 In.	748
Dresser Base, George III, Welsh, Oak, 8 Drawers, Arches, Stretcher Shelf, c.1790, 36 x 97 In...	2440
Dresser, Art Deco, Burl Veneer, Inlay, 2 Tiers, Carved, Royal Furniture, 56 x 38 x 20 In.......	780
Dresser, Chippendale Style, Mahogany, Various Size Drawers, Henkel Harris, 1900s, 34 x 66 In.	960
Dresser, Drexel Declaration, Walnut, Doors, 4 Drawers, Tapered Legs, 47 x 42 In. ....*illus*	502
Dresser, Empire, Mahogany, Mirror, Carved, Dolphin Supports, 7 Drawers, 73 x 45 In.	805
Dresser, Farmhouse, Walnut, Scalloped Top, Gold Accents, Dovetailed, 33 x 67 In................	192
Dresser, Hollywood Regency, Allover Mirror, 6 Drawers, Removable Console, 32 x 59 In......	156
Dresser, Mahogany, Mixed Wood, 12 Drawers, Scrolled Feet, Hickory Chair Co., 40 x 70 In.	144
Dresser, Parzinger, Faux Parchment Over Wood, Chrome Metal, 6 Drawers, 31 x 96 In.*illus*	9750
Dresser, Tiger Oak, Gallery Top, 3 Small Drawers Over 1 Long, 2 Doors, 35 x 21 x 41 In......	130
Dresser, Victorian, 3 Drawers, Burl Fronts, Carved Panels, Beveled Mirror, 84 x 52 x 23 In..... *illus*	308
Dresser, Victorian, Cherry, 5 Drawers, Wishbone Mirror, Glass Knob, 61 x 42 In....................	173
Dresser, Victorian, Shell Encrusted, Mirror, 3 Drawers, Drop Well, c.1870, 80 x 37 In. .*illus*	7625
Dresser, Welsh, Oak, Dovetailed Drawers, Pierced Corner Brackets, c.1800, 32 x 84 In. *illus*	2816
Dry Sink, Corner, Mixed Woods, Door, Shelves, Zinc Lined Well, Casters, 1850s, 43 x 50 In.	450
Dry Sink, Country, Pine, 3 Paneled Doors, Rectangular Well, Applied Feet, 1850s, 34 x 75 In. *illus*	1434
Dumbwaiter, Federal Style, 5 Tiers, Mahogany, Turned Supports, Casters, c.1950, 59 x 30 In.... *illus*	108
Dumbwaiter, George III, 3 Tiers, Mahogany, Round Shelves, Tripod Leg, 1800s, 51 x 20 In. ...	319
Dumbwaiter, George III, Mahogany, 3 Tiers, Casters, Recessed Holders, c.1790, 43 x 26 In.	504
Dumbwaiter, Regency, Mahogany, 3 Drop Leaf Tiers, Tripod Base, Wheels, c.1810, 48 In....	523
Easel, Renaissance Revival, Walnut, Folio, Flowers, Tripod Feet, c.1875, 80 x 37 x 23 In....... *illus*	3630
Easel, Victorian, Pine, White Paint, Shaped Crest, Gold Rosettes, 3 Legs, c.1880, 74 x 28 In.	450
Easel, Victorian, White Metal, Urn Shape Finial, Arching, White, 15 ½ x 8 x 9 In.................	94
Etagere, Arts & Crafts, Oak, Rectangular, 3 Tiers, Shelves, 2 Doors, 1900s, 48 x 37 x 11 In..	125
Etagere, Bamboo, Painted, 4 Tiers, Open Shelves, Spindles, 4 Legs, 1800s, 46 x 18 x 15 In..........	305
Etagere, Chinese, Bamboo, 4 Shelves, Scrolled Supports, Black Painted, 63 x 21 x 13 In., Pair....	1188
Etagere, Corner, Regency Style, Mahogany, 5 Shelves, Turned Supports, 1880s, 51 In..........	688
Etagere, Mahogany, 4 Tiers, 4 Open Shelves, Turned Posts, Drawer, 1800s, 54 x 18 x 14 In.. *illus*	1872
Etagere, Mahogany, Pierced Diapered Crest, Glazed Doors, Cabriole Legs, 78 x 35 ½ In.......	384
Etagere, Rosewood, Shelves, Openwork Gallery, Turned Supports, Drawer, England, 41 x 21 In.	702
Etagere, Victorian, Rosewood, 4 Shelves, Turned Finials, Paneled Back, 1800s, 40 x 39 In..	1521
Etagere, Victorian, Walnut, Shelves, Carved, Marble, Buckley & Bancroft, c.1860, 98 x 56 In.	1380
Etagere, Wall Unit, Chippendale Style, Mahogany, Shelves, Eng., c.1890, 80 x 65 x 10 In. ...	4538
Etagere, Walnut, Marble Top, Carved, Scrolling Crest, Mirror, c.1890, 100 x 50 x 20 In.	1029
Etagere, Walnut, Turnings, 2 Tiers, Drawers, Writing Surface, Continental, c.1890, 64 x 24 In. ..	1125
Etagere, William IV, Rosewood, 3 Tiers, Pierced Gallery, Inlay, Shelves, 1800s, 33 x 21 In...	488
Etagere, Wormley, Ash, Walnut, 5 Shelves, Drawer, Brass, Dunbar, 1967, 61 x 18 In. .... *illus*	4750
Footstool, Chippendale Style, Needlework, Upholstered, Carved, 1800s, 20 x 24 x 18 In.......	308
Footstool, Chippendale, Mahogany, Upholstered, Carved, Ball & Claw Feet,..........................	1250
Footstool, Dimitri Omersa, Bulldog Shape, Abercrombie & Fitch, c.1960, 17 x 29 In. ... *illus*	1000

Furniture, Dresser, Victorian,
3 Drawers, Burl Fronts, Carved Panels,
Beveled Mirror, 84 x 52 x 23 In.
$308

Apple Tree Auction Center

Furniture, Dresser, Victorian, Shell
Encrusted, Mirror, 3 Drawers, Drop Well,
c.1870, 80 x 37 In.
$7,625

Rafael Osona Nantucket Auctions

Furniture, Dresser, Welsh, Oak,
Dovetailed Drawers, Pierced Corner
Brackets, c.1800, 32 x 84 In.
$2,816

Brunk Auctions

This is an edited listing of current
prices. Visit **Kovels.com** to check thousands of prices from previous years and
sign up for free information on trends,
tips, reproductions, marks, and more.

F

Furniture, Dry Sink, Country, Pine, 3 Paneled Doors, Rectangular Well, Applied Feet, 1850s, 34 x 75 In.
$1,434

Jeffrey S. Evans & Associates

Furniture, Dumbwaiter, Federal Style, 5 Tiers, Mahogany, Turned Supports, Casters, c.1950, 59 x 30 In.
$108

Garth's Auctioneers & Appraisers

Furniture, Easel, Renaissance Revival, Walnut, Folio, Flowers, Tripod Feet, c.1875, 80 x 37 x 23 In.
$3,630

Fontaine's Auction Gallery

Furniture, Etagere, Mahogany, 4 Tiers, 4 Open Shelves, Turned Posts, Drawer, 1800s, 54 x 18 x 14 In.
$1,872

Thomaston Place Auction Galleries

Furniture, Etagere, Wormley, Ash, Walnut, 5 Shelves, Drawer, Brass, Dunbar, 1967, 61 x 18 In.
$4,750

Wright

Furniture, Footstool, Dimitri Omersa, Bulldog Shape, Abercrombie & Fitch, c.1960, 17 x 29 In.
$1,000

Eldred's

Furniture, Footstool, Roycroft, Mahogany, Leather, Brass Tacks, Carved Orb & Cross, 10 x 16 x 10 In.
$1,040

Toomey & Co. Auctioneers

Furniture, Footstool, Victorian, Bamboo Turnings, Round Top, Needlepoint, Tassels, 1800s, 18 In.
$832

Brunk Auctions

Furniture, Footstool, Victorian, Cast Iron, Needlepoint Top, Flowers, Black Paint, 14 x 11 x 9 In.
$53

Charleston Estate Auctions

Furniture, Frame, Rococo Revival, Giltwood, Carved, Pierced, Rocaille, Spandrels, Continental, 72 In.
$750

Neal Auction Company

Furniture, Frame, Victorian, Walnut, Giltwood, c.1880, 17 x 15 In., Pair
$84

Treasureseeker Auctions

Furniture, Hall Stand, Cast Iron, Mirror, Umbrella Stand, Painted, France, c.1900, 82 x 40 x 20 In.
$281

Charlton Hall Auctions

Furniture, Hall Stand, Victorian, Mahogany, Carved, Mirror, Compartment, Brass Hooks, 94 x 70 In.
$2,040

Alderfer Auction Company

Furniture, Hall Tree, Black Forest Style, Carved, Bear, Cubs Climbing, Umbrella Rack, 81 In.
$708

Copake Auction

Furniture, Hall Tree, Black Forest, Carved, Bear & Cub, Branches, Glass Eyes, c.1890, 75 x 26 x 21 In.
$3,933

Fontaine's Auction Gallery

Furniture, Highchair, Windsor, Comb Back, Turned Spindles, Knuckle Arm, 1800s, 37 In.
$375

Hindman

Furniture, Kneeler, Prie-Dieu, Rococo Revival, Rosewood, Carved, Cushion, Continental, c.1850, 38 In.
$475

Neal Auction Company

Furniture, Headboard, Italian Rococo, Parcel, Gilt, Ebonized, Las Palmas Design, King, 60 x 95 In.
$1,063

Andrew Jones Auctions

Furniture, Lap Desk, Burl, Mother-Of-Pearl & Wire Inlay, 5 ¼ x 13 x 9 ¼ In.
$65

Conestoga Auction Company

Furniture, Lap Desk, Satinwood, Brass, Hinged Top, Leather, Compartment Storage, 1800s, 7 x 14 x 10 In.
$488

Rafael Osona Nantucket Auctions

Furniture, Library Ladder, Putnam Oak, Iron Hand Rails, Roller Casters, 1900s, 73 x 18 x 44 In.
$938

Wiederseim Auctions

Footstool, French Provincial, Upholstered, Brass Tacks, Carved, 1800s, 19 x 21 x 20 In.......	176
Footstool, French Provincial, Walnut, Needlepoint Upholstery, France, 1700s, 13 x 20 In., Pair ..	1785
Footstool, George I Style, Mahogany, Upholstered, Paw Feet, 1800s, 20 x 23 In.....................	375
Footstool, Louis XV, Walnut, Leather Upholstery, Carved, Italy, 1900s, 19 x 17 In.	605
Footstool, Mission Style, Mixed Wood, Abstract Canvas, Drop-In Seat, 10 x 14 x 11 In.	183
Footstool, Neoclassical, Mahogany, Carved, Upholstered, Boston, Ma., c.1820, 15 x 21 x 14 In.	625
Footstool, Rocker, Oak, Leather Seat, Lakeside Craft Shop, Wisconsin, 17 x 16 x 13 In..........	422
Footstool, Roycroft, Mahogany, Leather, Brass Tacks, Carved Orb & Cross, 10 x 16 x 10 In.....*illus*	1040
Footstool, Victorian, Bamboo Turnings, Round Top, Needlepoint, Tassels, 1800s, 18 In...*illus*	832
Footstool, Victorian, Cast Iron, Needlepoint Top, Flowers, Black Paint, 14 x 11 x 9 In..*illus*	53
Footstool, Victorian, Oak, Leather, Tufted, Brass, Adjustable, c.1890, 15 x 24 x 14 In.	767
Footstool, Walnut, Carved, 4 Turned Legs, c.1890, 7 x 10 In...................................	126
Frame, Chrome Plate, Glass, Square, Claude De Muzac, France, c.1970, 13 x 7 x 2 In..........	4000
Frame, Flame Grain Painted, Red, Pennsylvania, Mid 1800s, 17 x 14 In.....................	139
Frame, Modernist, Purple Cabochon Border, Matl, Taxco, 3 x 2 In.	500
Frame, Rococo Revival, Giltwood, Carved, Pierced, Rocaille, Spandrels, Continental, 72 In..*illus*	750
Frame, Victorian, Walnut, Giltwood, c.1880, 17 x 15 In., Pair ....*illus*	84
Gun Case, On Stand, Mahogany, Brass Handle, Metal Edge, 1900s, 19 x 40 In.	378
Gun Rack, Mahogany, Turned Frame, Slotted Center Board, Trestle Base, c.1890, 38 x 28 In....	704
Hall Stand, Cast Iron, Mirror, Umbrella Stand, Painted, France, c.1900, 82 x 40 x 20 In....*illus*	281
Hall Stand, Oak, Beveled Mirror, Single Lift-Up Seat, Carved, 4 Hooks, 79 x 20 x 14 In.	286
Hall Stand, Victorian, Mahogany, Carved, Mirror, Compartment, Brass Hooks, 94 x 70 In....*illus*	2040
Hall Stand, Walnut, Mirror, Cane & Umbrella Stand, Marble Top, Drip Pan, 91 x 38 In.	350
Hall Tree, Black Forest Style, Carved, Bear, Cubs Climbing, Umbrella Rack, 81 In........*illus*	708
Hall Tree, Black Forest, Carved, Bear & Cub, Branches, Glass Eyes, c.1890, 75 x 26 x 21 In....*illus*	3933
Hall Tree, Black Forest, Carved, Standing Bear, Climbing Cub, Glass Eyes, 1900s, 77 x 20 x 21 In. .	1331
Hall Tree, R.J. Horner, Mahogany, Bench Seat, Arms, Scrollwork, Griffins, c.1890, 93 x 55 In. ..	1625
Hall Tree, Wood, Tree Shape, 8 Hooks, X-Shape Base, Early 1900s, 80 ½ In.	250
Headboard, Drexel, Declaration, Walnut, Sliding Doors, Porcelain Pulls, c.1950, 36 x 54 In.	59
Headboard, Italian Rococo, Parcel, Gilt, Ebonized, Las Palmas Design, King, 60 x 95 In....*illus*	1063
Highboy, Queen Anne, Walnut, Bonnet Top, Carved Shell & Plaque, c.1765, 85 x 40 In.	7380
Highchair, Sheraton, Green Paint, Flowers, New England, 1800s, 34 x 15 x 14 In.................	122
Highchair, Windsor, Comb Back, Turned Spindles, Knuckle Arm, 1800s, 37 In. ....*illus*	375
Highchair, Wood, Turned Spindles, Multicolor Painted Designs, 38 x 22 x 22 In.	75
Humidor, Marble Top, Drawer, 2 False Drawers, Fitted Interior, 32 x 14 x 17 In.	360
Huntboard, George III, Mahogany, Inlaid, Crossbanded Top, Bow Front, c.1820, 33 x 41 x 22 In. ..	750
Kneeler, Prie-Dieu, Rococo Revival, Rosewood, Carved, Cushion, Continental, c.1850, 38 In.*illus*	475
Kneeler, Wrought Iron, Leather Top, Horse Hair, Scrollwork, c.1920, 17 x 87 In...................	469
Lap Desk, Burl, Mother-Of-Pearl & Wire Inlay, 5 ¼ x 13 x 9 ¼ In. ....*illus*	65
Lap Desk, Camphorwood, Brass, Roll Top, Side Handles, Drawer, 1800s, 10 x 19 x 16 In.	497
Lap Desk, Roll Top, Mixed Wood, Burl, Brass Handle, Nameplate, Drawer, 1900s, 9 x 19 In.	563
Lap Desk, Satinwood, Brass, Hinged Top, Leather, Compartment Storage, 1800s, 7 x 14 x 10 In..*illus*	488
Lap Desk, Walnut, Inlay, Leather Writing Surface, Brass Lock, England, c.1810, 6 x 14 x 9 In....	300
Library Ladder, Green Leather, Folding, Studded Accents, England, 1900s, 93 x 12 ½ In....	3025
Library Ladder, Putnam Oak, Iron Hand Rails, Roller Casters, 1900s, 73 x 18 x 44 In.....*illus*	938
Library Steps, George III Style, Mahogany, 3 Steps, Hand Rail, 56 x 18 ½ In........................	420
Library Steps, Mahogany, 4 Spiral Steps, Gilt-Lined Green Leather, c.1910, 67 In.................	1750
Library Steps, Regency Style, Leather Clad, Folding, Brown, Brass Tacking, End Caps, 81 In......	1599
Library Steps, Walnut, 5 Steps, Turned Wood Handle, Carved Rail, 79 x 22 x 19 In.	531
Library Steps, Walnut, Turned Posts, Circular, 3 Steps, Faux Bamboo, 1900s, 23 x 31 In....*illus*	497
Library Steps, William IV Style, Mahogany, 3 Steps, Turned Feet, 1900s, 31 x 18 In....*illus*	688
Linen Press, Chippendale, Cherry, Doors, Shelves, Drawers, Bracket Feet, c.1790, 79 x 46 In.......	2813
Love Seat, Federal, Mahogany, Velvet Upholstery, Curved Arm, Carved, 35 x 73 In................	518
Lowboy, Chippendale Style, Mahogany, Drawers, Centennial, Ball & Claw Feet, c.1900s, 28 x 31 In...	127
Lowboy, Queen Anne, Cabriole Legs, Pad Feet, Maple, New England, c.1740, 30 x 34 In........	4500
Mirror, Adam Style, Oval, Carved Leaves, Giltwood Frame, 1900s, 51 x 23 ½ In....................	156
Mirror, Aventurine Frame, Sculpted Leaves & Flowers, Twisted Canes, Italy, 1900s, 47 x 28 In. ...	1188
Mirror, Baroque, Beveled, Giltwood, Carved, Leaves, Scrolls, Italy, c.1985, 55 x 40 In...........	512
Mirror, Baroque, Giltwood, Beads Design, Scrolled Edge, Italy, 1900s, 54 x 40 In. ....*illus*	750
Mirror, Baroque, Giltwood, Wall Mount, Continental, 1700s, 35 x 18 In., Pair..............*illus*	956

F

Mirror, Baroque, Urn Shape Top, Giltwood, Rectangular, 1900s, 60 x 20 In.	1125
Mirror, Bevel Plate, Giltwood, Frame, Victorian, 29 x 50 In.	136
Mirror, Blue Panels, Tiles, Rosette Decor, Segmented, Art Deco, 50¾ x 26¾ In.	1024
Mirror, Brass, Beveled Glass, Arms Crest Rail, Easel, Stamped, Continental, c.1915, 12 x 20 In.	48
Mirror, Cheval, Edwardian, Mahogany, Bentwood, c.1915, 71 x 43 x 22 In.	540
Mirror, Cheval, Federal Style, Mahogany, Inlay, Oval, 1800s, 65 x 28 x 25 In.	732
Mirror, Cheval, Federal Style, Mahogany, Pineapple Finials, Casters, 70 x 30 In.	469
Mirror, Cheval, Mahogany, Carved, Leaves & Crest, Cherub Head, c.1900, 78 x 32 In.	270
Mirror, Cheval, Neoclassical, Painted, Casters, 1800s, 74 x 31 x 20 In.	750
Mirror, Chippendale Style, Carved, Kinloch Woodworking Ltd., 2000, 43 x 22 In., Pair	406
Mirror, Chippendale Style, Leaf & Rocaille, Molded Composition, Wood, 1900s, 58 In.	738
Mirror, Chippendale Style, Mahogany, Molded Giltwood Eagle, 42 x 22 In.	281
Mirror, Chippendale, Giltwood, Carved, Leaf & Scrolled Crest, 1700s, 54 x 24 In.	2460
Mirror, Christian Dior, Faux Tortoiseshell, Painted, Brass, c.1975, 10 x 9 In.	280
Mirror, Chrome Plated Steel, Mirrored Glass, Art Deco, c.1935, 40 x 42 x ¾ In. *illus*	1250
Mirror, Claude Lalanne, Gilt Bronze, Dragonfly, France, 1985, 4 x 3 x 2 In.	20000
Mirror, Contemporary, Mahogany, Holton Studio, Calif., Signed, 1990s, 30 x 13 In.	554
Mirror, Dresser, Empire, Mahogany, Adjustable, 2 Candleholders, c.1830s, 29 x 26 In.	89
Mirror, Dressing, Federal, Mahogany, Scroll Supports, Drawers, Rufus Pierce, c.1827, 22 x 30 In.	2500
Mirror, Dressing, Mahogany, Tilting, Serpents, Drawer, Tabletop, 1860s, 17 x 13 In.	380
Mirror, Empire Style, Arrows Supports, Parcel Gilt, Metal Frame, 1900s, 30 x 16 In. *illus*	344
Mirror, Federal Style, Gold Eagle, Acanthus Leaves, 13 Balls, Convex, 1980s, 23 x 34 In.	1310
Mirror, Federal, Bull's-Eye, Eagle Finial, Scroll Candle Brackets, Boston, c.1810, 41 x 25 In.	2340
Mirror, Federal, Mahogany, Giltwood, Eagle Crest, c.1810, 20 x 42 In.	413
Mirror, Federal, Mahogany, Reverse Painted, Sailboat, House, 1800s, 40 x 19 In.	227
Mirror, Folk Art, Mahogany, Plaque, Carved, Eagle, Stars & Stripes Shield, 13 x 9 In.	761
Mirror, Foundry Shape, Red Paint, Circular, Wood Frame, 49 In.	375
Mirror, Giltwood, Arched Leafy Crest, Beveled, Swags, Continental, 1800s, 68 x 32 In.	360
Mirror, Giltwood, Carved, Beveled, Windsor Art & Mirror Co., 28 x 43 In.	395
Mirror, Giltwood, Coppertone Gesso, Butterfly Medallions, Braided Border, 43 x 28 In.	120
Mirror, Giltwood, Openwork, Square, Continental, 1900s, 42 In.	750
Mirror, Giltwood, Palladio, Column Sides, Figural & Floral Frieze, Italy, 1900s, 45 x 26 In.	150
Mirror, Girandole, Chippendale Style, Carved, Brass Candleholders, 1700s, 42 x 23 In. *illus*	2768
Mirror, Girandole, George II, Burl Walnut, Parcel Gilt, Eagle Finial, 1700s, 45 x 26 In.	1625
Mirror, Girandole, Giltwood, Convex, Carved, Leaves, Candleholders, c.1840, 33 x 20 In.	4270
Mirror, Glass Frame, Octagonal, Scalloped Scroll Crest, Bands, Rosettes, Murano, 44 x 25 In. *illus*	780
Mirror, Hardwood, Carved, Flowers, 1950, 67½ x 37 x 3¾ In. *illus*	500
Mirror, Italian Style, Giltwood, Shell Carved, Crest, Acanthus Leaf, 25 x 42 In.	65
Mirror, Kai Kristiansen, Teak, Silvered, Aksel Kjersgaard, Denmark, 1960s, 32 x 23 In.	343
Mirror, Keith Fritz, Trefoil, Gold Details, Ribbed, Signed, 2008, 38 In. *illus*	1152
Mirror, Le Mirophar, Chrome Plated Brass, Plastic, Tripod, Brot, France, c.1930, 53 x 16 In.	625
Mirror, Louis XVI Style, Giltwood, Carved, Scrolled Leaves, La Barge, 1950s, 49 x 28 In.	188
Mirror, Louis XVI, Giltwood, Beveled, 1800s, 48 x 32 In.	630
Mirror, Napoleon III, Giltwood, Beaded, Scrolls, Urns, Molded, Arched, 69 x 33 In.	1403
Mirror, Neoclassical Style, Ebonized, Giltwood, Griffins, Divided, 58 x 39 In.	384
Mirror, Neoclassical Style, Giltwood, Brown Paint, Ribbon Swag, Rosettes, 36 x 25 In.	125
Mirror, Neoclassical, Girandole, Giltwood, Carved, Metal Candle Arms, c.1820, 40 x 25 In. *illus*	3024
Mirror, Neoclassical, Medallions, Brass, Fluted Frame, Beveled Plate, 1900s, 31¾ x 38 x 2 In.	363
Mirror, Neoclassical, Reverse Painted, Parcel Gilt, House, New Eng., 1830s, 11 x 19 In. *illus*	72
Mirror, Neoclassical, Round, Carved, Giltwood, Ebonized, Beveled, 1810s, 28 In.	1792
Mirror, On Stand, Wood, Adjustable, Pedersen & Hansen Viby J., Denmark, 25 x 25 In. *illus*	375
Mirror, Oval, Grape & Vine, Ornate Gesso, 20 x 18 In.	45
Mirror, Paolo Venini, Millefiori, Murrine, Octagonal, Italy, 32 x 26 In. *illus*	10625
Mirror, Parzinger, Wood & Brass Frame, 54 x 36½ In.	2340
Mirror, Pier, Portrait, Landscape, Painted, Carved, Wood, England, 1800s, 74 x 25 In.	406
Mirror, Pier, Victorian, Giltwood, Ornate Crown, Woman's Head, c.1870, 96 x 37 In.	1150
Mirror, Queen Anne Style, Walnut, Cutout Crest, Shenandoah Valley, 1750s, 17 x 10 In.	72
Mirror, Regency Style, Giltwood, Carved, Grapevine, Flower Urn Top, 1800s, 78 x 41 In.	5000
Mirror, Renaissance Revival, Carved, Burled Pilasters, Ebonized, 1800s, 75 x 26 In.	450
Mirror, Rococo Revival, Etched Frame, Octagonal Plate, Venice, Late 1900s, 44 x 28 In.	594

Furniture, Library Steps, Walnut, Turned Posts, Circular, 3 Steps, Faux Bamboo, 1900s, 23 x 31 In.
$497

Thomaston Place Auction Galleries

Furniture, Library Steps, William IV Style, Mahogany, 3 Steps, Turned Feet, 1900s, 31 x 18 In.
$688

Hindman

F

Furniture, Mirror, Baroque, Giltwood, Beads Design, Scrolled Edge, Italy, 1900s, 54 x 40 In.
$750

Hindman

Furniture, Mirror, Baroque, Giltwood, Wall Mount, Continental, 1700s, 35 x 18 In., Pair
$956

Bonhams

Furniture, Mirror, Chrome Plated Steel, Mirrored Glass, Art Deco, c.1935, 40 x 42 x ¾ In.
$1,250

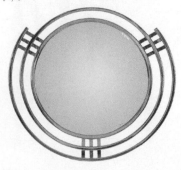

Wright

Furniture, Mirror, Empire Style, Arrows Supports, Parcel Gilt, Metal Frame, 1900s, 30 x 16 In.
$344

Hindman

Furniture, Mirror, Girandole, Chippendale Style, Carved, Brass Candleholders, 1700s, 42 x 23 In.
$2,768

Nadeau's Auction Gallery

Furniture, Mirror, Glass Frame, Octagonal, Scalloped Scroll Crest, Bands, Rosettes, Murano, 44 x 25 In.
$780

Alderfer Auction Company

Furniture, Mirror, Hardwood, Carved, Flowers, 1950, 67 ½ x 37 x 3 ¾ In.
$500

Andrew Jones Auctions

Furniture, Mirror, Keith Fritz, Trefoil, Gold Details, Ribbed, Signed, 2008, 38 In.
$1,152

Nadeau's Auction Gallery

Furniture, Mirror, Neoclassical, Girandole, Giltwood, Carved, Metal Candle Arms, c.1820, 40 x 25 In.
$3,024

Freeman's

Mirror, Rococo Revival, Gilt Metal, Oval, Flowers, Leaves, 41 x 25 In............................*illus* 154
Mirror, Rococo Style, Rectangular Shape, Gold Paint, 57 x 46 In. 191
Mirror, Rococo Style, Tiered Scallops, Gilt Metal Bands, Rectangular, 28 x 35 In. 125
Mirror, Shaving, Dresser Top, Revolving, Serpentine Base, 1800s, 19 x 17 In. 48
Mirror, Shaving, Federal, Walnut, Drawer, Brass Escutcheon, Bracket Feet, 21 x 13 In. 880
Mirror, Shaving, Georgian, Mahogany, Bracket Feet, Dovetailed Drawers, c.1815, 22 x 21 In. 168
Mirror, Shaving, Walnut, Veneer, Scroll Mounts, Drawers, England, c.1810, 23 x 23 In........ 250
Mirror, Tiger Maple, Square, Glass, 1800s, 20 x 15 In... 290
Mirror, Vanity, Art Nouveau, Bronze, Figural Pedestal, Oval, 1900s, 18 In....................... 219
Mirror, Vanity, Curved Top, Silver Plate, Emile Puiforcat, France, c.1920, 17 x 11 In. 510
Mirror, Venetian Glass Frame, Beveled Oval Center, Etched Mounts & Borders, 51 x 40 In. . 608
Mirror, Venetian, Blown Glass, Etched, Flower Crest, Spiral Trim, Rosettes, 70 x 30 In. 896
Mirror, Venetian, Octagonal, Smoked & Cut Panels, Bevele, Italy, 1900s, 51 x 35 In. 3630
Mirror, Victorian, Tartanware, Red Frame, Scotland, 1800s, 49 x 37 In............................ 576
Mirror, William & Mary Style, Chinoiserie, Etched Crown & Thistle, 48 x 19 In.................. 366
Ottoman, French Deco, Round, Upholstered, Black Piping, Footed, France, 16 x 18 In., Pair....... *illus* 761
Ottoman, Louis XV Style, Beech, Carved, Attached Cushion, Tassels, 1800s, 21 x 28 In........ 594
Ottoman, Neoclassical, Mahogany, Scroll Feet, Upholstered, American, c.1890, 13 x 29 In.. 240
Ottoman, Papa Bear, Wegner, Teak, Upholstered, A.P. Stolen, Denmark, 1950, 16 x 27 In. .. 3250
Ottoman, Rococo Style, Upholstered, Stacked Cushions, Green Base, 16 x 23 In.................. 188
Ottoman, Tray Top, Brass Casters, Upholstered, Oversized, 18 x 58 x 58 In................... *illus* 1280
Ottoman, Velvet Upholstery, Pleated Skirt, Round, 20 x 30 In. ....*illus* 431
Ottoman, Victorian, Mahogany, Needlepoint Upholstery, American, c.1890, 20 x 17 In.*illus* 120
Ottoman, William & Mary Style, Oak, Round, Haircalf Upholstery, Legs, 1900s, 19 x 35 In. 563
Overmantel Mirror, see Architectural category.
Pedestal, Brass, Renaissance Style, Scroll Base, Footed, Continental, 43 In 3854
Pedestal, Carved, Gilt, Leafy, Round Top, Turned Standard, Tripod, France, 15 x 40 In....... 354
Pedestal, Column, Marble Top, Brass Mounted, Continental, 39 In....................................... 125
Pedestal, Column, Marble, Swirl, Square Top, Brown & White, 43 x 16 x 13 In. 480
Pedestal, Fantasy, Mahogany, Carved, Scalloped Skirt, Legs & Boots, 1900s, 34 x 24 In...*illus* 875
Pedestal, Faux Malachite, Column, Iron Red Painted Metal, Italy, 1900s, 49 x 11 x 13 In..... 605
Pedestal, Figural, Mahogany, Carved Draped Female, Marble Top, Round Base, 43 In.......... 863
Pedestal, Figural, Putto, Carved Wood, Round Tray, Acanthus Leaf, Italy, 1800s, 43 x 11 In.. 305
Pedestal, Gothic Revival Style, Oak, Carved, Shelf, 3 Legs, Triangular, 45 x 13 In. 649
Pedestal, Leather Clad, Nailheads, Square Base, c.1900, 32 x 12 In...................................... 313
Pedestal, Louis XV Style, Bombe, Bronze, Marquetry, Parquetry, Marble Top, 48 In., Pair... 896
Pedestal, Louis XV Style, Marble Top, Gilt Metal, Splayed Legs, 1900s, 50 x 15 In., Pair........ 875
Pedestal, Louis XVI Style, Painted, Parcel Gilt, Tapered, Carved, Swags, 43 In., Pair............ 400
Pedestal, Mackenzie Child's Style, Plaster, Composition, Multicolor Capital, 29 x 13 ½ In... 250
Pedestal, Mahogany, Carved, Round, Egg & Dart Border, Griffin Heads, c.1890, 36 x 24 In. 4840
Pedestal, Neoclassical Style, Onyx, Gilt Metal, Marble Base, 45 x 13 x 13 In. 554
Pedestal, Onyx, Marble, Tapered, Bronze Mounts, Square Base, Italy, 43 x 16 In., Pair....*illus* 2805
Pedestal, P. Evans, Cityscape, Chrome, Patchwork, C-Shape, 48 x 15 x 15 In., Pair.......*illus* 2040
Pedestal, Rococo, Painted Scenes, Transfer Plates, Gold Bust Figures, France, 49 x 17 In.... 9775
Pedestal, Walnut, Black Leather, Brass Tacks, Continental, c.1925, 40 x 17 In. 219
Pedestal, Walnut, Figural, Male & Female, Draped, Square Top, Continental, 41 x 13 In...... 1024
Pedestal, Wood, Carved, Faux Marble, Painted, Greek Key, Continental, c.1890, 47 x 18 In....*illus* 219
Pedestal, Wood, Carved, Multicolor, Round Top, Flowers On Body, Hexagonal Base, 41 In. . 600
Pie Safe, Cypress, Stepped Edge, 2 Doors, 2 Drawers, Louisiana, c.1900, 73 x 41 In. 625
Pie Safe, Poplar, Drawer, Doors, Punched Tin Panels, Tulips, H.A., c.1830, 51 x 39 In.......... 1625
Pie Safe, Poplar, Punched Tin Panels, Star Pattern, Overhang Top, 1800s, 58 x 41 In. 531
Pie Safe, Softwood, Blue Paint, White Trim, Doors, Punched Tin Panels, 48 x 42 In....*illus* 354
Pie Safe, Tin, Punched Tin Panels, Embossed, Penn Treaty, Copper Steel, c.1900, 27 x 40 In.. 156
Pie Safe, Walnut, Doors, Punched Tin Panels, Hearts & Flowers, Shelves, 45 x 41 In. 1560
Pie Safe, Yellow Pine, Poplar, Punched Tin Panels, Shelves, Virginia, c.1850, 51 x 46 In...... 1135
Planter, Henredon, Georgian, Mahogany, Brass Band, Lion Shape Handles, Paw Feet, 16 ½ x 28 In... 281
Planter, Regency Style, Mahogany, Slatted Basket, Brass Liner, Dolphin Base, Ball Feet, 29 In., Pair... 1150
Rack, Baking, Brass, Metal Racks, 3 Levels, Glass Shelves, Dupic Dijon, France, 87 x 66 In....*illus* 1125
Rack, Bread, French Provincial, Fruitwood, Urn Finials, Lyre Door, Scroll, 1800s, 34 x 40 In.. 625
Rack, French Provincial, Open Shelves, Carved Front Rail, Continental, 1800s, 60 x 35 x 10 In. 480

Furniture, Mirror, Neoclassical, Reverse Painted, Parcel Gilt, House, New Eng., 1830s, 11 x 19 In.
$72

Jeffrey S. Evans & Associates

Furniture, Mirror, On Stand, Wood, Adjustable, Pedersen & Hansen Viby J., Denmark, 25 x 25 In.
$375

Palm Beach Modern Auctions

Furniture, Mirror, Paolo Venini, Millefiori, Murrine, Octagonal, Italy, 32 x 26 In.
$10,625

Palm Beach Modern Auctions

FURNITURE

Furniture, Mirror, Rococo Revival, Gilt Metal, Oval, Flowers, Leaves, 41 x 25 In.
$154

Auctions at Showplace, NYC

Furniture, Ottoman, French Deco, Round, Upholstered, Black Piping, Footed, France, 16 x 18 In., Pair
$761

Thomaston Place Auction Galleries

Furniture, Ottoman, Tray Top, Brass Casters, Upholstered, Oversized, 18 x 58 x 58 In.
$1,280

Nadeau's Auction Gallery

Furniture, Ottoman, Velvet Upholstery, Pleated Skirt, Round, 20 x 30 In.
$431

Brunk Auctions

Furniture, Ottoman, Victorian, Mahogany, Needlepoint Upholstery, American, c.1890, 20 x 17 In.
$120

Selkirk Auctioneers & Appraisers

Furniture, Pedestal, Fantasy, Mahogany, Carved, Scalloped Skirt, Legs & Boots, 1900s, 34 x 24 In.
$875

Fontaine's Auction Gallery

Furniture, Pedestal, Onyx, Marble, Tapered, Bronze Mounts, Square Base, Italy, 43 x 16 In., Pair
$2,805

Bonhams

Furniture, Pedestal, P. Evans, Cityscape, Chrome, Patchwork, C-Shape, 48 x 15 x 15 In., Pair
$2,040

Abington Auction Gallery

Furniture, Pedestal, Wood, Carved, Faux Marble, Painted, Greek Key, Continental, c.1890, 47 x 18 In.
$219

Charlton Hall Auctions

Furniture, Pie Safe, Softwood, Blue Paint, White Trim, Doors, Punched Tin Panels, 48 x 42 In.
$354

Conestoga Auction Company

Furniture, Rack, Baking, Brass, Metal Racks, 3 Levels, Glass Shelves, Dupic Dijon, France, 87 x 66 In.
$1,125

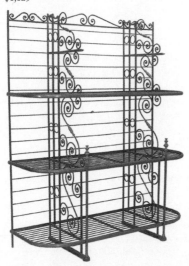

Susanin's Auctioneers & Appraisers

Furniture, Recamier, Sofa, Ebonized, Upholstered, Curved Legs, 1800s, 77 x 27 x 30 In.
$738

Copake Auction

Furniture, Rocker, Alpine Style, Headrest, Rawhide Back, Seat, Oversized, 56 x 34 x 22 In.
$469

Wiederseim Auctions

Furniture, Rocker, Horns, Velvet Upholstery, Folk Art, American, c.1890, 38 In.
$438

New Haven Auctions

Furniture, Rocker, Mission, Stickley Bros., 3-Slat Back, Flat Arms, Marked, 35 x 29 x 30 In.
$144

Alderfer Auction Company

Furniture, Rocker, Windsor, Comb Back, Writing Arm, Saddle Seat, Drawer, 1800s, 44 x 36 In.
$230

F

Merrill's Auctions

TIP
If you own a wicker chair that makes small popping noises when you sit in it, dampen it with water. It is too dry, and wicker may crack if not kept moist.

Furniture, Rocker, Windsor, Hoop Back, Elm, Saddle Seat, Stretchers, c.1790, 38 In.
$225

Neal Auction Company

Furniture, Room Divider, Wegner, Teak, Chrome Plated Steel, 4 Drawers, Denmark, c.1965, 81 x 122 In.
$7,500

Wright

Furniture, Screen, 3-Panel, Oil On Canvas, Fox Hunting, Roman Art Screen Co., c.1910, 72 x 60 In.
$1,107

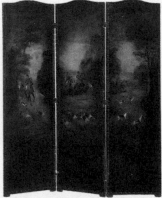

Pook & Pook

TIP
When cleaning mother-of-pearl inlay, use a weak solution of detergent, never an acid.

Furniture, Screen, 4-Panel, Wallpaper, Folding, Castle, People, Elephant, c.1950, 90 x 28 In.
$750

Hindman

Rack, Magazine, 2 Cylindrical Tubes, Rods, Enameled Steel, Ball Feet, c.1955, 19 x 14 In....	344
Rack, Magazine, Aesthetic Revival, Charred Bamboo, Lacquered, c.1890, 18 x 18 In.	225
Rack, Magazine, Art Deco, Cast Metal, Round Sides, Dog Leaping In Circle, 14 x 12 In.	345
Rack, Magazine, Arts & Crafts, Oak, Hanging, c.1910, 14 x 18 In....................................	123
Rack, Magazine, Brass, Flowing Plumes, Borzoi Hounds, Square Base, Art Deco, c.1920, 14 x 12 In. .	443
Rack, Magazine, Wormley, Mahogany, 5 Tiers, Tree Shape, Trestle, Dunbar, c.1950, 25 x 28 In....	1250
Rack, Quilt, Mahogany, 5 Spindles, Turned Side Supports, 27 x 8 x 35 In.	94
Rack, Riding, Boot & Whip, Mahogany, Finials, Shoe Trestle Foot, 47 x 27 x 14 In...............	497
Recamier, Sofa, Ebonized, Upholstered, Curved Legs, 1800s, 77 x 27 x 30 In............... *illus*	738
Rocker, Alpine Style, Headrest, Rawhide Back, Seat, Oversized, 56 x 34 x 22 In. .... *illus*	469
Rocker, G. Stickley, Oak, Leather Seat, Slat Back, Red Decal, 41 x 29 In.	1250
Rocker, Horns, Velvet Upholstery, Folk Art, American, c.1890, 38 In............................*illus*	438
Rocker, Hunzinger Style, Turned Stiles, Pieced Rug Upholstery, c.1890, Child's, 26 x 14 In.	48
Rocker, Leather, Oak, Slat Back, Arms, Oak Craft Shops, Portland, Mich., 34 In.................	375
Rocker, Limbert, Spade Cutout Sides, Leather Sides, c.1910, 37 x 39 In.........................	1968
Rocker, Mission, Stickley Bros., 3-Slat Back, Flat Arms, Marked, 35 x 29 x 30 In..........*illus*	144
Rocker, Nursing, Skull Of Baleen Back Splat, Whaler Made, Arms, c.1850, 27 x 18 In.	5795
Rocker, Sam Maloof, Walnut, Spindles, Leather, Arms, Marked, 45 In.........................	7500
Rocker, Windsor, Comb Back, Writing Arm, Saddle Seat, Drawer, 1800s, 44 x 36 In..... *illus*	230
Rocker, Windsor, Hoop Back, Elm, Saddle Seat, Stretchers, c.1790, 38 In. ....*illus*	225
Rocker, Wood Frame, Red Tufted, Upholstered Cushion, Seat, John Stuart, 29 In.................	375
Room Divider, Wegner, Teak, Chrome Plated Steel, 4 Drawers, Denmark, c.1965, 81 x 122 In..... *illus*	7500
Screen, 3-Panel, Folding, Brown Leather, Brass Bound, Bracket Feet, c.1900, 53 x 61 In......	438
Screen, 3-Panel, Folding, Chinoiserie Lithograph Design, 64 x 54 In.	76
Screen, 3-Panel, Oil On Canvas, Fox Hunting, Roman Art Screen Co., c.1910, 72 x 60 In. ...*illus*	1107
Screen, 3-Panel, Watercolor On Rice Paper, Bird, Tree, Black Characters, Japan, 59 x 75 In.	192
Screen, 4-Panel, Dressing, Oil On Canvas, Garden Scenes, Nailhead Trim, 73 x 78 In.	250
Screen, 4-Panel, Hand Painted, Court Scene, Chinese, 72 x 70 In..............................	406
Screen, 4-Panel, Lacquered Wood, Asian Figures, Garden Scenes, c.1950, 60 x 16 In............	240
Screen, 4-Panel, Oriental, Painted, Courtyard Scene, Family Dinner, 55 x 100 In.	768
Screen, 4-Panel, Paisley Upholstery, Tacks, 1700s, 67 x 78 In.	875
Screen, 4-Panel, Paper, Market Scene, Watercolor, Brocade Border, Kyoto, Japan, 36 x 73 In....	325
Screen, 4-Panel, Rosewood, Carved, Mother-Of-Pearl, Fretwork, Birds, Chinese, 78 x 76 In. .	900
Screen, 4-Panel, Tree, Flowers, Ink, Gold Leaf, Black Border, Signed, Japan, 36 x 65 In.......	240
Screen, 4-Panel, Wallpaper, Folding, Castle, People, Elephant, c.1950, 90 x 28 In. ....*illus*	750
Screen, 5-Panel, Rococo, Walnut, Pierced, Carved, Grapes & Vines, 1800s, 77 x 97 In.	2300
Screen, 6-Panel, Accordion Fold, Ink On Silk, Landscape Scenes, Japan, c.1950, 52 x 105 In........	180
Screen, 6-Panel, Black Lacquer, Cloisonne Inset, Chinese, 1900s, 72 x 105 In.	640
Screen, 6-Panel, Coromandel, Birds, 2-Sided, Chinese, 84 x 96 In..............................*illus*	1008
Screen, 6-Panel, Court Scenes, Story Of Genji, Multicolor, Japan, 1700s, 49 x 112 In............	1875
Screen, 6-Panel, Scroll Paintings, Buddhist Deities, Calligraphy, Chinese, 63 x 91 In.	295
Screen, 6-Panel, Watercolor, Gouache On Paper, Warriors, Horseback, Japan, 68 x 25 In....	188
Screen, 8-Panel, Coromandel, Black Lacquer, Painted, Village Scene, 84 x 128 In.	216
Screen, Cloisonne, Hardstone, Mother-Of-Pearl, Malachite, 2-Sided, Chinese, 42 In....*illus*	3660
Screen, Table, Agate, Stone Slab, Lattice Fretwork Frame, Chinese, c.1925, 26 x 22 In..........	720
Screen, Table, Embroidered, Birds, Mother-Of-Pearl, Black Lacquer Frame, Chinese, 30 x 23 x 9 In...	2880
Screens are also listed in the Architectural and Fireplace categories.	
Secretary, Arts & Crafts, Oak, Glass Doors, Drawers, England, 1900s, 78 x 30 In.	360
Secretary, Baroque, Painted, Scenes, Doors, Drawer, Italy, 72 x 36 x 19 In...........................	1920
Secretary, Chinoiserie, Drop Front, Finials, Drawers, Maitland-Smith, 1900s, 87 x 40 In....	1500
Secretary, Chippendale, Slant Front, Walnut, Carved, Philadelphia, Pa., c.1760, 97 x 40 In. ...	6300
Secretary, Drop Front, Mahogany, Fretwork, Doors, Drawers, Ireland, 1800s, 93 x 41 In....*illus*	2048
Secretary, Drop Front, Walnut, Glass Doors, Fitted Interior, Drawer, Doors, c.1870, 90 x 36 In.....*illus*	3388
Secretary, Eastlake, Cylinder, Walnut, 3 Drawers, 2 Glass Doors, Victorian, 94 x 44 In........	270
Secretary, George I, Drop Front, Walnut, Fitted Interior, Drawers, c.1710, 64 x 42 In.	1188
Secretary, George II Style, Mahogany, Gilt, Pigeonholes, Theo. Alexander, 98 In.	11495
Secretary, George II/III, Mahogany, Doors, Shelves, Drawers, Leather, c.1760, 92 In.	2952
Secretary, George III, Mahogany, Carved, Gothic Arch, Bracket Feet, c.1810, 94 x 44 In.*illus*	3250
Secretary, Gothic Revival, Drop Front, Mahogany, Arched Crest, Glass Doors, c.1850, 88 x 49 In. .	320

Furniture, Screen, 6-Panel, Coromandel, Birds, 2-Sided, Chinese, 84 x 96 In.
$1,008

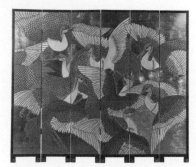

Pook & Pook

Furniture, Screen, Cloisonne, Hardstone, Mother-Of-Pearl, Malachite, 2-Sided, Chinese, 42 In.
$3,660

Neal Auction Company

Furniture, Secretary, Drop Front, Mahogany, Fretwork, Doors, Drawers, Ireland, 1800s, 93 x 41 In.
$2,048

Neal Auction Company

Furniture, Secretary, Drop Front, Walnut, Glass Doors, Fitted Interior, Drawer, Doors, c.1870, 90 x 36 In.
$3,388

Fontaine's Auction Gallery

Furniture, Secretary, George III, Mahogany, Carved, Gothic Arch, Bracket Feet, c.1810, 94 x 44 In.
$3,250

Charlton Hall Auctions

Furniture, Secretary, Hepplewhite, Mahogany, Tambours, Swift & Shearman, c.1808, 53 x 42 In.
$2,500

Eldred's

Furniture, Secretary, Meeks, Mahogany, Glass & Solid Doors, Stencil, Bronze, 1800s, 96 x 56 In.
$8,640

Neal Auction Company

Furniture, Semainier, Louis XVI Style, Mahogany, 7 Drawers, Metal Pulls, c.1890, 55 x 32 In.
$250

Hindman

Furniture, Server, Art Deco, Mahogany Veneer, Double Pedestal, Platform, Scroll Feet, 55 x 42 In.
$177

Conestoga Auction Company

Furniture, Server, Jacobean Style, 4 Drawers, 4 Doors, Tack Edge, 31 In.
$338

Nadeau's Auction Gallery

Furniture, Settee, Arne Jacobsen, Swan, Upholstered, Aluminum Base, Fritz Hansen, 1958, 30 x 56 In.
$5,000

Wright

Furniture, Settee, G. Stickley, No. 208, Quartersawn Oak, Back & Side Slats, c.1904, 29 x 72 In.
$938

Fontaine's Auction Gallery

Secretary, Hepplewhite, Mahogany, String Trim, Doors, Shelves, Drawers, 81 x 40 In.	878
Secretary, Hepplewhite, Mahogany, Tambours, Swift & Shearman, c.1808, 53 x 42 In. *illus*	2500
Secretary, Hepplewhite, Pedestal Crest, Inlaid Mahogany, Drawer, Doors, 76 x 21 In...........	761
Secretary, Japanned, 2 Glass Doors, 6 Drawers, Gilt, Splayed Legs, c.1890, 68 x 22 In.........	2583
Secretary, Kneehole, Painted, Scenes, Red Lacquer, Doors, Drawers, Chinese, 84 x 54 In. ..	976
Secretary, Lacquered, Landscape Scenes, Red Background, Japan, 89 x 39 x 15 In.	406
Secretary, Louis XV Style, Slant Front, Walnut, Drawer, Cabriole Legs, c.1910, 38 x 29 In.	810
Secretary, Louis XVI Style, Stand, Inlay, Panel Door, Fitted Interior, Gilt, 1900s, 71 x 38 In. ...	600
Secretary, Meeks, Mahogany, Glass & Solid Doors, Stencil, Bronze, 1800s, 96 x 56 In. *illus*	8640
Secretary, Neoclassical, Drop Front, Inlay, Seashell & Rosette, 59 x 36 In.	188
Secretary, Sheraton Style, Drop Front, Mahogany, Inlay, Pullouts, c.1850, 85 x 49 In.	1375
Secretary, Sheraton, 6 Drawers, 2 Glass Doors, Urn Finial, c.1825, 72 x 38 In......................	1375
Semainier, Louis XVI Style, Mahogany, 7 Drawers, Metal Pulls, c.1890, 55 x 32 In...... *illus*	250
Semainier, Louis XVI Style, Mahogany, Inlay, Faux Marble, Drawers, 50 x 14 In., Pair........	576
Server, Art Deco, Mahogany Veneer, Double Pedestal, Platform, Scroll Feet, 55 x 42 In..... *illus*	177
Server, Arts & Crafts, Oak, Backsplash, Drawers, Doors, Square Legs, 1900s, 41 x 40 In.	270
Server, Arts & Crafts, Oak, Mirror, Drawers, Stained Glass, c.1910, 56 x 38 x 17 In.	420
Server, Chippendale Style, Oak, 3 Drawers, Scalloped Skirt, Cabriole Legs, 31 x 60 In.	702
Server, Dunlap Style, Tiger Maple, Drawers, Carved, Eldred Wheeler, Mass., 1900s, 36 x 39 In.......	2000
Server, Federal Style, Back Splat, Inlay, Drawer, Potthast Brothers, 1900s, 38 x 42 In.	1020
Server, Federal, Mahogany, Drawers, Corner Shelves, Lower Shelf, N.Y., c.1815, 40 x 41 In...	3198
Server, Geometric Tile, Inlaid Top, 4 Drawers, 2 Compartments, 1900s, 36 x 71 x 18 In.	100
Server, Hepplewhite, Mahogany, Swell Front, Inlay, Cellarette Interior, 34 x 42 In.	540
Server, Jacobean Style, 4 Drawers, 4 Doors, Tack Edge, 31 In. .... *illus*	338
Server, Sheraton Style, Mahogany, Bowfront, Drawer, Lower Shelf, c.1930, 37 x 42 In.........	234
Server, Victorian, Faux Bamboo, Open Shelves, Drawer, Doors, Miniature, 14 x 8 x 23 In.....	443
Settee, Anglo-Indian, Rosewood, Carved, Triple Arched Pierced Back, 1800s, 34 x 72 In.	5185
Settee, Arne Jacobsen, Swan, Upholstered, Aluminum Base, Fritz Hansen, 1958, 30 x 56 In.... *illus*	5000
Settee, Chippendale Style, Camelback, Upholstered, Cushion, Scroll Arm, Tacks, 1900s, 32 x 58 In. ...	861
Settee, Elias Svedberg, Maple, Upholstered, Sweden, c.1955, 35 x 51 x 27 In., Pair	8750
Settee, Empire, Mahogany, Veneer, Upholstered, Fabric, Claw Feet, 1800s, 32½ x 86 x 26 In...	469
Settee, G. Stickley, No. 208, Quartersawn Oak, Back & Side Slats, c.1904, 29 x 72 In. .... *illus*	938
Settee, Georgian Style, High Back, Wing, Curved, Arms, Old Paint, c.1890, 67 x 68 In..........	570
Settee, Louis XV Style, Upholstered, Carved, Red Paint, Cabriole Legs, c.1890, 16 x 24 In. ...	497
Settee, Louis XVI Style, Giltwood, Tapestry Upholstery, Carved, 1900s, 41 x 52 In.	600
Settee, Louis XVI, Beech, Arched Crest, Pierced, 3 Cushions, Reeded Legs, 36 x 58 In., Pair.	512
Settee, Modern, Leather Cushions, Black Plastic Armrests, Chrome Plated Frame, c.1950, 32 x 44 In.	156
Settee, Modern, Rosewood, Rattan, Circular Arms, Trestle Feet, 31 x 52 x 25 In........... *illus*	840
Settee, Nancy Corzine, Upholstered, Loose Cushion, Tapered Legs, c.2003, 31 x 67 x 40 In. .	576
Settee, Pull-Out Trundle, Spindles, Turned Legs, Cannon Ball Finials, 1800s, 31 x 75 x 28 In...	390
Settee, Risom, 3 Sections, Pine, Nylon, Copper, Webbed, Knoll, c.1941, 31 x 63 In.................	1560
Settee, Tapestry Upholstery, Carved, Cartouche Panels, Arms, Germany, c.1890, 79 x 79 In.	3024
Settee, Thonet, Bentwood, Looped Back, Cane Seat, Splayed Legs, Child's, 26 x 33 In... *illus*	219
Settee, William IV, Mahogany, Brass, Inlay, Scroll Arms, Bending Feet, c.1835, 35 x 84 x 22 In. .... *illus*	688
Settle, Carved, Paneled, Square Back, Leaf Design, Turned Legs, England, 1600s, 40 x 48 In...	688
Settle, G. Stickley, No. 208, Oak, Leatherette, Red Decal, New York, 29 x 76 x 33 In.	2875
Settle, Windsor, Mixed Wood, Shaped Crest, Spindles, Bamboo Turnings, c.1825, 36 x 39 In. . *illus*	450
Shelf, Arts & Crafts, Oak, Paint Stained, 4 Open Shelves & Sides, 1900s, 33 x 18 x 10 In.	30
Shelf, Clock, Victorian, Wood, Carved, Eagle, 2 13-Star U.S. Flags, 15 x 16 In.	480
Shelf, Eames, Birch, Masonite, Steel, Laminate, Shelves, Drawers, Herman Miller, 59 x 47 In.	2305
Shelf, Hanging, Chippendale, Pine, Shelves, Red Wash, Scalloped Supports, c.1790, 35 x 32 In.	615
Shelf, Hanging, Mahogany, Whale Tail, 3 Shelves, Drawers, Mushroom Knobs, 33 x 27 In. .	380
Shelf, Hanging, Oak, 3 Cathedral Peaks, Devil Heads, Gothic Revival, 1800s, 46 x 36 x 8 In.....	1000
Shelf, Hanging, Oak, 4 Shelves, Carved, Board Construction, c.1650, 39 x 42 In....................	4973
Shelf, Hanging, Walnut, 3 Shelves, Shaped Sides, c.1900, 37½ x 30 In.................................	302
Shelf, Painted, Flower & Heart Design, Yellow Ground, Peter Hunt, 1900s, 30 x 40 In... *illus*	563
Shelf, Plate, Hanging, Mahogany, Carved, 1800s, 23 x 15 In., Pair................................. *illus*	1220
Shelf, Plate, Pine, Whale Ends, Plate Groove, Painted, Shelves, c.1985, 35 x 28 In.	192
Shelf, Scrolled Bronze, Red & Gray Marble, Bracket, 8 x 4 In., Pair...	277
Sideboard, Aesthetic Revival, Walnut, Ebony, Glass, Attrib. James Lamb, c.1885, 49 x 89 In.... *illus*	1250

Furniture, Settee, Modern, Rosewood, Rattan, Circular Arms, Trestle Feet, 31 x 52 x 25 In.
$840

Alderfer Auction Company

Furniture, Settee, Thonet, Bentwood, Looped Back, Cane Seat, Splayed Legs, Child's, 26 x 33 In.
$219

New Haven Auctions

Furniture, Settee, William IV, Mahogany, Brass, Inlay, Scroll Arms, Bending Feet, c.1835, 35 x 84 x 22 In.
$688

Andrew Jones Auctions

Furniture, Settle, Windsor, Mixed Wood, Shaped Crest, Spindles, Bamboo Turnings, c.1825, 36 x 39 In.
$450

Garth's Auctioneers & Appraisers

Furniture, Shelf, Painted, Flower & Heart Design, Yellow Ground, Peter Hunt, 1900s, 30 x 40 In.
$563

Eldred's

Furniture, Shelf, Plate, Hanging, Mahogany, Carved, 1800s, 23 x 15 In., Pair
$1,220

Rafael Osona Nantucket Auctions

Furniture, Sideboard, Aesthetic Revival, Walnut, Ebony, Glass, Attrib. James Lamb, c.1885, 49 x 89 In.
$1,250

Cowan's Auctions

Furniture, Sideboard, Federal Style, Mahogany, Inlay, Drawers, Doors, Tapered Legs, 40 x 64 In.
$945

Freeman's

Furniture, Sideboard, Hepplewhite
Style, Serpentine Front, Inlay, Drawers,
1800s, 36 x 54 In.
$1,000

F

Charlton Hall Auctions

Furniture, Sideboard, Majorelle Style,
Art Nouveau, Mahogany, Gilt Bronze,
Doors, 82 x 63 x 21 In.
$1,875

Fontaine's Auction Gallery

The Skyscraper
Paul T. Frankl, the American furniture designer, hired cabinetmakers to make his furniture. Pieces from the 1920s and '30s are rare and high-priced. Skyscraper bookcases can sell for over $50,000. In the late 1930s, he had his designs mass-produced, and these pieces are less expensive. His designs were often copied.

Sideboard, Arts & Crafts, Copper Faces, Mirror, Doors, Drawers, Eng., c.1905, 69 x 59 In.	1476
Sideboard, Arts & Crafts, Oak, Angled Sides, 2 Doors, Drawers, Back Rail, 39 x 78 In.	2700
Sideboard, Corner, Neoclassical, Mahogany, Carved, Drawers, Doors, 1810s, 40 x 79 In.	6710
Sideboard, Empire, Doors, Drawers, Barley Twist Columns, Original Pulls, Claw Feet, 44 x 55 In.	546
Sideboard, Federal Style, Mahogany, Inlay, Drawers, Doors, Tapered Legs, 40 x 64 In. *illus*	945
Sideboard, Federal, Mahogany, 3 Drawers, Doors, Inlay, Tapered Legs, c.1800s, 39 x 70 In. ..	7930
Sideboard, Federal, Mahogany, Beaded Edges, Doors, Drawers, Backsplash, 49 x 72 In.	1112
Sideboard, Federal, Tiger Maple, Walnut, Hinged Lid, Miniature, c.1830, 16 x 24 In.	4688
Sideboard, Frankl, Mahogany, Cork, Brass, Doors, Drawers, Johnson Co., 1940s, 32 x 72 In.	520
Sideboard, George III, Mahogany, Burl, Drawers, Doors, Shaped Front, c.1790, 37 x 72 In..	1088
Sideboard, Georgian Style, Mahogany, Carved, 8 Drawers, Ball & Claw Feet, c.1920, 40 x 79 In.	838
Sideboard, Hepplewhite Style, Serpentine Front, Inlay, Drawers, 1800s, 36 x 54 In. ...... *illus*	1000
Sideboard, Hepplewhite, 4 Drawers, Gallery, Brass Handles, Square Legs, c.1825, 43 x 77 In. .	813
Sideboard, Hepplewhite, Mahogany, Banding, Barber Pole Inlay, 1800s, 34 x 47 In.	2091
Sideboard, Kittinger, Federal, Brass, Drawer, Door, Tapered Legs, c.1950, 39 x 79 In.	330
Sideboard, Mahogany, Inlay, Brass Pulls, Hickory White, c.1950, 38 x 66 In.	570
Sideboard, Majorelle Style, Art Nouveau, Mahogany, Gilt Bronze, Doors, 82 x 63 x 21 In.. *illus*	1875
Sideboard, Marble Top, Carved, Stag Head, Bell Flower, Drawer, Victorian, 87 x 60 In.	4375
Sideboard, Neoclassical, Mahogany, Carved, Mirror, Acanthus Paw Feet, c.1825, 61 x 87 In.	1216
Sideboard, Neoclassical, Mahogany, Mirror, Bowfront, Columns, Gilt, c.1825, 70 x 81 In. ...	1280
Sideboard, Quartersawn Oak, 2 Doors, 4 Drawers, Gallery, Brass, 41 x 60 In.	201
Sideboard, Renaissance Revival, Burl Walnut, Inlay, Mirrors, Marble, c.1865, 107 x 72 In.	1220
Sideboard, Roycroft, Quartersawn Oak, Mirror, Drawers, Open Cupboards, c.1910, 53 x 56 In......	8125
Sideboard, Sheraton Style, Irving & Casson, Mahogany, A.H Davenport, Boston, c.1910, 38 x 60 In...	625
Sideboard, Slate Top, Rosewood, Veneer, Wall Mounted, Drawers, American, c.1985, 28 x 89 In. ..	2500
Sideboard, Stickley, Queen Anne Style, Mahogany, Drawers, Scalloped, c.1980, 34 x 62 In. ..	600
Sideboard, Victorian, Walnut, Marble Top, Carved, 2 Doors, 2 Drawers, 93 x 62 In.	489
Sideboard, Wegner, Sliding Doors, Turned Legs, Ry Mobler, Denmark, 1960, 31 x 79 In.	3125
Silver Chest, Reed & Barton, Cherry, Hand Crafted, Compartments, Hinged Lid, 15 x 11 x 6 In. ..	454
Sofa, Baker, Bolster Back, Upholstery, Walnut, 1958, 28 x 62 In., Pair	5460
Sofa, Charles Stewart, Down Pillows, Upholstered, 89 In................................	1320
Sofa, Chesterfield, Tufted Brown Leather Upholstery, Caster Feet, c.1910, 32 x 68 In..... *illus*	3750
Sofa, Chippendale Style, Camelback, Mahogany, Carved, Upholstered, 37 x 77 In.	472
Sofa, Chippendale Style, Camelback, Mahogany, Upholstered, 1900s, 33 x 86 In............	938
Sofa, Chippendale, Camelback, Mahogany, Upholstered, H-Stretcher, c.1780, 39 x 79 In. *illus*	2000
Sofa, Donghia, John Hutton, Block Island, Woven, Rattan, Cushions, 30 x 67 In..............	1800
Sofa, Dunbar Style, Upholstered, Tufted Button Back, 1945-69, 31 x 85 x 32 In.............. *illus*	1063
Sofa, Edwardian Style, Wood Trim, Upholstered, Carved, Scroll Arms, 30 x 86 In.	234
Sofa, Elm, Carved, Rolled Arms, Mortised Construction, Asia, c.1900, 36 x 90 In.	168
Sofa, Empire Style, Mahogany, Velvet Upholstery, Ogee Feet, c.1890, 34 x 84 In............	500
Sofa, Empire, Mahogany, Silk Upholstery, Acanthus Carved, Claw Feet, 35 x 91 In............	2070
Sofa, Johannes Andersen, Oak, Leather Upholstery, Denmark, c.1965, 32 x 95 x 36	10625
Sofa, Louis XV, Shaped Back, Painted, Needlepoint Tapestry, Brass Tacks, c.1750, 42 x 84 In.	4688
Sofa, Neoclassical, Mahogany, Upholstered, Downswept Arms, Casters, c.1850, 32 x 71 In. ..	1088
Sofa, Parlor, Karpen, Mahogany, Carved, Dragon, Dolphin Arms, Leather, 36 x 61 In.	2530
Sofa, Pine, Birch, Roped Seat, Rolled Arms, Upholstered, Mid 1800s, 18 x 80 In........... *illus*	2040
Sofa, Sheraton, Mahogany, Swan Arm, Arched Back, 8 Turned Legs, Upholstered................	1287
Sofa, Teak, Heavily Carved, Elephant Herd, Scroll Arms, Upholstered, c.1950, 31 x 69 In.	330
Sofa, Tuxedo, Contemporary, Bobby McAlpine, Manuel Canovas, 39 x 84 In..........................	896
Sofa, V. Kagan, Crescent, Brass, Upholstered, Brass, c.1970, 27 x 71 In........................ *illus*	5200
Sofa, V. Kagan, Purple Ultrasuede, Acrylic, Serpentine, Directional, c.1990, 27 x 93 In.	9170
Sofa, V-Shape, Custom Upholstered, Tufted Seats, 29 x 77 In., Pair	352
Stand, 2 Drawers, Molded Top, Lip Ends, Square Legs, Chinese, c.1870, 35 x 35 x 17 In.	510
Stand, Arne Vodder, Teak, Shelf Over Drawer, Sibast, Denmark, 1960s, 19 x 27 In., Pair......	1375
Stand, Arts & Crafts, Oak, Tapered Shape, Leather, Shelves, Carved, 44 x 12 x 13 In.	2040
Stand, Book, Florentine, Giltwood, Curved Feet, 1800s, 9 x 16 x 15 In.	813
Stand, Bridal, Victorian, Gilt Metal, Leaves, Cushion, Mirror, France, 1800s, 18 In..............	288
Stand, Bronze, 3 Figural Legs, Marble Top, Triangular Base, Tiffany & Co., 33 x 18 In.	3438
Stand, Brouer Mobelfabrik, Rosewood, Shelf, Drawer, Brass, Denmark, c.1960, 26 x 18 In., Pair ..	3250
Stand, Brushed Stainless Steel, Embossed Leather, Drawer, 18 x 18 x 24 In., Pair........ *illus*	7761

Furniture, Sofa, Chesterfield, Tufted Brown Leather Upholstery, Caster Feet, c.1910, 32 x 68 In.
$3,750

Hindman

Furniture, Sofa, Chippendale, Camelback, Mahogany, Upholstered, H-Stretcher, c.1780, 39 x 79 In.
$2,000

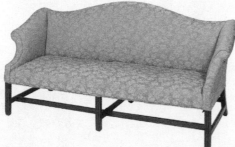

Eldred's

Furniture, Sofa, Dunbar Style, Upholstered, Tufted Button Back, 1945-69, 31 x 85 x 32 In.
$1,063

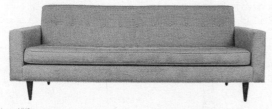

Auctions at Showplace, NYC

Furniture, Sofa, Pine, Birch, Roped Seat, Rolled Arms, Upholstered, Mid 1800s, 18 x 80 In.
$2,040

Garth's Auctioneers & Appraisers

Furniture, Sofa, V. Kagan, Crescent, Brass, Upholstered, Brass, c.1970, 27 x 71 In.
$5,200

Wright

Furniture, Stand, Brushed Stainless Steel, Embossed Leather, Drawer, 18 x 18 x 24 In., Pair
$7,761

Thomaston Place Auction Galleries

Furniture, Stand, Drum Shape, Wood, Carved, Porcelain Inset, Garden Scene, Painted, c.1890, 20 x 15 In.
$1,560

Garth's Auctioneers & Appraisers

Furniture, Stand, G. Stickley, Oak, 2 Drawers, Wood Knob, Tapered Legs, Signed, 29 x 20 In.
$1,040

Treadway

F

FURNITURE

Furniture, Stand, Magazine, Jens Nielsen, Teak, Plywood, X-Shape, Handle Hole, c.1965, 14 x 12 x 31 In.
$875

Wright

Furniture, Stand, Magazine, L. & J.G Stickley, Oak, Carved, Lower Shelf, New York, 34 x 14 In.
$4,225

Toomey & Co. Auctioneers

Furniture, Stand, Music, Lyre Shape, Openwork, Black Paint, Cast Iron, 1800s, 13 x 9 In.
$94

Hindman

Furniture, Stand, Octagonal, Bone Inlay, 2 Piece Top, Butterfly Support, Indonesia, 19 x 18 x 18 In.
$266

Conestoga Auction Company

Furniture, Stand, Plant, Neoclassical, Metal, Gilt, Copper Liner, Continental, 1900s, 41 x 19¾ In., Pair
$640

Brunk Auctions

Furniture, Stand, Plant, Onyx Top, Gilt Metal, Leafy, Brass Legs, Continental, c.1910, 30 x 15 In.
$210

Selkirk Auctioneers & Appraisers

Furniture, Stand, Plant, Painted, 3 Steps, Early 1900s, 39 x 48 In.
$302

Pook & Pook

Furniture, Stand, Plant, Red Marble Top, Reticulated Skirt, Sinuous Legs, Chinese, 1800s, 18 x 13 In.
$234

Thomaston Place Auction Galleries

Furniture, Stand, Shaving, Renaissance Revival, Walnut, Mirror, Drawers, Marble, Pedestal, 77 x 20 In.
$450

Michaan's Auctions

F

Stand, Bugatti, Sellette, Ebonized, Vellum, Tassels, Copper, Pewter Inlay, c.1902, 44 x 18 In. ..	8190
Stand, Butler's, Mahogany, 2 Doors, Scallop Gallery, 1800s, 29 x 22 x 18 In., Pair...............	1152
Stand, Card, Venetian, Figural, Blackamoor, Boy, Holding Tray, Carved, 1800s, 38 In..........	768
Stand, Drum Shape, Wood, Carved, Porcelain Inset, Garden Scene, Painted, c.1890, 20 x 15 In...*illus*	1560
Stand, Ebony, Rosewood, 6-Sided Top, Marble Panels, Carved, Ceylon, c.1850, 28 x 22 In., Pair ..	2340
Stand, Empire, Mahogany, Cylindrical, Marble Top, Door, 28 x 15 In.	448
Stand, Fern, Mahogany, Round, Carved Edge, 3 Legs, Reverse Scrolled Feet, 48 x 13 In.	293
Stand, G. Stickley, Oak, 2 Drawers, Wood Knob, Tapered Legs, Signed, 29 x 20 In. ....*illus*	1040
Stand, Georgian, Mahogany, 4 Drawers, Henredon Heritage, Drexel, 30 x 28 x 28 In., Pair .	180
Stand, Georgian, Mahogany, Gallery Top, Side Handles, Sliding Door, 29 x 19 x 17 In., Pair	2340
Stand, Hardwood, Round Top & Base, Carved, 5 Curved Legs, Chinese, 1900s, 39 x 15 In., Pair.....	2250
Stand, Hepplewhite, Maple, Fruitwood Inlay, Drawer, New Hampshire, c.1810, 26 x 17 In....	688
Stand, Magazine, Jens Nielsen, Teak, Plywood, X-Shape, Handle Hole, c.1965, 14 x 12 x 31 In...*illus*	875
Stand, Magazine, L. & J.G Stickley, Oak, Carved, Lower Shelf, New York, 34 x 14 In......*illus*	4225
Stand, Marble, Round Top, Pierced & Scrolled Brass, Victorian, 34 x 14 In...........................	177
Stand, Music, Brass, Lyre Shape, Ornately Cast Base, Owned By Frank Sinatra, 52 x 13 In..	2400
Stand, Music, Duet, Rosewood, Gilt, Lyre Shape Rest, Paw Feet, Early 1800s, 57 In...............	1152
Stand, Music, Lyre Shape, Openwork, Black Paint, Cast Iron, 1800s, 13 x 9 In. ....*illus*	94
Stand, Music, Renaissance Revival, Walnut, 2 Sections, Gilt, Bronze, c.1875, 49 x 26 In.	666
Stand, Octagonal Top, Marble Insert, Carved, Flowers, Openwork, Chinese, 36 x 18 In........	88
Stand, Octagonal, Bone Inlay, 2 Piece Top, Butterfly Support, Indonesia, 19 x 18 x 18 In.*illus*	266
Stand, Plant, 3 Tiers, Crinkle Wirework, Flower, Yellow Paint, France, 1800s, 60 x 40 x 2 In......	2925
Stand, Plant, Bird & Flower Inlay, Mother-Of-Pearl, Oval, Openwork, Korea, c.1950, 13 x 14 In.....	120
Stand, Plant, George III, Mahogany, Cabinet Door, Square Feet, c.1800, 31 x 14 In...............	340
Stand, Plant, Metal Wire, Black Painted Surface, c.1915, 35 x 47 x 15 In.	657
Stand, Plant, Neoclassical, Metal, Gilt, Copper Liner, Continental, 1900s, 41 x 19¾ In., Pair...... *illus*	640
Stand, Plant, Onyx Top, Gilt Metal, Leafy, Brass Legs, Continental, c.1910, 30 x 15 In...*illus*	210
Stand, Plant, Painted, 3 Steps, Early 1900s, 39 x 48 In..*illus*	302
Stand, Plant, Pine, Stained, 7 Tiers, Slat Tops, 1950, 31 x 33 x 12 In..................................	150
Stand, Plant, Red Marble Top, Reticulated Skirt, Sinuous Legs, Chinese, 1800s, 18 x 13 In....*illus*	234
Stand, Plant, Victorian, Brass, Cast Iron, Reeded Handles, American, Late 1800s, 31 ½ In..	120
Stand, Shaving, Renaissance Revival, Walnut, Mirror, Drawers, Marble, Pedestal, 77 x 20 In..... *illus*	450
Stand, Sheraton, Burl Walnut, Oval Top, Splay Leg, 1800s, 24 x 18 In.	2337
Stand, Sheraton, Cherry, Beaded Edge, Reeded Legs, Dovetailed Drawer, 1830s, 29 x 18 In.	300
Stand, Sheraton, Cherry, Drop Leaf, Drawer, Turned Legs, 1800s, 29 x 17 x 24 In...............	113
Stand, Sheraton, Drop Leaf, Dovetailed Drawers, Bennington Knobs, 1830s, 29 x 36 x 22 In.	450
Stand, Sheraton, Mahogany, Maple, Drop Leaf, 2 Drawers, American, 27 x 20 In.	585
Stand, Sheraton, Pine, Poplar, Dovetailed Drawer, 4 Turned Legs, 1830s, 28 x 19 x 26 In....	192
Stand, Sheraton, Pine, Soap Hollow Style Decoration, David T. Smith, 1835, 29 x 20 x 19 In.......	330
Stand, Sheraton, Poplar, Painted, Drawer, Philpott Top, Pennsylvania, 1800s, 31 x 22 In....	277
Stand, Sheraton, Tiger Maple, 2 Drawers, Dovetailed, 28 x 18 x 16 In................................	69
Stand, Smoking, Hollywood Regency, Marble, Pierced Metal Handle, 6-Footed Base, c.1910, 23 In.*illus*	300
Stand, Smoking, Victorian, Mahogany, Marble, Drawer, Door, c.1880, 35 x 17 In.................	360
Stand, Victorian Renaissance, Round Seat, Carved, Chains, Copper Medallion, 1870, 13 x 32 In. .	173
Stand, Walnut, Overhang, 3 Drawers, Paneled Sides, Turned Legs, 1800s, 29 x 16 In., Pair.	1521
Stand, Wrought Iron, Tripod, Floral Elements, Bell, Copper Basin, 1800s, 18 ½ In. ......*illus*	704
Stand, Wrought Iron, Wirework Basket, Green Paint, Patina, France, c.1890, 33 x 19 x 15 In.......	188
Stool, Arts & Crafts, Octagonal, Hand Carved, Snakes, Bird, Leaves, c.1905, 13 x 16 In.........	738
Stool, Birch Plywood, Steel, Removable Trays, Isokon Furniture Co., UK, c.1933, 17 x 13 In...*illus*	8750
Stool, Carved, Wood, Walnut, Winged Lion Shape, Platform Seat, 25 x 16 In...............*illus*	351
Stool, Empire Style, X-Shape Frame, Upholstered, Scroll Arms, 1900s, 24 x 15 x 26 In.	236
Stool, Figural, Prestige, Female Caryatid, Wood, Wrought Iron, Luba, Congo, 1900s, 6 x 10 In.....*illus*	563
Stool, Hardwood, Mellon Shape, Carved, Openwork, Chinese, 13 x 15 ½ In., Pair	813
Stool, L. & J.G. Stickley, Oak, Leather, X-Shape, Folding, Slat Legs, c.1910, 14 x 18 In....*illus*	2000
Stool, Piano, Round Wood Seat, Iron Base, Twisted Tripod Legs, Adjustable ....*illus*	150
Stool, Piet Hein, Chrome Plated Steel, Aluminum, Leather, Fritz Hansen, 1971, 31 In., 6 Piece	3000
Stool, Pine, Heart Shape Top, Blue Paint, 3 Scrolled Legs, Mid 1900s, 14 ½ In.	302
Stool, Poul Hundevard, Folding, Teak, Saddle Leather, Denmark, c.1948, 13 x 19 In....*illus*	2000
Stool, Queen Anne Style, Oval, Upholstered, Ball & Claw Feet, c.1900, 19 x 24 In.	75
Stool, Ria & Youri Augousti, Arched, Encrusted Eggshell Mosaic, UK, c.1991, 20 x 28 In.	1040

Furniture, Stand, Smoking, Hollywood Regency, Marble, Pierced Metal Handle, 6-Footed Base, c.1910, 23 In.
$300

Selkirk Auctioneers & Appraisers

Furniture, Stand, Wrought Iron, Tripod, Floral Elements, Bell, Copper Basin, 1800s, 18½ In.
$704

Brunk Auctions

Furniture, Stool, Birch Plywood, Steel, Removable Trays, Isokon Furniture Co., UK, c.1933, 17 x 13 In.
$8,750

Wright

FURNITURE

F

Furniture, Stool, Carved, Wood, Walnut, Winged Lion Shape, Platform Seat, 25 x 16 In.
$351

Thomaston Place Auction Galleries

Furniture, Stool, Piano, Round Wood Seat, Iron Base, Twisted Tripod Legs, Adjustable
$150

Donley Auctions

Furniture, Table, Art Deco, Edgar Brandt, Marble Top, Loops & Scrolls, Wrought Iron, 20 x 33 In.
$1,320

Nadeau's Auction Gallery

Furniture, Table, Art Deco, Metal Base, Green Glass Top, 3-Rod Pedestal, 3-Footed, c.1935, 20 x 20 In.
$750

New Haven Auctions

Get What You Pay For

Be sure you get what you pay for. Many designers created hand-made pieces, then had the designs mass-produced. If the furniture was very popular, it was often copied. Copies are worth much less than original works.

Furniture, Stool, Figural, Prestige, Female Caryatid, Wood, Wrought Iron, Luba, Congo, 1900s, 6 x 10 In.
$563

Wright

Furniture, Stool, L. & J.G. Stickley, Oak, Leather, X-Shape, Folding, Slat Legs, c.1910, 14 x 18 In.
$2,000

Fontaine's Auction Gallery

Furniture, Stool, Poul Hundevard, Folding, Teak, Saddle Leather, Denmark, c.1948, 13 x 19 In.
$2,000

Wright

Furniture, Stool, Thebes, Bamboo, Turned Up Corners, Traditional Spindled Style, 1800s, 17 x 15 In.
$448

Neal Auction Company

TIP
Be sure the big furniture you buy is small enough to go through the door into your room.

Furniture, Table, Center, Burl Walnut, Inset Marble Top, Carved Dog Heads, Burl Legs, 30 x 38 In.
$2,600

Woody Auction

Furniture, Table, Center, Hardwood, Carved, Openwork, Marble, 3 Legs, Chinese, c.1890, 32 x 33 In.
$2,440

CRN Auctions

Furniture, Table, Chris Wager, Adirondack, Curly Maple Top, Root Base, Yellow Birch, Antlers, 30 x 40 In.
$5,400

Blanchard's Auction Service LLC

Furniture, Table, Chrome Plated, 2 Tiers, Round Clear & Frosted Glass, 28 x 26 x 17 In.
$527

Thomaston Place Auction Galleries

Furniture, Table, Coffee, Bouillotte Style, Circular Marble Top, 2 Drawers, Brass Gallery, 21 x 36 In.
$413

Neue Auctions

TIP

To look best and work well, a coffee table should be two-thirds as wide as the sofa and a few inches lower than the 14- to 18-inch high seats.

Furniture, Table, Coffee, Richard Schultz, Petal, Wood, Aluminum, Knoll, 1960, 15 x 42 In.
$2,080

Wright

Furniture, Table, Console, Adam Style, Neoclassical, Mahogany, Marble, Demilune, 1900s, 34 x 52 In.
$2,178

Ahlers & Ogletree Auction Gallery

Furniture, Table, Console, Neoclassical, Carved, Giltwood, Marble, 3-Part Mirror, Italy, c.1890, 30 x 62 In.
$3,750

Hindman

Furniture, Table, Dining, G. Stickley, No. 656, Oak, Pedestal, 2 Leaves, Craftsman, c.1912, 30 x 54 In.
$625

Fontaine's Auction Gallery

Furniture, Table, Dining, Jacques Duval-Brasseur, Glass, Brass, Bejart Dancers Base, France, 30 x 98 In.
$5,313

Palm Beach Modern Auctions

Furniture, Table, Dining, Modern, Drop Leaf, Teak, Folding, Swing Legs, Marked, Sweden, 27 x 57 In.
$270

Alderfer Auction Company

Furniture, Table, Dining, Oak, Round, Carved Apron, Griffins, Turned Center Leg, c.1890, 30 x 60 In.
$5,445

Fontaine's Auction Gallery

Furniture, Table, Dining, Ship's Wheel, Inlaid Rim, Oak, Mahogany, Round Pedestal, c.1850, 29 x 73 In.
$4,270

Rafael Osona Nantucket Auctions

Furniture, Table, Dining, Widdicomb, Mahogany, Inlay, 2 Pedestals, Casters, c.1980, 30 x 46 x 78 In.
$1,680

Garth's Auctioneers & Appraisers

Furniture, Table, Drafting, Mahogany, Adjustable, Drawers, Turned Column, c.1880, 32 x 26 In.
$510

Garth's Auctioneers & Appraisers

Furniture, Table, Dressing, Queen Anne, Walnut, 5 Drawers, Stamped F. Burn, c.1760, 27 x 34 In.
$4,063

Hindman

Furniture, Table, Drop Leaf, Walnut, Pullout Supports, Turned Legs, Box Stretcher, 1700s, 27 x 42 In.
$2,223

Thomaston Place Auction Galleries

Furniture, Table, Egyptianesque, Bronze, Faux Porphyry, 3 Standing Pharaohs, Tripartite, 28 x 22 In.
$625

Neal Auction Company

Furniture, Table, Empire Style, Malachite Veneer, Gilt Bronze, Round, Winged Lion, 33 x 44 In.
$9,000

Michaan's Auctions

Furniture, Table, Figural Bronze Elephant, Standing, Square Glass Top, 26 x 20 In.
$234

Apple Tree Auction Center

> ### TIP
> Cigarette burns on wooden furniture are difficult to conceal. Rub the burn with scratch-cover polish. If that does not help, rub the burn with a paste of rottenstone (found in most hardware stores) and linseed oil.

Furniture, Table, Figural, 2 Cast Cement Atlas Supports, Marble Top, 1900s, 39 x 60 In.
$1,500

Fontaine's Auction Gallery

Furniture, Table, Frits Henningsen, Mahogany, Round, Pedestal, Splay Legs, Denmark, c.1940, 24 x 27 In.
$1,750

Wright

Stool, Tavern, Octagonal, Cutout In Seat, Turned Legs, Stretcher Base, England, 19 In., Pair	1375
Stool, Thebes, Bamboo, Turned Up Corners, Traditional Spindled Style, 1800s, 17 x 15 In... *illus*	448
Stool, Triangular, Subtle Incised, Posts, Spindles, England, 1700s, 21 x 21 In.	281
Stool, Vanity Seat, Walnut, Shell Shape, Carved, 23 x 15 x 19 In......	688
Table, Aesthetic Revival, Brass, Copper, Pastoral Painted Scene, Tubular Legs, 32 x 17 In. ..	610
Table, Art Deco, Edgar Brandt, Marble Top, Loops & Scrolls, Wrought Iron, 20 x 33 In. *illus*	1320
Table, Art Deco, Lacquered Wood, Glass, Aluminum, Black & Red, c.1935, 25 x 17 In.	625
Table, Art Deco, Metal Base, Green Glass Top, 3-Rod Pedestal, 3-Footed, c.1935, 20 x 20 In.. *illus*	750
Table, B. Mathsson, Annika, Teak, Laminated Beech, 3 Legs, c.1936, 19 x 33 In......	650
Table, Backgammon, John Vesey, Stainless Steel, Glass, Walnut, c.1960, 29 x 50 x 25 In.	390
Table, Book, Dividers On Top, Inlay, Slender Legs, Stretcher, Medial Shelf, c.1940s, 32 In....	24
Table, Card, Federal, Mahogany, Inlay, Boston, Massachusetts, c.1805, 29 x 36 x 17 In.	1500
Table, Card, Hepplewhite Style, Mahogany, Foldover Top, Inlay, Henkel-Harris, c.1985, 30 x 36 In. .	345
Table, Center, Burl Walnut, Inset Marble Top, Carved Dog Heads, Burl Legs, 30 x 38 In.*illus*	2600
Table, Center, Dodecagonal, Mahogany, Cyma Apron, Scroll Supports, 1810s, 28 x 36 In.	384
Table, Center, Ebonized, Bronze Mounts, Gilt, Marble, Pedestal, Italy, 34 x 45 In.	9760
Table, Center, Hardwood, Carved, Openwork, Marble, 3 Legs, Chinese, c.1890, 32 x 33 In. ... *illus*	2440
Table, Center, Mahogany, Round, Inlay, Medial Shelf, American, c.1940, 28 x 24 In.	72
Table, Center, Regency, Rosewood, Tilt Top, Gilt, Paw Feet, c.1810, 29 x 49 In.	2560
Table, Center, Rococo, Rosewood, White Marble Top, Carved Stretcher, 31 x 39 In.	518
Table, Center, Victorian, Rosewood, Marble, Turtle Top, Carved, Casters, c.1985, 29 x 39 In.	300
Table, Center, Victorian, Walnut, Marble Top, Carved, Shaped Legs, 1860s, 27 x 29 In......	132
Table, Center, Victorian, Walnut, Marble Turtle Top, Stretcher Base, 1800s, 29 x 41 x 28 In.	585
Table, Center, Walnut, Marble Top, Carved, 4 Part Base, Drop Finial, 1800s, 29 x 29 x 21 In..	210
Table, Charles X, Gothic Revival, Rosewood, Inlay, Octagonal, Casters, c.1830, 26 x 13 In. ...	1500
Table, Cherry, Round Top, 3 Reeded Legs, Ethan Allen, 26 x 28 In.	118
Table, Chinoiserie, Lacquered, Reverse Painted Top, Domed Base, 30 x 36 In......	275
Table, Chippendale Style, Inlaid Top, Councill Craftsman, Chinese, 27 x 15 x 54 In.	338
Table, Chippendale, Mahogany, Tilt Top, Partition Top, Claw Feet, Ireland, 1700s, 44 x 33 In.	3510
Table, Chris Wager, Adirondack, Curly Maple Top, Root Base, Yellow Birch, Antlers, 30 x 40 In.... *illus*	5400
Table, Chrome Plated, 2 Tiers, Round Clear & Frosted Glass, 28 x 26 x 17 In............... *illus*	527
Table, Cocktail, H. Probber, Walnut, Glass Top, Free Shape, c.1950, 12 x 62 x 42 In.	2750
Table, Coffee, Art Deco Style, Glass Top, Gilt Bronze Legs Resemble Bamboo, 17 x 44 In.	156
Table, Coffee, Bouillotte Style, Circular Marble Top, 2 Drawers, Brass Gallery, 21 x 36 In..... *illus*	413
Table, Coffee, Erik Van Buijtenen, Glass Top, Black Frame, Round, Nebu, Midcentury, 14 x 31 In.	440
Table, Coffee, I. Noguchi, Glass Top, 3 Curved Sides, Herman Miller, c.1950, 16 x 50 In.	1500
Table, Coffee, I. Noguchi, Rudder, Birch, Zinc-Plated Steel, Herman Miller, 15 x 50 x 35 In.	27500
Table, Coffee, Jansen Style, Beveled Glass, Brass Frame, 2 Tiers, 43 x 26 x 18 In............	572
Table, Coffee, Karl Springer, Parsons Style, Glass, Gunmetal, Black Oxide Finish, 72 In.	2520
Table, Coffee, Marble Top, Metal, Painted, Pietra Dura, Italy, 1900s, 20 x 61 x 24 In.	1211
Table, Coffee, Modernist, Oak, Travertine, 3 Legs, Tripod Base, Italy, 1900s, 17 x 60 x 40 In....	2000
Table, Coffee, P. Evans, Directional, Copper, Brass, Aluminum, Glass, c.1970, 42 x 42 In.	2000
Table, Coffee, Richard Schultz, Petal, Wood, Aluminum, Knoll, 1960, 15 x 42 In........... *illus*	2080
Table, Coffee, Robert Locher, Enameled Steel, Oval Glass Top, c.1939, 18 x 33 In.	1820
Table, Console, Adam Style, Neoclassical, Mahogany, Marble, Demilune, 1900s, 34 x 52 In. *illus*	2178
Table, Console, Eldred Wheeler, Cherry, Reeded Legs, 2 Drawers, c.1985, 30 x 36 In.	188
Table, Console, Federal Style, Mahogany, Inlaid Fan, Demilune, 31 x 30 In.	189
Table, Console, Georgian, Mahogany, Demilune, Carved, Inlay, c.1810, 28 x 41 In., Pair	1664
Table, Console, Imperial, Walnut, Hand Painted, Turned Feet, Curved Stretchers, 32 x 56 In.....	300
Table, Console, Iron, Marble Top, Pierced & Scrolling Base, Continental, 1900s, 33 x 51 In.	600
Table, Console, Louis XV Style, Faux Marble, Openwork, Continental, 31 x 36 In., Pair	768
Table, Console, Louis XV Style, Giltwood, Carved, Marble Top, c.1900, 32 x 18 In.	438
Table, Console, Louis XV, Mahogany, Parcel Gilt, Diminutive, Drawer, 1950, 22 x 24 x 13 In.	75
Table, Console, Mahogany, Rectangular, Drawer, Scroll Feet, c.1910, 33 x 45 In.	527
Table, Console, Neoclassical, Carved, Giltwood, Marble, 3-Part Mirror, Italy, c.1890, 30 x 62 In.*illus*	3750
Table, Console, Oak, Carved, Winged Griffins, Paw Feet, Drawer, c.1890, 37 x 40 In.	1250
Table, Console, Parzinger, Lacquered Wood, Black Marble, Drawers, c.1955, 30 x 78 In........	5200
Table, Console, Parzinger, Lacquered Wood, Marble, Brass, Drawers, 30 x 78 x 20 In.	5000
Table, Console, Serge Roche, Wrought Iron, Mirror, France, c.1940, 27 x 47 x 24 In.	8750
Table, Dining, Arts & Crafts Style, Oak, Round, Extendable, Split Pedestal, c.1915, 30 x 53 In.	3125

Furniture, Table, Game, George III, Herringbone Band, Foldover Felt Top, 29 x 35 In.
$1,188

Turner Auctions + Appraisals

Furniture, Table, Game, Mahogany, Half Round, Leather Top, 30 x 55 ½ In.
$339

Apple Tree Auction Center

TIP
Furniture casters were patented in 1876.

Furniture, Table, Game, Victorian, Walnut, Round, Printed Top Under Glass, Tripod, 28 x 25 In.
$556

Thomaston Place Auction Galleries

This is an edited listing of current prices. Visit **Kovels.com** to check thousands of prices from previous years and sign up for free information on trends, tips, reproductions, marks, and more.

Furniture, Table, George III Style, Walnut, Carved, Marble, Scroll Feet, 1900s, 35 x 65 In.
$1,250

Hindman

Furniture, Table, Hibachi, Glass Top, Copper, 2 Lidded Compartments, Japan, c.1950, 43 x 24 x 19 In.
$94

Charleston Estate Auctions

Furniture, Table, Jacobean Style, Rosewood, Mother-Of-Pearl & Brass Boulle Top, 1800s, 24 x 35 x 22 In.
$2,040

Alex Cooper Auctioneers

Furniture, Table, Library, Carved, Ribbed Skirt, Turned Legs, Full Length Stretcher, 1930s, 31 x 98 x 50 In.
$900

Selkirk Auctioneers & Appraisers

TIP

A white ring on a tabletop is in the finish; a black ring is in the wood. It is easier to remove a damaged finish than a wood stain.

Table, Dining, Danish Modern Style, Teak, Butterfly Drop Leaf, Meredew, Eng., 30 x 52 In..	430
Table, Dining, G. Nakashima, Walnut, Adjustable, Widdicomb, 1959, 28 x 71 In.	7500
Table, Dining, G. Stickley, No. 656, Oak, Pedestal, 2 Leaves, Craftsman, c.1912, 30 x 54 In....*illus*	625
Table, Dining, Georgian Style, Mahogany, 3 Pedestals, Inlay, Casters, 24-In. Leaves, 48 x 144 In..........	3250
Table, Dining, Glass Slab Top, 2 Plaster Column Supports, 29 x 77 x 39 In.	527
Table, Dining, Gustavian, Drop Leaf, Painted, Frieze, Iron Hooks, Sweden, 1700s, 29 x 53 In.......	976
Table, Dining, Jacques Duval-Brasseur, Glass, Brass, Bejart Dancers Base, France, 30 x 98 In...*illus*	5313
Table, Dining, Marble Top, Pietra Dura, Flowers, 2 Pedestals, 33 x 95 x 47 In.....................	3900
Table, Dining, Michael Taylor, Oak, 3 Leaves, Rolling Feet, Baker Furniture, 1960s, 60 x 38 In.	438
Table, Dining, Modern, Drop Leaf, Teak, Folding, Swing Legs, Marked, Sweden, 27 x 57 In....*illus*	270
Table, Dining, Oak, Round, Carved Apron, Griffins, Turned Center Leg, c.1890, 30 x 60 In....*illus*	5445
Table, Dining, Ship's Wheel, Inlaid Rim, Oak, Mahogany, Round Pedestal, c.1850, 29 x 73 In......*illus*	4270
Table, Dining, Tiger Maple, Dark Green Base, Cabriole Legs, David Smith, 1900s, 29 x 66 In...	2500
Table, Dining, Victorian, Walnut, 5 Skirted Leaves, Carved Pedestal, c.1870, 137 In.	2875
Table, Dining, W. McArthur, Namco, Round, Laminate, Aluminum Legs, c.1968, 29 x 30 In........	1063
Table, Dining, Walnut, 3 Pedestals, Carved, Gilt Dolphins, 1900s, 29 x 54 x 186 In.	1260
Table, Dining, Widdicomb, Mahogany, Inlay, 2 Pedestals, Casters, c.1980, 30 x 46 x 78 In. .....*illus*	1680
Table, Dining, Wood, Plank Top, Scrolling Wrought & Zinc Iron Base, 1900s, 87 x 39 In.	594
Table, Dining, Yellow Pine, 2 Tiers, Lazy Susan, Turned Legs, c.1890, 33 x 60 x 59 In.	2000
Table, Drafting, Mahogany, Adjustable, Drawers, Turned Column, c.1880, 32 x 26 In. .*illus*	510
Table, Dressing, Drawer, Shaped Backsplash, Later Green Paint, 1800s, 35 x 31 In.	202
Table, Dressing, Edwardian, Satinwood, Mahogany, Lift Lid, Hamilton & Co., 1910, 39 x 36 In....	4305
Table, Dressing, Queen Anne, Oak, Carved, 3 Drawers, Pad Feet, England, c.1740, 27 x 31 In.....	531
Table, Dressing, Queen Anne, Walnut, 5 Drawers, Stamped F. Burn, c.1760, 27 x 34 In.*illus*	4063
Table, Drop Leaf, Tiger Maple, 4 Square Tapered Legs, New England, c.1820, 27 x 37 In.	113
Table, Drop Leaf, Walnut, Pullout Supports, Turned Legs, Box Stretcher, 1700s, 27 x 42 In....*illus*	2223
Table, Egyptianesque, Bronze, Faux Porphyry, 3 Standing Pharaohs, Tripartite, 28 x 22 In...*illus*	625
Table, Empire Style, Gilt Bronze, Lapis Lazuli Veneer, Lozenges, Figural Legs, 1900s, 28 x 30 In.	2250
Table, Empire Style, Malachite Veneer, Gilt Bronze, Round, Winged Lion, 33 x 44 In....*illus*	9000
Table, Empire Style, Round, Ormolu, Stone, Gilt Bronze Frame, France, c.1910, 27 x 29 In..	4305
Table, Farm, French Provincial, Cherry, Walnut, Drawer, 1800s, 31 x 98 In.........................	2125
Table, Farm, Hepplewhite, Old Paint, 3-Board Top, Pegged, 32 x 59 In.	1140
Table, Federal Style, Irving & Casson, Mahogany, 2 Pedestals, A.H. Davenport & Co., 1900s, 65 In..	500
Table, Figural Bronze Elephant, Standing, Square Glass Top, 26 x 20 In.....................*illus*	234
Table, Figural, 2 Cast Cement Atlas Supports, Marble Top, 1900s, 39 x 60 In................*illus*	1500
Table, Folding, Steel, Polished, Ring Handle, Glass Top, Tripod Feet, 1950s, 23 x 14 In.........	125
Table, Frits Henningsen, Mahogany, Round, Pedestal, Splay Legs, Denmark, c.1940, 24 x 27 In...*illus*	1750
Table, G. Nakashima, Walnut, Single Slab Top, Free Edge, Tripod Legs, 1980, 17 x 23 In......	6250
Table, Galle, Art Nouveau, Mahogany, Inlay, 3 Tiers, Splayed Legs, Signed, 33 x 31 In..........	1875
Table, Game, Drop Leaf, Walnut, Wide Skirt, Tapered Legs, England, 1800s, 30 x 35 In.	410
Table, Game, Flame Mahogany, Column Base, Turned Legs, 29 x 48 x 24 In.	374
Table, Game, George I Style, Oak, Demilune, Cabriole Legs, Pad Feet, 1700s, 29 x 33 In........	594
Table, Game, George III, Herringbone Band, Foldover Felt Top, 29 x 35 In. ....*illus*	1188
Table, Game, Louis Philippe, Walnut, Stepped Top, Reverse Painted Chessboard, Tripod, 28 x 28 In...	690
Table, Game, Louis XV, Provincial, Fruitwood, Splayed Legs, 1700s, 27 x 30 x 31 In.	531
Table, Game, Mahogany, Half Round, Leather Top, 30 x 55 ½ In.................................*illus*	339
Table, Game, Mahogany, Reversible, Leather Top, Inlay, Molded Edge, Drawers, 30 x 46 In.	761
Table, Game, Mosaic Tile Top, Red & Black Squares, Hearts, Turned Legs, 1800s, 30 x 19 x 19 In.	100
Table, Game, Neoclassical, Mahogany, Swivel Top, Carved, Pedestal, 29 x 35 x 36 In............	480
Table, Game, Octagonal, White & Black Squares, Pewter Inlay, Splayed Legs, 1950s, 29 x 21 x 21 In.	125
Table, Game, Victorian, Walnut, Round, Printed Top Under Glass, Tripod, 28 x 25 In. .*illus*	556
Table, Game, Yellow Pine, Walnut, Checkerboard Top, Stamped, 1910s, 26 x 17 x 23 In.	191
Table, George II, Mahogany, Dovetailed Drawer, Brass, Carved Legs, c.1750, 27 x 34 In........	3998
Table, George III Style, Walnut, Carved, Marble, Scroll Feet, 1900s, 35 x 65 In. ....*illus*	1250
Table, Georgian Style, Inlay, Inset Top, Paw Feet, Herter Brothers, 29 x 33 x 26 In................	156
Table, Hibachi, Glass Top, Copper, 2 Lidded Compartments, Japan, c.1950, 43 x 24 x 19 In. ...*illus*	94
Table, Imari Style, Porcelain, Round, 3 Sections, Flowers, Geometrics, 22 x 25 In., Pair	360
Table, Inlaid Flower Design, Drawer, Slender Tapered Legs, Italy, 1800s, 29 x 18 In.............	265
Table, Inset Marble Top, Bead Trim, Leafy, Club Legs Shape, Chinese, 1800s, 17 x 17 In.	180
Table, Jacobean Style, Rosewood, Mother-Of-Pearl & Brass Boulle Top, 1800s, 24 x 35 x 22 In......*illus*	2040

F

Furniture, Table, Louis XVI Style, Drawers, Leather Top, Side Pullout, Krieger, Paris, 1800s, 30 x 51 In.
$896

Roland NY Auctioneers & Appraisers

Furniture, Table, Neo-Grec, Inlaid Bouquet, Leafy Scroll, Round, Pedestal, Bun Feet, 1800s, 29 x 27 In.
$840

Michaan's Auctions

Furniture, Table, Queen Anne Style, Mahogany, 3 Graduated Tiers, Round, Pedestal, 40 x 24 In.
$71

Conestoga Auction Company

TIP
Make your furniture multitask. A stool can double as a small side table, the right size for holding a drink or a small plate at a party.

Furniture, Table, Nesting, Regency Style, Mahogany Tone, Column Legs, 27 x 14 x 10 In., 4 Piece
$88

Greenwich Auction

Furniture, Table, R.J. Horner, Faux Bamboo, Drawers, Adjustable Mirror, 1800s, 59 x 42 x 20 In.
$3,438

Cowan's Auctions

Furniture, Table, Marble Top, Caryatid Bust Legs, Giltwood, Gesso, Continental, 1700s, 30 x 52 In.
$2,070

Merrill's Auctions

Furniture, Table, Parzinger, Square, Curved Legs, X-Stretcher, 21 x 27 In.
$780

Palm Beach Modern Auctions

Furniture, Table, Refectory, Shaped Legs, Elongated Stretcher, Continental, c.1900, 30 x 84 In.
$390

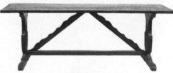

Selkirk Auctioneers & Appraisers

Furniture, Table, Mixing, Walnut, Marble, Tile Backsplash, Lower Door, Victorian, 48 x 41 In.
$295

Conestoga Auction Company

Furniture, Table, Pier, Giltwood, Figural Eagle Pedestal, Spread Wings, 1800s, 36 x 48 In.
$7,995

Pook & Pook

FURNITURE

F

Furniture, Table, Regency, Checkerboard Top, Malachite, Marble, Shelf, Gilt Legs, 32 x 29 x 32 In.
$1,610

Blackwell Auctions

Furniture, Table, Sewing, Federal, Mahogany, Drop Leaf, 3 Drawers, Arched Feet, c.1835, 28¾ x 30 In.
$188

Eldred's

> **TIP**
> *Do not put any furniture in front of a window if the room is small and dark. Let the sun shine in.*

Furniture, Table, Sewing, Mahogany, 2 Drawers, Pedestal Base, Casters, 24 x 16 x 31 In.
$144

Merrill's Auctions

Furniture, Table, Sewing, Maple, Cherry, Adjustable, 2 Candle Sockets, New Eng., c.1790, 37 In.
$984

Pook & Pook

Furniture, Table, Side, Pompeiian Style, Metal, Patina, 3 Figural Legs, Tripod Base, 1900s, 24 In.
$375

Hindman

Furniture, Table, Tavern, Pine, Birch, Scalloped Top, Tapered Legs, New England, c.1790, 27 x 35 In.
$2,460

Pook & Pook

Furniture, Table, Tea, Pine, Piecrust Top, Carved, Central Pedestal, Scroll Feet, Drexel
$234

Thomaston Place Auction Galleries

Furniture, Table, Tea, Tilt Top, Mahogany, Piecrust Edge, Tripod, New England, 1700s, 28 x 28 In.
$585

Thomaston Place Auction Galleries

Furniture, Table, Tray, Walnut, Glass Insert, Carved Scene, 4 Figural Legs, Italy, c.1910, 19 x 25 In.
$363

Fontaine's Auction Gallery

Table, John Boone, Brass, Mirror, Round, Pedestal, Adjustable, Pierced Gallery, 31 x 12 In. 1560
Table, Jupe, Mahogany, Santos, Rosewood, Crossbanded, Theo. Alexander, 1900s, 29 x 84 In. 5120
Table, Library, Carved, Ribbed Skirt, Turned Legs, Full Length Stretcher, 1930s, 31 x 98 x 50 In..*illus* 900
Table, Library, Pyrography Flowers, Red & Green, 2 Side Bookshelves, 1900s, 27 x 30 In. 180
Table, Library, Regency, Rosewood, Ormolu Mounts, Leather Top, 2 Drawers, 30 x 56 In..... 192
Table, Limbert, Oak, Round, X-Stretcher, Paper Label, Grand Rapids, 30 x 29 In................... 1250
Table, Louis Philippe, Mahogany, Round, Marble Top, Pedestal, Casters, c.1850, 30 x 39 In. 688
Table, Louis XV Style, Kingwood, Drawers, Gilt, Sevres Plaques, E.H. Baldock, c.1810, 51 In. 6300
Table, Louis XVI Style, Drawers, Leather Top, Side Pullout, Krieger, Paris, 1800s, 30 x 51 In..*illus* 896
Table, Louis XVI Style, Round, Marble Top, 2 Drawers, Doris Dessauer, 1900s, 29 x 21 x 16 In. 406
Table, Louis XVI Style, Walnut, Marble, Gallery Edge, Drawer, Pullout Shelves, 29 x 32 In... 1989
Table, Louis XVI, Mahogany, Rounds, Gilt Metal Mounted, Marble Top, c.1890, 28 x 25 In... 461
Table, Mangiarotti, Eros, Grigio Scogliera Marble, Skipper, Italy, 28 x 26 x 18 In................... 5313
Table, Marble Top, Caryatid Bust Legs, Giltwood, Gesso, Continental, 1700s, 30 x 52 In. *illus* 2070
Table, Mixing, Walnut, Marble, Tile Backsplash, Lower Door, Victorian, 48 x 41 In...... *illus* 295
Table, Monastery, French Provincial, Oak, Carved, Trestle Base, 1800s, 29 x 76 x 33 In. 1000
Table, Neo-Grec, Inlaid Bouquet, Leafy Scroll, Round, Pedestal, Bun Feet, 1800s, 29 x 27 In.*illus* 840
Table, Nesting, Regency Style, Mahogany Tone, Column Legs, 27 x 14 x 10 In., 4 Piece *illus* 88
Table, Oak, Drawer, Carved, Box Stretchers, Turned Legs, England, 1800s, 31 x 22 In. 236
Table, Oak, Drawer, Carved, Turned Legs, England, 1800s, 31 x 22 x 29 In.......................... 236
Table, Oscar Bach, Demilune, Black Marble Top, Iron Base, Bronze Scrollwork, 32 x 32 In. 300
Table, Parzinger, Square, Curved Legs, X-Stretcher, 21 x 27 In. ....*illus* 780
Table, Pembroke, Federal Style, Satinwood, String & Carrot Inlay, Drawer, 28 x 31 In.......... 120
Table, Pembroke, Hepplewhite, Mahogany, Tapered Legs, Drawer, 28 x 36 x 18 In. 330
Table, Pembroke, Mahogany, Drawer, Straight Legs, England, 1700s, 27 x 31 x 19 In. 375
Table, Pembroke, Sheraton, Mahogany, Drawer, Reeded Legs, Urn Foot, 29 x 30 x 20 In...... 439
Table, Pier, Giltwood, Figural Eagle Pedestal, Spread Wings, 1800s, 36 x 48 In............*illus* 7995
Table, Pier, Neoclassical, Mahogany, Carved, Marble, Columns, Mirror, 1800s, 36 x 42 In... 1150
Table, Pub, Cast Iron, Faux Marble Top, Caryatid Legs, Medial Shelf, 29 x 21 In. 366
Table, Queen Anne Style, Drop Leaf, Mahogany, 2 Drawers, 29 x 17 x 27 In. 475
Table, Queen Anne Style, Mahogany, 3 Graduated Tiers, Round, Pedestal, 40 x 24 In...*illus* 71
Table, R.J. Horner, Faux Bamboo, Drawers, Adjustable Mirror, 1800s, 59 x 42 x 20 In. . *illus* 3438
Table, Refectory, Shaped Legs, Elongated Stretcher, Continental, c.1900, 30 x 84 In..... *illus* 390
Table, Regency Style, Mahogany, Drum, Drawers, Yorkshire House, 1900s, 30 x 30 In.......... 256
Table, Regency, Checkerboard Top, Malachite, Marble, Shelf, Gilt Legs, 32 x 29 x 32 In....*illus* 1610
Table, Regency, Drop Leaf, Mahogany, Leather, Drawers, Pedestal, Casters, c.1940, 26 x 24 In... 150
Table, Renaissance Revival, Walnut, Round Marble Top, Gray, Carved, 1800s, 30 x 20 In. ... 1000
Table, Rohde, East Indian Laurel, Glass, Demilune, Steel, Herman Miller, c.1936, 19 x 24 In. 4160
Table, Round, Glass Top, Beveled, Wood Frame, Faux Marble, c.1985, 27 x 28 In., Pair 281
Table, Sawbuck, Contemporary, Pine, X Ends, Stretchers, c.1985, 30 x 95 In......................... 900
Table, Sewing, Federal, Cherry, Leaf Carved, 3 Drawers, Turned Legs, 27 x 21 x 18 In. 293
Table, Sewing, Federal, Mahogany, Drop Leaf, 3 Drawers, Arched Feet, c.1835, 28¾ x 30 In..*illus* 188
Table, Sewing, French Style, Rosewood, Gilt Design, Saber Feet, 24 x 16 In. 230
Table, Sewing, Louis XV, Ebonized Wood, Brass Inlay, France, 1800s, 29 x 17 x 25 In. 225
Table, Sewing, Mahogany, 2 Drawers, Pedestal Base, Casters, 24 x 16 x 31 In...............*illus* 144
Table, Sewing, Mahogany, Empire, Drop Leaf, Antebellum Home, 3 Thread Drawers, 29 x 18 x 18 In. 374
Table, Sewing, Mahogany, Sheraton, Reeded Legs, 4 Cherry Drawers, 1800s, 29 x 22 x 17 In.... 1830
Table, Sewing, Maple, Cherry, Adjustable, 2 Candle Sockets, New Eng., c.1790, 37 In....*illus* 984
Table, Sewing, Neoclassical, Mahogany, Lift Lids, Drawers, 1800s, 26 x 22 In...................... 369
Table, Sewing, Oak, Oval, Beaded, Molded Edge, 3 Drawers, Turned Legs, 30 x 37 In. 146
Table, Sewing, Regency Inlay, Satinwood, Octagonal Lift Top, Casters, Early 1800s, 27 x 19 In.......... 256
Table, Sewing, Walnut, Rosewood, Veneers, Drawers, 3 Legs, Eng., 1800s, 28 x 17 In........... 219
Table, Side, Chinese Style, Oak, Interlocking Circles, c.1950, 19 x 16 x 16 In.......................... 31
Table, Side, Contemporary, Sailor's Valentine In Frame, Octagonal, 16 x 22 In. 1708
Table, Side, Contemporary, Wood, Folding, Overhanging Top, Carved, Nepal, 21 x 17 In., Pair..... 351
Table, Side, Neoclassical, Mahogany, Round, Carved, Pedestal, Casters, c.1850, 26 x 24 In. . 594
Table, Side, Philip & Kelvin LaVerne, Bronze, Pewter, Chinoiserie, c.1960, 16 x 26 In., Pair . 3000
Table, Side, Philippe Hiquily Style, Geode Stone, Curved Chrome Base, 24 x 16 In., Pair...... 2520
Table, Side, Pompeiian Style, Metal, Patina, 3 Figural Legs, Tripod Base, 1900s, 24 In... *illus* 375
Table, Side, Round, Marble Top, 3 Iron Legs, Ball Feet, 1900s, 20 x 18 In. 325

Furniture, Table, Walnut, Glass Top, Round, 3 Curved Legs, 2000, 26 x 21 In. $1,040

Wright

Furniture, Table, Writing, Regency, Mahogany, Leather Top, Gilt Border, England, 1800s, 30 x 60 x 27 In. $1,342

Rafael Osona Nantucket Auctions

Furniture, Table, Wrought Iron, Tile Top, La Paloma Tableau, San Jose Pottery, c.1936, 22 x 34 In. $5,200

Toomey & Co. Auctioneers

Furniture, Tabouret, Moorish, Mother-Of-Pearl Inlay, 10-Sided, Arcade Base, 28 In., Pair $2,048

Neal Auction Company

225

TIP

Sap bleeds from the knots in old wood and it stains the paint. This discoloration is one way to determine if paint is old.

F

Furniture, Tea Cart, Ico Parisi, Mahogany, Brass, 2 Tiers, Wheels, De Baggis, c.1950, 32 x 35 In.
$295

Soulis Auctions

Furniture, Teapoy, Rococo Revival, Mahogany, Lift Top, Cabriole Legs, c.1850, 32 x 21 In.
$610

Neal Auction Company

Furniture, Tete-A-Tete, Mixed Wood, Spindles, Faux Skin Upholstery, Continental, 1800s, 27 x 53 In.
$281

Charlton Hall Auctions

Table, Side, Teak, Scroll Carved, Pinned Construction, Asian, 1900s, 18 x 38 x 20 In.	6250
Table, Side, Walnut, Carved Eagle Base, Marble Top, c.1910, 23 x 22 x 16 In.	666
Table, Tavern, Pine, Birch, Scalloped Top, Tapered Legs, New England, c.1790, 27 x 35 In. *illus*	2460
Table, Tavern, Pine, Drawer, Overhanging Top, Breadboard Ends, 1800s, 27 x 39 x 25 In.	1003
Table, Tavern, Queen Anne, Natural Wood Top, Painted Turned Legs, c.1750, 26 x 35 In.	480
Table, Tavern, Queen Anne, Tiger Maple, Carved, Oval, New Eng., 1700s, 27 x 18 In.	2016
Table, Tea, Chippendale, Mahogany, Piecrust Edge, Turkey Claw & Egg Foot, 28 x 30 In.	176
Table, Tea, George III Style, Mahogany, Tilt Top, Round, Tripod Leg, c.1790, 29 x 26 In.	319
Table, Tea, Pine, Piecrust Top, Carved, Central Pedestal, Scroll Feet, Drexel *illus*	234
Table, Tea, Queen Anne, Walnut, Tilt Top, Tripod Base, Pennsylvania, c.1770, 28 x 34 In.	1722
Table, Tea, Tilt Top, Mahogany, Piecrust Edge, Tripod, New England, 1700s, 28 x 28 In.*illus*	585
Table, Tea, Tilt Top, Tiger Maple, Urn Pedestal, Tripod, Cabriole Legs, 1700s, 42 x 31 In.	1287
Table, Tray, 4 Stacked Removable Trays, Round, Multicolor, Domed Base, c.1935, 23 x 14 In.	250
Table, Tray, Butler's, Chinese Chippendale Style, Inlay, Oval, Brass Handles, 34 x 22 In.	69
Table, Tray, Continental, Painted Flowers, Scroll Legs, Medial Shelf, 1800s, 27 x 22 In.	563
Table, Tray, Walnut, Glass Insert, Carved Scene, 4 Figural Legs, Italy, c.1910, 19 x 25 In. *illus*	363
Table, Trestle, Limbert, Chestnut, Cutout Sides, Paper Label, c.1902, 36 x 30 x 24 In.	3567
Table, Trestle, Maple, Oak, Rectangular, 2 Supports Joined, Shoe Feet, 1700s, 25 x 19 x 20 In.	313
Table, Victorian, Mahogany, Oval Top, Pedestal Base, 4 Scroll Feet, 29 x 54 x 41 In.	300
Table, Walnut, Glass Top, Round, 3 Curved Legs, 2000, 26 x 21 In. *illus*	1040
Table, Widdicomb, Walnut, Inlay, Upturned Legs, Basket In Legs, Emilio Terry, 28 x 29 In.	531
Table, Writing, Bonheur Du Jour, Kingwood, Porcelain Plaques, Gilt Bronze, c.1890, 48 x 31 In.	2662
Table, Writing, Regency, Mahogany, Leather Inset, Casters, 1800s, 29 x 54 x 36 In.	406
Table, Writing, Regency, Mahogany, Leather Top, Gilt Border, England, 1800s, 30 x 60 x 27 In. *illus*	1342
Table, Wrought Iron, Tile Top, La Paloma Tableau, San Jose Pottery, c.1936, 22 x 34 In.*illus*	5200
Tabouret, Moorish, Mother-Of-Pearl Inlay, 10-Sided, Arcade Base, 28 In., Pair *illus*	2048
Tea Cart, Ico Parisi, Mahogany, Brass, 2 Tiers, Wheels, De Baggis, c.1950, 32 x 35 In. *illus*	295
Tea Cart, William IV, Mahogany, Overhead Shelf, Cupboard Doors, Casters, c.1840, 45 x 41 In.	1000
Tea Server, Mahogany, 3 Tiers, Turned Post, 3 Pad Feet, England, 19th Century, 44½ x 24 In.	270
Teapoy, George III, Brass Inlay, Drawer, Fitted Interior, Coromandel, c.1790, 29 x 19 In.	10455
Teapoy, Rococo Revival, Mahogany, Lift Top, Cabriole Legs, c.1850, 32 x 21 In. *illus*	610
Tete-A-Tete, Mixed Wood, Spindles, Faux Skin Upholstery, Continental, 1800s, 27 x 53 In. *illus*	281
Tray Table, 2 Schooners, Mountainous Lake Scene, 1700s, 19 x 28 x 21 In.	854
Tray, On Stand, Bamboo Turnings, Tole, X-Stretcher Base, 19 x 32 In. *illus*	640
Tray, On Stand, Red Vinyl, Chrome Handles, Metal Tacks, Folding, c.1940, 40 x 28 In.	219
Umbrella Stand, Arts & Crafts, Ball Finial, Foot, Donut Shape, Metal Catch Tray, 1900s, 27 In.	300
Umbrella Stand, Arts & Crafts, Pyrography, Hexagonal-Sided, Cutouts, c.1905, 27 x 11 In.	492
Umbrella Stand, Blue & White, Mountainous Village Scene, Chinese, 18 x 11 In., Pair	313
Umbrella Stand, Blue Decorations, White Ground, Swan, Tree, Chinese, 1900s, 22½ In.	180
Umbrella Stand, Brass, Embossed Classical Figures, Egg & Dart Bands, Gilt, Paw Feet, 26 In.	110
Umbrella Stand, Brass, Peacock, Corner, Arts & Crafts, c.1900, 24 x 15 x 9 In. *illus*	984
Umbrella Stand, Brass, Multicolor Enamel Panels & Borders, Chinese, 20th Century, 24 x 8¾ In.	165
Umbrella Stand, Bronze, Bear, Standing, Black Forest Style, Footed Base, 1900s, 37 x 14 x 22 In.	660
Umbrella Stand, Cast Iron, Bear, Upright, Black Forest Style, Drip Well, Germany, 37 In.	685
Umbrella Stand, Dorothy Thorpe, Coiled Lucite, Cane, 22 In. *illus*	157
Umbrella Stand, Navy Blue Fabric, Rectangular, Square Base, 70 x 120 In.	738
Umbrella Stand, Sheet Iron, Fox, Painted, c.1950, 25 x 18 In. *illus*	738
Umbrella Stand, Stick & Ball, Wood, Gilt Metal Feet, Early 1900s, 29 x 9 In. *illus*	406
Valet, Brass, Hat Stand, Coat Rack, Pants Rail, Vide Poche Tray, Tripod Base, 54 x 18 In. *illus*	94
Valet, Wood, Brass Tray, Fluted Standard, Hangers, Circular Base, 1900s, 49 In.	96
Vanity, Arne Wahl Iversen, Rosewood, Mirror, Vinde Mobelfabrik, c.1960, 29 x 32 In.	875
Vanity, Brass Stand, Mirror, Pietra Dura, Cloisonne, Drawer, Shelves, c.1880, 52 x 15 In.	5000
Vitrine, Art Deco, Ruhlmann Style, Glass, Various Inlay, 68 x 48 In.	5120
Vitrine, Continental Style, Glass, Brass Mounts, Velour Interior Back, 58 x 26 In.	640
Vitrine, Louis XV Style, Curved Glass Door, Courtship Scene, Damask, 1900s, 77 x 43 In.	1512
Vitrine, Louis XV Style, Vernis Martin, Putti Crest, Glass Door, Inlay, c.1985, 75 x 32 x 16 In. *illus*	1250
Vitrine, Louis XV, Gilt Bronze Mounts, Painted Panels, 3 Shelf Sections, Spain, 60 x 27 In.	720
Vitrine, Louis XV/XVI, Transitional Style, Kingwood, Bombe, Gilt Metal, Glass, 1900s, 71 x 34 In.	344
Vitrine, Louis XVI Style, Burl Walnut, Glass, Mirror Back, Shelf, Spain, 44 x 33 In.	2550
Vitrine, Neoclassical Style, Giltwood, Wall Mounted, Italy, 1900s, 19 x 10 In., Pair	363

Furniture, Tray, On Stand, Bamboo Turnings, Tole, X-Stretcher Base, 19 x 32 In. $640

Neal Auction Company

Furniture, Umbrella Stand, Brass, Peacock, Corner, Arts & Crafts, c.1900, 24 x 15 x 9 In. $984

California Historical Design

Furniture, Umbrella Stand, Dorothy Thorpe, Coiled Lucite, Cane, 22 In. $157

Susanin's Auctioneers & Appraisers

Furniture, Umbrella Stand, Sheet Iron, Fox, Painted, c.1950, 25 x 18 In. $738

Pook & Pook

Furniture, Umbrella Stand, Stick & Ball, Wood, Gilt Metal Feet, Early 1900s, 29 x 9 In. $406

Hindman

Furniture, Valet, Brass, Hat Stand, Coat Rack, Pants Rail, Vide Poche Tray, Tripod Base, 54 x 18 In. $94

Auctions at Showplace, NYC

Furniture, Vitrine, Louis XV Style, Vernis Martin, Putti Crest, Glass Door, Inlay, c.1985, 75 x 32 x 16 In. $1,250

John Moran Auctioneers

Furniture, Wardrobe, Georgian Style, Palatial, Mahogany, Doors, Drawers & False Drawers, c.1910, 91 In. $545

Ahlers & Ogletree Auction Gallery

Furniture, Wardrobe, Wegner, Oak, Lacquered, Chrome Plated Steel, Johannes Hansen, c.1955, 80 x 23 In. $3,000

Wright

FURNITURE

Furniture, Washstand, Pine, Bowfront, Backsplash, Yellow Paint, Shelf, Drawer, c.1830, 36 x 18 In.
$644

Thomaston Place Auction Galleries

Furniture, Washstand, Sheraton, Pine, Mottled Paint, Bowl Hole, Shelf, Drawer, 1800s, 35 In.
$461

Pook & Pook

Furniture, Wastebasket, Brass, Reticulated, Hexagonal, Leaves, Rope Shape Rim & Base, 11½ x 9½ In.
$63

Greenwich Auction

Vitrine, Rococo, Walnut, 3 Glass Doors, Shelves, Continental, 101 x 103 x 26 In.	3050
Vitrine, Wood, Painted, Glass, Lower Drawer, 3 Glass Shelves, Electrified, 73 x 32 In.	281
Wall Bracket, Baroque, Pine, Dolphin Shape, Continental, c.1890, 19 x 17 x 9 In.	1500
Wall Unit, G. Nelson, CSS, Aluminum, Walnut, Steel, Herman Miller, c.1959, 108 x 33 In.	4000
Wardrobe, Georgian Style, Palatial, Mahogany, Doors, Drawers & False Drawers, c.1910, 91 In.. *illus*	545
Wardrobe, Wegner, Oak Veneer, Lacquered Wood, Steel, Johannes Hansen, c.1955, 81 x 24 In. .	3750
Wardrobe, Wegner, Oak, Lacquered, Chrome Plated Steel, Johannes Hansen, c.1955, 80 x 23 In. *illus*	3000
Washstand, Eastlake Style, Revolving Mirror, Marble, Cupboard Door, c.1890, 79 x 29 In...	270
Washstand, Federal, Mahogany, Backsplash, Lower Shelf, Drawer, Turned Legs, 34 x 17 In....	315
Washstand, Pine, Bowfront, Backsplash, Yellow Paint, Shelf, Drawer, c.1830, 36 x 18 In.. *illus*	644
Washstand, Pine, Gallery Top, Frieze Drawer, Turned Legs, Stretcher Shelf, 36 x 38 In.	640
Washstand, Sheraton, Pine, Mottled Paint, Bowl Hole, Shelf, Drawer, 1800s, 35 In...... *illus*	461
Washstand, Walnut, Marble Top, Shelves, Drawers, Doors, American, c.1890, 45 x 31 In.....	210
Wastebasket, Brass, Reticulated, Hexagonal, Leaves, Rope Shape Rim & Base, 11½ x 9½ In.. *illus*	63
Wastebasket, G. Stickley, Oak, Iron, Staves, Red Decal, Paper Label, N.Y., 14 In........... *illus*	5000
Whatnot Shelf, Mahogany, 4 Tiers, Drawer, Brass Casters, England, 1910s, 50 x 23 In........	625
Whatnot Shelf, Mahogany, Display, Lower Cabinet, Drawer, Caster Feet, c.1860, 63 x 20 In....	995
Window Seat, Claxton Chippendale Style, Upholstered, Turquoise, 25 x 53 x 18 In.............	240
Window Seat, Louis XVI Style, Gold Paint, Tufted Cushion, Italy, 1900s, 18 x 25 x 17 In., Pair......	313
Wine Cooler, Georgian Style, Mahogany, Octagonal, Brass, c.1910, 28 In. .... *illus*	450

G. ARGY-ROUSSEAU

G-ARGY-ROUSSEAU

G. Argy-Rousseau is the impressed mark used on a variety of glass objects in the Art Deco style. Gabriel Argy-Rousseau, born in 1885, was a French glass artist. In 1921, he formed a partnership that made pate-de-verre and other glass. The partnership ended in 1931 and he opened his own studio. He worked until 1952 and died in 1953.

Ashtray, Art Deco, Pate-De-Verre, Molded, Purple, c.1925, 5½ In.	1800
Veilleuse, Egg Shape, Rose, Pate-De-Verre, Wrought Iron, 1923, 6¾ In.	1084

GALLE

Galle

Galle was a designer who made glass, pottery, furniture, and other Art Nouveau items. Emile Galle founded his factory in France in 1874. After Galle's death in 1904, the firm continued to make glass and furniture until 1931. The *Galle* signature was used as a mark, but it was often hidden in the design of the object. Galle cameo and other types of glass are listed here. Pottery is in the next section. His furniture is listed in the Furniture category.

Jar, Egg Shape, Rooster, Fire Polished, Red Orange, Cameo, c.1900, 5¾ In. .... *illus*	3509
Perfume Bottle, Yellow Ground, Tulips, Cameo, Squeeze Bulb, Cord, Atomizer, c.1920, 7 In.. *illus*	420
Pillbox, Copper, Arts & Crafts Center Bands, Cameo, Late 1800s, 2 In.	182
Vase, Boat Shape, Ocean Scene, Red Orange, Cameo, c.1900, 5⅛ x 7¼ x 3 In.	2299
Vase, Bud, Bulbous, Carved Flowers, Cameo, Pink & Yellow Ground, Signed, 6 x 2 In..........	351
Vase, Bulbous, Lavender Flowers, Cameo, 5¼ In..	780
Vase, Cameo, Fire Polished, Morning Glory, Frosted White Ground, 7 In..........................	420
Vase, Cream To Peach, Yellow Overlay, Green & Brown Flowers, Bulbous, Signed, 9¾ x 6½ In. *illus*	6325
Vase, Cut Back, Leaves, Long Neck, Flared Rim, Cream Ground, Marked, 11 In....................	277
Vase, Cylindrical, Flowers, Ruby, Cameo, Bulbous Base, Flattened, 1800s, 17 In.......... *illus*	1260
Vase, Fire Polished Overlay, Broad Neck, Globular Body, Lotus Design, 14 In............... *illus*	3200
Vase, Frosted White, Orange Overlay, Carved Flowers, Cameo, Signed, 2½ x 2¾ In. ..... *illus*	202
Vase, Jug Shape, 2 Loop Handles, Pinecone, Branch, Ocher, Green, Cameo, 1904, 5¼ In.....	1063
Vase, Leaves, Beige Pink Ground, Silver Rim & Base, Cameo, c.1900, 4 In.	540
Vase, Leaves, Red, Clear Ground, Cameo, Signed, Nancy, France, 7 x 3 In.	2860
Vase, Pink & White Ground, Carved, Flower & Leaf Overlay, Cameo, 2 x 3 In.	350
Vase, Plums, Textured Leaves, Orange Shaded To Purple, Cameo, Oval, Flared Rim, Signed, 8 In...	1935
Vase, Red Flowers, Shaded Yellow, Cylindrical, Cameo, 1900s, 11¼ In.	1000
Vase, White To Green, Lavender Shade Overlay, Flowers & Leaves, Shouldered, Signed, 4¾ In. ..... *illus*	460

Furniture, Wastebasket, G. Stickley, Oak, Iron, Staves, Red Decal, Paper Label, N.Y., 14 In. $5,000

Toomey & Co. Auctioneers

Furniture, Wine Cooler, Georgian Style, Mahogany, Octagonal, Brass, c.1910, 28 In. $450

Garth's Auctioneers & Appraisers

Galle, Jar, Egg Shape, Rooster, Fire Polished, Red Orange, Cameo, c.1900, 5¾ In. $3,509

Fontaine's Auction Gallery

Galle, Perfume Bottle, Yellow Ground, Tulips, Cameo, Squeeze Bulb, Cord, Atomizer, c.1920, 7 In. $420

Treasureseeker Auctions

Galle, Vase, Cream To Peach, Yellow Overlay, Green & Brown Flowers, Bulbous, Signed, 9¾ x 6½ In. $6,325

Woody Auction

Galle, Vase, Cylindrical, Flowers, Ruby, Cameo, Bulbous Base, Flattened, 1800s, 17 In. $1,260

Brunk Auctions

Galle, Vase, Fire Polished Overlay, Broad Neck, Globular Body, Lotus Design, 14 In. $3,200

Nadeau's Auction Gallery

Galle, Vase, Frosted White, Orange Overlay, Carved Flowers, Cameo, Signed, 2½ x 2¾ In. $202

Woody Auction

Galle, Vase, White To Green, Lavender Shade Overlay, Flowers & Leaves, Shouldered, Signed, 4¾ In. $460

Woody Auction

229

Galle, Vase, White To Yellow, Cranberry Overlay, Cherry Branches, Short Neck, Cameo, Signed, 11¼ In.
$5,463

Woody Auction

Galle, Vase, White, Pink, Lavender Overlay, Leafy Branches, Stick, Squat Base, Signed, 11¼ In.
$460

Woody Auction

Galle Pottery, Figurine, Cat, Yellow, Green Glass Eyes, Blue & White Trim, Faience, Signed, E. Galle, 6 x 5 In.
$1,755

Thomaston Place Auction Galleries

Vase, White To Yellow, Cranberry Overlay, Cherry Branches, Short Neck, Cameo, Signed, 11¼ In. *illus*	5463
Vase, White, Pink, Lavender Overlay, Leafy Branches, Stick, Squat Base, Signed, 11¼ In. *illus*	460
Vase, Yellow, Red Overlay, Flowers, Cameo, Footed, 1900s, 7 x 5¼ In.	1658

GALLE POTTERY

Galle pottery was made by Emile Galle, the famous French designer, after 1874. The pieces were marked with the initials *E. G.* impressed, *Em. Galle Faiencerie de Nancy,* or a version of his signature. Galle is best known for his glass, listed above.

Cup & Saucer, Lid, Fruit Finial, Blue & Red Flowers & Birds, Twisted Handle, c.1870, 5 x 6 In.	219
Figurine, Cat, Yellow, Green Glass Eyes, Blue & White Trim, Faience, Signed, E. Galle, 6 x 5 In. *illus*	1755
Vase, Shaped Rim, Yellow & Brown Ground, Raised Bees, Flowers, Footed, c.1880, 11 x 11¾ In.	3438

GAME

Game collectors like all types of games. Of special interest are any board games or card games. Transogram and other company names are included in the description when known. Other games may be found listed under Card, Toy, or the name of the character or celebrity featured in the game. Gameboards without the game pieces are listed in the Gameboard category.

All Star Baseball, Green Playing Field, Multicolor, 3 Spinners, 1941, 19 x 12 In.	79
Backgammon Set, Inlaid Wood, Hinged Board, Lock Hook, 12 x 11⅞ In.	41
Basketball, Pinball, Plungers, Goal, Net, Wood Frame, France, 1930s-40s, 23 x 13 In.	118
Bowling, Puck Style, Formica, Black & White Tiles, United Supreme, 1970, 67 x 102 x 30 In. *illus*	633
Box, Poker Chips, Oak, Silver Trim, Enamel Horseshoe, Late 1800s, 3¾ x 13 x 11 In.	424
Bulls And Bears, McLoughlin Bros., Spinner, Play Money, Instructions, Board, 1883, 12 x 15 In. *illus*	6400
Chess Set, Box, Folding, Pieces, Holes, Miniature, 2½ x 7½ x 3½ In.	51
Chess Set, Civil War Generals, Board, Pieces, Hills National, Moroccan Leather, 1862, 14 x 15 In. *illus*	8125
Cribbage, Triangular Board, Inlaid, Some Playing Pins, Directions, 12½ In. *illus*	63
Dexterity, Desbeckers' Clothiers, Children Blowing Bubble, Pipes, Embossed, 2 In.	71
Dexterity, Man In The Moon, Courting Couple On Boat, Tin, Cardboard Back, Metal Frame, 2 In. *illus*	59
Dexterity, Scull's Coffee, Waiter, Orange Ground, 2 In.	59
Dexterity, Motorcycle, Norton, Metal Frame, Mirrored Back, England, 1937, 2 In. *illus*	207
Invasion Kit, Tiles, Red & White, Mounted, No. 13, Invader, Japan, 9¾ x 11¼ In.	6300
Mahjong, Set, Leather Case, Carved Tiles, Racks, 4 Dice, Key, Chinese, 1939, 11 x 11 x⅞ In.	201
Marbelator, Marble Roller, School House Shape, Black & Red, Steel, 22½ x 21 In., Pair	554
Parlor, Shooting Gallery, Indian Targets, Glass Top, Wood Base, Metal Figures & Gun, 12 x 3 In.	768
Puzzle, Block, Ball, Beech, Oak, Lacquered Wood, Sori Yanagi, Japan, c.1965, 4 x 4 x 4 In., Pair.	813
Puzzle, St. Nicholas, Santa & Reindeer, McLoughlin Bros., N.Y., Late 1800s, 12 x 9 In. *illus*	1625
Shooting Gallery, 7 Birds, Rack, Cast Iron, Painted, Carnival, 4 x 35½ x 2 In.	585
Steeple Chase, Spinners, Wood Tokens, Metal Pieces, McLoughlin Bros., Board, c.1900, 12 x 13 In.	565
Target, Cap & Ball, Clown, Children, Pitching, Die Cut, Chad Valley Works, England, Box, 10 x 14 In.	71

GAME PLATE

Game plates are plates of any make decorated with pictures of birds, animals, or fish. The game plates usually came in sets consisting of 12 dishes and a serving platter. These sets were most popular during the 1880s.

Game Birds, Set, Tray, Plates, Rose Border, Bavaria, 12½-In. Tray, 9-In. Plates, 15 Piece	300

GAMEBOARD

Gameboard collectors look for just the board without the game pieces. The boards are collected as folk art or decorations. Gameboards that are part of a complete game are listed in the Game category.

Automobile Race, McLoughlin Bros., Frame, Early 1900s, 31½ x 17 In.	469
Baseball, BOP, Wood Framework, Remco, 49 x 21 In. *illus*	73

Game, Bowling, Puck Style, Formica, Black & White Tiles, United Supreme, 1970, 67 x 102 x 30 In.
$633

Donley Auctions

Game, Bulls And Bears, McLoughlin Bros., Spinner, Play Money, Instructions, Board, 1883, 12 x 15 In.
$6,400

New Haven Auctions

Game, Chess Set, Civil War Generals, Board, Pieces, Hills National, Moroccan Leather, 1862, 14 x 15 In.
$8,125

Hindman

Game, Cribbage, Triangular Board, Inlaid, Some Playing Pins, Directions, 12 ½ In.
$63

Turner Auctions + Appraisals

Game, Dexterity, Man In The Moon, Courting Couple On Boat, Tin, Cardboard Back, Metal Frame, 2 In.
$59

Stony Ridge Auction

Game, Dexterity, Motorcycle, Norton, Metal Frame, Mirrored Back, England, 1937, 2 In.
$207

Stony Ridge Auction

Game, Puzzle, St. Nicholas, Santa & Reindeer, McLoughlin Bros., N.Y., Late 1800s, 12 x 9 In.
$1,625

Hindman

> **TIP**
> *Printed gameboards from the 1940s–60s fade very quickly. Older printing seems to be damaged less by exposure to ultraviolet light.*

G

Gameboard, Baseball, BOP, Wood Framework, Remco, 49 x 21 In.
$73

Hartzell's Auction Gallery Inc.

Gameboard, Checkers, Chess, Parcheesi, Red Geometric, White Ground, Folk Art, 20½ x 20 In.
$540

Alderfer Auction Company

Gameboard, Checkers, Pine, Octagonal, Tabletop, Painted, Green Squares, 1850s, 19½ x 27 In.
$330

Garth's Auctioneers & Appraisers

Gameboard, Chess, Checkers, Marbleized Slate, 4 Stars In Corners, Metal Frame, 22 x 22 In.
$254

Hartzell's Auction Gallery Inc.

Gameboard, Chinese Checkers, Wood, Painted, Multicolor, c.1900, 23 x 23 x 2 In.
$406

New Haven Auctions

Gameboard, Football, Linoleum, Stenciled Design, Multicolor, Frame, c.1915, 19 x 19 In.
$156

Garth's Auctioneers & Appraisers

Box, Checkerboard & Backgammon, Slide Out, Burl, Brass Handles, 1800s, 15 x 10 x 7 In...	505
Checkers, Chess, Parcheesi, Red Geometric, White Ground, Folk Art, 20 1/2 x 20 In......*illus*	540
Checkers, Folk Art, Slate, Red & Black Squares, Blue Border, Birds, c.1900, 20 x 20 In........	100
Checkers, Fox & Geese, Black & White, Reddish Brown Border, 1800s, 12 x 12 In................	500
Checkers, Painted, Mustard & Black Squares, Green Border, 19th Century, 16 x 16 In........	218
Checkers, Parcheesi, 2-Sided, Red & White Squares, Multicolor, Folk Art, 20 1/2 x 20 In......	565
Checkers, Pine, Octagonal, Tabletop, Painted, Green Squares, 1850s, 19 1/2 x 27 In......*illus*	330
Checkers, Pine, Sandy Red, Flat Black, Folk Art, Painted, JLT, 1800s, 30 x 20 In................	468
Chess, Checkers, Marbleized Slate, 4 Stars In Corners, Metal Frame, 22 x 22 In..........*illus*	254
Chess, Checkers, Round, Malachite, Marble, Brassbound, 1800s, 12 In...........................	244
Chess, Octagonal, Patchwork Inlay, Marble, Stone, Pietra Dura, Italy, Tabletop, 29 1/2 x 3/4 In. .	1989
Chinese Checkers, Painted, Slate, Brown Ground, c.1900, 17 x 17 In.	88
Chinese Checkers, Wood, Painted, Multicolor, c.1900, 23 x 23 x 2 In.........................*illus*	406
Cribbage, Hedgehog, Cast Iron, Stenciled, John Gill, c.1873, 2 x 11 3/4 In.	420
Football, Linoleum, Stenciled Design, Multicolor, Frame, c.1915, 19 x 19 In.................*illus*	156
Lion Coffee, Green Squares, Cream Ground, Wood, Frame, 1900s, 27 x 18 In.	188
Little Goldenlocks & The 3 Bears, McLoughlin Brothers, Frame, 20 1/2 x 21 1/2 In.	502
Numbers, Horse Heads In Corners, Painted, Laminated Panel, c.1900, 15 3/4 x 15 3/4 In.........	1188
Parcheesi, Checkers On Reverse, Folding, Wood Panels, Paint, Silver Leaf, 21 x 21 In.	1125
Parcheesi, Folding, Painted, Wood Panel, White Ground, c.1920, 24 x 23 In.	625
Parcheesi, Pine, Painted, Multicolor, Applied Border, Early 1900s, 16 x 18 In.	250
Parcheesi, Wood, Painted, 2-Sided, Multicolor Playing Fields, 1800s, 19 x 19 In....................	3068
Pinball, Arched, Painted, Multicolor, Geometric Design, Early 1900s, 30 x 15 In.	2125
Pine, Book Shape, Backgammon Interior, Checkerboard Exterior, Late 1800s, 3 x 19 x 9 In..	192
Red & Black Squares, Green Border, Painted, Drawer, Pieces, 1800s, 3 x 14 x 15 In.	594
Slate, Made From Tabletop, Egg & Dart Design, Oak Frame, 24 x 24 In.................................	100
Suit Of Cards, Cat, Circles, Hearts, Spades, Diamond, Club, Wood, A.K., 1910, 21 x 21 In. ...	406
Wood, Painted, Diamond, Triangle Border, Multicolor, Late 1800s, 36 1/2 x 22 3/4 In.	2520

GARDEN

Garden furnishings have been popular for centuries. The stone, cement, or metal statues, urns and fountains, sundials, small figurines, and wire, iron, or rustic furniture are included in this category. Many of the metal pieces have been made continuously for years.

Arbor, Seat, Arch, Curlicue, S-Scroll, Metal, 84 x 41 x 93 In.	2596
Armillary, Sphere, Man Carrying, Rings, Arrow, Cast Stone Base, 57 In......................*illus*	797
Basin, Tapered Sides, Archaic Dragon, Phoenix, Molded Base, Chinese, 11 x 13 In.......*illus*	1755
Bench, Back & Seat Slats, Square Feet, Teak, 64 In..	615
Bench, Backrest, Cast Birds, Arms, Wrought Iron, 48 x 18 x 37 In.	1121
Bench, Carved, Figural Bear Supports, Black Forest, Wood, 35 x 56 x 24 In., 3 Piece	688
Bench, Classical Style, Carved, Acanthus Leaves, Centaurs, Carrara Marble, 40 x 60 x 16 In........	7500
Bench, Leaves & Vines, White Paint, Openwork Back, Cast Iron, 37 x 69 x 18 In.	1610
Bench, Leaves, Flowers, Green, Cast Iron, 28 x 41 x 14 In...	748
Bench, Painted, Curtain Pattern, Rosette Crest, Arms, Iron, Late 1800s, 38 x 33 x 18 In., 3 Piece..	2813
Bench, Renaissance Revival, Scrolls, Female Mask, Cast Iron, Late 1800s, 32 x 44 In., Pair	2000
Bench, Sculptured Back, Curved Arms, Hairpin Legs, Wire, Late 1800s, 36 x 39 x 24 In.......	390
Bench, Slat Back, Black Paint, Stretcher Base, Square Legs, 35 x 75 x 20 1/2 In.	75
Bench, White Paint, Square Back, Pad Feet, Cast Iron, Victorian, 37 x 34 x 24 In.	878
Bench, Women's Heads Crest, Floral Backs & Ends, Slat Seat, Iron, c.1880, 17 x 34 x 47 In. ...*illus*	1440
Bench, Yellow Paint, Pleather Cushion, Wrought Iron, John Salterini, 30 x 54 x 32 In.	113
Birdbath, Round Basin, Pedestal, Granite, Rough Hewn, 2 Parts, 24 In. ....*illus*	2457
Birdbath, Tree Branches, Carved Stone, 1900s, 23 1/2 x 12 In.	478
Birdhouse, Cottage, Green, Silver Roof, 2 Openings, Chimney, Wood, 14 x 9 x 14 In....*illus*	55
Chair, Sunburst, Bronze, Spring Steel, Rolled Arms, Francois Carre, c.1930s, 30 In., Pair ...*illus*	1287
Chair, Sunwest, Rocking Swivel, Club, Ottoman, Wicker, Sunbrella Cushions, 34 x 35 x 36 In., Pair ...	1872
Chaise Longue, Painted, Sculptured Arms, Walnut Frame, Robert Mitchell, 1920s, 38 x 29 x 56 In....	120
Chaise Longue, Richard Schultz, Upholstered, Steel, Rubber Wheels, Knoll, c.1963, 14 x 77 x 29 In.	1063
Figure, Bear, Walking, Cast Concrete, c.1910, 11 x 6 x 8 1/2 In.	615
Figure, Bird, Standing, Painted, Iron, Early 1900s, 13 x 15 x 6 In..	826

Garden, Armillary, Sphere, Man Carrying, Rings, Arrow, Cast Stone Base, 57 In.
$797

Copake Auction

Garden, Basin, Tapered Sides, Archaic Dragon, Phoenix, Molded Base, Chinese, 11 x 13 In.
$1,755

Thomaston Place Auction Galleries

Garden, Bench, Women's Heads Crest, Floral Backs & Ends, Slat Seat, Iron, c.1880, 17 x 34 x 47 In.
$1,440

Garth's Auctioneers & Appraisers

Garden, Birdbath, Round Basin, Pedestal, Granite, Rough Hewn, 2 Parts, 24 In.
$2,457

Thomaston Place Auction Galleries

Garden, Birdhouse, Cottage, Green, Silver Roof, 2 Openings, Chimney, Wood, 14 x 9 x 14 In.
$55

Apple Tree Auction Center

Garden, Chair, Sunburst, Bronze, Spring Steel, Rolled Arms, Francois Carre, c.1930s, 30 In., Pair
$1,287

Thomaston Place Auction Galleries

Garden, Figure, Lion, White, Seated, Cast Cement, 21 x 12 In., Pair
$420

Nadeau's Auction Gallery

Garden, Figure, Rabbit, Lying Down, Lawn Ornament, Aluminum, Verde Antique Finish, 17 In.
$173

Merrill's Auctions

Garden, Fountain, Aqua Scape, Frogs, Water Lilies, Bronze, Patina, 17 x 13 x 10 In.
$819

Thomaston Place Auction Galleries

Garden, Fountain, Bronze, Guanyin Figure, Dragon Supports, Paw Feet, Chinese, 64 x 36 In.
$3,520

Roland NY Auctioneers & Appraisers

Garden, Fountain, Swan, Standing, Open Wings, Bronze, Patina, Shaped Base, 40 x 51 In.
$3,120

Abington Auction Gallery

Garden, Gate, Napoleon III Style, Latticework, Gilt Lions, Acanthus Scroll, Iron, 108 x 156 In., Pair
$2,440

Neal Auction Company

Figure, Boundary Marker, Carved, Folk Art, Stone, c.1900, 22½ x 7 x 5 In., Pair	875
Figure, Buddhistic Lion, Bronze, Green Patina, 1950s, 36 x 40 x 20 In., Pair	1500
Figure, Cherub, Green, Painted, Pedestal, Cast Iron, 2 Parts, 52½ In.	2223
Figure, Dog, Seated, Flower Basket, Cast Iron, England, 1900s, 24 In., Pair	1089
Figure, Dragonfly, Openwork, 4 Wings, Wrought Iron, 12 x 30 x 16 In.	50
Figure, Foo Dogs, White Marble, 18 x 7¼ In., Pair	720
Figure, Girl, Standing, Butterfly On Wrist, Lead, 43 In.	4500
Figure, Lion, Glazed, Signed, Amphora, Porcelain, c.1910, 14½ x 21 x 8½ In.	185
Figure, Lion, Lying Down, Rectangular Base, Stone, 11 x 8 x 17 In., Pair	156
Figure, Lion, Seated, Rectangular Base, Concrete, 13 In.	209
Figure, Lion, White, Seated, Cast Cement, 21 x 12 In., Pair......*illus*	420
Figure, Maiden, Bonnet, Rectangular Base, Iron, 53 x 32½ In.	200
Figure, Rabbit, Lying Down, Lawn Ornament, Aluminum, Verde Antique Finish, 17 In.*illus*	173
Figure, Sphinx, White Glaze, Base, Ceramic, Continental, 14¼ In.	375
Figure, Sprite, Boy, Playing Flute, Standing On Shell Base, Bronze, 53 In.	2160
Figure, Virgin Mary, Standing, Oxidized, Domed Base, Cast Iron, 22½ In.	244
Fountain, Aqua Scape, Frogs, Water Lilies, Bronze, Patina, 17 x 13 x 10 In.....*illus*	819
Fountain, Bronze, Guanyin Figure, Dragon Supports, Paw Feet, Chinese, 64 x 36 In..*illus*	3520
Fountain, Shell Shape Basin, 2 Dolphins Base, Marble, Carved, Bronze Boy, 3 Parts, 44 x 17 In.	1380
Fountain, Swan, Standing, Open Wings, Bronze, Patina, Shaped Base, 40 x 51 In.......*illus*	3120
Fountain, Wall, Central Shell, Cherub Supports, Bronze, France, 27½ x 51 In.	3456
Gate, Napoleon III Style, Latticework, Gilt Lions, Acanthus Scroll, Iron, 108 x 156 In., Pair..*illus*	2440
Gate, Scrolls, Square Posts, Serpentine Grid, Iron, America, Late 1800s, 72 x 35½ In.	688
Hitching Post, Gnome, Painted, Red Suit, Square Base, Cast Iron, 37 x 16 x 16 In. .....*illus*	5440
Hitching Post, Jockey, Holding Arm Out, Aluminum, Painted, Green Base, 1900s, 45 In..*illus*	1440
Jardiniere, Green Interior Glaze, Multicolor Exterior, Raised Vases, Pottery, 7 x 9 In.	246
Lawn Jockey, Holding Lantern, Square Base, Painted, Cast Metal, 46 In.	900
Love Seat, Plaque, Bird Lady, Black Paint, Openwork Back, Ball Finial, Cast Iron, 36 x 42 x 14 In.	1955
Ornament, Eagle, Spread Wings, Pedestal Support, Square Base, Concrete, 49½ x 3 x 33 In.	2040
Ornament, Griffin Shape, White Paint, Base Plinths, Concrete, c.1950, 56 x 24 x 18 In., Pair	480
Pedestal, Green Paint, Faces Design, Cylindrical, Iron, 1900s, 31¾ x 19 In.	125
Pedestal, Monkey, Seated, Circular Plinth Base, Cast Stone, c.1960, 25 In. ...*illus*	438
Plant Stand, see also Furniture, Stand, Plant	
Planter, Basket Style, Crossed Arrows, Stand, Circular Base, Wrought Iron, 51 x 12 In.	219
Planter, Fishbowl, Cherry Blossom, Blue & White, Chinese, 14½ x 12½ In.....*illus*	944
Planter, Frog Shape, Green Paint, Wirework, Mid 1900s, 21 x 32 x 32 In., Pair	2394
Planter, Pedestal, Flowerpots, Gothic Arches, Star Base, Cast Iron, 7 x 8 In., Pair	136
Planter, Pottery, Scratch Design, Brown Ground, David Cressey, c.1963, 11 In.	938
Planter, Rectangular, Metal Liners, Footed, Iron, 14½ x 34 In., Pair	500
Planter, Rectangular, Twisted Columns, Wrought Iron, c.1915, 31 x 44 x 17 In.....*illus*	1063
Planter, Stand, Pinecones, Twisted Branch Base, Arts & Crafts, Wood, 32 x 19 x 11 In.	1152
Planter, Turned Stem, Tripod Base, Scroll Feet, Bronze, 1700s, 28 x 15 In.	644
Porch Swing, Wood, Combination Swing & Cradle, Salesman's Sample, 15 x 6 x 6 In. *illus*	1800
Sculpture, Pecheur, Fisherman, Basket, Splayed Legs, Terra-Cotta, Eugene Blot, 9 x 6 x 7 In.	293
Sculpture, Sleeping Girl, Bed, Brown Ground, Concrete, 1900s, 16 x 24 x 14 In.	63
Sculpture, Young Man, Standing, Dog, Tree, Marble, 1900s, 34 x 13 x 7 In.	192
Seat, Bulbous, Scenic, Blue & White, Porcelain, Cantonese, Mid 1800s, 18 x 12 In.	1989
Seat, Drum Shape, Landscape, Multicolor, Porcelain, Chinese, Mid 1900s, 18 x 13 In., Pair	270
Seat, Elephant Shape, Porcelain, Chinese, Late 1800s, 22 x 25 x 10 In.	438
Seat, Elephant Shape, Standing, Trunk Down, Blanc De Chine, 21 x 17 In.	71
Seat, Elephant, Multicolor Glaze, Pottery, Chinese, 20 x 14½ In., Pair .....*illus*	1495
Seat, Flambe, Barrel Shape, Coin Medallions, Berry Glaze, Porcelain, Chinese, 12 x 14 In., Pair	300
Seat, Hexagonal Sides, Medallions, Brass, Chinese, c.1950, 15½ In. .....*illus*	259
Seat, Octagonal, White, Flowers & Birds, Chinese Blue, Porcelain, 1900s, 18 x 13 In., Pair	1658
Seat, Pale Tan, White, Crackle Glaze, Hexagonal, Pierced Design, Chinese, 17 x 12 x 11 In., Pair	156
Seat, Turquoise Glaze, Square Top, Open Sides, Pottery, Late 1900s, 18 x 12 x 12 In., Pair	406
Seat, White Flowers, Cobalt Blue Ground, Drum Shape, Porcelain, Chinese, 18 x 13 In.. *illus*	2160
Sphere, Stepped Base, Granite, 21 x 17 In., Pair	1024
Sprinkler, Duck Shape, White, Pink Beak & Feet, Painted, Cast Iron, Early 1900s, 8 x 13 In.....*illus*	250
Sprinkler, Hummingbird Design, Ornamental, Spikes, Copper, 33½ In.	30
Stool, Barrel Shape, Chinoiserie, Sgraffito, Scrolls, Lacquered, Black, 1900s, 17 x 9⅞ In.	163
Stool, Blue & White, Flowers, Leaves, Cylindrical, Porcelain, Chinese, 6 x 5 In.	63

Garden, Hitching Post, Gnome, Painted, Red Suit, Square Base, Cast Iron, 37 x 16 x 16 In.
$5,440

Rachel Davis Fine Arts

Garden, Hitching Post, Jockey, Holding Arm Out, Aluminum, Painted, Green Base, 1900s, 45 In.
$1,440

Selkirk Auctioneers & Appraisers

Garden, Pedestal, Monkey, Seated, Circular Plinth Base, Cast Stone, c.1960, 25 In.
$438

New Haven Auctions

Garden, Planter, Fishbowl, Cherry Blossom, Blue & White, Chinese, 14½ x 12½ In.
$944

Bunch Auctions

Garden, Planter, Rectangular, Twisted Columns, Wrought Iron, c.1915, 31 x 44 x 17 In.
$1,063

John Moran Auctioneers

Garden, Porch Swing, Wood, Combination Swing & Cradle, Salesman's Sample, 15 x 6 x 6 In.
$1,800

Chupp Auctions & Real Estate, LLC

Garden, Seat, Elephant, Multicolor Glaze, Pottery, Chinese, 20 x 14½ In., Pair
$1,495

Merrill's Auctions

TIP

Set heavy garden urns or statues on a foundation, usually a cement block set in the ground.

Garden, Seat, Hexagonal Sides, Medallions, Brass, Chinese, c.1950, 15½ In.
$259

Merrill's Auctions

Garden, Seat, White Flowers, Cobalt Blue Ground, Drum Shape, Porcelain, Chinese, 18 x 13 In.
$2,160

Abington Auction Gallery

Stool, Flowers, Multicolor, Enameled, Porcelain, Chinese, 12 x 12 x 18 In.	177
Sundial, Bronze, Octagonal Plate, Roman Numerals, Directional, Sun Face, c.1702, 5 In.	610
Sundial, Horizontal, Circular Base, Bronze, Adams London, England, 1700s, 9¾ In. *illus*	1320
Sundial, Orrery, Armillary, Orb Shape, Bent Metal Bands, Base, Roman Numerals, 44 x 51 In.	720
Sundial, Triangle, Roman Numerals, Circular Base, Iron, S. Moore, Kensington, Conn., 10 In.	983
Table, Dragon Legs, Tripod Feet, Cast Iron, 25½ x 20 In.	1265
Table, Round Stone Top, Iron Base, 3-Footed, 30 x 44 In. *illus*	1125
Urn, Blue Paint, Faces & Handles, On Base, Cast Iron, 41 x 19 In., Pair	690
Urn, Campana Form, Festoons, Wrought Iron, Early 1900s, 17½ x 13 In., Pair	270
Urn, Egg & Dart Border, Curved Rim, Black Ground, Stand Base, Cast Iron, 46 x 22 In., Pair	633
Urn, Egg & Dart, Flared Rim, Gray Paint, Square Base, Cast Iron, 32 x 25 In., Pair	563
Urn, Egyptian Revival, Nude Sphinxes, Lion's Mask, Square Base, Metal, 1800s, 33 x 34 In., Pair	2142
Urn, Leafy Vine, Berries, Textured Ground, Gilt, Ebonized, Cast Metal, 1800s, 9¾ In.	163
Urn, Majolica Style, Brown Glaze, Egg & Dart Base, Earthenware, 1900s, 53 In., Pair *illus*	3328
Urn, Neoclassical Shape, Melon Sided, Integral Square Base, Cast Iron, 18 x 13 In., Pair *illus*	497
Urn, Neoclassical, Campana Form, Hole For Drainage, Stone, Cast, 1950, 19 In., Pair	500
Urn, Neoclassical, Gadroon Borders, Elephant Handles, Iron, 1900s, 16 x 24 x 19 In., Pair	630
Urn, Oval, Lotus Leaves, Leafy, Reed Pedestal, Concrete, 1960s, 24 x 39 In.	360
Urn, With Bases, Old Painted Surface, Cast Iron, 1900s, 39½ x 28 In., Pair	1076

GAUDY DUTCH

Gaudy Dutch pottery was made in England for the American market from about 1810 to 1820. It is a white earthenware with Imari-style decorations of red, blue, green, yellow, and black. Only sixteen patterns of Gaudy Dutch were made: Butterfly, Carnation, Dahlia, Double Rose, Dove, Grape, Leaf, Oyster, Primrose, Single Rose, Strawflower, Sunflower, Urn, War Bonnet, Zinnia, and No Name. Other similar wares are called Gaudy Ironstone and Gaudy Welsh.

Grape pattern
1810–1820

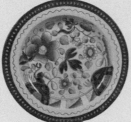
Single Rose pattern
1810–1820

War Bonnet pattern
1810–1820

Plate, Soup, War Bonnet, Soft Paste, Child's, 7 In.	212 to 354
Teapot, Lid, Double Rose, Pinched Handle, Square Base, Early 1800s, 6 In.	299
Waste Bowl, Leaf, Early 1800s, 3¼ x 6¼ In.	2749

GAUDY IRONSTONE

Gaudy ironstone is the collector's name for the ironstone wares with the bright patterns similar to Gaudy Dutch. It was made in England for the American market after 1850. There may be other examples found in the listing for Ironstone or under the name of the ceramic factory.

Tea Set, Seeing Eye, 2 Plates, 4 Cups & Saucers, 6 Piece	130

GAUDY WELSH

Gaudy Welsh is an Imari-decorated earthenware with red, blue, green, and gold decorations. Most Gaudy Welsh was made in England for the American market. It was made from 1820 to about 1860.

Coffeepot, Dome Lid, Urn Pattern, Red, Blue, Green, Gilt, Octagonal, Footed, 9 In.	12
Cracker Jar, Silvertone Lid & Bail, Red & Blue Flowers, Baluster Shape, Scalloped Base, 7 In.	18
Pitcher, Snake Handle, Red & Blue Flowers, Scalloped Rim, Octagonal, 5¾ In.	25

TIP
The optimum depth of a birdbath is 2½ inches.

G

Garden, Sprinkler, Duck Shape, White, Pink Beak & Feet, Painted, Cast Iron, Early 1900s, 8 x 13 In.
$250

Hindman

Garden, Sundial, Horizontal, Circular Base, Bronze, Adams London, England, 1700s, 9¾ In.
$1,320

Bonhams

Garden, Table, Round Stone Top, Iron Base, 3-Footed, 30 x 44 In.
$1,125

Nadeau's Auction Gallery

GEISHA GIRL

Garden, Urn, Majolica Style, Brown Glaze, Egg & Dart Base, Earthenware, 1900s, 53 In., Pair
$3,328

Ahlers & Ogletree Auction Gallery

TIP

Save your broken dishes, vases, and other decorative china to make mosaic stepping stones or tabletops for your garden. Chipped vases can still be turned upside down for toad homes.

Garden, Urn, Neoclassical Shape, Melon Sided, Integral Square Base, Cast Iron, 18 x 13 In., Pair
$497

Thomaston Placc Auction Galleries

G

GEISHA GIRL

Geisha girl porcelain was made for export in the late nineteenth century in Japan. It was an inexpensive porcelain often sold in dime stores or used as free premiums. Pieces are sometimes marked with the name of a store. Japanese ladies in kimonos are pictured on the dishes. There are over 125 recorded patterns. Borders of red, blue, green, gold, brown, or several of these colors were used. Modern reproductions are being made.

Dish, Lemon Shape, 2 Women, Green Scalloped Rim, 1920s, 6 ½ In.	13
Plate, Figures, Trees, Flowers, Multicolor, Red Rim, Wall Hanging, 1921, 9 ⅞ In.	15
Tea Set, Creamer, Green Rim & Handle, 1920s, 2 ¾ x 3 ½ x 4 In.	13

GEORG JENSEN

Georg Jensen (1866–1935) began his silver company in Copenhagen, Denmark, in 1904. He combined his training as a sculptor with metalsmithing to make objects that were both useful and original. There are now Georg Jensen stores in many countries. Georg Jensen Silversmiths merged with Royal Copenhagen in 1985. It was sold to Investcorp in 2012. The Georg Jensen company continues to make and sell silver, jewelry, watches, and high-end homewares.

Georg Jensen 1925–1932   Georg Jensen 1933–1944   Georg Jensen 1945–present

Asparagus Tongs, Silver, Acorn, c.1940, 7 ⅜ In. *illus*	2000
Bowl, Centerpiece, Silver, Deep, Footed, 3 x 13 In. *illus*	4182
Bowl, Silver, Shell Shape, Allan Scharff, 1900s, 4 In.	1375
Bracelet, Bangle, Silver, Smooth Undulating Shape, No. 501, 6 ¾ In.	397
Bracelet, Link, Silver, 5 Buds, Alternating Coral Cabochons, 7 ¼ In.	610
Bracelet, Link, Silver, 6 Beaded Buds, Straight Links, No. 100, 7 ¼ In.	183
Bracelet, Toggle, Silver, 6 Rounded Triangles, 3 Holes Each, Round Links, 7 In.	519
Candelabrum, 2-Light, Silver, Model 1296C, Granite Base, Jorgen Henrik Moller, 1986, 7 In. *illus*	3500
Candelabrum, 2-Light, Silver, Pomegranate, c.1920-27, 8 x 10 x 4 In.	4688
Cheese Plane, Silver, Acanthus, Stainless Steel Slit Blade, Johan Rohde, 8 In.	140
Cigarette Holder, Silver, Acorn, 1950s, 3 In.	250
Compote, Silver, Flared Rim, Mounted, Marked, 4 x 4 ½ In.	570
Dish, Silver, 2 Shell Shape Handles, Ring Feet, 1945, 6 ¼ In., Pair	344
Fish Set, Silver, Chased, Cutouts, 2 Fish On Handle, Mussel Ends, c.1914, 2 Piece	1380
Pepper Mill, Silver, Ebony Mounted Top, Henning Koppel, Copenhagen, c.1950, 3 ¼ In.	2000
Pepper Mill, Steel, Ebony, Henning Koppel, 1978, 2 ½ x 2 ½ In. *illus*	750
Pin, Butterflies, Flowers, Sterling Silver, Denmark, Marked, 2 ⅛ In.	281
Pitcher, Silver, Grapes, Ebony Handle, Footed, c.1950, 9 ⅜ In.	5313
Poultry Shears, Silver, Acorn, Weighted Handles, Stainless Blades, 10 In.	308
Ring, Lapis, Oval, Bezel Set, Sterling Silver, Raised Oval Disc, Denmark, 1970s, Size 6	250
Salad Set, Silver, Cactus Pattern, Black Horn Ends, c.1944, Fork 9 ⅜ In.	210
Salt Cellar, Shell Shape Handles, Marked, 3 In., Pair	330
Sauceboat, Stand, Silver, Johan Rohde, c.1950, 4 ½ x 6 ½ In. *illus*	1000
Serving Dish, Lid, Silver, Henning Koppel, c.1965, 4 ¼ x 11 ¾ In. *illus*	2813
Sugar Basket, Silver, Gold Wash, Floral Handle & Base, c.1925-31, 4 x 3 In.	510
Sugar Tongs, Silver, Cactus, Lever, 1945, 3 ½ In.	63
Teapot, Silver, Black Finial & Handle, Johan Rohde, c.1950, 10 In. *illus*	3750

GIBSON GIRL

Gibson Girl black-and-blue decorated plates were made in the early 1900s. Twenty-four different 10 ½-inch plates were made by the Royal

Georg Jensen, Asparagus Tongs, Silver, Acorn, c.1940, 7 3/8 In.
$2,000

Hindman

Georg Jensen, Bowl, Centerpiece, Silver, Deep, Footed, 3 x 13 In.
$4,182

Pook & Pook

Jensen Silver, Jewelry and Porcelain
The Georg Jensen company was founded in Denmark in 1904. In 1918, the shop in Paris opened, followed by London (1921), New York (1924), Brussels (1925), and Barcelona (1935). Georg Jensen Company is known for its hollow ware and jewelry.

Georg Jensen, Candelabrum, 2-Light, Silver, Model 1296C, Granite Base, Jorgen Henrik Moller, 1986, 7 In.
$3,500

Wright

Georg Jensen, Pepper Mill, Steel, Ebony, Henning Koppel, 1978, 2 1/2 x 2 1/2 In.
$750

Wright

Georg Jensen, Sauceboat, Stand, Silver, Johan Rohde, c.1950, 4 1/2 x 6 1/2 In
$1,000

G

Hindman

Georg Jensen, Serving Dish, Lid, Silver, Henning Koppel, c.1965, 4 1/4 x 11 3/4 In.
$2,813

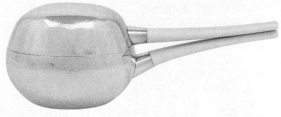

Hindman

Georg Jensen, Teapot, Silver, Black Finial & Handle, Johan Rohde, c.1950, 10 In.
$3,750

Hindman

Girl Scout, Doll, Georgene, Brownie, Cloth, Molded & Painted Face, Blond Braided Hair, 13 In.
$37

Ron Rhoads Auctioneers

Girl Scout, Doll, Terri Lee, Molded & Painted Face, Light Brown Braided Hair, 5-Piece Body, 16 In.
$107

Apple Tree Auction Center

Girl Scout, Pin, Figural, Scout Holding Flag, Green Uniform Dress, Brown Hair, Celluloid, 1940s
$14

Sabertooth Auctions

> **TIP**
> Glass becomes cloudy if not kept completely dry when not in use. That is why decanters and vases often discolor.

Glass-Art, Vase, Ribbed, Cut Velvet, White Interior, Pink Exterior, 4 x 5¾ In.
$150

Woody Auction

Glass-Blown, Ball, Gazing, Mercury Glass, Attached Stand, Shaped Base, 22½ In.
$1,230

Pook & Pook

Glass-Blown, Celery Vase, Pillar Mold, Baluster Stem, Disc Foot, Clear, Pittsburgh, c.1850, 9¾ In.
$150

Garth's Auctioneers & Appraisers

Glass-Art, Vase, Tree & Sailboat, Yellow & Orange Ground, Window Box Shape, 3 x 5 x 3 In.
$550

Woody Auction

Doulton pottery at Lambeth, England. These pictured scenes from the book *A Widow and Her Friends* by Charles Dana Gibson. Another set of twelve 9-inch plates featuring pictures of the heads of Gibson Girls had all-blue decoration. Many other items also pictured the famous Gibson Girl.

Plate, A Quiet Dinner With Dr. Bottles, White & Blue, Royal Doulton, 1815, 10¼ In............	89
Print, Portrait, Mixed Media Collage, Multicolor, On Canvas, 12 x 12 In................................	88
Print, Straight Through The Heart, Fencing, Black & White, Red Heart, 8 x 10 In...............	21

GIRL SCOUT

Girl Scout collectors search for anything pertaining to the Girl Scouts, including uniforms, publications, and old cookie boxes. The Girl Scout movement started in 1912, two years after the Boy Scouts. It began under Juliette Gordon Low of Savannah, Georgia. The first Girl Scout cookies were sold in 1928.

Calendar, 1964, Girl Scouts In Action..	43
Charm, Logo, Sterling Silver, ⅞ x ⅞ In.	32
Doll, Georgene, Brownie, Cloth, Molded & Painted Face, Blond Braided Hair, 13 In...... *illus*	37
Doll, Terri Lee, Molded & Painted Face, Light Brown Braided Hair, 5-Piece Body, 16 In.*illus*	107
Handbook, Hardcover, Intermediate Program, Green, Yellow, 1945	64
Pin, Figural, Scout Holding Flag, Green Uniform Dress, Brown Hair, Celluloid, 1940s.. *illus*	14

GLASS-ART

Art glass means any of the many forms of glassware made during the late nineteenth or early twentieth century. These wares were expensive when they were first made and production was limited. Art glass is not the typical commercial glass that was made in large quantities, and most of the art glass was produced by hand methods. Later twentieth-century glass is listed under Glass-Contemporary, Glass-Midcentury, or Glass-Venetian. Even more art glass may be found in categories such as Burmese, Cameo Glass, Tiffany, and other factory names.

Bowl, Abalone Shell Shape, Yellow, Late 1800s, 2 x 11 x 8 In...	63
Bowl, Iridescent, White & Brown, Swirl Design, 3 x 16 In...	25
Bowl, Lid, White Glass Stem Finial, Apple Shape, Tiffany Blue, Continental, 1900s, 7½ In..	121
Centerpiece, Ruffled Rim, Wide Cobalt Border, Gold Highlights, 24½ In.............................	96
Epergne, 7 Cameo Cut Vases, Etched Pink, Gilt Metal Frame, 13½ In., Pair	2304
Epergne, Brass, Flower Shape Rim, Clear Glass, 13 In...	173
Figurine, Egret, Clear Beak, Green, Yellow, Amethyst Legs, Italy, Mid 1900s, 19 x 19 In., Pair	102
Humidor, Lid, Three Guardsmen, Cream & Brown, 3 Bulldogs, Pipe Holder Rings, 7 x 5 In..	800
Jar, Lid, Shaped Base, Latticinio & Ribbon, Italy, 5 x 5½ In.	90
Pitcher, Water, Cranberry & White Spatter, Oval, Quatrefoil Rim, Clear Ribbed Handle, 8½ In..	70
Vase, Bottle, Waisted Shape, Gold Iridescent, Polished Rim, Gilt, c.1915, 6¼ In.	70
Vase, Carved, Etched, Red Flower, Flared Foot, France, c.1910s, 16¾ x 5¼ In.	2460
Vase, Iridescent, Dark Gold, Silver, Feather Decoration, 1900s, 5½ In.............................	923
Vase, Iridescent, Multicolor, Blown, Double Gourd, Peacock Feather, Bubbly Surface, 9 x 4 In...	7605
Vase, Multicolor Body, Flared Rim, Wrought Iron Cage, 1930s, 10 x 9 In.	250
Vase, Ribbed, Cut Velvet, White Interior, Pink Exterior, 4 x 5¾ In. .... *illus*	150
Vase, Tree & Sailboat, Yellow & Orange Ground, Window Box Shape, 3 x 5 x 3 In......... *illus*	550

GLASS-BLOWN

Blown glass was formed by forcing air through a rod into molten glass. Early glass and some forms of art glass were hand blown. Other types of glass were molded or pressed.

Amster Stocking Darner, Clear, Amethyst Tint, Sheared Mouth, c.1890, 5¼ In.................	60
Ball, Gazing, Mercury Glass, Attached Stand, Shaped Base, 22½ In............................ *illus*	1230
Bell Jar, Aromatherapy Candle, Glass Plant, Wax Fragrance, 10 x 6 In..................................	113
Cake Stand, Dome, Center Handle, Folded Bottom Rim, 9½ x 13 In.	158
Celery Vase, Pillar Mold, Baluster Stem, Disc Foot, Clear, Pittsburgh, c.1850, 9¾ In. ... *illus*	150

Imitation—The Sincerest Form of Flattery

Almost every known type of glassware—pressed, blown, colored, clear—has been reproduced or reissued since the nineteenth century. Some reissues are from original molds. Some repros have fake marks.

Glass-Blown, Salt, Sapphire Blue, 3-Piece Mold, Tooled Rim, Boston & Sandwich, 2⅜ In. $1,755

G

Norman C. Heckler & Company

Glass-Blown, Sugar, Dome Lid, Knob Finial, Footed, Amethyst, Milk Glass Loopings, 1830-50, 6¾ In. $4,680

Norman C. Heckler & Company

This is an edited listing of current prices. Visit **Kovels.com** to check thousands of prices from previous years and sign up for free information on trends, tips, reproductions, marks, and more.

Glass-Bohemian, Beaker, Lid, Red, Carved, Flowers, Ornate Designs, Bell Shape Base, c.1900, 15 In. $210

Treasureseeker Auctions

Glass-Bohemian, Compote, Gold, Enamel, Cranberry Case, Castellated Rim, Circular Base, c.1800, 7 x 6 In. $225

Woody Auction

Glass-Bohemian, Decanter, Cut Back, Deer Design, Silver Ground, Molded Base, Marked, 8 In., Pair $123

Apple Tree Auction Center

Compote, Pillar, Folded Rim, Baluster Stem, Baluster Stem, Pittsburgh, Mid 1800s, 7 x 9 In.	132
Decanter, Clear, Ball Stopper, Engraved Body, Pattern In Base, 1800s, 10 3/4 In., Pair	151
Dish, Green Aqua, Outward Folded Rim, Pontil, c.1830, 2 x 6 In.	330
Ewer, Ruby, Teardrop Body, Triangular Rim, Clear Handle, Continental, Late 1800s, 13 In., Pair	36
Globe, Hurricane, Etched, Colorless, Vining Blossoms, Dotted Borders, Early 1800s, 23 In., Pair	5938
Jar, Old Amber, Yellow Olive Tint, Swollen Shoulder, Wide Mouth, Flared Lip, c.1830, 7 In.	1680
Jar, Pink Lavender, Bucket Shape, Flared Rim, 1790-1820, 4 1/2 x 4 In.	330
Linen Smoother, Mushroom Shape, End Of Day, Multicolor, 4 1/2 In.	254
Pitcher, Twist, Blue Opalescent, Circular Tooled Rim, Late 1800s, 10 1/2 In.	449
Rolling Pin, Dark Olive Amber, White Flakes, Tapered Ends, 11 5/8 In.	132
Salt, Footed, Open, Opal Rim, Base Trim, Flared, Cylindrical, Cobalt Blue, 1800, 2 x 2 5/8 x 2 In.	380
Salt, Sapphire Blue, 3-Piece Mold, Tooled Rim, Boston & Sandwich, 2 3/8 In. ....*illus*	1755
Sock Darner, Yellow Amber, Round Top, Tapered Handle, Sheared End, 1840-70, 6 In.	60
Sugar, Dome Lid, Knob Finial, Footed, Amethyst, Milk Glass Loopings, 1830-50, 6 3/4 In...*illus*	4680
Vase, Figural, Man & Woman, Mold, Opaque, Painted, Ruffled Rim, 9 In., Pair	30
Vase, Opaque White, Pale Pink Ground, Multicolor, Enamel, Flowers, Gilt Rim, 1860s, 12 In.	120

GLASS-BOHEMIAN

Bohemian glass is an ornate overlay or flashed glass made during the Victorian era. It has been reproduced in Bohemia, which is now a part of the Czech Republic. Glass made from 1875 to 1900 is preferred by collectors.

Adolf Beckert
c.1914–1920s

Gräflich Schaffgotsch'sche
Josephinenhütte
c.1890

J. & L. Lobmeyr
1860+

Beaker, Clear, Etched, Engraved, Circular Base, 1700s, 6 In., Pair	366
Beaker, Lid, Red, Carved, Flowers, Ornate Designs, Bell Shape Base, c.1900, 15 In. ....*illus*	210
Centerpiece, Rococo Revival, Red Exterior, White Interior, Silver Base, Continental, 8 1/2 In.	150
Compote, Gold, Enamel, Cranberry Case, Castellated Rim, Circular Base, c.1800, 7 x 6 In....*illus*	225
Decanter, Clear, Enameled Case, Flowers, Leaves, White Opaque Oval, Mid 1800s, 13 In.	183
Decanter, Cut Back, Deer Design, Silver Ground, Molded Base, Marked, 8 In., Pair......*illus*	123
Jar, Vanity, Hinged Lid, Painted, Flowers, Gilt, Green Ground, c.1900, 3 1/2 In. ....*illus*	38
Pitcher, Silver Plate Rim & Spout, Iridescent Green, Gold, 10 x 4 1/2 In.	125
Pokal, Ruby Flash, Woodland Scene, Glass Lid, Continental, 1800s, 21 x 8 In.............*illus*	313
Teacup, Saucer, Cobalt Cut To Clear, Gilt Rim, Molded Handle, 3 1/4 In. ....*illus*	188
Urn, Flowers, Gilt Design, Amber Ground, Egg Shape Stopper, Circular Foot, 17 In.	38
Vase, Cobalt Blue, Gilt Metal, Painted, Flowers, Linear Shape, 14 1/2 In.	150
Vase, Cranberry, Pedestal, Hand Painted, Woman Gleaning In Field, 11 x 3 In.	80
Vase, Iridescent, Red Marbled, Multicolor, Pulled Feathers, Rindskopf, Germany, 10 In.*illus*	250
Vase, Long Neck, Spiral Melt Drop Design, Kralik, Austria, 12 1/2 x 4 1/2 In. ....*illus*	228
Vase, Orange Flower, Carved & Inlaid Glass, Harrach, c.1904, 7 1/2 x 5 In.	520
Vase, Ruby, Ornate Gilt, Porcelain Panels, Painted, Flowers, c.1900, 13 1/2 In.	330
Vase, Squat, Gilt Inlay, Rim & Base, Long Neck, Green Matte Ground, Heckert, 10 x 5 3/4 In.	406
Vase, White To Cranberry, Clear, Grapevine, Round Base, Late 1900s, 9 x 5 In., Pair	270
Wine, Flowers, Prunts, 4-Knop Stem, Multicolor, c.1880, 7 5/8 In. ....*illus*	129
Wine, Gilt Design, Blue, Unmarked, c.1900, 7 In., 14 Piece	625

GLASS-CONTEMPORARY

Glass-Contemporary includes pieces by glass artists working after 1970. Many of these pieces are free-form, one-of-a-kind sculptures. Paperweights by contemporary artists are listed in the Paperweight category. Earlier studio glass may be found listed under Glass-Midcentury or Glass-Venetian.

Bowl, Basket, Blue Rimmed Mouth, Opaque Orange, Round Foot, Dale Chihuly, 7 x 6 3/4 In...*illus*	3000
Bowl, Blown, Dolphin, Blue Rim, Point-Etched Signature, Malcolm Sutcliffe, c.1990, 3 1/2 x 6 In.	200

Glass-Bohemian, Jar, Vanity, Hinged Lid, Painted, Flowers, Gilt, Green Ground, c.1900, 3 ½ In.
$38

Greenwich Auction

Glass-Bohemian, Pokal, Ruby Flash, Woodland Scene, Glass Lid, Continental, 1800s, 21 x 8 In.
$313

John Moran Auctioneers

Glass-Bohemian, Teacup, Saucer, Cobalt Cut To Clear, Gilt Rim, Molded Handle, 3 ¼ In.
$188

Hindman

Glass-Bohemian, Vase, Iridescent, Red Marbled, Multicolor, Pulled Feathers, Rindskopf, Germany, 10 In.
$250

Treadway

TIP
Valuable glass should not be washed in a dishwasher.

Glass-Bohemian, Vase, Long Neck, Spiral Melt Drop Design, Kralik, Austria, 12 ½ x 4 ½ In.
$228

Treadway

Glass-Bohemian, Wine, Flowers, Prunts, 4-Knop Stem, Multicolor, c.1880, 7 ⅝ In.
$129

Jeffrey S. Evans & Associates

Glass-Contemporary, Bowl, Basket, Blue Rimmed Mouth, Opaque Orange, Round Foot, Dale Chihuly, 7 x 6 ¾ In.
$3,000

Michaan's Auctions

Glass-Contemporary, Bowl, Cypriot, Flowers, White Interior, Textured Exterior, Lotton, Late 1900s, 6 x 9 ½ In.
$1,200

Garth's Auctioneers & Appraisers

Glass-Contemporary, Bowl, Pink Anthuriums, Hand Blown, Daniel Lotton, 2008, 9 x 12¾ In.
$650

Wright

G

Glass-Contemporary, Figurine, Shoe Shape, Pulled Feather, Charles Lotton, 1988, 4 In.
$269

Jeffrey S. Evans & Associates

Glass-Contemporary, Sculpture, Aerolith, Cased, Venetian Red, Signed, Bernard Katz, 2004, 15 x 12 x 6 In.
$150

Woody Auction

Glass-Contemporary, Sculpture, Emergence, Multicolor, Blown, Dominick Labino, c.1978, 7¼ In.
$5,143

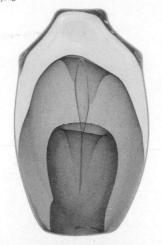

Fontaine's Auction Gallery

Glass-Contemporary, Vase, Blown, Multicolor, Black Tribe, Massimiliano Schiavon, 2008, 6¾ x 11 In.
$563

Hindman

Glass-Contemporary, Vase, Fan, Pulled Feather, Iridescent, Signed, Vandermark, Branchburg, N.J., c.1980, 14 x 9 In.
$410

Jeffrey S. Evans & Associates

Glass-Contemporary, Vase, Hawthorn, Millefiori, Golden Iridescent, Studio, Orient & Flume, Chico, Calif., 1980, 7 In.
$644

Jeffrey S. Evans & Associates

Glass-Contemporary, Vase, Orchids, Iridescent, Urn Shape, Greg Held & Bruce Sillars, Orient & Flume, 1984, 9 In.
$702

Jeffrey S. Evans & Associates

Glass-Midcentury, Decanter, Gray, Sphere Cork, Kaj Franck, Nuutajarvi Notsjo, Finland, 1962, 8 x 3 In.
$2,250

Wright

Bowl, Blue, Favrile Peacock Decoration, Flared Rim, Signed, C.S., 1984, 6 ½ In.		188
Bowl, Cypriot, Flowers, White Interior, Textured Exterior, Lotton, Late 1900s, 6 x 9 ½ In.	*illus*	1200
Bowl, Folded Rim, Feathered, Striped Ground, Signed, Charles Lotton, Dated, 1998, 7 x 15 In.		1140
Bowl, Iridescent Clear, Pink Pulled Feathers, Footed, Signed, Alberman, 1992, 5 x 13 In.		125
Bowl, Multicolor, Clear Case, Paperweight, Signed, Gary Beecham, 1988, 4 x 9 In.		468
Bowl, Pink Anthuriums, Hand Blown, Daniel Lotton, 2008, 9 x 12 ¾ In.	*illus*	650
Bowl, Sand Cast, Multicolor Swirls, Textured, Footed, Susan Gott, Fl., Late 1900s, 8 x 5 x 10 ⅞ In.		59
Bowl, White, Pink Flowers, Green Leaves, Folded Rim, Charles Lotton, 2001, 7 x 12 In.		2280
Figurine, Festive Pheasant, Hand Blown, Oiva Toikka, Iittala, Finland, 2007, 9 x 15 x 6 In.		2340
Figurine, Flamingo, Standing, Clear, Rosaline Accents, Swarovski, 2002, 6 In.		175
Figurine, Shoe Shape, Pulled Feather, Charles Lotton, 1988, 4 In.	*illus*	269
Goblet, Hand Blown, Blue Rim, William & Katherine Bernstein, 1990, 8 x 3 In., Pair		250
Salt, Master, Hand Blown, Blue Rim, Signed, Lundberg Studios, 2 x 3 ½ In.		48
Sculpture, Aerolith, Cased, Venetian Red, Signed, Bernard Katz, 2004, 15 x 12 x 6 In.	*illus*	150
Sculpture, Emergence, Multicolor, Blown, Dominick Labino, c.1978, 7 ¼ In.	*illus*	5143
Sculpture, Obelisk Shape, Clear, Sharp Pointed Top, Square Base, 30 x 5 In.		221
Sculpture, Red Squared, Clear, Laminated Glass, John Kuhn, 1990, 8 In.		2760
Sculpture, Ruffled Fan Shape, Multicolor, Copper & Gilt Inclusions, Munson, 2001, 11 x 25 x 7 In.		59
Vase, Blown, Multicolor, Black Tribe, Massimiliano Schiavon, 2008, 6 ¾ x 11 In.	*illus*	563
Vase, Blown, Rolled Rim, Tree & Mountains Scene, Blue Ground, Garry Nash, 18 x 13 x 4 In.		1053
Vase, Blue Lava Rim, Gold, Amethyst Iridescent, Signed, Lotton, Dated, 1973, 4 In.		510
Vase, Boat, Blue, Walnut Base, Bertil Vallien, c.1995, 3 ¼ x 11 ¾ x 3 ½ In.		1375
Vase, Bud, Studio, White, Blue & Brown Decoration, Polished Base, Terry Crider, 1980, 11 ½ In.		108
Vase, Cobalt Blue, White Flowers, Iridescent Interior, Charles Lotton, 1994, 10 In.		1020
Vase, Cylindrical, White Pulled Feather, Iridescent Gold, Flared Rim, 10 x 4 In.		60
Vase, Fan, Pulled Feather, Iridescent, Signed, Vandermark, Branchburg, N.J., c.1980, 14 x 9 In.	*illus*	410
Vase, Feather, Pulled, Iridescent, Studio, Stuart Abelman, Van Nuys, 1985, 6 ¼ x 9 ½ In.		129
Vase, Flowers, Red Ground, Black Rim, c.2000, R. Satava, 15 x 7 In.		461
Vase, Free Blown, Organic Shape, Multicolor, Signed, Tim Lazer, 13 ½ x 21 In.		94
Vase, Gold Iridescent, Stretched, Orange Flowers, Signed, Charles Lotton, Dated, 1979, 3 In.		204
Vase, Hand Blown, Red, Iridescent Gold Interior, Signed, Lundberg Studios, 1983, 6 x 7 In.		60
Vase, Hand Blown, Yellow Ground, Black Design, John Lotton, 1993, 16 x 11 In.		1125
Vase, Hawthorn, Millefiori, Golden Iridescent, Studio, Orient & Flume, Chico, Calif., 1980, 7 In.	*illus*	644
Vase, Jack-In-The-Pulpit, Red Ground, Cobalt, Signed, Charles Lotton, 1975, 12 ¼ In.		344
Vase, Merritt, Flowers, Blue, Red, Signed, Vandermark, c.1980s, 11 ½ x 4 ½ In.		277
Vase, Millefiori, Iridescent, Bulbous, Flared Rim, Black Ground, Vanderlaan, 1998, 4 x 6 In.		125
Vase, Orchids, Iridescent, Urn Shape, Greg Held & Bruce Sillars, Orient & Flume, 1984, 9 In.	*illus*	702
Vase, Oval, Pink Flowers, Iridescent Vines, Blue, Charles Lotton, 1987, 9 In.		761
Vase, Paperweight, Squared, Clear, Multicolor, Dominick Labino, 1973, 6 x 2 ¾ In.		422
Vase, Paperweight, Torchwork, Beta Fish, Orient & Flume, Scott Beyers, Chico, Calif., 1985, 9 In.		995
Vase, Pink & Clear Cased, Jack-In-The-Pulpit Flowers, Swollen, J. Lotton, 1996, 14 In.		1625
Vase, Prototype, Lava Shape Sides, Multicolor, Signed, Daniel Salazar, 1992, 8 ½ x 3 ½ In.		330
Vase, Red & Yellow Flowers, Signed, Charles Lotton, 1974, 8 ½ In.		512
Vase, Ruffled Rim, Red, Signed, Poschinger, Germany, 3 In.		45
Vase, Spherical, King Tut, Golden Iridescent, Studio, Correia, Santa Monica, Calif., c.1980, 6 In.		263
Vase, Urn Shape, Iridescent, Amethyst, Pulled Feather, Lundberg, Davenport, Calif., 1993, 11 In.		556
Vase, White, Tan, Gray, Dog, Stephen Dale Edwards, 1983, 11 x 9 In.		1000

GLASS-CUT, *see Cut Glass category.*

GLASS-DEPRESSION, *see Depression Glass category.*

GLASS-MIDCENTURY

Glass-Midcentury refers to art glass made from the 1940s to the early 1970s. Some glass factories, such as Baccarat or Orrefors, are listed under their own categories. Earlier glass may be listed in the Glass-Art and Glass-Contemporary categories. Italian glass may be found in Glass-Venetian.

Claret, Jug, Gilt Metal, Mounted, Animal Shape Spouts, Italy, 1950s, 9 ½ In., Pair		363
Churn, Devil's, Sand Blasted, Cut & Acid, Etched, Iittala, Timo Sarpaneve, Finland, 1955, 7 In.		688
Decanter, Gray, Sphere Cork, Kaj Franck, Nuutajarvi Notsjo, Finland, 1962, 8 x 3 In.	*illus*	2250

Glass-Midcentury, Platter, Multicolor, Michael & Frances Higgins, Higgins Glass Studio, c.1958, 17 ¼ In.
$188

Wright

Tapio Wirkkala

Tapio Wirkkala (1915–1985) was a Finnish designer of glassware, silver, ceramics, stoneware, cutlery, wooden ware, furniture, jewelry, textiles, and even banknotes. He was chief designer at Iittala glass-works from 1946 until 1985. He also designed for the German firm Rosenthal and Venini glassworks in Murano. His flowing, organic shapes were inspired by nature—leaves, seashells, birds, and fish.

Glass-Midcentury, Vase, Orchidea, Etched Signature, Timo Sarpaneve, Finland, c.1980, 11 x 3 ½ In.
$162

Toomey & Co. Auctioneers

Glass-Venetian, Aquarium, Multicolor
Fish, Murano, Elio Raffaeli, Italy,
6½ x 8 x 2 In.
$510

Abington Auction Gallery

G

Glass-Venetian, Bowl, Fasce Ritorte,
Multicolor Spirals, Fulvio Bianconi,
Vinini, Italy, c.1960, 1¼ x 4 In.
$813

Wright

Glass-Venetian, Bowl, Green Swirl,
Ridged, Shallow, Murano, Signed,
Alberto Dona, 5 x 16 In.
$128

Rachel Davis Fine Arts

Glass-Venetian, Figurine, Glove,
Lattimo, Amethyst Ribbon, Model 2981,
Italy, 1948, 2 x 8 x 4 In.
$4,688

Wright

Figurine, Musician, Standing, Yellow Trumpet, Frosted, Crystal Base, St. Louis, France, 6 In. ...		95
Platter, Multicolor, Michael & Frances Higgins, Higgins Glass Studio, c.1958, 17¼ In. *illus*		188
Vase, Orchidea, Etched Signature, Timo Sarpaneve, Finland, c.1980, 11 x 3½ In. .... *illus*		162
Vase, Savoy, Mold Blown, Alvar Aalto, Iittala, Finland, 1936, 6 x 8 x 7 In.		2000
Vase, Savoy, Mold Blown, Alvar Aalto, Iittala, Finland, c.1980, 12 x 12 x 10 In.		938

GLASS-PRESSED, *see Pressed Glass category.*

GLASS-VENETIAN

Venetian glass has been made near Venice, Italy, since the thirteenth century. Thin, colored glass with applied decoration is favored, although many other types have been made. Collectors have recently become interested in the Art Deco, 1950s, and contemporary designs. Glass was made on the Venetian island of Murano from 1291. The output dwindled in the late seventeenth century but began to flourish again in the 1850s. Some of the old techniques of glass-making were revived, and firms today make traditional designs and original modern glass. Since 1981, the name *Murano* may be used only on glass made on Murano Island. Other pieces of Italian glass may be found in the Glass-Contemporary and Glass-Midcentury categories of this book.

Aquarium, Multicolor Fish, Murano, Elio Raffaeli, Italy, 6½ x 8 x 2 In. .... *illus*		510
Bowl, Clear, Fluted, Glitter Edge, Pink Spiral Ribbon Design, 13 x 4 In.		98
Bowl, Fasce Ritorte, Multicolor Spirals, Fulvio Bianconi, Vinini, Italy, c.1960, 1¼ x 4 In. .....*illus*		813
Bowl, Filigrana, Figural, Leaf, Opal Loopings, Italy, 1900s, 3⅜ x 6¼ x 8¾ In.		263
Bowl, Fused, Transparent Murrine, Model 3914, Carlo Scarpa, Italy, c.1940, 4 x 7 In.		22500
Bowl, Green Swirl, Ridged, Shallow, Murano, Signed, Alberto Dona, 5 x 16 In. ....*illus*		128
Bowl, Shell Shape, Green Paint, Faux Malachite, Gold Accents, Italy, 9 x 10 x 4 In.		71
Bowl, Sommerso, Thick Sides, Semicircular, Cased Red & White, Murano, Italy, 4 x 6 In. ...		95
Bowl, Tear Shape, Multicolor, Murano, Signed, Alfredo Barbini, 2⅛ In.		90
Cornucopia, Gold Flakes, Scalloped Opening, Fruits, Murano, 20th Century, 5 x 7 x 4 In., Pair		225
Figurine, Clown, Standing, Holding Yo-Yo, A Simpler Life, Multicolor, Murano, 2005, 15¼ In...		94
Figurine, Glove, Lattimo, Amethyst Ribbon, Model 2981, Italy, 1948, 2 x 8 x 4 In. .... *illus*		4688
Figurine, Pulcini Bird, Sculpture, Blown, Blue Ground, Wire Legs, Vistosi, Murano, 6 x 8 x 4 In.		8190
Figurine, Shoe, Black, Lattimo Zanfirico Ribbon, Fulvio Bianconi, Italy, 1950, 6 x 6 x 3 In. .... *illus*		5000
Frame, Gilt Metal Leaves On Corners, Wood Stand, Fratelli Toso Murano, 12 x 14 In.		113
Mirror, Girandole, Ruffled Rim, Spiral Border, Yellow, Flower Finial, c.1935, 18 x 10 x 7 In., Pair...		438
Pitcher, Cylindrical, Swirled, Aventurine Spatter, Fratelli Toso, Murano, 1900s, 10½ In.		140
Sculpture, 2 Doves, Open Wings, Flowers, Branches, Giuseppe Armani, 13 x 14 In...............		35
Sculpture, Abstract, Clear, Orange, Green, Gino Cenedese, Murano, 1900s, 8¾ In.		1063
Sculpture, Amanti, Lovers, Hugging, Standing, Bicolor, Clear, Black, Formia Murano, 17 In. ...		83
Sculpture, Animal, Abstract, Multicolor Stripes, Cone Shape Base, Murano, 1900s, 11 x 19 In..		75
Sculpture, Aquarium, Oval Shape, Murano, Elio Raffaelli, 1980, 14 x 17 x 4¼ In.		3570
Sculpture, Teardrop Shape, Multicolor, Wavy Line, Murano, 6 x 3 x 12 In.		94
Vase, Abstract, Face, Multicolor, Stefano Toso, Murano, 17 x 9 x 6 In. .... *illus*		570
Vase, Amethyst Soffiato, Handles, Model 1765, Vittorio Zecchin, Italy, 1921, 9 x 7 In.		5000
Vase, Blue & Green, Signed, Seguso, Viro, Murano, 17 In................................. *illus*		160
Vase, Blue, Silver Aventurine, Air Bubbles, Maurizio Antoni, 19 x 14 In. .... *illus*		1000
Vase, Cordonato D'Oro, Clear, Blue, Ercole, Barovier & Toso, Murano, c.1955, 11 x 7 x 7 In..		910
Vase, Cylindrical, Swirled, Aventurine Spatter, Fratelli Toso, Murano, 1900s, 10½ In.		152
Vase, Delta PM, Amber, Taurillon Leather, Murano, Box, Hermes, 8½ x 9 In.		1188
Vase, Monumental, Mosaic, Murrine, Multicolor, Nicolo Barovier, Italy, c.1924, 8 x 15 In. ....*illus*		62500
Vase, Murano Style, Flared Rim, Diaper Pattern, Continental, 1900s, 9¾ In................*illus*		121
Vase, Nabuco, Multicolor, Patchwork, Pinwheel, Dino Martens, c.1950, 9½ x 9 x 3¾ In.		9375
Vase, Oxide Black, Gold Leaf, Fratelli Toso, c.1955, 10½ x 6 x 4 In..................................		3500
Vase, Sharp Point, Leone Panisson, Murano, 2013, 20 x 10 x 4¼ In.		531
Vase, Smoky Gray Coral, Red Bands, Decorated, Flavio Poli, Italy, c.1955, 13 x 4 In.		15000
Vase, Squat, Yellow, Bubbles, White Rim & Stick Figures, Murano, Robert Willson, 6 x 9 In........ *illus*		1800
Vase, Teardrop Shape, Red & Amber Glass, Luigi Onesto, Italy, 11 x 5 x 3 In................. *illus*		400
Vase, Zoomorphic Barbarico, Textured Surface, Ercoli Barovier, c.1950, 6 x 8 x 2 In.		3500
Wine, Blue, Clear & Gilt, Fish Stem, Disc Foot, Murano, 1900s, 8 In., 7 Piece ....*illus*		406

Glass-Venetian, Figurine, Shoe, Black, Lattimo Zanfirico Ribbon, Fulvio Bianconi, Italy, 1950, 6 x 6 x 3 In.
$5,000

Wright

Glass-Venetian, Vase, Abstract, Face, Multicolor, Stefano Toso, Murano, 17 x 9 x 6 In.
$570

Abington Auction Gallery

Glass-Venetian, Vase, Blue & Green, Signed, Seguso, Viro, Murano, 17 In.
$160

Nadeau's Auction Gallery

Glass-Venetian, Vase, Blue, Silver Aventurine, Air Bubbles, Maurizio Antoni, 19 x 14 In.
$1,000

Palm Beach Modern Auctions

Glass-Venetian, Vase, Monumental, Mosaic, Murrine, Multicolor, Nicolo Barovier, Italy, c.1924, 8 x 15 In.
$62,500

Wright

TIP
Italian glass from the 1920s to the 1970s is going up in price at auctions.

Glass-Venetian, Vase, Murano Style, Flared Rim, Diaper Pattern, Continental, 1900s, 9¾ In.
$121

Ahlers & Ogletree Auction Gallery

Glass-Venetian, Vase, Squat, Yellow, Bubbles, White Rim & Stick Figures, Murano, Robert Willson, 6 x 9 In.
$1,800

Abington Auction Gallery

G

Glass-Venetian, Vase, Teardrop Shape, Red & Amber Glass, Luigi Onesto, Italy, 11 x 5 x 3 In.
$400

Bruneau & Co. Auctioneers

Glass-Venetian, Wine, Blue, Clear &
Gilt, Fish Stem, Disc Foot, Murano,
1900s, 8 In., 7 Piece
$406

Hindman

See the Difference
Eyeglasses didn't have
widespread use until the
twentieth century. In England the National Health
Service started giving
glasses free in 1948, so
more people wanted them.
Designer glasses were
introduced in the 1960s.

Glasses, Lorgnette, Victorian, Openwork
Leaves, Engraved, 18K Gold, c.1885,
6¾ In.
$2,125

John Moran Auctioneers

TIP
*Use opaque window
shades or drapes so
the contents of your
rooms can't be seen
from outside.*

GLASSES
Glasses for the eyes, or spectacles, were mentioned in a manuscript in 1289
and have been used ever since. The first eyeglasses with rigid side pieces were made in
London in 1727. Bifocals were invented by Benjamin Franklin in 1785. Lorgnettes were
popular in late Victorian times. Opera Glasses are listed in their own category.

Lorgnette, Neoclassical Style, Leaves, Cornucopias, Monogram, 14K Gold, c.1900, 4¾ In...	592
Lorgnette, Victorian, Openwork Leaves, Engraved, 18K Gold, c.1885, 6¾ In...............*illus*	2125
Magnifying, Victorian, Silver, Parasol Handle, Late 1800s, 15½ In.	94
Sunglasses, Metal Frame, 4 Lenses, Octagonal, Blue, Pewter Case, Wool Lining, Pre-1860, 4¾ In.	188
Sunglasses, Purple Frame, Blues, Green, Gray Tinted Lens, Emilio Pucci, France, 1960s, 6 In..	250
Sunglasses, Ray-Ban, Aviator, Gold Frame, Brown, Leather Case, 2 x 5½ x 5¼ In.	75
Sunglasses, Tortoiseshell, Glass Butterfly At Temples, Judith Leiber......................................	36

GLIDDEN
Glidden Pottery worked in Alfred, New York, from 1940 to 1957. The pottery
made stoneware, dinnerware, and art objects.

Bowl, Double, Free-Form, Pink Exterior, Blue Interior, 7 x 12 In..	72
Bowl, Green Mesa, Boat Shape, Brown & Mustard Bands, Chow, c.1956, 4¾ x 18 In.	217
Candelabra, 3-Light, Blue Bands, Swollen Top, Openwork, 9½ x 8 x 4 In...........................	554
Planter, Gulfstream, Blue Violet, Wavy Band, Underplate, Fong Chow, 6 x 10¼ In.	1375
Vase, Gray, Brown & White Bands, Swollen Shoulders, Openwork, Shaped Rim, 14½ In.	431
Vase, Green Mesa, Abstract, Swollen Top, Openwork, Fong Chow, 10 x 10¼ In.	875
Wall Pocket, Gulfstream, Round, Blue, Concentric Circles, 10½ x 10½ In..................	185 to 375

GOEBEL
Goebel is the mark used by W. Goebel Porzellanfabrik of Oeslau,
Germany, now Rodental, Germany. The company was founded by Franz
Detleff Goebel and his son, William Goebel, in 1871. It was known as F&W Goebel.
Slates, slate pencils, and marbles were made. Soon the company began making
porcelain tableware and figurines. Hummel figurines were first made by Goebel in
1935. Since 2009 they have been made by another company. Goebel is still in business.
Old pieces marked Goebel Hummel are listed under Hummel in this book.

Figurine, Bugs Bunny, Elmer Fudd, Shotgun, Sitting, Trunk Wood, Malaysia, 1997, 5¾ In.	88
Figurine, Cat, Mitzi, White, Head Turned, Green Eyes, Last Bee Mark, West Germany, 3¼ In....	88
Figurine, Marvin The Martian, Aiming Gun, Helmet, Japanese Flag, Looney Tunes, 1997, 6½ In..	125
Figurine, Owl, Brown, White Face, Ear Tufts, Ruffled Feathers, Missing Bee Mark, 3¾ In. .	24
Figurine, Road Runner, Accelerath Incredibus, Fast & Furry-Ous Series, 1998, 5 In.	281
Figurine, Woman, Nude, Seated, Bisque, Three Line Mark, c.1970, 8½ In.	50

GOLDSCHEIDER
Goldscheider was founded by Friedrich Goldscheider in Vienna in 1885.
The family left Vienna in 1938 and the factory was taken over by the
Germans. Goldscheider started factories in England and in Trenton, New Jersey. It made
figurines and other ceramics. The New Jersey factory started in 1940 as Goldscheider-U.S.A.
In 1941 it became Goldscheider-Everlast Corporation. From 1947 to 1953 it was Goldcrest
Ceramics Corporation. In 1950 the Vienna plant was returned to Mr. Goldscheider,
but it closed in 1953. The Trenton, New Jersey, business, called Goldscheider of Vienna,
is a wholesale importer.

Bust, Young Woman, Classical Style, Wreath In Hair, Wood Base, Painted White, c.1920, 21 In.*illus*	480
Candelabrum, 3-Light, Blue Ring, Nude Woman, Dancing, Multicolor Base & Foot, 16 x 13 x 5 In. .	660
Clock, Woman, Seminude, Sitting, Dirty White Cloth, Gilt, 21½ In.	960
Figure, Moroccan Nude, Female Slave, Metal Cuffs & Chains, Terra-Cotta, c.1890, 30 In.....	1800

G

Goldscheider, Bust, Young Woman, Classical Style, Wreath In Hair, Wood Base, Painted White, c.1920, 21 In.
$480

Alex Cooper Auctioneers

Goldscheider, Figurine, Child, Lying On Open Book, Arm Around Rabbit, Marble, 4¾ x 9¾ x 5 In.
$64

I.M. Chait Gallery/Auctioneers

Goldscheider, Figurine, Woman, Dog, Borzoi, Red Dress & Hat, Flowers, Art Deco, Claire Weiss, 1920s, 16 In.
$1,375

Lion and Unicorn

Goldscheider, Mask, Wall, Double, Comedy & Tragedy, Brown, White, Numbered, VII, 10¾ In.
$1,042

Sworders

Goldscheider, Mask, Wall, Woman, Wearing Hat, Red Hair, Turquoise Scarf, 12 In.
$729

Sworders

Goldscheider, Mask, Wall, Woman, With Fan, Curly Yellow Hair, Pierced Eyes, 10¼ In.
$833

Sworders

G

Goss, Figure, Model Of Cheddar Cheese, Cylindrical, Gothic Lettering, 2 x 1¾ In. $24

Woody Auction

Goss, Model, Factory Oven, Red Brick, Gray Roof, 3 In. $48

Hannam's Auctioneers

TIP

Mother was right: Have a place for everything and everything in its place. Don't stack old dishes or crowd vases on a shelf. Proper spacing prevents nicks and breaks in pottery or porcelain.

Gouda, Charger, Folded Rim, Rust & Terra-Cotta Coloring, Neil Tetkowski, 4 x 35 In. $600

Bruneau & Co. Auctioneers

Figurine, Child, Lying On Open Book, Arm Around Rabbit, Marble, 4¾ x 9¾ x 5 In... *illus*	64
Figurine, Man & Woman, East Asian Dress, Lime Green, Blue, Square Base, Art Deco, 11 In., Pair	63
Figurine, Man, Blacksmith, Wearing Hat & Apron, Holding Tools, c.1900, 21 In.	1088
Figurine, Man, Violinist, Blue Wig & Coat, Flowered Vest, Scrolled Base, Everlast, 9 In.	32
Figurine, Pierrette, Woman, Sitting, Clown Costume, Ruffled Trim, Red & Blue Medallions, 8 In. .	1063
Figurine, Woman, Dancing, Multicolor Flowers, Holding Skirt Open, Art Deco, 15¼ In.	613
Figurine, Woman, Dog, Borzoi, Red Dress & Hat, Flowers, Art Deco, Claire Weiss, 1920s, 16 In.. *illus*	1375
Mask, Wall, Double, Comedy & Tragedy, Brown, White, Numbered, VII, 10¾ In. .... *illus*	1042
Mask, Wall, Woman, Profile, Wavy Turquoise Hair, 9¾ In....................................	382
Mask, Wall, Woman, Smelling Flower, Yellow, Turquoise Hair, 11 In.	1042
Mask, Wall, Woman, Wearing Hat, Red Hair, Turquoise Scarf, 12 In.......................... *illus*	729
Mask, Wall, Woman, With Bird, Orange Hair, Turquoise Cuff, Pierced Eyes, 12 In.	1649
Mask, Wall, Woman, With Fan, Curly Yellow Hair, Pierced Eyes, 10¼ In..................... *illus*	833
Mask, Wall, Woman, With Flower, Yellow, Curly Bronze Hair, Turquoise Collar, 10¼ In.	451
Plaque, Round, Woman, In Garden, Cockatoos, Terra-Cotta, Impressed Marks, 1800s, 18½ In. ..	313
Vase, Bottle Shape, Nude Woman & Man, Terra-Cotta, Art Nouveau, c.1890, 23½ In., Pair .	2048
Vase, Urn, Round, Square Neck & Foot, Brown, Blue Geometrics, Egyptian Revival, 12 x 8 x 3 In..	75

GOLF, *see Sports category.*

GONDER

Gonder Ceramic Arts, Inc., was opened by Lawton Gonder in 1941 in Zanesville, Ohio. Gonder made high-grade pottery decorated with flambe, drip, gold crackle, and Chinese crackle glazes. The factory closed in 1957. From 1946 to 1954, Gonder also operated the Elgee Pottery, which made ceramic lamp bases.

Jar, Black Lid, Celadon Glaze, Imperial, 3 Dragons, c.1950, 8 x 7 In.	36
Vase, Peacock, Royal Purple, Drip Glaze, 12 In..	25

GOOFUS GLASS

Goofus glass was made from about 1900 to 1930 by many American factories. It was originally painted gold, red, green, bronze, pink, purple, or other bright colors. Colors were cold painted or sprayed on, not fired on, and were not permanent. Many pieces are found today with flaking paint, and this lowers the value. Both goofus glass and carnival glass were sold at carnivals, but carnival glass colors are fired on and don't flake off.

Bowl, Apples & Pears, Gold, Clear Ground, Scalloped Rim, 9¾ In.	46
Bowl, Leaves, Gold, Footed, Opalescent Ruffle, 8½ In., Pair.................................	24

GOSS

Goss china has been made since 1858. English potter William Henry Goss first made it at the Falcon Pottery in Stoke-on-Trent. The factory name was changed to Goss China Company in 1934 when it was taken over by Cauldon Potteries. Production ceased in 1940. Goss China resembles Irish Belleek in both body and glaze. The company also made popular souvenir china, usually marked with local crests and names.

Figure, Model Of Cheddar Cheese, Cylindrical, Gothic Lettering, 2 x 1¾ In................ *illus*	24
Model, Factory Oven, Red Brick, Gray Roof, 3 In..*illus*	48

GOUDA

Gouda, Holland, has been a pottery center since the seventeenth century. Two firms, the Zenith pottery, established in 1749, and the Zuid-Hollandsche pottery, made the colorful art pottery marked *Gouda* from 1898 to about 1964. Other factories that made

"Gouda" style pottery include Regina (1898–1979), Schoonhoven (1920– present), Ivora (1630–1965), Goedewaagen (1610–1779), Dirk Goedewaagen (1779–1982), and Royal Goedewaagen (1983–present). Many pieces featured Art Nouveau or Art Deco designs. Pattern names in Dutch are often included in the mark.

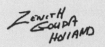
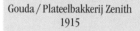

Gouda / Plateelbakkerij Zenith 1915	Gouda / Kon. Hollandsche Pijpen–en Aardewekfabriek Goedewaagen 1923–1928	Gouda / Zuid–Holland Platteelbakkerij 1926+

Charger, Folded Rim, Rust & Terra-Cotta Coloring, Neil Tetkowski, 4 x 35 In.............*illus*		600
Vase, Art Nouveau, Multicolor, Flowers, 2 Side Handles, Holland, 3 1/2 x 13 1/2 x 8 In.............		250
Vase, Emmy, Red, Yellow, Gold Borderlines, Blue Base, Holland, c.1920s, 10 x 3 3/4 In. ..*illus*		185

GRANITEWARE

Graniteware is enameled tin or iron used to make kitchenware since the 1870s. Earlier graniteware was green or turquoise blue, with white spatters. The later ware was gray with white spatters. Reproductions are being made in all colors.

Geuder, Paeschke & Frey Co. 1905–c.1972	Iron Clad Manufacturing Co. 1888–1913	Lalance & Grosjean Manufacturing Co. 1877–1955

Berry Bucket, Metal Lid, Wire Handle, Gray, Speckled, 6 In..	48
Coffeepot, Dome Lid, Metal, Bail Handle, Gray, Straight Spout, Horizontal Ridge, 13 x 12 In. ...	60
Coffeepot, Dome Lid, Metal, Hinged, Gray, Mottled, Large Straight Spout, 8 In.....................	36
Coffeepot, Hinged Enamel Lid, Open Finial, Straight Spout, Gray, 9 x 5 1/2 In.	24
Coffeepot, Hinged Metal Lid, Gooseneck Spout, Scroll Handle, White, Statue Of Liberty, 9 3/4 In..	38
Coffeepot, White Ground, Statue Of Liberty, Scenic, 9 3/4 x 7 3/4 x 5 1/4 In.......................*illus*	36
Cuspidor, Blue Green, White Ground, Flared Rim, c.1910, 5 x 9 1/2 In., Pair	125
Tray, Blue & White, Rectangular, Round Corners, 10 x 15 In.	177

GREENTOWN

Greentown glass was made by the Indiana Tumbler and Goblet Company of Greentown, Indiana, from 1894 to 1903. In 1899, the factory became part of National Glass Company. A variety of pressed glass was made. Additional pieces may be found in other categories, such as Chocolate Glass, Holly Amber, Milk Glass, and Pressed Glass.

Cactus, Tumbler, Chocolate Glass, 4 In..	50
Fleur-De-Lis, Tumbler, Chocolate Glass, 4 In.	60
Wheelbarrow, Salt, Open, Old Gold, Indiana Tumbler & Goblet Co., Early 1900s, 1 7/8 In......*illus*	187

GRUEBY

Grueby Faience Company of Boston, Massachusetts, was founded in 1894 by William H. Grueby. Grueby Pottery Company was incorporated in 1907. In 1909, Grueby Faience went bankrupt. Then William Grueby founded

Gouda, Vase, Emmy, Red, Yellow, Gold Borderlines, Blue Base, Holland, c.1920s, 10 x 3 3/4 In.
$185

California Historical Design

G

TIP

To clean an enamel or graniteware pan, fill it with water. Add the peel of an apple or some cut-up fresh rhubarb. Boil the mixture for 15 minutes.

Graniteware, Coffeepot, White Ground, Statue Of Liberty, Scenic, 9 3/4 x 7 3/4 x 5 1/4 In.
$36

Main Auction Galleries, Inc.

Greentown, Wheelbarrow, Salt, Open, Old Gold, Indiana Tumbler & Goblet Co., Early 1900s, 1 7/8 In.
$187

Jeffrey S. Evans & Associates

GRUEBY

Grueby, Paperweight, Scarab, Amber Matte Glaze, Yellow Orange, c.1910, 1 x 3⅞ x 3 In.
$750

Toomey & Co. Auctioneers

Grueby, Tile, Purple Grapes, Green Leaves, Tan Ground, Matte Glaze, Painted Mark, 6 x 6 x ¾ In.
$845

Toomey & Co. Auctioneers

Grueby, Vase, Melon Shape, Blue Matte Glaze, c.1905, 3½ x 4 In.
$2,952

California Historical Design

Grueby, Vase, Salt Glaze, Leaves, Russell Crook, c.1900, 7¾ x 5¼ In.
$3,198

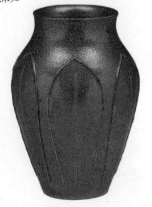

California Historical Design

G

the Grueby Faience and Tile Company. Grueby Pottery closed about 1911. The tile company worked until 1920. Garden statuary, art pottery, and architectural tiles were made until 1920. The company developed a green matte glaze that was so popular it was copied by many other factories making a less expensive type of pottery. This eventually led to the financial problems of the pottery. Cuerda seca (dry cord) decoration uses a greasy pigment to separate different glaze colors during firing. Cuenca (raised line) decorations are impressed, leaving ridges that separate the glaze colors. The company name was often used as the mark, and slight changes in the form help date a piece.

Paperweight, Scarab, Amber Matte Glaze, Yellow Orange, c.1910, 1 x 3⅞ x 3 In.	*illus*	750
Paperweight, Scarab, Blue Matte Glaze, Impressed Mark, 1½ x 2¾ In.		625
Paperweight, Scarab, Green Matte Glaze, c.1910, 1½ x 2¾ x 4 In.		625
Tile, Purple Grapes, Green Leaves, Tan Ground, Matte Glaze, Painted Mark, 6 x 6 x ¾ In.	*illus*	845
Tile, Sea Gull, Waves, Blue Matte Glaze, Signed, MM, c.1905, Frame, 6 x 6 In.		800
Tile, White Duck, Tan Matte Glaze, Wide Wood Frame, C. Pardee Works, N.J., c.1925, 4¼ In.		375
Vase, Bulbous, Flared Rim, Green Matte Glaze, Ribbed, Lillian Newman, Early 1900s, 6 x 9 In.		1404
Vase, Carved Leaves, Green Glaze, Earthenware, Initials Underside, 1800s, 7 In.		4193
Vase, Earthenware, Rolled Tips, Green Matte Glaze, c.1905, 9¼ x 7¼ In.		2000
Vase, Green Matte Glaze, Yellow Flowers, Incised Signature, Eva Russell, 10½ x 6¾ In.		4687
Vase, Hammered, Keswick School Of Industrial Arts, c.1900, 11⅜ x 4½ In.		923
Vase, Melon Shape, Blue Matte Glaze, c.1905, 3½ x 4 In.	*illus*	2952
Vase, Salt Glaze, Leaves, Russell Crook, c.1900, 7¾ x 5¼ In.	*illus*	3198

GUN. *Only toy guns are listed in this book. See Toy category.*

GUSTAVSBERG

Gustavsberg ceramics factory was founded in 1827 near Stockholm, Sweden. It is best known to collectors for its twentieth-century artwares, especially Argenta, a green stoneware with metallic silver inlay. The company broke up and was sold in the 1990s but the name is still being used.

Gustavsberg	Gustavsberg	Gustavsberg
1839–1860	1940–1970	1970–1990s

Bowl, Glazed Stoneware, Round Shape, Footed, Wilhelm Kage, c.1955, 3 x 3 In.	*illus*	1000
Vase, Farsta, Dark Blue Glaze, Earthenware, Wilhelm Kage, Argenta, c.1954, 7¾ In.	*illus*	4063
Vase, Farsta, Dragonfish, Glazed, Stoneware, Wilhelm Kage, 1954, 15 x 4 x 3 In.		9375
Vase, Glazed Stoneware, Eating Fish, Bubbles, 1900s, 10½ In.		548
Vase, Short Neck, Glazed Stoneware, Stig Lindberg, 1967, 15 x 7 x 6 In.		2210

HAEGER

Haeger Potteries, Inc., Dundee, Illinois, started making commercial artwares in 1914. Early pieces were marked with the name *Haeger* written over an *H*. About 1938, the mark *Royal Haeger* was used in honor of Royal Hickman, a designer at the factory. The firm closed in 2016. See also the Royal Hickman category.

Ashtray, Horseshoe Shape, Horse Heads, Green, White, Footed, 1940s, 8 x 7 In.	60
Figurine, Dog, Cocker Spaniel, Stretched Stance, Brown, c.1940, 9 x 7 In.	95
Table Lamp, 8-Sided, Pagoda Shape, Raised Fern Panels, Bracket Feet, Gray, 22½ In.	145
Vase, Round, Bulbous, Fluted Sides, Cranberry Glaze, 1950s, 6½ In.	45
Vase, Triple Cornucopia, Green Glaze, Leafy Base, 9 x 13 In.	89

HALF-DOLL, *see Pincushion Doll category.*

HALL CHINA

Hall China Company started in East Liverpool, Ohio, in 1903. The firm made many types of wares. Collectors search for the Hall teapots made from the 1920s to the 1950s. The dinnerware of the same period, especially Autumn Leaf pattern, is popular. Hall China Company merged with Homer Laughlin China Company in 2010. Hall China was bought by Steelite International, a British company that makes tableware for the hospitality industry, in 2020. Autumn Leaf pattern dishes are listed in their own category in this book.

HALL'S SUPERIOR QUALITY KITCHENWARE

Item	Price
Bank, Elephant, Standing, Trunk Up, Pink.................................*illus*	537
Bean Pot, Green, Lid, Spherical Body, Handle....................................	51
Blue Garden, Casserole, Lid, 8 In.	48
Blue Garden, Casserole, Lid, Loop Handle, Sundial Finial, c.1930, 8 x 5 In.	53
Cameo Rose, Bowl, Vegetable, Oval, 10 In.	14
Cameo Rose, Gravy Boat, Footed..	20
Cameo Rose, Plate, Dinner, 10 In.	21
Casserole, Lid, Pour Spout, Handles, Green	23
Cold Spot, Refrigerator Dish, Butter, Lid, Periwinkle & White, 1940s, 6 x 4 x 4 In.	24
Crocus, Plate, Bread & Butter, 6¼ In.	9
Crocus, Platter, Oval, 13 In.	31
French Daisy, Teapot, Ball Shape, 1950s, 4½ x 7 In.	42
Golden Glo, Casserole, Lid, Basketweave..	95
Jar, Lid, Dog Finial, Cylindrical, White, Pair	62
Orange Poppy, Coffeepot, 7½ In.	55
Orange Poppy, Plate, Dinner, 9½ In.	43
Orange Poppy, Platter, Oval, 13 In.	58
Orange Poppy, Sugar & Creamer	90
Phoenix, Pitcher, Blue, Stoneware, Westinghouse, c.1940, 5 x 10½ x 5 In..................*illus*	438
Red Poppy, Baker, Fluted, Silver Trim, 1950s, 7¾ In.....................	32
Red Poppy, Bowl, Cereal, Rim, 6 In.	18
Red Poppy, Platter, Oval, 13 In.	27
Red Poppy, Shaker, Teardrop, 2⅜ In.	14
Rose Parade, Casserole, Tab Handles, 2½ Qt.	62
Rose White, Jug, 5 In...	41
Rose White, Salt & Pepper, Handles, c.1940, 4½ In.	47
Rose White, Shaker...	14
Royal Rose, Salt & Pepper, Handles..	38
Teapot, Automobile, Figural, Art Deco Era, Cobalt Blue, 1930s, 9 x 4 x 4 In..................*illus*	156
Teapot, Everson, Ribbed, Handle, Monterey Green, Sample, Paper Label, 1952	367

HALLOWEEN

Halloween is an ancient holiday that has changed in the last 200 years. The jack-o'-lantern, witches on broomsticks, and orange decorations seem to be twentieth-century creations. Collectors started to become serious about collecting Halloween-related items in the late 1970s. Old costumes and papier-mache decorations, now replaced by plastic, are in demand.

Item	Price
Basket, Jack-O'-Lantern, Papier-Mache, Textured Orange, Paper Inserts, Wire Handle, 8 In......	220
Chimney Cover, 2 Children Holding Jack-O'-Lantern, Metal, c.1900, 8½ In.	150
Costume, Goldilocks, Vinyl Mask, Flame Retardant Dress, Ben Cooper, Child's, Medium Size 8-10.	55
Costume, Witch, Black, Laced Bodice, Cape, Pointy Hat, Black Cat, c.1940, Adult Size..........	95
Figure, Black Cat, Standing, Arched Back, Papier-Mache, Paint, Orange Base, 1940s, 13 In.	490
Jack-O'-Lantern, Parade, Candleholder, Tin Lithograph, Toledo Metal Sign Co., 1900s, 9½ In..*illus*	3000
Jack-O'-Lantern, Pumpkin, Glass, Orange, Light-Up, 1975, 6 In.	20
Lantern, Pumpkin, Jack-O'-Lantern, Paper Split Nose, Wire Handle, Germany, c.1920, 8½ In..*illus*	6600
Noisemaker, Tin, Cricket, Witch, Broom, US Metal Toy Mfg. Co., 1940-60, 2⅜ In.	18
Tambourine, Tin, Black Cat Face, Witch & Cat Faces, Clappers, T. Conn, Inc., 1940-60, 7 In.	60
Toy, Cat, On Wheels, Spring Necks, Fiddle, Jack-O'-Lantern, Tico Toys, 1940s, 9 In., Pair	1008
Witch, Riding Broom, Hat, Cardboard, Die Cut, 1920s, 10 In.	177

Gustavsberg, Bowl, Glazed Stoneware, Round Shape, Footed, Wilhelm Kage, c.1955, 3 x 3 In.
$1,000

Wright

Gustavsberg, Vase, Farsta, Dark Blue Glaze, Earthenware, Wilhelm Kage, Argenta, c.1954, 7¾ In.
$4,063

Wright

H

Hall, Bank, Elephant, Standing, Trunk Up, Pink
$537

Strawser Auction Group

Hall, Phoenix, Pitcher, Blue, Stoneware, Westinghouse, c.1940, 5 x 10½ x 5 In.
$438

Wright

Hall, Teapot, Automobile, Figural, Art Deco Era, Cobalt Blue, 1930s, 9 x 4 x 4 In.
$156

Potter & Potter Auctions

Halloween, Jack-O'-Lantern, Parade, Candleholder, Tin Lithograph, Toledo Metal Sign Co., 1900s, 9½ In.
$3,000

Morphy Auctions

Halloween, Lantern, Pumpkin, Jack-O'-Lantern, Paper Split Nose, Wire Handle, Germany, c.1920, 8½ In.
$6,600

Morphy Auctions

TIP

Be careful where you put a fresh pumpkin or gourd at Halloween or Thanksgiving. Put a plastic liner underneath it. A rotting pumpkin will permanently stain wood or marble.

HAMPSHIRE

Hampshire pottery was made in Keene, New Hampshire, between 1871 and 1923. Hampshire developed a line of colored-glaze wares as early as 1883, including a Royal Worcester–type pink, olive green, blue, and mahogany. Pieces are marked with the printed mark or the impressed name *Hampshire Pottery* or *J.S.T. & Co., Keene, N.H.* (James Scollay Taft). Many pieces were marked with city names and sold as souvenirs.

Mug, Green Matte Glaze, Signed, Jest & Co., Keene, N.H., c.1910s, 5½ x 4¼ x 3⅝ In., Pair... *illus*		185
Vase, Brown Ground, Molded Decor, Matte Glaze, Keene, Early 1900s, 7¼ In.		113
Vase, Green Matte Glaze, 2 Handles, Signed, c.1910, 5½ x 7½ In. ....*illus*		308

HANDBAG, *see Purse category.*

HANDEL

Handel glass was made by Philip Handel working in Meriden, Connecticut, from 1885 and in New York City from 1893 to 1933. The firm made art glass and other types of lamps. Handel shades were made not only of leaded glass in a style reminiscent of Tiffany but also of reverse painted glass. Handel also made vases and other glass objects.

Bookends, Green Patina, Bronzed Metal, 6 x 7 In..	488
Lamp, 2-Light, Scenic, Bronze, Sunset Pines, Slag Glass, Multicolor, 21 x 21 x 8 In...... *illus*	1170
Lamp, Arab & Camel, Desert Scene, Domed Shade, Patina, Metal Base, Early 1900s, 25¾ In....... *illus*	7563
Lamp, Bronze, Leaded Slag Glass, Yellow, Green, 30 x 26 In. ....*illus*	4225
Lamp, Bronze, Lily Pad Base, Slag Glass Shade, Maple Leaf, 14 x 17 x 7 In. ....*illus*	720
Lamp, Bronze, Patinated, Painted Scene, Venetian Dock, Late 1800s, 23½ In.	6400
Lamp, Bronze, Yellow Slag Glass, White Opaque, Water Lily, 13½ x 7 x 10 In..............*illus*	715
Lamp, Cattail Shade, 1900s, 24 x 18 In..	4500
Lamp, Flowers, Reverse Painted, Chipped Glass, Patinated Metal, Early 1900s, 24 In. .. *illus*	1250
Lamp, Hanging Shade, Painted Virginia Creeper Overlay, 13 x 24 x 22½ In..........................	552
Lamp, Hanging, Leaded Glass, Ball Shape, Signed, c.1910s, 13 x 10 In.................................	1476
Lamp, Overlay, Scenic Shade, Sunset, Slag Glass, Patinated Metal, Early 1900s, 64 x 22 In.	2500
Lamp, Piano, Leaded Glass, Green Rim, Round Base, c.1910, 11½ x 18½ x 8½ In.	1353
Lamp, Pink Chipped Ice Shade & Base, Frosted Stem, Brass Fittings, c.1915, 14 In.	480
Lamp, Reverse Painted, 6-Panel, Flowers, c.1910, 19 x 18 In. ....*illus*	1845
Lamp, Reverse Painted, Yellow Flowers, Hexagonal Shade, Patinated Metal, 1900s, 14 In.	1548
Lamp, Teroca, Leaves Design, Tube Shape, Patinated Metal, 8 x 15 In...................................	910
Lamp, Teroca, Sunset Palm, 3-Light, Slag Glass & Bronze Shade, Patina, 8½ x 20 In.	3240
Light, Leaded Glass, Spherical Ball, Hanging, Multicolor, c.1910, 11 x 14 x 40 In..........*illus*	6150
Sconce, Copper, Hammered, 6-Sided Shade, c.1910, 13 x 5½ x 6½ In., Pair ....*illus*	3690
Shade, Slag Glass, Light Brown Panels, Leaded, Domed, 4⅛ x 7 In......................................	33

HARDWARE, *see Architectural category.*

HARKER

Harker Pottery Company was incorporated in 1890 in East Liverpool, Ohio. The Harker family had been making pottery in the area since 1840. The company made many types of pottery but by the Civil War was making quantities of yellowware from native clays. It also made Rockingham-type brown-glazed pottery and whiteware. The plant was moved to Chester, West Virginia, in 1931. Dinnerware was made and sold nationally. In 1971 the company was sold to Jeannette Glass Company, and all operations ceased in 1972. For more prices, go to kovels.com.

Apple & Pear, Plate, Hotoven, 9¾ In...*illus*	15
Cameoware, Dainty Flower, Cake Plate, Tab Handles, Pink, White Flowers, 1940s, 12 In. ...	23

Hampshire, Mug, Green Matte Glaze, Signed, Jest & Co., Keene, N.H., c.1910s, 5 ½ x 4 ¼ x 3 ⅝ In., Pair
$185

California Historical Design

Hampshire, Vase, Green Matte Glaze, 2 Handles, Signed, c.1910, 5 ½ x 7 ½ In.
$308

California Historical Design

> **TIP**
> *Reverse-painted lamp-shades should never be washed. Just dust them.*

Handel, Lamp, 2-Light, Scenic, Bronze, Sunset Pines, Slag Glass, Multicolor, 21 x 21 x 8 In.
$1,170

Toomey & Co. Auctioneers

Handel, Lamp, Arab & Camel, Desert Scene, Domed Shade, Patina, Metal Base, Early 1900s, 25 ¾ In.
$7,563

Fontaine's Auction Gallery

Handel, Lamp, Bronze, Leaded Slag Glass, Yellow, Green, 30 x 26 In.
$4,225

Toomey & Co. Auctioneers

Handel, Lamp, Bronze, Lily Pad Base, Slag Glass Shade, Maple Leaf, 14 x 17 x 7 In.
$720

Main Auction Galleries, Inc.

Handel, Lamp, Bronze, Yellow Slag Glass, White Opaque, Water Lily, 13 ½ x 7 x 10 In.
$715

Toomey & Co. Auctioneers

Handel, Lamp, Flowers, Reverse Painted, Chipped Glass, Patinated Metal, Early 1900s, 24 In.
$1,250

Fontaine's Auction Gallery

Handel, Lamp, Reverse Painted, 6-Panel, Flowers, c.1910, 19 x 18 In.
$1,845

California Historical Design

Handel, Light, Leaded Glass, Spherical
Ball, Hanging, Multicolor, c.1910,
11 x 14 x 40 In.
$6,150

California Historical Design

H

Handel Marks

Handel lamp bases are
marked with the word
Handel. The glass shades
usually have a four-digit
number on the inside near
the rim. It is a design
number and can be looked
up in several books about
the lamps. A few are
marked on the inside of
the glass shade with the
name of an artist—Palme,
Runge, or Parlow.

Handel, Sconce, Copper, Hammered,
6-Sided Shade, c.1910,
13 x 5½ x 6½ In., Pair
$3,690

California Historical Design

Cameoware, Plate, Duck, Umbrella, Blue, 7 In.	12
Dainty Flower, Cameoware, Bowl, Blue, 12 In. *illus*	15
Petit Point Rose, Teapot, Oval, 1930s, 9 x 6 In.	35
Tulip, Mixing Bowl, Hotoven, 7 In. *illus*	40

HARLEQUIN

Harlequin dinnerware was produced by the Homer Laughlin Company from 1938 to 1964, and sold without trademark by the F. W. Woolworth Co. It has a concentric ring design like Fiesta, but the rings are separated from the rim by a plain margin. Cup handles are triangular in shape. Seven different novelty animal figurines were introduced in 1939. For more prices, go to kovels.com.

Gray, Pitcher, 5 In.	65
Green, Perfume Bottle, 2½ In. *illus*	277
Maroon, Salt & Pepper, Decal, Blond Woman With Headdress, Man With Chef's Hat.... *illus*	93
Mauve Blue, Butter, Cover, ½ Lb. *illus*	68
Red, Plate, Donkey Decal, 6 In. *illus*	80
Rose, Cup, Tankard. *illus*	148
Spruce Green, Tumbler, 4 In.	55
Turquoise, Relish, 2 Turquoise Inserts, 2 Rose Inserts, Unmarked *illus*	984
Turquoise, Water Pitcher, Ball Shape	70

HATPIN

Hatpin collectors search for pins popular from 1860 to 1920. The long pin, often over four inches, was used to hold the hat in place on the hair. The tops of the pins were made of all materials, from solid gold and real gemstones to ceramics and glass. Be careful to buy original hatpins and not recent pieces made by altering old buttons.

Brass, Insect, c.1910, 4½ In.	65
Enamel, Cabochon, Green, Faux Malachite, Silver Setting, Steel, The Rokesley Shop, 8 In... *illus*	487
Enamel, Cabochon, Turquoise, Ruskin, Silver, Steel, The Jarvie Shop, 10⅛ In.	390
Enamel, Pansy, Red, White, Blue, Glass Rhinestone, 6¼ In.	32
Silver, Flower, Art Nouveau, 1900s, 8 In.	90

HATPIN HOLDER

Hatpin holders were needed when hatpins were fashionable from 1860 to 1920. The large, heavy hat required special long-shanked pins to hold it in place. The hatpin holder resembles a large saltshaker, but it often has no opening at the bottom as a shaker does. Hatpin holders were made of all types of ceramics and metal. Look for other pieces under the names of specific manufacturers.

Porcelain, Obelisk, Art Deco, Silver Trim, Square Base, Marked, Belleek Sterling, 6½ x 2 In. *illus*	210
Porcelain, Painted Scene, Mill, Flying Swallows, Gilt, 6-Sided, Unmarked, Prussia, 4 x 2½ In.	150

HAVILAND

Haviland china has been made in Limoges, France, since 1842. David Haviland had a shop in New York City and opened a porcelain company in Limoges, France. Haviland was the first company to both manufacture and decorate porcelain. Pieces are marked *H & Co.*, *Haviland & Co.*, or *Theodore Haviland*. It is possible to match existing sets of dishes through dealers who specialize in Haviland china. Other factories worked in the town of Limoges making a similar chinaware. Those porcelains are listed in this book under Limoges.

Harker, Apple & Pear, Plate, Hotoven, 9¾ In.
$15

jamesandtheattic on eBay

Harker, Dainty Flower, Bowl, Cameoware, Blue, 12 In.
$15

ardonantiques on eBay

Harker, Tulip, Mixing Bowl, Hotoven, 7 In.
$40

popeirasplace on eBay

Harlequin, Green, Perfume Bottle, 2½ In.
$277

Strawser Auction Group

Harlequin, Maroon, Salt & Pepper, Decal, Blond Woman With Headdress, Man With Chef's Hat
$93

Strawser Auction Group

Dangerous Weapons—Hatpins

In the early 1900s, women began protecting themselves from male "mashers" by using their fashionable hatpins. In 1908, the nation began passing laws to ban hatpins longer than 9 inches. Other cities passed regulations requiring safety caps on the ends (nibs) to prevent an accidental stabbing.

Harlequin, Mauve Blue, Butter, Cover, ½ Lb.
$68

Strawser Auction Group

Harlequin, Red, Plate, Donkey Decal, 6 In.
$80

Strawser Auction Group

Harlequin, Rose, Cup, Tankard
$148

Strawser Auction Group

Harlequin, Turquoise, Relish, 2 Turquoise Inserts, 2 Rose Inserts, Unmarked
$984

Strawser Auction Group

Hatpin, Enamel, Cabochon, Green, Faux Malachite, Silver Setting, Steel, The Rokesley Shop, 8 In.
$487

Toomey & Co. Auctioneers

Hatpin Holder, Porcelain, Obelisk, Art Deco, Silver Trim, Square Base, Marked, Belleek Sterling, 6 ½ x 2 In.
$210

Woody Auction

Haviland Pottery, Pitcher, Bulbous, Narrow Neck, Aesthetic, Mottled Green, Branch, Red Berries, 7 ½ x 9 ½ In.
$508

Tremont Auctions

Hawkes, Goblet, Satin Iris, Faceted Stem, Square Foot, 7 In., 8 Piece
$787

Ahlers & Ogletree Auction Gallery

HAVILAND & Co Limoges	**Théo Haviland** Limoges FRANCE	**Haviland** France
Haviland and Co. 1876–1878; 1889–1931	Theodore Haviland 1893–early 1900s	Haviland and Co. c.1894–1931

Charger, Fish, Trout, Blue Green Ground, Hand Painted, Wood Frame, 19th Century, 16 In.	118
Charger, Red Poppies, Flying Bird, Light Blue Ground, Artist Signed, Limoges, c.1900, 15 ½ In.	154
Pitcher, 8-Sided, Red Flowers, Blue Flowers On Reverse, Molded, Gilt, Shreve & Co., c.1880, 8 In. .	462
Plate, Art Nouveau, Pink Passionflowers, Gilt Beaded Rim, France, 1920s, 9 In.	20
Plate, Dessert, Sea Life, Cobalt Rim, Gilt Flowers, France, Late 19th Century, 8 ½ In., 12 Piece	677
Plate, Fish, Crabs, Shells, Seaweed, Nets, Gilt Trim, Limoges, c.1920, 8 ½ In., 12 Piece.........	1054
Plate, Rose Vine Transfer, Gilt Trim, Scalloped Rim, Bailey, Banks & Biddle, 9 ¾ In., 11 Piece.....	369
Vase, Earthenware, High Glaze, Emile Justin Merlot, France, c.1875, 12 x 10 ½ x 4 In.	975

HAVILAND POTTERY

Haviland Pottery began in 1872, when Charles Haviland decided to make art pottery. He worked with the famous artists of the day and made pottery with slip glazed decorations. Production stopped in 1885. Haviland Pottery is marked with the letters *H & Co.* The Haviland name is better known today for its porcelain.

HAVILAND & Co Limoges	**H & Co** L	**C F H** **G D M** FRANCE
Haviland and Co. 1875–1882	Haviland and Co. 1875–1882	Charles Field Haviland 1891+

Jardiniere, Aesthetic, White Birds, Trees, Gilt, Stoneware, 14 ⅜ x 8 ¼ In., Pair.....................	1016
Pitcher, Bulbous, Narrow Neck, Aesthetic, Mottled Green, Branch, Red Berries, 7 ½ x 9 ½ In....*illus*	508
Vase, Barbotine, Rooster, Bottle Shape, Wide Collar, Signed, 19th Century, 13 x 7 ½ In........	532

HAWKES

Hawkes cut glass was made by T. G. Hawkes & Company of Corning, New York, founded in 1880. The firm cut glass blanks made at other glassworks until 1962. Many pieces are marked with the trademark, a trefoil ring enclosing a fleur-de-lis and two hawks. Cut glass by other manufacturers is listed under either the factory name or in the general Cut Glass category.

Bowl, Revere, Diamond, Chipped Ice Edge, Silver Stepped Foot, c. 1920, 4 ¼ In.	363
Candlestick, Grapevines, Circular Foot, c.1920, 12 In., Pair..	152
Goblet, Satin Iris, Faceted Stem, Square Foot, 7 In., 8 Piece ....*illus*	787
Vase, Flower Garland, Verre De Soie, Engraved, Polished Pontil Base, 10 x 5 In....................	60
Wine, Flowers, Topaz, Bucket Shape Bowl, Knop Stem, c.1915, 5 ⅞ In., Pair................*illus*	269

HEAD VASE

Head vases, generally showing a woman from the shoulders up, were used by florists primarily in the 1950s and 1960s. Made in a variety of sizes and often decorated with imitation jewelry and other lifelike accessories, the vases were manufactured in Japan and the U.S.A. Less elaborate examples were made as early as the 1930s. Religious themes, babies, and animals are also common subjects. Other head vases are listed under manufacturers' names and can be located through the index in the back of this book. Collecting head vases was a fad in the 1960s–1970s and prices rose. There is less interest now and only a few are high priced.

Baby, Blond Hair, Blue Eyes, White Dress & Bonnet, National Potteries, 6 In.	45

Girl, Orange Dress, Hair Bows, Pearl Earrings, Blond, Blue Eyes, Relpo, 1950s, 5½ In.	195
Madonna, Blue Robe, Looking Down, Gold Trim, Japan, 3⅞ In.	22
Teen, Blond Hair, Curls, Blue Eyes, Pearl Drop Earrings, Pink & White Top, Inarco, 5½ In. ...*illus*	95
Woman, Blond Hair, Rose In Hair, Hand On Face, Pearl Drop Earrings, c.1961, 4¾ In.	75
Woman, Blond Updo, Rose Headband, Pearls, Pink Lacy Dress, Raised Hand, Inarco, c.1961, 9½ In..	161
Woman, Debbie Reynolds, Blond, Blue Eyes, Pearls, Glove, Black Dress, Relpo, 7 In.....*illus*	75
Woman, Grace Kelly, Peach Turban & Dress, Pearl Earrings, Necklace, Napco, c.1960, 6 In.........	189
Woman, Green Dress, Pearls, White & Gold Flower In Hair, 5¼ In.	63

HEINTZ ART METAL SHOP

Heintz Art Metal Shop used the letters *HAMS* in a diamond as a mark. In 1902, Otto Heintz designed and manufactured copper items with colored enamel decorations under the name Art Crafts Shop. He took over the Arts & Crafts Company in Buffalo, New York, in 1903. By 1906 it had become the Heintz Art Metal Shop. It remained in business until 1930. The company made ashtrays, bookends, boxes, bowls, desk sets, vases, trophies, and smoking sets. The best-known pieces are made of copper, brass, and bronze with silver overlay. Similar pieces were made by Smith Metal Arts and were marked *Silver Crest*. Some pieces by both companies are unmarked.

Ashtray, Green Patina, Sterling On Bronze, c.1915, 3¾ x 8 In.	185
Frame, Silvercrest, Overlay, Deer, Picture, Sterling On Bronze, c.1920, 3½ x 3¾ x 3½ In. .	277
Humidor, Sea Gull, Signed, Sterling On Bronze, c.1915, 2½ x 8½ x 3½ In.	338
Inkwell, Leaf, Curled Feet, Sterling On Bronze, c.1907, 3¼ x 5¼ x 5¼ In. ....*illus*	215
Lamp, Helmet Shape Shade, Sterling On Bronze, Acid Etched, Paper Label, 14½ x 8 In.......	343
Lamp, Mica, Red Shade, Sterling On Bronze, c.1915, 11¾ x 9¾ In.	1169
Lamp, Poppies Shade, Sterling On Bronze, Paper Label, 10⅜ x 9 In.	715
Vase, Flowers, Green Ground, Sterling On Bronze, Early 1900s, 12¼ In.	303
Vase, Green Patina, Flower, Sterling On Bronze, Signed, c.1915, 5 x 5½ In.	369
Vase, Wheat, Molded Rim, Sterling On Copper, Impressed Mark, 11 x 4 In. ....*illus*	260

HEISEY

Heisey glass was made from 1896 to 1957 in Newark, Ohio, by A. H. Heisey and Co., Inc. The Imperial Glass Company of Bellaire, Ohio, bought some of the molds and the rights to the trademark. Some Heisey patterns have been made by Imperial since 1960. After 1968, they stopped using the *H* trademark. Heisey used romantic names for colors, such as Sahara. Do not confuse color and pattern names. The Custard Glass and Ruby Glass categories may also include some Heisey pieces.

Heisey 1900–1957	Heisey Paper label	Heisey Paper label

Animal, Airedale, Standing, Clear Glass, 6 x 7 In.	123
Animal, Flying Mare, Cobalt Blue, Dalzell, 9 In. ....*illus*	431
Animal, Mother Elephant, Raised Trunk, Blown Glass, Clear, 4 x 2 In.	59
Animal, Pouter Pigeon, Lavender Ice, Dalzell, 6½ In.	99
Bookends, Horse, Rearing, Lavender Ice, Dalzell, 8 In., Pair	277
Cherub, Candlestick, Flamingo, Orange, Frosted, Pair ....*illus*	554
Colonial, Candy Jar, Dome Lid, Clear, 9¾ In. ....*illus*	74
Colonial, Humidor, Removable Lid, Octagonal, 10 In.	74
Jar, Pretzel Lid, Club Drinking Scene, Etched, 9 In.	246
Lamp, Oil, Banquet, Pressed Bull's-Eye, Prism Drops, Square Foot, c.1900, 33 x 8 In..........	351
Orchid Etch, Urn, Vase, Square Plinth Base, 8½ In. ....*illus*	123
Warwick, Cornucopia Vase, Ruffled Rim, Cobalt Blue, 9 In.	123

Hawkes, Wine, Flowers, Topaz, Bucket Shape Bowl, Knop Stem, c.1915, 5⅞ In., Pair
$269

Jeffrey S. Evans & Associates

Head Vase, Teen, Blond Hair, Curls, Blue Eyes, Pearl Drop Earrings, Pink & White Top, Inarco, 5½ In.
$95

Ruby Lane

Head Vase, Woman, Debbie Reynolds, Blond, Blue Eyes, Pearls, Glove, Black Dress, Relpo, 7 In.
$75

Ruby Lane

This is an edited listing of current prices. Visit **Kovels.com** to check thousands of prices from previous years and sign up for free information on trends, tips, reproductions, marks, and more.

HEREND

Heintz Art, Inkwell, Leaf, Curled Feet, Sterling On Bronze, c.1907, 3¼ x 5¼ x 5¼ In.
$215

California Historical Design

Heintz Art, Vase, Wheat, Molded Rim, Sterling On Copper, Impressed Mark, 11 x 4 In.
$260

Treadway

Heisey, Animal, Flying Mare, Cobalt Blue, Dalzell, 9 In.
$431

Apple Tree Auction Center

HEREND

Herend is a mark used on porcelain made in Herend, Hungary. A pottery was established there in 1826. The pottery was bought by Moritz Fischer in 1839. Fischer made replacement pieces for German and Far Eastern dinnerware and later began making his own dinnerware patterns. Figurines were made beginning in the 1870s. The company became Herend Porcelain Works Co. in 1884. It was nationalized in 1948. Herend became an independent company in 1981. In 1993 it became Herend Porcelain Manufactory. It is the world's largest porcelain manufacturer.

Basket, Trinket, Rothschild Bird, Reticulated, 2 Handles, Marked, 2 x 6 In.	123
Bonbonniere, Lid, Strawberry Finial, Flowers, Spherical, 1900s, 4¾ In.	125
Bonbonniere, Reticulated, Openwork, Flowers, Multicolor, 4 x 4 In.	215
Box, Lid, Asparagus, White, Green Ends, Pink Tie, 3 x 5 x 2 In., Pair. *illus*	234
Casserole, Rothschild Bird, Scalloped Dish, Branch Shape Handles, Nut Baskets, 6 x 13 In.	450
Coffee Set, Rust Fortuna, Coffeepot, Sugar Bowl, Creamer, 3 Piece	360
Compote, Unicorn Shape, Blue Fishnet, Standing, Gilt Accent, 4 x 3 In.	201
Dish, 3 Sections, Queen Victoria, Flowers, Butterflies, Gilt Rim, 1900s, 4 x 11 In.	281
Dish, Figural, Dragon Shape, Hand Painted, Black Dynasty, Flowers, 3 x 11 x 4 In. *illus*	330
Figurine, Bear, Sitting, Hand Painted, Blue Fishnet, White Ground, 4¾ x 4½ x 5 In. *illus*	156
Figurine, Cat, Playing, Blue & White, Painted, Gilt Feet, Orange Ball, 5¼ In.	160
Figurine, Foo Dog, Famille Noire, Black Dynasty Series, Kramlik Ferncne, 6 x 6 x 3 In., Pair. *illus*	570
Figurine, Nude Woman, Crouching, Holding Goblet, Jozsef Gondos, 8½ In.	75
Figurine, Panther, Green Fishnet Design, Hand Painted, Gilt Paws & Nose, 6 x 18 x 4 In. *illus*	840
Figurine, Pig, Standing, Green Fishnet, Gilt Highlights, 3½ In.	94
Figurine, Rabbit, Seated, Green Fishnet, Gilt Nose & Feet, 1900s, 6 In.	188
Figurine, Rabbit, Sitting, Turquoise Fishnet, Gilt Nose & Feet Tips, Marked, 12 x 4½ In.	860
Figurine, Stallion, Running, Reddish Brown Fishnet, 7½ x 9¼ x 3½ In.	563
Pitcher, Flowers, Unique Shape, Lizard Figural Handle, 14 x 12 x 5 In. *illus*	540
Plate, Basket Weave Ground, Gilt, Scalloped Rim, Flowers, 7½ In., 5 Piece *illus*	219
Plate, Blue Garland, Reticulated Border, Painted, Scalloped Rim, 9½ In., Pair	500
Teapot, Flowers, Applied Handle, Gooseneck Spout, 9¼ x 14¾ In.	175
Trinket Box, Lid, Raspberry & Gilt Decoration, 2⅞ In.	41
Tureen, Dome Lid, Lemon Finial, White, Multicolor Flowers, Green Handles, 6¼ x 9 In. *illus*	531
Tureen, Dome Lid, Songbird Finial, Bamboo Shape Handles, Flora & Fauna, 11 x 13 In.	531
Tureen, Famille Noire, Gilt Edges, Half Lemon Finial, Miniature, 4 x 6 x 3 In. *illus*	120
Vase, Queen Victoria, Flowers, Butterflies, Flared Rim, 20 x 11 In.	406

HISTORIC BLUE, *see factory names, like Adams, Ridgway, and Staffordshire.*

HOBNAIL

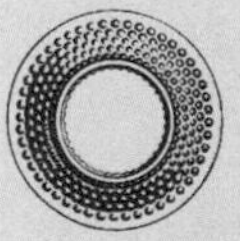

Hobnail glass is a style of glass with bumps all over. Dozens of hobnail patterns and variants have been made. Clear, colored, and opalescent hobnail have been made and are being reproduced. Other pieces of hobnail may also be listed in the Duncan & Miller and Fenton categories.

Bottle, Amethyst Glass, Lift Lid, Spiral Neck, c.1910, 8 In. *illus*	53
Bowl, Light To Dark Pink, Ruffled, Edge, Footed, 8 x 4 In.	20
Candy Dish, Tab Handles, Clear, 1950s, 6 x 4 In.	16
Cruet, Stopper, Blue Opalescent, Shouldered, c.1900, 5 In.	34
Pitcher, Cranberry, Clear Handle, Globular, Hobbs Brockunier, 7¾ x 7 In.	325
Vase, Green, Ball Shape, Czechoslovakia, 4 x 4 In.	175

HOLLY AMBER

Holly amber, or golden agate, glass was made by the Indiana Tumbler and Goblet Company of Greentown, Indiana, from January 1, 1903, to June 13, 1903. It is a pressed glass pattern featuring holly leaves in the amber-shaded glass. The glass was made with shadings that range from creamy opalescent to brown-amber.

Heisey, Cherub, Candlestick, Flamingo, Orange, Frosted, Pair
$554

Apple Tree Auction Center

Heisey, Colonial, Candy Jar, Dome Lid, Clear, 9¾ In.
$74

Apple Tree Auction Center

Heisey, Orchid Etch, Urn, Vase, Square Plinth Base, 8½ In.
$123

Apple Tree Auction Center

Herend, Box, Lid, Asparagus, White, Green Ends, Pink Tie, 3 x 5 x 2 In., Pair
$234

Thomaston Place Auction Galleries

Herend, Dish, Figural, Dragon Shape, Hand Painted, Black Dynasty, Flowers, 3 x 11 x 4 In.
$330

Alderfer Auction Company

Herend, Figurine, Bear, Sitting, Hand Painted, Blue Fishnet, White Ground, 4¾ x 4½ x 5 In.
$156

Auctions at Showplace, NYC

Herend, Figurine, Foo Dog, Famille Noire, Black Dynasty Series, Kramlik Ferncne, 6 x 6 x 3 In., Pair
$570

Alderfer Auction Company

Herend, Figurine, Panther, Green Fishnet Design, Hand Painted, Gilt Paws & Nose, 6 x 18 x 4 In.
$840

Alderfer Auction Company

Herend, Pitcher, Flowers, Unique Shape, Lizard Figural Handle, 14 x 12 x 5 In.
$540

Alderfer Auction Company

H

Herend, Plate, Basket Weave Ground, Gilt, Scalloped Rim, Flowers, 7½ In., 5 Piece
$219

Turner Auctions + Appraisals

Herend, Tureen, Dome Lid, Lemon Finial, White, Multicolor Flowers, Green Handles, 6¼ x 9 In.
$531

Hindman

Herend, Tureen, Famille Noire, Gilt Edges, Half Lemon Finial, Miniature, 4 x 6 x 3 In.
$120

Alderfer Auction Company

Hobnail, Bottle, Amethyst Glass, Lift Lid, Spiral Neck, c.1910, 8 In.
$53

Charleston Estate Auctions

Holly Amber, Sauce, Golden Agate, Beaded Rim, 1¾ x 4¼ In.
$150

Jeffrey S. Evans & Associates

Holly Amber, Tumbler, Golden Agate, Opalescent Rim, Vertical Panels, Bead Trim, 4 In.
$225

Jeffrey S. Evans & Associates

Sauce, Golden Agate, Beaded Rim, 1¾ x 4¼ In..*illus*   150
Tumbler, Golden Agate, Opalescent Rim, Vertical Panels, Bead Trim, 4 In. ....*illus*   225

HOLT-HOWARD

Holt-Howard was an importer that started working in New York City in 1949 and moved to Stamford, Connecticut, in 1955. The company sold many types of table accessories, such as condiment jars, decanters, spoon holders, and saltshakers. Its figural pieces have a cartoon-like quality. The company was bought out by General Housewares Corporation in 1968. Holt-Howard pieces are often marked with the name and the year or *HH* and the year stamped in black. The *HH* mark was used until 1974. The company also used a black and silver paper label. Holt-Howard production ceased in 1990 and the remainder of the company was sold to Kay Dee Designs. In 2002, Grant Holt and John Howard started Grant-Howard Associates and made retro pixie cookie jars marked *GHA* that sold from a mail-order catalog. Other GHA retro pixie pieces were made until 2006.

Dish, Tree Shape, Bell, Ivy, Pink Bow, Green Border, 1959, 9¾ x 5½ In.....................................   28
Salt & Pepper, Four Seasons, Blue, Brown, Cream, 4-Sided, c.1964.....................................   20
Stringholder, Cat Head, Green Eyes, Plaid Collar, c.1958, 5 x 4 x 3 In....................................   75

HOPALONG CASSIDY

Hopalong Cassidy was a character in a series of 28 books written by Clarence E. Mulford, first published in 1907. Movies and television shows were made based on the character. The best-known actor playing Hopalong Cassidy was William Lawrence Boyd. His first movie appearance was in 1919, but the first Hopalong Cassidy film was not made until 1934. Sixty-six films were made. In 1948, William Boyd purchased the television rights to the movies, then later made 52 new programs. In the 1950s, Hopalong Cassidy and his horse, named Topper, were seen in comics, records, toys, and other products. Boyd died in 1972.

Badge, 6-Sided Star, Metal, Portrait, 1950s, 2 In.   44
Book, Little Golden, Hopalong Cassidy & The Bar 20 Cowboy, 1952.......................................   25
Lapel Pin, Hoppy, Initials, Metal, 2 In.   59
Pennant, Hoppy On Horse, Gun Drawn, Name In Cowboy Rope, Felt, White On Black, 29 x 11 In. ...   68
Plate, Hoppy On Horse, Gun In Hand, Porcelain, 1950s, 9 In...   48
Slate, School Outfit, Transogram, 1 Old Man, Young Boy & Girl, 1950, Box   120

HORN

Horn was used to make many types of boxes, furniture inlays, jewelry, and whimsies. The Endangered Species Act makes it illegal to sell many of these pieces. See also Powder Horn.

Carving, Water Buffalo, God Of Longevity, Staff, Peach, Chinese, Late 1800s, 12½ In.   120
Centerpiece, 3 Horns, Gilt Metal Mounts, Scrolled Candlestick, Continental, 1800s, 16 In... *illus*   605
Cup, Rhinoceros, Carved, Horse's Head, Demon & Dragon Rim, Chinese, 1800s, 4¾ In.   4680
Figure, Man, Holding Fish, Children, Carved, Japan, 5½ In...*illus*   150

HOWDY DOODY

Howdy Doody and Buffalo Bob were the main characters in a children's series televised from 1947 to 1960. Howdy was a redheaded puppet. The series became popular with college students in the late 1970s when Buffalo Bob began to lecture on campuses.

Doll, Blue Striped Polo, Red Pants, Marked, Kagran Corp., Ideal, Box, 1952, 21 In. ....*illus*   704

Horn, Centerpiece, 3 Horns, Gilt Metal Mounts, Scrolled Candlestick, Continental, 1800s, 16 In.
$605

Ahlers & Ogletree Auction Gallery

Horn, Figure, Man, Holding Fish, Children, Carved, Japan, 5½ In.
$150

Treasureseeker Auctions

Howdy Doody, Doll, Blue Striped Polo, Red Pants, Marked, Kagran Corp., Ideal, Box, 1952, 21 In.
$704

Morphy Auctions

Howdy Doody, Doll, Ventriloquist, Cloth Body, Eegee Broadcasting Co., 1972, 32 In.
$86

Apple Tree Auction Center

Hull, Bowl, Cauliflower Shape, Snail Top, Green Leaves, Underplate, Bellevue, Faience, 12 x 13 In.
$469

Turner Auctions + Appraisals

Hummel, Figurine, No. 331, Crossroads, 2 Boys, Standing By Signpost, Halt, Last Bee, 1970s, 6 In.
$75

Lion and Unicorn

Doll, Ventriloquist, Cloth Body, Eegee Broadcasting Co., 1972, 32 In. .... *illus* 86
Lamp, Clarabell Clown, Orange Shade, Multicolor, Marked, Kagran, 1950, 13¼ In. 282
Wristwatch, Ingraham, Stand, Clear Plastic Case, Marked, Kagran, Box, 7 In. 450

HULL

Hull pottery was made in Crooksville, Ohio, from 1905. Addis E. Hull bought the Acme Pottery Company and started making ceramic wares. In 1917, A. E. Hull Pottery began making art pottery as well as the commercial wares. For a short time, 1921 to 1929, the firm also sold pottery imported from Europe. The dinnerware of the 1940s (including the Little Red Riding Hood line), the matte wares of the 1940s, and the high gloss artwares of the 1950s are all popular with collectors. The firm officially closed in March 1986.

Hull Pottery
c.1915

A.E. HULL U.S.A.

Hull Pottery
1930s

Hull Pottery
c.1950

Bowl, Cauliflower Shape, Snail Top, Green Leaves, Underplate, Bellevue, Faience, 12 x 13 In.....*illus* 469
Lavabo, Dolphin Shape, Cast Metal, Swirl, 25 x 16 x 7 In. 219

HUMMEL

Hummel figurines, based on the drawings of the nun M.I. Hummel (Berta Hummel), were made by the W. Goebel Porzellanfabrik of Oeslau, Germany, now Rodental, Germany. They were first made in 1935. The *Crown* mark was used from 1935 to 1949. The company added the *bee* marks in 1950. The *full bee* with variations, was used from 1950 to 1959; *stylized bee,* 1957 to 1972; *three line mark,* 1964 to 1972; *last bee,* sometimes called *vee over gee,* 1972 to 1979. In 1979 the V bee symbol was removed from the mark. *U.S. Zone* was part of the mark from 1946 to 1948; *W. Germany* was part of the mark from 1960 to 1990. The *Goebel W. Germany* mark, called the *missing bee* mark, was used from 1979 to 1990; *Goebel, Germany,* with the crown and *WG,* originally called the *new mark,* was used from 1991 through part of 1999. A new version of the bee mark with the word *Goebel* was used from 1999 to 2008. A special *Year 2000* backstamp was also introduced. Porcelain figures inspired by Berta Hummel's drawings were introduced in 1997. These are marked *BH* followed by a number. They were made in the Far East, not Germany. Goebel discontinued making Hummel figurines in 2008 and Manufaktur Rodental took over the factory in Germany and began making new Hummel figurines. Hummel figurines made by Rodental are marked with a yellow and black bee on the edge of an oval line surrounding the words *Original M.I. Hummel Germany.* The words *Manufaktur Rodental* are printed beneath the oval. Manufaktur Rodental was sold in 2013 and new owners, Hummel Manufaktur GmbH, took over. It was sold again in 2017, but figurines continue to be made in the factory in Rodental. Other decorative items and plates that feature Hummel drawings were made by Schmid Brothers, Inc. beginning in 1971. Schmid Brothers closed in 1995.

Hummel
1935–1949

Hummel
1950–1959

Hummel
2009–present

Figurine, No. 71, Stormy Weather, Girl & Boy Under Umbrella, Missing Bee, 6 In.	42
Figurine, No. 152/B, Umbrella Girl, Three Line Mark, 4¾ In.	238
Figurine, No. 170, School Boys, 3 Boys, Goebel Bee, 1982, 9½ In.	229
Figurine, No. 185, Accordion Boy, Stylized Bee, 5¼ In.	30
Figurine, No. 331, Crossroads, 2 Boys, Standing By Signpost, Halt, Last Bee, 1970s, 6 In. *illus*	75

HUTSCHENREUTHER

LORENZ
HUTSCHEN REUTER

GERMANY

Hutschenreuther Porcelain Factory was founded by Carolus Magnus in Hohenburg, Bavaria, in 1814. A second factory was established in Selb, Germany, in 1857. The company made fine-quality porcelain dinnerware, figurines, and plaques. The mark changed through the years, but the name and the lion insignia appear in most versions. Hutschenreuther became part of the Rosenthal division of the Waterford Wedgwood Group in 2000. Rosenthal became part of the Arcturus Group in 2009.

Plaque, Night, Woman Flying, Nude, Painted, Giltwood Frame, c.1915, 5 x 3 In. *illus*	250
Plaque, Portrait, Woman, Gilt Bronze, Frame, 9 x 6½ In. *illus*	570

ICON

Icons, special, revered pictures of Jesus, Mary, or a saint, are usually Russian or Byzantine. The small icons collected today are made of wood and tin or precious metals. Many modern copies have been made in the old style and are being sold to tourists in Russia and Europe and at shops in the United States. Rare, old icons have sold for over $50,000. The riza (oklad) is the metal cover protecting the icon. It is often made of silver or gold.

Mary Holding Jesus, Silver Oklad, Painted, Wood Panel, Late 1800s, 7 x 5 In.	273
Our Lady Of Kazan, Tempera On Panel, Gilt Repousse Riza, Cloisonne Enamel, 8⅞ x 7 In. *illus*	2048
St. Nicholas, Holding Bible, Silver, Embellished, Gilt Highlights, Russia, c.1893, 10 x 12 In.	908
Triptych, Gothic Style, Painted, Madonna & Child, Flanked By Saints, 3 Panels, 16 In.	250

IMARI

Imari is a porcelain design made in Japan and China beginning in the seventeenth century. In the eighteenth century and later, it was copied by porcelain factories in Germany, France, England, and the United States. It was especially popular in the nineteenth century and is still being made. Imari is decorated with stylized bamboo, floral, and geometric designs in orange, red, green, and blue. The name comes from the Japanese port of Imari, which exported the ware made nearby in a factory at Arita. Imari is now a general term for any pattern of this type.

Bowl, Phoenix Interior, Dragon, Floral Cartouches, Leaf Sprays Exterior, Japan, 1900s, 6 In. *illus*	384
Bowl, White Ground, Multicolor, Blue Lines, Scalloped Rim, Footed, 17 In.	75
Charger, Fan Design, Flowers, Figures, Landscape, 4-Character Mark, 12 In.	83
Charger, Painted, Gilt Accent, Multicolor, Japan, 1800s, 3 x 17¾ In.	215
Charger, People, Flowers, Multicolor, Gilt Rim, 15½ In.	219
Charger, Scalloped Rim, Trees, Leaves & Flowers, 13 In.	125
Dish, Running Horse, Flowering Trees & Plants, Diapered Borders, Chinese, c.1720, 1 x 9 In., Pair	488
Dish, Rural Scene, Pagoda, Clouds, Trees, Japan, 1868, 18¾ In. *illus*	638
Fishbowl, Floral Exterior, Carp Interior, c.1870s, 9 x 14 In.	570
Garden Seat, Cylindrical, Open Handle, Cherry Blossoms, White Ground, Japan, 19 x 10 In.	450
Garniture, Vase, Lid, Figural Cartouches, Japan, Late 1800s, 18 In. *illus*	188
Jar, Flowers, Red, Blue, Gilt Bronze Mounted, Paw Feet, 1700s, 24¼ In., Pair	6930
Jar, Lid, Flowers, Stems, Female Figure, Garden, Tezuka Kinsei, Japan, 1800s, 29 In.	570
Lamp, Tea Caddy Shape, Red & Blue Flowers, Wood Base, Ribbed Shade, Japan, 34 x 10 In.	192
Lamp, Vase, Bronze Ormolu Mounts, Lion's Head Handles, Tassel Rings, Japan, 1800s, 29 In.	199
Plate, Birthday, Blue Underglaze, Multicolor, Lingzhi Design, Chinese, c.1875, 9 In., Pair	244

Hutschenreuther, Plaque, Night, Woman Flying, Nude, Painted, Giltwood Frame, c.1915, 5 x 3 In.
$250

Hindman

Hutschenreuther, Plaque, Portrait, Woman, Gilt Bronze, Frame, 9 x 6½ In.
$570

I

Treasureseeker Auctions

Icon, Our Lady Of Kazan, Tempera On Panel, Gilt Repousse Riza, Cloisonne Enamel, 8⅞ x 7 In.
$2,048

Neal Auction Company

Imari, Bowl, Phoenix Interior, Dragon, Floral Cartouches, Leaf Sprays Exterior, Japan, 1900s, 6 In. $384

Neal Auction Company

Imari, Dish, Rural Scene, Pagoda, Clouds, Trees, Japan, 1868, 18 ¾ In. $638

Bonhams

Imari, Garniture, Vase, Lid, Figural Cartouches, Japan, Late 1800s, 18 In. $188

Charlton Hall Auctions

Plate, Black, Flowers, Gilt Borders, 1900s, 10 ⅝ In., 6 Piece	512
Umbrella Stand, Gilt, Highlight, Bamboo Decor, Gold, Flowers, Painted, Yellow, 18 In.	59
Vase, Bottle, Flowers, Blue, Red, Gold, Wood Stand, Japan, Late 1800s, 12 x 8 ¼ In., Pair	431
Vase, Bud, Floral Vases, Tree In Garden, Fukagawa, Late 1800s, 7 ½ In. ....*illus*	300
Vase, Dragon, Flared Rim, Figural Flowers, 2 Handles, Peonies, Mid 1800s, 8 ½ In.	240
Vase, Faceted Bottle Shape, Wood Base, Mounted As Lamp, Japan, 1900s, 39 ½ In. ....*illus*	960
Vase, Flowers, Flared Rim, White Ground, Blue Base, Japan, 1800s, 24 In.	290
Vase, Ginger Jar, Lobed Detail, Parcel Gilt Accent, Character Mark, Chinese, 14 ¾ x 11 ½ In.... *illus*	1000
Vase, Ribbed, Bird, Floral Cartouches, Flared Rim, Japan, 1900s, 11 ¾ In., Pair	244
Vase, Scalloped Edge, Flowers, Birds, Late 1800s, 18 In.	240

IMPERIAL GLASS

Imperial Glass Corporation was founded in Bellaire, Ohio, in 1901. It became a subsidiary of Lenox, Inc., in 1973 and was sold to Arthur R. Lorch in 1981. It was sold again in 1982, and went bankrupt in 1984. In 1985, the molds and some assets were sold. The Imperial glass preferred by the collector is freehand art glass, carnival glass, slag glass, stretch glass, and other top-quality tablewares. Tablewares and animals are listed here. The others may be found in the appropriate sections.

Imperial Glass 1911–1932

Imperial Glass 1913–1920s

Imperial Glass 1973–1981

Animal, Owl, Candy Dish, Lid, Brown, Gray, White, Slag Glass, 7 In.	30
Art Glass, Vase, Free Hand, Loops, Blue, Shoulders, Flared Neck, 6 ½ In.	200
Art Glass, Vase, Free Hand, Orange & Green Loops, Shoulders, Flared Neck, 8 In.	112
Heavy Grape, Bowl, Ruffled Rim, Purple, Carnival Glass, 10 ¼ In.	24
Love Birds, Dish, Lid, Pale Green Slag, 5 ½ In.	24
Scroll, Plate, Green Center, Marigold Edge, Octagonal, Scalloped	24
Windmill, Pitcher, Ruby Slag, 6 ½ In.	24

INDIAN

Indian art from North and South America has attracted the collector for many years. Each tribe has its own distinctive designs and techniques. Baskets, jewelry, pottery, and leatherwork are of greatest collector interest. Eskimo art is listed under Eskimo in this book.

Bag, Nez Perce, Thread Sewn, 2 Women Design, Floral, Multicolor, Late 1800s, 13 x 9 In....*illus*	5625
Bag, Potawatomie, Loom Beaded, Bandolier, Thread Sewn, Opaque Ground, c.1900, 37 ¾ In.	1250
Basket, Apache, Coiled, 5-Point Star Inside Larger Star, Round, 10 ¼ In.	170
Basket, Apache, White Mountain, Devil's Claw, 2-Color Design, 8 Floating Diamonds, 4 x 19 In.	2832
Basket, Pit River, Dark Brown, Tan, Zigzag Design, Northeastern California, c.1920s, 5 ½ x 7 ½ In.	677
Basket, Tlingit, Lift Lid, Rattle Top, Woven, Geometric Design, Early 1900s, 4 x 6 In.	2813
Basket, Tlingit, Spruce Root, Tapered, 2 Bands, Dark Brown & Orange, c.1900, 4 x 5 In.	322
Basket, Trinket, Penobscot, Lid, Porcupine Twists, Theresa Secord, 5 ½ x 4 In. ....*illus*	469
Basket, Wounaan, Woven, Parrot Design, Flared Rim, Oval Body, Panama Rainforest, 11 In...*illus*	813
Basket, Yokuts, Bowl Shape, Linear Designs, c.1910, 8 ¾ x 4 In.	800
Bear, San Ildefonso, Redware, Turquoise & Heishi, Russell Sanchez, Denver, 1963, 4 x 6 In. .. *illus*	3438
Belt Buckle, Navajo, Spider Web Design, 2 Spiders, Turquoise, Coral Bead Eyes, 2 ⅜ x 3 In.	440
Belt Buckle, Zuni, Bird Man, Inlay, Turquoise, Onyx, Coral, 2 x 1 ½ x ½ In...............*illus*	188
Blanket, Navajo, Red Field, Black & White Lattice, Zigzags, Wool, Hand Woven, 105 x 58 In.	2815
Blanket, Navajo, Sand Field, Central Medallion, Red & Green, Striped Ends, c.1900, 56 x 78 In.	497
Blanket, Navajo, Wool, Serrated Edge, Diamond Motifs, Red Field, Hand Woven, 105 x 58 In.. *illus*	2700
Bow, Mojave, Painted, Black, Red, White Diamond & Linear Design, Late 1800s, 35 ¾ In.	438
Bowl, Avanyu, San Ildefonso, Black On Black, 2 x 3 ⅝ In.	63
Bowl, Great Lakes, Ho-Chunk, Wood, Stylized Bird, Elongated Neck, Tail Handles, c.1860, 3 x 11 In.	2500

Bowl, Mata Ortiz, Signed, Tomasa Mora, Mexico, Late 1900s, 6 In.	56
Bowl, Pomo, Basketry, Whirling Geometric Design, c.1910, 5 x 20 In.	1003
Bowl, San Ildefonso, Black, Bird Design, Signed, Marie & Julian, c.1935, 10⅞ In.	1280
Bowl, San Ildefonso, Blackware, Carved, Birdlike Decor, Juanita & Wo-Peen Gonzales, 5¾ x 6 In.	187
Bowl, San Ildefonso, Blackware, Pollywog, Marie & Santana Martinez, 4 x 6 In.	281
Bowl, San Ildefonso, Feathers & Geometrics, Red Slip Exterior, Carmelita Dunlap, 3 x 14 In. *illus*	800
Bowl, Santa Clara Pueblo, Blackware, Bird, Signed, Luann Tafoya, 2⅞ x 5⅞ x 6¾ In.	260
Bowl, Southwest, Black Birds, Wheel, Cream Ground Interior, 3¼ In.	366
Bowl, Zuni Kiva, Horned Toad & Tadpoles, Dragonflies, 2 x 6 In. *illus*	313
Box, Lid, Tlingit, Bentwood, Painted, Fish, Side Tie Closure, 2⅞ x 4¼ In.	150
Box, Northwest Coast, Copper, Wood, Carved Face, c.1920s, 4 x 6 x 4 In.	1476
Candlestick, Massasoit, Standing, Gilt Metal, c.1890, 9⅞ In., Pair.	182
Canteen, San Ildefonso, Deer Design, Beads, Cornhusk Stopper, Russell Sanchez, 1963, 9 x 8 In.	11250
Cap, Naskapi, Beaded, Red & Black, Wool, Late 1800s, 9¾ In. *illus*	188
Charger, San Ildefonso, Blackware, Feather Design, Maria Montoya & Santana Martinez, 2 x 12 In.	2750
Cradle, Nez Perce, Contour, Hide, Beaded, Red Trade Cloth, Late 1800s, 39 x 14 In.	4375
Dagger, Chilanum, South, Forged Steel, Sculptural Hilt, Fuller Blade, 18 In.	900
Doll, Nakota, Male, Thread Sewn, Braided Pigtails, c.1900, 16 In. *illus*	2500
Dress, Sioux, Thread Sewn, Multicolor, Basket Beads, Brass Bells, Late 1800s, 25 x 24 In.	5000
Eye Dazzler, Navajo, Feather Design, Red, White, c.1930s, 57 x 35 In.	1353
Figure, Zuni, Mustached Male, Linear Elements, Multicolor, Pottery, 1930s, 10 x 8 In.	1063
Fish Hook, Halibut, Inuit, Wood, Bone Spur, Twine, Carved, Alaska, Early 1900s, 10 x 4 In.	410
Hat, Hupa, Woven, Hazelnut Warp, Pine Root Weft, Basketry, 5 x 8 In. *illus*	826
Hat, Pacific Northwest, Fiber, Multicolor Rims, Central Bands, Fish, Geometrics, 1900s, 15 In. *illus*	315
Hide Panel, Northern Cree, Beaded, Thread, Sinew Sewn, Floral Medallions, Early 1900s, 23 x 23 In.	313
Hide Scraper, Plains, Elk Antler, Steel Blade, c.1880, 12½ In.	594
Jar, Hopi, Ruins Design, Al Qoyawayma, Denver, 1938, 8 x 11 In. *illus*	7500
Jar, Hopi-Teva, Corn Device, Sienna Red, Brown, Star, Dextra Quotskuyva Nampeyo, 2⅝ In.	1280
Jar, Mata Ortiz, Blackware, Serpent, Jaeme Quezada, 10½ In. *illus*	288
Jar, Mata Ortiz, Fish, Red, Black, Signed, Roberto Banuelos, Contemporary, 8 x 4½ In.*illus*	308
Jar, Mata Ortiz, Tribal & Symbolic Design, Gregorio Goyo Silveira, 1900s, 12 In.	150
Jar, San Ildefonso, Blackware, Feather Design, Eagle, Marie & Santana Martinez, 4½ x 6 In.	1063
Jar, Santa Clara Pueblo, Redware, Melon Shape, Ribbed, Signed, Helen Shupla, c.1960, 9 x 12 In.	3445
Katsina, Hopi, Crow Mother, Gift For The Chief, Cottonwood, Carved & Painted, 12 In.	381
Katsina, Hopi, Dancer, Cottonwood, Carved, Multicolor, Signed, Roanna Jackson, 12 In. *illus*	203
Katsina, Hopi, Feathers, Fur, Copper, Marble Base, Signed, K. Bird, 2000s, 52 In.	240
Katsina, Hopi, Standing, Circular Base, Signed, Duwyenie Dawa, 6 In.	100
Moccasins, Cree, Beaded, Smoke Tanned, Thread Sewn, Floral, Late 1800s, 16 x 9½ In.	875
Moccasins, Iroquois Style, Fabric, Tan, Brown, Leather Sole, Bead Trim, Blue Tie, Child's, 6 In.	100
Model, Totem, Northwest Coast, Argillite, Animal & Human Faces, Tom Hans, Skidegate, 6½ In.	704
Olla, Acoma, Carved, Multicolor, Kokopelli, Fish, Turtle, Bear, 1900s, 10½ In. *illus*	256
Olla, Apache, Woven, Geometric Design, Brown, Round Top, 11 x 9 In. *illus*	132
Olla, Jemez, Birds, Flowers, Signed, Mary T. Magdalena, 7¼ x 8 In.	75
Parfleche, Lakota Sioux, Clothing Container, Painted Rawhide, c.1890, 28 x 16 x 4 In.	2223
Pipe, Southern Plains, Tamper, Osage Orange Wood, Curved Crescent Top, c.1880, 11½ In.	313
Plate, San Ildefonso, Pottery, Black, Feather Design, Signed, Maria Popovi, 1966, 6½ In.	1024
Plate, Santa Clara, Carved Red & Sienna, Nathan Youngblood, Denver, 1954, 13 In. *illus*	6875
Platter, San Ildefonso, Blackware, Feather Design, Signed Maria & Santana, 15 In.	630
Pot, Casas Grandes, Bulbous, Red & Black, Variegated Clay, Footed, Signed, 6 x 7 In.	293
Pot, Mata Ortiz, Blackware, Signed, Fernando Gonzales, Contemporary, 6¾ x 4¾ In.	431
Purse, Dine, Felt, Brass Buttons, Buffalo Tracks, Trade, Penny Singer, 1900s, 9 x 15 x 6 In.	94
Rattle, Sioux, Wood Handle & Hoop, Painted Rawhide, Leather Drop, c.1880, 15 In. *illus*	313
Rug, Navajo, Feather, Arrows, Geometric Pattern, Red, Black, c.1930s, 60 x 40 In. *illus*	1476
Rug, Navajo, Storm Pattern, Multicolor, Sand Field, Mid 1900s, 35 x 60 In.	878
Saddle Blanket, Anishinaabe, Floral Beadwork, Wool, c.1900, 29½ x 56 In.	1000
Saddle Blanket, Navajo, Tufted, White, Mid 1900s, 24 x 21 In.	615
Stole, Northeastern, Beaded, Embroidered, Flower & Cross Design, Early 1900s, 90 In.	219
Teepee, Arapaho, Wood Poles, Roundels & Drops, c.1900, 47 x 22 In. *illus*	2500
Totem, Haida, Bear, Man, Seal, Crow, Carved & Painted, Wood, Multicolor, 1800s, 25 In.	3510
Tray, Apache, Basketry, Round, Coiled, Brown Paint, Star, Animals, Figures, c.1910, 4 x 16 In.	3276

Imari, Vase, Bud, Floral Vases, Tree In Garden, Fukagawa, Late 1800s, 7½ In. $300

Alex Cooper Auctioneers

Imari, Vase, Faceted Bottle Shape, Wood Base, Mounted As Lamp, Japan, 1900s, 39½ In. $960

Neal Auction Company

Imari, Vase, Ginger Jar, Lobed Detail, Parcel Gilt Accent, Character Mark, Chinese, 14¾ x 11½ In. $1,000

Auctions at Showplace, NYC

Indian, Bag, Nez Perce, Thread Sewn, 2 Women Design, Floral, Multicolor, Late 1800s, 13 x 9 In.
$5,625

TIP
Never leave your house keys on your key chain when an attendant parks your car.

Indian, Bear, San Ildefonso, Redware, Turquoise & Heishi, Russell Sanchez, Denver, 1963, 4 x 6 In.
$3,438

Indian, Bowl, San Ildefonso, Feathers & Geometrics, Red Slip Exterior, Carmelita Dunlap, 3 x 14 In.
$800

Hindman

Hindman

Brunk Auctions

Indian, Bowl, Zuni Kiva, Horned Toad & Tadpoles, Dragonflies, 2 x 6 In.
$313

Indian, Basket, Trinket, Penobscot, Lid, Porcupine Twists, Theresa Secord, 5 ½ x 4 In.
$469

Indian, Belt Buckle, Zuni, Bird Man, Inlay, Turquoise, Onyx, Coral, 2 x 1 ½ x ½ In.
$188

Auctions at Showplace, NYC

Hindman

Hindman

Indian, Blanket, Navajo, Wool, Serrated Edge, Diamond Motifs, Red Field, Hand Woven, 105 x 58 In.
$2,700

Indian, Cap, Naskapi, Beaded, Red & Black, Wool, Late 1800s, 9 ¾ In.
$188

Indian, Basket, Wounaan, Woven, Parrot Design, Flared Rim, Oval Body, Panama Rainforest, 11 In.
$813

Hindman

Charlton Hall Auctions

Alderfer Auction Company

Indian, Doll, Nakota, Male, Thread Sewn, Braided Pigtails, c.1900, 16 In.
$2,500

Hindman

Indian, Hat, Hupa, Woven, Hazelnut Warp, Pine Root Weft, Basketry, 5 x 8 In.
$826

Soulis Auctions

Indian, Hat, Pacific Northwest, Fiber, Multicolor Rims, Central Bands, Fish, Geometrics, 1900s, 15 In.
$315

Brunk Auctions

Indian, Jar, Hopi, Ruins Design, Al Qoyawayma, Denver, 1938, 8 x 11 In.
$7,500

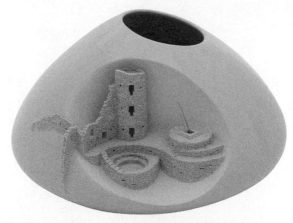

Hindman

Indian, Jar, Mata Ortiz, Blackware, Serpent, Jaeme Quezada, 10 ½ In.
$288

Merrill's Auctions

Indian, Jar, Mata Ortiz, Fish, Red, Black, Signed, Roberto Banuelos, Contemporary, 8 x 4 ½ In.
$308

California Historical Design

I

Indian, Katsina, Hopi, Dancer, Cottonwood, Carved, Multicolor, Signed, Roanna Jackson, 12 In.
$203

White's Auctions

Indian, Olla, Acoma, Carved, Multicolor, Kokopelli, Fish, Turtle, Bear, 1900s, 10 ½ In.
$256

Brunk Auctions

Indian, Olla, Apache, Woven, Geometric Design, Brown, Round Top, 11 x 9 In.
$132

Alderfer Auction Company

Indian, Plate, Santa Clara, Carved Red & Sienna, Nathan Youngblood, Denver, 1954, 13 In.
$6,875

Hindman

Indian, Rattle, Sioux, Wood Handle & Hoop, Painted Rawhide, Leather Drop, c.1880, 15 In.
$313

Hindman

Indian, Rug, Navajo, Feather, Arrows, Geometric Pattern, Red, Black, c.1930s, 60 x 40 In.
$1,476

California Historical Design

Trinket Box, Navajo, Hinged Lid, Silver, Chrysoprase Stone, Engraved Arrows, 5 x 3 x 2 In.	575
Vase, Mata Ortiz, Fish, Carved, Signed, Lconel Lopez Seanz, Contemporary, 7 x 4¾ In........	369
Vase, San Ildefonso, Pottery, Black, Scalloped Decor, Marie & Julian, c.1935, 3 In.................	512
Vest, Ogala Lakota, Leather, Beaded Medallion, 2 Warriors, Douglas Fast Horse, 1985, 22 x 42 In.	2000

INDIAN TREE

Indian Tree is a china pattern that was popular during the last half of the nineteenth century. It was copied from earlier Indian textile patterns that were very similar. The pattern includes the crooked branch of a tree and a partial landscape with exotic flowers and leaves. Green, blue, pink, and orange were the favored colors used in the design. Coalport, Spode, Johnson Brothers, and other firms made this pottery. Don't be confused by a pattern called India Tree made by Copeland.

Platter, Oval, Multicolor, Ironstone, 12 x 15 In..	83
Tureen, Lid, Underplate, Side Handles, Gilt Trim, Derby, c.1820, 9¼ x 15 In........................	1500
Tureen, Underplate, Dome Lid, Iron Red, Gilt, Derby, c.1820, 9 x 14¼ In. ....*illus*	1500
Waste Bowl, Multicolor, Gilt Trim, Coalport, 3¼ x 4¾ In.	12

INKSTAND

Inkstands were made to be placed on a desk. They held some type of container for ink, and possibly a sander, a pen tray, a pen, a holder for pounce, and even a candle to melt the sealing wax. Inkstands date to the eighteenth century and have been made of silver, copper, ceramics, and glass. Additional inkstands may be found in these and other related categories.

Brass Mounted, Bronze Serpent Handle, Ink Pots, Late 1800s, 5 x 10½ x 6½ In........*illus*	94
Bronze, Napoleon III, 2 Cut Glass Bottles, Cupid Center, Marble Base, 1800s, 7 x 13 x 6 In. *illus*	497
Fruitwood, Carved, Clear Glass, Lion's Paw Feet, 1800s, 3 x 12 x 9 In.	183
Mahogany, Boule, Brass Inlay, Paw Feet, Marquis Of Wellington, c.1915, 8 x 16 x 13 In.......	270
Porcelain, Flower Encrusted, Rectangular, Multicolor, Germany, 1800s, 12 In.....................	357
Porcelain, Green & White Sponge, Slanted Side, Dip Hole, Pen Rest, Art Deco, c.1920, 2½ In.....	150
Silver, Clock, Roman Numerals, Glass Insert, Circular Base, London, 1903, 5½ In.............	600
Silver, Edwardian Style, Gadroon Rim, Square Cut Glass, William Hutton & Sons, 1904, 9 x 6 In......	313
Silver, Orientalist, Palm Tree, G.R. Collis & Co., Birmingham, Victorian, 1847, 6 x 9 x 7 In.	1750
Silver, Race Car, Driver, Passenger, Shaped Base, Wilhelm Zwick, 1900s, 6 x 15½ x 8½ In.	847
Walnut, Ebonized, 2 Glass Inkwells, Fountain Pen, Victorian, England, 6 x 12 x 8 In.. *illus*	125
Walnut, Ebonized, Brass, 2 Glass Inkwells, Pen Tray, Bun Feet, 1800s, 4¾ x 12 In.	212

INKWELL

Inkwells, of course, held ink. Ready-made ink was first made about 1836 and was sold in bottles. The desk inkwell had a narrow hole so the pen would not slip inside. Inkwells were made of many materials, such as pottery, glass, pewter, and silver. Ink bottles are listed in the Bottle category.

Agate, Lion's Heads, Champleve, Cone Finial, France, 9 In..	60
Brass, Skull & Crossed Bones Shape, Hinged Face, Pottery Insert, 1880s, 3 In......................	390
Bronze, Art Nouveau, Nude, Woman, Long Hair, Sphinx Style, Figure Top, c.1890, 3½ x 6 In....	270
Bronze, Boar's Head, Head Flips Open, Signed, Barrie, 7 x 5 x 4 In............................*illus*	191
Bronze, Louis XVI Style, Gilt & Marble, 1800s, 4 x 13 In...	250
Bronze, Michelangelo, 2 Ink Pots, Pen Tray, Rouge Marble Base, c.1900, 12¾ In.	640
Bronze, Pen Tray, Art Nouveau, Patina, Gustav Gurschner, 4 x 11 x 7 In.	300
Cast Iron, Man In Barrel, Hinged Lid, Orange, Black, Blue, Brown, J. & E. Stevens, 3½ In. *illus*	780
Cranberry Glass, Iridescent, Pink, Web Design, Brass Flip Lid, Swirls, 2 x 5 In.................	200
Cut Glass, 8-Sided, Hobstar Base, Panel Cut, Silver Top, Monogram, Gorham, 2½ x 3½ In......	540
Gilt Bronze, Lion's Head, Roaring, Mouth Open, Glass Reservoir, Continental, 4 x 3½ In. .	125
Ivory, Porous Bone, Locomotive Shape, Carved, 3 Ornate Wheels, Dieppe, France, 3 x 4 x 1 In.	295
Metal, Lion, Standing, Full Mane, 1900s, 21 x 47 x 18 In., Pair.....................................*illus*	1260

Indian, Teepee, Arapaho, Wood Poles, Roundels & Drops, c.1900, 47 x 22 In.
$2,500

Hindman

Indian Tree, Tureen, Underplate, Dome Lid, Iron Red, Gilt, Derby, c.1820, 9 x 14¼ In.
$1,500

Hindman

Inkstand, Brass Mounted, Bronze Serpent Handle, Ink Pots, Late 1800s, 5 x 10½ x 6½ In.
$94

Auctions at Showplace, NYC

Inkstand, Bronze, Napoleon III, 2 Cut Glass Bottles, Cupid Center, Marble Base, 1800s, 7 x 13 x 6 In.
$497

Thomaston Place Auction Galleries

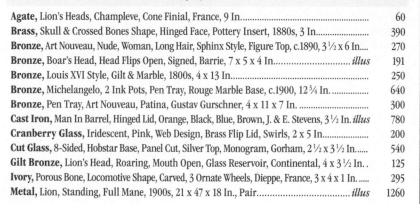

Inkstand, Walnut, Ebonized, 2 Glass Inkwells, Fountain Pen, Victorian, England, 6 x 12 x 8 In.
$125

Susanin's Auctioneers & Appraisers

A Standish

A *standish* is an inkstand to be used on a nieteenth-century desk. Most are figural with inkwells and containers for pens, blotting material, sealing wax, or other things needed to write a letter in the 1800s.

Inkwell, Bronze, Boar's Head, Head Flips Open, Signed, Barrie, 7 x 5 x 4 In.
$191

White's Auctions

Inkwell, Cast Iron, Man In Barrel, Hinged Lid, Orange, Black, Blue, Brown, J. & E. Stevens, 3 1/2 In.
$780

Bertoia Auctions

Ormolu, Rabbit, Double, Flower Shape Lid, Gilt, Cut Glass Inserts, 3 3/4 x 9 x 6 In.	63
Porcelain, Inkwell, Rococo Style, Sand Shaker, Purple & Blue, Gilt, Paris, 1800s, 8 x 9 In.	363
Porcelain, Mother, Daughters, Praying, Altar, Germany, 1800s, 10 1/2 In. *illus*	150
Porcelain, Soft Paste, Fruit Lid, Central Candleholder, Green & Red Borders, 1800s, 4 x 8 x 7 In.	122
Pressed Glass, Couch, Fine Cut & Button, Amber, Novelty, c.1915, 4 x 5 In.	140
Silver, Pen Rack, Glass Body, Weighted Bottom, Marked, L.B. Co., 4 In. *illus*	180
Silvered Metal, Pen Tray, Race Car, Driver, Navigator, Wilhelm Zwick, Kayser, c.1910, 15 3/4 In. *illus*	1440
Verde Marble, Spread Wing Figural Eagle, Paw Feet, Gilt, Early 1900s, 8 x 11 x 6 In. *illus*	295
Wood, Owl, Hinged Neck, Stone Shape Base, Black Forest, 6 1/2 In.	156

INSULATOR

Insulators of glass or pottery have been made for use on telegraph or telephone poles since 1844. Billions of insulators in hundreds of styles have been made. Most common glass insulators are clear or aqua; the most common porcelain ones are chocolate brown. The most desirable are the threadless types made from 1850 to 1870. Collectors identify insulators by their shape. Glass insulators are identified by their CD (Consolidated Design) numbers and porcelain insulators by their U (Unipart) numbers. Information about these numbering systems can be found online.

CD 102, Diamond, True Milky Mustard	1018
CD 104, New England Telegraph & Telephone Co., Yellow Green *illus*	352
CD 112, Brookfield, Bubble Dome, Light Blue *illus*	2255
CD 127.4, Dark Aqua, Patent Dec. 19, 1871, Attributed To Hemingray	1018
CD 257, Hemingray, Electric Blue, Milk Swirls	1815
CD 316, Brookfield, Deep Blue Aqua	1980
CD 701.6, Confederate Egg, Translucent Aqua	4510
CD 791, Baby Teapot, Dark Green, Damaged	4730

IRISH BELLEEK, *see Belleek category.*

IRON

Iron is a metal that has been used by man since prehistoric times. It is a popular metal for tools and decorative items like doorstops that need as much weight as possible. Items are listed here or under other appropriate headings, such as Bookends, Doorstop, Kitchen, Match Holder, or Tool. The tool that is used for ironing clothes, an iron, is listed in the Kitchen category under Iron and Sadiron.

Anvil, Bell Shape, 4-Sided Tip, 4 1/2 In.	90
Birdhouse, Wasp Nest Shape, Top Loop, Marked, Miller Iron Co., Prov., R.I., 1800s, 6 1/2 In. *illus*	1152
Book Press, Painted, Black & Gold, Scrolls, Number 4, Wheel, 1800s, 12 1/2 x 17 1/2 In.	213
Boot Scraper, Curled Extension, Black Paint, Stone Block, Wrought, 1800s, 33 x 15 1/2 In.	837
Boot Scraper, Dog, Dachshund, Long Body, Short Legs, 20 In.	180
Boot Scraper, Halloween Cat, Black Paint, Early 1900s, 16 In.	188
Boot Scraper, Pig, Standing, Curly Tail, Blue Paint, Base, 9 1/4 In. *illus*	236
Candleholder, U-Shape, Tapered Candlecup, Tripod Base, Penny Feet, Wrought, 1700s, 35 In.	531
Candlesnuffer, Extended Length, Scissor Handle, Cylindrical, Wrought, 1800s, 10 1/4 In.	155
Candlestand, Tabletop, Circular Brass Base, 3 Short Legs, Adjustable, 1800s, 22 3/4 x 8 3/4 In.	143
Compote, Arts & Crafts, Hand Forged, Red, Leaves, Square Base, Ball Feet, c.1910s, 13 x 14 1/2 In.	369
Escutcheon, Heart Shape, Wrought, c.1800, 8 1/2 In.	932
Figure, Bodhisattva, Goddess, Statue, Standing, Chinese, 1800s, 11 In.	1150
Figure, Buddha Head, Elongated Ears, Chinese, 1800s, 6 x 3 1/2 x 3 In.	120
Figure, Female, Raised Hand, Square Base, Art Nouveau, c.1905, 12 x 3 x 12 3/4 In.	400
Figure, Fuxi, Seated, Mythical Emperor, Long Hair, Leaf Wreathed Dress, Chinese, 8 1/4 In. *illus*	2280
Figure, Rooster, Brown, Standing, With Base, Newark, 22 In.	246
Horse Tether, Octagonal, Curved Handle, 1850s, 4 x 7 In. *illus*	360
Horse Tie, Head, Rings, Chain, Black Paint, Square Base Plate, 34 In.	210
Model, Ferris Wheel, Folk Art, Welded, Rectangular Wood Base, 1950, 24 x 17 x 8 In.	50
Padlock, Great Patina, Portico Front, Figural Key Device, Signed, 13 x 8 x 2 In.	2124

I

Inkwell, Metal, Lion, Standing, Full Mane, 1900s, 21 x 47 x 18 In., Pair
$1,260

Freeman's

Inkwell, Porcelain, Mother, Daughters, Praying, Altar, Germany, 1800s, 10½ In.
$150

Cottone Auctions

Inkwell, Silver, Pen Rack, Glass Body, Weighted Bottom, Marked, L.B. Co., 4 In.
$180

Richard Opfer Auctioneering, Inc.

Inkwell, Silvered Metal, Pen Tray, Race Car, Driver, Navigator, Wilhelm Zwick, Kayser, c.1910, 15¾ In.
$1,440

Cottone Auctions

Inkwell, Verde Marble, Spread Wing Figural Eagle, Paw Feet, Gilt, Early 1900s, 8 x 11 x 6 In.
$295

Soulis Auctions

Sewing Lamps and Insulators
Did you know Hemingray, the insulator company, also made sewing lamps? Eight designs are known.

Insulator, CD 104, New England Telegraph & Telephone Co., Yellow Green
$352

Bill and Jill Insulators

Insulator, CD 112, Brookfield, Bubble Dome, Light Blue
$2,255

Bill and Jill Insulators

Iron, Birdhouse, Wasp Nest Shape, Top Loop, Marked, Miller Iron Co., Prov., R.I., 1800s, 6½ In.
$1,152

Rachel Davis Fine Arts

Iron, Boot Scraper, Pig, Standing, Curly Tail, Blue Paint, Base, 9¼ In.
$236

Copake Auction

273

Iron, Figure, Fuxi, Seated, Mythical Emperor, Long Hair, Leaf Wreathed Dress, Chinese, 8¼ In.
$2,280

Michaan's Auctions

TIP
Beware of using some rust and stain removers on iron-stone. The chemical could remove both the rust and the glaze, ruining the piece. It can also seep into the glaze and make the piece unfit for use with food.

Iron, Sculpture, Eagle In Flight, Welded, Designed To Hang, 15 x 50 In.
$780

Michaan's Auctions

Iron, Horse Tether, Octagonal, Curved Handle, 1850s, 4 x 7 In.
$360

Garth's Auctioneers & Appraisers

Iron, Safe, Wells Fargo & Co. Express, Combination, Black, Caster Feet, 20 x 24 x 31 In.
$677

Morphy Auctions

Iron, Sculpture, Wall Plaque, Horse Head, Painted, Brown, 1900s, 29 x 13 x 21 In., Pair
$4,160

Brunk Auctions

TIP
To clean small pieces of iron, try soaking them in white vinegar for 24 to 48 hours.

Iron, Stringholder, Man's Face, 2-Piece Ball Shape, Red Paint, Pedestal, 1900s, 8 x 7 In.
$826

Soulis Auctions

Iron, Windmill Weight, Eagle, 2-Sided, Flattened, Full Body, Old Black Paint, c.1900, 15½ In
$1,053

Jeffrey S. Evans & Associates

Plaque, Shield Shape, Greek Warriors, Neoclassical, Wall Mounted, 1800s, 24 x 17 In.	165
Safe, Black, Mountain Lake Scene, Locking Door, Small Compartment, 18 x 18 x 26 In.	897
Safe, Mosler Safe Co., Gold & Black Paint, Combination, Caster Feet, c.1900, 22 x 15 x 16 In..	878
Safe, Wells Fargo & Co. Express, Combination, Black, Caster Feet, 20 x 24 x 31 In........*illus*	677
Sculpture, 5 Elephants, Leaning, Stacked, Walter Dahn, 84 x 24 x 14 In.............................	536
Sculpture, Eagle In Flight, Welded, Designed To Hang, 15 x 50 In.............................*illus*	780
Sculpture, Kingdom Style, Julius Schmidt, 1963, 9 x 21 x 13 In...	2813
Sculpture, Stag Head, Wall Hanging, 7 ½ x 12 In..	590
Sculpture, Sting Ray, Pointed Tail, Patina, Chase Allen, 30 x 18 In.	100
Sculpture, Wall Plaque, Horse Head, Painted, Brown, 1900s, 29 x 13 x 21 In., Pair .....*illus*	4160
Seat, Wall Mount, Vine Design, Round Seat, Oak, 18 x 17 In., Pair...................................	443
Stand, Pot, Scrollwork, Forged, Tripod Feet, Late 1700s, 17 In..	468
Stringholder, Man's Face, 2-Piece Ball Shape, Red Paint, Pedestal, 1900s, 8 x 7 In.....*illus*	826
Target, Shooting Gallery, Cossack, Openwork, Saddle, Sword, Signed, A.J. Smith, 7 x 6 In...	708
Windmill Weight, Chicken Shape, Rectangular, Base, Patina, 15 ½ In.	938
Windmill Weight, Eagle, 2-Sided, Flattened, Full Body, Old Black Paint, c.1900, 15 ½ In...*illus*	1053
Windmill Weight, Horse, Standing, Mounted, Metal Box Base, 22 x 17 x 5 ¾ In...................	288
Wine Cradle, Bottle Shape, Mechanical, Black Base, Ball Feet, Marked, Saint Hilaire, 10 x 12 In.	469

IRONSTONE

Ironstone china was first made in 1813. It gained its greatest popularity during the mid-nineteenth century. The heavy, durable, off-white pottery was made in white or was decorated with any of hundreds of patterns. Much flow blue pottery was made of ironstone. Some of the decorations were raised. Many pieces of ironstone are unmarked, but some English and American factories included the word *Ironstone* in their marks. Additional pieces may be listed in other categories, such as Chelsea Grape, Chelsea Sprig, Flow Blue, Gaudy Ironstone, Mason's Ironstone, Moss Rose, Staffordshire, and Tea Leaf Ironstone. These three marks were used by companies that made ironstone.

TJ & J Mayer's	W. Baker & Co. (Ltd.)	Wood & Son(s) (Ltd.)
1842–1855	1893+	1910+

Cheese Dome, Hunt Scene, Blue & White, 9 x 6 In...*illus*	106
Plate, Border Of 10 Turkeys, Separated By Trees, Crackle Glaze, 1910s, 10 In.	180
Plate, Blue Spatter, Dahlia Center, Green Sprigs, Paneled Rim, 9 ¼ In.........................*illus*	165
Plate, Red Spatter, Acorn Center, Paneled Rim, White Ground, Chinese, 9 ¼ In.	59
Platter, Meat, Well & Tree, Floral Sprays, White Ground, Gilt, Flutter Rim, Footed, 1800s, 21 In. ..	70
Platter, Scalloped Rim, Flow Blue Transfer, Multicolor Highlights, Mid 1800s, 16 x 13 In. ..	72
Tureen, Blue, Crown Top, Lift Lid, Underplate, Ladle, J.E. Coburg, 12 x 9 x 11 In.................	278
Tureen, Dome Lid, Underplate, Imari, Blue Ground, Gilt, Ashworth, 11 x 14 x 10 In. ....*illus*	219
Urn, White Ground, Flowers, 2 Handles, 1800s, 10 ½ x 14 In.	51

IVORY

Ivory from the tusk of an elephant is thought by many to be the only true ivory. To most collectors, the term *ivory* also includes such natural materials as walrus, hippopotamus, or whale teeth or tusks, and some of the vegetable materials that are of similar texture and density. Other ivory items may be found in the Scrimshaw and Netsuke categories. Collectors should be aware of the recent laws limiting the buying and selling of elephant ivory and scrimshaw. Many auctions list ivory as bone.

Box, Cricket, Carved, Reticulated, Dragons, Molded Lid & Base, Chinese, 1800s, 3 ½ x 5 x 4 In......	410
Box, Lid, Carved, 3 Dormice, In Garden, Fruit, Vegetables, Oval, Japan, 1800s, 3 x 4 x 3 ¼ In.. *illus*	1755
Case, Calling Card, Relief Carved, Figures, Gardens, Monogram, 1800s, 3 x 2 x 5 In.	644

Ironstone, Cheese Dome, Hunt Scene, Blue & White, 9 x 6 In.

$106

Charleston Estate Auctions

Ironstone, Plate, Blue Spatter, Dahlia Center, Green Sprigs, Paneled Rim, 9 ¼ In.

$165

Conestoga Auction Company

Ironstone, Tureen, Dome Lid, Underplate, Imari, Blue Ground, Gilt, Ashworth, 11 x 14 x 10 In.

$219

Greenwich Auction

Ivory, Box, Lid, Carved, 3 Dormice, In Garden, Fruit, Vegetables, Oval, Japan, 1800s, 3 x 4 x 3¼ In.
$1,755

Thomaston Place Auction Galleries

Ivory, Figurine, Monk, Standing, Long Beard, Carved, Bone, Wood Base, Chinese, 8½ In.
$344

New Haven Auctions

Ivory, Figurine, Mother, Baby, Lightweight Robe, Seated, Porcelain Barrel, Chinese, 1800s, 7½ In.
$2,340

Thomaston Place Auction Galleries

Cigar Cutter, Lion Head Handle, Carved, Solingen Steel, Germany, 6½ In.	293
Figurine, Aphrodite Rising, Carved, Woman & Child, Naked, Ludwig Walther, c.1920	2925
Figurine, Gaijin Traveler, Elderly Man, Hunched Shoulders, Beard, Turban, Japan, 1800s, 11 In.	1521
Figurine, Guanyin, Carved, Bouquet, Bamboo Staff, Lacquered Base, Chinese, Early 1900s, 11 In.	510
Figurine, Monk, Standing, Long Beard, Carved, Bone, Wood Base, Chinese, 8½ In. ..... *illus*	344
Figurine, Mother, Baby, Lightweight Robe, Seated, Porcelain Barrel, Chinese, 1800s, 7½ In. ..... *illus*	2340
Figurine, Okimono, Carved, Man, Tethered Crane, Basket, Serpentine Dragon, Japan, 7¾ In.	240
Figurine, St. George, Riding Horse, Dragonslayer, Rosewood Base, Continental, 1800s, 6 x 8 In.	4680
Figurine, Woman Artist, Holding Palette & Brush, Wood Base, Chinese, 1800s, 9 In.	644
Figurine, Palanquin, 4 Bearers, Boy Reading Book, India, 1800s, 3 x 5 x 2 In.	468
Handle, Walking Stick, Carved, Hand Holding Ball, Folk Art, Screw, 1800s, 4¼ In. .... *illus*	410
Okimono, Dragon Boat, 6 Musicians, Hotei Buddha, Japan, 1800s, 13 In.	556
Okimono, Old Man, Basket, Holding Stalk Of Corn, Pipe, Plants, Japan, 1900s, 5½ In. ..... *illus*	840
Okimono, Fisherman, Standing, Catch & Basket Slung Over Shoulder, Japan, 1800s, 6 In. .	702
Okimono, Woman Holding Child, Sling Rope, 2 Puppies, Slatted Platform, Japan, 1900s, 8¼ In.	1020
Pie Crimper, Walrus Bone, Bird Shape, Attached Wings, Contemporary, 5 In.	469
Pie Crimper, Whale & Snake, Baleen Eyes, Human Torso, Curling Neck, 5 In.	212
Pie Crimper, Whalebone, Carved & Pierced, Tapered Handle, Pique Borders, 1830s, 7 In. ..	2500
Plaque, Carved, King Louis XIV & Wife, Shallow Convex, 2 Leaves, Wire Hinge, 2 x 1 In.	468
Plaque, Carved, Screaming Monkey, Wasp, Bas Relief, On Rosewood Panel, 1800s, 6 x 4 In.	761
Tusk, Ancient, Figure Stand, Sack, Busy, Birds At Top, Chinese, 1900s, 10¼ In. .... *illus*	540
Walrus, Skull Snout, Tusks, Mounted, Oak Plaque, 14 x 10 x 5 In.	1112
Whale, Document Seal, Turned Knop & Stem, Brass End, 1800s, 2 In.	469

J P. JACOB PETIT

Jacob Petit (1796–1868) was a porcelain painter who worked for the Sevres factory in France. He opened his own shop near Paris sometime after 1830 and took over a nearby factory in about 1834. The factory made ornamental vases, statues, clocks, inkwells, and perfume bottles. A specialty were figural veilleuses shaped like sultans or fortune tellers. These were meant for use in the bedroom. He used the cobalt blue initials *J.P.* as his mark, but many of his pieces were not marked. His customers wanted "antique" style china, so he made copies of Sevres vases, Meissen figurines, many patterns of English dinnerware, Chinese export porcelain, and more. Petit sold his factory to one of his employees in 1862, but he continued to work in Paris until 1866.

Candleholder, Figural, Sultana, Sitting, Turban, White Glaze, 1900s, 5 In. .... *illus*	225
Clock, Cartel, Rococo, Bronze, Acanthus, Flowers, Marked, France, 1800s, 19 x 12 x 4 In. ...	320
Vase, Cornucopia, Blue Ground, Gilt Floral Sprays, c. 1835, 10 x 8 x 6 In., Pair............. *illus*	330
Vase, Woman, Holding Flower, Painted, Gilt, Footed, 1900s, 11 In. .... *illus*	281

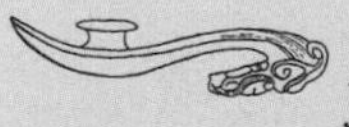

JADE

Jade is the name for two different minerals, nephrite and jadeite. Nephrite is the mineral used for most early Oriental carvings. Jade is a very tough stone that is found in many colors from dark green to pale lavender. Jade carvings are still being made in the old styles, so collectors must be careful not to be fooled by recent pieces. Jade jewelry is found in this book under Jewelry.

Box, Gilt Butterfly, Silver Hinge, Stepped Panels, 6 x 4¼ x 1¾ In.	570
Censer, Curling Lid, 3 Handles, Ring, Paw Foot, Lion Mask, Wood Base, 1900s, 5 In. .... *illus*	256
Cup, Spinach Jade, Light Transparent Ground, Wood Stand, Chinese, 1800s, 3 x 2½ In., Pair...	416
Disk, Spinach Jade, Carved, Dark Green, Dragon Bands, Geometric Patterns, 12 In.	216
Figurine, Dragon, Snake Shape, 4 Legs, Base, Chinese, 1900s, 8 x 5¾ In.	115
Figurine, Serpentine, Guanyin, Cradling Ruyi, Lacquered Base, Southeast Asia, 1900s, 10 In...	1140
Figurine, Vaudhara, Seated, Dragon, Ocean Waves, Celadon, 1900s, 15¾ In. .... *illus*	468
Figurine, White, Celadon, Goat, Lingzhi Mushroom, Jaw, 2⅜ x 1¼ In. .... *illus*	1152
Jar, Lid, White, Archaic Shape, Dragon & Reek Key Band, 9½ x 11 In.	2340

Ivory, Handle, Walking Stick, Carved, Hand Holding Ball, Folk Art, Screw, 1800s, 4 ¼ In.
$410

Thomaston Place Auction Galleries

Ivory, Okimono, Old Man, Basket, Holding Stalk Of Corn, Pipe, Plants, Japan, 1900s, 5 ½ In.
$840

Selkirk Auctioneers & Appraisers

Ivory, Tusk, Ancient, Figure Stand, Sack, Busy, Birds At Top, Chinese, 1900s, 10 ¼ In.
$540

Selkirk Auctioneers & Appraisers

Jacob Petit, Candleholder, Figural, Sultana, Sitting, Turban, White Glaze, 1900s, 5 In.
$225

Lion and Unicorn

Jacob Petit, Vase, Cornucopia, Blue Ground, Gilt Floral Sprays, c. 1835, 10 x 8 x 6 In., Pair
$330

Michaan's Auctions

Jacob Petit, Vase, Woman, Holding Flower, Painted, Gilt, Footed, 1900s, 11 In.
$281

Lion and Unicorn

Jade, Censer, Curling Lid, 3 Handles, Ring, Paw Foot, Lion Mask, Wood Base, 1900s, 5 In.
$256

Brunk Auctions

Jade, Figurine, Vaudhara, Seated, Dragon, Ocean Waves, Celadon, 1900s, 15 ¾ In.
$468

Thomaston Place Auction Galleries

Jade, Figurine, White, Celadon, Goat, Lingzhi Mushroom, Jaw, 2 ⅜ x 1 ¼ In.
$1,152

Brunk Auctions

277

JADE

Jade, Vase, Applied Flowers Side, Carved, Wood Base, Chinese, 5³/₈ x 5 x 4 In.
$500

New Haven Auctions

Jewelry, Bracelet, Cuff, Baker, Brass, Silver Wire, Acid Washed, Modernist, Art Smith, c.1955, 6 In.
$20,312

Bonhams

Jewelry, Bracelet, Cuff, Brass, 6-Sided, Pleated Form, Modernist, Marked, Art Smith, c.1950, 5¹/₂ In.
$3,825

Bonhams

Jar, Lid, Wolf Howl, Elongated, Carved, Birds, Flower, Chinese, 1800s, 5 x 3 In. 960
Page Turner, Spinach Green, Silver, Mounted, Engraved, Monogram, Continental, 1889, 9 In. 832
Teapot, Lid, White, Reeded, Footed Lacquered Wood Base, Miniature, Chinese, 1800s, 2¹/₂ In... 450
Vase, 3 Pinched Graduated Tiers, Foo Dogs, Dragons, Rings, Wooden Base, Chinese, 14 x 10 In. 750
Vase, Applied Flowers Side, Carved, Wood Base, Chinese, 5³/₈ x 5 x 4 In. ....*illus* 500
Vase, Lid, Chained Finial, Serpentine, Carved, Wood Stand, Mid 1900s, 8³/₄ In. 210

🏺 JAPANESE CORALENE

Japanese Coralene is a ceramic decorated with small raised beads and dots. It was first made in the nineteenth century. Later wares made to imitate coralene had dots of enamel. There is also another type of coralene that is made with small glass beads on glass containers.

Vase, Women, Flowers, Palace Size, 1900s, 32¹/₂ x 13 In., Pair.. 500

JAPANESE WOODBLOCK PRINTS *are listed in this book in the Print category under Japanese.*

🏺 JASPERWARE

Jasperware can be made in different ways. Some pieces are made from a solid-colored clay with applied raised designs of a contrasting colored clay. Other pieces are made entirely of one color clay with raised decorations that are glazed with a contrasting color. Additional pieces of jasperware may also be listed in the Wedgwood category or under various art potteries.

Box, Lid, White Raised Relief, Cherub, Blue & Green Tones, 1 x 4 In. 20

📿 JEWELRY

Jewelry, whether made from gold and precious gems or plastic and colored glass, is popular with collectors. Values are determined by the intrinsic value of the stones and metal and by the skill and fame of the craftsmen and designers. Although costume jewelry has been made since the 17th century, it became fashionable in the 1920s. Victorian and older jewelry has been collected since the 1950s. Edwardian and Art Deco jewelry were copied in the first half of the 1900s, then Modernist jewelry designs appeared. Bakelite jewelry was a fad from the 1930s to the 1990s. Copies of almost all styles are being made. American Indian jewelry is listed in the Indian category in this book. Tiffany jewelry is listed here.

Belt Buckle, Silver, 3 Lines, Bands, Hector Aquilar, Taxco, Mexico, 1⁵/₈ x 1³/₄ In. 94
Bracelet, Bakelite, Bangle, Carved, Ivory Color 72
Bracelet, Bakelite, Charm, Seeds & Nuts, Multicolor, Goldtone Metal Link Chain................. 60
Bracelet, Bangle, Bakelite, Opaque Amber, Carved Flower & Leaves, 3-In. Diam. 38
Bracelet, Bangle, Bakelite, Yellow, Faceted Edge, 2¹/₂ In. 25
Bracelet, Bangle, Flower, Diamond, Blue Enamel, 18K White Gold, La Nouvelle Bague, Italy, 7 In..... 403
Bracelet, Bangle, Onyx & 14K Gold Ropetwist, 2 Flower Bands, Art Nouveau, 7 In............... 610
Bracelet, Bangle, Penguins, Blue Landscape, Enamel, Goldtone, Hinged, Marked, Hermes, 6¹/₄ In..... 512
Bracelet, Bangle, Wide, Silver, Black Leather, Stamped Beaded Squares, Bottega Veneta, 8 In... 85
Bracelet, Charm, Bear, Stroller, Tricycle, Drums, Plane, 7 Charms, 18K Gold, Child's, Cartier, 7 In. . 4000
Bracelet, Cuff, Baker, Brass, Silver Wire, Acid Washed, Modernist, Art Smith, c.1955, 6 In...*illus* 20312
Bracelet, Cuff, Brass, 6-Sided, Pleated Form, Modernist, Marked, Art Smith, c.1950, 5¹/₂ In......*illus* 3825
Bracelet, Cuff, Hinged, Silver, Black Enamel, Gold Beaded Bands, Onyx Tips, Caviar, Lagos, 7 In. 207
Bracelet, Cuff, Lava, Abstract, Brass On Copper, Modernist, Marked, Art Smith, c.1945, 5³/₄ In.....*illus* 16562
Bracelet, Cuff, Silver, Repousse Pansies, Beaded Edge, Danecraft, Width 1 In. 63
Bracelet, Mesh Band, 14K Gold, 20 Pearls In Raised Mounts, 1960s, 7⁷/₈ In. 1464
Bracelet, Silver, Beaded Double Book Links, Articulated, Safety Chain, Marked Taxco, 8 In. 156
Bracelet, Silver, Flower, Leaf, Green Hardstone, Mexico, 2¹/₄ In. 125

Bracelet, Silver, Openwork, Pastes, 6 Ruby Glass Jewels, Art Deco, France, 1920s, 7 In. *illus*	750
Charm, Bank, Lucky Charms, 14K Gold, Jewel, Mink Meadows, Vineyard Haven, Mass., ¾ In.	531
Charm, Padlock, Wrapped With Bow, Sterling Silver, Marked, Tiffany & Co., ¾ In.	37
Charm, Skull, Memento Mori, Sterling Silver, Round Bail, ½ In.	50
Charm, West Chop Lighthouse, Vineyard Haven, 14K Gold, Mink Meadows, ¾ In.	406
Clip, Fur, Bakelite, Butterscotch, Leaf Shape, Carved, Pair	24
Clip, Shield, Silver, Center Crystal, Eisenberg Original, 2¼ x 2 In. *illus*	625
Clip, Undulating Strip, Engine Turned Stripes, 14K Gold, Marked, Cartier, c.1960, 2 In.	305
Cuff Links, 2 Bloodstone Circles, Diamond Centers, 18K Gold Wire Frame, c.1900, ½ In.	488
Cuff Links, Fluted Double Bars, 18K Gold, Band Of Square-Cut Rubies, 1950s, 1 x ¾ In.	1750
Cuff Links, Muses' Heads, Flower Headdress, 14K Gold, Art Nouveau, ¾ x ½ In.	220
Cuff Links, Onyx & Sterling Silver Ball Ends, Marked, Tiffany & Co., 1¼ In.	100
Cuff Links, Triangle, 18K Gold, Black Enamel, Marina B, 1987, ½ x ¾ In.	793
Earrings, 2 Blue Opals, Oval, 18K Gold Textured Branch Mount, 1970s, ¾ x ½ In.	366
Earrings, 4 Flowers, Fluted Petals, Beaded Stamens, 14K Gold, Tiffany, 1950s, 1 In.	1037
Earrings, Citrine Block, 18K Gold Cable Wrap, Diamond Band, Marked, David Yurman, ⅜ In.	915
Earrings, Cluster, Green Lucite Leaves, Iridescent Rhinestones, Goldtone, Lisner, 1½ In.	12
Earrings, Drop, Cameo, Pink Coral, Classical Women's Profile, 18K Gold, Beaded, c.1880, 2 In.	732
Earrings, Green Beryl Cabochon, 14K Gold Shredded Ribbon Mount, 1970s, 1 In.	671
Earrings, Sterling Silver, Black Enamel, Abstract Heart, Andy Warhol, R.L. Morris Studio, 2 In.	50
Earrings, Turquois Disc, 8-Sided Frame, Diamonds, 18K Gold, Marked, Cellino, ¾ In.	2196
Hatpins are listed in this book in the Hatpin category.	
Locket, 2 Art Nouveau Flowers, Trailing Stems, Garnet Centers, Round, c.1900, 1½ In.	113
Locket, Chinoiserie Grasses, Sterling Silver, 2 Gold Birds, Shakudo, Oval, 1800s, 2 In.	113
Locket, Heart, Crescent Moon, Seed Pearls, Garnet Set Star, Hinged, c.1890, 1¼ In.	110
Locket, Horseshoe, 6 Inset Paste Stones, Gold, Square, Riding Crop Bail, 1800s, 1 In.	75
Necklace, Bead, Amber, Faceted, Various Shapes & Shading, 1920s, 56 In.	275
Necklace, Bead, Rock Crystal, Melon Shape, Graduated, 14K White Gold Clasp, c.1900, 19 In.	113
Necklace, Choker, Half & Half, Brass Sheet & Wire, Marked, Art Smith, c.1950, 13½ In. *illus*	8925
Necklace, Friendship, Beads, Green, Purple, Malinda Norton, Aurora, Ohio, 1833, 56 In.	384
Necklace, Leaves, Green Lucite, Goldtone, Iridescent Rhinestones, Marked, Lisner, 17 In.	50
Necklace, Link Circle, 18K Gold, Citrine Dangle, Silk Cord, Marked LV, Louis Vuitton, 21 In.	732
Necklace, Link, Pairs Of Overlapping Leaves, Sterling Silver, Anton Michelsen, 16 In.	1040
Necklace, Link, Straight, Chunky, Hammered 18K Gold, Marked, Henry Dunay, 16 In.	4026
Necklace, Pendant, Jasperware, Black Disc, Gold Pharaoh Bust, Chain, Wedgwood, 25 In.	38
Necklace, Pendant, Mother-Of-Pearl Plaque, Diamond & Seed Pearl Frame, c.1890, 18 In.	854
Necklace, Pendant, Onyx, Black Enamel, Inset Pearl, 6 Rose-Cut Diamonds, c.1885, 3 In.	390
Necklace, Pendant, Paste, Rhinestones, Emerald Green Crystals, Georgian, 18½ In. *illus*	1250
Necklace, Pendant, Theater Masks, Joy & Sorrow, Link Chain, 14K Gold, Italy, c.1975, 20 In.	410
Necklace, Pendant, Watch, 18K Gold, Engine Turned, Diamonds, Chain, Longines, 20 In.	1625
Necklace, Pin & Earrings, Vine, Berries, Silver, Clip-On Earrings, Mary Gage, c.1990, Necklace 30 In.	1125
Necklace, Turquoise Chunks, Shell Disc Beads, 2 Jaclas, Southwest, 15¼ In.	313
Pendant, Amber, Carved, Birds, Farmer, Chinese, 2½ x 2 x 3 In.	1020
Pendant, Bow, White & Black Diamonds, Dangling Pearls, 18K Gold, La Nouvelle Bague, 2⅜ In.	2125
Pendant, Cameo, Mars & Venus, Love & War, Shell, 14K Bicolor Gold Frame, 2¼ In.	594
Pendant, Carnelian, Intaglio, Carved Classical Bust, Gold Ropetwist Frame, 1800s, 1¼ In.	113
Pendant, Dice, Textured Gold, Glossy Gold Pips, 1800s, ¾ In.	75
Pendant, Egg, Green, Diamond Zigzag, Rubies, 14K Gold, H. Wigstrom, Faberge, c.1915, 1 In.	5125
Pendant, Fob, Square Citrine, 14K Gold, Repousse Flowers, Scrolls, c.1890, 1½ In.	1342
Pendant, Hamsa, Stylized Hand Shape, Judaica, Silver, 1⅜ x ⅞ In. *illus*	63
Pendant, Heart, Puffy, Black Enamel, 6-Point Star, Diamonds, 14K Gold Bail, Victorian, ⅞ In.	580
Pendant, Heart, Puffy, Woven, 18K Gold, Marked, Tiffany & Co., 1 x ¾ In.	915
Pendant, Jade, Medallion, Carved, White, Lavender, Celadon, Fighting Tigers, 2 In.	175
Pendant, Mourning, 6 Woven Hair Wreaths, Old Ropetwist & Beaded Frame, c.1890, 2½ In.	188
Pendant, Portrait, Woman In Black Mantilla, 3 Diamonds, Porcelain, Coral Bead Rim, 1¾ In.	732
Pendant, Rooster In Circle, Diamond Eye, 18K Gold, Cutout Chanticler Capri, Italy, 2 In.	366
Pendant, Spinner, Apple, 6 Slices Joined In Center, Double C's, 18K Gold, Cartier, 1 In.	1586
Pendant, Starburst, 12-Point Star, Chain Link Circle Inside, Garnet Center, 1800s, 1 In.	219
Pendant, Zodiac, Sagittarius, Intaglio, Faceted Glass, Round 14K Gold Frame, c.1920, ⅝ In.	146

Jewelry, Bracelet, Cuff, Lava, Abstract, Brass On Copper, Modernist, Marked, Art Smith, c.1945, 5¾ In.
$16,562

Bonhams

Jewelry, Bracelet, Silver, Openwork, Pastes, 6 Ruby Glass Jewels, Art Deco, France, 1920s, 7 In.
$750

Ripley Auctions

Jewelry, Clip, Shield, Silver, Center Crystal, Eisenberg Original, 2¼ x 2 In.
$625

Ripley Auctions

JEWELRY

Jewelry, Necklace, Choker, Half & Half, Brass Sheet & Wire, Marked, Art Smith, c.1950, 13 ½ In.
$8,925

Bonhams

Jewelry, Necklace, Pendant, Paste, Rhinestones, Emerald Green Crystals, Georgian, 18 ½ In.
$1,250

Ripley Auctions

Jewelry, Pendant, Hamsa, Stylized Hand Shape, Judaica, Silver, 1 ⅜ x ⅞ In.
$63

Auctions at Showplace, NYC

Jewelry, Pin & Earrings, Hand, Figural, Holds Diamond, Celluloid, Coral Color, 19th Century, 2 ¼ In.
$244

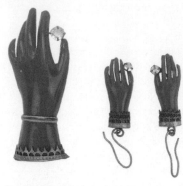

Rachel Davis Fine Arts

Jewelry, Pin, Bakelite, Dangling Balls In Circles, Butterscotch, 1930s
$120

Taranova Auctions Inc.

Jewelry, Pin, Bakelite, Dangling Heart, Red, 1930s
$72

Taranova Auctions Inc.

TIP
Periodically check your jewelry for loose stones.

Jewelry, Pin, Bakelite, Horse's Head, Red, Carved, Brass Bridle & Reins
$84

Taranova Auctions Inc.

TIP
Bakelite jewelry can be cleaned with a soft damp cloth and a mild abrasive cleaner such as a car-body polish. After cleaning, rub on bees-wax polish.

Jewelry, Pin, Bakelite, Swordfish, Marbled Green, Lucite Fin
$144

Taranova Auctions Inc.

Jewelry, Pin, Bee, 14K Gold, Openwork Body, Diamond, Sapphire & Ruby Wings, 1 ¾ In.
$540

Alderfer Auction Company

Pin & Earrings, Hand, Figural, Holds Diamond, Celluloid, Coral Color, 19th Century, 2¼ In... *illus* 244
Pin, 14 Opals, Scrolling 14K Gold Mount, Opal Drop, c.1885, 1½ x 1⅝ In. 488
Pin, 2 Swallows In Flight, 18K Textured Gold, Pink Stone Eyes, Diamond On Beak, Guyot, 1¾ In.... 1260
Pin, 4 Bursting Flowers, 3-Diamond Centers, Textured 14K Gold Petals, 1960s, 1⅝ In......... 854
Pin, Bakelite, Cherries, Dangling From Branch, Red, Brown, Green Stems 72
Pin, Bakelite, Dangling Balls In Circles, Butterscotch, 1930s.. *illus* 120
Pin, Bakelite, Dangling Heart, Red, 1930s.. *illus* 72
Pin, Bakelite, Horse's Head, Red, Carved, Brass Bridle & Reins................................... *illus* 84
Pin, Bakelite, Swordfish, Marbled Green, Lucite Fin .... *illus* 144
Pin, Bee, 14K Gold, Openwork Body, Diamond, Sapphire & Ruby Wings, 1¾ In. .... *illus* 540
Pin, Bee, 14K Gold, Textured Wings, 18 Round Sapphires, ½ x ¾ In. 259
Pin, Biomorphic, Stylized Lightning Bolt, Brass, Art Smith, 4½ In.............................. *illus* 1657
Pin, Bow, Ribbon, 14 Loops, Green & Red Enamel, Goldtone, Marked, Joan Rivers, 2½ In. .. 13
Pin, Cameo, Opal, Woman's Profile, Oval Gold Frame With 16 Diamonds, c.1900, 2 In......... 1188
Pin, Cameo, Victorian Woman, Shell, Carved, Oval, 18K Gold, 1¾ x 1¼ In. .... *illus* 230
Pin, Circle, 14 Opal Cabochons, Pear Shape, Spiral Twist 14K Gold Frame, Retro, 1¼ In..... 315
Pin, Circle, 3 Concentric, Emeralds & Diamonds, Diamond Center, 14K Gold, c.1900, 1 In... 1342
Pin, Citrine, Faceted Oval, Goldtone Scroll Frame, Split Pearls, Rubies, Regency Period, 1 In..... 260
Pin, Clubs Suit Symbol, 18K Gold Bar, 3 Black Pearls, Diamond, France, Victorian, 1½ In.. 375
Pin, Dragonfly, 4 Mother-Of-Pearl Wings, Movable Jadeite Tail, 18K Gold, Victorian, 2 In.... 915
Pin, Entwined Comma & Swirl, Yellow Enamel, Diamond Strip, Marked SCH, Norway, 2 In. 38
Pin, Firebird, Glass Gemstones, Red Eye, Green & Blue Plumes, 1964, 4½ In............... *illus* 1320
Pin, Flower, 3 Diamonds, 5 Round Emeralds, 18K Gold, Retro, 3½ x 1¾ In...................... 1053
Pin, Flower, 5 Petals, Lucite, Glass Center, Velvet Pouch, Alexis Bittar, 4 In.................. *illus* 63
Pin, Frog, Playing Guitar, 14K Textured Gold, Green Enamel, Emerald Eye, 1 x 1 In. 228
Pin, Frog, Silver, Green Enamel, Glass Eyes, Mexican Hallmarks, 1½ x 1¾ In................... 63
Pin, Golf Bag, Clubs, 18K Textured Gold, Diamonds, Ruby, Emerald, Sapphire, Hermes, 2 x 1 In. 3100
Pin, Grasshopper Playing Lute, 18K Gold, Enamel, Ruby Eyes, Marked Italy, 1960s, 2 x 1½ In.. 940
Pin, Koi Fish, Pave Rhinestones, Blue & Green Enamel, Red Glass Eyes, Jomaz, 2¾ In. 75
Pin, Lizard, 18K Gold, Orange & Black Enamel, Ruby Eyes, Italy, 1½ x ¾ In...................... 330
Pin, Mourning, Woman's Portrait, Reverse Painted Glass, Rose Gold, Woven Hair, c.1890, 2 x 2 In. 375
Pin, Mourning, Woven Hair, Gold Frame, Black Enamel, Gilt Initials, Glass, c.1880, 1 x 1¼ In...... 100
Pin, Owl's Face, Figural, Sterling Silver, Yellow & Black Glass Eyes, Unger Bros., 1¾ In. 344
Pin, Rooster, 14K Textured Gold, Glossy Comb, Pearl Body, Ruby Eye, 1960s, 1¼ In.......... 244
Pin, Rose, Carved Coral, 14K Gold Frame, Navette Shape, Openwork Leaves, 1960s, 1½ In. 488
Pin, Starfish, 18K Textured Gold, Turquoise Bead, Stars, Sapphires, Tiffany & Co., Italy, 2 In.... 2100
Pin, Stylized Frog, Carved Lucite, Green Body, Red Legs, Black Eyes, 1950s, 2¼ In. 38
Pin, Tassel, Art Deco, Joseff Of Hollywood, 6 In. .... *illus* 688
Pin, Tree Frog, Round Brilliant Diamond, Red Stone Eyes, 18K Gold, Stamped, Guyot, 1½ In. 1105
Pin, Turtle, 18K Gold, Textured Shell, Turquoise Beads, Diamonds, Marked, Neiman Marcus, 2 In. 1700
Ring, 5 Opals, 5 Diamonds, Abstract Textured Bark Mount, 14K Gold, 1970s, Size 5 488
Ring, 18K Gold, Coral Wrap, Band Of 12 Diamonds, Van Cleef & Arpels, Size 6½ 2318
Ring, 40 Small Pearls, 18K Gold Bead Centers & Band, Marked, Me & Ro, Top ⅝ In. Wide... 488
Ring, Band, Goldtone, Inset Woven Hair, Engraved JCD To LR, Victorian, Width ¼ In........... 190
Ring, Class, United States Military Academy, 14K Gold, Gem Set, 1949, ¾ In........................ 2125
Ring, Dangling Gemstones, Opal, Pearl, Tourmaline, Peridot, 18K Gold, Marked, Tous, Size 9.. 488
Ring, Diamond & Sapphire Strips, Shaped Beaded Platinum Mount, Art Deco, Size 7 1037
Ring, Dome, Gray & Black Pearls, 14K Gold, Black Niello, Victorian, Size 8, 1 In.......... *illus* 1000
Ring, Hercules Knot, Sterling Silver, One Side Ribbed, Marked, Lalaounis, Greece, Size 5¼ 183
Ring, Insect, Opal Body, Emerald & Diamond Wings, Ruby Eyes, Victorian, 1 In. Long........ 915
Ring, Oval Citrine, Textured 14K Gold Free-Form Mount, Modernist, 1970s, ¾ In. 488
Ring, Serpent, Entwined, Diamond Head & Rattler, 18K Gold, c.1900, Size 6½..................... 1220
Ring, Trinity, 3 Entwined Bands, 18K Tricolor Gold, Cartier, Size 6 610
Ring, Undulation, 3 Stones, Rhodochrosite, Turquoise, Amethyst, Silver, Art Smith, Size 6¼ *illus* 4080
Stick Pin, Green Tourmaline, Elongated Oval, 18K Gold, 9 Diamond Leaves, 2¼ In. 549
Stick Pin, Intaglio, Carved Classical Figure With Sword On Horse, Horseshoe Shape, 3 In. . 38
Stick Pin, Opal, Teardrop Shape, 14K Gold Pin, c.1890, 3 In. 134
Stick Pin, Pansy, Purple Shaded To Yellow, Diamond Center, 18K Gold, c.1890, 2½ In........ 550
Stickpin, Black Opal End, Pear Cut, Diamond Connector, 14K Gold Pin, Edwardian, 2½ In... 565

Jewelry, Pin, Biomorphic, Stylized Lightning Bolt, Brass, Art Smith, 4½ In. $1,657

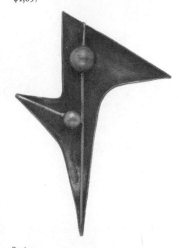

Bonhams

Jewelry, Pin, Cameo, Victorian Woman, Shell, Carved, Oval, 18K Gold, 1¾ x 1¼ In. $230

J

Blackwell Auctions

Jewelry, Pin, Firebird, Glass Gemstones, Red Eye, Green & Blue Plumes, 1964, 4½ In. $1,320

Taranova Auctions Inc.

JEWELRY

Jewelry, Pin, Flower, 5 Petals, Lucite, Glass Center, Velvet Pouch, Alexis Bittar, 4 In.
$63

Auctions at Showplace, NYC

Jewelry, Pin, Tassel, Art Deco, Joseff Of Hollywood, 6 In.
$688

Ripley Auctions

Jewelry, Ring, Dome, Gray & Black Pearls, 14K Gold, Black Niello, Victorian, Size 8, 1 In.
$1,000

Ripley Auctions

Jewelry, Ring, Undulation, 3 Stones, Rhodochrosite, Turquoise, Amethyst, Silver, Art Smith, Size 6 ¼
$4,080

Bonhams

John Rogers, Group, The Photographer, The Sitter, Man With Camera, Woman With Child, 1878, 19 In., Pair
$953

Tremont Auctions

Judaica, Cup, Elijah, Lid, Silver, Passover Scenes, Handles, Amethysts, R. Hendery & Co., 11 ¾ In.
$2,160

Auctions at Showplace, NYC

Judaica, Cup, Kiddush, Hebrew Lettering, Scroll Designs, Leaf Trim Base, 1800s, Germany, 3 ¼ In.
$256

Roland NY Auctioneers & Appraisers

Judaica, Magillah, Esther Bible Scroll, Ink On Parchment, Handwritten, 7 ¼ x 76 In.
$1,020

Auctions at Showplace, NYC

Judaica, Menorah, 9-Light, Regency Style, With Oil Pitcher, Hazorfim, Israel, 22 ¾ x 14 ¾ In.
$1,920

Michaan's Auctions

Watch Chain, Hair Art, Woven, Toggle, Gold Filled End Caps, Centerpiece, Etched, Victorian, 13 In.... 108
Watches are listed in their own category.
Wristwatches are listed in their own category.

JOHN ROGERS

John Rogers statues were made from 1859 to 1892. The originals were bronze, but the thousands of copies made by the Rogers factory were of painted plaster. Eighty different figures were created. Similar painted plaster figures were produced by some other factories. Rights to the figures were sold in 1893, and the figures were manufactured until about 1895 by the Rogers Statuette Co. Never repaint a Rogers figure because this lowers the value to collectors.

Group, A Matter Of Opinion, 2 Men Standing, Seated Woman, Plaster, 21½ x 17 In.............	154
Group, Council Of War, Brown Patina, 24 In.	875
Group, Courtship In Sleepy Hollow, Painted, Multicolor, Plaster, 17 x 15½ x 10 In..............	63
Group, Fetching The Doctor, Man & Boy On Galloping Horse, 16 In.	60
Group, The Photographer, The Sitter, Man With Camera, Woman With Child, 1878, 19 In., Pair. *illus*	953
Group, The Picket Guard, 3 Figures, Painted, Plaster, 14 x 10 In...	156
Group, The School Examination, Standing Woman & Girl, Seated Man, Plaster, 20 x 12 In.......	155
Group, We Boys, 2 Boys On Horseback, Painted, Plaster, 17 x 14 In...	256

JOSEF ORIGINALS

Josef Originals ceramics were designed by Muriel Joseph George. The first pieces were made in California from 1945 to 1962. They were then manufactured in Japan. The company was sold to George Good in 1982 and he continued to make Josef Originals until 1985. The company was sold two more times. The last owner went bankrupt in 2011.

Figurine, Dog, Dalmatian, Sitting, Raised Paw, Paper Label, 3½ In.	32
Figurine, Frog, Mushroom, Ladybug, Foil Label, c.1950, 3½ x 3½ In............................	14
Figurine, Woman, Blond, Brown Dress & Bonnet, International Series, England, 4 In.	80
Figurine, Woman, Pink Gown, Holding Letter, Romance Series, Love Story, 8 In..................	226

JUDAICA

Judaica is any memorabilia that refers to the Jews or the Jewish religion. Interests range from newspaper clippings that mention eighteenth- and nineteenth-century Jewish Americans to religious objects, such as menorahs or spice boxes. Age, condition, and the intrinsic value of the material, as well as the historic and artistic importance, determine the value.

Cup, Elijah, Lid, Silver, Passover Scenes, Handles, Amethysts, R. Hendery & Co., 11¾ In.....*illus*	2160
Cup, Kiddush, Hebrew Lettering, Scroll Designs, Leaf Trim Base, 1800s, Germany, 3¼ In..*illus*	256
Cup, Kiddush, Silver, Blue & Green Glass Grapes, Hebrew Letters, Gilt, Dugma, Israel, 3¼ In. ...	160
Cup, Kiddush, Silver, Relief Flower Garlands, Gold Interior, Topazio, Portugal, 5¾ In.	330
Cup, Kiddush, Silver, Repousse Grapevines, Flared Rim, Baluster Stem, Round Foot, 9½ In........	900
Etrog Container, Citron Fruit Shape, Repousse Fruit & Leaf Lid, 4 Ball Feet, 1900s, 4 x 6 x 3 In.	375
Etrog Container, Hinged Lid, Oval, Repousse Fruits, Silver, Continental, 4 x 7 x 4½ In.	660
Kovsh, Jade, 14K Gold, Enamel, Diamond & Paste, Cypher Handle, Russia, 1900s, 3 x 7 In..	1625
Magillah, Esther Bible Scroll, Ink On Parchment, Handwritten, 7¼ x 76 In. ....*illus*	1020
Manuscript, Illuminated, Pictorial Panels, Horseback, Modern Frame, India, 1800s, 10 x 6 In., Pair	407
Menorah, 9-Light, Regency Style, With Oil Pitcher, Hazorfim, Israel, 22¾ x 14¾ In...*illus*	1920
Menorah, Brass, Oil, Open Scrollwork Back, 2 Deer Figures, Poland, 12½ x 11 x 5 In........	1792
Menorah, Bronze, Modular, 9 Stylized Elephants, Michael Ende, 3-In. Elephants...............	385
Menorah, Candelabragram, Mixed Media, Angled Arms, Kinetic, Yaacov Agam, 9 x 14½ In.....	2489
Menorah, Silver, 8 Cups, Star Of David, Shield, 4-Footed, Early 1900s, 8½ x 9½ In...*illus*	381
Menorah, Silver, Tree Of Life, Shamash Holder, Bird Finial, Repousse Foot, 10¾ x 11 In....	2040

Judaica

Judaica (items made by Jews or made for Jewish religious ceremonies) is collected. The pieces often are influenced by events of the time. A silver spice container from Poland made in the late 1800s was in the shape of the newly invented steam engine. The spice container was used during the Havdalah service that closes Sabbath every week.

Judaica, Menorah, Silver, 8 Cups, Star Of David, Shield, 4-Footed, Early 1900s, 8½ x 9½ In.
$381

Tremont Auctions

Judaica, Spice Box, Besamim, Slide Lid, 4-Footed, German Silver, 1½ x ½ x 2½ In.
$576

Roland NY Auctioneers & Appraisers

This is an edited listing of current prices. Visit **Kovels.com** to check thousands of prices from previous years and sign up for free information on trends, tips, reproductions, marks, and more.

Jukebox, Rock-Ola, Model 1422, Art Deco Design, Scrolled Front, Chrome Grill, 1946, 59 x 28 x 26 In. $2,640

Morphy Auctions

Jukebox, Wurlitzer, Model 1015, Bubbler, One More Time, 100 CDs, Wood Case, 1947, 60 x 32 In. $3,456

Neal Auction Company

Kelva, Bonbon, Pink Poppies, Mottled Green Ground, Gilt Metal Rim & Handle, 2 x 6 In. $150

Woody Auction

Mezuzah, Silver, Cloisonne Enamel, Multicolor Flowers, Russia, 6 9/16 In.	160
Sculpture, Hamsa, Hand, Cityscape, Hinged Door, Lettering, Marked, Karshi, 11 1/2 x 6 x 3 3/4 In.	600
Spice Box, Besamim, Silver, Tower, Flag On Spire, 6-Sided Filigree Center, Round Foot, 7 3/4 In.	160
Spice Box, Besamim, Slide Lid, 4-Footed, German Silver, 1 1/2 x 1/2 x 2 1/2 In. .... *illus*	576

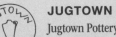

JUGTOWN POTTERY

Jugtown Pottery refers to many pottery pieces made in North Carolina as far back as the 1750s. In 1915, Juliana and Jacques Busbee set up a training and sales organization for what they named Jugtown Pottery. In 1921, they built a shop at Jugtown, North Carolina, and in 1923 hired Ben Owen as a potter. The Busbees moved the village store where the pottery was sold to New York City. Juliana Busbee sold the New York store in 1926 and moved into a log cabin near the Jugtown Pottery. The pottery closed in 1959. It reopened in 1960 and is still working near Seagrove, North Carolina.

Bowl, Mottled, Green & Brown Glaze, Ringed Foot, Indentations, c.1920s, 5 x 3 In.	125
Pitcher, Green Frogskin Glaze, Concentric Lines, 7 3/4 In.	35
Pitcher, Orange, Strap Handle, Flared Rim, 4 3/4 In.	68
Platter, Orange, Marked, 10 x 8 3/4 In.	68
Porringer, Brown Mottled Glaze, Strap Handle, 4 1/2 In.	55
Sugar & Creamer, Orange Glaze	44

JUKEBOX

Jukeboxes play records. The first coin-operated phonograph was demonstrated in 1889. In 1906 the Automatic Entertainer appeared, the first coin-operated phonograph to offer several different selections of music. The first electrically powered jukebox was introduced in 1927. Collectors search for jukeboxes of all ages, especially those with flashing lights and unusual design and graphics.

Rock-Ola, Model 1422, Art Deco Design, Scrolled Front, Chrome Grill, 1946, 59 x 28 x 26 In..... *illus*	2640
Rock-Ola, Model 1422, Swirls, Bars, Multicolor, Wood Case, c.1946, 58 x 30 x 25 In.	1573
Seeburg, Model 220 SR, Speaker Grill, Colored Lights, 100 Selections, c.1958, 55 1/2 x 34 In.	3690
Wurlitzer, Model 600, Wood Cabinet, Light-Up Plastics, Bubble Tubes, 1938, 54 x 31 x 25 In.	3198
Wurlitzer, Model 1015, Bubbler, One More Time, 100 CDs, Wood Case, 1947, 60 x 32 In. ..*illus*	3456

KAY FINCH CERAMICS

Kay Finch
CALIFORNIA Kay Finch Ceramics were made in Corona del Mar, California, from 1935 to 1963. The hand-decorated pieces often depicted whimsical animals and people. Pastel colors were used.

Figurine, Baby Bird, Chocolate Brown, 1940s, 4 In.	65
Figurine, Pig, Whimsical, Dimple On Nose, Blue Ears, 3 1/2 x 4 1/2 In.	49
Figurine, Praying Angel, White Dress, Blue Collar & Wings, Blond Hair, 3 3/4 In.	12

KAYSERZINN, *see Pewter category.*

KELVA

KELVA
Kelva glassware was made by the C. F. Monroe Company of Meriden, Connecticut, about 1904. It is a pale, pastel-painted glass decorated with flowers, designs, or scenes. Kelva resembles Nakara and Wave Crest, two other glasswares made by the same company.

Bonbon, Pink Poppies, Mottled Green Ground, Gilt Metal Rim & Handle, 2 x 6 In. .... *illus*	150
Dresser Box, 12-Sided, Mottled Blue Ground, Pink & White Flowers, Gilt Collar, Silk Lining, 6 In..	469
Jewelry Box, 6-Sided, Mottled Brown Ground, Flowers, White Bead Trim, Gilt Collar & Feet, 4 In.	216
Vase, Pink Flowers, Mottled Green Ground, Gilt Metal Handles & Feet, 14 x 7 In..........*illus*	250
Vase, Pink Roses, Mottled Blue Ground, Gilt Collar, Scroll Handles, Ruffled Light Blue Base, 17 In.	506

COLLECTING TRENDS:
TWENTIETH-CENTURY STUDIO CERAMICS

By Al Eiber

Collecting contemporary studio ceramics, art made from shaping clay, has never been more popular. Major auctions, extensive contemporary ceramic collections, and a major donation of more than 600 pieces by Robert P. Ellison to the Metropolitan Museum in New York City have only fueled the excitement for ceramics collecting.

"Contemporary studio ceramics" can be defined as a blend of art, design, and function using traditional, modern, or experimental techniques. Artists are seen as breathing new life into an age-old tradition of making functional pottery. They are pursuing new shapes and expressions rather than the typical rounded or oval utilitarian shapes.

As with collecting anything, learning about studio ceramics is important. Study books, websites, and museum collections to familiarize yourself with the subject matter and to see what you like. Go to antique shows as well as galleries that specialize in ceramics. Dealers and gallery owners have a wealth of information that they usually are willing to share.

Try to buy the best you can afford. Try to focus on one great piece instead of many less desirable examples. Condition is particularly important, especially for resale. Damage or restoration will decrease the price of a piece, which may be the only way to afford very collectible artists, but it will also make them less desirable on the resale market.

Collecting should always be fun. The thrill of discovering new material or a new artist is the most exciting aspect of collecting. Here are twelve of the most sought-after contemporary studio ceramicists in the antiques and collectible world today.

British Studio Ceramics

Hans Coper (1920–1981) was born in Germany and became an important studio potter based out of Britain. His work is often coupled with fellow British potter Lucie Rie because of their close association, but their best-known works are quite different in style. Rie's work is considered to be less sculptural whereas Coper created much more abstract forms. Coper preferred textured surfaces using black and white slip, and he frequently put different forms together in the same piece.

Right: Hans Coper "Spade" form, 1969, stoneware, black glaze, textured and incised, impressed artist's seal, 9¼ in.

Phillips

Albert Eiber is a retired physician and Miami Beach resident. He is a board member of the Cooper Hewitt Smithsonian Design Museum and has served on the vetting committee for Design Miami and Design Miami/Basel for many years.

Left: Hans Coper tall bottle vase, c.1967, glazed stoneware, impressed initials "HC" on bottom, 10 in. by 3½ in.

Right: Hans Coper pot, c.1965, glazed stoneware, impressed initials "HC" on bottom, 6½ in. by 4½ in.

Wright

Wright

Bernard Leach (1887–1979) was a British studio potter and art teacher. He was born in Hong Kong, studied in London, and went back to Hong Kong in 1909. He is considered the "Father of British studio pottery." Exposure to the ancient pottery tradition of Japan impacted his artistic development, and he is known for merging the East and the West. Leach used Western slipware and salt glaze on simple and precise forms with Eastern brushwork and aesthetics. During his career, Leach created an astounding body of work intersected with various influences, contexts, and ideas.

Right: Bernard Leach vase, c.1959, glazed stoneware, flattened form, stamped mark, St. Ives Pottery, England, 7¾ in. by 5 by 3 in.

Far Right: Bernard Leach vase, 1970s, stoneware, Tenmoku glaze, stamped mark, Leach Pottery, St. Ives, England, 14 in. by 6 in.

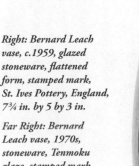

Rago Arts and Auction Center

Rago Arts and Auction Center

Lucie Rie (1902–1995) was an Austrian-born British ceramic artist. Rie's work usually consists of hand-thrown pots, bottles, and bowl shapes. They are noteworthy for their Modernist forms, minimal decoration, and use of bright colors.

Phillips

Above: Lucie Rie footed bowl, c.1978, porcelain, yellow glaze with golden manganese drip, impressed artist's seal on bottom, 3½ in. by 3¾ in.

Right: Lucie Rie vase, late 1970s, glazed and incised porcelain, impressed artist's seal on bottom, 10 in. by 5½ in.

Far Right: Lucie Rie vase, c.1980, glazed stoneware, artist's seal on bottom, 11½ in. by 4¾4 in. by 3½ in.

Rago Arts and Auction Center

Rago Arts and Auction Center

American Studio Ceramics

Claude Conover (1907–1994) studied at the Cleveland Institute of Art. He was employed as a commercial designer for decades before teaching himself pottery in the late 1950s and embarking on a second career. His seven-day work schedule is legendary: from rolling slabs on Monday to finishing his sawtooth blade surface decorations on Sunday and putting into the vase a clear plastic flower frog to contain dried stalks or branches. Conover's disciplined production resulted in six pots a week, 250 a year, and 3,500 by the time he retired in the 1980s.

Right: Claude Conover Ukukci vessel, glazed stoneware with engobe decoration, signed and titled "Claude Conover 'Ukukci'" on bottom, 16½ in. by 13 in.

Far Right: Claude Conover Ablil vessel, glazed stoneware with engobe decoration, signed and titled "Claude Conover 'Ablil'" on bottom, 21½ in. by 12½ in.

Wright

Wright

Rago Arts and Auction Center

Above: Maija Grotell charger wall hanging, c.1940, glazed stoneware, incised initials "MG" on bottom, 2½ in. by 12 in.

Maija Grotell (1899–1973), a Finnish American, began teaching ceramics at Cranbrook in Bloomfield Hills, Michigan, in 1938. The program was unstructured, and students were mainly there to learn the rudimentary basics of pottery after working in what were considered to be more serious artistic mediums. Eventually, the program Grotell developed became known for producing celebrated ceramic artists like, Richard DeVore, Howard Kottler and Toshiko Takaezu.

Wright

Above: George Ohr pitcher, 1897–1900, earthenware with cobalt, emerald, and gunmetal glazes, impressed signature " G. E. OHR, Biloxi, Miss." on bottom, 2¾ in. by 5 by 3 in.

George Ohr (1857–1918) was a transformational figure in contemporary ceramics even though he worked decades before many of the other contemporary potters were even born. Called "The Mad Potter of Biloxi (Mississippi)," he made most of his pots between 1895 and 1905. Today he is hailed as a "clay prophet" and "the Picasso of art pottery." His pots were twisted, folded, and crimped clay, forms that are frequently not reproducible. He also made some realistic objects such as hats, animals, and houses, and decorated his unique shapes with realistic snakes or lizards. Unappreciated by the art world in his day, Ohr is now considered to be the father of contemporary ceramics.

Left: George Ohr vase, 1898–1910, earthenware with gunmetal and brown glazes, two handles, one crimped, one ear-shaped, incised signature "G E Ohr" on bottom, 3¾ in. by 7½ in. by 4½ in.

Below: George Ohr vase, pink and gunmetal glazes, crimped and folded rim, 7 in. by 5½ in.

Wright

Left: Maija Grotell vase, c.1945, glazed stoneware, incised initials "MG" on bottom along with "CA" for Cranbrook Academy, 8¼ in. by 4 in.

Private Collection

Wright

Ken Price (1935–2012) was influenced by the progressive ceramist Peter Voulkos, who taught him at Otis Art Institute in Los Angeles. Price and Voulkos applied contemporary styles to ceramic forms, and played with the balance between fine art and crafting work. Price was a frequent surfer and his work was influenced by the ocean, as well as by the Mexican pottery he came across during various surfing trips. As his career progressed, Price's pieces grew in scale and their subject matter became more abstract. Price was unwavering in his refusal to explain the meaning behind his works, and he felt that the spectator should be left to reach their own understanding of his often complex and sensual forms.

Below: Suite of four works by Ken Price, 1991, cast and glazed earthenware, individually titled Mildred, California Cup, Fireworm Cup, and Chet, each signed "Kenneth Price" and numbered on the bottom, 4 in. by 6 in. by 3½ in.

Wright

Left: Ken Price Mickelos sculpture, 1987, hand-built slab earthenware, painted and sanded, 11 in. by 11 in. by 17 in.

Wright

Axel Salto (1889–1961), a Danish ceramics master, pushed the limits of ceramic art by bringing together rich glazes and organic, and oftentimes abstract, shapes that evoke living forms. His famous Solfatara glaze is known for its green and yellow hue, which could sometimes create startling color variations. Although it was developed at Royal Copenhagen, the Solfatara glaze takes its name from an Italian volcano.

Right: Axel Salto vase, 1963, glazed stoneware, incised "Salto" on bottom with a glazed three-line wave mark and Royal Copenhagen stamp, 8¾ in. by 5½ in. dia.

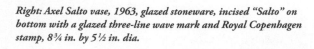

Rago Arts and Auction Center

Rago Arts and Auction Center

Edwin (1910–2008) and **Mary Scheier** (1908–2007) collaborated on most of their pieces, with Mary creating the forms and Edwin glazing and decorating them. Edwin rarely made preliminary drawings for his decorations. As a result, their designs are imaginative and impulsive, showing the influence of late surrealism and abstract expressionism art. In the 1950s, the Scheiers took an interest in the forms and decorations of pre-Columbian pottery.

Far Left: Edwin and Mary Scheier chalice form, 1966, glazed stoneware, incised signature and date "Scheier 66" on bottom, 20 in. by 10 in. by 8½ in.

Left: Edwin and Mary Scheier chalice form, 1991, glazed stoneware, incised signature and date "Scheier 91" on bottom, 13½ in. by 12 in.

Rago Arts and Auction Center

Wright

Toshiko Takaezu (1922–2011) was one of the twentieth century's foremost abstract artists. Known as a visionary with immense amounts of drive and determination, she took inspiration from her own cultural background as an American artist of Japanese descent (hailing from Hawaii) and combined it with ideas pulled from contemporary painting and sculpture to create a unique form of expression that was all her own. In addition to her ceramic art, Takaezu was also a painter, a sculptor, and an educator, and she became known for her rounded, closed forms that represented ceramics as a fine art, and as more than just functional vessels.

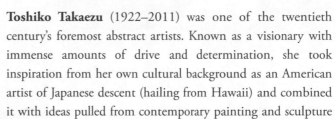

Above Left: Toshiko Takaezu closed form, glazed earthenware, incised initials TT on bottom, 10 in. by 7½ in.

Left: Toshiko Takaezu closed form with rattle, glazed earthenware, 8 in. by 8 in.

Wright

Rago Arts and Auction Center

Peter Voulkos (1924–2002) used radical methods and ideas that fundamentally transformed his field in ways that are still being felt today. Originally trained as a functional potter, Voulkos defied midcentury craft principles of proper technique and form. In 1955 he began to experiment with increasingly unconventional works inspired by a variety of influences including Abstract Expressionism, Japanese pottery, and the artworks of Franz Kline, Henri Matisse, and Pablo Picasso.

Rago Arts and Auction Center

Left: Peter Voulkos Untitled Stack, 1973, gas-fired glazed stoneware with pass-throughs and slashes, glazed signature and date "Voulkos 73" on bottom, 33¾ in. by 11 in.

Above: Peter Voulkos Untitled Plate, 1973, glazed, gouged, incised, and gas-fired stoneware with clear glaze and porcelain pass-throughs, glazed signature and date "Voulkos 73" on bottom, 18½ in. by 3 in.

Betty Woodman (1930–2018) was a leading ceramist whose inventive forms and painter's use of color have won her international renown. Woodman began her career making simple, functional pottery. Although her ambitious experiments with clay resulted in profound changes in her work, it still appears functional even if her baroque, expressive forms are not. Woodman's art was inspired by diverse sources, from Etruscan, Greek, and Asian cultures to majolica ceramics.

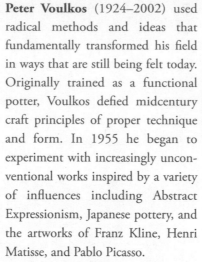

Rago Arts and Auction Center

Above: Betty Woodman Pillow Pitcher, c.1975, glazed earthenware, squat pillow form, flattened handle, impressed "Woodman" near base, 15 in. by 15 in. by 11 in.

Left: Betty Woodman platter, c.2000, glazed earthenware, impressed "Woodman" on bottom, 27 in. by 12½ in. by 2½ in.

Right: Betty Woodman platter, 2004, glazed earthenware, glazed signature and date "Betty Woodman '04" on bottom, 15½ in. by 23½ in. by 2½ in.

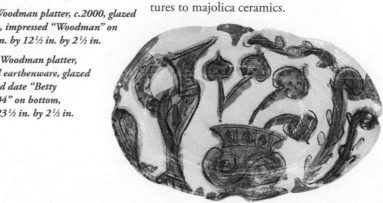

Wright

Wright

KEW BLAS

Kew Blas is a name used by the Union Glass Company of Somerville, Massachusetts. The name refers to an iridescent golden glass made from the 1890s to 1924. The iridescent glass was reminiscent of the Tiffany glass of the period.

Basket, Ruffled Dish, Gold Iridescent, Gilt Metal Handle, Leaves & Flowers, 5 x 7 In.	100
Finger Bowl, Underplate, Gold Iridescent, Art Glass, Ribbed, Ruffled Rim, Signed, 2 x 6 In....... *illus*	250
Vase, Gold Iridescent, Orange, Flower Shape, Flared Lip & Base, Round Foot, 8 1/4 x 4 In......	240
Vase, White, Green Pulled Feather, Squat, Flared Lip, Round Foot, 4 1/4 x 7 3/4 In....................	60

KEWPIE

Kewpies, designed by Rose O'Neill (1874–1944), were first pictured in the *Ladies' Home Journal.* The figures, which are similar to pixies, were a success, and Kewpie dolls and figurines started appearing in 1911. Kewpie pictures and other items soon followed. Collectors search for all items that picture the little winged people. They are still popular with collectors.

Bisque, Broom, Dust Pan, 4 1/2 In.	225
Bisque, Pink Tint, Blue Wings, Seated, Hands On Chin, 1 7/8 In.	45
Book, Primer, Illustrations, Stokes Publication, 1916	325
Cabinet Plate, Children Holding Bouquets, Love To You, 1978, 8 In.	18
Chocolate Mold, Baby Biting Fingers, Metal, 12 In.........................*illus*	74
Composition, Jointed Arms, Heart Label, 11 In....................................	55
Felt, Holding Teddy Bear, Green Hat, Limited Edition, R. John Wright, Box, 1999, 6 1/4 In.....*illus*	210
Print, Kewpie Hatching From Egg, Frame, Signed, 6 1/2 x 4 1/4 In.	22
Salt & Pepper, Looking Down, Silver Plate, Sheffield, 3 In.	160
Spoon, Figural Kewpie Finial, Sterling Silver, Germany, 4 5/8 In.	38
Tobacco Felt, Leapfrog, c.1914, 5 x 6 In.	62

KITCHEN

Kitchen utensils of all types, from eggbeaters to bowls, are collected today. Handmade wooden and metal items, like ladles and apple peelers, were made in the early nineteenth century. Mass-produced pieces, like iron apple peelers and graniteware, were made in the nineteenth century. Also included in this category are utensils used for other household chores, such as laundry and cleaning. Other kitchen wares are listed under manufacturers' names or under Advertising, Iron, Tool, or Wooden.

Baking Pan, Cast Iron, Deep, Elongated Shape, Griswold Erie, No. 8, c.1915, 2 5/8 x 21 In. ...	448
Basket, Rice, Carved, Character Marks, Brass Mounts, 1800s, 6 x 16 x 12 In..............*illus*	63
Blender, Milkshake, Porcelain, Mint Green, Chrome, Hamilton, 18 x 8 x 7 In.............*illus*	150
Blender, Model 702A, Peter Muller-Munk, Chrome Plate, Waring Products, 1948, 14 x 6 1/2 In...*illus*	1250
Board, Cutting, Pig, Wood, Relief Carved, Oval, Folk Art, 1910s, 10 x 21 In...................*illus*	644
Bowl, Dough, Burl, Turned & Incised, 1800s, 13 3/4 In. ....*illus*	688
Bowl, Krenit, Enameled Steel, Herbert Krenchel, Torben Orskov & Co., Denmark, 1953, 5 x 10 In.	195
Box, Food, Lid, Octagonal, Brass Hardware, Fish Locks, Key, Chinese, 1900s, 18 1/4 In., Pair.	84
Bread Box, Metal, Kreamer, French Bread, Hinged Lid, Painted, c.1910, 13 1/2 x 27 x 10 1/2 In.....*illus*	108
Broom, Splint, Thin Handle, Trevor Shreves, 2000s, 54 In.	813
Butcher's Block, Thick Seat, 4 Short Feet, Brown, 32 x 24 x 24 In. ....*illus*	428
Butter Paddle, Burl, Wood, Hole Handle, Varnished, 1800s, 8 In.	180
Butter Press, Pine, Hinged, Nailed, Rectangular Base, The Handy Print, 13 x 17 1/2 In........	126
Butter Stamp, Carved, Tulip Design, Wood, Round, 1800s, 4 1/2 In. ....*illus*	861
Butter Stamp, Lollipop Shape, Carved, Duck, Flower, Wheat, 5 x 6 In.	367
Butter Stamp, Whalebone, Ropework Border, Shielded Eagle, 8-Point Star, 1800s, 3 1/4 In..	6875
Cabbage Cutter, Pierced Heart, Scandinavia, Dated 1850, 17 1/2 In.	227
Cabinet, Chrome Steel, Sliding Door, 2 Shelves, Salesman's Sample, c.1940, 17 x 17 x 7 In..	188

Kelva, Vase, Pink Flowers, Mottled Green Ground, Gilt Metal Handles & Feet, 14 x 7 In.
$250

Woody Auction

Kew Blas, Finger Bowl, Underplate, Gold Iridescent, Art Glass, Ribbed, Ruffled Rim, Signed, 2 x 6 In.
$250

K

Woody Auction

Kewpie, Chocolate Mold, Baby Biting Fingers, Metal, 12 In.
$74

Apple Tree Auction Center

Kewpie, Felt, Holding Teddy Bear, Green Hat, Limited Edition, R. John Wright, Box, 1999, 6¼ In.
$210

Potter & Potter Auctions

Kitchen, Basket, Rice, Carved, Character Marks, Brass Mounts, 1800s, 6 x 16 x 12 In.
$63

K

Greenwich Auction

Kitchen, Blender, Milkshake, Porcelain, Mint Green, Chrome, Hamilton, 18 x 8 x 7 In.
$150

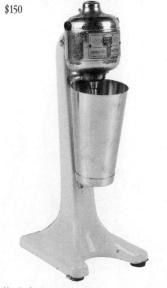

Morphy Auctions

Cake Board, Maple, Carved, Flowers, Leaves, Heart, Hanging Ring, 1800s, 10 x 9½ In. *illus*	923
Carrier, Cutlery, Silverware Tray, Cherry, Shaped Handle, Dovetailed, 6 x 13 x 9 In.	1053
Cauldron, Cast Iron, 3-Footed, Upside-Down Heart, Handles, Marked, 7½ x 10 In.	500
Chest, Sugar & Flour, Tulip, Flowers, Painted, Bracket Feet, Continental, 1782, 19 x 49 x 20 In. ..	1534
Churn, Double, Wood, Brass, Plaque, Engraved, C.H. Arnold, 1846, 13 x 8½ In...................	875
Churn, Lid, Glass Jar, Cast Iron & Tin Mill, Wood Handle, Dazey, No. 30, 13 In............ *illus*	84
Churn, Lid, Treen, Metal Bands, Original Dasher, Mellow Color, Late 1800s, 37 In.	120
Churn, Painted, Salmon Surface, New Hampshire, 1800s, 16½ x 14½ x 11 In............. *illus*	738
Churn, Silver Lid, Glass, Wood Handle, Hand Crack, Dandy, Gal....................................	74
Coffee Grinders are listed in the Coffee Mill category.	
Coffee Machine, Aluminum, Plastic, Stainless, Richard Sapper, Alessi, 1998, 16 x 9 x 13 In. *illus*	188
Coffee Mills are listed in their own category.	
Colander, Brass, Circular, Side Handles, Small Holes, Footed, England, 1800s, 5 x 16 In.....	281
Cookie Board, Carved Lion, Wood, Hanging, c.1900, 11¼ x 17¼ In.............	315
Cookie Board, Swan, Impressed, Pottery, Wood Frame, 19th Century, 9 x 10½ In..............	150
Cookie Cutter, Heart Within Rectangle, Swing Handle, 1800s, 20 x 9¾ In.	1084
Cookie Cutter, Rabbit, Iron, Tinned Sheet, 1800s, 8 x 12 In................................ *illus*	308
Cupboard, 2 Parts, Walnut, Wavy Glass, 2 Drawers, 1800s, 85 x 61 x 21 In.	5490
Cutlery Tray, Carved, Scroll Cut Divider, 2 Compartments, Etched, 1800s, 6 x 11 x 7 In......	201
Cutlery Tray, Pine, Canted Sides, Heart Shape Handle, Dovetailed, Mid 1800s, 5 x 14 x 11 In...... *illus*	168
Cutlery Tray, Pine, Dovetailed, Scroll Edges, Cutout Handles, Wire Nails, 6 x 13 x 9 In.	204
Dough Box, Cherry, Rectangular Top, Shaped Feet, Pennsylvania, 38 x 20 x 26 In.	130
Dough Box, Lid, Pine, Alligatored Paint, Applied Wood Handles, 1800s, 29 x 37 x 18 In. .....*illus*	885
Dough Box, Lift Lid, Pine, Primitive, Canted Sides, Mid 1800s, 15 x 33 x 15 In.	108
Dough Box, Pine, White Paint, Canted Dovetailed Case, Turned Legs, c.1850, 28 x 48 x 30 In. ...	360
Dough Box, Poplar, Canted Sides & Splayed, Turned Legs, Red Wash, 1830s, 28 x 34 x 17 In.....	156
Dough Box, Provincial Style, Walnut, 2 Cabinet Doors, Scroll Feet, 37 x 47 x 21 In.	610
Duck Press, Mechanical Wheel, Chrome Plated, Cast Iron, Wood Base, 1800s, 23 In...*illus*	1125
Duck Press, Silver Plate, Wheel, Inverted U-Shape, France, c.1960s, 20 x 12¼ x 8 In. .*illus*	4800
Dutch Oven, Removable Lid, Loop Handle, Black, Griswold, No. 4....................................	281
Flour Container, Tin, Removable Lid, Lug Handles, Green Paint, 26 In.............................	68
Food Chopper, Fox Shape, Wood Handle, Steel Blade, 1800s, 11½ In.........................*illus*	219
Food Chopper, Iron, Mounted, Wood Handle, Rectangular Base, 15 x 10¾ In......................	88
Food Chopper, Whalebone Handle, Heart Shape Mount, Late 1800s, 3¼ In.	469
Frying Pan, Milled Bottom, Cast Iron, Griswold, 15 x 14½ In.	2938
Grater, Nutmeg, Figural, Painted, Brass Crank, Boar's Head Spout, Pheasant Cap, 1800s, 10 In..*illus*	192
Holder, Utensil, Hanging, Varying Knot Design, Painted Wreaths, Late 1800s, 32 x 20 In. ...	366
Hoosier Cabinet, Oak, Enamel Shelf, Tambour Doors, Cooking Hints, 2 Parts, 62 x 41 In..	465
Ice Bucket, Taitu, Wood Carving, Stetson Hat Shape, Italy, 10½ x 20 x 13 In.	281
Ice Cream Freezer, White Mountain Junior, Wood, Metal, Qt.....................................*illus*	480
Ice Crusher, Enameled Steel, Plastic, Wood, Jean Otis Reinecke, Dazey, c.1938, 10¼ x 5½ In.....*illus*	455
Icebox, 3 Doors, Oak, Zinc Lining, Brass Hardware, 29 x 15 x 39 In............................*illus*	400
Iron, Charcoal, Strijk Lustig, Brass Iron, Wood Handle, Front Latch, Dutch, 7 x 7¾ x 3½ In. .....*illus*	3108
Iron, Fluter, Handle, Lever, Separate Rolls, Round Hat Base, 12½ x 5 x 7½ In......................	3673
Iron, Goffering, Miniature, White Steel Base, Brass Barrel, Ball Feet, England, 4¼ x 3 In...	622
Iron, Pressing Box, Cast Iron, Ornate Scrollwork, 1800s, 6½ In......................................	1638
Iron, Slug, Flat, Brass Heart, Ebony Handle, Swing Gate, AM & RI, Germany, 1749, 6 x 5 x 3¾ In.	3673
Ironing Board, Pine, Elongated Paddle Shape, 1850s, 60 x 15 In...................................	96
Juicer, Aluminum, Citrus Squeezer, Space Age Shape, Philippe Starck, 1900s, 11½ In.	240
Kettle, Candy, Copper, Looped Handle, Elongated Cutout Handle, 36 In.	510
Kettle, Candy, Copper, Rolled Rim, Cast Handles, Original Rivets, 7 x 17 In.	55
Kettle, Lid, Scrollwork Handle, Brass, 12 x 12 In..	35
Knife Sharpener, Carved, Wood, Flat Stone Inset, Folk Art, Jamesn Rosser, 1826, 2½ x 14 In.	438
Ladle, Carved Handle, Pewter Mounts, Stamped, Ball, Hand, 1800s, 14½ In.......................	277
Ladle, Wrought Iron, Tooled Eagle, Tulips & Stars, Signed, Cy. Crites, Dated 1848, 21 In.	1680
Laundry, Washing Bat, Blue Paint, Kissing Swans, Necks Shape A Heart, Germany, 1700s, 16 x 7 In. .	1469
Lazy Susan, Georgian, Mahogany, Scalloped Rim, Early 1800s, 5 x 21 In..........................	738
Mangle Board, Hand Carved, Vegetation, Lion Handle, Brown, Green, Norway, 1700s, 30 x 3 In..	1921
Mangle Board, Horse Handle, Carved, Geometric Pattern, 27 In. ....*illus*	147
Mangle Board, Horse Shape Grip, Punched Stars, Painted, Scandinavia, 1800s, 33¾ In. ..	391

Kitchen, Blender, Model 702A, Peter Muller-Munk, Chrome Plate, Waring Products, 1948, 14 x 6½ In.
$1,250

Wright

Kitchen, Board, Cutting, Pig, Wood, Relief Carved, Oval, Folk Art, 1910s, 10 x 21 In.
$644

Jeffrey S. Evans & Associates

Kitchen, Bowl, Dough, Burl, Turned & Incised, 1800s, 13¾ In.
$688

Hindman

Kitchen, Bread Box, Metal, Kreamer, French Bread, Hinged Lid, Painted, c.1910, 13½ x 27 x 10½ In.
$108

Main Auction Galleries, Inc.

Kitchen, Butcher's Block, Thick Seat, 4 Short Feet, Brown, 32 x 24 x 24 In.
$428

Pook & Pook

Kitchen, Butter Stamp, Carved, Tulip Design, Wood, Round, 1800s, 4½ In.
$861

Pook & Pook

Kitchen, Cake Board, Maple, Carved, Flowers, Leaves, Heart, Hanging Ring, 1800s, 10 x 9½ In.
$923

Pook & Pook

Kitchen, Churn, Lid, Glass Jar, Cast Iron & Tin Mill, Wood Handle, Dazey, No. 30, 13 In.
$84

Alderfer Auction Company

Kitchen, Churn, Painted, Salmon Surface, New Hampshire, 1800s, 16½ x 14½ x 11 In.
$738

Pook & Pook

Kitchen, Coffee Machine, Aluminum, Plastic, Stainless, Richard Sapper, Alessi, 1998, 16 x 9 x 13 In.
$188

Wright

K

Kitchen, Cookie Cutter, Rabbit, Iron, Tinned Sheet, 1800s, 8 x 12 In.
$308

Pook & Pook

Kitchen, Cutlery Tray, Pine, Canted Sides, Heart Shape Handle, Dovetailed, Mid 1800s, 5 x 14 x 11 In.
$168

Garth's Auctioneers & Appraisers

K

Kitchen, Dough Box, Lid, Pine, Alligatored Paint, Applied Wood Handles, 1800s, 29 x 37 x 18 In.
$885

Soulis Auctions

Kitchen, Duck Press, Mechanical Wheel, Chrome Plated, Cast Iron, Wood Base, 1800s, 23 In.
$1,125

Neal Auction Company

Kitchen, Duck Press, Silver Plate, Wheel, Inverted U-Shape, France, c.1960s, 20 x 12 ¼ x 8 In.
$4,800

Michaan's Auctions

Kitchen, Food Chopper, Fox Shape, Wood Handle, Steel Blade, 1800s, 11 ½ In.
$219

New Haven Auctions

Kitchen, Grater, Nutmeg, Figural, Painted, Brass Crank, Boar's Head Spout, Pheasant Cap, 1800s, 10 In.
$192

Nadeau's Auction Gallery

Kitchen, Ice Cream Freezer, White Mountain Junior, Wood, Metal, Qt.
$480

Chupp Auctions & Real Estate, LLC

Kitchen, Ice Crusher, Enameled Steel, Plastic, Wood, Jean Otis Reinecke, Dazey, c.1938, 10 ¼ x 5 ½ In.
$455

Wright

Kitchen, Icebox, 3 Doors, Oak, Zinc Lining, Brass Hardware, 29 x 15 x 39 In.
$400

Apple Tree Auction Center

Kitchen, Iron, Charcoal, Strijk Lustig, Brass Iron, Wood Handle, Front Latch, Dutch, 7 x 7¾ x 3½ In.
$3,108

Hartzell's Auction Gallery Inc.

Kitchen, Mangle Board, Horse Handle, Carved, Geometric Pattern, 27 In.
$147

Hartzell's Auction Gallery Inc.

Kitchen, Mold, Food, Redware, Fluted, Lead Glaze, J.S. Henne, Berks County, c.1860, 3½ x 7 In.
$900

Crocker Farm, Inc.

Kitchen, Mold, Pig's Head Shape, Wall Hanging, 2 Handles, Cast Iron, 11 In.
$270

Chupp Auctions & Real Estate, LLC

Kitchen, Mortar & Pestle, Painted, Shaped Base, Blue Surface, 1800s, 7½ In.
$517

Pook & Pook

Kitchen, Mortar, Cylindrical, Flared Rim, Concentric Bands, Square Handles, Bronze, Stand, 5⅞ In.
$80

Neal Auction Company

Kitchen, Pantry Box, Folk Art, Bentwood, Scroll Cut, Figural Bird, Flowers, Round, 1800s, 6 x 9 In.
$118

Soulis Auctions

Size Matters

Size makes a difference when pricing cast iron cookware. Very small and very large pieces sell for higher prices than medium-sized pans. A Griswold No. 1 can be worth over $3,000.

Kitchen, Peel, Wrought Iron, Square Shape Plate, Round Shaft, Ipswich, Mass., Late 1700s, 64 x 8 x 9 In.
$120

Jeffrey S. Evans & Associates

Kitchen, Pie Plate, Redware, Coggled Rim, Yellow Linear Slip, Mid 1800s, 9 In. **$270**

Garth's Auctioneers & Appraisers

Kitchen, Sadiron, Figural, Swan Handle, Patina, 1800s, 6 x 9 x 2 In. **$4,248**

Soulis Auctions

Kitchen, Scoop, Ice Cream, Heart Shape, Nickel Over Brass, Manos Novelty Co., Toronto **$4,800**

Rich Penn Auctions

Kitchen, Spice Box, Walnut, Dovetailed Case, Arched Back, 1850s, 5 x 14¼ x 7½ In. **$203**

Jeffrey S. Evans & Associates

> **TIP**
> Keep basement windows locked at all times.

Mangle Board, Mermaid Handle, Carved, Painted, Wood, Norway, 21¼ In.	1375
Match Holders can be found in their own category.	
Match Safes can be found in their own category.	
Mixer, Mayonnaise & Cream Whipper, Universal, Landers, Frary & Clark, Early 1900s, 12 x 5 In.	156
Mixer, Milk Shake, Hamilton Beach, Light Green, Electric	120
Molds may also be found in the Pewter and Tinware categories.	
Mold, Cake, Walnut, American Eagle, Patriotic Shield, Wood Stand, c.1818, 24 x 12 x 11 In.	5670
Mold, Food, Redware, Fluted, Lead Glaze, J.S. Henne, Berks County, c.1860, 3½ x 7 In. *illus*	900
Mold, Pig's Head Shape, Wall Hanging, 2 Handles, Cast Iron, 11 In. *illus*	270
Mold, Turk's Head, Ivory Rim, Mottled Green & Orange, Shenandoah Valley, Mid 1800s, 3 x 9 In.	450
Mold, Candle, see Tinware category.	
Mold, Ice Cream, see also Pewter category.	
Mortar & Pestle, Painted, Shaped Base, Blue Surface, 1800s, 7½ In. *illus*	517
Mortar, Cylindrical, Flared Rim, Concentric Bands, Square Handles, Bronze, Stand, 5⅞ In. *illus*	80
Pan, Loaf, Redware, Semi Round Shape, Yellow, Slip Grid, Coggled Edge, 1800s, 11 x 14 In.	283
Pantry Box, Bentwood, Painted, Round, Late 1800s, 3¼ x 8 In.	227
Pantry Box, Folk Art, Bentwood, Scroll Cut, Figural Bird, Flowers, Round, 1800s, 6 x 9 In. *illus*	118
Pantry Box, Lid, Bentwood, Round, Lapped Seams, Copper Tacks, 1850s, 4 x 7 In.	150
Pantry Box, Lid, Pine, Maple, Stag, Landscape, Maine, Paint, Oblong, 1800s, 1½ x 4¾ x 3¾ In.	531
Peel, Wrought Iron, Square Shape Plate, Round Shaft, Ipswich, Mass., Late 1700s, 64 x 8 x 9 In. *illus*	120
Pie Plate, Redware, Coggled Rim, Yellow Linear Slip, Mid 1800s, 9 In. *illus*	270
Press, Citrus, Silver Plate, Curved Arm Support, Green, Marble Base, 11¾ In.	366
Rack, Pot, Scalloped Edges, Pinwheels, Flowers, Green Ground, 1800s, 11 x 84½ In.	4428
Rack, Pot, Wrought Iron, Hanging, Late 1700s, 8 x 18½ In.	344
Reamers are listed in their own category.	
Roaster, Coffee Bean, Slide Lid, Rattail, Wrought Iron, Late 1700s, 23¼ In.	120
Roaster, Lift Lid, Wrought Iron, Penny Feet Front, Mid 1800s, 25 x 19 x 13 In.	180
Sadiron, Box Type, Cast Iron, Turned Oak Handle, Brass Supports, Continental, c.1835, 8 In.	85
Sadiron, Figural, Swan Handle, Patina, 1800s, 6 x 9 x 2 In. *illus*	4248
Salt & Pepper Shakers are listed in their own category.	
Scoop, Ice Cream, Heart Shape, Nickel Over Brass, Manos Novelty Co., Toronto *illus*	4800
Scoop, Maple, Carved, Bird In Hand Grip, 1800s, 12½ In.	984
Shelf, 3 Shelves, Painted, Red & Gold, Teapot Shape Ends, Wood, c.1950, 21 x 25 x 5 In.	125
Shelf, 4 Tiers, Art Deco, Demilune, Chrome, Glass, Black Base, c.1935, 31¾ In.	344
Skillet, Bronze, Wages Of Sin Is Death, Tripod Feet, 1700s, 6½ x 16 x 7 In.	1512
Skimmer, Milk, Shell Shape, Cherrywood, Polished, 1800s, 5¾ x 5¼ In.	156
Smoothing Stone, Sphere, Black Glass, Hand Blown, Polished, 3½ In.	90
Spatula, Wrought Iron, Short Handle, Hearth Peel, Circular Shape Plate, 1800s, 11⅞ x 7¾ In.	167
Spice Box, Circular, Green Paint, Flowers, Removable Lid, 5⅝ In.	156
Spice Box, Tin, 8 Drawers, Metal Knob, Green Paint, Spiral Finial, 1800s, 10 x 7 x 3 In.	188
Spice Box, Walnut, Dovetailed Case, Arched Back, 1850s, 5 x 14¼ x 7½ In. *illus*	203
Spoon Rack, Pine, Carved, Pinwheel Decor, New Jersey, Dated 1752, 21 x 10 In. *illus*	10455
Spoon Rack, Pine, Scalloped Back, 15 Hooks, Square Nail Pegs, Continental, 1900s, 5 x 47 In.	72
Spoon Rack, Tiger Maple, Hanging, Brown, 1800s, 3½ x 13½ In. *illus*	246
Spoon Rest, Art Nouveau, Metal, Woman, Long Hair, c.1900s, 2 x 3¾ x 2¼ In.	185
Strainer, Cheese, Tin, Heart Shape, Wood Knob, Pennsylvania, 1800s, 2 x 6 In. *illus*	1230
Strawholder, Flora Dora, Red Flashed, Gilt, Footed, c.1900, 12 In. *illus*	1320
Sugar Nippers, Iron, Heart Shape Handle Tips, 1785, 4 In. *illus*	1260
Teakettle, Gooseneck, Swing Handle, Copper, 10 x 10 In. *illus*	51
Teapot, Sepik, Spherical, Lid, Handle, Black, Blue, Marco Zanini, Italy, 1983, 8¾ x 12½ x 7¾ In.	250
Teapot, Spice O'Life, Corning Ware, 1970s, 6 Cup	18
Toaster, Electric, Art Deco Style, Sides Drop Down, Manning-Bowman, 1920-30	50
Trammel, Wrought Iron, Painted Green, Hook, Ring, 1800s, 24½ In. *illus*	151
Trivet, see Trivet category.	
Waffle Iron, Cast Iron, Metal Handle, 2 Wood Handles, Stover Junior, No. 8, 7 In. *illus*	45
Waffle Iron, Wrought, Masonic Symbols, Heart Shape, 1800s, 29 In. *illus*	214
Wash Stick, Wood, Heart, Diamond, Clover, Carved Sawtooth, 25¾ In.	124
Washboard, Pine, Canted Side Joints, Staright Back Edge, Early 1800s, 25 In.	200

K

Kitchen, Spoon Rack, Pine, Carved, Pinwheel Decor, New Jersey, Dated 1752, 21 x 10 In.
$10,455

Pook & Pook

Kitchen, Spoon Rack, Tiger Maple, Hanging, Brown, 1800s, 3 1/2 x 13 1/2 In.
$246

Pook & Pook

Kitchen, Strainer, Cheese, Tin, Heart Shape, Wood Knob, Pennsylvania, 1800s, 2 x 6 In.
$1,230

Pook & Pook

Kitchen, Strawholder, Flora Dora, Red Flashed, Gilt, Footed, c.1900, 12 In.
$1,320

Garth's Auctioneers & Appraisers

Kitchen, Sugar Nippers, Iron, Heart Shape Handle Tips, 1785, 4 In.
$1,260

Freeman's

Kitchen, Teakettle, Gooseneck, Swing Handle, Copper, 10 x 10 In.
$51

Hartzell's Auction Gallery Inc.

Kitchen, Trammel, Wrought Iron, Painted Green, Hook, Ring, 1800s, 24 1/2 In.
$151

Pook & Pook

Kitchen, Waffle Iron, Cast Iron, Metal Handle, 2 Wood Handles, Stover Junior, No. 8, 7 In.
$45

Hartzell's Auction Gallery Inc.

Kitchen, Waffle Iron, Wrought, Masonic Symbols, Heart Shape, 1800s, 29 In.
$214

Pook & Pook

K

Knife, Dagger, Carved, Green, Russet Jade, Organic Leaf Design, Lotus Petals, India, 1800s, 6 x 2 In.
$150

Bruneau & Co. Auctioneers

Knife, Dagger, Inuit, Carved, Bone, Walrus Shape Handle, Sheath, 1900s, 11 In.
$666

Fontaine's Auction Gallery

Knife, Switchblade, 2 Blades, Automatic, Push Button, Schrade Cut Co., Walden, 1906, 2⅝ In.
$230

Blackwell Auctions

TIP

Always dust from the top down. The dust falls.

Kosta, Sculpture, Abstract, Meeting, Brain Series, Bartil Vallien, 2006, 7⅞ In.
$176

Jeffrey S. Evans & Associates

KNIFE

Knife collectors usually specialize in a single type. In the 1960s, the United States government passed a law that required knife manufacturers to mark their knives with the country of origin. This seemed to encourage the collectors, and knife collecting became an interest of a large group of people. All types of knives are collected, from top quality twentieth-century examples to old bone- or pearl-handled knives in excellent condition.

Combat Master, Stainless Steel, Molded Handle, Blackie Collins, 1980s, 12 In.	177
Dagger, Carved, Green, Russet Jade, Organic Leaf Design, Lotus Petals, India, 1800s, 6 x 2 In.....*illus*	150
Dagger, Inuit, Carved, Bone, Walrus Shape Handle, Sheath, 1900s, 11 In. ...*illus*	666
Dagger, Luftwaffe, Nickel Plated Blade, Steel Scabbard, Aluminum Chain & Hook, 18 In.	780
Draw, Folding Hand, 2 Handles, Lever Screw, Cutting Edge, J. Wilkinson & Co., 8 In.	120
Hunting, Curved Blade, Wood Grip, Finger Guard, Stamped Russell, 1800s, 10½ In.	215
Silver, Curved Blade, Rolling Waves, Gilt Carp On Handle, 17 In.	531
Steel, Flensing, Hardwood Handle, Pointless Tip, Mid 1800s, 31¼ In.	1063
Switchblade, 2 Blades, Automatic, Push Button, Schrade Cut Co., Walden, 1906, 2⅝ In.....*illus*	230

KNOWLES, *Taylor & Knowles items may be found in the KTK and Lotus Ware categories.*

KOSTA

Kosta, the oldest Swedish glass factory, was founded in 1742. During the 1920s through the 1950s, many pieces of original design were made at the factory. Kosta and Boda merged with Afors in 1964 and created the Afors Group in 1971. In 1976, the name Kosta Boda was adopted. The company merged with Orrefors in 1990 and is still working.

Bowl, Can Can, Opaque, Blue Rim, Base, Kjell Engman, Late 1900s, 10¼ x 12¼ In.	156
Charger, Koi Fish, Sun Ceramics, Japan, 12½ In., 6 Piece	246
Sculpture, Abstract, Meeting, Brain Series, Bartil Vallien, 2006, 7⅞ In. ...*illus*	176
Sculpture, Whale, Jonah, Clear & Etched Glass, Vicke Lindstrand, 7 x 16 x 2 In. ...*illus*	527
Vase, Aphrodite, Blown, Bartil Vallien, c.1985, 8 x 10 x 7½ In.	390
Vase, Bluish Gray, Pedestal Base, Ellis Bergh, Early 1900s, 10 In.	30
Vase, Bud, Elongated Bottle Shape, Clear, Marked, 10¼ x 3 In.	125
Vase, Clear, Flat Lozenge Shape, Spiral Amethyst, Vicke Lindstrand, 1950s, 8¼ In. ...*illus*	156
Vase, Zebra Design, Red, Hand Blown, Vicke Lindstrand, c. 1955, 6 x 4 x 2 In. ...*illus*	688

KPM

KPM refers to Berlin porcelain, but the same initials were used alone and in combination with other symbols by several German porcelain makers. They include the Konigliche Porzellan Manufaktur of Berlin, initials used in mark, 1823–1847; Meissen, 1723–1724 only; Krister Porzellan Manufaktur in Waldenburg, after 1831; Kranichfelder Porzellan Manufaktur in Kranichfeld, after 1903; and the Krister Porzellan Manufaktur in Scheibe, after 1838.

Casket, Lid, Cherub Handle, Gilt Bronze Mounted, 1800s, 14 x 14 In. ...*illus*	3188
Figurine, Woman, Standing, Holding Bouquet Of Flowers, Blue Dress, Flowers, 1900s, 8¼ In...*illus*	13
Lithophane, see also Lithophane category.	
Plaque, Angel, Hand Painted, Gilt & Velvet Frame, 10 x 9 In.	445
Plaque, Daphne, Giltwood Frame, Late 1800s, 10¾ In.	150
Plaque, Nymph, Hand Painted, Enamel Decorated, 1900s, 6 x 12 In.	4063
Plaque, Orpheus & Eurydice, Holding Harp, Blue Frame, 12⅞ x 7⅞ In.	4538
Plaque, Young Girl, Playing, Toy, Painted, Gilt Frame, Signed, Franz Till, 1800s, 6½ x 4 In. ...*illus*	900
Plate, Portrait, Woman, Scepter & Beehive Marks, 1900s, 10¼ In., 4 Piece ...*illus*	5143
Tureen, Dome Lid, Rakes's Progress, Figural Finial, Gilt, Flowers, 12 x 10 In. ...*illus*	375
Urn, Dome Lid, Flowers, Courtship Scene, Eagle On Top, Gold Meander Body, 1800s, 14 x 8 In., Pair	1625

Kosta, Sculpture, Whale, Jonah, Clear & Etched Glass, Vicke Lindstrand, 7 x 16 x 2 In.
$527

Thomaston Place Auction Galleries

Kosta, Vase, Clear, Flat Lozenge Shape, Spiral Amethyst, Vicke Lindstrand, 1950s, 8¼ In.
$156

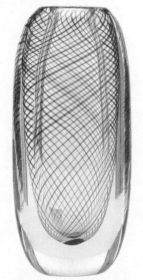

Garth's Auctioneers & Appraisers

Kosta, Vase, Zebra Design, Red, Hand Blown, Vicke Lindstrand, c. 1955, 6 x 4 x 2 In.
$688

Wright

KPM, Casket, Lid, Cherub Handle, Gilt Bronze Mounted, 1800s, 14 x 14 In.
$3,188

Bonhams

KPM, Figurine, Woman, Standing, Holding Bouquet Of Flowers, Blue Dress, Flowers, 1900s, 8¼ In.
$13

Lion and Unicorn

KPM, Plaque, Young Girl, Playing, Toy, Painted, Gilt Frame, Signed, Franz Till, 1800s, 6½ x 4 In.
$900

Treasureseeker Auctions

KPM, Plate, Portrait, Woman, Scepter & Beehive Marks, 1900s, 10¼ In., 4 Piece
$5,143

Fontaine's Auction Gallery

KPM, Tureen, Dome Lid, Rakes's Progress, Figural Finial, Gilt, Flowers, 12 x 10 In.
$375

Hindman

KPM, Vase, Floor, Gilt, Flower Head Medallions, Abstract Design, 26 x 11 In.
$4,484

Soulis Auctions

K

Kutani, Jar, Lid, Foo Dog Finial, Flowers, Iron Red, Gilt, Signed, Late 19th Century, 18 ½ In.
$330

Leland Little Auctions

Kutani, Platter, Round, Figures Around Table, Enjoying Tea & Fruit, 1800s, 14 In.
$320

Brunk Auctions

Kutani, Vase, Chrysanthemum, Figures, Landscape, Foo Dog Handles, Stepped Foot, c.1900, 14 In., Pair
$155

DuMouchelles

Urn, Lid, Leaf Shape Finial, Scrolling Dragon, Scepter Mark, White, 1900s, 20 ½ In., Pair ..	1024
Vase, Floor, Gilt, Flower Head Medallions, Abstract Design, 26 x 11 In......................... *illus*	4484

KTK

K.T.&K. CHINA

KTK are the initials of the Knowles, Taylor & Knowles Company of East Liverpool, Ohio, founded by Isaac W. Knowles in 1853. The company made many types of utilitarian wares, hotel china, and dinnerware. It made belleek and the fine bone china known as Lotus Ware from 1891 to 1896. The company merged with American Ceramic Corporation in 1928. It closed in 1934. Lotus Ware is listed in its own category in this book.

Chop Plate, Flowers, Blue, Peach, White, Gold Swag Rim, 1920s	19
Cup, Green, Peach Highlights, Dome Swirls, Vines, Flowers	165
Dish, Woman's Profile, Ruffled Collar, Shell Shape, Gold Trim, 5 x 5 In................................	99
Pitcher, Moss Rose Pattern, c.1879, 6 ½ In.	79

KUTANI

Kutani porcelain was made in Japan after the mid-seventeenth century. Most of the pieces found today are nineteenth century. Collectors often use the term *Kutani* to refer to just the later, colorful pieces decorated with red, gold, and black pictures of warriors, animals, and birds.

Box, Lid, Round, Samurai, Geisha, Red Scrolls, Multicolor Medallions, 6-Character Mark, 5 x 6 In. ...	24
Candlestick, Bottle Shape, Flowers, Birds, 3 Scrolled Feet, Late 1800s, 11 In., Pair..............	188
Cup & Saucer, Flowers, Blue & Gold Rim, Red Medallions, Utsukushi Yamasei, 2 ½ x 4 ¾ In......	32
Jar, Lid, Foo Dog Finial, Flowers, Iron Red, Gilt, Signed, Late 19th Century, 18 ½ In..... *illus*	330
Plate, Multicolor Scene, Ducks At Pond, Flowers, Clouds, Scalloped Rim, Seal Mark, 10 ¼ In..	59
Platter, Round, Figures Around Table, Enjoying Tea & Fruit, 1800s, 14 In................... *illus*	320
Punch Bowl, Gilt Dragon, Flowers, Clouds, Stand, Stone, Wood, Japan, c.1800s, 6 ¾ x 14 ¼ In. ...	1845
Urn, Palace, Garden Scenes, Multicolor Flower Ground, Flared Ruffled Rim, 1800s, 35 In., Pair...	480
Vase, 8 Immortals, Blue & Green Ground, Gilt, Handles, Animal Head Terminals, 10 ½ In.	300
Vase, Bottle Shape, Red & Gold Flowered Neck, Scenic, Figures, Seaside, 1800s, 11 ¾ In., Pair	225
Vase, Chrysanthemum, Figures, Landscape, Foo Dog Handles, Stepped Foot, c.1900, 14 In., Pair. *illus*	155
Vase, Foo Dog, Phoenix, Moth, Chrysanthemums, Gilt Accents, Red Ground, 15 x 5 In.........	240

L.G. WRIGHT

W

L.G. Wright Glass Company of New Martinsville, West Virginia, started selling glassware in 1937. Founder "Si" Wright contracted with Ohio and West Virginia glass factories to reproduce popular pressed glass patterns like Rose & Snow, Baltimore Pear, and Three Face, and opalescent patterns like Daisy & Fern and Swirl. Collectors can tell the difference between the original glasswares and L.G. Wright reproductions because of colors and differences in production techniques. Some L.G. Wright items are marked with an underlined *W* in a circle. Items that were made from old Northwood molds have an altered Northwood mark—an angled line was added to the *N* to make it look like a *W*. Collectors refer to this mark as "the wobbly W." The L.G. Wright factory was closed and the existing molds sold in 1999. Some of the molds are still being used.

Daisy & Fern, Tumbler, Blue Opalescent, Factory Polished Rim, 3 ¾ In., 4 Piece	125
Daisy & Fern, Water Set, Cranberry Opalescent, Ball Pitcher With Ruffled Rim, 7 Piece	212
Daisy & Fern, Water Set, Vaseline Opalescent, Ball Pitcher With Ruffled Rim, 7 Piece *illus*	200

LACQUER

Lacquer is a type of varnish. Collectors are most interested in the Chinese and Japanese lacquer wares made from the Japanese varnish tree. Lacquer

wares are made from wood with many coats of lacquer. Sometimes the piece is carved or decorated with ivory or metal inlay.

Box, Bento, Landscape Scene, 3 Tiers, 14 In.	59
Box, Black & Gold, Stacking, Chinese, 17 1/2 x 16 In., Pair	492
Box, Black, 3 Maidens, Dancing, Flute Players, Russia, 1800s, 1 3/4 x 3 x 5 1/2 In. ....*illus*	60
Box, Coffin Lid, Travelers, Exotic Animals, Multicolor, Persia, 5 x 8 x 5 In.	380
Box, Hinged Lid, Troika Scene, Painted, Imperial Seal, Russia, 2 x 8 x 5 In. ....*illus*	142
Box, On Stand, Black, Chinese, Late 1800s, 21 x 26 x 17 In.	219
Box, Red, Lobed Flower Shape, Landscapes, Chinese, 5 1/4 x 21 3/4 In. ....*illus*	1024
Box, Table, Cranes, Deer Panels, Gilt, Black Ground, Japan, 9 x 8 x 16 In.	113
Box, Tea, Pewter Compartment, Trading Scenes, Chinese, Early 1900s, 8 x 13 x 10 In.	250
Cabinet, Document, Mountain Scene, 2 Doors, Drawers, Stand, Japan, 1700s, 51 x 37 x 21 In. ...*illus*	2925
Cabinet, Octagonal, Hinged Top, Black, Landscapes, 16 Drawers, 2 Doors, 1800s, 44 x 17 x 12 In.	1220
Chest, Vermilion Red & Black Trunk, Metal Hardware, Japan, Late 1800s, 27 x 37 x 30 3/8 In.	570
Lap Desk, Gilt, Painted, 2 Brass-Topped Ink Jars, 1800s, 7 3/4 x 15 1/2 x 12 1/2 In.	384
Screen, Coromandel, 5-Panel, Black, Hardstone Inlay, Giltwood Mounts, 1900s, 75 x 106 In.	500
Shrine, Butsudan, Cabinet, 2 Sliding Doors, Gilt Metal Trim, Japan, 1930s, 82 x 24 x 21 In.	500
Shrine, Wood, Carved, Red & Black, 3 Drawers, 1800s, 48 x 33 x 19 In. ....*illus*	854
Tray, Black Ground, Metallic Gold Leaves, Curved Edges, 1800s, 33 x 24 In.	125
Tray, Chinoiserie, Wood, Black, Gilt, Continental, Early 1900s, 19 1/4 x 30 In.	242
Tray, Square, Flower Design, Raised Feet, Japan, 2 x 10 3/4 In. ....*illus*	125
Trunk, Black, Brass, Gilt, Chrysanthemum-Mon, Ginkgo Leaves, Late 1900s, 14 x 23 1/4 In.	305

LADY HEAD VASE, *see Head Vase.*

LALIQUE

Lalique glass and jewelry were made by Rene Lalique (1860–1945) in Paris, France, between the 1890s and his death in 1945. Beginning in 1921 he had a manufacturing plant in Alsace. The glass was molded, pressed, and engraved in Art Nouveau and Art Deco styles. Most pieces were marked with the signature *R. Lalique.* Lalique glass is still being made. Most pieces made after 1945 bear the mark *Lalique.* After 1978 the registry mark was added and the mark became *Lalique ® France.* In the prices listed here, this is indicated by Lalique (R) France. Some pieces that are advertised as ring dishes or pin dishes were listed as ashtrays in the Lalique factory catalog and are listed as ashtrays here. Names of pieces are given here in French and in English. The Lalique brand was bought by Art & Fragrance, a Swiss company, in 2008. Lalique and Art & Fragrance both became part of the Lalique Group in 2016. Lalique glass and jewelry are still being made. Jewelry made by Rene Lalique and the company is listed in the Jewelry category.

R.LALIQUE.FRANCE	LALIQUE FRANCE	Lalique® France
Lalique	Lalique	Lalique
c.1925–1930s	1945–1960	1978+

Bookends, Enfants, Children, Standing, Frosted, Circular Base, Marked, 8 x 6 1/4 x 3 In.	900
Bookends, Reverie, Kneeling Nude Woman, Clear, 1900s, 8 x 5 x 3 In. ....*illus*	650
Bowl, Champs Elysees, Stylized Leaves, Frosted & Clear, 1950s, 7 3/4 x 17 3/4 In. ....*illus*	1063
Bowl, Clear, 2 Amber Serpents, Intertwined, 3 x 8 In.	450
Bowl, Contemporary, Frosted, Horizontal Lines, Marked Lalique, (R), France, 3 1/4 x 12 In.	192
Bowl, Coupe Angelots, Frosted Angel Column, Footed, Signed, Lalique France, 1900s, 6 x 9 In.	200
Bowl, Fleurons, Flowers, Opalescent & Clear, Floret Swirls, R. Lalique, 3 x 8 In.	270
Bowl, Lierre, Ivy, Applied Leaves, Pale Green, Clear, Molded Rim, 3 x 9 In.	625
Bowl, Marguerite, Daisies, Clear, Frosted, 2 1/2 x 12 1/2 In.	187
Bowl, Nemours, Clear, Deep Molded Daisies, Black Enamel Centers, c.1978, 3 x 10 In. .*illus*	594
Bowl, Nonnettes, Lovebirds, 3 Pairs, 2 1/4 x 8 1/2 In.	390
Bowl, Oeillets, Carnations, Opalescent & Clear, Signed, R. Lalique France, 1932, 2 x 14 In. *illus*	485

L.G. Wright, Daisy & Fern, Water Set, Vaseline Opalescent, Ball Pitcher With Ruffled Rim, 7 Piece
$200

Jeffrey S. Evans & Associates

Lacquer, Box, Black, 3 Maidens, Dancing, Flute Players, Russia, 1800s, 1 3/4 x 3 x 5 1/2 In.
$60

Alderfer Auction Company

Lacquer, Box, Hinged Lid, Troika Scene, Painted, Imperial Seal, Russia, 2 x 8 x 5 In.
$142

Soulis Auctions

Lacquer, Box, Red, Lobed Flower Shape, Landscapes, Chinese, 5 1/4 x 21 3/4 In.
$1,024

Neal Auction Company

L

Lacquer, Cabinet, Document, Mountain Landscape, 2 Doors, Drawers, Stand, Japan, 1700s, 51 x 37 x 21 In.
$2,925

Thomaston Place Auction Galleries

Lacquer, Shrine, Wood, Carved, Red & Black, 3 Drawers, 1800s, 48 x 33 x 19 In.
$854

Rafael Osona Nantucket Auctions

Lacquer, Tray, Square, Flower Design, Raised Feet, Japan, 2 x 10¾ In.
$125

Auctions at Showplace, NYC

Lalique, Bookends, Reverie, Kneeling Nude Woman, Clear, 1900s, 8 x 5 x 3 In.
$650

Bruneau & Co. Auctioneers

Lalique, Bowl, Champs Elysees, Stylized Leaves, Frosted & Clear, 1950s, 7¾ x 17¾ In.
$1,063

Hindman

Lalique, Bowl, Nemours, Clear, Deep Molded Daisies, Black Enamel Centers, c.1978, 3 x 10 In.
$594

John Moran Auctioneers

Lalique, Bowl, Oeillets, Carnations, Opalescent & Clear, Signed, R. Lalique France, 1932, 2 x 14 In.
$485

Bonhams

Lalique, Bowl, Pinson, Finches, Bird & Leaves Relief, Signed, 3¾ x 9 In.
$180

Alderfer Auction Company

Lalique, Bowl, Verone, Birds, Frosted & Clear, Scrolled, Footed, Late 1900s, 7½ In.
$605

Ahlers & Ogletree Auction Gallery

Lalique, Dresser Box, Coppelia, Roses, Frosted, Brass, Hinged Lid, Late 1900s, 3½ x 6¾ In.
$273

Ahlers & Ogletree Auction Gallery

Lalique, Figurine, Bear Ursus, Standing, Amber, Inscribed Lalique France, 4 x 7 x 3 In.
$330

Treasureseeker Auctions

Lalique, Figurine, Leopard, Stretching, Etched, Black Spotted Glass, 4 x 14 x 2 In.
$900

Abington Auction Gallery

Lalique, Figurine, Sidonie, Turtle, Frosted, Etched Lalique, 1900s, 3 In.
$344

Lion and Unicorn

Lalique, Figurine, Sparrow, Wings Out, Frosted, Signed, Lalique France, 1950s, 3 In.
$96

Garth's Auctioneers & Appraisers

Lalique, Paperweight, Elephant, Frosted, Signed, 6 ¼ In.
$150

Nadeau's Auction Gallery

Lalique, Vase, Bacchantes, Encircling Female Nudes, Frosted, Crystal, 9 ½ x 7 ½ In.
$1,250

Greenwich Auction

Lalique, Vase, Dampierre, Protruding Birds, Frosted & Clear, Marked, 4 ¾ In.
$185

Nadeau's Auction Gallery

Lalique, Vase, Esterel, Leaves & Branches, Amber, Rene Lalique, 1923, 6 ¼ In.
$1,694

Ahlers & Ogletree Auction Gallery

> **TIP**
> *Install locks on all garage doors and windows.*

Lalique, Vase, Dahlias, Chinese Wood Stand, Silver Inlay, c.1923, 5 x 7 In.
$1,950

Toomey & Co. Auctioneers

L

Lalique, Vase, Formose, Swirling Carp, Spherical, Emerald Green, c.1924, 6½ In.
$6,435

Jeffrey S. Evans & Associates

Lalique, Vase, Marrakech, Palm Leaves, Amber, Molded Handle, Rene Lalique, 1900s, 12 In.
$1,210

Fontaine's Auction Gallery

Lamp, Aladdin, Student, Harvard, Butterscotch Ribbed Shade, Wick Knob, c.1880, 21 In.
$660

Garth's Auctioneers & Appraisers

Bowl, Pinson, Finches, Bird & Leaves Relief, Signed, 3¾ x 9 In. ....*illus*	180
Bowl, Roses, Flowers On Vine, Frosted, Square, Late 1900s, 3 x 9½ In.	545
Bowl, Verone, Birds, Frosted & Clear, Scrolled, Footed, Late 1900s, 7½ In. ....*illus*	605
Candlestick, Mesanges, Band Of Birds, Clear, Frosted, Flowers, 6¾ x 5½ In., Pair............	1046
Chandelier, 6-Light, Champs Elysees, Leaves, Brass Frame, Hexagonal Bottom Pane, 1900s, 22 In....	5313
Compote, Aries, Ram's Head, Frosted, Clear Bowl, Round Foot, 8 x 7 In............	200
Compote, Nogent, 4 Birds, Frosted, Clear Bowl, Circular Base, 3½ x 5½ In.	113
Dresser Box, Coppelia, Roses, Frosted, Brass, Hinged Lid, Late 1900s, 3½ x 6¾ In. ...*illus*	273
Dresser Jar, Lid, Frosted, Jay Thorpe, Stamped Jaytho, c.1928, 2⅞ In............	468
Figurine, Bear Ursus, Standing, Amber, Inscribed Lalique France, 4 x 7 x 3 In. ....*illus*	330
Figurine, Chrysalide, Winged Female Fairy, Standing, Frosted & Clear, 1950s, 9½ In.	625
Figurine, Chrysis, Nude Woman, Kneeling, Arched Back, Round Base, Frosted, 5 x 6 x 2 In..	531
Figurine, Cygne, Tete Haute, Swan, Head Up, Frosted, 9½ x 12 In.	1680
Figurine, Deux Cygnes, 2 Swans, Frosted, Circular Plinth Base, Signed, 3 In............	38
Figurine, Deux Poissons, 2 Fish, Swimming, Clear, Circular Base, 1950s, 11 In............	1063
Figurine, Leopard, Stretching, Etched, Black Spotted Glass, 4 x 14 x 2 In. ....*illus*	900
Figurine, Sidonie, Turtle, Frosted, Etched Lalique, 1900s, 3 In. ....*illus*	344
Figurine, Sparrow, Wings Out, Frosted, Signed, Lalique France, 1950s, 3 In. ....*illus*	96
Figurine, Tete De Cheval, Horse's Head, Clear, Circular Black Base, 17 x 15 x 6 In............	5313
Hood Ornament, Coq Nain, Rooster, Frosted, Etched, Post 1978, 8½ In............	120
Lamp, Mesanges, Band Of Birds, Wreath Stem, Metal Socket, Hexagonal Base, 1950s, 6½ In..	375
Paperweight, Bull, Pawing Ground, Frosted, Rectangular Base, Etched, Sticker, Post 1945, 3 In..	84
Paperweight, Elephant, Frosted, Signed, 6¼ In. ....*illus*	150
Perfume Bottle, 2 Overlapping Anemone, Beaded Centers, Frosted & Clear, 1935, 4 In.	125
Perfume Bottle, Clairefontaine, Floral Stopper, Clear Base, 4 x 3 In.	275
Perfume Bottle, Grande Pomme, Apple, Frosted, Stopper, Clear Stem & Leaves, 5 In.	205
Powder Box, Lid, Cleones, Beetles, Opalescent, Signed, 2 x 7 In............	944
Powder Box, Trois Figurines, 3 Figures, Frosted, c.1925, 1½ x 3¾ In............	105
Trinket Box, Duncan, Embossed Nude, Beveled, Frosted, Post 1945, 2¼ In.	210
Vase, Bacchantes, Encircling Female Nudes, Frosted, Crystal, 9½ x 7½ In. ....*illus*	1250
Vase, Bagatelle, Relief Birds & Leaves, Frosted, 6¾ x 4¾ In.	563
Vase, Coeur De Jeanette, Flowers & Leaves, Frosted, 4 x 5 In.	210
Vase, Dahlias, Chinese Wood Stand, Silver Inlay, c.1923, 5 x 7 In. ....*illus*	1950
Vase, Dampierre, Protruding Birds, Frosted & Clear, Marked, 4¾ In. ....*illus*	185
Vase, Dryades, Nymphs, Frosted & Clear, Signed, R. Lalique, France, c.1937, 8½ In............	5000
Vase, Esterel, Leaves & Branches, Amber, Rene Lalique, 1923, 6¼ In. ....*illus*	1694
Vase, Formose, Swirling Carp, Spherical, Emerald Green, c.1924, 6½ In. ....*illus*	6435
Vase, Frosted Glass, Corkscrew, Leaf Accent, Etched, Post 1945, 6 In.	150
Vase, Ispahan, Roses, Etched, Frosted & Clear, Signed, 9 x 7 In.	468
Vase, Marrakech, Palm Leaves, Amber, Molded Handle, Rene Lalique, 1900s, 12 In. ...*illus*	1210
Vase, Mossi, Protruding Discs, Kaleidoscopic, Frosted & Clear, R. Lalique, 1933, 8¼ In.	594
Vase, Nymphale, Butterflies, Cobalt Blue, Globular, Fluted Rim, 8¾ x 7 In............	1500
Vase, Sylvie, 2 Entwined Doves, Clear, Etched, Marked, 8 In............	118

LAMP

Lamps of every type, from the early oil-burning Betty and Phoebe lamps to the recent electric lamps with glass or beaded shades, interest collectors. Fuels used in lamps changed through the years; whale oil (1800–1840), camphene (1828), Argand (1830), lard (1833–1863), solar (1843–1860s), turpentine and alcohol (1840s), gas (1850–1879), kerosene (1860), and electricity (1879) are the most common. Early solar or astral lamps burned fat. Modern solar lamps are powered by the sun. Other lamps are listed by manufacturer or type of material.

2-Light, Porcelain, Crane, Fabric Shade, Metal Base, Manifattura Artistica Le Porcellane, 34 x 23 In.	938
2-Light, Porcelain, Gilt Bronze, Mounted, Acorn Finial, Square Base, Continental, Late 1800s, 33 In.	250
3-Light, Bronze, Peacock Shape Base, Gilt, Bronze Conical Shade, 16 x 10 In.	1800
Aladdin, 2-Light, No. 1247, Venetian Art-Craft, Red, Brass, 1931, 23¾ In.	299
Aladdin, Student, Electric, Model 4, Brass, Weighted Base, 75th Anniversary, 30 x 16 x 8 In.......	117

L

Aladdin, Student, Harvard, Butterscotch Ribbed Shade, Wick Knob, c.1880, 21 In. ..... *illus*	660
Argand, Electric, Gilt Bronze, Clear Prisms, Vase Shape Font, Paw Feet, 19 In......................	800
Astral, Oil, Brass, Marble Base, Etched Glass Globe, Columnar, Cornelius & Co., c.1845, 25 x 9 In..	630
Astral, Oil, Figural, Woman, Brass, Marble Base, Gold, Black, Chimney, Cornelius, 34 In. .*illus*	1380
Banquet, Kerosene, Figural, Cherub, Metal Base, Glass Shade, Sunflower Decal, 32 x 11 In. *illus*	200
Banquet, Kerosene, Junior, Blown Glass, Conical, Spar Brenner Burner, c.1880, 14⅜ x 4 In...	187
Banquet, Kerosene, Onyx & Cut Glass, Gilt Bronze Mounts, 1800s, 46 x 13 In.......................	3025
Banquet, Oil, Monumental, Owl Shade & Base, Blue, Purple, 28 In...........	1093
Banquet, Oil, Silver Plate, Corinthian, Cut Glass, Victorian, 1800s, 24 In.	64
Bouillotte, 2-Light, Bronze Dore, Flower Design, Black Shade, 28 x 15¼ In.....................	320
Bouillotte, 2-Light, Empire Style, Brass, Openwork Base, Tole Shade, 1900s, 29 In.	188
Bouillotte, 2-Light, Tin, Painted, Candles, Ring Top, Old Red Surface, 1900s, 19 In............	189
Bouillotte, Gilt Bronze, Porcelain, Red Shade, Beaux Arts, Sterling Bronze Co., c.1910, 24 In. ..... *illus*	200
Bradley & Hubbard lamps are included in the Bradley & Hubbard category.	
Bronze, Figural, Woman, Diaphanous Dress, Favrile Glass Flower, France, 1900s, 27 x 8 In..	450
Candle, Bronze, Iridescent Yellow Shade, Flared Top, Round Base, 21 x 5 In.	300
Candle, Etched Hurricane Chimney, Flared Rim, Flowers, c.1880, 20 x 8 In., Pair.................	281
Candle, Tripod Legs, Socket, Adjustable, Spring Mechanism, Wrought Iron, 1800s, 23½ In....	531
Candlestick, Brass, Empire Shade, Turned Finial, 1930s, 33½ x 12 In., Pair	132
Ceiling, 4-Light, Inverted Umbrella, Glass, Metal, Poliarte, Italy, 28 x 11 In. .... *illus*	375
Ceiling, Aluminum, Brass, Beehive Design, White & Gold, Alvar Aalto, Finland, c.1975, 11 x 13 In.	5000
Ceiling, Aluminum, Glass, Round, Henry Dreyfuss, c.1938, 5 x 12 In.	1000
Ceiling, Bronze, Glass Domed Shade, Frame, 9 x 20 In.	625
Ceiling, Brutalist, Brass, Steel, Chrome Plated, Enameled, Frosted Glass, c.1965, 11 x 19 In. *illus*	1250
Ceiling, Idman, Brass, Enameled Steel, Glass Shade, Paavo Tynell, Finland, c.1945, 16 x 22 In.	3000
Chandelier, 2 Tiers, Swan, Gilt Bronze, Reddish Brown Alabaster, Early 1900s, 60 x 35 In., Pair	1936
Chandelier, 2-Light, Black Forest, Carved, Multicolor, Antlers, Woman, 1900s, 25 In...........	563
Chandelier, 3-Light, Kerosene, Brass, Colored Ruffled Glass Shades, 1800s, 67 x 27 In. ..*illus*	908
Chandelier, 3-Light, Oak, Slag Glass, Hanging, W.B. Brown, c.1910, 24 In.........................	1353
Chandelier, 4 Tiers, Brass, Hanging, Glass Swags, Flowers, 28 In.	252
Chandelier, 4-Light, Brass, Lanterns, Square, Arts & Crafts, c.1910s, 33½ x 18 x 18 In.*illus*	1107
Chandelier, 4-Light, Candle, Brass, Detachable Arms, Spindle Base, Dutch, 1700s, 10 x 15½ In.	468
Chandelier, 4-Light, Neoclassical Style, Silver Plate, 38 x 28 In..........................	192
Chandelier, 5-Light, Clear, Glass Body & Arms, Venetian, 1900s, 26 x 28 In.........................	750
Chandelier, 5-Light, Georgian Style, Cut Glass, Hanging Prisms, 3 Tiers, 1900s, 30 In.	469
Chandelier, 5-Light, Hanging Pendants, Copper, Glass Shades, Metal Frame, 4 x 4 In...........	600
Chandelier, 6-Light, Brass & Black Metal, Rectangular Canopy, Stilnovo, Italy, 28 x 14 x 47 In. ...	813
Chandelier, 6-Light, Bronze, Candlearms, Glass Prisms, Brass Frame, 1900s, 41 x 25 In. ....*illus*	768
Chandelier, 6-Light, Bronze, Colored Glass, Basket Shape, Flowers, 36 In.	960
Chandelier, 6-Light, Bronze, Parcel Gilt, Nude, White Flowers, Continental, Early 1900s, 34 In.	5625
Chandelier, 6-Light, Candle Shape Socket, Green Paint, Leafy Center, Italy, c.1950, 18 x 16 In....	1250
Chandelier, 6-Light, Cast Metal, Matte Patina, Cut Glass, Continental, Late 1800s, 33 x 22 In. .	750
Chandelier, 6-Light, Cut Glass, Regency Style, Ralph Lauren, 35 x 30 In............................	406
Chandelier, 6-Light, Empire Style, Faceted Glass Beads, Pendant, 42 x 33 x 33 In...............	219
Chandelier, 6-Light, Empire Style, Gilt, Patinated Bronze, 26 x 22 In................................	638
Chandelier, 6-Light, Gilt Metal, Glass Pear Drops, Clusters, 23 x 22 In.	576
Chandelier, 6-Light, Iron, Wood, Chamfered Post, Hook, Scrolled Candlearms, 1700s, 29 x 20 In.	1000
Chandelier, 6-Light, Louis XV, Gilt, Scrolled Leafy Arms, Black Painted Disc, 14½ x 24 In.	225
Chandelier, 6-Light, Louis XVI Style, Crystal, Hanging Prisms, Gilt Arms, 1900s, 38 In.	625
Chandelier, 7-Light, Brass, Regency Style, 14 x 14 x 27 In.	130
Chandelier, 8-Light, Candlecups, Multicolor, Flowers, Drop Chains, Murano, c.1950, 35 x 36 In. .	1063
Chandelier, 8-Light, Gilt Brass, Chains, Hans-Agne Jakobsson, Sweden, c.1965, 56 x 19 In.	650
Chandelier, 9-Light, 2 Tiers, Mixed Metal, Cut Glass, Prisms, 1910s, 18 x 29 In. ....*illus*	1303
Chandelier, 9-Light, Brass, Bottle Shape Glass, Hans-Agne Jakobsson, Markaryd, 36 x 33 In.	938
Chandelier, 10-Light, Prisms, Scroll Arms, Candlestick Shape, Continental, 1960s, 22 x 31 In.	540
Chandelier, 12-Light, Brass, Candle Socket, Masks, Gilt, 1900s, 24 x 24 x 34 In.	454
Chandelier, 12-Light, Bronze, Central Flowers, Acanthus Scroll Arms, Late 1800s, 23 In. ...	1800
Chandelier, 12-Light, Empire, Gilt Bronze, Cut Glass, Fruit Basket, c.1840, 48 x 34 In. *illus*	4375
Chandelier, 12-Light, Georgian Style, Cut Glass, Hanging Prisms, 1900s, 38 x 35 In.	438

Lamp, Astral, Oil, Figural, Woman, Brass, Marble Base, Gold, Black, Chimney, Cornelius, 34 In.
$1,380

Stevens Auction Co.

Lamp, Banquet, Kerosene, Figural, Cherub, Metal Base, Glass Shade, Sunflower Decal, 32 x 11 In.
$200

Woody Auction

L

This is an edited listing of current prices. Visit **Kovels.com** to check thousands of prices from previous years and sign up for free information on trends, tips, reproductions, marks, and more.

Lamp, Bouillotte, Gilt Bronze, Porcelain, Red Shade, Beaux Arts, Sterling Bronze Co., c.1910, 24 In.
$200

Neal Auction Company

Lamp, Ceiling, 4-Light, Inverted Umbrella, Glass, Metal, Poliarte, Italy, 28 x 11 In.
$375

Palm Beach Modern Auctions

Lamp, Ceiling, Brutalist, Brass, Steel, Chrome Plated, Enameled, Frosted Glass, c.1965, 11 x 19 In.
$1,250

Wright

Lamp, Chandelier, 3-Light, Kerosene, Brass, Colored Ruffled Glass Shades, 1800s, 67 x 27 In.
$908

Fontaine's Auction Gallery

Lamp, Chandelier, 4-Light, Brass, Lanterns, Square, Arts & Crafts, c.1910s, 33 ½ x 18 x 18 In.
$1,107

California Historical Design

Lamp, Chandelier, 6-Light, Bronze, Candlearms, Glass Prisms, Brass Frame, 1900s, 41 x 25 In.
$768

Brunk Auctions

Lamp, Chandelier, 9-Light, 2 Tiers, Mixed Metal, Cut Glass, Prisms, 1910s, 18 x 29 In.
$1,303

Hindman

Lamp, Chandelier, 12-Light, Empire, Gilt Bronze, Cut Glass, Fruit Basket, c.1840, 48 x 34 In.
$4,375

Hindman

Chandelier, 12-Light, Scrolls, Gilt, Candlearms, Drops, Beaded, Venetian, 1900s, 36 In., Pair...	2460
Chandelier, 18-Light, Gilt Bronze, Baluster Urn Shape, Celeste Blue, c.1980, 41 x 36 In.	2125
Chandelier, 18-Light, Hanging Prisms, Flower Shape Socle, Gilt, 36 In.	1380
Chandelier, 24-Light, Sputnik, Bronze Ball, White Enamel Shades, Italy, 1960s, 58 x 62 In.	1250
Chandelier, Aluminum, Chrome Plated Brass, Steel, Brass, Acrylic, Italy, c.1970, 48 x 39 In. ......*illus*	910
Chandelier, Artichoke, Copper, Aluminum, Poul Henningsen, Louis Poulsen, 1975, 22 x 29 In. .	5625
Chandelier, Artichoke, Copper, Steel, Poul Henningsen, Louis Poulsen, 1957, 25 x 31 In. ...*illus*	8750
Chandelier, Brass Fittings, Scrolled Candles, Glass Drops, Swags, 1800s, 32 In.	3528
Chandelier, Brass, Cut Glass Drops, Electrified, 46 x 29 In.	2375
Chandelier, Brass, Opalescent Chunk Glass, Koloman Moser, Austria, c.1902, 36 x 12 In. ..*illus*	3750
Chandelier, Central Stem, Candlearms, Scrolled, 1900s, 22 In.	256
Chandelier, Fairy, Burmese Glass, Brass Buttons, Thomas Webb & Sons, c.1880, 17 x 12 In. ..	1872
Chandelier, Rock Crystal, French Rococo, Gilt Bronze, 1800s, 45 x 33 In.	6000
Chandelier, Stained Glass, Green, Caramel, Red, Jeweled Centers, c.1900, 15 x 10 In. .*illus*	150
Conch Shell, Cameo, Carved, Neoclassical Scene, Wood Stand, 1800s, 8¾ In. ....*illus*	787
Cylindrical, Marble, White Shade, Brass Base, 1900s, 48 In.	250
Desk, Electric, Chrome, Weighted, Cylindrical Shade, 34 x 23 x 9 In., Pair ....*illus*	380
Desk, Electric, Steel, Enameled Aluminum, Brass, Kurt Versen, Inc., c.1955, 14 x 6 x 16 In..	1063
Electric, 2 Tiers, Bronze, Applied Flowers, Gilt Angel Faces, Footed, 1901, 30 x 17 In. ..*illus*	546
Electric, 2-Light, 6 Bent Petal Shade Panels, Caramel Slag, Metal Base & Frame, 23 x 17 In......	600
Electric, 2-Light, Art Nouveau, Bronze, 6-Panel Slag Glass Shade, Metal Base, 22 x 18 In. ..	224
Electric, 2-Light, Brass, Quezal Shades, Circular Base, 4 In. ....*illus*	806
Electric, 2-Light, Brass, Wrought Iron Cup Holders, Adjustable, Tripod Legs, 1900s, 22¾ In......	568
Electric, 2-Light, Famille Rose, Ormolu Mount, Classical Scenes, Chinese Export, 27½ x 9 In., Pair	984
Electric, 2-Light, Gold Cherry Blossom, Domed Shade, Carl Radke, 2002, 19 x 12 In.	1200
Electric, 2-Light, Green Glaze, Gilt Brass Base, Converted From Vase, Chinese 28 In............	1536
Electric, 2-Light, Satin Nickel Finish, Shallow Shade, 48½ x 15 In., Pair	130
Electric, 3-Light, Brass, Fasces Shape, Wood Base, Black Fringe, Continental, Late 1900s, 53 In.	121
Electric, 3-Light, Bronze, Leaded Glass Shade, Grapes, Geometrics, Gorham, 22 x 15 In. ...*illus*	4800
Electric, 3-Light, Lily, Patinated Bronze Base, Iridescent Glass Shades, 19 In.	188
Electric, 3-Light, Metal, Hammered, Silvered, Candlestick Shape, Caldwell, 26½ In., Pair ...*illus*	1024
Electric, 3-Light, Rock Crystal, Giltwood Base & Trim, Paw Feet, 35 x 6½ In.	1680
Electric, 4-Light, Enamel on Steel, Cylindrical Shade, Tommi Parzinger, 60 x 13 In.	1950
Electric, 4-Light, Figural, Satyr, Gilt Bronze, Cornucopia, Flowers, Linke, c.1900, 27 x 17 In. ......*illus*	1800
Electric, 5-Light, Brass, Lucerne, Pivoting Shade, 1800s, 28 In., Pair...............................	488
Electric, 12-Light, Chandelier, Gaetano Sciolari, 4 Arms, Polished Brass Tubes, c.1970, 20 x 24 In.	1000
Electric, 16-Light, 3 Tiers, Metal & Wood, T.H. Robsjohn-Gibbings, 72 x 26 x 26 In.............	8125
Electric, Acrylic, Book Shape, Red & White, Pierre Cardin, France, c.1975, 7 x 8 x 5 In.	875
Electric, Acrylic, Enameled Aluminum, S-Shape Curve, Artemide, Italy, c.1966, 31 x 8 x 7 In....	1105
Electric, Airplane Shape, Chrome, Blue Glass, Mounted, c.1940, 12 In. ....*illus*	531
Electric, Aluminum, Frosted Glass, Egg Shape, Hans-Agne Jakobsson, c.1960, 10 x 16 In. ......*illus*	1875
Electric, Art Nouveau, Bronze, Frog, Umbrella Shade, Glass Jewels, Early 1900s, 10½ In. ...*illus*	2988
Electric, Arts & Crafts, Copper, Patinated, Bean Pot, Mica Lamp Co., 18 x 17 In.	438
Electric, Arts & Crafts, Oak, Mica Lamp Co., 57 x 20 x 20 In.	832
Electric, Babadul, Paper, Enameled Steel, Silicone, Ingo Maurer & Dagmar Mombach, 1998, 53 In...	2500
Electric, Banker's, Emeralite, Multicolor Shade, Flowers & Rocaille Design, 16 x 8 In.	1180
Electric, Blue, White Glaze, Landscape, Circular Wood Base, Chinese,16½ In., Pair...........	369
Electric, Boudoir, Iridescent Glass, Heart Shape Leaves, Pink, Daniel Lotton, 1986, 10 In. ..	570
Electric, Boudoir, Iron, Pink Molded Glass Shade, Floral Swags, Art Nouveau, R.B. Co., 14 x 7 In.	59
Electric, Boudoir, Metal Base, Orange Glass Shade, Landscape Scene, Deguy, 14½ x 6 In. .*illus*	108
Electric, Brass, Bronze Rectangular Shade, Visual Comfort, Thomas O'Brien Dixon, 20 In.	153
Electric, Brass, Chrome Plated, Lighthouse, On Rocky Base, 12 In.	322
Electric, Brass, Chrome Plated, Lock & Key, Stacked Box Leather, 15 x 10 In. ....*illus*	8750
Electric, Brass, Hammered, Cutout, Lion's Head, Square Base, Arts & Crafts, c.1910, 22 x 16 In.	3567
Electric, Brass, Lacquered, Fiberglass Shade, c.1970, 22 x 17 In.	455
Electric, Brass, Lion Supports, Multicolor Jeweled Shade, 21 x 13 In. ....*illus*	2415
Electric, Brass, Stained Glass Shade, Multicolor, Footed, Mid 1900s, 26 In.	270
Electric, Brass, Steam Whistle Shape, Handle, Switch, 9 In.	120

Lamp, Chandelier, Aluminum, Chrome Plated Brass, Steel, Brass, Acrylic, Italy, c.1970, 48 x 39 In.
$910

Wright

Lamp, Chandelier, Artichoke, Copper, Steel, Poul Henningsen, Louis Poulsen, 1957, 25 x 31 In.
$8,750

Wright

Lamp, Chandelier, Brass, Opalescent Chunk Glass, Koloman Moser, Austria, c.1902, 36 x 12 In.
$3,750

Toomey & Co. Auctioneers

Lamp, Chandelier, Stained Glass, Green, Caramel, Red, Jeweled Centers, c.1900, 15 x 10 In.
$150

Treasureseeker Auctions

Lamp, Conch Shell, Cameo, Carved, Neoclassical Scene, Wood Stand, 1800s, 8¾ In.
$787

Fontaine's Auction Gallery

Lamp, Desk, Electric, Chrome, Weighted, Cylindrical Shade, 34 x 23 x 9 In., Pair
$380

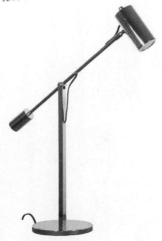

Thomaston Place Auction Galleries

Electric, Bronze, 3 Female Figures, Stepped & Shaped Base, France, 23 x 13 In., Pair	1287
Electric, Bronze, Figural, Monkey, On Book Base, Pen Shell Shade, Maitland-Smith, 25 In.	1936
Electric, Bronze, Figural, Slag Glass, Marked, Behrens, 1900s, 29½ In. ..... *illus*	2903
Electric, Bronze, Figural, Un Courrier, Au Maroc, Man, Running, France, 9 x 14 x 37 In.	797
Electric, Bronze, Figural, Young Woman, Long Dress, Marble Base, Late 1900s, 37½ In. . *illus*	840
Electric, Bronze, Satin Glass Shade, Rivers & Dirt Paths, Early 1900s, 17 x 10 In.	300
Electric, Cast Resin, Figural, Fox, Red Coat, Faux Candle, Bill Huebbe, 1980s, 22 In., Pair..	543
Electric, Ceramic, Double Baluster, Flared Cup Top, Blue Bands, Bitossi, Italy, c.1950, 23 In., Pair	940
Electric, Cobra Shape, Steel, Chrome Plated, Greta Magnusson Grossman, 1950, 54 x 11 x 28 In.	563
Electric, Corinthian Column Base, Domed Shade, Etched Glass, Prisms, 31 x 10 In.	120
Electric, Cut Glass, Pinwheel, Jewel Shade, Brass Trim, 31 In.	1035
Electric, Figural, 3 Nudes, Bronze, Multicolor, Slag Glass Shade, Gustav Gurshave, 35 In.	540
Electric, Figural, Bronze, Spanish Conquistador, Frosted Flame Shade, La Tremouille, 50 x 15 In.	960
Electric, Figural, Cast Metal, Mermaid, Nautilus, Glass Shade, Art Nouveau Style, 19 In.	903
Electric, Figural, Frog & Toadstool, Bronze, McClelland Barclay, c.1930s, 12 x 8 In.	322
Electric, Figural, Globe, Statue Girl, Hood, Marble Base, 10 x 4 x 9 In. ..... *illus*	443
Electric, Figural, Lighthouse, Rock Shape Base, Cast Metal, Patina, 1940s, 13 x 7 In.	330
Electric, Fish, Twisted Tail, Tripod Base, Sea Creature Feet, Gold, Copper, 1900s, 61 In.	554
Electric, Football Shape, Frosted Glass, Matteo Thun, Arteluce, Italy, c.1990, 13 x 7½ In.	875
Electric, Gilt Bronze, Cone Shape Shade, De Wael, Fondica, France, 52½ x 10 x 7 In.	2750
Electric, Gilt, Leaded Glass Shade, Flowers, Unique Art Glass & Metal Co., Early 1900s, 23 In.	1089
Electric, Glass & Cast Metal, Painted, Perforated Mesh Shade, Contemporary, Late 1900s, 21 In.	72
Electric, Glass, Black Base, Deep Amethyst & Frosted Shade, Correia, 1989, 18 In. ..... *illus*	450
Electric, Glass, Brass, White Lattice, Gold Flecked, Amber Ground, Wood Base, Murano, 23 In.	125
Electric, Glass, Frosted, Mushroom Shape, Chrysanthemums, Pittsburgh Lamp, 12 x 11 In. . *illus*	357
Electric, Glass, Scallop Shape, Filled With Seashells, Beige Fabric, Flared Shades, 24 In., Pair ..	125
Electric, Hanging, Slag Glass, Bell Shape, 8-Sided, 40 x 22 In. ..... *illus*	2700
Electric, Italian Marble, Cylindrical, Brown, White, Black, Late 1900s, 21 x 5 In., Pair	1000
Electric, Jefferson, Bronze Base, Glass Shade, Reverse Painted, Landscape, 23 x 16 In.	688
Electric, Karl Springer, Wood, Lacquered Vellum, Brass, American, c.1970, 24 x 16 In.	1875
Electric, Leaded Glass Shade, Multicolor, Duffner Kimberly, New York, c.1910, 28 x 21½ In..	9225
Electric, Leaded Glass Shade, Patinated Metal, Unique Art Glass & Metal Co., Early 1900s, 25 In..	2000
Electric, Loetz Glass Shade, Flower Shape, Figural Stem, Metal, Art Nouveau, 21 x 5 In. *illus*	1063
Electric, Mahogany, Georgian, Adjustable, Candlestand, Oval Top, 51 x 16 x 16 In., Pair	2750
Electric, Metal & Glass, Peacock, Spread Tail, Czechoslovakia, 16 x 15 In. ..... *illus*	1250
Electric, Metal Base, Umbrella Shade, Amber Slag, Flower Pattern, Miller Lamp Co., c.1919, 22 In.	69
Electric, Metal, Copper Shade, Marked, Bronstein, 25½ x 5 In. ..... *illus*	469
Electric, Metal, Figural, Sphinx, Tripod Base, Egyptian Revival, 71½ x 14 In.	344
Electric, Metal, Half Round Shade, Silver Gray Finish, Circular Base, 54 x 9 In., Pair . *illus*	263
Electric, Mica, Hammered, Early John L. Wilcox, Russia, c.1910, 20½ x 19 In. ..... *illus*	7995
Electric, Neoclassical, Decorative Crafts, Trophy Shape, Late 1900s, 37 x 9 In., Pair	160
Electric, Nickeled Bronze & Lucite, Circular Base, c.1935, 64 In.	281
Electric, Nightmare Before Christmas, 10th Anniversary, Umbrella Shades, Skeleton, Child's, 24 In.	570
Electric, Oak, Copper, Pine Branch, Cone, Arts & Crafts, Mica Lamp Co., 59 x 20 x 26 In. .. *illus*	487
Electric, Oak, Slag Glass, Double Base, Green, Prairie School, c.1910, 20 x 25 x 16¾ In. *illus*	3567
Electric, Painted, Octagonal Shade, Arab Rug Merchant Base, Austria, c.1915, 15 In.	240
Electric, Porcelain, Baluster Shape, Flowers, Pierced Foot, Herend, 1900s, 23 x 16 In. ..... *illus*	100
Electric, Porcelain, Foo Dog Shape, Iron Red & White Glaze, Lucite Base, 27 In.	308
Electric, Porcelain, Light Green, Gilt Bronze, Bacchus Mask Handles, Continental, 1900s, 26 x 11 In.	242
Electric, Porcelain, Snake Shape Handles, Openwork Rim, Robin's-Egg Blue Vase, France, 41 x 10 In.	704
Electric, Quilted Blown Glass, Diamond Cut, Brass, Barovier & Toso, Italy, 31½ x 7 In., Pair .... *illus*	1875
Electric, Slag Glass Panels, Filigree, Grapevine Design, c.1902, 21 x 14 In.	6250
Electric, Stained Glass, Flowers, Multicolor, Contemporary, 17 x 16½ x 15 In.	115
Electric, Steel, Hammered, Round Lobed Base, Cast Glass, Blossom & Fruits Top, Frosted, 7 x 8 In.	819
Electric, Tin, Daisy Minnow Bucket, Green Ground, Geometric Shade, c.1915, 21 In.	660
Electric, Tole, Drum Shape Base, Multicolor, Birds & Flowers, Octagonal Foot, 1800s, 25 In., Pair..	305
Electric, Torchiere, Chrome, Bakelite Base, Inverted Domed Shade, Art Deco, c.1930, 68 x 15 In., Pair	585
Electric, Torchiere, Metal Stem, Red Enamel, Reverse Domed Shade, W. Von Nessen, 72 x 10 In.	375
Electric, Turned Wood, Cylindrical Fabric Shade, Simon Blake Interiors, 9 x 21 x 15 In.	176

L

Lamp, Electric, 2 Tiers, Bronze, Applied Flowers, Gilt Angel Faces, Footed, 1901, 30 x 17 In.
$546

Stevens Auction Co.

Lamp, Electric, 2-Light, Brass, Quezal Shades, Circular Base, 4 In.
$806

Pook & Pook

Lamp, Electric, 3-Light, Bronze, Leaded Glass Shade, Grapes, Geometrics, Gorham, 22 x 15 In.
$4,800

Treasureseeker Auctions

Lamp, Electric, 3-Light, Metal, Hammered, Silvered, Candlestick Shape, Caldwell, 26½ In., Pair
$1,024

Nadeau's Auction Gallery

Lamp, Electric, 4-Light, Figural, Satyr, Gilt Bronze, Cornucopia, Flowers, Linke, c.1900, 27 x 17 In.
$1,800

Treasureseeker Auctions

Lamp, Electric, Airplane Shape, Chrome, Blue Glass, Mounted, c.1940, 12 In.
$531

New Haven Auctions

Lamp, Electric, Aluminum, Frosted Glass, Egg Shape, Hans-Agne Jakobsson, c.1960, 10 x 16 In.
$1,875

Wright

Lamp, Electric, Art Nouveau, Bronze, Frog, Umbrella Shade, Glass Jewels, Early 1900s, 10½ In.
$2,988

Jeffrey S. Evans & Associates

Lamp, Electric, Boudoir, Metal Base, Orange Glass Shade, Landscape Scene, Deguy, 14½ x 6 In.
$108

Richard Opfer Auctioneering, Inc.

L

Lamp, Electric, Brass, Chrome Plated, Lock & Key, Stacked Box Leather, 15 x 10 In.
$8,750

Wright

Lamp, Electric, Brass, Lion Supports, Multicolor Jeweled Shade, 21 x 13 In.
$2,415

Stevens Auction Co.

Lamp, Electric, Bronze, Figural, Slag Glass, Marked, Behrens, 1900s, 29 ½ In.
$2,903

Cowan's Auctions

Lamp, Electric, Bronze, Figural, Young Woman, Long Dress, Marble Base, Late 1900s, 37 ½ In.
$840

Selkirk Auctioneers & Appraisers

Lamp, Electric, Figural, Globe, Statue Girl, Hood, Marble Base, 10 x 4 x 9 In.
$443

Copake Auction

Lamp, Electric, Glass, Black Base, Deep Amethyst & Frosted Shade, Correia, 1989, 18 In.
$450

Garth's Auctioneers & Appraisers

Lamp, Electric, Glass, Frosted, Mushroom Shape, Chrysanthemums, Pittsburgh Lamp, 12 x 11 In.
$357

Toomey & Co. Auctioneers

Lamp, Electric, Hanging, Slag Glass, Bell Shape, 8-Sided, 40 x 22 In.
$2,700

Nadeau's Auction Gallery

Lamp, Electric, Loetz Glass Shade, Flower Shape, Figural Stem, Metal, Art Nouveau, 21 x 5 In.
$1,063

Treadway

Electric, Venini Glass, Fungo, White, Green, Massimo Vignelli, Italy, 10 x 8 ½ In. .... *illus*	1000
Electric, Walnut, Holly, Fiberglass, G. Nakashima, 58 x 16 In.	62500
Electric, White Marble, Cylinder On Block, Tapered Sharkskin Shade, Italy, c.1950, 20 In...	470
Electric, Wood, Goose, Carved, Cream Shade, Rectangular Base, c.1940, 7 x 9 In. .... *illus*	125
Fat, Wrought Iron, Wrigglework Bird Design, 1800s, 8 In. .... *illus*	400
Fluid, Shaped Base, White & Blue, Clear Glass, Polka Dot Design, c.1860, 23 In.	185
Gas, Brass, Domed Base, Glass Shade, Sherwood & Son, Birmingham, 14 In., Pair.............	101
Gasolier, 4-Light, Gilt Brass, Rococo, Cut Glass Shades, Cornelius & Baker, Electrified, 1800s, 74 In.	2048
Handel lamps are included in the Handel category.	
Hanging, 2-Light, Copper Body, Embossed, Opalescent Swirl Shades, 20 x 22 In.	90
Hanging, 4-Light, Bronze, Cherubs, Floral Shades, 30 x 23 x 12 In., Pair	1320
Hanging, 4-Light, Rod, Clear Glass, Black, 4 x 15 x 15 In.	156
Hanging, 6-Light, Chrome, Red Ball Shape Shade, Gilt Chain, 21 In. .... *illus*	625
Hanging, 8-Light, Oak Frame, Green Stained Glass, Arts & Crafts, 1900s, 43 x 38 In. . *illus*	1375
Hanging, Blown Glass, Massimo Vignelli, Italy, 1954, 14 x 5 ½ In..........................	1500
Hanging, Brass, Jewels, Chain, Swirl Base Cap, Stand, Late 1800s, 23 In.	329
Hanging, Cast Iron, Horned Owl Shape, Openwork, Japan, 22 In................................	201
Hanging, Enamel Steel, Pendant, Preben Dahl, Hans Folsgaard, Denmark, 16 In. ...... *illus*	813
Hanging, Gilt Bronze, Owls On Shade, Clear Prism, Scrollwork, Chain, Victorian, 30 x 14 In.	805
Hanging, Marble Shade, Ornate Brass Collar, 3 Twist Cords, c.1920, 21 x 16 In.................	84
Hanging, Oil, 3-Light, Bronze, Grand Tour, Central Urn, 8 ¼ x 12 In........................	768
Hanging, Oil, Cast Iron, Painted Glass, Adjustable, Victorian, Late 1800s, 36 x 14 In.	156
Hanging, Oil, Polished Brass, Ratchet Post, Electrified, 1800s, 23 In........................	224
Hanging, Steel, Domed Shade, Chain, Acrylic, George Nelson, Nessen Studio, c.1969, 12 x 14 In. *illus*	1625
Hanging, Tavern, 9-Light, Candle, Wrought Iron, Hand Forged, 1800s, 26 x 32 In.	848
Hanging, Wire Wrapped, Metal Birdcage, Balloon Shape, Blue Bird, 19 In...........................	352
Hurricane, 3-Light, Silvered Metal, Glass Shade, 1800s, 24 In., Pair.................................	1573
Hurricane, Clear Glass, Ruffled Rim, Prisms, Square Base, 9 x 22 In., Pair......................	201
Hurricane, Tole, 3 Removable Candlesticks, Glass Chimney, Square Base, 22 x 8 ¾ In., Pair	832
Jefferson, Metal Base, Patina, Stippled Shade, Reverse Painted, Flowers, 22 x 18 In.............	600
Kerosene, Diamond Thumbprint, Stand, Boston & Sandwich Glass Co., 1850, 11 ½ x 4 In..	94
Kerosene, Gone With The Wind, Painted, Owls Top & Bottom, Brass Trim, Clear Chimney, 24 In. .	1725
Kerosene, Gone With The Wind, Red Satin, White Enamel, Flowers, Electrified, 23 x 9 In...	175
Kerosene, Marble Base, Lithophane Shade, Blue, Clear, Electrified, 1800s, 12 x 4 In...........	702
Kerosene, Student, Weighted Base, Cylindrical Teal Glass, Manhattan Brass Co., c.1881, 20 In...	168
Kerosene, Triform Stem, Acanthus Leaves, Optic Shade, Continental, Early 1900s, 37 ½ In.......	191
Lard, Sheet Iron, Green, Gold Stencil, On Stand, Saucer Base, Samuel Davis, c.1856, 7 x 6 In. *illus*	143
Lighthouse Shape, Copper, Glass Globe, 1900s, 16 In..	438
Metal Arms, Mushroom Shade, Iridescent Glass, Feather Decoration, John Cook, 22 x 13 In.	1680
Oil, Blue Milk Glass, Parker Clock Set In Stem, 1883, 16 ½ In................................ *illus*	1216
Oil, Bronze, Brass Column, Cranberry Glass, White Overlay, Marble Base, 1800s, 24 In.*illus*	320
Oil, Gilt Bronze, Dragon Handle, Square Base, Continental, 1800s, 16 x 15 x 7 In. .... *illus*	2250
Oil, Glass, Domed Shade, Blue To Cream, Morning Glories, Victorian, 17 In.	244
Oil, Grand Tour, Bronze, Palmette Design, Scrolling Handle, Cherub, Swan, 6 ¼ x 9 ½ In...	492
Oil, Incised Figures, Fisherman Catches Mermaid, Footed, India, Early 1900s, 12 x 13 x 5 In.	200
Oil, Iron, Glass, Wood Handle, Russell Patent, 1973, 7 ¾ In.	1808
Oil, Ornate Tinware Arm, Turned Wood, Glass Shade, Wick Hole, c.1840, 22 ½ In. ...... *illus*	240
Oil, Victorian, Pink Flowers, Green Ground, Globe Shade, Painted, Electrified, 1800s, 22 In.	188
Oil, Whale, Brass, Dolphin Handles, Fluted Columnar Posts, 1800s, 7 ¼ In...........................	594
Pairpoint lamps are in the Pairpoint category.	
Peg, Silver Plate Stick, Satin Glass, Square Base, 18 ½ In. .... *illus*	210
Pharmacy, Library, Brass, Adjustable, Semicircular Shade, 1950s, 48 ½ In.	424
Piano, Brass, Orange, Jeweled Glass Shade, Gilt, Marble Base, Late 1800s, 36 ¼ In. ...... *illus*	1452
Pressed Glass, Bigler Pattern, Sapphire Blue, Brass Collar, New England, 10 In..........*illus*	2106
Sconce, 2-Light, Bagues Style, Gilt Metal, Rock Crystal, Glass, 31 x 16 x 9 In., Pair.............	3570
Sconce, 2-Light, Brass, Glass, Hanging Prisms...	100
Sconce, 2-Light, Brass, Rock Crystal, Flower Shape, 11 x 19 ½ In., Pair	250
Sconce, 2-Light, Bronze, Etched Mirror, 1920s-30s, 17 In., Pair	354
Sconce, 2-Light, Bronze, Marble, Goat Shape, Round, 10 x 6 In.	352

Lamp, Electric, Metal & Glass, Peacock, Spread Tail, Czechoslovakia, 16 x 15 In. $1,250

Treadway

Lamp, Electric, Metal, Copper Shade, Marked, Bronstein, 25 ½ x 5 In. $469

Auctions at Showplace, NYC

Lamp, Electric, Metal, Half Round Shade, Silver Gray Finish, Circular Base, 54 x 9 In., Pair $263

Thomaston Place Auction Galleries

L

Lamp, Electric, Mica, Hammered, Early John L. Wilcox, Russia, c.1910, 20 ½ x 19 In.
$7,995

California Historical Design

Lamp, Electric, Oak, Copper, Pine Branch, Cone, Arts & Crafts, Mica Lamp Co., 59 x 20 x 26 In.
$487

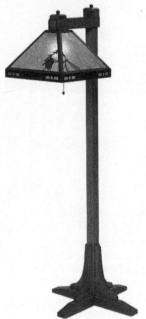

Toomey & Co. Auctioneers

Lamp, Electric, Oak, Slag Glass, Double Base, Green, Prairie School, c.1910, 20 x 25 x 16 ¾ In.
$3,567

California Historical Design

Lamp, Electric, Porcelain, Baluster Shape, Flowers, Pierced Foot, Herend, 1900s, 23 x 16 In.
$100

Bruneau & Co. Auctioneers

Lamp, Electric, Quilted Blown Glass, Diamond Cut, Brass, Barovier & Toso, Italy, 31 ½ x 7 In., Pair
$1,875

Palm Beach Modern Auctions

Lamp, Electric, Venini Glass, Fungo, White, Green, Massimo Vignelli, Italy, 10 x 8 ½ In.
$1,000

Auctions at Showplace, NYC

Lamp, Electric, Wood, Goose, Carved, Cream Shade, Rectangular Base, c.1940, 7 x 9 In.
$125

New Haven Auctions

Lamp, Fat, Wrought Iron, Wrigglework Bird Design, 1800s, 8 In.
$400

Pook & Pook

Lamp, Hanging, 6-Light, Chrome, Red Ball Shape Shade, Gilt Chain, 21 In.
$625

New Haven Auctions

Lamp, Hanging, 8-Light, Oak Frame, Green Stained Glass, Arts & Crafts, 1900s, 43 x 38 In.
$1,375

Hindman

TIP
Use a soft-bristle paintbrush to dust lampshades.

Lamp, Hanging, Enamel Steel, Pendant, Preben Dahl, Hans Folsgaard, Denmark, 16 In.
$813

Clars Auction Gallery

Lamp, Hanging, Steel, Domed Shade, Chain, Acrylic, George Nelson, Nessen Studio, c.1969, 12 x 14 In.
$1,625

Wright

Lamp, Lard, Sheet Iron, Green, Gold Stencil, On Stand, Saucer Base, Samuel Davis, c.1856, 7 x 6 In.
$143

Jeffrey S. Evans & Associates

Lamp, Oil, Blue Milk Glass, Parker Clock Set In Stem, 1883, 16½ In.
$1,216

Rachel Davis Fine Arts

Lamp, Oil, Bronze, Brass Column, Cranberry Glass, White Overlay, Marble Base, 1800s, 24 In.
$320

Neal Auction Company

Lamp, Oil, Gilt Bronze, Dragon Handle, Square Base, Continental, 1800s, 16 x 15 x 7 In.
$2,250

Hindman

Lamp, Oil, Ornate Tinware Arm, Turned Wood, Glass Shade, Wick Hole, c.1840, 22½ In.
$240

Selkirk Auctioneers & Appraisers

Lamp, Peg, Silver Plate Stick, Satin Glass, Square Base, 18½ In.
$210

Nadeau's Auction Gallery

Lamp, Piano, Brass, Orange, Jeweled Glass Shade, Gilt, Marble Base, Late 1800s, 36 ¼ In.
$1,452

Fontaine's Auction Gallery

Lamp, Pressed Glass, Bigler Pattern, Sapphire Blue, Brass Collar, New England, 10 In.
$2,106

Norman C. Heckler & Company

Lamp, Sconce, 2-Light, Wood, Gesso, Figural Medallion, 19 x 13 In., Pair
$352

Nadeau's Auction Gallery

Lamp, Sconce, 3-Light, Bronze, Mask Wall Bracket, Gilt Berries, Circular Band, 14 x 14 ½ In.
$640

Nadeau's Auction Gallery

Lamp, Sconce, 3-Light, Louis XV Style, Gilt Bronze, Cherub, Leaves, c.1915, 18 x 15 In., Pair
$2,500

Hindman

Lamp, Sconce, 5-Light, Louis XVI Style, Gilt Bronze, Scroll Arms, Acanthus Leaf, France, 32 x 18 In.
$256

Roland NY Auctioneers & Appraisers

Lamp, Sconce, Brass, Neoclassical, Cast, Ball Top Finials, Fluted Column, 17 x 11 x 5 In., Pair
$72

Main Auction Galleries, Inc.

Lamp, Sconce, Figural, Bronze, Octagonal Backplate, Crown Shape, Candlecup, 11 In., Pair
$384

Neal Auction Company

Lamp, Sconce, Louis XV, Dore Bronze, Gilt, Putti Musicians, Sunflower Shape Socket, 15 In., Pair
$780

Treasureseeker Auctions

308

Sconce, 2-Light, Bronze, Metal Mounted, Wood, Mirrored Glass, Galleon, c.1880, 13 x 9 x 7 In., Pair .	4575
Sconce, 2-Light, Gilt Bronze, Scrolls, Ram's Face, Louis XV, 16¾ x 8¾ x 6¾ In., Pair.........	406
Sconce, 2-Light, Gilt Metal, Clear Flowers, Urn Base, 16 In., Pair...	896
Sconce, 2-Light, Gilt, Carved, Flame Torch, Leaf Scroll Candleholders, c.1890, 26 x 20 In., Pair..	610
Sconce, 2-Light, Giltwood, Candle, Rococo, Scroll Arms, Italy, 1900s, 17 x 10 x 3¾ In., Pair......	363
Sconce, 2-Light, Mahogany, Carved, Brass, Glass Shades, 22 x 16 x 11 In., Pair	1152
Sconce, 2-Light, Wood, Gesso, Figural Medallion, 19 x 13 In., Pair .... illus	352
Sconce, 2-Light, Wrought Iron, Drip Pan, Scrollwork, Flowers, 1900s, 24 In., Pair	250
Sconce, 3-Light, Brass, Mesh Metal, Diamond Shape Frames, Midcentury, 28 x 12 x 9 In., Pair.	160
Sconce, 3-Light, Bronze, Mask Wall Bracket, Gilt Berries, Circular Band, 14 x 14½ In. . illus	640
Sconce, 3-Light, Gilt Bronze, Empire, E.F. Caldwell & Co., N.Y., Early 1900s, 26 x 15 x 10 In., Pair.	2420
Sconce, 3-Light, Gilt Bronze, Round Mirror, Carved Wood Plaque, Baroque, 18 x 12 x 9 In., Pair .	938
Sconce, 3-Light, Gilt, Black Composite, Floral Shade, 37 In., Pair...	130
Sconce, 3-Light, Louis XV Style, Gilt Bronze, Cherub, Leaves, c.1915, 18 x 15 In., Pair ..illus	2500
Sconce, 3-Light, Louis XV Style, Gilt Bronze, Leaf Shape Drip Pan, c.1870, 11 x 15 x 10 In., Pair....	500
Sconce, 5-Light, Gilt Bronze, Cloisonne, Floral Festoons, Acanthus Arms, c.1915, 42 x 25 In., Pair	1250
Sconce, 5-Light, Louis XVI Style, Gilt Bronze, Lyre Back, Wall Mount, 53 x 22 In., Pair........	1020
Sconce, 5-Light, Louis XVI Style, Gilt Bronze, Scroll Arms, Acanthus Leaf, France, 32 x 18 In. ..... illus	256
Sconce, American Sheet Iron, Wall Candle, Crimped Edges, c.1815, 13¾ x 4⅝ In., Pair......	239
Sconce, Arts & Crafts, Copper, Hammered, Amber Glass, Porch, c.1920, 10 x 4½ x 8 In.......	584
Sconce, Brass, Candle, Scroll Arms, Removable, Circular Plates, Shaped Hangers, 1700s, 10 In..	1875
Sconce, Brass, Neoclassical, Cast, Ball Top Finials, Fluted Column, 17 x 11 x 5 In., Pair .....illus	72
Sconce, Brass, Pricket, Hook Shape, France, 34¼ x 18 In., Pair..	185
Sconce, Candle, Brass, Drip Pan, Curved Stem, Round Wall Plaque, Germany, 1700s, 5 x 9 x 5 In..	334
Sconce, Candle, Brass, Repousse, 1 Arm, 3 Taper Holders, 1800s, 23 x 18 In., Pair	984
Sconce, Candle, Mirrored, Tin, Piecrust Shape, Crimped Bobeches, 1910s, 9 x 8 x 4¾ In., Pair...	263
Sconce, Copper, Hammered, Michael Adams, Aurora Studios, Harvey Ellis, 22½ In.	2583
Sconce, Figural, Bronze, Octagonal Backplate, Crown Shape, Candlecup, 11 In., Pair illus	384
Sconce, Frosted Glass, Brass, Marked Shade, c.1925, 25 In., Pair..	6875
Sconce, Kerosene, 2-Light, Brass, Flowers, Elbow Globes, Angle Lamp Co., c.1915, 8⅞ In. ...	777
Sconce, Louis XV, Dore Bronze, Gilt, Putti Musicians, Sunflower Shape Socket, 15 In., Pair ..illus	780
Sconce, Machine Age, Frosted Glass, Chrome Plated Steel, c.1935, 6 x 12 In., Pair	625
Sconce, Pine, Brass, Carved Eagle On Corbel, Iron Arms & Cups, Late 1800s, 24 x 9 x 7 In.	84
Sconce, Polished Brass, Half Dome, Lucite Prisms, Karl Springer, 20th Century, 15 x 7 In., Pair	540
Sconce, Silvered Wood, Carved, Shell Teardrop, Scrolled, Metal Arms, Italy, 15 x 20 x 5 In..	36
Sconce, Tulip Design, 6 Leaded Glass Panes, Gooseneck Arm, 13 x 7 In...............................	660
Sconce, Wood, Rococo Revival, Candle, Painted, Flowers, Rocaille, 21 x 12½ x 5 In., Pair..	492
Searchlight, Silver, Tripod Base, Ralph Lauren Montauk, 65 In. ....illus	2331
Solar, Fluted Column, Hanging Prisms, Cut Glass Shade, Gold Paint, Marble Base, c.1850, 23 In. illus	510
Solar, Gilt Brass, Engraved Shade, Prisms, Marble Base, Electrified, 18 In............................	400
Student, 2-Light, Harvard, Brass, Yellow Shades, Plume & Atwood, Late 1800s, 21¾ x 22 In. illus	1452
Tiffany lamps and Tiffany style lamps are listed in the Tiffany category.	
Torchere, 5-Light, Brass, Adjustable, Flame Shape Shades, Molded Base, c.1910, 75 In., Pair.....	325
Torchere, Gilt Metal, Glass, Round Dome Base, Seguso Murano, c.1930, 74 In., Pair............	2500
Torchere, Louis XVI Style, Giltwood, Verte Marble Top, Guilloche Frieze, Hoof Feet, 43½ In.	1024
Torchere, Wrought Iron, Twisted Vine Around Body, 3 Legs, 57 x 21 In.	120
Urn, 2-Light, French Marble, 4 Brass Candelabra Arms, Brass Mounts, Finial, 34 In.	128

LAMP BASE

Electric, 2-Light, Porcelain, Blue & White, Flowers, Chinese, 12½ In. ....illus	4500
Electric, 2-Light, Pottery, Flowers, Metal Base, 22½ In..	219
Electric, Black Marble, Gilt Metal Mounts, Footed, Continental, Early 1900s, 25 In., Pair....	500
Electric, Marble, Female Figure, Hands Folded, Column Pedestal, 74 x 13 x 13 In.	660
Electric, Porcelain Jar, Famille Rose, Phoenix, Peonies, Wood Base, Chinese, c.1840, 9 In..	450
Electric, Redware, Jar, Black & Green Band, Slip, Turtle Creek, Signed, David T. Smith, 26 In.....	450
Electric, Temple Jar, Cobalt Blue, White Ground, Teak Base, Chinese, 1900s, 18 x 11 In., Pair .....illus	732
Figural, Kingfisher, Porcelain, Multicolor, Flower On Base, Continental, 19th Century, 10½ In.. illus	384
Jug, 2 Gal., Converted To Lamp, Cobalt Blue Design, Stoneware, Wood Base, 13¼ In............	252
Silver Plate, Candlestick Shape, Carlyle Hotel Monogram, Gorham, 1900s, 20½ In., Pair..	847

Lamp, Searchlight, Silver, Tripod Base, Ralph Lauren Montauk, 65 In.
$2,331

Pook & Pook

Lamp, Solar, Fluted Column, Hanging Prisms, Cut Glass Shade, Gold Paint, Marble Base, c.1850, 23 In.
$510

Garth's Auctioneers & Appraisers

Lamp, Student, 2-Light, Harvard, Brass, Yellow Shades, Plume & Atwood, Late 1800s, 21¾ x 22 In.
$1,452

Fontaine's Auction Gallery

L

309

LAMP BASE

Lamp Base, Electric, 2-Light, Porcelain, Blue & White, Flowers, Chinese, 12½ In.
$4,500

Cottone Auctions

Lamp Base, Electric, Temple Jar, Cobalt Blue, White Ground, Teak Base, Chinese, 1900s, 18 x 11 In., Pair
$732

Rafael Osona Nantucket Auctions

Lamp Base, Figural, Kingfisher, Porcelain, Multicolor, Flower On Base, Continental, 19th Century, 10½ In.
$384

Rachel Davis Fine Arts

Silver, Candlestick, Converted, Marble Base, James Dixon & Son, Sheffield, 1897, 29 In.	1353
Stoneware, Turquoise Glaze, Lucite Base, Chinese, 20 x 4¾ x 4¾ In., Pair .... *illus*	270
Stoneware, White Ground, Blue Design, Glazed, Fog & Morup, Denmark, c.1960, 19 x 6 In., Pair	2125

LAMPSHADE

Aladdin, Opaque White, Glass, No. 501-11, c.1915, 7 In., Pair .... *illus*	120
Glass, Ruffled Rim, Apricot, Acid Cut Flowers, 5 x 8 x 4 In.	125
Leaded Glass, Flowers, Pink, Yellow, Unique Art Glass & Metal Co., Early 1900s, 16 In. .... *illus*	1331

LANTERN

Lanterns are a special type of lighting device. They have a light source, usually a candle, totally hidden inside the walls of the lantern. Light is seen through holes or glass sections.

Brass, 3-Light, Prairie School, Caramel Slag Glass, Montana, c.1906, 36½ x 30 x 14 In. ...*illus*	1625
Bronze, 3-Light, Regency, Glass Hall, Hexagonal, England, 1900s, 26 x 16 x 16 In. ...... *illus*	363
Bronze, 6-Light, Louis XV Style, Frosted Glass Panels, Leaves, 54 x 29 In.	2684
Bronze, Leaded Glass, Egg Shape, Hooks On Top, Jeweled Glass, 20 x 8 In. .... *illus*	8400
Candle, Arts & Crafts Style, Square, Ring Finial, c.1980s, 7½ x 6 x 6 In.	123
Candle, Cherry, Front & Side Doors, Mirror Back, Dome Top, 1700s, 19 x 12½ x 9 In. ..*illus*	1952
Candle, Wood, Spindles Joining Circular, Movable Platform, Early 1800s, 12 x 7 In.	2750
Carriage, Copper & Tin, Glass, Chimney, Ring Hoop, 1800s, 18 In., Pair	188
Hanging, 3-Light, Clear Glass, Gilt Metal, Chain, 1900s, 17½ In.	250
Hanging, 3-Light, Glass, Brass, Phoenix Head Mount, Electrified, 1800s, 23 In., Pair .*illus*	1845
Hanging, 3-Light, Glass, Candle Sockets, Grapevine, Metal Band, Federal, c.1800, 23 In.	702
Hanging, Arts & Crafts, Copper, Amber Glass Shade, 1910, 22½ In.	369
Hanging, Arts & Crafts, Wrought Iron, Mica, Cylindrical, 46 x 21½ In. .... *illus*	1062
Hanging, Arts & Crafts, Yellow, Leaded, Stained Glass, Copper, Chain, 33 x 10 In.	1690
Hanging, Blown Glass & Smoke Bell, Folded Rim, Grapevine, Anglo-Indian, Late 1800s, 23 In.....	270
Hanging, Blown Glass, Oak Leaf, Acorn, Obelisk Cut, Phoenix Head, 1800s, 28 In.	4410
Hanging, Brass, Hexagonal, Fitted For Candle, Swing Handle, Early 1900s, 20 In................	531
Hanging, Bronze, Fleur-De-Lis Corona, Shell, Flowers, Bud Pendants, Early 1900s, 27 In. ..	976
Hanging, Classical, Blown Glass, Pressed Metal, Mounted, Chains, c.1840, 10 In.................	469
Hanging, Galvanized Steel, Painted, Clear Glass Lens, Glasgow, 21 In.	244
Hanging, Glass, Brass, Leafy Band, Eagle Head Hooks, 17 In., Pair	400
Hanging, Las Palmas, Puccini, Indoor, 25 x 19 x 19 In.	100
Hanging, Neoclassical Style, Gilt, Pentagon, Painted Wood, 39 In., Pair	701
Hanging, Tole, Leaded Glass Panels, Leaves, Flowers, Spiral Design, Chain, 1800s, 22 x 15 In. .. *illus*	375
Miner's, Brass, Wolf's Safety Lamp, Glass Lens, Hook On Top, 10 In.	150
Pendant, Arts & Crafts, Copper, Hammered, Mica, Hanging, Cutouts, c.1910, 12 x 6½ x 6½ In. *illus*	615
Pine, Clear Glass Sides, Swing Handle, Painted, Early 1800s, 9 x 5 In...................	492
Skater's, Brass, Deep Ruby Globe, Bail Handle, Gilt Band, Early 1900s, 11½ x 7 x 3 In. *illus*	1554
Tin, Painted, Punched, Old Green Surface, Cylindrical, 1800s, 14 In. .... *illus*	984
Tin, Punched, Lines & Dots, Hinged Door, O.H. Fusselman, Lower Sandusky, c.1850, 12 In. ..*illus*	1375
Tin, Punched, Ring Handle, Black Paint, Round Base, 1900s, 15 In......................	120
Tole, Glass, Flower & Leaf Design, Italy, 22 x 9 In., Pair...........................	512
Wall, Black Painted Iron, Hexagonal Shape, Scrolls & Leaves, Early 1900s, 41 x 13 x 24 In.	640
Wood, Electric, Pagoda Style, Roof, 4-Sided, Base Stand, Japan, 36 In. .... *illus*	336
Wood, Glass Panel, Swing Handle, Hinged Door, 15 x 6 x 6 In.	156
Wood, Moon Shape Design, Drawer, Handle, Black, Red, Japan, 1800s, 14 In.	163
Wood, Pentagon, Glass Panels On Each Side, 1800s, 11 x 8 In.	594

LE VERRE FRANCAIS

Le Verre Francais is one of the many types of cameo glass made by the Schneider Glassworks in France. The glass was made by the C. Schneider factory in Epinay-sur-Seine from 1918 to 1933. It is a mottled glass, usually decorated with floral designs, and bears the incised signature *Le Verre Francais*.

Lamp, Boudoir, Digitale, Stylized Flowers, Etched Base, c.1920, 7¼ In............................	896

Lamp Base, Stoneware, Turquoise Glaze, Lucite Base, Chinese, 20 x 4¾ x 4¾ In., Pair
$270

Main Auction Galleries, Inc.

> **TIP**
> *Parchment lampshades can be cleaned with a cloth soaked in milk. Then wipe dry with a clean cloth.*

Lampshade, Aladdin, Opaque White, Glass, No. 501-11, c.1915, 7 In., Pair
$120

Jeffrey S. Evans & Associates

Lampshade, Leaded Glass, Flowers, Pink, Yellow, Unique Art Glass & Metal Co., Early 1900s, 16 In.
$1,331

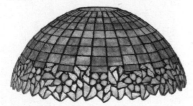

Fontaine's Auction Gallery

Lantern, Brass, 3-Light, Prairie School, Caramel Slag Glass, Montana, c.1906, 36½ x 30 x 14 In.
$1,625

Toomey & Co. Auctioneers

Lantern, Bronze, 3-Light, Regency, Glass Hall, Hexagonal, England, 1900s, 26 x 16 x 16 In.
$363

Ahlers & Ogletree Auction Gallery

Lantern, Bronze, Leaded Glass, Egg Shape, Hooks On Top, Jeweled Glass, 20 x 8 In.
$8,400

Nadeau's Auction Gallery

Lantern, Candle, Cherry, Front & Side Doors, Mirror Back, Dome Top, 1700s, 19 x 12½ x 9 In.
$1,952

CRN Auctions

Lantern, Hanging, 3-Light, Glass, Brass, Phoenix Head Mount, Electrified, 1800s, 23 In., Pair
$1,845

Brunk Auctions

Lantern, Hanging, Arts & Crafts, Wrought Iron, Mica, Cylindrical, 46 x 21½ In.
$1,062

Toomey & Co. Auctioneers

L

Lantern, Hanging, Tole, Leaded Glass Panels, Leaves, Flowers, Spiral Design, Chain, 1800s, 22 x 15 In.
$375

New Haven Auctions

Lantern, Pendant, Arts & Crafts, Copper, Hammered, Mica, Hanging, Cutouts, c.1910, 12 x 6½ x 6½ In.
$615

California Historical Design

Lantern, Skater's, Brass, Deep Ruby Globe, Bail Handle, Gilt Band, Early 1900s, 11½ x 7 x 3 In.
$1,554

Jeffrey S. Evans & Associates

Lantern, Tin, Painted, Punched, Old Green Surface, Cylindrical, 1800s, 14 In.
$984

Pook & Pook

Lantern, Tin, Punched, Lines & Dots, Hinged Door, O.H. Fusselman, Lower Sandusky, c.1850, 12 In.
$1,375

Hindman

Lantern, Wood, Electric, Pagoda Style, Roof, 4-Sided, Base Stand, Japan, 36 In.
$336

CRN Auctions

Le Verre Francais, Vase, Lavender, Art Deco & Art Nouveau Features, 13 x 9 In.
$1,920

Abington Auction Gallery

Leather, Address Book, Canvas, Monogram, 6-Ring Binder, Louis Vuitton, c.1980s, 5½ x 4 In.
$125

Auctions at Showplace, NYC

Leather, Basket, Key, Tooled, Oval, Cutout Hearts & Tulips Band, Vine, c.1850, 7 x 3 x 6 In.
$7,605

Jeffrey S. Evans & Associates

Vase, Digitale, Stylized Flowers, Opal Ground, Ogee Bowl, Footed, 1925, 9 x 6 ¾ In.	585
Vase, Digitale, Stylized Flowers, Rolled Rim, Shaped Handles, Paris, 12 x 7 In.	975
Vase, Lavender, Art Deco & Art Nouveau Features, 13 x 9 In. .... *illus*	1920
Vase, Stylized Mushrooms, Dark To Light Cranberry, Footed, 12 x 7 ¼ In.	480

LEATHER

Leather is tanned animal hide and has been used to make decorative and useful objects for centuries. Leather objects must be carefully preserved with proper humidity and oiling or the leather will deteriorate and crack. This damage cannot be repaired.

Address Book, Canvas, Monogram, 6-Ring Binder, Louis Vuitton, c.1980s, 5 ½ x 4 In. *illus*	125
Bag, Tooled, Painted, Bronze Dragons, Bone Hand Button, Japan, 4 In.	225
Basket, Key, Tooled, Oval, Cutout Hearts & Tulips Band, Vine, c.1850, 7 x 3 x 6 In........ *illus*	7605
Briefcase, Newsbag, Red Box Leather, Gold Plated Brass, Hermes, France, 2002, 12 x 16 x 2 In.....	1300
Flag Carrier, Red, Brass Flag Mount, CW. Mutell, Springfield, Mass., 22 ¼ In.	750
Harness, Horse, Brass, Engraved, Stamped J. Schaffer, Pischelsdorf, Germany, 1800s, 49 In.	125
Mask, Masquerade, Gold, Red, Painted Accents, Tassel, Wood, Brass Stand, 1900s, 9 In. ..... *illus*	492
Saddle, Brown, Marked, Blevins Buckle, Pat. Pend., Wheatland, Wyo., 1900s, 35 x 26 x 19 In. ... *illus*	212
Saddle, Brown, Pommel Bags, Hand Tooied, Flowers, Geometric Border, 17 x 10 x 4 In.	780
Saddle, High Fork, Belt, Strap, Wood Stand, 1900s, 25 In...	1211
Saddle, Western, Tooled, Brown, Hand Engraved, Silver Fitting, Mid 1900s, 27 In.	313

LEEDS

LEEDS POTTERY

Leeds pottery was made at Leeds, Yorkshire, England, from 1774 to 1878. Most Leeds ware was not marked. Early Leeds pieces had distinctive twisted handles with a greenish glaze on part of the creamy ware. Later ware often had blue borders on the creamy pottery. A Chicago company named Leeds made many Disney-inspired figurines. They are listed in the Disneyana category.

Basket, Chestnut, Creamware, Reticulated, Beaded Rim & Foot, England, c.1775, 7 In. ....*illus*	1521
Bowl, Flowers, Flowers & Stems On Exterior, 4 Colors, Soft Paste, 4 ¼ x 9 In. .... *illus*	136
Charger, Blue Feather Edge, Scalloped Rim, Flower Urn, c.1800, 13 In. .... *illus*	300
Coffeepot, Lid, Pearlware, Flower Basket, Bird, Blue On Cream, Brown Trim, c.1810, 10 ¾ In. ..	100
Cup & Saucer, 4-Point Star Center, Tulips Around Rim, 3 Colors, Handleless, Soft Paste, 5 In.	87
Cup & Saucer, Cottage, Sponge Trees, Brown Rim, 5 Colors, Handleless, Soft Paste, 5 ¼ In. .. *illus*	339
Cup & Saucer, Strawberry, Handleless, Brown Stripe Borders, Soft Paste, 5 ½ In.	62
Cup & Saucer, Tulip, Vine Border, 3 Colors, Handleless, Soft Paste, 5 ½ In.	87
Mug, Flower Basket, Flower & Leaf Spray On Reverse, Brown Bands, Soft Paste, Child's, 2 ¾ In. *illus*	277
Plate, Bird On Branch, 4 Colors, Blue Feather Edge, Scalloped Rim, Soft Paste, 7 In.	339
Plate, Blue Feather, Scalloped Edge, American Eagle, Early 1800s, 8 In. .... *illus*	390
Plate, Cottage, Sponge Trees, 5 Colors, Multicolor Rim, Soft Paste, 8 In................................	400
Plate, Peafowl, On Branch, Feather Edge, Cream Ground, Soft Paste, 10 In............................	177
Plate, Peafowl, On Bridge, Sponge Leaves, Blue Feather Edge, Scalloped Rim, Soft Paste, 7 In.	308
Plate, Star Flower Center, Sprigs & Flowers Surrounding, Blue Feather Edge, Soft Paste, 7 In...	123
Platter, Feather Edge, Flowers, Multicolor, 1800s, 11 x 9 In. .... *illus*	416
Teapot, Lid, Basket Of Flowers, 3 Colors, Soft Paste, Child's, 3 ½ In.	62
Vase, Tulip, 5 Spouts, Flowers, Feather Edge, Scalloped Rim, Oblong Foot, Soft Paste, 7 ½ In. 148 to 431	

LEFTON

Lefton is a mark found on pottery, porcelain, glass, and other wares imported by the Geo. Zoltan Lefton Company. The company started in 1941. George Lefton died in 1996 and members of the family continued to run the company. Lefton was sold to OMT Enterprises of Gardena, California, in 2005 and is now a division of that company. The name "Lefton" is still used. The company mark has changed through the years and a mark is usually used for a long period of time.

Leather, Mask, Masquerade, Gold, Red, Painted Accents, Tassel, Wood, Brass Stand, 1900s, 9 In.
$492

Brunk Auctions

Leather, Saddle, Brown, Marked, Blevins Buckle, Pat. Pend., Wheatland, Wyo., 1900s, 35 x 26 x 19 In.
$212

Fontaine's Auction Gallery

Leeds, Basket, Chestnut, Creamware, Reticulated, Beaded Rim & Foot, England, c.1775, 7 In.
$1,521

Jeffrey S. Evans & Associates

L

Leeds, Bowl, Flowers, Flowers & Stems On Exterior, 4 Colors, Soft Paste, 4¼ x 9 In.
$136

Conestoga Auction Company

Leeds, Charger, Blue Feather Edge, Scalloped Rim, Flower Urn, c.1800, 13 In.
$300

Garth's Auctioneers & Appraisers

TIP
Visit thrift stores frequently. The more you go, the more bargains you will find.

Leeds, Cup & Saucer, Cottage, Sponge Trees, Brown Rim, 5 Colors, Handleless, Soft Paste, 5¼ In.
$339

Conestoga Auction Company

Lefton China 1948–1953	Lefton China 1950–1955	Lefton China 1949–2001

Figurine, Woman, Standing, Holding Parasol, Dress, Ruffled, Gold Trim, Japan, 1900s, 7¾ In. . *illus* ... 19
Plaque, Mermaid, Holding Fish, Carved, Signed, Ellen McCaleb, 18 x 57 In. .... *illus* ... 1525

LEGRAS

Legras was founded in 1864 by Auguste Legras at St. Denis, France. It is best known for cameo glass and enamel-decorated glass with Art Nouveau designs. Legras merged with Pantin in 1920 and became the Verreries et Cristalleries de St. Denis et de Pantin Reunies.

Vase, Art Glass, Floral Cameo, Carved, Gold, Olive Green Acid Cut Ground, 9 x 3 In....... *illus* ... 350
Vase, Purple Leaves, Frosted Ground, Cylindrical, Tapered, Triangular Rim, Signed, 16¾ In...... 660

LENOX

Lenox porcelain is well-known in the United States. Walter Scott Lenox and Jonathan Coxon founded the Ceramic Art Company in Trenton, New Jersey, in 1889. In 1896 Lenox bought out Coxon's interest, and in 1906 the company was renamed Lenox, Inc. The company makes porcelain that is similar to Irish Belleek. In 2009, after a series of mergers, Lenox became part of Clarion Capital Partners. The marks used by the firm have changed through the years, so collectors can date the ceramics. Related pieces may also be listed in the Ceramic Art Co. category.

Candlestick, Versailles, Fluted Column, Pierced Base, 11 In., Pair 18
Chip & Dip Plate, Greenfield Pattern, Leaf Design, 24K Gold Trim, 10 In. 45
Dish, Swan Shape, Green Mark, 4½ x 2 In. 15
Figurine, Black Cat, Standing, Blue Eyes, Strass Stones Necklace, 1900s, 5 In. 75
Figurine, Elephant Calf, Twisting Trunk, Sitting, Grayish Brown, 1991, 6 In. 113
Trinket Box, Heart Shape, Red Rose, Embossed Rose Border, 24K Gold Trim, 5 x 5 x 2 In... 20

LETTER OPENER

Letter openers have been used since the eighteenth century. Ivory and silver were favored by the well-to-do. In the late nineteenth century, the letter opener was popular as an advertising giveaway and many were made of metal or celluloid. Brass openers with figural handles were also popular.

Bronze, Rose, Clemens Friedell, Pasadena Rotary Club, c.1915, 8⅝ In................... 308
Copper, Hammered, Signed, Nuke, Norman Dekalb Edwards, c.1920s, 9 In......... 246
Fish, Bronze, Elsie Greene, Artistic Co., Bridgeport, Connecticut, 1931, 7 x 2 x 5 In. ..... *illus* ... 65
Olive Wood, Copper, Shells, Cattails, Elizabeth Eaton Durton, California, 13 x 2 In. ... *illus* ... 1250

LIBBEY

Libbey Glass Company has made many types of glass since 1888, including the cut glass and tablewares that are collected today. The stemwares of the 1930s and 1940s are once again in style. The Toledo, Ohio, firm was purchased by Owens-Illinois in 1935 and is still working under the name Libbey Inc. Maize is listed in its own category.

Bowl, Bread, Cut Glass, Flowers & Thistle, Nailhead Diamond Center, Signed, 2 x 12 x 7 In. ... 175
Bowl, Salad Underplate, Corona, Cut Glass, 7 x 11 In. 800
Carafe, Harvard Pattern, Cut Glass, 8 x 6 In. 125
Compote, Amberina, Art Glass, 4 x 6¼ In. 540

Leeds, Mug, Flower Basket, Flower & Leaf Spray On Reverse, Brown Bands, Soft Paste, Child's, 2¾ In.
$277

Conestoga Auction Company

Leeds, Plate, Blue Feather, Scalloped Edge, American Eagle, Early 1800s, 8 In.
$390

Garth's Auctioneers & Appraisers

Leeds, Platter, Feather Edge, Flowers, Multicolor, 1800s, 11 x 9 In.
$416

Pook & Pook

TIP
For a pollution-free glass cleaner, use a mixture of white vinegar and water.

TIP
Never put your name on your mailbox. Put the street number in reflecting numerals more than 3 inches high, and be sure the numbers are in clear view. Make it easy for the police and fire departments to find your house.

Lefton, Figurine, Woman, Standing, Holding Parasol, Dress, Ruffled, Gold Trim, Japan, 1900s, 7¾ In.
$19

Lion and Unicorn

Letter Opener, Fish, Bronze, Elsie Greene, Artistic Co., Bridgeport, Connecticut, 1931, 7 x 2 x 5 In.
$65

Toomey & Co. Auctioneers

Lefton, Plaque, Mermaid, Holding Fish, Carved, Signed, Ellen McCaleb, 18 x 57 In.
$1,525

Rafael Osona Nantucket Auctions

Legras, Vase, Art Glass, Floral Cameo, Carved, Gold, Olive Green Acid Cut Ground, 9 x 3 In.
$350

Woody Auction

Letter Opener, Olive Wood, Copper, Shells, Cattails, Elizabeth Eaton Durton, California, 13 x 2 In.
$1,250

Toomey & Co. Auctioneers

Lighter, Butterscotch Cube, Art Deco, Resin, Greco-Roman Relief, Metal Cameos, 1900s, 4 x 2 In.
$180

Selkirk Auctioneers & Appraisers

Lighter, Cigar, Citizen's Club, Tin Punched Shade, Patina, Square Base, Footed, 11 x 7 x 7½ In.
$900

Morphy Auctions

Lighter, Dunhill, Aquarium, Lucite & Chrome, Beveled Edges, England, Table, 3½ x 4 x 2 In.
$2,880

Abington Auction Gallery

LIGHTER

Lighters for cigarettes and cigars are collectible. Cigarettes became popular in the late nineteenth century, and with the cigarette came matches and cigarette lighters. All types of lighters are collected, from solid gold to the first disposable lighters. Most examples found were made after 1940.

Butterscotch Cube, Art Deco, Resin, Greco-Roman Relief, Metal Cameos, 1900s, 4 x 2 In. ..*illus*	180
Cigar, Citizen's Club, Tin Punched Shade, Patina, Square Base, Footed, 11 x 7 x 7½ In. *illus*	900
Cigar, Figural, Boy, Metal, Cast, Miniature, Marked, Deerste Proef, c.1880, 7 x 2 In.............	187
Cigar, Silver, Whale's Tooth, Marked, London, c.1900, 7 x 3 In.	2623
Dunhill, Aquarium, Lucite & Chrome, Beveled Edges, England, Table, 3½ x 4 x 2 In. *illus*	2880
Dunhill, Silver Plate, Marked, Switzerland, 2 x 1¼ x ¼ In.	108
Pistol, Tinder, Iron & Walnut, Engraved Trigger Guards, Candlecup, 1800s, 7 In. ......*illus*	1107
Ronson, Touch Tip, Chrome Plated Brass, Enameled, Art Metal Works Inc., c.1925, 3 x 2 x 4 In.	195

LIGHTNING ROD AND LIGHTNING ROD BALL

Lightning rods and lightning rod balls are collected. The glass balls were at the center of the rod that was attached to the roof of a house or barn to avoid lightning damage. The balls were made in many colors and many patterns. Collectors prefer examples made before 1940.

LIGHTNING ROD

Copper, Aluminum Arrow, Blue Milk Glass Ball, 4 Stars, 27½ x 23 In..........................*illus*	369
Copper, Sailboat, Quilted Glass Globe, 4-Footed Stand, 83 x 26½ In.......................................	336
Milk Glass Ball, Blue Green Patina, Tripod Base, 63 In...	84
Milk Glass Ball, Spiked Finial, Tripod Base, 37 In.	90

LIGHTNING ROD BALL

Green Glass, Vertical Seam	120
Milk Glass, Faceted, Embossed, Patent Applied For, Diamond Mark, Metal Bands, 5¼ x 3½ In.	30
Red Glass, Arrow, Kite Tail, White Snowflake, Reyburn Hunter Co., 34 In. ....*illus*	369

LIMOGES

Limoges porcelain has been made in Limoges, France, since the mid-nineteenth century. Fine porcelains were made by many factories, including Haviland, Ahrenfeldt, Guerin, Pouyat, Elite, and others. Modern porcelains are being made at Limoges. The word *Limoges* as part of the mark is not an indication of age. Porcelain called "Limoges" was also made by Sebring China in Sebring, Ohio, in the early 1900s. The company changed its name to American Limoges China Company after the Limoges Company in France threatened to sue. American Limoges China Company went out of business in 1955. Haviland, one of the Limoges factories, is listed as a separate category in this book. These three marks are for factories in Limoges, France.

A. Klingenberg
c.1880s–1890s

D & Co.
c.1881–1893

M. Redon
c.1882–1896

Box, Lid, Orange Pastel Tones, Wild Flowers, Gold Trim, Round, Signed, E.S.B., 4 x 7 In......	175
Box, Lid, Women, Fountain Scene, Blue Ground, Signed, Gamet, c.1900, 5 In. ....*illus*	480
Cachepot, Flowers, Gilt, White Ground, Painted, Octagonal Base, 1900s, 5 x 6 In.	250
Cachepot, Pondichery, Flowers, Multicolor, Marked, Bernardaud, 6 x 6¼ In., Pair..............	861

Candlestick, Gilt Floral Overlay, Black Base, Marked, B & Co., 8½ In., Pair.............	244
Charger, Dogs, Landscape Scene, Gilt Rim, Signed, C. Golse, Early 1900s, 11½ In., Pair.....	545
Compote, Bronze Mounts, Robin's-Egg Blue, Rose, Gilt, Copie Dancien, 8 x 8½ In.	130
Cooler, Wine, Gilt, Painted, 2 Handles, Flowers, Red, Marked, 7 x 9½ In.	63
Perfume Bottle, Hand Painted, Flowers, Gilt Accents, 1900s, 4 In...	63
Pitcher, Grapes, Signed, Wanda, 10-26-27, 5½ x 8 x 7 In..*illus*	185
Pitcher, Grapevine, Lattice Pattern, Cylindrical, Arched Handle, Jape Limoges, 13 x 6 In....	79
Plaque, Game Bird, Chucker Partridge, Silvered Metal, Oval, Late 1800s, 19 x 14 In.	188
Plaque, Napoleon, Gilt, White Ground, Late 1800s, 5 In.	96
Plaque, Portrait, Woman, Blue Cloth, Red Background, Frame, c.1890s, 6¼ x 5⅜ In. *illus*	615
Plate, Flower, Gilt Rim, White Ground, Porcelain, Marked, W.G. & Co., 9½ In., 12 Piece	787
Plate, Octagonal, Floral & Fauna, White Ground, Raynaud & Cie, 9 In., 4 Piece	100
Punch Bowl, Hand Painted, Fruits, Footed, Dated 1901, 7 x 16 In. ....*illus*	288
Punch Bowl, Multicolor, Grapes, Vines, Green Foot, 7 x 14¼ In...	139
Tankard, Painted, Monk, Keg Transfer, Scalloped Rim, Dragon Handle, Jean Pouyat, 15 In.	72
Trinket Box, Hinged Lid, Figural, Monkey Reading Book, Bananas, Painted, 1900s, 2 In. ...	75
Trinket Box, Turquoise, Yellow Lovebirds, Marked, Mid 1900s, 1 x 3 In. ....*illus*	120
Urn, Gilt, Flowers, Swan Shape Handles, Plinth Base, 18 In	375
Urn, Lid, Portrait, Bust, Woman, Hand Painted, Reticulated, William Guerin, France, 1900, 19 In.	468
Vase, Cobalt Blue, Gilt Accents, Flowers, 1900s, 2 x 4 In...	50

LITHOPHANE

Lithophanes are porcelain pictures made by casting clay in layers of various thicknesses. When a piece is held to the light, a picture of light and shadow is seen through it. Most lithophanes date from the 1825–1875 period. A few are still being made. Many lithophanes sold today were originally panels for lampshades.

Lamp, Globe Shade, Hunting Scenes, Reverse Painted, 2-Tier Base, 3-Footed, Electrified, 63⅞ In.	826
Lamp, Hanging, 4-Sided, Domestic Scenes, Red Glass Corners, Tin Frame, Electrified, 19 x 8 In.	216
Window, 2 Young Women, Veiled Older Woman, Leaded Glass Frame, 10¾ x 10 In. .....*illus*	60

LIVERPOOL

Liverpool, England, has been the site of many pottery and porcelain factories since the eighteenth century. Color-decorated porcelains, transfer-printed earthenware, stoneware, basalt, figurines, and other wares were made. Sadler and Green made print-decorated wares starting in 1756. Many of the pieces were made for the American market and feature patriotic emblems, such as eagles and flags. Liverpool pitchers are called Liverpool jugs by collectors.

Basin, Creamware, Flower Spray Rim, 3-Masted Sailing Ship In Center, Late 1700s, 2 x 16 In.....	1112
Bowl, Susan's Farewell, Black Transfer, Creamware, Early 19th Century, 4¾ x 11 In.	157
Bowl, Water Scene, House, Blue & White, Chinoiserie, Flowers Reverse, 1800s, 3¾ x 8⅝ In....	135
Dish, Cordwainers Arms & Motto, Black Transfer, Blue Shell Rim, Herculaneum, 10 In.	416
Jug, Boston Packet, Ship, Washington Portrait On Reverse, Multicolor Transfer, c.1800, 11 In. .. *illus*	1875
Jug, George Washington Memorial, America Lamenting, Black Transfer, c.1805, 6 x 3½ In.. *illus*	2500
Jug, Ireland, Maps, Mottos, Brown Ridged Neck, Satyr's Mask Spout, c.1800, 16 In.	5000
Jug, James Madison Portrait, Peace Plenty & Independence On Reverse, Black Transfer, 7 In..	3000
Jug, Putting Off, Apotheosis On Reverse, U.S. Seal, Black Transfer, Creamware, c.1800, 11 In. ..*illus*	3500
Jug, Ship, Cumberland, Multicolor, Farmer's Arms On Reverse, Black Transfer, c.1800, 9½ In....	1125
Jug, Ship, U.S. Seal On Reverse, Flower Sprigs, Black Transfer, Creamware, 7½ In..............	1188
Jug, Success To America, Soldier, 2 Portraits On Reverse, Creamware, c.1802, 10 In. ...*illus*	4160
Jug, The Sailor's Farewell, Success To Trade On Reverse, c.1800, 8¾ In.	100
Plate, Ship, American Flag, Monogram Underneath, Flowers Around Rim, Multicolor, 10 In.....	750
Teapot, Dome Lid, Multicolor Flowers, Leafy Arches, Philip Christian & Co., c.1775, 7¼ In.	315
Teapot, Lid, Palm Leaf & Column Molding, Roses, Philip Christian & Co., c.1775, 7 In.	315

Lighter, Pistol, Tinder, Iron & Walnut, Engraved Trigger Guards, Candlecup, 1800s, 7 In.
$1,107

Pook & Pook

Lightning Rod, Copper, Aluminum Arrow, Blue Milk Glass Ball, 4 Stars, 27½ x 23 In.
$369

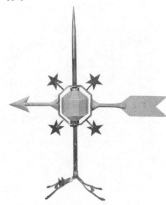

Rich Penn Auctions

Lightning Rod Ball, Red Glass, Arrow, Kite Tail, White Snowflake, Reyburn Hunter Co., 34 In.
$369

Rich Penn Auctions

Limoges, Box, Lid, Women, Fountain Scene, Blue Ground, Signed, Gamet, c.1900, 5 In.
$480

Treasureseeker Auctions

Limoges, Pitcher, Grapes, Signed, Wanda, 10-26-27, 5 ½ x 8 x 7 In.
$185

California Historical Design

Limoges, Plaque, Portrait, Woman, Blue Cloth, Red Background, Frame, c.1890s, 6 ¼ x 5 ⅜ In.
$615

California Historical Design

Limoges, Punch Bowl, Hand Painted, Fruits, Footed, Dated 1901, 7 x 16 In.
$288

Stevens Auction Co.

Limoges, Trinket Box, Turquoise, Yellow Lovebirds, Marked, Mid 1900s, 1 x 3 In.
$120

Garth's Auctioneers & Appraisers

Lithophane, Window, 2 Young Women, Veiled Older Woman, Leaded Glass Frame, 10 ¾ x 10 In.
$60

Martin Auction Co.

Liverpool, Jug, Boston Packet, Ship, Washington Portrait On Reverse, Multicolor Transfer, c.1800, 11 In.
$1,875

Eldred's

Liverpool, Jug, George Washington Memorial, America Lamenting, Black Transfer, c.1805, 6 x 3 ½ In.
$2,500

Early American History Auctions

Liverpool, Jug, Putting Off, Apotheosis On Reverse, U.S. Seal, Black Transfer, Creamware, c.1800, 11 In.
$3,500

Early American History Auctions

Liverpool, Jug, Success To America, Soldier, 2 Portraits On Reverse, Creamware, c.1802, 10 In.
$4,160

Nye & Company

Lladro, Bottle, Liquor, Botella Licor, Cuarentay Tres, Flowers, No. 7516, 1992-2002, 9 ½ x 3 ½ In.
$1,188

Lion and Unicorn

LLADRO

Lladro is a Spanish porcelain. Brothers Juan, Jose, and Vicente Lladro opened a ceramics workshop in Almacera in 1951. They soon began making figurines in a distinctive, elongated style. In 1958 the factory moved to Tabernes Blanques, Spain. The company makes stoneware and porcelain figurines and vases in limited and unlimited editions. Dates given are first and last years of production. Marks since 1977 have the added word *Daisa,* the acronym for the company that holds the intellectual property rights to Lladro figurines.

LLADRÓ®

Bottle, Liquor, Botella Licor, Cuarentay Tres, Flowers, No. 7516, 1992-2002, 9 ½ x 3 ½ In. ....*illus*	1188
Bust, Nautical Watch, Woman Hugging Child, Gres Finish, No. 2134, Jose Puche, 1984-88, 12 ½ In....	594
Candleholder, Angel With Tambourine, No. 5950, Jose Puche, 1992-97, 11 In.......................	75
Chalice, Grapes & Leaves, Matte Finish, No. 5263, Jose Roig, 1984-89, 3 In...........................	75
Figurine, Bust, Victory, Arms Raised, Triumphant, Black, No. 3531, Jose Puche, 1983, 25 In........	1625
Figurine, Chinese Farmer, Old, Robe, Holding Staff, No. 2065, Jose Roig, 1977-85, 19 ¾ In.	594
Figurine, Don Quixote, Letters To Dulcinea, No. 3509, Salvador Debon, 1978-97, 15 ¼ x 20 In. ...*illus*	2750
Figurine, Fairy Of The Butterflies, Wood Base, No. 1850, 1999-2000, 17 x 13 In. ....*illus*	1035
Figurine, Flowers Of Peace, Angel, Bouquet, No. 2145, Virginia Gonzalez, 2001-04, 13 In. ..*illus*	1500
Figurine, Harpooner, Spear, Boat Head, Gres Finish, No. 2121, 1980-87, 20 In.......................	330
Figurine, Heaven & Earth, Cherubs, Hugging, Wood Base, No. 1824, 1998-99, 12 x 5 ½ In..	431
Figurine, Holy Mary, Wood Base, No. 1832, Signed, Francisco Catala, 1982, 15 x 7 In. *illus*	938
Figurine, Mystical Garden, Young Woman, Flowers, Wood Base, No. 6686, 2000-02, 13 ¾ x 6 ¾ In.....	634
Figurine, New Horizons, Woman, Raised Hand, Birds, Glazed, No. 6570, 1999-2000, 14 ½ In. ..*illus*	360
Figurine, Nude With Rose, Sitting, No. 2079, 1978-79, 17 x 11 In. ....*illus*	118
Figurine, Quiet Moment, Woman, Seated, Glazed, No. 6384, Box, 1999, 11 In.......................	173
Figurine, Spring Shepherdess, Hat, Carrying Hay, No. 2133, Francisco Catala, 1983-85, 17 ¾ In...	1250
Group, Family Roots, Grandmother, Reading To 2 Children, No. 5371, 1986-2007, Box, 10 ¾ In. ..	360
Group, Graceful Duo, Thai Dancers, Female, No. 2073, Vincente Martinez, 1977-94, 22 In..	1125
Group, Road To Mandalay, Men, Woman, On Elephant, No. 3556, Vicente Martinez, 1982-88, 22 In.	3000
Group, True Affection, Mother, Child, Kiss, No. 3019, Fulgencio Garcia, 1988-97, 26 ½ x 12 ¼ In..	1375
Vase, Pastoral Vase, Human Image, Sitting, Flowers, No. 1122, Julio Fernandez, 1971-75, 9 In. ..	688

LOETZ

Loetz glass was made in many varieties. Johann Loetz bought a glassworks in Klostermuhle, Bohemia (now Klastersky Mlyn, Czech Republic), in 1840. He died in 1848 and his widow ran the company; then in 1879, his grandson took over. Most collectors recognize the iridescent gold glass similar to Tiffany, but many other types were made. *Richard* was the mark used on acid-etched cameo glass vases, bowls, night-lights, and lamps made by Loetz after 1918. The pieces were very similar to the French cameo glasswares made by Daum, Galle, and others. The firm closed during World War II.

Loetz Austria

Atomizer, Carved Holly Overlay, Green, Yellow Ground, Cameo, Signed, Richard, 8 x 2 In...	225
Bowl, Green Iridescent, Star Crimped Edge, Signed, 2 x 5 In.	60
Compote, Green Iridescent, Glass & Metal, Triangular Base, c.1910s, 6 ¼ x 5 ½ In..............	246
Compote, Red, Acid Cut, Black Flower Bands, Flared, Marked Czecho Slovakia, 4 ¾ x 7 ¾ In. *illus*	358
Vase, Brown, 3 Foldover Handles, Yellow Green Prunts & Threading, Tapered, Art Deco, 7 In. ...*illus*	585
Vase, Cream, Acid Cutback Bands, Blackish Red Rim, 4 Buttressed Handles, Tapered, 4 x 7 In..	2000
Vase, Glass, Silver Rim, Signed, English Hallmarks, RP, c.1910s, 6 ¾ x 2 ½ In........................	369
Vase, Iridescent Blue & Mauve Swirls, Ruffled Rim, Czechoslovakia, c.1910, 6 ¾ In..............	405
Vase, Iridescent, Brain Design, Art Glass, Flared Rim, 5 x 3 In. ....*illus*	550
Vase, Medici, Phanomen Genre, Blue & Gold Iridescent, Lady's-Leg Neck, 6 ½ x 4 ½ In.......	4875
Vase, Medici, Phanomen Genre, Iridescent, Spreading Chestnut, Flared Rim, c.1900, 4 x 3 In. *illus*	688
Vase, Nautilus, Candia Martele, Applied Blue & Gold Prunts, Tadpoles, c.1903, 7 x 6 ½ In. .*illus*	1625
Vase, Nautilus, Textured White Body, Gold Prunts, 2 ¾ x 2 ¼ In...	225
Vase, Pampas, Green Iridescent, 4 Handles, c.1899, 11 x 6 ½ In. ....*illus*	813
Vase, Pampas, Wavy Rim, Drop Painted, Cobalt Blue, c.1899, 4 ½ x 5 In. ....*illus*	875
Vase, Pink & Blue Iridescent, Silver Overlay, Stems & Leaves, Shouldered, Flared Rim, 6 In. .....*illus*	1040

Lladro, Figurine, Don Quixote, Letters To Dulcinea, No. 3509, Salvador Debon, 1978-97, 15 ¼ x 20 In. $2,750

Lion and Unicorn

Lladro, Figurine, Fairy Of The Butterflies, Wood Base, No. 1850, 1999-2000, 17 x 13 In. $1,035

Blackwell Auctions

Lladro, Figurine, Flowers Of Peace, Angel, Bouquet, No. 2145, Virginia Gonzalez, 2001-04, 13 In. $1,500

Lion and Unicorn

Lladro, Figurine, Holy Mary, Wood Base, No. 1832, Signed, Francisco Catala, 1982, 15 x 7 In.
$938

Lion and Unicorn

Lladro, Figurine, New Horizons, Woman, Raised Hand, Birds, Glazed, No. 6570, 1999-2000, 14½ In.
$360

Alex Cooper Auctioneers

Lladro, Figurine, Nude With Rose, Sitting, No. 2079, 1978-79, 17 x 11 In.
$118

Soulis Auctions

Loetz, Compote, Red, Acid Cut, Black Flower Bands, Flared, Marked Czecho Slovakia, 4¾ x 7¾ In.
$358

Treadway

Loetz, Vase, Brown, 3 Foldover Handles, Yellow Green Prunts & Threading, Tapered, Art Deco, 7 In.
$585

Treadway

Loetz, Vase, Iridescent, Brain Design, Art Glass, Flared Rim, 5 x 3 In.
$550

Woody Auction

Loetz, Vase, Medici, Phanomen Genre, Iridescent, Spreading Chestnut, Flared Rim, c.1900, 4 x 3 In.
$688

Treadway

Loetz, Vase, Nautilus, Candia Martele, Applied Blue & Gold Prunts, Tadpoles, c.1903, 7 x 6½ In.
$1,625

Treadway

Loetz, Vase, Pampas, Green Iridescent, 4 Handles, c.1899, 11 x 6½ In.
$813

Treadway

Vase, Platinum Decoration, Hand Blown, Unmarked, 1900s, 5⅜ In.	1408
Vase, Swirl Design, Rainbowlike, 6½ x 4½ In.	4875
Vase, Tree Trunk, Gold Iridescent, 3 Pierced Knots, 10½ In. .... *illus*	406
Vase, Yellow Iridescent, Silvered Design, c.1900, 8¼ In.	2662

LONE RANGER

Lone Ranger, a fictional character, was introduced on the radio in 1932. Over three thousand shows were produced before the series ended in 1954. In 1938, the first Lone Ranger movie was made. The latest movie was made in 2013. Television shows were started in 1949 and are still seen on some stations. The Lone Ranger appears on many products and was even the name of a restaurant chain from 1971 to 1973 that gave out silver bullets and other souvenirs.

Comic Book, Dell, Volume 1, Number 43, 1952	9
Tie Rack, Wood, Lone Ranger, Silver, 1940s, 12 x 6 In.	35
Toy, Lone Ranger & Silver, Tin, Windup, Lasso, Marx, 1938, 8½ In.	370

LONGWY WORKSHOP

Longwy Workshop of Longwy, France, first made ceramic wares in 1798. The workshop is still in business. Most of the ceramic pieces found today are glazed with many colors to resemble cloisonne or other enameled metal. Many pieces were made with stylized figures and Art Deco designs. The factory used a variety of marks.

Longwy Faience Co.
1880–1939

Longwy Faience Co.
1890–1948

Longwy Faience Co.
1951–1962

Cachepot, Cherry Blossoms, Blue Ground, Stoneware, Bronze Rim, Handles, Footed, 4½ In.	187

LONHUDA

Lonhuda Pottery Company of Steubenville, Ohio, was organized in 1892 by William Long, W. H. Hunter, and Alfred Day. Brown underglaze slip-decorated pottery was made. The firm closed in 1896. The company used many marks; the earliest included the letters *LPCO.*

Vase, Brown, Silver Overlay, Shaped Spout, c.1900, 7 x 4¼ In.	585
Vase, Pillow, Leaves, Standard Brown Glaze, Footed, Impressed Mark, 8½ x 7¾ In.	188

LOSANTI

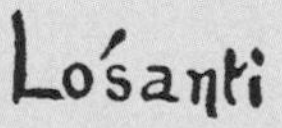

Losanti was made by Mary Louise McLaughlin in Cincinnati, Ohio, about 1899. It was a hard-paste decorative porcelain. She stopped making it in 1906.

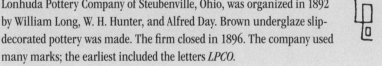

Vase, Grain-De-Riz, Rice Grain, Carved, Glazed, Signed, MCL 154, 3½ x 3¼ In.	11250
Vase, Green, Carved Leaves, Signed, MCL 11, 2½ x 3¾ In.	2750

LOTUS WARE

Lotus Ware was made by the Knowles, Taylor & Knowles Company of East Liverpool, Ohio, from 1890 to 1900. Lotus Ware, a thin porcelain that resembles Belleek, was sometimes decorated outside the factory. Other types of ceramics that were made by the Knowles, Taylor & Knowles Company are listed under KTK.

Dish, Shell Shape, Portrait, Woman In Profile, 5 x 5 x 1¼ In.	99
Vase, Green, White Relief Flowering Vines, Branch Handles, 8 In.	660

Loetz, Vase, Pampas, Wavy Rim, Drop Painted, Cobalt Blue, c.1899, 4½ x 5 In. $875

Treadway

Loetz, Vase, Pink & Blue Iridescent, Silver Overlay, Stems & Leaves, Shouldered, Flared Rim, 6 In. $1,040

Treadway

Loetz, Vase, Tree Trunk, Gold Iridescent, 3 Pierced Knots, 10½ In. $406

Susanin's Auctioneers & Appraisers

This is an edited listing of current prices. Visit **Kovels.com** to check thousands of prices from previous years and sign up for free information on trends, tips, reproductions, marks, and more.

L

Lunch Box Thermos, Milltown, Ind., Steel, Catalin, Model 370, Henry Dreyfuss, American Bottle Co., 1937, 14 In.
$750

Wright

Luneville, Sculpture, Lion, Lying Down, Head Raised, Tail Curled, Faience, 1700s, 14 x 17 ¼ x 8 ¾ In.
$540

Michaan's Auctions

Luster, Copper, Pitcher, Andrew Jackson, Beaded Rim, Molded Spout, Staffordshire, c.1825, 6 ½ In.
$995

Jeffrey S. Evans & Associates

LOW

J.&J.G.LOW

Low art tiles were made by the J. and J. G. Low Art Tile Works of Chelsea, Massachusetts, from 1877 to 1902. A variety of art and other tiles were made. Some of the tiles were made by a process called "natural," some were hand-modeled, and some were made mechanically.

Tile, Flowering Vine, Yellow Glaze, Shaded Brown Ground, Wood Frame, c.1890, 7¾ x 7¾ In.	94
Tile, Monks, Gothic Cathedral, Yellow, Arthur Osborne, Fabric Covered Frame, 1881, 13 x 8 In......	3328
Tile, Scenic, 3 Figures In Rowboat, Green Glaze, Round, Frame, c.1890, 4¼ In.	157
Tile, Stove, Cast Iron, Brown Tiles, Putti On Front, North Wind On Sides, 1800s, 34 x 19 x 12 In....	688

LUNCH BOX

Lunch boxes and lunch pails have been used to carry lunches to school or work since the nineteenth century. Today, most collectors want either early tin tobacco advertising boxes or children's lunch boxes made since the 1930s. These boxes are made of metal or plastic. Vinyl lunch boxes were made from 1959 to 1982. Injection molded plastic lunch boxes were made beginning in 1972. Legend says metal lunch boxes were banned in Florida in 1972 after a group of mothers claimed children were hitting each other with them and getting injured. This is not true. Metal lunch boxes stopped being made in the 1980s because they were more expensive to make than plastic lunch boxes. Boxes listed here include the original Thermos bottle inside the box unless otherwise indicated. Movie, television, and cartoon characters may be found in their own categories. Tobacco tin pails and lunch boxes are listed in the Advertising category.

G.I. Joe, Spaceship, Blue, Plastic, Aladdin, c.1992..	25
Grizzly Adams, Dome Top, Grizzly & Animal Friends, Metal, Aladdin, 1977, 9 x 7 x 4 In.	165
Lance Link, Secret Chimp, Monkeys, Metal, Thermos, 1970s, 9 x 6 x 4 In.............................	79
Roy Rogers & Dale Evans, Horseback, Cattle, Double R Bar Ranch, Metal, 1950s, 8 In.	79
Sesame Street, Alphabet, Characters, Red Lid, Aladdin, 1980s....................................	15
Tom Corbett Space Cadet, Metal, Glass Liner, Yellow Plastic Lid, Aladdin, 1952, 6 In.	135

LUNCH BOX THERMOS

Milltown, Ind., Steel, Catalin, Model 370, Henry Dreyfuss, American Bottle Co., 1937, 14 In.	*illus*	750

LUNEVILLE

Luneville

Luneville, a French faience factory, was established about 1730 by Jacques Chambrette. It is best known for its fine bisque figures and groups and for large faience dogs and lions. The early pieces were unmarked. The firm was acquired by Keller and Guerin and is still working.

Platter, Fishing Village Scene, Fruit & Vegetable Handles, 10 x 21 In.		431
Sculpture, Lion, Lying Down, Head Raised, Tail Curled, Faience, 1700s, 14 x 17¼ x 8¾ In.	*illus*	540
Vase, 3 Fins, Lotus Flower, Glaze, Enameled, Keller & Guerin, France, 13½ x 7 In.		325

LUSTER

Luster glaze was meant to resemble copper, silver, or gold. The term *luster* includes any piece with some luster trim. It has been used since the sixteenth century. Some of the luster found today was made during the nineteenth century. The metallic glazes are applied on pottery. The finished color depends on the combination of the clay color and the glaze. Blue, orange, gold, and pearlized luster decorations were used by Japanese and German firms in the early 1900s. Fairyland Luster was made by Wedgwood in the 1900s. Copies made by modern methods started appearing in 1990. Tea Leaf pieces have their own category.

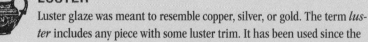

Copper, Pitcher, Andrew Jackson, Beaded Rim, Molded Spout, Staffordshire, c.1825, 6½ In.	*illus*	995

Fairyland Luster is included in the Wedgwood category.

Pink, Creamer, Maritime Scene, Black Transfer, 1910s, 5½ In. .... *illus* 875

Sunderland Luster pieces are in the Sunderland category.

LUSTRES

Lustres are mantel decorations or pedestal vases with many hanging glass prisms. The name really refers to the prisms, and it is proper to refer to a single glass prism as a lustre. Either spelling, luster or lustre, is correct.

Amber, Cut To Clear, Drop Prisms, Bohemian Style, 13 x 6½ In., Pair .... *illus*	300
Amber, Ruffled Rim, Prisms, Round Base, Bohemia, 12 x 7 In., Pair	633
Cranberry, Shah's Portrait, Baccarat Candlestick, Medallion, Moser, Early 1900s, 22 In., Pair ...	3750
Dark Ruby, Flowers, Gilt Trim, 16 Saber Prisms, Stepped Round Base, Victorian, 14 In., Pair	523
Emerald, Flowers, Gilt, Scalloped Rim, Spear & Pendalogue Prisms, Late 1800s, 14½ In., Pair .	339
Flowers, Scrolling Decor, Hanging Prisms, Metal Bases, Electrified, c.1915, 18 In., Pair.......	118
Gilt, Scalloped Rim, Enamel, White Overlay, Long Prisms, Bohemia, 1900s, 12½ In., Pair..... *illus*	531
Green Cut To Clear, Thumbprint, Gold Trim, Notched, Spear Prisms, Bohemia, c.1910, 11 In., Pair .	440
Green Opaline, Lobed Bowl, Frosted Stem, Gilt Trim, Clear Prisms, 19th Century, 9 In., Pair...	313
Opaque Blue, Gold Stencil, Scalloped Rim, Stepped Base, 2 Rows Of Prisms, 14½ In., Pair ..... *illus*	240
Pink, Cut Prisms, Flowers, Victorian, 14 x 7 In., Pair..	518
Pink, Flowers, Ruffled Rim, White Interior, Prisms, Round Base, 9 x 5 In., Pair	81
Ruby Cut To Clear, Frosted Leaves, Diamond, 10 Prisms, 15 In., Pair...................................	390
Ruby, White Flowers & Butterflies, Gilt, Clear Prisms, Fluted Rim, 14¼ In., Pair.................	100
White, Cut To Clear, Flared Fluted Rim, Gilt Trim, Clear Prisms, Bohemia, 19th Century, 10¼ In....	346
White, Cut To Emerald, Multicolor Flowers, Gilt Trim, Clear Prisms, Bohemia, 12¾ In., Pair ...	125
White, Salmon, Multicolor Flowers, Victorian, Hand Painted, 13 In., Pair .... *illus*	230

MACINTYRE, *see Moorcroft category.*

MAJOLICA

Majolica is a general term for any pottery glazed with an opaque tin enamel that conceals the color of the clay body. It has been made since the fourteenth century. Today's collector is most likely to find Victorian majolica. The heavy, colorful ware is rarely marked. Some famous makers include George Jones & Sons, Ltd.; Griffen, Smith and Hill; Joseph Holdcroft; and Minton. Majolica made by Wedgwood is listed in the Wedgwood category. These three marks can be found on majolica items.

George Jones, George Jones & Sons, Ltd. 1861–1873	Griffen, Smith and Hill c.1879–1889	Joseph Holdcroft, Sutherland Pottery 1865–1906

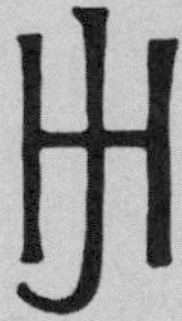

Basket, Centerpiece, Fruit & Flowers, White Glaze, Italy, 11 x 7 x 8 In.	53
Bottle, Earthenware, Bulbous, Blue & White, Flowers & Vines, 8 x 5 In. .... *illus*	527
Bowl, Dragonfly, Green Interior, Brown Glaze, 3½ x 11 In.	96
Candleholder, Art Nouveau, Multicolor, Flowers, Brown Ground, France, 8¼ In.	31
Centerpiece, Empire, Female Figures, Malachite Veneer Base, Gilt Bronze, 35 In., Pair *illus*	10800
Charger, Portrait, Man, River Scene, Blue Ground, Cantagalli, Italy, 1800s, 18 In...............	406
Charger, Traders At Port, Masks Border, Mythological Beasts, Italy, Late 1700s, 18¼ In. .... *illus*	660
Cheese Dish, Dome Lid, Flowers, Black Ground, Brown Handle, 11 x 12 In.	288
Compote, Shell Shape, Scalloped Bowl, Petal Stand, 12 x 16 In. .... *illus*	600
Dish, Pie, Lid, Fox, Game, George Jones, 1800s, 7 x 10½ In. .... *illus*	2400
Dish, Trompe L'Oeil, Fish, Brown Ground, Glazed, Marked, Minton, 13⅝ In........................	384
Egg Caddy, 3 Cups, Pineapple, Green, Gold, Pink Glaze, Rope Shape Loop Handle, 5½ In..	130

Luster, Pink, Creamer, Maritime Scene, Black Transfer, 1910s, 5½ In.
$875

Eldred's

Lustres, Amber, Cut To Clear, Drop Prisms, Bohemian Style, 13 x 6½ In., Pair
$300

Alex Cooper Auctioneers

Lustres, Gilt, Scalloped Rim, Enamel, White Overlay, Long Prisms, Bohemia, 1900s, 12½ In., Pair
$531

Hindman

M

Lustres, Opaque Blue, Gold Stencil, Scalloped Rim, Stepped Base, 2 Rows Of Prisms, 14½ In., Pair
$240

Woody Auction

Lustres, White, Salmon, Multicolor Flowers, Victorian, Hand Painted, 13 In., Pair
$230

Stevens Auction Co.

Majolica, Bottle, Earthenware, Bulbous, Blue & White, Flowers & Vines, 8 x 5 In.
$527

Thomaston Place Auction Galleries

Jar, Apothecary, Round Rim, Multicolor, Flowers, Blue Ground, Italy, 1600s, 12 In.	..... *illus*	2500
Jar, Bust Portrait, Helmeted Warrior, Flowers, Multicolor, 1700s, 10 x 6 In.		761
Jardiniere, Cobalt Blue & Gold, Hand Painted, Footed, England, 15 x 17 x 14 In.		345
Jardiniere, Cottura, Zigzag, Blue, Yellow Rim & Base, Contemporary, Italy, 12 x 8¾ In.		154
Jardiniere, Figural, Putti, Pink, Oval, Side Handles, Minton, 1800s, 17¾ x 9 In.	.... *illus*	1872
Jardiniere, Flared Rims, Leaves, Multicolor, Ribbed Base, Italy, 15 x 15 In., Pair		468
Jardiniere, Flowers, Leaves, Mottled Brown, Oval, Lion's Mask Handles, France, c.1890, 10 x 17 In.		630
Jardiniere, Lion's Mask Medallions, Fruit, Multicolor, Continental, Mid 1900s, 21 x 13 In.		180
Jardiniere, Pedestal, Brown & Green Ground, Embossed Flowers, c.1900, 31 In.		203
Jardiniere, Pedestal, Flowers, Brown, Green, Red, 22½ In.		125
Jardiniere, Putti Handles, Lion's Head, Blue, Base, Minton, 1800s, 10¾ In.	.... *illus*	660
Lamp, 2-Light, Figural, Blackamoor, Brass Base, 34 In.		1024
Plaque, Earthenware, Biblical, Castelli, Hand Painted, Italy, Frame, 1800s, 14½ x 11½ In.	..... *illus*	644
Plate, Asparagus, Barbotine, Art Nouveau Style, Scallop Shell Design, France, c.1890s, 9 x 9 In.		94
Plate, Oiseaux De Paradis, White Ground, Gian, France, 10 In., 14 Piece		469
Plate, Spiny Lobster, Crabs, Shrimp, Barnacles, Mossy Ground, Portuguese, c.1890, 4 x 12 In.	.... *illus*	1220
Sardine Box, Dome Lid, Underplate, Seaweed, Yellow Rim, Green Leaves, George Jones, 4 x 8 x 8 In.		570
Server, Eggplant Shape, Snail Finial, Leaf Base, Bellevue Pottery, Hull, 4 x 8 In.	.... *illus*	469
Server, Pastry, Curved Rim, Leaves, Painted, 1800s, 4 x 12 x 8 In.		244
Table, Baroque, Figural Fish, Painted, Italy, 1900s, 18 x 27 In.	.... *illus*	213
Tureen, Lid, Figural, Boar's Head, Earthenware, Portuguese, c.1900, 8 x 16 x 8 In.	.... *illus*	1525
Umbrella Stand, Iris, Mottled Brown, Green Glaze, Art Nouveau, c.1915, 19⅞ In.		108
Urn, Relief Masks, Latin Text, Berries & Pomegranates, White Ground, Porcelain, 19 In.	....	150
Vase, Child Smelling Flowers, Aesthetic Movement, Late 1800s, 29¾ x 12 x 11 In.	....	187

MALACHITE

Malachite is a green stone with unusual layers or rings of darker green shades. It is often polished and used for decorative objects. Most malachite comes from Siberia or Australia. Copies are made of molded glass.

Box, Hinged Lid, Jeweled, Portrait Mount, Stand, Russia, 35½ x 16 x 12 In.	....	3570
Box, Lid, Micro Mosaic, Tiger Plaque, Gilt Metal, Early 1800s, 1¼ x 5⅜ x 3¾ In.	....	9375
Frame, Mirror, Carved Wood, Brass, 44 x 31½ In.	.... *illus*	3188
Frame, Silvered Metal Portraits, Relief, Profile, Man, Woman, 10 x 8 In., Pair	....	701
Obelisk, 4-Sided, Pillar, Pyramid Shape Top, Square Base, 32 In., Pair	....	1785
Sculpture, Guitar, 6-String, Curved Waist, Silver Design, 29 x 10 In.	....	960
Snuff Bottle, Turquoise Green, Rectangular, Stone Matrix, 1850, 2½ In.	.... *illus*	2040

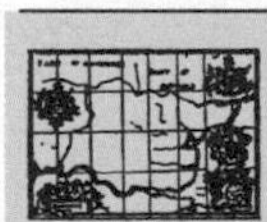

MAP

Maps of all types have been collected for centuries. The earliest known printed maps were made in 1478. The first printed street map showed London in 1559. The first road maps for use by drivers of automobiles were made in 1901. Collectors buy maps that were pages of old books, as well as the multifolded road maps popular in the twentieth century. Terrestrial globes are spherical maps of the earth. Celestial globes show the position of the stars and the constellations in the sky.

Boston, Adjacent Cities, Colton's General Atlas, 1800s, 23 x 20 In.	....	281
Boston, Pictorial, The Colour Of An Old City, Edwin Olsen, Houghton Mifflin, 1926, 28 x 38 In.	. *illus*	561
Britannia, Kings Of 5th-7th Centuries Vignettes, Jan Jansson, Amsterdam, c.1646	..... *illus*	1024
Cape Cod, Pictorial, Myles Standish, Wood Frame, Coulton Waugh, 1926, 17½ x 21 In.	......	594
Chart, Waterways, Bottom Of North Sea, Signed, Oster & Son, 1808, 40 x 26 In.	....	165
Connecticut, Stanley Factory, Seymour Park, New Britain, Frame, 1902, 22 x 28 In.	....	60
Globe, Celestial, Brass Meridian, Horizontal Ring, Tripod Stand, J. & W. Cary, England, 1800s, 25 In.		2991
Globe, Celestial, Star Globe, Mahogany Case, Kelvin & Hughes Ltd., England, c.1950, 7¼ In.	.... *illus*	880
Globe, Celestial, Steel Stand, Ernst Schotte & Co., Berlin, Early 1900s, 9 x 9 In.	.... *illus*	750
Globe, Celestial, Table, Brass Meridian, Tripod Stand, Benjamin Martin, England, 1700s, 17½ In.		12317
Globe, Lunar, Iron Tripod Base, Copper Flash, Late 1900s, 20 x 12 In.	....	502

M

Majolica, Centerpiece, Empire, Female Figures, Malachite Veneer Base, Gilt Bronze, 35 In., Pair
$10,800

Michaan's Auctions

Majolica, Charger, Traders At Port, Masks Border, Mythological Beasts, Italy, Late 1700s, 18 ¼ In.
$660

Alderfer Auction Company

Majolica, Compote, Shell Shape, Scalloped Bowl, Petal Stand, 12 x 16 In.
$600

Woody Auction

Majolica, Dish, Pie, Lid, Fox, Game, George Jones, 1800s, 7 x 10 ½ In.
$2,400

Cottone Auctions

Majolica, Jar, Apothecary, Round Rim, Multicolor, Flowers, Blue Ground, Italy, 1600s, 12 In.
$2,500

Hindman

Majolica, Jardiniere, Figural, Putti, Pink, Oval, Side Handles, Minton, 1800s, 17 ¾ x 9 In.
$1,872

Thomaston Place Auction Galleries

Majolica, Jardiniere, Putti Handles, Lion's Head, Blue, Base, Minton, 1800s, 10 ¾ In.
$660

Cottone Auctions

Majolica, Plaque, Earthenware, Biblical, Castelli, Hand Painted, Italy, Frame, 1800s, 14 ½ x 11 ½ In.
$644

Jeffrey S. Evans & Associates

Majolica, Plate, Spiny Lobster, Crabs, Shrimp, Barnacles, Mossy Ground, Portuguese, c.1890, 4 x 12 In.
$1,220

Rafael Osona Nantucket Auctions

Majolica, Server, Eggplant Shape, Snail Finial, Leaf Base, Bellevue Pottery, Hull, 4 x 8 In.
$469

Turner Auctions + Appraisals

M

TIP
An old majolica pitcher has a small hole inside where the handle meets the body. A new pitcher will not have this hole but will often have a large hole in the base.

Majolica, Table, Baroque, Figural Fish, Painted, Italy, 1900s, 18 x 27 In.
$213

Lion and Unicorn

Majolica, Tureen, Lid, Figural, Boar's Head, Earthenware, Portuguese, c.1900, 8 x 16 x 8 In.
$1,525

Rafael Osona Nantucket Auctions

Malachite, Frame, Mirror, Carved Wood, Brass, 44 x 31 ½ In.
$3,188

Bonhams

Malachite, Snuff Bottle, Turquoise Green, Rectangular, Stone Matrix, 1850, 2 ½ In.
$2,040

Bonhams

Map, Boston, Pictorial, The Colour Of An Old City, Edwin Olsen, Houghton Mifflin, 1926, 28 x 38 In.
$561

Copake Auction

Map, Britannia, Kings Of 5th-7th Centuries Vignettes, Jan Jansson, Amsterdam, c.1646
$1,024

Neal Auction Company

Map, Globe, Celestial, Steel Stand, Ernst Schotte & Co., Berlin, Early 1900s, 9 x 9 In.
$750

Eldred's

Map, Globe, Terrestrial, Cast Iron Stand, Tripod Feet, Merriam & Moore, 1800s, 14 In.
$384

Neal Auction Company

> **TIP**
> *Wash your hands or wear cotton gloves before handling books, textiles, or paper artifacts.*

Map, Globe, Celestial, Star Globe, Mahogany Case, Kelvin & Hughes Ltd., England, c.1950, 7 ¼ In.
$880

Bonhams

M

Globe, Terrestrial, Brass Meridian, Mahogany Stand, John Senex, England, c.1740, 18 In. ..	8798
Globe, Terrestrial, Cardboard, Hand Colored, Folding, David Townsend, G.M. Smith, 1869, 6 In. ..	1664
Globe, Terrestrial, Cast Iron Stand, Tripod Feet, Merriam & Moore, 1800s, 14 In. ....*illus*	384
Globe, Terrestrial, Collapsible, Silk, Metal Frame, Box, John Betts, c.1850, 3 x 29 In.............	576
Globe, Terrestrial, Cut Glass, Sawtooth, Latitude & Longitude Lines, Waterford, c.1980, 11 In. .... *illus*	204
Globe, Terrestrial, Diamond Marquise, Silvered, Lucite, Midcentury Modern, Replogle, 16 x 12 In.	288
Globe, Terrestrial, Library, Walnut Stand, Cram's Imperial, 1970, 20 x 33 In........................	144
Globe, Terrestrial, Mahogany Stand, Paw Feet, Replogle, 44 x 21 ½ In.............................	375
Globe, Terrestrial, Metal Stand, Replogle World Classic, Series 16, 41 In.	246
Globe, Terrestrial, Pocket, Fishskin Case, Inner Hemispheres, J. & W. Cary, 1800s, 3 In. *illus*	11437
Globe, Terrestrial, Pocket, Fishskin Case, Newton & Son, London, 1910s, 3 In.	5625
Globe, Terrestrial, School, Writing Surface, Rotating, Metal Post, Round Base, 1960s, 51 In.	240
Globe, Terrestrial, Sheet Metal, Lithograph, Wood Handle, Germany, 10 ½ In......................	116
Great Britain, Pocket, Folding, Black Frame, William Faden, 1795, 31 x 25 In.	468
Hampshire, England, Mahogany Frame, Joan Blaeu, Amsterdam, 1645, 21 x 25 In.	176
Imperial Turkey, Colored, Abraham Ortelius, 1573, 15 ½ x 20 In. ....*illus*	1063
Lincoln County, Maine, Vignettes, C.M. Hopkins, Plexiglas, Frame, 1857, 62 x 63 In...........	1404
Maine, Varnished Lithograph, H.F. Halling & J. Chase Jr. Co., Portland, 1862, 64 x 61 In. ...*illus*	936
Petrus Montanus, Novi Belgii, New England, Virginia, Hand Colored, John Ogilby, 1671, 11 x 14 In..	1093
South America, Hand Colored, Thomas Bowen, Frame, 1789, 23 x 18 In.	127
United States, Hand Colored, Margins Cut, Carey & Sons, John Mellish, 1821, 16 x 21 In....	978
Western Switzerland, Das Wiflispurgergow, Gilt Frame, Willem Janszoon Blaeu, c.1650, 25 x 31 In.	120

MARBLE

Marble collectors pay highest prices for glass and sulphide marbles. The game of marbles has been popular since the days of the ancient Romans. American children were able to buy marbles by the mid-eighteenth century. Dutch glazed clay marbles were least expensive. Glazed pottery marbles, attributed to the Bennington potteries in Vermont, were of a better quality. Marbles made of pink marble were also available by the 1830s. Glass marbles seem to have been made later. By 1880, Samuel C. Dyke of South Akron, Ohio, was making clay marbles and The National Onyx Marble Company was making marbles of onyx. The Navarre Glass Marble Company of Navarre, Ohio, and M. B. Mishler of Ravenna, Ohio, made glass marbles. Ohio remained the center of the marble industry, and the Akron-made Akro Agate brand became nationally known. Other pieces made by Akro Agate are listed in this book in the Akro Agate category. Sulphides are glass marbles with frosted white figures in the center.

Clambroth, White & Red Bands, Black Base, ⅝ In. ....*illus*	1353
Joseph Coat, White, Blue, Orange, Red & Green, 1 ⁹⁄₁₆ In.	800
Onionskin, Mica, Red & Turquoise Spotting, White Base, 2 ¼ In.	2640
Sulphide, Dog Center, Seated, Clear, Air Bubbles, 2 ⁷⁄₁₆ In. ....*illus*	338
Swirl, White Solid Core, Pink, Yellow, Green, Red, 3-Stage, 2 ³⁄₁₆ In. ....*illus*	861

MARBLE CARVING

Marble carvings, such as large or small figurines, groups of people or animals, and architectural decorations, have been a special art form since the time of the ancient Greeks. Reproductions, especially of large Victorian groups, are being made of a mixture using marble dust. These are very difficult to detect and collectors should be careful. Other carvings are listed under Alabaster.

Bust, African Man, Portrait, Shona Greenstone, Signed, Nicholas Tandi, 14 x 8 x 6 In.	527
Bust, Beatrice, Love Of Dante's Life, Grand Tour, Italy, 1800s, 15 x 15 x 7 In.........................	761
Bust, Franz Schubert, Base, Brown, Carrara, Italy, 10 In.	120
Bust, Mercury, Head, Wings, Gray, Tadolini Roma, Italy, 1800s, 25 x 34 In. ....*illus*	3570

Map, Globe, Terrestrial, Cut Glass, Sawtooth, Latitude & Longitude Lines, Waterford, c.1980, 11 In.
$204

Garth's Auctioneers & Appraisers

Map, Globe, Terrestrial, Pocket, Fishskin Case, Inner Hemispheres, J. & W. Cary, 1800s, 3 In.
$11,437

Bonhams

Map, Imperial Turkey, Colored, Abraham Ortelius, 1573, 15 ½ x 20 In.
$1,063

New Haven Auctions

M

> **TIP**
> *If you want to keep your collections free from harm, always clean and dust them yourself.*

Map, Maine, Varnished Lithograph, H.F. Halling & J. Chase Jr. Co., Portland, 1862, 64 x 61 In.
$936

Thomaston Place Auction Galleries

Marble, Clambroth, White & Red Bands, Black Base, ⅝ In.
$1,353

Morphy Auctions

Marble, Sulphide, Dog Center, Seated, Clear, Air Bubbles, 2⁷⁄₁₆ In.
$338

Morphy Auctions

Marble, Swirl, White Solid Core, Pink, Yellow, Green, Red, 3-Stage, 2³⁄₁₆ In.
$861

Morphy Auctions

Bust, Napoleon, Wearing Hat & Coat, Cream Ground, Socle Base, 31 In. ....*illus*	3712
Bust, The Nazarene, Carved, Head, Face, White, Robert Merrell Gage, 1961, 19¾ In. ..*illus*	536
Bust, Woman, Hair Tied, Smiling, Signed, A. Piazza, Carrara, 17 In.	531
Bust, Woman, Head Turned, Wearing Pearl Necklace, Socle Base, 1800s, 29 In.	1875
Bust, Woman, Patinated Bronze, Carrara Head, Affortunato Gory, Paris, 21 x 14 x 8 In. ....*illus*	3803
Bust, Woman, Signed Verso, Emilio P. Fiaschi, 26½ x 16 x 8 In.	780
Cassoulet, Louis XVI Style, Bronze Mounted, Flower Finial, Ram's Head Handles, 21 In., Pair	896
Centerpiece, Empire Style, Bronze Mounted, Flame Finials, Leaves, Ribbon, 12 In. ....*illus*	704
Column, Grand Tour, Gilt Bronze, Stepped Base, 1800s, 10¼ In.	625
Compote, Birdbath Shape, Doves, Raised Bowls, Plinth Base, Italy, 10½ In., Pair ....*illus*	625
Head, Man, Wreath, Mounted, Carved Wood Column, 1800s, 6⅞ In.	531
Jardiniere, Bowl, 3 Bearded Men, Leaves, 2 Birds, Gilt Bronze, Tripod Feet, Late 1800s, 43 In..*illus*	6050
Medici Lion, Standing, Foot On Ball, Flaminio Vacca, Italy, 1800s, 11 x 14 x 4 In.	2074
Obelisk, Variegated, Beige, Monument, Pedestal Base, Continental, 1900s, 16¾ In., Pair .....*illus*	375
Pedestal, Black, Aesthetic, Bronze Mounted, Molded Square Top, 43 x 16 x 16 In.	1280
Pedestal, Carved & Fluted, Painted, Square Base, c.1900, 32 In.	250
Pedestal, Carved, Chamfered Corners, Molded Base, Italy, Late 1800s, 42 x 9 In.	531
Pedestal, Column, Red, Brown, Green, Cream Onyx, Square Plinth Base, 1900s, 32 x 14 x 14 In..	556
Pedestal, Gray & White, Gadroon Stem, Octagonal, 30 x 12 In.	633
Pedestal, Green, Ormolu Mounted, Paw Feet, 40 x 12 x 12 In.	1408
Pedestal, Green, Twisted, Columnar, Circular Top & Base, 33 x 14 x 16 In. ....*illus*	300
Pedestal, Louis XV, Sienna, Dore Bronze Mounted, France, 40 x 16 x 16 In., Pair	2280
Pedestal, Neoclassical, Fluted, Green Ground, Octagonal Base, 1800s, 42¾ In.	406
Pedestal, Neoclassical, White & Gray, Circular Top, Stepped Base, 1800s, 43½ In.	500
Pedestal, Round Top, Acanthus Leaves, 3 Dolphins Base, Claw Feet, Late 1800s, 32 x 18 x 16 In .*illus*	1210
Plaque, Mother & Daughters, Curved, Cream Ground, 1800s, 26 x 18½ 9 In.	188
Plaque, Relief, Oval, Louis Alexandre Bottee, France, Frame, Late 1800s, 11¾ x 8¾ In.	738
Plaque, Susan B. Anthony, Facing Left, Ruffled Collar, Frame, Late 1800s, 20 x 15¾ In..*illus*	125
Sink, Shell, Pedestal, Cut Glass Faucets, Ribbon & Reed Spout, Sherle Wagner, 39½ In. .....*illus*	3538
Statue, Bust, Rebecca, Curly Hair, Circular Base, 18 In. ....*illus*	177
Statue, Elderly Woman, Headscarf, Boy, Seated, 16 x 13 x 9 In.	300
Statue, Fawn, Standing, Head Down, Holding Grapes, White, 1800s, 36 In.	6325
Statue, Indian Woman, Sitting, Dream Catcher, Green, Pedestal Stand, 1800s, 21 In.	1785
Statue, Reclining Nude, Woman, White, M. Bouraine, 1946, 17 x 38 In.	1403
Statue, Roman Man, Neoclassical, Carved, Carrara, Italy, 63 x 21 x 17 In., Pair	7800
Statue, Venus Vitrix, Chaise Longue, Wood Base, M. Passini, 15 x 20 In.	688
Tazza, Black, Brass Mounted, Continental, c.1900, 11 In.	100
Toilet Casing, Scroll & Flourish, Giltwood Lid, Sherle Wagner, 21 x 23 In.	3660
Torso, Aphrodite, Female Nude, Mounted, Hexagon Plinth Base, 1800s, 18 In.	313
Urn, Bell Shape, Flared Rim, Circular Socle, Square Base, 1950s, 19 x 13 In., Pair	875
Urn, Green, Mottled, Garland, Mermaid Handles, Ram's Heads, 17½ x 9 x 7 In., Pair .*illus*	8750
Urn, Green, Silver Plate Mounted, Winged Cherub Handles, 16½ x 7 In., Pair	224

MARBLEHEAD POTTERY

Marblehead Pottery was founded in 1904 by Dr. J. Hall as a rehabilitative program for the patients of a Marblehead, Massachusetts, sanitarium. Two years later it was separated from the sanitarium and it continued operations until 1936. Many of the pieces were decorated with marine motifs.

Basket, Hanging, Green Matte Glaze, 3 Handles, c.1910, 3⅝ x 5¼ In. ....*illus*	185
Bowl, Gray Matte Glaze, Speckled, Closed, c.1910, 3¼ x 4½ In.	312
Chamberstick, Blue Matte Glaze, Flared Rim, 4 In., Pair	406
Tile, Galleon Ship, Shaded Blue Ground, Blue Border, c.1910, 6 x 6 In.	500
Tile, Galleon Ship, White, Blue Ground, Rope Twist Border, c.1910, 9½ x 9½ In.	250
Vase, Blue Matte Glaze, Mottled, Shoulders, Sea Gull Mark, 6 In.	1188
Vase, Brown Matte Glaze, Mottled, Cylindrical, Tapered, c.1910, 5 In.	219
Vase, Cream Ground, Incised, Bird Mosaic Band, Multicolor, c.1913, 9¼ In.	12500
Vase, Gray Matte Glaze, Lemon Tree, Hennessey & Tutt, Tall Ship Mark, 4½ In.	2921
Vase, Squat, Stylized Trees, Olive Green Ground, Hennessey & Tutt, 1908-16, 3¾ In.	17500

M

Marble Carving, Bust, Mercury, Head, Wings, Gray, Tadolini Roma, Italy, 1800s, 25 x 34 In.
$3,570

Bonhams

TIP
Marble will scorch. A marble statue very close to the heat of a 100-watt lightbulb may be damaged.

Marble Carving, Bust, Napoleon, Wearing Hat & Coat, Cream Ground, Socle Base, 31 In.
$3,712

Neal Auction Company

Marble Carving, Bust, The Nazarene, Carved, Head, Face, White, Robert Merrell Gage, 1961, 19¾ In.
$536

Bonhams

Marble Carving, Bust, Woman, Patinated Bronze, Carrara Head, Affortunato Gory, Paris, 21 x 14 x 8 In.
$3,803

Thomaston Place Auction Galleries

Marble Carving, Centerpiece, Empire Style, Bronze Mounted, Flame Finials, Leaves, Ribbon, 12 In.
$704

Neal Auction Company

Marble Carving, Compote, Birdbath Shape, Doves, Raised Bowls, Plinth Base, Italy, 10½ In., Pair
$625

Neal Auction Company

Marble Carving, Jardiniere, Bowl, 3 Bearded Men, Leaves, 2 Birds, Gilt Bronze, Tripod Feet, Late 1800s, 43 In.
$6,050

Fontaine's Auction Gallery

M

329

Marble Carving, Obelisk, Variegated, Beige, Monument, Pedestal Base, Continental, 1900s, 16¾ In., Pair
$375

Neal Auction Company

Marble Carving, Pedestal, Green, Twisted, Columnar, Circular Top & Base, 33 x 14 x 16 In.
$300

Alderfer Auction Company

> ### TIP
> It is best to wash marble with distilled water. Any trace of acid or iron in the water will cause deterioration or stains. Use soft soap, a bit of ammonia, and a plastic container.

Marble Carving, Pedestal, Round Top, Acanthus Leaves, 3 Dolphins Base, Claw Feet, Late 1800s, 32 x 18 x 16 In
$1,210

Fontaine's Auction Gallery

Marble Carving, Plaque, Susan B. Anthony, Facing Left, Ruffled Collar, Frame, Late 1800s, 20 x 15¾ In.
$125

Auctions at Showplace, NYC

Marble Carving, Sink, Shell, Pedestal, Cut Glass Faucets, Ribbon & Reed Spout, Sherle Wagner, 39½ In.
$3,538

Neal Auction Company

Marble Carving, Statue, Bust, Rebecca, Curly Hair, Circular Base, 18 In.
$177

Copake Auction

Marble Carving, Urn, Green, Mottled, Garland, Mermaid Handles, Ram's Heads, 17½ x 9 x 7 In., Pair
$8,750

Susanin's Auctioneers & Appraisers

Marblehead, Basket, Hanging, Green Matte Glaze, 3 Handles, c.1910, 3⅝ x 5¼ In.
$185

California Historical Design

MARDI GRAS

Mardi Gras, French for "Fat Tuesday," was first celebrated in seventeenth-century Europe. The first celebration in America was held in Mobile, Alabama, in 1703. The first krewe, a parading or social club, was founded in 1856. Dozens have been formed since. The Mardi Gras Act, which made Fat Tuesday a legal holiday, was passed in Louisiana in 1875. Mardi Gras balls, carnivals, parties, and parades are held from January 6 until the Tuesday before the beginning of Lent. The most famous carnival and parades take place in New Orleans. Parades feature floats, elaborate costumes, masks, and "throws" of strings of beads, cups, doubloons, or small toys. Purple, green, and gold are traditional Mardi Gras colors. Mardi Gras memorabilia ranges from cheap plastic beads to expensive souvenirs from early celebrations.

Charm, Mask, Silver, Tag, New Orleans, Signed, JMF...	18
Doubloon, Krewe Of Iris, Silver, 1983..	75
Necklace, Silver Chain, Pearlescent Purple, Green & Gold Beads, Mask Pendant, 31 In.	20
Pin, Doubloon, Gilt Ground, Cloisonne, 2 Tragedy Masks, New Orleans, 1½ x 1¾ In.	15
Pin, Rex Ball, Gold Crown, White Enamel, Green, Gold & Purple Ribbon, Favor, 1998, 1½ x 2¼ In....	32
Tray, Invitation, Krewe Of Nereus, Oliver, Porcelain, 1981, 7 x 5 In..	15

MARTIN BROTHERS

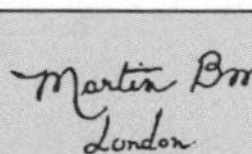

Martin Brothers of Middlesex, England, made Martinware, a salt-glazed stoneware, between 1873 and 1915. Many figural jugs and vases were made by the four brothers. Of special interest are the fanciful birds, usually made with removable heads. Most pieces have the incised name of the artists plus other information on the bottom.

Flask, Face, Cork Stopper, Silver Finial, Handles, R.W. Martin, 1901, 8¾ x 6½ In........ *illus*	12300
Jar, Lid, Figural, Bird, Grotesque, Green, Blue, Cream, Signed, 1907, 9½ In.................. *illus*	45000
Jug, Round Shoulders, Blue Flowers, Monogram, Brown Trim, Signed, 5 x 6¼ x 4½ In.	615
Pitcher, Herons, Palm Trees, Blue, Brown Trim, Cream Ground, R.W. Martin, 1881, 8½ In. ..	3250
Pitcher, Incised, Marsh, Ducks, Pelicans, Cylindrical, Cream Ground, Signed, 1894, 9½ In.	6250
Stand, Round, Fish & Kelp Around Edge, Green, Cream Ground, Signed, 1890, 10 In...........	475
Vase, Bottle, Blue, Cream, Brown, Leafy Scrolls, Abstract Flowers, Signed, 1888, 9¼ In.......	938
Vase, Incised, Grotesque Masks, Scrolls, Dark Brown Ground, Shoulders, c.1890, 8¼ In.	5000

MARY GREGORY

Mary Gregory is the name used for a type of glass that is easily identified. White figures were painted on clear or colored glass as the decoration. The figures chosen were usually children at play. The first glass known as Mary Gregory was made in about 1870. Similar glass is made even today. The traditional story has been that the glass was made at the Boston & Sandwich Glass Company in Sandwich, Massachusetts, by a woman named Mary Gregory. Recent research has shown that none was made at Sandwich. In fact, all early Mary Gregory glass was made in Bohemia. Beginning in 1957, the Westmoreland Glass Co. made the first Mary Gregory–type decorations on American glassware. These pieces had simpler designs, less enamel paint, and more modern shapes. France, Italy, Germany, Switzerland, and England, as well as Bohemia, made this glassware. Children standing, not playing, were not pictured until after the 1950s.

Bell, Girl, Holding Bird, Ruby Red, Clear Handle, 6 In.	25
Epergne, Girl & Birds, Cranberry, Trumpet Shape, Silver Plated Base, 23 In.	863
Tumbler, Girl, Holding Flowers, Green, Ribbed, c.1900, 3¾ In..	50
Vase, Girl, Playing Tennis, Trees, Marigold, Flared, Footed, 10½ In.	350

MASONIC, *see Fraternal category.*

Martin Brothers, Flask, Face, Cork Stopper, Silver Finial, Handles, R.W. Martin, 1901, 8¾ x 6½ In. $12,300

Neue Auctions

TIP
Some repairs make the sale of an antique very difficult and lower the price. Don't buff pewter. Don't wash ivory. Don't repaint old toys. Don't tape old paper. Don't wash oil paintings.

M

Martin Brothers, Jar, Lid, Figural, Bird, Grotesque, Green, Blue, Cream, Signed, 1907, 9½ In. $45,000

Heritage Auctions

Massier, Urn, Turquoise Glaze, 2 Open Loop Handles, 20 x 15 In., Pair
$1,664

Nadeau's Auction Gallery

Massier, Vase, 4 Handles, Flowers, Spider, Hand Painted, Stoneware, c.1900s, 4 x 5 In. Diam.
$282

Wright

Massier, Vase, Art Nouveau, Gold Iridescent, 3 Handles, Flowers & Stems Scene, Delphin, 13 In.
$600

Treasureseeker Auctions

MASON'S IRONSTONE

Mason's Ironstone was made by the English pottery of Charles J. Mason after 1813. Mason, of Lane Delph, was given a patent for this improved earthenware. He usually called it *Mason's Patent Ironstone China*. It resisted chipping and breaking, so it became popular for dinnerware and other table service dishes. Vases and other decorative pieces were also made. The ironstone was decorated with orange, blue, gold, and other colors, often in Japanese-inspired designs. The firm had financial difficulties, but the molds and the name *Mason* were used by many owners through the years, including Francis Morley, Taylor Ashworth, George L. Ashworth, and John Shaw. Mason's joined the Wedgwood group in 1973 and the name was used for a few years and then dropped.

Bowl, Blue, Cream, Red, White, Chinoiserie Pattern, c.1815, 15 x 4½ In.	1195
Bowl, Wood Pigeon Pattern, Fruit & Flower Vines, Multicolor, 10 In.	145
Dish, Flowers, Red, Green, Beige, Curved Sides, Bittersweet, 6½ x 4 In.	29
Dish, Mandarin Pattern, Flower Border & Interior, Gilt, 7¾ In.	75
Dish, Multicolor Flowers, Green Scalloped Rim, c.1830, 9 In.	325
Jug, Schoolhouse Pattern, Lizard Shape Handle, Paneled, Blue, Orange, c.1825, 9 In.	425
Plate, Chinoiserie Pattern, Couple In Garden, Flower Border, c.1820, 8 In.	85
Plate, Huntsman, Winged Eagle, Sheaf Of Wheat, Green Flowered Border, 1838, 9 In.	199
Plate, Salad, Vista Pattern, Landscape, Leaves, Red, Pink, 7 In.	18
Platter, Stoneware, Flower Pattern, Leaves, Imari, 1800s, 17 x 13½ In.	266
Platter, Watteau Pattern, Brown & Cream Transfer, Round, 13 In.	95
Syrup, Pewter Lid, Mottled Blue, Yellow Ocher, Ribbed, Marked, M. & Co., 9 In.	39
Tea Caddy, Flowers, Leaves, Yellow, Brown, Ascot, Hexagonal, Footed, 6½ x 4 In.	35
Vase, Tipped Basket, Fruits, Harvest Gold, Footed, 4⅝ In.	24
Vase, Yellow, Cobalt Blue Dragons, Beaker Shape, c.1830, 6 x 3¾ In., Pair	303

MASSIER

J.Massier fils

Massier, a French art pottery, was made by brothers Jerome, Delphin, and Clement Massier in Vallauris and Golfe-Juan, France, in the late nineteenth and early twentieth centuries. It has an iridescent metallic luster glaze that resembles the Weller Sicardo pottery glaze. Most pieces are marked *J. Massier*. Massier may also be listed in the Majolica category.

Urn, Turquoise Glaze, 2 Open Loop Handles, 20 x 15 In., Pair .... *illus*	1664
Vase, 4 Handles, Flowers, Spider, Hand Painted, Stoneware, c.1900s, 4 x 5 In. Diam..... *illus*	282
Vase, Art Nouveau, Gold Iridescent, 3 Handles, Flowers & Stems Scene, Delphin, 13 In. *illus*	600

MATCH HOLDER

Match holders were made to hold the large wooden matches that were used in the nineteenth and twentieth centuries for a variety of purposes. The kitchen stove and the fireplace or furnace had to be lit regularly. One type of match holder was made to hang on the wall, another was designed to be kept on a tabletop. Of special interest to collectors today are match holders that have advertisements as part of the design.

Advertising, Coal Bucket, J. Robbins & Co., East Boston, Cast Iron, 5¼ In.	79
Bear, Walking, Hole On Top, Patina, Metal, Gilt Liner, c.1890, 4¼ x 8½ In. ...... *illus*	182
Boot, Figural, Cast Iron, Wall Hanging, Black, 6½ In. .... *illus*	47
Face, Closed Eyes, Cast Iron, Gothic Type, Triangular Gable, 8 In. .... *illus*	325
Indian Head, Ashtray, Striker, Bronze, 3¾ In.	68
Reindeer, Standing, Silver, Colored Stone Collar, Oblong Base, Continental, 10 x 4½ In. ...... *illus*	2280

M

MATCH SAFE

Match safes were designed to be carried in the pocket or set on a table. Early matches were made with phosphorus and could ignite unexpectedly. The matches were safely stored in the tightly closed container. Match safes were made of sterling silver, plated silver, or other metals. The English call these "vesta boxes."

Frog, Cast Iron, Advertising, Garland, Michigan Stove Co., 4 1/4 In.. 150
Tennis Player, Embossed, Silver, Striker On Base, 1 5/8 x 1 1/4 In. .... *illus* 77

McCOY

McCoy pottery was made in Roseville, Ohio. Nelson McCoy and J.W. McCoy established the Nelson McCoy Sanitary and Stoneware Company in Roseville, Ohio, in 1910. The firm made art pottery after 1926. In 1933 it became the Nelson McCoy Pottery Company. Pieces marked *McCoy* were made by the Nelson McCoy Pottery Company. Cookie jars were made from about 1940 until December 1990, when the McCoy factory closed. Since 1991 pottery with the McCoy mark has been made by firms unrelated to the original company. Because there was a company named Brush-McCoy, there is great confusion between Brush and Nelson McCoy pieces. See Brush category for more information.

Cookie Jar, Dog In Basket, Basketweave, Black & White, 1950s, 10 In. 65
Pitcher, Green, Ribbed Body, 5 1/2 In.. 125
Planter, Boat, Fisherman, Playing Guitar, Brown, 11 1/2 x 4 x 6 In. 125
Planter, Koi Fish, Pink, Tail Up, 12 In. 58
Planter, Quilted Diamond Pattern, Turquoise, 3 1/2 In. 35
Sugar & Creamer, Brown Drip Glaze 28
Vase, Grapes & Leaves, Green, Brown, Base, Marked, 9 1/4 In. 70
Vase, Green, Handles, Knot Tie Design, Footed, 8 In. 79
Vase, Lilies, Leaves, Base, Yellow, Green, Brown, c.1940, 6 3/4 x 6 3/4 In. 80
Vase, Orchid Glaze, Swirl, Pedestal Foot, 4 1/4 In. 35

McKEE

McKee is a name associated with various glass enterprises in the United States since 1836, including J. & F. McKee (1850), Bryce, McKee & Co. (1850 to 1854), McKee and Brothers (1865), and National Glass Co. (1899). In 1903, the McKee Glass Company was formed in Jeannette, Pennsylvania. It became McKee Division of the Thatcher Glass Co. in 1951 and was bought out by the Jeannette Corporation in 1961. Pressed glass, kitchenwares, and tablewares were produced. Jeannette Corporation closed in the early 1980s. Additional pieces may be included in the Custard Glass and Depression Glass categories.

McKee	PRESCUT	McK
McKee Glass Co. c.1870	McKee Glass Co. c.1904–1935	McKee Glass Co. 1935–1940

Bowl, Jade, Scalloped, 8 In... 68
Cake Stand, Ruby, Pedestal, Octagonal Foot, 1920s, 11 x 2 1/4 In............................. 125
Goblet, Rock Crystal Pattern, Octagonal Foot, 6 1/4 In., 11 Piece.................... *illus* 50
Refrigerator Dish, Milk Glass, Clear Lid, Red Sailboat, 3 x 5 In.................... *illus* 94
Salt & Pepper, Rock Crystal, Green, Silver Plate Lid, 3 1/2 In.................... *illus* 105
Sherbet, Laurel, 3 1/2 In... 5

MECHANICAL BANKS *are listed in the Bank category.*

Match Holder, Bear, Walking, Hole On Top, Patina, Metal, Gilt Liner, c.1890, 4 1/4 x 8 1/2 In.
$182

Fontaine's Auction Gallery

Match Holder, Boot, Figural, Cast Iron, Wall Hanging, Black, 6 1/2 In.
$47

Copake Auction

Match Holder, Face, Closed Eyes, Cast Iron, Gothic Type, Triangular Gable, 8 In.
$325

Copake Auction

M

Match Holder, Reindeer, Standing, Silver, Colored Stone Collar, Oblong Base, Continental, 10 x 4½ In.
$2,280

Abington Auction Gallery

Match Safe, Tennis Player, Embossed, Silver, Striker On Base, 1⅝ x 1¼ In.
$77

Rachel Davis Fine Arts

McKee, Goblet, Rock Crystal, Octagonal Foot, 6¼ In., 11 Piece
$50

Hartzell's Auction Gallery Inc.

MEDICAL

Medical office furniture, operating tools, microscopes, thermometers, and other paraphernalia used by doctors are included in this category. Veterinary collectibles are also included here. Medicine bottles are listed in the Bottle category. There are related collectibles listed under Dental.

Cabinet, Apothecary, 3 Drawers Over Drop Front, Carved, 1700s, 34 x 29 x 12 In.	1250
Cabinet, Apothecary, 18 Drawers, Porcelain Pulls, Wood, Early 1900s, 12 x 26 x 8⅞ In.	125
Chest, Apothecary, Brass Handle, 2 Doors, Mahogany, Dinneford, England, c.1850, 10½ In. *illus*	1496
Chest, Apothecary, Brass Handle, Hinged Lid, Glass Bottles, Mahogany, England, c.1850, 12 In.	1232
Chest, Apothecary, Mahogany, Brass Bail Handle, Mid 1800s, 10½ x 11½ In.	2375
Chest, Apothecary, Tiger Maple, 15 Drawers, Wood Pulls, 1800s, 32 x 41 x 12 In.	4388
Chest, Apothecary, Traveling, Regency, Brass, Mahogany, 2 Doors, Drawer, 1800s, 15 x 13 x 8 In.	813
Chest, Doctor's, Fitted Interior, Brass, Wood, 1810s, 9 x 13 x 9 In.	250
Cupboard, Apothecary, 2 Parts, Pine, 50 Drawers, Painted, New England, 1800s, 58 x 35 x 9 In.	1722
Diathermy Machine, Short Wave, Hogan Brevatherm, Western Electric Co. Inc., 22 x 22 x 14 In.	90
Fleet's Spinal Demonstrator, Model No. 9, Aluminum, Rubber, Adjustable, c.1939, 36 x 9 x 11 In.	2340
Head, Phrenology, Glass Eyes, Ceramic, Fowler's, 9½ In. *illus*	5313
Leech Jar, Blown Glass, Ribbed Rim, Hollow Baluster Stem, Circular Feet, 1850, 10 In. *illus*	360
Leech Jar, Glass, Round, Blue Trim, Pedestal Base, 11½ x 8 In. *illus*	608
Microscope, Shutter Plate, Reflector, Projection Tube, Dollond Solar, England, 1800s, 11 In.	2639
Quack Device, Classic Oak Case, Bracket Feet, Drawer, 2 Doors, 50 x 18 x 18 In. *illus*	266
Quack Device, Violetta, Violet Ray, Electro Therapy, Case, Early 1900s, 9 x 14 x 3 In.	64
Saw, Amputation, Metal Handle, Fine Teeth, Armstrong & Co., 12 In.	54
Sign, Apothecary, Hanging, Multicolor, Glass Jewels, Brass, c.1900, 10½ x 8 In. *illus*	1063
Splint, Leg, Molded, Mahogany, Plywood, Charles & Ray Eames, 1943, 42 x 8 x 4 In. *illus*	813
Surgeon's Kit, Bone Saws, Brass, Cloth Tourniquet, Mahogany Case, Lesueur, France, 1800s, 19 In.	2111

MEISSEN

Meissen is a town in Germany where porcelain has been made since 1710. Any china made in the town can be called Meissen, although the famous Meissen factory made the finest porcelains of the area. The crossed swords mark of the great Meissen factory has been copied by many other firms in Germany and other parts of the world. Pieces of Meissen dinnerware in the Onion pattern are listed in their own category in this book.

Box, Hinged Lid, Harlequin Design, Gilt Metal, Mounted, 3¾ In.	120
Box, Hinged Lid, Scene, People, Horses, Angels, Bronze Mounts, Late 1800s, 11 x 7 x 5 In.	4375
Box, Sugar, Lid, Painted Garden Scenes, Gilt Bands, Octagonal, K.P.M. Mark, c.1724, 4½ In.	31500
Candlestick, Urn Shape Bobeche, Drip Pan, Gilt, 1900s, 11½ In., Pair *illus*	125
Cane Handle, Horn Shape, Chamois Goat's Head, 2 Figures, Dog, Silver Mounted, c.1730, 2¾ In.	12600
Clock, Shelf, 2 Women, Gilt, Blue & White, Roman Numerals, Footed, c.1815, 14 x 12 x 5 In. *illus*	3750
Clock, Shelf, 4 Seasons, Blue & White, Flowers, Cherubs, Footed, 1800s, 18 x 12 In.	1375
Clock, Shelf, Multicolor, Luster, Gilt Bronze Mount, Barrey a Paris Movement, 1700s, 17 In. *illus*	1593000
Cup & Saucer, Cartouche, Figures In Garden, Yellow Ground, Augustus Rex, c.1727, 5 In.	60480
Dish, Kakiemon, 12-Sided, Hob In The Well, Flowers, Leaves, Dreher Mark, c.1730, 9½ In.	25200
Figurine, 2 Cupids, Embracing, Flowers, Multicolor, Crossed Swords Mark, 7½ x 6 In.	58
Figurine, Boy, Standing, Holding Basket Of Grapes, Square Base, 3¾ In.	88
Figurine, Dancing Man, Holding Tankard & Hat, Blanc De Chine, 1900s, 9 In.	250
Figurine, Female Gardener, Flower Basket, Flowers In Hand, Marcolini, 14 In. *illus*	240
Figurine, Lioness, White Glaze, Rectangular Base, August Gaul, c.1930, 12 x 14 x 4½ In. *illus*	936
Figurine, Loie Fuller, Dancer, White Flowing Dress, c.1910, 10½ x 10½ x 7 In.	2600
Figurine, Monkey, Band Conductor, Standing, Gilt, Round Base, Germany, 1900s, 7 In.	644
Figurine, Parrot, Perched On Branch Post, Blue Crossed Swords Mark, 1900s, 6 In.	594
Group, Satyr, Mother, Fauns, Leopard Pelt, Tambourine, Pan Flute, 11 x 9 In.	431
Group, Shepherdess, Lamb, Tree Stump, Blue Crossed Swords Mark, Late 1800s, 7¼ In.	469
Group, Silenus, Bacchus & Bacchante, Donkey, Gilt, Multicolor, 1800s, 8½ In.	448
Jug, Milk, Lid, Purple, Chinoserie Cartouches, Children, Dreher Mark, c.1730, 6¼ In. *illus*	18900
Nodder, Woman, Seated, Hand Painted, Wood Base, Germany, 1800s, 6 x 5½ x 5¼ In. *illus*	4305
Serving, Dish, Dome Lid, Figural Finial, Blue & White, Footed, 1900s, 8 x 13⅜ In.	375

M

McKee, Refrigerator Dish, Milk Glass, Clear Lid, Red Sailboat, 3 x 5 In.
$94

Ruby Lane

McKee, Salt & Pepper, Rock Crystal Pattern, Green, Silver Plate Lid, 3 ½ In.
$105

Ruby Lane

Mad Medicine

A strange item used in early days to cure rabies, snakebites, and other ailments is called a "madstone." It is not a stone but a calcified blob from a deer's stomach, the equivalent of a human gallstone. The madstone was put on the patient's body to magically cure the problem.

Medical, Head, Phrenology, Glass Eyes, Ceramic, Fowler's, 9 ½ In.
$5,313

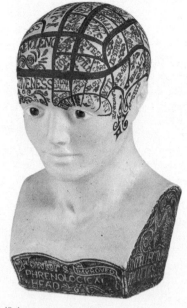

Hindman

Medical, Leech Jar, Blown Glass, Ribbed Rim, Hollow Baluster Stem, Circular Feet, 1850, 10 In.
$360

Garth's Auctioneers & Appraisers

Medical, Chest, Apothecary, Brass Handle, 2 Doors, Mahogany, Dinneford, England, c.1850, 10 ½ In.
$1,496

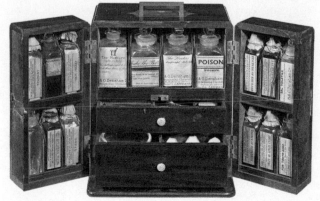

Bonhams

Medical, Leech Jar, Glass, Round, Blue Trim, Pedestal Base, 11 ½ x 8 In.
$608

Rachel Davis Fine Arts

Medical, Quack Device, Classic Oak Case, Bracket Feet, Drawer, 2 Doors, 50 x 18 x 18 In.
$266

Soulis Auctions

Medical, Sign, Apothecary, Hanging, Multicolor, Glass Jewels, Brass, c.1900, 10 ½ x 8 In.
$1,063

New Haven Auctions

M

Medical, Splint, Leg, Molded, Mahogany, Plywood, Charles & Ray Eames, 1943, 42 x 8 x 4 In.
$813

Clars Auction Gallery

Meissen, Candlestick, Urn Shape Bobeche, Drip Pan, Gilt, 1900s, 11 1/2 In., Pair
$125

Hindman

Meissen, Clock, Shelf, 2 Women, Gilt, Blue & White, Roman Numerals, Footed, c.1815, 14 x 12 x 5 In.
$3,750

Hindman

Tea & Coffee Set, Armorial, Pots, Tea Canister, Sugar Box, Tea Bowls & Saucers, Waste Bowl, 1731	1351000
Tea Canister, Lid, 6-Sided, Chinoiserie Panels, Gilt Trim, Baluster Shape, 1725-30, 4 In. ..*illus*	4095
Tea Set, Flowers, Birds, Pink, Orange, Gilt, Miniature, 6 Cups & Saucers, 13-In. Tray	535
Teacup, Scallop Shape Body, Gilt, Flower Bough, Marked, 1900s, 2 In.	36
Tureen, Lid, Flower Encrusted, Painted, Figural Knops, 1800s, 7 1/4 x 11 In., Pair ....*illus*	570
Vase, Blue & White, Beaker Shape, Flared Rim, Augustus Rex, c.1725, 12 In. ....*illus*	478800
Waste Bowl, Gilt, Chinoiserie, Scrolled Edges, Short Foot, Hausmaler, Swuter Workshop, 6 3/4 In. .	10800

MERRIMAC POTTERY

Merrimac Pottery Company was founded by Thomas Nickerson in Newburyport, Massachusetts, in 1902. The company made art pottery, garden pottery, and reproductions of Roman pottery. The pottery burned to the ground in 1908.

Jar, Lid, Earthenware, 3 Stubby Handles, Blue Matte Glaze, c.1903, 6 1/8 x 6 In.	552
Vase, Black Highlights, Matte Glaze, Red, Orange, Green, 4 x 5 In. ....*illus*	687
Vase, Squat, 2 Handles, Green Matte Glaze, Newburyport, Mass., Early 1900s, 4 1/2 x 4 In.	568

METLOX POTTERIES

Metlox Potteries was founded in 1927 in Manhattan Beach, California. Dinnerware was made beginning in 1931. Evan K. Shaw purchased the company in 1946 and expanded the number of patterns. Poppytrail (1946–1989) and Vernonware (1958–1980) were divisions of Metlox under Shaw's direction. The factory closed in 1989.

Homestead Provincial, Pitcher, Brown, 16 Oz., 6 In.	38
Poppy Trail, Bowl, Serving, 9 x 4 In.	26
Sculptured Grape, Pitcher, Water, 2 Qt., 8 3/4 In.	52

METTLACH

Mettlach, Germany, is a city where the Villeroy and Boch factories worked. Steins from the firm are marked with the word *Mettlach* or the castle mark. They date from about 1842. *PUG* means painted under glaze. The steins can be dated from the marks on the bottom, which include a date-number code that can be found online. Other pieces may be listed in the Villeroy & Boch category.

Charger, Cherub & Fairy, Mushrooms, Gilt Borders, Heinrich Schlitt, 17 In.	1900
Charger, Stoneware, Circular Shape, Butterflies & Moth, Signed, Heinrich Schlitt, 17 1/2 In. ..*illus*	3186
Plaque, No. 2749, Sunrise Scene, Church, Water, Trees, Late 1800s, 19 3/4 In.	837
Stein, Art Nouveau, Mosaic, Flowers, White Stems, Metal Lid, Late 1800s, 12 1/2 In.	227
Stein, No. 1946, Pewter Hinge, Courting Couple Scene, Lovebird On Lid, 9 In.	123
Stein, No. 2721, Occupational, Carpenter, Etched, Musical, Lid Inlay, Porcelain Disc, 8 In. .	921
Stein, Painted, Blue Ground, Loop Handle, Owl On Hinged Lid, 6 x 5 x 4 In. ....*illus*	1250
Stein, Pug, Hinged Pewter Lid, Multicolor, Print, Vikings Drinking, Germany, 15 1/2 In.	200
Vase, No. 2535, Slate Blue Ground, Poppy Flowers, Red Trim, Shoulders, 11 In.	201
Vase, Square, White Relief, Woman, Watering, Bow & Arrows, Grapes, Blue & Green, 12 x 4 In.	100

MILK GLASS

Milk glass was named for its milky white color. It was first made in England during the 1700s. The height of its popularity in the United States was from 1870 to 1880. It is now correct to refer to some colored glass as blue milk glass, black milk glass, etc. Reproductions of milk glass are being made and sold in many stores. Related pieces may be listed in the Cosmos, Vallerysthal, and Westmoreland categories.

Box, Lion Finial, Scrolled Scalloped Edge, c.1890, 5 x 3 x 4 In.	75
Dish, Lid, Dove In Hand, Red Stone Ring, Glass Eye, Reticulated Rim, Footed, c.1889, 5 x 8 In.	63
Epergne, Blue, Ribbed, Fluted Dish, Scalloped Rim, 2 Piece, 9 x 6 1/4 In.	96
Paperweight, Continental Cut, Rococo, Engraved Knife Shape, Monogram, 1800s, 16 3/4 In.	480

Meissen, Clock, Shelf, Multicolor, Luster, Gilt Bronze Mount, Barrey a Paris Movement, 1700s, 17 In.
$1,593,000

Meissen, Jug, Milk, Lid, Purple, Chinoserie Cartouches, Children, Dreher Mark, c.1730, 6¼ In.
$18,900

Meissen, Tureen, Lid, Flower Encrusted, Painted, Figural Knops, 1800s, 7¼ x 11 In., Pair
$570

Michaan's Auctions

Meissen, Vase, Blue & White, Beaker Shape, Flared Rim, Augustus Rex, c.1725, 12 In.
$478,800

Sotheby's

Meissen, Figurine, Female Gardener, Flower Basket, Flowers In Hand, Marcolini, 14 In.
$240

Sotheby's

Meissen, Nodder, Woman, Seated, Hand Painted, Wood Base, Germany, 1800s, 6 x 5½ x 5¼ In.
$4,305

Michaan's Auctions

Meissen, Figurine, Lioness, White Glaze, Rectangular Base, August Gaul, c.1930, 12 x 14 x 4½ In.
$936

Brunk Auctions

Meissen, Tea Canister, Lid, 6-Sided, Chinoiserie Panels, Gilt Trim, Baluster Shape, 1725-30, 4 In.
$4,095

Sotheby's

Merrimac, Vase, Black Highlights, Matte Glaze, Red, Orange, Green, 4 x 5 In.
$687

Thomaston Place Auction Galleries

Doyle

Toomey & Co. Auctioneers

Mettlach, Charger, Stoneware, Circular Shape, Butterflies & Moth, Signed, Heinrich Schlitt, 17 ½ In.
$3,186

Neue Auctions

Mettlach, Stein, Painted, Blue Ground, Loop Handle, Owl On Hinged Lid, 6 x 5 x 4 In.
$1,250

New Haven Auctions

Milk Glass, Vase, Portrait, Indian, Painted, Light Brown Ground, c.1910, 11 ⅜ In.
$121

Fontaine's Auction Gallery

Pitcher, Footed, Jenny Lind, Fostoria, 1950s, 8 ½ In.	60
Plate, Angel Playing Harp, Open Heart Border, 7 ½ In.	26
Platter, Dog Swimming, Lily Pond, Duck, Leaf Border, 13 x 9 In.	135
Trinket Dish, Open Hand, Flowers At Wrist, 5 In.	14
Vase, Bud, Hobnail, Bulbous, 7 In.	13
Vase, Portrait, Indian, Painted, Light Brown Ground, c.1910, 11 ⅜ In. *illus*	121

MILLEFIORI

Millefiori means, literally, a thousand flowers. Many small pieces of glass resembling flowers are grouped together to form a design. It is a type of glasswork popular in paperweights and some are listed in that category.

Flask, Filigree Twists, Blue, White, Pink, Green, Murano, Italy, 1900s, 4 ⅜ x 3 In. *illus*	117
Lamp, Glass Shade, Mushroom Shape, Mounted, Brass, Murano, 1930s, 18 ¼ In.	545
Vase, Side Handles, Multicolor, 14 In.	277

MINTON

Minton china was made in the Staffordshire region of England beginning in 1796. The firm became part of the Royal Doulton Tableware Group in 1968, but the wares continued to be marked *Minton*. In 2009 the brand was bought by KPS Capital Partners of New York and became part of WWRD Holdings. The company no longer makes Minton china. Many marks have been used. The word *England* was added in 1891. Minton majolica is listed in this book in the Majolica category.

Minton c.1822–1836	 Minton c.1863–1872	Minton 1951–c.2009

Figurine, Guinevere & The Tree Of Life, Hand Painted, John Ablitt, c.1994, 8 x 13 In.	1063
Jardiniere, 4 Tiles, Family, Square Shape, Blue, Ball Finial, c.1900, 9 ½ x 9 x 9 In.	2583
Plaque, Made In England, White, Green Letters, 1900s, 3 In.	88
Plate, Denmark Pattern, White, Red Flowers, Scrolls, 8-Sided, Marked, 10 ½ In., 12 Piece	565
Vase, Lid, Bicentenary, Cupid, Nymph, Handle, Alboin Birks, 1992, 14 ¼ In., Pair *illus*	3875
Vase, Pate-Sur-Pate, Figure, Bronze, Gilt, Fretwork, Mounted As Lamp, Late 1800s, 24 ½ In. *illus*	666

MIRRORS *are listed in the Furniture category under Mirror.*

MOCHA

Mocha pottery is an English-made product that was sold in America during the early 1800s. It is a heavy pottery with pale coffee-and-cream coloring. Designs of blue, brown, green, orange, black, or white were added to the pottery and given fanciful names, such as Tree, Snail Trail, or Moss. Mocha designs are sometimes found on pearlware. A few pieces of mocha ware were made in France, the United States, and other countries.

Bowl, Cat's-Eye, Deep, Shaped Base, White Ground, 3 x 5 ½ In.	523
Bowl, Earthworm, Blue Ground, Brown, Black, White, Green Rim, Footed, 3 ¾ x 7 ½ In.	1197
Coffeepot, Lid, Tree, Orange Slip Field, Blue Rim, Early 1800s, 10 ¾ In.	406
Mug, Combed, Marbleized Glaze, Multicolor, Painted, 2 In. *illus*	800
Mug, Fans, Yellow Ground, Black Border, White Rim & Handle, 4 ¾ In. *illus*	1599
Mug, Seaweed, Creamware, Gray & Brown Slip Bands, c.1820, 4 ¾ In.	281
Pepper Pot, Cat's-Eye, Narrow Bands, Blue & Brown Slip, Early 1800s, 4 ¼ In.	200
Pitcher, Bands, Blue, Brown, Green, Black Trees, 9 x 5 ½ In. *illus*	678
Pitcher, Cat's-Eye, Light Blue Ground, Black Stripes, 4 ½ In. *illus*	347
Pitcher, Earthworm, Twig, Tulip, Brown, Blue, Black, Bulbous, Footed, 8 ½ In.	13530
Pitcher, Milk, Seaweed, White Bands, Mocha Stripes, Brown & Blue, Loop Handle, 7 ½ In.	502
Pitcher, Trees, Orange Ground, 2 Brown Slip Bands, c.1820, 8 In.	875
Pot, Cat's-Eye, Twig, Blue Ground, Black Bands, Flared Rim, Handle, 5 ½ x 8 ½ In. *illus*	378

M

Millefiori, Flask, Filigree Twists, Blue, White, Pink, Green, Murano, Italy, 1900s, 4⅜ x 3 In
$117

Jeffrey S. Evans & Associates

Minton, Vase, Lid, Bicentenary, Cupid, Nymph, Handle, Alboin Birks, 1992, 14¼ In., Pair
$3,875

Lion and Unicorn

Minton, Vase, Pate-Sur-Pate, Figure, Bronze, Gilt, Fretwork, Mounted As Lamp, Late 1800s, 24½ In.
$666

Ahlers & Ogletree Auction Gallery

Mocha, Mug, Combed, Marbleized Glaze, Multicolor, Painted, 2 In.
$800

Pook & Pook

Don't Take Your Car to a Flea Market

Take your van, truck, or station wagon when you go to a farm auction, flea market, or out-of-town show. You never know when you'll find the dining room table of your dreams.

Mocha, Mug, Fans, Yellow Ground, Black Border, White Rim & Handle, 4¾ In.
$1,599

Pook & Pook

Mocha, Pitcher, Bands, Blue, Brown, Green, Black Trees, 9 x 5½ In.
$678

Hartzell's Auction Gallery Inc.

Mocha, Pitcher, Cat's-Eye, Light Blue Ground, Black Stripes, 4½ In.
$347

Pook & Pook

Mocha, Pot, Cat's-Eye, Twig, Blue Ground, Black Bands, Flared Rim, Handle, 5½ x 8½ In.
$378

Pook & Pook

Mocha, Sugar, Lid, Seaweed, Light Blue Ground, Green Band, White Handles & Finial, 5¼ In.
$1,134

Pook & Pook

M

TIP
Do not put water in a pottery container with an unglazed interior. The water will be absorbed and eventually stain the container.

TIP

A vase that has been drilled for a lamp, even if the hole for the wiring is original, is worth 30 percent to 50 percent of the value of the same vase without a hole.

Moorcroft, Bowl, Wheat, Light Brown Ground, Circular Base, 4 x 8 ½ In. $125

Turner Auctions + Appraisals

Moorcroft, Compote, Tudric Pewter Base, Hammered, William Moorcroft, Liberty & Co., 8 x 9 In. $156

Alderfer Auction Company

Moorcroft, Jar, Oil, Orchid, Ball Shape Stopper, Light Green Ground, 6 In. $344

Turner Auctions + Appraisals

Sugar, Lid, Seaweed, Light Blue Ground, Green Band, White Handles & Finial, 5 ¼ In. *illus*	1134
Vase, Marbleized, Deep, Multicolor, Shaped Base, 4 In.	615

MONT JOYE, *see Mt. Joye category.*

MOORCROFT

Moorcroft pottery was first made in Burslem, England, in 1913. William Moorcroft had managed the art pottery department for James Macintyre & Company of England from 1898 to 1913. The Moorcroft pottery continues today, although William Moorcroft died in 1945. The earlier wares are similar to the modern ones, but color and marking will help indicate the age.

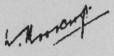

W. Moorcroft Ltd. 1898–c.1905   W. Moorcroft Ltd. 1898–1913   W. Moorcroft Ltd. 1928–1978

Bowl, Hazeldene, Trees, Landscape, Green, 1919, 13 ¼ In.	2250
Bowl, Wheat, Light Brown Ground, Circular Base, 4 x 8 ½ In. *illus*	125
Compote, Tudric Pewter Base, Hammered, William Moorcroft, Liberty & Co., 8 x 9 In. *illus*	156
Creamer, Daisies & Poppies, Pointed Spout, Curved Handle, 5 In.	344
Jar, Lift Lid, Pomegranate, Painted, Marked, William Moorcroft, 6 x 4 In.	240
Jar, Oil, Orchid, Ball Shape Stopper, Light Green Ground, 6 In. *illus*	344
Lamp, Mushroom, Fairy Ring, Electric, 1900s, 8 ¾ In.	531
Saucer, Peaches & Berries, Dark Blue Ground, 5 ½ In.	38
Sugar, Stylized Blue & Yellow Flowers, Green & Cobalt Ground, Footed, Marked, 4 In.	65
Vase, Dawn, Landscape, Trees, Mountains, Dark Outlines, Orange & Cobalt Glaze, Swollen, 9 In.	3750
Vase, Hidden Dreams, Flared Rim, Flowers, Scene, Emma Bossons, 2006, 26 ½ In. *illus*	1188
Vase, Owl On Branch, Leaves, Acorns, Crescent Moon, Glossy Blue Ground, S. Tuffin, 12 In.	440
Vase, Pomegranate, Painted, Footed, Signed, William Moorcroft, 9 x 5 In.	330
Vase, Pomegranate, Tube Lined, Grapes, Green Ground, 1900s, 16 In.	1250
Vase, Tudric, Blue Glaze, Liberty & Co, Pilkington, c.1905, 6 x 3 ¼ In.	492
Vase, White & Orange Tulips, Dark Blue Ground, Glaze, 4 ½ In.	88

MORGANTOWN GLASS WORKS

Morgantown Glass Works operated in Morgantown, West Virginia, from 1900 to 1974. Some of their wares are marked with an adhesive label that says Old Morgantown Glass.

El Mexicano, Decanter, Stopper, No. 1933, Opaque, Seaweed Green, c.1930, 8 ¼ In.	225
Goblet, Ruby Red, Pineapple Stems, Round Base, No. 8224, 6 Piece *illus*	74

MORIAGE

Moriage is a special type of raised decoration used on some Japanese pottery. Sometimes pieces of clay were shaped by hand and applied to the item; sometimes the clay was squeezed from a tube the way we apply cake frosting. One type of moriage is called Dragonware by collectors.

Planter, 2 Handles, Footed, Miyako, Satsuma, 5 x 10 x 8 In.	309
Vase, Cylindrical, Snow Geese In Flight, 2 Handles, Turquoise Ground, Nippon, 9 x 5 In. *illus*	600
Vase, Multicolor, Brushstrokes, Flowers, Satsuma, 1920s, 17 In.	130
Vase, Oval, Lipped Rim, Short Neck, Figures, Early 1900s, 18 In. *illus*	96

MOSAIC TILE COMPANY

Mosaic Tile Company of Zanesville, Ohio, was started by Karl Langerbeck and Herman Mueller in 1894. Many types of plain and ornamental tiles

were made until 1959. The company closed in 1967. The company also made some ashtrays, bookends, and related giftwares. Most pieces are marked with the entwined MTC monogram.

Ceiling Light, Amber Glass Shade, Arts & Crafts, 40 x 25 In. 1408
Tile, Turtle, Green Ground, Glazed, Wood Frame, 9 ½ x 9 ½ In. .... *illus* 455

MOSER

Moser glass is made by a Bohemian glasshouse founded by Ludwig Moser in 1857. Art Nouveau–type glassware and iridescent glassware were made. The most famous Moser glass is decorated with heavy enameling in gold and bright colors. The firm, Moser Glassworks, is still working in Karlovy Vary, Czech Republic. Few pieces of Moser glass are marked.

Bowl, Fairytale Scenes, Castle, Horseback, Knight's Head, 1920, 5 x 11 ½ In. 173
Pokal, Elaborate, Green Shade, Gold Enamel Schoolwork, Petal Design, c.1900, 16 In. 250

MOTHER-OF-PEARL GLASS

Mother-of-pearl glass, or pearl satin glass, was first made in the 1850s in England and in Massachusetts. It was a special type of mold-blown satin glass with air bubbles in the glass, giving it a pearlized color. It has been reproduced. Mother-of-pearl shell objects are listed under Pearl.

Ewer, Rainbow, Herringbone, Applied Frosted Handle, 7 x 4 In. 550
Vase, Victorian, Pale Blue Ground, Cranberry Vertical Stripes, c.1880, 9 ½ In. .... *illus* 132

MOTORCYCLE

Motorcycles and motorcycle accessories of all types are being collected today. Examples can be found that date back to the early twentieth century. Toy motorcycles are listed in the Toy category.

Hat, Leather, Black, Visor, Enamel Pin, Eight, 10 ½ In. 181
Watch Fob, Indian Motorcycle, Arrow Shape, Bastian Bros Rochester, N.Y., c.1920s, 2 x ½ In. 277

MOUNT WASHINGTON, *see Mt. Washington category.*

MOVIE

Movie memorabilia of all types are collected. Animation Art, Games, Sheet Music, Toys, and some celebrity items are listed in their own section. A lobby card is usually 11 by 14 inches, but other sizes were also made. A set of lobby cards includes seven scene cards and one title card. An American one sheet, the standard movie poster, is 27 by 41 inches. A three sheet is 40 by 81 inches. A half sheet is 22 by 28 inches. A window card, made of cardboard, is 14 by 22 inches. An insert is 14 by 36 inches. A herald is a promotional item handed out to patrons. Press books, sent to exhibitors to promote a movie, contain ads and lists of what is available for advertising, i.e., posters, lobby cards. Press kits, sent to the media, contain photos and details about the movie, i.e., stars' biographies and interviews.

Lobby Card, Forbidden Planet, Flying Saucer, MGM, No. 8, 11 x 14 In. .... *illus* 603
Lobby Card, Son Of The Sheik, Rudolph Valentino, Vilma Banky, United Artists, 11 x 14 In. 191
Lobby Card, The 3 Outlaws, Neville Brand, Alan Hale, Bruce Bennett, 1956, 14 x 11 In. 30
Lobby Card, The Light Touch, Stewart Granger, Pier Angeli, George Sanders, 1950s, 17 x 14 In. ... 21
Lobby Card, Wizard Of Oz, Cast, Marked MGM Silver Anniversary, No. 2, 1949, 11 x 14 In. ... 254
Mask, Makeup, Face Shape, Plaster, Brown Glaze, Humphrey Bogart, c.1950, 14 x 7 ½ In. 330
Poster, Citizen Kane, It's Terrific, Orson Welles, Color Lithograph, 1941, 35 x 23 In. 38
Poster, Gone With The Wind, Clark Gable, Vivien Leigh, Leslie Howard, c.1980, 29 x 20 In. .. 38

Moorcroft, Vase, Hidden Dreams, Flared Rim, Flowers, Scene, Emma Bossons, 2006, 26 ½ In. $1,188

Wright

Morgantown, Goblet, Ruby Red, Pineapple Stems, Round Base, No. 8224, 6 Piece $74

Apple Tree Auction Center

Moriage, Vase, Cylindrical, Snow Geese In Flight, 2 Handles, Turquoise Ground, Nippon, 9 x 5 In. $600

Woody Auction

This is an edited listing of current prices. Visit **Kovels.com** to check thousands of prices from previous years and sign up for free information on trends, tips, reproductions, marks, and more.

M

Moriage, Vase, Oval, Lipped Rim, Short Neck, Figures, Early 1900s, 18 In.
$96

Selkirk Auctioneers & Appraisers

Mosaic Tile Co., Tile, Turtle, Green Ground, Glazed, Wood Frame, 9½ x 9½ In.
$455

Treadway

Mother-Of-Pearl, Vase, Victorian, Pale Blue Ground, Cranberry Vertical Stripes, c.1880, 9½ In.
$132

Jeffrey S. Evans & Associates

Poster, Run Silent Run Deep, Clark Gable & Burt Lancaster, Frame, 27 x 33 In.	120
Poster, Theatre Geant Columbia, La Maison Qui Brule, Lithograph, France, 51 x 36½ In.	517
Poster, Toy Story Mania, On Plywood, Disneyland, 48 x 40 In.	1125
Prop, Lunar Excursion Module Hatch, Fiberglass Cover, Apollo 13, 1997, 9½ x 27½ In.	2000

MT. JOYE

Mt. Joye is an enameled cameo glass made in the late nineteenth and twentieth centuries by Saint-Hilaire Touvier de Varraux and Co. of Pantin, France. This same company made De Vez glass. Pieces were usually decorated with enameling. Most pieces are not marked.

Vase, Cameo, Acid Etched, Gilt, Chestnut, Marked, Early 1900s, 13½ x 6 In.	832
Vase, Clear To Purple, Multicolor, Flowers, Leaves, 11½ In. .... *illus*	219
Vase, Dandelion, Cameo Glass, Square, Marked, 12½ x 5 In.	738
Vase, Jack-In-The-Pulpit, Amethyst, White & Yellow Flowers, Gilt, 23½ In., Pair .... *illus*	1397
Vase, Poppy, Clear Acid Cut Ground, Enamel Highlights, 4 x 3 In.	175

MT. WASHINGTON

Mt. Washington Glass Works started in 1837 in South Boston, Massachusetts. In 1870 the company moved to New Bedford, Massachusetts. Many types of art glass were made there until 1894, when the company merged with Pairpoint Manufacturing Co. Amberina, Burmese, Crown Milano, Cut Glass, Peachblow, and Royal Flemish are each listed in their own category.

Flower Holder, Mushroom, Pink & White Tones, Gilt Metal Rim, Footed, 2 x 4 In. ......*illus*	50
Mustard, Silver Plate Lid & Handle, Flowers, White Tones, 2 x 3 In. .... *illus*	40
Pitcher, Water, Enameled, Holly Leaf, Red Berry Jewels, Cream, Rope Handle, 8 x 7 In. *illus*	1600
Rose Bowl, Multicolor Pansies, White Ground, Cream Tones, 5 x 5½ In.	125
Salt & Pepper, Fig Shape, Cranberry, Enameled, Flowers, 2 x 2 In. .... *illus*	200
Salt & Pepper, Opaque White, Multicolor, Pinecone Design, 1893, 2¾ In.	96
Sugar Shaker, Branch & Blossoms, Egg Shape, 4¼ x 3¼ In.	125
Sugar Shaker, Cherries, Blue & White, Egg Shape, 4 x 3 In. .... *illus*	50
Vase, Swirl, Yellow Tones, Flower Blossoms, Pulled Ears Rim, 3 x 4 In.	175
Vase, Sicilian, Blown, Enameled, Lava, Black Ground, Footed Base, 1878, 8¾ x 9 In.	2318

MULLER FRERES

Muller Freres, French for Muller Brothers, made cameo and other glass from about 1895 to 1933. Their factory was first located in Luneville, then in nearby Croismare, France. Pieces were usually marked with the company name.

Bowl, 2 Hunters, Elephant, Pink Ground, Signed, France, 1920s, 13 In.	2200
Lamp, Carved Roses, Multicolor, Cameo, Contemporary, Signed, 1950s, 20 x 7 x 8 In.	3120
Lamp, Luneville, Orange Mottled Glass Shade, Bronze Base, c.1920, 13½ In.	330
Lamp, Luneville, Pink & Blue, White Frosted Ground, Dome Shape Shade, Mottled Glass, 13 In. *illus*	360
Lamp, Rose, Red, Yellow & Amber Overlay, Carved Roses, Cameo, Signed, 20 In.	3250
Vase, Blue, 4 Rectangular Handles, Luneville, France, c.1900, 7 x 9 In.	1500
Vase, Landscape, Enameled, Etched, Tree, Cameo, 5 In. .... *illus*	572
Vase, Red Poppies, Leafy Stems, Yellow Ground, Cameo, Luneville, 9 In.	2198

MUNCIE

Muncie Clay Products Company was established by Charles Benham in Muncie, Indiana, in 1918. The company made pottery for the florist and gift-shop trade. Art pottery was made beginning in 1922. Rombic is pottery made by this company and Ruba Rombic is glass made by the Consolidated Glass Company. Both were designed by Reuben Haley. The company closed by 1939. Pieces are marked with the name *Muncie* or just with a system of numbers and letters, like *1A*.

Movie, Lobby Card, Forbidden Planet, Flying Saucer, MGM, No. 8, 11 x 14 In.
$603

White's Auctions

Mt. Joye, Vase, Clear To Purple, Multicolor, Flowers, Leaves, 11½ In.
$219

Treadway

Mt. Joye, Vase, Jack-In-The-Pulpit, Amethyst, White & Yellow Flowers, Gilt, 23½ In., Pair
$1,397

Tremont Auctions

Mt. Washington, Flower Holder, Mushroom, Pink & White Tones, Gilt Metal Rim, Footed, 2 x 4 In.
$50

Woody Auction

Mt. Washington, Mustard, Silver Plate Lid & Handle, Flowers, White Tones, 2 x 3 In.
$40

Woody Auction

Mt. Washington, Pitcher, Water, Enameled, Holly Leaf, Red Berry Jewels, Cream, Rope Handle, 8 x 7 In.
$1,600

Woody Auction

Mt. Washington, Salt & Pepper, Fig Shape, Cranberry, Enameled, Flowers, 2 x 2 In.
$200

Woody Auction

Mt. Washington, Sugar Shaker, Cherries, Blue & White, Egg Shape, 4 x 3 In.
$50

Woody Auction

Muller Freres, Lamp, Luneville, Pink & Blue, White Frosted Ground, Dome Shape Shade, Mottled Glass, 13 In.
$360

Treasureseeker Auctions

Muller Freres, Vase, Landscape, Enameled, Etched, Tree, Cameo, 5 In.
$572

White's Auctions

M

Music, Autoharp, Appalachian Style, Spruce Top, Ash Back & Sides, Oscar Schmidt, 1970s
$84

Alderfer Auction Company

Music, Box, Bird, Rectangular, Oval Hinged Lid, Silver Case, Avian Design, c.1880, 1 x 3 x 2 In.
$1,375

John Moran Auctioneers

Music, Box, Polyphon, Walnut Inlay, Double Comb, Disc, Late 1800s, 13 x 23 x 20 In.
$2,375

Fontaine's Auction Gallery

Vase, Bud, Peachskin, 4¾ In.	120
Vase, Ruba Rombic, Star, Black, Reuben Haley, 1928, 4½ x 5 In.	595
Vase, Ruba Rombic, Star, Geen Over Pumpkin, Reuben Haley, 5 In.	352

MURANO, *see Glass-Venetian category.*

MUSIC

Music boxes and musical instruments are listed here. Phonograph records, jukeboxes, phonographs, and sheet music are listed in other categories in this book.

Accordion, Piano, Artist Galanti, Deluxe New York, Mother-Of-Pearl Case, c.1930	230
Amplifier, MA5100, Black, Glass Front Panel, McIntosh, 5 x 16 x 14 In.	900
Amplifier, Stereo Power, 100 Watts Output, Mahogany Case, McIntosh, 9 x 17 x 15 In.	1755
Autoharp, Appalachian Style, Spruce Top, Ash Back & Sides, Oscar Schmidt, 1970s .... *illus*	84
Banjo, 5-String, Long Neck, Grade 2, Ode, Hardshell Case, 1964	688
Banjo, Irish Tenor, Mahogany, Ivorine Rim & Tuners, Paragon, Black Nylon Case, 1930s, 32½ In.	439
Banjo, Minstrel Face, Painted, Cartoon Dog, Case, 1920, 33½ In.	354
Box, Birch Plywood, Chromolithograph, Monkey Grinder, Children, Mid 1900s, 13 x 8 x 4 In.	84
Box, Bird, Rectangular, Oval Hinged Lid, Silver Case, Avian Design, c.1880, 1 x 3 x 2 In. *illus*	1375
Box, Criterion, Disc, Tabletop, Serial Number 3684, c.1905, 11½ In.	329
Box, Cylinder, 8 Tunes, Musical Vignette Inlay, Rosewood Case, Swiss, 1800s, 5 x 15½ x 7 In.	384
Box, Cylinder, 8 Tunes, Rosewood Case, Dustcover, Pad Feet, Swiss, 1881, 10 x 32 x 16 In.	1989
Box, Cylinder, 12 Tunes, Hinged Lid, Austria, Late 1800s, 7 x 21½ x 9¾ In.	594
Box, Cylinder, Bedplate, Double Comb, Fruitwood Case, Henri Metert, Swiss, c.1850, 14½ In.	792
Box, Cylinder, Hinged Lid, Inlaid Burl Case, 6 Bells & Drums, Swiss, 15 x 25 In.	840
Box, Cylinder, Key Wind, Bedplate, Tune Sheet, Veneered Wood Case, Swiss, c.1850, 15¾ In.	1056
Box, Cylinder, Marquetry, Harpe, Harmonique, Piccolo, Swiss, c.1850, 8 x 30 x 12 In.	406
Box, Cylinder, Tune Sheet, Veneered Wood Case, Lock, Key, Swiss, Late 1800s, 20 In.	792
Box, Olympia, Cabinet, Mahogany Case, F.G. Otto & Sons, 2 Piece, c.1890, 45 x 23 x 21 In.	4388
Box, Polyphon, Single Comb, Walnut & Mahogany Case, 18 x 20 In.	570
Box, Polyphon, Walnut Inlay, Double Comb, Disc, Late 1800s, 13 x 23 x 20 In. .... *illus*	2375
Box, Regina Style, 17A, Mahogany Case, 30 Discs, Double Comb, Upright, c.1910, 20 x 19 x 12 In.	2299
Box, Regina, Coffintop, Brass, Stand, Quartersawn, Oak, 42 x 32 x 22 In.	3267
Box, Regina, Double Comb, Disc, Cabinet, 1897, 25½ x 22 x 23 In. .... *illus*	3000
Box, Regina, Mahogany Case, Hinged Lid, Serpentine Sides, Reeded Legs, Early 1900s, 42 x 19 In.	2832
Box, Regina, No. 66635, Disc, Gilt Lock, Mahogany Case, 8 x 12½ x 9¾ In.	944
Box, Singing Bird, Book Shape, Silver Filigree, Germany, Late 1800s, 2 x 4 x 3 In. .... *illus*	2500
Box, Singing Bird, Brass, Footed Base, Karl Griesbaum, 9 x 4¾ In. .... *illus*	3510
Box, Singing Bird, Gilt, Enameled, Landscape, Windup, Continental, Early 1900s, 2 x 4 x 2 In. .	3125
Box, Singing Bird, Perched, Gilt Metal Cage, France, c.1900, 11 In.	688
Box, Singing Bird, Silvered Metal, Karl Griesbaum, Early 1900s, 4 x 3 x 2 In. .... *illus*	7865
Box, Singing Bird, Tortoiseshell, Tulip Stamp, Freres Rochat, Swiss, c.1830, 3¾ In. ..... *illus*	12317
Box, Stella, Mahogany Case, Carved, Flowers, Disc, 1800s, 22 x 18 x 12 In.	635
Box, Stella, Mahogany, Lid, Carved, Side Crank, 15 Discs, Swiss, 13½ x 19½ x 22 In.	1625
Box, Symphonion, Black, Wood Case, Double Comb, Disc, Late 1800s, 7 x 13 x 13 In. .. *illus*	563
Box, Veneer, Walnut, Fruitwood Inlay, Flower, Swiss, Late 1800s, 6 x 20 x 8 In.	531
Bugle, Copper, Brass Highlights, 7th Calvary Insignia, Gold Threaded Bulb Tassel, 1900s, 11 In.	84
Cabinet, Mahogany, Satinwood, Splayed Legs, R.J. Horner & Co., Early 1900s, 38 x 23 x 15 In. . *illus*	2662
Cabinet, Regency Style, Pewter Inlaid, Marble Top, Frieze Drawer, Bracket Corners, 40 In., Pair	1586
Clarinet, Gilt & Black, Buffet, No. 65161, Wood Case, 27 In.	469
Drum, Red Lacquer, Leather Top & Bottom, Metal Tack Trim, Chinese, Early 1800s, 16 x 19 In. .	96
Drum, Snare, Black Chrome, White, Gretsch, Signed, 6 x 14 In.	84
Dulcimer, 23-String, Wood, Scheitholt, Continental, 1800s, 32 In.	179
Dulcimer, Mahogany, Veneer, Hammered, Dovetailed, Early 1900s, 15 x 39 x 4 In. ..... *illus*	72
Dulcimer, Walnut, Wood, Painted, Warren A. May, Appalachian Mountains	192
Euphonium, Brass, 5 Piston Valves, Case, C.G. Conn. Ltd., Elkhart, 9 x 21 x 13 In. ..... *illus*	216
Guitar, Acoustic, 6-String, Black, White & Orange, Stella Harmony, Case, 36 In.	63
Guitar, Acoustic, 6-String, Painted Flowers, Regal, c.1920, 37 In. .... *illus*	270
Guitar, Electric, Comb Converter, 12-String, Rickenbacker	3900
Guitar, Electric, Epiphone, Special II, Artist Autographs, Soft Case	339

M

Music, Box, Regina, Double Comb, Disc, Cabinet, 1897, 25 ½ x 22 x 23 In.
$3,000

Alderfer Auction Company

Music, Box, Singing Bird, Book Shape, Silver Filigree, Germany, Late 1800s, 2 x 4 x 3 In.
$2,500

Hindman

Music, Box, Singing Bird, Brass, Footed Base, Karl Griesbaum, 9 x 4¾ In.
$3,510

Thomaston Place Auction Galleries

Music, Box, Singing Bird, Silvered Metal, Karl Griesbaum, Early 1900s, 4 x 3 x 2 In.
$7,865

Fontaine's Auction Gallery

Music, Box, Singing Bird, Tortoiseshell, Tulip Stamp, Freres Rochat, Swiss, c.1830, 3¾ In.
$12,317

Bonhams

Music, Box, Symphonion, Black, Wood Case, Double Comb, Disc, Late 1800s, 7 x 13 x 13 In.
$563

Fontaine's Auction Gallery

345

MUSIC

Music, Cabinet, Mahogany, Satinwood, Splayed Legs, R.J. Horner & Co., Early 1900s, 38 x 23 x 15 In.
$2,662

Fontaine's Auction Gallery

TIP
Never hang a stringed instrument by the neck.

Music, Dulcimer, Mahogany, Veneer, Hammered, Dovetailed, Early 1900s, 15 x 39 x 4 In.
$72

Jeffrey S. Evans & Associates

Music, Euphonium, Brass, 5 Piston Valves, Case, C.G. Conn. Ltd., Elkhart, 9 x 21 x 13 In.
$216

Alderfer Auction Company

Music, Guitar, Acoustic, 6-String, Painted Flowers, Regal, c.1920, 37 In.
$270

Selkirk Auctioneers & Appraisers

TIP
Be sure that any restorer, refinisher, or upholsterer working on your antique is insured.

Music, Harp, Black Frame, Gilt, Claw Feet, Lyon & Healy, 1900s, 64 In.
$1,875

Hindman

Music, Organ, Hurdy-Gurdy, Hand Crank, 5 Discs, Wheels, Child's, 23 x 12 x 19 In.
$330

Chupp Auctions & Real Estate, LLC

Music, Piano, Baby Grand, Steinway, Model S, Ebonized, 1936, 39 x 61 x 55 In.
$5,120

Roland NY Auctioneers & Appraisers

Music, Saxophone, Eb Alto, Largebore, Silver Plate, Henri Selmer, Case, 1920, 6 x 24 x 10 In.
$1,872

Thomaston Place Auction Galleries

M

Guitar, Electric, Les Paul Style, Cherry Sunburst, Allman Brothers, 39 In.	360
Guitar, Mahogany Body, Ebony Neck, Classical, Goya G-30, Hard Shell Case, 1970	460
Guitar, Parlor, Ebonized Neck, Ice Cream Cone Heel, Coffin Case, Evansville, Wis., c.1890	344
Harp, Black Frame, Gilt, Claw Feet, Lyon & Healy, 1900s, 64 In. .... *illus*	1875
Harp, Parcel Gilt, Engraved, Schimmeyer, Late 1800s, 74½ x 33 x 17½ In.	4410
Harpsichord, Wood, Walnut Keys, Music Stand, Wittmayer, Germany, Mid 1900s, 33 x 60 x 28 In.	260
Mandolin, 8-String, Painted, Red To Sunburst, Kay, Pitch Pipe & Picks	108
Organ, Concert, Roller, Walnut, Ebonized & Gilt, Autophone Co., c.1900, 13 x 18 x 17 In.	212
Organ, Hurdy-Gurdy, Hand Crank, 5 Discs, Wheels, Child's, 23 x 12 x 19 In. ...... *illus*	330
Piano, Baby Grand, Baldwin, Walnut, 7 Octaves, 38 x 58 x 63 In.	875
Piano, Baby Grand, Steinway & Sons, No. 265459, Mahogany, Marked, 76 x 56 In.	4688
Piano, Baby Grand, Steinway, Brown Mahogany, Matching Bench, 1947, 38 x 58 x 65 In.	6400
Piano, Baby Grand, Steinway, Model A-1, Straight Bridge, Mahogany Case, c.1905	8775
Piano, Baby Grand, Steinway, Model S, Ebonized, 1936, 39 x 61 x 55 In. ...... *illus*	5120
Piano, Grand, Steinway, Model M, Mahogany, Bench, c.1930, 53 x 38 In.	8775
Piano, Player, Baby Grand, Brambach Co., Mahogany, Stool, 41 x 55 x 62 In.	288
Piano, Player, Baby Grand, Mason & Hamlin, No. A32971, Black	1560
Piano, Player, W. Hoffmann, Upright, Walnut, Carved, Bench, Berlin, c.1900, 56 x 59 x 27 In.	750
Piano, Spinet, John Broadwood, George III, Mahogany, Satinwood, London, c.1786, 30 x 63 x 21 In.	1125
Saxophone, Alto, Low Pitch, Mouthpiece, Ligature, Martin, Hard Case	216
Saxophone, Eb Alto, Largebore, Silver Plate, Henri Selmer, Case, 1920, 6 x 24 x 10 In. *illus*	1872
Saxophone, Elkhart Soprano, Silver Plate, Buescher, No. 218530, c.1920s, 26 In.	540
Saxophone, Gilt, Conical Body, Mouthpiece, Buescher, Case, 6 x 26 x 10 In.	281
Trumpet, Pocket, Kuhnl & Hoyer, 9 x 3 In.	489
Ukulele, Soprano, 4-String, Wood, Weymann, Philadelphia	300
Viola, Scroll, F Holes, Joseph Quarnerius, Cremonensis Faciebat Anno, Czechoslovakia, 1737	563
Violin, 4-String, 1-Piece Back, Painted, 2 Bows, John Juzek, Prague	1560
Violin, Antonius Stradivarius, Johann Gottfried Liebich, Mittenwald, Germany, c.1910	563

MUSTACHE CUP

Mustache cups were popular from 1850 to 1900 when the large, flowing mustache was in style. A ledge of china or silver held the hair out of the liquid in the cup. This kept the mustache tidy and also kept the mustache wax from melting. Old left-handed mustache cups are rare and have been reproduced since the 1960s.

Christmas Holly & Berry, Saucer, Germany, c.1900, 5 x 3 In.	100
Morning Glories, White, Shaded Brown Ground, Stick Handle, Victorian, 3⅝ In. ...... *illus*	14
Pink Roses, Leaves, Germany, 3 x 3¼ In.	28
Swirled, Purple, Flowers, Austria, 3½ In.	71
Yellow & Pink Flowers, Pink To White Ground, Swirl Mold, Prussia, 2½ x 4 In. ...... *illus*	12

MZ AUSTRIA

MZ Austria

MZ Austria is the wording on a mark used by Moritz Zdekauer on porcelains made at his works in Altrolau, Austria, from 1884 to 1909. The mark was changed to *MZ Altrolau* in 1909, when the firm was purchased by C.M. Hutschenreuther. The firm operated under the name Altrolau Porcelain Factories from 1909 to 1945. It was nationalized after World War II. The pieces were decorated with lavish floral patterns and overglaze gold decoration. Full sets of dishes were made as well as vases, toilet sets, and other wares.

Butter, Dome Cover, White, Gold Trim, 7¾ x 4 In.	40
Hair Receiver, Flower Band, Blue, Pink, Yellow, 3-Footed, 4½ x 3 In.	16
Sugar & Creamer, Holly & Berry Pattern, Scalloped Feet, Ornate Handles, Gold Trim	169

NAILSEA

Nailsea glass was made in the Bristol district in England from 1788 to 1873. The name also applies to glass made by many different factories, not just the

Mustache Cup, Morning Glories, White, Shaded Brown Ground, Stick Handle, Victorian, 3⅝ In.
$14

Ruby Lane

Mustache Cup, Yellow & Pink Flowers, Pink To White Ground, Swirl Mold, Prussia, 2½ x 4 In.
$12

Woody Auction

Nailsea, Bell, Light Brown, White Rim, Clear Handle, Red & Blue Twist, No Ringer, Victorian, 11½ In.
$108

Turner Auctions + Appraisals

N

TIP

Don't talk or use social media, especially Facebook, to tell when you are going on vacation.

Nailsea, Decanter, White Loops, Pear Shape, Footed, Applied Beads, Victorian, 17 In.

$120

Turner Auctions + Appraisals

Nakara, Dresser Box, Lid, Pink & Purple Flowers, Gilt Collar, Marked, 3 ½ x 5 ½ In.

$96

Nadeau's Auction Gallery

Nakara, Jewelry Box, Hinged Lid, Orange, Pink Flowers, White Beads, Bishop's Hat Mold, 3 ¾ x 4 In.

$180

Woody Auction

Nailsea Glass House. Many pieces were made with loopings of either white or colored glass as decoration.

Bell, Amber, Pale Yellow Handle With Stepped End, Victorian, 12 ½ In.	96
Bell, Aqua, Purple Rim & Applied Rosettes, Clear Handle, No Ringer, Victorian, 13 ½ In.	120
Bell, Cranberry, Clear Handle, Cobalt Blue Beads, Victorian, 11 In.	96
Bell, Light Brown, White Rim, Clear Handle, Red & Blue Twist, No Ringer, Victorian, 11 ½ In. ...*illus*	108
Bell, Multicolor Spatter, Clear Handle, No Ringer, Victorian, 11 In.	96
Bell, Purple, Clear Rim, Clear Handle With Purple Ribbon Twist, No Ringer, Victorian, 14 In.	120
Decanter, White Loops, Pear Shape, Footed, Applied Beads, Victorian, 17 In. ...*illus*	120
Fairy Lamp, Cranberry, White Loopings, Ruffled Rim, Clear Insert, Late 1800s, 6 ¾ In., Pair...	819

NAKARA

NAKARA Nakara is a trade name for a white glassware made about 1900 by the C. F. Monroe Company of Meriden, Connecticut. It was decorated in pastel colors. The glass was very similar to another glass, called Wave Crest, made by the company. The company closed in 1916. Boxes for use on a dressing table are the most commonly found Nakara pieces. The mark is not found on every piece.

Biscuit Jar, Maroon & Cream Tones, Pink Flowers, Metal Lid & Base, 7 x 6 In.	100
Bonbon, Green, Pink, White Scallops, Pink Flowers, Gilt Collar, Bail Handle, Marked, 2 x 6 In.	84
Dresser Box, Hinged Lid, Courting Couple, Blue, Pink Flowers, Beaded, Gilt, c.1900, 4 x 6 In. .	179
Dresser Box, Lid, Pink & Purple Flowers, Gilt Collar, Marked, 3 ½ x 5 ½ In. ...*illus*	96
Ferner, Cream To Green, Pansies, Molded Borders, Gilt Collar & Stand, Stamped Mark, 6 ¼ x 7 In.	108
Humidor, Hinged Lid, Shaded Blue Ground, Pink Gladiola, Cigars In Gilt, Stamped, 5 ½ x 4 In.	714
Jewelry Box, Hinged Lid, Blue To Cream, 2 Pink Flowers, Round, Gilt Collar, 2 ½ x 4 ½ In.	210
Jewelry Box, Hinged Lid, Orange, Pink Flowers, White Beads, Bishop's Hat Mold, 3 ¾ x 4 In. *illus*	180
Jewelry Box, Hinged Lid, Orange, Yellow, White Beads, 6-Sided, Gilt Collar & Base, 3 ¾ In.	150
Match Holder, Gilt Rim & Handles, Rust & Pink, White Enamel Beaded, 1 ¾ x 3 ¼ In.	100
Toothpick Holder, Green & Pinks, Flowers, Gilt Metal Handles, 2 x 2 In. ...*illus*	175
Vase, Cream To Blue, Yellow Roses, Beaded Lip, Gilt Base, 4-Footed, Stamped, c.1900, 17 ¼ In...	952
Vase, Green, Pink & White Flowers, Scrolled Gilt Fittings, 4-Footed, c.1900, 17 ¼ x 10 ½ In.	1547

NANKING

Nanking is a type of blue-and-white porcelain made in China from the late 1700s to the early 1900s. It was shipped from the port of Nanking. It is similar to Canton wares (listed here in the Canton category). The blue design was almost the same: a landscape, building, trees, and a bridge. But a person was often on the bridge on a Nanking piece. The "spear and post" border was used, sometimes with gold added.

Basket, Chestnut, 2 Handles, Blue & White, Landscape, c.1770, 4 x 6 In.	1464
Basket, Chestnut, Reticulated, Flared Rim, Square Handles, Leafy Terminals, c.1770, 4 x 7 In.	1524
Bowl, Houses On Shore, Boat In Water, Blue Scalloped Rim, Shallow, Mid 1800s, 7 In., Pair	88
Pitcher, Cider, Blue & White, Foo Dog Finial, Twisted Handle, Late 1700s, 10 x 7 x 5 In. *illus*	3050
Platter, Meat, Oval, Person On Bridge, Well & Tree, c.1800, 11 ⅛ x 14 ½ In.	512
Platter, Meat, Oval, Riverscape, Pavilions, Scalloped Rim, c.1770, 10 ½ x 13 ½ In., Pair	2540
Platter, Octagonal, Person On Bridge, Diaper & Flower Band, Flowers, Late 1700s, 11 x 14 In. .	512
Platter, Oval, Riverscape, Pavilions, Person On Bridge, Dot & Dagger, Late 1700s, 16 x 19 In. ...*illus*	635
Tea Bowl & Saucer, Pagoda In Landscape, Nanking Cargo, c.1752, 1 ⅝ x 4 ⅝ In., Pair	320
Trinket Box, Bamboo Design, Marked Bottom, 2 ½ x 3 ½ In.	160
Tureen, Lid, Oval, Blue & White, River Landscape, Spearhead Borders, c.1820, 5 x 12 x 9 In...	244
Tureen, Shaped Rim, Inverted Handles, Person On Bridge, Round Foot, 5 x 12 x 7 In.	113

NAPKIN RING

Napkin rings were in fashion from 1869 to about 1900. They were made of silver, porcelain, wood, and other materials. They are still being made

N

today. Collectors pay the highest prices for the silver plated figural examples. Small, realistic figures were made to hold the ring. Good and poor reproductions of the more expensive rings have been made since the 1950s and collectors must be very careful.

Bakelite, Penguin, Butterscotch, Brown Beak, Painted Eyes, Rectangular Base, 2¾ x 2⅛ In.		50
Figural, Bronze, Dog, Pug, Next To Ring, Marked, Franz Bermann, 1½ In..........................		125
Figural, Silver Plate, Cat & Dog On Ring, Round Base, Meriden, Late 1800s, 3½ In.		345
Glass, Medusa Head, Frosted, Marked Rosenthal, Versace, 2 x 2¼ x 1¾ In. ....*illus*		94

NATZLER

G + O
NATZLER

Natzler pottery was made by Gertrud Amon and Otto Natzler. They were born in Vienna, met in 1933, and established a studio in 1935. Gertrud threw thin-walled, simple, classical shapes on the wheel, while Otto developed glazes. A few months after Hitler's regime occupied Austria in 1938, they married and fled to the United States. The Natzlers set up a workshop in Los Angeles. After Gertrud's death in 1971, Otto continued creating pieces decorated with his distinctive glazes. Otto died in 2007.

Bowl, Blue & White Crystalline Interior, Brown Exterior, Short Pedestal, 2½ x 3¾ In. *illus*	875
Bowl, Crater Glaze, White & Brown, Footed, Terra-Cotta, 1965, 2¾ x 5 In. ....*illus*	3825
Bowl, Flaring, Cat's-Eye Reduction Glaze, Ash Deposits, Fire Marks, Fissures, 1967, 3 x 6 In.	4750
Bowl, Textured, Thick Walls, Steel Blue Matte Glaze, Signed, 1962, 3¼ x 3½ In.	3500
Dish, Rolled Rim, Dark To Light Red, Marked, 7 In. ....*illus*	2080
Vase, Black Glaze, Cylindrical, Asymmetrical Rim, Short Foot, 1985, 7¼ x 2¾ In..............	896
Vase, Bottle, Squat, Flange Rim, Mottled Brown, Gray Green & Sang Nocturne, 1974, 3 x 4 In...	3500
Vase, Lens Shape Body, Cylindrical Neck & Pedestal, Mottled Green, 1984, 15 x 10½ In.......	2600
Vase, Tapered, Green & Blue Mariposa Reduction Glaze, Melt Fissures, 1963, 12¾ x 6 In.	11875
Wind Chime, Narrow Cone, Textured, Terra-Cotta, Slip Signed, c.1965, 13½ x 5 In.	3250

NAUTICAL

Nautical antiques are listed in this category. Any of the many objects that were made or used by the seafaring trade, including ship parts, models, and tools, are included. Other pieces may be found listed under Scrimshaw.

Anchor, Grappling Hook, Retractable Prongs, Brass, 14½ In.........................*illus*	330
Becket, Carved, Chamfered Block, Stars, Macrame & Leather Rings, c.1850, 8 x 2 In., Pair .... *illus*	1830
Binnacle, Brass, Lifeboat Compass, Gimbaled Liquid, Oil Burner, Circular Base, 10 x 10 In.	854
Binnacle, Copper, U.S Navy, Corsair Compass, Lionel Corp., N.Y., 1940s, 10 x 9 x 7½ In......	125
Boots, Diving, U.S. Navy, Mark 12, No. 2, Rubber, Servus, 1980s, Size 10.....................*illus*	660
Box, Library, Sailor's, Pine, 6-Board, Stenciled Door, Shelf, c.1890, 20 x 14 In......................	313
Chest, Painted, Carved, Dovetailed, Becket Handles, New England, Early 1800s, 16 x 35 x 15 In....	3125
Chest, Pine, Hinged Lid, Green Paint, Whale, Rope Handle, 1800s, 16 x 40 x 17 In.	878
Chest, Sea, 6-Plank Pumpkin Pine, Dovetailed, Iron Strap Hinges, 1800s, 16 x 37 x 16 In.........	819
Chest, Sea, Dovetailed Case, Green Paint, Shaped Base Moldings, c.1840, 15 x 40 x 16 In. ...	305
Chest, Sea, Hinged Lid, Blue Green Paint, Dovetailed, 1800s, 16 x 44 In..............................	1063
Chest, Sea, Pine, Blue Paint, Rope Beckets, Iron Lid Lift, 1800s, 18½ x 40¾ x 21½ In.	585
Chest, Sea, Pine, Footboard, William Lysander Conrad, Nova Scotia, c.1910, 15 x 35 x 17 In. *illus*	1521
Chronometer, Brass, Mahogany Box, Silver Dial, Signed, B.F. & T.M. Davis, 1800s, 7 x 6 x 6 In.	4484
Chronometer, Deck, 2-Day, Silver Matte, Arabic Dial, Hamilton, Model 22, Lancaster, 2 In.	1188
Chronometer, Elgin, 2-Day, Silver, Model 600, 3-Tier Mahogany Box, 7½ In........................	5000
Chronometer, Elgin, Gimbaled, Display Table, Mahogany, 4 Glass Panels, Parts, 34 x 34 x 16 In. .	1063
Chronometer, Gimbal, Brass Mounted, Silvered Dial, Mahogany Box, Thomas Mercer, 6 x 7 x 7 In...	840
Chronometer, Marine, 2-Day, Mahogany, Brass, Frodsham & Son, London, c.1870, 7 x 6 In.	2125
Chronometer, Marine, Rosewood Case, Gimbaled, Hewitt & Son, London, Mid 1800s, 6½ x 6¾ In...	1638
Chronometer, Vertical, Burl Walnut Case, Thomas Mercer, 11½ x 10 x 5 In. ....*illus*	4688
Clock, Chelsea, Ship's Bell, Mahogany, Gilt, Brass, 1900s, 13 x 20 x 5 In. ....*illus*	1375
Clock, Chelsea, Ship's Bell, Mariner Yacht Wheel, Brass, Mahogany Base, 10 x 8 x 4 In........	1112
Clock, Ship's Bell, Seth Thomas, Corsair, Brass, Silvered Dial, Glass Bezel, Marked, 3 x 6 In. ..*illus*	351
Clock, Ship's Bell, Brass, Mahogany Stand, Chelsea, 5½ In.......................................	1063

Nakara, Toothpick Holder, Green & Pinks, Flowers, Gilt Metal Handles, 2 x 2 In.
$175

Woody Auction

> **TIP**
> *Cups are best stored by hanging them on cup hooks. Stacking cups inside each other can cause chipping.*

Nanking, Pitcher, Cider, Blue & White, Foo Dog Finial, Twisted Handle, Late 1700s, 10 x 7 x 5 In.
$3,050

Rafael Osona Nantucket Auctions

Nanking, Platter, Oval, Riverscape, Pavilions, Person On Bridge, Dot & Dagger, Late 1700s, 16 x 19 In.
$635

Rafael Osona Nantucket Auctions

Napkin Ring, Glass, Medusa Head, Frosted, Marked Rosenthal, Versace, 2 x 2 ¼ x 1 ¾ In.
$94

Auctions at Showplace, NYC

Natzler, Bowl, Blue & White Crystalline Interior, Brown Exterior, Short Pedestal, 2 ½ x 3 ¾ In.
$875

Ripley Auctions

Natzler, Bowl, Crater Glaze, White & Brown, Footed, Terra-Cotta, 1965, 2 ¾ x 5 In.
$3,825

Bonhams

Natzler, Dish, Rolled Rim, Dark To Light Red, Marked, 7 In.
$2,080

Treadway

Clock, Ship's Bell, Chelsea, Bronze, Yacht Wheel, Wood Base, Waves, 11 x 13 x 3 In...... *illus*	660
Clock, Ship's Bell, Chelsea, Yacht Wheel, 6 x 17 In.	1495
Clock, Ship's, Brass, Smith's Astral, England, Early 1900s, 10 In.	150
Clock, Ship's, Second, Minute, Hour Hands, Metal Dial, Brass, Ashcroft Mfg. Co., 10 ¾ x 4 In.	472
Compass, Case, Top Handle, Attached Lantern, U.S. Navy, Lionel, 10 x 7 x 7 ½ In.	244
Compass, Fitted Wood Box, North Marker, Fleur-De-Lis, Oval Ink Stamp, England, 1900s, 6 x 10 In.	210
Compass, Floating, Illuminated, Negus, N.Y., 12 In. *illus*	154
Diorama, Clipper Ship, Sobraon, Carved, Painted, Glazed Oak Case, Late 1800s, 11 x 16 x 8 In. . *illus*	1464
Diorama, Ship, Off Shore, Painted Sea, Carved Sails & Hull, Late 1800s, 21 x 28 x 4 In.	1500
Figurehead, Ship's, Viking, Carved, Painted, Giltwood, Late 1900s, 17 x 11 x 21 In. ..... *illus*	380
Fog Horn, Lothrop's, Painted, Marked, Early 1900s Patent, 11 ½ x 8 ½ In.	563
Half-Model, Caroline Nesmith, Wood, 1800s, 19 ¾ x 85 x 8 In.	1500
Half-Model, Cat Boat, Sea Bisquet, Multi Wood, 24 x 7 In.	275
Half-Model, Coast Guard Cutter, CR96-99, Plating, Gibbs & Cox, 1942, 14 x 70 In.	1170
Half-Model, Sailboat, SS Fantasia J.F.K., Wood Plaque, 2007, 9 ¼ x 24 ½ In.	36
Half-Model, Sailing Sloop, Mahogany Backboard, Bowknot, Late 1800s, 13 x 35 x 5 In.	1170
Half-Model, SS Nigel, Mahogany & Glass Case, Wood Stand, 1910s, 19 x 12 x 81 In.	7560
Harpoon, Sperm Whale, Toggle, Carved, Rope Border, Wrapped Board, 22 x 47 In. .... *illus*	92
Helm, Brass, Faintly Marked, 8-Spoke Wheel, 1910s, 51 x 42 In. .... *illus*	2250
Helmet, Diving, U.S. Navy, Mark 12, Yellow Fiberglass, Breech Ring, Rockland, Mass., 1983... *illus*	6300
Helmet, Diving, U.S. Navy, Mark V, 1943 .... *illus*	21600
Lantern, Mast, Copper, Pale Green Glass, Rod Cage, Loop Handle, Electric, 1800s, 22 x 10 In., Pair..	527
Lantern, Mast, Oil, Copper, Fresnel Lens, Red Paint, Seahorse, Great Britain, 18 x 10 ¾ In.	497
Light, Masthead, Brass, Copper, Marked, Meteorite, Fresnel Lens, Early 1900s, 25 x 12 In....	688
Model, Albatross, Painted, Wood & Glass Case, 1900s, 32 x 45 x 15 In. .... *illus*	938
Model, Barque, Domed Glass, Molded Wood Base, Signed, Jim Plante, c.2006, 4 x 5 In.........	610
Model, Cargo Ship, Excalibur, Glass, Brass & Wood Case, 18 x 40 In. .... *illus*	575
Model, Clipper Ship, Rigged, Painted, Wood Cradle, 1960, 25 x 10 In.	594
Model, Cutty Sark, Mosaic Style, Painted, Plexiglas & Wood Case, Marked, Robert V. Reid, 30 x 40 In.	228
Model, Pond Boat, Hollow, Weighted Hull, Painted, Wood Cradle, Early 1900s, 39 In............	219
Model, Racing Yacht, Mahogany Deck, Coppered Hull, Full Sails, 1800s, 41 x 49 x 8 In. *illus*	1638
Model, Sailboat, Radio Controlled, Multicolor, Victoria, 48 In.	86
Model, Sailboat, Silver, Mounted On Fabric Stand, Chinese, 1800s, 6 In.	125
Model, Sailing Ship, Carved & Rigged, Mounted, Cast Metal, Red & Black Paint, 31 x 42 x 7 In.	75
Model, Sailing Ship, Smuggler, Glass Case, 33 ½ x 40 x 11 In.	1625
Model, Schooner, Sailor Made, 2-Masted, Wood Spar, Painted, Early 1900s, 31 x 32 In.	375
Model, Schooner, Yacht Atlantic, 1903, Planked Deck, 3-Masted, Rigging, Cloth Sails, 32 x 37 In..	185
Model, Ship, HMS Victory, 108 Guns, White Sails, Flat Base, 1805, 32 x 37 In.	330
Model, Ship, Queen Hatshepsut, Full Sail, Paddles, Glass Case, 64 ¾ x 28 x 18 In.	313
Model, Ship, Square Rigger, Painted, Brass Details, Wood Base, 1800s, 23 x 30 x 4 In.	349
Model, Steamship, New Haven Line, Richard Peck, Wood Base, V. Niedermertl, 18 ¾ x 41 x 9 In. *illus*	216
Model, Whaling Ship, Charles W. Morgan, 3-Masted, Rowboats, Glass Case, 23 x 28 x 12 In..	1521
Model, Whaling Ship, Whalebone, Wood Hull, Oval Base, 1800s, 14 In.	8750
Paddle, Canoe, Wood, Treasure Island, Camping Trip, Port Jervis, 1963, 59 In. .... *illus*	124
Plaque, Wessex-Bristol, Half-Hull, Hanging, Black Ground, 1861, 20 In.	94
Quarterboard, Nantucket, Hand Carved, Wood, Painted, Yellow & Blue, 44 x 5 In.	275
Sailor's Valentine, 2-Sided, Hinged, Octagonal, Center Tintype, Man, Woman, 1800s, 9 x 18 In.	1680
Sailor's Valentine, Bouquet Of Flowers, Shells, Multicolor, 9 x 9 In.	1525
Sailor's Valentine, Box, Hinged Lid, Barber Pole Trim, c.1880, 3 x 13 x 9 In.	3660
Sailor's Valentine, Double, Shells, Present From Barbados, Octagonal, Wood, 1800s, 2 x 9 x 8 In.	2457
Sailor's Valentine, Double, Shells, Rose, Hinged, Octagonal, Wood Case, 1800s, 9 In. *illus*	3965
Sailor's Valentine, Geometric Design, Shells, Multicolor, Octagonal, Wood Case, 15 x 15 In.	688
Sailor's Valentine, Heart Center, Shell Rosettes, Octagonal, Wood, 12 In.	1708
Sailor's Valentine, Spring, Heart, Multicolor Shells, Octagonal, Sandy Moran, 1944, 7 ½ In.	1625
Sextant, Box, Hinged Lid, Brass & Wood, Ross, London, 3 x 5 x 6 In. .... *illus*	192
Sextant, Case, Retailed By Husan, Henry Hughes & Son, London, 1900s, 5 ¼ x 11 x 10 In...	250
Sextant, Royal Navy, Brass, Fitted Case, Henry Hughes & Son., London, 5 ½ x 11 x 9 ¾ In. .	288
Shell, Carved Conch, Cameo, Classical Scene, Cybele, Chariot, Lions, 5 ½ x 4 ¼ x 4 In.	188
Ship Model, see Nautical, Model.	
Ship's Wheel, 8 Spokes, Brass & Mahogany, John Hastie & Co., Scotland, 1800s, 36 In........	793

N

Nautical, Anchor, Grappling Hook, Retractable Prongs, Brass, 14 ½ In.
$330

Nation's Attic

Nautical, Becket, Carved, Chamfered Block, Stars, Macrame & Leather Rings, c.1850, 8 x 2 In., Pair
$1,830

Rafael Osona Nantucket Auctions

Nautical, Boots, Diving, U.S. Navy, Mark 12, No. 2, Rubber, Servus, 1980s, Size 10
$660

Nation's Attic

Nautical, Chest, Sea, Pine, Footboard, William Lysander Conrad, Nova Scotia, c.1910, 15 x 35 x 17 In.
$1,521

Thomaston Place Auction Galleries

Nautical, Chronometer, Vertical, Burl Walnut Case, Thomas Mercer, 11 ½ x 10 x 5 In.
$4,688

Wiederseim Auctions

Nautical, Clock, Chelsea, Ship's Bell, Mahogany, Gilt, Brass, 1900s, 13 x 20 x 5 In.
$1,375

Hindman

TIP
If you discover a cache of very dirty antiques and you are not dressed in work clothes, make yourself a temporary cover-up from a plastic garbage bag.

Nautical, Clock, Ship's Bell, Seth Thomas, Corsair, Brass, Silvered Dial, Glass Bezel, Marked, 3 x 6 In.
$351

Thomaston Place Auction Galleries

Nautical, Clock, Ship's Bell, Chelsea, Bronze, Yacht Wheel, Wood Base, Waves, 11 x 13 x 3 In.
$660

Abington Auction Gallery

N

Nautical, Compass, Floating, Illuminated, Negus, N.Y., 12 In.
$154

Rachel Davis Fine Arts

TIP
Check stored items once a year to be sure there is no deterioration or bugs.

Nautical, Diorama, Clipper Ship, Sobraon, Carved, Painted, Glazed Oak Case, Late 1800s, 11 x 16 x 8 In.
$1,464

Rafael Osona Nantucket Auctions

TIP
Never leave a note outside explaining that you are not at home.

Nautical, Figurehead, Ship's, Viking, Carved, Painted, Giltwood, Late 1900s, 17 x 11 x 21 In.
$380

Thomaston Place Auction Galleries

Nautical, Harpoon, Sperm Whale, Toggle, Carved, Rope Border, Wrapped Board, 22 x 47 In.
$92

Rafael Osona Nantucket Auctions

Nautical, Helm, Brass, Faintly Marked, 8-Spoke Wheel, 1910s, 51 x 42 In.
$2,250

Eldred's

Nautical, Helmet, Diving, U.S. Navy, Mark 12, Yellow Fiberglass, Breech Ring, Rockland, Mass., 1983
$6,300

Nation's Attic

Nautical, Helmet, Diving, U.S. Navy, Mark V, 1943
$21,600

Nation's Attic

Nautical, Model, Albatross, Painted, Wood & Glass Case, 1900s, 32 x 45 x 15 In.
$938

Hindman

Nautical, Model, Cargo Ship, Excalibur, Glass, Brass & Wood Case, 18 x 40 In.
$575

Ron Rhoads Auctioneers

Nautical, Model, Racing Yacht, Mahogany Deck, Coppered Hull, Full Sails, 1800s, 41 x 49 x 8 In.
$1,638

Thomaston Place Auction Galleries

Nautical, Model, Steamship, New Haven Line, Richard Peck, Wood Base, V. Niedermertl, 18¾ x 41 x 9 In.
$216

Michaan's Auctions

Nautical, Paddle, Canoe, Wood, Treasure Island, Camping Trip, Port Jervis, 1963, 59 In.
$124

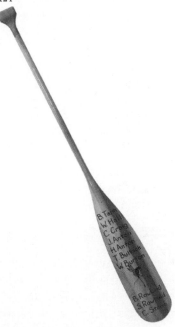

Hartzell's Auction Gallery Inc.

Nautical, Sailor's Valentine, Double, Shells, Rose, Hinged, Octagonal, Wood Case, 1800s, 9 In.
$3,965

CRN Auctions

Nautical, Sextant, Box, Hinged Lid, Brass & Wood, Ross, London, 3 x 5 x 6 In.
$192

Alderfer Auction Company

Nautical, Ship's Wheel, 8 Turned Spokes, Mahogany, Brass Rim & Hub, 31¾ In.
$878

Thomaston Place Auction Galleries

Nautical, Signal Cannon, Naval, Oak Base & Carriage, Cutaway Deck, Brass, 1779, 7 x 17 x 8 In.
$5,558

Thomaston Place Auction Galleries

Nautical, Suit, Diving, U.S. Navy, Mark 12, Blue, Yellow Stripes, No. 3, Breech Ring, Harness, Weights
$1,140

Nation's Attic

Nautical, Telegraph, Ship's, Brass, Marked, Staten Island, N.Y., Late 1800s, 47½ In.
$2,500

Eldred's

Nautical, Trunk, Sea Captain's, Pine, Hinged Lid, R. Foster, 1815, 16 x 35 x 15 In.
$1,872

Thomaston Place Auction Galleries

Netsuke, Inro, Black Lacquer, Gold Scene, Kyoyu & Sofu, Ox, 4-Case, Signed, Kahei, 1700s, 3¼ In.
$978

Bonhams

Netsuke, Inro, Gold Lacquer, Naval Scene, 4 Compartments, Signed, Shojosai Roshu Saku, 1900s, 4 In.
$8,006

Bonhams

Netsuke, Inro, Red & Black Lacquer, Peony, Vase On Reverse, 2-Case, Signed, Yoyusai, 1800s, 2 In.
$1,779

Bonhams

Ship's Wheel, 8 Spokes, Mahogany Handle, Brass Hub, 29 In.		610
Ship's Wheel, 8 Turned Spokes, Mahogany, Brass Rim & Hub, 31¾ In. .... *illus*		878
Ship's Wheel, 12 Spokes, Walnut, Brass Hub, 1900s, 78 In.		563
Ship's Wheel, Carved, Turned Wood, Steel, 38 In.		188
Sign, Texaco Marine Lubricants, Boats, Sea Gulls, Logos, Enameled Metal, 1950s, 15 x 30 In.		1020
Signal Cannon, Naval, Oak Base & Carriage, Cutaway Deck, Brass, 1779, 7 x 17 x 8 In.*illus*		5558
Spyglass, Nickel Plated, Woven Black Leather, Turk's Head Macrame, c.1850, 1 x 17 x 23 In.		439
Suit, Diving, U.S. Navy, Mark 12, Blue, Yellow Stripes, No. 3, Breech Ring, Harness, Weights *illus*		1140
Telegraph, Engine Room, Iron, 3 Knobs, Battleship Gray Paint, Red Glass, 1930, 55 x 16 x 15 In.		1755
Telegraph, Ship's, Brass, Marked, Staten Island, N.Y., Late 1800s, 47½ In. .... *illus*		2500
Telegraph, Wheel, Brass, 5 Sections, Jos. Harper & Son Co., New York, 25 x 9½ x 6½ In.		469
Telescope, Sighting, Brass, Power 7, No. 269, W. Ottaway & Co., 24 In.		180
Timer, Glass, White Sand, Wood, 4 Turned Columns, Mid 1900s, 24¾ In.		202
Trophy, Bronze, America's Cup Yacht, Columbia, Gold Tournament, Duxbury, 1902, 3½ In.		219
Trunk, Sea Captain's, Pine, Hinged Lid, R. Foster, 1815, 16 x 35 x 15 In. .... *illus*		1872
Wall Pocket, Ship, Half-Model, Sailor Made, Carved, Wood, Flowers & Vines, 1800s, 10 x 18 In.		549
Yacht Light, Interior, Cast Nickel, Glass Dome Lenses, Electrified, 3½ x 4¼ In., Pair		344

NETSUKE

Netsukes are small ivory, wood, metal, or porcelain pieces used as toggles on the end of the cord that held a Japanese money pouch or inro. The earliest date from the sixteenth century. Many are miniature carved works of art. This category also includes the ojime, the slide or string fastener that was used on the inro cord. There are legal restrictions on the sale of ivory. Check the laws in your state.

Inro, Black Lacquer, Gold Scene, Kyoyu & Sofu, Ox, 4-Case, Signed, Kahei, 1700s, 3¼ In. .. *illus*	978
Inro, Black Lacquer, Inlaid Cherry Tree, Gold, Pewter, Shell, 5-Case, Toju, c.1800, 3¾ In.	3914
Inro, Black Lacquer, Pewter & Shell Cranes, 5-Case, Kajikawa Shoshin, 1800s, 3¼ In.	978
Inro, Black Lacquer, Pigeon Scene, Silver, Brown, 3-Case, Signed, Koma Yasutada, 1800s, 3 In.	6227
Inro, Black Lacquer, Sheath, Erotic Scene, 3-Case, Kanshosai Toyo, 1800s, 2⅜ In.	29494
Inro, Gold Lacquer, Buddhist Acolyte, Foo Dog, Red Interior, Signed, Toyo, c.1779, 3½ In.	3202
Inro, Gold Lacquer, Naval Scene, 4 Compartments, Signed, Shojosai Roshu Saku, 1900s, 4 In. ... *illus*	8006
Inro, Lacquer, Panels, Chinese Zodiac Symbols, Wood Ojime, Japan, 1800s, 3 x 2½ In.	840
Inro, Rattan, Black Lacquer Over Gold, Shell Inlay, 2-Case, Signed, Urin, 1700s, 3⅝ In.	622
Inro, Red & Black Lacquer, Peony, Vase On Reverse, 2-Case, Signed, Yoyusai, 1800s, 2 In. ..*illus*	1779
Inro, Wood, Bamboo Inlay, Gold Crab & Rock, 5 Drawers, 1800s, 3⅜ In.	1957
Inro, Wood, Pouch Form, Rectangular Plaque, 3 Interior Drawers, Late 1900s, 4½ In.	563
Ivory, Samurai, Dynamic Figure, Carved, Full Dress, Oval Base, 2¾ In. .... *illus*	180
Ivory, Spotted Cat, Brocade Ball, Inlaid Horn Eyes, 1800s, 1½ In.	438
Lacquer, Lion Dancer, Red Hair, Gold Mask, Black & Gold Costume, 1800s, 1½ In. .... *illus*	469
Shakudo, Shishi Mask, Foo Dog, Cloud, Wood, Gilt Metal, Manju, 1800s, 1 In.	313
Staghorn, Seated Monkey, Double Gourd Bottle, Signed, 1800s, 1½ In. .... *illus*	4375
Wood, Carved, Animal, Frog Body, Turtle Shell, Monkey Face, 1 x 2 x 1 In.	31

New Hall ## NEW HALL

New Hall Porcelain Works was in business in Shelton, Hanley, Staffordshire, England, from 1781 to 1835. Simple decorated wares were made. Between 1810 and 1825, the factory made a glassy bone porcelain sometimes marked with the factory name. Do not confuse New Hall porcelain with the pieces made by the New Hall Pottery Company, Ltd., a twentieth-century firm working from 1899 to 1956 at the New Hall Works.

Bowl, Boy In Window, Multicolor, Chinoiserie, Blue & Red Inner Rim, 1800s, 6 In. ...... *illus*	88
Coffee Can, Vine Leaves, Gilt Rim & Base, Curved Handle, No. 558, 1800, 2 x 2½ In.	110
Cream Jug, Pink Flowers & Ribbon, No. 186, Curved Handle, Wide Spout, c.1795, 5 x 3 x 5 In.	122
Teapot, Lid, Floral, Basket, Red Trim, Curved Handle, Wavy Base, 1790, 6¼ x 9¾ In.	150
Teapot, Lid, Flower Sprigs, Pink Trim, Hand Painted, Straight Sides, Lobed, 1780-1815, 5 x 6 In.	38

N

NEWCOMB POTTERY

Newcomb Pottery was founded at Sophie Newcomb College, New Orleans, Louisiana, in 1895. The work continued through the 1940s. Pieces of this art pottery are marked with the printed letters *NC* and often have the incised initials of the artist and potter as well. A date letter code was printed on pieces made from 1901 to 1941. Most pieces have a matte glaze and incised decoration. From 1942 to 1952 the Newcomb mark was revived and put on pieces of pottery from the college. New names were used.

Bowl, Jonquil, Blue & Green Matte Underglaze, Anna Frances Simpson, 1923, 4 In. 640
Bowl, Purple Matte Glaze, Thin Band Of Flowers, Earthenware, 1926, 3 1/2 x 8 3/4 In. ...*illus* 1250
Chamberstick, Ring Handles, Let's To Bed, 3 Children, Sadie Irvine, 1903, 6 7/8 x 5 In. *illus* 3770
Tile, Commemorative, Episcopal Triennial, The Church, Crusader, Cross, L.N., 1925, 3 3/4 x 3 5/8 In.... 422
Tyg, Copper, Iridescent Glaze, Flowers, Katherine Louise Wood, 1901, 5 5/8 In. .... *illus* 4480
Vase, Blue & Green, Flowers, Signed, Anna Frances Simpson, c.1914, 3 x 6 In. 1100
Vase, Blue, White, Crackle Ground, Marked, Emilie Leblanc, 3 x 3 1/4 In. ....*illus* 8750
Vase, Carved, Matte, Blue & Green Underglaze, Anna Frances Simpson, 1929, 5 In. ......*illus* 1920
Vase, Earthenware, Matte Glaze, Carved, Anna Frances Simpson, Louisiana, 1930, 5 3/4 x 4 1/8 In. . 4225
Vase, Flowers, Blue Ground, Sadie Irvine, 1922, 5 x 4 3/4 In.................................... 1722
Vase, Iris, White, Green Leaves, High Glaze, Marie De Hoa Leblanc, 1903, 6 1/2 x 4 In. ..*illus* 10625
Vase, Scenic, Glazed Earthenware, Blue, Incised Emu Underside, 1900s, 3 1/2 In.................... 1664
Vase, Star Jasmine, Relief Carved, Blue & Green Matte, Anna Frances Simpson, 1922, 3 5/8 In. 640

NILOAK POTTERY

Niloak Pottery (*Kaolin* spelled backward) was made at the Hyten Brothers Pottery in Benton, Arkansas, between 1910 and 1947. Although the factory did make cast and molded wares, collectors are most interested in the marbleized art pottery line made of colored swirls of clay. It was called Mission Ware. By 1931 the company made castware, and many of these pieces were marked with the name *Hywood*.

NILOAK	NILOAK POTTERY	NILOAK
Niloak 1910	Niloak c.1910–1920s	Niloak 1930s–1947

Figurine, Airplane, Mottled Pink & Blue Green Glaze, c.1940, 1 3/4 x 4 3/4 x 4 In. .... *illus* 63
Pitcher, Marbleized Red, Brown, Cream, Blue Swirl, Paper Label, 5 1/2 In. .... *illus* 358
Vase, Bottle Shape, Marbleized, 6 1/2 x 3 3/4 In.................................*illus* 54
Vase, Marbleized, Ball Shape, Marked, Paper Label, 10 1/2 x 10 1/2 In............................*illus* 840
Vase, Marbleized, Handles, c.1915, 23 1/2 In...*illus* 12,500

NIPPON

Nippon porcelain was made in Japan from 1891 to 1921. *Nippon* is the Japanese word for "Japan." The McKinley Tariff Act of 1891 mandated that goods imported to the United States had to be marked with the country of origin. A few firms continued to use the word *Nippon* on ceramics after 1921 as a part of the company name and not to identify things as made in Japan. More pieces marked *Nippon* will be found in the Dragonware, Moriage, and Noritake categories.

| Nitto 1890–1921 | Nippon 1894–1920 | Morimura/Noritake c.1911–1921 |

Ashtray, Dog, Scenic, Blown Mold, Multicolor, 2 x 5 In.. 90
Jar, Incense, Lid, Egyptian Scene, Moriage Highlights, Internal Lid, Marked, 6 x 3 In. 150

Netsuke, Ivory, Samurai, Dynamic Figure, Carved, Full Dress, Oval Base, 2 3/4 In.
$180

Selkirk Auctioneers & Appraisers

Netsuke, Lacquer, Lion Dancer, Red Hair, Gold Mask, Black & Gold Costume, 1800s, 1 1/2 In.
$469

Eldred's

N

Netsuke, Staghorn, Seated Monkey, Double Gourd Bottle, Signed, 1800s, 1 1/2 In.
$4,375

Eldred's

New Hall, Bowl, Boy In Window, Multicolor, Chinoiserie, Blue & Red Inner Rim, 1800s, 6 In.
$88

Hudson Valley Auctions

Newcomb, Bowl, Purple Matte Glaze, Thin Band Of Flowers, Earthenware, 1926, 3 ½ x 8 ¾ In.
$1,250

Toomey & Co. Auctioneers

Newcomb, Chamberstick, Ring Handles, Let's To Bed, 3 Children, Sadie Irvine, 1903, 6 ⅞ x 5 In.
$3,770

Toomey & Co. Auctioneers

TIP
The surface of Niloak marbleized pottery is porous. Oil from skin, glue from sticky labels, and other types of oil will make marks.

Newcomb, Tyg, Copper, Iridescent Glaze, Flowers, Katherine Louise Wood, 1901, 5 ⅝ In.
$4,480

Neal Auction Company

Newcomb, Vase, Blue, White, Crackle Ground, Marked, Emilie Leblanc, 3 x 3 ¼ In.
$8,750

Treadway

Newcomb, Vase, Carved, Matte, Blue & Green Underglaze, Anna Frances Simpson, 1929, 5 In.
$1,920

Neal Auction Company

Newcomb, Vase, Iris, White, Green Leaves, High Glaze, Marie De Hoa Leblanc, 1903, 6 ½ x 4 In.
$10,625

Toomey & Co. Auctioneers

Niloak, Figurine, Airplane, Mottled Pink & Blue Green Glaze, c.1940, 1 ¾ x 4 ¾ x 4 In.
$63

California Historical Design

Niloak, Pitcher, Marbleized Red, Brown, Cream, Blue Swirl, Paper Label, 5 ½ In.
$358

Treadway

Plate, Portrait, Woman, Green & White Border, Pink, Green, Jewels, Gold Trim, 9¾ In.	200
Vase, Grapevine, Hexagonal, Multicolor, 14 In.	144
Vase, Green Ground, Roses, Gold, White, Medallions, 3 Handles, 8¾ x 6 In.	100
Vase, Yellow Ground, Flowers, Birds, Crowns, 4¾ x 3½ x 3½ In.	108
Whiskey Jug, Painted, Scenic, Pink & Black Border, Gold Stencil, 4-Sided, 7 x 4 In. ...*illus*	175

NODDER

Nodders, also called nodding figures or "pagods," are figures with heads and hands that are attached to wires. Any slight movement causes the parts to move up and down. They were made in many countries during the eighteenth, nineteenth, and twentieth centuries. A few Art Deco designs are also known. Copies have been made. A more recent type of nodder is made of papier-mache or plastic. These often represent sports figures or comic characters. Sports nodders are listed in the Sports category.

Armadillo, Clay, Mexico, 5¼ In.	30
Child, Sitting On Potty Chair, Nightshirt & Cap, Scarf, Bisque, Germany, 4½ In.	144
Girl Duck, Yellow, Bonnet, Scarf, Hollow Textured Plaster, 6½ In.	48
Happy Hooligan, Bobble, Red Hat, Candy Box Base, Prewar, 7¼ In. ....*illus*	60
Hula Girl, Black Hair, Grass Skirt, Leis, Ceramic, Japan, 1950s, 6½ In.	72
Salt & Pepper Shakers are listed in the Salt & Pepper category.	
Santa Claus, Holding Lantern & Tree, Windup, Germany, c.1900, 27½ In. ....*illus*	6875

NORITAKE

Noritake porcelain was made in Japan after 1904 by Nippon Toki Kaisha. A maple leaf mark was used from 1891 to 1911. The best-known Noritake pieces are marked with the *M* in a wreath for the Morimura Brothers, a New York City distributing company. This mark was used primarily from 1911 to 1921 but was last used in the early 1950s. The *N* mark was used from 1940 to the 1960s, and *N Japan* from 1953 to 1964. Noritake made dinner sets with pattern names. Noritake Azalea is listed in the Azalea category in this book.

Bowl, Cereal, Good Times, 5½ In.	8
Bowl, Cereal, Lugged, Century, 6⅝ In.	12
Bowl, Fruit, Adagio, 5½ In.	20
Butter, Cover, Homecoming	35
Butter, Cover, Mardi Gras	21
Casserole, Lid, Blue Haven, 2 Qt.	55
Creamer, Milburn, 3¾ In.	8
Cup & Saucer, Angela	6
Cup & Saucer, Colburn	12
Cup & Saucer, Sunny Side	6
Dish, Soup, Goldston, 7½ In.	7
Dish, Vegetable, Oval, Selby, 10 In.	35
Dish, Vegetable, Split, Harley, 10 In.	21
Figurine, Bird, Crane, Mother & Baby, Bone China, Glossy, c.1970, 6½ In. ....*illus*	175
Gravy Boat, Dutch Treat	28
Gravy Boat, Handle, Pacific	19
Plate, Bread & Butter, Arabesque, 6 In.	7
Plate, Bread & Butter, Bright Side, 6¼ In.	8
Plate, Bread & Butter, Tressa, 6 In.	5
Plate, Dinner, Blue Moon, 10 In.	17
Plate, Dinner, Flower Time, 10½ In.	10
Plate, Dinner, Willowbrook, 10 In.	35
Plate, Salad, Laurel, 8 In.	7
Platter, Berries 'N Such, 13 In.	15
Platter, Desert Flowers, 14 In.	20

Niloak, Vase, Bottle Shape, Marbleized, 6½ x 3¾ In.

$54

Cordier Auctions

Niloak, Vase, Marbleized, Ball Shape, Marked, Paper Label, 10½ x 10½ In.

$840

Soulis Auctions

Niloak, Vase, Marbleized, Handles, c.1915, 23½ In.

$12,500

N

Rago Arts and Auction Center

Nippon, Whiskey Jug, Painted, Scenic, Pink & Black Border, Gold Stencil, 4-Sided, 7 x 4 In.
$175

Woody Auction

Nodder, Happy Hooligan, Bobble, Red Hat, Candy Box Base, Prewar, 7 ¼ In.
$60

Morphy Auctions

Nodder, Santa Claus, Holding Lantern & Tree, Windup, Germany, c.1900, 27 ½ In.
$6,875

Hindman

Noritake, Figurine, Bird, Crane, Mother & Baby, Bone China, Glossy, c.1970, 6 ½ In.
$175

Lion and Unicorn

Norse, Jug, Earthenware, Snake, Stopper, Matte Cold Painted, c.1910, 8 x 5 ½ x 5 In.
$325

Toomey & Co. Auctioneers

North Dakota, Bowl, Earthenware, Praire Rose Decoration, Matte Glaze, M. Cable, c.1935, 2 ⅜ x 6 In.
$422

Toomey & Co. Auctioneers

North Dakota, Candleholder, Earthenware, Carved Leaf Design, M. Dowhower, c.1945, 3 ¾ x 5 In.
$325

Toomey & Co. Auctioneers

North Dakota, Lamp, Earthenware, 3 Parts, Crows, High Glaze, Freida Louise Hammers, c.1929, 10 ¾ x 6 In.
$625

Toomey & Co. Auctioneers

North Dakota, Vase, Earthenware, Spotted Cats Encircling Shoulder, Julia Mattson, c.1943, 2 ½ x 3 In.
$585

Toomey & Co. Auctioneers

NORSE POTTERY

Norse Pottery Company started in Edgerton, Wisconsin, in 1903. In 1904 the company moved to Rockford, Illinois. The company made a black pottery, which resembled early bronze relics of the Scandinavian countries. The firm went out of business in 1913.

Jug, Earthenware, Snake, Stopper, Matte Cold Painted, c.1910, 8 x 5 ½ x 5 In. ....*illus*		325
Vase, Squat, Lindworm Handles, Footed, Cold Painted, 3⅞ x 7 x 6 In.		910

NORTH DAKOTA SCHOOL OF MINES

North Dakota School of Mines was established in 1898 at the University of North Dakota. A ceramics course was established in 1910. Students made pieces from the clays found in the region. Although very early pieces were marked *U.N.D.*, most pieces were stamped with the full name of the university. After 1963 pieces were only marked with students' names.

U.N.D.

North Dakota School of Mines
1910–1963

North Dakota School of Mines
c.1913–1963

Bowl, Earthenware, Praire Rose Decoration, Matte Glaze, M. Cable, c.1935, 2⅜ x 6 In. *illus*		422
Candleholder, Earthenware, Carved Leaf Design, M. Dowhower, c.1945, 3¾ x 5 In. ....*illus*		325
Lamp, Earthenware, 3 Parts, Crows, High Glaze, Freida Louise Hammers, c.1929, 10¾ x 6 In. ...*illus*		625
Pitcher, Lid, Wisteria, Gray Shaded To Pink, Hildegarde Fried, c.1920, 14 x 7¾ x 4 In.........		325
Vase, Cream Glaze, Carved Wavy Lines, Greenish Interior, 1954, 2 x 3 ½ In.		406
Vase, Earthenware, Carved Swans, High Glaze, Julia Mattson, c.1937, 3 x 4 In......................		593
Vase, Earthenware, Spotted Cats Encircling Shoulder, Julia Mattson, c.1943, 2½ x 3 In. ...*illus*		585
Vase, Lamp, Incised Butterflies, Green Matte, Dorothy Sullivan Olson, c.1950, 6⅞ x 4 In. ...		375
Vase, Prairie Dog, Margaret Cable, c.1930s, 5¼ x 3¼ In..		1230

NORTHWOOD

Northwood glass was made by one of the glassmaking companies operated by Harry C. Northwood. His first company, Northwood Glass Co., was founded in Martins Ferry, Ohio, in 1887 and moved to Ellwood City, Pennsylvania, in 1892. The company closed in 1896. Later that same year, Harry Northwood opened the Northwood Co. in Indiana, Pennsylvania. Some pieces made at the Northwood Co. are marked "Northwood" in script. The Northwood Co. became part of a consortium called the National Glass Co. in 1899. Harry left National in 1901 to found the H. Northwood Co. in Wheeling, West Virginia. At the Wheeling factory, Harry Northwood and his brother Carl manufactured pressed and blown tableware and novelties in many colors that are collected today as custard, opalescent, goofus, carnival, and stretch glass. Pieces made between 1905 and about 1915 may have an underlined *N* trademark. Harry Northwood died in 1919, and the plant closed in 1925.

Northwood Glass Co.
1905–c.1915

Northwood Glass Co.
1905–c.1915

Northwood Glass Co.
1905–c.1915

Chrysanthemum Swirl, Pitcher, Cranberry Graniteware, Applied Handle, 9 x 6 In. ..*illus*		350
Chrysanthemum Swirl, Syrup, Lid, Blue, Opal Frit, Applied Handle, c.1890, 6⅞ In.		144
Daisy & Fern, Pickle Castor, Swirl, Blue Opalescent, Silver Plated Stand, c.1894, 14½ In. *illus*		1195

Northwood, Chrysanthemum Swirl, Pitcher, Cranberry Graniteware, Applied Handle, 9 x 6 In.
$350

Woody Auction

Northwood, Daisy & Fern, Pickle Castor, Swirl, Blue Opalescent, Silver Plated Stand, c.1894, 14½ In.
$1,195

Jeffrey S. Evans & Associates

N

Northwood, Spanish Lace, Biscuit Jar, Opaline Brocade, Vaseline, Silver Plated Collar, 1899, 10 In.

$419

Jeffrey S. Evans & Associates

Nutcracker, Press, Blue Onion, Stirrup, Iron, Porcelain, Meissen, 4 ½ x 6 In.

$113

Hartzell's Auction Gallery Inc.

Nutcracker, Squirrel, Seated, Tail Up, Cast Iron, Wood Base, Humphrey, Worcester, 1878, 7 x 7 In.

$226

Hartzell's Auction Gallery Inc.

Leaf Mold, Sugar Shaker, Cranberry, White Cased Spatter Glass, 3 x 3 In.	150
Leaf Umbrella, Syrup, Lid, Pink, Applied Handle, No. 263, 1889, 6 ¾ In.	239
Spanish Lace, Biscuit Jar, Opaline Brocade, Vaseline, Silver Plated Collar, 1899, 10 In. *illus*	419
Sugar Shaker, Lid, Twist, 9-Panel Mold, 1892, 4 ¾ In.	156

NUTCRACKER

Nutcrackers of many types have been used through the centuries. At first the nutcracker was probably strong teeth or a hammer. But by the nineteenth century, many elaborate and ingenious types were made. Levers, screws, and hammer adaptations were the most popular. Because nutcrackers are still useful, they are still being made, some in the old styles.

Press, Blue Onion, Stirrup, Iron, Porcelain, Meissen, 4 ½ x 6 In. *illus*	113
Squirrel, Seated, Tail Up, Cast Iron, Wood Base, Humphrey, Worcester, 1878, 7 x 7 In. *illus*	226

NYMPHENBURG, *see Royal Nymphenburg.*

OCCUPIED JAPAN

Occupied Japan was printed on pottery, porcelain, toys, and other goods made during the American occupation of Japan after World War II, from 1947 to 1952. Collectors now search for these pieces. The items were made for export. Ceramic items are listed here. Toys are listed in the Toy category in this book.

Casserole, Lid, Scalloped Band Of Flowers, Scroll Handles, Adline China, 10 x 8 In.	45
Figurine, Girl, Basket Of Flowers, Yellow & Red Dress, 5 ½ In.	28
Plate, Fruit, Reticulated Fleur-De-Lis Glaze, 10 In.	14

OFFICE TECHNOLOGY

Office technology includes office equipment and related products, such as adding machines, calculators, and check-writing machines. Typewriters are in their own category in this book.

Adding Machine, Champion, 10 Keys, Prints, Gray Case, Victor, 5 x 12 x 9 In.	19
Adding Machine, Mechanical Accountant, J.A. Turck, Steel, c.1920, 5 ½ x 13 x 5 ½ In.	246
Calculator, 9 Digits, Displays Total, Prints, Black Case, Burroughs, Early 1900s, 13 x 13 x 22 In.	360
Calculator, ANITA Mark VIII, Bell Punch Co., England, 1961, 9 ¼ x 15 x 18 In. *illus*	7463
Calculator, Fuller, Scale Of Sines & Logs, Bakelite, Brass, Wood Case, W.F. Stanley, c.1930	330
Calculator, TI-30, Red LED, Gray Fabric Case, Texas Instruments, 1970s, 3 ½ x 6 ½ In.	31
Calculator, Webb Adder, 2 Number Wheels, Figure 8 Shape, c.1890, 6 ¼ x 4 ⅜ In. *illus*	125
Desk Organizer, 3 Cylinders, Carved Dolphin & Seal, Mahogany, c.1890, 4 x 13 x 8 ½ In.	88
Desk Organizer, Figural, Elephant, Letter Slots, Penholders, Marble, Midcentury, 3 x 5 x 1 In.	18
Desk Organizer, Maple, Steel, 2 Drawers, P. McCobb, Planner Group, Winchendon, 1949, 16 In.	1875
Desk Organizer, Ventotene, Model 3054A, Stainless Steel, Enzo Mari, Danese Milano, 1962.	132
Keyboard, Computer, Apple Design M2980, Cord, Signed By Steve Wozniak, Apple	303
Paper Tray, 2 Tiers, Teak, Sweden, Rainbow Wood Products, Midcentury, 5 x 15 x 10 In.	150
Small Letter Punch Set, Stamps, Display Case, L.G. Smith, 5 x 5 x 5 ½ In.	420
Stapler, Zephyr, 101A, Steel, Nickel Plate, Enamel, R. Heller, Hotchkiss, 1938, 3 ½ x 8 In.	375

OHR

Ohr pottery was made in Biloxi, Mississippi, from 1883 to 1906 by George E. Ohr, a true eccentric. The pottery was made of very thin clay that was twisted, folded, and dented into odd, graceful shapes. Some pieces were lifelike models of hats, animal heads, or even a potato. Others were decorated with folded clay "snakes." Reproductions and reworked pieces are appearing on the market. These have been reglazed, or snakes and other embellishments have been added.

Mechanical Bank, Barrel, Novelty, Earthenware, 3 ⅞ x 3 ½ In.	910

Mechanical Bank, Novelty, Moorish, Bisque, Onion Dome, 3 7/8 x 2 1/2 In.		585
Pot, Mustard Interior, Raspberry, Dark Blue Sponge Spattered Glaze, 1899, 2 5/8 In. *illus*		4160
Vase, Barrel Shape, Brown Mottled Glaze, Earthenware, 9 x 5 In. *illus*		1287
Vase, Manganese Speckled Lead Glaze, Folded Rim, Late 1800s, 4 x 3 In.		4183

OLD PARIS, *see Paris category.*

OLD SLEEPY EYE, *see Sleepy Eye category.*

OLYMPICS

Olympics memorabilia include commemorative pins, posters, programs, patches, mascots, and other items from the Olympics, even the torch carried before the games. The Olympics are thought to have started as a religious festival held in Olympia, Greece, in 776 BC. It included a foot race in the stadium. After that games were held every four years until 393 AD and more athletic events were added. The games were revived in 1896 when the first modern Olympics were held in Athens, Greece, with fourteen countries participating. The Olympics were held only in the summer until 1924 when the first Winter Olympics were held in Chamonix, France. The current schedule of an Olympics every two years, alternating between Summer and Winter Olympics, began in 1994. The Olympic flag was introduced in 1908; official Olympics posters were first commissioned in 1912; the Olympic torch first appeared in 1928; and the first relay to light the torch was held in 1936 at the Olympics in Berlin.

Button, Winter Games, Austria, 1976, Silver, Loop Shanks, Buildings, 7/8 In., 5 Piece	35
Jacket, Montreal, 1976, Green & White Stripes, Nigerian Basketball Team	144
Medal, Participant's, Summer, Berlin, 1936, Silver, Art Deco Style, 1 1/2 In.	275
Pin, Torch Bearer, Greek Myth, Prometheus, Nude, Running, 18K Gold, 2002, 1 3/4 x 1 3/16 In.	399
Poster, Lake Placid, 1980, Winter Scene, Mountains, John Gallucci, Frame, 40 1/2 x 27 1/2 In. *illus*	127
Poster, Los Angeles, 1932, Indians, Hernando Gonzallo Villa, Santa Fe RR, 26 x 19 In.	5980
Venue Fragment, Los Angeles, 1984, Architectural, Cylinder, Black & White Stripes, 82 x 12 In.	250

ONION PATTERN

Onion pattern, originally named bulb pattern, is a white ware decorated with cobalt blue or pink designs of a vine with buds that look like onions. Although it is commonly associated with Meissen, other companies made the pattern in the late nineteenth and the twentieth centuries. A rare type is called *red bud* because there are added red accents on the blue-and-white dishes.

Bowl, Lozenge Shape, Reticulated, Blue, Flowers & Leaves, Meissen, 1700s, 9 x 7 In.	125
Pitcher, Lid, Bud Finial, 2 Spouts & Handles, Flowers, c.1850, 5 1/4 x 6 3/4 In.	184
Platter, Blue & White, Oval, Scalloped Rim, Meissen, 17 1/2 x 23 1/4 In.	352
Platter, Blue, Flowers & Leaves, White Ground, Meissen, 1815, 20 x 14 x 2 In.	649
Serving Dish, Divided, Wavy Rim, Blue Flowers, 13 3/4 In.	325

OPALESCENT GLASS

Opalescent glass is translucent glass that has the tones of the opal gemstone. It originated in England in the 1870s and is often found in pressed glassware made in Victorian times. Opalescent glass was first made in America in 1897 at the Northwood glassworks in Indiana, Pennsylvania. Some dealers use the terms *opaline* and *opalescent* for any of these translucent wares. More opalescent pieces may be listed in Hobnail, Pressed Glass, and other glass categories.

Big Windows, Sugar Shaker, Blue, Period Metal Lid, Buckeye, c.1880, 4 3/4 In. *illus*		132
Bubble Lattice, Pickle Castor, Blue, Hinged Lid, Stand, Buckeye Glass Co., c.1889, 8 3/4 In. *illus*		419
Bubble Lattice, Sugar Shaker, Lid, Blue, Buckeye Glass Co., c.1889, 5 1/4 In.		168
Coinspot, Bowl, Hemispherical, Quadruple Plate Stand, Webster Mfg. Co., Late 1800s, 8 In.		84

Office, Calculator, ANITA Mark VIII, Bell Punch Co., England, 1961, 9 1/4 x 15 x 18 In.
$7,463

RR Auction

Office, Calculator, Webb Adder, 2 Number Wheels, Figure 8 Shape, c.1890, 6 1/4 x 4 3/8 In.
$125

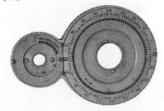

Fairfield Auction

TIP

Art pottery fakes are sold on eBay by an American company. It's selling copies, some very bad, of Pillin, Natzler, and Ohr pottery. The Ohr pottery has stilt marks on the bottom, not seen on real Ohr.

Ohr, Pot, Mustard Interior, Raspberry, Dark Blue Sponge Spattered Glaze, 1899, 2 5/8 In.
$4,160

Neal Auction Company

This is an edited listing of current prices. Visit **Kovels.com** to check thousands of prices from previous years and sign up for free information on trends, tips, reproductions, marks, and more.

Ohr, Vase, Barrel Shape, Brown Mottled Glaze, Earthenware, 9 x 5 In. **$1,287**

Thomaston Place Auction Galleries

Olympics, Poster, Lake Placid, 1980, Winter Scene, Mountains, John Gallucci, Frame, 40½ x 27½ In. **$127**

Tremont Auctions

Opalescent, Big Windows, Sugar Shaker, Blue, Period Metal Lid, Buckeye, c.1880, 4¾ In. **$132**

Jeffrey S. Evans & Associates

Coinspot, Sugar Shaker, Lid, Ruby, Hobbs, Brockunier & Co., c.1880, 5½ In.	156
Cranberry, Vase, Stripe, Ruffled Rim, Fenton, 11 In.	123
Double Greek Key, Butter, Dome Cover, Nickel Plate Glass Co., c.1892, 5 In. *illus*	192
Seaweed, Bottle, Bitters, Blue, Tapered Shape, Ceramic Spout, Late 1800s, 7¾ In.	156

OPALINE

Opaline, or opal glass, was made in white, green, and other colors. The glass had a matte surface and a lack of transparency. It was often gilded or painted. It was a popular mid-nineteenth-century European glassware.

Cachepot, Green, Gilt Metal, Hanging, Chain Decoration, Paw Feet, 1900s, 6½ x 6¾ In. ... *illus*	1188
Lamp, Oil, Portrait, Man, Gilt, Blue Leaves & Flowers, Persian Market, Late 1800s, 21 In., Pair . *illus*	1875
Vase, Gilt Bands, Greek Key, Flared Rim, Footed, 11⅞ In., Pair	750

OPERA GLASSES

Opera glasses are needed because the stage is a long way from some of the seats at a play or an opera. Mother-of-pearl was a popular decoration on many French glasses.

Enameled, Cherubs, Musical Instruments Scene, Gilt, LeClerc, Paris, c.1900, 4 x 1¾ In.	150
Mother-Of-Pearl, St. Louis, A.S. Aloe, Gilt Metal, Leaves, Enameled, c.1890, 2 x 4 In. . *illus*	390

ORPHAN ANNIE

Orphan Annie first appeared in the comics in 1924. The last strip ran in newspapers on June 13, 2010. The redheaded girl, her dog Sandy, and her friends were on the radio from 1930 to 1942. The first movie based on the strip was produced in 1932. A second movie was produced in 1938. A Broadway musical that opened in 1977, a movie based on the musical and produced in 1982, and a made-for-television movie based on the musical produced in 1999 made Annie popular again, and many toys, dishes, and other memorabilia have been made. An adaptation of the movie based on the musical opened in 2014.

Badge, Decoder, Radio, Goldtone, Wreath & Star, 1938. *illus*	13
Button, Pinback, Some Swell Sweater, Annie, Yellow Sweater, Celluloid, 1928	95
Decoder Badge, Rotating Numbers & Letters, 1938	48
Doll, Annie, Molded Face & Hair, Red Dress, Sandy, Sitting, Box, 13¼ x 12 In. *illus*	510
Mug, Annie & Sandy, Glasbake, 1975, 3¼ In.	12
Mug, Shake-Up, Leapin' Lizards, Annie, Sandy, Ovaltine, Wander Co., 1930s, 4 In.	40
Toothbrush Holder, Annie & Sandy, Bench, Bisque, Japan, 1930s, 3 x 3 In.	55

ORREFORS

Orrefors

Orrefors Glassworks, located in the Swedish province of Smaaland, was established in 1898. The company is still making glass for use on the table or as decorations. There is renewed interest in the glass made in the modern styles of the 1940s and 1950s and after. In 1990, the company merged with Kosta Boda and is still working as Orrefors. Most vases and decorative pieces are signed with the etched name *Orrefors*.

Vase, Clear, Engraved Romeo & Juliet, Signed, 7¾ x 5 In.	50
Vase, Clear, Curvy Sides, Nils Landberg, 8 In. *illus*	94
Vase, Etched Glass, Vicke Lindstrand, c.1940, 7¾ x 4½ In.	438
Vase, Glass, Blue & White, Round, Ingeborg Lundin, 1959, 5 x 6 In.	1750
Vase, Hand Blown Glass, Green, Apple Shape, Ingeborg Lundin, 1957, 15 x 13 In.	3500
Vase, Pearl Diver, Etched Glass, Vicke Lindstrand, c.1938, 11 x 6 In.	2080
Vase, Rose Bowl, Smoked, Optic Ripple, Edvard Hald, 1930, 6 x 7 In.	113
Vase, Square Inner Rim, Flared Outer Rim, Ridged Body, 10½ x 6 x 3½ In.	75

O

Opalescent, Bubble Lattice, Pickle Castor, Blue, Hinged Lid, Stand, Buckeye Glass Co., c.1889, 8¾ In.
$419

Jeffrey S. Evans & Associates

Opalescent, Double Greek Key, Butter, Dome Cover, Nickel Plate Glass Co., c.1892, 5 In.
$192

Jeffrey S. Evans & Associates

Opaline, Cachepot, Green, Gilt Metal, Hanging, Chain Decoration, Paw Feet, 1900s, 6½ x 6¾ In.
$1,188

Hindman

Opaline, Lamp, Oil, Portrait, Man, Gilt, Blue Leaves & Flowers, Persian Market, Late 1800s, 21 In., Pair
$1,875

Hindman

Opera Glasses, Mother-Of-Pearl, St. Louis, A.S. Aloe, Gilt Metal, Leaves, Enameled, c.1890, 2 x 4 In.
$390

Selkirk Auctioneers & Appraisers

TIP
If you are remodeling, think about antiques displayed in the work area. A worker will hammer on a wall without worrying about the shelves on the other side.

Orphan Annie, Badge, Decoder, Radio, Goldtone, Wreath & Star, 1938
$13

Mid-Hudson Auction Galleries

Orphan Annie, Doll, Annie, Molded Face & Hair, Red Dress, Sandy, Sitting, Box, 13¼ x 12 In.
$510

Morphy Auctions

Orrefors, Vase, Clear, Curvy Sides, Nils Landberg, 8 In.
$94

Charleston Estate Auctions

Ott & Brewer, Cup & Saucer, Cream Luster, Ridged, Gilt Trim, American Belleek, 1 1/2 x 4 1/2 In.
$88

Lion and Unicorn

Overbeck, Bowl, Lid, Pink Band With Blue & Yellow Flowers, Coiled, Mary Frances, 5 1/4 x 8 1/2 In.
$4,248

McMurray Antiques & Auctions

Overbeck, Vase, The Sower, Stylized Figure, Yellow Ground, Elizabeth & Mary Frances, c.1920, 10 1/4 x 6 In.
$43,750

Rago Arts and Auction Center

Owens, Vase, Green, 2 Handles, Impressed Mark, 6 1/2 In.
$780

Treadway

OTT & BREWER

Ott & Brewer Company operated the Etruria Pottery at Trenton, New Jersey, from 1871 to 1892. It started making belleek in 1882. The firm used a variety of marks that incorporated the initials *O & B*.

Cup & Saucer, Cream Luster, Ridged, Gilt Trim, American Belleek, 1 1/2 x 4 1/2 In........ *illus*	88
Pitcher, Lily Bud Handle, Painted, Pink Lotus, Ivory Ground, c.1883, 9 In.	2078
Vase, Tree Stump Shape, Gilt, Scalloped, Oak Leaves, c.1883, 5 In.	500

OVERBECK POTTERY

Overbeck Pottery was made by four sisters named Overbeck at a pottery in Cambridge City, Indiana. They started in 1911. They made all types of vases, each one of a kind. Small, hand-modeled figurines are the most popular pieces with today's collectors. The factory continued until 1955, when the last of the four sisters died.

Bowl, Lid, Pink Band With Blue & Yellow Flowers, Coiled, Mary Frances, 5 1/4 x 8 1/2 In. *illus*	4248
Pin, Pink Flower, Yellow Center, 2 Green Leaves, Glossy Glaze, 1 1/2 In., Pair	256
Vase, Pink, Raised Orange Flower Band, Earthenware, Elizabeth & Hannah, 5 In.	8125
Vase, The Sower, Stylized Figure, Yellow Ground, Elizabeth & Mary Frances, c.1920, 10 1/4 x 6 In. *illus*	43750

OWENS POTTERY

Owens Pottery was made in Zanesville, Ohio, from 1891 to 1928. The first art pottery was made after 1896. Utopian Ware, Cyrano, Navarre, Feroza, and Henri Deux were made. Pieces were usually marked with a form of the name *Owens*. The company continued to make tiles but production of art pottery was discontinued about 1907 and the company was sold. The new owners went bankrupt in 1909. J.B. Owens started the J.B. Owens Floor & Wall Tile Company in 1909. It closed in 1928.

Owens Pottery
1896–1907

Owens Pottery
1896–1907

Owens Pottery
1905+

Humidor, Dome Lid, Squat, Opalescent, Flowers, Silver Plate Mounts, c.1915, 6 In.	300
Jardiniere, Pedestal, Autumn Leaves, Dark Brown Ground, Salesman's Sample, 12 1/4 In.	180
Pitcher, Green Matte Glaze, Molded Leaves & Berries, Cylindrical, 8 5/8 In.	72
Pitcher, Utopian, Brown To Green Ground, Yellow & Red Pears, Cylindrical, 13 In.	61
Pitcher, Utopian, Round, Shaded Brown Ground, Thorny Vine, Scrolled Handle, 7 1/2 In.	157
Tile, Grapevine, Border, Green Ground, Pink, Brown, c.1910s, 9 x 6 In.	246
Vase, Green Matte Glaze, Textured, Cylindrical, Flared Base, Stamped Owensart, 6 3/4 In.	98
Vase, Green Matte, Pierced Shoulders, Incised Geometrics, Tapered Neck, Marked, 7 1/2 x 5 1/2 In.	840
Vase, Green, 2 Handles, Impressed Mark, 6 1/2 In. *illus*	780
Vase, Mottled Brown Ground, Incised Flowers, 13 5/8 In.	360
Vase, Sudanese, 2 Fish, Seaweed, Ebony Ground, Pearl Highlights, Marked 220, c.1900, 8 3/4 In. *illus*	540

OYSTER PLATE

Oyster plates were popular from 1840 to 1900. Each course at dinner was served in a special dish. The oyster plate had indentations shaped like oysters. Usually six oysters were held on a plate. There is no greater value to a plate with more oysters, although that myth continues to haunt antiques dealers. There are other plates for shellfish, including cockle plates and whelk plates. The appropriately shaped indentations are part of the design of these dishes.

5 Wells, Coral, Seaweed, Gilt Fishnet, Turquoise, Turkey Style, Scalloped Edge, 9 In.	282
5 Wells, Flowers, Gold Trim, Theodore Haviland, Limoges, Early 1900s, 8 3/8 In., 6 Piece *illus*	469

O

5 Wells, White Shells, Blue Dividers, Pink Flowers, Gilt, 8 ½ In., 12 Piece 313
6 Wells, Alternating White & Yellow, Multicolor Flowers, Courting Scenes, Gilt, 9 In., Pair .. 250
6 Wells, Majolica, White Scallop Shell Shape, Green Basket Weave Ground, c.1890s, 9 In. .. *illus* 201
6 Wells, Pink Shaded Edge, Blue Shaded Center, Gilt Flowers, Porcelain, France, c.1920, 10 In., Pair .. 87
6 Wells, Purple Ground, Multicolor Shading In Shells, Paris Porcelain, 9 In. 175
6 Wells, White, Scalloped Rim, Limoges, Early 20th Century, 10 ¼ In., 18 Piece 1046

PAIRPOINT

Pairpoint Manufacturing Company was founded by Thomas J. Pairpoint in 1880 in New Bedford, Massachusetts. It soon joined with the glassworks nearby and made glass, silver-plated pieces, and lamps. Reverse-painted glass shades and molded shades known as "puffies" were part of the production until the 1930s. The company reorganized and changed its name several times. It became the Pairpoint Glass Company in 1957. The company moved to Sagamore, Massachusetts, in 1970 and now makes luxury glass items. Items listed here are glass or glass and metal. Silver-plated pieces are listed under Silver Plate. Three marks are shown here.

Pairpoint Corp.
1894–1939

Gunderson–Pairpoint Glass
Works
1952–1957

Pairpoint Manufacturing Co.
1972–present

Ladle, Cut Glass, Silver Plate, Scalloped Shape, Curved Handle, 17 In. .... *illus* 59
Lamp, Aesthetic, Metal, Dragonflies, Birds, White Glass Globe, Wood Feet, 30 In. 238
Lamp, Bronze, Reverse Painted Shade, Octagonal Marble Base, 25 ½ x 16 In. 625
Lamp, Electric, Art Nouveau, Reverse Painted, Glass, Gilt Metal, Early 1900s, 23 x 14 In. 1250
Lamp, Puffy Torino, Flowers, Painted, Gilt, Octagonal Base, Early 1900s, 21 ¾ In. .... *illus* 2904
Lamp, Puffy, Flowers, Grapes, Yellow, Red, Green, c.1910s, 21 x 13 In. 1353
Lamp, Puffy, Rare Palermo Shade, Multicolor Tulips, Marked, 21 x 14 In. .... *illus* 6000
Lamp, Radio, Seascape, Painted, Gilt Metal Base, Decagon, Early 1900s, 9 x 9 ¼ In. 1815
Paperweight, Pedestal, Crimped Rose, Fuchsia, Grapevine, Engraved, 1950s, 4 ¼ x 2 ⅞ In. 152
Vase, Art Glass, Flared Rim, Clear Controlled Bubble Stem, Selenium Red, Disc Foot, 13 x 6 In. 100
Vase, Fan, Cranberry, Jewels, Figures, Gold Decor, Mosier, 15 x 8 ½ In. 288
Vase, Urn Shape, Ruby, Controlled Bubble Stem, Folded Rim, Circular Foot, c.1915, 11 ⅞ In. *illus* 117

PALMER COX, *Brownies, see Brownies category.*

PAPER

Paper collectibles, including almanacs, catalogs, children's books, some greeting cards, stock certificates, and other paper ephemera, are listed here. Paper calendars are listed separately in the Calendar category. Paper items may be found in many other sections, such as Christmas and Movie.

Book, Common Prayer, Rites & Ceremonies, Church, Gilt, Brass Clasps, 1893, 14 x 10 In. ... 448
Certificate, 25-Year Club, Jos. H. Rider & Son, Disston, 1927, 12 ½ x 15 In. 30
Drawing, Architectural, Army-Navy Bowl, Watercolor & Pencil, Signed, LR, Frame, 1933, 39 x 60 In. 469
Drawing, Ram's Head, Curly Horns, Chalk, Graphite, American School, 26 x 32 ½ In. 295
Fraktur, Birth & Baptism, Watercolor, Ink On Paper, Frame, Scalloped Edges, c.1782, 12 x 10 In.. *illus* 418
Fraktur, Birth & Christening, Robed Figures, Flowers, Fruit, Butterfly, 1815, 15 x 12 In....... 288
Fraktur, Birth, Printed, Hand Colored, Carl Egelmann, Frame, 1838, 12 x 9 ½ In................ 101
Fraktur, Family Record, Garland, Fruit, Flowers, Birds, Grau, Frame, 1800s, 16 x 23 In...... 167
Fraktur, Family Record, Watercolor, James H. Frederick, Wood Frame, 1826, 12 x 15 ¼ In.. 563
Fraktur, Marriage, Flowers, Diamond Border, Swags, Tassels, Painted, Frame, 1831, 14 x 18 In. *illus* 23040
Fraktur, Watercolor, Flowers & Vines, German Text, Painted, Frame, 20 ½ x 24 ½ In.......... 469
Fraktur, Watercolor, Printed, German Text, G.S Peters, Harrisburg, Pa., c.1840, 10 ½ x 15 ½ In... 281

Owens, Vase, Sudanese, 2 Fish, Seaweed, Ebony Ground, Pearl Highlights, Marked 220, c.1900, 8 ¾ In. $540

Leland Little Auctions

Oyster Plate, 5 Wells, Flowers, Gold Trim, Theodore Haviland, Limoges, Early 1900s, 8 ⅜ In., 6 Piece $469

Hindman

Oyster Plate, 6 Wells, Majolica, White Scallop Shell Shape, Green Basket Weave Ground, c.1890s, 9 In. $201

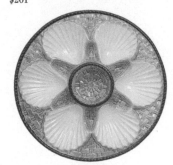

Charleston Estate Auctions

PAPER

Pairpoint, Ladle, Cut Glass, Silver Plate, Scalloped Shape, Curved Handle, 17 In.
$59

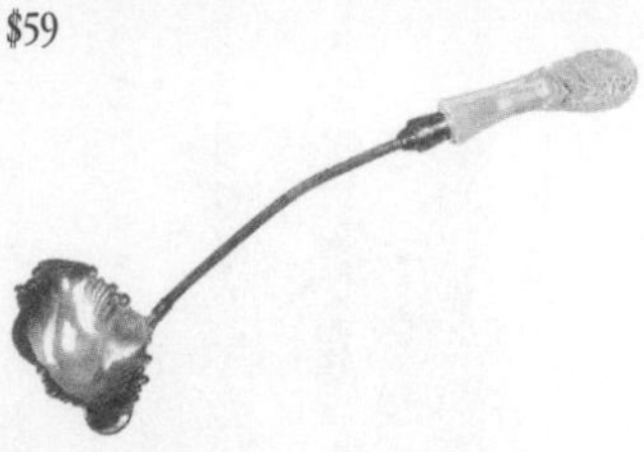

Bunch Auctions

Pairpoint, Lamp, Puffy Torino, Flowers, Painted, Gilt, Octagonal Base, Early 1900s, 21 3/4 In.
$2,904

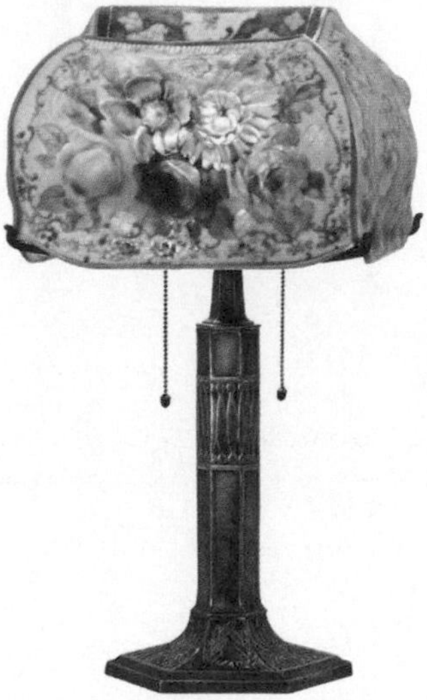

Fontaine's Auction Gallery

Pairpoint, Lamp, Puffy, Rare Palermo Shade, Multicolor Tulips, Marked, 21 x 14 In.
$6,000

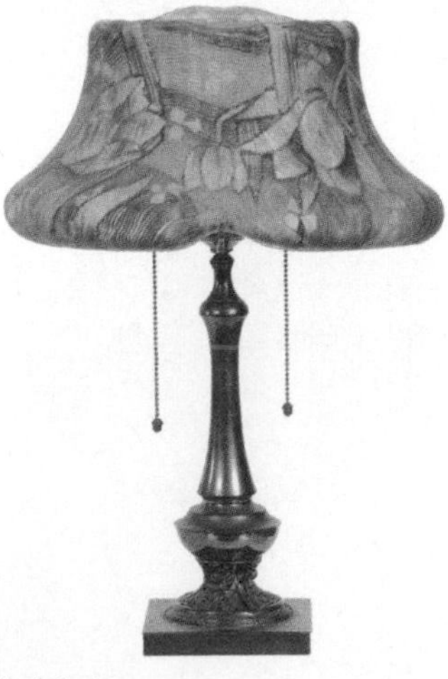

Woody Auction

P

Invitation, Armistice Day, November 11, 1945, Jerusalem District, 3 1/8 x 4 3/4 In. 80
Magazine Cover, New Year's Baby, Baby Angel On Globe, Saturday Evening Post, Jan. 2, 1932, 13 In. 55
Manuscript Leaf, Gilt, Carved Frame, Illuminated, Death Of Mary, 11 3/4 x 9 In. 640
Promissory Note, Handwritten, William Gibson & John McComb, Lancaster, Pa., 1750...... 443

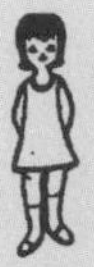

PAPER DOLL

Paper dolls were probably inspired by the pantins, or jumping jacks, made in eighteenth-century Europe. By the 1880s, sheets of printed paper dolls and clothes were being made. The first paper doll books were made in the 1920s. Collectors prefer uncut sheets or books or boxed sets of paper dolls. Prices are about half as much if the pages have been cut.

Doll, Betty & Jack, 6 Outfits, Mary Nye Marshall, c.1920, Uncut.......... 95
Princess Diana, 8 Outfits, World International Publishing, c.1980, 4 Pages, Uncut............ 44
Thumbelina, Newborn, Whitman, 1969, 6 Pages, Uncut.......... 30

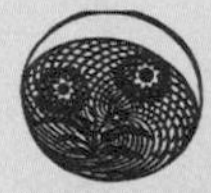

PAPERWEIGHT

Paperweights must have first appeared along with paper in ancient Egypt. Today's collectors search for every type, from the very expensive French weights of the nineteenth century to the modern artist weights or advertising pieces. The glass tops of the paperweights sometimes have been nicked or scratched, and this type of damage can be removed by polishing. Some serious collectors think this type of repair is an alteration and will not buy a repolished weight; others think it is an acceptable technique of restoration that does not change the value. Printie is the flat or concave surface formed when a paperweight is shaped on a grinding wheel. Baccarat paperweights are listed separately under Baccarat.

Acrylic, 5 Stacks Of 1 Dollar Bills, 1969, 7 1/4 x 3 1/2 In.......... 540
Anvil, Nickeled Cast Iron, Detroit Stove Works, 2 1/4 x 4 1/4 In. .... *illus* 136
Brass, Figural, Bird, Standing On Oval Base, 3 x 4 In.......... 147
California Art Tile Co., Flower, Red, Brown, Round, Signed, c.1910, 4 In.......... 185
Cast Iron, Black Racehorse, Jockey, Painted White & Orange, Hubley, 4 3/4 In. 180
Claycraft Potteries, Scarab, Uranium, Orange, Signed, c.1920s, 3 x 2 1/2 x 1 1/4 In. 923
Gillinder & Sons, Pressed Glass, Abraham Lincoln, Centennial, Philadelphia, c.1880, 3 1/4 In. ... *illus* 176
Glass, 5-Petal Flower, Green Leaves, Multicolor, Stone Ground, 1900s, 5 3/4 x 6 3/4 In. 182
Glass, Feathered Design, Signed, Cisch, Black, White, 2 3/4 x 3 In.......... 38
Glass, Teardrop Shape, Blue Green, Pink Flower At Bottom, 5 x 6 In.......... 55
Kaziun, Charles Jr., Pedestal, Lampwork, Crimp, Rose, Massachusetts, 1980, 3 1/8 x 2 In..... *illus* 497
Lotton, David, Magnum, White Flowers, Variegated Leaves, Blue, Crete, Il, 1982, 6 In.......... 187
Lotton, John, Magnum, Clear, White Jack-In-The-Pulpits, 1999, 8 In.......... *illus* 900
Lundberg, Steven, Sculpture, Aquarium, Lampwork, Calif., 1994, 3 1/4 x 2 7/8 x 4 1/4 In. . *illus* 702
Lundberg, World Globe, Blue Oceans, Green Continents, White Arctic, 1988, 4 1/2 In. 281
Panda, Black & White Glass, Sitting, Raising Hand, Marcolin, Sweden, 1 x 3 x 6 In. 83
Perthshire, Millefiori, Mushroom Shape, Pedestal, Signed, 1990, 3 3/4 In. .... *illus* 1024
St. Louis, Basket, Millefiori, Super Magnum, Concentric, Canes, Garlands, 1991, 7 3/4 x 9 In...... 4680
St. Louis, Millefiori, Paneled, Close Pack, Stardust Cane, Opaque Twist, c.1848, 2 5/8 In...... *illus* 4680
St. Louis, Piedouche, Millefiori, Close Pack, Filigree Twists, 1953, 2 7/8 x 2 5/8 In.......... 2106
Stankard, Paul, Cube, Lampwork, Bouquet, Honeycomb, Botanical, Late 1900s, 3 x 2 1/2 In... *illus* 4095
Stankard, Paul, Flowers, Fruit, Bee, White Glass, Orb, New Jersey, 5 In. .... *illus* 5166

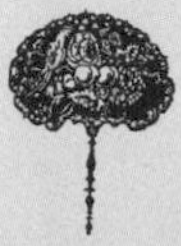

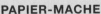

PAPIER-MACHE

Papier-mache is made from paper mixed with glue, chalk, and other ingredients, then molded and baked. It becomes very hard and can be painted. Boxes, trays, and furniture were made of papier-mache. Some of the nineteenth-century pieces were decorated with mother-of-pearl. Papier-mache is still being used to make small toys, figures, candy containers, boxes, and other giftwares. Furniture made of papier-mache is listed in the Furniture category.

Pairpoint, Vase, Urn Shape, Ruby, Controlled Bubble Stem, Folded Rim, Circular Foot, c.1915, 11 7/8 In.
$117

Jeffrey S. Evans & Associates

Paper, Fraktur, Birth & Baptism, Watercolor, Ink On Paper, Frame, Scalloped Edges, c.1782, 12 x 10 In.
$418

Jeffrey S. Evans & Associates

Paper, Fraktur, Marriage, Flowers, Diamond Border, Swags, Tassels, Painted, Frame, 1831, 14 x 18 In.
$23,040

Rachel Davis Fine Arts

Paperweight, Anvil, Nickeled Cast Iron, Detroit Stove Works, 2 1/4 x 4 1/4 In.
$136

Hartzell's Auction Gallery Inc.

Paperweight, Gillinder & Sons, Pressed Glass, Abraham Lincoln, Centennial, Philadelphia, c.1880, 3 1/4 In.
$176

Jeffrey S. Evans & Associates

Paperweight, Kaziun, Charles Jr., Pedestal, Lampwork, Crimp, Rose, Massachusetts, 1980, 3 1/8 x 2 In.
$497

Jeffrey S. Evans & Associates

Paperweight, Lotton, John, Magnum, Clear, White Jack-In-The-Pulpits, 1999, 8 In.
$900

Garth's Auctioneers & Appraisers

Paperweight, Lundberg, Steven, Sculpture, Aquarium, Lampwork, Calif., 1994, 3 1/4 x 2 7/8 x 4 1/4 In.
$702

Jeffrey S. Evans & Associates

Paperweight, Perthshire, Millefiori, Mushroom Shape, Pedestal, Signed, 1990, 3 3/4 In.
$1,024

Nadeau's Auction Gallery

Paperweight, St. Louis, Millefiori, Paneled, Close Pack, Stardust Cane, Opaque Twist, c.1848, 2 5/8 In.
$4,680

Jeffrey S. Evans & Associates

P

Paperweight, Stankard, Paul, Cube, Lampwork, Bouquet, Honeycomb, Botanical, Late 1900s, 3 x 2½ In.
$4,095

Jeffrey S. Evans & Associates

Paperweight, Stankard, Paul, Flowers, Fruit, Bee, White Glass, Orb, New Jersey, 5 In.
$5,166

Pook & Pook

TIP

If your papier-mache doll heads or furniture are cracking, you might try arresting the cracks with a thin coat of white household glue.

Papier-Mache, Dresser Box, Painted Top, Children, Garden Set, Pearl, Silk Lined, England, c.1900, 4 x 11 In.
$120

Selkirk Auctioneers & Appraisers

Dresser Box, Painted Top, Children, Garden Set, Pearl, Silk Lined, England, c.1900, 4 x 11 In.... *illus*	120
Figure, Woman, Bottle Shape, Holding Bird, Carved, Blue, Black, 14½ x 3½ In.	31
Head, Display, Millinery, Woman, Flower, Painted, France, c.1900, 16 In. ...... *illus*	717
Parrot, On Swing, Signed, Sergio Bustamante, Mexico, 56 x 13 In.	300
Plaque, Clown Face, Smiling, Painted, Multicolor, c.1940, 24 x 19 x 5 In.	188
Plaque, Portrait, Marquess & Marchioness, Gilt Floral Border, 1800s, 14 In., Pair .... *illus*	244
Snuffbox, Hinged Lid, Faux Tortoiseshell Exterior, Vernon, 1700s, 1 x 3½ x 1⅞ In. .... *illus*	936
Tray, Landscape, Painted, Oval, 1800s, 26 x 20 In.	325
Tray, Oval, Landscape, Painted, Marked Clay Patent, 1800s, 26 x 20 In.	325

PARASOL, *see Umbrella category.*

PARIAN

Parian is a fine-grained, hard-paste porcelain named for the marble it resembles. It was first made in England in 1846 and gained favor in the United States about 1860. Figures, tea sets, vases, and other items were made of Parian at many English and American factories.

Figure, Boy, Sitting, Reading Book, Footed Base, 13 x 5⅝ x 7 In. .... *illus*	58
Figurine, Goddess, Laetitia, Leaning On Pillar, Circular Plinth, France, c.1900, 18 x 8¾ In.	375
Garniture, Lid, Ridged, Swirl Neck & Foot, Bronze Mounted, Leafy Handles, 22 x 8 In., Pair	375
Group, 4 Dancing Cherubs, Holding Basket, Oval Base, Signed, Andre, 9 x 14 x 10 In.	87

PARIS

Paris, Vieux Paris, or Old Paris, is porcelain ware that is known to have been made in Paris in the eighteenth or early nineteenth century. These porcelains often have no identifying mark but can be recognized by the whiteness of the porcelain and the lines and decorations. Gold decoration is often used.

Basket, Cobalt Blue, Gilt, White Ground, Reticulated, Square Base, c.1850, 8¾ In.	320
Bowl, Ships Flying British Flags, c.1875, 5½ x 11 In., Pair	188
Cachepot, Peach, Stylized Gilt Border, Drainage Holes, Pedestal Stand, 1900s, 9 In., Pair ... *illus*	960
Centerpiece, Reticulated Basket, Cherub Supports, Paw Foot Base, 12 x 12 x 6½ In.... *illus*	416
Cuspidor, Urn Shape, Leaves, Painted Gold, Blue, White Ground, 6 x 8 In.	144
Sculpture, Modernist, Wood & Stone, Standing, Dated '83, 83½ In.	88
Urn, Campana Form, Gilt, Landscapes, Castles, Hunters, Masque Handles, 13⅛ In., Pair ..... *illus*	550
Urn, Portrait, Man & Woman, Flowers, Gilt Ground, Mask Handles, 1800s, 13¾ In., Pair....	525
Urn, Unglazed Faces, Deep, Square Base, 8½ x 6¼ In., Pair..................................	240
Vase, 2 Handles, Gilt Accents, Flowers, Dogs, France, 1800s, 10 In.	424
Vase, Bisque, Mint Green Ground, Molded, Acanthus Leaves, White Psyche, c.1850, 14 In., Pair ...	576
Vase, Courting Scene, Black Border, Hand Painted, Late 1700s, 13 x 11 In., Pair	100
Vase, Hand Painted, Label, L. Rihouet, 1800s, 18¾ In., Pair	1134
Vase, Mantel, Royal Blue Ground, Gold Decoration, Roses, Pink, 1800s, 17 x 8 In., Pair.......	2415

PATE-DE-VERRE

Pate-de-verre is an ancient technique in which glass is made by blending and refining powdered glass of different colors into molds. The process was revived by French glassmakers, especially Galle, around the end of the nineteenth century.

Compote, Mottled Yellow Green, Rows Of Leaf Shapes, Dark Olive Foot, France, 4 x 10¼ In.	3200
Sculpture, Bowl, 3 Frogs, Pink To Green, Lost Wax Cast, Charles Miner, 6¾ x 11 In...........	4200
Sculpture, Relief Cable Car Scene, Blue, Signed, 9¾ x 8 In.....................................	308
Sculpture, Waiting For The Train, Woman Standing, Wendy Saxon-Brown, 1997, 17 x 9¾ In. ...	938
Vase, Blue Cameo, Lake Scene, Fisherman, Signed, Michna, Austria, 9 In.................... *illus*	144
Vase, Figural, Barrel, Bird & Grape Bunch On Rim, Shaded Yellow, Signed, A. Felicio, 8 x 6 In. .	130
Vase, Misshapen, Mottled Cream, Painted Flowers & Shells, Early 1900s, 10 x 8½ In.	125

P

Papier-Mache, Head, Display, Millinery, Woman, Flower, Painted, France, c.1900, 16 In.
$717

Jeffrey S. Evans & Associates

Parian, Figure, Boy, Sitting, Reading Book, Footed Base, 13 x 5⅝ x 7 In.
$58

Blackwell Auctions

Paris, Centerpiece, Reticulated Basket, Cherub Supports, Paw Foot Base, 12 x 12 x 6½ In.
$416

Roland NY Auctioneers & Appraisers

Paris, Urn, Campana Form, Gilt, Landscapes, Castles, Hunters, Masque Handles, 13⅛ In., Pair
$550

Neal Auction Company

Papier-Mache, Plaque, Portrait, Marquess & Marchioness, Gilt Floral Border, 1800s, 14 In., Pair
$244

Neal Auction Company

Papier-Mache, Snuffbox, Hinged Lid, Faux Tortoiseshell Exterior, Vernon, 1700s, 1 x 3½ x 1⅞ In.
$936

Thomaston Place Auction Galleries

Paris, Cachepot, Peach, Stylized Gilt Border, Drainage Holes, Pedestal Stand, 1900s, 9 In., Pair
$960

Brunk Auctions

Pate-De-Verre, Vase, Blue Cameo, Lake Scene, Fisherman, Signed, Michna, Austria, 9 In.
$144

Pasarel Auctions

P

Patent Model, Washing Machine, Softwood, F.C. Walker, Nov. 29, 1864, Original Tags, 11 x 9 x 5 In. $761

Thomaston Place Auction Galleries

Paul Revere, Pitcher, Blue, House, Trees, Signed, Fannie Levine, 1920, 5 x 6 In. $738

California Historical Design

Paul Revere, Vase, Earthenware, Stylized Flower, Blue Matte Glaze, 1924, 8⅜ x 7¼ In. $845

Toomey & Co. Auctioneers

PATENT MODEL

Patent models were required as part of a patent application for a United States patent until 1880. In 1926 the stored patent models were sold by the U.S. Patent Office. Some were given to the Smithsonian, some were returned to inventors' descendants, and the rest were sold as a group. As groups changed hands in later years in unsuccessful attempts to start a museum, individual models started appearing in the marketplace. A model usually has an official tag.

Brake, Car, Walnut, Wood Wheels, Brass Coupler, 6½ x 12 In.	295
Churn, Double, Wood, Brass Plaque, C.H. Arnold, 1846, 12¾ x 8½ In.	875
Loom, Blind Weaving, Shuttle Driving Mechanism, Metal Gears, Jeremiah Stever, 1870, 7 In.	720
Paper Pulp Engine, Wood, Tin, Brass, Tags, M.R. Bonju, March 1, 1875, 4 x 12½ x 8 In.	900
Revolving Retort, Apparatus For Manufacturing Gas, Brass, J. Hanlon, Dec 15th, 1874, 5 x 7 x 3 In.	840
Steam Boiler, Double, Tin, T. Champion, Washington, D.C., June 26th, 1855, 6¾ x 9 x 6½ In.	360
Ticket Case, Railroad Coupons, Pine, Hinged Door, Tags, S. Simons, March 21, 1876, 12 x 7 x 3 In.	600
Washing Machine, Softwood, F.C. Walker, Nov. 29, 1864, Original Tags, 11 x 9 x 5 In. *illus*	761
Washing Machine, Wood, J.R. Underwood, Label, April 9, 1878, 10 x 9½ x 6 In.	660
Washing Machine, Wood, Octagonal Case, G.H. Ashworth & A.F. Van Voorhis, 1872, 3 In.	660
Whitman Weeder, Adjustable Lever, Late 19th Century, 16 In.	1188

PAUL REVERE POTTERY

Paul Revere Pottery was made at several locations in and around Boston, Massachusetts, between 1906 and 1942. The pottery was operated as a settlement house program for teenage girls. Many pieces were signed *S.E.G.* for Saturday Evening Girls. The artists concentrated on children's dishes and tiles. Decorations were outlined in black and filled with color.

Pitcher, Blue, House, Trees, Signed, Fannie Levine, 1920, 5 x 6 In. *illus*	738
Plate, Green Trees, White Ground, Blue, 1928, 8¼ In.	369
Vase, Earthenware, Stylized Flower, Blue Matte Glaze, 1924, 8⅜ x 7¼ In. *illus*	845
Vase, Orange Ground, Trees, Fannie Levine, 1917, 2¼ x 4¼ In. *illus*	3690

PEACHBLOW

Peachblow glass was made by several factories beginning in the 1880s. New England Peachblow is a one-layer glass shading from red to white. Mt. Washington Peachblow shades from pink to bluish-white. Hobbs, Brockunier and Company of Wheeling, West Virginia, made Coral glass that it marketed as Peachblow. It shades from yellow to peach and is lined with white glass. Reproductions of all types of peachblow have been made. Related pieces may be listed under Webb Peachblow.

Ewer, Pink Satin, Clear Handle, Twisted Rim, 1800s, 9½ x 4 x 3½ In., Pair	205
Pitcher, J.H. Hobbs, Brockunier & Co., 7¼ x 7⅜ x 5¼ In. *illus*	130
Vase, Amberina, Long Neck, Wheeling, West Virginia, 8¾ x 3¼ In.	895
Vase, Gilt, Insect, Floral & Leaves, Ruffled Rim, Tripod Base, Glass Feet, Harrach, 5 x 5 In.	108

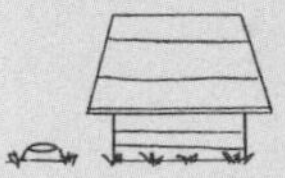

PEANUTS

Peanuts is the title of a comic strip created by cartoonist Charles M. Schulz (1922–2000). The strip, drawn by Schulz from 1950 to 2000, features a group of children, including Charlie Brown and his sister Sally, Lucy Van Pelt and her brother Linus, Peppermint Patty, and Pig Pen, and an imaginative and independent beagle named Snoopy. The Peanuts gang has also been featured in books, television shows, and a Broadway musical. The comic strip is being rerun in some newspapers. Original "Peanuts" art sells for very high prices.

Doll, Cloth, Lucy, Blue Dress, Holding Book, 13 In.	14

Ornament, Charlie Brown Holding Kite, Porcelain, 4 In.	....	20
Pin, Linus, Holding Yellow Blanket, Sucking Thumb, Plastic, c.1972, 2 In.	....	10
Plate, Good Grief, Lucy, Charlie, Snoopy, Danbury Mint, 8 In.	....	18
Puzzle, Charlie & Friends, Ice Cream Shop, 250 Pieces, Milton Bradley, 1982	....	15
Tie, Snoopy Playing Soccer, Red, Silk, United Feature Syndicate, 56 x 4 In.	....	20

PEARLWARE

Pearl

Pearlware is an earthenware made by Josiah Wedgwood in 1779. It was copied by other potters in England. Pearlware is only slightly different in color from creamware and for many years collectors have confused the terms. Wedgwood pieces are listed in the Wedgwood category in this book. Most pearlware with mocha designs is listed under Mocha.

Bowl, Center Peafowl, Geometrics & Leaves On Rim, Flower, c.1800, 4 x 9¾ In.	.... *illus*	561
Cup, Motto, Multicolor Transfer, Honest John Barley Corn, Pink Luster Band, 3¾ In.	....	155
Figurine, Goat, Standing, Kid, Lying Down, Black Spots, On Leafy Ledge, Bocage, 6¾ x 5 x 3½ In.	...	192
Jug, Arms Of The United States, Luster Rim, Staffordshire, Early 1800s, 6 x 5 x 7 In.	... *illus*	1071
Lantern, Painted Flowers & Vines, Arched Top, Handle, Glass Front Window, Early 1800s, 8 x 5 In.	..	2875
Mug, Dark Brown Ground, Yellow & Orange Flowers, Multicolor Trim, 3¾ In.	.... *illus*	279
Mug, Peafowl, Green Sponge Branch, Multicolor, 2 Handles, c.1815, 4 In.	....	380
Mug, Workers In Field, Dr. Franklin's Maxims, Staffordshire, Child's, c.1820, 2¾ x 3 In.	......	264
Pitcher, Barrel Shape, Black Bands, White Links, Blue & Yellow Borders, Slip Decorated, 7 In.		1500
Pitcher, George Washington Memorial, Black Transfer, c.1800, 8½ In.	....	704
Pitcher, Slip Bands, Dark Brown, Rust, Blue, Applied Handle, Early 1800s, 9½ In.	....	1125
Punch Bowl, Chinoiserie, Blue & White, Brown Trim, Verse, Staffordshire, Early 1800s, 5⅝ x 14 In.		512
Punch Pot, Lid, Slip, Speckled, Checkered, Extruded Handle, Blue, 1800s, 7½ In.	....	469
Teapot, Lid, King's Rose, Pink & White, Bulbous, 4¾ x 9½ In.	....	99
Teapot, Lid, Straight-Sided, Ocher Brown & White Fans, Slip, Gooseneck, Marked, Shorthose, 4¼ In.		4375
Vase, 5 Spouts, Blue & White, Flowers, Molded Feathers, Rectangular Base, c.1815, 7 In.	......	498

PEKING GLASS

Peking glass is a Chinese cameo glass first made popular in the eighteenth century. The Chinese have continued to make this layered glass in the old manner, and many new pieces are now available that could confuse the average buyer.

Bowl, Ruby Red, White Peony, Branch Design, Chinese, Late 1800s, 2½ x 6¼ In., Pair	*illus*	270
Snuff Bottle, Large Embossed Turtle, Red Dome Lid, Amber, 2½ In.	.... *illus*	688
Snuff Bottle, Red Seaweed, Frosted & Cracked Ground, Bronze Cap, Ropework, 3 x 1½ In.		300
Vase, Nesting Birds, Peony Branches, Green, White, Chinese, Late 1800s, 9 In., Pair	... *illus*	240
Vase, Opaque Ground Vase, Green, Crane, Flowers, Chinese, 14 x 5½ In.	....	120

PEN

Pens replaced hand-cut quills as writing instruments in 1780, when the first steel pen point was made in England. But it was 100 years before the commercial pen was a common item. The fountain pen was invented in the 1830s but was not made in quantity until the 1880s. All types of old pens are collected, everything from quill pens to fountain pens. Float pens feature small objects floating in a liquid as part of the handle. Advertising pens are listed in the Advertising section of this book.

Fountain, 14K Yellow Gold, Engraved, Art Deco, Case Marked T, c.1930, 4⅞ In.	.... *illus*	388
Montblanc, Fountain, Blue Boheme, Sapphire, Sterling Silver, 4⅞ In.	.... *illus*	540
Montblanc, Fountain, Meisterstuck, No. 149, Piston Fill, Black, Gold Plated, Germany, 5¾ In.		438

PEN & PENCIL

Cross, Ballpoint Pen, Mechanical Pencil, Silver, Green Case, Marshall Field, 5¼ In.	....	106
Sheaffer, Fountain Pen, Mechanical Pencil, 14K Gold, Case, 5¼ In.	....	1188

Paul Revere, Vase, Orange Ground, Trees, Fannie Levine, 1917, 2¼ x 4¼ In. $3,690

California Historical Design

Peachblow, Pitcher, J.H. Hobbs, Brockunier & Co., 7¼ x 7⅜ x 5¼ In. $130

Toomey & Co. Auctioneers

Pearlware, Bowl, Center Peafowl, Geometrics & Leaves On Rim, Flower, c.1800, 4 x 9¾ In. $561

Jeffrey S. Evans & Associates

> **TIP**
> *Before you store an old fountain pen, empty the ink bladder. Wash the bladder out with lukewarm water.*

P

Pearlware, Jug, Arms Of The United States, Luster Rim, Staffordshire, Early 1800s, 6 x 5 x 7 In.
$1,071

Freeman's

Pearlware, Mug, Dark Brown Ground, Yellow & Orange Flowers, Multicolor Trim, 3¾ In.
$279

John McInnis Auctioneers

Peking Glass, Bowl, Ruby Red, White Peony, Branch Design, Chinese, Late 1800s, 2½ x 6¼ In., Pair
$270

Selkirk Auctioneers & Appraisers

TIP
Never allow water to evaporate in a glass vase. It will leave a white residue that may be impossible to remove.

Peking Glass, Snuff Bottle, Large Embossed Turtle, Red Dome Lid, Amber, 2½ In.
$688

Turner Auctions + Appraisals

Peking Glass, Vase, Nesting Birds, Peony Branches, Green, White, Chinese, Late 1800s, 9 In., Pair
$240

Selkirk Auctioneers & Appraisers

Pen, Fountain, 14K Yellow Gold, Engraved, Art Deco, Case Marked T, c.1930, 4⅞ In.
$388

Jeffrey S. Evans & Associates

Pen, Montblanc, Fountain, Blue Boheme, Sapphire, Sterling Silver, 4⅞ In.
$540

Cottone Auctions

TIP
If a vintage fountain pen cap or barrel is discolored, the pen has little value.

Pencil Sharpener, Electric, Bakelite, Adjustable Knob, Burt M. Morris Co., Los Angeles, 6 x 8 x 7 In.
$240

Morphy Auctions

Pencil Sharpener, Hand Crank, Automatic Metal Pencil Sharpener Co., New York, Wood Base, Original Label
$360

Chupp Auctions & Real Estate, LLC

PENCIL

Pencils were invented, so it is said, in 1565. The eraser was not added to the pencil until 1858. The automatic pencil was invented in 1863. Collectors today want advertising pencils or automatic pencils of unusual design. Boxes and sharpeners for pencils are also collected. Advertising pencils are listed in the Advertising category. Pencil boxes are listed in the Box category.

Retractable Lead, 18K Gold, Blue Enamel, Sapphire Cabochons, Square End, France, 3 ⅝ In. ..	1190
Set, Silver Cylinder, 3 Retractable Pencils, Red, Blue, Green, Chain, Late 1800s, 2 ¾ In.	89

PENCIL SHARPENER

Electric, Bakelite, Adjustable Knob, Burt M. Morris Co., Los Angeles, 6 x 8 x 7 In. .... *illus*	240
Hand Crank, Automatic Metal Pencil Sharpener Co., New York, Wood Base, Original Label..*illus*	360
Hand Crank, Black Paint, Table Clamp, Universal Sharpening Machine Co., Late 1800s, 11 In..	94

PEPSI-COLA

Pepsi-Cola, the drink and the name, was invented in 1898 but was not trademarked until 1903. The logo was changed from an elaborate script to the modern block letters in 1963. Several different logos have been used. Until 1951, the words *Pepsi* and *Cola* were separated by two dashes. These bottles are called "double dash." In 1951 the modern logo with a single hyphen was introduced. All types of advertising memorabilia are collected, and reproductions are being made.

Clock, Diet Pepsi, Teardrop Numbers, Light-Up, 1960s, 18 In...	150
Clock, Wall, Victorian Woman, Wood, Glass, Battery Operated, 1973, 13 x 9 x 2 In.	67
Menu Board, Pepsi, Tin, Red, Blue & Black, Yellow Border, 1950s, 19 x 30 In.	165
Poster, There's Pep In Pepsi-Cola, Race Drivers, 1956, 18 x 14 In......................................	175
Rack Stand, Bottle, 3 Tiers, Red & Black, Metal, 2-Sided Sign Top, 19 x 19 x 53 In....... *illus*	960
Sign, Drink Pepsi-Cola Iced, Yellow Ground, Porcelain, 24 x 12 In.......................................	1440
Sign, Enjoy Pepsi, Flange, Spinner, Yellow Ground, 1960s, 15 x 20 In........................... *illus*	2400
Tray, Victorian Woman, Drinking Pepsi, Bar, 1970s, 14 ½ x 11 ½ In.	23

PERFUME BOTTLE

Perfume bottles are made of cut glass, pressed glass, art glass, silver, metal, jade, enamel, and even plastic or porcelain. Although the small bottle to hold perfume was first made before the time of ancient Egypt, it is the nineteenth- and twentieth-century examples that interest today's collector. DeVilbiss Company has made atomizers of all types since 1888 but no longer makes the perfume bottle tops so popular with collectors. These were made from 1920 to 1968. The glass bottle may be by any of many manufacturers even if the atomizer is marked *DeVilbiss*. The word *factice,* which often appears in ads, refers to large store display bottles. Glass or porcelain examples may be found under the appropriate name such as Lalique, Czechoslovakia, Glass-Bohemian, etc.

Bohemian Glass, Garnet Cut To Clear, Tapered, Footed, Atomizer, Owned By Vivian Leigh	440
Cameo Glass, Cranberry, Silver Lid, Carved Flowers, Gorham, 6 x 1 In. .... *illus*	2000
Cut Glass, Amethyst Cut To Clear, Lay Down, Silver Cap, Roses, T.B. Starr, 4 In.	565
Daniel Lotton, Blue, Iridescent Feathers, Teardrop Stopper, 2007, 11 In.	390
Glass, Pulpit Type Flowers, Black Ground, Signed, Scott Bayless Lotton, 2000, 6 In.............	144
Passion, Elizabeth Taylor, Amethyst, Stepped Fan Body, Gilt Diamond, Factice, 12 In..........	375
Red, Twist Stopper, Bulbous Bottom, Crosshatch Design, Bohemian, 12 In.................. *illus*	108

PETERS & REED

Peters & Reed Pottery Company of Zanesville, Ohio, was founded by John D. Peters and Adam Reed in 1897. Chromal, Landsun, Montene, Pereco, and Persian are some of the art lines that were made. The company, which

Pepsi-Cola, Rack Stand, Bottle, 3 Tiers, Red & Black, Metal, 2-Sided Sign Top, 19 x 19 x 53 In.
$960

Morphy Auctions

Pepsi-Cola, Sign, Enjoy Pepsi, Flange, Spinner, Yellow Ground, 1960s, 15 x 20 In.
$2,400

Morphy Auctions

> **TIP**
> *Tin signs and cans will fade from the ultraviolet rays coming in a window or from a fluorescent light. Plexiglas UF-1 or UF-3 will cover the window and keep the rays away from your collection. There are also plastic sleeves to cover fluorescent tubes.*

Perfume Bottle, Cameo Glass, Cranberry, Silver Lid, Carved Flowers, Gorham, 6 x 1 In.
$2,000

Woody Auction

Perfume Bottle, Red, Twist Stopper, Bulbous Bottom, Crosshatch Design, Bohemian, 12 In.
$108

Treasureseeker Auctions

Pewabic, Vase, Black Satin Glaze, Angled Handles Join Rim, Mary Chase Perry, 1903-18, 11 x 7 In.
$3,720

DuMouchelles

---

became Zane Pottery in 1920 and Gonder Pottery in 1941, closed in 1957. Peters & Reed pottery was unmarked.

Jardiniere, Moss Aztec, 1920s, 7 x 11 ½ In.		468
Vase, Chromal, Green Matte Glaze, Long Cylindrical Neck, c.1910, 7 x 2 ¾ In.		219
Vase, Green Matte Glaze, Ribbed, 2 Handles, Earthenware, 13 ½ In.		130

PETRUS REGOUT, *see Maastricht category.*

PEWABIC POTTERY

Pewabic Pottery was founded by Mary Chase Perry and Horace Caulkins in 1903 in Detroit, Michigan. The company made many types of art pottery, including pieces with matte green glaze and an iridescent crystalline glaze. Mary married William Stratton in 1918. After she died in 1961, her secretary, Ella Peters, managed the pottery. Horace Caulkins's son gave the building to Michigan State University in 1967. Ella and her husband, Ira, continued to made pottery with Pewabic glazes in their home studio until 1969. The Pewabic Society, Inc., a non-profit organization, took ownership of the pottery in 1981 and resumed production. Architectural tiles, bowls, vases, lamps, and other pottery items are still being made.

Tile, Paperweight, Round, Airplane, Iridescent, Blue Sky, High Glaze, c.1930, 3 In.		162
Vase, Black Satin Glaze, Angled Handles Join Rim, Mary Chase Perry, 1903-18, 11 x 7 In.	*illus*	3720
Vase, Blue Iridescent Glaze, Flared Rim, Circular Mark, 4 ¾ x 5 In.		800
Vase, Lava Glaze, Copper Iridescent Over Blue, Blistered, Bottle Shape, 1906-18, 11 x 6 In.	*illus*	6820

PEWTER

Pewter is a metal alloy of tin and lead. Some of the pewter made after 1840 has a slightly different composition and is called Britannia metal. This later type of pewter was worked by machine; the earlier pieces were made by hand. In the 1920s pewter came back into fashion and pieces were often marked *Genuine Pewter.* Eighteenth-, nineteenth-, and twentieth-century examples are listed here. Marks used by three pewter workshops are pictured.

Thomas Danforth
1727–1733

Timothy Boardman
1822–1825

William Will
1764–1798

Beaker, Samuel Danforth, Cylindrical, Hartford, Connecticut, c.1805, 5 In.	*illus*	441
Bedpan, Boardman & Hall, Turned Rim, Baluster Handle, Philadelphia, c.1845, 17 ½ x 12 In.		90
Box, Charles Fleetwood Varley, Tudric, Liberty & Co., Enamel, Garden Scene, 2 x 4 ½ In.	*illus*	1690
Champagne, Glass Flutes, Banded, Woodland Scenes, Domed Base, 9 In., 3 Piece		63
Charger, Temperantia, Grand Tour Style, Classical Figures, Continental, 1800s, 17 In.		320
Coffeepot, Boardman, Lighthouse Shape, Hinged Lid, Stamped XX, New York, Mid 1800s, 12 In.		61
Coffeepot, John Munson, Lighthouse Shape, Hinged Dome Lid, c.1850, 10 x 10 x 6 In.	*illus*	293
Dish, Osiris, Isis, Gilt, Patinated, 3 Handles, Art Nouveau, Germany, Early 1900s, 8 ½ x 3 In.		120
Figurine, Tang Horse, Galloping, Saddle, Gump's, 19 x 6 x 17 In.		59
Flagon, Communion, Hinged Lid, John Gardner, Scotland, c.1781, 10 ¾ In.	*illus*	313
Flagon, Dome Lid, Boardman & Co., Touchmark, 1800s, 12 In., Pair		738
Lamp, Whale Oil, Circular Base, Mid 1800s, 11 In., Pair	*illus*	369
Lamp, Whale Oil, Trumpet Vase, 2-Tube Burner, 1830, 9 In., Pair		295
Measure, Curved Handle, Circular Foot, Guernsey Channel Island, Mid 1700s, 11 ½ x 5 ½ In.		179
Mug, Tudric, Liberty & Co., Hammered, Signed, England, c.1920s, 4 ¾ x 5 ¼ x 3 ¼ In.		92
Pot, Israel Trask, Hinged Lid, Bright Cut Band, Wood, Wafer Finial, Marked, 12 In.	*illus*	420
Tankard, Hinged Lid, Monumental, Heraldic Dragons, Germany, 20 x 8 In.		313
Tankard, Thomas Danforth III, Cylindrical, Scroll Handle, 5 In.	*illus*	2160
Tea Set, Royal Holland, Wood Veneer, 2 Pots, Sugar & Creamer, Tray, Modernist, 20 x 12 ½ In.		345

Pewabic, Vase, Lava Glaze, Copper Iridescent Over Blue, Blistered, Bottle Shape, 1906-18, 11 x 6 In.
$6,820

DuMouchelles

Pewter, Beaker, Samuel Danforth, Cylindrical, Hartford, Connecticut, c.1805, 5 In.
$441

Pook & Pook

Pewter, Box, Charles Fleetwood Varley, Tudric, Liberty & Co., Enamel, Garden Scene, 2 x 4½ In.
$1,690

Treadway

Pewter, Coffeepot, John Munson, Lighthouse Shape, Hinged Dome Lid, c.1850, 10 x 10 x 6 In.
$293

Thomaston Place Auction Galleries

Pewter, Flagon, Communion, Hinged Lid, John Gardner, Scotland, c.1781, 10¾ In.
$313

Hindman

Pewter, Lamp, Whale Oil, Circular Base, Mid 1800s, 11 In., Pair
$369

Pook & Pook

Pewter, Pot, Israel Trask, Hinged Lid, Bright Cut Band, Wood, Wafer Finial, Marked, 12 In.
$420

Garth's Auctioneers & Appraisers

TIP
To clean pewter, rub it with fresh cabbage leaves.

Pewter, Tankard, Thomas Danforth III, Cylindrical, Scroll Handle, 5 In.
$2,160

Garth's Auctioneers & Appraisers

Pewter, Teapot, George Richardson, Hinged Lid, Footed, Massachusetts, c.1830
$239

Pook & Pook

P

Phonograph, Edison, Amberola, Oak Cabinet, Cylinder, SM-8899, 80 Records, 41 In.
$172

Phonograph, Kammer & Reinhardt, Gramophone, Hand Wind, Horn, Berliner Patent, c.1891, 13 x 7 In.
$57,500

Phonograph, Victor Victrola, XX VTLA, Side Crank, Cabinet, Red Mahogany, Refinished
$2,760

Donley Auctions

Phonograph, Victor IV, Disc, Morning Glory Horn, Painted, Blue, Pink Flowers, Mahogany Cabinet, c.1908
$1,495

Apple Tree Auction Center

Phonograph, Edison, Cylinder, Oak Case, Horns, No. H184210, Dated 1901, 12 x 16 x 9 In.
$472

Donley Auctions

Phonograph, Victor Victrola, Model II, Soundbox, Brass Horn, Wood Base, No. 9130A
$960

Donley Auctions

Phonograph Needle Case, Songster, Bird On Branch, Sun Rays, Yellow, Orange, Hinged Lid, 1920s, 1 7/8 x 1 3/8 In.
$27

chateaucurios on Etsy

Soulis Auctions

Alderfer Auction Company

TIP
Big dogs seem scary, but small dogs bark more. It's the bark that discourages a burglar.

P

Teapot, George Richardson, Hinged Lid, Footed, Massachusetts, c.1830......................*illus*	239
Teapot, Richard King, Hinged Lid, Wood Scroll Handle, England, c.1770, 5 In.......................	615
Teapot, William McQuilkin, Gooseneck Spout, Scrolled Handle, Philadelphia, 10½ x 11 In.	158
Tray, Tudric, Archibald Knox, Liberty & Co., 2 Handles, England, c.1905, ¾ x 18 x 9 In.	688
Tray, Tudric, Liberty & Co., Center Handle, London, England, 4⅞ x 9¾ x 7 In....................	130
Vase, Kayserzinn, Fish, 2 Handles, Signed, c.1910, 6½ x 6 In..	369
Vase, Protruding Woman's Face, Flowers, Shaped Handle & Base, Art Nouveau, c.1900, 15½ In..	150
Vase, Raised Band, 4 Handles, Molded Rim, Signed CB, 1900s, 9⅜ In..................................	344

PHOENIX GLASS

Phoenix Glass Company was founded in 1880 in Pennsylvania. The firm made commercial products, such as lampshades, bottles, and glassware. Collectors today are interested in the "Sculptured Artware" made by the company from the 1930s until the mid-1950s. Some pieces of Phoenix glass are very similar to those made by the Consolidated Lamp and Glass Company. Phoenix made Reuben Blue, lavender, and yellow pieces. These colors were not used by Consolidated. In 1970 Phoenix became a division of Anchor Hocking. It was sold to the Newell Group in 1987 and resold several times after that. Phoenix glass is no longer being made.

Pitcher, Air Trap, Mother-Of-Pearl, Duck-Billed Rim, Applied Handle, c.1880, 8¾ In.	192
Vase, White, Plants & Birds Relief, Mint Green Ground, 1900s, 24 In.	88

PHONOGRAPH

Phonographs, invented by Thomas Edison in 1877, have been made by many firms. This category also includes other items associated with the phonograph. Jukeboxes and Records are listed in their own categories.

Edison, Amberola, Oak Cabinet, Cylinder, SM-8899, 80 Records, 41 In........................*illus*	172
Edison, Cylinder, Oak Case, Horns, No. H184210, Dated 1901, 12 x 16 x 9 In. ....*illus*	472
Edison, Standard, Cylinder, Black & Brass Bell Horn, Windup Spring Motor, 6 Records, c.1900.	288
Edison, Standard, Cylinder, Morning Glory Horn, Dome Lid, Decal, 5 Cylinder Records	390
Kammer & Reinhardt, Gramophone, Hand Wind, Horn, Berliner Patent, c.1891, 13 x 7 In..... *illus*	57500
Puritan, Bombay, No. 7475, Disc, Crank Arm, Caster Feet, 53 Records, 1910, 22 x 22 x 46 In.	288
Regina, Hexaphone, Model 101, Quartersawn Oak, Cast Iron, Cabriole Legs, 70 x 26 x 19 In.	8470
Regina, Reginaphone, No. 240, Mahogany Case, Carved Lion's Heads, Caster Feet, 51 x 23 x 20 In....	6353
Victor III, Oak, Wood Horn, Cabinet Base, Gilt, Nipper Decal, 1911, 21½ x 23 In..................	3738
Victor IV, Disc, Morning Glory Horn, Painted, Blue, Pink Flowers, Mahogany Cabinet, c.1908... *illus*	1495
Victor Victrola, Model II, Soundbox, Brass Horn, Wood Base, No. 9130A......................*illus*	960
Victor Victrola, Model VV-IX, Hinged Lid, Disc, Mahogany, Crank, Footed, 15 x 17 x 20 In.   115 to 207
Victor Victrola, Model VV-XVI, Talking Machine Co., Mahogany Case, 1906-29, 48 x 23 x 24 In...	230
Victor Victrola, XX VTLA, Side Crank, Cabinet, Red Mahogany, Refinished.................*illus*	2760

PHONOGRAPH NEEDLE CASE

Phonograph needle cases of tin are collected today by music and phonograph enthusiasts and advertising addicts. The tins are very small, about 2 inches across, and often have attractive graphic designs lithographed on the top and sides.

Fidelitone Master, Red, Gold, Round, 2 In.	13
Golden Pyramid, Pyramid Shape, Embossed, British Needle Co., 1900s, 2½ In.	95
Songster, Bird On Branch, Sun Rays, Yellow, Orange, Hinged Lid, 1⅞ x 1⅜ In............*illus*	27
Victor, Nipper Logo, 200 Needles, Hinged Lid, Blue, England	28

PHOTOGRAPHY

Photography items are listed here. The first photograph was a view from a window in France taken in 1826. The commercially successful photograph started with the daguerreotype introduced in 1839. Today all sorts of photographs and photographic equipment are collected. Albums were popular in Victorian times.

Photography, Albumen, Ulysses S. Grant & Staff, Cold Harbor, Virginia, Washington, 1864, 8 x 5 In.
$2,813

Cowan's Auctions

Photography, Cabinet Card, Chang & Eng Bunker, Siamese Twins, JH Blakemore, Mt. Airy, 1839, 6 x 4 In.
$504

Pook & Pook

Photography, Cabinet Card, Sioux Chief Long Soldier, Bismarck, D.T., Dakota Territory, D.F. Barry, 4 x 7 In.
$932

Pook & Pook

P

Photography, Camera Obscura, Rotating Prism, Glass Screen, Elongated Shape, France, 1800s, 10 In.
$540

Cottone Auctions

Digital Date

The first digital or "film-less" camera was invented in 1975 by Steven Sasson of Eastman Kodak.

Photography, Camera, Graphic Press, Graflex Crown, Optar, Wollensak
$259

Blackwell Auctions

Photography, Camera, Leica, Model A, Elmax, Flat Eyepiece, Baseplate, c.1925
$12,317

Bonhams

Cartes de visite, popular after 1854, were mounted on 2½-by-4-inch cardboard. Cabinet cards were introduced in 1866. These were mounted on 4¼-by-6½-inch cards. Stereo views are listed under Stereo Card. Stereoscopes are listed in their own section.

Albumen, Capt. Frank B. Schaffer, 1st Pa. Light Artillery, Gilt Frame, 1860, 9⅝ x 12½ In..	213
Albumen, Ulysses S. Grant & Staff, Cold Harbor, Virginia, Washington, 1864, 8 x 5 In. *illus*	2813
Ambrotype, Ruby, 2 Men Imbibing, Raising Glasses For A Toast, ⅙ Plate	238
Ambrotype, Ruby, CSA Private John D. Fly, 1st Bn., Mississippi Sharpshooters, 1860, ⅙ Plate	5000
Cabinet Card, Chang & Eng Bunker, Siamese Twins, JH Blakemore, Mt. Airy, 1839, 6 x 4 In.. *illus*	504
Cabinet Card, Geronimo, His Son & 2 Picked Braves, C.S. Fly, Arizona, 1886, 5 x 8½ In. ...	3465
Cabinet Card, Sioux Chief Long Soldier, Bismarck, D.T., Dakota Territory, D.F. Barry, 4 x 7 In.... *illus*	932
Cabinet Card, Union Officers, Camp, 13 Men, Albumen, c.1860, 4½ x 6½ In.	406
Camera Obscura, Rotating Prism, Glass Screen, Elongated Shape, France, 1800s, 10 In.... *illus*	540
Camera, Daguerreotype, Circular Base, Rocket Shape, Metal, Voigtlander, 1939, 34 In.	840
Camera, Ernst Leitz Wetzlar, Model 668 003, Leather Case, Germany, 3 x 5¾ x 2¾ In.	563
Camera, Graphic Press, Graflex Crown, Optar, Wollensak *illus*	259
Camera, Leica, Model A, Elmax, Flat Eyepiece, Baseplate, c.1925 *illus*	12317
Camera, Leica, Ms. Minoctar, 9.6mm Digital Lens, Wood Case, Minox	136
Camera, Nikon F5, 35mm, AF Nikkor 1:3.5-4.5 Lens, No. 3045256	277
Carte De Visite, Crew, Cannon, Docked Steamship, McPherson & Oliver, c.1860, 3⅝ x 2¼ In....	406
Carte De Visite, Marine Corps Musicians, Barracks, Civil War, Cardstock, 2¼ x 3⅝ In..	438
Daguerreotype, Woman Of Means, Brass Mat & Glass, Gilt Frame, Full Plate *illus*	281
Opalotype, Portrait, Gen. Lovell Harrison Rousseau, Oval, 1860, 3 x 2½ In., ⅙ Plate	125
Photograph, Miss America, 64 Contestants, Panoramic, Atlantic City, Frame, 1925, 10 x 40 In.. *illus*	680
Photograph, Model In White Turban, Digital Print, Richard Avedon, 1960s, 19½ x 16½ In.....	64
Photograph, Police, Group, Panorama, S.H. Beck, St. Petersburg, Florida, Frame, 1900s, 20 x 8 In.	173
Photograph, Workers, Cigar Store Indian, Charles S. McCaughan, Indiana, 4¾ x 6¾ In...	454
Photogravure, Canon De Chelly, Edward Sheriff Curtis, Woodgrain, 1904, 12 x 14 In.........	3600
Photogravure, Flute Boys, Priest, Hopi Farmers, Tawapa Spring, E.S. Curtis, 1908, 5½ x 7 In...	500
Photogravure, Schatten, Shadows, Aquatint, Markus Raetz, Frame, 1991, 73 x 30 In.	1020
Photogravure, Winter Camp, Apsaroke, On Rice Paper, Edward S. Curtis, 1908, 18 x 15½ In..	420
Silver Print, Dunes Oceano, Pencil Signed, Edward Weston, 1934, 8 x 9¾ In......................	8400
Silver Print, Hunting Ground, Indian, Montana, Roland Reed, 1912, 9 x 16 In.	2625
Tintype, Civil War Soldier, Standing, Shell Jacket, Holding Musket, Frame, 3 x 2 In.	381
Tintype, Mining Scene, Box Sluice, Entryway, ¼ Plate, 3¼ x 4¼ In.............................*illus*	605
Tintype, Police Officer, Tinted Pink Cheek, Peaked Cap, ⅙ Plate	150

PIANO BABY

Piano baby is a collector's term. About 1880, the well-decorated home had a shawl on the piano. Bisque figures of babies were designed to help hold the shawl in place. They usually range in size from 6 to 18 inches. Most of the figures were made in Germany. Reproductions are being made. Other piano babies may be listed under manufacturers' names.

Baby, Sitting, Dress, Bonnet, Pastel Colors, Gold Highlights, Bisque, Germany, 7 x 4 x 5 In...........*illus*	58
Baby, Sitting, Legs Crossed, Hands To Mouth, Blond Hair, Intaglio Eyes, Gebruder Heubach, 6 In.	107

PICKARD

Pickard China Company was started in 1893 by Wilder Pickard. Hand-painted designs were used on china purchased from other sources. In the 1930s, the company began to make its own china wares in Chicago, Illinois. The company made a line of limited edition plates and bowls in the 1970s and 1980s. It now makes many types of porcelains.

Pickard/Edgerton Art Studio
1893–1894

Pickard/Pickard Studios, Inc.
1925–1930

Pickard, Inc.
1938–present

Photography, Daguerreotype, Woman Of Means, Brass Mat & Glass, Gilt Frame, Full Plate
$281

Cowan's Auctions

Piano Baby, Sitting, Dress, Bonnet, Pastel Colors, Gold Highlights, Bisque, Germany, Victorian, 7 x 4 x 5 In.
$58

ardonantiques on eBay

Pickard, Basket, Rose, White Ground, Gold Trim, 3 Handles, 10 x 6 In.
$90

Woody Auction

Photography, Photograph, Miss America, 64 Contestants, Panoramic, Atlantic City, Frame, 1925, 10 x 40 In.
$680

Pook & Pook

Pickard, Jar, Lid, Flowers, Black Band, Gold, 2 Handles, Signed, Maxwell Rean Klipphahn, 9 x 4 In.
$150

Photography, Tintype, Mining Scene, Box Sluice, Entryway, ¼ Plate, 3 ¼ x 4 ¼ In.
$605

Pook & Pook

Don't Say "Cheese"

A smile may help date an old photograph. A smile expressed excessive familiarity. It was considered inappropriate and unbecoming to smile in a photograph in the days of daguerreotypes, tintypes, and even platinum prints. Having a picture taken was an important event. Clothing, background, posture, and expression were all serious and well-planned decisions.

Woody Auction

Pickard, Vase, Roses, Flared Rim, Leaves, Signed, Dominick Campana, 14 x 9 In. $6,500

Woody Auction

Picture, Calligraphy, Lion, Standing, Steel Nibbed Pen, Ink On Paper, Frame, c.1850, 21 ½ x 26 ¾ In. $2,691

Thomaston Place Auction Galleries

Picture, Diorama, Family, Outdoors, Trees, House, Mixed Media, Frame, Victorian, 20 x 30 In. $384

Rachel Davis Fine Arts

Basket, Rose, White Ground, Gold Trim, 3 Handles, 10 x 6 In.........................*illus*	90
Bowl, Grapes, Red & Green Swirl, Round, Pedestal, Limoges Blank, Signed Breidel, 4 x 9 In......	80
Cup & Saucer, Metallic Grapes, Black, Gold Decoration, Signed, RH, 2 x 4 In., Pair.............	100
Jar, Lid, Flowers, Black Band, Gold, 2 Handles, Signed, Maxwell Rean Klipphahn, 9 x 4 In. ....*illus*	150
Jug, Whiskey, Ears Of Corn, Bulbous, Dark Red Ground, Handle, Signed, Vokral, 6 x 5 In.	150
Pitcher, Aura Argenta Linear Pattern, 6-Sided, Handle, Limoges Blank, Signed, Hiecke, 8 ½ In.	125
Vase, Roses, Flared Rim, Leaves, Signed, Dominick Campana, 14 x 9 In. ....*illus*	6500

PICTURE

Pictures, silhouettes, and other small decorative objects framed to hang on the wall are listed here. Some other types of pictures are listed in the Print and Painting categories.

Aquatint, California Poppies, Signed & Numbered, Mark Adams, 1981, 15 x 16 In................	540
Calligraphy, Lion, Standing, Steel Nibbed Pen, Ink On Paper, Frame, c.1850, 21 ½ x 26 ¾ In. ....*illus*	2691
Calligraphy, Lord's Prayer, Marbled Paper, German Text, William H. Riegal, Frame, 1837, 8 x 6 In.....	508
Charcoal, Portrait, Woman, Thinking Position, Harvey Dinnerstein, Frame, 21 ¾ x 17 ½ In. ...	113
Charcoal, Sandpaper, Beacon Hill, Park Street, Boston Commons, Mid 1800s, 14 x 17 ½ In.	875
Diorama, Family, Outdoors, Trees, House, Mixed Media, Frame, Victorian, 20 x 30 In.*illus*	384
Drawing, Cattle Market, Charcoal & Ink, Frame, Willem Van Den Berg, Dutch, 48 x 38 In.	240
Drawing, Pencil, Seated Man, Miniature, Frame, P.M. Crowley, c.1830s, 2 In........................	572
Engraving, Lieutenant General George Washington, Hand Colored, Wood Frame, 13 x 10 In....	219
Engraving, The Baron, Gentlemen, Steel Plate, Frame, Gualoh Lubeck, 1800s, 10 ¼ x 9 ¼ In...	59
Etching, Cardigan Pier, Gilt Frame, James McNeill Whistler, Frame, 12 x 13 ⅜ In........*illus*	813
Etching, Landscape, On Paper, Signed, Rene Carcan, Frame, 1980, 20 ¾ x 24 ½ In.	125
Feather, 4 Hummingbirds, Flowering Branch, Victorian, Frame, 16 ½ x 13 ¾ In.	192
Gouache, Landscape, On Paper, Signed, W.H. Chafin Jr., Frame, 1961, 5 x 6 ¾ In.	666
Graphite, 2 Cats, Sleeping On Sheet, Henry Jarvis Peck, Walnut Stick Frame, 14 x 10 In......	234
Lithograph, Good Dog Bad Dog, Wood Frame, Stephen Huneck, 1997, 27 x 31 In.................	219
Lithograph, Steam Fire Engines, Wood Frame, Amoskeag Mfg. Co., c.1870, 27 x 34 In.	3630
Mechanical, Charley's Hat, Man & Dog Chase Hat, Clockwork, Schoenhut, Frame, 18 In.	570
Mechanical, Dog & Cat, Dancing, Monkey & Man, Playing Music, Clockwork, Frame, 16 In.	2040
Mechanical, Noah's Ark, Animals, Lithographed Paper, Crank Operated, Frame, 13 x 15 In.	4800
Mechanical, President & Mrs. Cleveland Fishing,Paper Litho, Clockwork, J. Ottmann, 18 In. ..	360
Mechanical, School Days, Teacher, Students, Paper Lithograph, Clockwork, Schoenhut, 21 x 25 In...	1800
Mechanical, The Tailor, Apprentice Pokes Tailor, Clockwork, Schoenhut, Frame, 13 ½ x 18 In. .	1320
Miniature, 2 Cupids, Putti Charging Arrows, Oil On Ivory, Brass Bezel, 1800s, 6 x 8 In.......	585
Needlework, British Warship, Inset, 3 Tintypes, Sailors, Woolwork, 1800s, 18 x 21 In.*illus*	813
Needlework, Embroidered, Sailing Ship, Wool, Gilt Frame, Late 1800s, 13 ¾ x 17 In. ..*illus*	188
Needlework, Embroidery, Christ In Prayer, Oval, Wood Frame, Continental, 1800s, 18 x 14 In...	425
Needlework, Embroidery, Flowers, Silk, Carved Wood, Square Frame, 1800s, 12 ½ x 14 In. ..	239
Needlework, Embroidery, Koi Fish, Lily Pads, White Flowers, Frame, Chinese, 28 x 28 In. ..	51
Needlework, Embroidery, Linen, Handwoven, Flowers, Repeat Border, Frame, 18 x 20 In. ..	120
Needlework, Embroidery, Whole Damn Family, Watercolor, On Fabric, Frame, c.1920, 23 x 23 In..	156
Needlework, Handmade Silk, Patriotic Design, Black Ground, 1900s, 20 ½ x 26 ½ In. *illus*	500
Needlework, Memorial, Silk Threads, Linen Ground, New England, c.1815, 15 ½ x 16 ¾ In. .	625
Needlework, Moses In The Bulrushes, Charles I, Gilt Frame, 1700s, 19 ½ x 22 ⅝ In	1875
Needlework, Mourning, Woman, Standing, Tombstone, Gilt, Gesso Frame, c.1799, 17 x 21 In.*illus*	2040
Needlework, Phoenix, Multicolor, Silk On Silk, Gilt, Molded Frame, c.1810, 14 x 20 In........	410
Needlework, Silkwork, Shepherdess, Snail, Bee & Fungus, Vine Border, 1700s, 11 x 12 In.*illus*	1000
Needlework, Stumpwork, Carrots, White, Brown, Oval, Frame, Victorian, 13 x 10 In...*illus*	384
Needlework, Stumpwork, Courtship, Plants, Animals, Shadowbox Frame, 1700s, 11 x 15 In.*illus*	9945
Needlework, Stumpwork, Dogs, Needlepoint, Trees, Shadowbox Frame, Victorian, 19 x 18 In.....*illus*	576
Needlework, Stumpwork, Friendship, 2 Women, Cream Ground, c.1700, 12 x 17 ½ In.........	1375
Needlework, Stumpwork, Parrot, Flowers, Beaded, Shadowbox Frame, Victorian, 20 x 16 In......	231
Needlework, Stumpwork, Biblical Scene, Wood Panel, England, 1600s, 16 x 12 In. .....*illus*	837
Pastel, Monterey Cypress, Signed, Esterberg, California, Frame, 1921, 11 x 14 In................	246
Plaque, Pietra Dura, 2 Parrots, Seated, Branch, Giltwood Frame, 10 ¼ x 8 ¼ In..................	216
Print, Bowle's Moral, Poor Richard's Almanac, 29 Colored Vignettes, Frame, c.1795-96, 30 x 24 In.	300
Scroll, Watercolor, Man, Woman, Below Tree, Chinese, 84 x 33 ¼ In. ....*illus*	1375

Picture, Etching, Cardigan Pier, Gilt Frame, James McNeill Whistler, Frame, 12 x 13⅜ In.
$813

New Haven Auctions

Picture, Needlework, British Warship, Inset, 3 Tintypes, Sailors, Woolwork, 1800s, 18 x 21 In.
$813

Eldred's

Picture, Needlework, Embroidered, Sailing Ship, Wool, Gilt Frame, Late 1800s, 13¾ x 17 In.
$188

Hindman

Picture, Needlework, Handmade Silk, Patriotic Design, Black Ground, 1900s, 20½ x 26½ In.
$500

Eldred's

Picture, Needlework, Mourning, Woman, Standing, Tombstone, Gilt, Gesso Frame, c.1799, 17 x 21 In.
$2,040

Alderfer Auction Company

Picture, Needlework, Silkwork, Shepherdess, Snail, Bee & Fungus, Vine Border, 1700s, 11 x 12 In.
$1,000

Hindman

TIP
Pictures above a bed or sofa should fill about two-thirds of the space. Hang a large picture or a group of small ones.

Picture, Needlework, Stumpwork, Carrots, White, Brown, Oval, Frame, Victorian, 13 x 10 In.
$384

Rachel Davis Fine Arts

Picture, Needlework, Stumpwork, Courtship, Plants, Animals, Shadowbox Frame, 1700s, 11 x 15 In.
$9,945

Thomaston Place Auction Galleries

Picture, Needlework, Stumpwork, Dogs, Needlepoint, Trees, Shadowbox Frame, Victorian, 19 x 18 In.
$576

Rachel Davis Fine Arts

P

Picture, Needlework, Stumpwork, Biblical Scene, Wood Panel, England, 1600s, 16 x 12 In.
$837

Jeffrey S. Evans & Associates

Picture, Scroll, Watercolor, Man, Woman, Below Tree, Chinese, 84 x 33 ¼ In.
$1,375

Andrew Jones Auctions

Picture, Serigraph, San Gabriel Mountains, Trees, Fred Grayson Sayre, Frame, c.1910, 18 x 25 ½ In.
$923

California Historical Design

Picture, Shadowbox, Specimen Eggs, Gilt Liner, Oval, 21 x 17 In.
$915

Rafael Osona Nantucket Auctions

Picture, Silhouette, Man & Woman, Side View, Gilt, Brass Frame, c.1835, 5 ¼ x 4 ½ In., Pair
$438

New Haven Auctions

Picture, Wax, Bowl Of Fruit, Multicolor, Oval Shadowbox Frame, Victorian, 30 x 26 In.
$1,216

Rachel Davis Fine Arts

P

Serigraph, American Girl, Nude, William Nelson Copley, 1973, 26 x 19 ½ In.	544
Serigraph, San Gabriel Mountains, Trees, Fred Grayson Sayre, Frame, c.1910, 18 x 25 ½ In.....*illus*	923
Shadowbox, Specimen Eggs, Gilt Liner, Oval, 21 x 17 In..*illus*	915
Silhouette, Family, Coaching Scene, Rearing Horses, Wood Frame, c.1900, 24 x 43 In.	120
Silhouette, Man & Woman, Side View, Gilt, Brass Frame, c.1835, 5 ¼ x 4 ½ In., Pair ...*illus*	438
Silhouette, Portrait, Robert Morris AE 50, American School, Frame, 1800s, 8 x 10 In.	2268
Silkwork, Multicolor, Flowers, 4 Swastika, Dark Blue Boarder, Faux Bamboo Frame, 44 x 60 In..	2340
Watercolor, La Bretagne, French School Ship, Moored, Ross Sterling Turner, 1913, 26 x 34 In.	556
Watercolor, On Paper, Address To Sons Of Temperance, Urns, Flowers, Columns, 1800s, 15 x 11 In.	810
Wax Portrait, King Louis XVI, Profile, Black & Gold Shadowbox, France, Early 1800s, 5 x 5 In.	410
Wax, Bowl Of Fruit, Multicolor, Oval Shadowbox Frame, Victorian, 30 x 26 In. ....*illus*	1216

PICTURE FRAMES *are listed in this book in the Furniture category under Frame.*

PILLIN

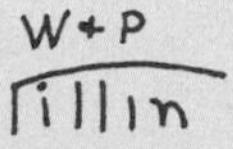

Pillin pottery was made by Polia (1909–1992) and William (1910–1985)
Pillin, who set up a pottery in Los Angeles in 1948. William shaped, glazed, and fired
the clay, and Polia painted the pieces, often with elongated figures of women, children,
flowers, birds, fish, and other animals. The company closed in 2014. Pieces are marked
with a stylized Pillin signature.

W + P
Ṗillin

Vase, Cylindrical, 3 Women, Multicolor, Horizontal Stripes, 10 x 3 ½ In..................................	469
Vase, Cylindrical, Black Decoration, Pinched Neck, Rolled Rim, 14 ½ x 5 In.	1300
Vase, Inverted Cone, Painted Horses, Multicolor Glaze, Signed, 5 x 5 In.	384
Vase, Oval, Brown Tones, Figure, Child's Portrait, 7 ⅛ x 4 ⅝ In....................................*illus*	254
Vase, Portrait, 3 Horses, Ballet Dancer, Blue Ground, Glaze, Polia Pillin, 8 ½ In..................	900
Vase, Square, Woman With Bird, Blue & Red Tones, Signed, c.1966, 10 ¼ x 3 ½ In.	1438

PINCUSHION DOLL

Pincushion dolls are not really dolls and often were not even pincushions. Some
collectors use the term "half-doll." The top half of each doll was made of porcelain. The edge of the half-doll was made with several small holes for thread, and
the doll was stitched to a fabric body with a voluminous skirt. The finished figure
was used to cover a hot pot of tea, powder box, pincushion, whiskbroom, or lamp. They
were made in sizes from less than an inch to over 9 inches high. Most date from the early
1900s to the 1950s. Collectors often find just the porcelain doll without the fabric skirt.

Baby, Arms Away, Curly Blond Hair, Blue Headband, Flowers, Germany, 2 ½ In.	14
Woman, Flapper, Pink Jacket, Multicolor Collar & Cuffs, Brown Hair, Hands Out, Art Deco, 6 In. .	446
Woman, Gray Hair, Yellow Bow, Head Turned, Arms Away, Nude, Marked, Dressel & Kister, 7 In...	275
Woman, Molded Black Hair, Blue Eyes, Pink Roses, Half Arms, Nude, Germany, c.1880, 5 In. .	230
Woman, Multicolor Hat, Hands Folded, Fabric Bow, Tea Cozy, Yellow, Checkered Panel, Early 1900s...	34

PIPE

Pipes have been popular since tobacco was introduced to Europe. Carved
wood, porcelain, ivory, and glass pipes and accessories may be listed here.

Applewood, Turned Wood Handle, Brass Collar, Steel Shaft, Hearts, France, 1831, 11 ¼ In.	509
Box, Wall Hanging, Pine, Scroll Cut, 1 Drawer, New England, 16 x 4 x 4 In...........................	531
Meerschaum, Bicycle Rider, Carved, Black Case, 5 ½ In..*illus*	156
Meerschaum, Erotic, Nude, Woman, Fitted Leather Case, 3 ½ In.	156
Pipe Rest, Figural, Head Shape, Open Mouth, Composition, Signed, 9 In. ....*illus*	150
Redware, Shaped Bowl, Person's Face, Wood Stem, 1850s, 8 In...	330
Water, Paktong, Opium, Engraved, Chinese, Early 1900s, 14 ¾ x 3 x 1 ½ In.	125
Wood, Dark, Carved, Folk Art, Bone Mouthpiece, George Benton, 5th Connecticut, 1863, 3 ½ In...	2500

Pillin, Vase, Oval, Brown Tones, Figure,
Child's Portrait, 7 ⅛ x 4 ⅝ In.
$254

Michaan's Auctions

Pipe, Meerschaum, Bicycle Rider,
Carved, Black Case, 5 ½ In.
$156

New Haven Auctions

Pipe, Pipe Rest, Figural, Head Shape,
Open Mouth, Composition, Signed, 9 In.
$150

Selkirk Auctioneers & Appraisers

This is an edited listing of current
prices. Visit **Kovels.com** to check thousands of prices from previous years and
sign up for free information on trends,
tips, reproductions, marks, and more.

P

Planters Peanuts, Tin, Pennant Brand, Salted Peanuts, 10 Lbs., 9¾ x 8½ In. $84

Cordier Auctions

Plastic, Bowl, Spaghetti, Resin Strands, Gaetano Pesce, Italy, 2013, 7 x 16½ In. $531

Palm Beach Modern Auctions

Plastic, Pitcher, Burrite, Model 123, Red, Disc, Clarence M. Burroughs, Los Angeles, 1948, 8½ In. $375

Wright

Plastic, Sculpture, Pumpkin, Resin, Red, White, Painted, Yayoi Kusama, Japan, 4 x 3¼ In. $390

Treadway

PIRKENHAMMER

Pirkenhammer is a porcelain manufactory started in 1803 by Friedrich Holke and J. G. List. It was located in Bohemia, now Brezova, Czech Republic. The company made tablewares usually decorated with views and flowers. Lithophanes were also made. It became Manufaktura Pirkenhammer I.S. Original Porcelan Fabrik Brezova s.r.o. in 2002. The mark of the crossed hammers is easy to remember as the Pirkenhammer symbol.

Bowl, Basket Weave, Multicolor Flowers, 2 Open Handles, Gold Trim, 10¼ In.	35
Plate, Dinner, Fruit Design, Light Pink Border, Gold Flowers & Trim, Epiag, Early 1900s, 9¾ In.	30
Teacup & Saucer, Pink Rose, Green Leaves, Scalloped Rim, Gold Trim, 2¼ x 6 In.	37
Vase, Cobalt Blue, Gilt Rim & Handles, Bird, Flowers & Leaves, 10¼ x 5¼ In.	329

PISGAH FOREST

Pisgah Forest Pottery was made in North Carolina beginning in 1926. The pottery was started by Walter B. Stephen, who had been making pottery in that location since 1914. The pottery continued in operation after his death in 1961. It closed in 2014. The most famous Pisgah Forest ware are the turquoise crackle glaze wares and the cameo type with designs made of raised glaze.

Pisgah Forest Pottery 1926+

Pisgah Forest Pottery Late 1940s

Pisgah Forest Pottery 1961+

Teapot, Lid, Turquoise, Pink Interior, Lipped Opening, Strainer Holes In Spout 1942, 4½ In.	75
Vase, Mottled Green, Tan Inside, Oval, Curved Shoulder, 3 Strap Handles, Marked, Late 1920s, 14 In.	500

PLANTERS PEANUTS

Planters peanuts memorabilia are collected. Planters Nut and Chocolate Company was started in Wilkes-Barre, Pennsylvania, in 1906. The Mr. Peanut figure was adopted as a trademark in 1916. National advertising for Planters Peanuts started in 1918. The company was acquired by Standard Brands, Inc., in 1961. Standard Brands merged with Nabisco in 1981. Nabisco was bought by Kraft Foods in 2000. Kraft merged with H.J. Heinz Company in 2015. Planters brand is now owned by Kraft Heinz. Some of the Mr. Peanut jars and other memorabilia have been reproduced and, of course, new items are being made.

Jar, Display, Slanted, Logo, Embossed, c.1937, 9 x 5 x 7 In.	99
Jar, Lid, Peanut Finial, Pennant, 5 Cent, 8-Sided, Glass	180
Knife & Fork, Child's, Carlton Silver Plate	28
Mechanical Pencil, Yellow, Blue, Gold	20
Mug, Figural Head, Monocle, Top Hat, Tan, Plastic, 1960s, 8 Oz.	12
Salt & Pepper, Figural, Crossed Leg, Plastic, 1940s, 3½ In.	32
Tin, Pennant Brand, Salted Peanuts, 10 Lbs., 9¾ x 8½ In. ....*illus*	84

PLASTIC

Plastic objects of all types are being collected. Some pieces are listed in other categories; gutta-percha cases are listed in the Photography category. Celluloid is in its own category. Some bakelite may also be found in the Jewelry category.

Bowl, Fruit, Molded Acrylic, Dansk Acryl Teknik, Denmark, c.1988, 4 x 20 x 17 In.	313
Bowl, Spaghetti, Resin Strands, Gaetano Pesce, Italy, 2013, 7 x 16½ In. ....*illus*	531
Ice Bucket, Lucite, Midcentury Modern, Thick Form, Oval Interior, Swing Lid, 1950s, 9 x 7 In.	145
Pitcher, Burrite, Model 123, Red, Disc, Clarence M. Burroughs, Los Angeles, 1948, 8½ In. .....*illus*	375

P

Sculpture, Acrylic, Untitled, Michael Wehstedt, 1900s, 37 x 12½ x 7½ In.	240
Sculpture, Fiberglass & Resin, Light Blue, Pink Top, Tom Butter, c.1982, 72 x 32 In.	2125
Sculpture, Lucite, Tree Shards, Group Of Narrow Peaks, Lillian Florsheim, 37 x 14 x 13 In.	2500
Sculpture, Monumental, Abstract, Check Shape, Resin, Louis Von Koelnau, 1986, 31 x 18 x 14 In. ...	2000
Sculpture, Pumpkin, Resin, Red, White, Painted, Yayoi Kusama, Japan, 4 x 3¼ In. .....*illus*	390
Sculpture, Woman, Nude Figure, Hair, Acrylic, Signed Hart, Frederick Elliott, 15 x 17 In. ....*illus*	2040
Tray, Sea Things, Transfer Print, Charles & Ray Eames, Waverly Products, c.1954, 1 x 20 x 13 In. ..	625
Tumbler, Engraved Skeleton, Prison Art, Practice Tattoo, White Ground, 6 x 2 In.	63

PLATED AMBERINA

Plated amberina was patented June 15, 1886, by Joseph Locke and made by the New England Glass Company. It is similar in color to amberina, but is characterized by a cream colored or chartreuse lining (never white) and small ridges or ribs on the outside.

Spooner, Ribbed, Waisted, Mahogany Rim, Cream Base, 4¼ In. ....*illus*	1500
Syrup, Silver Plate Lid & Dish, Signed, Pairpoint, 6 In. ....*illus*	2375
Tumbler, Ribbed, 3¾ In.	1080 to 1625
Vase, Trumpet, 3-Petal Rim, Clear Amber Foot, 9 In.	2700

POLITICAL

Political memorabilia of all types, from buttons to banners, are collected. Items related to presidential candidates are the most popular, but collectors also search for material related to state and local offices. Memorabilia related to social causes, minor political parties, and protest movements are also included here. Many reproductions have been made. A jugate is a button with photographs of both the presidential and vice presidential candidates. In this list a button is round, usually with a straight pin or metal tab to secure it to a shirt. A pin is brass, often figural, sometimes attached to a ribbon.

Badge, Teddy Roosevelt, Eagle, Rough Rider Club, Campaign, 1900, 3½ x 5 In.	502
Banner, Harrison & Morton, American Flag, Stars Border, Wood Frame, 1888, 19 x 19 In... *illus*	875
Bust, Thomas Jefferson, Plaster, Shoulder, White, Plinth, 28 In.	620
Button, Lincoln, For President, Ferrotype, Gilt Brass Frame, Round, Embossed, 1864, 1 In. *illus*	480
Candy Container, McKinley, Pail, Full Dinner, Albert Pick & Co., Chicago, 1900, 5½ x 4 x 2½ In.	222
Drum, Parade, Patriotic, 2 Sticks, Painted, Admiral George Dewey, Victorian, 8⅝ x 12 In. .	563
Flag, American, Shotgun Shells, Red, White & Blue, Wood Frame, 1900s, 13¼ x 21½ In. .... *illus*	84
Horn, Parade, Toleware, Thin To Thick, Yellow, Flower Design, 1900s, 26 In.	189
Match Safe, George Washington, Profile, Ax Shape, Inauguration, Spelter, 1789, 9 In. *illus*	47
Plate, McKinley, Roosevelt, Post, Taft & Bryan, Flower Rim, Opaque White, Early 1900s, 8¼ In....	199
Poster, Angela Davis, Flag, Rifle, Psychedelic Lettering, Yvonne Lawson, 17½ x 23 In.	290
Poster, Edward M. Kennedy, He Can Do More, Portrait, For U.S. Senator, Frame, 22½ x 14½ In. .	177
Poster, Russian Propaganda, 3 Grenadiers, V.N. Deni, Frame, 20 x 16 x 28 In. .... *illus*	281
Textile, Teddy Roosevelt, Progressive Battle Flag, Frame, 1912, 27 x 29½ In.	236
Ticket, Andrew Johnson, Impeachment, Black Text, Orange Ground, April 2, 1868, 3 x 3½ In.	576
Tray, Sherman, Taft, Our Candidates, Eagle, Elephant, Gilt Decoration, c.1915, 8 x 11 In. ...	70
Watch Fob, Woodrow Wilson, Charles E. Hughes, Portrait, 1916, 2 x 1½ In., Pair........ *illus*	236

POMONA

Pomona glass is a clear glass with a soft amber border decorated with pale blue or rose-colored flowers and leaves. The colors are very, very pale. The background of the glass is covered with a network of fine lines. It was made from 1885 to 1888 by the New England Glass Company. First grind was made from April 1885 to June 1886. It was made by cutting a wax surface on the glass, then dipping it in acid. Second grind was a less expensive method of acid etching that was developed later.

Plastic, Sculpture, Woman, Nude Figure, Hair, Acrylic, Signed Hart, Frederick Elliott, 15 x 17 In.
$2,040

Michaan's Auctions

Plated Amberina, Spooner, Ribbed, Waisted, Mahogany Rim, Cream Base, 4¼ In.
$1,500

Jaremos

Plated Amberina, Syrup, Silver Plate Lid & Dish, Signed, Pairpoint, 6 In.
$2,375

Jaremos

Political, Banner, Harrison & Morton, American Flag, Stars Border, Wood Frame, 1888, 19 x 19 In.
$875

Hindman

Political, Poster, Russian Propaganda, 3 Grenadiers, V.N. Deni, Frame, 20 x 16 x 28 In.
$281

Greenwich Auction

Political, Button, Lincoln, For President, Ferrotype, Gilt Brass Frame, Round, Embossed, 1864, 1 In.
$480

Rachel Davis Fine Arts

Political, Watch Fob, Woodrow Wilson, Charles E. Hughes, Portrait, 1916, 2 x 1½ In., Pair
$236

Copake Auction

Pomona, Teapot, Dome Lid, Botanical Garden, Curved Handle, Portmeirion, 10 x 9 In.
$63

Greenwich Auction

Political, Flag, American, Shotgun Shells, Red, White & Blue, Wood Frame, 1900s, 13¼ x 21½ In.
$84

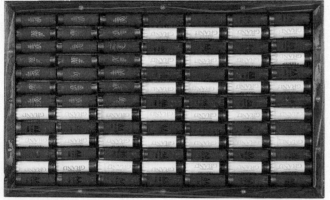

Selkirk Auctioneers & Appraisers

Popeye, Toy, Airplane, Eccentric, Tin Lithograph, Windup, Marx, Box, 1940, 7 In.
$800

Morphy Auctions

Political, Match Safe, George Washington, Profile, Ax Shape, Inauguration, Spelter, 1789, 9 In.
$47

Copake Auction

TIP

Condition, size, and small details determine the value of political buttons. To be sure the description is accurate for buying, selling, or insurance, just put the buttons on the glass top of a photocopying machine. Make copies of both the front and the back.

Bowl, Fluted, Amber Glass, Polished Pontil, 2½ x 5¼ In. 105
Teapot, Dome Lid, Botanical Garden, Curved Handle, Portmeirion, 10 x 9 In............. *illus* 63

PONTYPOOL, *see Tole category.*

POOLE POTTERY

Poole Pottery was founded by Jesse Carter in 1873 in Poole, England, and has operated under various names since then. The pottery operated as Carter & Co. for several years and established Carter, Stabler & Adams as a subsidiary in 1921. The company specialized in tiles, architectural ceramics, and garden ornaments. Tableware, bookends, candelabra, figures, vases, and other items have also been made. *Poole Pottery Ltd.* became the name in 1963. The company went bankrupt in 2003 but continued under new owners. Poole Pottery became part of Burgess & Leigh Ltd. in 2012. It is still in business, now making pottery in Middleport, Stoke-on-Trent.

Poole Pottery
1921–1924

POOLE ENGLAND

Poole Pottery
1924–1950

Poole *handpainted*

Poole Pottery Ltd.
1990–1991

Charger, Delphis, Red Ground, Green & Orange Quatrefoil, 16 In. 66
Ginger Jar, Lid, African Sky, Red Ground, Landscape Silhouette, 12 In. 60
Serving Bowl, Rectangular, Yellow & Orange Ground, Dark Blue & Turquoise Rectangles, 20 In..... 60
Vase, Atlantis, Relief Thistles, Gray Ground, Guy Sydenham, 10½ In.................................... 77
Vase, Calypso, Luster Glaze, Mottled Black & Gray, Oval, 6¼ In. 30
Vase, Matte Black, Freeform, Peanut Shape, Cream Interior, 11 In.. 59

POPEYE

Popeye was introduced to the Thimble Theatre comic strip in 1929. The character became a favorite of readers. In 1932, an animated cartoon featuring Popeye was made by Paramount Studios. The cartoon series continued and became even more popular when it was shown on television starting in the 1950s. The full-length movie with Robin Williams as Popeye was made in 1980. KFS stands for King Features Syndicate, the distributor of the comic strip.

Game, Pinball, Tin Lithograph, Vegetables, Durable Toy & Novelty Corp., 1935, 23 x 14 In... 400
Toy, Airplane, Eccentric, Tin Lithograph, Windup, Marx, Box, 1940, 7 In......................*illus* 800
Toy, Popeye The Pilot, Airplane, Tin, Multicolor, Large Wheels, Windup, Marx, 1930s, 7 In. 1020
Toy, Popeye, Carrying Parrot Cages, Tin Lithograph, Windup, Marx, Box, 8½ In................. 960
Toy, Popeye, Drummer, Multicolor, Chein, 7 In. ....*illus* 1320
Toy, Turnover Tank, Popeye, Tin Lithograph, Windup, Marx, Mexico, 4 x 3 In. ....*illus* 615
Toy, Van, Tractor Trailer, Popeye Transit Co., Tin Lithograph, Friction, Linemar, 4¼ x 13 In.. *illus* 861

PORCELAIN

Porcelain factories that are well known are listed in this book under the factory name. This category lists pieces made by the less well-known factories. Additional pieces of porcelain are listed in this book in the categories Porcelain-Asian, Porcelain-Chinese, Porcelain-Contemporary, Porcelain-Midcentury, and under the factory name.

Basin, Foot, Transferware, Blue & White, Flowers, 9 x 19 x 13 In. 305
Basket, Flowers, Leaves, Butterfly, Multicolor, Zigzag, 3½ x 12½ In. 126
Basket, Openwork, Blue & White, Gilt Rim, Shape Handle, Stamped, Walter, Germany, 4 x 7 In. .. 281
Bottle, Lid, Carriage, Omnibus & Coupe, White Ground, Lift Lid, 11 In., Pair........................ 164

Popeye, Toy, Popeye, Drummer, Multicolor, Chein, 7 In.
$1,320

Bertoia Auctions

Popeye, Toy, Turnover Tank, Popeye, Tin Lithograph, Windup, Marx, Mexico, 4 x 3 In.
$615

Morphy Auctions

Popeye, Toy, Van, Tractor Trailer, Popeye Transit Co., Tin Lithograph, Friction, Linemar, 4¼ x 13 In.
$861

Morphy Auctions

Porcelain, Bowl, Reticulated, Hand Painted, Multicolor Flowers, Plaue Schierholz, 2¼ x 11 In.
$94

Auctions at Showplace, NYC

P

Porcelain, Charger, Plate, Koi Fish, Blue & White, Dansk International Designs, Japan, 1½ x 12 In.
$63

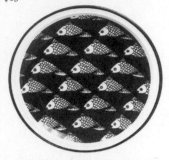

Auctions at Showplace, NYC

Porcelain, Compote, Figural, Dancing Figures, Marked, Germany, 1817, 20½ In., Pair
$512

Nadeau's Auction Gallery

Porcelain, Compote, Oval, Figures, Floral Interior, Mask Handles, Art Nouveau, Late 1800s, 12 x 18 In.
$1,188

John Moran Auctioneers

Porcelain, Fernery, Bright Blue Ground, Flowers, Leaves, Russia, c.1780s, 7½ x 12½ In.
$650

Woody Auction

Bowl, Reticulated, Hand Painted, Multicolor Flowers, Plaue Schierholz, 2¼ x 11 In. ... *illus*	94
Box, Lid, Hand Painted, Flowers, Hearts, Round, C.S. Babcock, c.1910, 5 x 2½ In.	215
Casket, Louis XV Style, Garden Scene, Gilt, Bronze, Scrollwork, Late 1800s, 14 x 14 x 10 In.	3933
Centerpiece, 12 Geese, Ring Style, Yellow Beak, Bellini, Italy, 7½ x 12 In.	63
Centerpiece, Basin Shape Top, Column, Cherubs, Flowers, Plaue Schierholtz, 1800s, 15 In. .	200
Centerpiece, Louis XV, Figural, Hand Painted, Basket Top, Top Shape Feet, 1900s, 27 x 14 In., Pair..	1638
Charger, Butterflies, Insects, Multicolor, Gilt Border, Wing Highlights, 1800s, 2¼ In.	431
Charger, Louis XVI, Painted, Blue Border, Gilt, Vienna, Late 1800s, 16⅝ In	500
Charger, Plate, Koi Fish, Blue & White, Dansk International Designs, Japan, 1½ x 12 In. ...*illus*	63
Charger, Royal Vienna, Hand Painted, Signed, Joseph Nigg, Austria, Late 1800s, 18¾ In. ...	2223
Compote, Figural, Dancing Figures, Marked, Germany, 1817, 20½ In., Pair. *illus*	512
Compote, Oval, Figures, Floral Interior, Mask Handles, Art Nouveau, Late 1800s, 12 x 18 In. *illus*	1188
Cooler, Wine, Hand Painted, Flowers, Leaves, Multicolor, 1800s, 7¾ In.	252
Cup & Saucer, Painted Flowers, Lobed, Wishbone Handle, Blue Mark, Vincennes, c.1750, 4¼ In.	4725
Cup & Saucer, Painted, Branches, Flowers, Kakiemon Colors, Scalloped Rim, St. Cloud, c.1740, 5 In.	1638
Cup, Pudding, Dome Lid, Gilt, Floral Finial, Richard Ginori, Italy, 4 x 3½ In., 7 Piece	188
Cup, Pudding, Dome Lid, Mushroom Shape Finial, Apilco, France, 4 x 3½ In., 6 Piece	63
Dish, Reticulated, Footed, Flowers, Multicolor, 2¼ x 9¼ In., Pair	128
Egg, Hinged Lid, Green Ground, Gilt, Flowers, Silver Mounted, Round Base, 7 In.	384
Fernery, Bright Blue Ground, Flowers, Leaves, Russia, c.1780s, 7½ x 12½ In. ... *illus*	650
Figurine, Bird, Toucan, Brass Base, Le Porcellane Manifattura Artistica, 1900s, 17 In.	938
Figurine, Courbette, Lipizzaner Horse, Rider, Jumping, Augarten, Vienna, c.1926, 11¼ In.	470
Figurine, Dancer, Wearing Green Vest & Pants, Mounted, Schaubach Kunst, 9½ In.	108
Figurine, Die Frucht, Nude, Art Deco, Gustav Oppel, Schwarzburger, Germany, 1921, 15 x 6 In., Pair .	260
Figurine, Dog, Seated, Gilt & Blue Collar, Rock Shape Base, Korzec, c.1790, 10¼ In.	1625
Figurine, Fish, Pink, Gilt Scales, Stand, No. 2476, Manifattura Porcellane, Italy, 12½ In.... *illus*	750
Figurine, Knight, Red, Blue, Black, Gilt Accents, Signed, M.J. Sutty, 1900s, 13¼ In.	2125
Figurine, Mother, Sitting, Holding Child, Wood Base, Florence Giuseppe Armani, Italy, 1900s, 12 In..	188
Figurine, Royal Officer, Man, Standing, Tricorn Hat, Tie, Schierholz Plaue, Germany, 1907, 8 In.*illus*	75
Figurine, Woman, Country Dress, Pink, White, Vincenzo Bertolotti, Italy, 1900s, 13½ In...	163
Figurine, Woman, Dancer, Raised Arm, Long Lacy Dress, Franz Witter, Germany, 1900s, 9½ In.	100
Figurine, Woman, Sitting, Dress, Chords, Cello Player, Luigi Fabris, Italy, 1900s, 7¾ In. ...	688
Group, Man, Sword, Woman, Flowers, Sideway, Ride, Gray Horse, Sitzendorf, Germany, 1900s, 11 In.	175
Group, Woman, Sitting, Playing Harp, Cherub, Gilt Base, G. Calle, Italy, 1900s, 10¼ In.	281
Jar, Oval, Fluted Gilt, Green Border, Molded, Wreath Center, 1900s, 12 In.	378
Jar, Yellow Glaze, Crackle, Carved, Teak Lid & Stand, Late 1800s, 7 x 6¾ In. ... *illus*	1521
Jardiniere, Famille Verte, Molded, Dragon Design, Octagonal, 6¾ x 9⅝ In., Pair	1200
Jardiniere, Flowers, Blue & White Design, Castle Mark, Gien, 12 x 13½ In. ... *illus*	236
Lavabo, Dolphin Spout, 2-Tail Merman, Italy, 1900s, 33 x 20 x 12 In.	325
Mirror, Flower Decorated Frame, 2 Putti, Oval Cartouche Crest, Italy, 1900s, 52 x 28 x 8 In.*illus*	480
Obelisk, Blue, Applied Vines, White Ground, Square Base, Continental, c.1900, 25 In., Pair	875
Obelisk, Multicolor, Neoclassical Decoration, Continental, 25 x 6 In., Pair	344
Pedestal, Minton Style, Cobalt Blue, Ceramic Top, Tripod Base, France, 1800s, 43 x 15 x 11 In. ...	275
Pitcher, Arts & Crafts, Hand Painted, Signed, Ivy Owens, Austria, c.1910, 8 x 8 x 4 In. ... *illus*	185
Pitcher, White Flowers, Multicolor, Ernst Wahliss, Late 1800s, 9¼ In. *illus*	545
Plaque, Courting Scene, Man, Woman, Gilt, Wood Frame, Signed, L. Coussy, France, 14 x 10 In...	350
Plaque, Enameled, Birds, Flowers, Frame, 1900s, 28½ x 8½ In., 4 Piece *illus*	1403
Plaque, Madonna & Child, Magnificat, Gilt Details, Botticelli, Frame, 13¾ In.	300
Plaque, Miniature, Portrait, Young Woman, Ivory Inlay, Continental, Frame, 1800s, 4 x 3½ In...	150
Plaque, Portrait, Indian Chief, Circular, Gilt, Metal Frame, c.1900, 7½ x 6 In.	121
Plaque, Round, Flowers & Phoenix, Multicolor, Enameled, 20 In.	1440
Plaque, Urn, Stone Shelf, Rose, Carnation, Fuchsia, C. Brown, England, Frame, c.1825, 10 x 8 In.	1196
Plaque, Woman, Giltwood Frame, Wagner, Swain, Shonau Co., Germany, c.1920, 12 x 10 In.*illus*	322
Plate, Flowers, Gilt, Scalloped Rim, White Ground, Continental, 1800s, 11 In.	375
Plate, Fruit & Leaves, Pierced Border, Green Rim, Schumann, Germany, 7½ In., 6 Piece ...	50
Plate, Multicolor, Flowers, Wavy Rim, Signed, Allen Louverstoft, 8 In., 9 Piece	72
Plate, Portrait, Woman, Pierce Carved, Giltwood Frame, Germany, Late 1800s, 9 x 9 In.	1500
Plate, Tiger Raj, Lynn Chase Design, White Ground, Green & Brown Border, 11 In., 8 Piece	875
Plate, White Ground, Gilt Rim, Blue Border, Lomonosov, 1900s, 12¼ In. ... *illus*	125

P

Porcelain, Figurine, Fish, Pink, Gilt Scales, Stand, No. 2476, Manifattura Porcellane, Italy, 12 ½ In.
$750

Lion and Unicorn

Porcelain, Figurine, Royal Officer, Man, Standing, Tricorn Hat, Tie, Schierholz Plaue, Germany, 1907, 8 In.
$75

Lion and Unicorn

Porcelain, Jar, Yellow Glaze, Crackle, Carved, Teak Lid & Stand, Late 1800s, 7 x 6 ¾ In.
$1,521

Thomaston Place Auction Galleries

Porcelain, Jardiniere, Flowers, Blue & White Design, Castle Mark, Gien, 12 x 13 ½ In.
$236

Copake Auction

Porcelain, Mirror, Flower Decorated Frame, 2 Putti, Oval Cartouche Crest, Italy, 1900s, 52 x 28 x 8 In.
$480

Selkirk Auctioneers & Appraisers

Porcelain, Pitcher, Arts & Crafts, Hand Painted, Signed, Ivy Owens, Austria, c.1910, 8 x 8 x 4 In.
$185

California Historical Design

Porcelain, Pitcher, White Flowers, Multicolor, Ernst Wahliss, Late 1800s, 9 ¼ In.
$545

Fontaine's Auction Gallery

Porcelain, Plaque, Enameled, Birds, Flowers, Frame, 1900s, 28 ½ x 8 ½ In., 4 Piece
$1,403

Bonhams

TIP
Dust the backs of your framed pictures once a year.

P

Porcelain, Plaque, Woman, Giltwood Frame, Wagner, Swain, Shonau Co., Germany, c.1920, 12 x 10 In.
$322

Jeffrey S. Evans & Associates

PORCELAIN

Porcelain, Plate, White Ground, Gilt Rim, Blue Border, Lomonosov, 1900s, 12 1/4 In.
$125

Hindman

Porcelain, Plate, White, Wide Border Of Roses, Morning Glory, Leaves, Swansea, 1815, 8 1/2 In.
$6,492

Bonhams

Porcelain, Platter, Shell Decoration, Seaweed, Oval, Marked Vietri, 14 x 19 In.
$122

Rafael Osona Nantucket Auctions

Porcelain, Pot, Crocus, Flowers, Gilt, White Ground, c.1810, 5 x 9 In., Pair
$1,599

Pook & Pook

Porcelain, Potpourri, Louis XV, Rococo, Green, Gilt, Scrolled Feet, France, 1800s, 7 x 12 x 8 1/2 In.
$787

Ahlers & Ogletree Auction Gallery

Porcelain, Urn, Gilt, Landscape, 2 Side Handles, Square Base, France, 1800s, 15 In., Pair
$938

New Haven Auctions

Porcelain, Urn, Lake, Trees & Swans, Courting, Transfer, Pink Border, Gilt, Sevres Style, 21 x 8 In.
$250

Woody Auction

Porcelain, Vase, Flared Rim, Parcel Gilt, Molded, 2 Handles, Footed, Continental, 1800s, 6 In.
$219

Hindman

Porcelain, Vase, Goofy, Painted, 2 Loop Handles, Asymmetric Lid, 18 In.
$531

Potter & Potter Auctions

Plate, White, Wide Border Of Roses, Morning Glory, Leaves, Swansea, 1815, 8½ In....... *illus*	6492
Platter, Oval, Figures, Flowers, Landscape, Gildea & Walker, 16 x 13 In.	35
Platter, Shell Decoration, Seaweed, Oval, Marked Vietri, 14 x 19 In. ....*illus*	122
Pot, Blanc De Chine, Lid, Floral Finial, Relief, Prunus Branches, 1700s, 2⅞ In., Pair	225
Pot, Crocus, Flowers, Gilt, White Ground, c.1810, 5 x 9 In., Pair.....................................*illus*	1599
Potpourri, Louis XV, Rococo, Green, Gilt, Scrolled Feet, France, 1800s, 7 x 12 x 8½ In....... *illus*	787
Punch Bowl, Blue Band, White Ground, Fruit, Leaves, Footed, 7¼ In.	250
Punch Bowl, Fuchsia, White Leafy Cartouches, Footed, Vine Around Base, Gilt Trim, 9 x 18 In..	180
Punch Bowl, Gilt Rim, Grapes, Fitted Base, Marked, 15 In.	360
Serving Dish, Double Bowls, Ruffled Rims, Fruit, Art Nouveau, Continental, 1950s, 4 x 13 In.	438
Sugar, Lid, Pinecone Finial, Marshall Field & Co., Swiss, c.1800, 4 In.	125
Tazza, Pastry, 3 Tiers, White & Gold Highlights, Marked, Portugal, 23 x 15 In......................	244
Tea Bowl, Painted, Flowers, Tree, Fence, Iron Red, Crossed Z Mark, Zurich, 1760s, 1¾ x 3 In., Pair..	284
Teapot, Lid, Blanc De Chine, Barrel Shape, Flowers, Metal Strainer, Bottger, c.1715, 5¼ x 6 In.....	4950
Teapot, Lift Lid, Painted, Arms Of High, 1700s, 5 x 7 In.	1586
Tureen, Lift Lid, Mermaids, Dolphins, Putti, Swans, Woman In Chariot, 4-Footed, 16 x 15 x 11 In.	240
Urn, Bisque, Bronze Mounted, Neoclassical Design, France, 9 x 13 x 10 In..........................	406
Urn, Dome Lid, Multicolor, Flowers, Gilt Metal Mounted, Tiche, 1900s, 23 In., Pair..............	313
Urn, Faux Malachite, Gilt, Lion Shape Handles, Paw Feet, 18 x 15½ In.	615
Urn, Gilt, Landscape, 2 Side Handles, Square Base, France, 1800s, 15 In., Pair..............*illus*	938
Urn, Lake, Trees & Swans, Courting, Transfer, Pink Border, Gilt, Sevres Style, 21 x 8 In...*illus*	250
Urn, Lid, Spiral Bands, Flowers, Gilt Metal, Cobalt Blue Neck & Foot, France, 21¼ In., Pair	420
Urn, Sevres Style, Courting Scene, Gilt Metal, Mounted, Signed, Lyse, 27¼ In., Pair..........	1063
Urn, Sevres Style, Lid, Bronze, Cobalt Blue Ground, Landscape, Maiden Handles, 1800s, 29 In., Pair..	5760
Vase Stand, Putti, Acanthus, Vienna Style, Painted, Flared Rims, Germany, 9 x 8 In., Pair ...	660
Vase, Art Nouveau, Figural, Blue & White Glaze, Richard Forster, 8 x 6 In.	84
Vase, Baluster Shape, Enamel Gilt, Celeste Ground, Footed, Late 1800s, 11 x 7 x 6 In., Pair.	1000
Vase, Butterfly, Swans, Hand Painted, Makkum Tichelaar, Dutch, 8½ x 5 In.	94
Vase, Chinese Style, Dark Blue, Bats, White Ground, Franz Mehlem, Germany, c.1900, 13½ In.	600
Vase, Doucai, Dragon, Gilt Bronze Base, Globular Body, Pale White Ground, 5½ x 4¾ In...	2040
Vase, Figural, Rabbits, Holding Hands, Wearing Clothes, Multicolor, Fitz & Floyd, 9 x 7 x 12 In.	59
Vase, Flared Rim, Parcel Gilt, Molded, 2 Handles, Footed, Continental, 1800s, 6 In............. *illus*	219
Vase, Goofy, Painted, 2 Loop Handles, Asymmetric Lid, 18 In. ....*illus*	531
Vase, Gorham, Gilt, Enamel Flowers, Marked, Jane Hutchinson, 16 x 11 In..................*illus*	384
Vase, Irises, Cream Ground, Gilt Top, Double Handles, Narrow Neck, Art Nouveau, 10 In.....	180
Vase, KPM Style, Gilt Ground, Flowers, Flared Rim, Figural Handles, 23¾ In., Pair.............	896
Vase, Limoges Style, Gilt, Pink Ground, Flowers, Swan Handles, Socle Plinth, 1900s, 12¾ In., Pair.....	242
Vase, Nude, Leaves Handle, Gilt, Marbleized, Art Nouveau, Jugendstil, 10 x 5 In. .... *illus*	240
Vase, Painted, Woman, Yellow Flower, Leaves, Signed, E. Simchen, Vienna, 7 In.	126
Vase, Turquoise, Green, Gilt Art, Landscape Scene, Painted Accent, 1900s, 13 In., Pair	256
Vase, Vienna Secessionist, Squares, Multicolor, Impressed Numbers, c.1900s, 10 x 4 In.. *illus*	677
Vase, Young Girl, Hand Painted, Champleve Top & Foot, Pedestal, France, 6 x 2 In..............	70

Porcelain-Asian includes pieces made in Japan, Korea, and other Asian countries. Asian porcelain is also listed in Canton, Chinese Export, Imari, Japanese Coralene, Moriage, Nanking, Occupied Japan, Porcelain-Chinese, Satsuma, Sumida, and other categories.

Centerpiece, Lid, Gilt, Multicolor, Dragon Handles, Shishi Lion Knob, Japan, 1900s, 12 x 14 In..	500
Charger, Blue & White, Leaping Fish, Swamp Grass, Geometric Rim, Vietnam, 1700s, 2 x 10 In.	1287
Dish, Diamond Shape, Paulownia Designs, Blue & White, Japan, Early 1900s, 6½ In., Pair	88
Dish, Peach, Leafy Branches, Footed, Japan, 1800s, 5¾ In., Pair...	201
Fishbowl, Blue & White, Flowers, Japan, 1800s, 15 x 17 In..*illus*	270
Incense Burner, Foo Dog Shape, Blue On White, Flowers, Spiral Highlights, Japan, 1900s, 5 In.	108
Jardiniere, Blue & White, Hexagonal, Bird, Floral Landscape, Japan, Meiji Period, 14 x 18 In...	250
Urn, Craquelure, Scenic, 2 Handles, Blue, White, 12½ In., Pair...	189
Vase, 2 Handles, Urn Shape, Serpentine Dragon, Decorated, Relief Scales, Greek Key, Japan, 10 In.	120
Vase, Cherry Blossoms, Tree, Blue, White, Fluted, Ruffled, Wood Base, Japan, 25½ In.	153
Vase, Dark Coal Glaze, Mallet Shape, 6-Character Mark, Japan, 1900s, 19 In.	60

Porcelain, Vase, Gorham, Gilt, Enamel Flowers, Marked, Jane Hutchinson, 16 x 11 In.
$384

Nadeau's Auction Gallery

Porcelain, Vase, Nude, Leaves Handle, Gilt, Marbleized, Art Nouveau, Jugendstil, 10 x 5 In.
$240

Alderfer Auction Company

P

Porcelain, Vase, Vienna Secessionist, Squares, Multicolor, Impressed Numbers, c.1900s, 10 x 4 In.
$677

California Historical Design

Porcelain-Asian, Fishbowl, Blue & White, Flowers, Japan, 1800s, 15 x 17 In.
$270

Michaan's Auctions

Porcelain-Asian, Vase, Dark Orange, Floral Ground, Landscape Scene, Samurai, Woman, 1800s, 24 In.
$960

Brunk Auctions

Porcelain-Chinese, Bowl, Flowers, Dragon Design, Yellow Ground, Republic Period, 33 In., Pair
$625

Charlton Hall Auctions

Porcelain-Chinese, Charger, Ming Style, Blue & White, Birds, Waterscape, Pine & Rock, 1900s, 8½ In.
$384

Neal Auction Company

TIP

Don't soak old ceramic pieces in water for a long time. Old repairs may be loosened.

Porcelain-Chinese, Cooler, Fruit, Dome Lid, Painted, Flowers, Gilt Rim, Blue Ground, 6 x 7 In., Pair
$1,200

Richard Opfer Auctioneering, Inc.

Porcelain-Chinese, Cup, Doucai, Dragon, Auspicious Emblems, Blue Underglaze, Yongzheng Mark, 2¾ In., Pair
$540

Michaan's Auctions

Porcelain-Chinese, Dish, Shallow, Blue, Island & Flags Scene, White Ground, Ming Dynasty, 5¼ In.
$995

Thomaston Place Auction Galleries

Porcelain-Chinese, Figurine, Guanyin, White, Flowing Robe, Lotus Blossom, Fish, Waves, Blue, 29 x 14 In.
$344

Auctions at Showplace, NYC

Porcelain-Chinese, Ginger Jar, Lid, Knob Finial, Red, Blue, Flowers, 14 x 8 In.
$448

Roland NY Auctioneers & Appraisers

Vase, Dark Orange, Floral Ground, Landscape Scene, Samurai, Woman, 1800s, 24 In.. *illus* 960

Vase, Painted, Paneled Sides, Vignettes, People, Garden Scenes, 11 ½ In., Pair...................... 660

Porcelain-Chinese is listed here. See also Canton, Chinese Export, Imari, Moriage, Nanking, and other categories.

Bottle Stand, Pompadour, 2 Cups, Conjoined Handles, Eagle, Fish Cartouches, 1745, 3 x 8 x 4 In.. 2700

Bowl, Chrysanthemums, Enameled, Wood Stand, Jiaqing, 5 ¼ x 9 In. 390

Bowl, Famille Rose, Boys Playing, Outdoor Setting, 6-Character Mark, 4 In., Pair.............. 1140

Bowl, Famille Verte, Fish, People, Garden Pavilions, Green Ground, Wood Stand, 1900s, 30 In...... 183

Bowl, Flared Rim, White Ground, Blue Flying Horses & Crabs, 1368-1644, 3 x 7 In. 7605

Bowl, Flowers, Dragon Design, Yellow Ground, Republic Period, 33 In., Pair................ *illus* 625

Bowl, Qingbai, Conical, Carved Interior, Glazed, White Ground, 2 ⅞ x 8 ¼ In. 854

Bowl, Red, White, Flowers, Marked, 2 x 4 In.. 438

Box, Lid, Figural, Goose, Turquoise & Green, c.1970, 16 x 9 x 15 In. 130

Charger, Figural, Blue & White, Round Panel, Natural Scene, Dragons, Phoenixes, 12 In... 1440

Charger, Ming Style, Blue & White, Birds, Waterscape, Pine & Rock, 1900s, 8 ½ In...... *illus* 384

Charger, Pink Ground, Bird On Branch, Black Rim, Multicolor Flowers, 20th Century, 18 In.... 26

Cooler, Fruit, Dome Lid, Painted, Flowers, Gilt Rim, Blue Ground, 6 x 7 In., Pair......... *illus* 1200

Cup, Doucai, Dragon, Auspicious Emblems, Blue Underglaze, Yongzheng Mark, 2 ¾ In., Pair.... *illus* 540

Dish, Shallow, Blue, Island & Flags Scene, White Ground, Ming Dynasty, 5 ¼ In.......... *illus* 995

Dish, Square, Blue & White, Scalloped Edge, Central Foo Dog, Flowers, 2 x 11 In. 180

Figurine, Buddhist, Guanyin, Sitting, Blanc De Chine, Dragon, 1900s, 32 In. 255

Figurine, Guanyin, Goddess Of Mercy, Holding Vase, Multicolor, Wood Platform Base, 25 In..... 189

Figurine, Guanyin, White, Flowing Robe, Lotus Blossom, Fish, Waves, Blue, 29 x 14 In.. *illus* 344

Figurine, Parrot, Standing, On Rocks, Red Glazed, 1800s, 9 In., Pair 938

Figurine, Phoenix Bird, Perched, Tree, 1800s, 24 In. 1188

Figurine, Seated, 2-Lotus Base, Blanc De Chine Guanyin, 1000 Arms, 10 In........................ 180

Flask, Ming Style, Moon, Blue & White, Dragon, Rolling Waves Handles, 18 x 13 x 4 In. 270

Ginger Jar, Dragons & Phoenix, Red & Blue, White Ground, Early 1800s, 7 x 6 In. 400

Ginger Jar, Lid, Knob Finial, Red, Blue, Flowers, 14 x 8 In. .... *illus* 448

Ginger Jar, Lid, Multicolor, Painted, Flower Lappets, Orange Beast Heads, 26 In. 480

Ginger Jar, Women, Children, Playing, Courtyard, Blue White, Mid 1700s, 11 ¾ x 9 ½ In. .. 3690

Group, Blanc De Chine, 8 Classical Figures, Boat, 1800s, 10 ¾ x 10 ½ x 5 In............... *illus* 484

Hat Stand, Vase, Famille Rose, Yellow Ground, Leafy Lotus Flowers, 11 In. 540

Incense Burner, Famille Rose, Gilt Bronze, Figural, Mounted, Late 1700s, 6 ½ x 6 x 4 In., Pair........ 4410

Jar, Lid, Baluster, Flowers & Fruit, Yellow Ground, Early 1900s, 15 In............................ *illus* 100

Jar, Lid, Glazed, Figural Designs, Foo Dog Finial, Square Tapered Bodies, 14 x 4 x 4 In., Pair....... 1088

Jar, Lid, Kangxi, Court Garden, Double Ring Underside, 1900s, 11 In., Pair 1250

Planter, Blue Flowers & Panels, White Ground, Landscape Scenes, 13 x 16 In....................... 1080

Planter, Koi Fish, Birds, Flowers, Multicolor, 14 ½ x 16 ½ In., Pair...................................... 192

Planter, Koi Fish, Flowers, Leaves, Multicolor, 1800s, 19 x 18 ½ In. 1664

Planter, Narcissus, Ge Type, Creamy Glaze, Dark Crackle, 4 Ruyi Shape Feet, Chinese, 6 ½ In.... 720

Planter, Red Glaze, White Interior, 12 x 9 ½ In., Pair.. 154

Planter, Tobacco Leaf Pattern, White Ground, 11 x 12 ½ In. 384

Planter, Tray, Blue & White Floral Ground, Oval Medallion, Landscape, 7 x 10 In., Pair...... 2160

Plaque, Famille Rose, Hardwood, Painted, Couple In Garden Scene, 48 x 14 x 1 In............. 454

Plate, Friendship, Crossed Flags, Blue Rim, White Ground, c.1912, 9 In. 854

Platter, Hundred Antiques Pattern, Oval, 1700s, 14 ½ x 11 In. 3750

Punch Bowl, Hand Painted, Butterflies, Flowers, Brass Stand, Macau, 1900s, 12 x 12 x 5 In. ....*illus* 153

Sculpture, Cat, Sleeping, White & Orange Stripes, 1900s, 3 x 8 x 5 In. 50

Teapot, Frog Finial Lid, Earthenware, Crackle Glaze, Bamboo Handle, 7 x 5 In........... *illus* 438

Vase, Blanc De Chine, Latticework Design, c.1900s, 13 ½ x 7 In. .... *illus* 125

Vase, Caramel, Brown Hombre, Cylindrical Neck, Bulbous Pear Shape, Ring Foot, 1900s, 10 In. 150

Vase, Celadon Handle, Blue Calligraphy, Landscape, Late 1700s, 15 x 8 In. 100

Vase, Chrysanthemums, Blue & White, Narrow Neck, 2 Rings, 13 ⅞ In. 1920

Vase, Cobalt Blue, White Crackle Glaze, Bottle Shape, 14 x 8 In... 60

Vase, Double Gourd, Yellow Ground, 2 Dragons, White Flowers, 7 In. 813

Vase, Famille Rose, Hexagonal, Nobles, Landscape, Celadon Ground, 1900s, 18 ¾ In., Pair. 671

Porcelain-Chinese, Group, Blanc De Chine, 8 Classical Figures, Boat, 1800s, 10 ¾ x 10 ½ x 5 In.
$484

Fontaine's Auction Gallery

Porcelain-Chinese, Jar, Lid, Baluster, Flowers & Fruit, Yellow Ground, Early 1900s, 15 In.
$100

Turner Auctions + Appraisals

P

Porcelain-Chinese, Punch Bowl, Hand Painted, Butterflies, Flowers, Brass Stand, Macau, 1900s, 12 x 12 x 5 In.
$153

Charleston Estate Auctions

Porcelain-Chinese, Teapot, Frog Finial Lid, Earthenware, Crackle Glaze, Bamboo Handle, 7 x 5 In.
$438

Auctions at Showplace, NYC

Porcelain-Chinese, Vase, Blanc De Chine, Latticework Design, c.1900s, 13 ½ x 7 In.
$125

P

Woody Auction

Porcelain-Chinese, Vase, Flowers, Birds, 2 Foo Dog Handles, Multicolor, White Ground, 1800s, 16 ½ In.
$545

Fontaine's Auction Gallery

Porcelain-Chinese, Vase, Sages, Scholars In Garden, Fish Scale, Multicolor, 18th Century, 16 In.
$330

Alex Cooper Auctioneers

Porcelain-Chinese, Water Dropper, Buddhist Lion, Lying Down, Brocade, Ball, Multicolor, 2 In.
$250

Neal Auction Company

Porcelain-Contemporary, Epergne, Chinoiserie, 2 Tiers, Male Figure, Baskets, Vista Alegre, 16 ½ In.
$2,057

Ahlers & Ogletree Auction Gallery

Porcelain-Midcentury, Decanter, Napoleon, Cork Stopper, Matte Glaze, Robj, Paris, France, c.1930, 10 x 4 x 3 ½ In.
$375

Toomey & Co. Auctioneers

Porcelain-Midcentury, Figurine, Dog, Pekingese, No. 1003, Seated, Brown & White, Dahl Jensen, Denmark, 5 ¼ In.
$113

Lion and Unicorn

Vase, Famille Verte, Birds, Landscapes, Flared Edges, Woven Baskets, 1722, 14 In., Pair.......	5985
Vase, Flambe, Flared Rim, Lavender, Molded Foot, 21¼ In., Pair..	750
Vase, Flowers, Birds, 2 Foo Dog Handles, Multicolor, White Ground, 1800s, 16½ In. ..... *illus*	545
Vase, Flowers, Birds, Long Neck, Gilt Rim, White Ground, 8½ In..	219
Vase, Flowers, Butterflies, 6 Children, Climbing, Black Ground, 1970s, 9 x 9 x 14 In.	59
Vase, Koi Fish, Water Lily, Cloisonne, 14½ In., Pair	1658
Vase, Meiping, Black Dragon, Crackle White Ground, 1800s, 16¾ In.	726
Vase, On Stand, Square, Multicolor, Flowers, Red Mark, 12 x 7 x 5 In.	5440
Vase, Reticulated, Flowers, White Ground, Greek Key Design Top & Bottom, 2 x 2 x 4 In.	4200
Vase, Ruyi Scepter, 2 Handles, Birds, Flowers, 14 x 5¼ In.	3438
Vase, Sages, Scholars In Garden, Fish Scale, Multicolor, 18th Century, 16 In.............. *illus*	330
Vase, Sang De Boeuf, Glaze, Wide Shoulder, Narrow Neck, 15 x 7 In., Pair	125
Vase, Tied Satchel Form, Etched Dragons, Yellow Glaze, Rope Twist Neck, 1800s, 7 In.	370
Vase, White Ground, Courtyard, Tattoo Ceremony, Flowers, Ruyi Border, 1644, 9½ In.	512
Vase, Yen Yen Shape, Pine Design, Orange Peel Texture, Blue, White, 1644, 14½ x 10 In.....	2337
Water Dropper, Buddhist Lion, Lying Down, Brocade, Ball, Multicolor, 2 In. .... *illus*	250

Porcelain-Contemporary lists pieces made by artists working after 1975.

Cachepot, Vista Alegre, Yellow, Cream, Gilt Highlights, Mottahedeh, 7½ x 6½ In., Pair	118
Dish, Rythme, White & Red, Rectangular, Hermes, France, 6¼ x 4¾ In., Pair	363
Epergne, Chinoiserie, 2 Tiers, Male Figure, Baskets, Vista Alegre, 16½ In. .... *illus*	2057
Figurine, Florence Comet, Woman, Shooting Star, Giuseppe Armani, Limited Edition, 1998, 15 In.....	3500

Porcelain-Midcentury includes pieces made from the 1930s to about 1975.

Decanter, Napoleon, Cork Stopper, Matte Glaze, Robj, Paris, France, c.1930, 10 x 4 x 3½ In.. *illus*	375
Figurine, Dog, Pekingese, No. 1003, Seated, Brown & White, Dahl Jensen, Denmark, 5¼ In.*illus*	113
Figurine, Horse, Rider, Titled, Hufourg Wien, Oval Base, Vienna, 1930s, 9½ In........... *illus*	344
Figurine, Little Nell, White Ground, Base, Viktor Schreckengost, Cleveland, c.1930, 5 x 4 x 3 In. *illus*	1875
Figurine, Seated, Stamped, Painted, Walter Bosse, 7 x 6 In.. *illus*	2813
Vase, Cobalt Blue Ground, Flower Decor, Gilt, 2 Handles, Maurice Pinon, c.1930, 17¾ In., Pair.	182
Vase, Collina, 4 Parts, Modular, Black Glaze, Sergio Asti, Italy, c.1965, 9 x 16 x 17 In............	688
Vase, Hand Painted, Birds & Flowers, Loop Handles, On Stand, Signed, Alton, 19 x 10 In.	58

POSTCARD

Postcards were first legally permitted in Austria on October 1, 1869. The United States passed postal regulations allowing the card in 1872. Most of the picture postcards collected today date after 1910.

The amount of postage can help to date a card. The rates are: 1872 (1 cent), 1917 (2 cents), 1919 (1 cent), 1925 (2 cents), 1928 (1 cent), 1952 (2 cents), 1958 (3 cents), 1963 (4 cents), 1968 (5 cents), 1971 (6 cents), 1973 (8 cents), 1975 (7 cents), 1976 (9 cents), 1978 (10 cents), March 1981 (12 cents), November 1981 (13 cents), 1985 (14 cents), 1988 (15 cents), 1991 (19 cents), 1995 (20 cents), 2001 (21 cents), 2002 (23 cents), 2006 (24 cents), 2007 (26 cents), 2008 (27 cents), 2009 (28 cents), 2011 (29 cents), 2012 (32 cents), 2013 (33 cents), 2014 (34 cents), 2016 (35 cents beginning January 17 and back to 34 cents beginning April 10, 2016), 2018 (35 cents beginning January 21, 2018). Collectors search for early or unusual postmarks, picture postcards, or important handwritten messages (that includes celebrity autographs). While most postcards sell for low prices, a small number bring high prices. Some of these are listed here.

Christmas, Santa, Smoking Pipe, Child With Wings, Embossed, Merry Xmas, 1910	35
Couple, Table, Victorian Dress, Lithograph, Greetings From Coney Island, c.1910	15
Native American Indians, Tama, Iowa, 1940s	5
Prince Andrew, Miss Sarah Ferguson, Reproduction Of Stamp, 1986...................................	20
Sabine River, At Orange, Texas, 1917	10
Thanksgiving Day, Boy Riding Turkey, Holding Reins, Multicolor, Gilt, Divided Back, 1917.	15

Porcelain-Midcentury, Figurine, Horse, Rider, Titled, Hufourg Wien, Oval Base, Vienna, 1930s, 9½ In.
$344

Eldred's

Porcelain-Midcentury, Figurine, Little Nell, White Ground, Base, Viktor Schreckengost, Cleveland, c.1930, 5 x 4 x 3 In.
$1,875

Wright

P

Porcelain-Midcentury, Figurine, Seated, Stamped, Painted, Walter Bosse, 7 x 6 In.
$2,813

Nadeau's Auction Gallery

Poster, 3rd Exposition De Bellas Artes, Barcelona, 2 Women, Art Nouveau, Frame, 1896, 8 x 13 In.
$185

California Historical Design

Poster, Allman Brothers, Dreams, Lithograph, Lorraine Klotz, Polygram Records, 1989, 36 x 24 In.
$500

Turner Auctions + Appraisals

Poster, Circus, Walter L. Main, 3 Ring Trained Wild Animal Shows, Woman, Tigers, 26 x 40 In.
$391

Pook & Pook

TIP
Never store paper items with any metal staples or paper clips. They may rust.

POSTER

Posters have informed the public about news and entertainment events since ancient times. Nineteenth-century advertising and theatrical posters and twentieth-century movie and war posters are of special interest today. The price is determined by the artist, the condition, and the rarity. Posters may also be listed in Movie, Political, World War I and II, and other categories in this book.

31st Annual Grammy Awards, Rainbow Gramophone, Signed, Peter Max, 24 In.	800
3rd Exposition De Bellas Artes, Barcelona, 2 Women, Art Nouveau, Frame, 1896, 8 x 13 In. *illus*	185
Allman Brothers, Dreams, Lithograph, Lorraine Klotz, Polygram Records, 1989, 36 x 24 In. *illus*	500
Cafe Liqueur, Lithograph, Yellow, Brown, Custom Frame, 41 ½ x 32 x 33 In.	176
Circus, Carnival & Fun Fair, Clown, Bump Car, Wood, Frame, 44 x 38 ⅜ In.	38
Circus, Ringling Bros. & Barnum & Bailey, Greatest Show On Earth, Lou Jacobs, c.1960, 50 x 28 In.	150
Circus, Ringling Bros. & Barnum & Bailey, Masonite Board, 38 x 42 In.	241
Circus, Walter L. Main, 3 Ring Trained Wild Animal Shows, Woman, Tigers, 26 x 40 In. *illus*	391
Concert, Billy Joel, Moore Theater, Seattle, November 1976, Portrait, White, Black, 22 In.	425
Concert, Dance, Zachary Richards, Sun Dogs MoFessions, Mark Henson, 1996, 13 x 19 In.	88
Concert, Lightning Hopkins, Kaleidoscope At The Straight, Lithograph, C. Braga, 1967, 22 x 16 In.	344
Concert, Olympia, Grand Ballet, Brighton, Pal, Jean De Paleologue, 1893, 48 x 30 In. *illus*	1040
Concert, Willie Nelson, Listen To These Lyrics, Offset Lithograph, 1975, 23 x 17 ½ In.	219
Dance, Erry & Merry, Walter Schnackenberg, 1912, 49 x 37 In. *illus*	8750
Exhibition, Jasper Johns, Whitney Museum, Savarin Coffee Can, Litho, Frame, 1977, 30 x 46 In.	345
J.A. Coburn's Great Minstrels, La Raub & Scottie, Donaldson Lithograph Co., Ky., 34 x 47 In.	63
L'Emeraude, Lithograph, Precious Stones, Alphonse Mucha, F. Champenois, Paris, 1902, 38 x 15 In.	7800
Olympia, Grand Ballet, Brighton, Lithograph, Jean De Paleologue, Paris, 55 x 37 In.	688
Opera, Life & Death, Chromolithograph, Montague Chatterton & Co., Frame, Late 1800s, 29 x 19 In.	63
Political, 500 Anos Terrorismo Plan Columbina, Offset Lithograph, 72 x 16 In.	38
Theater, Jane Marny, Woman's Face, H. Chachoin, Paris, Frame, c.1930, 65 ½ x 49 ½ In. *illus*	666
Theater, Mikado, D'Oily Carte's Opera Co., Lithograph, J. Stetson, London, 1885, 29 ½ x 29 ½ In.	780
Travel, California, Color, Screenprint, Mario, 1979, 24 x 18 In. *illus*	38
Window Card, Carter The Great, Carter Beats The Devil, Litho, Frame, 19 x 13 In. *illus*	125

POTLID

Potlids are just that, lids for pots. Transfer-printed potlids had their heyday from the 1840s to the early 1900s. The English Staffordshire potteries made ceramic containers with decorative lids for bear's grease, shrimp or meat paste, cold cream, and toothpaste. Printed advertising and pictures of historical events, portraits of famous people, or scenic views were designed in black and white or color. Reproductions have been made.

Celebrated Heal-All Ointment, Mrs. Ellen Hale's, Woman's Portrait, London	35
Cherry Tooth Paste, Patronized By The Queen, John Gosnell & Co., c.1880, 3 In. *illus*	132

POTTERY

Pottery and porcelain are different. Pottery is opaque; you can't see through it. Porcelain is translucent. If you hold a porcelain dish in front of a strong light, you will see the light through the dish. Porcelain is colder to the touch. Pottery is softer and easier to break and will stain more easily because it is porous. Porcelain is thinner, lighter, and more durable. Majolica, faience, and stoneware are all pottery. Additional pieces of pottery are listed in this book in the categories Pottery-Art, Pottery-Chinese, Pottery-Contemporary, Pottery-Midcentury, and under the factory name. For information about pottery makers and marks, see *Kovels' Dictionary of Marks—Pottery & Porcelain: 1650–1850* and *Kovels' New Dictionary of Marks—Pottery & Porcelain: 1850 to the Present*, or go to Kovels.com.

Bowl, Deep, Mottled Glaze, Multicolor, 4 x 9 In.	84

Poster, Concert, Olympia, Grand Ballet, Brighton, Pal, Jean De Paleologue, 1893, 48 x 30 In.
$1,040

Poster, Theater, Jane Marny, Woman's Face, H. Chachoin, Paris, Frame, c.1930, 65 ½ x 49 ½ In.
$666

Poster, Travel, California, Color, Screenprint, Mario, 1979, 24 x 18 In.
$38

Turner Auctions + Appraisals

Swann Auction Galleries

Fontaine's Auction Gallery

Poster, Window Card, Carter The Great, Carter Beats The Devil, Litho, Frame, 19 x 13 In.
$125

Poster, Dance, Erry & Merry, Walter Schnackenberg, 1912, 49 x 37 In.
$8,750

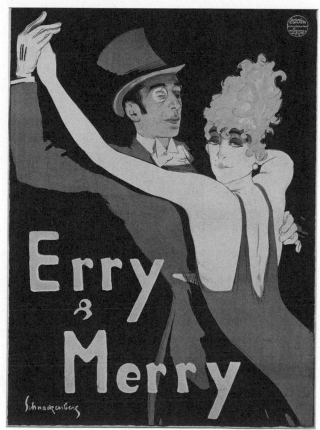

Swann Auction Galleries

Hindman

Potlid, Cherry Tooth Paste, Patronized By The Queen, John Gosnell & Co., c.1880, 3 In.
$132

Milestone Auctions

397

POTTERY

Pottery, Charger, Sunflowers, Hand Painted, Wall Hung, Marked, Pinder Bourne & Company, 19 ½ In.
$704

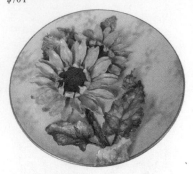

Nadeau's Auction Gallery

Pottery, Jardiniere, Ivory Color, Arts & Crafts, Carved, 10 x 10 x 9 In.
$106

Charleston Estate Auctions

Pottery, Pitcher, Portrait, Indian Chief, W.H. Tatler Decorating Co., c.1900, 12 ⅜ In.
$121

Fontaine's Auction Gallery

TIP

If you have a lightweight vase that tips easily, fill it with sand.

Pottery, Vase, Arts & Crafts, Sand Ground, Glazed, 8 In.
$125

New Haven Auctions

Pottery-Art, Figurine, Ram, Curled Horn, Black & White, Glazed, Stamped, Vietre, 12 x 17 In.
$150

Selkirk Auctioneers & Appraisers

Pottery-Art, Jardiniere, Standard Glaze, Grapes, Hand Painted, c.1915, 12 x 14 ⅝ In.
$96

Jeffrey S. Evans & Associates

Pottery-Art, Vase, Brown Glaze, Stylized Squirrels, Stoneware, C. J. Van Der Hoef, Haga, Dutch, c.1904, 14 In.
$516

Bonhams

Pottery-Art, Vase, Butterfly & Insect, Shape Handles, Enamel, Green Ground, Glaze, 7 ½ In.
$35

Conestoga Auction Company

P

Charger, Delft Style, Scalloped Rim, Blue & White, Glazed Earthenware, 1800s, 14 In......... 94
Charger, Sunflowers, Hand Painted, Wall Hung, Marked, Pinder Bourne & Company, 19 ½ In. *illus* 704
Dish, Game, Lid, Animals Design, Caneware Removable Liner, 11 In................................... 353
Dish, Serving, 2 Parts, Brown Slip Glaze, Parallel Lines Interior, 1800s, 11 ⅛ In. 125
Figurine, Man, Standing, Blue Attire, Feathered Hat, Moriyama Pottery, Japan, 1900s, 12 ½ In.. 63
Jar, Globular, Orchids, Yellow Ground, John Bennett, c.1880, 5 x 7 In........................... 1755
Jar, Olive, 3 Loop Handles, Molded, Concentric Bands, Earthenware, 44 In........................ 1408
Jardiniere, Earthenware, Cream Ground, Glazed, Flared Rim, 19 In................................ 450
Jardiniere, Ivory Color, Arts & Crafts, Carved, 10 x 10 x 9 In.....................*illus* 106
Jardiniere, Square Rim, Multicolor Glaze, Uzes, France, 1900s, 13 x 16 In. 1125
Pitcher, Blue & White Salt, Melon Shape Body, Neck Handle, Westerwald, Germany, 12 x 6 In. 63
Pitcher, Portrait, Indian Chief, W.H. Tatler Decorating Co., c.1900, 12 ⅜ In..................*illus* 121
Plaque, Oval, Glazed, Multicolor, Flowers, Dog, Seated, Center, 17 ½ x 12 In..................... 250
Plate, Native Birds, Multicolor Leaves, Black Lines Ground, Gien, France, 11 In., 6 Piece 875
Tureen, Dome Lid, Flower Basket, Stone Plinth, Lysaght Service, Square, c.1817, 9 ½ In. 11960
Vase, 4 Handles, Green Matte Glaze, 1900s, 11 ⅝ In..................................... 2706
Vase, Arts & Crafts, Sand Ground, Glazed, 8 In......................................*illus* 125
Vase, Blue & White Glaze, Signed, G. Scott, Dated 1921, 4 ¾ x 5 ¼ In. 70
Vase, Dark Blue, Glazed Earthenware, Willem Coenraad Brouwer, Dutch, c.1915, 6 In. 563
Vase, Earthenware, 4 Women, Muse, Art Deco, Edgardo Simone, Illinois, c.1940, 19 ¾ x 4 ⅜ In.. 3375
Vase, Green Crystalline, Cryptic Glaze, Stilt Pulls, Thomas Gotham, c.1927, 8 ¼ x 4 ½ In.... 1845
Vase, Jardiniere, Pot Shape, Cobalt Blue Glaze, Optical Swirl, 1900s, 20 x 17 x 10 In., Pair .. 550
Vase, Red, Chinese Oxblood Glaze, Robertson Hollywood, c.1920s, 5 ¼ x 3 In................... 431

Pottery-Art. Art pottery was first made in America in Cincinnati, Ohio, during the 1870s. The pieces were hand thrown and hand decorated. The art pottery tradition continued until studio potters began making different artistic wares about 1930. American, English, and Continental art pottery by less well-known makers is listed here. Most makers listed in Kovels' American Art Pottery, such as Arequipa, Ohr, Rookwood, Roseville, and Weller, are listed in their own categories in this book. More recent pottery is listed under the name of the maker or in Pottery-Contemporary or Pottery-Midcentury.

Basket, Green Matte Glaze, Squares, Hanging, Arts & Crafts, c.1910, 4 ¼ x 6 In. 123
Bowl, Console, Domed Flower Frog, Light Blue, Scalloped Rim, 15 ½ In................................. 53
Bowl, Shades Of Brown, Green, High Glaze, Signed, Auguste Delaherche, France, 1903, 1 ½ x 5 In. 312
Charger, Round, Glazed, Multicolor, Signed, David McDonald, 3 x 15 In. 281
Face Jug, Olive Glaze, Kaolin Eyes, Broken China Teeth, Strap Handles, B.B. Craig, 17 In..... 700
Figurine, Ram, Curled Horn, Black & White, Glazed, Stamped, Vietre, 12 x 17 In........*illus* 150
Jardiniere, Stand, Nude Female Handles, Leaves Base, Red Ground, Putti, Ohio, c.1915, 44 In... 660
Jardiniere, Standard Glaze, Grapes, Hand Painted, c.1915, 12 x 14 ⅝ In.....................*illus* 96
Vase, Aesthetic Movement, Bretby, Floor, Oxblood Glaze, Chinoiserie, England, c.1890, 26 x 17 In. 300
Vase, Bottle, Mission, Swirl, Blue, White, Ozark, c.1930s, 11 x 5 ½ In. 123
Vase, Brown Glaze, Stylized Squirrels, Stoneware, C. J. Van Der Hoef, Haga, Dutch, c.1904, 14 In...*illus* 516
Vase, Butterfly & Insect, Shape Handles, Enamel, Green Ground, Glaze, 7 ½ In...........*illus* 35
Vase, Cabinet, Santa Barbara, Signed, Fredrick Rhead, c.1913, 3 ¼ x 3 ¼ In.................*illus* 615
Vase, Flambe, Patterned Design, Oval Body, Bernard Moore Pottery, England, 1900s, 8 ½ In...*illus* 938
Vase, Green Matte Glaze, Alexander W. Robertson, Alberhill, 1914, 5 x 3 1/4 In. 1968
Vase, High Choke, Green & Black, Metal Tendril Handles, 1900s, 17 x 22 In. 125
Vase, Red, White, Santa Barbara Design, Frederick Rhead, c.1913, 6 ½ x 5 1/4 In.........*illus* 1968
Vase, Squat, Matte Green, Glazed, Merrimac Pottery, Early 1900s, 4 x 3 ½ In..............*illus* 468
Vase, Tapered Neck, Bulbous Base, Domenico Zumbo, Arenes De Frejus, France, 6 ¾ x 3 ¾ In. 227

Pottery-Asian includes pieces made in Japan, Korea, and other Asian countries. Asian pottery is also listed in Canton, Chinese Export, Imari, Japanese Coralene, Moriage, Nanking, Occupied Japan, Pottery-Chinese, Satsuma, Sumida, and other categories.

Bowl, Amphora, Terra-Cotta Red, Round Bottom, Metal Stand, Ban Chiang, 21 x 16 In....... 885

Pottery-Art, Vase, Cabinet, Santa Barbara, Signed, Fredrick Rhead, c.1913, 3 ¼ x 3 ¼ In.
$615

California Historical Design

Pottery-Art, Vase, Flambe, Patterned Design, Oval Body, Bernard Moore Pottery, England, 1900s, 8 ½ In.
$938

Lion and Unicorn

Pottery-Art, Vase, Red, White, Santa Barbara Design, Frederick Rhead, c.1913, 6 ½ x 5 ¼ In.
$1,968

California Historical Design

P

This is an edited listing of current prices. Visit **Kovels.com** to check thousands of prices from previous years and sign up for free information on trends, tips, reproductions, marks, and more.

Pottery-Art, Vase, Squat, Matte Green, Glazed, Merrimac Pottery, Early 1900s, 4 x 3½ In.
$468

Thomaston Place Auction Galleries

Pottery-Chinese, Figurine, Foo Dog, Seated, White Clay, Yellow Glaze, Integral Base, 18 x 6 x 6 In.
$351

Thomaston Place Auction Galleries

P

Pottery-Chinese, Figurine, Foo Dog, Sitting, Earthenware, Glazed, Lotus Base, 22 In.
$634

Bonhams

Tile, Square, Green Slip, Potter's Mark, Japan, 1900s, 11 x 11 In.	63
Vase, Enamel Metal, Pattern, Dragon, Phoenix, Japan, c.1950, 8 x 9½ In.	120
Vase, Sand Glazed Ground, Flying Bird, Flared Rim, Footed, Japan, 12¼ In.	63

Pottery-Chinese is listed here. See also Canton, Chinese Export, Imari, Moriage, Nanking, and other categories.

Brushpot, Carved, Mountain Landscape, Ox, Men Working, Brown, 7¾ x 5¾ In.	369
Figurine, Foo Dog, Seated, White Clay, Yellow Glaze, Integral Base, 18 x 6 x 6 In. .... *illus*	351
Figurine, Foo Dog, Sitting, Earthenware, Glazed, Lotus Base, 22 In. .... *illus*	634
Ginger Jar, Double Happiness, Blue & White Glaze, Oval, 6¼ x 4 In., Pair	108
Vase, Han Style, Cocoon, Melon Shape, Concentric Bands, 11¼ In.	122
Vase, Mirror Black Glaze, Blue Accents, Bulbous, Elongated Neck, Flared Rim, 14 x 8 In.	490
Vase, Yellow Crackle Glaze, Bulbous Shape, 11 x 5¼ In., Pair	216

Pottery-Contemporary lists pieces made by artists working about 1975 and later.

Basket, Nantucket, Lightship, Signed, George Davis, 1985, 6 x 9 x 8 In.	488
Basket, Woven Clay, Amorphous, Painted, Metallic, Susan Margin, 2003, 9¾ x 13 x 11 In..	195
Bird, Glazed, Engobe Design, Signed, Claude Conover, 14 x 4 x 6 In.	12500
Bowl, Angular, Tricolor, Abstract, Banded, Bisque Ground, Stoneware, Signed, Makoto Yabe, 4 x 13 In.	625
Bowl, Bitossi, Glazed, Ettore Sottsass, Italy, 1¾ x 6½ In. .... *illus*	313
Bowl, Blackware, Shallow, Fitted Mesh, Wire Stand, Reynoldo Quezada, 3½ x 12 In.	224
Bowl, Footed, Glazed Earthenware, Beatrice Wood, 3½ x 10 In.	813
Bowl, Oxblood Glaze, Toini Muona, 2 x 8 In. .... *illus*	450
Box, Lid, Bumble Bees, Red Designs, Round, Etched Date 2006, 4¼ x 2¼ In.	92
Chalice, Beatrice Wood, Narrow, Round Foot, Iridescent Glaze, Copper Tone, Beato, 4¼ x 4 In.	1080
Charger, Blue & Orange, Turquoise Glaze, Stoneware, Signed, Makoto Yabe, 16 In.	875
Charger, Turquoise & Oxblood Glaze, Toini Muona, 15 In. .... *illus*	840
Egg, With 4 Owls, Multicolor, Signed, Sergio Bustamante, 12 In.	896
Face Jug, Alkaline Glaze, Clay Eyes, Strap Handle, Stoneware, Meaders Family, 1996, 5 x 5 In... *illus*	222
Face Jug, Blank Eyes, Porcelain Teeth, Orange Glaze, Signed, M.L. Owens, N. Carolina, 5 x 4 In...	150
Face Jug, Grotesque, Manganese Glazed, Marked, James Seagreaves, 6 In.	561
Jar, Mishima, White, Wood Ash Glaze, Stoneware, Signed, Makoto Yabe, 9½ In.	813
Jug, 2 Faces, Blue Dripped Base, Randy Tobias, Cullowhee, N.C., Late 1900s, 14 In.	167
Jug, Rattlesnake, Alkaline Glaze, Handle, Stoneware, Michael & Melvin Crocker, 13 x 9 In. ..... *illus*	1872
Planter, Glazed Earthenware, Flowers, Face, Bjorn Wiinblad, Denmark, 1953, 20 x 17 x 14 In.*illus*	1875
Pumpkin, Earthenware, Removable Lid, Orange, Mary Kirk Kelly, 10 In. .... *illus*	896
Sake Pot, Black, Gilt, Lacquer, Flowers, Japan, 8½ x 9½ x 7 In., Pair	75
Tureen, Cabbage Shape, Underplate, Continental, 9½ x 16½ In. .... *illus*	484
Vase, Brown Glaze, Otto & Vivika Heino, Stoneware, 19 In. .... *illus*	1188
Vase, Carrot, Blue, Multicolor, Memphis Milano, Nathalie Du Pasquier, 1985, 12 x 5¼ In...... *illus*	375
Vase, Luster Glaze, Signed, Beato, Beatrice Wood, Ojai, California, c.1970, 3⅞ x 3 In... *illus*	750
Vase, Mask Series, Glazed Earthenware, Johanna Grawunder, 2002, 13 x 12 In.	500
Vase, Nudes In The Garden, Cream Ground, JoAnn Greenberg, 9 In. .... *illus*	320

Pottery-Midcentury includes pieces made from the 1930s to about 1975.

Bowl, Trees, Matte Glaze, Painted, Waylande Gregory, Warren, New York, c.1950, 5 x 9⅛ In. ..	125
Cup, 2 Faces, Flared Rim, Blue & White, Signed, Christian Dior, Paris, c.1950, 6 In...... *illus*	188
Figure, Man, Dog, Arctic Series, Earthenware, Waylande Gregory, c.1940, 17 x 8 x 9 In.*illus*	520
Figure, Polar Bear, Stoneware, Gordon Newell, Architectural Pottery, c.1950, 7 x 26 x 6 In.	5250
Plate, Bouquet, Faience, Madoura, Empreinte Originale, Pablo Picasso, 1955, 14 x 11⅞ In...*illus*	10000
Plate, Centaure, Round, Engobe Design, Pablo Picasso, 15 x 21 In.	5100
Plate, Face No. 111, Glazed Earthenware, Engobe Decoration, Pablo Picasso, 1881, 1½ x 10 In... *illus*	9375
Plate, Jouer De Flute Et Cavaliers, White Earthenware, Pablo Picasso, 1956, 14 x 14 x 1 In..	8750
Tureen, Lid, Underplate, Cabbage Shape, Lettuce Ware, Dodie Thayer, 6 x 8 In. .... *illus*	2040
Vase, Black Glaze, Polished, Avanyu Encircling Shoulder, Signed Maria Popovi, c.1969, 5 In..... *illus*	2176
Vase, Chouetton, Owl, Terre De Faience, Brown & White, Earthenware, Picasso, 1952, 10 In. *illus*	8125
Vase, Earthenware, 4 Panels, Potter, Wheel, Maija Grotell, Michigan, c.1945, 7½ x 7 In.... *illus*	1625
Vase, Sculptural, Slab, Multicolor, Rudy Autio, c.1950, 34½ In. .... *illus*	6250

Pottery-Contemporary, Bowl, Bitossi, Glazed, Ettore Sottsass, Italy, 1 ¾ x 6 ½ In.
$313

Treadway

Pottery-Contemporary, Bowl, Oxblood Glaze, Toini Muona, 2 x 8 In.
$450

Alderfer Auction Company

Pottery-Contemporary, Charger, Turquoise & Oxblood Glaze, Toini Muona, 15 In.
$840

Alderfer Auction Company

Pottery-Contemporary, Face Jug, Alkaline Glaze, Clay Eyes, Strap Handle, Stoneware, Meaders Family, 1996, 5 x 5 In.
$222

Jeffrey S. Evans & Associates

Pottery-Contemporary, Jug, Rattlesnake, Alkaline Glaze, Handle, Stoneware, Michael & Melvin Crocker, 13 x 9 In.
$1,872

Thomaston Place Auction Galleries

Pottery-Contemporary, Planter, Glazed Earthenware, Flowers, Face, Bjorn Wiinblad, Denmark, 1953, 20 x 17 x 14 In.
$1,875

Wright

P

Pottery-Contemporary, Pumpkin, Earthenware, Removable Lid, Orange, Mary Kirk Kelly, 10 In.
$896

Neal Auction Company

Pottery-Contemporary, Tureen, Cabbage Shape, Underplate, Continental, 9 ½ x 16 ½ In.
$484

Ahlers & Ogletree Auction Gallery

Pottery-Contemporary, Vase, Brown Glaze, Otto & Vivika Heino, Stoneware, 19 In.
$1,188

Clars Auction Gallery

Pottery-Contemporary, Vase, Carrot, Blue, Multicolor, Memphis Milano, Nathalie Du Pasquier, 1985, 12 x 5 ¼ In.
$375

Palm Beach Modern Auctions

Pottery-Contemporary, Vase, Luster Glaze, Signed, Beato, Beatrice Wood, Ojai, California, c.1970, 3 ⅞ x 3 In.
$750

Toomey & Co. Auctioneers

Pottery-Contemporary, Vase, Nudes In The Garden, Cream Ground, JoAnn Greenberg, 9 In.
$320

Neal Auction Company

Pottery-Midcentury, Cup, 2 Faces, Flared Rim, Blue & White, Signed, Christian Dior, Paris, c.1950, 6 In.
$188

Hindman

Pottery-Midcentury, Figure, Man, Dog, Arctic Series, Earthenware, Waylande Gregory, c.1940, 17 x 8 x 9 In.
$520

Toomey & Co. Auctioneers

P

Pottery-Midcentury, Plate, Bouquet, Faience, Madoura, Empreinte Originale, Pablo Picasso, 1955, 14 x 11 ⅞ In.
$10,000

Susanin's Auctioneers & Appraisers

Pottery-Midcentury, Plate, Face No. 111, Glazed Earthenware, Engobe Decoration, Pablo Picasso, 1881, 1 ½ x 10 In.
$9,375

Wright

Pottery-Midcentury, Tureen, Lid, Underplate, Cabbage Shape, Lettuce Ware, Dodie Thayer, 6 x 8 In.
$2,040

Abington Auction Gallery

Pottery-Midcentury, Vase, Black Glaze, Polished, Avanyu Encircling Shoulder, Signed, Maria Popovi, c.1969, 5 In.
$2,176

Brunk Auctions

Pottery-Midcentury, Vase, Chouetton, Owl, Terre De Faience, Brown & White, Earthenware, Picasso, 1952, 10 In.
$8,125

Eldred's

Pottery-Midcentury, Vase, Earthenware, 4 Panels, Potter, Wheel, Maija Grotell, Michigan, c.1945, 7 ½ x 7 In.
$1,625

Toomey & Co. Auctioneers

P

Pottery-Midcentury, Vase, Sculptural, Slab, Multicolor, Rudy Autio, c.1950, 34½ In.
$6,250

Clars Auction Gallery

Powder Flask, Copper, Embossed Leaves, Stags, Foxes, G. & J. W. Hawksley, 1830-50s, 8½ In.
$71

Stony Ridge Auction

Powder Flask, Leather, Brown, Pear Shape, Metal Nozzle, c.1800, 10 In.
$375

Early American History Auctions

POWDER FLASK AND POWDER HORN

Powder flasks and powder horns were made to hold the gunpowder used in antique firearms. The early examples were made of horn or wood; later ones were of copper or brass.

POWDER FLASK

Bamboo, Double Gourd, Incised Basketweave Bands, Lid Attached By Rope, Japan, 1900s, 5½ In..	250
Bone, Incised, Metal Trim, Morocco, Early 20th Century, 12½ x 8 x 2½ In.	128
Coconut Shell, Bugbear, Hand Carved, Coat Of Arms, Ship, Silver Mount, 1859, 7 x 3¼ In.	240
Copper, Embossed Leaves, Stags, Foxes, G. & J. W. Hawksley, 1830-50s, 8½ In.............*illus*	71
Copper, Pear Shape, Ridged, Brass Head, Patina, James Dixon & Son, Sheffield, 1800s, 8 In.	96
Gun Stock, Fary Benham, c.1860, 8½ In.	352
Leather, 2 Pouches, Brass Heads, Connecting Strap, Late 19th Century, 14 In.	62
Leather, Brown, Pear Shape, Metal Nozzle, c.1800, 10 In............*illus*	375
Leather, Pear Shape, Embossed Bird Dog, Brass Head, A.M. Flask & Cap Co., 5½ In.	60

POWDER HORN

Brass, Bulb Shape, Birds, Animals, Flowers, Embossed	69
Cow Horn, Wood Plug, Nail Fastened, Mid 19th Century, 6½ In.	36
Engraved, Circus Scene, Eagle On Reverse, E. Pluribus Unum, Signed, Peacham, 1849, 12 In.	640
Engraved, Figures, Buildings, Flowers, Animals, WEM, Brass Base & Spout, 1800s, 17½ In........	2000
Engraved, Liberty Eagle, Ships, Sailor, Tavern, Wood Plug, J.L. Carman, 1845, 7½ In. *illus*	381
Engraved, Village Scene, Church, Tree, Fish, Birds, c.1800, 7½ In.	640
Grid Patterns, Scalloped Metal Ends, 2-Color String Loop, Arabic, 13 In.	123
Raised Panel, Rectangular, Inscribed Warrin, April 15, 1777, Stylized Horse, 1900s, 8¼ In.	250
Scrimshaw, Clipper Ship, Figures, Geometrics, Snake, William Scott, Joseph Scott, 1867, 15 In...*illus*	953
Scrimshaw, House, Barn, Ship, Bird, James Hoff, Nov. 4, 1847, Malden, Ulster Co., N.Y., 13½ In.	369
Scrimshaw, House, Road, Fort, Tomahawk, Initials JE, Wood Plug, Iron Ring, c.1800, 14 In.....	148
Scrimshaw, Pierced Flowerpot, Carved Moon Face, Fish, E. Rose, XXIM, Truncated, 7¼ In.	508
Scrimshaw, Wood Plug, Iron Ring, Hand Carved, Initials JE, Late 1700s, 14 In.	138
Stars, Stylized Shapes, Alternating Nails & Domed Studs Around Base, Dated, 1779, 11 In..	113
White Overlay, Pierced Circles, Brown Stepped Tip, Signed, Joe E. Neale, Woolwich, Maine, 11 In.	242

PRATT

Pratt ware means two different things. It was an early Staffordshire pottery, cream colored with colored decorations, made by Felix Pratt during the late eighteenth century. There was also Pratt ware made with transfer designs during the mid-nineteenth century in Fenton, England. Reproductions of the transfer-printed Pratt are being made.

Box, Money, Figural, Clock, Dog, Man & Woman, Multicolor, Open Top, 1800s, 9 x 5¾ x 3 In. *illus*	1183
Figure, Female Archer, Standing, Arrows, White Square Base, 12 In......................................	94
Jug, Group, Boy Reading, Multicolor, Raised Stylized Leaves, Brown Trim, 1800s, 9 x 8½ In.	378

PRESSED GLASS

Pressed glass, or pattern glass, was first made in the United States in the 1820s after the invention of glass pressing machines. Hundreds of patterns of pressed glass were made in complete table settings. Although the Boston and Sandwich Works was the most famous of the pressed glass factories, there were about sixteen other factories making pressed glass from 1830 to 1850, and still more from 1850 to 1900, when pressed glass reached its greatest popularity. It is now being widely reproduced. The pattern names used in this listing are based on the information in the book *Pressed Glass in America* by John and Elizabeth Welker. There may be pieces of pressed glass listed in this book in other categories, such as Lamp, Ruby Glass, Sandwich Glass, and Souvenir.

Aquarium, Pitcher, Water, Clear, Footed, Applied Handle, U.S. Glass Co., c. 1908, 9 x 4 In...	94

Argus, Compote, Open, Early Thumbprint, Bakewell, Pears & Co., Pittsburgh, Pa, 1860s, 9 x 9 x 6 In.	70
Bowl, Deep Violet Blue, 16 Vertical Ribs, Funnel Foot, Stiegel, 1770-74, 3¼ In.	1080
Button Panel, Punch Bowl, Scalloped Rim, Clear, Duncan Sons & Co., c.1900, 7 x 14 In.	35
Civil War, Tumbler, Union For Ever, Clasped Hands, American Flag, 1860s, 3¼ x 2¾ In.	263
Cosmos pattern is listed in this book as its own category.	
Dakota, Cake Stand, Lid, Leaf & Berry Design, Clear, Ripley & Co., 13 x 6 x 9 In. .... *illus*	702
Diamond Point, Pitcher, Water, Solid Handle, New England Glass & Co., 1860s, 9½ In.	12
Dish, Clamshell, Lid, Figural, Clear, 4-Footed, Novelty, Early 1900s, 4 x 5 x 7 In.	263
Dispenser, Windmill, Amethyst, 9 Panels, Embossed Swirls, Silver Plate Lid, Novelty, 1900s, 8¾ In.	105
Gonterman, Goblet, Clear, Frosted, Amber Stained, Duncan & Sons, 6¼ In. .... *illus*	878
Historical, Tray, Pacific Fleet, Busts, Admirals Sperry, Evans, c.1908, 8⅛ x 11⅛ In.	35
Hobnail pattern is in this book as its own category.	
Jar, Humidor, Cigar Storage, Seal Lid, Clear, Eugene Vallens & Co., c.1915, 5 x 5 In.	47
Liberty Bell, Mug, Snake Handle, Clear, Gillinder & Sons, c.1876, 3½ x 3⅜ x 2⅜ In.	222
Moon & Stars, Creamer, Miniature, Blue, Signed, Robert Hansen, Texas	75
Squirrel, Goblet, Stepped Base, Circular, Colorless, c.1880, 6 In.	380
Three Face, Compote, Clear, Frosted, Circular Plinth Base, Duncan & Sons Co., 1878, 8 x 7 In.	2106
Thumbprint, Ale, Cylindrical, Bulbed Stem, Circular Foot, Cobalt Blue, 1860s, 7⅛ In.	176
Wedding Ring, Syrup, Period Lid, Applied Handle, Opaque White, 1860s, 7 In.	70

PRINT

Print, in this listing, means any of many printed images produced on paper by one of the more common methods, such as lithography. The prints listed here are of interest primarily to the antiques collector, not the fine arts collector. Many of these prints were originally part of books. Other prints will be found in the Advertising, Currier & Ives, Movie, and Poster categories.

Audubon bird prints were originally issued as part of books printed from 1826 to 1854. They were issued in two sheet sizes, 26½ inches *J.W.Audubon* by 39½ inches and 11 inches by 7 inches. The height of a picture is listed before the width. The quadrupeds were issued in 28-by-22-inch prints. Later editions of the Audubon books were done in many sizes, and reprints of the books in the original sizes were also made. The words *After John James Audubon* appear on all of the prints, including the originals, because the pictures were made as copies of Audubon's original oil paintings. The bird pictures have been so popular they have been copied in myriad sizes using both old and new printing methods. This list includes originals and later copies because Audubon prints of all ages are sold in antiques shops.

Audubon, Black & Yellow Warbler, Birds Of America, R. Havell, 1833, 15½ x 19 In.	584
Audubon, Black Guillemot, R. Havell, J. Whatman Watermark, 1834, 18¾ x 22¾ In.	625
Audubon, Carolina Pigeon Or Turtle Dove, R. Havell, 1827, Frame, 49 x 36 In.	5040
Audubon, Carolina Turtle Dove, Birds, Dogwood, Princeton Edition, Frame, 44 x 32 In.	410
Audubon, Cervus Virginianus, Common Or Virginia Deer, J.T. Bowen, 1848, 29½ x 35 In.	3780
Audubon, Ferruginous Thrush, The Birds Of America, R. Havell, 1831, 37⅝ x 25 In.	5985
Audubon, Great-Footed Hawk, R. Havell, J. Whatman Watermark, 1820, Frame, 36 x 49 In.	3438
Audubon, Marsh Hawk, R. Havell, J. Whatman Watermark, 1837, Frame, 49½ x 35⅞ In.	3276
Audubon, Musk Ox, North American Quadrupeds, Wove Paper, J.T. Bowen, 20 x 27 In. *illus*	1170
Audubon, Red-Tailed Hawk, R. Havell, 1829, J. Whatman Watermark, Frame, 47 x 34 In.	1240
Audubon, Rose-Breasted Grosbeak, R. Havell, 1833, 15½ x 19 In.	1107
Audubon, Semipalmated Snipe Or Willet, R. Havell, 1835, Frame, 28½ x 41½ In.	1920
Audubon, Smew Or White Nun, R. Havell, J. Whatman Watermark, 1834, 28 x 24 In.	813
Audubon, Stanley Hawk, R. Havell, J. Whatman Watermark, 1836, Frame, 49 x 35⅝ In.	1890
Audubon, The Wolverine, Hand Colored, Pumpkin Pine Mitered Frame, 26 x 32 In.	1404
Audubon, White-Crowned Pigeon, R. Havell, 1833, 15½ x 19 In.	984
Audubon, Yellow Shank Or Lesser Yellowlegs, R. Havell, 1836, Frame, 33 x 43 In.	8400
Calder, Alexander, Cibles Variables, Lithograph, Color, Signed, Frame, 1969, 28 x 40 In. *illus*	6250

Powder Horn, Engraved, Liberty Eagle, Ships, Sailor, Tavern, Wood Plug, J.L. Carman, 1845, 7½ In.
$381

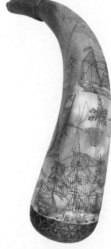

Rafael Osona Nantucket Auctions

Powder Horn, Scrimshaw, Clipper Ship, Figures, Geometrics, Snake, William Scott, Joseph Scott, 1867, 15 In.
$953

Tremont Auctions

Pratt, Box, Money, Figural, Clock, Dog, Man & Woman, Multicolor, Open Top, 1800s, 9 x 5¾ x 3 In.
$1,183

Jeffrey S. Evans & Associates

P

Pressed Glass, Dakota, Cake Stand, Lid, Leaf & Berry Design, Clear, Ripley & Co., 13 x 6 x 9 In.
$702

Jeffrey S. Evans & Associates

Pressed Glass, Gonterman, Goblet, Clear, Frosted, Amber Stained, Duncan & Sons, 6¼ In.
$878

Jeffrey S. Evans & Associates

Print, Audubon, Musk Ox, North American Quadrupeds, Wove Paper, J.T. Bowen, 20 x 27 In.
$1,170

Thomaston Place Auction Galleries

Print, Calder, Alexander, Cibles Variables, Lithograph, Color, Signed, Frame, 1969, 28 x 40 In.
$6,250

Charlton Hall Auctions

Calder, Alexander, Sky Swirl, Flying Colors, Lithograph, 1974, 25 x 19½ In.	320
Calder, Alexander, Stylized Flowers, Horizontal Lines, Lithograph, 22½ x 18¾ In.	2432
Currier & Ives prints are listed in the Currier & Ives category.	
Dali, Salvador, Petite Chouette, Etching, Color, Frame, 1968, 14½ x 12 In.	5100
Deines, H., Mother's Horseshoe Geranium, Wood Engraving, Frame, c.1950, 23 x 19 In.	1060
Erte, Les Bijoux De Perle, Serigraph, Silkscreen On Paper, Frame, 33½ x 26½ In. ......*illus*	443
Erte, Letter R, Alphabet Suite, Silkscreen, Paper, Signed, Frame, 1900s, 14 x 20 In. .....*illus*	250

Icart prints were made by Louis Icart, who worked in Paris from 1907 as an employee of a postcard company. He then started printing magazines and fashion brochures. About 1910 he created a series of etchings of fashionably dressed women, and he continued to make similar etchings until he died in 1950. He is well known as a printmaker, painter, and illustrator. Original etchings are much more expensive than the later photographic copies.

Icart, 2 Art Deco Women, Cats, Spilled Milk, Etching, Signed, Frame, 32 x 32 In.	813
Icart, Art Deco Woman, 3 Cats, Etching, Black & White, Frame, 16 x 16 In.	375
Icart, Clown, Etching, Signed, Frame, 19 x 22½ In.	492
Icart, Dancing 10, Chorus Line Girls, Etching, Color, Signed, 1938, 7 x 5½ In.	3250
Icart, Dancing 12, Man & Woman, Etching, Color, Signed, 1938, 7 x 5½ In.	2625
Icart, Eve, Lounging Nude, Serpentine Cuff, Etching, Signed in Crayon, 13 x 19 In.	1920
Icart, Faust, Windmill Mark, Arched Velvet Mat, Frame, 1928, 28 x 20 In.	469
Icart, La Tosca, Etching, Color, Aquatint, Windmill Stamp, Frame, 1928, 27 x 20 In.	281
Icart, Laziness, Drypoint, Color, Hand Signed, 1925, 15 x 19 In.	1000
Icart, Little Book, Etching, Black & White, Signed, 1925, 17 In.	1625
Icart, Nude Art Deco Woman, 2 Birds, Etching, Black & White, Frame, 16 x 16 In.	475
Icart, Sleeping, Art Deco Nude, Lithograph, Signed In Pencil, Frame, 25 x 51 In.	4250
Icart, Snack, Art Deco Woman, Ducks, Etching, Color, Signed, 1927, 18½ x 13 In.	1125
Icart, Spanish Dancer, Titled, Hand Signed, Matted, Frame, 1928, 21 x 14 In.	375
Icart, Swing, Etching, Color, Aquatint, Signed, Windmill Stamp, 1928, 20 x 14 In.	1000
Icart, Symphony In Blue, Etching, Watercolor, Hand Signed, 1936, 22⅝ x 19 In.	1000

Jacoulet prints were designed by Paul Jacoulet (1902–1960), a Frenchman who spent most of his life in Japan. He was a master of Japanese woodblock print technique. Subjects included life in Japan, the South Seas, Korea, and China. His prints were sold by subscription and issued in series. Each series had a distinctive seal, such as a sparrow or butterfly. Most Jacoulet prints are approximately 15 x 10 inches.

Jacoulet, Jeu Princier, Mongol, Woodblock, Color, France, Frame, 15 x 11½ In. ....*illus*	1080
Jacoulet, La Statuette Thang, Woodblock, Color, France, Frame, 15¼ x 11½ In.	1080

Japanese woodblock prints are listed as follows: Print, Japanese, name of artist, title or description, type, and size. Dealers use the following terms: *Tate-e* is a vertical composition. *Yoko-e* is a horizontal composition. The words *Aiban* (13 by 9 inches), *Chuban* (10 by 7½ inches), *Hosoban* (13 by 6 inches), *Koban* (7 by 4 inches), *Nagaban* (20 by 9 inches), *Oban* (15 by 10 inches), *Shikishiban* (8 by 9 inches), and *Tanzaku* (15 by 5 inches) denote approximate size. Modern versions of some of these prints have been made. Other woodblock prints that are not Japanese are listed under Print, Woodblock.

Japanese, Hasui, Kawase, Hiejin Shrine Snow, Color, Watanabe, 1946-51, 15 x 10 In.	748
Japanese, Hasui, Kawase, Kasuga Shrine At Nara, Color, Watanabe, 1933, 15 x 10 In.	1610
Japanese, Hasui, Kawase, Lingering Snow At Hikone Castle, Color, Watanabe, Seal, 1934, 14 x 9 In.	875
Japanese, Hasui, Kawase, Miyajima By Moonlight, Color, Watanabe, 1947, 15 x 10 In.	690
Japanese, Hasui, Kawase, Moon Over Arakawa River, Bokashi Shading, 1929, 15 x 10 In.	1265
Japanese, Hasui, Kawase, Morning Nijubashi Bridge, Color, Watanabe, 1930, 15 x 10 In.	690
Japanese, Hasui, Kawase, Spring Evening Otemon Gate, Color, 1st Edition, 1952, 15 x 10 In.	1265

Print, Erte, Les Bijoux De Perle, Serigraph, Silkscreen On Paper, Frame, 33 ½ x 26 ½ In. $443

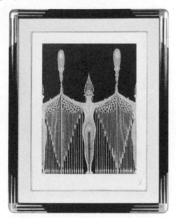

Bunch Auctions

Print, Erte, Letter R, Alphabet Suite, Silkscreen, Paper, Signed, Frame, 1900s, 14 x 20 In. $250

Andrew Jones Auctions

Print, Jacoulet, Jeu Princier, Mongol, Woodblock, Color, France, Frame, 15 x 11 ½ In. $1,080

Alex Cooper Auctioneers

Print, Japanese, Koitsu, Tsuchiya, Benkei Bridge, Gauffrage, c.1963, 10 ¾ x 15 ¾ In. $1,035

Ukiyoe Gallery: Japanese Woodblock Prints

TIP

Spray glass cleaner on a cloth, then wipe the glass on a framed print. Do not spray the glass because the liquid may drip and stain the mat or print.

Print, Lithograph, Continental Divide, Abstract, Red, Blue, Yellow, Paul Jenkins, 1981, 38 x 29 In. $544

Rachel Davis Fine Arts

Print, Lithograph, L'Amethyste, Color, Alphonse Mucha, F. Champenois, Paris, 1902, 38 x 15 In. $6,000

Michaan's Auctions

Print, Parrish, Lute Players, Trees & Rocks, Shaped Frame, Convex Glass, 18 x 12 In. $508

White's Auctions

Print, Sternberg, Harry, David Burliuk, Man At Easel, Serigraph, 1944, 12 x 13 ½ In. $218

Rachel Davis Fine Arts

Print, Woodblock, Forty Niners Inn, Franz Geritz, Signed, Frame, 1925, 7 x 11 In.
$400

California Historical Design

Print, Woodblock, Rain Blossoms, Umbrellas, Lilian Miller, Signed, Frame, 1928, 9½ x 14 In.
$615

California Historical Design

Necessaire

A necessaire is an expensive vanity case used for formal events. The case, usually silver and enamel, had compartments for powder, rouge, lipstick, and cigarettes. They were popular from 1915 into the 1930s.

Purse, Basket, Nantucket, Oval, Swing Handle, Hinged Lid, Mike Kane, 1974, 6¾ x 10 In.
$2,000

Eldred's

Japanese, Hasui, Kawase, Snow At Miyajima, Red Tilted Seal, 1955-58, 15¾ x 10¾ In.	1610
Japanese, Koitsu, Kangetsu Bridge, Shimonoshi Early Autumn Evening, 1936, 10 x 16 In.	2070
Japanese, Koitsu, Tsuchiya, Benkei Bridge, Gauffrage, c.1963, 10¾ x 15¾ In. ....*illus*	1035
Japanese, Koitsu, Twilight, Imamiya Street, Color, Gauffrage, Watanabe, Seal, c.1947, 15 x 10 In.	460
Japanese, Koson, Ohara, Crow On Cherry Branch, Moon, Color, 1910-20, 13 x 6¾ In.	748
Japanese, Saito, Kiyoshi, Tea House, 1965, 15 x 20½ In.	390
Japanese, Shotei, Takahashi, Tama Cat, Color, Gauffrage, Seal, 1946-57, 10 x 14 In.	1265
Japanese, Tanaka, M., Landscape, Birds, Tree, Sun, 4 Colors, Signed, Late 1900s, 12 x 17½ In.	188
Japanese, Tokuriki, Tomikichiro, Night Vendor, Noodle Cart, Color, Frame, 1950s, 15 x 20 In.	95
Japanese, Yoshida, Hiroshi, Calm Wind, Boat, Sailing, Signed, Frame, 11¾ x 8¾ In.	1107
Japanese, Yuhan, Ito, Cherry Blossoms, Castle, Color, 1930s, 16 x 11 In.	805
Johnson, Lester Frederick, Man, Women, Serigraph, Signed, Maple Frame, c. 1985, 38 x 30 In.	234
Kloss, Gene, Pueblo Leader, Indian Man, Drypoint Etching, Titled, Signed, Frame, c.1950, 25 x 22 In.	1770
Landon, Edward, Time Silhouette, Green & Orange, Black Shapes, Serigraph, 1969, 18 x 9 In.	288
Leger, Fernand, Still Life, Shapes, Green, Orange, Black, White, Serigraph, 1952, 8¾ x 11½ In.	154
Lithograph, Continental Divide, Abstract, Red, Blue, Yellow, Paul Jenkins, 1981, 38 x 29 In. .....*illus*	544
Lithograph, Honorary Degree, 3 Men In Academic Robes, Signed, Grant Wood, 1938, 22 x 17 In.	1770
Lithograph, Kegon Falls, Offset, After Hiroshi Sugimoto, 1977, 21 x 26¼ In.	650
Lithograph, L'Amethyste, Color, Alphonse Mucha, F. Champenois, Paris, 1902, 38 x 15 In.....*illus*	6000
Lithograph, Mexican War, Hand Colored, Sarony & Major, N.Y., Dated 1847, 13½ x 18 In.	60
Lithograph, Rhythms, Color, Arches Paper, Max Ernst, 1950, 22¼ x 14¾ In.	390
Lithograph, Seated Woman, R.C. Gorman, Frame, 1971, 20½ x 21 In.	125
Lithograph, Sir Robert Ball, Globe, Vanity Fair, Popular Astronomy, London, 1905, 15 x 10 In.	13
Lithograph, The Musicians, 3 Figures, Multicolor, Graciela Rodo Boulanger, 2¾ x 4½ In.	64
Meredith, Maggie, Happiness Is Nantucket, 2 Whales, Eating Lobster, Signed, Frame, 22 x 15 In.	250
Morning Cup, Woman, Black Dog, Drypoint, Color, Signed, Windmill Stamp, 20 x 18 In.	1024

Wallace Nutting **Nutting** prints are popular with collectors. Wallace Nutting is known for his pictures, furniture, and books. Collectors call his pictures Nutting prints although they are actually hand-colored photographs issued from 1900 to 1941. There are over 10,000 different titles. Wallace Nutting furniture is listed in the Furniture category.

Nutting, A Garden Of Larkspur, Hand Colored, Titled, Signed, 18¾ x 15¾ In.	48
Nutting, A Perkiomen October, Hand Colored, Signed, Frame, 9½ x 11¾ In.	113
Nutting, Birches In June, Hand Colored, Titled & Signed, Frame, 9½ x 7 In.	63
Nutting, By The Wayside, Sheep, Hand Tinted, Titled, Signed, Frame, 10½ x 15½ In.	44
Nutting, Grace, Birch Trees Next To Placid Lake, Carved Wood Frame, 13 x 10 In.	48
Nutting, The Old Homestead, Hand Tinted, Titled, Signed, 19¾ x 23¾ In.	136

Maxfield Parrish **Parrish** prints are wanted by collectors. Maxfield Frederick Parrish was an illustrator who lived from 1870 to 1966. He is best known as a designer of magazine covers, posters, calendars, and advertisements. His prints have been copied in recent years. Some Maxfield Parrish items may be listed in Advertising.

Parrish, An Ancient Tree, Signed, 1940, 15¾ x 12¾ In.	531
Parrish, Day Break, Frame, 22 x 34 In.	94
Parrish, Day Dream, Lithograph On Paper, Signed In Corner, Frame, 20 x 32 In.	531
Parrish, Dinky Bird, Swinging Over Water, Foggy Night, Castle, Frame, 17¾ x 13 In.	200
Parrish, Lute Players, Trees & Rocks, Shaped Frame, Convex Glass, 18 x 12 In...........*illus*	508
Parrish, Stars, Nude Woman Looking At Night Sky, Frame, c.1930, 22 x 14 In.	688
Parrish, Stars, Nude Woman, Seated On Rock, Wood Frame, 12 x 16 In.	286
Parrish, The Canyon, Barefoot Robed Woman Hiking, 16½ x 13½ In.	281
Redoute, Pierre-Joseph, Ornithogalum Nutans, Ornithogale Penche, Mat, Frame, 20 x 13 In.	313
Sternberg, Harry, David Burliuk, Man At Easel, Serigraph, 1944, 12 x 13½ In............*illus*	218
Sternberg, Harry, Evening, Young Woman, Turquoise Blue Dress, Holds Flower, Serigraph, 8 x 5 In.	141
Watanabe, Sadao, Kappazuri, People, Buildings, Stencil, Frame, 1971, 35 x 29½ In.	313
Wayne, June Claire, A Little Nothing, Serigraph, Bronze Frame, Signed, 16 x 30 In.	380

Woodblock prints that are not in the Japanese tradition are listed here. Most were made in England and the United States during the Arts and Crafts period. Japanese woodblock prints are listed under Print, Japanese.

Woodblock, Forty Niners Inn, Franz Geritz, Signed, Frame, 1925, 7 x 11 In.............. *illus*	400
Woodblock, Nishijin Roofs, Clifton Karhu, Signed In Pencil, 1983, 22½ x 37 In.	1800
Woodblock, Rain Blossoms, Umbrellas, Lilian Miller, Signed, Frame, 1928, 9½ x 14 In.*illus*	615

PURINTON

Purinton Pottery Company was incorporated in Wellsville, Ohio, in 1936. The company moved to Shippenville, Pennsylvania, in 1941 and made a variety of hand-painted ceramic wares. By the 1950s Purinton was making dinnerware, souvenirs, cookie jars, and florist wares. The pottery closed in 1959.

Purinton Pottery

Apple, Canister Set, Lids, 5 Piece	67
Fruit, Canister, 4 Sections, Flour, Sugar, Tea, Coffee, Round Wood Base & Top, 9¼ x 10¼ In.	19
Open Apple, Snack Plate, Cup..	36

PURSE

Purses have been recognizable since the eighteenth century, when leather and needlework purses were preferred. Beaded purses became popular in the nineteenth century, went out of style, but are again in use. Mesh purses date from the 1880s and are still being made. How to carry a handkerchief, lipstick, and cell phone is a problem today for every woman, including the Queen of England.

Alligator, Handbag, Black, Goldtone Hardware, Interior Pockets, Judith Leiber, 19½ In.	486
Basket, Nantucket, Bentwood Handle, Signed, Albert Farnum Cleaveland, c.1970, 9 x 7 In..	644
Basket, Nantucket, Friendship, Braided Leather Shoulder Strap, Jose Formoso Reyes, c.1962, 6 In..	4575
Basket, Nantucket, Lightship, Swing Handle, Oak Ribs, David E. Ray, c.1870, 7 In.............	4062
Basket, Nantucket, Oval, Swing Handle, Hinged Lid, Mike Kane, 1974, 6¾ x 10 In....... *illus*	2000
Basket, Nantucket, Scrimshaw, Ducks, Carved Whales, Signed, Farnum, c.1970, 10 In.	143
Basket, Nantucket, Swing Handle, Hinged Lid, Signed, Bill & Judy Sayle, Dated 1988, 7¼ In. .	1250
Basket, Nantucket, Woven, Leather Front Flap, Brass Hasp & Loop, Sherwin Boyer, c.1950, 9 x 7 In...	819
Beaded, Mary Golay Lake Scene, Multicolor, Knitted, Brass Chain, Gemstones, c.1920, 13 x 9 In. *illus*	525
Beaded, Oval, Blue, Abstract Leaves, Wrist Strap, Silk Crepe Lining, c.1920, 10⅜ x 4 In.*illus*	99
Beaded, Parrot, Flowers, Multicolor, Linen, Nickeled Silver Bail & Chain, 1900s, 9½ x 3¼ In.. . *illus*	298
Beaded, Steel Beads, Multicolor, Woven, Brass Bail & Chain, Gemstones, c.1920, 9¾ x 6 In...*illus*	128
Boy Bag, Chanel, Black Quilted Caviar Calfskin, Leather & Gold Chain, Logo, 10 x 4 In.	3438
Canvas, Saint Cloud, Slip Pocket, Cross Body, Monogrammed, Louis Vuitton, 9 x 9½ In.....	500
Canvas, Supreme Tote, Monogrammed, Black Topstitched Leather, Label, Gucci, 11 x 18 In........	615
Clutch, Crocodile, Pochette Box, Knot, Brown, Bottega Veneta, 4 x 6 x 1 In................. *illus*	1375
Clutch, Embroidered, Flowers, Crystal Detail, Judith Leiber, 4½ x 6½ x 2 In. .... *illus*	281
Clutch, Leather, Evening, Quilted, Envelope, Velvet, Pink, Chanel, France, 1900s, 5½ x 8 x 1 In...	640
Clutch, Leather, Intrecciato Woven, Metallic, Zipered Pocket, Bottega Veneta, 4 x 9¼ x 4 In......	219
Clutch, Stingray, Purple, Silvertone Frame, Retractable Shoulder Chain, Judith Leiber, 5 x 9 In. ..	1125
Coin, Leather, Arts & Crafts, Hand Tooled, Strap, c.1915, 6½ x 6 In.	123
Crystal Beads, Minaudiere, Silvertone Hardware, Removable Chain Strap, Judith Leiber, 6½ In...	732
Fiber, Bag, Woven, Seashells, Beads & Feathers, 1900s, 10 x 9 x 3 In............................*illus*	250
Leather, Bowler Bag, Interlocking G Logo, Pebbled Black, 2 Rolled Handles, Gucci, 10½ x 17 x 6 In...	550
Leather, Burgundy, Loop Handle, Christian Dior, c.1998, 19½ In..	976
Leather, Flap Bag, Blue & Black, 2 Rolled Handles, Silvertone Keyhole, Prada, 9 x 10 In.	330
Leather, Handbag, Black, Nylon, Bamboo Design, Diamante Fabric, Gucci, 2¾ x 6¾ x 4 In. *illus*	63
Leather, Lakota, Ledger Style Drawing, Thomas Red Owl Haukaas, 1950, 14 x 15 In............	219
Leather, Ostrich Skin, Handle, Lock, Selliers Du Marais, 9 x 12¼ x 4½ In. .... *illus*	250
Leather, Vespa PM, Tan, Gold Metal Chain & Bar, Pocket, Shoulder Strap, Hermes, 11 x 11 In.......	885
Lizardskin, Kelly, Black, Handle, Silvertone Hardware, Argentina, 8 x 9½ x 3¼ In.	219
Mesh, Art Deco, Clasp Lock, Flowers, Chain Sling, 6 In...*illus*	88

Purse, Beaded, Mary Golay Lake Scene, Multicolor, Knitted, Brass Chain, Gemstones, c.1920, 13 x 9 In.
$525

Quittenbaum Kunstauktionen GmbH

Purse, Beaded, Oval, Blue, Abstract Leaves, Wrist Strap, Silk Crepe Lining, c.1920, 10⅜ x 4 In.
$99

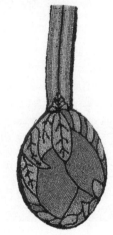

Quittenbaum Kunstauktionen GmbH

Purse, Beaded, Parrot, Flowers, Multicolor, Linen, Nickeled Silver Bail & Chain, 1900s, 9½ x 3¼ In.
$298

Quittenbaum Kunstauktionen GmbH

P

Purse, Beaded, Steel Beads, Multicolor, Woven, Brass Bail & Chain, Gemstones, c.1920, 9¾ x 6 In.
$128

Quittenbaum Kunstauktionen GmbH

Purse, Clutch, Crocodile, Pochette Box, Knot, Brown, Bottega Veneta, 4 x 6 x 1 In.
$1,375

Hindman

Purse, Clutch, Embroidered, Flowers, Crystal Detail, Judith Leiber, 4½ x 6½ x 2 In.
$281

Auctions at Showplace, NYC

Purse, Fiber, Bag, Woven, Seashells, Beads & Feathers, 1900s, 10 x 9 x 3 In.
$250

John Moran Auctioneers

Purse, Leather, Handbag, Black, Nylon, Bamboo Design, Diamante Fabric, Gucci, 2¾ x 6¾ x 4 In.
$63

Auctions at Showplace, NYC

Purse, Leather, Ostrich Skin, Handle, Lock, Selliers Du Marais, 9 x 12¼ x 4½ In.
$250

Auctions at Showplace, NYC

Purse, Mesh, Art Deco, Clasp Lock, Flowers, Chain Sling, 6 In.
$88

Turner Auctions + Appraisals

Purse, Satin, Black, Convertible, Crystal, Clutch, Flower Clasp, Judith Leiber, 6 x 8¼ x 2 In.
$156

Auctions at Showplace, NYC

Purse, Silver, Minaudiere, Cat, Red Eyes, Kuppenheim, 2 x 3½ In.
$1,536

Nadeau's Auction Gallery

Nylon, Braided, Leather Handles, Red Interior, Dooney & Bourke, 17 x 12 In.	12
Ostrich, Taupe, 2 Handles, Goldtone Clasp, Pouch, Mirror, Metal Tag, Judith Leiber, 8 x 11 In. .	275
Ostrich, Tote, Tan, Woven, Intrecciato, 2 Top Handles, Bottega Veneta, 16 x 15 x 3 In.	2125
Patent Leather, Handbag, Lady Dior, Black, Cannage Quilted, Christian Dior, 8 x 9 ½ In. .	925
Satin, Black, Convertible, Crystal, Clutch, Flower Clasp, Judith Leiber, 6 x 8 ¼ x 2 In. ...*illus*	156
Silver, Minaudiere, Cat, Red Eyes, Kuppenheim, 2 x 3 ½ In...*illus*	1536
Tote, Panier Straw, Leather Handles, Black, Saint Laurent, 11 x 16 ½ x 10 In.......................	813
Wallet, Crocodile, Dogon Duo, Silvertone Clou De Selle Closure, Hermes, 5 x 7 x 1 ¼ In.	4688
Wallet, Leather, Metallic, Silvertone, Snap Closure, Card Holder, Logo Plaque, Prada, 3 x 4 In.....	94
Wood, Dachshund, Carved, Black Cord Shoulder Strap, Timmy Woods, Beverly Hills, 9 In. .	230

PYREX

pyrex

Pyrex glass baking dishes were first made in 1915 by the Corning Glass Works. Pyrex dishes are made of a heat-resistant glass that can go from refrigerator or freezer to oven or microwave and are nice enough to put on the table. Clear glass dishes were made first. Pyrex Flameware, for use on a stovetop burner, was made from 1936 to 1979. A set of four mixing bowls, each in a dfferent color (blue, red, green, and yellow), was made beginning in 1947. The first pieces with decorative patterns were made in 1956. After Corning sold its Pyrex brand to World Kitchen LLC in 1998, changes were made to the formula for the glass.

Bowl, Mixing, Blue Exterior, White Interior, Band Rim, 3 ¼ x 6 In.	25
Bowl, Mixing, Gooseberry Pattern, Cinderella Style, White & Black, Flowers, 7 ½ In.	32
Carafe, Lemonade, Clear, Yellow Stopper, 10 ½ In.	20
Cup, Measuring, Red Marking, Clear, Pour Spout, 7 ½ x 5 ¼ In.	35

QUEZAL

Quezal

Quezal glass was made from 1901 to 1924 at the Queens, New York, company started by Martin Bach. Other glassware by other firms, such as Loetz, Steuben, and Tiffany, resembles this gold-colored iridescent glass. Martin Bach died in 1921. His son-in-law, Conrad Vahlsing Jr., went to work at the Lustre Art Company about 1920. Bach's son, Martin Bach Jr., worked at the Durand Art Glass division of the Vineland Flint Glass Works after 1924.

Bowl, Golden Iridescent, Bronze & Purple Pulled Feather, Flared Rim, 2 x 5 In.	1800
Compote, Yellow & Marigold Iridescent, Green Pulled Feather, Free Shape Edge, 4 x 5 In....	200
Globe, Lighting, Gold Iridescent, Green Pulled Feather Design, Signed, 3 x 6 In............*illus*	225
Lampshade, White Iridescent, Gold Heart, Applied Threading, 5 x 3 In.	150
Salt Cellar, Gold Iridescent, Ribbed, Strap Style Rim, 1 x 2 In., Pair.....................................	175
Shade, Pulled Feather, Scalloped White Rim, Gold Interior, 4 x 5 ½ In., 5 Piece	960
Vase, Blue Iridescent, Round Base, 7 x 3 In..*illus*	350
Vase, Green & Gold Iridescent, Pulled Feather, Trefoil Rim, Circular Base, 6 x 3 In.............	650
Vase, Uncased Vase, Green Iridescent, Silvery Blue, Pulled Feather,1900s, 4 ¾ In.................	1152
Vase, Wavy Rim, Cream Ground, Flowers, Gilt, Domed Base, 9 x 6 In.	1750

QUILT

Quilts have been made since the seventeenth century. Early textiles were very precious and every scrap was saved to be reused. A quilt is a combination of fabrics joined to a filler and a backing by small stitched designs known as quilting. An appliqued quilt has pieces stitched to the top of a large piece of backing fabric. A patchwork, or pieced, quilt is made of many small pieces stitched together. Embroidery can be added to either type.

Amish, Baby Blocks, Hand Stitched, Maroon, Navy, Black Fabrics, Crib, 1950s, 39 x 45 In....	448
Amish, Diamond, Sawtooth, Dark Red Ground, Blue Border, Lancaster, 79 x 81 ½ In.	281
Appliqued, Christmas, Lily, Flowers, Multicolor, Carolina, 1900s, 84 x 82 In. ....*illus*	313

Quezal, Globe, Lighting, Gold Iridescent, Green Pulled Feather Design, Signed, 3 x 6 In.
$225

Woody Auction

Quezal, Vase, Blue Iridescent, Round Base, 7 x 3 In.
$350

Woody Auction

TIP
Forged glass signatures, including Steuben, Quezal, and Tiffany, are being faked. Do not trust a signature. Be sure the glass is the proper shape to have been made by the original factory or artist. Fake marks are written with a diamond-tipped drill or are acid-stamped. All look real.

Q

Quilt, Appliqued, Christmas, Lily, Flowers, Multicolor, Carolina, 1900s, 84 x 82 In.
$313

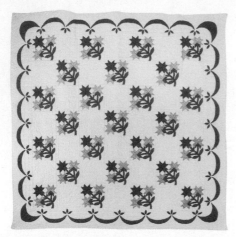

Eldred's

Quilt, Appliqued, Princess Feather, White Ground, Green Leaves, Red Border, 76 x 79 ¼ In.
$406

New Haven Auctions

Quilt, Crazy, Masonic Knights Templar, St. Elmo Commandery, 1885, 56 x 64 In.
$313

Auctions at Showplace, NYC

Quilt Trim
Black buttonhole stitching outlining an appliqué on a quilt was popular from 1925 to 1950. Earlier quilts sometimes had tan or white buttonhole trim for the appliqué.

Quilt, Mennonite, Trip Around The World, Lancaster, Pennsylvania, c.1910, 82 x 82 In.
$281

New Haven Auctions

Quilt, Patchwork & Appliqued, The Lily, Hand & Machine Stitched, Pennsylvania, 1910s, 73 x 87 In.
$143

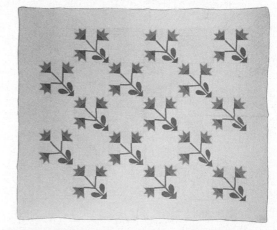

Jeffrey S. Evans & Associates

TIP
Hanging textiles should be given a rest from time to time. The weight of the hanging causes strain on the threads. If the textile is taken down and stored for a few months, the threads will regain some strength.

Appliqued, Hand Sewn, Pink & White, Toothed Border, Floral Quilting, 71 x 68 In.		47
Appliqued, Hand Stitched, Basket Pattern, Sawtooth Wave, 76 x 74 In.		254
Appliqued, Oak Leaf Pattern, Blue Oak Leaves, 84 x 84 In.		188
Appliqued, Princess Feather, White Ground, Green Leaves, Red Border, 76 x 79 ¼ In.	*illus*	406
Appliqued, Tripe Irish Chain, Hand Stitched, Red, Green, Yellow, White Fabric, c.1870, 87 x 88 In.		269
Crazy, Masonic Knights Templar, St. Elmo Commandery, 1885, 56 x 64 In.	*illus*	313
Mennonite, Trip Around The World, Lancaster, Pennsylvania, c.1910, 82 x 82 In.	*illus*	281
Patchwork & Appliqued, The Lily, Hand & Machine Stitched, Pennsylvania, 1910s, 73 x 87 In.	*illus*	143
Patchwork, 8-Point Star, Multicolor, Yellow Border, 80 x 74 In.		148
Patchwork, 8-Point Star, Red, Print & Plain Blocks, Arrows Border, 1800s, 81 x 93 In.		384
Patchwork, Cradle, Bear Paw, Yellow, Red, Charles Leroy Kline, Pennsylvania, 1908, 40 x 42 In.		302
Patchwork, Double Wedding Ring, Feedsack Fabrics, Scalloped Border, 1930-50s, 76 x 91 In.		177
Patchwork, Geometrical Square Pattern, Sawtooth Border, Red, Pink, Green, 75 x 80 In.		339
Patchwork, Hand & Machine Stitched, Multicolor, Triangle, Squares, Cotton, 1930s, 72 x 74 In.		600
Patchwork, Rank Post G.A.R. No. 534, Gnadenhutten, 67 Panels, Ink Inscriptions, 76 x 65 In.		500
Whole Cloth, Olive, Linsey Woolsey, Floral Pattern, 1700s, 87 x 97 In.		1063

QUIMPER

Quimper pottery has a long history. Tin-glazed, hand-painted pottery has been made in Quimper, France, since the late seventeenth century. The earliest firm was founded in 1708 by Pierre Bousquet. In 1782, Antoine de la Hubaudiere became the manager of the factory and the factory became known as the HB Factory (for Hubaudiere-Bousquet), de la Hubaudiere, or Grande Maison. Another firm, founded in 1772 by Francois Eloury, was known as Porquier. The third firm, founded by Guillaume Dumaine in 1778, was known as HR or Henriot Quimper. All three firms made similar pottery decorated with designs of Breton peasants and sea and flower motifs. The Eloury (Porquier) and Dumaine (Henriot) firms merged in 1913. Bousquet (HB) merged with the others in 1968. The group was sold to an American holding company in 1984. More changes followed, and in 2011 Jean-Pierre Le Goff became the owner and the name was changed to Henriot-Quimper.

Centerpiece, Swan Shape, Bent Neck, Green, Blue, Yellow, Signed, Henriot Quimper, 8½ x 15 In.		92
Figurine, Mythical Beast, Multicolor Wings, Brown Ground, Italy, 1700s, 6 In.	*illus*	3125
Vase, Multicolor, 3 Women, 2 Men On Reverse, Figures In Background, Jim E. Sevellec, 6¾ In.		488
Vase, Multicolor, Geometrics, Curves, Spots Spirals, Rene Beauclair, Midcentury, 6¾ x 9 In.		438
Wall Pocket, Bagpipe Shape, Group At Front, Auvergne, Crest, Flowers, Scrolls, Blue Bows, 11½ In.		76

RADFORD

RADURA.

Radford pottery was made by Alfred Radford in Broadway, Virginia; Tiffin and Zanesville, Ohio; and Clarksburg, West Virginia, from 1891 until 1912. Jasperware, Ruko, Thera, Radura, and Velvety Art Ware were made. The jasperware resembles the famous Wedgwood ware of the same name. Another pottery named Radford worked in England and is not included here.

Vase, Radura, Green Matte, 4 Handles, Teco Pottery Shape, c.1910, 14 x 7½ In.		1968

RADIO

Radio broadcast receiving sets were first sold in New York City in 1910. They were used to pick up the experimental broadcasts of the day. The first commercial radios were made by Westinghouse Company for listeners of the experimental shows on KDKA Pittsburgh in 1920. Collectors today are interested in all early radios, especially those made of Bakelite plastic or decorated with blue mirrors. Figural advertising radios and transistor radios are also collected.

Fada, Model 1000, Bullet, Maroon & Butterscotch, Catalin, 9 In.		912
Philco Jr., Model 80, Wood Exterior, Cloth Cover, Horseshoe Shape, Table		58

Quimper, Figurine, Mythical Beast, Multicolor Wings, Brown Ground, Italy, 1700s, 6 In.
$3,125

Hindman

Radio, Sparton, Midnight Blue, Tufflex Mirrored Glass, Sparks Withington Co., c.1936, 9 x 17 x 8 In.
$1,040

Wright

Early Transistor Radios
The first American transistor radio was the Regency TR-1 made in 1954. The best color is red or black; the least expensive is ivory or gray.

Railroad, Broadside, C.&N.W. Ry., Short Line, Oak Frame, c.1880s, 34¾ x 29 In.
$10,030

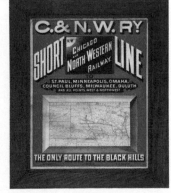

Soulis Auctions

Railroad, Ice Bucket, Overland Route Logo, Ring Handles, Union Pacific, 8½ x 8½ In.
$1,298

Soulis Auctions

Railroad, Lamp, Electric, Non Sweating, Caboose, Adlake, 16 In.
$185

Apple Tree Auction Center

Railroad, Lantern, Orange Glass Globe, Swing Handle, Adams & Westlake Co., 9½ x 6½ In.
$115

Donley Auctions

Railroad, Lantern, Yellow, White Reflectors, Amber Lenses, Adams & Westlake, Adlake, 18 In.
$177

Stony Ridge Auction

Railroad, Sign, Erie, Porcelain, Black & White, Enameled, Beveled Edge, 14 x 14 In.
$826

Soulis Auctions

Railroad, Sign, Little Silver Station, Jersey Central R.R., Cocktail Lounge, Tombstone Top, 49 x 34 In.
$1,287

Thomaston Place Auction Galleries

Philco, Slant Front, Wood, Table, 12 x 19 In.	56
RCA Victor, Model T62, Curved Edge, Wood Case, 19¼ x 8 In.	58
Sparton, Bluebird, Round, Painted Wood, Blue Mirror, Walter Dorwin Teague, 1934, 14 In. Dia.	1875
Sparton, Midnight Blue, Tufflex Mirrored Glass, Sparks Withington Co., c.1936, 9 x 17 x 8 In.*illus*	1040
Zenith, Guardian Ear, Enameled Steel, Isamu Noguchi, c.1937, 6 x 4 x 8 In.	813
Zenith, Model 6D030, Walnut, Brass, Bakelite, Charles & Ray Eames, 1946, 7 x 13 x 6 In.	293

RAILROAD

Railroad enthusiasts collect any train memorabilia. Everything is wanted, from oilcans to whole train cars. The Chessie system has a store that sells many reproductions of its old dinnerware and uniforms.

Barber Chair, Pennsylvania RR, Cast Iron, Porcelain, Red Leather, 41 x 27 x 43 In.	960
Box, Ticket Agent's, Pennsylvania Railroad, Tin, Yellow Lettering, 10 x 16 x 10½ In.	130
Bread Tray, Canadian Pacific Logo, Silver Plate, Signed, 2 x 9 x 6¾ In.	106
Broadside, C.&N.W. Ry., Short Line, Oak Frame, c.1880s, 34¾ x 29 In. *illus*	10030
Broadside, Lithograph, Advertising Short Line, Chicago, 1800s, 16¾ x 6¾ In.	413
Brochure, Pullman, Pleasant View, Passenger Coach, c.1920s, 6¾ x 35½ In.	130
Cup, Wabash, Flag Design, Double Egg, Signed, 3 In.	383
Dish, Pudding, A.T.& S.F., Atchison, Topeka, & Santa Fe, Chinese, 1½ x 4½ In.	266
Ice Bucket, Overland Route Logo, Ring Handles, Union Pacific, 8½ x 8½ In. *illus*	1298
Lamp, Electric, Non Sweating, Caboose, Adlake, 16 In. *illus*	185
Lamp, Switch Stand, 4 Blue & Red Glass Lenses, Swing Handle, Dressel, 16½ x 10 In.	104
Lantern, Black Painted, Marked Osmeka, 1900s, 36 In.	191
Lantern, L & N, Kerosene, Brass, Glass Globe, Swing Handle	74
Lantern, Orange Glass Globe, Swing Handle, Adams & Westlake Co., 9½ x 6½ In. *illus*	115
Lantern, Projector, British Railways, Western, Kerosene, Double Bull's-Eye, Marked, 17 x 9 In.	127
Lantern, Switch, Gray-Boston, Electric, 4-Sided, Red & Green Lights, Red Top, Embossed, 20 In.	205
Lantern, Yellow, White Reflectors, Amber Lenses, Adams & Westlake, Adlake, 18 In. *illus*	177
Poster, Black & Red, Slogan, Frame, Santa Fe, 28½ x 34 In.	266
Sign, American Railway Express, Black Sanded Ground, Gilt Letters, Frame, Late 1800s, 11 x 71 In.	900
Sign, Erie, Porcelain, Black & White, Enameled, Beveled Edge, 14 x 14 In. *illus*	826
Sign, Little Silver Station, Jersey Central R.R., Cocktail Lounge, Tombstone Top, 49 x 34 In. *illus*	1287
Sign, SEPTA, Trenton Station, R7, Fiberglass, Chestnut Hill East, 1970s, 5 x 19⅞ In.	41
Sign, Train, Cross-Buck Form, Black Painted Locomotive, Triangular, First Half 1900s, 24 In.	329
Step Box, Northern Pacific, Steel, Embossed Monad Logo, Rubber Pads, 11 x 20 In.	531
Strong Box, Railway Express Agency, Wood, Painted, Red, Black, Canvas Mail Bag, 18 x 33 x 18 In.	1006
Whistle, Train, Brass, Lunkenheimer, Steam, Switch Handle, 9 x 2 In. *illus*	420

RAZOR

Razors were used in ancient Egypt and subsequently wherever shaving was in fashion. The metal razor used in America was made in Sheffield, England, until about 1870. After 1870, machine-made hollow-ground razors were made in Germany or America. Plastic or bone handles were popular. The razor was often sold in a set of seven, one for each day of the week. The set was often kept by the barber who shaved the well-to-do man each day in the shop.

Ever Ready Deluxe, Metal Chromed Handle, 6-Sided, Blade Holder, Bakelite Clamshell Case, 1940s.	74
Straight, Celluloid Handle, Nude, Raised Arms, Wadsworth Razor Co., 6 In.	125
Straight, Solingen, Germany, Box, 9 In.	79
Straight, Uncle Sam On Blade, Celluloid, Moshy & Rahaim, 1920s	48

REAMER

Reamers, or juice squeezers, have been known since 1767, although most of those collected today date from the twentieth century. Figural reamers are among the most prized.

Figural, Clown, Blue, Orange & Yellow Accents, Japan, 4½ In.	35

Railroad, Whistle, Train, Brass, Lunkenheimer, Steam, Switch Handle, 9 x 2 In.
$420

Chupp Auctions & Real Estate, LLC

TIP

For emergency repairs to chipped pottery, try coloring the spot with a wax crayon or oil paint. It will look a little better.

Reamer, Porcelain, Figural, Clown, Seated, Orange Suit, White Hat & Ruff, 2 Piece, Japan, 5 x 4 In.
$60

R

Woody Auction

Record, Berliner, Disc, No. 114,
Gutta-Percha, E. Berliner's
Grammophon, Germany, 5 In.
$3,738

Donley Auctions

Red Wing, Crock, Cobalt Blue Slip,
Stylized Flower, Albany, N.Y., 1800s,
11¾ In.
$270

Selkirk Auctioneers & Appraisers

Redware, Bank, Presentation, Bird
Finial, Multicolor, Glossy, 1909, 7 In.
$406

New Haven Auctions

Glass, Crisscross Square Pattern, Pour Spout, Handle, 7 x 6 x 2 In.	29
Glass, Spout, Tab Handle, Embossed Manny's, c.1898, 6 x 3 In.	12
Lusterware, Plastic, Green Turquoise, USA, 1950s, 6 In.	12
Milk Glass, Ridged Sides, Handle, Footed, Federal Glass, 1930s, 8 x 6 In.	95
Porcelain, Figural, Clown, Seated, Orange Suit, White Hat & Ruff, 2 Piece, Japan, 5 x 4 In. *illus*	60
Porcelain, Lemon Base & Lid, Handle, Yellow, 5½ x 5 In.	30
Sterling Silver, Gold Wash, Beaded Rim, Handle, Fuchs, 4¾ In.	550

RECORD

Records have changed size and shape through the years. The cylinder-shaped phonograph record for use with the early Edison models was made about 1889. Disc records were first made by 1894, the double-sided disc by 1904. High-fidelity records were first issued in 1944, the first vinyl disc in 1946, the first stereo record in 1958. The 78 RPM became the standard in 1926 but was discontinued in 1957. In 1932, the first 33⅓ RPM was made but was not sold commercially until 1948. In 1949, the 45 RPM was introduced. Compact discs became available in the United States in 1982 and many companies began phasing out the production of phonograph records. Vinyl records are popular again. People claim the sound is better on a vinyl recording, and new recordings are being made. Some collectors want vinyl picture records. Vintage albums are collected for their cover art as well as for the fame of the artist and the music.

Berliner, Disc, No. 114, Gutta-Percha, E. Berliner's Grammophon, Germany, 5 In. *illus*	3738
Glen Campbell, Wichita Lineman, Capitol Records, 33⅓ RPM, 1968	30
Hank Williams, Honky Tonkin', 45 RPM, MGM Records, 1956	77
John Lennon, Stand By Me, Apple Records, 45 RPM, 1975	10
Peter, Paul & Mary, Album 1700, 33⅓ RPM, 1967	45
Rolling Stones, Emotional Rescue, 33⅓ RPM, 1980	43

RED WING

Red Wing Pottery of Red Wing, Minnesota, was a firm started in 1877. The company first made utilitarian pottery, including stoneware jugs and canning jars. In 1906, three companies combined to make the Red Wing Union Stoneware Company and began producing flowerpots, vases, and dinnerware. Art pottery was introduced in 1926. The name of the company was changed to Red Wing Potteries in 1936. Many dinner sets and vases were made before the company closed in 1967. R. Gillmer bought the company in 1967 and operated it as a retail business. The name was changed again, to Red Wing Pottery. The retail business closed in 2015. Red Wing Stoneware Company was founded in 1987. It was sold to new owners in 2013. They bought Red Wing Pottery and combined the two companies to become Red Wing Stoneware & Pottery. The company makes stoneware crocks, jugs, mugs, bowls, and other items with cobalt blue designs. Rumrill pottery made by the Red Wing Pottery for George Rumrill is listed in its own category. For more prices, go to kovels.com.

Bowl, Brown, Green Interior, Narcissus Pattern, 1930s, 9½ In.	75
Bowl, Spongeware, Molded Rings, 7¼ x 4¼ In.	62
Crock, Cobalt Blue Slip, Stylized Flower, Albany, N.Y., 1800s, 11¾ In. *illus*	270
Cup & Saucer, Capistrano Pattern	14
Plate, Ducks In Flight, 10 In., Pair	139
Plate, Quail, Baby Chicks, Brown, Turquoise, 8 In.	25
Vase, Flowers, Leaves, Relief, Green, No. 203, 1929, 12 In.	202
Vase, Star Shape, 8-Sided, Gray, Coral Interior, 9½ In.	25
Wall Pocket, Green, Brown, Birds, 10¼ x 4 x 3 In.	140

R

REDWARE

Redware is a hard, red stoneware that has been made for centuries and continues to be made. The term is also used to describe any common clay pottery that is reddish in color. American redware was first made about 1625.

Bank, Presentation, Bird Finial, Multicolor, Glossy, 1909, 7 In.	*illus*	406
Basin, Stylized Flowers, Slip Zigzag Bands, Tapered, Tab Handles, Dated 1822, 5 x 18 In.		125
Bottle, Manganese Flecks, Yellow Slip, 2 Birds & 2 Tulips, 1910s, 5 In.	*illus*	6600
Bowl, Turtle Creek, Square, Rounded Corners, Chris Woods, Ohio, Dated 2000, 2 x 11 x 11 In.		132
Bride's Basket, Openwork, Curved Handle, Loop Finial, Flowers Decor, France, 1800s, 6¼ In.	*illus*	281
Canister, Octagonal, Lid, Manganese Splash Decoration, 1800s, 8¾ In.	*illus*	554
Charger, Sgrafitto, Bird, Flowers & Leaves, Orange Ground, Breininger, 1984, 14 In.		165
Charger, Yellow Slip Design, Red Ground, Pennsylvania, 1800s, 13 In.		3690
Crock, Deep, Multicolor, Mottled Glaze, Pennsylvania, 1800s, 8 In.	*illus*	1476
Crock, Wide Mouth, Tapering Foot, Lead Glaze, Shenandoah Valley, Virginia, 1820s, 3 In.		299
Crock, Yellow Glaze, Deep, Pennsylvania, 1800s, 4¾ In.		431
Cuspidor, Streaked Manganese, Footed Base, John Bell, Waynesboro, Pa., c.1850-80, 4¼ In.		180
Dish, Loaf, Yellow, Green Slip, Pennsylvania, 1800s, 10½ x 16½ In.		2337
Dish, Octagonal, Slip, Molded, Coggled Edge, Philadelphia, Pa., 1810s, 2⅞ In.		5100
Ewer, Narrow Mouth, Striped Glaze Decor, Ribbed Handle, Footed Base, 1810s, 8 In.	*illus*	2040
Face Jug, 2 Front Teeth, Eyes Wide Open, Green Glaze, Southern, 1800s, 8 x 6½ In.		4688
Figurine, Dog, Spaniel, Mirrored, Black Glaze, Gold Collars, Glass Eyes, 1850s, 14 In., Pair		330
Figurine, Lion, Standing, Yellow, Spaghetti Style Brown Hair & Tail, Breininger, 1985, 8 x 9 In.		224
Figurine, Yellow Lion, Curly Hair, Lester Breininger, 8 In.	*illus*	353
Jar, Brown, Molded Rim, A.H. Shepard, 1800s, 5¼ In.		151
Jar, Lid, Button Knop, Darker Splotch, Light Orange, Brown Glaze, 9 In.		250
Jar, Lid, Turtlecreek Potters, Glazed, Lobbed Handles, 14½ In.		252
Jar, Manganese, Flared Rim, Footed Base, William Jackson, c.1811, 9 In.		4200
Jug, Devil Face, Grotesque, Glazed, James Seagreaves, 5¾ In.		502
Jug, Storage, Orange Body, Brown Speckles, Applied Handle, 11¾ In.		124
Pitcher, Lead & Manganese Glaze, Shenandoah Valley Of Virginia, Earthenware, 9 x 5 In.		4388
Plate, Multicolor Glaze, Slip Decor, Round Shape, Continental, 1800s, 11½ In.		139
Plate, Round, Yellow & Green Slip, 1800s, 8½ In.		738
Plate, Round, Yellow Slip Design, Red Ground, Pennsylvania, 1800s, 9 In.		615
Shaving Mug, Manganese Splash, Glaze, Pennsylvania, 4¼ In.		338
Sugar, Dome Lid, Mottle Glaze, Molded Base, Pennsylvania, 1800s, 4¼ x 4½ In.		148

REGOUT, *see Maastricht category.*

RICHARD, *see Loetz category.*

RIDGWAY

Ridgway pottery has been made in the Staffordshire district in England since 1792 by a series of companies with the name Ridgway. The company began making bone china in 1808. Ridgway became part of Royal Doulton in the 1960s. The transfer-design dinner sets are the most widely known product. Other pieces of Ridgway may be listed under Flow Blue.

Creamer, Oriental Design, Red, Transferware, Ribbed, 3¾ In.		20
Mug, Coaching Days, Brown, c.1900, 4 In.		53
Pitcher, Relief, Pub Scene, Thistle Garland Around Rim, Yellow Glaze, c.1900, 9 In.	*illus*	75
Plate, Pomerania, Brown, Transferware, c.1835, 10¼ In.		50
Platter, Blue Transfer, Rural Courtship, Flowers Around Rim, Well & Tree, 15 x 19 In.	*illus*	62
Platter, English Garden, Flowers, 13 x 10 In.		98
Teapot, Flowers, Gilt Highlights, c.1830, 10¾ x 7 In.		275
Tureen, Blue & White, Alms House, Boston, Beauties Of America, Footed, c.1820, 8 x 15 In.	*illus*	688

RIFLES *that are firearms made after 1900 are not listed in this book. BB guns and air rifles are listed in the Toy category.*

Redware, Bottle, Manganese Flecks, Yellow Slip, 2 Birds & 2 Tulips, 1910s, 5 In.
$6,600

Garth's Auctioneers & Appraisers

Redware, Bride's Basket, Openwork, Curved Handle, Loop Finial, Flowers Decor, France, 1800s, 6¼ In.
$281

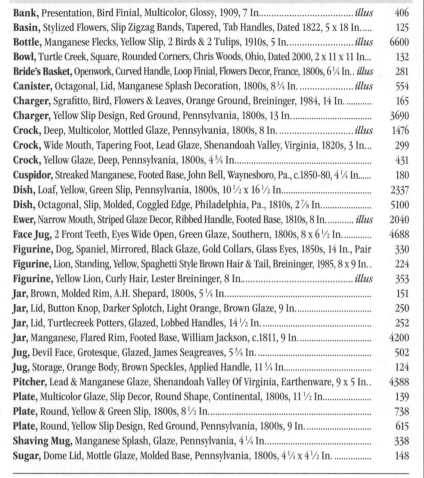

Hindman

Redware, Canister, Octagonal, Lid, Manganese Splash Decoration, 1800s, 8¾ In.
$554

R

Pook & Pook

Redware, Crock, Deep, Multicolor, Mottled Glaze, Pennsylvania, 1800s, 8 In.
$1,476

Pook & Pook

Redware, Ewer, Narrow Mouth, Striped Glaze Decor, Ribbed Handle, Footed Base, 1810s, 8 In.
$2,040

Crocker Farm, Inc.

Redware, Figurine, Yellow Lion, Curly Hair, Lester Breininger, 8 In.
$353

Pook & Pook

Ridgway, Pitcher, Relief, Pub Scene, Thistle Garland Around Rim, Yellow Glaze, c.1900, 9 In.
$75

DuMouchelles

Ridgway, Platter, Blue Transfer, Rural Courtship, Flowers Around Rim, Well & Tree, 15 x 19 In.
$62

John McInnis Auctioneers

Ridgway, Tureen, Blue & White, Alms House, Boston, Beauties Of America, Footed, c.1820, 8 x 15 In.
$688

Garth's Auctioneers & Appraisers

RIVIERA

Riviera dinnerware was made by the Homer Laughlin Co. of Newell, West Virginia, from 1938 to 1950. The pattern was similar in coloring to Fiesta and Harlequin. The Riviera plates and cup handles were square. For more prices, go to kovels.com.

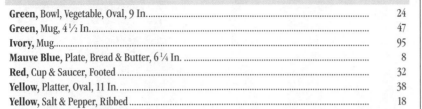

Green, Bowl, Vegetable, Oval, 9 In.	24
Green, Mug, 4½ In.	47
Ivory, Mug.	95
Mauve Blue, Plate, Bread & Butter, 6¼ In.	8
Red, Cup & Saucer, Footed	32
Yellow, Platter, Oval, 11 In.	38
Yellow, Salt & Pepper, Ribbed	18

ROCKINGHAM

Rockingham, in the United States, is a pottery with a brown glaze that resembles tortoiseshell. It was made from 1840 to 1900 by many American potteries. Mottled brown Rockingham wares were first made in England at the Rockingham factory. Other types of ceramics were also made by the English firm. Related pieces may be listed in the Bennington category.

Cuspidor, Mottled Brown, Dark Blue Glaze, Octagonal, Mid 1800s, 4⅝ x 8 In.	120
Figurine, Dog, Spaniel, Seated, Brown Glazed, Plinth Base, 11 In.	99
Figurine, Lion, Lying Down, Brown Glaze, Oval Base, Late 1800s, 9 x 10 In., Pair........ *illus*	438
Flask, Book Shape, Flint Enamel, Ladies Companion, Unmarked, c.1850, 4 Qt., 10¾ x 8⅜ In... *illus*	4669
Mixing Bowl, Spongeware, Textured Exterior, Flared Lip, 4¼ x 10 In.	25
Pitcher, Deer Hunt, Leafy Borders, Twig Handle, Footed, Mocha, 1800s, 9 x 9 x 7½ In.	90
Pitcher, Hound Handle, Harker, East Liverpool, Oh., c.1850, 11½ In. .... *illus*	688
Pitcher, Hunting Scene, Branch Shape Handle, Footed, 7¾ In.	36
Plate, Primrose Leaves, Flower Vase, Basket, Flower, Stone Ledge, Edwin Steele, 1830, 10 In., Pair..	1879
Toby Jug, Man In Tricorn, Scroll Handle, Yellowware, American Pottery Co., N.J., c.1840, 6 In.	191

ROGERS, *see John Rogers category.*

ROOKWOOD

Rookwood pottery was made in Cincinnati, Ohio, beginning in 1880. All of this art pottery is marked, most with the famous flame mark. The *R* is reversed and placed back to back with the letter *P*. Flames surround the letters. After 1900, a Roman numeral was added to the mark to indicate the year. The company went bankrupt in 1941. It was bought and sold several times after that. For several years various owners tried to revive the pottery, but by 1967 it was out of business. The name and some of the molds were bought by a collector in Michigan in 1982. A few items were made beginning in 1983. In 2004, a group of Cincinnati investors bought the company and 3,700 original molds, the name, and trademark. Pottery was made in Cincinnati again beginning in 2006. Today the company makes architectural tile, art pottery, and special commissions. New items and a few old items with slight redesigns are made. Contemporary pieces are being made to complement the dinnerware line designed by John D. Wareham in 1921. Pieces are marked with the RP mark and a Roman numeral for the four-digit year date. Mold numbers on pieces made since 2006 begin with 10000.

ROOKWOOD
1882

Rookwood
1882–1886

$\mathcal{R}\!\!\!\mathcal{P}$

Rookwood
1886

Rookwood
1901

Rockingham, Figurine, Lion, Lying Down, Brown Glaze, Oval Base, Late 1800s, 9 x 10 In., Pair
$438

Hindman

Rockingham, Flask, Book Shape, Flint Enamel, Ladies Companion, Unmarked, c.1850, 4 Qt., 10¾ x 8⅜ In.
$4,669

Jeffrey S. Evans & Associates

Rockingham, Pitcher, Hound Handle, Harker, East Liverpool, Oh., c.1850, 11½ In.
$688

Hindman

This is an edited listing of current prices. Visit **Kovels.com** to check thousands of prices from previous years and sign up for free information on trends, tips, reproductions, marks, and more.

R

TIP
*Rub white toothpaste
on crayon marks on the
wall to remove
the marks.*

Rookwood, Bookends, Horse, White Glaze, William P. McDonald, Cincinnati, 1943, 6 ¼ x 5 ¼ In.
$500

Treadway

Rookwood, Bookends, Shirayamadani Fruit, Brown, Tan Matte Glaze, 1937, 3 x 5 x 2 ¼ In.
$360

Main Auction Galleries, Inc.

Rookwood, Bowl, Flowers, Yellow Blue Ground, Vellum, Lenore Asbury, 1921, 2 In.
$1,920

Garth's Auctioneers & Appraisers

Rookwood, Ewer, Standard Glaze, Coreopsis, Sara Sax, 1899, 10 ¼ x 7 In.
$531

Toomey & Co. Auctioneers

Rookwood, Jar, Lid, Dull Finish, Glaze, Honeysuckle, Artus Van Briggle, 1869, 5 x 4 x 6 In.
$650

Toomey & Co. Auctioneers

Rookwood, Mug, Indian Portrait, Little Soldier, Standard Glaze, Edward Timothy Hurley, 4 In.
$2,360

Soulis Auctions

Rookwood, Mug, Puzzle, Portrait, William Shakespeare, Rounded Rim, Standard Glaze, 5 In.
$600

Treasureseeker Auctions

TIP
Install motion detector lights to guard your yard at night.

Rookwood, Paperweight, Dog, Painted, Brown, Seated, Square Base, 1930, 4 ¾ x 6 x 3 ½ In.
$461

California Historical Design

Rookwood, Plaque, Vellum, Mt. Tamalpais, California, Carl Schmidt, Frame, 1916, 9 ¼ x 14 ½ In.
$9,840

California Historical Design

Bookends, Figural, Penguins, Ocher & Gray, Paper Label, Factory Marks, c.1910, 5¾ x 2½ In.		675
Bookends, Figural, Trees, Signed, William P. McDonald, Dated 1929, 5 x 5 In., Pair		350
Bookends, Horse, White Glaze, William P. McDonald, Cincinnati, 1943, 6¼ x 5¼ In.. *illus*		500
Bookends, Shirayamadani Fruit, Brown, Tan Matte Glaze, 1937, 3 x 5 x 2¼ In. *illus*		360
Bookends, Woman, Blue Matte Glaze, Louise Abel, c.1925, 6½ In.		388
Bowl, Berries, Vine, Orange Leaves, Dark Brown Glaze, 3½ x 5½ In.		156
Bowl, Flowers, Yellow Blue Ground, Vellum, Lenore Asbury, 1921, 2 In. *illus*		1920
Bowl, Green Matte Glaze, Flower Frog, 1914, 2¾ x 6¾ In.		400
Bowl, Green, Black Glaze Exterior, 1928, 2¾ x 9¾ x 11 In.		120
Candlestick, Figural, Juggler, Lying Down, Holds Cup With Feet, Gray, Haswell, 1916, 7½ In.		290
Ewer, Standard Glaze, Coreopsis, Sara Sax, 1899, 10¼ x 7 In. *illus*		531
Figurine, Leopard, Standing, William P. McDonald, Cincinnati, 1946, 3 x 6 In.		344
Figurine, Rooster, Standing, Platform, William P. McDonald, Cincinnati, 1943, 4¾ x 3¼ In.		390
Humidor, Glazed Earthenware, Date Mark, Artist Monogram, 1929, 5 In.		688
Jar, Lid, Dull Finish, Glaze, Honeysuckle, Artus Van Briggle, 1869, 5 x 4 x 6 In. *illus*		650
Mug, Green Matte Finish, Embossed Corn Design, Dated 1905, 5 x 5 In.		200
Mug, Indian Portrait, Little Soldier, Standard Glaze, Edward Timothy Hurley, 4 In. *illus*		2360
Mug, Puzzle, Portrait, William Shakespeare, Rounded Rim, Standard Glaze, 5 In. *illus*		600
Paperweight, Dog, Painted, Brown, Seated, Square Base, 1930, 4¾ x 6 x 3½ In. *illus*		461
Paperweight, Figural, Fox, Lying Down, Blue Matte Glaze, 1¾ x 5¾ x 2½ In.		219
Pin Tray, Man, Sitting, Flamboyant Costume, Hat, Sallie Toohey, Cincinnati, 1930, 4 x 6 In.		293
Pitcher, Earthenware, Sea Green Glaze, 4 Swimming Fish, E.T. Hurley, 1900, 7 x 3¼ x 3 In.		1250
Plaque, Across The Lake, Landscape, Glazed, Earthenware, Gilt Frame, c.1927, 10 x 12 In.		2178
Plaque, Earthenware, Vellum Glaze, Full Moon, Kataro Shirayamadani, 1865, 13 x 16 x 1 In.		6875
Plaque, Earthenware, Vellum, Tonalist Landscape, E.T. Hurley, 1917, 14¼ x 16½ x 2 In.		3000
Plaque, Vellum, Mt. Tamalpais, California, Carl Schmidt, Frame, 1916, 9¼ x 14½ In. *illus*		9840
Sculpture, Woman, Art Deco, Ivory Matte Glaze, Louise Abel, 1930, 11½ x 5 x 4 In.		480
Stein, Wiedemann Brewing Co., Eagle, Metal Lid, Brown Ground, 1948, 5½ In.		180
Tile, Fish, Blue Ground, Wood Frame, 11½ x 11½ In.		1000
Tile, Trivet, Parrot, Green, Yellow, Blue, Circular Design, 1925, 5¾ x 5¾ In. *illus*		154
Tray, Earthenware, Owl, Red, Tan Glaze, 1905, 4⅛ x 6¾ x 5½ In.		260
Trivet, Basket Of Flowers & Butterflies, Blue, Yellow, White, 1943, 5¾ x 5¾ In.		120
Trivet, Tile, Parrot, Flowers, Multicolor, 1922, 5¾ x 5¾ In.		215
Tyg, Earthenware, Standard Glaze, High Bear Sioux, Adeliza Drake Sehon, 6 x 7 x 6 In.		2125
Vase, Black Glaze, RP Logo, Shape Number 6749, 1939, 6 x 4 In.		96
Vase, Blue Matte Glaze, Flowers, Red, Lorinda Epply, 1918, 11½ x 5½ In. *illus*		984
Vase, Blue Matte Glaze, Stamped Mark, 1928, 5½ x 3½ In.		188
Vase, Blue Matte, 2 Handles, Signed, XXVII 63, 1927, 4½ x 4¼ In.		154
Vase, Flowers, Blue & Beige Ground, Molded Rim, Vellum, Ed Diers, 1917, 7½ In.		480
Vase, Flowers, Charles S. Todd, Cylindrical, 1886, 3 x 5 In.		357
Vase, Flowers, Dark Brown Glaze, Earthenware, Albert R. Valentien, c.1899, 14½ In. *illus*		968
Vase, Flowers, Purple, Blue, Pink Tones, Janet Harris, Signed, JH, 1928, 5 x 5 In.		316
Vase, Globular, Mahogany Glaze, Geraniums, Albert Robert Valentien, 1889, 10 In.		819
Vase, Handle, Vine Design, Glazed, Silver, M. Nourse, Cincinnati, 1893, 5½ x 4¾ In.		1250
Vase, Hudson, Earthenware, Trillium, Dorothy England, 4 x 8 In. *illus*		162
Vase, Iris, Multicolor Glaze, No. 821B, 12 In.		338
Vase, Leaf & Berry, Brown Glazed, Bulbous, Round Rim, 6¾ In.		254
Vase, Multicolor, Glazed, Flowers, E.T. Hurley, 6 In. *illus*		677
Vase, Scenic, 2 Pheasant Cocks, Hen, Pine Tree, Arthur Conant, 1919, 6¼ x 5½ In. *illus*		3375
Vase, Scenic, Forest, Vellum Glaze, Tapered, Flared Rim, F. Rothenbusch, 1920, 7¾ In.		685
Vase, Scenic, Vellum, Artist Initialed ED, Ed Diers, Dated 1915, 9¾ In.		706
Vase, Squeezebag, Heart Shape Leaves, Berries, Mottled Tan, Swollen, W. Hentschel, 1929, 10 In.		2770
Vase, Vellum, Roses, Glazed Earthenware, Date Mark, Initials, 1932, 6 In.		375
Vase, Vellum, Scenic, Trees, Cylindrical, Signed, Sally E. Coyne, Dated 1915, 7 x 3 In.		700

RORSTRAND

Rorstrand was established near Stockholm, Sweden, in 1726. By the nineteenth century Rorstrand was making English-style earthenware, bone china, porcelain, ironstone china, and majolica. The three-crown mark has been used since

Rookwood, Tile, Trivet, Parrot, Green, Yellow, Blue, Circular Design, 1925, 5¾ x 5¾ In.

$154

California Historical Design

Rookwood, Vase, Blue Matte Glaze, Flowers, Red, Lorinda Epply, 1918, 11½ x 5½ In.

$984

California Historical Design

Rookwood, Vase, Flowers, Dark Brown Glaze, Earthenware, Albert R. Valentien, c.1899, 14½ In.

$968

Fontaine's Auction Gallery

Rookwood, Vase, Hudson, Earthenware, Trillium, Dorothy England, 4 x 8 In.
$162

Toomey & Co. Auctioneers

Rookwood, Vase, Multicolor, Glazed, Flowers, E.T. Hurley, 6 In.
$677

Apple Tree Auction Center

Rookwood, Vase, Scenic, 2 Pheasant Cocks, Hen, Pine Tree, Arthur Conant, 1919, 6 1/4 x 5 1/2 In.
$3,375

Toomey & Co. Auctioneers

1884. Rorstrand became part of the Hackman Group in 1991. Hackman was bought by Iittala Group in 2004. Fiskars Corporation bought Iittala in 2007 and Rorstrand is now a brand owned by Fiskars.

Jardiniere, Cream Ground, Ross, On Stand, Signed, Art Nouveau, 48 In., Pair 4560
Pitcher, Dark Red, Waisted, Slanted Rim, Midcentury, 10 In. 42
Vase, Bulbous, Reclining Nudes, Trees, Blue Geometric Borders, Signed, NTE, early 1900s, 8 In.. 750
Vase, Carved, Painted, Roses, Stems, Karl Larsen, c.1925, 10 3/8 x 3 3/4 In. ..... *illus* 487
Vase, Long Neck, Glazed Stoneware, Gunnar Nylund, c.1950, 14 x 5 In. ..... *illus* 2500

ROSALINE, *see Steuben category.*

ROSE BOWL

Rose bowls were popular during the 1880s. Rose petals were kept in the open bowl to add fragrance to a room, a popular idea in a time of limited personal hygiene. The glass bowls were made with crimped tops, which kept the petals inside. Many types of Victorian art glass were made into rose bowls.

Art Glass, Yellow To White, Applied Amber Branch & Pink Flowers, 5 3/4 x 6 1/2 In. ..... *illus* 48
Cranberry Glass, Opalescent Swirl, Crimped Rim, 4 1/4 In. 52
Glass, Honey Yellow, Blown, Small Opening, Signed, Peter Bramhall, 10 x 8 In. 293
Glass, Iridescent Yellow Leaves, Handblown, Signed, Peter Bramhall, 1984, 8 1/2 In. 300
Mother-Of-Pearl, Satin Moire, Lavender To White, 3 x 3 In. 1800
Panel Optic, Enamel & Gilt, Late 1800s, 8 3/4 In. ..... *illus* 108
Porcelain, Yellow, White, Roses, Gilt, Molded Scrolls, Scalloped Rim, Marked, Vienna, 4 3/4 x 5 In. 30

ROSE CANTON

Rose Canton china is similar to Rose Mandarin and Rose Medallion, except that no people are pictured in the decoration. It was made in China during the nineteenth and twentieth centuries in greens, pinks, and other colors.

Barrel Seat, Hexagonal, 19 x 9 1/2 In. 628
Plate, Center Medallion, Unidentified Armorial, c.1860s, 9 1/2 In. 150

ROSE MANDARIN

Rose Mandarin china is similar to Rose Canton and Rose Medallion. If the main design pictures only people in scenes, often in a garden, and is framed with a border of flowers, birds, insects, fruit, or fish, it is Rose Mandarin.

Cup, Cann, Court Scene, Floral Banded Rim, Twist Handles, c.1840, 5 In. 540
Jar, Lid, Urn Shape, Chrysanthemum Finial, Peacock & Flower Design, 20 1/4 In. 2723
Plate, Flowers, Butterfly, Banded Border, Figures, Garden Scene, 1842, 9 3/4 In. ..... *illus* 450
Punch Bowl, Scenic Panels, Flower & Butterfly, Courtyard, Wood Stand, 19th Century, 7 x 16 In. 1230
Vase, Court Scenes, Figures, Greek Key Border, c.1840, 10 1/2 In. 300
Vase, Iron Red, Palette Lobed, Mounted As Lamp, Landscape Scenes, 11 1/2 x 4 1/2 In. ..... *illus* 666
Vase, Oval, Wide Petal Rim, Qilong At Neck & Shoulder, 1800s, 17 In., Pair 1500

ROSE MEDALLION

Rose Medallion china was made in China during the nineteenth and twentieth centuries. It is a distinctive design with four or more panels of decoration around a central medallion that includes a bird or a peony. The panels show combinations of birds, people, flowers, fish, fruit, or insects. The panels have border designs of tree peonies and leaves. Pieces are colored in greens, pinks, and other colors. It is similar to Rose Canton and Rose Mandarin.

Basket, Stand, Pierced, Reticulated, Flared Rim, Underplate, 4 x 10 x 11 In. 250
Bowl, Centerpiece, White Ground, Flowers, Court Scene, 4 x 11 In. 240

Rorstrand, Vase, Carved, Painted, Roses, Stems, Karl Larsen, c.1925, 10 3/8 x 3 3/4 In.
$487

Toomey & Co. Auctioneers

Rorstrand, Vase, Long Neck, Glazed Stoneware, Gunnar Nylund, c.1950, 14 x 5 In.
$2,500

Wright

Rose Bowl, Art Glass, Yellow To White, Applied Amber Branch & Pink Flowers, 5 3/4 x 6 1/2 In.
$48

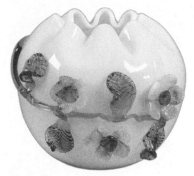

Woody Auction

Rose Bowl, Panel Optic, Enamel & Gilt, Late 1800s, 8 3/4 In.
$108

Jeffrey S. Evans & Associates

Rose Mandarin, Plate, Flowers, Butterfly, Banded Border, Figures, Garden Scene, 1842, 9 3/4 In.
$450

Alex Cooper Auctioneers

Rose Mandarin, Vase, Iron Red, Palette Lobed, Mounted As Lamp, Landscape Scenes, 11 1/2 x 4 1/2 In.
$666

Ahlers & Ogletree Auction Gallery

TIP
Always wash antique china in a sink lined with a rubber mat or towels. This helps prevent chipping. Wash one piece at a time. Rinse and let it air dry. If you suspect a piece has been repaired, do not wash it. Clean with a soft brush dampened in a solution of ammonia and water.

Rose Medallion, Garden, Seat, Drum Shape, People, Floral, Multicolor, White Ground, 18 1/2 In.
$450

Neal Auction Company

Rose Medallion, Garden Seat, Flowers, Gilt Bosses, Hexagonal, c.1870, 19 In.
$1,875

Eldred's

R

423

Rose Medallion, Jardiniere, People, Court, Flowers, Square Rim, Gilt, 1900s, 12 x 14 In.

$250

Hindman

Rose Medallion, Platter, Serving, People, Birds, Flowers, Scenic, Chinese, 1800s, 2¼ x 14½ In.

$259

Merrill's Auctions

Rose Medallion, Punch Bowl, Multicolor, People, Birds, Butterfly, Flowers, Leaves, 1800s, 7 In.

$875

Charlton Hall Auctions

TIP

It is easy to glue pieces of broken china. Use a new fast-setting but not instant glue. Position the pieces correctly, then use tape to hold the parts together. If the piece needs special support, lean it in a suitable position in a box filled with sand.

Bowl, Flowers, Deep, 1800s, 5 x 13 In.	492
Charger, Scholar Scene, Tree, Lanterns, Table, Multicolor, 14½ In.	1000
Fishbowl, Flowers, Carved Base, 19 x 22 In.	160
Garden Seat, Drum Shape, People, Floral, Multicolor, White Ground, 18½ In. *illus*	450
Garden Seat, Flowers, Gilt Bosses, Hexagonal, c.1870, 19 In. *illus*	1875
Ginger Jar, Lid, Bird & Warrior Scenes, Lion Mounted Tops, c.1970s, 32 x 15 In.	576
Jardiniere, People, Court, Flowers, Square Rim, Gilt, 1900s, 12 x 14 In. *illus*	250
Lamp, Central Medallion, Roses, Butterflies, Birds, Carved Wood Base, 1900s, 30½ In., Pair	893
Plate, Phoenix, Shield, Latin Motto, Chinese Scenes, 1800s, 10 In.	220
Platter, Oval, Court Scenes, Multicolor, Birds, Butterflies, Flowers, Fruit, 8 x 15 In.	120
Platter, Serving, People, Birds, Flowers, Scenic, Chinese, 1800s, 2¼ x 14½ In. *illus*	259
Pot, Molded, 2 Handles, Foo Dog, Flowers, Multicolor, 7¼ x 8 In.	384
Punch Bowl, Multicolor, People, Birds, Butterfly, Flowers, Leaves, 1800s, 7 In. *illus*	875
Punch Bowl, People, Courtyard, Flowers & Leaves, Round Foot, Late 1800s, 4 x 11 In.	313
Teapot, Flowers, Multicolor, Wrought Iron Handle, 7 x 4 x 5 In.	53
Tureen, Lid, 2 Handles, Oblong Shape, 1850, 11 x 14 x 9 In.	469
Umbrella Stand, Ribbed Body, Interior Scene, Bird, Flower, 3 Tiers, 1900s, 24 x 9 In.	563
Vase, Bronze, Mounted, Pine Cone Finial, Allover Crackle Glaze Design, Multicolor, 18 x 12 In.	118
Vase, Foo Dogs, Gilt, Floral Rim, c.1875, 14 In.	500
Vase, Gilt Elephant Trunk, 2 Handles, 1800s, 12 x 3½ In., Pair	1875
Vase, Hu Shape, Flared Rim, Flowers, Multicolor, Mid 1800s, 12½ In. *illus*	219
Vase, Lid, Gourd, Figure, Flowers, Bird, Insect, 1800s, 10 In., Pair	448
Vase, Lion Handles, Salamanders, Enameled, Flowers, Birds, Butterflies, 10 In., Pair	847
Vase, Lion Mask Handle, Gilt, Figures, Flowers, Scenes, Cylindrical, 9 x 5 x 4 In.	556
Vase, Painted, Applied, Foo Dogs & Dragons Handles, Curved Rim, 24 In.	168
Vase, People, Flowers, Yellow Ground, Flared Rim, Wood Base, 36 In.	256
Vase, Scalloped Ring, Court Scene, Chilong Dragons, Wood Stand, 1644, 25½ In., Pair	3840

ROSE O'NEILL, *see Kewpie category.*

ROSE TAPESTRY

Rose Tapestry porcelain was made by the Royal Bayreuth factory of Tettau, Germany, during the late nineteenth century. The surface of the porcelain was pressed against a coarse fabric while it was still damp, and the impressions remained on the finished porcelain. It looks and feels like a textured cloth. Very skillful reproductions are being made that even include a variation of the Royal Bayreuth mark, so be careful when buying.

Basket, Green, Pink Roses, Gilt, Scalloped Rim, Marked, Royal Bayreuth Style, 1900s, 5½ In. *illus*	50
Bonbon, Wavy Rim, 2 Open Handles, Gold Trim, Paragon, 6 x 4 In.	30
Dresser Box, Removable Lid, Clam Shell Shape, Pink & Yellow Roses, 5¼ x 3¼ x 2 In.	150
Pitcher, Pink Roses, Handle & Spout, Signed, c.1880, 4 x 4¾ In.	395
Pitcher, Rose Blossoms, Yellow, Pink, White, Sculptured Handle, 3¾ In.	98

ROSENTHAL

Rosenthal porcelain was made at the factory established in Selb, Bavaria, in 1891. The factory is still making fine-quality tablewares and figurines. A series of Christmas plates was made from 1910. Other limited edition plates have been made since 1971. Rosenthal became part of the Arcturus Group in 2009.

Rosenthal China
1891–1904

Rosenthal China
1928

Rosenthal China
1948

Figurine, Child With Chicks, 4¾ In.	125

Figurine, Dog, Irish Setter, Sitting, Open Mouth, 6¾ In.	295
Figurine, Dog, Poodle, White, Green Collar, Standing, 8 x 7 In.	150
Figurine, Squirrel, Plume Tail, Pointed Ears, Clutching Walnut, Kunstabteilung Selb, 6 In.	212
Figurine, Tschaikiun Sword Dancer, Constantin Holzer-Defanti, Bavaria, c.1925, 13½ x 5 In. *illus*	1000
Gravy Boat, Underplate, Orange Flowers, Maria, 1930s	87
Plate, Pink Roses, Beaded Sterling Silver Rim, 6 In.	65
Vase, Footed Cup Shape, Gilt Floral, Bjorn Wiinblad, 1918-2006, 5 x 6 In.	180

ROSEVILLE

Roseville Pottery Company was organized in Roseville, Ohio, in 1890. Another plant was opened in Zanesville, Ohio, in 1898. Many types of pottery were made until 1954. Early wares include Sgraffito, Olympic, and Rozane. Later lines were often made with molded decorations, especially flowers and fruit. Most pieces are marked *Roseville*. Many reproductions made in China have been offered for sale since the 1980s.

Roseville Pottery Company 1914–1930	Roseville Pottery Company 1935–1954	Roseville Pottery Company 1939–1953

Aztec, Vase, Light Green, White Flowers, Dark Green Trim, 9 x 4½ In.	375
Basket, Green Matte Glaze, Hanging Chain, c.1910, 4½ x 7¼ In. *illus*	523
Basket, Green Matte Glaze, Hanging, Stylized Rim, c.1910s, 6 x 9 In.	246
Blackberry, Jardiniere, Pedestal, Embossed, Flowers, Leaves, Green Ground, 1930s, 28 In. *illus*	1440
Carnelian II, Vase, Pink, Drip, Round Body, Long Neck, Fins, Footed, 16 In. *illus*	1000
Cherry Blossom, Jardiniere, Pedestal, Tan Ground, White Blossoms, Stripes, 29 x 13 In. *illus*	618
Cherry Blossom, Vase, Squat, Pink Flowers, Tree Branches, c.1932, 3⅞ In.	131
Chloron, Wall Pocket, Earthenware, Green Matte Glaze, c.1905, 10 x 6¼ x 2⅛ In. *illus*	357
Clematis, Jardiniere, Pedestal, Brown & Green Tones, 24 x 12 In. *illus*	225
Clematis, Jardiniere, Pedestal, Multicolor, 17 x 8 In. *illus*	338
Crystalis, Vase, Cylindrical, Flaring Base, Green Matte Glaze, Rozane, 1906, 13⅞ In.	3346
Dahlrose, Vase, Squat, Arched Handle, 8½ x 5¼ In. *illus*	344
Dahlrose, Wall Pocket, 2 Handles, Green, Brown, c.1920s, 8½ x 6¾ In.	123
Della Robbia, Vase, Rozane, Brown Ground, 10 x 4½ In.	2470
Donatello, Jardiniere, Green, Brown & White Tones, Figures, 6 x 5 In. *illus*	70
Florane, Vase, Orange Matte Glaze, Tapered Foot, Marked, RV, c.1920, 12 In. *illus*	191
Freesia, Lamp, Blue Ground, 2 Side Handles, Brass, 24 In., Pair	492
Freesia, Vase, Blue Ground, White Floral, Green Leaves, 2 Handles, Footed, 1940s, 7½ In.	100
Futura, Candlestick, Aztec Woman, Matte Glaze, 4¹/₁₆ x 3¼ In., Pair *illus*	487
Imperial II, Vase, Green, Semigloss, c.1924, 19⅜ x 12½ In. *illus*	2625
Jonquil, Vase, Flowers, Loop Handles, Multicolor, 8 In.	148
Luffa, Vase, Green & Brown Shaded Ground, Angular Handles, 8 x 8 In. *illus*	195
Pauleo, Vase, Orange Iris, Ream Background, Green Banding, c.1914, 18 In. *illus*	1440
Pinecone, Vase, Blue Ground, Shaped Rim & Handles, Pedestal Base, 10½ x 8 In. *illus*	293
Pinecone, Vase, Green Glaze, Handle, Stepped Base, 10½ x 8½ In.	215
Pinecone, Vase, Green Ground, Branch Shape Handles, Foil Label, 11¾ In.	470
Rozane, Vase, Flared Rim, 2 Handles, Falstaff Portrait, c.1915, 21 In.	780
Sunflower, Vase, 2 Handles, Unmarked, 5¼ x 5 In. *illus*	358
Umbrella Stand, Green Matte, Embossed Asiatic Lilies, 8 Panels, c.1910, 23 x 10⅜ In.	650
Umbrella Stand, Strap Rim, 2 Handles, Tan Ground, Domed Base, 1930s, 20¼ In.	270
Vase, Cream Ground, Green, Slatted, Molded Rim, Round Base, 9 In.	62
Velmoss, Jardiniere, Tulip, Green & Turquoise Matte Glaze, Oh, c.1916, 9 x 10 In.	837
Water Lily, Vase, Flowers, Painted, Blue Ground, 2 Handles, 1940s, 11 x 8 x 15 In.	127
White Rose, Vase, Green Ground, Satin Matte Finish, c.1940, 9¼ In., Pair	131
Wisteria, Vase, Purple, Green, Matte Glaze, Marked, Silver Foil Label, 15¼ x 7 In. *illus*	975

Rose Medallion, Vase, Hu Shape, Flared Rim, Flowers, Multicolor, Mid 1800s, 12½ In.
$219

Eldred's

Rose Tapestry, Basket, Green, Pink Roses, Gilt, Scalloped Rim, Marked, Royal Bayreuth Style, 1900s, 5½ In.
$50

Lion and Unicorn

Rosenthal, Figurine, Tschaikiun Sword Dancer, Constantin Holzer-Defanti, Bavaria, c.1925, 13½ x 5 In.
$1,000

Toomey & Co. Auctioneers

R

ROSEVILLE

Roseville, Basket, Green Matte Glaze, Hanging Chain, c.1910, 4 1/2 x 7 1/4 In.
$523

California Historical Design

Roseville, Blackberry, Jardiniere, Pedestal, Embossed, Flowers, Leaves, Green Ground, 1930s, 28 In.
$1,440

Garth's Auctioneers & Appraisers

Roseville, Carnelian II, Vase, Pink, Drip, Round Body, Long Neck, Fins, Footed, 16 In.
$1,000

Treadway

Roseville, Cherry Blossom, Jardiniere, Pedestal, Tan Ground, White Blossoms, Stripes, 29 x 13 In.
$618

Treadway

Roseville, Chloron, Wall Pocket, Earthenware, Green Matte Glaze, c.1905, 10 x 6 1/4 x 2 1/8 In.
$357

Toomey & Co. Auctioneers

TIP

When you can't decide whether or not to buy a treasure at a show or flea market, remember the classic slogan, "Buy now or cry later."

Roseville, Clematis, Jardiniere, Pedestal, Brown & Green Tones, 24 x 12 In.
$225

Woody Auction

Roseville, Clematis, Jardiniere, Pedestal, Multicolor, 17 x 8 In.
$338

Apple Tree Auction Center

TIP

If you use valuable pottery vases like Roseville for flowers, use dried plants unless you protect the vase. Put a slightly smaller glass vase inside to hold the water and the flowers. "Hard" water will leave a stain on pottery or glass.

Roseville, Dahlrose, Vase, Squat, Arched Handle, 8 ½ x 5 ¼ In.
$344

Treadway

Roseville, Donatello, Jardiniere, Green, Brown & White Tones, Figures, 6 x 5 In.
$70

Woody Auction

Roseville, Florane, Vase, Orange Matte Glaze, Tapered Foot, Marked, RV, c.1920, 12 In.
$191

Jeffrey S. Evans & Associates

Roseville, Futura, Candlestick, Aztec Woman, Matte Glaze, 4 ¹⁄₁₆ x 3 ¼ In., Pair
$487

Toomey & Co. Auctioneers

Roseville, Imperial II, Vase, Green, Semigloss, c.1924, 19 ³⁄₈ x 12 ½ In.
$2,625

Toomey & Co. Auctioneers

Roseville, Luffa, Vase, Green & Brown Shaded Ground, Angular Handles, 8 x 8 In.
$195

Treadway

Roseville, Pauleo, Vase, Orange Iris, Ream Background, Green Banding, c.1914, 18 In.
$1,440

Garth's Auctioneers & Appraisers

Roseville, Pinecone, Vase, Blue Ground, Shaped Rim & Handles, Pedestal Base, 10 ½ x 8 In.
$293

Treadway

Roseville, Sunflower, Vase, 2 Handles, Unmarked, 5 ¼ x 5 In.
$358

Treadway

Roseville, Wisteria, Vase, Purple, Green, Matte Glaze, Marked, Silver Foil Label, 15 ¼ x 7 In.
$975

Toomey & Co. Auctioneers

Roy Rogers, Holster Set, 2 Guns, Red Plastic Bullet, Black & Silver, Box, c.1955
$456

Weiss Auctions

Royal Bayreuth, Vase, Tapestry Finish, Green Tones, White & Lavender Flowers, 7 x 4 In.
$80

R

Woody Auction

ROWLAND & MARSELLUS

Rowland & Marsellus Company is part of a mark that appears on historical Staffordshire dating from the late nineteenth and early twentieth centuries. *Rowland & Marsellus* is the mark used by an American importing company in New York City. The company worked from 1893 to about 1937. Some of the pieces may have been made by the British Anchor Pottery Co. of Longton, England, for export to a New York firm. Many American views were made. Of special interest to collectors are the plates with rolled edges, usually blue and white.

Beaker, Views Of Seattle, Waterfront, Mt. Ranier, 4 In.	100
Bowl, Valley Forge, 6 Cartouches, Washington Scenes, 10 In.	89
Plate, Landing Of Hendrick Hudson, Rolled Edge, 10 In.	77
Plate, Souvenir Of Niagara Falls, Vignettes Of Area, Rolled Edge, 10 In.	105

ROY ROGERS

Roy Rogers was born in 1911 in Cincinnati, Ohio. His birth name was Leonard Slye. In the 1930s, he made a living as a singer; in 1935, his group started work at a Los Angeles radio station. He appeared in his first movie in 1937. He began using the name Roy Rogers in 1938. From 1952 to 1957, he made 101 television shows. The other stars in the show were his wife, Dale Evans, his horse, Trigger, and his dog, Bullet. Rogers died in 1998. Roy Rogers memorabilia, including items from the Roy Rogers restaurants, are collected.

Bobble Head, Duck, Red & White Uniform, Cardinals, Sports Specialties, Los Angeles, 7 In.	90
Holster Set, 2 Guns, Red Plastic Bullet, Black & Silver, Box, c.1955 .... *illus*	456

ROYAL BAYREUTH

Royal Bayreuth is the name of a factory that was founded in Tettau, Bavaria, in 1794. The factory closed in 2019. The marks have changed through the years. A stylized crest, the name Royal Bayreuth, and the word *Bavaria* appear in slightly different forms from 1870 to about 1919. Later dishes may include the words *U.S. Zone* (1945–1949), the year of the issue, or the word *Germany* instead of *Bavaria.* Related pieces may be found listed in the Rose Tapestry, Snow Babies, and Sunbonnet Babies categories.

Royal Bayreuth
1887–1902

Royal Bayreuth
c.1900+

Royal Bayreuth
1968+

Ashtray, Young Woman, Herding Geese, Green Border, Marked, 4 x 4 In.	35
Bowl, Little Boy Blue, Boy On Hay Pile, Verse, Marked, 5 ⅞ In.	380
Charger, Roses, Pink, Yellow, Lavender, Gold Central Ring & Trim, 12 In.	180
Hair Receiver, Roses, Yellow, Peach, Creamy Ground, Gilt, 3 Leaf Feet, c.1902, 4 x 2 In.	89
Humidor, Peasant Musician, Tripod Feet, Gilt Lid & Handles, 6 Panel Base, c.1910, 8 x 6 In.	150
Mustache Cup, 6-Sided, Old Castle Scenes, Gilt Handle, c.1890, 3 ¼ In.	110
Nappy, Roses, Scalloped Edge, Gold Trim, Raised Dots, Handle, Marked, 7 x 5 In.	32
Pitcher, Rooster, Figural, White Feather, Red, Marked, c.1910, 5 In.	195
Plate, Jack & Jill, Verse, Brown & Green Ground, Marked, c.1900, 6 ¼ In.	48
Vase, Swans, Blue & Pink Sky, Oval, Shouldered, Ornate Molding, 7 In.	115
Vase, Tapestry Finish, Green Tones, White & Lavender Flowers, 7 x 4 In. .... *illus*	80

ROYAL BONN

Royal Bonn is the nineteenth- and twentieth-century trade name used by Franz Anton Mehlem, made in Bonn, Germany, from 1836 to 1931. Porcelain and earthenware were made. Royal Bonn also made cases for Ansonia clocks. The factory was purchased by Villeroy & Boch in 1921 and closed in 1931. Many marks were used, most including the name *Bonn,* the initials *FAM,* and a crown.

Clock, Hand Painted Landscape, Cupid, Gilt Scrolls, French Movement, 10¼ x 12½ In.	984
Urn, Pedestal, 1 Door, Lid, Rectangular Base, Ribbon Design, 65 In.	448
Vase, Cylindrical, Hand Painted, Multicolor, Meissonier, H. Wallraff, Germany, Late 1800s, 7¼ In.	59
Vase, Sailor, Smoking Pipe, Painted, Gilt Rims, Leaves, Signed, E. Volk, 9 x 4 In.	168
Vase, White, Blue Lattice, Roses & Tulips, Signed, W. Euskirchen, 8 x 8 In. .... *illus*	200

ROYAL COPENHAGEN

Royal Copenhagen porcelain and pottery have been made in Denmark since 1775. The Christmas plate series started in 1908. The figurines with pale blue and gray glazes have remained popular in this century and are still being made. Many other old and new style porcelains are made today. In 2001 Royal Copenhagen became part of the Royal Scandinavia Group owned by the Danish company Axcel. Axcel sold Royal Copenhagen to the Finnish company Fiskars in December 2012.

Royal Copenhagen
1892

Royal Copenhagen
1894–1900

Royal Copenhagen
1935–present

Bowl, Black & White, Glazed Stoneware, Axel Salto, c.1940, 6 x 11 In. .... *illus*	4063
Bowl, Blue & White, Fluted, Half Lace, Reticulated, Marked, 2½ x 7⅜ In. .... *illus*	224
Bowl, Dome Lid, White Ground, Blue Onion Pattern, Side Handles, 7 x 11 In.	344
Bowl, Glazed Stoneware, Axel Salto, c.1965, 2 x 6 In. ...... *illus*	1875
Charger, Flora Danica, Reticulated Edge, Painted, Flowers, Dated 1971, 13 In.	960
Chop Plate, Flora Danica, Round, Painted, Flowers & Leaves, White Ground, 1950s, 12 In.	570
Dish, Pickle, Flora Danica, Handle, Luzula Arcuata Wahlenb, 6¼ In.	375
Dish, Square, Flora Danica, Painted, Flowers, White Ground, 1950s, 9 In. .... *illus*	1320
Figurine, Bear, Standing, Glazed, Stoneware, Knud Kyhn, Denmark, 1952, 10 x 5 x 4 In.	438
Figurine, Dog, Wire Haired Fox Terrier, White Fur, Brown Spots, 1900s, 4 In.	75
Figurine, Henrik & Else, Standing, Multicolor, Circular Base, 17 x 8½ In. .... *illus*	281
Figurine, Mermaid, Nude, Seated, Rock Shape Base, 1900s, 9 In.	94
Figurine, Nathan The Wise, Standing, Headdress, Robe, 14¼ In.	63
Figurine, Shepherd, Wearing Hat, Glazed, Oval Base, Signed, 8 x 5 In.	63
Platter, Fish, Oval, Elongated, Gilt Rim, Half Lace, Blue, Late 1800s, 23 x 9½ In. .... *illus*	702
Platter, Flora Danica, Botanical, Gilt Notched Rim, c.1965, 16 x 12 In.	2125
Platter, Oval, Flora Danica, Painted, Flowers, White Ground, 1950s, 15 x 12 In.	2040
Tureen, Sauce, Floral Danica, Applied Flowers On Handle, 5 x 6 In.	2706
Vase, Little Mermaid, Black Top, Vibrant Colors, Crab, Seaweeds, Elisabete Gomes, 16 In. .... *illus*	1188
Vase, Sea Eagle, High Glaze, Vilhelm Theodor Fischer, c.1920, 19⅜ x 12¼ In.	2340
Vase, Stoneware, Maroon Glaze, Gerd Bogelund, 1962, 8 x 4 In.	2750
Vase, Stoneware, Matte Glaze, Painted, Jorgen Mogensen, c.1960, 7⅜ x 6 x 6 In. .... *illus*	195

ROYAL CROWN DERBY

Royal Crown Derby Company, Ltd., is a name used on porcelain beginning in 1890. There is a complex family tree that includes the Derby, Crown Derby, and Royal Crown Derby porcelains. *Derby* has been marked on porcelain and bone china made in the city of Derby, England, since about 1750 when Andrew Planche and William Duesbury

Royal Bonn, Vase, White, Blue Lattice, Roses & Tulips, Signed, W. Euskirchen, 8 x 8 In.
$200

Woody Auction

Royal Copenhagen, Bowl, Black & White, Glazed Stoneware, Axel Salto, c.1940, 6 x 11 In.
$4,063

Clars Auction Gallery

Royal Copenhagen, Bowl, Blue & White, Fluted, Half Lace, Reticulated, Marked, 2½ x 7⅜ In.
$224

Nadeau's Auction Gallery

Royal Copenhagen, Bowl, Glazed Stoneware, Axel Salto, c.1965, 2 x 6 In.
$1,875

R

Wright

Royal Copenhagen, Dish, Square, Flora Danica, Painted, Flowers, White Ground, 1950s, 9 In.
$1,320

Garth's Auctioneers & Appraisers

Royal Copenhagen, Figurine, Henrik & Else, Standing, Multicolor, Circular Base, 17 x 8 ½ In.
$281

R

Greenwich Auction

Royal Copenhagen, Platter, Fish, Oval, Elongated, Gilt Rim, Half Lace, Blue, Late 1800s, 23 x 9 ½ In.
$702

Jeffrey S. Evans & Associates

Royal Copenhagen, Vase, Little Mermaid, Black Top, Vibrant Colors, Crab, Seaweeds, Elisabete Gomes, 16 In.
$1,188

Potter & Potter Auctions

Royal Copenhagen, Vase, Stoneware, Matte Glaze, Painted, Jorgen Mogensen, c.1960, 7 ⅜ x 6 x 6 In.
$195

Toomey & Co. Auctioneers

Royal Crown Derby, Cann, Painted, Fruit, On Stone Shelf, George Complin, 1791, 2 ½ In.
$2,563

Bonhams

Royal Crown Derby, Cup, Chocolate, Bucket Shape, Lid, Entwined Handles, Classical Woman, Reading, 1790, 5 ¼ In.
$5,126

Bonhams

Royal Crown Derby, Plate, Rural Landscape, Blue Border, Star, Dots, Zachariah Boreman, c.1790, 9 ¼ In.
$1,367

Bonhams

Royal Crown Derby, Vase, Campana Form, Tulip, Roses, Chrysanthemums, William Quaker Pegg, c.1815, 12 ¾ In.
$5,126

Bonhams

established the first china factory in Derby. In 1775, King George III honored the company by granting them a patent to use the royal crown in their backstamp and the company became known as *Crown Derby*. Pieces are marked with a crown and the letter *D* or the word *Derby*. When the original Derby factory closed in 1848, some of its former workers opened a smaller factory on King Street, Derby, and used Crown Derby's original molds and patterns. About 1876 the present company was formed when another factory opened under the name Derby Crown Porcelain Co. (1876–1890). Queen Victoria granted Derby Crown Porcelain a royal warrant in 1890 and the name became Royal Crown Derby Porcelain Co. Finally, in 1935 Royal Crown Derby bought the King Street factory, which brought Derby china under one company again. The Royal Crown Derby mark includes the name and a crown. The words *Made in England* were used after 1921. The company became part of Allied English Potteries Group in 1964 and then merged into Royal Doulton Tableware. Royal Crown Derby Co. Ltd. was acquired by Steelite International in 2013. Kevin Oakes bought Royal Crown Derby in 2016. The company is still in business.

Royal Crown Derby
1877–1890

Royal Crown Derby
1890–1940

Royal Crown Derby
c.1976–2014

Bowl, Flowers, Gilt, Holes Rim, Footed, Shaped Base, 1800s, 4 x 4 In., Pair	406
Cann, Painted, Fruit, On Stone Shelf, George Complin, 1791, 2 1/2 In. *illus*	2563
Cup, Chocolate, Bucket Shape, Lid, Entwined Handles, Classical Woman, Reading, 1790, 5 1/4 In. *illus*	5126
Jug, Milk, Bucket Shape, Angular Handle, Naval Warfare, Stormy Seas, Geo. Robertson, 1800s, 4 In.	1709
Plate, Kings Pattern, Flowers, Leaves, Bloor, 1800s, 1 x 10 In., 17 Piece	625
Plate, Kings Pattern, Imari, Blue Rim, Gilt Trim, Painted Crown Mark, 8 3/4 In., 5 Piece	87
Plate, Rural Landscape, Blue Border, Star, Dots, Zachariah Boreman, c.1790, 9 1/4 In. *illus*	1367
Plate, Snowballing, Winter Season, Tree, Cloudy Sky, Rural, William Corden, 1825, 9 1/2 In.	2734
Platter Set, Imari, Scalloped Rim, Gilt Trim, Graduated Sizes, c.1916, 6 Piece	500
Relish, Gilt & Iron Red, Flowers, Tree, Wavy Rim, White Ground, c.1820, 9 In., Pair	281
Tea Set, Blue & Orange Flowers, Gilt, Teapot, Coffeepot, Sugar & Creamer, Cup & Saucer, 28 Piece	640
Vase, Campana Form, Tulip, Roses, Chrysanthemums, William Quaker Pegg, c.1815, 12 3/4 In. *illus*	5126

ROYAL DOULTON

Royal Doulton is the name used on Doulton and Company pottery made from 1902 to the present. Doulton and Company of England was founded in 1853. Pieces made before 1902 are listed in this book under Doulton. Royal Doulton collectors pay high prices for the out-of-production figurines, character jugs, vases, and series wares. Some vases and animal figurines were made with a special red glaze called flambe. Sung and Chang glazed pieces are rare. The multicolored glaze is very thick and looks as if it were dropped on the clay. Bunnykins figurines were first made by Royal Doulton in 1939. In 2005 Royal Doulton was acquired by the Waterford Wedgwood Group. It was bought by KPS Capital Partners of New York in 2009 and became part of WWRD Holdings. WWRD was bought by Fiskars Group in 2015. Beatrix Potter bunny figurines were made by Beswick and are listed in that category.

Royal Doulton
1902–1922, 1927–1932

Royal Doulton
1922–1956

Royal Doulton
c.2000–present

Royal Doulton, Bowl, Lid, Dogwood Blossoms, Flambe Design, Harry Nixon, 1900s, 3 3/4 x 5 In.
$938

Lion and Unicorn

Royal Doulton Marks
Royal Doulton collectors can easily identify character jugs and figurines made before 1984. That year the words *hand made* and *hand decorated* were added above the lion and crown mark, in the shape of an arch.

Royal Doulton, Character Jug, Capt. Scott, Cream Balaclava, Goggles, David B. Biggs, D 7116, 1998, 7 In.
$128

Lion and Unicorn

Royal Doulton, Character Jug, Clown, D 6384, Green Cap, Yellow Bowtie, Stanley J. Taylor, 1989, 6 1/2 In.
$100

Lion and Unicorn

Royal Doulton, Character Jug, George Washington, D 6660, Stanley Taylor, 1982, 7 In.
$469

Lion and Unicorn

Royal Doulton, Charger, Giraffes, D 6366, Pastel, Sepia, African Series Ware, Backstamp, 1900s, 13 ¼ In.
$75

Lion and Unicorn

Royal Doulton, Figurine, Aria, Venetian Masquerade Ball, HN 4504, Shane Ridge, 2005, 12 In.
$2,875

Lion and Unicorn

Ashtray, Character Bird, HN 284, Green Head, Orange Beak, Art Deco, 1922, 2 ¼ x 3 In.	688
Bottle, Night Watchman, Dewar's Scotch, Kingsware, Brown, 10 ¾ In.	375
Bowl, Lid, Dogwood Blossoms, Flambe Design, Harry Nixon, 1900s, 3 ¾ x 5 In. ....*illus*	938
Candlestick, Battle Of Hastings, Multicolor, Beige Pillar Background, Square Base, 1900s, 6 In.	63

 Royal Doulton character jugs depict the head and shoulders of the subject. They are made in four sizes: large, 5 ¼ to 7 inches; small, 3 ¼ to 4 inches; miniature, 2 ¼ to 2 ½ inches; and tiny, 1 ¼ inches. Toby jugs portray a seated, full figure.

Character Jug, Bacchus, Old Man, Grapes On Head, Max Henk, D 6499, 1959, 7 In.	50
Character Jug, Beefeater, Wearing Hat, Black Bird, Timothy Potts, D 7299, 2010, 7 In.	63
Character Jug, Beethoven, Feather & Notcholder, Stanley J. Taylor, D 7021, 1996, 7 In.	50
Character Jug, Capt. Scott, Cream Balaclava, Goggles, David B. Biggs, D 7116, 1998, 7 In. .*illus*	128
Character Jug, Clown, D 6384, Green Cap, Yellow Bowtie, Stanley J. Taylor, 1989, 6 ½ In...*illus*	100
Character Jug, Charlie Chaplin, Black Hat, Multicolor Tie, William K. Harper, D 6949, 1993, 7 In.	75
Character Jug, George Washington, D 6660, Stanley Taylor, 1982, 7 In. ....*illus*	469
Character Jug, Mephistopheles, D 5757, Red, Brown, Charles Noke, 1937, 7 x 6 In.	375
Character Jug, Santa Claus, D 6794, Red Cap, White Fur Trim, Wreath Handle, 1980s, 7 In.	190
Character Jug, Wizard, D 6862, Black Coat, Red Collar, Stanley J. Taylor, 1990, 6 ¾ In.	68
Charger, Giraffes, D 6366, Pastel, Sepia, African Series Ware, Backstamp, 1900s, 13 ¼ In..*illus*	75
Figurine, Amanda, Young Girl In White Dress, HN 2996, Robert Tabbenor, 1986, 5 In.	63
Figurine, Ann, Multicolor Dress, Swaying, Douglas V. Tootle, HN 3259, 1990, 8 In.	113
Figurine, Aria, Venetian Masquerade Ball, HN 4504, Shane Ridge, 2005, 12 In............*illus*	2875
Figurine, Broken Lance, Knight On Horseback, HN 2041, 1949-75, 8 ¾ x 7 ¾ x 4 ¼ In.	123
Figurine, Bunnykins, Daisie Spring Time, Sitting, Blue Dress, 1900s, 3 ¼ In.	25
Figurine, Bunnykins, Grandpa's Story, Sitting, Cross-Legged, Reading Book, DB14, 1900s, 4 In.	50
Figurine, Bunnykins, Halloween, Mouse In Jack-O'-Lantern, DB 132, 1993-97, 3 ¼ In.	60
Figurine, Bunnykins, Making Cupcakes, Pink Dress, Neil Faulkner, DB 500, 2016, 4 In.	1375
Figurine, Dauphin, Mermaid, Holding Shell, Alan Maslankowski, HN 4694, 2005, 8 In.	2875
Figurine, Father Christmas, Santa, Green Coat, Gilt Fur, Scroll, HN 3399, 9 In.	2875
Figurine, Jackpoint, Multicolor Jester, Gilt Bells, HN 3920, Charles Noke, 1996, 17 In.	625
Figurine, King Wenceslas, Multicolor, Glazed Finish, HN 2118, 1953-76, 1900s, 9 In.	63
Figurine, Mardi Gras, Carmen, Masked Woman, Shane Ridge, HN 4964, 2006, 12 In..*illus*	3125
Figurine, Moorish Minstrel, Stylized Stacked Base, HN 797, Charles Noke, 1926, 13 ½ In. ...	4375
Figurine, Poke Bonnet, Yellow Dress, Green Shawl, HN 0612, Charles Noke, 1924, 9 In.	1500
Figurine, Snake Charmer, Glossy Finish, HN 1317, 1929, 5 ¼ In. ....*illus*	4750
Figurine, Spook, Yellow Orange Robe, Blue Cap, HN 625, Marked, 1900s, 7 In............*illus*	6563
Figurine, Toucan, Santa Claus Hat, Guinness, Is Good For Yule, Martyn Alcock, 2002, 5 ¾ In. ...	125
Figurine, Williamsburg, Soldiers Of The Revolution, 3rd New Jersey Reg., HN 2752, c.1975, 10 In.	179
Figurine, Wandering Minstrel, HN 1224, Leslie Harradine, 1927, 7 ¼ In.	750
Flask, Kingsware, Dewars Whisky, Bonnie Prince Charlie, c.1900, 7 x 4 ¾ x 3 ¾ In.	62
Jardiniere, Oyama Pattern, Dragon Design, Ornate Bands, Marked, c.1910, 12 In.......*illus*	281
Jug, Dickens Dream, Handle, Faces, Charles Noke, 1936, 10 ¾ In. ....*illus*	1500
Jug, Treasure Island, 2 Pirates, Treasure Chest, Charles Noke, Harry Fenton, 1934, 7 In. .....*illus*	1750
Jug, Watchman, Lantern, Green, White, Gilt Rim, D 1494, 1900s, 7 In.	38
Loving Cup, George Washington, Baluster Form, Green Handles, Signed, Noke, 1932, 8 In.	6125
Medallion, Wall, Face, Neoclassical, Sculptured, Doulton Lambeth, 1900s, 16 In.........*illus*	6000
Plaque, Cavaliers In Relief, Dark Brown, 1900s, 12 In.	813
Plaque, Dealer's, Marks, Multicolor, Oval, 1900s, 4 x 3 In.	100
Plate, Tiff, Cat Fight, Woman's Faces, Art Nouveau Style, Henry Souter, 1900s, 9 ¼ In..*illus*	531
Platter, Fox Hunting, Trees, Mountains, Green Rim, Multicolor, 14 In.	136
Punch Bowl, City Street, Queen, Litter, Leafy Borders, 1900s, 9 ⅛ In.	246
Punch Bowl, Hunting Scene, Cream Ground, Socle Base, 7 x 12 In.	339
Shaker, Silver Lid, Men, Riding Horse, Multicolor Glaze, 9 In.	677
Tobacco Jar, Lid, Kingsware Novelty, Smoking Pipe Shape, Charles Noke, 1900s, 12 ¼ In. ..*illus*	1500
Toby Jug, King George V, Royal Navy Fleet Admiral Uniform, Globe, 1915-19, 12 In.	1250
Urn, Kingsware, Dark Brown Glaze, Witch, Scalloped Spout, c.1930s, 16 ¼ In.	813
Vase, Blue Ground, White Design, Gold Shoulder, Square Rim, 11 ⅛ In., Pair	94
Vase, Green Ground, Brown Trim, Green Leaves, Marked, 8 ¾ x 4 ¾ In.	60

R

Royal Doulton, Figurine, Mardi Gras, Carmen, Masked Woman, Shane Ridge, HN 4964, 2006, 12 In.
$3,125

Lion and Unicorn

Royal Doulton, Figurine, Snake Charmer, Glossy Finish, HN 1317, 1929, 5 ¼ In.
$4,750

Lion and Unicorn

Royal Doulton, Figurine, Spook, Yellow Orange Robe, Blue Cap, HN 625, Marked, 1900s, 7 In.
$6,563

Lion and Unicorn

Royal Doulton, Jardiniere, Oyama Pattern, Dragon Design, Ornate Bands, Marked, c.1910, 12 In.
$281

Charlton Hall Auctions

Royal Doulton, Jug, Dickens Dream, Handle, Faces, Charles Noke, 1936, 10 ¾ In.
$1,500

Lion and Unicorn

Royal Doulton, Jug, Treasure Island, 2 Pirates, Treasure Chest, Charles Noke, Harry Fenton, 1934, 7 In.
$1,750

Lion and Unicorn

Royal Doulton, Medallion, Wall, Face, Neoclassical, Sculptured, Doulton Lambeth, 1900s, 16 In.
$6,000

Lion and Unicorn

Royal Doulton, Plate, Tiff, Cat Fight, Woman's Faces, Art Nouveau Style, Henry Souter, 1900s, 9 ¼ In.
$531

Lion and Unicorn

Royal Doulton, Tobacco Jar, Lid, Kingsware Novelty, Smoking Pipe Shape, Charles Noke, 1900s, 12 ¼ In.
$1,500

Lion and Unicorn

R

Royal Doulton, Vase, Titianian Ware, Mottled Blue Ground, Bird Of Paradise In Flight, c.1925, 7 In.
$344

Lion and Unicorn

Royal Doulton, Wall Mask, Jester, Crazy Hat, Winking, Smiling, HN 1611, 1900s, 3 In.
$438

Lion and Unicorn

Royal Dux, Compote, Centerpiece, Figural, Woman, 2 Cherubs, 19 x 15 In.
$225

Woody Auction

Vase, Painted, Old Ruins, Flared Rim, Yellow, Gold Highlights, 2 Handles, Footed, 9 x 4 In., Pair..	350
Vase, Titianian Ware, Mottled Blue Ground, Bird Of Paradise In Flight, c.1925, 7 In...... *illus*	344
Wall Mask, Jester, Crazy Hat, Winking, Smiling, HN 1611, 1900s, 3 In........................*illus*	438
Water Filter, Stoneware, Relief, Central Band Of Flowers, 1800s, 14 In.................................	531

ROYAL DUX

Royal Dux is the more common name for the Duxer Porzellanmanufaktur, which was founded by E. Eichler in Dux, Bohemia (now Duchcov, Czech Republic), in 1860. By the turn of the twentieth century, the firm specialized in porcelain statuary and busts of Art Nouveau–style maidens, large porcelain figures, and ornate vases with three-dimensional figures climbing on the sides. The firm is still in business. It is now part of Czesky Porcelan (Czech Porcelain).

Bowl, Figural, Maiden, Art Nouveau, c.1900, 8 x 16 x 7¾ In...	62
Compote, Centerpiece, Figural, Woman, 2 Cherubs, 19 x 15 In....................................*illus*	225
Figurine, Cat, Modernist, Stretching, Black, White, 12½ In...*illus*	250
Figurine, Cockatoo, Standing, White, Pink, Brown Feet, Czechoslovakia, 1900s, 6¾ In.	63
Figurine, Woman, Topless, Water Carrier, Jug, Bohemia, Czechoslovakia, 7½ In.................	213
Group, Afternoon Tea, Man, Woman, Sitting, Drinking Tea, 1800s, 13 In....................*illus*	344
Group, Orientalist, 2 Men, Camel, Shaped Base, Czechoslovakia, 1900s, 23 x 18 x 9 In........	250
Vase, Maiden Musicians, Tambourine, Mandolin, Bohemia, 12½ x 4 x 4½ In., Pair...........	188

ROYAL FLEMISH

Royal Flemish glass was made during the late 1880s in New Bedford, Massachusetts, by the Mt. Washington Glass Works. It is a colored satin glass decorated with dark colors and raised gold designs. The glass was patented in 1894. It was supposed to resemble stained glass windows.

Condiment Set, Cruet, Salt & Pepper, Textured, Flowers, Pairpoint Silver Plate Frame, 9½ x 10 In. ..	2975
Vase, Convex Stick Neck, Red, Squat Body, Cherry Blossoms, Medallions, 11 x 7 In. ..... *illus*	1126
Vase, Oval, Red & Orange Panels, Rampant Griffin, Dragon Head On Reverse, 7½ In.	2000

ROYAL HAEGER, *see Haeger category.*

ROYAL HICKMAN

Royal Hickman designed pottery, glass, silver, aluminum, furniture, lamps, and other items. From 1938 to 1944 and again from the 1950s to 1969, he worked for Haeger Potteries. Mr. Hickman operated his own pottery in Tampa, Florida, during the 1940s. He moved to California and worked for Vernon Potteries. During the last years of his life he lived in Guadalajara, Mexico, and continued designing for Royal Haeger. He died in 1969. Pieces made in his pottery listed here are marked *Royal Hickman* or *Hickman*.

Compote, Swan Shape, Brown Ground, Iridescent, Sea Foam Green, c.1950, 5 x 19 x 8 In. ...	245
Dish, Lobster Shape, 2 Bowls, Aluminum, Bruce Fox, 1960s, 3¼ x 14 x 9 In.........................	78
Pitcher, Yellow, Left Molded Handle, Wide Spout, Late 1940s, 3½ x 3 In...............................	45
Vase, Oil Jar Shape, Long Neck, Tan, Sea Foam Green, Petty Crystal Glaze, c.1930, 8 In.	125

ROYAL NYMPHENBURG

Royal Nymphenburg is the modern name for the Nymphenburg porcelain factory, which was established at Neudeck ob der Au, Germany, in 1753 and moved to Nymphenburg in 1761. The company is still in existence. Marks include a checkered shield topped by a crown, a crowned *CT* with the year, and a contemporary shield mark on reproductions of eighteenth-century porcelain.

Figurine, Cherub, Seated, Nude, Holding Flower, 1900s, 5⅝ In., Pair .... *illus*   188
Figurine, Niki, Dog, Fox Terrier, Seated, No. 493, Willy Zugel, 12½ x 9 x 5 In......................   1440
Vase, Cylindrical, Flared Mouth, Medallions, Gray Black, Gold Rim, Bavarian Royal Service, 7¾ In.   812

ROYAL RUDOLSTADT, *see Rudolstadt category.*

ROYAL VIENNA, *see Beehive category.*

ROYAL WORCESTER

Royal Worcester is a name used by collectors. Worcester porcelains were made in Worcester, England, from about 1751. The firm went through many periods and name changes. It became the Worcester Royal Porcelain Company, Ltd., in 1862. Today collectors call the porcelains made after 1862 "Royal Worcester." In 1976, the firm merged with W.T. Copeland to become Royal Worcester Spode. The company was bought by the Portmeirion Group in 2009. Some early products of the factory are listed under Worcester. Related pieces may be listed under Copeland, Copeland Spode, and Spode.

Royal Worcester
1862–1875

Royal Worcester
1891

Royal Worcester
c.1959+

Ewer, Snowflakes Design, Pink Ground, Gilt, Painted, c.1887, 10 x 6 x 6 In............................   125
Figurine, Equestrian, White Horse, 2 Hound Dogs, Green Base, Doris Linder, 9½ In... *illus*   390
Figurine, King Henry VIII, Red, Gold, Square Base, After Holbein, 1900s, 9½ In.   375
Figurine, Lara, Christmas Morning, Les Petites, Red Jacket, Muff, Limited Edition, 7 In.*illus*   188
Figurine, Women, Curly Hair, Half Naked, Barefoot, Late 1800s, 14 x 4 x 4 In., Pair   438
Lamp, Kerosene, 3 Spherical Vases, Enameled, Umbrella Shape Shade, 12¾ In.......... *illus*   956
Plaque, Rural Landscape, Woman, Child Walking, Boat, Harry Davis, c.1969, 6 x 4 In.   3417
Vase, Figural, Nautilus Shell, Shaped Base, 9 x 6½ In... *illus*   50
Vase, Highland Cattle, 2 Handles, Porcelain, Signed, John Stinton, Late 1800s, 14¾ In.   281
Vase, Oval, Cobalt Blue Ground, Square Base, Frederick H. Chivers, Early 1900s, 10½ In. ...*illus*   702
Vase, Tusk, Ivory Stain, Marching Frogs, Leafy Branches, 886, 7⅞ In...................................   313

ROYCROFT

Roycroft products were made by the Roycrofter community of East Aurora, New York, from 1895 until 1938. The community was founded by Elbert Hubbard, famous philosopher, writer, and artist. The workshops owned by the community made furniture, metalware, leatherwork, embroidery, and jewelry. A print-shop produced many signs, books, and the magazines that promoted the sayings of Elbert Hubbard. Furniture by the Roycroft community is listed in the Furniture category.

Bookends, Owl, Copper, Hammered, Rectangular Base, c.1920s, 3⅞ x 6⅜ In.   492
Bowl, Brass, Hammered, Molded Rim, Tripod Feet, 4⅛ x 9¼ In................................ *illus*   531
Bowl, Copper, Hammered, Curled Rim, c.1920s, 2¼ x 6½ In... *illus*   277
Calendar, Desk, Copper, Hammered, Brown Patina, c.1920s, 4¾ x 3¾ x 2 In. .... *illus*   308
Card Tray, Copper, Hammered, 3 Dots, Brown Patina, Signed, R, c.1920, 6¾ In.   400
Goodie Box, Poplar, Mahogany Finish, Copper, Carved Orb & Cross, 9½ x 26 x 12 In.. *illus*   1250
Humidor, Copper, Hammered, Stamped Orb & Cross, Tobacco Bowl, c.1920, 3⅝ x 5 In.*illus*   390
Lamp, Copper, Hammered, Helmet, Ball Finial, Stepped Base, c.1920, 13½ x 6 In...............   3198
Lamp, Copper, Hammered, Mica, Helmet, Ball Finial, Square Base, 13½ x 7¼ In....... *illus*   3690
Letter Rack, Copper, Hammered, Trifoil, Brown Patina, Signed R, c.1920s, 4¼ x 4 x 2¼ In. ..... *illus*   461
Napkin Ring, Copper, Hammered, Clip Shape, Signed, c.1920, 2¾ In.   125
Tray, Copper, Hammered, Brass, Overlay, Green Patina, Etruscan, c.1920s, 1¾ x 8 In. *illus*   1353
Vase, Copper, American Beauty, Stamped Orb & Cross, 21⅜ x 7¾ In. .... *illus*   2990

Royal Dux, Figurine, Cat, Modernist, Stretching, Black, White, 12½ In.
$250

Eldred's

Royal Dux, Group, Afternoon Tea, Man, Woman, Sitting, Drinking Tea, 1800s, 13 In.
$344

Lion and Unicorn

Royal Flemish, Vase, Convex Stick Neck, Red, Squat Body, Cherry Blossoms, Medallions, 11 x 7 In.
$1,126

Matthew Bullock Auctioneers

Royal Nymphenburg, Figurine, Cherub, Seated, Nude, Holding Flower, 1900s, 5⅝ In., Pair
$188

Hindman

Royal Worcester, Figurine, Equestrian, White Horse, 2 Hound Dogs, Green Base, Doris Linder, 9 ½ In.
$390

Alderfer Auction Company

Royal Worcester, Figurine, Lara, Christmas Morning, Les Petites, Red Jacket, Muff, Limited Edition, 7 In.
$188

Lion and Unicorn

Royal Worcester, Lamp, Kerosene, 3 Spherical Vases, Enameled, Umbrella Shape Shade, 12 ¾ In.
$956

Jeffrey S. Evans & Associates

Royal Worcester, Vase, Figural, Nautilus Shell, Shaped Base, 9 x 6 ½ In.
$50

Woody Auction

Royal Worcester, Vase, Oval, Cobalt Blue Ground, Square Base, Frederick H. Chivers, Early 1900s, 10 ½ In.
$702

Jeffrey S. Evans & Associates

Roycroft, Bowl, Brass, Hammered, Molded Rim, Tripod Feet, 4 ⅛ x 9 ¼ In.
$531

New Haven Auctions

Roycroft, Bowl, Copper, Hammered, Curled Rim, c.1920s, 2 ¼ x 6 ½ In.
$277

California Historical Design

Roycroft, Calendar, Desk, Copper, Hammered, Brown Patina, c.1920s, 4 ¾ x 3 ¾ x 2 In.
$308

California Historical Design

Roycroft, Goodie Box, Poplar, Mahogany Finish, Copper, Carved Orb & Cross, 9 ½ x 26 x 12 In.
$1,250

Toomey & Co. Auctioneers

Roycroft, Humidor, Copper, Hammered, Stamped Orb & Cross, Tobacco Bowl, c.1920, 3 ⅝ x 5 In.
$390

Toomey & Co. Auctioneers

Vase, Copper, Hammered, Flared Rim, c.1920s, 4½ x 2½ In.		369
Vase, Copper, Hammered, Revival, Elongated Shape, Leaves, 12 x 4½ In.		480
Vase, Copper, Hammered, Signed Walter Jennings, c.1915, 4¼ x 2¾ In.		1107

ROZANE, *see Roseville category.*

ROZENBURG

Rozenburg worked at The Hague, Holland, from 1890 to 1914. The most important pieces were earthenware made in the early twentieth century with pale-colored Art Nouveau designs.

Charger, Wall, Earthenware, Butterfly, Flowers, Den Haag, 15 In.	*illus*	625
Plate, Wall, Yellow Ground, Abstract Bird & Flowers, Art Nouveau, The Hague, 1901, 10¾ In.	*illus*	1203
Vase, Twin Handles, Chrysanthemums, Samuel Schellink, 1907, 8 x 4 x 3 In.	*illus*	3900

RRP

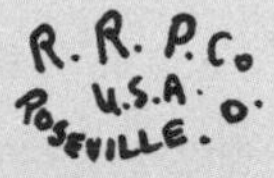

RRP, or RRP Roseville, is the mark used by the firm of Robinson-Ransbottom. It is not a mark of the more famous Roseville Pottery. The Ransbottom brothers started a pottery in 1900 in Ironspot, Ohio. In 1920, they merged with the Robinson Clay Product Company of Akron, Ohio, to become Robinson-Ransbottom. The factory closed in 2005.

Bowl, Yellow, Flared Rim, Banded, 10 x 5 In.		46
Cookie Jar, Apples, Leaves, Red, Green, Yellow, Handles, Pedestal Foot, 8½ x 9 In.		48
Cookie Jar, Chef, Hat, Blue Scarf, Holding Spoon & Plate, 1957, 11 In.		150
Crock, Spongeware, Blue & Tan, Tab Handles, Lid, 8 In.		38
Jardiniere, Green & Brown, Flower, Leaf, Pedestal, 7⅝ x 13⅞ In.		281
Jardiniere, Sun & Stars, Green, Brown, White Accents, 6 x 5 In.		29
Vase, Amphora Shape, Buff Clay, Green Mottled Glaze, 1950s, 25 In.	*illus*	60

RS GERMANY

RS Germany is part of the wording in marks used by the Tillowitz, Germany, factory of Reinhold Schlegelmilch from 1914 until about 1945. The porcelain was sold decorated and undecorated. The Schlegelmilch families made porcelains marked in many ways. See also ES Germany, RS Poland, RS Prussia, RS Silesia, RS Suhl, and RS Tillowitz.

Bowl, Centerpiece, White Flowers, 9 x 4 In.		69
Creamer, Flowers, Leaves, Gold Handle, 5½ x 2¼ In.		35
Plate, Scalloped Rim, Pink Roses, Gold Trim, 6¼ In.		18
Platter, Morning Glories, White, Leaves, Open Handles, 10 In.		125
Tray, Handles, Pheasants, Meadow, House, 9 x 4 In.		135

RS POLAND

RS Poland (German) is a mark used by the Reinhold Schlegelmilch factory at Tillowitz from about 1946 to 1956. After 1956, the factory made porcelain marked *PT Poland*. This is one of many of the RS marks used. See also ES Germany, RS Germany, RS Prussia, RS Silesia, RS Suhl, and RS Tillowitz.

RS Poland
c.1945–1956

PT Tulowice
After 1945–1956

Vase, Cylindrical, Round Rim, Black Swan Scene, Dark To Light Brown Ground, 7 x 3 In.	*illus*	450

Roycroft, Lamp, Copper, Hammered, Mica, Helmet, Ball Finial, Square Base, 13½ x 7¼ In.
$3,690

California Historical Design

Roycroft, Letter Rack, Copper, Hammered, Trifoil, Brown Patina, Signed R, c.1920s, 4¼ x 4 x 2¼ In.
$461

California Historical Design

R

Roycroft, Tray, Copper, Hammered, Brass, Overlay, Green Patina, Etruscan, c.1920s, 1¾ x 8 In.
$1,353

California Historical Design

Roycroft, Vase, Copper, American Beauty, Stamped Orb & Cross, 21 3/8 x 7 3/4 In.
$2,990

Toomey & Co. Auctioneers

Rozenburg, Charger, Wall, Earthenware, Butterfly, Flowers, Den Haag, 15 In.
$625

Susanin's Auctioneers & Appraisers

Rozenburg, Plate, Wall, Yellow Ground, Abstract Bird & Flowers, Art Nouveau, The Hague, 1901, 10 3/4 In.
$1,203

Bonhams

Rozenburg, Vase, Twin Handles, Chrysanthemums, Samuel Schellink, 1907, 8 x 4 x 3 In.
$3,900

Toomey & Co. Auctioneers

RRP, Vase, Amphora Shape, Buff Clay, Green Mottled Glaze, 1950s, 25 In.
$60

Garth's Auctioneers & Appraisers

RS Poland, Vase, Cylindrical, Round Rim, Black Swan Scene, Dark To Light Brown Ground, 7 x 3 In.
$450

Woody Auction

RS Prussia, Biscuit Jar, Lid, Icicle Mold, Water Lilies, Cream & Green Ground, Gilt Trim, 7 1/2 In.
$108

Woody Auction

TIP
When cleaning or repairing antiques, remember less is more.

RS Prussia, Bowl, Melon Eater, Ribbon & Jewel Mold, Green Ground, Marked, 3 x 5 In.
$200

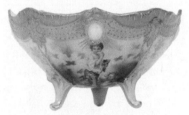

Woody Auction

RS Prussia, Cup & Saucer, Lily Of The Valley, Leaf Mold, Gilt Trim, Satin Finish, 3 1/2 x 4 1/2 In.
$60

Woody Auction

R

RS PRUSSIA

RS Prussia appears in several marks used on porcelain before 1917. Reinhold Schlegelmilch started his porcelain works in Suhl, Germany, in 1869. See also ES Germany, RS Germany, RS Poland, RS Silesia, RS Suhl, and RS Tillowitz.

RS Prussia	RS Prussia
Late 1880s–1917	c.1895–1917

Biscuit Jar, Lid, Icicle Mold, Water Lilies, Cream & Green Ground, Gilt Trim, 7½ In.... *illus*	108
Bowl, Melon Eater, Ribbon & Jewel Mold, Green Ground, Marked, 3 x 5 In.................... *illus*	200
Bowl, Portrait, Madame Le Brun, Green & Yellow Ground, Iridescent Border, 10½ In.	225
Bowl, Red & White Roses, c.1900, 10¾ x 3 In.	110
Bowl, Red Roses, Stepped Dome, Vertical Lines, c.1900, 10½ In..............................	175
Bowl, Roses, Hydrangeas, Scalloped Rim, 9¼ In.	38
Bowl, White Poppies, Cream Ground, Pink & Blue Shaded Rim, Purple Inner Band, Satin, 10 In.	30
Creamer, Cobalt Blue & Black, Gold Stencil, Iris Mold, 2½ In.	100
Cup & Saucer, Lily Of The Valley, Leaf Mold, Gilt Trim, Satin Finish, 3½ x 4½ In...... *illus*	60
Cup, Coffee, Green, White, Purple, Gilt, Sunflower Mold, Satin Finish, 2¾ x 4½ In..... *illus*	60
Hair Receiver, Cream To Blue, Pink Roses, Gilt Trim, 4 Lobes, Scalloped Base, 2½ x 3¾ In. ...	24
Hatpin Holder, 3 Handles, Purple Ground, White Flowers, Green Base, Gilt, 4 x 3¾ In.*illus*	48
Pitcher, Pink & Yellow Roses, Shaded Green & Brown Ground, Gold Leaf Handle, 13½ In.....*illus*	188
Plate, Summer, Woman With Pink Poppies, Ruffled Rim, Gilt, Red & Green Mark, 8¾ In.....*illus*	370
Shaving Mug, Fleur-De-Lis Mold, Blue & White Tones, Poppies, 3½ In...................... *illus*	50
Shaving Mug, Green, White, Pink, Round Inset Mirror, Floral Mold, 3 x 4 In.............. *illus*	36
Sugar & Creamer, Lid, Winter Scene, Blond Woman, Gilt Flowers, Red & Green Mark, 5 In...... *illus*	180
Tankard, Fall Season Portrait, Cream & Peach Satin, Flowers, Marked, 14 In.	1000
Toothpick Holder, Green & White Tones, Flowers Decor, 2¼ In.........................	250

RS SILESIA

RS Silesia appears on porcelain made at the Reinhold Schlegelmilch factory in Tillowitz, Germany, from the 1920s to the 1940s. The Schlegelmilch families made porcelains marked in many ways. See also ES Germany, RS Germany, RS Poland, RS Prussia, RS Suhl, and RS Tillowitz.

Candy Dish, Rose Blossoms, Leaves, Flared, Oval, Reticulated Handles, 10 x 6 In.	84
Sugar & Creamer, Pink Flowers, Gold Handles	195
Tray, Pink Flowers, Leaves, Handles, 16 x 5 In...	225

RS SUHL

RS Suhl is a mark used by the Reinhold Schlegelmilch factory in Suhl, Germany, between 1900 and 1917. The Schlegelmilch families made porcelains in many places. See also ES Germany, RS Germany, RS Poland, RS Prussia, RS Silesia, and RS Tillowitz.

Sugar & Creamer, Cream To Pale Green, Flowers, Ribbed.......................................	100
Vase, Bowling Pin Shape, Woman, Palm Leaves, Red & Green Neck, 7 In.............................	174
Vase, Melon Eaters, Bowling Pin Shape, Shaded Green, Red Border, Gilt, 6¼ In. .... *illus*	120
Vase, Napoleon Bonaparte, Portrait, c.1900, 7¼ In...	165
Vase, Portrait, Woman With Dandelion, Black & White, Shaded Blue Reverse, Gilt Trim, 7 In. *illus*	1140

RS TILLOWITZ

RS Tillowitz was marked on porcelain by the Reinhold Schlegelmilch factory at Tillowitz from the 1920s to the 1940s. Table services and ornamental pieces were made. See also

---

RS Prussia, Cup, Coffee, Green, White, Purple, Gilt, Sunflower Mold, Satin Finish, 2¾ x 4½ In.
$60

Woody Auction

RS Prussia, Hatpin Holder, 3 Handles, Purple Ground, White Flowers, Green Base, Gilt, 4 x 3¾ In.
$48

Matthews Auctions, LLC

RS Prussia, Pitcher, Pink & Yellow Roses, Shaded Green & Brown Ground, Gold Leaf Handle, 13½ In.
$188

California Historical Design

This is an edited listing of current prices. Visit **Kovels.com** to check thousands of prices from previous years and sign up for free information on trends, tips, reproductions, marks, and more.

R

RS Prussia, Plate, Summer, Woman With Pink Poppies, Ruffled Rim, Gilt, Red & Green Mark, 8¾ In.
$370

Jeffrey S. Evans & Associates

RS Prussia, Shaving Mug, Fleur-De-Lis Mold, Blue & White Tones, Poppies, 3½ In.
$50

Woody Auction

RS Prussia, Shaving Mug, Green, White, Pink, Round Inset Mirror, Floral Mold, 3 x 4 In.
$36

Woody Auction

RS Prussia, Sugar & Creamer, Lid, Winter Scene, Blond Woman, Gilt Flowers, Red & Green Mark, 5 In.
$180

Cottone Auctions

ES Germany, RS Germany, RS Poland, RS Prussia, RS Silesia, and RS Suhl.

RS Tillowitz
1920s–1940s

RS Tillowitz
1932–1983

Pitcher, Parrots & Grapes, 5 In.	295
Plate, 24K Gold, Flowers, Center Courting Scene, Green Inner Border, Pedestal Base, 8¾ In. .... *illus*	108
Plate, Central Flowers, Multicolor, Gold Handles, 6 In.	125
Serving Plate, Tiered, Flowers, Red, Blue, Purple, 9½ In.	195
Syrup, Underplate, Berry & Vine, 4 In.	245

 RUBINA

Rubina is a glassware that shades from red to clear. It was first made by George Duncan and Sons of Pittsburgh, Pennsylvania, in about 1885. This coloring was used on many types of glassware.

Barber's Bottle, Red To Clear, Metal Top, 8 In.	62
Biscuit Jar, Silver Plate Lid & Bail, Enameled Daisy, 8 x 6 In. .... *illus*	450
Celery Vase, Clear To Cranberry, Flowers, Ruffled Rim, Rockford Silver Plate Frame, 8 x 5¼ In. .	96
Dish, Sweetmeat, Cranberry To Clear, Applied Vaseline Rigaree, Silver Plate Frame, 6½ x 6 In. .... *illus*	150
Pitcher, Water, Coin Spot, Pink To Clear, Flowers, Pleated Rim, Clear Ribbed Handle, 10 x 7 In. .	60
Pitcher, Water, Pink To Clear, Ruffled Rim, Molded Threaded Body, Ribbed Handle, 9 x 6¾ In. . *illus*	60
Rose Bowl, Pink To Clear, Optic Rib Swirl, Threaded Interior, 5½ x 6 In.	60
Salt & Pepper, Cranberry To Clear, Enamel Butterflies, Wilcox Silver Holder, Victorian, 5 x 3½ In.	108

 RUBINA VERDE

Rubina Verde is a Victorian glassware that was shaded from red to green. It was first made by Hobbs, Brockunier and Company of Wheeling, West Virginia, about 1890.

Decanter, Cranberry To Clear, Round Emerald Foot, Optic Rib Body, Clear Stopper, 11¼ x 3½ In.	60
Pitcher, Milk, Cranberry Opal To Vaseline, Lobed Round Body, Ribbed Handle, 6¾ x 5½ In.	238
Pitcher, Water, Cranberry To Vaseline, Inverted Thumbprint, Hobb's, 8 x 7½ In.	209
Vase, Enameled Dragonflies & Flowers, Shoulders, Square Crimped Rim, 7½ x 6 In. ... *illus*	180
Vase, Optic Rib, Flared, Scalloped Rim, Enameled Girl, Petal Foot, Rossler, 9 In., Pair. *illus*	300
Vase, Optic Rib, Gold Enameled Flowers, Ruffled Rim, Round Foot, 16½ In., Pair .... *illus*	210

RUBY GLASS

Ruby glass is the dark red color of a ruby, the precious gemstone. It was a popular Victorian color that never went completely out of style. The glass was shaped by many different processes to make many different types of ruby glass. There was a revival of interest in the 1940s when modern-shaped ruby table glassware became fashionable. Sometimes the red color is added to clear glass by a process called flashing or staining. Flashed glass is clear glass dipped in a colored glass, then pressed or cut. Stained glass has color painted on a clear glass. Then it is refired so the stain fuses with the glass. Pieces of glass colored in this way are indicated by the word *stained* in the description. Related items may be found in other categories, such as Cranberry Glass, Pressed Glass, and Souvenir.

Drink Glass, Stem, Cased, Musketeer Portrait, Clear Base, Gilt Trim, Weighted, 8¾ In. .... *illus*	72
Pitcher, Water, Greek Key Band, Gold Stencil, Baluster Shape, Ridged Handle, 10 In. .... *illus*	36
Vase, Trumpet, Faceted, Scalloped Rim, Wood Base, Black Forest Carved, 13½ In., Pair .... *illus*	38

R

TIP

China can be washed in warm water with mild soapsuds. The addition of ammonia to the water will add that extra sparkle.

RS Suhl, Vase, Melon Eaters, Bowling Pin Shape, Shaded Green, Red Border, Gilt, 6¼ In.
$120

Woody Auction

RS Suhl, Vase, Portrait, Woman With Dandelion, Black & White, Shaded Blue Reverse, Gilt Trim, 7 In.
$1,140

Woody Auction

RS Tillowitz, Plate, 24K Gold, Flowers, Center Courting Scene, Green Inner Border, Pedestal Base, 8¾ In.
$108

Woody Auction

Rubina, Biscuit Jar, Silver Plate Lid & Bail, Enameled Daisy, 8 x 6 In.
$450

Woody Auction

Rubina, Dish, Sweetmeat, Cranberry To Clear, Applied Vaseline Rigaree, Silver Plate Frame, 6½ x 6 In.
$150

Woody Auction

Rubina, Pitcher, Water, Pink To Clear, Ruffled Rim, Molded Threaded Body, Ribbed Handle, 9 x 6¾ In.
$60

Woody Auction

Rubina Verde, Vase, Enameled Dragonflies & Flowers, Shoulders, Square Crimped Rim, 7½ x 6 In.
$180

Woody Auction

Rubina Verde, Vase, Optic Rib, Flared, Scalloped Rim, Enameled Girl, Petal Foot, Rossler, 9 In., Pair
$300

Woody Auction

R

Rubina Verde, Vase, Optic Rib, Gold Enameled Flowers, Ruffled Rim, Round Foot, 16 ½ In., Pair
$210

Woody Auction

Ruby Glass, Drink Glass, Stem, Cased, Musketeer Portrait, Clear Base, Gilt Trim, Weighted, 8¾ In.
$72

Woody Auction

Ruby Glass, Pitcher, Water, Greek Key Band, Gold Stencil, Baluster Shape, Ridged Handle, 10 In.
$36

Woody Auction

RUDOLSTADT

Rudolstadt was a faience factory in the Thuringia region of Germany from 1720 to about 1791. In 1854, Ernst Bohne began working in the area. From about 1887 to 1918, the New York and Rudolstadt Pottery made decorated porcelain marked with the RW and crown familiar to collectors. This porcelain was imported by Lewis Straus and Sons of New York, which later became Nathan Straus and Sons. The word *Royal* was included in their import mark. Collectors often call it "Royal Rudolstadt." Most pieces found today were made in the late nineteenth or early twentieth century. Additional pieces may be listed in the Kewpie category.

Bust, Woman, Bonnet, Ruffled, Signed, Royal, Germany, Victorian, 17 x 13 In.	863
Oyster Plate, 5 Wells, Square, Scalloped Rim, Red, Yellow, Gilt, 8⅝ In. .... *illus*	213
Vase, Angel Handles, Green Ground, Dragon Around Pedestal, Gilt, Pink, 1895-1924, 14½ In. .. *illus*	1375
Vase, Ball Shape, Flower, Footed Base, 2 Handles, Hand Painted, Purple Iris, 7 In.	24

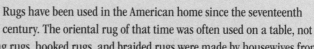

RUG

Rugs have been used in the American home since the seventeenth century. The oriental rug of that time was often used on a table, not on the floor. Rag rugs, hooked rugs, and braided rugs were made by housewives from scraps of material. American Indian rugs are listed in the Indian category.

Afghan Bokhara, 9 Octagonal Guls, Navy Blue, Red Field, Diamond Border, 3 Ft. 4 In. x 5 Ft... *illus*	644
Afshar, Scatter, Red Medallion, Blue Flowers, Ivory Vines, Camel Hair Field, 1930s, 3 x 3 Ft.	156
Ardabil, Tree Of Life, Ivory Field, Rust, Gold, Midnight Blue, Palmette Border, 4 Ft. 2 In. x 6 Ft. 2 In...	527
Ardebil, Dark Blue Abrash Field, Red Medallions, Late 1900s, Runner, 4 Ft. 2 In. x 10 Ft. 8 In.	84
Aubusson, Cream Ground, Multicolor, Flowers & Leaves, White Border, 14 x 30 Ft.	5463
Aubusson, Green Ground, Rust Border, Central Medallion, Leaves, 16 Ft. 8 In. x 20 Ft. 5 In.	2560
Bakhtiari, Pictorial, Grid, Flowers, Birds, Animals, Cream Main Border, 9 Ft. 9 In. x 6 Ft. 11 In...	480
Bakhtiari, Rosette Medallion, Midnight Blue, Red Field, Ivory, Leaf Border, 4 Ft. 10 In. x 6 Ft....... *illus*	351
Beshir, Octagonal Star, Medallion, Palmettes, Diamonds, Blue & Red Field, 5 Ft. 8 In. x 11 Ft... *illus*	2106
Bidjar Kilim, Center Diamond, Red & Yellow Flowers, Early 1900s, 7 Ft. x 4 Ft. 6 In.	768
Bidjar, Herati Pattern, Blue, Flowers, Repeat Design, Border, 11 x 16 Ft.	4880
Bokhara, Diamond Center, Cream Field, Blue, Red Borders, Tan Fringe, 2 Ft. 9 In. x 5 Ft. 6 In.	130
Bokhara, Runner, Geometric Red, Hand Knotted, Red, Woven, Pakistan, 9 Ft. 7 In. x 2 Ft. 8 In. ..	115
Bokhara, Runner, Wool, Column Design, Hand Knotted, Persian, 9 Ft. 6 In. x 3 Ft. 2 In.	281
Caucasian, Kazak, 3 Central Medallions, Blue Ground, Red Main Border, 4 Ft. 4 In. x 3 Ft. 5 In.	240
Caucasian, Kazak, Blue, Multicolor, 8-Point Star Border, c.1890, 6 Ft. 2 In. x 3 Ft. 10 In....	495
Caucasian, Kazak, Hall, Geometric Medallions, Navy, Flower Vines, 1900s, 7 Ft. 2 In. x 5 Ft. *illus*	600
Caucasian, Medallion, Blue Ground, Red Borders, Flowers, Wool, Early 1900s, 9 Ft. 4 In. x 6 Ft...	1375
Caucasian, Runner, Wool, Geometrics, Flowers, Red, Blue Border, Fringe, 9 Ft. 4 In. x 3 Ft.	938
Chinese, Art Deco, Brown, Lilac Border, Flowers, Birdcage, Vase, 8 Ft. 10 In. x 11 Ft. 8 In. ..*illus*	640
Chinese, Art Deco, Multicolor, Leaves, Floral, Black Border, 8 Ft. 10 In. x 11 Ft.	2750
Chinese, Figural, Women, Blue, Flowers, Bamboo, Nichols, c.1930, 11 Ft. 4 In. x 8 Ft. 10 In.	7500
Chinese, Flowers, Light Blue, Red Ground, Black Border, Peking Wool, c.1910, 7 Ft. x 4 Ft. 3 In...	438
Ege Rya, Abstract Shapes, Red Shades, Denmark,1970s, 14 x 10 Ft.	1216
Ege Rya, Abstract Stripes With Ragged Ends, Multicolor, Denmark, 1970s, 11 x 8 Ft. .... *illus*	960
Fereghan Sarouk, Room Size, Flowers, Geometric Design, c.1910, 11 Ft. 8 In. x 9 Ft. 2 In..*illus*	2151
Grenfell, Harbor, Sailing Ship, 2 Houses, Mountains, Frame, Gilt Liner, 2 Ft. 4 In. x 2 Ft. 9 In... *illus*	1170
Hamadan, Blue Field, Flowers, Vine, Pink Spandrels, 1900s, 6 Ft. 2 In. x 3 Ft. 11 In............	1230
Hamadan, Carpet, Rosettes, Flowering Vines, Palmette Border, Northwest Persia, 8 Ft. 8 In. x 11 Ft. ..	2574
Hamadan, Flower Medallions, Blue Field, Green Corners, c.1910, 4 Ft. x 6 Ft. 9 In.	630
Hamadan, Flowers, Vines, Rosettes, Blue, Ivory, Red Field, Palmette Border, 3 Ft. 6 In. x 5 Ft.	351
Hamadan, Ivory, Crimson, Red Fields, Navy Blue Border, 1930s, 3 Ft. 7 In. x 5 Ft. .... *illus*	500
Hamadan, Serabend, Palace, Carpet, Boteh Design, Red, Multi-Tier Guards, 20 Ft. 2 In. x 14 Ft. 6 In.	1200
Hereke, Silk, Ivory, Beige Border, Celadon Highlight, Turkey, Frame, 1900s, 4 Ft. 1 In. x 2 Ft. 7 In.	210
Heriz, Blue, Square Medallion, Pendant, Flowering Vines, Gold Palmettes, 9 Ft. x 11 Ft. 8 In. .	1170
Heriz, Geometric & Flower Medallions, Red, Cream, Wool, Runner, 1900s, 15 Ft. 10 In. x 2 Ft. 5 In.*illus*	375
Heriz, Red, Geometric Flowers, Dark Blue Ground, Wool, 10 Ft. 3 In. x 8 Ft. 6 In.	1125

Ruby Glass, Vase, Trumpet, Faceted, Scalloped Rim, Wood Base, Black Forest Carved, 13½ In., Pair
$38

Jaremos

Rudolstadt, Oyster Plate, 5 Wells, Square, Scalloped Rim, Red, Yellow, Gilt, 8⅝ In.
$213

Strawser Auction Group

Rudolstadt, Vase, Angel Handles, Green Ground, Dragon Around Pedestal, Gilt, Pink, 1895-1924, 14½ In.
$1,375

Lion and Unicorn

Rug, Afghan Bokhara, 9 Octagonal Guls, Navy Blue, Red Field, Diamond Border, 3 Ft. 4 In. x 5 Ft.
$644

Thomaston Place Auction Galleries

Rug, Bakhtiari, Rosette Medallion, Midnight Blue, Red Field, Ivory, Leaf Border, 4 Ft. 10 In. x 6 Ft.
$351

Thomaston Place Auction Galleries

Rug, Beshir, Octagonal Star, Medallion, Palmettes, Diamonds, Blue & Red Field, 5 Ft. 8 In. x 11 Ft.
$2,106

Thomaston Place Auction Galleries

R

Rug, Caucasian, Kazak, Hall, Geometric Medallions, Navy, Flower Vines, 1900s, 7 Ft. 2 In. x 5 Ft.
$600

Selkirk Auctioneers & Appraisers

TIP
Put a pad under any small rug to keep it from slipping. The pad also protects it from wear.

Rug, Chinese, Art Deco, Brown, Lilac Border, Flowers, Birdcage, Vase, 8 Ft. 10 In. x 11 Ft. 8 In.
$640

R Neal Auction Company

Rug, Ege Rya, Abstract Stripes With Ragged Ends, Multicolor, Denmark, 1970s, 11 x 8 Ft.
$960

Hunt & Peck Auctions, LLC

Rug, Fereghan Sarouk, Room Size, Flowers, Geometric Design, c.1910, 11 Ft. 8 In. x 9 Ft. 2 In.
$2,151

Jeffrey S. Evans & Associates

Rug, Grenfell, Harbor, Sailing Ship, 2 Houses, Mountains, Frame, Gilt Liner, 2 Ft. 4 In. x 2 Ft. 9 In.
$1,170

Thomaston Place Auction Galleries

Rug, Hamadan, Ivory, Crimson, Red Fields, Navy Blue Border, 1930s, 3 Ft. 7 In. x 5 Ft.
$500

Eldred's

Rug, Heriz, Geometric & Flower Medallions, Red, Cream, Wool, Runner, 1900s, 15 Ft. 10 In. x 2 Ft. 5 In.
$375

Hindman

Rug, Heriz, Room Size, Center Medallion, Geometric Patterns, Red Field, 12 Ft. 2 In. x 8 Ft.
$594

Wiederseim Auctions

Rug, Hooked, 2 Rabbits, Carrot, Multicolor, Mounted, Frame, Late 1800s, 22 x 36 In.
$563

Hindman

Heriz, Room Size, Center Medallion, Geometric Patterns, Red Field, 12 Ft. 2 In. x 8 Ft.....*illus*	594
Hooked, 2 Canada Geese, Flying Position, Turquoise Sky, 29 x 42 In..........................	293
Hooked, 2 Rabbits, Carrot, Multicolor, Mounted, Frame, Late 1800s, 22 x 36 In........... *illus*	563
Hooked, 2 Sea Gulls, 4 Stars, White On Blue Ground, Red Trim, 17 ½ x 33 In............... *illus*	170
Hooked, Afghan War, Knotted Wool, Tribal Art, Grenade Borders, Helicopter, 32 x 25 In..*illus*	863
Hooked, Brown Dog, Standing, Dreamy Setting, 24 x 44 In.	113
Hooked, Clipped, Rectangular, Cross, Flower, Mauve Ground, 1910s, 40 x 27 In.	60
Hooked, Cow, Cream Ground, Multicolor Border, Early 1900s, 16 ½ x 26 ½ In.....................	344
Hooked, Demilune, Doormat, Welcome, Sailboat, Lighthouse, Whale, c.1930, 14 x 30 In............ *illus*	313
Hooked, Flowers, Central Medallion, Tan Field, Fern Border, Waldoboro, Maine, c. 1900, 28 x 59 In.	380
Hooked, Flowers, Strawberry, Leaves, Multicolor, 1900s, 30 x 46 In.	378
Hooked, Folk Art, Block Design, Geometric Design, Mid 1900s, 24 x 36 In.	156
Hooked, Gray Cat, Seated, Striated Ground, Geometric Border, Early 1900s, 36 x 39 In.	204
Hooked, Horse, Running, Multicolor Zigzag Border, Signed, PL, Dated '89, 25 x 36 In.	500
Hooked, Lion, Cream Ground, Multicolor, Flower Border, Late 1800s, 52 x 34 In.	406
Hooked, Peacock, Blue & Red, Light Blue Ground, Vine, Black Border, 19th Century, 25 x 43 In.....	116
Hooked, Pig, Leaves, Berries, Green Ground, Wool, Claire Murray, 1900s, 26 x 41 In...... *illus*	281
Hooked, Sailing Ship, 2 Masts, Full Sail, Choppy Sea, Twisted Rope, Ship's Wheels, 33 x 31 In.	285
Hooked, Schooner, 2 Masts, Black Figure, Tan Field, Lattice Frame, 30 x 45 In. .... *illus*	322
Hooked, Shore, House, Tree, Dog, Whale In Water, Initials L.M. 99, Late 1800s, 26 x 48 In.. *illus*	480
Hooked, Starfish, Shells, Rectangular, Border Design, 1900s, 28 x 36 In.	431
Hooked, U.S. Map, Earth Tones On Blue, For Peter Stone On His 5th Birthday, Nov. 1940, 27 x 41 In...	470
Hooked, Woman, Man, Riding Tandem Bicycle, Dorothy Strauser, 16 x 15 In.......................	537
India, Peace, Rust Red Field, 7 Columns, Religious Symbols, Cream Fringe, 3 x 5 Ft....*illus*	702
Indo-Persian, Cypress Trees, Gold, Brick Red, Camel, Beige, Blue Meander Border, 3 Ft. 2 In. x 5 Ft..	702
Indo-Persian, Flowers, Navy Blue Border, Guard, c.1920s, 6 Ft. 9 In. x 3 Ft. 9 In...................	420
Indo-Persian, Nain, Blue, Red Leafy Medallion, Ivory Field, Round, 1900s, 4 Ft. Diam.......	180
Indo-Persian, Red, Navy Corners, Ivory Border, Leafy Vine, Persia, c.1920, 5 Ft. 11 In. x 5 Ft. 2 In.	240
Indo-Persian, Sawtooth Border, 2 Diamond Shapes, Navy Medallion, c.1900, 6 Ft. 9 In. x 4 Ft. 3 In. .	360
Indo-Persian, Stylized Geometric Pattern, Multicolor, Turkey, 1900s, 5 Ft. 5 In. x 3 Ft. 9 In.. *illus*	150
Iranian, Ivory Field, Multicolor Flower Sprays, Kermen Gallery, c.1950, 13 Ft. 5 In. x 5 Ft. 10 In. ..	405
Isfahan, Flowers & Leaves, Birds, Dark Blue Field, Red Border, Wool, c.1970, 5 Ft. 5 In. x 3 Ft. 7 In.....	375
Karabagh, Abrashed, Crimson Field, Animals, Roses, 1800s, 3 Ft. 9 In. x 8 Ft. 5 In. .....*illus*	813
Karaja, Medallions, Red, 3 Borders, Ivory, Navy, Red, Persia, 1900s, 3 Ft. 10 In. x 2 Ft. 6 In. .	210
Karaja, Mat, Geometric Medallions, Ivory Outline, Flowers, Leaves, Red, Blue, 1930s, 2 x 3 Ft...	50
Kashan, Blue, Pink Border, Flowers, Fringe, Wool, Manchester, c.1920, 16 Ft. x 10 Ft. 9 In.....*illus*	5313
Kashan, Medallion, Anchor Pendants, Flowering Vines, Blue, Rose Border, 4 Ft. 6 In. x 7 Ft. 8 In.	1404
Kashan, Garden, Red Field, Blue & Beige Borders, 3 Ft. 3 In. x 4 Ft. 8 In.................................	510
Kashan, Lattice, Vines, Palmettes, Rosettes, Persian & Midnight Blue, 8 Ft. 6 In. x 11 Ft. 5 In. ..	1638
Kazak, Karachoph, Starburst Medallion, Octagonal, Ivory, Pakistan, 6 Ft. 6 In. x 9 Ft. 4 In. ...	702
Kazak, Kilim, Flat Woven, Lion, Sword Motifs, Turkey, Late 1900s, 3 Ft. 9 In. x 5 Ft. 6 In....	259
Kerman, Floral Medallion, Persian Blue, Sage Green Field, Ivory Turtle Border, 10 Ft. x 14 Ft. 6 In.....	702
Kerman, Ivory Field, Flowers, Blue Border, Persia, Mid 1900s, 4 Ft. 9 In. x 2 Ft. 9 In.	96
Kerman, Oval Floral Medallion, Sky Blue Field, Floral Sprays, Tan Gold Border, 7 Ft. 8 In. x 10 Ft......	1755
Kerman, Red Ground, Central Medallion, Floral Border, Persia, 10 Ft. x 13 Ft. 10 In...*illus*	4063
Kilim, Aqua Field, Geometric Design, Striped Clusters, 2000s, 6 Ft. 9 In. x 9 Ft. 7 In. ...*illus*	594
Kilim, Geometrics, Flat Woven, Red, White, Black, Orange, Tan, Morocco, 6 Ft. 8 In. x 3 Ft. 8 In.	259
Lavar Kerman, Palace Carpet, Central Blue, Red Medallion, Flower Clusters, c.1930, 22 x 12 Ft.....	6000
Lillihan, Pink Field, Multicolor, Geometric Medallions, Runner, c.1930, 2 Ft. 8 In. x 10 Ft. 6 In...*illus*	469
Mahal, Herati, Diamonds, Blue Field, Tan Border, Persia, Early 1900s, 10 Ft. 6 In. x 12 Ft.......*illus*	3218
Malayer, Blue Ground, Red Border, Flowers, Wool, c.1920, 7 Ft. 5 In. x 5 Ft. 6 In.	1625
Modern, Verner Panton, Geometric, Wool, Unika Vaev, Denmark, c.1960, 4 Ft. 6 In. x 7 Ft. 5 In..*illus*	563
Needlepoint, Aubusson, Palatial, Hand Woven, Green, Pink, France, 1900s, 7 Ft. x 4 Ft. 1 In..	2420
Oriental, Geometric Pattern, Blue, Coral, Cream, Wool, Hand Knotted, 3 Ft. 9 In. x 5 Ft. 5 In.	168
Oriental, Geometric Pattern, Red Field, Cream Border & Fringe, Runner, 2 Ft. 3 In. x 8 Ft. 10 In.	590
Oriental, Medallion, Border, Geometric Design, 9 Ft. 5 In. x 18 Ft.................................	1534
Oushak, Beige Ground, Green & Gold, Flowers & Leaves, White Fringe, 18 x 12 Ft.	863
Oushak, Cream Ground, Flowers, Salmon, Blue & Yellow, Fringe, 12 Ft. x 14 Ft. 10 In.	3584
Pakistan, Flowers, Border, Runner, 12 Ft. 5 In. x 2 Ft. 7 In.	156

Rug, Hooked, 2 Sea Gulls, 4 Stars, White On Blue Ground, Red Trim, 17 ½ x 33 In.
$170

Hartzell's Auction Gallery Inc.

Rug, Hooked, Afghan War, Knotted Wool, Tribal Art, Grenade Borders, Helicopter, 32 x 25 In.
$863

Blackwell Auctions

Rug, Hooked, Demilune, Doormat, Welcome, Sailboat, Lighthouse, Whale, c.1930, 14 x 30 In.
$313

Eldred's

Rug, Hooked, Pig, Leaves, Berries, Green Ground, Wool, Claire Murray, 1900s, 24 x 41 In.
$281

Eldred's

R

Rug, Hooked, Schooner, 2 Masts, Black Figure, Tan Field, Lattice Frame, 30 x 45 In.
$322

Thomaston Place Auction Galleries

Tongue Rugs
Some early rugs in America were made from fabric scraps. Tongue rugs were made from tongue-shaped pieces of cloth overlapped and sewn to the backing. The tongues completely covered the backing.

Rug, Hooked, Shore, House, Tree, Dog, Whale In Water, Initials L.M. 99, Late 1800s, 26 x 48 In.
$480

Rachel Davis Fine Arts

Rug, India, Peace, Rust Red Field, 7 Columns, Religious Symbols, Cream Fringe, 3 x 5 Ft.
$702

Thomaston Place Auction Galleries

Penny, Multicolor, Felt Cutouts, Black Tab Ends, c.1950, 1 Ft. 1 In. x 2 Ft. 8 In. .... *illus*	150
Perepedil, Dark Blue Field, Flowers, Barber Pole Design, Late 1800s, 3 Ft. 8 In. x 5 Ft.	2875
Persian, Blue Diamond, Red Field, Stepped Edge Spandrels, c.1910, 12 Ft. 3 In. x 8 Ft. 6 In.	6735
Persian, Central Medallion, Red Ground, Flower Sprays, Blue Spandrels, 11 Ft. x 6 Ft. 8 In... *illus*	300
Persian, Cream Ground, Central Medallion, Multicolor, Leaves, Flowers, 8 Ft. 10 In. x 11 Ft. 10 In....	549
Persian, Floral Medallion, Navy Blue Field, Animal Motifs, Hand Knotted, 1900s, 9 Ft. 4 In. x 6 Ft.	270
Persian, Hamadan, Red Ground, Flowers, Geometric Border, 5 Ft. x 10 Ft. 2 In.	531
Persian, Heriz, Handmade, Red Ground, Green, Beige, Iran, 9 Ft. 8 In. x 13 Ft. 4 In.	978
Persian, Heriz, Polygonal Medallion, Geometric Design, White Field, Mid 1900s, 6 Ft. x 4 Ft. 8 In. .	1476
Persian, Heriz, Reds, Rust & Blues, Angular Lines, Geometrical Design, 6 Ft. 2 In. x 9 Ft. 7 In.	2520
Persian, Medallion Center, Flowers, Red Ground, Blue & Gold, Cream Fringe, 7 Ft. 8 In. x 4 Ft. 8 In...	230
Persian, Nain, Medallion, Flowers, Cream Blue, Fringe, Wool, Round, c.1950, 4 Ft. 10 In. Diam. ..	344
Persian, Navy, Vine, 3 Ivory & Red Medallions, Ivory Border, 1900s, 11 Ft. 10 In. x 2 Ft. 6 In.	390
Persian, Pole Medallion, Red, Ivory Panels, Columnar Separations, 1900s, 12 Ft. 3 In. x 8 Ft. 7 In. ..	150
Persian, Red Ground, Blue Border, Leaves, Cream Fringe, 4 Ft. x 5 Ft. 10 In.	300
Persian, Red Ground, Circular Medallion, Flowers, Cream Border, 10 Ft. 10 In. x 14 Ft. 7 In.	4800
Persian, Serapi, Salmon Ground, Blue Border, Leaves Design, 9 Ft. 10 In. x 9 Ft. 8 In.. *illus*	6100
Persian, Silk, Central Medallion, Multiple Borders, 6 Ft. 2 In. x 4 Ft. 1 In.	2280
Prayer, Vines, Palmettes, Deer & Birds, Navy Blue Field, Northwest Persia, 5 x 10 Ft. .... *illus*	556
Prayer, Sino-Kirman, Navy Blue Field, Multicolor, Flowers, 1980s, 4 x 6 Ft...........................	531
Qashqai, 3 Stepped Diamond Medallions, Ivory, Red Field, Serpent Head Border, 6 Ft. x 7 Ft. 2 In.....	410
Qashqai, Sawtooth Medallions, Geometrics, Red Field, Persia, c.1820s, 5 Ft. 4 In. x 3 Ft. 10 In....	120
Rya, Abstract Sun, Orange, Yellow, Red, White, Galaxy Collection, Denmark, 1970s, 11 x 8 Ft.... *illus*	768
Rya, Abstract, Purple, Hojer Eksport Wilton, Denmark, 1970s, 10 x 6½ Ft.................. *illus*	1280
Rya, Circles & Stripes, Brown, Yellow, Orange, Dania Taepper, Denmark, 1970s, 11 x 8 Ft...*illus*	640
Rya, Concentric Rectangles, Blue Shades, Hojer Eksport Wilton, Denmark, 9 x 6 Ft. ..... *illus*	1792
Rya, White, Irregular Stripes, Black, Orange, Hojer Eksport Wilton, Denmark, 10 x 6 Ft......	1408
Sarouk, Burgundy Ground, Overall Pattern, Blue Border, 1900s, 17 Ft. x 10 Ft. 6 In.	4200
Sarouk, Floral Medallion, Gold, Red, Brown, Blue, Vase, Palmette Border, 4 Ft. 5 In. x 5 Ft. 4 In.	410
Sarouk, Center Hall, Red Field, Floral Patterns, 6 Ft. 4 In. x 4 Ft.................................*illus*	344
Sarouk, Flower Vines, Rosettes & Palmettes, Multicolor, 4 Ft. 6 In. x 6 Ft. 10 In....................	936
Sarouk, Flowers, Deep Blue Ground, Borders, 1900s, 4 Ft. 3 In. x 6 Ft. 8 In.	344
Sarouk, Flowers, Red Field, Blue, Yellow, Multiple Borders, Wool, c.1920, 6 Ft. 4 In. x 5 Ft. 2 In.	500
Sarouk, Ivory Medallion, Floral, Geometric Line, Farahan, Persia, c.1920, 4 Ft. 10 In. x 3 Ft. 6 In. .	330
Sarouk, Red Field, Flower Clusters, Multicolor, Late 1900s, Runner, 2 Ft. 6 In. x 9 Ft. 10 In.	156
Sarouk, Red Ground, Multicolor, Flowers, Cream Fringe, Wool, c.1920, 11 Ft. 7 In. x 8 Ft. 8 In.	1250
Sarouk, Rose Medallion, Anchor Pendants, Spandrels, Palmette Border, 12 x 16 Ft.	1170
Serapi, Collar Medallion, Ivory, Salmon, Blue Border, Hand Knotted, Runner, 11 Ft. 9 In. x 2 Ft...	270
Serapi, Overlapping Gold, Gabled Medallions, Traditional Bold Elements, 2000s, 10 x 14 Ft... *illus*	3375
Serapi, Salmon Pink, Gold Spandrels, Ivory Field, Green & Gray Border, 2000s, 8 x 10 Ft....	1125
Shiraz, Pictorial, Camels, Elephants, Horses, Tigers, Blue, Green, Tan, Yellow, 7 Ft. 2 In. x 4 Ft.. *illus*	288
Sultanabad, Red Ground, Dark Blue Main Border, Flower Design, Pakistan, 11 Ft. 10 In. x 9 Ft..*illus*	1440
Tabriz, Center Medallion, Ivory Field, Flowers, White Fringe, Silk, 1900s, 6 Ft. 6 In. x 4 Ft. 8 In.	875
Tabriz, Blue Medallion, Red Ground, Flowers, Triple Borders, 7 Ft. 8 In. x 11 Ft. 3 In.	360
Tabriz, Central Oval Medallion, Blue Field, Vine & Floral Motifs, White Border, 8 Ft. x 10 Ft. 4 In.	585
Tabriz, Flowers, Medallions, Cream Ground, Multicolor, Wool, 1950s, 7 Ft. 4 In. x 4 Ft. 6 In.. *illus*	344
Tabriz, Flowers, Medallions, Multicolor, Wool, Hadji Jalili, Late 1800s, 9 Ft. 7 In. x 13 Ft. 10 In.	4063
Tabriz, Lobed Medallion, Layered Corners, Guard Borders, India, 1900s, 12 x 9 Ft....................	450
Tabriz, Persian, Silk Blend, Medallion, Flowers, Trees, Red Field, Iran, 1900s, 10 Ft. 4 In. x 6 Ft.	2016
Tabriz, Pictorial, Monochrome, Trees, Animals, Tan, Brown, Gold, 1800s, 4 Ft. 10 In. x 6 Ft. 7 In. *illus*	1170
Tibetan, 2 Skeletal Figures, Red Ground, Greek Border, 7 Ft. 2 In. x 3 Ft. .... *illus*	390
Tibetan, Sino, 3 Medallion Panels, Multicolor, Runner, 6 Ft. 7 In. x 2 Ft. 2 In......................	360
Turkish, Caucasian, Lesghi Star, Ivory Field, Zigzag Design, Red, Blue, 1950s, 3 Ft. 3 In. x 3 Ft. 8 In.	63
Turkish, Flatweave, Geometric Designs, Ivory, Red, Black, Turkey, 1900s, 7 Ft. 9 In. x 5 Ft. 7 In.	210
Turkish, Silk, Maroon, Spider Shape Border, Flowers, Fringe, Frame, 1900s, 3 Ft. x 16 In. ....*illus*	250
Turkish, Tribal, Carpet, Red, Blue, Yellow, Geometric Border, 4 Ft. 2 In. x 5 Ft. 4 In.	750
Ushak, Tan Ivory Field, Geometric, Plant, Blue Spandrels, Rosette Border, 8 Ft. x 10 Ft. 6 In..*illus*	1112
Wool, Flatweave, Blue Ground, Fringe, Woven, Sweden, c.1950, 2-Sided, 4 Ft. 6 In. x 6 Ft. 5 In. .....*illus*	3250
Wool, Pile, Hand Knotted, Nude Ground, Morocco, 1900s, 13 Ft. 8 In. x 17 Ft. 7 In.	8750

R

Rug, Indo-Persian, Stylized Geometric Pattern, Multicolor, Turkey, 1900s, 5 Ft. 5 In. x 3 Ft. 9 In.
$150

Selkirk Auctioneers & Appraisers

Rug, Karabagh, Abrashed, Crimson Field, Animals, Roses, 1800s, 3 Ft. 9 In. x 8 Ft. 5 In.
$813

Eldred's

Rug, Kashan, Blue, Pink Border, Flowers, Fringe, Wool, Manchester, c.1920, 16 Ft. x 10 Ft. 9 In.
$5,313

Hindman

Rug, Kerman, Red Ground, Central Medallion, Floral Border, Persia, 10 Ft. x 13 Ft. 10 In.
$4,063

Neal Auction Company

Orientals on the Wall

There is a modern safe way to hang an antique Oriental rug on the wall. Put a strip of 2-inch-wide Velcro on a strip of wood. Mount the wood on the wall. Hang the rug directly on the Velcro. The rug will stay in place and can be pulled loose to be cleaned.

Rug, Kilim, Aqua Field, Geometric Design, Striped Clusters, 2000s, 6 Ft. 9 In. x 9 Ft. 7 In.
$594

Eldred's

Rug, Lillihan, Pink Field, Multicolor, Geometric Medallions, Runner, c.1930, 2 Ft. 8 In. x 10 Ft. 6 In.
$469

Eldred's

Rug, Mahal, Herati, Diamonds, Blue Field, Tan Border, Persia, Early 1900s, 10 Ft. 6 In. x 12 Ft.
$3,218

Thomaston Place Auction Galleries

R

Rug, Modern, Verner Panton, Geometric, Wool, Unika Vaev, Denmark, c.1960, 4 Ft. 6 In. x 7 Ft. 5 In.
$563

Wright

Rug, Penny, Multicolor, Felt Cutouts, Black Tab Ends, c.1950, 1 Ft. 1 In. x 2 Ft. 8 In.
$150

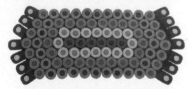

Garth's Auctioneers & Appraisers

Rug, Persian, Central Medallion, Red Ground, Flower Sprays, Blue Spandrels, 11 Ft. x 6 Ft. 8 In.
$300

Michaan's Auctions

TIP
Vacuum the top of an Oriental rug at least once a week. Turn it over and vacuum the bottom once a year.

Rug, Persian, Serapi, Salmon Ground, Blue Border, Leaves Design, 9 Ft. 10 In. x 9 Ft. 8 In.
$6,100

Neal Auction Company

Rug, Prayer, Vines, Palmettes, Deer & Birds, Navy Blue Field, Northwest Persia, 5 x 10 Ft.
$556

Thomaston Place Auction Galleries

Rug, Rya, Abstract Sun, Orange, Yellow, Red, White, Galaxy Collection, Denmark, 1970s, 11 x 8 Ft.
$768

Hunt & Peck Auctions, LLC

Rug, Rya, Abstract, Purple, Hojer Eksport Wilton, Denmark, 1970s, 10 x 6½ Ft.
$1,280

Hunt & Peck Auctions, LLC

Rug, Rya, Circles & Stripes, Brown, Yellow, Orange, Dania Taepper, Denmark, 1970s, 11 x 8 Ft.
$640

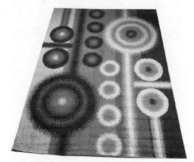

Hunt & Peck Auctions, LLC

Rug, Rya, Concentric Rectangles, Blue Shades, Hojer Eksport Wilton, Denmark, 9 x 6 Ft.
$1,792

Hunt & Peck Auctions, LLC

R

Rug, Sarouk, Center Hall, Red Field, Floral Patterns, 6 Ft. 4 In. x 4 Ft.
$344

Wiederseim Auctions

Rug, Serapi, Overlapping Gold, Gabled Medallions, Traditional Bold Elements, 2000s, 10 x 14 Ft.
$3,375

Eldred's

Rug, Shiraz, Pictorial, Camels, Elephants, Horses, Tigers, Blue, Green, Tan, Yellow, 7 Ft. 2 In. x 4 Ft.
$288

Blackwell Auctions

Rug, Sultanabad, Red Ground, Dark Blue Main Border, Flower Design, Pakistan, 11 Ft. 10 In. x 9 Ft.
$1,440

Michaan's Auctions

Rug, Tabriz, Flowers, Medallions, Cream Ground, Multicolor, Wool, 1950s, 7 Ft. 4 In. x 4 Ft. 6 In.
$344

Hindman

Fringe Determines the Value

If the border of a rug is badly frayed or missing, it dramatically lowers the value. A rug with a good fringe could be worth $1,500; without a border, the same rug could be worth only $100.

Rug, Tabriz, Pictorial, Monochrome, Trees, Animals, Tan, Brown, Gold, 1800s, 4 Ft. 10 In. x 6 Ft. 7 In.
$1,170

Thomaston Place Auction Galleries

Rug, Tibetan, 2 Skeletal Figures, Red Ground, Greek Border, 7 Ft. 2 In. x 3 Ft.
$390

Michaan's Auctions

Rug, Turkish, Silk, Maroon, Spider Shape Border, Flowers, Fringe, Frame, 1900s, 3 Ft. x 16 In.
$250

Hindman

R

Rug, Ushak, Tan Ivory Field, Geometric, Plant, Blue Spandrels, Rosette Border, 8 Ft. x 10 Ft. 6 In.
$1,112

Thomaston Place Auction Galleries

Rug, Wool, Flatweave, Blue Ground, Fringe, Woven, Sweden, c.1950, 2-Sided, 4 Ft. 6 In. x 6 Ft. 5 In.
$3,250

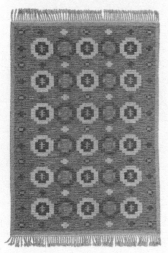

Wright

Russel Wright, Aluminum, Ice Bucket, Lid, Chrome Plate, Glass, c.1935, 8 ½ In.
$2,375

Wright

RUMRILL

RumRill

Rumrill Pottery was designed by George Rumrill of Little Rock, Arkansas. From 1933 to 1938, it was produced by the Red Wing Pottery of Red Wing, Minnesota. In January 1938, production was transferred to the Shawnee Pottery in Zanesville, Ohio. It was moved again in December of 1938 to Florence Pottery Company in Mt. Gilead, Ohio, where Rumrill ware continued to be manufactured until the pottery burned in 1941. It was then produced by Gonder Ceramic Arts in South Zanesville until early 1943.

Vase, Apple Blossom Glaze, Saucer Shape Bottom, Graduated Neck, Handles, 8 In.	195
Vase, Pillow Form, Fluted Sides, Hip Hugging Handles, Green Glaze, Yellow Interior, 6 x 6 x 2 In.	75
Vase, Rust Over Green Matte Glaze, Dancing Nudes, Leaf Handles, 7 ½ In.	350

RUSKIN

Ruskin is a British art pottery of the twentieth century. The Ruskin Pottery was started by William Howson Taylor, and his name was used as the mark until about 1899. The factory, at West Smethwick, Birmingham, England, stopped making new pieces in 1933 but continued to glaze and sell the remaining wares until 1935. The art pottery is noted for its exceptional glazes. They also made ceramic "stones" with the famous glaze to be used in jewelry.

Inkwell, Blue Glaze, Silver Lid, Hallmark, Liberty & Co., 1902, 2 x 2 ⅛ In.	455
Vase, Iridescent Purple, Cone Shape, Cylindrical Neck, 1922, 8 ¼ In.	256

RUSSEL WRIGHT

Russel Wright designed dinnerware in modern shapes for many companies. Iroquois China Company, Harker China Company, Sterling China Co., Steubenville Pottery, and Justin Tharaud and Sons made dishes marked *Russel Wright*. The Steubenville wares, first made in 1938, are the most common today. Wright was a designer of domestic and industrial wares, including furniture, aluminum, radios, interiors, and glassware. A new company, Bauer Pottery Company of Los Angeles, is making Russel Wright's American Modern dishes using molds made from original pieces. Pieces are marked *Russel Wright by Bauer Pottery California USA.* Russel Wright dinnerware and other original pieces by Wright are listed here. For more prices, go to kovels.com.

STERLING CHINA
by
Russel Wright

Russel Wright
1948–1950

JUSTIN THARALD & SON
Russel Wright
MADE IN U.S.A.

Russel Wright
1948–1953

Russel Wright
FLAIR
BOSTON 27

Russel Wright
1959–1960

Aluminum, Ice Bucket, Lid, Chrome Plate, Glass, c.1935, 8 ½ In. *illus*	2375
American Modern, Casserole Dish, Coral, Removable Lid, Steubenville, Late 1930s, 11 x 8 x 4 In.	39
American Modern, Celery Dish, Black Chutney, Steubenville, 1 ¼ x 13 x 3 ½ In.	50
Chrome, Syrup Pourer, Loop Handle, Long Spout, 1940s, 5 ½ x 6 In.	89
Glass, Warming Tray, Round, Wood Base, Electriglas, 1950s, 19 ½ x 17 x 2 In.	104
Iroquois Casual, Platter, Lettuce Green, c.1946, 12 ½ x 10 In.	65
Iroquois, Pitcher, Water, Painted, Multicolor, Flowers, Curved Handle, Signed, 1948, 9 In.	219
Woodfield, Salad Plate, Coral Pink, Triangular Rim, Steubenville, 1940s, 8 ½ In., Pair	47

SABINO

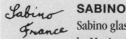
Sabino France

Sabino glass was made in the 1920s and 1930s in Paris, France. Founded by Marius-Ernest Sabino (1878–1961), the firm was noted for Art Deco lamps, vases, figurines, and animals in clear, colored, and opalescent glass. Production

stopped during World War II but resumed in the 1960s with the manufacture of nude figurines and small opalescent glass animals. Pieces made in recent years are a slightly different color and can be recognized. Only vintage pieces are listed here.

Bowl, Ballerines, Molded, Opalescent, Brass, Twist Rim, Pierced Handles, 3 x 13¾ In.........	480
Bowl, Faceted, 3 Clamshell Shape Feet, Opalescent, Art Deco, 4 x 9¼ In..............................	154
Figurine, Pekinese Dog, Opalescent, 4 x 3 In..*illus*	94
Vase, Cotes, Herringbone, Frosted, c.1915, 12¾ In...	439

SALESMAN'S SAMPLES *may be listed in the Advertising or Stove category. Some are considered toys and are listed in the Toy category.*

SALT AND PEPPER SHAKERS

Salt and pepper shakers in matched sets were first used in the nineteenth century. Collectors are primarily interested in figural examples made after World War I. Huggers are pairs of shakers that appear to embrace each other. Many salt and pepper shakers are listed in other categories and can be located through the index at the back of this book.

Bakelite, Art Deco, Half Cylinder, Mottled Orange, Black & Orange Tops, 1920s, 1¾ x 1½ In.	315
Cranberry Opalescent, Hobnail, Fenton	50
Liberty Bell Shape, Blue Glass, 3 In.	8
Mammy, Black Woman, Mobcap, Molded Plastic, Luzianne, 5⅛ In., Pair	68
Mice, Bows Around Neck, Clear Lucite Plastic, Hong Kong, 2⅞ In......................................	12
Penguin, Blue, Yellow, Orange, Ceramic, Japan, 2½ In.	15
Pottery, Red & White Stripes, Tapered, Bulbous, Yona, Japan, 5 In..	72
White Ducks, Pink Bandannas, Cork Stoppers, 3 In.	19

SALT GLAZE

Salt glaze has a grayish white surface with a texture like an orange peel. It is a method of decoration that has been used since the eighteenth century. Salt-glazed pieces are still being made.

Pitcher, Bacchanalian Scene, Leaf Shape, Pewter Lid, Charles Meigh, 1800s, 19¼ In., Pair..*illus*	246

SAMPLER

AB CDE

Samplers were made in America from the early 1700s. The best examples were made from 1790 to 1840 on homemade fabrics. Long, narrow samplers are usually older than square ones. Early samplers just had stitching or alphabets. The later examples had numerals, borders, and pictorial decorations. Those with mottoes are mid-Victorian. A revival of interest in the 1930s produced simpler samplers, using machine-made textiles, usually with mottoes.

Adam & Eve, Angels, Snake, Birds, Plants, Tree Of Life, Cross-Stitch, 1774, Frame, 18 x 16 In.... *illus*	826
Alphabet, Flowers, Vines, Bird, Poem, Embroidered, Maria Watkins, Silk, c.1821, 20 x 12 In...... *illus*	250
Alphabet, Hearts, Deer, Flowers, Jane Rich, 1824, Cotton Thread, Linen, Frame, 18 x 19 In.	72
Alphabet, Inscribed Wrought By Lucy Stone, Aged 11 Years, 1829, 8 x 8½ In.	1625
Alphabet, Lower & Upper Case, Tamson Heverly, 1829, Wool On Linen, Wood Frame, 18 x 15 In..*illus*	585
Alphabet, Numbers, Birds, Leaves, 1832, Wood Frame, 12⅝ x 15¼ In.................................	594
Alphabet, Numbers, Cross-Stitch, Sagnes R. Dadley, Aged 11 Years, 1880, Frame, 19 x 15 In......	118
Alphabet, Numbers, Verse, Mary Elizabeth Hartzman, 1846, Wood Frame, 17 x 8 In.	300
Alphabet, Panel, Cross, Flowers, Embroidered, Ecole Corneille, Annee, 1907, 29 x 22 In.	63
Alphabet, Poem, Embroidered, Margaret Branch, 1769, Frame, 15 x 12 In. ....*illus*	375
Alphabet, Prayer, Floral Vine & Pine Frond Border, Sarah Ann Baker, 1814, Frame, 21 x 18 In. ..	585
Alphabet, Reading, Flower, Vine, Bird, Tree, Animal, Verse, 1800s, 15½ x 16½ In.	83
Alphabet, Scattered Design, L. Garcia, Mexico, Ano 1826, Linen, Frame, 10¾ x 14¾ In...... *illus*	270
Alphabet, Upper & Lower Case, Mary Jenkins, 1817, Linen, Wood Frame, 14 x 14½ In.........	204
Alphabet, Verse, Flowers, Scroll Border, Catherine Kelly, 7 Years, 1848, 18 x 15½ In............	154

Sabino, Figurine, Pekinese Dog, Opalescent, 4 x 3 In.
$94

Charleston Estate Auctions

Salt Glaze, Pitcher, Bacchanalian Scene, Leaf Shape, Pewter Lid, Charles Meigh, 1800s, 19¼ In., Pair
$246

Brunk Auctions

Sampler, Adam & Eve, Angels, Snake, Birds, Plants, Tree Of Life, Cross-Stitch, 1774, Frame, 18 x 16 In.
$826

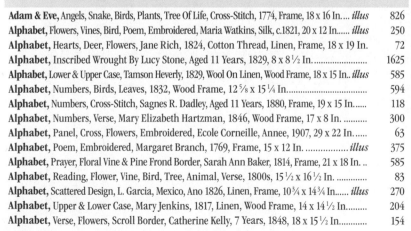

Soulis Auctions

S

Sampler, Alphabet, Flowers, Vines, Bird, Poem, Embroidered, Maria Watkins, Silk, c.1821, 20 x 12 In.
$250

Hindman

Sampler, Alphabet, Lower & Upper Case, Tamson Heverly, 1829, Wool On Linen, Wood Frame, 18 x 15 In.
$585

Thomaston Place Auction Galleries

Sampler, Alphabet, Poem, Embroidered, Margaret Branch, 1769, Frame, 15 x 12 In.
$375

Hindman

Sampler, Alphabet, Scattered Design, L. Garcia, Mexico, Ano 1826, Linen, Frame, 10¾ x 14¾ In.
$270

Michaan's Auctions

Sampler, Church, Tree, People, Isabella McNaughton, Silk On Linen, Frame, 1800s, 16 x 17 In.
$428

Pook & Pook

Sampler, Family Record, Flowers, House, Dodge Family, Ashtabula County, 1851, Frame, 16½ x 21 In.
$704

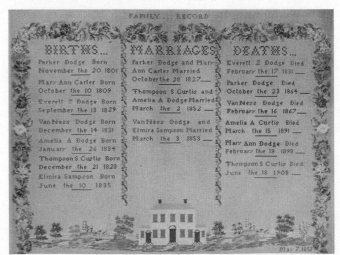

Rachel Davis Fine Arts

Sampler, Homestead Scene, Horses, Silhouette Cut, Folk Art, Frame, 13 x 13 In.
$266

Soulis Auctions

Sampler, Mourning, Charlotte Weeping, Verse, Elizabeth Fry, 1819, Silk On Silk, Frame
$9,600

Alderfer Auction Company

Church, Tree, People, Isabella McNaughton, Silk On Linen, Frame, 1800s, 16 x 17 In......*illus* ... 428
Family Record, Flowers, House, Dodge Family, Ashtabula County, 1851, Frame, 16½ x 21 In... *illus* ... 704
Family Record, Names, Births, Deaths, Mehitable Griffin, 1774-1829, Silk, Connecticut, 17 x 29 In... ... 921
Homestead Scene, Horses, Silhouette Cut, Folk Art, Frame, 13 x 13 In. ....*illus* ... 266
Mourning, Charlotte Weeping, Verse, Elizabeth Fry, 1819, Silk On Silk, Frame............*illus* ... 9600
Needlework, Garden Design, Frame, Rebecca Webster, 1800, 19 x 20 In. 406
Pastoral Scene, Prayer, Polly Ayer, Massachusetts, c.1792, 17 x 12 In. 625

SAMSON

Samson and Company, a French firm specializing in the reproduction of collectible wares of many countries and periods, was founded in Paris in the early nineteenth century. Chelsea, Meissen, Famille Verte, and Chinese Export porcelain are some of the wares that have been reproduced by the company. The firm used fake marks similar to the real ones on the reproductions. It closed in 1969.

Tureen, Lid, Handle, Painted, Gilt, 10 x 15 x 9 In... ... 125
Urn, Lid, Chinese Export, Late 1800s, 32 In., Pair ....*illus* ... 4725
Vase, Animals, Birds, Leaves, Turquoise Ground, Silver Rim, Iranian Style, c.1880, 21 In., Pair. *illus* ... 1586
Vase, Flowers, Scrolling Acanthus Handle, 1800s, 21 x 10½ In., Pair 688

SANDWICH GLASS

Sandwich glass is any of the myriad types of glass made by the Boston & Sandwich Glass Company of Sandwich, Massachusetts, between 1825 and 1888. It is often very difficult to be sure whether a piece was really made at the Sandwich factory because so many types were made there and similar pieces were made at other glass factories. Additional pieces may be listed under Pressed Glass and in other related categories.

Cologne Bottle, Milk Glass, Fiery Opalescent, 12-Sided, 1850-70, 5⅝ In. 1140
Diamond Thumbprint, Wine, Clear, Plain Base, Boston & Sandwich, 1850, 4⅜ x 2 x 2⅛ In...... ... 129
Lamp, Oil, Amethyst Glass, 7 Panels, Applied Handle, Pewter Collar, 1800s, 3 In. 315
Vase, Tulip, Emerald Green, Hexagonal Base c.1855, 10½ In., Pair ....*illus* ... 2375
Vase, Vaseline, Thumbprint, Waffle, Scalloped Rim, Flared Base, Yellow, c.1840, 11½ In. 469

SARREGUEMINES

Sarreguemines is the name of a French town that is used as part of a china mark for Utzschneider and Company, a porcelain factory that made ceramics in Sarreguemines, Lorraine, France, from about 1775. Transfer-printed wares and majolica were made in the nineteenth century. The nineteenth-century pieces, most often found today, usually have colorful transfer-printed decorations showing peasants in local costumes.

Mantel Set, Clock, 2 Vases, Woman & Dog, Royal Blue, Yellow Trim, Marked, Art Deco, 3 Piece 567
Plate, Strawberry Vine Around Rim, Fruit, Blossoms, Light Blue Ground, Marked, 10 In.*illus* ... 120
Platter, Majolica, Oval Shape, Quail, Wheat, 1800s, 24 x 17 In. 4200
Tureen, Sauce, Lid, Attached Underplate, Fruit Finial, Multicolor, 1800s, 7½ x 7 In............ ... 192

SASCHA BRASTOFF

Sascha Brastoff made decorative accessories, ceramics, enamels on copper, and plastics of his own design. He headed a factory, Sascha Brastoff of California, Inc., in West Los Angeles, from 1953 until about 1973. He died in 1993. Pieces signed with the signature *Sascha Brastoff* were his work and are the most expensive. Other pieces marked *Sascha B.* or with a stamped mark were made by others in his company.

Ashtray, Chi Chi Birds, Foot Shape, Off-White Ground, 8 x 6 x 1⅜ In. 36
Box, Gray, Kneeling Figure, Metallic Gold, Dancers Series, 5 x 3⅝ In.................................... ... 49

Samson, Urn, Lid, Chinese Export, Late 1800s, 32 In., Pair
$4,725

Freeman's

Samson, Vase, Animals, Birds, Leaves, Turquoise Ground, Silver Rim, Iranian Style, c.1880, 21 In., Pair
$1,586

Neal Auction Company

Sandwich Glass, Vase, Tulip, Emerald Green, Hexagonal Base c.1855, 10½ In., Pair
$2,375

New Haven Auctions

Sarreguemines, Plate, Strawberry Vine Around Rim, Fruit, Blossoms, Light Blue Ground, Marked, 10 In.
$120

Pasarel Auctions

Satsuma, Bowl, Bell Shape, Bamboo Decor, Tozan, Early 1900s, 4¾ In.
$31

Eldred's

Satsuma, Bowl, Gilt, Panoramic Design, Painters, Artisans, Enameled, Yabu Meizan, 2½ In. Diam.
$3,300

Alderfer Auction Company

Satsuma, Plate, Imperial, Bustling Market Scene, Trees, Cherry Blossoms, 1800s, 8 In.
$6,000

Bruneau & Co. Auctioneers

Satsuma, Vase, Double Gourd, Gilt Handles, Multicolor, Butterflies, 7½ In.
$120

Treasureseeker Auctions

Satsuma, Vase, Gilt, Panoramic Scene, Fishing Village, Flowers, Earthenware, Yabu Meizan, 2 x 2 In.
$1,680

Alderfer Auction Company

Satsuma, Vase, Miniature, Gourd Shape, Painted, Figural Design, 3 In.
$125

Auctions at Showplace, NYC

Satsuma, Vase, Octagonal, People, River Scene, Flared Rim, Wood Stand, c.1900, 18½ In.
$510

Treasureseeker Auctions

Satsuma, Vase, Painted, Samurai & Garden Scene, Gilt Rim, 9¾ In.
$960

Richard Opfer Auctioneering, Inc.

Scale, Balance, Beam, Pointer, Base, Brass, Cast Iron, F. Meyers & Co., 42 x 27 In.
$360

Chupp Auctions & Real Estate, LLC

S

Lamp, Horses, Metallic Highlights, Rectangular Base, c.1960, 29 x 11 x 5 In., Pair	4500
Pitcher, Snowing Scene, Caparisoned Camels, 1950, 7 x 5 x 6 In.	145
Sculpture, Wall, Free-Form, Brutalist, Iron, Unsigned, 38 x 45 In.	344
Tea Set, White Ground, Marbled, Purple, Gray, Gilt, Teapot, Sugar, Creamer, 17-In. Tray, 4 Piece.	64
Vase, Unicorn & Genie, Signed, 9 1/2 x 5 In.	495

SATSUMA

Satsuma is a Japanese pottery with a distinctive creamy beige crackled glaze. Most of the pieces were decorated with blue, red, green, orange, or gold. Almost all Satsuma found today was made after 1860, especially during the Meiji Period, 1868–1912. During World War I, Americans could not buy undecorated European porcelains. Women who liked to make hand-painted porcelains at home began to decorate white undecorated Satsuma. These pieces are known today as "American Satsuma."

Bowl, Bell Shape, Bamboo Decor, Tozan, Early 1900s, 4 3/4 In. .... *illus*	31
Bowl, Gilt, Panoramic Design, Painters, Artisans, Enameled, Yabu Meizan, 2 1/2 In. Diam... *illus*	3300
Cup, Gilt, Multicolor, Court Figures, Interior Text, 1900s, 4 1/4 In.	62
Plate, Imperial, Bustling Market Scene, Trees, Cherry Blossoms, 1800s, 8 In. .... *illus*	6000
Urn, Foo Dog Finial, Navy Blue & Gold, Square Baluster Shape, 8 x 5 x 17 In.	543
Vase, Double Gourd, Gilt Handles, Multicolor, Butterflies, 7 1/2 In. .... *illus*	120
Vase, Dragons, Figures, Gold Ground, Flared Rim, 2 Handles, 1800s, 8 x 4 x 4 In., Pair	219
Vase, Enameled, Figural, Bird, Flowers, Gilt Ground, Late 1900s, 18 In., Pair	610
Vase, Gilt, Panoramic Scene, Fishing Village, Flowers, Earthenware, Yabu Meizan, 2 x 2 In. *illus*	1680
Vase, Long Neck, Bulbous, Flared Rim, Floral, Blue Ground, 1800s, 30 x 11 In.	351
Vase, Miniature, Gourd Shape, Painted, Figural Design, 3 In. .... *illus*	125
Vase, Multicolor, Figure, Landscape, Gilt Rim & Base, 19 x 10 In.	260
Vase, Octagonal, People, River Scene, Flared Rim, Wood Stand, c.1900, 18 1/2 In. .... *illus*	510
Vase, Painted, Samurai & Garden Scene, Gilt Rim, 9 3/4 In. .... *illus*	960
Vase, Pottery, Flowers, Multicolor, Heart Shape, 1850s, 14 3/4 In.	1512
Vase, Relief Dragons, Shimazu Family Crest, Signature Plaque, 1900s, 12 1/4 In.	406
Vase, Ruffled Rim, Bulbous Vase, Foo Dog Handles, Glaze, Flowers, Japan, 1900s, 18 x 14 In.	100

SATURDAY EVENING GIRLS, *see Paul Revere Pottery category.*

SCALE

Scales have been made to weigh everything from babies to gold. Collectors search for all types. Most popular are small gold dust scales, special grocery scales, and tall figural scales for people to use to check their weight.

Balance, Beam, Pointer, Base, Brass, Cast Iron, F. Meyers & Co., 42 x 27 In. .... *illus*	360
Balance, Steelyard, Anchor, Eagle, Red Wood Display Rack, J.S. Trowbridge & Co., 17 In.	122
Candy, Dayton, No. 166, Stenciled, Brass, Computing Scale Co., Early 1900s, 16 1/2 In. . *illus*	847
Candy, National, Fan Shape, Round Glass Tray, Red Ground, Lancaster, Pa., 9 x 10 x 4 In. .	570
Candy, Pennsylvania National Store Specialty Co., Cast Iron, Fan Shape Gauge	660
Weighing, Lollipop, 300 Pound Capacity, John Chatillon & Sons, 68 x 11 In. .... *illus*	58
Weighing, Lollipop, Jennings, 1 Cent, Drug Store, Porcelain, 70 x 20 In.	316
Weighing, Lollipop, Toledo, White Porcelain, Cast Iron, Platform Base, 70 x 31 x 19 In. *illus*	492
Weighing, Watling, Questions & Answers, Mirror, Green, Yellow, Porcelain, 66 x 17 x 27 In... *illus*	320

SCHAFER & VATER

Schafer & Vater, makers of small ceramic items, are best known for their amusing figurals. The factory was located in Volkstedt-Rudolstadt, Germany, from 1890 to 1962. Some pieces are marked with the crown and *R* mark, but many are unmarked.

Figurine, Comical Figure, Bulging Eyes, Mouth Agape, Keep Your Hair On!, Early 1800s, 3 1/2 In. .	185
Figurine, Happy Scot, Gray Puppy, Blond Beard, Early 1800s, 5 1/2 In.	135
Vase, Figural, Scotsman, Mind Your Own Business, c.1930, 5 1/2 In.	99

Scale, Candy, Dayton, No. 166, Stenciled, Brass, Computing Scale Co., Early 1900s, 16 1/2 In.
$847

Fontaine's Auction Gallery

Scale, Weighing, Lollipop, 300 Pound Capacity, John Chatillon & Sons, 68 x 11 In.
$58

Ron Rhoads Auctioneers

Scale, Weighing, Lollipop, Toledo, White Porcelain, Cast Iron, Platform Base, 70 x 31 x 19 In.
$492

Morphy Auctions

S

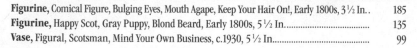

SCHEIER POTTERY

Scale, Weighing, Watling, Questions & Answers, Mirror, Green, Yellow, Porcelain, 66 x 17 x 27 In.
$320

Morphy Auctions

Scheier, Pot, Sgraffito Figures & Fish, Brown Glaze, Stoneware, c.1955, 4¾ x 6 In.
$5,313

Rago Arts and Auction Center

Scheier, Vase, Chalice Shape, Raised Facial Features, Glazed, Stoneware, Signed, 1966, 22¼ x 13 In.
$20,000

Rago Arts and Auction Center

Schneider, Vase, Art Deco, Clear Thick Glass, Applied Handles, Signed, 7½ In.
$330

Treasureseeker Auctions

Scientific Instrument, Armillary Sphere, Charles Delamarche, Horizon Ring, Latitude, Longitude, c.1835, 18 In.
$5,279

Bonhams

Scientific Instrument, Compass, Stockert, Sundial, Brass Gnomon, Paper Dial, Glass Dome, Wood Case, 1¾ In.
$1,024

Rachel Davis Fine Arts

Scientific Instrument, Microscope Lamp, Bench, Glass Oil Reservoir, Adjustable Stand, England, c.1880, 12½ In.
$528

Bonhams

Scientific Instrument, Microscope, Ocular Lens, Tripod Base, Baker Binocular Compound, England, 1800s, 14 In.
$440

Bonhams

Scientific Instrument, Model, Steam Traction Engine, Doll & Co., Crank, Feedwater Pump, Germany, 13 x 6 x 16 In.
$4,320

Morphy Auctions

S

SCHEIER POTTERY

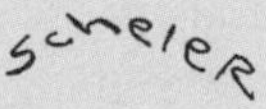

Scheier pottery was made by Edwin Scheier (1910–2008) and his wife, *Scheier*
Mary (1908–2007). They met while they both worked for the WPA, and married in
1937. In 1939, they established their studio, Hillcrock Pottery, in Glade Spring, Virginia.
Mary made the pottery and Edwin decorated it. From 1940 to 1968, Edwin taught at
the University of New Hampshire and Mary was artist-in-residence. They moved to
Oaxaca, Mexico, in 1968 to study the arts and crafts of the Zapotec Indians. When the
Scheiers moved to Green Valley, Arizona, in 1978, Ed returned to pottery, making some
of his biggest and best-known pieces.

Bowl, Blue Matte Glaze, Sgraffito Figure & Faces, Pink Glazed Bottom, c.1960, 10¾ In.	1188
Bowl, Blue Stylized Figures, Connected Hands & Feet, Textured Brown Glaze, Marked, 8 x 7 In.	1750
Bowl, Conical, Footed, Ocher Mouth Rim, Dark Glaze, Late 1900s, 3¾ x 6⅜ In.	163
Bowl, Pink & White Glaze, Stylized Face, Stoneware, c.1950, 12¾ In.	938
Bowl, Sgraffito Bands & Faces, Glazed, Stoneware, Signed, c.1960, 6 x 8¼ In.	6875
Bowl, Sgraffito, Abstract Design, Green Glaze, Short Foot, Marked, 1950s, 9 x 13 In.	2750
Bowl, Sgraffito, Dark Brown Glaze, Stoneware, c.1950, 4¾ x 8½ In.	3250
Chalice, Raised Stylized Figures, Dark Brown Glaze, Dark Blue, Signed, 1986, 10 x 10½ In.	4688
Pot, Sgraffito Figures & Fish, Brown Glaze, Stoneware, c.1955, 4¾ x 6 In. .... *illus*	5313
Vase, Chalice Shape, Raised Facial Features, Glazed, Stoneware, Signed, 1966, 22¼ x 13 In. ...... *illus*	20000
Vase, Dark Brown Glaze, Sgraffito Faces, Stoneware, Signed, 1948, 10 x 9 In.	10000

SCHNEIDER GLASSWORKS

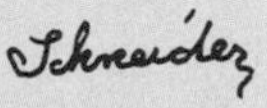

Schneider Glassworks was founded in 1917 at Epinay-sur-Seine, *Schneider*
France, by Charles and Ernest Schneider. Art glass was made between 1918 and 1933.
The company went bankrupt in 1939. Charles Schneider and his sons opened a new
glassworks in 1949. Art glass was made until 1981, when the company closed. See also
the Le Verre Francais category.

Vase, Art Deco, Clear Thick Glass, Applied Handles, Signed, 7½ In. .... *illus*	330
Vase, Multicolor Mottled Design, Round Base, 9 x 4 In.	450

SCIENTIFIC INSTRUMENT

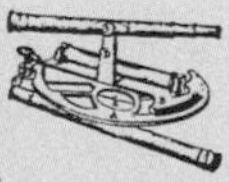

Scientific instruments of all kinds are included in this category. Other
categories such as Barometer, Binoculars, Dental, Medical, Nautical, and
Thermometer may also price scientific apparatus.

Armillary Sphere, Charles Delamarche, Horizon Ring, Latitude, Longitude, c.1835, 18 In. *illus*	5279
Cabinet, Electrotherapy, Wall Mount, Oak, Carved, Door, Beveled Glass, 1890s, 43 x 20 In..	561
Compass, Brinton, Brass, Thos J. Evans, London, 1862, 3 In.	600
Compass, Stockert, Sundial, Brass Gnomon, Paper Dial, Glass Dome, Wood Case, 1¾ In... *illus*	1024
Encryption Machine, L.C. Smith & Corona Typewriter Inc., M-209-B, c.1950, 7 In.............	1760
Kaleidoscope, Chesnik-Koch, Brass Body, 2 Wheels, Textured Glass, Wood Stand, 11 In.	156
Magnifying Glass, Cloisonne Handle, Multicolor, Flowers, Japan, c.1900, 10¼ x 3 In..........	150
Magnifying Glass, Turned Frame, Hinged, Mirror, Pillar, Mahogany, Marble Base, 1800s, 22 In..	1875
Measuring Device, Square Cherry Wood Shaft, Scrimmed Bone, Folk Art, 1800s, 15 In.	325
Microscope Lamp, Bench, Glass Oil Reservoir, Adjustable Stand, England, c.1880, 12½ In... *illus*	528
Microscope, A. Picart, Field, Brass, Mounted, Walnut Case, Signed, Paris, 1800s, 3 x 5 x 7 In. ..	240
Microscope, Carl Zeiss, Binocular, Brass, Square Stage, Mono, Jena, 7 x 5 x 13 In.	153
Microscope, Monocular, Ernst Leitz Wetzlar, Wood Case, Electric Light, Germany...............	115
Microscope, Ocular Lens, Tripod Base, Baker Binocular Compound, England, 1800s, 14 In....... *illus*	440
Model, Steam Engine, Bing, Vertical, Spoked Wheel, Brass Style Stack, Germany, 11⅝ In...	330
Model, Steam Traction Engine, Doll & Co., Crank, Feedwater Pump, Germany, 13 x 6 x 16 In..... *illus*	4320
Nocturnal, Boxwood, Square Brass Hub Nut, Pierced Heart Design, c.1680, 4½ In.	6875
Orrery, George Philips & Sons, Patented, Pine Case, Marked, London, c.1890, 10 x 19 In. ...	3000
Pantograph, Hermes, Gold Taurillon, Leather, LED Lamps, Italy, Box, 38 In.............. *illus*	5625
Periscope, Carl Zeiss, Pedestal, Steel & Brass Metals, Germany, 28 x 28 x 85 In........... *illus*	2750

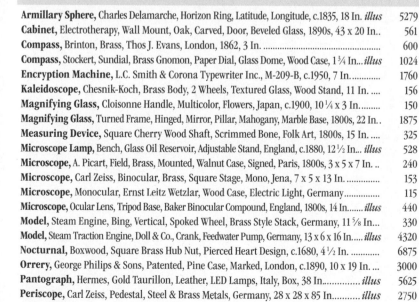

SCIENTIFIC INSTRUMENT

Scientific Instrument, Pantograph,
Hermes, Gold Taurillon, Leather, LED
Lamps, Italy, Box, 38 In.
$5,625

Clars Auction Gallery

Scientific Instrument, Periscope, Carl
Zeiss, Pedestal, Steel & Brass Metals,
Germany, 28 x 28 x 85 In.
$2,750

Morphy Auctions

Scientific Instrument, Planetarium,
Sun, 6 Planets, Mechanical, Paper Litho,
Months, Zodiac Signs, Murdock, 20 In.
$19,200

Rachel Davis Fine Arts

This is an edited listing of current
prices. Visit **Kovels.com** to check thousands of prices from previous years and
sign up for free information on trends,
tips, reproductions, marks, and more.

S

SCIENTIFIC INSTRUMENT

Scientific Instrument, Telescope, Brass, Leather Celestial, Mounted On Oak Tripod, 44 x 3 In.
$936

Thomaston Place Auction Galleries

Scientific Instrument, Telescope, Collapsible Wood & Brass, Painted, 1800s, 14 In.
$153

Charleston Estate Auctions

Scientific Instrument, Telescope, John Cuthbert, Gregorian, Star Finder, Tripod Base, Brass, England, c.1830, 18 In.
$6,686

Bonhams

Planetarium, Sun, 6 Planets, Mechanical, Paper Litho, Months, Zodiac Signs, Murdock, 20 In.. *illus*	19200
Planetarium, Trippensee, Earth & Moon, Chain & Gear Drive, Pedestal, Saginaw, 12¼ In.	288
Polyhedral Dial, 8-Sided, Paper Litho, Gnomons, Inset Compass, Turned Pedestal Base, 7 In.	1356
Spyglass, Brass, Leather, Adjustable, Stamped, Made In France, 1800s, 28¾ In.	120
Spyglass, Negretti & Zambra, Wrapped, Leather, Single Draw, Marked, London, 1894, 56½ In.	125
Telescope, A. Bardou, Refractor, Brass, Library, Tripod Base, Paris, 1800s, 39 In.	369
Telescope, Bausch & Lomb, Brass, Mahogany, Tripod Base, 59 x 48 In.	500
Telescope, Brass Tube, Hardwood, Tripod Base, 29 In.	160
Telescope, Brass, Leather Celestial, Mounted On Oak Tripod, 44 x 3 In. *illus*	936
Telescope, Brass, Oak Barrel, Sunshade, Tripod Stand, Mid 1800s, 60 x 37 In.	488
Telescope, Brass, Slender Barrel, Pivot Mount, Tripod Oak Stand, Continental, 1900s	180
Telescope, Brass, Tabletop, Tripod, 18½ x 26¼ In.	125
Telescope, Collapsible Wood & Brass, Painted, 1800s, 14 In. *illus*	153
Telescope, Dollond, Refracting, Rack, Pinion Focus, Lens Lid, Tripod Base, England, 1800s, 29 In..	792
Telescope, John Cuthbert, Gregorian, Star Finder, Tripod Base, Brass, England, c.1830, 18 In.. *illus*	6686
Telescope, Rosewood, Brass Lens, Tripod Stand, c.1830, 14 In.	1008
Telescope, Steinheil, Brass, Tripod Base, Wood Stand, Munchen, 1800s, 72 In. *illus*	1275
Telescope, Terrestrial, Brass, Wood, Leather, Tripod Stand, Dark Brown, 38 In. *illus*	427
Telescope, Unitron, 5 Lenses, Accessories, Custom Fitted Case, Folding Wood Tripod, 45½ In.	180
Telescope, Wm. Parris & Co., Desk, Brass, Marked, Tripod, England, 1800s, 18 x 38 In.	750
Tellurium, Fr. J. Berg, Globe, Orbiting Moon, Astrological Wheel, Stockholm, 1800s, 16 x 21 In.. *illus*	1725
Transit, Keuffel & Esser, Telescope, Brass Fittings, Tripod, c.1939, 8 x 12 x 9½ In.	893
Transit, Pine, Chamfered Tripod Legs, Pegged Construction, Red Paint, Early 1800s, 53 In.	780

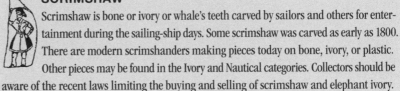

SCRIMSHAW

Scrimshaw is bone or ivory or whale's teeth carved by sailors and others for entertainment during the sailing-ship days. Some scrimshaw was carved as early as 1800. There are modern scrimshanders making pieces today on bone, ivory, or plastic. Other pieces may be found in the Ivory and Nautical categories. Collectors should be aware of the recent laws limiting the buying and selling of scrimshaw and elephant ivory.

Bodkin, Whale Ivory, Tapered Shaft, Faceted Terminal, Inlaid Dots, Mid 1800s, 6 In.	1125
Box, Bald Eagle, Rough Legged Falcon, Signed, JMC, 3½ In.	378
Box, Mahogany, Hinged Lid, Geometric Whale Ivory Inlay, Sailor Made, 1800s, 4 x 13 x 5 In.	427
Box, Salt, Whalebone, Brass, Hinged Oval Top, Carved Oak Base, c.1850, 5 x 7 x 5 In. .. *illus*	3355
Busk, Fan Design, 2 Intersecting Hearts, 2 Phases Of The Moon, Multicolor, 1800s, 12¼ In.. *illus*	4688
Busk, Geometric, Whale Hunting Scene, c.1850, 13⅝ In.	500
Busk, Whalebone, Corset, Flowers, Heart Shape Top, Mid 1800s, 13 In.	2745
Busk, Whalebone, Sailor Made, Whaling Ship, Game Board, Bicorn Hat, Early 1800s, 1 x 12 In.	497
Cribbage Board, Walrus Tusk, Carved, Holes Design, 16 In. *illus*	254
Cup, Horn, Flowers Decoration, Deep, Dated 1808, 4½ In.	800
Dipper, Rum, Coconut Cup, Whale Ivory Ring, Heart Shape Fastener, Mid 1800s, 15 In.. *illus*	2318
Ditty Box, Oval, Removable Lid, Panbone, Engraved, Patriotic Eagle, c.1850, 1¾ x 4½ In.	11875
Fid, Whalebone, 3 Sailing Vessels, Geometric Border, Mid 1800s, 9¼ In.	688
Fid, Whalebone, Round Grip, 7 Scribe Lines, c.1840, 20 x 2 In.	610
Group, Egg Shape, Elephants, Carved, Walking, Jungle, Stand, 2½ In.	120
Rattle, Whistle Handle, Carved, Brass Balls, c.1800s, 4½ In. *illus*	125
Seam Rubber, Bone, Turned Post, Cap End, Shield, Star, Heart, 4½ x 1½ In. *illus*	622
Seam Rubber, Exotic Wood, Golden Hardwood, Faceted Knop, Dated 1868, 4½ In.	406
Swift, Whalebone, Carved Clamp, Dog Head, Birds, Inlaid Onyx Heart, 1800s, 12¾ x 17 In. *illus*	2806
Swift, Whalebone, Red Banding, Cylindrical Clamp, Fitted Wood Box, Mid 1800s, 14½ In..	1375
Tusk, Engraved, Scotsman, Woman, Man With Sword, 1800s, 20½ In.	519
Tusk, Walrus, Eagle Head, Pearl Eye, Bristles Base, c.1875, 4½ In. *illus*	625
Walking Stick Top, Semi-Closed Hand, Carved, Whale's Tooth, Tropical Wood, c.1860, 36 In. .	976
Whale's Tooth, Sailing Ship, Rachel, Sailor Carved, 4¼ In. *illus*	1357
Whale's Tooth, Bull, Portrait Of Franklin, Flag, Pen, Wood Mount, Ambassador Watson, 8 In.	2106
Whale's Tooth, Hercules, Cretan Bull, Woman, Wearing Tiara, 1860s, 5¾ In.	2000
Whale's Tooth, Nantucket, 5 Boats, Cpt. H. Pease, 1800s, 6 x 1 In.	7930
Whale's Tooth, Portrait, Mother, Young Daughter, 1800s, 6¼ In.	594

Scientific Instrument, Telescope, Steinheil, Brass, Tripod Base, Wood Stand, Munchen, 1800s, 72 In.
$1,275

Bonhams

Scientific Instrument, Telescope, Terrestrial, Brass, Wood, Leather, Tripod Stand, Dark Brown, 38 In.
$427

Rafael Osona Nantucket Auctions

Scientific Instrument, Tellurium, Fr. J. Berg, Globe, Orbiting Moon, Astrological Wheel, Stockholm, 1800s, 16 x 21 In.
$1,725

Merrill's Auctions

Scrimshaw, Box, Salt, Whalebone, Brass, Hinged Oval Top, Carved Oak Base, c.1850, 5 x 7 x 5 In.
$3,355

Rafael Osona Nantucket Auctions

Scrimshaw, Busk, Fan Design, 2 Intersecting Hearts, 2 Phases Of The Moon, Multicolor, 1800s, 12 ¼ In.
$4,688

Eldred's

Scrimshaw, Cribbage Board, Walrus Tusk, Carved, Holes Design, 16 In.
$254

White's Auctions

Scrimshaw, Dipper, Rum, Coconut Cup, Whale Ivory Ring, Heart Shape Fastener, Mid 1800s, 15 In.
$2,318

Rafael Osona Nantucket Auctions

TIP
Trim shrubs near the house so they don't hide burglars trying to break in basement or first-floor windows.

Scrimshaw, Rattle, Whistle Handle, Carved, Brass Balls, c.1800s, 4 ½ In.
$125

Potter & Potter Auctions

S

Scrimshaw, Seam Rubber, Bone, Turned Post, Cap End, Shield, Star, Heart, 4 ½ x 1 ½ In.
$622

Hartzell's Auction Gallery Inc.

Scrimshaw, Swift, Whalebone, Carved Clamp, Dog Head, Birds, Inlaid Onyx Heart, 1800s, 12¾ x 17 In. $2,806

CRN Auctions

Scrimshaw, Tusk, Walrus, Eagle Head, Pearl Eye, Bristles Base, c.1875, 4½ In. $625

Eldred's

Scrimshaw, Whale's Tooth, Portrait, Woman & Dog, Wearing Dress, Multicolor, c.1830, 7 In. $1,625

Hindman

Scrimshaw, Whale's Tooth, Sailing Ship, Rachel, Sailor Carved, 4¼ In. $1,357

Stony Ridge Auction

Whale's Tooth, Portrait, Woman & Dog, Wearing Dress, Multicolor, c.1830, 7 In.......... *illus*	1625
Whale's Tooth, Sailing Ship, Shore, 2 Whales, Wave, Mountain, Palm Tree, Moon, 1900s, 5 In....	240
Whale's Tooth, Sailor, Cutlass, Wood Stand, 1800s, 6 x 4½ x 2¼ In..........................	1170
Whalebone, Inuit, Vertebrae, Sculpture, Walrus Head, Anorak Hoods, 7 x 16 x 9 In.	585

SEG, *see Paul Revere Pottery category.*

SEVRES

Sevres porcelain has been made in Sevres, France, since 1769. Many copies of the famous ware have been made. The name originally referred to the works of the Royal Porcelain factory. The name now includes any of the wares made in the town of Sevres, France. The entwined lines with a center letter used as the mark is one of the most forged marks in antiques. Be very careful to identify Sevres by quality, not just by mark.

Bowl, Birds, Tree Center, White, Sky Blue Border, Gilt Rim, 1800s, 12 In., Pair.....................	219
Bowl, Blue, Oxblood Flambe Glaze, Signed, Taxile Maximin Doat, 2¼ x 4 In. .... *illus*	520
Bowl, Flowers, Blue Ground, Gilt, Scroll Handles, Bronze Stand, 1800s, 10 In.	384
Bowl, Oval, Blue Ground, Gilt Leaves, Flowers, 1900s, 9⅝ In..........................	313
Bowl, Potpourri, Serenade Scene, Porcelain, Rococo Style 2 Handles & Base, 1900s, 13 In..	1188
Bowl, Putti, Blue Ground, Gilt, Mounted, Metal Stand, Late 1800s, 6 x 12 In.	438
Box, Hinged Lid, Couple, Blue Ground, Gilt Scrolls, Signed, Kownacki, c.1900, 3 x 8 x 5 In..*illus*	780
Box, Hinged Lid, Napoleon Scene, Marked, 2 x 3 In..........................	512
Cachepot, Flower Band, 2 Handles, c.1940, 4¾ x In., Pair..........................	484
Cachepot, Painted Bird Design, Footed, Augustus Rex, 5¾ x 5¼ In., Pair	768
Casket, Hinged Lid, 2 Woman, Lake Scene, Gilt, 1800s, 6 In.	219
Centerpiece, Napoleon III, Bronze, Bleu Celeste, Greek Key Handles, 1800s, 20 In....... *illus*	2806
Dish, Painted, Castle, Couple, Cobalt Blue Ground, Gilt, Bronze, Tripod Feet, Ovington, 4 x 6 In. ..	270
Plaque, Portrait Medallion, Napoleon, Bisque, Bertrand Andrieu, 5⅛ In. .... *illus*	862
Plate, Salad, Vines & Flowers, Musical Design, Medallions, 1800s, 8⅞ In., 12 Piece..... *illus*	1521
Urn, Cobalt Blue, Courting Scene, Gold Stencil Highlights, Matte Finish, Plinth Base, 14 x 4 In.....	225
Urn, Lid, Acorn Finial, Flowers, Blue Ground, Gilt, Painted, 1800s, 14¾ In., Pair......... *illus*	677
Urn, Lid, Blue Flambe, Gilt Bronze Base & Finial, Paul Milet, Early 1900s, 15 In., Pair. *illus*	1830
Vase, Art Nouveau, New Chevilly Paste, Alexandre Sandier, c.1900, 9 x 3½ x 2½ In. ....*illus*	4225
Vase, Irises, Silver Overlay, Footed, Signed, Sarock, Early 1900s, 9½ In........................ *illus*	1936
Vase, Lid, Gilt, Mask Handle, Painted, Wooded Landscape, J. Bailley, Late 1800s, 19 x 9 In., Pair.	3276
Vase, Maidens, Cherubs, Landscape Scene, Gilt, Bronze, Footed Base, 1900s, 13 In., Pair.....	1625
Vase, Scenic, Hand Painted, Flowers, Gilt Borders, Oval, Mid 1800s, 18¼ In........................	896

SEWER TILE

Sewer tile figures were made by workers at the sewer tile and pipe factories in the Ohio area during the late nineteenth and early twentieth centuries. Figurines, small vases, and cemetery vases were favored. Often the finished vase was a piece of the original pipe with added decorations and markings. All types of sewer tile work are now considered folk art by collectors.

Figure, Deer, Doe, Lying Down, Brown Glaze, Signed, R.L., Ohio, 1910s, 10 x 12 x 5 In. *illus*	180
Figure, Dog, Spaniel, Seated, Black Design, Orange Ground, Stamped, BCUW, 7 In.............	50
Figure, Dog, Spaniel, Seated, Mottled Brown Glaze, c.1900, 5 In.	63
Figure, Eagle, Open Wings, Head Turned, Glazed, Shaped Base, Ohio, Late 1800s, 22 In., Pair.. *illus*	2813
Figure, Foot Shape, Dark Brown Glaze, Late 1800s, 3 x 8¼ In.	688
Jardiniere, 2 Applied Handles, Claysville, Pa., Late 1800s, 21 x 22¾ In.	330
Planter, Tree Stump Shape, Grape Cluster, Ohio, Late 1800s, 9⅜ In..........................	344

SEWING

Sewing, knitting, and weaving equipment of all types is collected, from sewing birds that held the cloth to tape measures, needle books, and old wooden spools. Sewing machines are included here. Needlework pictures are listed in the Picture category.

S

Sevres, Bowl, Blue, Oxblood Flambe Glaze, Signed, Taxile Maximin Doat, 2 ¼ x 4 In.
$520

Toomey & Co. Auctioneers

Sevres, Box, Hinged Lid, Couple, Blue Ground, Gilt Scrolls, Signed, Kownacki, c.1900, 3 x 8 x 5 In.
$780

Treasureseeker Auctions

Sevres, Centerpiece, Napoleon III, Bronze, Bleu Celeste, Greek Key Handles, 1800s, 20 In.
$2,806

Neal Auction Company

Sevres, Plaque, Portrait Medallion, Napoleon, Bisque, Bertrand Andrieu, 5 ⅛ In.
$862

Neal Auction Company

Sevres, Plate, Salad, Vines & Flowers, Musical Design, Medallions, 1800s, 8 ⅞ In., 12 Piece
$1,521

Thomaston Place Auction Galleries

> **TIP**
> *Early plates often have no rim on the bottom.*

Sevres, Urn, Lid, Acorn Finial, Flowers, Blue Ground, Gilt, Painted, 1800s, 14 ¾ In., Pair
$677

Brunk Auctions

Sevres, Urn, Lid, Blue Flambe, Gilt Bronze Base & Finial, Paul Milet, Early 1900s, 15 In., Pair
$1,830

Neal Auction Company

Sevres, Vase, Art Nouveau, New Chevilly Paste, Alexandre Sandier, c.1900, 9 x 3 ½ x 2 ½ In.
$4,225

Toomey & Co. Auctioneers

S

> **TIP**
> *Doors from a garage should have inside locks. Get a strong door. We know someone who came home to find a burglar had used an axe to "open" the door.*

Sevres, Vase, Irises, Silver Overlay, Footed, Signed, Sarock, Early 1900s, 9 ½ In.
$1,936

Fontaine's Auction Gallery

Sewer Tile, Figure, Deer, Doe, Lying Down, Brown Glaze, Signed, R.L., Ohio, 1910s, 10 x 12 x 5 In.
$180

Crocker Farm, Inc.

Sewer Tile, Figure, Eagle, Open Wings, Head Turned, Glazed, Shaped Base, Ohio, Late 1800s, 22 In., Pair
$2,813

Hindman

Basket, Woven Splint, Painted, Bentwood Loop Handles, Southern Appalachian, c.1915, 8 ¼ In. . . *illus*	4418
Basket, Woven, Straw, Handle, 3 Slats, Curved, 25 x 15 ½ In.	63
Bird, Cast Fire Gilt, Brass, Pincushion Top, 1850s, 7 In. . . *illus*	168
Box, Hinged Lid, Mother-Of-Pearl, Carved, Silver Needle Case, Compartments, 4 x 2 x 2 In. . . *illus*	1220
Box, Lacquer, 2 Hinged Cabana Shape Lid, River Landscape, Japan, 11 x 13 x 12 In.	275
Box, Pagoda Lid, Mother-Of-Pearl Inlay, Tortoiseshell, William IV, 1800s, 6 x 10 x 8 In.	3840
Cabinet, Walnut, 8-Sided, 8 Spool Holders, Drawers In Base, Inset Shields, Victorian, 10 x 9 In. *illus*	352
Cabinet, Spool, see also the Advertising category under Cabinet, Spool.	
Caddy, Mahogany, Pincushion Top, Turned Column, Spool Racks, 3 Drawers, c.1870, 16 x 7 In.	595
Caddy, Mahogany, Pine, Multicolor Pincushion, Spool Holders, Late 1800s, 8 ½ x 7 ¾ In.	100
Caddy, Mahogany, Tiger Maple, Hatpin Spool Holders, Dovetailed Case, Drawer, Mid 1800s, 7 x 5 In.	132
Caddy, Peaseware, Urn Finial, 3 Parts, Wrought Iron, Ohio, 1850s, 9 In. . . *illus*	192
Caddy, Thread, Circular 3 Tiers, 8 Ivory, 8 Spool Legs, 4 Ball Feet, c.1850, 7 x 4 In.	1220
Chest, Hinged Lid, Rosewood, Lacquered Wood, Upholstered, c.1960, 15 x 27 x 16 In. . . *illus*	1560
Chest, Mahogany & Pine, Dovetailed, 5 Drawers, Pincushion Top, Mid 1800s, 13 x 15 ¼ In.	218
Clamp, Maple, Chip Carved, Punched Hex Symbols, Double Stepped Riser, Etched, 1837, 5 x 8 In.	267
Clamp, Metal, Butterfly Figure, Pincushion, 4 x 3 x 2 In.	625
Kit, Figural, Round Hut, Thatched Roof, Napoleonic Bees, Basket, Marble Base, France, 5 ¼ In. . . *illus*	576
Machine, Singer, No. AL-392829, Featherweight, Black, Foot Pedal, Electric. . . *illus*	339
Machine, Willcox & Gibbs, Black Paint, Wood Base, Late 1800s, 10 x 12 x 8 In.	188
Machine, Willcox & Gibbs, Oak Case, Cast Iron, Treadle Base, 1900s, 39 x 28 x 16 In.	96
Pincushion Dolls are listed in their own category.	
Pincushion, Beadwork, Flowers, Crown, Dirty White Ground, 1800s, 6 x 8 In.	252
Sock Darner, Rouge Flambe, Glossy Handle, 1900s, 7 ⅜ In.	185
Spool Cabinets are listed here or in the Advertising category under Cabinet, Spool.	
Spool Holder, Strawberry Pincushions, 4 Tiers, Spool Column, Pewter Head Spindles, 12 In. *illus*	288
Spool Holder, Walnut, Bird Finial, 3 Graduated Tiers, Caroline, Oh., Mid 1800s, 12 x 9 In.	244
Spool Rack, 5 Rods, Shaped Sides, Turned Feet, Regency, Early 1800s, 12 ½ In. . . *illus*	640
Stringholder, Sewing Machine, Winder, Cast Iron, E.G. Zimmerman, 6 x 7 ½ x 5 In.	147
Swift, Tiger Maple, On Stand, Pennsylvania, 1800s, 19 In.	113
Tape Loom, Standing, Pegged To The Post, Cross Base, 1700s, 32 In.	1250
Tape Measure, Abbott's Ice Cream, Woman Carrying Tray, Celluloid, Round, ½ x 1 ¾ In.	120
Thread Holder, Walnut, Stepped, Mirror, 2 Pincushions, Stand, Victorian, 13 x 12 x 8 In. . . *illus*	128
Winder, 2 Spools, T-Shape Base, Pointed, Brown, 1800s, 49 In.	438
Yarn Winder, Wood, Red Painted, 1800s, 43 In.	139
Yarn Winder, Wood, Tabletop, Hand Crank, Painted, 1800s, 24 x 17 In.	861

SHAKER

Shaker items are characterized by simplicity, functionalism, and orderliness. There were many Shaker communities in America from the eighteenth century to the present day. The religious order made furniture, small wooden pieces, and packaged medicines, herbs, and jellies to sell to "outsiders." Other useful objects were made for use by members of the community. Shaker furniture is listed in this book in the Furniture category.

Basket, 4-Finger, Maple, Ash, Pine, Yellow Paint, Copper Tacks, Handle, c.1890, 7 x 11 In.	1125
Box, Lid, Oval, Bentwood, Gothic Fingers, Copper Tacks, 1850s, 2 x 5 ½ In. . . *illus*	420
Box, Sewing, 4-Finger, Lid, Painted, Oval, Bail Handle, 7 x 5 x 2 In.	127
Carrier, Berry Basket, Painted Pine, Old Blue Surface, 1900s, 11 x 20 In.	340
Churn, Painted, Wood, Orange Surface, 1800s, 41 ½ In. . . *illus*	615
Dust Pan, Tin, Painted, Yellow Ground, Contemporary, 15 x 12 In.	151
Pantry Box, Lid, Gothic Arch Fingers, Copper Tacks, 1850s, 4 x 11 In.	420

SHAVING MUG

Shaving mugs were popular from 1860 to 1900. Many types were made, including occupational mugs featuring pictures of men's jobs. There were scuttle mugs, silver-plated mugs, glass-lined mugs, and others.

Holly & Berry, 8-Sided, Footed, Bavaria, c.1900, 3 ⅝ In.	122
Jasperware, Barbershop Scenes, Schafer & Vater, 3 In.	189

Sewing, Basket, Woven Splint, Painted, Bentwood Loop Handles, Southern Appalachian, c.1915, 8 ¼ In.
$4,418

Jeffrey S. Evans & Associates

Sewing, Bird, Cast Fire Gilt, Brass, Pincushion Top, 1850s, 7 In.
$168

Garth's Auctioneers & Appraisers

Sewing, Box, Hinged Lid, Mother-Of-Pearl, Carved, Silver Needle Case, Compartments, 4 x 2 x 2 In.
$1,220

Rafael Osona Nantucket Auctions

Sewing, Cabinet, Walnut, 8-Sided, 8 Spool Holders, Drawers In Base, Inset Shields, Victorian, 10 x 9 In.
$352

Rachel Davis Fine Arts

Sewing, Caddy, Peaseware, Urn Finial, 3 Parts, Wrought Iron, Ohio, 1850s, 9 In.
$192

Garth's Auctioneers & Appraisers

Sewing, Chest, Hinged Lid, Rosewood, Lacquered Wood, Upholstered, c.1960, 15 x 27 x 16 In.
$1,560

Wright

Sewing, Kit, Figural, Round Hut, Thatched Roof, Napoleonic Bees, Basket, Marble Base, France, 5 ¼ In.
$576

Rachel Davis Fine Arts

Sewing, Machine, Singer, No. AL-392829, Featherweight, Black, Foot Pedal, Electric
$339

Apple Tree Auction Center

Sewing, Spool Holder, Strawberry Pincushions, 4 Tiers, Spool Column, Pewter Head Spindles, 12 In.
$288

Rachel Davis Fine Arts

S

Sewing, Spool Rack, 5 Rods, Shaped Sides, Turned Feet, Regency, Early 1800s, 12 ½ In. $640

Neal Auction Company

Sewing, Thread Holder, Walnut, Stepped, Mirror, 2 Pincushions, Stand, Victorian, 13 x 12 x 8 In. $128

Rachel Davis Fine Arts

Shaker, Box, Lid, Oval, Bentwood, Gothic Fingers, Copper Tacks, 1850s, 2 x 5 ½ In. $420

Garth's Auctioneers & Appraisers

TIP
A two-finger Shaker box really has three. Two are on the bottom; one is on the lid.

TIP
Your collectibles will live best at the temperature and humidity that is comfortable for you. Not too hot, cold, wet, or dry.

Shaker, Churn, Painted, Wood, Orange Surface, 1800s, 41 ½ In. $615

Pook & Pook

Shaving Mug, Odd Fellows, 3 Chain Links Over Eye, Personalized, Gilt, Austria, c.1900, 3 ½ In. $63

Potter & Potter Auctions

Shearwater, Bowl, Sea Foam, Green Glaze, Molded Rim, 3 ¼ In. $475

Neal Auction Company

Shearwater, Figurine, Horse, Standing, Alkaline Blue Glaze, Peter Anderson, c.1940, 12 In. $3,416

Neal Auction Company

Shearwater, Vase, Woman, Bird, Flowers, Sun, Molded Rim, Patricia Anderson Findeisen, 2004, 9 In. $512

Neal Auction Company

Mr. & Mrs. Garfield, Ivy Sprays, Laurel Leaves, Ring Handle, Opaque White, 2¾ x 3¼ x 5 In.	187
Occupational, Engineer, Train, C.C. McKinley, 3⅜ In.	75
Occupational, Ice Man, Horse Drawn Wagon, John Hudson Moore Co., 3¾ In.	45
Occupational, Woodworker Design, Cabinetmaker, Ring Handle	450
Odd Fellows, 3 Chain Links Over Eye, Personalized, Gilt, Austria, c.1900, 3½ In. .... *illus*	63
Yellow Rose, Red Center, Leaves, Vines, Loop Handle, Gilt Rim, Germany, 4 In.	225

SHAWNEE POTTERY

Shawnee Pottery was started in Zanesville, Ohio, in 1937. The company made vases, novelty ware, flowerpots, planters, lamps, and cookie jars. Three dinnerware lines were made: Corn, Lobster Ware, and Valencia (a solid color line). White Corn pattern utility pieces were made in 1945. Corn King was made from 1946 to 1954; Corn Queen, with darker green leaves and lighter colored corn, from 1954 to 1961. Shawnee produced pottery for George Rumrill during the late 1930s. The company closed in 1961.

Cookie Jar, Corn King, 10 In.	52
Planter, Fish, Green, Open Mouth, 3½ x 4½ In.	26

SHEARWATER POTTERY

Shearwater Pottery is a family business started in 1928 by Peter Anderson, with the help of his parents, Mr. and Mrs. G.W. Anderson Sr. The local Ocean Springs, Mississippi, clays were used to make the wares in the 1930s. The company was damaged by Hurricane Katrina in 2005 but was rebuilt and is still in business, now owned by Peter's four children.

Bowl, Sea Foam, Green Glaze, Molded Rim, 3¼ In. *illus*	475
Candlestick, Horse, Sitting, Antique Green Glaze, Peter Anderson, c.1940, 8¾ In.	768
Figurine, Duck, Long Neck, Green Glaze, c.1935, 5¾ In.	384
Figurine, Horse, Standing, Alkaline Blue Glaze, Peter Anderson, c.1940, 12 In. *illus*	3416
Figurine, Sea Gull, Stylized, Brown Glaze, 2-Tone, Walter Inglis Anderson, c.1945, 5¾ In.	610
Plate, Nude Female & Fish, Patricia Anderson Findeisen, 2004, 10¾ In.	244
Sculpture, Bust Of Allison, Double-Blue Glaze, Walter Inglis Anderson, c.1935, 9 In.	366
Vase, Duck, Blue Green Glaze, Walter Inglis Anderson, 1930, 7⅛ In.	2048
Vase, Geometric, Rectangular, Triple Glaze, Brown, Walter Inglis Anderson, c.1940, 4 x 2¾ In.	2304
Vase, Woman, Bird, Flowers, Sun, Molded Rim, Patricia Anderson Findeisen, 2004, 9 In. *illus*	512

SHEET MUSIC

Sheet music from the past centuries is now collected. The favorites are examples with covers featuring artistic or historic pictures. Early sheet music covers were lithographed, but by the 1900s photographic reproductions were used. The early sheet music pages were larger than more recent sheets, and you must watch out for examples that were trimmed to fit in a twentieth-century piano bench and should be lower priced.

Bonanza Theme, Actor Portraits, Henry Mancini, 1959, 12 x 9 In.	27
Herman's Hermits On Tour, I'm Henry VIII, Fred Murray & R.P. Weston, 1965	12
I Know What It Means To Be Lonesome, Woman, Kendis, Brockman & Vincent, 11 x 8 In. *illus*	10
Love Story, Carl Sigman, Francis Lai, 1971	9
My Love, Paul McCartney & Linda McCartney, 1973	17
Phonograph, Blue Cover, Woman With Record, Charles D. Blake, Frame, 1878, 17½ x 13½ In. *illus*	84
The Big Red Motor & The Little Blue Limousine, Jerome H. Remick & Co., Detroit, Mich.	13
When Johnny Comes Marching Home, Stars, Civil War, Louis Lambert, 1863, 13 x 10 In. *illus*	500
Where The Black-Eyed Susans Grow, Al Jolson, 13 x 10 In.	25
Yes We Have No Bananas, Frank Silver & Irving Cohn, c.1923, 12 x 9 In.	8

SHEFFIELD *items are listed in the Silver Plate and Silver-English categories.*

Sheet Music, I Know What It Means To Be Lonesome, Woman, Kendis, Brockman & Vincent, 11 x 8 In.
$10

Ruby Lane

Sheet Music, Phonograph, Blue Cover, Woman With Record, Charles D. Blake, Frame, 1878, 17½ x 13½ In.
$84

Donley Auctions

Sheet Music, When Johnny Comes Marching Home, Stars, Civil War, Louis Lambert, 1863, 13 x 10 In.
$500

Early American History Auctions

S

Shelley, Cup & Saucer, Pole Star, Blue Interior, Lobed, Scalloped Saucer, Bone China, 3 x 5 ½ In.
$32

Lion and Unicorn

Shirley Temple, Doll, Baby, Mohair Wig, Glass Flirty Eyes, Cloth Body, Composition Arms & Legs, 22 In.
$554

Apple Tree Auction Center

TIP
Don't keep identifi-cation on your key ring. If it is lost, it's an invitation for burglars to visit.

Silver Deposit, Jug, Lid, Handle, Lilies, Green, Sterling Silver Overlay, Art Nouveau, 1900s, 8 x 4 ¼ In.
$875

Treadway

S

 ## SHELLEY

Shelley first appeared on English ceramics about 1912. The Foley China Works started in England in 1860. Joseph Ball Shelley joined the company in 1862 and became a partner in 1872. Percy Shelley joined the firm in 1881. The company went through a series of name changes and in 1910 the then Foley China Company became Shelley China. In 1929 it became Shelley Potteries. The company was acquired in 1966 by Allied English Potteries, then merged with the Doulton group in 1971. Shelley is no longer being made. Trio is the name for a cup, saucer, and cake plate set.

Cup & Saucer, Pole Star, Blue Interior, Lobed, Scalloped Saucer, Bone China, 3 x 5 ½ In. *illus*	32
Cup & Saucer, Primrose, Chintz, Cobalt Blue, Yellow Flowered Interior, Gilt, 3 x 6 In.	38
Cup & Saucer, Rosebud, Pink Roses, Blue Flowers, Green Trim & Handle, 2 ¼ x 5 ½ In.	25

 ## SHIRLEY TEMPLE

Shirley Temple, the famous movie star, was born in 1928. She made her first movie in 1932. She died in 2014. Thousands of items picturing Shirley have been and still are being made. Shirley Temple dolls were first made in 1934 by Ideal Toy Company. Millions of Shirley Temple cobalt blue glass dishes were made by Hazel Atlas Glass Company and U.S. Glass Company from 1934 to 1942. They were given away as premiums for Wheaties and Bisquick. A bowl, mug, and pitcher were made as a breakfast set. Some pieces were decorated with the picture of a very young Shirley, others used a picture of Shirley in her 1936 Captain January costume. Although collectors refer to a cobalt creamer, it is actually the 4 ½-inch-high milk pitcher from the breakfast set. Many of these items have been reproduced and are being sold today.

Doll, Baby, Mohair Wig, Glass Flirty Eyes, Cloth Body, Composition Arms & Legs, 22 In. *illus*	554
Doll, Vinyl, Red Dress, Apron, Red Shoes, Sleep Eyes, Ideal, 1959, 15 In.	99
Playing Cards, USPC, United States Playing Card Co., c.1935	35
Sheet Music, Rebecca Of Sunnybrook Farm, Toy Trumpet, 1938, 9 x 12 In.	27
Token, Shirley Temple's Storybook, Plastic, Goldtone, Nov. 12, 1958, 1 ¼ In.	18
Trunk, Brass Hinge, Drawer, Portrait, Our Little Girl, 1930s, 16 In.	225

SHRINER, *see Fraternal category.*

 ## SILVER DEPOSIT

Silver deposit glass was first made during the late nineteenth century. Solid sterling silver is applied to the glass by a chemical method so that a cutout design of silver metal appears against a clear or colored glass. It is not the same as silver overlay, which is thin designs of sheet metal applied over glass or ceramics.

Jar, Glass Urn Shape, Decanter, Ribbed Body, Flower, 4 Panels, Continental, 1900s, 8 In.	48
Jug, Lid, Handle, Lilies, Green, Sterling Silver Overlay, Art Nouveau, 1900s, 8 x 4 ¼ In. *illus*	875

SILVER FLATWARE

Silver flatware includes many of the current and out-of-production sterling silver and silver-plated flatware patterns made in the past 125 years. Other silver is listed under Silver-American, Silver-English, etc. Most silver flatware sets that are missing a few pieces can be completed through the help of a silver matching service. Three U.S. silver company marks are shown here.

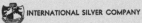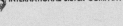 

International Silver Co.
1928+

Reed & Barton
c.1915+

Wallace Silversmiths, Inc.
1871–1956

Silver Flatware Plated, Berwick, Serving Spoon, Wm. Rogers, 1904, 11 In.
$13

Lion and Unicorn

Silver Flatware Plated, Cluny, Asparagus Server, Pierced, Christofle, 9 ¼ In.
$62

Kodner Galleries, Inc.

Silver Flatware Plated, Louis, Serving Set, Knife, Spoon, Velvet Lined Box, Lee & Wigfull
$39

Nye & Company

Silver Flatware Plated, Pearl, Nut Pick, Art Nouveau, Reed & Barton, Wood Box, c.1898, 4 ⅞ In., 8 Piece
$154

Charleston Estate Auctions

Silver Flatware Sterling, Love Disarmed, Macaroni Server, Reed & Barton, 11 ½ In.
$768

Alex Cooper Auctioneers

Silver Flatware Sterling, Phoebe, Almond Scoop, Repousse, Nude On Handle, Pierced Bowl, Cherub, 6 In.
$307

Charleston Estate Auctions

Silver Flatware Sterling, Server, Dutch Style & Motifs, Openwork Blade, Tavern Scene Handle, Figural Neck, 10 In.
$120

Richard Opfer Auctioneering, Inc.

S

Silver Flatware Sterling, Shell & Thread, Victorian, Fish Slice, William Eaton, London, 1840, 12½ In.
$156

Eldred's

Silver Flatware Sterling, St. Cloud, Tablespoon, Gorham, 7⅞ In., Pair
$168

Leland Little Auctions

Silver Plate, Biscuit Jar, Swan, Pelican Mark, Thomas Wilkinson, England, c.1850, 8 x 6½ In.
$270

Selkirk Auctioneers & Appraisers

SILVER FLATWARE PLATED

Berwick, Serving Spoon, Wm. Rogers, 1904, 11 In.	*illus*	13
Cluny, Asparagus Server, Pierced, Christofle, 9¼ In.	*illus*	62
Louis, Serving Set, Knife, Spoon, Velvet Lined Box, Lee & Wigfull	*illus*	39
Pearl, Nut Pick, Art Nouveau, Reed & Barton, Wood Box, c.1898, 4⅞ In., 8 Piece	*illus*	154

SILVER FLATWARE STERLING

Chrysanthemum, Salad Server, Gold Wash, White & Green Enamel, Durgin, 1800s, 9 In.		500
Francis I, Serving Utensil, Repousse, Flowers Handle, Curved Bowl, Reed & Barton, 8 In.		38
Louis XV, Cocktail Fork, Shaped Handle, Monogram, Whiting, 5½ In., 12 Piece		240
Love Disarmed, Macaroni Server, Reed & Barton, 11½ In.	*illus*	768
Phoebe, Almond Scoop, Repousse, Nude On Handle, Pierced Bowl, Cherub, 6 In.	*illus*	307
Punch Ladle, Flowers, Thin Handle, Wavy Cup, Gorham, c.1905, 12 x 4 In.		366
Repousse, Tablespoon, Flowers Handle, Monogram, D.B.L., Kirk, 6½ In., 8 Piece		360
Rose, Butter Knife, Repousse, Flowers Handle, Shaped Blade, Monogram, Stieff, 5 In., 11 Piece		192
Rose, Ice Cream Fork, Repousse, Floral, Monogram, Stieff, 5¾ In., 10 Piece		216
Server, Dutch Style & Motifs, Openwork Blade, Tavern Scene Handle, Figural Neck, 10 In.	*illus*	120
Shell & Thread, Victorian, Fish Slice, William Eaton, London, 1840, 12½ In.	*illus*	156
Sovereign, Fish Serving Set, 2-Tine Fork, Oblong Spoon, Gorham 10½ In.		175
St. Cloud, Tablespoon, Gorham, 7⅞ In., Pair	*illus*	168
Stieff Rose, Berry Spoon, Shaped Bowl, Embossed Fruit, Flowers Handle, Kirk, 9 In.		270

SILVER PLATE

Silver plate is not solid silver. It is a ware made of a metal, such as nickel or copper, that is covered with a thin coating of silver. The letters *EPNS* are often found on American and English silver-plated wares. *Sheffield* is a term with two meanings. Sometimes it refers to sterling silver made in the town of Sheffield, England. Sometimes it refers to an old form of plated silver made in England. Here are marks of three U.S. silver plate manufacturers.

Barbour Silver Co.	J.W. Tufts	Meriden Silver Plate Co.
1892–1931	1875–c.1915	1869–1898

Biscuit Jar, Swan, Pelican Mark, Thomas Wilkinson, England, c.1850, 8 x 6½ In.	*illus*	270
Bowl, Figural Handles, Flowers, Footed, 12 In.		250
Bowl, Leaf Shape, Applied Snails, Gabriella Crespi, Italy, c.1970, 4 x 13 x 9 In.	*illus*	1440
Bowl, Vegetable, Lid, Shaped Handle, Potter, Sheffield, 11 x 8 x 6 In., Pair		53
Box, Enamel, Velvet Lined, Removable Lid, Reed & Barton, 2 x 6 x 5 In.		63
Bun Warmer, Lid, Revolving, Flower, Embossed, Ram's Head Legs, Hoof Feet, 10 x 8 x 7 In.	*illus*	153
Bun Warmer, Revolving Lid, Removable Liner, Openwork Legs, Late 1800s, 9 x 14 In.	*illus*	132
Cake Stand, Bride's, Gadroon, Signed, Scotch Bakery, Victorian, 7 x 14½ In.		920
Candleholder, Hurricane Shade, Rosewood Base, Puiforcat, Late 1900s, 9 x 6 In., Pair		1000
Centerpiece, Art Nouveau, 2 Women, Handles, Glass Insert, WMF, Early 1900s, 6 x 20 x 11 In.	*illus*	545
Centerpiece, Boat Shape, Cherub, Eagle, Shells, Footed Base, Worn Patina, 13 x 12½ In.		207
Centerpiece, Brass, Footed, Ward Bennett, c.1970, 9 x 13 In.		1875
Champagne Bucket, Turned Hardwood, Pedestal Stand, Royal Castle, Sheffield, 22¾ In.		813
Citrus Press, Curved Arm Support, Wood, Mounted, Marble Base, 12½ In.	*illus*	250
Cocktail Shaker, Fire Extinguisher Shape, 10 In.		281
Cocktail Shaker, Lighthouse Shape, Marked, Late 1900s, 14 In.		406
Cocktail Shaker, Lighthouse Shape, Solar Valve, Gallery, Windows, 14½ In.	*illus*	438
Coffee Urn, Dome Lid, Lion & Ring Handles, Square Base, Ball Feet, England, c.1800, 13 In.	*illus*	344
Coffeepot, Dome Lid, Octagonal, Wood Handle, Footed, Argentina, 1800s, 7¾ In.	*illus*	188
Coffeepot, Dome Lid, Wood Handle, Matthew Boulton, Birmingham, George III, Late 1700s, 7¾ In.		281
Coffeepot, Lid, Cream Handle, Britannia, Nathaniel Lock, London, George I, 1716, 10½ In.		5000
Cornucopia, Horn, Mounted, Bicycle Racer, Continental, Early 1900s, 19½ In.		500

S

Silver Plate, Bowl, Leaf Shape, Applied Snails, Gabriella Crespi, Italy, c.1970, 4 x 13 x 9 In.
$1,440

Abington Auction Gallery

Silver Plate, Bun Warmer, Lid, Revolving, Flower, Embossed, Ram's Head Legs, Hoof Feet, 10 x 8 x 7 In.
$153

Bunch Auctions

Silver Plate, Bun Warmer, Revolving Lid, Removable Liner, Openwork Legs, Late 1800s, 9 x 14 In.
$132

Garth's Auctioneers & Appraisers

Silver Plate, Centerpiece, Art Nouveau, 2 Women, Handles, Glass Insert, WMF, Early 1900s, 6 x 20 x 11 In.
$545

Fontaine's Auction Gallery

Silver Plate, Citrus Press, Curved Arm Support, Wood, Mounted, Marble Base, 12½ In.
$250

Neal Auction Company

Silver Plate, Cocktail Shaker, Lighthouse Shape, Solar Valve, Gallery, Windows, 14½ In.
$438

Eldred's

Silver Plate, Coffee Urn, Dome Lid, Lion & Ring Handles, Square Base, Ball Feet, England, c.1800, 13 In.
$344

Hindman

Silver Plate, Coffeepot, Dome Lid, Octagonal, Wood Handle, Footed, Argentina, 1800s, 7¾ In.
$188

Hindman

Silver Plate, Decanter Set, Vase Form, Cut Glass, Flowers, Figural Cherub, Germany, c.1890s, 11 In.
$450

Selkirk Auctioneers & Appraisers

Silver Plate, Epergne, 3-Light, Scroll Arms, Openwork Socles, Tripod Feet, c.1830, 17 In.
$219

Hindman

S

SILVER PLATE

Silver Plate, Kettle, Lid, Flower Finial, Spigot & Burner Base, Stand, 18 x 11 In.
$128

Silver Plate, Samovar, Persian Style, Teapot, Receptacle & Tray, 12 In.
$300

Silver Plate, Tureen, Dog Chasing Rabbit, Gadroon Border, Elkington, Mid 1800s, 11 ¼ x 17 x 10 ½ In.
$441

Brunk Auctions

Silver Plate, Wine Coaster, Grapevine Shape, Wooden Bottom, Marked S, England, 1800s, 3 ¼ x 6 ¾ In.
$847

Roland NY Auctioneers & Appraisers

Treasureseeker Auctions

Ahlers & Ogletree Auction Gallery

Silver Plate, Lid, Dome, Snake Finial, Burwash & Sibley, London, George III, 1810, 6 x 9 In.
$1,125

Silver Plate, Sugar Shaker, Figural, Mouse, Standing, Victorian, 1800s, 2 ½ In., Pair
$425

Silver Plate, Wine Cooler, 2 Handles, Sheffield, 1761, 9 ½ In.
$480

Hindman

Leland Little Auctions

Nadeau's Auction Gallery

Silver Plate, Platter, Dome Lid, Melon Finial, Sheffield, Venison, A.B. Savory & Sons, London, 10 In.
$549

Silver Plate, Tray, Oval, Loop Handles, Grapevine Border & Feet, 31 ⅝ In.
$200

Neal Auction Company

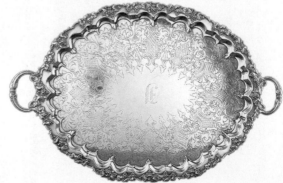

Neal Auction Company

S

Cover, Meat, Rope Twist Handle & Borders, Scroll Feet, England, 1800s, 15 ½ x 25 ⅜ In......	1024
Decanter Set, Vase Form, Cut Glass, Flowers, Figural Cherub, Germany, c.1890s, 11 In.*illus*	450
Epergne, Clear Pattern Glass Bowl & Lily, On Stand, 10 x 9 In.	80
Epergne, 3-Light, Scroll Arms, Openwork Socles, Tripod Feet, c.1830, 17 In................*illus*	219
Epergne, Cast Leaves & Fruit, 4 Removable Candle Arms, Sheffield, Mid 1800s, 22 x 14 In..	330
Figurine, Ostrich, Brass, Murano Glass Egg Body, Gabriella Crespi, Italy, c. 1970, 18 x 6 x 9 In.	3000
Hot Water Urn, Dolphin Spout, Acanthus Feet, Sheffield, England, 1830s, 21 ¾ In.	545
Hot Water Urn, Lid, 2 Handles, Spigot, Square Base, Ball Feet, England, c.1800, 20 ¼ x 13 In. .	375
Kettle, Lid, Flower Finial, Spigot & Burner Base, Stand, 18 x 11 In..............................*illus*	128
Lid, Dome, Ring Finial, Plated, Gadroon Rim, Engraved, Lion, Sheffield, 1800s, 10 x 16 In........	406
Lid, Dome, Snake Finial, Burwash & Sibley, London, George III, 1810, 6 x 9 In. ....*illus*	1125
Nut Dish, Vertigo Pattern, 3 Sections, Wavy Ring Handle, Christofle, France, 4 x 9 In.........	345
Plateau, Mirrored, Gadroon Border, Paw Feet, George III, c.1800, 50 ½ x 16 x 2 In.	2016
Platter, Dome Lid, Melon Finial, Sheffield, Venison, A.B. Savory & Sons, London, 10 In.*illus*	549
Platter, Dome Lid, Shell, William Hutton & Sons, Sheffield, c.1900s, 13 x 18 x 15 In.	625
Platter, Meat, Well, Sheffield, Egg & Dart Border, Scroll Feet, James Dixon & Sons, 21 x 16 In. ..	366
Platter, Shallow Center, Square Rim, Christofle, 1900s, 11 ⅞ In., 10 Piece	1750
Salver, Round, 3 Stars & Birds, Oval, Tripod Feet, Sheffield, 12 ½ x 16 In.	88
Samovar, Flowers, Leaves, Chased, Late 1800s, 31 In.	210
Samovar, Persian Style, Teapot, Receptacle & Tray, 12 In. ....*illus*	300
Spoon, Souvenir, see Souvenir category.	
Steak Knife, Albi Pattern, Blades Marked Christofle, France, 9 ¼ In., 12 Piece	530
Sugar Shaker, Figural, Mouse, Standing, Victorian, 1800s, 2 ½ In., Pair....................*illus*	425
Tea Urn, Lid, Shell Finial, 2 Handles, Spigot, Splayed Legs, Ball Feet, 1800s, 16 ½ In.	469
Tray, Buttercup, Cutout Handles, Raised Flowers, Gorham, 1930s, 1 x 22 ¼ x 16 In.	151
Tray, Dome Lid, Beaded Trim, Loop Handle, Christofle, France, 1800s, 7 ½ x 10 In.............	315
Tray, Flowers, Leafy Scroll, Reticulated Border, 2 Handles, Footed, 28 x 17 In.	88
Tray, Oval, Loop Handles, Grapevine Border & Feet, 31 ⅝ In. ....*illus*	200
Tray, Rosewood, Curved Side, Puiforcat, 1900s, 12 ¾ In...	375
Tray, Serving, Old Sheffield, Armorial, Footed, Oval, Paw Feet, 1800s, 22 ½ In.......................	545
Tray, Serving, Oval, Reeded Border, Tinned Back, Footed, Georgian, Sheffield, 1700s, 20 ⅛ In..	366
Tureen, Dog Chasing Rabbit, Gadroon Border, Elkington, Mid 1800s, 11 ¼ x 17 x 10 ½ In..*illus*	441
Tureen, Flower Strap, Leaf Bands, Engraved Heraldic Device, England, 1800s, 12 x 14 x 8 In....	531
Tureen, Soup, Acorn & Oak Leaves, Scroll Feet, Rolled Edges, Sheffield, 1800s, 11 ⅜ In.	640
Tureen, Soup, Bead & Scroll, Lobed Body, Acanthus, Classical, 12 x 15 x 9 In.	188
Vase, 2 Handles, Footed Base, Meriden Silver Co., 8 ½ x 6 ¾ In.	31
Vase, Bud, Winged Streamliner Zephyr Logo, Signed, 6 ¾ In.......................................	3776
Waiter, Rococo Border, Grapevine, Flowers, 2 Handles, Bun Feet, 1900s, 2 x 32 x 19 In........	375
Wine Coaster, Circular Gadroon Shape, Mahogany Base, Sheffield, c.1810, 5 ¾ In., Pair...........	142
Wine Coaster, Grapevine Shape, Wooden Bottom, Marked S, England, 1800s, 3 ¼ x 6 ¾ In...*illus*	847
Wine Coaster, Scroll Border, Rolled Edge, Turned Wood Base, Sheffield, 1800s, 2 x 7 In., 4 Piece	384
Wine Cooler, 2 Handles, Sheffield, 1761, 9 ½ In...*illus*	480
Wine Cooler, Armorial, Alte Volat, Sheffield, England, Regency, 1900s, 10 x 7 ½ In., Pair ...	1573
Wine Cooler, Bucket Shape, Stirrup Handles, Christofle, 1900s, 11 In...............................	406
Wine Cooler, Classic Campana Form, Shell Rim, Family Crest, Early 1800s, 9 x 9 In., Pair	561
Wine Cooler, Stag's Head Handles, Removable Liner, Royal Castle, Sheffield, 10 ½ In., Pair..*illus*	1408

SILVER-AMERICAN

American silver is listed here. Coin and sterling silver are included. Most of the sterling silver listed in this book is subdivided by country. There are also other pieces of silver and silver plate listed under special categories, such as Candelabrum, Napkin Ring, Silver Flatware, Silver Plate, Silver-Sterling, and Tiffany Silver. The meltdown price determines the value of solid silver items. Coin silver sells for less than sterling silver.

Gorham & Co.	INTERNATIONAL SILVER CO.	Reed & Barton Co.
1865+	International Silver Co.	1824–2015
	1898–present	

TIP
Do not have old monograms removed from silver. It lowers the value. If it bothers you to have an old initial, don't buy the piece. We like to tell people it belonged to a great aunt with that initial.

Silver Plate, Wine Cooler, Stag's Head Handles, Removable Liner, Royal Castle, Sheffield, 10 ½ In., Pair
$1,408

Neal Auction Company

Silver-American, Beaker, Round Rim, Repousse, Follies, Garden Scene, Floral Sprays, Coin, 1800s, 3 ½ In.
$313

Hindman

Silver-American, Bowl, Art Deco, Monogram, Footed, Gorham, 11 x 11 x 3 In.
$248

Charleston Estate Auctions

Silver-American, Bowl, Brass Flower Frog Lid, Pierced, Clarence A. Vanderbilt, N.Y., Late 1800s, 6 x 11 In.
$313

Hindman

Silver-American, Bowl, Central Flower, Repousse Design, Ball Feet, S. Kirk & Son, 2 ½ In.
$448

Brunk Auctions

Silver-American, Bowl, Flared Rim, John Ewan, Coin, Charleston, South Carolina, Mid 1800s, 5 x 9 ½ In.
$7,995

Brunk Auctions

Silver-American, Bowl, Fluted Swirled Interior, Floral Rim, Dominick & Haff, 15 In.
$1,573

Ahlers & Ogletree Auction Gallery

Silver-American, Bowl, Lobed, Applied E Monogram, Kalo Shop, Illinois, 1912, 2 ⅜ x 8 ⅞ In.
$531

Toomey & Co. Auctioneers

Silver-American, Bowl, Repousse, Marked, Eagle-R-Lion, Reed & Barton, Early 1900s, 3 x 17 x 12 In., Pair
$3,509

Fontaine's Auction Gallery

Silver-American, Bread Tray, Puritan Pattern, Oblong, Gorham, 1 ¾ x 12 x 6 In.
$156

Susanin's Auctioneers & Appraisers

Silver-American, Butter, Dome Cover, Cow Finial, Chased, Pierced Liner, R. & W. Wilson, 1825-46, 7 In.
$2,313

Leland Little Auctions

Silver-American, Cake Basket, Oval, Rope Twist Handle, Flared Rim, Footed, William Gale & Son, 1856, 9 In.
$640

Neal Auction Company

Silver-American, Cake Cutter, Flower Handle, Marked Schneider-Toledo Pat., S. Kirk & Sons
$84

Main Auction Galleries, Inc.

Silver-American, Card Tray, Rectangular, Engraved E.R. Monogram, Kalo Shop, Illinois, c.1905, ⅜ x 8 x 5 In.
$375

Toomey & Co. Auctioneers

Silver-American, Cigarette Box, Rectangular, Inscribed, Initials, Date 1959, Caldwell, 10 In.
$300

Richard Opfer Auctioneering, Inc.

S

Bank, Still, Royalty, Nursery Rhymes, Bailey, Banks & Biddle, Victorian, 2¾ In.	300
Basket, Cut Glass Vase, Shaped Base, Marked, J.E. Caldwell, 17½ x 9¾ In.	270
Beaker, Round Rim, Repousse, Follies, Garden Scene, Floral Sprays, Coin, 1800s, 3½ In. .. *illus*	313
Blotter Corners, Repousse, Masks, 4 Winds, Scrolls, Gorham, 3½ x 3½ In., 4 Piece	448
Bonbon, Oval, Scalloped Rim, Orchids, Reed & Barton, 1950s, 10 x 7 x 1¾ In.	230
Bonbon Spoon, Reticulated, Shell Shape, Seaweed Handle, Marshall Field, Early 1900s, 11 In., Pair.	970
Bowl, Art Deco, Monogram, Footed, Gorham, 11 x 11 x 3 In. ....*illus*	248
Bowl, Baby's, Underplate, Octagonal, Barbour Silver Co., Hartford, Conn., 1913, 2¼ x 6⅞ In.	375
Bowl, Brass Flower Frog Lid, Pierced, Clarence A. Vanderbilt, N.Y., Late 1800s, 6 x 11 In..*illus*	313
Bowl, Cartouche & Scroll Shape, Footed, Reed & Barton, 10 In.	266
Bowl, Central Flower, Repousse Design, Ball Feet, S. Kirk & Son, 2½ In. ....*illus*	448
Bowl, Flared Rim, John Ewan, Coin, Charleston, South Carolina, Mid 1800s, 5 x 9½ In. .... *illus*	7995
Bowl, Flared Scalloped Ring, Tapered Round Foot, Wallace, 4½ x 10 In.	660
Bowl, Fluted Swirled Interior, Floral Rim, Dominick & Haff, 15 In........*illus*	1573
Bowl, Footed Base, 3-Letter Monogram, J.E. Caldwell & Co., 8 x 4 In.	236
Bowl, Fruit, Arts & Crafts, Hammered, Handles, Barbour Silver Co., c.1920s, 3½ x 13 x 10 In.	308
Bowl, Leaf Shape, Tripod Feet, Alfredo Sciarrotta, 4 In.	854
Bowl, Lobed, Applied E Monogram, Kalo Shop, Illinois, 1912, 2⅜ x 8⅞ In........*illus*	531
Bowl, Monteith, Embossed Flowers, Hand Chased, Castle Turret Top Edge, S. Kirk & Son, 7 x 9½ In.	2280
Bowl, Openwork Cornice, Multiple Beaded Borders, Square Foot, J.E. Caldwell, 4½ x 6 In.	360
Bowl, Ornate Rim, Raised Scrolls & Designs, Marked, Black, Starr & Frost, 10¾ x 2¼ In.	270
Bowl, Oval, Embossed Rim & Base, Scrolled Feet, Theodore Starr, 5½ x 12 In.	1320
Bowl, Pierced Flower, Tulip Holder, Center, Dominick & Haff, 4½ x 12 In.	469
Bowl, Pierced, Larkspur Pattern, Wallace, 10 In.	180
Bowl, Repousse, Flowers & Leaves, Shaped Base, S. Kirk & Son, Early 1800s, 4 x 10 In.	350
Bowl, Repousse, Marked, Eagle-R-Lion, Reed & Barton, Early 1900s, 3 x 17 x 12 In., Pair...*illus*	3509
Bowl, Revere, Wallace, Engraved, W.B.F. Jr., 5 x 9 In.	544
Bowl, Scroll Handles, Leaves, Pods, Art Deco, Gorham, c.1930, 5¼ In.	1159
Bowl, Tulip, Ribbon Border, Floral Base, 4-Footed, Black, Starr & Frost, Late 1800s, 4 x 15 In. ..	1875
Bowl, Underplate, Openwork, Leaves & Floral Rim, Bailey, Banks & Biddle, 8½ In.	660
Bread Tray, Puritan Pattern, Oblong, Gorham, 1¾ x 12 x 6 In........*illus*	156
Bread Tray, Ribbed Borders, Marked, Herschede Co., 10½ x 6¾ In.	144
Butter, Dome Cover, Acorn Finial, Repousse, Flowers, Ball, Tompkins & Black, 4½ In.	480
Butter, Dome Cover, Cow Finial, Chased, Pierced Liner, R. & W. Wilson, 1825-46, 7 In. *illus*	2313
Cake Basket, Oval, Rope Twist Handle, Flared Rim, Footed, William Gale & Son, 1856, 9 In.*illus*	640
Cake Compote, Repousse, Embossed Flowers, Hand Chased, Monogram, Schofield, 2 x 11 In. .	1080
Cake Cutter, Flower Handle, Marked Schneider-Toledo Pat., S. Kirk & Sons ....*illus*	84
Candelabra are listed in the Candelabrum category.	
Candlesticks are listed in their own category.	
Candy Dish, Repousse, Fruit, Flowers, Ball Feet, S. Kirk & Son, 1900s, 5 In.	108
Card Tray, Rectangular, Engraved E.R. Monogram, Kalo Shop, Illinois, c.1905, ⅜ x 8 x 5 In. *illus*	375
Centerpiece, 2 Handles, International, 5 x 8 In.	437
Centerpiece, Classic Figure, Circular Bowl, Ball, Black & Company, N.Y., c.1910s, 9¾ In. ...	600
Centerpiece, Griffin Handles, Marked, Ball, Black & Co., c.1860-75, 11 x 17 x 12 In.	3509
Cigarette Box, Rectangular, Inscribed, Initials, Date 1959, Caldwell, 10 In........*illus*	300
Cigarette Case, Gold Color Interior, Basket Weave, Rectangular, Evans, 5 x 3 In.	122
Cigarette Case, Plain Interior, Scrolling Etched Strap, c.1950, 3¼ x 7¼ In.	180
Cigarette Case, Silver & 18K Gold, Rectangular, Cartier, 4 x 2⅝ In.	1320
Coffeepot, Swing Lid, Wood Handle, Engraved, Stand, Paw Feet, Philip Oriel, 8 In. ......*illus*	938
Compote, Bowl Shape Top, Domed Base, Crighton Bros., 5 x 5⅜ In., Pair	375
Compote, Gadroon Rim, Feather Decor Posts, Weighted, Black, Starr & Frost, 6½ x 6 In., Pair	160
Compote, Repousse Flowers & Leaves, Theodore B. Starr, Early 1900s, 4 x 10 In., Pair	1815
Compote, Reticulated, Cabriole Legs, Paw Feet, Frank M. Whiting, 1900s, 4½ x 5 In...*illus*	363
Cordial, Flared Rims, No Monogram, Marked Gorham, 1900s, 2⅞ In., 12 Piece	431
Coupe, 3 Giraffe Shape Supports, Standing, Ring Base, Gorham, 3 x 4 In..............*illus*	1920
Coupe, Neoclassical Style, Pierced, 2 Strap Handles, Footed, Gorham, 1¾ x 5½ In., 6 Piece	281
Cream Jug, Lid, Oval, Urn Shape Finial, Coin, Joel Sayre, N.Y., Early 1800s, 6¼ In.	439
Creamer, Repousse Flowers, Long Spout, Footed, Baltimore Silver Co., c.1900, 4 In.	570
Cup, Masonic Interest, Chased Flowers, Scrollwork, Coin, Wood & Hughes, New York, 4⅝ In.*illus*	388
Cup, Parcel Gilt, Handle, Engraved Fielding Hight, Base, Reed & Barton, 1951, 3½ In.	150

Silver-American, Coffeepot, Swing Lid, Wood Handle, Engraved, Stand, Paw Feet, Philip Oriel, 8 In.
$938

New Haven Auctions

Silver-American, Compote, Reticulated, Cabriole Legs, Paw Feet, Frank M. Whiting, 1900s, 4½ x 5 In.
$363

Ahlers & Ogletree Auction Gallery

TIP
Never wear rubber gloves when cleaning silver.

Silver-American, Coupe, 3 Giraffe Shape Supports, Standing, Ring Base, Gorham, 3 x 4 In.
$1,920

S

Michaan's Auctions

Silver-American, Cup, Masonic Interest, Chased Flowers, Scrollwork, Coin, Wood & Hughes, New York, 4⅝ In. $388

Leland Little Auctions

> **TIP**
> To clean crevices in old silver, use a cotton-tipped cuticle stick.

Silver-American, Frame, Hammered, Monogram, MHL, Clemens Friedell, Pasadena, Calif., 12 x 8½ In. $780

Treasureseeker Auctions

Silver-American, Gravy Boat, Arc Handle, Undertray, Reed & Barton, Windsor, 1945-46, 3 x 5 x 7 In. $563

Leland Little Auctions

Cup, Shaped Spout, Tapered Body, Scrolled Handle, Samuel Edwards, Boston, c.1730, 3 x 4 In.	5040
Dish, Leaf Shape, Chased Design, Marked, Reed & Barton, Dated 1934, 11 x 11 In.	375
Dish, Sculpted Rim, Rectangular Shape, Wallace, 6½ x 4½ In.	96
Ewer, Embossed Flowers, Hand Chased, Wide Spout, S. Kirk & Son, 10 In.	660
Ewer, Urn Shape, Pearl Border, Rim, Applied Handle, Base, Gorham, Providence, 1896, 13½ In.	1375
Frame, Hammered, Monogram, MHL, Clemens Friedell, Pasadena, Calif., 12 x 8½ In.*illus*	780
Frame, Picture, Flowers, Engraved, Script Monogram, 11 x 9 In.	384
Glove Stretcher, Hammered, Sea Creatures, Beaded, Monogram FA, Whiting, c.1890, 9 In.	125
Goblet, Engraved, Engine Turned, Circular Base, 1800s, 5 In.	165
Goblet, Flared Rim, Mirrored Base, Monogram, Stieff Co., Baltimore, 1900s, 6 In., 6 Piece .	625
Gravy Boat, Arc Handle, Undertray, Reed & Barton, Windsor, 1945-46, 3 x 5 x 7 In.....*illus*	563
Hair Comb, 17 Teeth, Engraved, May, Coin, S. Kirk & Son, Baltimore, c.1850, 2 x 2 In. *illus*	439
Jar, Dresser, Embossed, Castle Scene, Flowers, S. Kirk & Son, 4 In.	570
Jardiniere, Underplate, Reticulated, Curved Rim, Theodore B. Starr, Early 1900s, 8 x 12 In.*illus*	2420
Julep Cup, Cylindrical, Monogram, 1900s, 3 x 2 In., Pair	956
Julep Cup, Kentucky, Cylindrical, Flared Lip, Banded Foot, Marked, E.C. Garner, 1800s, 3 In.*illus*	1192
Kettle, Lid, Bud Shape Finial, Scroll Handle, Repousse Flowers, Shell Shape Feet, Stand......	1287
Ladle, Elongated Handle, Hallmark, Coin, Thomas Daniel, 1812, 14½ In.	125
Ladle, Fiddle Handle, Coin, Frederick Marquand, 13⅜ In.	366
Ladle, Monogram HJS, Coin, William H. Ewan, Charleston, South Carolina, Mid 1800s, 13 In.*illus*	861
Loving Cup, Concave Body, 3 Loop Handles, Ribbed Base, Gorham, Dated 1895, 7 x 25 In. .	540
Loving Cup, Repousse, 2 Loop Handles, Flowers, Round Base, Hennegan & Bates, 9 x 8 In.	1310
Loving Cup, Structures & Trees, 3 Handles, Marked, Woodside, 8 x 7 In.	472
Loving Cup, Vase Shape, 2 Scrolling Handles, Whiting, 7¼ x 9 x 5 In. ....*illus*	640
Mirror, Hand, Embossed, Couple Swinging, Foster & Bailey, Art Nouveau, 7½ In.............*illus*	219
Mirror, Hand, Shield Shape, Strapwork & Flowers Handle, Foster & Bailey, 11¼ In .....*illus*	70
Mirror, Heart Shape, Openwork, Cupids, Flowers, Easel Back, Dominick & Haff, 18 x 14 In.*illus*	480
Mug, Monogram Emma, Coin, Gregg, Hayden & Co., Charleston, S.C., Mid 1800s, 3¼ In.....*illus*	492
Mug, Shaped Handle, Cottage Landscape, Coin, Gorham, c.1852, 4 In.	1375
Napkin Rings are listed in their own category.	
Pitcher, Baluster, Leaves Scroll Handle, Molded Foot, International, 8⅞ In.	610
Pitcher, Beer, Cylindrical, Wood Grain Texture, Rivet Bands, Coin, Bailey & Co., c.1850, 9 x 6 In. .	3803
Pitcher, Classical Style, Starr & Frost, Cast Flowers, Scroll Handle, Early 1900s, 7 x 14 In....*illus*	1440
Pitcher, Figural Handle, Wide Spout, Coin, Lion-Anchor-G Mark, Gorham, c.1870, 11 In. ...	2420
Pitcher, Flower, Ribbon, Lebkuecher & Co., J.E. Caldwell, New Jersey, 1896, 10 In.	625
Pitcher, Oval Body, Acanthus Leaf, Flowers, Repousse, 1861, 8½ In.	4305
Pitcher, Pear Shape, Coin, Samuel Wilmot Jr., Charleston, South Carolina, Mid 1800s, 5½ In..*illus*	3444
Pitcher, Presentation, Repousse, Twisted Handle, Coin, Lincoln & Foss, Boston, 1848, 6½ In...	375
Pitcher, Pyriform, Wide Spout, Flowers, Shell & Scroll Feet, Coin, Lewes Owen & Co., 9⅜ In......	4575
Pitcher, Repousse Flowers, Coin, Hyde & Goodrich, New Orleans, Mid 1800s, 12 In.............	861
Pitcher, Repousse, Castle, Flowers, Leaves, S. Kirk & Son, Baltimore, Md., 1850s, 8 In.	2500
Pitcher, Water, Classical, Thomas Charles Fletcher, Philadelphia, Pa., Early 1800s, 10 x 21 In.	2520
Pitcher, Water, Flowers, Script Monogram, 4 Bracket Feet, Gorham, 1898, 9 In.	719
Pitcher, Water, Hand Chased Design, Base, Grainger Hannan Co., 1900s, 9½ x 10 In.........	1080
Pitcher, Water, Hand Wrought, Stamped Marks, Kalo Shop, Illinois, 1912, 8 x 6⅝ x 5½ In.......	1250
Pitcher, Water, Hand Wrought, Wide Spout, Shaped Handle, Kalo, 9 x 7½ In. ....*illus*	1140
Pitcher, Water, Repousse, Flowers & Leaves, Whiting Mfg. Co., New York, N.Y., Late 1800s, 7½ In.	2813
Pitcher, Water, Urn Shape, Arc Handle, Footed Base, Frank M. Whiting, 9¼ In.	413
Plate, Beaded Rim, Gorham, Providence, 1921, 10 In., 12 Piece	3825
Plate, Service, Wedgwood Pattern, International, 10⅝ In., 12 Piece	4800
Platter, Leaves Rim, Black, Starr & Frost, New York, 13½ x 18 In.	907
Platter, Oval, Script, Monogram, Plymouth, Gorham, 18 x 12½ In.	781
Platter, Tree & Well, 4 Scrolled Feet, Gorham, c.1950, 20 In. ....*illus*	1140
Porringer, Pierced Handle, George Hanners Sr., Boston, Mass., c.1720, 2 x 8 x 5 In. .....*illus*	5040
Porringer, Repousse Bowl, Floral, Openwork Handle, S. Kirk & Son, 7½ In.	600
Porringer, Repousse, Floral, Leaves, Openwork Handle, Coin, Samuel Kirk, c.1830, 8 In.....	531
Punch Ladle, Shell Shape, Joseph Richardson Jr., Philadelphia, Pa., c.1750, 14½ In.........	2250
Punch Ladle, Spiral Twist Handle, Coin, Henry Muhr & Son, Late 1800s, 12½ In..............	375
Punch Strainer, Shaped Handles, Benjamin Burt, Boston, Mass., c.1760, 1¼ x 11 x 4¾ In..*illus*	2772
Salt Cellar, Cut Glass, Silver Frame, No. 2735, Gorham, 2 x 3 In. ....*illus*	150

S

Silver-American, Hair Comb, 17 Teeth, Engraved, May, Coin, S. Kirk & Son, Baltimore, c.1850, 2 x 2 In.
$439

Jeffrey S. Evans & Associates

Silver-American, Jardiniere, Underplate, Reticulated, Curved Rim, Theodore B. Starr, Early 1900s, 8 x 12 In.
$2,420

Fontaine's Auction Gallery

Silver-American, Julep Cup, Kentucky, Cylindrical, Flared Lip, Banded Foot, Marked, E.C. Garner, 1800s, 3 In.
$1,192

Charleston Estate Auctions

Silver-American, Ladle, Monogram HJS, Coin, William H. Ewan, Charleston, South Carolina, Mid 1800s, 13 In.
$861

Brunk Auctions

Silver-American, Loving Cup, Vase Shape, 2 Scrolling Handles, Whiting, 7 ¼ x 9 x 5 In.
$640

Roland NY Auctioneers & Appraisers

> **TIP**
> *Rub silverware length-wise when cleaning.*

Silver-American, Mirror, Hand, Embossed, Couple Swinging, Foster & Bailey, Art Nouveau, 7 ½ In.
$219

New Haven Auctions

Silver-American, Mirror, Hand, Shield Shape, Strapwork & Flowers Handle, Foster & Bailey, 11 ¼ In
$70

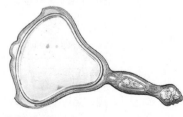

Neal Auction Company

Silver-American, Mirror, Heart Shape, Openwork, Cupids, Flowers, Easel Back, Dominick & Haff, 18 x 14 In.
$480

Richard Opfer Auctioneering, Inc.

Silver-American, Mug, Monogram Emma, Coin, Gregg, Hayden & Co., Charleston, S.C., Mid 1800s, 3 ¼ In.
$492

Brunk Auctions

Silver-American, Pitcher, Classical Style, Starr & Frost, Cast Flowers, Scroll Handle, Early 1900s, 7 x 14 In.
$1,440

Garth's Auctioneers & Appraisers

S

Silver-American, Pitcher, Pear Shape, Coin, Samuel Wilmot Jr., Charleston, South Carolina, Mid 1800s, 5 ½ In.
$3,444

Brunk Auctions

Silver-American, Pitcher, Water, Hand Wrought, Wide Spout, Shaped Handle, Kalo, 9 x 7 ½ In.
$1,140

Alderfer Auction Company

Silver-American, Platter, Tree & Well, 4 Scrolled Feet, Gorham, c.1950, 20 In.
$1,140

Alderfer Auction Company

TIP
The English use this old system for cleaning silver: Put the silver in a bowl, cover it with sour milk, and let it stand overnight. Rinse it in cold water the next morning; dry with a soft cloth.

Silver-American, Porringer, Pierced Handle, George Hanners Sr., Boston, Mass., c.1720, 2 x 8 x 5 In.
$5,040

Freeman's

Silver-American, Punch Strainer, Shaped Handles, Benjamin Burt, Boston, Mass., c.1760, 1 ¼ x 11 x 4 ¾ In.
$2,772

Freeman's

Silver-American, Salt Cellar, Cut Glass, Silver Frame, No. 2735, Gorham, 2 x 3 In.
$150

Woody Auction

Silver-American, Scale, Bird, Repousse Flowers, Hanging Hook, Gorham, 2 Oz.
$378

Pook & Pook

Silver-American, Serving Spoon, Openwork Leaves, S. Kirk & Son, 9 ¼ In.
$120

Cottone Auctions

Silver-American, Sugar, Handles, Swirl Design, Scalloped Rim, 4 ¼ x 4 ¾ In.
$120

Main Auction Galleries, Inc.

TIP
Use your silver. If it is used, then washed and dried immediately, it rarely needs tarnish removal.

S

Salver, Chippendale, Shaped Rim, Poole, 1950s, 11¾ In.	787
Salver, Square, Footed, Engraved Border, Paw Feet, Bailey, Banks & Biddle, 1 x 12 x 12 In..	1188
Sauceboat, Undertray, Repousse, Grapes, Gilt Interior, Peter L. Krider Co., c.1900s, 4¼ In.	976
Scale, Bird, Repousse Flowers, Hanging Hook, Gorham, 2 Oz. ....*illus*	378
Sculpture, Fighting Bull, Bear, White Marble Base, S. Kirk & Son, 1900s, 3 x 5½ x 2½ In.	1750
Serving Bowl, Chrysanthemum, Floral Border, Cursive Script, Gorham, c.1900, 2½ x 9 In.	288
Serving Bowl, Shell Shape, Footed, Theodore Starr, c.1910, 9 x 9 x 2 In., Pair	94
Serving Spoon, 3-Letter Script, Monogram, Reed & Barton, 10⅜ In.	344
Serving Spoon, Leaf & Tendrils Terminal Handle, Flowers, Wood & Hughes, c.1870s, 11 In. ..	366
Serving Spoon, Openwork Leaves, S. Kirk & Son, 9¼ In. ....*illus*	120
Spoon, Carved Underside, Handle, Ephraim Brasher, N.Y., 1774, 8¼ In.	491
Spoon, Long Neck, Heart Shape Bowl, Hand Hammered, Kalo, Chicago, 13¾ x 1½ In........	219
Spoon, Pineapple, Leaves, Oblong Bowl, Gorham, 1870, 8½ In	1094
Sugar, Handles, Swirl Design, Scalloped Rim, 4¼ x 4¾ In...............................*illus*	120
Sugar Shaker, Trophy Shape, Black, Starr & Frost, Square Base, 7 In.	140
Sugar Urn, Lid, Engraved, Monogram, Hallmark, Coin, John Vernon, 1795, 9 x 4 In...*illus*	1063
Tablespoon, Trifid End, Beaded Rattail, Jeremiah Dummer, Boston, c.1685, 1½ x 7 In......*illus*	3780
Tankard, Dome Lid, Molded Foot, Scrolled Handle, Ephraim Brasher, N.Y., c.1780, 9 x 7 In...*illus*	7560
Tazza, Gilt, Tripartite, Serpent Shape Base, Monogram, Dominick & Haff, N.Y., 1891, 3 x 9 In., Pair...	1875
Tazza, Pierced Rim, Meriden Britannia, 2¾ x 8 In....................................	182
Tazza, Poppy, Gold Washed, Hammered, Clemes Friedell, 4½ x 5½ In., Pair.................	2040
Tazza, Poppy, Handwrought, Clemens Friedell, 4⅝ In., Pair	1408
Tazza, Repousse, Grapes & Vines, Molded Rim, Domed Base, 4¼ In............................*illus*	1375
Teapot, Dome Lid, Wood Handle, John Wanamaker, 1900s, 5½ In............................	188
Teapot, Grape Cluster Finial, Ram's Head Handle, S. Kirk & Son, 7 In.......................*illus*	2904
Teaspoon, Fiddle Thread, Cursive Script, Coin, Jones, Ball & Poor, Boston, c.1850, 6 In., 9 Piece ..	230
Tray, Center Monogram, Etched, Footed, Coin, Gorham, 12 x 12 x 1 In..........................	661
Tray, Engraved, Signatures & Commemorative Dates, Gorham, 23 In.......................	2125
Tray, Golfer, Carrying Clubs, Knickers, Cap, Flag, Trees, Oval, Beaded, Unger Bros., 10 In....	335
Tray, Outcurved Rim, Shell Border, Dominick & Haff, 1893, 15 x 10 In.	610
Tray, Repousse, Flowers, Art Nouveau, Square, Black, Starr & Frost, 7 In......................	660
Tray, Shell Shape, Scalloped Edge, Monogram, Gorham, 1 x 9 x 9⅜ In.......................*illus*	344
Tray, St. Dunstan Pattern, Oval, Scrolls, Tab Handles, Marked, Gorham, 1929, 14 In.	690
Trophy, Colt, Vice President's, Central Branch, Handles, Wallace, 1925, 15 x 12 x 8 In..*illus*	1200
Trophy, Loving Cup, 2 Handles, Repousse Sides, Marked Christmas, 1896, 7¼ x 10 In.	660
Trophy, Loving Cup, Convention Contest, Scroll Handles, Wm. B. Kerr & Co., 9¾ In.	554
Trophy, Pitcher, Northwestern Regatta Association, Kalo Shop, Illinois, c.1911, 7 x 6 x 4 In.	750
Tureen, Lid, Classical, Soldered, Urn Shape, Wide Handle, Gorham, Late 1800s, 9⅞ x 15 In.....	303
Tureen, Repousse, Flowers, 4 Volute Feet, Dominick & Haff, New York, N.Y., 1880, 8¾ x 14 In...	5000
Urn, Dome Lid, Pod Finial, Acanthus Handles, Scroll Feet, Coin, Baldwin Gardiner, 13¼ In...*illus*	2196
Vase, Flared Top, Castle & Flowers, Embossed, No. 38, Domed Base, S. Kirk & Son, 12 In..... *illus*	1800
Vase, Repousse, Fruit, Flower, Pedestal Base, Scalloped Rim, Loring Andrews, 13 x 5½ In..	2040
Vase, Trumpet, Chased Shells, Leaves, Swirl Texture, Art Nouveau, Shreve & Co., 22½ x 7 In......	3600
Vase, Trumpet, Hammered, Weighted Base, Marked Shreve & Company, c.1900, 9¾ In.......	281
Vase, Trumpet, Weighted Base, Marked, Engraved Initial D, Reed & Barton, 15½ In............	594
Wine, Flared Rim, Shaped Base, Monogram, S. Kirk & Son, 6¾ In., 6 Piece........................	780

SILVER-ASIAN

Bowl, Gold Wash, Embossed, Garden Scenes, Elephant, Leaves, Mandalay, Burma, 1906, 5 In...*illus*	1140
Bowl, Reticulated, 8 Cartouches, Repousse Figures, Engraved, Thailand, 6 In.............*illus*	938
Tureen, Chased & Repousse Flowers, Bodhisattva Figures, 12 x 12¼ In.	780

SILVER-AUSTRIAN

Cup, Gilt, Etched Rock, Marked, Karl Rossler, Vienna, Late 1800s, 5 x 4 x 3½ In.	3780

SILVER-AUSTRO-HUNGARIAN

Box, Hinged Lid, Oval, Embossed, 4 Children, Leaves & Flowers Border, 1800s, 1½ x 3⅛ In......	156
Gravy Boat, 2 Spouts, 2 Handles, Vermeil Interior, Attached Undertray, 5 x 11 In........*illus*	270

SILVER-BELGIAN

Necessaire, Hinged Lid, Engraved Design, Molded Base, c.1850, 5½ In.......................*illus*	250

Silver-American, Sugar Urn, Lid, Engraved, Monogram, Hallmark, Coin, John Vernon, 1795, 9 x 4 In.
$1,06?

Auctions at Showplace, NYC

Silver-American, Tablespoon, Trifid End, Beaded Rattail, Jeremiah Dummer, Boston, c.1685, 1½ x 7 In.
$3,780

Freeman's

Silver-American, Tankard, Dome Lid, Molded Foot, Scrolled Handle, Ephraim Brasher, N.Y., c.1780, 9 x 7 In.
$7,560

Freeman's

S

TIP
The acid or sulfur in eggs, onions, mayonnaise, tart salad dressing, and salt will corrode the surface of the silver or silver plate.

Silver-American, Tazza, Repousse, Grapes & Vines, Molded Rim, Domed Base, 4 ¼ In.
$1,375

Neal Auction Company

Silver-American, Teapot, Grape Cluster Finial, Ram's Head Handle, S. Kirk & Son, 7 In.
$2,904

Fontaine's Auction Gallery

Silver-American, Tray, Shell Shape, Scalloped Edge, Monogram, Gorham, 1 x 9 x 9 ⅜ In.
$344

Hindman

Silver-American, Trophy, Colt, Vice President's, Central Branch, Handles, Wallace, 1925, 15 x 12 x 8 In.
$1,200

Morphy Auctions

Silver-American, Urn, Dome Lid, Pod Finial, Acanthus Handles, Scroll Feet, Coin, Baldwin Gardiner, 13 ¼ In.
$2,196

Neal Auction Company

Silver-American, Vase, Flared Top, Castle & Flowers, Embossed, No. 38, Domed Base, S. Kirk & Son, 12 In.
$1,800

Richard Opfer Auctioneering, Inc.

Silver-Asian, Bowl, Gold Wash, Embossed, Garden Scenes, Elephant, Leaves, Mandalay, Burma, 1906, 5 In.
$1,140

Richard Opfer Auctioneering, Inc.

Silver-Asian, Bowl, Reticulated, 8 Cartouches, Repousse Figures, Engraved, Thailand, 6 In.
$938

Charlton Hall Auctions

Silver-Austro-Hungarian, Gravy Boat, 2 Spouts, 2 Handles, Vermeil Interior, Attached Undertray, 5 x 11 In.
$270

Garth's Auctioneers & Appraisers

Silver-Belgian, Necessaire, Hinged Lid, Engraved Design, Molded Base, c.1850, 5 ½ In.
$250

Hindman

SILVER-BURMESE

Bowl, Repousse, 6 Panels, Praying Buddha, Leaves, 5 1/8 x 2 1/2 In. 173

SILVER-CHINESE

Box, Hinged Lid, Flowers, Letter D, Marked, Early 1900s, 3 3/4 x 2 7/8 x 1 In. 125
Cigarette Box, Allover Design, Gold Mount, Marked Mithanh, 3 x 4 In. 640
Vase, Dragon, Flared Top, 2 Handles, Scroll Designs, Tripod Base, 8 1/2 In. .... *illus* 1408

SILVER-CONTINENTAL

Basket, Wavy Rim, Openwork, 3 Cherubs, Flowers, Hoof Feet, 3 7/8 x 9 1/2 In. 281
Bowl, Rococo, Repousse Center, Gilt Accents, Cartouche Panel, 1900s, 4 x 16 1/2 x 10 In. 545
Candlestand, Art Nouveau, 3 Branch Candlesticks, Marked 835, Germany, 8 x 10 In., Pair 240
Centerpiece, Etched Glass Bowl, 2 Scrolling Handles, 2 Putti, Early 1900s, 9 x 19 x 9 In.*illus* 2662
Creamer, Lid, 2 Griffins Facing, Central Lyre, Wood Finial & Handle, c.1915, 5 3/4 In. 250
Ewer, Ram's Head, Cherubs, Scrollwork, Glass, Figural Finial, 1800s, 8 1/4 In. .... *illus* 1331
Ladle, Pointed Handle, Vermeil Bowl, Gold, Marked IV & C.G., Continental, c.1910, 15 In..... 144
Salt, Master, Open Top, Ornate Border & Pedestal Base, Hallmark, 1700s, 3 1/4 x 5 In.. *illus* 450
Sconce, 2-Light, Ecclesiastic, Repousse, Angels, 1700s, 20 x 16 1/4 In., Pair........................... 3438
Spice Tower, 4 Flags, Filigree Center, Engraved Designs, 10 In. 480
Sprinkler, Water, Rose, Flared Top, Mounted, Underplate, Early 1900s, 11 1/4 In. .... *illus* 424
Tankard, Hinged Lid, Floral Repousse, Lion Feet, 1800s, 6 3/4 In. .... *illus* 1331
Tray, Rectangular, Shaped Border, 2 Handles, Eagle & Star, Marked, 14 x 23 In. 1058
Tray, Scrollwork Border, 2 Handles, Paw Feet, Marked, P.L., M.K., 1800s, 23 x 28 x 19 In. 5143
Vase, Scalloped Rim, Footed, Late 1800s, 6 x 2 In. 100

SILVER-DANISH

Bowl, Oval, Applied Wire Rim, Grapes, Marked E. Dragsted, Late 1900s, 2 3/4 x 6 1/4 In. 225
Candlestick, 2-Light, S-Shape Base, Eigil Jensen, A. Michelsen, c.1950, 4 x 5 x 6 In., Pair... 1125
Georg Jensen silver is listed in the Georg Jensen category in this book.
Stamp Box, Hinged Lid, Embossed, Woman, Pandora, 2 Compartments, 1 x 3 x 2 1/4 In. ...... *illus* 167

SILVER-DUTCH

Basket, Oval, Openwork, Cast Scroll Handles, 1948, 5 1/2 x 16 1/2 x 10 1/2 In. 738
Bowl, Repousse Filigree, Cherubs, Flowers, 2 Handles, Early 1700s, 3 x 10 x 5 In.......... *illus* 688
Creamer, Figural, Cow, Hinged Lid, Fly Finial, Tail Handle, Red Glass Eyes, c.1905, 5 x 8 In. 1370
Dresser Box, Religious & Hunting Panels, Shaped Feet, Hallmark, 2 x 6 x 2 In. .... *illus* 330
Sugar, Repousse, Scale Design, Shaped Handles, Footed, Amsterdam, 1700s, 7 1/4 In., Pair.. 469
Wine Coaster, Pierced Sides, Stamped, AB, Den Bosch, Netherlands, Late 1700s, 1 1/2 x 5 In., Pair 1755

SILVER-ENGLISH

English sterling silver is marked with a series of four or five small hallmarks. The standing lion mark is the most commonly seen sterling quality mark. The other marks indicate the city of origin, the maker, the year of manufacture, and the king or queen. These dates can be verified in many good books on silver. These prices are partially based on silver meltdown values.

Standard quality mark

City mark – London

Date letter mark

Maker's mark

Sovereign's head mark

Basket, 3-Legged, Scalloped Rim, Leafy, Adie Brothers Ltd., Sheffield, George V, 1922, 1 x 5 In.. 88
Basket, Boat Shape, Footed, Martin, Hall & Co., George V, 1911, 4 1/2 x 10 x 6 In.......... *illus* 787
Basting Spoon, Engraved Crown, Eagle Crest, Hester Bateman, London, George III, 1785, 12 In. 936
Berry Spoon, Shell Shape Bowl, Sculpted Handle, London, 1786, 7 In...................................... 128
Bowl, Hammered, Reticulated, Repousse, Bird Figurehead, Josiah Williams & Co., c.1884, 7 x 7 In..... 576
Bowl, Oval, 2 Loop Handles, Lion Passant & Head, John Samuel Hunt, 1800s, 5 x 12 x 8 In. 540
Bowl, Pedestal, Hammered, Walker & Hall, Birmingham, Arts & Crafts, 1889, 5 3/4 x 8 In.... 313

Silver-Chinese, Vase, Dragon, Flared Top, 2 Handles, Scroll Designs, Tripod Base, 8 1/2 In.
$1,408

Roland NY Auctioneers & Appraisers

Silver-Continental, Centerpiece, Etched Glass Bowl, 2 Scrolling Handles, 2 Putti, Early 1900s, 9 x 19 x 9 In.
$2,662

Fontaine's Auction Gallery

Silver-Continental, Ewer, Ram's Head, Cherubs, Scrollwork, Glass, Figural Finial, 1800s, 8 1/4 In.
$1,331

Fontaine's Auction Gallery

Silver-Continental, Salt, Master, Open Top, Ornate Border & Pedestal Base, Hallmark, 1700s, 3 ¼ x 5 In.
$450

Treasureseeker Auctions

Silver-Continental, Sprinkler, Water, Rose, Flared Top, Mounted, Underplate, Early 1900s, 11 ¼ In.
$424

Fontaine's Auction Gallery

Silver-Continental, Tankard, Hinged Lid, Floral Repousse, Lion Feet, 1800s, 6 ¾ In.
$1,331

Fontaine's Auction Gallery

Silver-Danish, Stamp Box, Hinged Lid, Embossed, Woman, Pandora, 2 Compartments, 1 x 3 x 2 ¼ In.
$167

Rachel Davis Fine Arts

Silver-Dutch, Bowl, Repousse Filigree, Cherubs, Flowers, 2 Handles, Early 1700s, 3 x 10 x 5 In.
$688

Fontaine's Auction Gallery

Silver-Dutch, Dresser Box, Religious & Hunting Panels, Shaped Feet, Hallmark, 2 x 6 x 2 In.
$330

Alderfer Auction Company

TIP

It is said you can clean silver with a banana peel mashed in a blender.

Silver-English, Basket, Boat Shape, Footed, Martin, Hall & Co., George V, 1911, 4 ½ x 10 x 6 In.
$787

Ahlers & Ogletree Auction Gallery

Silver-English, Bowl, Reticulated, 2 Ram's Head Handles, Domed Base, 1800s, 7 ½ x 12 ¼ In.
$3,025

Fontaine's Auction Gallery

Silver-English, Brandy Warmer, Reverse Engraved, Laurel Wreath, Hester Bateman, George III, 1787, 4 In.
$563

Eldred's

S

Bowl, Reticulated, 2 Ram's Head Handles, Domed Base, 1800s, 7½ x 12¼ In. ....*illus*	3025
Brandy Warmer, Reverse Engraved, Laurel Wreath, Hester Bateman, George III, 1787, 4 In.*illus*	563
Butter, Round, Swanlike Image, Glass, Pewter, Archibald Knox, 2¼ x 6½ In.	531
Cake Basket, Armorial, Samuel Hennell, London, George III, 1811, 9½ x 13 x 10⅜ In......*illus*	1287
Candelabra are listed in the Candelabrum category.	
Candlesticks are listed in their own category.	
Centerpiece, Shell Shape, Figural, 3 Dolphin Feet, Garrard & Co. Ltd., 1900s, 9 x 11 x 10 In.	3933
Coffeepot, Baluster Shape, Graduated Beading, Spout Ending, Shell On Body, London, 11 In.*illus*	472
Cup, Shaped Handle, Lobed Base, Footed, Monogram, Paul Storr, 1821, 3½ In............*illus*	2500
Dish Cross, James White, London, George III, 1816, 14 In.	750
Dish, Sweetmeat, Petal Fluted, Marked, Harry Freeman, London, George V, 1921, 8 In., Pair.	854
Epergne, 4-Light, Leaves, Paw Feet, Robert Gainsford, Sheffield, George III, c.1818, 17 x 19 In... *illus*	7560
Epergne, 5 Glass Bowls, 4-Legged, Sheffield, Israel Freeman & Son, 12 x 19 In.....................	615
Epergne, Knopped Column, Scrolling Leaves, 3 Branched Arms, Footed Base, Sheffield, 19 x 17 In.	3125
Gravy Boat, Oblong, Handle, Robert Hennell I, Mary Lee, London, 6 x 8 In.	563
Hot Water Urn, Presentation, Andrew Fogelberg, London, George III, 1776, 21¾ x 10 x 11 In. ...	8820
Jug, Dome Lid, Flame Finial, Pear Shape, Gadroon Border, Ivory Handle, 1744, 8½ In. ...*illus*	923
Jug, Urn Shape, Scroll Handle, Blossom Finial, Ivory Spacer, 7½ In..........................	677
Ladle, Engraved Handle, Outstretched Arm, Dagger, George Smith IV, 1800s, 13¼ In.	805
Ladle, Round Handle & Bowl, Hester Bateman, London, George III, 1787, 13 In...........*illus*	492
Marrow Scoop, Shaped Handle, Jane Lambe, George I, Early 1770s, 8¾ In........................	527
Muffineer, Floral Repousse, Henry Wilkinson & Co., London, 1895, 7 In.	305
Muffineer, Pierced, Stepped Foot, Richard Comyns, London, 1924, 6½ In. ....*illus*	156
Napkin Rings are listed in their own category.	
Nutmeg Grater, Hinged Lid, Engraved, Rectangular, Marked TPER, 1829, 2 x 1 x 1 In....*illus*	450
Plateau Mirror, Round, Bead & Floral Scrollwork, 3 Ornate Feet, 1910s, 5 In.............*illus*	688
Porringer, Hammered, Openwork Handle, Monogram, Tessiers Ltd., 7½ In. ....*illus*	168
Punch Bowl, Grapevine Rim, Fluted Base, Foot, John & Frank Pairpoint, London, 1900, 5¾ x 8 In.	702
Rattle, Bells & Whistle, Coral Teether, Hester Bateman, Georgian, 5¾ In.	1063
Rattle, Coral Teether, Squared Baluster, 2 Rows Of 4 Bells, Whistle, 6 In. ....*illus*	305
Rattle, Whistle Component, White Curved Handle, 6 x 1 In...*illus*	250
Salt, Lobed, Scroll Handles, Footed, Peter & Ann Bateman, George III, 1700s, 4 x 2 x 2 In., Pair...*illus*	201
Salt, Master Repousse, Gilt Wash Interiors, Mask Feet, John Bridge, George IV, 1824, 2 In., Pair..	448
Salver, Crest, Eagle, Shell & Scroll Border, Ball & Claw Feet, London, 8 In.................	295
Salver, Flowers, Footed, Samuel Smily, Goldsmiths Alliance Ltd., London, Victorian, 1872, 11 In..	1020
Salver, Gadroon Edge, Coat Of Arms Center, Ball & Claw Feet, 1½ x 12 In.	720
Salver, Gadroon Rim, Shell Shape Feet, Richard Rugg II, London, George III, 1776, 2 x 17 In....	2340
Salver, Georgian Border, Deer Hoof Feet, Marked London 1732, 6 In.	320
Salver, Leaf, Flower Border, Scrolling Feet, S.C. Younge & Co, Sheffield, George IV, 1826, 1 In....	813
Salver, Presentation, Scalloped Rim, Charles Reily, George Storer, London, 1840, 1½ x 14 In. ....*illus*	5355
Salver, Rococo, Repousse Band, Incised Herald, William Eley, London, George III, 1778, 8 In.	688
Salver, Shell & Scroll Border, 3 Hoof Feet, George III, c.1762, 10 In.	2135
Sculpture, Eagle, Spread Wings, Garrard & Co., London, c.1990s, 12 x 21½ x 6 In.............	2560
Serving Dish, Repousse, Hallmark, Charles Stuart Harris, London, 1896, 9½ In., Pair......	360
Skewer, William Eaton, London, George III, 1832, 14 In.	228
Soup Ladle, Onslow, Shell Shape, Thomas Ellis, George III, 1769, 13⅝ In.	320
Stuffing Spoon, Shaped Handle, Threaded, Marked N, 1910s, 15 In.	96
Sugar Tongs, Figural Lid, Bowl, Spoon, Arthur Sibley, 1857, 4 In.	600
Sugar, Urn Shape, Dome Lid, Repousse, Flowers, Pedestal Base, Mid 1700s, 5½ In.	857
Tankard, Hinged Lid, Handle, John Langlands, 1757, 7¼ In..*illus*	1440
Tankard, Hinged Lid, Souvenir, Coat-Of-Arms, Amsterdam, Chester, 1910, 8 In.	469
Teapot, Floral Finial, Richard William Atkins, William Nathaniel Somersall, 1829, 9 x 10 In....*illus*	570
Teapot, Hinged Lid, Wood Side Handle, Individual, 4½ In., Pair..............................	270
Teapot, Oval Fluted Shape, Ivory Finial, Crispin Fuller, London, George III, 1793, 6 x 11 x 4 In....*illus*	1053
Teapot, Scalloped Body, Engraved Band, Wood Handle & Finial, 1700s, 4½ x 9½ In.	2000
Teapot, Warwick Vase, Robert Hennell, London, George III, 1779, 6 x 12 In..........................	5000
Teapot, Wood Handle & Knop, Lion Passant, George III, Early 1700s, 4⅜ x 9 In..........*illus*	270
Teapot, Wood Handle, Sword Shape Finial, Lid, Monogram, Flowers, Leaves, Early 1800s, 13 Oz..	302
Tray, Armorial, John Crouch I & Thomas Hannan, London, George III, 1791, 11 x 8 In., Pair......	2520
Tray, Chippendale Pattern, Scalloped Edge, Poole, 9⅞ x 10 In....................................	469
Tray, Shell & Scroll Rim, Leaf & Bun Feet, Thomas Wallis II, London, George III, 1800, 12 In.....	527

Silver-English, Cake Basket, Armorial, Samuel Hennell, London, George III, 1811, 9½ x 13 x 10⅜ In.
$1,287

Thomaston Place Auction Galleries

Silver-English, Coffeepot, Baluster Shape, Graduated Beading, Spout Ending, Shell On Body, London, 11 In.
$472

Soulis Auctions

Silver-English, Cup, Shaped Handle, Lobed Base, Footed, Monogram, Paul Storr, 1821, 3½ In.
$2,500

Hindman

This is an edited listing of current prices. Visit Kovels.com to check thousands of prices from previous years and sign up for free information on trends, tips, reproductions, marks, and more.

S

Silver-English, Epergne, 4-Light, Leaves, Paw Feet, Robert Gainsford, Sheffield, George III, c.1818, 17 x 19 In.
$7,560

Freeman's

Jug, Dome Lid, Flame Finial, Pear Shape, Gadroon Border, Ivory Handle, 1744, 8½ In.
$923

Brunk Auctions

Silver-English, Ladle, Round Handle & Bowl, Hester Bateman, London, George III, 1787, 13 In.
$492

Brunk Auctions

Silver-English, Muffineer, Pierced, Stepped Foot, Richard Comyns, London, 1924, 6½ In.
$156

Alderfer Auction Company

Silver-English, Nutmeg Grater, Hinged Lid, Engraved, Rectangular, Marked TPER, 1829, 2 x 1 x 1 In.
$450

Garth's Auctioneers & Appraisers

Silver-English, Plateau Mirror, Round, Bead & Floral Scrollwork, 3 Ornate Feet, 1910s, 5 In.
$688

Charlton Hall Auctions

Silver-English, Porringer, Hammered, Openwork Handle, Monogram, Tessiers Ltd., 7½ In.
$168

Richard Opfer Auctioneering, Inc.

Silver-English, Rattle, Coral Teether, Squared Baluster, 2 Rows Of 4 Bells, Whistle, 6 In.
$305

Rafael Osona Nantucket Auctions

Silver-English, Rattle, Whistle Component, White Curved Handle, 6 x 1 In.
$250

New Haven Auctions

S

Silver-English, Salt, Lobed, Scroll Handles, Footed, Peter & Ann Bateman, George III, 1700s, 4 x 2 x 2 In., Pair
$201

Charleston Estate Auctions

Lock Your Doors

In half of all burglaries, the thief came in through an unlocked window or door.

Silver-English, Salver, Presentation, Scalloped Rim, Charles Reily, George Storer, London, 1840, 1 x 14 In.
$5,355

Freeman's

Silver-English, Tankard, Hinged Lid, Handle, John Langlands, 1757, 7¼ In.
$1,440

Cottone Auctions

Silver-English, Teapot, Floral Finial, Richard William Atkins, William Nathaniel Somersall, 1829, 9 x 10 In.
$570

Alderfer Auction Company

Silver-English, Teapot, Oval Fluted Shape, Ivory Finial, Crispin Fuller, London, George III, 1793, 6 x 11 x 4 In.
$1,053

Thomaston Place Auction Galleries

Silver-English, Teapot, Wood Handle & Knop, Lion Passant, George III, Early 1700s, 4⅜ x 9 In.
$270

Michaan's Auctions

Silver-English, Trophy Cup, Lid, Richmond Horse Show, June 1899, Mappin & Webb, London, 14 x 9 In.
$750

Charlton Hall Auctions

S

Silver-French, Bowl, Shell Shape, Gilt Wash, First Standard, Early 1900s, 7¾ x 10 x 6¼ In.
$1,250

Andrew Jones Auctions

Silver-French, Brandy Warmer, Flared Rim, Black Handle, C.M. Granger, Paris, c.1810, 2¾ x 11½ In.
$281

Hindman

> **TIP**
> Beware of clinging plastic wrap if your storage area is a hot attic!
> We have seen pieces of silver or other metals with melted plastic stuck to the metal.
> It must be professionally removed.

Silver-French, Cigarette Case, Blue & White, Enamel Border, Hand Chased, Hallmark, 4 x 3 In.
$204

Alderfer Auction Company

Silver-French, Coffeepot, Dome Lid, Flower Bud Finial, Scroll Handle, Footed, c.1900, 11 In.
$469

Hindman

Silver-French, Pie Server, Weighted Handle, Blade, Marked, Christofle, 10¾ In.
$125

Auctions at Showplace, NYC

Silver-French, Tray, Side Handles, Raised Rim, Stamped, Cartier, 29 x 18 In.
$4,329

Thomaston Place Auction Galleries

Silver-French, Tureen, Dome Lid, Undertray, 2 Handles, Footed, Art Deco, Early 1900s, 9 x 12 x 12 In.
$3,630

Fontaine's Auction Gallery

Silver-French, Wine Taster, Gadroon Bowl, Spiral, Serpent Shape Handle, Late 1700s, 1 x 4½ x 3½ In.
$497

Thomaston Place Auction Galleries

Silver-German, Centerpiece, Cobalt Blue Glass Bowl, Gilt, Grapevine Band, Putti Base, Baroque, 1800s, 10 In.
$790

Thomaston Place Auction Galleries

Trophy Cup, Lid, Richmond Horse Show, June 1899, Mappin & Webb, London, 14 x 9 In. *illus*	750
Waiter, Engraved Coat Of Arms, Rococo Border, George II, c.1748, 7 In., Pair......................	1169
Waiter, Oval, Coat Of Arms Center, Marked IM, London, George III, 1806, 11 In., Pair.........	1625
Wine Bottle Holder, Etched Glass Insert, Tripod Feet, Hallmarks, c.1920s, 1 ½ x 3 ¾ In......	308

SILVER-FRENCH

Beaker, Banded Rim, Engraved, Amy R, Theodor Tonnelier, Paris, c.1810, 3 ½ x 3 ¼ In......	250
Bowl, Console, Removable Liner, Deep, Marked Paris, 4 ¼ x 14 In.	688
Bowl, Shell Shape, Gilt Wash, First Standard, Early 1900s, 7 ¾ x 10 x 6 ¼ In................ *illus*	1250
Brandy Warmer, Flared Rim, Black Handle, C.M. Granger, Paris, c.1810, 2 ¾ x 11 ½ In....... *illus*	281
Cigarette Case, Blue & White, Enamel Border, Hand Chased, Hallmark, 4 x 3 In......... *illus*	204
Claret Jug, Hinged Lid, Glass Body, Repousse, Leaves, Shaped Handle, c.1880, 8 In..............	938
Coffeepot, Dome Lid, Flower Bud Finial, Scroll Handle, Footed, c.1900, 11 In.............. *illus*	469
Epergne, Flute Vase, Bowl, 3 Gryphons, Paw Foot, c.1910s, 19 ½ In..........................	330
Lipstick Case, Openwork, Gem Set, Engraved Butterfly, Flowers, Boucheron, France, 2 ¼ In.	906
Loving Cup, Gilt, Vermeil Finish, 2 Handles, Leon Maeght, Paris, 3 In..........................	192
Pie Server, Weighted Handle, Blade, Marked, Christofle, 10 ¾ In. .... *illus*	125
Sugar, Dome Lid, Acorn Finial, Embossed Design, Footed, 6 ½ In..............................	375
Tray, Serving, Rectangular, Leaf Shape Handles, Conforming Rim, 4 Shells, Late 1800s, 27 ½ In.	4688
Tray, Side Handles, Raised Rim, Stamped, Cartier, 29 x 18 In............................... *illus*	4329
Tureen, Dome Lid, Undertray, 2 Handles, Footed, Art Deco, Early 1900s, 9 x 12 x 12 In. *illus*	3630
Wine Taster, Gadroon Bowl, Spiral, Serpent Shape Handle, Late 1700s, 1 x 4 ½ x 3 ½ In. ....*illus*	497

SILVER-GERMAN

Basket, Centerpiece, Openwork Rinceau, Bird, Floral Swags, Putti, Early 1900s, 7 x 13 In...	531
Bowl, Classical Figures, Scrolling, Candlearm Handles, Continental, Late 1800s, 10 In.	4160
Bowl, Coin Inset Design, Beaded, Scalloped Rim, Marked Obscured, 1900s, 3 ¾ x 13 In.	750
Bowl, Repousse, Cherubs Scene, Curved Feet, 1800s, 2 ½ In., Pair..............................	144
Box, Tobacco, Hinged Lid, Smoking Scene, Flowers, Fruit, Oval, Hanau, 1900s, 4 ½ In.	125
Centerpiece, Cobalt Blue Glass Bowl, Gilt, Grapevine Band, Putti Base, Baroque, 1800s, 10 In....*illus*	790
Centerpiece, Swan, Swim Position, Frosted, Glass Insert, Marked, 1900s, 9 x 5 x 10 In...*illus*	2813
Cigar Cutter, Boar's Tusk, Fox Head, Gilt, Mounted, Gold Plated, Donatus, Solingen, 6 In..	497
Claret Jug, Neoclassical Style, Cut Glass, Joseph Netter, Late 1800s, 11 In., Pair..................	640
Coffeepot, Dome Lid, Repousse, Flowers, Birds, Wood Handle, Pad Feet, Late 1800s, 6 In....	407
Cup, Traubenpokal, Grapes, Flower Finial, Scrolled Stem, Circular Foot, 1600s, 10 ½ In.	1815
Cup, Traveling, Repousse, Flowers, Leaves, Late 1800s, 5 ¾ In., Pair............................ *illus*	281
Decanter, Etched Glass, Cherubs Playing, Dramatic Mask, Musical Instruments, 1874-1926, 11 In. ...	438
Dish, Sweetmeat, Hanau, Side Handles, B. Neresheimer & Sohne, 1800s, 7 x 8 x 3 In., Pair.	497
Figure, Peacock, Standing, Tail Shape Bowl, Wings Lift, Drawer Base, 11 In................ *illus*	192
Gravy Boat, Undertray, Scalloped Rim & Base, Lazarus Posen, Early 1900s, 6 ½ In.	1029
Jardiniere, Floral Garland, Ribbons, 4 Figures, Medallion, Footed, Late 1800s, 6 x 15 x 8 In...	2299
Kettle, Lid, Finial, Burner Stand, Simon Rosenau, Bad Kissengen, Early 1900s, 14 In.. *illus*	1098
Pokal, Lid, Roman Centurion Finial, Repousse, Classical, 1800s, 20 ¾ x 5 ½ In.	5265
Salt, 2 Shell Shape Bowls, Mermonkey Stem, Domed Base, 1800s, 5 ¾ In..................... *illus*	563
Sauceboat, Underplate, 2 Handles, Oval Base, Margraf & Co., 1914-36, 10 ½ x 7 In.	295
Stein, Hinged Lid, Bas Relief, Satyrs, Cupids, Ram, Dancing, Seminude Women, 1800s, 11 x 7 In.	8190
Tureen, Dome Lid, Lobed, Fruits Finial, 2 Handles, Footed, 9 ½ x 12 In. .... *illus*	1125
Vase, Trumpet Shape, Circular Stepped Base, Art Nouveau, 14 ¼ In............................	938

SILVER-INDIAN

Tankard, Dome Lid, Horse Finial, Reed Banded, Hamilton & Co., Calcutta, c.1850, 7 In..*illus*	1375

SILVER-IRISH

Bowl, 2 Handles, Celtic Engraving, Footed, Edmond Johnson Ltd., Dublin, 1923, 5 ½ In.	250
Dish, Sideboard, Beaded Rim, John Smith, Dublin, Victorian, 1869, 16 In.	4688
Lemon Strainer, Shaped Handle, Thomas Isaacs, Dublin, George II, 1736, 9 ⅞ In...... *illus*	2944
Marrow Scoop, Thistle Crest, Joseph Cullen, Dublin, George III, c.1765...................... *illus*	625
Potato Ring, Buildings, Animals, Blue Glass Insert, Thomas Weir, Dublin, 4 ½ x 7 ¼ In.	594
Salver, Gadroon Rim, Rocaille, Matthew West, Dublin, George III, 1794, 7 In.	438
Sauceboat, Repousse, Birds & Flowers, Curved Handle, Tripod Feet, Georgian, 1700s, 5 ½ In.	500
Spoon, Christening, Figural Handle, Charles Lamb, Dublin, Victorian, 1901, 7 ¾ In.	281
Sugar Basket, Oval Bowl, Floral Swags, Jos. Jackson, Dublin, George III, 1790, 7 In....*illus*	2000

Silver-German, Centerpiece, Swan, Swim Position, Frosted, Glass Insert, Marked, 1900s, 9 x 5 x 10 In. $2,813

Hindman

> **TIP**
> *Don't use silver polish that has dried up. The hard polish has too much abrasive in it and will scratch your silver. Splurge. Buy a new supply.*

Silver-German, Cup, Traveling, Repousse, Flowers, Leaves, Late 1800s, 5 ¾ In., Pair $281

Hindman

S

Silver-German, Figure, Peacock, Standing, Tail Shape Bowl, Wings Lift, Drawer Base, 11 In. $192

Richard Opfer Auctioneering, Inc.

Silver-German, Kettle, Lid, Finial, Burner Stand, Simon Rosenau, Bad Kissengen, Early 1900s, 14 In.
$1,098

Neal Auction Company

Silver-German, Salt, 2 Shell Shape Bowls, Mermonkey Stem, Domed Base, 1800s, 5 3/4 In.
$563

Hindman

Silver-German, Tureen, Dome Lid, Lobed, Fruits Finial, 2 Handles, Footed, 9 1/2 x 12 In.
$1,125

Hindman

Silver-Indian, Tankard, Dome Lid, Horse Finial, Reed Banded, Hamilton & Co., Calcutta, c.1850, 7 In.
$1,375

Hindman

Silver-Irish, Lemon Strainer, Shaped Handle, Thomas Isaacs, Dublin, George II, 1736, 9 7/8 In.
$2,944

Neal Auction Company

Silver-Irish, Marrow Scoop, Thistle Crest, Joseph Cullen, Dublin, George III, c.1765
$625

Hindman

Silver-Irish, Sugar Basket, Oval Bowl, Floral Swags, Jos. Jackson, Dublin, George III, 1790, 7 In.
$2,000

Hindman

Silver-Italian, Bowl, Hammered, Oval Lobed Body, Flared Foot, Buccellati, 1950s, 4 x 10 In.
$1,375

John Moran Auctioneers

Silver-Italian, Dish, Shell Shape, Footed, DeBoni Carla For Buccellati, Padua, 1944, 9 In.
$5,100

Bonhams

TIP

When cleaning silver, be careful of pieces like candlesticks or hollow knife handles that could hold the remains of chemical cleaner. Use a polish that is made to be used dry and wiped off.

S

Tazza, Cherub Masks, Stippled Crest, Wm. Nelson, Dublin, George IV, 1828, 6 x 10 In., Pair ... 4063

SILVER-ITALIAN

Bowl, Hammered, Oval Lobed Body, Flared Foot, Buccellati, 1950s, 4 x 10 In. .... *illus* 1375
Bowl, Lobed, Shaped Handles, Leaves, Scrollwork Feet, 1900s, 7 x 21¾ x 9½ In. 1815
Box, Chestnut, Marked Underside, Buccellati, Italy, c.1940, 3 x 6 x 4¼ In. 2304
Card Case, Hinged Lid, Rectangular, Marked, Cartier, Italy, Late 1800s, 3¾ In. 375
Dish, Shell Shape, Footed, De Boni Carla For Buccellati, Padua, 1944, 9 In. .... *illus* 5100
Goblet, Hammered Finish, Malachite Accents, Buccellati, 6½ x 3¼ In., Pair 1968
Serving Spoon, Neoclassical Style, Chased Handle, Conforming Stem, 1900s, 8½ In. 210
Teapot, Hinged Dome Lid, Shaped Handle, Gooseneck Spout, 4-Footed, 7 In. .... *illus* 156
Tray, 3 Leaf Shape, Marked, Buccellati, Italy, 1900s, 2¾ x 16¼ x 17 In. .... *illus* 3630
Vase, Urn Shape, Flared Rim, Acanthus leaves, Footed, Marked, Buccellati, 1900s, 14½ In. 3185

SILVER-JAPANESE

Cocktail Shaker, Acanthus, Engraved, Ivy Vine Handle, Yuchang, Early 1900s, 11½ In.*illus* 861
Teapot, Lid, Removable Spout, Round, Side Engraved, Crest, 3 Leaves, 4 x 8 x 5¾ In. 156

SILVER-MEXICAN

Silver objects have been made in Mexico since the days of the Aztecs. These marks are for three companies still making tableware and jewelry.

ChATo CASTillo STERLING MEXICO	Matl STERLING MEXICO 925	SANBORN'S STERLING H MADE IN MEXICO
Jorge "Chato" Castillo 1939+	Matilde Eugenia Poulat 1934–1960	Sanborn's 1931–present

Cachepot, Octagonal, Square Rim, 2 Handles, Removable Drip Pan, Ortega, 1900s, 5¼ x 8¼ In. . 438
Cigar Box, Hinged Lid, Mixed Metal, Relief Figures On Lid, 1½ x 6¼ In. 176
Coffeepot, Hinged Lid, Loop Handle, Signed, P. Lopez G, 10 x 10 x 5 In. .... *illus* 732
Dish, Shell Shape, Scalloped Edge, Handle, Engraved, Monogram, 4¼ In., 8 Piece 250
Pitcher, Melon Shape Body, Applied Leaves Rim & Base, 11 In. .... *illus* 840
Pitcher, Shaped Handle, Flared Rim, Myers, Mexico City, 1900s, 5¾ In. 313
Salt & Pepper, Blue Ceramic Ground, Emilia Castillo, 2⅞ x 1⅞ In., Pair 94
Spurs, Striped Inlay, Rowels & Jingle Bobs, Mexico, Early 1900s, 8 In., Pair 168
Tray, Oval, Petal Shape Border, 20 x 14½ In. .... *illus* 1500
Tray, Oval, Scalloped Edge, Relief Roses, Marked, Sanborns, 8 x 11½ In. 340
Tray, Serving, Shell & Scrolled Border, Open Side Handles, 34 In. 2760
Vase, Scalloped Rim, Footed, Signed, Ortega, Mid 1900s, 5 x 7 In., Pair 813

SILVER-PERSIAN

Box, Lid, Pierced Top, Decorated Finial, Flowers, Bird Base, 4 x 9 In. .... *illus* 832
Tray, Allover Incised Design, Corner Flowers, 14 x 10 In. 896
Vase, Fluted, Tapered Body, Chrysanthemums, 9½ In. 384

SILVER-PERUVIAN

Charger, 6-Lobed Dish, Coat Of Arms, 2 Eagles, Leafy Border, 16½ x 16½ In. 1080
Dish, Leaf Shape, Carved, Wood Handle, Footed, 1½ x 10 x 3½ In. 113

SILVER-PORTUGUESE

Tray, Scalloped Border, Hallmark, Porto, 1900s, 18½ In. 1063

SILVER-RUSSIAN

Russian silver is marked with the Cyrillic, or Russian, alphabet. The numbers 84, 88, or 91 indicate the silver content. Russian silver may be higher or lower than sterling standard. Other marks indicate maker, assayer, or city of manufacture. Many pieces of silver made in Russia are decorated with enamel. Faberge pieces are listed in their own category.

TIP

Eighteenth- and nine-teenth-century Irish silver is more valuable than English because it is rarer.

Silver-Italian, Teapot, Hinged Dome Lid, Shaped Handle, Gooseneck Spout, 4-Footed, 7 In.
$156

Alderfer Auction Company

Silver-Italian, Tray, 3 Leaf Shape, Marked, Buccellati, Italy, 1900s, 2¾ x 16¼ x 17 In.
$3,630

Fontaine's Auction Gallery

Silver-Japanese, Cocktail Shaker, Acanthus, Engraved, Ivy Vine Handle, Yuchang, Early 1900s, 11½ In.
$861

Brunk Auctions

Silver-Mexican, Coffeepot, Hinged Lid, Loop Handle, Signed, P. Lopez G, 10 x 10 x 5 In. $732

Rafael Osona Nantucket Auctions

Silver-Mexican, Pitcher, Melon Shape Body, Applied Leaves Rim & Base, 11 In. $840

Richard Opfer Auctioneering, Inc.

TIP

Store silver, sterling or plated, away from high humidity. The ideal humidity is 40 to 45 percent. You can keep small pieces in a glassed-in cupboard with anti-tarnish paper or camphor balls (moth balls). Big pieces can be kept in tarnish-preventing bags that can be found at department and jewelry stores or online.

Silver–Russian
Silver content numbers

Silver–Russian
1741–1900+

Silver–Russian
1896–1908

Beaker, Shaded Enamel, Blue, Leaves, Flowers, Syemyen Yegornov, Moscow, 1896, 2¼ In.*illus*	1250
Belt, Caucasian, Engraved, Niello, Hooked Buckle, Moscow Kokoshnik, 1800s, 35 In.	250
Bowl, Enamel Decoration, Multicolor, Ivan Sazikov, Moscow, Late 1800s, 1⅛ In.	344
Cigar Box, Horse-Drawn Carriage, 3 People, Dog, Monogram, Niello, Moscow, 1878, 3½ In.	500
Cigarette Box, Trompe L'Oeil, Alexander Moskvin, Moscow, Tabletop, 1899, 2 x 4 x 3 In.	2375
Cigarette Case, 2 Polar Bears, Scene, Emerald Inset, G.R., Moscow, Late 1800s, 4 In.*illus*	875
Jar, Dome Lid, Enameled, White Ground, Footed, Feodor Ruckert, Moscow, Late 1800s, 3½ In.	2500
Kovsh, Gilt, Shaded Enamel, Flowers, M. Chirkov, Moscow, c.1900, 4 x 8 In.	6875
Kovsh, Leafy Handle, Scrolls, Alexander Benediktovich Lyubavin, St. Petersburg, c.1900, 6 x 14 In.	5938
Samovar, Imperial, Square Base, Kokoshnik Marks, Mikhail Ovchinnikov, 19 x 12½ x 10½ In.	7380
Skewer, Gilt, Figural Heraldic Symbol, 2-Headed Eagle, Moscow, c.1900, 5⅛ In., 6 Piece	1125
Spoon, Gilt, Blue, Red, White, Stamped, Gustav Klingert, Moscow, 1870s, 7 In.	409
Spoon, Gold Wash, Rolled Handle, Hallmark, Moscow, 1889, 4¾ In., 12 Piece	210
Spoon, Niello, Gilt, Kremlin & St. Basil's Cathedral, Vasili Semenov, Moscow, 1869, 9 In., Pair	3125
Sugar Tongs, Swirl, Enameled, Multicolor Design, 4 In.	466
Vodka Cup, Cobalt Blue Ground, Flowers, Multicolor, 2 x 1½ In.*illus*	500

SILVER-SCOTTISH

Bowling Ball, Presentation, Leather Case, Muirhead & Arthur, Glasgow, 1870, 2⅞ In.	768
Salver, Engraved, Crest, Shaped Rim, Tripod, Pad Feet, c.1780, 8 In.	375
Spoon, Serving, William Dempster, Edinburgh, George III, 1761, 7½ In., 6 Piece	313
Tray, Round, Scroll, Waves, Engraved, Edinburgh, 1840, 18¼ In.	3444

SILVER-SPANISH

Cocktail Shaker, Dome Lid, Ball Shape Finial, Domenech & Soler Cabot, 1900s, 8¾ In.*illus*	847
Dish, Sweetmeat, Empire, Gadroon Rim, Damian De Castro, Cordoba, 1700s, 7½ In., Pair	188
Finial, Processional, Cruciform Top, Knopped Stem, 4 Bells, Colonial, c.1768, 7½ In.	531

SILVER-STERLING

Sterling silver is made with 925 parts silver out of 1,000 parts of metal. The word *sterling* is a quality guarantee used in the United States after about 1860. The word was used much earlier in England and Ireland. Other pieces of sterling quality silver are listed under Silver-American, Silver-English, etc.

Bowl, Deep, Repousse Border, Shaped Rim, 10⅜ In.	270
Bowl, Ornate, Scalloped Borders, Flowers, Marked, 10 In. *illus*	228
Bowl, Vegetable, Dome Lid, Flower Design, Oval Base, 5½ x 11 In.	567
Box, Hinged Lid, Embossed Design, Frog Feet, 1⅝ x 4 x 3 In.	313
Box, Square, Courting Scene, Couple, Floral Composition, Velvet Lined, 3 x 9½ x 9½ In.	813
Candelabra are listed in the Candelabrum category.	
Candlesticks are listed in their own category.	
Chocolate Pot, Demitasse, Urn Shape, Engraved, Ebony Handle, Neoclassical, 1920, 9 x 7 In.*illus*	230
Cigarette Box, Hinged Lid, Topaz Stone Finial, Wood Liner, Late 1800s, 2 x 11 x 3¾ In.*illus*	425
Coaster Set, Silver Caddy, Glass Coasters, Marked, 1900s, 3 In., 6 Piece	30
Figurine, Pheasant, Standing, Tabletop, Marked, 5½ x 14 In. *illus*	1024
Figurine, Vermeil Knight, Jewel Armor, Standing, Jewels Mounted On Base, 11½ In.	1476
Holder, Calendar & Watch, Splayed Feet, Art Nouveau, 5¼ x 4 In.	688
Ladle, Embossed Woman's Head, Flower, Victorian, 9¼ In.	420
Napkin Rings are listed in their own category.	
Pitcher, Mineola Horse Show, Wide Spout, Loop Handle, 1912, 7 In.	438
Punch Bowl, Presentation, Princeton Tiger Inn, Ring Handles, 1928, 7⅜ In.	2048
Rattle, Dumbbell Shape, Marked, MPLY, c.1950	72
Salver, Rococo Revival Style, Repousse Rim, Curved Feet, Victorian, 1907, 9 In.	375

Silver-Mexican, Tray, Oval, Petal Shape Border, 20 x 14 ½ In.
$1,500

New Haven Auctions

Silver-Persian, Box, Lid, Pierced Top, Decorated Finial, Flowers, Bird Base, 4 x 9 In.
$832

Roland NY Auctioneers & Appraisers

Silver-Russian, Beaker, Shaded Enamel, Blue, Leaves, Flowers, Syemyen Yegornov, Moscow, 1896, 2 ¼ In.
$1,250

Hindman

Silver-Russian, Cigarette Case, 2 Polar Bears, Scene, Emerald Inset, G.R., Moscow, Late 1800s, 4 In.
$875

Hindman

Silver-Russian, Vodka Cup, Cobalt Blue Ground, Flowers, Multicolor, 2 x 1 ½ In.
$500

Woody Auction

> **TIP**
> *Silver kept in direct sunlight will tarnish more quickly than pieces stored in the dark.*

Silver-Spanish, Cocktail Shaker, Dome Lid, Ball Shape Finial, Domenech & Soler Cabot, 1900s, 8 ¾ In.
$847

Fontaine's Auction Gallery

Silver-Sterling, Bowl, Ornate, Scalloped Borders, Flowers, Marked, 10 In.
$228

Main Auction Galleries, Inc.

Silver-Sterling, Chocolate Pot, Demitasse, Urn Shape, Engraved, Ebony Handle, Neoclassical, 1920, 9 x 7 In.
$230

Merrill's Auctions

Silver-Sterling, Cigarette Box, Hinged Lid, Topaz Stone Finial, Wood Liner, Late 1800s, 2 x 11 x 3 ¾ In.
$425

Fontaine's Auction Gallery

Silver-Sterling, Figurine, Pheasant, Standing, Tabletop, Marked, 5 ½ x 14 In.
$1,024

Nadeau's Auction Gallery

S

Silver-Sterling, Vase, Trumpet Shape, Weighted Base, Monogram, 12 In. $188

Turner Auctions + Appraisals

TIP
Have an inventory of your collections and adequate insurance.

Silver-Swedish, Compote, Hand Hammered, Flared Fluted Rim & Base, Repousse Flower, c.1915, 6 x 12 In. $585

Thomaston Place Auction Galleries

Silver-Swedish, Tankard, Hinged Lid, Ball Feet, Coin Inset, C.G. Hallberg, Stockholm, 1952, 5 ¼ In. $406

Hindman

Spoon, Souvenir, see Souvenir category.	
Tray, Rococo Design, Repousse Floral Border, 14 In..	750
Vase, Trumpet Shape, Weighted Base, Monogram, 12 In.............................*illus*	188

SILVER-SWEDISH
Compote, Hand Hammered, Flared Fluted Rim & Base, Repousse Flower, c.1915, 6 x 12 In. *illus*	585
Tankard, Hinged Lid, Ball Feet, Coin Inset, C.G. Hallberg, Stockholm, 1952, 5 ¼ In......*illus*	406

SILVER-THAI
Box, Figural, Pumpkin Shape, Stem & Leaf Finial, Flowers, Wood Stand, 1900s, 5 x 9 In.....	100

SILVER-TURKISH
Centerpiece, 2 Handles, Putti Playing Trumpets, Baroque Style, Lale, Istanbul, 1900s, 19 x 29 In..	6120

SINCLAIRE

Sinclaire cut glass was made by H.P. Sinclaire and Company of Corning, New York, between 1904 and 1929. He cut glass made at other factories until 1920. Pieces were made of clear glass as well as amber, blue, green, or ruby glass. Only a small percentage of Sinclaire glass is marked with the *S* in a wreath.

Bowl, Green Rim, Etched Grapes, 2 ¼ x 5 In.	59
Cologne Bottle, Fan & Miter, Stopper, Ray Cut Base, Signed, 6 x 5 In.	175
Ice Bucket, Hobstar, Strawberry Diamond, Fan, Engraved Flowers, Silver Plate Liner, 6 x 5 In..	210
Ice Tub, Strawberry Diamond & Fan Design, Hobstar, Flowers Border, Signed, 6 x 5 In.	175
Vase, Black Amethyst, Etched Dragons & Clouds, c.1915, 8 ⅝ In............................*illus*	400

SKIING, *see Sports category.*

SLAG GLASS

Slag glass resembles a marble cake. It can be streaked with different colors. There were many types made from about 1880. Caramel slag is the incorrect name for chocolate glass made by Imperial Glass. Pink slag was an American product made by Harry Bastow and Thomas E.A. Dugan at Indiana, Pennsylvania, about 1900. Purple and blue slag were made in American and English factories in the 1880s. Red slag is a very late Victorian and twentieth-century glass. Other colors are known but are of less importance to the collector. New versions of chocolate glass and colored slag glass have been made.

Beige, Brown, Lamp, Hanging, Leaded, Beaded Border, 1900s, 22 ½ In....................	150
Orange, Vase, Flared Shaded Base, Asymmetrical Top, Midcentury, 38 x 10 x 10 In.............	95
Bittersweet Orange, Candy Dish, Lid, Raised Ovals, Lobed Foot, L.E. Smith, 10 x 6 In.	30
Swirl, Ashtray, Car, Blue & Cream, Agate, 3 x 1 ¾ In....................................*illus*	48

SLEEPY EYE

Sleepy Eye collectors look for anything bearing the image of the nineteenth-century Indian chief with the drooping eyelid. The Sleepy Eye Milling Co., Sleepy Eye, Minnesota, used his portrait in advertising from 1883 to 1921. It offered many premiums, including stoneware and pottery steins, crocks, bowls, mugs, pitchers, and many advertising items, all decorated with the famous profile of the Indian. The popular pottery was made by Weir Pottery Co. from c.1899 to 1905. Weir merged with six other potteries and became Western Stoneware in 1906. Western Stoneware Co. made blue and white Sleepy Eye from 1906 until 1937, long after the flour mill went out of business in 1921. Reproductions of the pitchers are being made today. The original pitchers came in only five sizes: 4 inches, 5 ¼ inches, 6 ½ inches, 8 inches, and 9 inches. The Sleepy Eye image was also used by companies unrelated to the flour mill.

Pitcher, Blue & White, Profile, Landscape, Trees, Teepees, Blue Rim, 8 In...................*illus*	188

Sinclaire, Vase, Black Amethyst, Etched Dragons & Clouds, c.1915, 8 5/8 In.
$400

Sleepy Eye, Sign, Indian, Profile, Self-Framed, Rectangular, Tin Lithograph, c.1900, 24 x 20 In.
$3,300

Cottone Auctions

Heritage Auctions

Slag Glass, Swirl, Ashtray, Car, Blue & Cream, Agate, 3 x 1 3/4 In.
$48

Matthew Bullock Auctioneers

Sleepy Eye, Pitcher, Blue & White, Profile, Landscape, Trees, Teepees, Blue Rim, 8 In.
$188

Pottery Padded the Price
Old Sleepy Eye stoneware pitchers were put in bags of flour sold by the Sleepy Eye Milling Company. But the government made the company stop the practice. The pottery was so heavy that the customers did not get the full weight of flour they paid for.

Sleepy Eye, Vase, Indian, Profile, Cattails On Reverse, 8 1/2 In.
$219

New Haven Auctions

Hindman

S

Smith Brothers, Biscuit Jar, Cream Tones, Pansies, Lid, 6 x 4 In. $200

Woody Auction

Smith Brothers, Vase, Bottle Shape, Twisted Mold, Cream, Blue Flowers, Leafy Vines, Gilt, Marked, 7 In. $87

Neue Auctions

Snuffbox, Silver, Hinged Lid, Oval, Monogram, William Seal, Philadelphia, Pa., c.1815, 3 In. $1,625

Hindman

Sign, Indian, Profile, Self-Framed, Rectangular, Tin Lithograph, c.1900, 24 x 20 In. .... *illus*	3300
Vase, Indian, Profile, Cattails On Reverse, 8½ In. .... *illus*	219

SLOT MACHINES *are included in the Coin-Operated Machine category.*

SMITH BROTHERS

Smith Brothers glass was made from 1874 to 1899. Alfred and Harry Smith had worked for the Mt. Washington Glass Company in New Bedford, Massachusetts, for seven years before going into their own shop. They made many pieces with enamel decoration.

Biscuit Jar, Cream Tones, Pansies, Lid, 6 x 4 In. .... *illus*	200
Biscuit Jar, Melon Ribbed, Autumn Acorn Branch, Cream Tones, Gilt Lid, 6 x 7 In.	300
Bowl, Melon Ribbed, Acorn Branch, Silver Plate Rim, Cream Tones, 4 x 8½ In.	50
Sugar & Creamer, Melon Ribbed, Yellow Flowers, Silver Plate Lid, Marked, 3¼ x 3 In.	120
Vase, Bottle Shape, Twisted Mold, Cream, Blue Flowers, Leafy Vines, Gilt, Marked, 7 In. *illus*	87
Vase, Cream, Blue Flowers, 3-Sided, Gilt Rim, Enameled Beads, Marked, 4¾ x 3¾ In.	72

SNOW BABIES

Snow Babies, made from bisque and spattered with glitter sand, were first manufactured in 1864 by Hertwig and Company of Thuringia. Other German and Japanese companies copied the Hertwig designs. Originally, Snow Babies were made of candy and used as Christmas decorations. There are also Snow Babies tablewares made by Royal Bayreuth. Copies of the small Snow Babies figurines are being made today, and a line called "Snowbabies" was introduced by Department 56 in 1987. Don't confuse these with the original Snow Babies.

Figurine, Baby, Carrying Skis, Hertwig & Company, 2 x 2¼ In.	166
Cake Topper, 2 Babies Playing On World War I Tank, 2 x 2 In.	130

SNUFF BOTTLES *are listed in the Bottle category.*

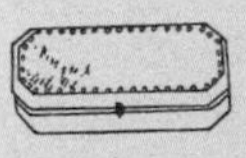

SNUFFBOX

Snuffboxes held snuff. Taking snuff was popular long before cigarettes became available. The gentleman or lady would take a small pinch of the ground tobacco or snuff in the fingers, then sniff it and sneeze. Snuffboxes were made of many materials, including gold, silver, enameled metal, and wood. Most snuffboxes date from the late eighteenth or early nineteenth centuries.

Agate, Painted Plaque, Gold, Mounts, Continental, Early 1800s, 1 x 2⅜ x 1¾ In.	4410
Brass, Hinged Lid, Engraved, Shell Bottom, Dutch, 1700s, 3¼ x 4 In.	214
Guilloche, Hinged Lid, Lavender, Silver Trim, Gold 2-Headed Eagle, Jewels, c.1908, 1 x 2 In.	2125
Silver, Foo Dog, Etched Erotic Scenes, Oval, Chinese, 1800s, 3 x 2¾ In.	2040
Silver, Hinged Lid, Oval, Monogram, William Seal, Philadelphia, Pa., c.1815, 3 In. ...... *illus*	1625
Silver, Octagonal, Hinged Slide Out, Chinese Export, Late 1800s, ¾ x 2 In. .... *illus*	205
Wood, Hinged Lid, Carved, Man O' War Ship Shape, Military Officer Figure, 1800s, 3 In.	295

SOAPSTONE

Soapstone is a mineral that was used for foot warmers or griddles because of its heat-retaining properties. Soapstone was carved into figurines and bowls in many countries in the nineteenth and twentieth centuries. Most of the soapstone collectibles seen today are from Asia. It is still being carved in the old styles.

Figurine, Ruyi Scepter, Carved, Koi Fish, Lacquered Wood Base, Chinese, Late 1800s, 17 In..	210

SOFT PASTE

Soft paste is a name for a type of pottery. Although it looks very much like porcelain, it is a chemically different material. Most of the soft-paste wares were made in the early nineteenth century. Other pieces may be listed under Gaudy Dutch or Leeds.

Figure, Elephant, White Glaze, Pink Roses, c.1930, 6 ½ x 9 ½ In.		188
Jar, Lid, Molded Flowers, Cream Glaze, Marked, St. Cloud, 18th Century, 4 ⅝ In.		688
Jug, British Ship, U.S. Seal On Reverse, Black Transfer, Raised Bands, Early 1800s, 9 ¼ In.....*illus*		1125
Pitcher, Squat, Grapes, Pinecones, Leaves, Gilt, Footed, Marked, Oxford, Austria, 14 ¾ x 8 In....		60
Plate, 2-Masted British Ship, White, Black Design, 1910s, 9 ¼ In..		188
Tray, Mauve Flowers, Gilt, 4-Footed, Vincennes, France, c.1750, 1 ¼ x 6 ¾ x 4 ¼ In..............		300
Work Basket, Underplate, Green Bands, Flowers, Pierced, Creamware, England, 4 x 10 ½ In.*illus*		125

SOUVENIR

Souvenirs of a trip—what could be more fun? Our ancestors enjoyed the same thing and souvenirs were made for almost every location. Most of the souvenir pottery and porcelain pieces of the nineteenth century were made in England or Germany, even if the picture showed a North American scene. In the early twentieth century, the souvenir china business seems to have been dominated by the manufacturers in Japan, Taiwan, Hong Kong, England, and the United States. Souvenir china was also made in other countries after the 1960s. Another popular souvenir item is the souvenir spoon, made of sterling or silver plate. These are usually made in the country pictured on the spoon. Related pieces may be found in the Coronation, Olympics, and World's Fair categories.

Charm, Chicago On Banner, Cutout Skyline, Pearl Moon, Fluted Edge, 14K Gold, 1 ½ In. ...		610
Coin, Pilgrim Half Dollar, Pilgrim Man With Prayer Book, Mayflower Reverse, 1620-1920 ..		300
Paddle, Canoe, Adirondack, Wood, Carved, Indian Chief Transfer, 1930s, 28 In., Pair		427
Pennant, Wool, Battle Of Gettysburg, 50th Anniversary, Reunion Encampment, 1913, 22 ½ In. *illus*		594
Sign, Societe St. Jean Baptiste, 50th Anniversary, Reverse Painted Glass, Gilt Frame,1914, 38 x 44 In. .		563

SPATTERWARE

Spatterware and spongeware are terms that have changed in meaning in recent years, causing much confusion for collectors. It is a type of ceramic. Some say that *spatterware* is the term used by Americans, *sponged ware* or *spongeware* by the English. The earliest pieces were made in the late eighteenth century, but most of the spatterware found today was made from about 1800 to 1850. Early spatterware was made in the Staffordshire district of England for sale in America. Collectors also use the word *spatterware* to refer to kitchen crockery with added spatter made in America during the late nineteenth and early twentieth centuries. Spongeware is very similar to spatterware in appearance. Designs were applied to ceramics by daubing the color on with a sponge or cloth. Many collectors do not differentiate between spongeware and spatterware and use the names interchangeably. Modern pottery is being made to resemble old spatterware and spongeware, but careful examination will show it is new.

Bowl, Thistle, Multicolor, Painted, Red Sponge, Footed, England, 1830s, 4 x 8 In.		527
Crock, Lid, Elongated Shape, Blue, Brown, Pink Sponge, 9 ¼ x 9 ½ In.........................*illus*		68
Pitcher, Primrose, Octagonal Panels, Blue Ground, Multicolor, England, 1830s, 10 In.*illus*		380
Plate, Bull's-Eye, Green & Blue, White Ground, 1800s, 9 In. ....*illus*		1968
Plate, Rabbitware, Rabbits & Frogs Center, Red Rim, Ironstone, 9 In., 6 Piece		510
Plate, Rainbow, Red & Green, White Ground, 8 ½ In...*illus*		1599
Plate, Thistle, Multicolor, Painted, Flower, Yellow Sponge Border, England, 1830s, 9 In.*illus*		527
Platter, Octagonal, Vertical Bands, Blue, Green & Red Sponge, England, 1830s, 12 x 9 In. *illus*		4680
Platter, Rainbow, Red & Green, White, Octagonal, 12 x 15 ¾ In. ....*illus*		1230

Snuffbox, Silver, Octagonal, Hinged Slide Out, Chinese Export, Late 1800s, ¾ x 2 In.
$205

Thomaston Place Auction Galleries

TIP
Don't store ceramic dishes or figurines for long periods of time in old newspaper wrappings. The ink can make indelible stains on china.

Soft Paste, Jug, British Ship, U.S. Seal On Reverse, Black Transfer, Raised Bands, Early 1800s, 9 ¼ In.
$1,125

Eldred's

S

Soft Paste, Work Basket, Underplate, Green Bands, Flowers, Pierced, Creamware, England, 4 x 10 ½ In.
$125

Carlsen Gallery

Souvenir, Pennant, Wool, Battle Of Gettysburg, 50th Anniversary, Reunion Encampment, 1913, 22 ½ In.
$594

Hindman

Spatterware, Crock, Lid, Elongated Shape, Blue, Brown, Pink Sponge, 9 ¼ x 9 ½ In.
$68

Hartzell's Auction Gallery Inc.

Spatterware, Pitcher, Primrose, Octagonal Panels, Blue Ground, Multicolor, England, 1830s, 10 In.
$380

Jeffrey S. Evans & Associates

Spatterware, Plate, Bull's-Eye, Green & Blue, White Ground, 1800s, 9 In.
$1,968

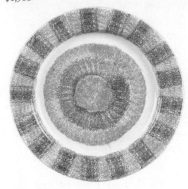

Pook & Pook

Spatterware, Plate, Rainbow, Red & Green, White Ground, 8 ½ In.
$1,599

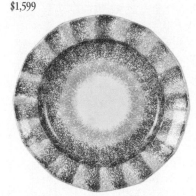

Pook & Pook

Spatterware, Plate, Thistle, Multicolor, Painted, Flower, Yellow Sponge Border, England, 1830s, 9 In.
$527

Jeffrey S. Evans & Associates

Spatterware, Platter, Octagonal, Vertical Bands, Blue, Green & Red Sponge, England, 1830s, 12 x 9 In.
$4,680

Jeffrey S. Evans & Associates

Spatterware, Platter, Rainbow, Red & Green, White, Octagonal, 12 x 15 ¾ In.
$1,230

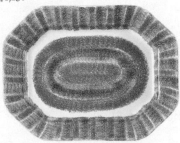

Pook & Pook

Spelter, Sculpture, Woman & Child, Standing On Roof, Peering Into Distance, 31 In.
$120

Garth's Auctioneers & Appraisers

S

SPELTER

Spelter is a synonym for a zinc alloy. Figurines, candlesticks, and other pieces were made of spelter and given a bronze or painted finish. The metal has been used since about the 1860s to make statues, tablewares, and lamps that resemble bronze. Spelter is soft and breaks easily. To test for spelter, scratch the base of the piece. Bronze is solid; spelter will show a silvery scratch.

Garniture, Clock, Figural, Woman, Seated, Writing Position, Oblong Base, Footed, 11 ½ In.	153
Sculpture, Cast Metal, Viking Warrior, Horse, Ax, Shield, 9 ½ In.	25
Sculpture, Chasseur, Man Standing Holding Bow, Patina, Wood Base, 24 In.	94
Sculpture, Man, Standing, Arm Raised, Dog, Victorian, 18 ½ x 8 x 5 In.	63
Sculpture, Young Boy, Standing, Naked, Raising Hands, With Base, 20 In.	74
Sculpture, Woman & Child, Standing On Roof, Peering Into Distance, 31 In. .... *illus*	120

SPINNING WHEEL

Spinning wheels in the corner have been symbols of earlier times for the past 150 years. Although spinning wheels date back to medieval days, the ones found today are rarely more than 150 years old. Because the style of the spinning wheel changed very little, it is often impossible to place an exact date on a wheel. There are different types for spinning flax or wool.

Beech, Treadle, Pedal Mechanism, French Provincial, 19th Century, 40 x 16 ½ x 27 In. *illus*	250
Castle, Flyer, Turned Post, Wood, Late 1700s, 18 x 15 x 37 In.	58
Mixed Wood, Bentwood Wheel, Walking, Yarn Winder, 3 Legs, 19th Century, 55 x 66 In..*illus*	63
Mixed Wood, Castle, Tabletop, Early 19th Century, 32 In. .... *illus*	92

SPODE

Spode pottery, porcelain, and bone china were made by the Stoke-on-Trent factory of England founded by Josiah Spode about 1770. The firm became Copeland and Garrett from 1833 to 1847, then W.T. Copeland or W.T. Copeland and Sons until 1976. It then became Royal Worcester Spode Ltd. The company was bought by the Portmeirion Group in 2009. The word *Spode* appears on many pieces made by the factories. Most collectors include all the wares under the more familiar name of Spode. Porcelains are listed in this book by the name that appears on the piece. Related pieces may be listed under Copeland, Copeland Spode, and Royal Worcester.

SPODE	COPELAND & GARRETT LATE SPODE	ROYAL WORCESTER SPODE
Spode c.1770–1790	Copeland & Garrett c.1833–1847	Royal Worcester Spode Ltd. 1976–c.2009

Ginger Jar, Lid, Chinoiserie, Multicolor, Flowers, Shima, 5 x 5 x 7 In., Pair	59
Planter, Fluted, Flowers, 8 x 8 x 7 In., Pair	59
Plate, King William IV, Queen Adelaide, Lion, Unicorn, 1830, 10 In. .... *illus*	2734

SPONGEWARE, *see Spatterware category.*

SPORTS, *Cards are listed in the Card category*

SPORTS

Sports equipment, sporting goods, brochures, and related items are listed here. Items are listed by sport. Other categories of interest are Bicycle, Card, Fishing, Sword, Toy, and Trap.

Baseball, Ball, Autographed, Mickey Mantle, Rawlings, 3 x 3 ¼ x 3 ¼ In. .... *illus*	352
Baseball, Ball, Autographed, White, Ford Frick, New York Giants, 1952	180

Spinning Wheel, Beech, Treadle, Pedal Mechanism, French Provincial, 19th Century, 40 x 16 ½ x 27 In. $250

Crescent City Auction Gallery

Spinning Wheel, Mixed Wood, Bentwood Wheel, Walking, Yarn Winder, 3 Legs, 19th Century, 55 x 66 In. $63

Garth's Auctioneers & Appraisers

Spinning Wheel, Mixed Wood, Castle, Tabletop, Early 19th Century, 32 In. $92

Conestoga Auction Company

Spode, Plate, King William IV, Queen Adelaide, Lion, Unicorn, 1830, 10 In.
$2,734

Bonhams

Sports, Baseball, Ball, Autographed, Mickey Mantle, Rawlings, 3 x 3 ¼ x 3 ¼ In.
$352

Morphy Auctions

Sports, Baseball, Box, Cereal, Wheaties, Lou Gehrig, Orange & Blue Graphics
$7,680

Julien's Auctions

Sports, Baseball, Button, Mickey Mantle, Red, White, Blue Ribbon, Bat & Ball Charms, 1950s
$96

Alderfer Auction Company

Sports, Baseball, Doll, Jackie Robinson, Brooklyn Dodgers, c.1950, 13 x 6 x 4 In.
$1,024

Morphy Auctions

Sports, Baseball, Figure, Chief Wahoo, Chalkware, Cleveland Indians, Mazzolini Artcraft, 8 In.
$90

Hartzell's Auction Gallery Inc.

Sports, Baseball, Figure, Roger Maris, Swinging Bat, Home Plate, Hartland, 7 In.
$57

Hartzell's Auction Gallery Inc.

Sports, Basketball, Ashtray, Hawks Championship, Porcelain, Denver M. Wright Jr. Co., c.1958, 6 In.
$240

Selkirk Auctioneers & Appraisers

Sports, Boxing, Gloves, Red Leather, Everlast, Autographed, Muhammad Ali, 1994, Pair
$2,070

Blackwell Auctions

TIP
Game-worn All-Star uniforms and shoes are the best things to collect from an All-Star Game. Other collectibles are mass-produced and widely available.

Baseball, Ball, St. Louis Cardinals, National League, 1961	288
Baseball, Bat, Commemorative, 1980 All Star Game, Autographs, Hillerich, Bradsbury, 1977, 34 In.	30
Baseball, Box, Cereal, Wheaties, Lou Gehrig, Orange & Blue Graphics .... *illus*	7680
Baseball, Button, Mickey Mantle, Red, White, Blue Ribbon, Bat & Ball Charms, 1950s *illus*	96
Baseball, Doll, Jackie Robinson, Brooklyn Dodgers, c.1950, 13 x 6 x 4 In...................... *illus*	1024
Baseball, Figure, Chief Wahoo, Chalkware, Cleveland Indians, Mazzolini Artcraft, 8 In......*illus*	90
Baseball, Figure, Roger Maris, Swinging Bat, Home Plate, Hartland, 7 In. .... *illus*	57
Baseball, Newspaper, Champs, Mets, Tom Seaver, Ed Kranepool, Autographs, Frame, 1969	85
Basketball, Ashtray, Hawks Championship, Porcelain, Denver M. Wright Jr. Co., c.1958, 6 In.....*illus*	240
Boxing, Gloves, Red Leather, Everlast, Autographed, Muhammad Ali, 1994, Pair..........*illus*	2070
Football, Jersey, Alonzo Spellman, Orange & Blue, Chicago Bears, 1994, 48 In.	2375
Hockey, Stick, Willie O'Ree, San Diego Gulls, Game Issued, Northland, 1970s, 54 In.	460
Pool, Table, Barney Bellinger, Adirondack, Oil Paintings, Slate Top, Sampson Bog Studios.. *illus*	61200
Pool, Table, Hudson, Walnut, Brunswick-Balke-Collender Co., c.1920, 32 x 59 x 110 In........ *illus*	4688
Tennis, Racket, Wood, Oversize, Red, Black, White, 54 x 19 In., Pair	610

Sports, Pool, Table, Barney Bellinger, Adirondack, Oil Paintings, Slate Top, Sampson Bog Studios
$61,200

Blanchard's Auction Service LLC

Sports, Pool, Table, Hudson, Walnut, Brunswick-Balke-Collender Co., c.1920, 32 x 59 x 110 In.
$4,688

Hindman

STAFFORDSHIRE

Staffordshire, England, has been a district making pottery and porcelain since the 1700s. Thousands of types of pottery and porcelain have been made in the many factories that worked in the area. Some of the most famous factories have been listed separately, such as Adams, Davenport, Ridgway, Rowland & Marsellus, Royal Doulton, Royal Worcester, Spode, Wedgwood, and others. Some Staffordshire pieces are listed under categories like Fairing, Flow Blue, Mulberry, Shaving Mug, etc.

Coffeepot, Lift Lid, Lafayette, Blue, Flowers, 11 In..*illus*	328
Creamer, Cow, White, Pink Flowers, Basket, 5 x 7 x 3 In.	63
Creamer, Sprig Molded Flower, Vines, Strap Handle, Tortoiseshell Glaze, 1760s, 3 ¼ In.	281
Figurine, Dog, Afghan, Blond, Limited Edition, With Certificate, 1900s, 8 ½ x 7 ¼ In.	75
Figurine, Dog, Red Spaniel, Royal Child Riding, c.1870, 9 x 7 x 3 In., Pair	156
Figurine, Dog, Spaniel, Black & White, Gilt Collar, 10 x 7 In., Pair.............................*illus*	81
Figurine, Dog, Spaniel, Seated, White Glaze, Black Nose, 13 x 12 x 5 In., Pair ....*illus*	173
Figurine, Dog, Spaniel, Standing, Brown & White, Glass Eyes, 1800s, 11 x 16 x 4 In., Pair ..	406
Figurine, Lion, Lying Down, Inset Glass Eyes, Gilt Highlights Base, 9 ½ x 12 ½ In., Pair	300
Figurine, Lion, Standing, Ball, Painted, Glass Eyes, 11 ½ x 12 In., Pair......................*illus*	153
Figurine, Lion, Standing, Orange & Brown Glaze, Glass Eyes, 10 x 14 In., Pair	130
Figurine, Robert Burns, Standing, Multicolor, Base, c.1860, 13 ½ In............................*illus*	63
Figurine, Rooster, White Crackle Ground, Red Comb & Wattle, Black Beak, 2 x 9 x 5 In., Pair ..	660
Figurine, Sailor, Standing, Painted, White & Black, Oval Base, 1800s, 13 In. ....*illus*	1525
Group, Band Of Hope, Woman & Child, Uniform, Flowered Dress, Multicolor, 1800s, 14 In.	156
Group, Vicar & Moses, In Pulpit, Sleeping, Red & Black Pulpit, 1800s, 9 ¼ In.	60
Jar, Rangoon, Lift Lid, Crown Top, Dragon Design, 7 x 7 x 13 In.	83
Lamp Base, 2-Light, Figural, Courtship Scene, Woman & Man, Tree, Wood Base, 22 x 10 In.	38
Panel, Stylized Grapevine, Rectangular, Hanging Chains, 1900s, 4 Ft. x 12 In., Pair...........	1045
Pitcher, Animals, Cyan Color, Transferware, Late 1800s, 8 In.	592
Pitcher, Cow Shape, Purple & Orange Sponge, Standing, Platform Base, England, 1800s....	108
Pitcher, Landing Of Lafayette, Ribbed Body, Blue, 7 ¾ In.	800
Plate, Cherubs, Adams, Scalloped Rim, White Ground, Blue Transfer, 10 ¼ In.............*illus*	83
Plate, La Grange, Residence Of Marquis De Lafayette, Pine Trees, Blue Transfer, 10 In.	136
Plate, Niagara Falls, Shell Border, Blue Transfer, Oval, Enoch Wood, c.1829, 15 In.	565
Plate, Toddy, Welcome Lafayette, Portrait Of Man, Blue, White Ground, 5 In. ....*illus*	923
Platter, Curvy Edge, Flowers, Blue & White, Leaves, 1800s, 16 x 20 In.	151
Platter, Fair Mount Near Philadelphia, Dark Blue, Joseph Stubbs, c.1820, 20 x 16 In............	702
Platter, Landing Of Lafayette, Flowers, Blue, 13 x 17 In..*illus*	984
Platter, Oval, River, Thomas & Benjamin Godwin, Burslem, New Wharf, c.1809, 21 x 17 In..	250
Platter, Peace On Earth, Millennium, Mulberry Transfer, Ironstone, 17 x 13 ¾ In.	390
Platter, State House, Boston, Flowers, Eagle Border, Blue & White, Rogers, 1830s, 12 x 14 In.*illus*	420
Salt Cellar, Landing Of Lafayette, Blue, Shaped Base, 2 x 3 In.	677

Staffordshire, Coffeepot, Lift Lid, Lafayette, Blue, Flowers, 11 In.
$328

Pook & Pook

Staffordshire, Figurine, Dog, Spaniel, Black & White, Gilt Collar, 10 x 7 In., Pair
$81

Stevens Auction Co.

Staffordshire, Figurine, Dog, Spaniel, Seated, White Glaze, Black Nose, 13 x 12 x 5 In., Pair
$173

Stevens Auction Co.

Staffordshire, Figurine, Lion, Standing, Ball, Painted, Glass Eyes, 11 ½ x 12 In., Pair
$153

Bunch Auctions

Staffordshire, Figurine, Robert Burns, Standing, Multicolor, Base, c.1860, 13 ½ In.
$63

Hindman

Staffordshire, Figurine, Sailor, Standing, Painted, White & Black, Oval Base, 1800s, 13 In.
$1,525

Rafael Osona Nantucket Auctions

Staffordshire, Plate, Cherubs, Adams, Scalloped Rim, White Ground, Blue Transfer, 10 ¼ In.
$83

Conestoga Auction Company

Staffordshire, Plate, Toddy, Welcome Lafayette, Portrait Of Man, Blue, White Ground, 5 In.
$923

Pook & Pook

Staffordshire, Platter, Landing Of Lafayette, Flowers, Blue, 13 x 17 In.
$984

Pook & Pook

Staffordshire Colors

Blue Staffordshire patterns were the earliest, with both black and blue transfer designs used during the eighteenth century. Pink, green, or brown transfer designs were used about 1830, and the combination of several colors began about 1850.

Staffordshire, Platter, State House, Boston, Flowers, Eagle Border, Blue & White, Rogers, 1830s, 12 x 14 In.
$420

Garth's Auctioneers & Appraisers

Staffordshire, Teapot, Lift Lid, Landing Of Lafayette, Blue Transfer, 5 ¾ x 9 ¾ In.
$431

Pook & Pook

S

Tea Caddy, Cut Glass Decanters, Brick House, Dragon, Dog, 1800s, 8 ¼ In.	540
Tea Caddy, Rectangular Body, Canted Corners, Tortoiseshell Glaze, 1760s, 4 ½ In.	200
Teapot, Lift Lid, Landing Of Lafayette, Blue Transfer, 5 ¾ x 9 ¾ In. .... *illus*	431
Teapot, Stoneware, Globular Shape, Crabstock Handle & Spout, Salt Glaze, Mid 1700s, 3 ¼ In. .	563
Tobacco Jar, Man, Seated, Wearing Blue Shirt, Orange Pants, Yellow Hat, c.1870, 8 ¼ In. ...*illus*	125
Toby Jugs are listed in their own category.	
Tureen, Alms House, Boston, Blue & White, Scrolled Handles, Footed, c.1815, 8 x 15 ½ In...	660
Watch Stand, 3 Women, Wearing Dresses, Multicolor, Flowers, c.1860, 11 x 8 In. .... *illus*	125

STAINLESS STEEL

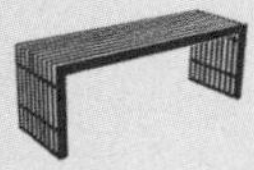

Stainless steel became available to artists and manufacturers about 1920. They used it to make flatware, tableware, and many decorative items.

Sculpture, Clarissa, Welded, Cylindrical, Gary Martin, 29 ¼ In.	425
Sculpture, Synergy, Abstract, Square Base, Boris Kramer, 2002, 15 ½ x 3 ½ x 3 ½ In.. *illus*	128

STANGL POTTERY

Stangl Pottery traces its history back to the Fulper Pottery of New Jersey. In 1910, Johann Martin Stangl started working at Fulper. He left to work at Haeger Pottery from 1915 to 1920. Stangl returned to Fulper Pottery in 1920, became president in 1926, and changed the company name to Stangl Pottery in 1929. Stangl bought the firm in 1930. The pottery is known for dinnerware and a line of bird figurines. Martin Stangl died in 1972 and the pottery was sold to Frank Wheaton Jr. of Wheaton Industries. Production continued until 1978, when Pfaltzgraff Pottery purchased the right to the Stangl trademark and the remaining inventory was liquidated. A single bird figurine is identified by a number. Figurines made up of two birds are identified by a number followed by the letter *D* indicating Double.

Stangl	Stangl	Stangl
1926–1930	1940s–1978	1949–1953

Bird, Duck, Flying, No. 3443, Blue Green, 9 x 13 ½ In. .... *illus*	36
Bird, Hen, No. 3446, Yellow, Red, Green Base, 1940s, 7 In.	46
Bird, No. 3581, Green, Yellow, Black, Brown, c.1950, 6 x 8 In..	125
Bowl, No. 3785, Handle, Eggplant Shape, Gray, Green, c.1955, 6 ½ In.	25
Cigarette Box, No. 3793, Double, Flowers, Leaves, Red, c.1947, 7 x 2 In.............................	95
Dish, Divided, Square, Blue Green, 8 In., Pair... *illus*	26
Oyster Plate, 5 Wells, Pink Ground, Turkey Style, Marked, Port Norris Oyster Co., 9 In.*illus*	320
Pitcher, Golden Harvest, Daffodils, Yellow White, Gray Ground, 5 ½ In.	16

STAR TREK AND STAR WARS

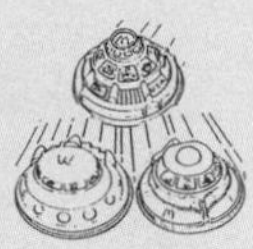

Star Trek and Star Wars collectibles are included here. The original *Star Trek* television series ran from 1966 through 1969. The series spawned an animated TV series, three TV sequels, and a TV prequel. The first Star Trek movie was released in 1979 and eleven others followed, the most recent in 2016. The movie *Star Wars* opened in 1977. Sequels were released in 1980 and 1983; prequels in 1999, 2002, and 2005. *Star Wars: Episode VII* opened in 2015, which increased interest in Star Wars collectibles. *Star Wars: The Last Jedi* opened in 2017. *Star Wars: Episode IX* was released in 2019. Star Wars characters also appeared in *Rogue One: A Star Wars Story* (2016) and *Solo: A Star Wars Story* (2018). Other science fiction and fantasy collectibles can be found under Batman, Buck Rogers, Captain Marvel, Flash Gordon, Movie, Superman, and Toy.

Staffordshire, Tobacco Jar, Man, Seated, Wearing Blue Shirt, Orange Pants, Yellow Hat, c.1870, 8 ¼ In.
$125

Hindman

Staffordshire, Watch Stand, 3 Women, Wearing Dresses, Multicolor, Flowers, c.1860, 11 x 8 In.
$125

Hindman

Stainless Steel, Sculpture, Synergy, Abstract, Square Base, Boris Kramer, 2002, 15 ½ x 3 ½ x 3 ½ In.
$128

Roland NY Auctioneers & Appraisers

S

Stangl, Bird, Duck, Flying, No. 3443, Blue Green, 9 x 13 ½ In.
$36

Cordier Auctions

Stangl Birds

Stangl Pottery birds have been made since 1939. During the 1940s, thousands were made. The figurines were based on illustrations in James Audubon's *Birds of America* and Alexander Wilson's *American Ornithology.*

Stangl, Dish, Divided, Square, Blue Green, 8 In., Pair
$26

Roland NY Auctioneers & Appraisers

Stangl, Oyster Plate, 5 Wells, Pink Ground, Turkey Style, Marked, Port Norris Oyster Co., 9 In.
$320

Nye & Company

Star Trek, Comic Book, No. 9, Spock, Kirk, Gold Key Comics, Feb. 1971, 13 x 8 In.
$138

Bruneau & Co. Auctioneers

Star Wars, Comic Book, No. 1, Marvel Comics, July 1977, 13 x 8 In.
$3,875

Bruneau & Co. Auctioneers

Star Wars, Toy, Wampa, Luke Skywalker, Uniform, Lightsaber, Holster, Blaster, Hasbro, 1997, 14 In.
$38

Lion and Unicorn

Stein, Character, Hinged Lid, Drunken Monkey, Beer, Signed, Musterschutz, 7 In.
$192

Alderfer Auction Company

Stereo Card, Daguerreotype, Hand Colored, Woman, Standing, Folio, Alexandre Bertrand, France, 3 x 6 In.
$1,180

Soulis Auctions

Stereo Card, Deadwood, S.D., Consolidated Tank Line Co., Wagons, Tanker, Barn, 1887, 8 x 10 In.
$479

Pook & Pook

TIP

Wave and call good-bye to "Grandma and the kids" when leaving in a cab for the airport. Make it sound as if the house is occupied.

S

STAR TREK

Comic Book, No. 9, Spock, Kirk, Gold Key Comics, Feb. 1971, 13 x 8 In........................*illus*   138

STAR WARS

Action Figure, C-3PO, Kenner, Box, 1979, 12 In...   282
Comic Book, No. 1, Marvel Comics, July 1977, 13 x 8 In. ....*illus*   3875
Poster, Revenge Of The Jedi, Saga Continues, Darth Vader's Head, Lucas Films, 1982, 41 x 27 In. .   750
Toy, Chewbacca, Body Hair, Wookiee Warrior, Weapon, Bag, Kenner, 13 In..........................   20
Toy, Wampa, Luke Skywalker, Uniform, Lightsaber, Holster, Blaster, Hasbro, 1997, 14 In.*illus*   38

STEIN

Steins have been used by beer and ale drinkers for over 500 years. They have been made of ivory, porcelain, pottery, stoneware, faience, silver, pewter, wood, or glass in sizes up to nine gallons. Although some were made by Mettlach, Meissen, Capo-di-Monte, and other famous factories, most were made by less important German potteries. The words *Geschutz* or *Musterschutz* on a stein are the German words for "patented" or "registered design," not company names. Steins are still being made in the old styles. Lithophane steins may be found in the Lithophane category.

Character, Hinged Lid, Drunken Monkey, Beer, Signed, Musterschutz, 7 In.................*illus*   192
Character, Mephistopheles, Glass, Metal Lid, Porcelain Insert, S. Reich & Co., c.1880, 8 In.   47
Character, Nun, Black Habit, Girl & Dog, Porcelain, Lithophane Base, Germany, ½ L., 7 In.   180
Cornell, Musical Notes, Verse, Loop Handle, Pewter Owl Thumblift, Villeroy & Boch, 9 x 11 In....   281
Mettlach steins are listed in the Mettlach category.
Regimental, Hinged Lid, Imperial, Men In Uniform, Lithophane, Germany, 9 In.   192
Regimental, Lithophane, Infantry Reg. 11th Co., Munchen, 1903-05, Injured Soldier, Germany, 11 In.   25

STEREO CARD

Stereo cards that were made for stereoscope viewers became popular after 1840. Two almost identical pictures were mounted on a stiff cardboard backing so that, when viewed through a stereoscope, a three-dimensional picture could be seen. Value is determined by maker and by subject. These cards were made in quantity through the 1930s.

Daguerreotype, Hand Colored, Woman, Standing, Folio, Alexandre Bertrand, France, 3 x 6 In..*illus*   1180
Deadwood, S.D., Consolidated Tank Line Co., Wagons, Tanker, Barn, 1887, 8 x 10 In..*illus*   479
Lou Gehrig, New York Yankees, 1932 World Series, Black & White, Keystone................*illus*   460

STEREOSCOPE

Stereoscopes were used for viewing stereo cards. The hand viewer was invented by Oliver Wendell Holmes, although more complicated table models were used before his was produced in 1859. Do not confuse the stereoscope with the stereopticon, a magic lantern that used glass slides.

Graphoscope, Wood, Tabletop, Inlay, Ebony Border, Hinged Card Stand, 1800s, 10 x 7 x 4 In....*illus*   236

STERLING SILVER, *see Silver-Sterling category.*

STEUBEN

Steuben glass was made at the Steuben Glass Works of Corning, New York. The factory, founded by Frederick Carder and T.G. Hawkes Sr., was purchased by the Corning Glass Company in 1918. Corning continued to make glass called Steuben. Many types of art glass were made at Steuben. Aurene is an iridescent glass. Schottenstein Stores Inc. bought 80 percent of the business in 2008. The factory

Stereo Card, Lou Gehrig, New York Yankees, 1932 World Series, Black & White, Keystone
$460

Blackwell Auctions

Stereoscope, Graphoscope, Wood, Tabletop, Inlay, Ebony Border, Hinged Card Stand, 1800s, 10 x 7 x 4 In.
$236

Soulis Auctions

TIP
You can remove stickers from most things by spraying them with a lubricant.

Steuben, Bowl, Flared Rim, Disc Foot, Gold Iridescent, Aurene, 3¼ x 6 In.
$313

Turner Auctions + Appraisals

This is an edited listing of current prices. Visit **Kovels.com** to check thousands of prices from previous years and sign up for free information on trends, tips, reproductions, marks, and more.

Steuben, Bowl, Medallion & Flowers, Plum Jade, Double Acid Etched, 4 x 8 In. $900

Woody Auction

Steuben, Bowl, Shallow, Wide Inverted Mouth, Curved Sides, 3 Round Tapered Feet, Aurene, 8⅜ In. $330

Michaan's Auctions

> **TIP**
>
> If you receive a package of glass antiques during cold weather, let it sit inside for a few hours before you unpack it. The glass must return to room temperature slowly or it may crack.

Steuben, Candlestick, Art Glass, Green Jade, Alabaster, Twist Stem, 10 x 4¼ In., Pair $175

Woody Auction

closed in 2011. In 2014 the Corning Museum of Glass took over the factory and is reproducing some tableware, paperweights, and collectibles. Additional pieces may be found in the Cluthra and Perfume Bottle categories.

Atomizer, Gilt Metal Cap, Round Foot, Blue Aurene, 9½ x 3½ In.	423
Basket, Flared, Ruffled Edge, Arched Handle, Amber Iridescent, Aurene, c.1915, 17 x 11 In.	625
Bowl, Amethyst, Flared, Ribbed Sides, Folded Rim & Foot, 4 x 9¾ In.	115
Bowl, Calcite, Gold Aurene Interior, 4⅞ x 12 In.	130
Bowl, Clear, Raised Base, Snail Feet, John Dreves, c.1942, 7 x 9 In.	854
Bowl, Clear, Scroll Footed, John Dreves, Signed, 3 x 7 In.	91
Bowl, Clear, Sunflower, Shape Base, Signed, Eric Hilton, 15 In.	488
Bowl, Flared Rim, Disc Foot, Gold Iridescent, Aurene, 3¼ x 6 In. ....*illus*	313
Bowl, Green Jade, Square, Slightly Wavy Sides, Carder, c.1915, 3½ x 8 In.	345
Bowl, Medallion & Flowers, Plum Jade, Double Acid Etched, 4 x 8 In. ....*illus*	900
Bowl, Shallow, Wide Inverted Mouth, Curved Sides, 3 Round Tapered Feet, Aurene, 8⅜ In. *illus*	330
Bowl, Shell Shape, Disc Foot, Ivrene, Signed, 6½ x 13¾ In.	293
Candlestick, Art Glass, Green Jade, Alabaster, Twist Stem, 10 x 4¼ In., Pair ....*illus*	175
Candlestick, Mushroom Shape, Gold Calcite, 6 x 5 In., Pair	225
Candy Dish, Lid, Ram's Head Finial, Irene Benton, c.1970, 2½ In.	273
Centerpiece, Flared Rim, Column Stem, Domed Base, F. Carder, 1950s, 6¼ In.	363
Champagne, Yellow, Black Thread, Flared Lip, Hand Blown, Frederick Carder, 6½ x 4 In., 8 Piece	625
Cocktail Shaker, Clear, Bubble In Stopper, Signed, Donald Russell, 10 In. ....*illus*	333
Cocktail Shaker, Clear, Teardrop In Stopper, Signed, Donald Russell, 6 In.	427
Compote, Gold, Shaped Stem, Disc Foot, Aurene, Signed, Early 1900s, 8 x 6 In.	363
Compote, Swirled Jade, Alabaster, 6-Corner Footed, Glass, Unmarked, 1900s, 3⅝ In.	65
Compote, Wavy Rim, Twisted Stem, Disc Foot, Gold Aurene, 6¼ In. ....*illus*	358
Decanter, Black, Diamond Shape Stopper, Thread Decoration, 1900s, 10 x 5½ In., Pair	250
Figurine, Apple Of Eden, Clear Bubbles, 18K Yellow Gold Serpent, John Houston, 1971, 5 x 4 In... *illus*	1440
Figurine, Elephant, Trumpeting, Clear, James Houston, c.1964, 8 In.	305
Figurine, Gazelle, Leaping, Frosted, Carder, Sidney Waugh, 1933, 6½ In.	273
Figurine, Koala Bear, Sitting, Clear, Signed, 6 In. ....*illus*	427
Figurine, Long Neck, Round Domed Base, Signed & Numbered, 16 In.	320
Figurine, Rooster, Standing, Curved Base, Signed, Donald Pollard, c.1980, 10¼ In..... *illus*	484
Jar, Potpourri, Removable Lid, Domed Base, Gold Aurene, 6 x 3½ In.	219
Paperweight, Partridge In Pear Tree, Clear, 18K Gold Bird & Tree, Lloyd Atkins, 6 x 3 x 2 In.*illus*	2106
Paperweight, Pharaoh's Horses, 3 Horse Heads, Engraved, Max Erlacher, 1969, 1 x 3 In. ...	850
Perfume Bottle, Gold Aurene, Atomizer Nozzle, Carder, Early 1900s, 7¼ In.	363
Pitcher, Bulbous, Flared Lip, Handle, Clear, Signed, 9 In.	488
Salt, Round Rim, Aurene, Gold Iridescent, Signed, 1 x 2 In. ....*illus*	90
Sculpture, Arctic Fisherman, Drilling Ice, Glass, Silver, James Houston, 1970, 6 x 6 x 2 In.	4463
Sculpture, Clear, 18K Yellow Gold Eagle, Spread Wings, James Houston, 5 x 4 In.	2223
Sculpture, Clear, Triangular, Engraved Schooner, 7 x 9 x 4 In.	4973
Sculpture, Excalibur, Sword Trapped, Silver, Gold, Glass Base, 1900s, 8½ In.	3720
Shade, Pulled Feather, Unmarked, 1900s, 4½ In., Pair. ....*illus*	219
Vase, Alabaster, Art Glass, Optic Rib Design, White Glaze, 4 x 5 In.	70
Vase, Amphora Shape, Flared Rim, 2 Scrolled Handles, 9½ x 7½ In.	390
Vase, Bud, Cylindrical, Circular Foot, Gold Aurene, Early 1900s, 10 x 3 In., Pair	410
Vase, Bud, Etched, Gold Iridescent, Aurene, 5½ x 2¼ In.	125
Vase, Clear, Deep, Shaped Base, 11 x 6 In.	183
Vase, Fan Shape, White Leaf & Vine, Blue, Aurene, Signed, 9 x 7 In. ....*illus*	2000
Vase, Flared Rim, Pinched Neck, Blue Iridescent, Aurene, 5½ In.	563
Vase, Flower, Intertwined Stem, George Thompson, c.1990, 8½ In.	212
Vase, Gold Aurene, Marked, 1900s, 9¾ In.	387
Vase, Horn Shape, Disc Foot, Gold Aurene, Signed, Carder, 5 In.	240
Vase, Rosaline, Fan Shape, Pink & White, 8 x 6 In.	125
Vase, Triangular Shape, Cluthra, Oval Base, 1903, 10¼ In.	424
Vase, Trumpet Shape, Gold, Bulbous Base, Aurene, 6 x 4 In.	325

Steuben, Cocktail Shaker, Clear, Bubble In Stopper, Signed, Donald Russell, 10 In.
$333

Rafael Osona Nantucket Auctions

Steuben, Compote, Wavy Rim, Twisted Stem, Disc Foot, Gold Aurene, 6 ¼ In.
$358

Treadway

Steuben, Figurine, Apple Of Eden, Clear Bubbles, 18K Yellow Gold Serpent, John Houston, 1971, 5 x 4 In.
$1,440

Abington Auction Gallery

Steuben, Figurine, Koala Bear, Sitting, Clear, Signed, 6 In.
$427

Rafael Osona Nantucket Auctions

Steuben, Figurine, Rooster, Standing, Curved Base, Signed, Donald Pollard, c.1980, 10 ¼ In.
$484

Ahlers & Ogletree Auction Gallery

Steuben, Paperweight, Partridge In Pear Tree, Clear, 18K Gold Bird & Tree, Lloyd Atkins, 6 x 3 x 2 In.
$2,106

Thomaston Place Auction Galleries

S

Steuben, Salt, Round Rim, Aurene, Gold Iridescent, Signed, 1 x 2 In. $90

Woody Auction

TIP
Shallow nicks and rough edges on glass can sometimes be smoothed off with fine emery paper.

Steuben, Shade, Pulled Feather, Unmarked, 1900s, 4 1/2 In., Pair $219

Cowan's Auctions

Steuben, Vase, Fan Shape, White Leaf & Vine, Blue, Aurene, Signed, 9 x 7 In. $2,000

Woody Auction

STEVENGRAPH

Stevengraphs are woven pictures made like fancy ribbons. They were manufactured by Thomas Stevens of Coventry, England, and became popular in 1862. Most are marked *Woven in silk by Thomas Stevens* or were mounted on a cardboard that tells the story of the Stevengraph. Other similar ribbon pictures have been made in England and Germany.

Bookmark, Morning Hymn, Light Blue Ground, Red & Yellow, Tassel, 1850, Frame, 7 In....	50
Bookmark, USA Centennial, George Washington Portrait, Yellow Tassel, 1876, 13 x 3 In. ...	120
Picture, Horse Race, The Start, The Struggle, Woven, Silk, Frame, 7 x 9 1/2 In., Pair	48
Picture, Lady Godiva Procession, Called To The Rescue, Embroidered, Frame, 7 x 10 In., Pair .	32

STEVENS & WILLIAMS

Stevens & Williams of Stourbridge, England, made many types of glass, including layered, etched, cameo, cut, and art glass, between the 1830s and 1930s. Some pieces are signed *S & W.* Many pieces are decorated with flowers, leaves, and other designs based on nature.

Compote, Pink Opaline, Clambroth Stem & Foot, England, 5 x 10 In.......................................	40
Finger Bowl, Rococo, Engraved, Flowers, Feather & Crosshatch, Cranberry To Clear, 2 x 5 In....	175
Vase, White Ground, Amber Acorns, Ruffled Rim, 7 In., Pair	50

STONE

Stone includes those articles made of stones, coral, shells, and some other natural materials not listed elsewhere in this book. Micro mosaics (small decorative designs made by setting pieces of stone into a pattern), urns, vases, and other pieces made of natural stone are listed here. Stoneware is pottery and is listed in the Stoneware category. Alabaster, Jade, Malachite, Marble, and Soapstone are in their own categories.

Brush Washer, Fluorite, Oval Basin, Carved, Dragon, Clear Green, Lavender Stone, 3 In.... *illus*	123
Carving, Dark Amber, 2 Lions, Medallion, Square Sides, Landscape, Scroll, 2 5/8 x 2 5/8 In. ..	64
Carving, Lion, Crouching, Black, Brown, Chinese, 1900s, 2 x 3 1/2 In.	56
Carving, Serpentine, Head, Taino Style, Painted, Red Mouth, Dominican Republic, 10 x 7 x 6 In.	936
Carving, Skull, Rhodochrosite, Human, Teeth, 7 1/4 In..	893
Centerpiece, Flowers, Green Base, Asian, 1900s, 12 x 24 x 12 In..	406
Chalice, Agate, Gem Set, Silver Mounts, Masked Faces & Putti, Hexagonal Base, 1800s, 7 x 3 In.. *illus*	1200
Figure, Angelfish, Seahorses, Coral, Hardstone, Chinese, 9 x 11 x 4 In.	128
Figure, Bear, Carved, Tribal, Mahogany Base, Signed, Victor Vigil, Dated 2002, 6 In............	445
Figure, Bird, Carved, Ribbon Tail, Rock, Spinach Green, Wood Stand, Chinese, 8 1/4 In........	163
Figure, Black Hardstone, Square Beige Base, John McIntire, 15 x 7 x 8 In.....................*illus*	900
Figure, Blade Shape, Archaic, Carved, Drilled Hole, Mottled, Metal Stand, Chinese, 10 3/4 In.	125
Figure, Buddha, Seated, Hands On Lap, Amethyst, Semiprecious, 1900s, 7 In..............*illus*	351
Figure, Buddha, Seated, Zoisite, Carved Ruby, Chinese, 14 1/2 In....................................*illus*	1320
Figure, Carved, 5 Buddhist Monks, Stele, Sitting, Open Hand, Chinese, 5 x 7 3/8 In.	570
Figure, Carved, Head Of Pharaoh, On Stand, Square Base, 12 x 7 3/4 x 4 1/4 In.	813
Figure, Cat, Persian, Seated, Pink Chalcedony, Red Cabochon Eyes, Box, 2 1/4 x 2 3/4 x 2 In. .	527
Figure, Coral, Carved, Dressed Guanyin, Laughing Child, Flowers, 5 1/2 x 3 In. ....*illus*	960
Figure, Dog, Carved, Standing, Light Brown, Ruby Eyes, Russia, 4 1/2 In.	1188
Figure, Dove, Perched, Cast, White Paint, Black Square Base, 9 In.	313
Figure, Duck, Swimming, Hardstone, Carved, Green, Brown, Wood Stand, 7 1/2 x 11 x 4 In.	1088
Figure, Elephants, Rock Crystal, Carved, Lacquered Base, Pierced, Chinese, Early 1900s, 4 3/4 x 7 In...	330
Figure, Gautama Buddha, Hardstone, Amber Finish, Composition Base, Chinese, 1800s, 18 In..	1125
Figure, Hotai, With Staff, Hardstone, Green, Carved, Stand, Chinese, 8 1/2 x 5 x 3 In............	64
Figure, Phoenix, Mythical Bird, Flowering Lotus, Hardstone, Carved, Chinese, 9 1/4 x 8 1/2 In...	75
Head, Buddha, Gray Schist, Carved, Hair In Bun, Base Stand, Gandhar, 12 x 5 x 4 In..........	688
Head, Buddha, Wood Base, Sino-Tibetan, 16 1/2 In..	1452

S

Stone, Brush Washer, Fluorite, Oval Basin, Carved, Dragon, Clear Green, Lavender Stone, 3 In.
$123

Brunk Auctions

Stone, Chalice, Agate, Gem Set, Silver Mounts, Masked Faces & Putti, Hexagonal Base, 1800s, 7 x 3 In.
$1,200

Abington Auction Gallery

Stone, Figure, Black Hardstone, Square Beige Base, John McIntire, 15 x 7 x 8 In.
$900

Abington Auction Gallery

Stone, Figure, Buddha, Seated, Hands On Lap, Amethyst, Semiprecious, 1900s, 7 In.
$351

Thomaston Place Auction Galleries

Stone, Figure, Buddha, Seated, Zoisite, Carved Ruby, Chinese, 14½ In.
$1,320

Michaan's Auctions

Stone, Figure, Coral, Carved, Dressed Guanyin, Laughing Child, Flowers, 5½ x 3 In.
$960

Michaan's Auctions

Stone, Jardiniere, Carved Exterior, Celtic Knots, Continental, 14 x 18 In.
$244

Neal Auction Company

Stone, Sculpture, Lion On Rock, Orange Alabaster, Milt Eisenhower, 1900s, 17 x 33 In.
$300

Garth's Auctioneers & Appraisers

TIP
The best burglary protection is a dog. Inmates from three Ohio prisons were surveyed and said timed lights, dead-bolt locks, and alarms are deterrents; but the thing most avoided by a professional thief is a noisy dog.

S

Stoneware, Bank, Lion, Lying Down, Dark Brown Ground, Ohio, 1800s, 4⅜ x 8 In.
$375

Hindman

Stoneware, Batter Pail, Cobalt Blue Flowers, Bail Handle, Sipe, Nichols & Co., c.1875, Gal., 8 In.
$1,080

Crocker Farm, Inc.

Stoneware, Bowl, Blue Tulip, Cowden & Wilcox, Harrisburg, 5¼ x 10½ In.
$215

Hartzell's Auction Gallery Inc.

Stoneware, Chicken Waterer, Fitted Lower Plate, Blue Highlights, 1910s, 9¼ In.
$210

Selkirk Auctioneers & Appraisers

Stoneware, Crock, Cobalt Blue Lioness, Lug Handles, F. Stetzenmeyer & Co., Rochester, N.Y., c.1860, 6 Gal.
$6,000

Crocker Farm, Inc.

Stoneware, Crock, Cobalt Blue Paddletail Bird, Lug Handles, N.A. White & Son, c.1885, 5 Gal., 12½ In.
$800

Pook & Pook

Jardiniere, Carved Exterior, Celtic Knots, Continental, 14 x 18 In. ....*illus*	244
Obelisk, Rock Crystal, 4-Sided, Rectangular Pillar, Pyramid Top, Square Base, 21 In., Pair..	2295
Obelisk, Rock Crystal, Pointed Top, Square Base, Continental, 1900s, 23½ In., Pair	3294
Pedestal, Onyx, Bronze Mounted, Square Top, Musical Trophy, Square Base, Continental, 43½ In.	704
Pedestal, Onyx, Column, White, Brown Veins, Square Top & Base, 20th Century, 36 x 14 In.	850
Plaque, Temple Relief, Carved, Fierce Guardian Figures, 28 x 34 In.	4130
Sculpture, Buddha, Standing, Lohan, Elongated Ears, Square Base, Chinese, 39 x 9 x 5¾ In.	240
Sculpture, Gargoyle, Hands On Chin, 25½ x 14 x 14 In.	625
Sculpture, Lion On Rock, Orange Alabaster, Milt Eisenhower, 1900s, 17 x 33 In..........*illus*	300
Sphere, Neoclassical, Polished, Socle Base, Black, 13½ x 9 In.	246
Vase, Agate, Pot, Yellow Polished, Orange & White Tone, Striation, Asia, 1900s, 15 x 9 In.	125

STONEWARE

Stoneware is a coarse, glazed, and fired potter's ceramic that is used to make crocks, jugs, bowls, etc. It is often decorated with cobalt blue decorations. In the nineteenth and early twentieth centuries, potters often decorated crocks with blue numbers indicating the size of the container. A *2* meant 2 gallons. Stoneware is still being made. American stoneware is listed here.

Bank, Lion, Lying Down, Dark Brown Ground, Ohio, 1800s, 4⅜ x 8 In. ....*illus*	375
Batter Jug, Cobalt Blue Stenciled, Slip, F.H. Cowden, Harrisburg, Pa., 1½ Gal., 9 In............	826
Batter Jug, Tin Lid, Swing Handle, Cobalt Blue Design, F.H. Cowden, Harrisburg, Pa., c.1880......	563
Batter Pail, Cobalt Blue Flowers, Bail Handle, Sipe, Nichols & Co., c.1875, Gal., 8 In.... *illus*	1080
Bowl, Blue Tulip, Cowden & Wilcox, Harrisburg, 5¼ x 10½ In. ....*illus*	215
Bowl, Budding, Solfatara Glaze, Axel Salto, Denmark, 1965, 2¾ x 5 In.................................	3000
Bowl, Scalloped Rim, Brown Glaze, Arne Bang, Denmark, c.1935, 4 x 9 In.	2250
Charger, Dark Blue, Child, Dancing, Cream Ground, c.1995, 1¾ x 15 In.	63
Chicken Waterer, Chocolate Brown, Glaze, Knob Finial, Lug Handles, 13 In.....................	113
Chicken Waterer, Fitted Lower Plate, Blue Highlights, 1910s, 9¼ In.........................*illus*	210
Churn, Cobalt Blue Dancing Man, Tooled Shoulder, Flared Rim, Ohio, 1860s, 4 Gal., 16 In.	2040
Churn, Cobalt Blue Flower & Leaves, Arched Handles, Strap Rim, 1800s, 5 Gal., 16½ In.....	156
Churn, Cobalt Blue Flower, 1800s, 5 Gal., 16¾ In..	277
Churn, Cobalt Blue Tulips, 2 Applied Handles, Marked, TH Gunther, Sheboygan, Wis., c.1860, 17 In.	390
Crock, 2 Handles, Mustard, Green, Brown, W.R. Addington, Maysville, Ga., 10½ x 7½ In...	219
Crock, Blue Band, Gray, 1900s, 12 Gal., 18 x 17 In..	48
Crock, Blue Bird, Molded Rim & Handle, Light Brown Ground, Ottman Bros., 13¼ In., 6 Gal...	500
Crock, Cobalt Blue Crow's Foot, Narrow Neck, Mid 1800s, 19 In.	168
Crock, Cobalt Blue Decoration, Baltimore, Cylindrical, 2 Gal., 13 In.	441
Crock, Cobalt Blue Design, Applied Handle, Marked, S. Hart, Oswego Falls, c.1832, 12 In.....	330
Crock, Cobalt Blue Design, Applied Handles, Wisconsin, 1841, 10¾ In................................	660
Crock, Cobalt Blue Design, Flat Lid, Tab Handles, Peter Hermann, Maryland, c.1850, 6 Gal., 21 In.	500
Crock, Cobalt Blue Flower, Flat Top Rim, Arched Handles, Penn Yan, N.Y., 1800s, 2 Gal., 10 In..	313
Crock, Cobalt Blue Flowers, 1800s, 3 Gal., 12½ In..	202
Crock, Cobalt Blue Flowers, Late 1800s, 3 Gal., 9 x 11 In.	188
Crock, Cobalt Blue Flowers, Tab Handles, A.O. Whittemore, Havana, N.Y., 2 Gal., 10¼ In. ...	201
Crock, Cobalt Blue Lettering, Hamilton & Jones, Flat Top Rim, Arched Handles, 1800s, 10 Gal..	1250
Crock, Cobalt Blue Lioness, Lug Handles, F. Stetzenmeyer & Co., Rochester, N.Y., c.1860, 6 Gal.....*illus*	6000
Crock, Cobalt Blue Paddletail Bird, Lug Handles, N.A. White & Son, c.1885, 5 Gal., 12½ In. *illus*	800
Crock, Crown, 12, Wire Handles, Cylindrical, 12 Gal., 19 x 15 In.	60
Crock, Demuth's Snuff, Orange Lid, Dark Blue Text, Lancaster, Pa., 1770, Gal., 8½ In.	177
Crock, Freehand Cobalt Blue Apples, Molded Rim, Arched Handles, 1800s, 3 Gal., 15 In.	500
Crock, J. Reitzel, Newark, N.J., Blue Script, Cylindrical, 9 In. ....*illus*	480
Crock, Pickle, Octagonal Glass Lid, Metal Fastener, Reid, Murdoch & Co.	780
Crock, Salt Glaze, Lug Handles, Paul Cushman, Albany, Early 1800s, 11 x 9 In.....................	3218
Cuspidor, Cobalt Blue Design, Leafy Spray, Rockingham Glaze, 1800s, 6½ In.	139
Figure, Dog, Spaniel, Seated, Albany Slip Glaze, A.J. Vermilyer, c.1870, 6⅞ In..................	1800
Figure, Grotesque Frog, Green & Brown Glaze, Andrew Hull, Cobridge Stoneware, 7½ In...	1875
Figure, Lion, Buddhist, Seated, On Haunches, Glazed, Brown Face, Black & White, 10 In., Pair	576
Figure, Owl Watch, Mother Shielding Chick, Andrew Hull Pottery, England, 2009, 12 In..*illus*	1625

Stoneware, Crock, J. Reitzel, Newark, N.J., Blue Script, Cylindrical, 9 In. $480

Hartzell's Auction Gallery Inc.

Stoneware, Figure, Owl Watch, Mother Shielding Chick, Andrew Hull Pottery, England, 2009, 12 In. $1,625

Lion and Unicorn

Stoneware, Figure, Tortoise, Head Out, Green, Andrew Hull Pottery, England, 1900s, 5¼ In. $1,250

Lion and Unicorn

S

Stoneware, Flowerpot, Ocher Wreath, Saucer, Ft. Edward, N.Y., 1868, 7 ½ x 8 ½ In. $780

Crocker Farm, Inc.

Stoneware, Jar, Lid, Memory, Pottery Shards, Salt Glaze, Lug Handles, Mid Atlantic, c.1890, 16 x 10 In. $322

Jeffrey S. Evans & Associates

Stoneware, Jug, Bellarmine, Beardman, Tooled Mouth, Medallion, Frechen, Germany, 1700s, 13 ½ In. $600

Crocker Farm, Inc.

Stoneware, Jug, Cobalt Blue Bird, Molded Handle, Rogers & Co., Boston, Mass., 1800s, 3 Gal., 16 In. $375

Hindman

Stoneware, Jug, Face, Alkaline Glaze, Kaolin Eyes, Lanier Meaders, Cleveland, Ga., c.1980, 9 ¾ In. $720

Crocker Farm, Inc.

Stoneware, Jug, Face, Eyes, Mouth, Teeth, Molded Ears, Dark Brown Glazed, Anita Meaders, 5 ¾ In. $188

New Haven Auctions

Stoneware, Jug, Flowering Urn, Tooled Spout, West Troy, N.Y., c.1875, 5 Gal., 19 ¼ In. $10,800

Crocker Farm, Inc.

Stoneware, Pitcher, Cobalt Blue Leaves, Molded Rim & Base, Applied Handle, Pennsylvania, 7 ⅜ In. $875

New Haven Auctions

Stoneware, Pitcher, Brown, Sand Glaze, Marguerite Wildenhain, Pond Farm, 11 ½ In. $1,000

Clars Auction Gallery

Figure, Rooster, 2-Headed, With Rattlesnake, Alkaline Glaze, 19¾ In.	384
Figure, Toad, Bumpy Texture, Speckled, Glazed, 4½ x 5½ x 6½ In.	188
Figure, Tortoise, Head Out, Green, Andrew Hull Pottery, England, 1900s, 5¼ In. .... *illus*	1250
Flagon, Olive Green Glaze, Flat Top Mouth, Oval, Beaded Ring, Strap Handle, 1800s, 12 In.	120
Flowerpot, Ocher Wreath, Saucer, Ft. Edward, N.Y., 1868, 7½ x 8½ In. .... *illus*	780
Jar, Blue Leaves, Molded Handle, Brown Ground, Buchanan & McClure, Philadelphia, 4 Gal., 14 In. ..	625
Jar, Cobalt Blue Bird, Round Rim, Mottled Glaze, Applied Handles, 1830s, 4 Gal., 13 In.	360
Jar, Cobalt Blue Flowers, Cylindrical, Molded Rim, Mid Atlantic, 1800s, 10 In.	290
Jar, Fahua, Figural, Wooden Lid, Elegant Scholar Scene, Ruyi, Broad Lappets, 18 In.	390
Jar, Freehand Cobalt Blue, Buff Clay, Applied Handles, c.1880, 15 x 21 In.	144
Jar, Lid, Memory, Pottery Shards, Salt Glaze, Lug Handles, Mid Atlantic, c.1890, 16 x 10 In. ....*illus*	322
Jar, R. Peet 21 Diamond, Cobalt Blue Slip Line, Pittsburgh, Pa., c.1865, 10½ In.	767
Jar, Salt Glaze, Oval, Squared Rim, Arched Handles, Stanford Perry, 1830s, 4 Gal., 15 In.	131
Jar, Wine, Dark Brown Flowers, Buff Glaze, Ribbed Neck, c.1730, 15 x 8 In.	1404
Jug, Acid Etched, Stag Hunt, Charles Graham Pottery, New York, c.1885, 7½ x 5 In.	130
Jug, Bellarmine, Beardman, Tooled Mouth, Medallion, Frechen, Germany, 1700s, 13½ In....*illus*	600
Jug, Bellarmine, Salt Glaze, Applied Handle, 17½ In.	188
Jug, Bird On Branch, Handle, Brady & Ryan, Ellenville, 2 Gal., 14 In.	254
Jug, Blue, 3 Flowers, Incised Neck, Arc Handle, 2 Gal., 14 In.	106
Jug, C.W. Schomp, Dover, N.J., Blue Script, Handle, 14¼ In.	424
Jug, Cobalt Blue Bird, Handle, Incised Neck, Ottman Brothers & Co., 14 x 9 In.	188
Jug, Cobalt Blue Bird, Molded Handle, Rogers & Co., Boston, Mass., 1800s, 3 Gal., 16 In. *illus*	375
Jug, Cobalt Blue Bird, On Branch, Cream Ground, Handle, 2 Gal., 15 In.	344
Jug, Cobalt Blue Design, Cylindrical, E.S. & B., Pennsylvania, 4 Gal., 16 In.	108
Jug, Cobalt Blue Flower, Norton & Co., Worcester, 1800s, 14 x 9 In.	230
Jug, Cobalt Blue Flowers, I. Seymour, Troy Factory, New York, Late 1800s, 13¼ In.	406
Jug, Cobalt Blue Flowers, J. Mantell, Penn Yan, 2 Gal., 13½ In.	266
Jug, Cobalt Blue Grapes, Tapered Spout, Cowden & Wilcox, Harrisburg, Pa., c.1865, 3 Gal., 14¾ In. ..	3000
Jug, Cobalt Blue Lettering, John F. Weiler, Allentown, Pa., 2 Gal., 12 In.	480
Jug, Cobalt Blue Pheasant, Haxstun Ottman & Co., Ft. Edward, N.Y., c.1875, 4 Gal., 17 In.....	4800
Jug, Cobalt Blue, R. Macdonald, New York Grocery, Plainfield, N.J., Handle, 11 In.	283
Jug, Face, Alkaline Glaze, Flared Spout, 2 Handles, B.B. Craig, Vale, N.C., c.1975, 15½ In.	270
Jug, Face, Alkaline Glaze, Kaolin Eyes, Lanier Meaders, Cleveland, Ga., c.1980, 9¾ In. *illus*	720
Jug, Face, Bristol Glaze, Blue Swirls, 2 Spouts, Signed, B.B. Craig, Henry, N.C., 1950s, 11 In. ...	410
Jug, Face, Concentric Rings, White Kaolin Ceramic Teeth, 2 Handles, Signed, 19 x 12 x 14 In. .	708
Jug, Face, Eyes, Mouth, Teeth, Molded Ears, Dark Brown Glazed, Anita Meaders, 5¾ In....*illus*	188
Jug, Face, White Eyes, Teeth, Runny Olive Glaze, Cleater & Billie Meaders, Georgia, 1993, 22 In.	406
Jug, Flowering Urn, Tooled Spout, West Troy, N.Y., c.1875, 5 Gal., 19¼ In. .... *illus*	10800
Jug, Gray Alkaline Glaze, Kaolin Eyes, Large Nose, Ears, Broken Teeth, Burton Craig, 13 In. .	1230
Jug, Harvest, Applied Leaves, Branch Shape Handle, Marked, C.L., Ohio, c.1885, 10½ In.	1320
Jug, Harvest, Lines, Branch Shape Handle, Signed, Stookey, Late 1800s, 9 In.	1750
Jug, Lid, Cobalt Blue Flowers, F. Stetzenmeyer & Co., Rochester, N.Y.,1800s, 3 Gal.,16¾ In...	6765
Jug, Molded Bearded Face, Leaf & Coin Design, Loop Handle, Germany, 1700s, 9 x 7 In.	2875
Jug, Oval, Applied Handle, Cobalt Blue Highlights, c.1840s, 11 In.	144
Jug, Oval, Strap Handle, Cobalt Blue Flowers, JB & A Maxfield, Milwaukee, 1850s, 13 In.......	900
Jug, Salt Glaze, Cobalt Blue, Tobacco Spit, c.1880, 17 In.	96
Jug, Salt Glaze, Light To Dark Brown, Strap Handle, Scratched Design, 15 In.	96
Loving Cup, Salt Glaze, Hound Handles, Silver Plate Rim, Wadham College Regatta, 1887, 6 In...	108
Pitcher, Cobalt Blue Leaves, Molded Rim & Base, Applied Handle, Pennsylvania, 7⅜ In....*illus*	875
Pitcher, Brown, Sand Glaze, Marguerite Wildenhain, Pond Farm, 11½ In..................*illus*	1000
Pitcher, Cobalt Blue Flowers, Baltimore, 1800s, 2 Gal., 14 In..	813 to 1599
Pitcher, Dark Brown, Alkaline Glaze, Squat, Round Rim, Pinched Spout, Late 1800s, 9 In.	120
Pitcher, Handle, Black & White Stripe, Glazed, Vallauris, France, c.1950, 15 x 7 x 6 In.........	1690
Pitcher, Slight Tapering, Floral Ring Borders, Rose Images, Basket Weave, 1800s, 9¼ In. ..	60
Tureen, Lift Lid, Salt Glaze, Grotesque Mask Feet, Late 1700s, 8 x 11 In.	492
Vase, Blue & White Glaze, Scholars Landscape, Flowers, Chinese, 8¼ x 7 In................*illus*	96
Vase, Closed Shape, Dark Brown Matte, American Studio, 1900s, 11 In.	250
Vase, Fahua Decor, Meiping Shape, Flowers, Butterflies, Waves, Phoenix Birds, Chinese, 13 x 7 In..	1638
Vase, Glazed, Shaped Base, Georges Jouve, France, c.1956, 10 x 5 In.	3500
Vase, Green Crystalline Matte Glaze, Grand Feu, California, c.1912, 5⅝ x 6½ In.........*illus*	1875

Stoneware, Vase, Blue & White Glaze, Scholars Landscape, Flowers, Chinese, 8¼ x 7 In.

$96

Main Auction Galleries, Inc.

Stoneware, Vase, Green Crystalline Matte Glaze, Grand Feu, California, c.1912, 5⅝ x 6½ In.

$1,875

Toomey & Co. Auctioneers

Stoneware, Water Cooler, Cobalt Blue Flower, Tab Handles, B.C. Milburn, Alexa, c.1850, 6 Gal., 17 In.

$10,200

Crocker Farm, Inc.

What's a Can Without an Opener?

The can opener was invented 48 years after the can.

Stoneware, Water Cooler, Crock, Lid, Slack & Brownlow, Tan, Manchester, 1830
$210

Chupp Auctions & Real Estate, LLC

Store, Bag Holder, Wood, Fan Shape, 6 Slots, Stenciled Sides, Cast Iron Stringholder, 22 x 16 x 8 In.
$461

Route 32 Auctions

Vase, Lobed, Pinched Overlapping Sides, Bisque Ground, Makoto Yabe, Boston, 1947, 3 x 9 In.	313
Vase, Melon Shape, Green Striped Glaze, Harrison McIntosh, Claremont, Calif., 1950, 18½ In.	1875
Vase, Pepper Shape, Glazed, Molded Rim, Arne Bang, Denmark, c.1930, 5¼ In.	2250
Water Cooler, Cobalt Blue Clover, Open Strap Handles, Baltimore, c.1860, 4 Gal., 13½ In..	14400
Water Cooler, Cobalt Blue Federal Eagle, Squared Rim, Bunghole, Liberty, 1853, 3 Gal., 13½ In.	2160
Water Cooler, Cobalt Blue Flower, Tab Handles, B.C. Milburn, Alexa, c.1850, 6 Gal., 17 In..... *illus*	10200
Water Cooler, Crock, Lid, Slack & Brownlow, Tan, Manchester, 1830 ....*illus*	210
Water Cooler, Lid, Cheavin's Saludor, Water Filter, Molded Handles, Late 1700s, 19 In.	185
Water Cooler, Lid, Painted, Blue Horse Design, Silver Faucet, M.A. Hadley, 12 In.	86
Water Cooler, Polar Bear, Light Blue To White Ground, Early 1900s, 15½ x 11¼ In.	182

STORE

Store fixtures, cases, cutters, and other items that have no company advertising as part of the decoration are listed here. Most items found in an old store are listed in the Advertising category in this book.

Bag Holder, Wood, Fan Shape, 6 Slots, Stenciled Sides, Cast Iron Stringholder, 22 x 16 x 8 In..... *illus*	461
Bin, Pine, Beadboard, Slant Lid, Blue Green Paint, Strap Hinges, Mid 1800s, 32 x 50 x 18 In......	390
Bin, Spice, Hinged Lid, Tin, Red, Gold Stencil, Woman's Portrait, Late 1800s, 9 x 7¾ In., Pair...	345
Cabinet, Cigar, Walnut, Carved, Leaves, 4 Revolving Doors, Black Forest, 10 In. ....*illus*	325
Cabinet, Display, 2 Hinged Doors, Old Surface, c.1915, 63¼ x 16½ x 6¼ In.	5975
Cabinet, Display, Pocket Watch, Hinged Lid, Rosewood, Velvet Tray, Drawers, 44 x 44 x 27 In....	813
Cabinet, Hardware, Rotating, Red Paint, A.R. Brown, Erwin, Tenn., Early 1900s, 50x 25 In. .	594
Candy Jar, Cranberry Purple, Glass, Lift Lid, Clear Base, 13 In.	74
Case, Display, Door, 3 Drawers, Glass Panels, Mixed Wood, Counter, 32 x 18 In.....................	492
Case, Display, Glass, Brass Mounted, Dragon, Leafy Wreath, France, 12 x 14 x 11 In.............	813
Case, Display, Mahogany, Square Top, Beveled Mirror, Glass Sides, Late 1900s, 23 x 16 In. ..	84
Case, Display, Nickel, Hinged Glass Door, Glass Shelves, Early 1900s, 42 x 23 x 9 In............	708
Case, Display, Oak, Glass, Curved Front, Blue, Mirror Back, J. Riswig, Chicago, 13 x 19 x 9 In. *illus*	276
Case, Display, Oak, Glass, Slant Front, Carved, J.W. Winchester & Co., Counter, 11 x 19 x 18 In.....	500
Case, Display, Sargent, 4-Sided, 2 Hinged Doors, Glass, Oak, 17 x 9 x 18 In...........................	150
Case, Display, Sloping Glass Front, Hinged Back, Counter, 9¼ x 31 In................................	150
Case, Display, Victorian Style, Walnut, Mahogany, Coffer Top, Sliding Doors, Mirrors, 74 x 62 In...	360
Case, Display, Wood, Glass Sides, Top & Door, Square Shape, Brown, 15 x 15 x 10 In.	62
Case, Display, Wood, Hinged Glass Door, Sides, Mirror Back, Shelves, 27 x 10½ x 6 In.........	113
Chest, Apothecary, Oak, 12 Drawers, Cast Iron Pulls, Inset Labels, c.1915, 35 x 45 x 15 In.*illus*	359
Cigar Cutter, Antler, Carved, Tiger, Gem Set Eyes, Marked, Donatus, Solingen, 1900s, 8 In.	363
Cigar Cutter, Hops & Malt, Barrel Shape, Mounted, Cast Iron...	300
Coffee Grinders are listed in the Coffee Mill category.	
Cutter, Curved Blade, Wood Handle, Chopping, Repurposed Metal File, 1800s, 5 x 12½ x 5 In. .... *illus*	68
Desk, Clerk's, Gallery Back, Hinged Slant Lid, Dovetailed Case, Counter, 1830s, 8 x 18 x 20 In...	120
Dispenser, Hot Toddy, Glass Globe, Faucet, Superior Electric, 1900s, 18 x 9 x 9½ In............	277
Display, Esquire Man Esky, Painted, Plaster Advertisement, Wood, 1940, 13 In.	295
Display, Safety Pin, Gilt, Brass, Signed, Mid 1900s, 35½ In..*illus*	1000
Figure, Cowboy, Standing, Guns & Ammunition, Wood, Wheels, 58 In....................................	3188
Jar, Soda Fountain, Dome Lid, Nickel Plate, Glass, Chrome Ice Cream Rack, 14 x 6½ In.....	180
Mannequin, Bust, Wax, Glass Eyes, Wood Faux Marble Stand, P. Imans, France, c.1920, 26 In...*illus*	2500
Mannequin, Dress Shape, 3-Quarter, Painted, Tripod Stand, London, Late 1800s, 66 In.............*illus*	1220
Rack, Disston, Metal, Includes Saws, 37 x 19 In..	480
Showcase, 4-Sided Glass, 3 Shelves, Magnet Close Door, Oak, 10½ x 10½ x 16 In.	210
Showcase, Box Gable Design, Wood & Glass, Counter, 20 x 20 x 25 In.................................	600
Showcase, Mahogany, Nickel Plated, Mt. Jackson, Virginia, Dated 1879, Counter, 8 x 27½ In.....	1016
Sign, Coffeepot Shape, Fresh Ground Coffee, Painted, Wood, 2-Sided, 21½ x 17 x 4 In. *illus*	2457
Sign, Eye Doctor, Glasses, Blue Eyes, White Text, Painted, 19 x 8 In.	50
Sign, Fish, Flounder, Wood, Carved, Painted, Iron Hangers, Slate Center For Prices, 35 x 57 In......	2574
Sign, Fishing Tackle, Fish Shape, Carved, Painted, 1900s, 16¼ x 38½ In............................	750
Sign, Lingerie, Script, Rose, Neon, Famous & Barr, 1960s, 39 x 20 x 42 In.	180
Sign, Melons, Watermelon As Letter O, Pink, Green, Pine, 1910s, 11 x 60 In.........................	510

Store, Cabinet, Cigar, Walnut, Carved, Leaves, 4 Revolving Doors, Black Forest, 10 In.
$325

Neal Auction Company

Store, Case, Display, Oak, Glass, Curved Front, Blue, Mirror Back, J. Riswig, Chicago, 13 x 19 x 9 In.
$276

Route 32 Auctions

> **TIP**
> *Display groups of at least three of your collectibles to get decorating impact.*

Store, Chest, Apothecary, Oak, 12 Drawers, Cast Iron Pulls, Inset Labels, c.1915, 35 x 45 x 15 In.
$359

Jeffrey S. Evans & Associates

Store, Cutter, Curved Blade, Wood Handle, Chopping, Repurposed Metal File, 1800s, 5 x 12½ x 5 In.
$68

Hartzell's Auction Gallery Inc.

Store, Display, Safety Pin, Gilt, Brass, Signed, Mid 1900s, 35½ In.
$1,000

New Haven Auctions

Store, Mannequin, Bust, Wax, Glass Eyes, Wood Faux Marble Stand, P. Imans, France, c.1920, 26 In.
$2,500

Hindman

Store, Mannequin, Dress Shape, 3-Quarter, Painted, Tripod Stand, London, Late 1800s, 66 In.
$1,220

Rafael Osona Nantucket Auctions

Store, Sign, Coffeepot Shape, Fresh Ground Coffee, Painted, Wood, 2-Sided, 21½ x 17 x 4 In.
$2,457

Thomaston Place Auction Galleries

S

Store, Sign, No Beer Sold To Indians, Printed Broadside, Cardstock, 11 x 7 In. $375

No Beer
SOLD TO
INDIANS

Cowan's Auctions

Store, Sign, Rabbits For Sale, Dressed Or Alive, Painted, Wood, 1900s, 21 ½ x 30 In. $469

RABBITS·FOR·SALE
DRESSED·OR·ALIVE

Hindman

Store, Sign, Shirts 10 Cents, Painted, Red Ground, Tin, Wood Frame, 2-Sided, c.1920, 23 x 29 In. $469

SHIRTS
10¢

New Haven Auctions

Store, Sign, Smith Bro's, Tin, Black, White Wood Letters, c.1920, 25 x 43 In. $508

SMITH
BRO'S

Jeffrey S. Evans & Associates

Sign, No Beer Sold To Indians, Printed Broadside, Cardstock, 11 x 7 In. ....*illus*	375
Sign, Propeller, Neon, Circular Back Plate, 4 Tubes, Mid 1900s, 22 x 30 x 19 In.	885
Sign, Rabbits For Sale, Dressed Or Alive, Painted, Wood, 1900s, 21 ½ x 30 In..............*illus*	469
Sign, Shirts 10 Cents, Painted, Red Ground, Tin, Wood Frame, 2-Sided, c.1920, 23 x 29 In..*illus*	469
Sign, Smith Bro's, Tin, Black, White Wood Letters, c.1920, 25 x 43 In...........................*illus*	508
Stringholder, Cast Iron, Blade On Top, 10 x 7 In...*illus*	300

STOVE

Stoves have been used in America for heating since the eighteenth century and for cooking since the nineteenth century. Most types of wood, coal, gas, kerosene, and even some electric stoves are collected. Salesman's samples may be listed here or in Toy.

Cook, Charcoal, Pentagon Shape, Wire Bail Handle, France, 11 ½ x 10 x 10 In.	1243
Heater, Gas Rocker, Howling Wolf, 2 Irons, Tilt Mechanism, Germany, 11 ½ x 7 ½ x 5 ¼ In..	904
Parlor, Cast Iron, Heating, Salesman's Sample, Store Display, 1860s, 10 ¼ x 8 ¼ x 5 In.*illus*	277
Parlor, Eriez Stove & Mfg. Co., Gas, Cast Iron, Erie, Pa., 37 x 23 ½ x 16 In...........................	384
Parlor, Faience, Kachelofen, Terra-Cotta, Green Glaze, Finial, Late 1800s, 83 ½ In. .....*illus*	960
Potbelly, Caboose Train, Cameron Stove Co., Model A90, Pipe, Brass Wall Plate, c.1900*illus*	345
Stove Plate, Cast Iron, Arched Columns, Tulip, Hearts, Bucks Co., Pa., 1756, 23 x 35 In.	878

SUMIDA

Sumida is a Japanese pottery that was made from about 1895 to 1941. Pieces are usually everyday objects—vases, jardinieres, bowls, teapots, and decorative tiles. Most pieces have a very heavy orange-red, blue, brown, black, green, purple, or off-white glaze, with raised three-dimensional figures as decorations. The unglazed part is painted red, green, black, or orange. Sumida is sometimes mistakenly called Sumida gawa, but true Sumida gawa is a softer pottery made in the early 1800s.

Brush Washer, Log, Monkey Family, Wearing Jackets, Mother Eating Peach, Stamped, 7 In.	127
Vase, Anthropomorphic Animals & People Walking, Cliff Path, 20 ½ x 12 In.	3200
Vase, Seated Figure, Relief Decoration, Signed, Banni, 6 ¾ In.	77

SUNBONNET BABIES

Sunbonnet Babies were introduced in 1900 in the book *The Sunbonnet Babies*. The stories were by Eulalie Osgood Grover, illustrated by Bertha Corbett. The children's faces were completely hidden by the sunbonnets. The children had been pictured in black and white before this time, but the color pictures in the book were immediately successful. The Royal Bayreuth China Company made a full line of children's dishes decorated with the Sunbonnet Babies. Some Sunbonnet Babies plates have been reproduced, but they are clearly marked.

Baby Plate, Wednesday, Mending, 7 In.	25
Bell, Friday, Sweeping, 3 Looped Handles, 4 In.	100
Bowl, Nut, Sunday, Fishing, Crimped Gilt Rim, 3-Footed, 4 x 2 In..	89
Candleholder, Shield Back, Tuesday, Ironing...	165
Creamer, Laundry	28
Mug, Friday, Sweeping, 2 ¾ In.	40
Plate, Saturday, Baking, 7 In.	32
Plate, Sunday, Fishing, 7 In.	20
Plate, Tuesday, Ironing, 7 ½ In.	35
Plate, Tuesday, Ironing, Octagonal, Bedonna, 1976, 8 In.	75
Postcard, Tuesday, Ironing..	7
Sugar, Wednesday, Mending	30

S

SUNDERLAND LUSTER

Sunderland luster is a name given to a special type of pink luster made by Leeds, Newcastle, and other English firms during the nineteenth century. The luster broth glaze is metallic and glossy and appears to have bubbles in it. Other pieces of luster are listed in the Luster category.

Jug, Clipper Ship, Loop Handle, 1800s, 9 x 11 x 8 In. 427
Jug, Pearlware, Sailboats, Pink Luster Band, England, c.1812, 7¼ x 6 x 8½ In. 1386

SUPERMAN

Superman was created by two seventeen-year-olds in 1938. The first issue of Action Comics had the strip. Superman remains popular and became the hero of a radio show in 1940, cartoons in the 1940s, a television series, and several major movies.

Bank, ½ Body, Ceramic, Red, Blue, Yellow, Enesco Corp., 6 x 6½ In. 125
Doll, Plush, Vinyl Head, Flying Stance, Kelly Toys, 16 In. 12
Lamp, Hands On Waist, Ceramic, Red, Blue, 1970s, 15 In. 225
Ring, Gold Finish, Red S, Yellow Ground, DC Comics, 1976, Adjustable 45
Ring, S Symbol, Sterling Silver, Size 14 100
Toy, Action Figure, Closed Fist, Presents, Hamilton Gifts, 15 In. 25

SUSIE COOPER

Susie Cooper (1902–1995) began as a designer in 1925 working for the English firm A.E. Gray & Company. She left to work on her own as Susie Cooper Productions in 1929, decorating white ware bought from other potteries. In 1931 she formed Susie Cooper Pottery, Ltd. and moved her studio to Wood & Sons Crown Works. In 1950 it became Susie Cooper China, Ltd., and the company made china and earthenware. She bought Crown Works in 1959. It became part of the Wedgwood Group in 1966. Wedgwood closed Crown Works in 1979 and Cooper moved her studio to Adams & Sons. In 1986 she moved to the Isle of Man and worked as a free-lance designer. The name *Susie Cooper* appears with the company names on many pieces of ceramics.

A.E. Gray & Co.
c.1925–1931

Susie Cooper
1932–1956

Susie Cooper
1932–1964

Jar, Honey, Lid, Underplate, Tan, Brown & Turquoise Circles, c.1940, 4 x 3½ x 5 In. 95
Platter, Meat, Feather Design, Light Pink Border, c.1930, 14 x 11 In. 106
Teacup & Saucer, Raspberry Pink, Scalloped Edge, Flowers, White Ground 40

SWORD

Swords of all types that are of interest to collectors are listed here. The military dress sword with elaborate handle is probably the most wanted. A tsuba is a hand guard fitted to a Japanese sword between the handle and the blade. Be sure to display swords in a safe way, out of reach of children.

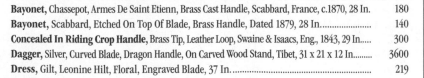

Bayonet, Chassepot, Armes De Saint Etienn, Brass Cast Handle, Scabbard, France, c.1870, 28 In. 180
Bayonet, Scabbard, Etched On Top Of Blade, Brass Handle, Dated 1879, 28 In. 140
Concealed In Riding Crop Handle, Brass Tip, Leather Loop, Swaine & Isaacs, Eng., 1843, 29 In. 300
Dagger, Silver, Curved Blade, Dragon Handle, On Carved Wood Stand, Tibet, 31 x 21 x 12 In. 3600
Dress, Gilt, Leonine Hilt, Floral, Engraved Blade, 37 In. 219

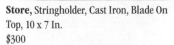

Store, Stringholder, Cast Iron, Blade On Top, 10 x 7 In.
$300

Chupp Auctions & Real Estate, LLC

Stove, Parlor, Cast Iron, Heating, Salesman's Sample, Store Display, 1860s, 10¼ x 8¼ x 5 In.
$277

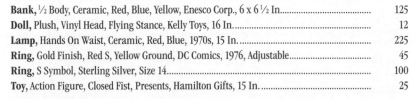

Jeffrey S. Evans & Associates

Stove, Parlor, Faience, Kachelofen, Terra-Cotta, Green Glaze, Finial, Late 1800s, 83½ In.
$960

S

Selkirk Auctioneers & Appraisers

SWORD

Stove, Potbelly, Caboose Train, Cameron Stove Co., Model A90, Pipe, Brass Wall Plate, c.1900
$345

Donley Auctions

Sword, Naval Officer, Double Fuller Blade, Etched, Gilt, Brass Hilt, Black Leather Scabbard, 38 In.
$944

Soulis Auctions

Syracuse, Plate, Commodore Perry, Ship, Gold Banner, Red Rim, Marked G-8, 10¼ In.
$83

Stony Ridge Auction

Dress, Officer's, Single Edge, Fuller Blade, Steel Scabbard, Wilkinson, London, 1900s, 32 x 39 In.	360
Naval Officer, Double Fuller Blade, Etched, Gilt, Brass Hilt, Black Leather Scabbard, 38 In.... *illus*	944
Saber, Cavalry, Leather Grip, Iron Scabbard, Shadowbox Frame, Early 1800s, 15½ In. x 43 In...	384
Yataghan, Ottoman, Curved Blade, Scabbard, Shadowbox Frame, Early 1800s, 12 x 40 In.	1664

SYRACUSE

Syracuse is one of the trademarks used by the Onondaga Pottery of Syracuse, New York. They also used O.P. Co. The company was established in 1871. The name became the Syracuse China Company in 1966. Syracuse China closed in 2009. It was known for fine dinnerware and restaurant china.

Syracuse China, Corp.
1871–1873

Syracuse China, Corp.
1892–1895

Syracuse China, Corp.
1966–1970

Bowl, Thistle, Footed, Scalloped Rim & Base, Gilt Trim, Green Inner Rim, c.1900, 3 x 6½ In....	4
Cup & Saucer, Old Ivory, Flower Clusters, Green Panels, Gilt Trim, Pair...............................	13
Plate, Commodore Perry, Ship, Gold Banner, Red Rim, Marked G-8, 10¼ In. ....*illus*	83
Platter, Western Longhorn, Brown, Oval, Econo-Rim, Restaurant Ware, c.1950, 10½ x 13 In...	36

TAPESTRY, *Porcelain, see Rose Tapestry category.*

TEA CADDY

Tea caddy is the name for a small box made to hold tea leaves. In the eighteenth century, tea was very expensive and it was stored under lock and key. The first tea caddies were made with locks. By the nineteenth century, tea was more plentiful and the tea caddy was larger. Often there were two sections, one for green tea, one for black tea.

Bird's-Eye Maple, 2 Compartments, Paneled Top, Knob Handles, Bun Feet, 1800s, 7 x 13 x 7 In..	488
Bird's-Eye Maple, Hinged Lid, Hardwood Inlay, Painted, Brass Cover Strap, c.1840, 6 x 14 x 6 In...	488
Burl Walnut, Hinged Lid, Octagonal, Keyhole, England, 1800s, 4¾ x 8¼ In. ....*illus*	600
Burl, Hinged Lid, 2 Compartments, Cross Banding, Brass Ball Feet, 1800s, 6 x 8 x 5 In........	305
Burl, Hinged Lid, Brass, Lion Mask Handles, 1800s, 8 x 13 In. ....*illus*	215
Fruitwood, Hinged Lid, Apple Shape, Foil Lined Interior, England, 4½ x 4½ In..................	367
Fruitwood, Hinged Lid, Apple Shape, Lined Interior, Lock & Key, Stem Finial, 1800s, 5 x 4 In.... *illus*	944
Fruitwood, Hinged Lid, Apple Shape, Metal Lock Escutcheon, Early 1800s, 5 x 4 In.............	2340
Fruitwood, Hinged Lid, Pear Shape, Ivory Escutcheon, England, 1800s, 8 In. ....*illus*	1375
Fruitwood, Hinged Lid, Pear Shape, Stem, Carved, Lined Interior, Horn Escutcheon, 1800s, 7½ In...	767
Lacquer, Black, Gilt, Silver, Figural Scenes, Dragon Wing Feet, Chinese Export, 1700s, 5 In..*illus*	305
Mahogany Veneer, Fruitwood Inlay, 3 Compartments, England, 1800s, 6 x 9 x 5 In.................	625
Mahogany, Canted Sides, Turned Knobs, Bun Feet, Federal, 7 x 12 x 6 In............................	761
Mahogany, Hinged Lid, 3 Compartments, Oval Shape Panels, Button Feet, 6 x 12 x 6 In.	1521
Mahogany, Hinged Lid, Bombe, Brass Handle, Escutcheon, Fitted Interior, Kittinger, 6 x 10 x 6 In....	240
Mahogany, Hinged Lid, Brass Handles, Bracket Feet, George III, Early 1800s, 7 x 11 x 6 In.	500
Mahogany, Hinged Lid, Brass, Canted Corners, Compartments, George III Style, 1700s, 5 x 7 x 4 In...	375
Mahogany, Hinged Lid, Floral Garlands, Shell Inlays, George III, Late 1700s, 5 x 9 In.........	1599
Mahogany, Hinged Lid, Inlaid, Floral Medallions, 3 Compartments, England, c.1825, 5 x 9 x 5 In.	1000
Mahogany, Hinged Lid, Inlaid, Coffin Shape, Bun Feet, Georgian, 1910s, 5 x 8 x 5 In.	313
Mahogany, Hinged Lid, Metal Handle, Ball Feet, George III, 1700s, 5 x 10 x 5 In..............*illus*	250
Mahogany, Hinged Lid, Regency Inlay, Banded, Fan, Ball Feet, Georgian, Early 1800s, 6 x 10 x 5 In.......	492
Mahogany, Hinged Lid, Satinwood Inlay, Ebony Trim & Escutcheon, 4¾ x 7 x 4¾ In.........	113
Mahogany, Mixing Bowl, 2 Lidded Interior Compartments, Flat Ball Feet, William IV, 7½ In..*illus*	250

Tea Caddy, Burl Walnut, Hinged Lid, Octagonal, Keyhole, England, 1800s, 4¾ x 8¼ In.
$600

Cottone Auctions

Tea Caddy, Burl, Hinged Lid, Brass, Lion Mask Handles, 1800s, 8 x 13 In.
$215

Pook & Pook

> **TIP**
> *If your tea caddy or knife box has a silver or brass keyhole, don't use a metal cleaner. The cleaner will damage the wood.*

Tea Caddy, Fruitwood, Hinged Lid, Apple Shape, Lined Interior, Lock & Key, Stem Finial, 1800s, 5 x 4 In.
$944

Soulis Auctions

Tea Caddy, Fruitwood, Hinged Lid, Pear Shape, Ivory Escutcheon, England, 1800s, 8 In.
$1,375

Eldred's

Tea Caddy, Lacquer, Black, Gilt, Silver, Figural Scenes, Dragon Wing Feet, Chinese Export, 1700s, 5 In.
$305

Neal Auction Company

Tea Caddy, Mahogany, Hinged Lid, Metal Handle, Ball Feet, George III, 1700s, 5 x 10 x 5 In.
$250

Hindman

Tea Caddy, Mahogany, Mixing Bowl, 2 Lidded Interior Compartments, Flat Ball Feet, William IV, 7½ In.
$250

Neal Auction Company

Tea Caddy, Marquetry, Hinged Lid, Diamond Shape Keyhole, George III, c.1790, 5¾ x 5 x 5 In.
$125

Hindman

Tea Caddy, Porcelain, Lid, Blue & White, Square, Landscapes, Chinese Export, 12 In., Pair
$1,037

Neal Auction Company

T

Tea Caddy, Rolled Paper, Hinged Lid, Oval, Painted, Scroll Design, George III, c.1790, 6 x 5 x 3 In.
$1,500

Charlton Hall Auctions

Tea Caddy, Satinwood, Hinged Lid, Inlaid Panels, Chinese Paper Lining, Octagonal, 1790, 4 ½ x 5 x 3 In.
$531

Wiederseim Auctions

Tea Caddy, Silver, Hinged Lid, Thomas Bradbury & Sons, London, Georgian, 1892, 6 x 4 ½ x 2 ¾ In.
$787

Ahlers & Ogletree Auction Gallery

Tea Caddy, Tortoiseshell, Hinged Lid, 2 Compartments, Serpentine Front, Regency, 1800s, 4 x 7 x 4 In.
$1,830

Rafael Osona Nantucket Auctions

Tea Caddy, Tortoiseshell, Hinged Lid, Mother-Of-Pearl, Coffin Shape, Regency, c.1815, 5 x 7 In.
$2,745

Rafael Osona Nantucket Auctions

Tea Caddy, Tortoiseshell, Hinged Lid, William IV, Bombe, 2 Compartments, Ball Feet, 1800s, 5 x 6 x 4 In.
$1,920

Neal Auction Company

T

Mahogany, Painted, Scenic, Banks Of Allan Water, Scotland, 1800s, 24 x 23 x 22 In.		406
Marquetry, Hinged Lid, Diamond Shape Keyhole, George III, c.1790, 5¾ x 5 x 5 In.	*illus*	125
Porcelain, Lid, Blue & White, Square, Landscapes, Chinese Export, 12 In., Pair	*illus*	1037
Porcelain, Lift Lid, Foo Dog Finial, Arms Of Fearon, Multicolor, c.1750, 4 x 2 x 2 In.		976
Rolled Paper, Hinged Lid, Oval, Painted, Scroll Design, George III, c.1790, 6 x 5 x 3 In.	*illus*	1500
Rosewood, Center Glass Bowl, Compartments, Flat Bun Feet, Regency Style, c.1830, 6 x 11 x 5 In.		375
Rosewood, Hinged Lid, Coffin Shape, Sapwood Line, Ball Feet, Mid 1800s, 5 x 8 x 4 In.		108
Satinwood, Hinged Lid, Floral Inlay, Boxwood, Paterae, 1800s, 5 x 10 x 5 In.		1521
Satinwood, Hinged Lid, Inlaid Panels, Chinese Paper Lining, Octagonal, 1790, 4½ x 5 x 3 In.	*illus*	531
Shell, Hinged Lid, Compartments, Ball Feet, Georgian, 5½ x 7¼ x 4 In.		1708
Silver, Elephant Finial, Floral & Leaves, Volute Feet, Marked, AP, Vienna, Late 1800s, 6¼ In.		1000
Silver, Gilt, Chinoiserie Figures, Rocaille, C-Scroll & Lion Mask, Dutch, c.1790, 5¾ In.		2375
Silver, Hinged Lid, Coconut Shell, 4 Whale's Teeth Legs, Swag Designs, 1910s, 8 In.		875
Silver, Hinged Lid, Thomas Bradbury & Sons, London, Georgian, 1892, 6 x 4½ x 2¾ In.	*illus*	787
Silver, Oval, Beaded Rims, Engraved Crest, Hester Bateman, 5½ x 5½ In.		1180
Tiger Maple, Hinged Lid, Rosewood Trim, Metal, Ball Feet, c.1840, 8 x 15 x 8½ In.		2691
Tortoiseshell, Hinged Lid, 2 Compartments, Serpentine Front, Regency, 1800s, 4 x 7 x 4 In.	*illus*	1830
Tortoiseshell, Hinged Lid, Mother-Of-Pearl, Coffin Shape, Regency, c.1815, 5 x 7 In.	*illus*	2745
Tortoiseshell, Hinged Lid, Pagoda Shape, Serpentine Front, Ball Feet, George III, 1800s, 6 x 8¼ In.		3712
Tortoiseshell, Hinged Lid, William IV, Bombe, 2 Compartments, Ball Feet, 1800s, 5 x 6 x 4 In.	*illus*	1920
Wood, Dome Top, Hinged Lid, Brass & Bone Mounted, Silk Lining, England, 6 x 9 x 5¾ In.		125
Wood, Hinged Lid, Octagonal, Satinwood Inlaid Butterfly, George III, 4 x 5 x 4 In.		854

TEA LEAF IRONSTONE

Tea leaf ironstone dishes are named for their decorations. There was a superstition that it was lucky if a whole tea leaf unfolded at the bottom of your teacup. This idea was translated into the pattern of dishes known as "tea leaf." By 1850 at least 12 English factories were making this pattern, and by the 1870s it was a popular pattern in many countries. The tea leaf was always a luster glaze on early wares, although now some pieces are made with a brown tea leaf. There are many variations of tea leaf designs, such as Teaberry, Pepper Leaf, and Gold Leaf. The designs were used on many different white ironstone shapes, such as Bamboo, Lily of the Valley, Empress, and Cumbow.

Butter, Cover, Footed, Domed, Drainer, Handles, Alfred Meakin, 4 x 4 x 4 In.		79
Chamber Pot, Lid, Handle, Footed, A.J. Wilkinson, 7 In.	*illus*	75
Mug, Paneled Body, Leaf & Berry Relief Handle, Anthony Shaw, 3½ In.		68
Relish, Mitten Shape, Anthony Shaw, c.1875, 5¼ In.		45
Tureen, Lid, Footed, Wedgwood, c.1900, 10 x 5 x 6¾ In.		259

TECO

Teco is the mark used on the art pottery line made by the American Terra Cotta and Ceramic Company of Terra Cotta and Chicago, Illinois. The company was an offshoot of the firm founded by William D. Gates in 1881. The Teco line was first made in 1885 but was not sold commercially until 1902. It continued in production until 1922. Over 500 designs were made in a variety of colors, shapes, and glazes. The company closed in 1930.

Vase, Blue, Monumental, Drilled Hole, W.B. Mundie, 19 x 28 In., Pair		6250
Vase, Green Matte Glaze, 2 Handles, W.D. Gates, 8½ x 3¾ In.	*illus*	552
Vase, Green Matte Glaze, 4 Handles, Buttress, c.1910, 7½ x 4¼ In.		3075
Vase, Green Matte Glaze, Arts & Crafts, Marked, c.1910, 1 x 9 In.		450
Vase, Pink Matte Glaze, 4 Buttress Handles, c.1910, 6¼ x 2½ In.	*illus*	2337
Vase, Tall, Calla Lily, Green Matte Glaze, Fritz Albert, 13 x 5½ In.		750

Tea Leaf Ironstone, Chamber Pot, Lid, Handle, Footed, A.J. Wilkinson, 7 In. **$75**

Pook & Pook

Teco, Vase, Green Matte Glaze, 2 Handles, W.D. Gates, 8½ x 3¾ In. **$552**

Toomey & Co. Auctioneers

Teco, Vase, Pink Matte Glaze, 4 Buttress Handles, c.1910, 6¼ x 2½ In. **$2,337**

California Historical Design

Teddy Bear, Dehaven Originals, Wally, Alpaca Wool, Felt Paw Pods, Pajamas, 1992, 15 In.
$50

Lion and Unicorn

Teddy Bear, Schuco, Tricky, Mohair, Light Brown, Jointed, Stitched Claws, Tail Operates Head, 1950s
$216

White's Auctions

Teddy Bear, Steiff, Growler, Standing, Metal Frame, Wood Wheels, 24 x 7 x 18 In.
$443

Copake Auction

Teddy Bear, Steiff, Mohair, Fully Jointed, Brown, Button In Ear, 6½ In.
$72

Jaremos

TIP

If you buy an old teddy bear at a garage sale, bring it home and put it in a plastic bag with some mothballs for a few weeks. Don't let the mothballs touch the bear. The fur and stuffing of old bears attract many types of hungry insects.

Teddy Bear, Steiner, Heidi, Mohair, Brown, Glass Eyes, Burgundy Bow, 19 In.
$86

Apple Tree Auction Center

Teddy Bear Paws
Early teddy bears had felt or cotton paws. Later ones had paws of velvet, plush, or leather. By the 1970s, the paws were ultra-suede.

T

TEDDY BEAR

Teddy bears were named for a president of the United States. The first teddy bear was a cuddly toy said to be inspired by a hunting trip made by President Theodore Roosevelt in 1902. He was praised because he saw a bear cub but did not shoot it. Morris and Rose Michtom started selling their stuffed bears as "teddy bears" and the name stayed. The Michtoms founded the Ideal Novelty and Toy Company. The German version of the teddy bear was made about the same time by the Steiff Company. There are many types of teddy bears and all are collected. The old ones are being reproduced. Other bears are listed in the Toy section.

Apple Whimsy, Thanksgiving Pilgrim, Fruit Basket, Hat, Donna Yackey, 1993, 18 In.	106
Dehaven Originals, Wally, Alpaca Wool, Felt Paw Pods, Pajamas, 1992, 15 In. .... *illus*	50
Donna Hodges, Bearons Of La Jolla, Magician, Musical, Mohair, 1900s, 16 In.	44
Dream Time, Santa Claus, Morning After, Red Robe, Eyeglasses, B. Lewis, 1993, 14 In.	31
Mac Animals, Attic Teddy, English Mohair, Shoebutton Eyes, Lace Collar, Tag, 1999, 16 In.	50
Schuco, Tricky, Mohair, Light Brown, Jointed, Stitched Claws, Tail Operates Head, 1950s...... *illus*	216
Schuco, Yes-No, Turning Tail, Golden Brown, Black Button Eyes, Floss Nose & Mouth, 1920s, 17 In. ..	75
Steiff, Ballerina, Plush, Cream, Pink Hairband, Dress & Shoes, Carrying Case, In.	62
Steiff, First American Teddy, Brown, Bow & Hat, Box, 16 In.	74
Steiff, Growler, Standing, Metal Frame, Wood Wheels, 24 x 7 x 18 In. .... *illus*	443
Steiff, Mohair, Brown, Glass Eyes, Wheel Base, Pull Toy, 5 x 6½ In.	428
Steiff, Mohair, Fully Jointed, Brown, Button In Ear, 6½ In. .... *illus*	72
Steiner, Heidi, Mohair, Brown, Glass Eyes, Burgundy Bow, 19 In. .... *illus*	86
Timbears, Bull Rider, Mohair, Glass Eyes, Bandanna, Mary Timma, Timbears, 1994, 14 In. ..	44
Wilder Cubs, Fil Prince, Mohair, Leather Paws, Shoes, Cathy Wilder, 1991, 8 In.	31
Winnie The Pooh, Pocket Pooh, Mohair Plush, Glass Bead Eyes, R. John Wright, 5 In........	135

TELEPHONE

Telephones are wanted by collectors if the phones are old enough or unusual enough. The first telephone may have been made in Havana, Cuba, in 1849, but it was not patented. The first publicly demonstrated phone was used in Frankfurt, Germany, in 1860. The phone made by Alexander Graham Bell was shown at the Centennial Exhibition in Philadelphia in 1876, but it was not until 1877 that the first private phones were installed. Collectors today want all types of old phones, phone parts, and advertising. Even recent figural phones are popular.

American Electric Co., Wall, Wood, Adjustable Mouthpiece, 2 Bells, c.1900, 31½ In.. *illus*	545
Automatic Electric Co., Payphone, Dial, Black Ground, Chrome, 18 x 7 x 8 In....................	246
Intercom, La Jollan Hotel, Black Ground, Domed Base, 24 x 16 x 12 In........................ *illus*	800
Kellogg, Wall, Cabinet Base, Earpiece, Wood, Stamped 2811H	81
Northern Electric, Wall, Oak, Cast Iron, Nickel Plated Brass, Cleveland, O., c.1900, 26 x 8 x 12 In....	190
Sign, White Text, Black Ground, Electric, 21 In., 2-Sided... *illus*	438

TELEVISION

Television sets are twentieth-century collectibles. Although the first television transmission took place in England in 1925, collectors find few sets that pre-date 1946. The first sets had only five channels, but by 1949 the additional UHF channels were included. The first color television set became available in 1951. Props used on television shows are also listed here.

Emerson, Model 621A, Restored, 1949-50	500
Philco Predicta, 1959...	570
Prop, Camera, Hasselblad, Rubber, Hard Foam, From The Earth To The Moon, HBO, 1997, 5 x 8 In...	406
Prop, Cookie, Parade Float, Cookie Monster, Sesame Street, Universal Studios, Japan, 8¼ In.	238
Prop, Poco Pirate Flag, Allegra's Window, Season 2, Nickelodeon, 1995, 13¼ x 19 In...........	63
Prop, Turtle, Gullah Gullah Island, Eric Baker, Nickelodeon, 1994, 3¾ x 9½ x 5½ In.	125
Prop, Upside-Down Compass, Legends Of The Hidden Temple, Nickelodeon, 1995, 2⅜ x 6 In....	313

Telephone, American Electric Co., Wall, Wood, Adjustable Mouthpiece, 2 Bells, c.1900, 31½ In.
$545

Fontaine's Auction Gallery

Telephone, Intercom, La Jollan Hotel, Black Ground, Domed Base, 24 x 16 x 12 In.
$800

Morphy Auctions

Telephone, Sign, White Text, Black Ground, Electric, 21 In., 2-Sided
$438

New Haven Auctions

This is an edited listing of current prices. Visit **Kovels.com** to check thousands of prices from previous years and sign up for free information on trends, tips, reproductions, marks, and more.

TIP

Modern bleach can damage eighteenth-century and some nineteenth-century dishes. To clean old dishes, try hydrogen peroxide or bicarbonate of soda. Each removes a different type of stain.

TEPLITZ

Teplitz refers to art pottery manufactured by a number of companies in the Teplitz-Turn area of Bohemia during the late nineteenth and early twentieth centuries. Two of these companies were the Alexandra Works founded by Ernst Wahliss, and the Amphora Porcelain Works, run by Riessner, Stellmacher, and Kessel.

Bowl, Flowers In Relief, Blue Matte Glaze, Reticulated Gilt Rim, Amphora, Mark, 3 x 7 In...	750
Bust, Woman, Green Hat & Shirt, Art Nouveau, Amphora, Signed, Stellmacher, 17 x 14 In. ....*illus*	450
Bust, Woman, Hat, Ribbon, Leaves & Grapes, Pink & White, Early 1900s, 14 In.	125
Ewer, Cylindrical, Cobalt Blue, Flowers, Gold Trim, Handle, 7 x 5 In.	70
Group, Man & Woman, Standing, Classical Clothes, Late 1800s, 23 In.......................*illus*	344
Humidor, Figural, Jester, Holding Globe, Hat Atop, Amphora, c.1900, 8 x 13 x 7 In.......*illus*	484
Urn, Pedestal, Lid, Woman & Cherub, Maroon & Green, Ernst Wahliss, 23 x 7 In..................	600
Vase, 2-Sided Octopus, Black Matte Glaze, Eduard Stellmacher, c.1905, 9 x 8½ In....*illus*	3250
Vase, 4 Handles, Glazed, Earthenware, Amphora, Paul Dachsel, Early 1900s, 13 In......*illus*	605
Vase, Figural, Woman, Iris, Riessner, Stellmacher & Kessel, Amphora, c.1900, 22 In.	2178
Vase, Flowers, Flared Rim, Bulbous, Multicolor, Amphora, Early 1900s, 8 x 8 In.	563
Vase, Pinecones, Glazed, Amphora, Paul Dachsel, 5½ x 5 In.......................................*illus*	469
Vase, Potbelly, Glazed, Amphora, Art Nouveau, Marked Campina, Austria, 7 x 8½ In.	64
Vase, Woman's Face, Art Nouveau, Crown Oak Ware, Grumbach, Bernard Bloch, 13 In......*illus*	380

TERRA-COTTA

Terra-cotta is a special type of pottery. It ranges from pale orange to dark reddish-brown in color. The color comes from the clay, which is fired but not always glazed in the finished piece.

Bowl, Archaic, Half Spherical Shape, Flat Rim, Round Bottom, 5¼ x 10½ In.	176
Bust, Madame Recamier, Gilt, Painted, Charles Jonchery, 1800s, 22 x 11 x 9 In...........*illus*	288
Bust, Man, Revolutionary, Multicolor, Directoire, 1700s, 13¾ In................................*illus*	383
Ewer, Classical Style, Figural, Merman, Riding Dolphin, Plinth Base, 25½ In.	150
Figurine, Bulldog, On Stand, Spiky Choker, 1900s, 13 x 16 In..	265
Figurine, Dwarf, Standing, Smiling, Beard, Hatchet, 1800s, 28 In. ....*illus*	2250
Figurine, Eagle, Bronze Tint, 1900s, 20 x 10½ x 12 In.	175
Figurine, Farm Girl, Standing, Holding Basket, France, 1800s, 30½ In.................................	188
Figurine, Goddess, Votive Figure, Offering Hole, 6¾ In.	300
Figurine, Lion, Lying Down, Bundled Laurel Base, Italy, 1983, 16 x 30¾ x 15 In. ....*illus*	272
Figurine, Putti, Seated, Holding Bunch Of Grapes, Urn Shape Base, 1900s, 31 x 25 In., Pair...*illus*	688
Figurine, Warrior, Standing, Square Base, Liu Fenghua, c.2005, 14½ In.	375
Figurine, Woman, Standing, Holding Knife, Side Face, Base, 1900s, 14½ In.	219
Group, 2 Cherubs, Standing & Seated, Kissing, Scroll Mark, France, 17½ In..............*illus*	350
Lion's Head, Roaring, Glazed, Yellow Gold, Italy, 18½ x 14 x 8 In.	500
Plaque, Medallion, Portrait, Benjamin Franklin, Jean-Baptiste Nini, France, 1777, 4¾ In....*illus*	3024
Plaque, Medallion, Portrait, Louis XVI, After Jean-Baptiste Nini, France, 1900s, 3¾ In.......	182
Roundel, Heraldic, Tin Glaze, After Della Robbia, Italy, 1900s, 30½ In.	750
Sculpture, Female Herm, Head, Torso, Square Base, Continental, 1900s, 57½ In...............	1875
Sculpture, Horse, Removable Head, Rectangular Base, White Pigment, Chinese, 50 x 42 x 13 In.*illus*	240
Sculpture, Venus, Square Base, John Marriott, Blashfield, Stamford, 1800s, 42 x 14 x 13 In.	4680
Sculpture, Woman, With Flower Basket, Standing, 46½ In.	270
Vase, Figural, Maiden, Holding Flower, Cylindrical, Bulbous Base, Art Nouveau, c.1900, 25 In...	570
Vase, Flared Mouth, Lion Mask, Raised Foot, White Matte Glaze, Italy, 1900s, 11½ x 7¼ In.	70
Vase, Mythological, Copper Tone, Signed, Dini E. Cellai, 5 x 5 In. ....*illus*	108

TEXTILE

Textiles listed here include many types of printed fabrics and table and household linens. Some other textiles will be found under Clothing, Coverlet, Rug, Quilt, etc.

Banner, Metallic Thread, Embroidery, Medallion, Angels, Dark Blue, Fringe, c.1750, 92 x 48 In..*illus*	1063

Teplitz, Bust, Woman, Green Hat & Shirt, Art Nouveau, Amphora, Signed, Stellmacher, 17 x 14 In.
$450

Treasureseeker Auctions

Teplitz, Group, Man & Woman, Standing, Classical Clothes, Late 1800s, 23 In.
$344

Hindman

Teplitz, Humidor, Figural, Jester, Holding Globe, Hat Atop, Amphora, c.1900, 8 x 13 x 7 In.
$484

Fontaine's Auction Gallery

Teplitz, Vase, 2-Sided Octopus, Black Matte Glaze, Eduard Stellmacher, c.1905, 9 x 8½ In.
$3,250

Toomey & Co. Auctioneers

Teplitz, Vase, 4 Handles, Glazed, Earthenware, Amphora, Paul Dachsel, Early 1900s, 13 In.
$605

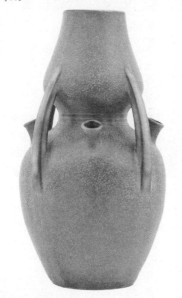

Fontaine's Auction Gallery

Teplitz, Vase, Pinecones, Glazed, Amphora, Paul Dachsel, 5½ x 5 In.
$469

Treadway

Teplitz, Vase, Woman's Face, Art Nouveau, Crown Oak Ware, Grumbach, Bernard Bloch, 13 In.
$380

Jeffrey S. Evans & Associates

Terra-Cotta, Bust, Madame Recamier, Gilt, Painted, Charles Jonchery, 1800s, 22 x 11 x 9 In.
$288

Roland NY Auctioneers & Appraisers

Terra-Cotta, Bust, Man, Revolutionary, Multicolor, Directoire, 1700s, 13¾ In.
$383

Bonhams

Terra-Cotta, Figurine, Dwarf, Standing, Smiling, Beard, Hatchet, 1800s, 28 In.
$2,250

Fontaine's Auction Gallery

Terra-Cotta, Figurine, Lion, Lying Down, Bundled Laurel Base, Italy, 1983, 16 x 30¾ x 15 In.
$272

Ahlers & Ogletree Auction Gallery

T

Terra-Cotta, Figurine, Putti, Seated, Holding Bunch Of Grapes, Urn Shape Base, 1900s, 31 x 25 In., Pair
$688

Hindman

Terra-Cotta, Group, 2 Cherubs, Standing & Seated, Kissing, Scroll Mark, France, 17 1/2 In
$350

Neal Auction Company

Terra-Cotta, Plaque, Medallion, Portrait, Benjamin Franklin, Jean-Baptiste Nini, France, 1777, 4 3/4 In.
$3,024

Freeman's

Terra-Cotta, Sculpture, Horse, Removable Head, Rectangular Base, White Pigment, Chinese, 50 x 42 x 13 In.
$240

Michaan's Auctions

Terra-Cotta, Vase, Mythological, Copper Tone, Signed, Dini E. Cellai, 5 x 5 In.
$108

Main Auction Galleries, Inc.

Grand Old Flag

If your American flag is tattered and can no longer be used be sure to dispose of it the official way. Give it to a Boy Scout, Girl Scout, American Legion post, or the U.S. military. They can do the official ceremony that includes burning the old flag.

Textile, Banner, Metallic Thread, Embroidery, Medallion, Angels, Dark Blue, Fringe, c.1750, 92 x 48 In.
$1,063

Hindman

Textile, Blanket, Camp, Stripes, Wool, Glacier Park, Hudson Bay, Pendleton, Contemporary, 80 x 78 In.
$259

Merrill's Auctions

Textile, Flag, American, 14 Stars, Cotton, Cowpens, 3rd Maryland Regiment, 1876, 62 x 104 In.
$3,276

Freeman's

T

Textile, Panel, Brocade, Red Ground, Children Playing Scene, 4 Roundel Birds, 64 x 28 ½ In.
$780

Michaan's Auctions

TIP

Don't send out your antique white linen or cotton items to be dry-cleaned. The chemicals will yellow the fabric. Hand wash them in soap, non-chlorine bleach, and tepid water. Be sure to rinse until all soap is removed.

Textile, Panel, Silk, Embroidery, Bird, Flowers, Mythical Animals, Frame, Chinese, 46 x 56 In.
$6,050

Ahlers & Ogletree Auction Gallery

Textile, Pillow Cover, Patchwork, Bolster, Multicolor, Pennsylvania, Early 1900s, 23 x 50 In.
$365

Pook & Pook

Textile, Pillow, Embroidery, Flower, Arts & Crafts, c.1910, 17 x 19 In.
$215

California Historical Design

Textile, Placemat, Linen, Embroidery, Oval, Flowers, Pink, c.1910s, 12 ½ x 5 ½ In., Pair
$123

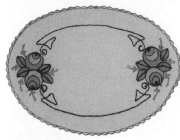

California Historical Design

Textile, Table Cover, Linen, Silk, Embroidered, Framed, May Morris, c.1880, 42 ½ x 40 In.
$227

Toomey & Co. Auctioneers

Textile, Table Runner, Cigar Ribbons, Silk, Pieced, Embroidery, Tassel Border, Victorian, 33 x 33 In.
$563

Wiederseim Auctions

Textile, Tapestry, Figures, Trees, Flowers, Landscape Scene, Cream Ground, Black Border, 78 x 70 In.
$275

Neal Auction Company

T

Textile, Tapestry, Needlepoint, Renn-Style Dinner Table, 5 People, Rod, 48 x 60 In.
$544

Roland NY Auctioneers & Appraisers

Textile, Tapestry, Wedding Day, Hand Woven, Wool, Signed, Genaro De Carvalho, 36 x 48 In.
$5,080

White's Auctions

Textile, Thangka, Red Tara, Multicolor, Gilt Ink Detailing, Silk Brocade, 1800s, 22 x 16 In.
$8,610

Auctions at Showplace, NYC

Banner, New Testament Church, Established A.D. 33., Cotton, c.1910-20, 66½ x 92 In.	710
Blanket, Camp, Stripes, Wool, Glacier Park, Hudson Bay, Pendleton, Contemporary, 80 x 78 In. *illus*	259
Blanket, Green Ground, Geometric, 3 Bands, Hudson Bay, 1800s, 62 x 56 In.	75
Blanket, Saddle, U.S. Marine Corps, Canvas, Leather Edge, Early 1900s, 30 x 21 In.	1020
Blanket, Wool, Cotton, No. 1, Red, Yellow, Black Border, Dale Chihuly, Pendleton, 2002, 78 x 64 In.	845
Blanket, Woven, Red, Blue & White Stripes, 2 Panel, 72 x 99 In.	188
Flag, American, 14 Stars, Cotton, Cowpens, 3rd Maryland Regiment, 1876, 62 x 104 In. *illus*	3276
Flag, American, 35 Stars, Cotton, Wool, Brass Grommet, 1863, 97 x 74 In.	2750
Flag, American, 47 Stars, Cotton, c.1912, 80 x 44 In.	188
Flag, Colorado, Centennial State, 38 Stars, 1976, 20 x 35 In.	953
Flower Arrangement, Felted, Multicolor, Under Glass Dome, Victorian, 15½ In.	141
Fragment, Embroidery, Boat, House, Tree, Birds, Japan, 53 x 70 In.	75
Hammock, Balloons, Hand Woven, Cotton, Alexander Calder, Nicaragua, 1975, 22 x 132 x 44 In.	6250
Mat, Braided, Blue, Red, Black, Pink, Crocheted Border, Oval, 50 x 31 In.	164
Panel, Brocade, Red Ground, Children Playing Scene, 4 Roundel Birds, 64 x 28½ In. *illus*	780
Panel, Imperial, Kesi, Dragon, Pale Orange Ground, Lingzhi Shape Clouds, Chinese, 20½ x 20 In.	660
Panel, Metal Thread, Silk, Embroidery, Chinese, 59¾ x 21¾ In.	813
Panel, Silk, Embroidery, Bird, Flowers, Mythical Animals, Frame, Chinese, 46 x 56 In. *illus*	6050
Panel, Silk, Bands, Dragons, Rust Ground, Republic Period, Frame, Chinese, 99 x 38 In., Pair	938
Pillow Cover, Patchwork, Bolster, Multicolor, Pennsylvania, Early 1900s, 23 x 50 In. *illus*	365
Pillow Sham, Patchwork, Multicolor, Geometric Design, Pa., Early 1900s, 19 x 26½ In., Pair	428
Pillow Sham, Persian, Woven Wool Cover, Insert, Middle Eastern, 1900s, 18 x 18 In., Pair	212
Pillow, 2 Hermes Scarves, Equestrian Theme, Silk, Tassels, 27 x 24 In.	320
Pillow, Embroidery, Flower, Arts & Crafts, c.1910, 17 x 19 In. *illus*	215
Pillow, Throw, Wool Needlepoint, Nautical Theme, 3 Sailing Ships, 15 x 11 In., Pair	263
Placemat, Linen, Embroidery, Oval, Flowers, Pink, c.1910s, 12½ x 5½ In., Pair *illus*	123
Sculpture, Fish Shape, Geometric, Multicolor, Button Eyes, Dahlov Ipcar, c.1970s-80, 17 In.	3218
Table Cover, Linen, Silk, Embroidered, Framed, May Morris, c.1880, 42½ x 40 In. *illus*	227
Table Runner, Cigar Ribbons, Silk, Pieced, Embroidery, Tassel Border, Victorian, 33 x 33 In. *illus*	563
Table Runner, Embroidery, Daisies, Yellow, Arts & Crafts, c.1910, 51 x 17 In.	185
Table Runner, Embroidery, Flowers, White, Yellow, Orange, Arts & Crafts, c.1910, 56 x 23 In.	246
Table Runner, Wool, Black, White, Gray Shade, 90 x 14 In	53
Table Scarf, Embroidery, Butterflies, Linen, Round, Arts & Crafts, c.1910s, 36 In.	185
Tablecloth, Dragon, Yellow Ground, Black Border, Red Back, Chinese, 18th Century, 70 x 73 In.	5120
Tablecloth, Scrolled Leaves, Orange, Tan, Blue, Fortuny, Importe D'Italie, 93¼ x 47½ In.	531
Tapestry, Birds, Hand Knotted, Wool, Evelyn Akerman, c.1965, 46¾ x 15¾ In.	2500
Tapestry, Figures, Trees, Flowers, Landscape Scene, Cream Ground, Black Border, 78 x 70 In. *illus*	275
Tapestry, Flemish, Woven, Mule, Lion, Poppies, Roses, Leaves, 1700s, 28¼ x 22 In.	420
Tapestry, Jacquard, Outdoor Dance, House, Tree, Continental, 19th Century, 75 x 49 In.	384
Tapestry, Machine Made, Wall Hanging, Wood Rod, 53 x 45½ In.	13
Tapestry, Medallion, Red & Green, Multicolor, Flowers, Gold Border, 156 x 96 In.	259
Tapestry, Needlepoint, Landscape, Courting Scene, Gilt Rod, 85 In.	281
Tapestry, Needlepoint, Renn-Style Dinner Table, 5 People, Rod, 48 x 60 In. *illus*	544
Tapestry, Pink Ground, Vase, Flowers, Leafy Scrolls, Peach Border, France, 1700s, 66 x 90 In.	115
Tapestry, Wedding Day, Hand Woven, Wool, Signed, Genaro De Carvalho, 36 x 48 In. *illus*	5080
Tapestry, Wool, Oak, Stallion, Green Ground, Evelyn Akerman, ERA Industrials, 1965, 43 x 30 In.	1500
Tapestry, Woven, Wool, Stripes, Dyed, Tomisita, 99 x 41 In.	188
Thangka, Red Tara, Multicolor, Gilt Ink Detailing, Silk Brocade, 1800s, 22 x 16 In. *illus*	8610
Wall Hanging, Abstract, Red, Black, White, Burlap Sleeve, Chile, 1972, 57 x 78 In.	293

THERMOMETER

Thermometer is a name that comes from the Greek word for heat. The thermometer was invented in 1731 to measure the temperature of either water or air. All kinds of thermometers are collected, but those with advertising messages are the most popular.

Abbott's Angostura Bitters, Wood, Wall Hung, 9 x 48 In.	780
Baker-Evans Ice Cream Co., P.H. Baker, Black Lithograph, Wood, Working, 14 x 4 In.	80
Chew Mail Pouch Tobacco, Dark Blue Ground, 39 x 8 In.	50
Ex-Lax, Chocolated Laxative, Porcelain, Blue Ground, Glass Tube, 36¼ x 8¼ In. *illus*	1107

Fahrenheit & Reaumur Scale, Ebonized, Bronze Mounted, Continental, 1800s, 15 ½ x 3 x 2 In..		303
Hires Root Beer, Bottle Shape, Red, Orange, c.1950, 29 x 9 ½ In.		115
Hires Root Beer, Tin, Painted, Orange, Red & Black, 1950s, 7 x 22 In.		318
Lighthouse, Industrial, Gilt, Silvered Brass, 2 Candle Arms, Turret, Late 1800s, 30 In. *illus*		1210
Mail Pouch, Chewing Tobacco Tin, Treat Yourself To The Best, 1930s, 39 In.		155
Ramon's Brownie Pills, Mounted, Wood, Early 1900s, 21 In. *illus*		875
Red Crown Gasoline, For Power Mileage, Polarine, Porcelain, 72 x 17 ½ In.		4320

TIFFANY

Tiffany is a name that appears on items made by Louis Comfort Tiffany, the American glass designer who worked from about 1879 to 1933. His work included iridescent glass, Art Nouveau styles of design, and original contemporary styles. He was also noted for stained glass windows, unusual lamps, bronze work, pottery, and silver. Tiffany & Company, often called "Tiffany," is also listed in this section. The company was started by Charles Lewis Tiffany and John B. Young in 1837 in New York City. In 1853 the name was changed to Tiffany & Company. Louis Tiffany (1848–1933), Charles Tiffany's son, started his own business in 1879. It was named Louis Comfort Tiffany and Associated American Artists. In 1902 the name was changed to Tiffany Studios. Tiffany & Company is a store and is still working today. It is best known for silver and fine jewelry. Louis worked for his father's company as a decorator in 1900 but at the same time was working for his Tiffany Studios. Other types of Tiffany are listed under Tiffany Glass, Tiffany Gold, Tiffany Porcelain, Tiffany Pottery, or Tiffany Silver. The famous Tiffany lamps are listed in this section. Tiffany jewelry is listed in the Jewelry and Wristwatch categories. Some Tiffany Studio desk sets have matching clocks. They are listed here. Clocks made by Tiffany & Co. are listed in the Clock category. Reproductions of some types of Tiffany are being made.

L.C. Tiffany
1848–1933

TIFFANY STUDIOS
Tiffany Studios
1902–1919

TIFFANY STUDIOS NEW YORK.
Tiffany Studios
1902–1922+

Ash Stand, Bowl, Bronze, Patinated, Green Glass Liner, Tiffany Studios, 1910, 27 ½ x 8 In....*illus*		1020
Ashtray, Match Holder, Chinese Style Decoration, Tiffany Studios, 3 x 7 In....*illus*		390
Blotter Ends, Ninth Century, Gilt Bronze, Applied Glass Jewels, 17 ½ x 2 In., Pair		219
Blotter Ends, Venetian, Bronze, Impressed Tiffany Studios, No. 1696, 19 x 2 ½ In., Pair		325
Blotter, Bronze, Rolling, Rectangular, Signed, Tiffany Studios, c.1910, 2 ½ x 5 ½ x 2 ¾ In....*illus*		185
Bookrack, Grapevine, Bronze, Caramel Slag Glass, Adjustable, Early 1900s, 6 ½ x 13 ⅞ In.		819
Bookrack, Grapevine, Bronze, Green Slag Glass, Adjustable, c.1910, 6 x 14 x 6 ½ In. ....*illus*		1694
Box, Card, Grapevine, Bronze, Patina, Green Slag Glass, c.1910, 4 x 3 x 1 ¼ In.		1210
Box, Stamp, Venetian, Gilt Bronze, Carved, Tiffany Studios, 2 x 4 In....*illus*		1063
Candelabrum, 2-Light, Silver Plate, Neoclassical Style, Scroll Arm, Tiffany & Co., 11 ½ In., Pair		100
Candelabrum, 3-Light, Rings, Chain, Circular Base, Bronze, Tiffany Studios, 14 x 10 In., Pair....		6500
Candlestick, Bronze, Bamboo Shape Stem, Naturalistic Flared Root Base, Marked, 10 ¼ In.		1353
Candlestick, Bronze, Tripod, Bowl Shape, Seal, Tiffany Studios, 1906, 7 ½ x 4 ½ In., Pair .		878
Candlestick, Cobra, Standing, Bronze, Brown Patina, Tiffany Studios, 1900s, 7 In., Pair......*illus*		1440
Candlestick, Lily Pad, Bronze, Patina, Favrile Glass, Gold Iridescent, Late 1800s, 18 x 5 In. ...		2125
Cigar Box, Venetian, Hinged Lid, Bronze, Impressed Tiffany Studios, No. 1680, 2 x 5 ½ In....*illus*		2340
Clock, Desk, Venetian, Dial, Bronze, Tiffany Studios, 1879, 2 x 4 x 4 In....*illus*		1875
Clock, Shelf, Porcelain, Never Wind, Pillared Body, Cobalt Blue, Yellow Glaze, Venus, 12 x 9 In. ..		120
Clock, Venetian, Arched, Gilt, Bronze, Tiffany Studios, 1851, 5 ¾ x 4 ½ In.		1560
Fan, Courtyard Scene, Women, Hand Painted, Mother-Of-Pearl, Tiffany & Co., 1800s, 11 ½ In.. *illus*		307
Frame, Grapevine, Bronze, Glass, Marked Tiffany Studios, New York, 10 x 8 In.		1152
Humidor, Bronze, Dragon Handles, Tiffany Studios, New York, 7 ½ x 6 ¾ In.		3900

Thermometer, Ex-Lax, Chocolated Laxative, Porcelain, Blue Ground, Glass Tube, 36 ¼ x 8 ¼ In.
$1,107

Morphy Auctions

Thermometer, Lighthouse, Industrial, Gilt, Silvered Brass, 2 Candle Arms, Turret, Late 1800s, 30 In.
$1,210

Fontaine's Auction Gallery

Thermometer, Ramon's Brownie Pills, Mounted, Wood, Early 1900s, 21 In.
$875

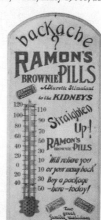

Hindman

Tiffany, Ash Stand, Bowl, Bronze, Patinated, Green Glass Liner, Tiffany Studios, 1910, 27 ½ x 8 In.
$1,020

Bonhams

Tiffany, Ashtray, Match Holder, Chinese Style Decoration, Tiffany Studios, 3 x 7 In.
$390

Treadway

Tiffany, Blotter, Bronze, Rolling, Rectangular, Signed, Tiffany Studios, c.1910, 2 ½ x 5 ½ x 2 ¾ In.
$185

California Historical Design

Tiffany, Bookrack, Grapevine, Bronze, Green Slag Glass, Adjustable, c.1910, 6 x 14 x 6 ½ In.
$1,694

Fontaine's Auction Gallery

Tiffany, Box, Stamp, Venetian, Gilt Bronze, Carved, Tiffany Studios, 2 x 4 In.
$1,063

Treadway

Tiffany, Candlestick, Cobra, Standing, Bronze, Brown Patina, Tiffany Studios, 1900s, 7 In., Pair
$1,440

Cottone Auctions

Tiffany, Cigar Box, Venetian, Hinged Lid, Bronze, Impressed Tiffany Studios, No. 1680, 2 x 5 ½ In.
$2,340

Treadway

Tiffany, Clock, Desk, Venetian, Dial, Bronze, Tiffany Studios, 1879, 2 x 4 x 4 In.
$1,875

Treadway

Tiffany, Fan, Courtyard Scene, Women, Hand Painted, Mother-Of-Pearl, Tiffany & Co., 1800s, 11 ½ In.
$307

Conestoga Auction Company

Tiffany, Inkwell, Cut Glass, Clear, Silver Hinged Lid, Tiffany & Co., 2 ½ x 4 In.
$188

New Haven Auctions

Tiffany, Inkwell, Pine Needle, Bronze, Round, Reticulated, Tiffany Studios, 4 x 7 In.
$813

Treadway

Tiffany, Inkwell, Venetian, Double, Bronze Dore, Stamped Tiffany Studios, 1900s, 2 ¾ x 5 x 3 In.
$1,125

Cowan's Auctions

TIP

Be careful removing a lightbulb from an old lamp with a glass shade. The Tiffany lily-shaped shades and others are made so that the shade is held in place by a screw-in bulb.

Tiffany, Lamp, 6-Light, Domed Glass Shade, Tulips, Bronze Bamboo Shape Stem, c.1910, 63 x 22 In.
$184,500

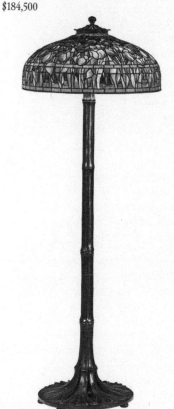

Brunk Auctions

Tiffany, Lamp, Balance Ball, Yellow & Green Iridescent Shade, Bronze, Favrile, 15 x 7 In.
$8,125

Treadway

Tiffany, Lamp, Desk, Gold Iridescent Shade, Bronze Domed Base, Ball Feet, Tiffany Studios, 13 ½ In.
$1,375

Turner Auctions + Appraisals

Tiffany, Lamp, Desk, Green Iridescent Shade, Pulled Feather, Bronze Base, 13 x 8 In.
$1,100

Woody Auction

Tiffany, Lamp, Hanging, Favrile Glass Prisms, Upside-Down Compote Style, Bronze, c.1910, 16 In.
$9,378

Fontaine's Auction Gallery

Tiffany, Letter Rack, Grapevine, Bronze, Verdigris Patina, 3 Compartments, c.1902, 8 x 12 x 3 In.
$1,625

John Moran Auctioneers

Tiffany, Magnifying Glass, American Indian, Gilt Bronze, Flat Handle, c.1910, 8 ½ x 4 ¼ In.
$1,029

Fontaine's Auction Gallery

T

Tiffany, Pen Tray, American Indian, Bronze, Rectangular, Tiffany Studios, 11 x 4 In.
$125

Treadway

Tiffany, Picture Frame, Abalone Pattern, Gilt Bronze, Tiffany Studios, 1910, 13 x 11 ¼ x 14 In.
$4,388

Thomaston Place Auction Galleries

Tiffany Glass, Bowl, Centerpiece, Gold Favrile, Gilt Bronze, Louis C. Tiffany Furnaces, Early 1900s, 5 x 12 In
$968

Fontaine's Auction Gallery

Pringles Can as Burial Wrap

The designer of the container for Pringles potato chips died in 2008, and as he requested, part of his ashes were buried in a Pringles can. The rest of his remains were put into urns given to family members.

Inkwell, Bronze, Dolphin, Scallop Shell, Marble Base, Neoclassical Style, 6 In. 500
Inkwell, Bronze, Patina, Butterfly, Favrile Glass Liner & Lid, Tiffany Studios, c.1905, 2 ¾ x 5 In. 9680
Inkwell, Bronze, Reticulated, Craquelure Design, Favrile Glass, Tiffany Studios, c.1900s, 3 x 4 In. 4063
Inkwell, Cut Glass, Clear, Silver Hinged Lid, Tiffany & Co., 2 ½ x 4 In. .... *illus* 188
Inkwell, Pine Needle, Bronze, Round, Reticulated, Tiffany Studios, 4 x 7 In. .... *illus* 813
Inkwell, Venetian, Bronze, Hinged Lid, Square Base, 3 ½ x 9 ¾ In. 780
Inkwell, Venetian, Double, Bronze Dore, Stamped Tiffany Studios, 1900s, 2 ¾ x 5 x 3 In. .... *illus* 1125
Inkwell, Zodiac, Gilt Bronze, Clear Glass Insert, Hexagonal, c.1910, 3 x 6 In. 281
Lamp, 3-Light, Domed Shade, Bronze, Flower Form, Silver Interior, Tiffany Studios, c.1910, 9 ¾ In. 2325
Lamp, 6-Light, Domed Glass Shade, Tulips, Bronze Bamboo Shape Stem, c.1910, 63 x 22 In. .... *illus* 184500
Lamp, Balance Ball, Yellow & Green Iridescent Shade, Bronze, Favrile, 15 x 7 In. .... *illus* 8125
Lamp, Bronze, Leaded Glass Shade, Green, Pink, Purple Flowers, 23 x 16 In. 1625
Lamp, Desk, Abalone, Linenfold Shade, Frosted Glass, Tiffany Studios, 1900s, 16 x 9 In. 5558
Lamp, Desk, Gold Iridescent Shade, Bronze Domed Base, Ball Feet, Tiffany Studios, 13 ½ In. .... *illus* 1375
Lamp, Desk, Green Iridescent Shade, Pulled Feather, Bronze Base, 13 x 8 In. .... *illus* 1100
Lamp, Desk, Wave Pattern Shade, Iridescent, Zodiac Base, Bronze, 13 x 7 ⅛ In. 2880
Lamp, Gold Favrile Shade, Gilt Bronze, Circular Base, 1900s, 13 ½ In. 5120
Lamp, Hanging, Favrile Glass Prisms, Upside-Down Compote Style, Bronze, c.1910, 16 In. .... *illus* 9378
Lamp, Hanging, Leaded Glass, Bronze, Acorn Shade, Tiffany Studios, New York, 27 In. 4375
Lamp, Lily, 3-Light, Favrile Shades, Gilt Bronze, Reeded Base, Early 1900s, 12 In. 1920
Lamp, Long Tube, Circular Shade, 5-Legged, Tiffany Studios, 57 x 15 ¼ In. 8750
Lamp, Student, 2-Light, Cased Emerald Overlay Shades, Brass, 19 ½ In. 832
Lamp, Student, Green, Favrile Glass Shade, Bronze, Patina, Adjustable, c.1905, 20 ½ In. 6353
Lamp, Weight Balance, Damascene Shade, Favrile Glass, Tiffany Studios, 1900s, 15 ¾ In. 6875
Letter Opener, Venetian, Bronze, 2-Sided Blade, Impressed Tiffany Studios, No. 1633, 9 ½ x 1 In. 358
Letter Rack, Grapevine, Bronze, Verdigris Patina, 3 Compartments, c.1902, 8 x 12 x 3 In. .... *illus* 1625
Magnifying Glass, American Indian, Gilt Bronze, Flat Handle, c.1910, 8 ½ x 4 ¼ In. .... *illus* 1029
Magnifying Glass, Zodiac, Round Frame, Convex Lens, Carved Handle, 9 x 4 In. 780
Napkin Ring, Wave Edge Pattern, Inscribed Amelia Haselton, Tiffany & Co., 1884, 1 ½ x 1 ⅞ In. 395
Notepad Holder, Zodiac, Bronze, Patina, Tiffany Studios, 3 ½ x 6 In. 531
Paperweight, Gilt Bronze, Lion, Lying Down, Marked Tiffany Studios, 2 x 5 ¼ In. 600
Paperweight, Wave, Favrile Glass, Bronze, Patina, Tiffany Studios, Early 1900s, 3 ¾ In. 2057
Pen Tray, American Indian, Bronze, Rectangular, Tiffany Studios, 11 x 4 In. .... *illus* 125
Pen Tray, Grapevine, Bronze, Slag Glass, Caramel, Bun Feet, ¾ x 2 ¾ x 9 ¾ In. 219
Picture Frame, Abalone Pattern, Gilt Bronze, Tiffany Studios, 1910, 13 x 11 ¼ x 14 In. *illus* 4388
Sconce, 3-Light, Pulled Feather Shades, Bronze, Tiffany Studios, 1900s, 19 x 16 In. 16800
Thermometer, Dore Bronze, Red Glass, Byzantine, Attached Stand, New York, c.1915, 7 ½ x 3 In. 2000
Thermometer, Pine Needle, Gilt, Bronze, Caramel Stained Glass, Tiffany Studios, 3 x 8 In. 840
Thermometer, Venetian, Bronze, Carved, Geometric Design, Patina, 8 x 4 In. 1300
Utility Box, Pine Needle, Bronze, Glass, Stamped, 1900s, 1 ½ x 4 ½ x 3 In. 645
Vase, Bud, Glass, Bronze Base, Dore, Tiffany Studios, 1900s, 22 ½ In. 813
Vase, Flower Shape, Feather Design, Tall Stem Holding, Bronze Base, Tiffany Studios, 16 x 5 In. 2500
Vase, Tel El Amarna, Favrile Glass, Cream Ground, Dark Blue Base, c.1910, 6 ¾ In. 2420
Vase, Tulip, Art Glass, Green, Pulled Feather Cup, Gold Iridescent Base, 13 ½ In. 3625
Walking Stick, Silver, Bear Handle, Wood Shaft, Tiffany & Co., 34 In. 8400

TIFFANY GLASS

Bowl, Centerpiece, Gold Favrile, Gilt Bronze, Louis C. Tiffany Furnaces, Early 1900s, 5 x 12 In. .... *illus* 968
Bowl, Centerpiece, Gold Iridescent, Holes, Signed L.C.T. Favrile, c.1920s, 2 ⅝ x 3 ½ In. 400
Bowl, Clear Graduation, Onionskin Rim, Optical Base, Favrile, c.1892, 3 x 12 In. 938
Bowl, Gold Favrile, Flared Rim, Etched Grape Leaf & Vines, Cameo, 1900s, 3 x 9 In. 550
Bowl, Gold Iridescent, Flared Rim, Engraved, Leaves, Favrile, Signed, L.C. Tiffany, 3 x 9 In. 700
Bowl, Opalescent, Yellow Scalloped, Triangular Panels, Favrile, L.C.T., c.1915s, 3 x 8 In. 375
Bowl, Ribbed Optic, Green Opaque Leaf, Blossoms, Footed, Favrile, Signed, L.C. Tiffany, 4 x 8 In. 2750
Candle Lamp, Domed Shade, Twisted Stem, Gold Favrile, Engraved, L.C.T., c.1910, 11 ½ In. 1936
Candle Lamp, Gold Iridescent, Chimney, Twirl Base, Favrile, Tiffany Studios, 13 x 7 In. .... *illus* 1625
Candlestick, Gold Iridescent, Engraved, Vines, Favrile, Signed, L.C.T., 1927, 4 x 4 In. 350
Candlestick, Iridescent, 6-Lobed Base, Flared Cup, L.C.T. Favrile, c.1915, 10 ½ In., Pair 875
Compote, Opalescent, Flared Cranberry Color, White Leaf Design, Favrile, L.C.T., c.1902, 8 x 9 In. 688

Tiffany Glass, Candle Lamp, Gold Iridescent, Chimney, Twirl Base, Favrile, Tiffany Studios, 13 x 7 In.
$1,625

Treadway

Tiffany Lamps

Since about 1970, the phrase "Tiffany lamp" has been misused. You see it in ads and stores to describe modern lamps with stained glass shades. A true Tiffany lamp was made by Louis Comfort Tiffany at his studio from 1891 to 1928.

Tiffany Glass, Compote, Stretched, Geometric Stars, Disc Base, Favrile, L.C.T., 1893, 3 ½ x 6 ¾ In.
$180

Richard Opfer Auctioneering, Inc.

Tiffany Glass, Finger Bowl, Underplate, Gold Iridescent, Pulled Loop Design, Signed, L.C.T., 2 x 6 In.
$350

Woody Auction

Tiffany Glass, Lampshade, Pink, Favrile, Inside Edge Marked Tiffany Studios, 1900s, 5 ⅜ In.
$1,677

Cowan's Auctions

Tiffany Glass, Vase, Baluster Shape, Leaf & Vine Design, Gold Iridescent, Favrile, L.C. Tiffany, 10 x 4 In.
$2,250

John Moran Auctioneers

Tiffany Glass, Vase, Blue, Rosebud Shape, Favrile, L.C. Tiffany, 1900s, 9 x 3 ½ In.
$1,320

Cottone Auctions

Tiffany Glass, Vase, Gold Iridescent, Green Pulled Feather, Long Neck, Favrile, Signed, L.C. Tiffany, 12 x 4 In.
$550

Woody Auction

Tiffany Glass, Vase, Tiered, Vertical Banding, Footed, Gold Favrile, 4 ½ x 3 ½ In.
$360

Alderfer Auction Company

T

Tiffany Gold, Cigarette Case, Tufted, 14K Yellow Gold, Stamped Tiffany & Co., 3¼ In.
$4,920

Brunk Auctions

Tiffany Silver, Asparagus Tray, Chrysanthemum, Handles, Tiffany & Co., 1892, 2½ x 12½ x 10 In.
$2,560

Brunk Auctions

Tiffany Silver, Baby Spoon, Baseball Bat, Glove & Ball Handle, Cloth Case, Tiffany & Co., 6 In.
$108

Treasureseeker Auctions

Tiffany Silver, Chafing Dish, Rinceau Band, Warming Stand, Pad Feet, Tiffany & Co., c.1900, 9¼ x 12½ In.
$2,500

T

Hindman

Compote, Stretched, Geometric Stars, Disc Base, Favrile, L.C.T., 1893, 3½ x 6¾ In.....*illus*	180
Decanter, Gold Favrile, Double Gourd, Lily Pads, Tiffany Glass & Decorating Co., c.1900s, 9 In. ...	790
Finger Bowl, Underplate, Gold Iridescent, Pulled Loop Design, Signed, L.C.T., 2 x 6 In.*illus*	350
Lampshade, Brick Pattern, Geometric, Leaded, 14 Rows, Marked Tiffany Studios, 20 In.....	6875
Lampshade, Iridescent, Dome Shape, Favrile, Fitter Rim, Louis Comfort Tiffany, 4½ x 7 In.	8125
Lampshade, Pink, Favrile, Inside Edge Marked Tiffany Studios, 1900s, 5⅜ In............*illus*	1677
Lampshade, Pulled Feather, Threaded, Gold Favrile, L.C.T., 6¼ x 1½ In.........................	313
Open Salt, Gold, Pink, Ruffled Rim, Favrile, Tiffany Studios, 1 x 2¾ In.	156
Paperweight, Star Shape, Award, Tiffany & Co., 6 x 4½ x 3 In..	31
Perfume Bottle, Gold Iridescent, Tadpole Tendrils, Favrile, Tiffany Studios, 5½ In...........	1200
Sherbet, Underplate, Gold Iridescent, Garland Border, Engraved, Favrile, Signed, L.C.T., 3 x 6 In.	300
Vase, Baluster Shape, Leaf & Vine Design, Gold Iridescent, Favrile, L.C. Tiffany, 10 x 4 In. .....*illus*	2250
Vase, Blue, Handle, Circular Base, Favrile, Etched L.C. Tiffany, 6¼ x 4¾ In.........................	938
Vase, Blue, Rosebud Shape, Favrile, L.C. Tiffany, 1900s, 9 x 3½ In. ....*illus*	1320
Vase, Cylindrical, Green Pulled Feather, Favrile, Tiffany Studios, c.1902, 14 x 3 In.	2125
Vase, Double Gourd, Flower, L.C. Tiffany, Favrile, 1900s, 11 x 4½ In.	6300
Vase, Flower Shape, Feather Design Bowl, Saucer Shape Foot, Favrile, c.1910, 15 x 6 In........	1053
Vase, Gold Iridescent, Green Pulled Feather, Long Neck, Favrile, Signed, L.C. Tiffany, 12 x 4 In....*illus*	550
Vase, Stick, Favrile, Gilt Bronze Base, Tiffany & Co., 1910, 13¼ x 5 In.	701
Vase, Tiered, Vertical Banding, Footed, Gold Favrile, 4½ x 3½ In. ....*illus*	360

TIFFANY GOLD

Cigarette Case, 14K, Platinum, Engine Turned, Monogram, Hinged, Openwork, Tiffany & Co., 4 In.	4410
Cigarette Case, Tufted, 14K Yellow Gold, Stamped Tiffany & Co., 3¼ In.....................*illus*	4920

TIFFANY POTTERY

Figurine, Rabbit, Hand Painted, Flowers, Tiffany & Co., Sintra, Portugal, 6¾ x 4½ x 8 In.	219

TIFFANY SILVER

Asparagus Tray, Chrysanthemum, Handles, Tiffany & Co., 1892, 2½ x 12½ x 10 In..*illus*	2560
Baby Spoon, Baseball Bat, Glove & Ball Handle, Cloth Case, Tiffany & Co., 6 In. ....*illus*	108
Basket, Bail Handle, Paw Feet, Tiffany & Co., c.1907-47, 11 x 13 x 11 In.	2420
Basket, Oval, Bead Border, Bail Handle, Floral Swag, Coin, Tiffany & Co., c.1854, 9¾ In.....	1230
Bowl, Flower Shape, Petal Rim, Footed, Tiffany & Co., Early 1900s, 4 x 9 In.	300
Bowl, Footed, Beaded Trim, Collared Base, Art Deco, Tiffany & Co., Early 1900s, 6 x 9 In. ...	640
Bowl, Hammered, Applied Insects & Leaves, Mixed Metal, Handles, Gilt Interior, 1873, 2 x 4 x 3 In. ..	2091
Bowl, Mooresque, Scrolled Handles, Monogram, Tiffany & Co., c.1854, 5 In.	1089
Bowl, Square, Round Edges, Leafy Beaded Border Rim, Tiffany & Co., 1907-47, 8⅞ In.	875
Bread Tray, Neoclassical Style, Cornucopias, Monogram, Tiffany & Co., 1911, 12¾ In........	640
Bread Tray, Oval, Openwork Ends, Tiffany & Co., 2 x 14 x 6½ In.	320
Candlestick, Leaves, Geometric Trim, 4 Paw Feet, 9½ In., Pair..	840
Candlestick, Round Stepped Base & Top, Engraved Cartouche, Tiffany & Co., 1902, 5½ In., Pair	431
Candlestick, Square Top, Cylindrical Shaft, Weighted Base, Tiffany & Co., 1907, 8 x 4 In., 4 Piece	2457
Chafing Dish, Rinceau Band, Warming Stand, Pad Feet, Tiffany & Co., c.1900, 9¼ x 12½ In.. *illus*	2500
Creamer, Folded Rim, Arc Handle, Molded Foot, Monogram, Tiffany & Co., 1898, 4 In.	219
Cup, Shaped Handle, Square Rim, Repousse Base, Tiffany & Co., c.1900, 6⅛ In.	750
Dispenser, Lid, Vermouth, Oil Can Shape, Domed Base, Stamped Tiffany, Sterling, 2 x 3½ In.. *illus*	125
Mustard Pot, Lid, Neoclassical Design, Glass Liner, Tiffany & Co., 6 In.......................*illus*	438
Pillbox, Hinged Lid, Gift Box Shape, Bow, Tiffany & Co., 1¼ x 1¼ x 1¼ In.	219
Pitcher, Aesthetic Movement, Hammered, Tiffany & Co, c.1880s, 9¼ x 7¼ In.	3998
Pitcher, Applied Handle, Bands, Relief Shell, Scroll Decoration, Tiffany & Co., 6 x 5 In.	1250
Pitcher, Water, Wide Spout, Shaped Handle, Carved, Flowers, Tiffany & Co., 9⅞ In.	2500
Salt Spoon, Chrysanthemum, Gilt Bowl, Blue Dust Bag, 2¼ In., 12 Piece	940
Salt, Shell Form, Ball Feet, Marked, 2¾ x 2¼ In., 4 Piece...	395
Salver, Scalloped Edge, Marked Tiffany & Co., 12 In..	875
Tazza, Round, Enamel Design, Domed Foot, Tiffany & Co., 7 In.	1625
Teapot, Pear Shape, Acanthus, Monogram, Grosjean & Woodward, Tiffany & Co., 1854, 8 In..	1230
Tray, Repousse, Floral & Berry Rim, Grapevine Handles, Tiffany & Co., c.1870, 16 x 10 In., Pair.	4095
Trophy, Horse Racing, San Fernando Stakes, Gilt, Handles, Tiffany & Co., c.1995, 11 In.	1397
Trophy, Tennis, Huggy Bears Invitational, Scalloped Border, Tiffany & Co., 1999, 12¼ In..	640

Tureen, Circular Finial, Classic Design, Open Handles, Base Oval, Tiffany & Co., 12 x 15 In......	2196
Tureen, Lid, Boar's Head, Footed, Oval, Steer Head Handles, Tiffany & Co., 1854-69, 11 x 15 x 9 In.....	7020
Vase, Amphora Shape, Scroll Handle, Chase Wavy, Footed Base, Tiffany & Co., 1891, 16¾ In.	1053
Vase, Trumpet, Banded Waist, Pedestal Foot, c.1947, 17 x 7 In.	1375
Wine Cooler, Lion Head Ring Handles, Greek Key, Beaded Base, Tiffany & Co., c.1854-70, 10 In.	3933

TIFFIN

Tiffin Glass Company of Tiffin, Ohio, was a subsidiary of the United States Glass Co. of Pittsburgh, Pennsylvania, in 1892. The U.S. Glass Co. went bankrupt in 1963, and the Tiffin plant employees purchased the building and the inventory. They continued running it from 1963 to 1966, when it was sold to Continental Can Company. In 1969, it was sold to Interpace, and in 1980, it was closed. The black satin glass, made from 1923 to 1926, and the stemware of the last 20 years are the best-known products.

Twilight, Compote, Amethyst Base, Controlled Bubbles, 1950s, 6½ x 8 In............................	36
Vase, Blue Satin Glass, Poppies, Raised Relief, 5¼ x 6¼ In.	54

TILE

Tiles have been used in most countries of the world as a sturdy building material for floors, roofs, fireplace surrounds, and surface toppings. The cuerda seca (dry cord) technique of decoration uses a greasy pigment to separate different glaze colors during firing. In cuenca (raised line) decorated tiles, the design is impressed, leaving ridges that separate the glaze colors. Many of the American tiles are listed in this book under the factory name.

2 Fish, Hand Carved, Brown Ground, c.1990s, 5½ x 5½ In...	92
Flowers, Bird, Multicolor, Gilt Frame, Perisa, 12¾ x 10½ In.	41
Little Miss Muffet, Nursery Rhyme, American Encaustic Tiling Co., Ohio, c.1910, 4⅛ In...	375
Mission, Santa Barbara, Red, Green, Signed, Bengur, c.1920s, 7 x 7 In.........................*illus*	461
Mural, Lisbon In 1500, 35 Blue & White Tiles, F. St. Anna, Wood Board, Frame, 32 x 43 In.	1016
Nursery Rhyme, Jack Horner, Seated, Blue, Yellow, 1914, 4 x 4 In.	215
Plaque, Koi Fish, Cement, Outdoor, 10 x 17 In.......................................*illus*	30
Roof, Figural, Chinese Man, Multicolor, On Stand, 7¾ x 4¾ x 3 In...............*illus*	25
Roof, Foo Dog, Green Ground, Rectangular Base, Terra-Cotta, 26 x 22 x 6 In.	250
Scene, Trees, Coppery Glaze, Green Patina, Beaver Falls Art Tile Co., c.1910, 6 In.........*illus*	750
Ship, Galleon, Mosaic Frieze, Multicolor, Round, Mueller, c.1905, 37 In. ....*illus*	9225
Sunburst, Matte Glaze, Flower, Vine, California Clay Product, 12 x 11⅞ In.	195

TINWARE

Tinware containers for household use have been made in America since the seventeenth century. The first tin utensils were brought from Europe, but by 1798 tin plate was imported and local tinsmiths made the wares. Painted tin is called tole and is listed separately. Some tin kitchen items may be found listed under Kitchen. The lithographed tin containers used to hold food and tobacco are listed in the Advertising category under Tin.

Aquarium Scenery, Anemones & Coral On Rocks, Multicolor, Cut, Painted, 1800s, 16 In...	1408
Barn Star, 10-Point, Old Paint, Iron Rod, Star Counterweight, Weathered, Late 1800s, 32 x 45 In...	3125
Birdcage, House Shape, Sheet Metal, Green Paint, Late 1900s, 20 x 14 x 12 In......................	60
Horn, Stage Coach, Sheet Iron, Conical Shape, Rectangular Handle, Mid 1800s, 37 In.	359
Mold, Candle, 6 Tube, Canted Shape, Strap Handle, Square Top & Base, c.1850, 7 In.... *illus*	168
Watch Hutch, Curved Door, Punched Arcs, Blue & Black Paint, Hanging, c.1850, 9¾ x 6¾ In...	1190

TOBACCO CUTTERS *may be listed in either the Advertising or Store categories.*

Tiffany Silver, Dispenser, Lid, Vermouth, Oil Can Shape, Domed Base, Stamped Tiffany, Sterling, 2 x 3½ In. $125

Greenwich Auction

Tiffany Silver, Mustard Pot, Lid, Neoclassical Design, Glass Liner, Tiffany & Co., 6 In. $438

Turner Auctions + Appraisals

Tile, Mission, Santa Barbara, Red, Green, Signed, Bengur, c.1920s, 7 x 7 In. $461

California Historical Design

Tile, Plaque, Koi Fish, Cement, Outdoor, 10 x 17 In.
$30

Bunch Auctions

Tile, Roof, Figural, Chinese Man, Multicolor, On Stand, 7¾ x 4¾ x 3 In.
$25

Andrew Jones Auctions

Tile, Scene, Trees, Coppery Glaze, Green Patina, Beaver Falls Art Tile Co., c.1910, 6 In.
$750

Toomey & Co. Auctioneers

Tile, Ship, Galleon, Mosaic Frieze, Multicolor, Round, Mueller, c.1905, 37 In.
$9,225

California Historical Design

Tinware, Mold, Candle, 6 Tube, Canted Shape, Strap Handle, Square Top & Base, c.1850, 7 In.
$168

Garth's Auctioneers & Appraisers

Toby Jug, Colonial Man, Blue Jacket & Hat, Holding Pitcher, Staffordshire, 8¼ In.
$31

Nadeau's Auction Gallery

Tole, Basin, Foot, Loop Handle, Continental, 12 In.
$550

Neal Auction Company

Tole, Box, Dome Lid, Wire Handle & Tin Hasp, Flowers, Black Ground, c.1840s, 5 x 9 In.
$720

Garth's Auctioneers & Appraisers

Tole, Coal Scuttle, Hinged Lid, Stenciled, Tin Liner, Curule Frame, 1800s, 16 x 17 x 14 In.
$502

Soulis Auctions

Toby Jugs

The Toby jug shaped like a seated man was named for Toby Philpot, a notorious drinker mentioned in a song written in 1761. Toby jugs were popular from 1776 to 1825, but many later versions have been made.

TOBACCO JAR

Tobacco jar collectors search for those made in odd shapes and colors. Because tobacco needs special conditions of humidity and air, it has been stored in humidors and other special containers since the eighteenth century. Some may be found in Advertising, Silver, or ceramic categories in this book.

Bear, Standing, Removable Head, Nottingham, Stoneware, c.1935, 4½ x 2 x 3 In.................	1550
Bull Dog, Wearing Red Fez Hat, Smoking Jacket, 1800s	160
Figural, Western Businessman, Seated, Tree Stump, Reading Newspaper, Bernard Bloch, 9¼ In.	650
Humidor, Glass, Dodecagon, Gray Tint, Removable Lid, c.1920, 5 x 6¾ In.	90

TOBY JUG

Toby jug is the name of a very special form of pitcher. It is shaped like the full figure of a man or woman. A pitcher that shows just the top half of a person is not correctly called a toby. It is often called a character jug. More examples of toby jugs can be found under Royal Doulton and other factory names. Some may be found in Advertising in this book.

Colonial Man, Blue Jacket & Hat, Holding Pitcher, Staffordshire, 8¼ In...................... *illus*	31
General Eisenhower, Military Uniform, Barrington, 7¼ x 4¼ In.	115
Hearty Good Fellow, Holding Pipe & Tankard, Painted, Pearlware, England, c.1810, 11 In.	250

TOLE

Tole is painted tin. It is sometimes called japanned ware, pontypool, or toleware. Most nineteenth-century tole is painted with an orange-red or black background and multicolored decorations. Many recent versions of toleware are made and sold. Related items may be listed in the Tinware category.

Basin, Foot, Loop Handle, Continental, 12 In..*illus*	550
Box, Document, Swing Handle, Blue Ground, New England, 7 x 9 x 6 In...............................	438
Box, Dome Lid, Wire Handle & Tin Hasp, Flowers, Black Ground, c.1840s, 5 x 9 In.......*illus*	720
Box, Hinged Dome Lid, Swags, Leaves, Shells, Twist Closure, Loop Handle, c.1860, 7 x 10 In.	280
Chandelier, 4-Light, Parcel Gilt, Black, Scrolled Arms, Baroque, France, 1800s, 29½ x 21 In...	1210
Coal Scuttle, Hinged Lid, Stenciled, Tin Liner, Curule Frame, 1800s, 16 x 17 x 14 In...*illus*	502
Coffeepot, Tapered Body, Flowers, Strap Handle, Pa., Early 1800s, 9 x 9 In.................*illus*	384
Jardiniere, Gilt, Metal, Urn Shape, Continental, Neoclassical, Late 1900s, 14½ x 17½ In., Pair.	272
Jardiniere, Musical Trophee, Torch Reserves, Paw Feet, Block Bases, 11 In., Pair.................	300
Lamp, 2-Light, Leaves, Yellow Ground, Acorn Finial, 33 x 9 x 6 In................................	113
Lamp, Rumford, Black, Gilt, Scrolled Flowers, Trophies, Square Base, England, 1900s, 14½ In...*illus*	484
Lamp, Tea Canister, Electrified, Chinese Characters, J. Maund, England, 1800s, 34¼ In....*illus*	242
Lantern, Tinted, Textured, Flowers, Leafy Details, 1900s, 24 x 12 In.	213
Pail, Metal, Bail Handle, Footed Brazier, Tripod, Flowers, 7 x 9 In.	165
Sconce, 3-Light, Basket Shape, Candle, Flowers, Italy, 1900s, 19½ x 13½ x 7 In., Pair........	1029
Sconce, Gilt Bust, Wheat, French Empire, Neoclassical, 1800s, 19 x 3 x 7 In., Pair..........*illus*	2520
Shield, Plaque, Metal, Armorial Scenes, Continental, Frame, Late 1800s, 14 x 13 In., Pair..	91
Sugar, Lid, Gold Swags, Leaves, Red Rays Inside Triangles, Tapered Shape, 3 x 4 In.............	145
Tea Caddy, Hinged Lid, Red, Yellow Trim, Bee Skep, Green Leaves, 1800s, 5¼ x 4 x 3 In...*illus*	288
Tray, 2 Tiers, Stone Steps, Woman Drawing Water, Reticulated Rim, England, c.1900, 16 x 17 In.	365
Tray, Black Ground, Red White & Blue Shield, Inscription, Liverpool, Oh., 1800s, 16 x 22 In.	352
Tray, Black, Yellow, Flowers, Faux Bamboo Stand, Victorian, Late 1800s, 17 x 24 x 19 In..*illus*	594
Tray, Floral Garland, Ebonized Ground, Victorian, 28 In.	113
Tray, Fruit, Side Handles, Rectangular, 1800s, 30 x 21½ In.	688
Tray, Landscape, Lake, Boatman, Cracked Surface, France, 1800s, 21 x 26½ In.	201
Tray, Peace & Commerce For America, Clipper Ship, Oval, Late 1800s, 25 x 20 In................	281
Tray, Red Ground, Gilt Basket, Fruit, Leaves, Curved Ends, Handles, 1800s, 14 x 20 In. *illus*	128
Tray, Red Ground, Rectangular, Flowers, Pine Trees, 1800s, 28½ In.	214
Tray, Rural House, Trees, Landscape, Gilt Leaf, 26 x 19 In.	59
Urn, Chestnut, Lift Lid, Scenes, Swing Handles, Oval, 1900s, 7 x 7 x 18 In., Pair..........*illus*	177
Vase, Cherub, Gold, Paw Feet, Square Base, Early 1900s, 9¾ In., Pair.........................	94

Tole, Coffeepot, Tapered Body, Flowers, Strap Handle, Pa., Early 1800s, 9 x 9 In. $384

Soulis Auctions

Tole, Lamp, Rumford, Black, Gilt, Scrolled Flowers, Trophies, Square Base, England, 1900s, 14½ In. $484

Ahlers & Ogletree Auction Gallery

Tole, Lamp, Tea Canister, Electrified, Chinese Characters, J. Maund, England, 1800s, 34¼ In. $242

Ahlers & Ogletree Auction Gallery

Tole, Sconce, Gilt Bust, Wheat, French Empire, Neoclassical, 1800s, 19 x 3 x 7., Pair
$2,520

Abington Auction Gallery

Tole, Tea Caddy, Hinged Lid, Red, Yellow Trim, Bee Skep, Green Leaves, 1800s, 5¼ x 4 x 3 In.
$288

Rachel Davis Fine Arts

Tole, Tray, Black, Yellow, Flowers, Faux Bamboo Stand, Victorian, Late 1800s, 17 x 24 x 19 In.
$594

Hindman

Tole, Tray, Red Ground, Gilt Basket, Fruit, Leaves, Curved Ends, Handles, 1800s, 14 x 20 In.
$128

Rachel Davis Fine Arts

Tole, Urn, Chestnut, Lift Lid, Scenes, Swing Handles, Oval, 1900s, 7 x 7 x 18 In., Pair
$177

Charleston Estate Auctions

Tool, Book Press, Oak, Turned Screw, Ball Shape Finial, c.1800s, 15 x 10 x 9 In.
$554

Pook & Pook

Tool, Box, Hinged, Stanley, No. 800, Cherry Wood, Brass Tag, Leather Handle, 22 x 6 x 12 In.
$420

Chupp Auctions & Real Estate, LLC

Tool, Brace, Corner Bit, Stanley, No. 992, Wood Handle, 8-In. Sweep
$60

Chupp Auctions & Real Estate, LLC

Tool, Cabinet, Stanley, No. 850, Roll-Up Front, Oak, Handle, Key Lock, 26 x 9 x 31 In.
$300

Chupp Auctions & Real Estate, LLC

T

TOOL

Tools of all sorts are listed here, but most are related to industry. Other tools may be found listed under Iron, Kitchen, Tinware, and Wooden.

Adze, Carved, Rattan Wrapped, Polished Stone, Papua New Guinea, 1910s, 20 x 25 In.	188
Book Press, Oak, Turned Screw, Ball Shape Finial, c.1800s, 15 x 10 x 9 In.................*illus*	554
Box, Carpenter's Tote, Walnut, Dovetailed, J. Frank Dellinger, Virginia, c.1880, 6 x 23 In.....	538
Box, Hinged, Stanley, No. 800, Cherry Wood, Brass Tag, Leather Handle, 22 x 6 x 12 In.*illus*	420
Brace, Bit, Ratchet, Mephisto, 10-In. Sweep..	30
Brace, Bit, Stanley, No. 923, Wood Handle, 10 In., Pair...	30
Brace, Corner Bit, Stanley, No. 992, Wood Handle, 8-In. Sweep.........................*illus*	60
Cabinet, Stanley, No. 850, Roll-Up Front, Oak, Handle, Key Lock, 26 x 9 x 31 In...........*illus*	300
Carrier, Pine, Carved, Painted, Later Decoration, 1800s, 8 x 27 x 12 In......................*illus*	113
Chest, Drawers, Hinged Lid, Handle, Lock, Wood, Model 041, H. Gerstner & Sons, 16 x 8 x 13 In..*illus*	420
Chest, Hinged Lid, Starrett, Vernier Height Gauge, Wood, Dovetailed, 23 x 4¼ x 7 In.	60
Chest, Wood, Old Red Paint, Rectangular Box, c.1900, 13 x 33½ In.	38
Cream Separator, DeLaval, Junior No. 2, Hand Crank, Metal Tag, 22½ Lb., 21 x 16 In........*illus*	39
Drilling Machine, Jackson's Patent, Wheel, Oak, No Belts, Salesman's Sample, 11 x 11 x 8 In..*illus*	1200
Flax Break, Wood, Rectangular Frame, 2 Hinged Blades, Trestle Feet, England, 1800s, 15 x 19 In.	250
Hacksaw, Disston, Wood Handle, 10-In. Blade ....*illus*	30
Hacksaw, Millers Falls, No. 014, Tall Frame, Woodworking Plane, 13-In. Blade	42
Hatchel, Iron & Wood, Hex Sign, Old Surface, Warm Color, 1800s, 4 x 21 In.................*illus*	179
Hatchet, Pexto Broad, Wood Handle, Carved, 4¼ In.	120
Hatchet, Stanley, No. 21, Four Square, Wood Handle, Hammer, Cutting Edge, 3½ In.	24
Hedge Trimmer, Detco Manufacturing Company, Little Wonder, Metal & Wood, c.1914, 64 In...*illus*	60
Inclinometer, L.L. Davis, Tall Frame, Carved Vines, Filigree, Adjustable Level, 24 In.	150
Inclinometer, Queen & Co., Double Plumb, Cast Iron, 18 In.................................	3600
Knife Sharpener, Hand Crank, Floor Mount, Wood, Cast Iron, Kent	480
Level, Bench, Sawyer Tool Co., Cast Iron, Black, 6 In...*illus*	300
Level, L.S. Starrett, Electrician's, Solid Brass, Display Case, Frame, 8 In. ....*illus*	210
Level, Plumb, Davis & Co., Cast Iron, Water To Win, 12 In....................................	390
Pitchfork, Wood, Patriotic, White & Blue, Stars, Thin Handle, c.1900, 58 In....................	540
Plane, Jack, Sargent, No. 411C, Corrugated Bottom, Iron, 11½ In....................................	78
Plane, Jack, Sargent, No. 718, Auto Set, Iron, Black Paint, 18 In. ....*illus*	150
Plane, Molding, H. Chapin, Oak, Adjustable, 2 Blades, Late 1800s, 6 x 9 In...........................	72
Plane, Plow, Hezekiah Niles, Wood, Philadelphia, Late 1700s, 14 In.	101
Plane, Smoothing, Millers Falls, No. 9, Chrome Plated, Wood Handle, 9 In.	72
Plumb & Level, Davis Level & Tool Co., Cast Iron, Vines Design, 18 In..............................	270
Ruler, Norvell-Shapleigh Hardware Co., Diamond Edge, Wood, 12 In.	12
Saw, Buck, I. Sorby Sheffield, Cast Steel, Wood Handle, 8 In...................................	180
Saw, George H. Bishop & Co., Handy, Duplex, Display Case, Frame, 17¾ In.	90
Screwdriver, Long Shaft, Flathead, Hardwood Handle, Steel, 29 In.	60
Screwdriver, Stanley, Wood Handle, Flat Blade, Alloy Steel, 6 In., 6 Piece	210
Scythe, Seymour, No. 1, 2 Handles, Metal Blade..	69
Sickle, Wrought Iron, Reaping Hook, Wood Handle, Christian Funk Sr., Pa., 1850s, 24 In.*illus*	155
Square, Try, St. Johnbury Tool Co., Patented, 6-In. Blade	102
Vise, Stanley, No. 766, Removable Jaw, 3 In.	48
Wheelbarrow, Painted, Wood, 1 Wheel, Grip Handle, 1800s, 17 x 37 In....................*illus*	252
Workbench, Sweetheart Folding, Stanley Works, No. 859, Wood, Angle Bar, 49 x 48 x 20 In.	330
Wrench, Pipe, Ampco, No. 214, Straight, Bronze, Adjustable, 24 In.	42

TOOTHBRUSH HOLDER

Toothbrush holders were part of every bowl and pitcher set in the late nineteenth century. Most were oblong covered dishes. About 1920, manufacturers started to make children's toothbrush holders shaped like animals or cartoon characters. A few modern toothbrush holders are still being made.

Dog, Bonzo, Paw On Chest, Japan, 5½ In..	125
Pinocchio, Pottery, California Cleminsons, Wall Mount, 1950s, 9 x 4 In.........................	55

Tool, Carrier, Pine, Carved, Painted, Later Decoration, 1800s, 8 x 27 x 12 In.
$113

Pook & Pook

Tool, Chest, Drawers, Hinged Lid, Handle, Lock, Wood, Model 041, H. Gerstner & Sons, 16 x 8 x 13 In.
$420

Chupp Auctions & Real Estate, LLC

Tool, Cream Separator, DeLaval, Junior No. 2, Hand Crank, Metal Tag, 22½ Lb., 21 x 16 In.
$39

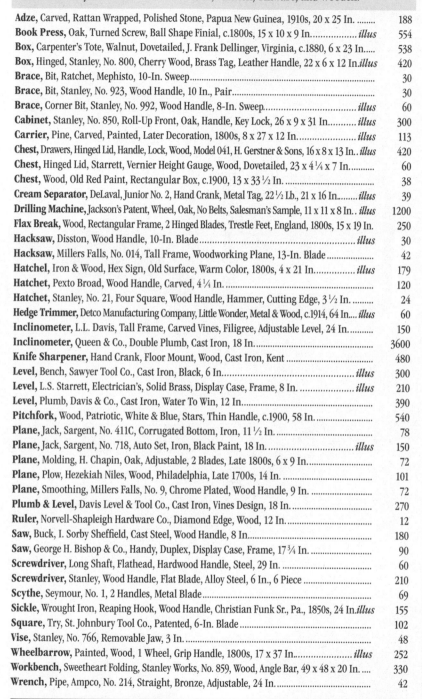

Rachel Davis Fine Arts

T

Tool, Drilling Machine, Jackson's Patent, Wheel, Oak, No Belts, Salesman's Sample, 11 x 11 x 8 In.
$1,200

Chupp Auctions & Real Estate, LLC

Tool, Hacksaw, Disston, Wood Handle, 10-In. Blade
$30

Chupp Auctions & Real Estate, LLC

Tool, Hatchel, Iron & Wood, Hex Sign, Old Surface, Warm Color, 1800s, 4 x 21 In.
$179

Jeffrey S. Evans & Associates

Tool, Hedge Trimmer, Detco Manufacturing Company, Little Wonder, Metal & Wood, c.1914, 64 In.
$60

Nadeau's Auction Gallery

Tool, Level, Bench, Sawyer Tool Co., Cast Iron, Black, 6 In.
$300

Chupp Auctions & Real Estate, LLC

Tool, Level, L.S. Starrett, Electrician's, Solid Brass, Display Case, Frame, 8 In.
$210

Chupp Auctions & Real Estate, LLC

Tool, Plane, Jack, Sargent, No. 718, Auto Set, Iron, Black Paint, 18 In.
$150

Chupp Auctions & Real Estate, LLC

Tool, Sickle, Wrought Iron, Reaping Hook, Wood Handle, Christian Funk Sr., Pa., 1850s, 24 In.
$155

Jeffrey S. Evans & Associates

Tool, Wheelbarrow, Painted, Wood, 1 Wheel, Grip Handle, 1800s, 17 x 37 In.
$252

Pook & Pook

Toothpick Holder, Hinged Lid, Bezel Set Ship, Piquet, Gold Stars, France, 1700s, 3 ¼ In.
$854

Rafael Osona Nantucket Auctions

TIP

To clean tortoiseshell, rub it with a mixture of jeweler's rouge and olive oil.

Tortoiseshell, Etui, Dark Brown, Silver Pique, Cylindrical, Pushbutton, Continental, 1700s, 4 x 1 ¼ In.
$351

Thomaston Place Auction Galleries

T

| Porcelain, Green, 5 Holders, Cup, Footed, 6 In. | 45 |
| Spider Man, Figural, Avon, 1979, 3 1/2 x 5 In. | 35 |

TOOTHPICK HOLDER

Toothpick holders are sometimes called *toothpicks* by collectors. The variously shaped containers used to hold small wooden toothpicks are made of glass, china, or metal. Most of the toothpick holders are made of Victorian glass. Additional items may be found in other categories, such as Bisque, Silver Plate, Slag Glass, etc.

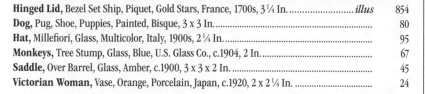

Hinged Lid, Bezel Set Ship, Piquet, Gold Stars, France, 1700s, 3 1/4 In. .... *illus*	854
Dog, Pug, Shoe, Puppies, Painted, Bisque, 3 x 3 In.	80
Hat, Millefiori, Glass, Multicolor, Italy, 1900s, 2 1/4 In.	95
Monkeys, Tree Stump, Glass, Blue, U.S. Glass Co., c.1904, 2 In.	67
Saddle, Over Barrel, Glass, Amber, c.1900, 3 x 3 x 2 In.	45
Victorian Woman, Vase, Orange, Porcelain, Japan, c.1920, 2 x 2 1/4 In.	24

TORTOISESHELL

Tortoiseshell is the shell of the tortoise. It has been used as inlay and to make small decorative objects since the seventeenth century. Some species of tortoise are now on the endangered species list, and old or new objects made from these shells cannot be sold legally. There is also a Victorian glass that looks like a tortoise shell and is called tortoiseshell glass.

Case, Hinged, Lid, Fitted, Blond, Rectangular, Engraved, 1910s, 5 x 3 1/2 In.	1890
Etui, Dark Brown, Silver Pique, Cylindrical, Pushbutton, Continental, 1700s, 4 x 1 1/4 In. *illus*	351
Jewelry Box, Dore Bronze Mounted, Escutcheon & Handle, 4 x 8 x 4 In.	1850
Pitcher, Brown & Amber, Pulled Handle, Christian Dior, c.1960, 7 x 4 3/8 x 12 In.	1950
Tea Caddy, Mother-Of-Pearl, George IV, Serpentine Front, Ball Feet, 1800s, 5 x 8 In. .... *illus*	1920

TORTOISESHELL GLASS

Tortoiseshell glass was made during the 1800s and after by the Sandwich Glass Works of Massachusetts and some firms in Germany. Tortoiseshell glass is, of course, named for its resemblance to real shell from a tortoise. It has been reproduced.

Bowl, Molded, Ridged, Side Handles, Scalloped Base, 4 x 8 1/2 In.	52
Bride's Basket, Ruffled Rim, Gilt, Silver Plate Frame, Pierced Feet, Monarch, 16 In.	180
Goblet, Cone Shape Cup, Clear Stem & Foot, 20th Century, 7 In., 14 Piece	1625
Perfume Bottle, Baluster Shape, Goldtone Top, Black Atomizer, Tassel, 7 1/4 In.	13
Vase, Cased, Satin, Enamel Flying Bird & Flowering Branches, Square Mouth, 10 In., Pair. *illus*	540
Vase, Light & Dark Brown, Flared Rim, 7 3/4 x 4 1/4 In.	35

TOTE, *see Purse category.*

TOY

Toy collectors have special clubs, magazines, and shows. Toys are designed to entice children, and today they have attracted new interest among adults who are still children at heart. All types of toys are collected. Tin toys, iron toys, battery-operated toys, and many others are collected by specialists. Penny toys are inexpensive tin toys made in Germany from the 1880s until about 1914. Some salesman's samples may be listed here. Dolls, Games, Teddy Bears, Bicycles, and other types of toys are listed in their own categories. Other toys may be found under company or celebrity names.

Action Figure, Amazing Spider Man, Red & Blue, Mego, Box, Unopened, 1977, 12 In.	384
Adam The Porter, Tin Lithograph, Windup, 2 Wheel Dolly, Lehmann, c.1900, 8 x 7 1/2 In. *illus*	330
Airplane, Biplane, Barnstormer, Jenny JN-7H, Red, Yellow & Blue, 7 x 21 x 30 1/2 In.	88
Airplane, Biplane, Yellow, Folding Wings, Clockwork, Tipp & Co., Germany, c.1930, 11 x 17 In.	210

TIP

To restore the sheen to a tortoiseshell box, rub it with a cloth dipped in lemon juice and salt. Rinse it with cold water, dry. Sometimes rubbing yogurt on the shell will help.

Tortoiseshell, Tea Caddy, Mother-Of-Pearl, George IV, Serpentine Front, Ball Feet, 1800s, 5 x 8 In.
$1,920

Neal Auction Company

Tortoiseshell Glass, Vase, Cased, Satin, Enamel Flying Bird & Flowering Branches, Square Mouth, 10 In., Pair
$540

Woody Auction

T

This is an edited listing of current prices. Visit **Kovels.com** to check thousands of prices from previous years and sign up for free information on trends, tips, reproductions, marks, and more.

Toy, Adam The Porter, Tin Lithograph, Windup, 2 Wheel Dolly, Lehmann, c.1900, 8 x 7½ In.
$330

Garth's Auctioneers & Appraisers

Toy, Airplane, Mail, 3 Wheels, Painted, Yellow, Kenton, 8 In.
$960

Bertoia Auctions

TIP

If your heavy cast-iron toy has rubber tires, display it on a partial stand so there is no pressure on the tires.

Toy, Ambulance, Blue Paint, Metal Driver, Disc Wheels, Cast Iron, Kenton, 4 x 7 x 3 In.
$780

Morphy Auctions

Airplane, Black Fuselage, Orange Wings & Tail, Chrome Propeller, Late 1900s, 8 x 10 In....	420
Airplane, Driver, Wings, Red & Yellow, Tin Lithograph, Gunthermann, 5½ x 8 In..............	532
Airplane, Great American Flying Machine, Wood, Ride On, 26¾ x 31 x 15½ In..................	41
Airplane, Mail, 3 Wheels, Painted, Yellow, Kenton, 8 In. ....*illus*	960
Ambulance, Blue Paint, Metal Driver, Disc Wheels, Cast Iron, Kenton, 4 x 7 x 3 In.......*illus*	780
Ambulance, Figure, Steering Wheel, Cream, Cast Iron, Paint, Kenton, Late 1800s, 7¼ In. .	375
Armoire, Doll's, Faux Bamboo, Beveled Glass, Mirror, Door, Drawer, France, 1800s, 22 x 14 x 7 In.	125
Bears are also listed in the Teddy Bear category.	
Bear, Smoking Papa Bear, Battery Operated, Remote Control, Marusan Toys, Japan, Box....	60
Bell Ringer, 2 Clowns, Tumbler, 4 Side Wheels, 1 Center Wheel, Painted, Watrous, 10 In.	1320
Bell Ringer, Elephant, 4 Wheels, Pull Toy, N.N. Hill Brass Co., c.1905, 4½ x 7 In. ....*illus*	272
Bell Ringer, Grindstone, Man Sharpens Tool, 4 Wheels, Hand Painted, Bergmann	1440
Bell Ringer, Jonah & Whale, Cast Iron, Painted, Multicolor, NH Hill Brass Co., 5 In.	1560
Bell Ringer, Landing Of Columbus, 3 Men, 3 Wheels, Painted, J. & E. Stevens, 7 In.....*illus*	1140
Bell Ringer, Red Cart, Monkey Strikes Bell, Pull Toy, Kyser & Rex, 7½ In............................	4500
Bicycles that are large enough to ride are listed in the Bicycle category.	
Bird, Flying, Paper Wings, Mechanical, Multicolor, Lehmann, 7 In. ....*illus*	120
Bird, Stoopy Storky, Critters, Popup, Paddle Shape Base, Fisher-Price, No. 407, 1931, 5 In. ..	330
Boat, Motor, Red & Black, Windup, Lindstrom, 15 In...	108
Boat, Ocean Liner, Leviathan, 3 Stacks, Masts, Flags, Tin Lithograph, Bing, Germany, 9 x 13 In..*illus*	660
Boat, Steamboat, H.E. Barracuda, Brass, 4-Cylinder, Boucher Engine, Stand, 1920s, 49 x 12 x 12 In.	2048
Boy, On Scooter, Painted, Disc Wheels, Tin, Windup, France, Prewar, 9 x 9 x 3 In.	1320
Building, Burning, Firemen, Woman, Ladder, Hose, Carpenter, 17 In.........................*illus*	15600
Bull, Growler, Mohair, Moo Sound, String Operated, Bell, Glass Eyes, 1950s, 13 x 10 In.	254
Bus, Double-Decker, Green & Orange Paint, Driver, 4 Passengers, Kenton, 7¼ In.................	450
Bus, Double-Decker, Pascall The Novelty House, Wright's Coal Tar Soap, Bing, 8 In.	2700
Bus, Greyhound, It's Such A Comfort To Take The Bus, Metal, Hinged Door, Japan, 1950s, 11 In.	75
Bus, RCA Victor, NBC Television, Man, Camera, Battery Operated, Yonezawa, 1950s, 6 x 9 In..*illus*	720
Bus, Seeing New York, Driver, 4 Passengers, Painted, Kenton, 10 In..........................*illus*	1680
Car, Armored, Camouflage Paint, Revolving Turret, Tin, Key Wind, Marklin, 1930s, 7 x 14 In...	880
Car, Circus, Sensation, Attraction, Blue, Orange, White, Painted Figures, Distler, 6 In..........	960
Car, Citroen, Red, Black, Spare Tire, License Plate, Clockwork, France, c.1930, 7 x 16 x 6 In..*illus*	1320
Car, Duesenberg, 20 Grand Model, Swarovski Crystals, Franklin Mint, 1933, 9 In..............	360
Car, Hand Crank, Orange & Black, Gilbert American Flyer, No. 740, Box, 1950.............*illus*	69
Car, Maroon, Driver, Rubber Wheels, Tom Sehloff, Box, 1900s, 4 x 11 In..............................	960
Car, Mystery, Driver, Tin, Multicolor, Battery Operated, Japan	50
Car, Plymouth Duster, Doors, Hood, & Trunk Open, Die Cast, 1971, 11¼ In.	31
Car, Racing, Driver, 4 Wheels, Painted, Multicolor, Fischer, Penny Toy, 4 In.	210
Car, Racing, Duesenberg, Stewart Special, 2 Drivers, Balloon Tires, Late 1900s, 10¾ In.*illus*	600
Car, Racing, Mercedes, Driver, Painted, Silver, Rubber Wheels, 12 x 25 x 11 In....................	88
Car, Roadster, Driver, Yellow, Maroon Wheels, A.C. Gilbert Stutz, 9½ In.	840
Car, Roadster, Red & Yellow Paint, Pressed Steel, Rubber Wheels, Wyandotte, 1930s, 13 In.*illus*	480
Car, Sedan, Gold Color Allover, Friction, Marusan, Japan, c.1951, 11 In.	1020
Car, Sedan, Red, Pathe News Camera On Roof, Folding Tripod Stand, Marx, c.1930s, 9 x 9½ In..*illus*	780
Car, Tin Lizzie, 4 Composition Figures, Remote Control, Arnold, Box, 9½ In.	360
Car, Touring, Sheet Metal, Leather Seats, E.C. Spurin's Manufactory, Windup, 1900s, 21 x 28 In...	239
Carousel, Horses, Gondolas, Girl At Center, Hand Painted, Althof Bergmann, 19 x 20 In. .....*illus*	4200
Carriage, Cycle, Umbrella Top, Open Car, Driver, Valet, Tin Lithograph, Lehmann, 1930s, 5 x 5 In.....	330
Carriage, Doll's, Stenciled, Red Paint, Black Running Stag, Parasol, Late 1800s, 22 In.......	25
Carriage, Horseless, Coachman, Blue Paint, 4 Wheels, Meier, Penny Toy, 3¼ In.	1080
Carriage, Open, 3 Wheels, Driver, Valet, Umbrella, Tin Litho, Windup, Lehmann, c.1935, 5 x 5 In..	345
Carriage, Spoked Wheels, Lamp, Blue, Red & Yellow Paint, Rock & Graner, Germany, 12 x 21 x 9 In.	3198
Carriage, Wicker, With Doll, Sleep Eyes, Open Mouth, Simon & Halbig, c.1910, 24 x 27 In.....*illus*	125
Cart, Farm, Oxen Drawn, Driver, Red, Yellow, Brown, Black, Ives, 14 In.	1200
Cart, Horse Drawn, Driver, Hose Reel, 2 Wheels, Shimmer, 10 In.	960
Cat, Felix, Chasing Mice, Disc Wheeled Platform, Pull Toy, Nifty, 8 In.	480
Cat, Felix, The Movie Cat, Painted, Windup, Nifty, Fischer, Germany, Box, 7 x 5 In.......*illus*	3360
Cat, Garfield, Stuffed Animal, White Bunny Shoes, Nightcap, Paws Inc., Indonesia, 1994, 17 In.	20
Cat, Minka, Gray, Glass Eyes, Red Ribbon, Steiff, 10 In...	111
Cat, Mohair, Sitting, Light Brown, Green Eyes, Swivel Head, Stitched Nose & Mouth, Steiff, 6 In...*illus*	1024

T

SELECTED TOY MARKS WITH DATES USED

Gebruder Bing
1902–1934
Nuremburg, Germany

Gebruder Bing Co.
c.1923–1924
Nuremberg, Germany

F.A.O. Schwarz
1914
New York, N.Y.

Louis Marx & Co.
1920–1977
New York, N.Y.

Ernst Lehmann Co.
1881–c.1947, 1951–2006
Brandenburg, Germany; Nuremburg,
Germany

Ernst Lehmann Co.
1915
Brandenburg, Germany

Gebruder Marklin & Co.
1899+
Goppingen, Germany

Nomura Toy Industrial Co., Ltd.
1940s+
Tokyo, Japan

Meccano
1901+
Liverpool, England

Georges Carette & Co.
1905–1917
Nuremburg, Germany

Joseph Falk Co.
1895–1934
Nuremburg, Germany

H. Fischer & Co.
1908–1932
Nuremburg, Germany

Lineol
c. 1906–1963
Bradenburg, Germany

Blomer and Schüler
1919–1974
Nuremberg, Germany

Yonezawa Toys Co.
1950s–1970s
Tokyo, Japan

T

Toy, Bell Ringer, Elephant, 4 Wheels, Pull Toy, N.N. Hill Brass Co., c.1905, 4 1/2 x 7 In.
$272

Fontaine's Auction Gallery

Toy, Bell Ringer, Landing Of Columbus, 3 Men, 3 Wheels, Painted, J. & E. Stevens, 7 In.
$1,140

Bertoia Auctions

Toy, Bird, Flying, Paper Wings, Mechanical, Multicolor, Lehmann, 7 In.
$120

Bertoia Auctions

Toy, Boat, Ocean Liner, Leviathan, 3 Stacks, Masts, Flags, Tin Lithograph, Bing, Germany, 9 x 13 In.
$660

Morphy Auctions

Cat, Sitting, Carved, Choker, On Platform, Pull Toy, Smith & Shrode, 1800s, 8 x 12 In.	202
Cat, Tricky Tommy, Cymbals, Paper On Wood, Push Toy, Fisher-Price, No. 470, 1936, 9 1/2 In.	832
Cats & The Fiddle, Sheet Iron & Wood, Painted, Turbine Operated, Windup, c.1910, 11 In.	370
Chair, Doll's, Chippendale, Mahogany, Upholstered, Ball & Claw Feet, 20 x 13 x 10 In.. *illus*	144
Chair, Doll's, Primitive, Thin Shaped Boards, Wire Nails, Painted, Late 1800s, 12 In.	228
Chair, Doll's, Recamier, Oak, Carved, Upholstered, Armrest, 11 x 21 In.	76
Chest, Doll's, Mirror, Flowers, 2 Drawers, c.1865, 15 x 9 x 4 In.	88
Chest, Doll's, Pine, Stained, 4 Drawers, Turned Feet, 15 In.	160
Chime Roller, Horse Drawn, Man On Platform, Ornate Spoke Wheels, Merriam Miner, 10 In. .	3000
Clown, Magician, Jacob's Ladder, Battery Operated, Cragstan, Japan, 1950s, 12 1/2 In... *illus*	210
Covered Wagon, Metal, Canvas Cover, 2 Lithographed Horses, 18 In.	180
Cow, Brown & Cream Upholstery, Leather Collar, Bell, 4 Wheels, Pull Toy, Late 1800s, 15 x 19 In. *illus*	625
Cupboard, Doll's, Stepback, Intricate Design, Dark Wood, Brittany, 14 1/2 In.	197
Cupboard, Victorian, Walnut, Doll, White Handles, Drawer, Slate Top, 17 1/2 x 14 1/2 In.	126
Dog, Flipo, See My Jump, Black & White, Red Collar, Louis Marx & Co., 3 In.	60
Dog, German Shepherd, Standing, Mohair, Button In Ear, Steiff, 15 x 17 In. *illus*	156
Dog, Hexie, Dachshund, Standing, Red Collar, Mohair, Golden Brown, Steiff, 6 In.	71
Dog, Odie Dog, Stuffed Animal, Nightcap, Garfield Slippers, Paws Inc., Indonesia, 1994, 23 In.	28
Dog, Scottie, Red Shoe, Black Cloth Skin, Orange Collar, Tin, Windup, 5 1/4 In.	66
Dog, Tyrus, Dirty White, Walker, Lithographed, Lehmann, 6 1/2 In.	480
Dolls are listed in the Doll category.	
Dollhouse Furniture, Piano, Grand, Bench, Blue Paint, Folding Music Stand, Arcade, 6 In.	150
Dollhouse, 2 Story, American Flag, Angel Gabriel Weathervane, Bliss, c.1910, 24 x 19 x 14 In.*illus*	500
Dollhouse, 2 Story, Red Roof, R. Bliss Mfg., Pawtucket, R.I., c.1910, 29 x 15 x 16 In. .... *illus*	1063
Dollhouse, 2 Story, Wood, White Curtains, Various Furnishings, Early 1900s, 25 x 25 x 13 1/2 In.	365
Dollhouse, 2 1/2 Story, Red Roof, Blue Trim, Balcony, Sides Open, Bliss, 29 x 20 x 18 In.	585
Dollhouse, 3 Story, Wood, Paint, Arched Windows, 2nd Floor Porch, Craftsman Style, 24 x 20 In.	135
Dollhouse, Townhouse, 3 Story, Lithograph Brick Front, Painted Sides & Back, Victorian, 24 In.	923
Dollhouse, Victorian Style, Stained Glass Window, Electric, Paul Brouder, c.1970, 60 x 27 In... *illus*	1024
Donkey, Circus, Painted Eyes, Ears, Mane & Tail, Wood, Schoenhut, 1900s, 7 In.	62
Erector Set, Gilbert No. 10083, Amusement Park Rides, Sound Effects, Original Box, 1950s	175
Ferris Wheel, Hercules, 6 Gondolas, Windup, Tin Lithograph, No. 172, Chein, 17 In.... *illus*	330
Figure, Jiminy Cricket, Painted, Wood, Movable Head, Felted Hat Brim & Collar, c.1940, 8 In.*illus*	344
Fire Engine, T.F.D. No. 5, Life Net, Pressed Steel, Ladder Raises & Lowers, Tonka, c.1957, 32 In.	235
Fire Truck, Fireman, Ladder, Head Lamp, Tin Litho, Windup, Georg Fischer, Germany, 4 1/2 In.. *illus*	270
Fire Truck, Hess, 2 Removable Hoses, Ladder, Decals, Marx, Hong Kong, Box, 1970	600
Fire Truck, Ladder, Aerial, Orange, Silver Tires, Buddy L, 29 In.	277
Fire Truck, Pressed Steel, Aerial, Bell, Nickel Ladder, Painted, Red, Buddy L, 38 1/4 In.	625
Fire Truck, Pumper, Cast Iron, Painted, Fireman, 3 Horses, 2 Rubber Hoses, 8 x 21 In.	240
Fire Truck, Pumper, Wood, Painted, 4 Wheels, 20 x 25 In. *illus*	265
Fire Truck, Red, Ladder, 4 Wheels, Pressed Steel, 11 x 32 1/2 x 7 In. *illus*	219
Fire Wagon, Front & Back Drivers, Holding Ladder, 3-Horse Team, Wheels, c.1950, 9 x 29 In..	72
Football Kicker, Red & Yellow, Orange Ball, Green Base, Right Leg Moves, Woolsey, 8 In.	440
Foxy Grandpa, Skates, Scissor-Action Legs, Hand Painted, Issmayer, Germany, c.1910, 8 In. *illus*	720
Funny Face, Harold Lloyd, Walker, Holding Cane, Windup, Marx, 10 1/2 In. *illus*	660
Games are listed in the Game category.	
Gas Station, Gas Pump, Service, Liberty Bus, Tin Lithograph, Marx, 1930s, 3 1/2 In.	210
Godzilla, Shogun Warriors, Green, Yellow, Launches Claw, Tongue Flames, Box, Mattel, 1977, 21 In..	900
Grasshopper, Green Paint, 2 Wheels, Pull Toy, Hubley, 13 In. *illus*	660
Gun, Cork, 2 Barrels, Wood Comb, Metal, Daisy Mfg. Co., 21 In.	120
Hobbyhorse, Pine, Mane, Skirt, Bridle, Saddle, Rocking, Mid 1900s, 42 1/2 x 65 In.	139
Hobbyhorse, Wood, Carved, Painted, Lou Schifferl, 1800s, 31 In. *illus*	239
Honeymoon Express, Flag Man, Stop Watch, Train, Round Track, Tin, Marx, Box	120
Horse, Cloth, Brown Leather, Wood Base, Metal Wheels, 16 1/2 In.	246
Horse, Pony, Fabric Coat, Leather Saddle, Hansa, Thomas Boland & Co., 1900s, 48 x 58 In.	406
Horse, Rocking, Black & White Paint, Gray Hair, Saddle, Platform, Late 1800s, 38 x 44 x 16 In.	313
Horse, Rocking, Folk Art, Carved, Multicolor, Painted, Walter J. Gottshall, 8 x 10 1/2 In.	325
Horse, Rocking, Laminated Wood, Modernist, Creative Playthings, Mid 1900s, 17 x 11 3/4 In.*illus*	250
Horse, Rocking, White Hair Tail, Leather Saddle, Carved, Painted, Wood, Early 1800s, 37 x 58 In. .	938
Horse, Rocking, Wood, Carved, Painted, Pinstripes, Stenciled, 28 x 36 x 12 In. *illus*	384

T

Toy, Building, Burning, Firemen, Woman, Ladder, Hose, Carpenter, 17 In.
$15,600

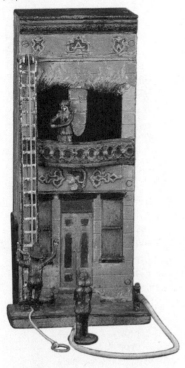

Bertoia Auctions

Toy, Bus, RCA Victor, NBC Television, Man, Camera, Battery Operated, Yonezawa, 1950s, 6 x 9 In.
$720

Selkirk Auctioneers & Appraisers

TIP

Don't let plastic toys or dishes touch each other. Different types of plastic may react to each other and be damaged.

Toy, Bus, Seeing New York, Driver, 4 Passengers, Painted, Kenton, 10 In.
$1,680

Bertoia Auctions

Toy, Car, Citroen, Red, Black, Spare Tire, License Plate, Clockwork, France, c.1930, 7 x 16 x 6 In.
$1,320

Morphy Auctions

Toy, Car, Hand Crank, Orange & Black, Gilbert American Flyer, No. 740, Box, 1950
$69

Donley Auctions

Toy, Car, Racing, Duesenberg, Stewart Special, 2 Drivers, Balloon Tires, Late 1900s, 10 ¾ In.
$600

Selkirk Auctioneers & Appraisers

Toy, Car, Roadster, Red & Yellow Paint, Pressed Steel, Rubber Wheels, Wyandotte, 1930s, 13 In.
$480

Garth's Auctioneers & Appraisers

Toy, Car, Sedan, Red, Pathe News Camera On Roof, Folding Tripod Stand, Marx, c.1930s, 9 x 9 ½ In.
$780

Selkirk Auctioneers & Appraisers

T

Toy, Carousel, Horses, Gondolas, Girl At Center, Hand Painted, Althof Bergmann, 19 x 20 In.
$4,200

Toy, Clown, Magician, Jacob's Ladder, Battery Operated, Cragstan, Japan, 1950s, 12 ½ In.
$210

Potter & Potter Auctions

Bertoia Auctions

Toy, Cow, Brown & Cream Upholstery, Leather Collar, Bell, 4 Wheels, Pull Toy, Late 1800s, 15 x 19 In.
$625

Toy, Carriage, Wicker, With Doll, Sleep Eyes, Open Mouth, Simon & Halbig, c.1910, 24 x 27 In.
$125

Toy, Cat, Mohair, Sitting, Light Brown, Green Eyes, Swivel Head, Stitched Nose & Mouth, Steiff, 6 In.
$1,024

Hindman

Toy, Dog, German Shepherd, Standing, Mohair, Button In Ear, Steiff, 15 x 17 In.
$156

Eldred's

Rachel Davis Fine Arts

Toy, Cat, Felix, The Movie Cat, Painted, Windup, Nifty, Fischer, Germany, Box, 7 x 5 In.
$3,360

Toy, Chair, Doll's, Chippendale, Mahogany, Upholstered, Ball & Claw Feet, 20 x 13 x 10 In.
$144

Wiederseim Auctions

Morphy Auctions

Stevens Auction Co.

Toy, Dollhouse, 2 Story, American Flag, Angel Gabriel Weathervane, Bliss, c.1910, 24 x 19 x 14 In.
$500

Hindman

Toy, Dollhouse, 2 Story, Red Roof, R. Bliss Mfg., Pawtucket, R.I., c.1910, 29 x 15 x 16 In.
$1,063

Hindman

Toy, Dollhouse, Victorian Style, Stained Glass Window, Electric, Paul Brouder, c.1970, 60 x 27 In.
$1,024

Morphy Auctions

Toy, Ferris Wheel, Hercules, 6 Gondolas, Windup, Tin Lithograph, No. 172, Chein, 17 In.
$330

Morphy Auctions

Toy, Figure, Jiminy Cricket, Painted, Wood, Movable Head, Felted Hat Brim & Collar, c.1940, 8 In.
$344

Potter & Potter Auctions

Toy, Fire Truck, Fireman, Ladder, Head Lamp, Tin Litho, Windup, Georg Fischer, Germany, 4 ½ In.
$270

Selkirk Auctioneers & Appraisers

Toy, Fire Truck, Pumper, Wood, Painted, 4 Wheels, 20 x 25 In.
$265

Pook & Pook

Toy, Fire Truck, Red, Ladder, 4 Wheels, Pressed Steel, 11 x 32 ½ x 7 In.
$219

New Haven Auctions

Toy, Foxy Grandpa, Skates, Scissor-Action Legs, Hand Painted, Issmayer, Germany, c.1910, 8 In.
$720

Bertoia Auctions

T

Toy, Funny Face, Harold Lloyd, Walker, Holding Cane, Windup, Marx, 10 ½ In.
$660

Bertoia Auctions

Toy, Grasshopper, Green Paint, 2 Wheels, Pull Toy, Hubley, 13 In.
$660

Bertoia Auctions

> **TIP**
> If you have a battery-operated 1940s toy such as "Smoking Grandpa" or "McGregor" you might want to replenish the smoke-maker when it wears out. Put a few drops of sewing machine oil into the smoking tube. An electric spark in the toy causes the oil to smoke and allows the toy to seem to puff on a cigarette, pipe, or cigar.

Toy, Hobbyhorse, Wood, Carved, Painted, Lou Schifferl, 1800s, 31 In.
$239

Pook & Pook

Toy, Horse, Rocking, Laminated Wood, Modernist, Creative Playthings, Mid 1900s, 17 x 11 ¾ In.
$250

Eldred's

Toy, Horse, Rocking, Wood, Carved, Painted, Pinstripes, Stenciled, 28 x 36 x 12 In.
$384

Soulis Auctions

Toy, Horse, Running, Black Body, White Legs, Brown Saddle, Wood, Late 1800s, 17 ½ x 34 In.
$156

Hindman

Slinky
The original Slinkys had sharp ends. Modern Slinkys with crimped ends are safer.

Toy, Jumper, Girl, Holding Rope, Wood Box Side, Clockwork, Jubilee, Ives, 11 In.
$1,320

Bertoia Auctions

Toy, Lamb, Wooly Sheep, Wood Wheels, Metal Frame, Pull Toy, 14 x 15 In.
$738

Stony Ridge Auction

Horse,	Rocking, Wood, Painted, Leather Ears, Inserted Seat Back, B. Crandall, c.1850, 22 x 41 In.	1875
Horse,	Running, Black Body, White Legs, Brown Saddle, Wood, Late 1800s, 17½ x 34 In..*illus*	156
Horse,	Running, Green Cart, Tin, Painted, 2 Wheels, Pull Toy, 6 In.	83
Horse,	Standing, Wood Base, Iron Wheels, Pull Toy, Germany, c.1900, 24 x 25 x 11 In.	121
Horse,	Standing, Wood, Painted, Multicolor, Black Hoofs, 36 x 36 In.	156
Horse,	Tan Paint, Milk Wagon, Articulated Cast Metal Legs, Early 1900s, 8 x 24 In.	330
Iron,	Swan Shape, Handle, Cast Iron, Green Paint, 1⅜ x 2¼ In.	68
Jeep,	Trailer, Pressed Steel, Red & Yellow, 4½ x 5½ x 11 In.	38
Joker,	Mechanical, Tin Lithograph, Multicolor, Windup, Billiken, Box, 8 In.	120
Jumper,	Girl, Holding Rope, Wood Box Side, Clockwork, Jubilee, Ives, 11 In. ....*illus*	1320
Jungle Jim Playset,	Tin Lithograph Structures, Plastic Figures, Series 1000, Marx, c.1960s .	780
Ladder,	Fire Escape, Sheet Steel, Wheels, Red, England, Salesman's Sample, 1910s, 61 x 37 x 12 In...	780
Lamb,	Wooly Sheep, Wood Wheels, Metal Frame, Pull Toy, 14 x 15 In.............*illus*	738
L'il Abner Dogpatch Band,	Tin Lithograph, Windup, Box, c.1945 ....*illus*	318
Magic Wheel,	Phenakistoscope, Disc Shape, J. Bradburn, New York, Late 1800s, 9½ x 9½ In..	1140
Mail Cart,	4 Wheels, 2 Irishmen, Sitting, Hand Painted, Mangold, 6 In.................*illus*	1200
Man On Bicycle,	High Wheel, With Dog, Painted, Windup, Gunthermann, 11 In. ....*illus*	3900
Merry-Go-Round,	Buster Brown Bread, 4 Pedal Horses, Wheels, Track, 72 In. ....*illus*	450
Mobile Space TV Unit,	Trailer, Rotating Camera Lenses, Tin, Battery, Nomura, Box, 10½ In. ..	2160
Model,	4-6-2 Locomotive, Brass, Wood, Glass Cased, 1900s, 11 x 31 x 12 In.	1000
Model,	Airplane, Biplane, Flying Circus, Yellow & Red, Curtiss Jenny, 7 x 20 x 31 In............	100
Model,	Tank, Brass, Treads, 16 Wheels, World War II Style, 4½ x 6 In.	224
Model,	Train, Steam Engine, Painted Wood, Iron Accents, c.1950, 26 In.	300
Monkey,	On Velocipede, Articulated Legs, Bell, Cast Iron, J. & E. Stevens, 8 x 8 x 4 In...*illus*	1353
Monkey,	Riding Tricycle, Peddling, Front Wheel Rotates, Rubber Tires, Hubley, 6½ In.	1920
Mother Goose,	Witch, Holding Rope, Multicolor, Cat, Windup, Marx, 9 In...................*illus*	540
Motorcycle,	Police Officer, Tin Lithograph, Balloon Tires, Marx, 9 In.	180
Motorcycle,	Red & Black, Yellow Driver, 2 Center Wheel, CKO, Penny Toy, 2¾ In.	570
Musicians,	Violinist, Harpist, Cellist, Round Base, Multicolor, Tin, Windup, 6 x 9½ In....*illus*	2176
Pail,	Sand, Bail Handle, Teddy Roosevelt Band, 1900s, 4¾ x 3½ In.	354
Pajama Bag,	Dog, Removable Head, Glass Eyes, Zipper, Mohair, Papier-Mache, France, 11 x 18 In. .	210
Pedal Car,	Airplane, Steel, Star Decals, 3 Wheels, Restored, Murray Steelcraft, 26 x 45½ x 35 In.	835
Pedal Car,	Fire Department, Ladder Truck, Pressed Steel, Rear Seat & Step, Bell, c.1935, 20 x 50 In....	510
Pedal Car,	Jeep, Utility, Wood, Pressed Steel, Steger, 21 x 17 x 43 In.	338
Pedal Car,	Tractor, John Deere, Model 4020, Ertl, 23 x 18 x 33 In..	492
Pedal Cart,	Horse Drawn, Stenciled Joy, Painted, Wood & Metal, 1800s, 22 x 47 In......*illus*	688
Piano,	Schoenhut, Germany, Child's, c.1950, 20 x 16 x 10 In.	24
Piano,	Woman, Plays, Turns Head, Clockwork, Secor, c.1885, 10 x 6 x 10 In. ....*illus*	1440
Pig,	Carved, Painted, Leather Covered Body & Ears, Pull Toy, 1800s, 10½ 14 In.	3444
Policeman,	Mechanical, Raises Arm, Sign Turns, Tin Lithograph, Marx, c.1930s, 5½ In.....*illus*	210
Puppet,	Pinocchio, Wood, Paper-Mache, Painted, Red, Yellow, Black, Pelham, UK, 26 In....	219
Rabbit,	Rises From Cabbage, Musical, Clockwork, Key Wind, Austria, c.1930, 7 x 6 x 7 In......*illus*	4248
Range Rider,	Cowboy, Horse, Lasso, Rocker Base, Tin Lithograph, Windup, Marx, 11 In.....	264
Robot,	Astronaut, Holds Walkie Talkie, Tin, Rubber Hands, Battery, Rosko-Nomura, Box, 14 In.	2400
Robot,	Earth Man, Walks, Shoots Ray Gun, Tin, Battery Operated, Nomura, Box, 9 In.	1020
Robot,	Electro Man, Arms & Legs Rotate, Chest Lights Up, Tin Litho, Battery, SY, Japan, Box, 10¾ In.	100800
Robot,	Mighty, Tin Lithograph, Battery Operated, Yoshiya, Japan, Box, 12 In. ....*illus*	1680
Robot,	Pug Robby, Piston Action, Remote Control, Gold Version, TN, Japan, Box, 9 In..........	1440
Robot,	Space Man, Walks, Helmet Lights Up, Gun Raises, Tin Lithograph, Cragstan, Box, 11 In.	1080
Robot,	Sparky Robot, Walks, Eyes Emit Rays, Tin, Windup, Ko, Japan, Box, 8 In..................	780
Robot,	Tin Lithograph, Directional Action, Battery, Yonezawa, Box, 11 In.	1680
Rocket Jet,	Nose Cone, Mounted, Wall Hanging & Light, Disneyland, 1990s, 11 In.	180
Rocket,	Sparkling, Z-18- The Moon, Tin, Spring Action Pull Toy, Marsan, Box, 9 In............	720
Room Box,	Castle, Fireplace, Limestone Floor, Wired, 15 x 18½ x 12 In.	250
Room Box,	Kitchen, Wallpaper, Cabinets, Cupboard, Table, 2 Chairs, 10 x 20 x 11 In.	86
Royal Carriage,	Figural Stagecoach, Yellow, Black & Red, Biscuit Tin, Pull Toy, Crawford, c.1930...	210
Rudy The Ostrich,	Standing, Pink, Blue, White Tail, Open Red Beak, Nifty, 9 In.................	780
Sailor,	Dancing, Tin, Clothing, Columbia On Cap, Windup, Lehmann, Box, 8 x 3 In....*illus*	540
Sheep,	Painted White, Carved, 4 Wheels, Pull Toy, Signed, Schifferl, 7 x 8¾ In.	290
Sheep,	Papier-Mache, Articulated Head, Tree Stump, Green Platform, Wheels, 7 x 10 x 3½ In.. *illus*	480

Toy, L'il Abner Dogpatch Band, Tin Lithograph, Windup, Box, c.1945
$318

White's Auctions

Toy, Mail Cart, 4 Wheels, 2 Irishmen, Sitting, Hand Painted, Mangold, 6 In.
$1,200

Bertoia Auctions

Legos

You can combine six eight-stud Lego blocks of the same color 102,981,500 different ways.

Toy, Man On Bicycle, High Wheel, With Dog, Painted, Windup, Gunthermann, 11 In.
$3,900

Bertoia Auctions

Toy, Merry-Go-Round, Buster Brown Bread, 4 Pedal Horses, Wheels, Track, 72 In.
$450

Chupp Auctions & Real Estate, LLC

TIP
Reproduction cast-iron toys and banks are heavier and thicker than the originals.

Toy, Monkey, On Velocipede, Articulated Legs, Bell, Cast Iron, J. & E. Stevens, 8 x 8 x 4 In.
$1,353

Morphy Auctions

Toy, Mother Goose, Witch, Holding Rope, Multicolor, Cat, Windup, Marx, 9 In.
$540

Bertoia Auctions

Toy, Musicians, Violinist, Harpist, Cellist, Round Base, Multicolor, Tin, Windup, 6 x 9 ½ In.
$2,176

Rachel Davis Fine Arts

Toy, Pedal Cart, Horse Drawn, Stenciled Joy, Painted, Wood & Metal, 1800s, 22 x 47 In.
$688

Hindman

Toy, Piano, Woman, Plays, Turns Head, Clockwork, Secor, c.1885, 10 x 6 x 10 In.
$1,440

Bertoia Auctions

TIP
Take batteries with you to toy sales if you plan to buy a battery-operated toy. Check to see if the toy really works.

Toy, Policeman, Mechanical, Raises Arm, Sign Turns, Tin Lithograph, Marx, c.1930s, 5 ½ In.
$210

Selkirk Auctioneers & Appraisers

Toy, Rabbit, Rises From Cabbage, Musical, Clockwork, Key Wind, Austria, c.1930, 7 x 6 x 7 In.
$4,248

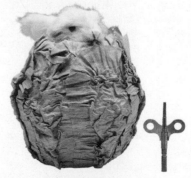

Soulis Auctions

T

Toy, Robot, Mighty, Tin Lithograph, Battery Operated, Yoshiya, Japan, Box, 12 In.
$1,680

Morphy Auctions

Toy, Sailor, Dancing, Tin, Clothing, Columbia On Cap, Windup, Lehmann, Box, 8 x 3 In.
$540

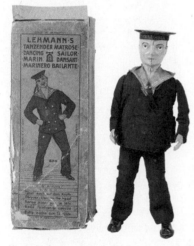

Morphy Auctions

Toy, Sheep, Papier-Mache, Articulated Head, Tree Stump, Green Platform, Wheels, 7 x 10 x 3½ In.
$480

Rachel Davis Fine Arts

Toy, Sled, Miniature, Yellow, Flower Designs, Painted, Late 1800s, 14 In.
$391

Pook & Pook

Toy, Soldier, 2 Bayonets, Articulated Lever, Painted, Fischer, Penny Toy, 3 In.
$780

Bertoia Auctions

Toy, Station Wagon, Black, Red & Blue Interior, 4 Doors, Asahi, Japan, c.1962, 12 In.
$660

Selkirk Auctioneers & Appraisers

Toy, Steam Engine, Brass Plate, Gauge, Cast Iron, Wood Base, Cretors & Co., 26 x 10 x 12 In.
$7,380

Morphy Auctions

Toy, Stove, Mt. Penn, Royal Esther, Nickel, Cast Iron, Salesman's Sample, 16 x 15 x 8 In.
$565

Hartzell's Auction Gallery Inc.

Fisher-Price
Fisher-Price toys were made of wood from 1931 to 1950. Some plastic was used in the 1950s. By 1964 the toys were almost entirely plastic.

Toy, Taxi, Yellow Cab, Driver, Orange & Black, Cast Iron, Arcade, c.1930, 4½ x 9 In.
$657

Jeffrey S. Evans & Associates

T

Toy, Theater, Punch & Judy, Biscuit Tin, A.M. Wilkin Ltd., England, c.1930, 8 In. $420

Bertoia Auctions

TIP

Replacement parts for many toys can be found on eBay ads.

Toy, Toonerville Trolley, Red, Blue & Brown, Tin, Windup, Fontaine Fox, 1922, 7¼ In. $240

Garth's Auctioneers & Appraisers

Sheep, White Wool, Glass Eyes, Leather Collar, Bell, Platform, 4 Wheels, Pull Toy, 1900s, 12 x 13 In.	1750
Skier, Woman, Standing, Painted, George Levy, Penny Toy, 2 In.	360
Sled, Maple, Maroon Ground, Yellow, Blue & White, Steel Runners, c.1900, 4 x 10 x 44 In.	192
Sled, Miniature, Yellow, Flower Designs, Painted, Late 1800s, 14 In. *illus*	391
Sled, Painted Panel, Horse, Wood, Border Lines, 1800s, 16 x 18¾ In.	400
Sled, Painted, Curved Base, Wood, Early 1900s, Child's, 37 x 16 In.	125
Sled, Red, Blue, Cast Iron, Steven Mfg., 8 In.	1020
Sled, Rocket, Red Paint, Stenciled, White Text, Wood, Early 1900s, 42 In.	344
Sled, Wood, Painted, Flowers, Yellow Ground, Victorian, Child's, 34 x 10½ In.	215
Sleigh, Wood, Arched Head & Foot Boards, Shaped Sides, Marked Hutton & Co., 15 x 30 In.	63
Soldier Set, Royal Mounted Artillery Wagon, Cannon, 6 Horses, 3 Men, Alymer, Spain, 1900s	108
Soldier, 2 Bayonets, Articulated Lever, Painted, Fischer, Penny Toy, 3 In. *illus*	780
Soldier, Wood, Carved, Painted Surface, Circular Base, England, 1800s, 14 x 5 In., Pair	1197
Space Race Car, Tin Lithograph, Friction, Yanoman, Box, 9 In.	1680
Space Racer, King Jet, No. 8, Tin, Plastic Dome, Friction, Taniguchi, Japan, Box, 12 In.	3000
Spaceship, Galactic Patrol, Lensman, Britannia II, Tomy, 1984, Box, 11 In.	150
Spaceship, No. X-5, Sparking, Tin, Friction, Modern Toys, Japan, Box, 12 In.	1200
Spaceship, X-2, Sparking, Tin, Friction, Modern Toys, Japan, Prewar, Box, 7½ In.	390
Station Wagon, Black, Red & Blue Interior, 4 Doors, Asahi, Japan, c.1962, 12 In. *illus*	660
Station, Facade, 2 Flags, France, Austria, Multicolor, Issmayer, 7 In.	570
Steam Accessory, Wind & Water Mill, Painted, Brick Style Base, Germany, 14 x 10 x 6 In.	315
Steam Engine, Brass Plate, Gauge, Cast Iron, Wood Base, Cretors & Co., 26 x 10 x 12 In. *illus*	7380
Steam Engine, Eureka, No. 32, Overtype, Safety Valve, Weeden, 15 x 7¾ x 4½ In.	384
Steam Shovel, Buddy L, Cletrac, Pressed Steel, T-Reproductions, 17 x 22 In.	923
Stove, Crescent, Grey Iron Casting Co., Accessories, Salesman's Sample, Box, 11½ x 9 In.	65
Stove, Mt. Penn, Royal Esther, Nickel, Cast Iron, Salesman's Sample, 16 x 15 x 8 In. *illus*	565
Stroller, Doll's, Wicker, Painted, Gilt, Swan Neck Crest, 4 Wheels, c.1900, 25 In.	328
Taxi, Coupe De Ville, Tin Lithograph, Driver, Painted, Multicolor, Gunthermann, 11 In.	2160
Taxi, Tricky, Yellow & Red, Limo LM0771, Tin, Windup, Marx, Box, 4½ In.	108
Taxi, Yellow Cab, Driver, 4 Seater, Painted, Black & Yellow, Arcade, 9 In.	660
Taxi, Yellow Cab, Driver, Orange & Black, Cast Iron, Arcade, c.1930, 4½ x 9 In. *illus*	657
Teddy Bears are also listed in the Teddy Bear category.	
Theater, Punch & Judy, Biscuit Tin, A.M. Wilkin Ltd., England, c.1930, 8 In. *illus*	420
Thresher, McCormick-Deering, Cast Iron, Arcade, 12 In.	210
Tool Box, Hinged Lid, Boys Favorite Tool Chests, Wood, Dovetailed, 14½ x 7½ x 5 In.	120
Toonerville Trolley, Red, Blue & Brown, Tin, Windup, Fontaine Fox, 1922, 7¼ In. *illus*	240
Tractor, Caterpillar, Diesel, Driver, Yellow, Cast Iron, Arcade, Box, 1930, 6 x 5 x 8 In. *illus*	2400
Tractor, Ford 7710, Blue, Pressed Steel, Rubber Tires, National Farm Toy Show, 1983, Box, Ertl. *illus*	242
Tractor, International Harvester, McCormick Farmall, Red, Die-Cast Metal, Box, Ertl. *illus*	963
Tractor, John Deere 730, Industrial Diesel Standard, Industrial Yellow, Plastic, Yoder Models *illus*	94
Tractor, John Deere 7020, Die Cast Metal, Central Ohio Farm Toy Show, 1990, Box *illus*	990
Tractor, John Deere WA-14, Open Station, Green, Metal, Rubber Tires, Eldon Trumm *illus*	4400
Tractor, Steam, Brass Boiler, Scratch Made, Wood & Metal, Early 1900s, 8 x 13 x 6 In.	375
Train Accessory, American Flyer, Newsstand, Darker Blue, 2 Windows, Door, Box	204
Train Accessory, American Flyer, Station, Red Suburban, Oak Park, S Gauge, Box	144
Train Accessory, Issmayer, Hill Climber, Trolley, Terminal, Tin Litho, Windup, O Gauge, 5 In. *illus*	3000
Train Accessory, Kibri, Shoeshine Man, Sitting Under Lamppost, Nigrin Sign, 6 In. *illus*	1200
Train Accessory, Lionel, Diner, Multicolor, 2 Stairs & Doors, Rectangular, Box *illus*	276
Train Accessory, Lionel, Switch Tower, Painted, Multicolor, Box	264
Train Accessory, Lionel, Tunnel, Brass, Hand Painted, Houses On Each Side, Box	96
Train Accessory, Marklin, Cafe Station, Hand Painted, Multicolor, 16 x 11 In.	11400
Train Accessory, Marklin, Crossing House, Halt Sign, Bell, Hand Painted, Multicolor, 5 In.	510
Train Accessory, Marklin, Freight Station, Blue Roof, Hand Painted, Gauge 2, 17 In. *illus*	3000
Train Accessory, Marklin, Guard House, Bell, Semaphore, Multicolor, 8 In.	480
Train Accessory, Marklin, Signal Bridge, 3 Lights, Stairs Each Side, 17 In.	660
Train Accessory, Marklin, Snowplow, 3 Passengers, Hand Painted, Multicolor, 2 In.	960
Train Accessory, Marklin, Station, Central-Bahnhof, Arched Windows, Turkish Flag, 14 In. *illus*	1560
Train Accessory, Marklin, Station, Central-Bahnhof, Onion Dome, No. 2140/1, c.1904, 22 In. *illus*	3000
Train Accessory, Marklin, Station, Gare Centrale, Multicolor, 3 Buildings, c.1902, 26 x 13 In. *illus*	18000
Train Accessory, Marklin, Station, Passenger, No. 2008, O Gauge, c.1912, 11 x 14 In. *illus*	7200

T

Toy, Tractor, Caterpillar, Diesel, Driver, Yellow, Cast Iron, Arcade, Box, 1930, 6 x 5 x 8 In.
$2,400

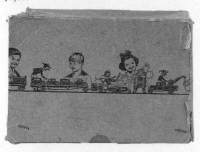

Morphy Auctions

Toy, Tractor, Ford 7710, Blue, Pressed Steel, Rubber Tires, National Farm Toy Show, 1983, Box, Ertl
$242

Girard Auction & Land Brokers, Inc.

Toy, Tractor, International Harvester, McCormick Farmall, Red, Die-Cast Metal, Box, Ertl
$963

Girard Auction & Land Brokers, Inc.

TIP
Remove the batteries from a stored toy.

Toy, Tractor, John Deere 730, Industrial Diesel Standard, Industrial Yellow, Plastic, Yoder Models
$94

Girard Auction & Land Brokers, Inc.

Toy, Tractor, John Deere 7020, Die Cast Metal, Central Ohio Farm Toy Show, 1990, Box
$990

Girard Auction & Land Brokers, Inc.

Toy, Tractor, John Deere WA-14, Open Station, Green, Metal, Eldon Trumm
$4,400

Girard Auction & Land Brokers, Inc.

Toy, Train Accessory, Issmayer, Hill Climber, Trolley, Terminal, Tin Litho, Windup, O Gauge, 5 In.
$3,000

Bertoia Auctions

Hot Wheels
The number on the base of a Hot Wheels car is the year it was copyrighted, not the year the car was made.

Toy, Train Accessory, Kibri, Shoeshine Man, Sitting Under Lamppost, Nigrin Sign, 6 In.
$1,200

Bertoia Auctions

Toy, Train Accessory, Lionel, Diner, Multicolor, 2 Stairs & Doors, Rectangular, Box
$276

Weiss Auctions

Toy, Train Accessory, Marklin, Freight Station, Blue Roof, Hand Painted, Gauge 2, 17 In.
$3,000

Bertoia Auctions

Toy, Train Accessory, Marklin, Station, Central-Bahnhof, Arched Windows, Turkish Flag, 14 In.
$1,560

Bertoia Auctions

Toy, Train Accessory, Marklin, Station, Central-Bahnhof, Onion Dome, No. 2140/1, c.1904, 22 In.
$3,000

Bertoia Auctions

TIP

If you want to use your old sled, yet keep it in the best possible condition as a collectible, coat it with a liquid furniture wax, then buff it, then a few days later coat it with paste furniture wax. Even the metal can be waxed after you remove the rust—and the waxing should make the sled slide even faster.

Toy, Train Accessory, Marklin, Station, Gare Centrale, Multicolor, 3 Buildings, c.1902, 26 x 13 In.
$18,000

Bertoia Auctions

Toy, Train Accessory, Marklin, Station, Passenger, No. 2008, O Gauge, c.1912, 11 x 14 In.
$7,200

Bertoia Auctions

Train Car, American Flyer, Chemical Tank, Green, Satin Patina, Stairs, Gilbert, Box	216
Train Car, American Flyer, Locomotive & Tender, New York Central, Box	144
Train Car, Bing, Schlitz Beer, Black & Yellow, Lithograph, 5 In.	450
Train Car, Buddy L, Boxcar, Outdoor Railroad, Red, Steel, Couplers, Decals, 22 In.	324
Train Car, Ernst Plank, Locomotive, Live Steam, Attached Tender, Multicolor, 5 In.	660
Train Car, Lionel, Caboose, Rescue Unit, U.S.M.C., Box	456
Train Car, Lionel, Pennsylvania, Dual Motors, Yellow Stripes, Black Ground, Decals, Box	1860
Train Car, Lionel, Tender, Pennsylvania, Silver Letters, Black Ground, 1950, Box	252
Train Car, Locomotive & Coal Car, Brass Sunset Model, Gresley A-4 Mallard, 12½ x 7¼ In...*illus*	1416
Train Car, Marklin, Crane, Wrecking Ball, Hand Painted, Multicolor, c.1908, 9 In. ..... *illus*	11400
Train Car, Marklin, Locomotive & Tender, Clockwork, Hand Painted, Multicolor, 7 In.*illus*	1320
Train Car, Marklin, Locomotive & Tender, Stork Leg Wheel, Hand Painted, 6 In.	1920
Train Car, Marklin, Veranda, Hand Painted, Multicolor, c.1904, 5 In. *illus*	3900
Train Set, Marklin, Locomotive & Tender, Clockwork, Hand Painted, Red & Black, 12 In.	9000
Train, Carette, Locomotive & Tender, Multicolor, 8 Wheels, 6 In.	1560
Train, Ernst Plank, Electric, Leipzig Sign, Hand Painted, Multicolor, c.1895, 7 In. *illus*	4800
Train, Karl Bub, Circus, 5 Cars, Multicolor, Track, Animals, 5-In. Locomotive	3900
Train, Lionel, Engine, Santa Fe Model, Red, Silver, Yellow *illus*	316
Train, Lionel, Locomotive, Lackawanna, Fairbanks-Morse Trainmaster, c.1950	210
Train, Marklin, Electric, Hand Painted, Multicolor, 4 Wheels, c.1904, 9 In.	10800
Train, Pratt & Letchworth, Locomotive, 6 Wheels, Painted, Multicolor, Clockwork, 9 In.	1920
Tram, 2 Gondolas, Flags, Steam Accessory, Painted, Doll & Co., 15 x 4 x 13 In.	608
Tram, Rack, Railway, Tunnel, Lithograph, Windup, Schumann, 4 In.	2040
Trolley, Belt Line 1492, Wood, Tin, Bench Seats, Old Paint, Spoke Wheels, c.1900, 12 x 28 In.	750
Trolley, Double-Decker, Yellow, People In Window, Windup, England, 5 In.	1020
Trolley, Electric, Pay As You Enter, Yellow & Green, Electric, Bing, 8 In.	1440
Trolley, Horse Drawn, 2 Horses, Hand Painted, Clerestory At Top, Hull & Stafford, 13 In.	1140
Trolley, Marklin, Electric Tramway, Hand Painted, Multicolor, c.1904, 6 In. *illus*	18000
Trolley, Municipal Tramways, Double-Decker, Electric Headlights, Bing, 9 In.	3600
Trolley, Painted, CR, Made In France, Charles Rossignol, Penny Toy, 3 In.	480
Trolley, Sliding Doors, Multicolor, Figures In Window, Windup, Orobr, 4 In.	1680
Trolley, United Electric Tramways, Double-Decker, Yellow & Red, No Roof, Windup, 5 In.	1920
Truck, Auto Transport, Red Trailer, 2 Cars, Yellow & Blue, Marx, c.1930s, 22 In.	210
Truck, Circus, Red, Driver, Platform Roof, Cage, Lion, Kenton Overland, c.1920s, 4 x 7 In.....*illus*	570
Truck, Dump, Green Cab, Red Dump Body, Pressed Steel, Wyandotte, c.1930s, 4 x 11½ In..	210
Truck, Inter City Delivery Service, Tin Lithograph, Marx Lumar, c.1950s, 16 In. ....*illus*	48
Truck, Pickup, Firecracker, Red, Action Figure, Mask, Kenner, Box, 1986	324
Truck, Railway Express, Pressed Steel, Gate, Buddy L, c.1920s, 24½ x 9 x 12 In. ....*illus*	500
Truck, Stake, Freeport Motor Express, Red & White, Steel, Structo, 13 In.	48
Truck, Tanker, Hess, Decals, Marx, Box, 1964	3240
Trunk, Doll's, Leather & Brass, Brown Leather Exterior, Trim, Blue Silk, Lithographed, 1800s, 6 In.	75
Trunk, Doll's, Wood, Dome Top, Stenciled Paper, Metal Mounts, Leather Handles, 11 x 16 In.	23
Trunk, Dome Top, Wood, Metal Covered, Leather Handles, Late 1800s, 16½ x 9½ In..*illus*	108
Van, Delivery, AHA, Driver, Bench Seat, Green Wheels, Red & Yellow, Lehmann, 5½ In	390
Vehicle, Live Steam, Stenciled Boston, Rubber Tubing, Green Paint, 15 x 5 x 5 In........*illus*	1440
Wagon, Black Mule, Red Frame, Cast Steel, 2 Wheels, Hubley, 1900s, 5 x 10 In.	420
Wagon, Circus, Man, Horses, Bears, Royal Circus, Cast Iron, Hubley, 9 x 16 x 3½ In. ..*illus*	313
Wagon, Express, Wood, 40 In.	600
Wagon, Farm, Anniversary Special, Wood, Metal Wheels, John Deere, 20 x 18 x 39 In.	246
Wagon, Horse Drawn, Carved, Painted, Folk Art, Early 1900s, 12 In.	88
Wagon, Horse Drawn, Rich Milk & Cream, 4 Wood Milk Bottles, Pull Toy, 1920, 27 In. *illus*	216
Wagon, Horse Drawn, U.S. Mail, Federal Shield, Tin Lithograph, Pull Toy, 12 In.	148
Wagon, Pine, Brown Wash, Yellow Pinstripes, Iron Spoke Wheels, Victorian, c.1890, 16 x 10 In.	560
Wagon, Red, Oval Bed, Art Deco Wheel Covers, c.1950, 7 x 40 In.	330
Wagon, Tin, Wood, Painted, Iron Wheels, Pull Handle, 1800s, 16 x 30 x 18 In.	254
Wagon, Wagner Coaster, Wood, Wagner Mfg. Co., Cedar Falls, Iowa, 16 x 38 x 14 In.....*illus*	531
Wagon, Water Tanker, Horse Drawn, Tin, Hand Painted, Bing, 16 In.	1020
Wheelbarrow, Oak, Pine, Chamfered Edges, Steel Tire, Red Paint, Child's, c.1900, 19 x 18 x 41 In.	180
Wheelbarrow, Painted, Wood, Stenciled Horse, c.1900, 28 In.	50
Wheelbarrow, Pressed Steel, Red Paint, Wood Frame, Metal Wheels, Daton Mfg., 1930s, 31 In..	47

Toy, Train Car, Locomotive & Coal Car, Brass Sunset Model, Gresley A-4 Mallard, 12½ x 7¼ In.
$1,416

Soulis Auctions

The First Roller Skates
The four-wheel roller skate was made in 1863. It was invented by James L. Pimpton, a Massachusetts inventor.

Toy, Train Car, Marklin, Crane, Wrecking Ball, Hand Painted, Multicolor, c.1908, 9 In.
$11,400

Bertoia Auctions

Toy, Train Car, Marklin, Locomotive & Tender, Clockwork, Hand Painted, Multicolor, 7 In.
$1,320

Bertoia Auctions

Toy, Train Car, Marklin, Veranda, Hand Painted, Multicolor, c.1904, 5 In.
$3,900

Bertoia Auctions

T

Toy, Train, Ernst Plank, Electric, Leipzig Sign, Hand Painted, Multicolor, c.1895, 7 In.
$4,800

Bertoia Auctions

TIP
Keep lead soldiers away from fresh paint, oak and other fresh wood, paper, and cardboard. All of these emit acidic vapors that attack the lead and cause corrosion.

Toy, Train, Lionel, Engine, Santa Fe Model, Red, Silver, Yellow
$316

Donley Auctions

Toy, Trolley, Marklin, Electric Tramway, Hand Painted, Multicolor, c.1904, 6 In.
$18,000

Bertoia Auctions

Toy, Truck, Circus, Red, Driver, Platform Roof, Cage, Lion, Kenton Overland, c.1920s, 4 x 7 In.
$570

Selkirk Auctioneers & Appraisers

Toy, Truck, Inter City Delivery Service, Tin Lithograph, Marx Lumar, c.1950s, 16 In.
$48

Selkirk Auctioneers & Appraisers

Toy, Truck, Railway Express, Pressed Steel, Gate, Buddy L, c.1920s, 24½ x 9 x 12 In.
$500

Potter & Potter Auctions

TIP
Old metal toy trucks were made of iron or tin, not brass or aluminum, the metals favored by some reproductions.

Toy, Trunk, Dome Top, Wood, Metal Covered, Leather Handles, Late 1800s, 16 ½ x 9 ½ In.
$108

Jeffrey S. Evans & Associates

Toy, Vehicle, Live Steam, Stenciled Boston, Rubber Tubing, Green Paint, 15 x 5 x 5 In.
$1,440

Morphy Auctions

Toy, Wagon, Circus, Man, Horses, Bears, Royal Circus, Cast Iron, Hubley, 9 x 16 x 3 ½ In.
$313

Wiederseim Auctions

Toy, Wagon, Horse Drawn, Rich Milk & Cream, 4 Wood Milk Bottles, Pull Toy, 1920, 27 In.
$216

White's Auctions

Toy, Wagon, Wagner Coaster, Wood, Wagner Mfg. Co., Cedar Falls, Iowa, 16 x 38 x 14 In.
$531

Hindman

Toy, Wheelbarrow, Wood, Yellow Painted Horses, c.1880, 9 ½ x 33 In.
$120

Jeffrey S. Evans & Associates

Toy, Woman, Maid Chasing Mouse With Broom, Painted, Issmayer, Germany, 7 In.
$660

Bertoia Auctions

Toy, Zeppelin, Pressed Steel, Akron On Side, Steelcraft, Pull Toy, 1920, 7 x 25 x 6 In.
$688

Wiederseim Auctions

T

Tramp Art, Cabinet, Hanging, Hinged, Heart Shape Door, Carved, c.1900, 16¾ x 14 x 5 In.
$328

Pook & Pook

Tramp Art, Frame, Crown Of Thorns, Crest, Extended Corners, 22 x 22 x 4½ In.
$384

Rachel Davis Fine Arts

Trench Art, Vase, Brass, 105 mm Shell, Ruffled Rim, Shoulders, Footed, c.1945, 12¾ In., Pair
$144

Milestone Auctions

Wheelbarrow, Wood, Yellow Painted Horses, c.1880, 9½ x 33 In. .... *illus*	120
Woman, Maid Chasing Mouse With Broom, Painted, Issmayer, Germany, 7 In. .... *illus*	660
Woman, Old Dutch, Cast Iron, Painted, Multicolor, Pull Toy, Hubley, 9 In.	2160
Yogi Bear, Hopping, Tin Lithograph, Windup, Linemar, Box, 1961, 4 x 3 In........................	525
Zeppelin, Pressed Steel, Akron On Side, Steelcraft, Pull Toy, 1920, 7 x 25 x 6 In........... *illus*	688

TRAMP ART

Tramp art is a form of folk art made since the Civil War. It is usually made from chip-carved cigar boxes. Examples range from small boxes and picture frames to full-sized pieces of furniture. Collectors in the United States started collecting it about 1970, and examples from other countries, especially Germany, were imported and sold by antiques dealers.

Box, Wall, Chip Carved, Stacked Hearts, Stars, Shelf, Drawer, 6-Sided Mirror, 42 x 12 x 5 In.	354
Cabinet, Hanging, Hinged, Heart Shape Door, Carved, c.1900, 16¾ x 14 x 5 In............. *illus*	328
Cabinet, Spice, Pine, Chip Carved, Flowers, Star Flowers, 9 Drawers, c.1915, 18 x 8 x 3 In....	390
Dresser Box, Chip Carved, Green Felt Panels, 2 Drawers, Lion Pulls, 5½ x 10 x 6 In.	148
Dresser Box, Heart & Shield Design, Red, Green, Brown, Rectangular, c.1900, 7¾ x 16 In.	139
Dresser, Carved, Round Mirror, 4 Drawers, Child's, 1800s, 21½ x 11½ x 33 In....................	295
Frame, Chip Carved, Applied Pinecones & Acorns, 5 Layers, 27 x 22 In.	105
Frame, Crown Of Thorns, Crest, Extended Corners, 22 x 22 x 4½ In.......................... *illus*	384
Mirror, Heart Shape, 2 Drawers, Kissing Doves, John Zadzora, 28 x 16 In.......................	848
Shelf, 6 Stepped Pyramids, Hanging Hooks, Carved Slat Apron, c.1900, 7½ x 20 In.	411
Shelf, Hanging, A-Frame, 3 Shelves, Chip Carved, Mirror Insets, 29½ x 30½ In.................	185
Stand, Drawer, Chip Carved, Square Base, Old Black Paint Over Red, 33 x 14½ x 13½ In..	250

TRAP

Traps for animals may be handmade. One of the most unusual is the mousetrap made so that when the mouse entered the trap, it was hit on the head with a mallet. Other traps were commercially manufactured and often are marked with the name of the manufacturer. Many traps were designed to be as humane as possible, and they would trap the live animal so it could be released in the woods.

Mouse, Wire, Die-Pressed Tin, Oval, Open End, Spring Trap, Maine, c.1900, 5 x 8 x 6 In.	240
Wasp, Glass, Beehive Shape, Purple Glass, Wire Hanger, 3 Knobs On Bottom, 5⅛ x 3¾ In.	15

TREEN, *see Wooden category.*

TRENCH ART

Trench art is a form of folk art made by soldiers. Metal casings from bullets and mortar shells were cut and decorated to form useful objects, such as vases. Coins and other things were used to make jewelry.

Ashtray, Brass, Tab Handle, Slanted Opening, 40 mm Shell, 5 x 4½ In.	30
Brass Knuckles, Wood Handle, U.S. Military, World War I, 2½ x 4 In.	130
Shell Casing, Memorial, Sword, Helmet, Leaves, Ruffled Rim, Inscribed, Reims, 13¾ In. ..	200
Shell Casing, Stylized U.S. Seal, Shield On Reverse, Leaves, Crimped Base, 1917, 8¾ In......	144
Vase, Brass, 105 mm Shell, Ruffled Rim, Shoulders, Footed, c.1945, 12¾ In., Pair....... *illus*	144

TRIVET

Trivets are now used to hold hot dishes. Most trivets of the late nineteenth and early twentieth centuries were made to hold hot pressing irons. Iron or brass reproductions are being made of many of the old styles.

Brass, Wood Handle, Hairy Paw Feet, Copper Underlay, Brass, Germany, 13 In.	311
Silver Plate, Rococo Style, Tapering Legs, Christofle, 3½ x 13 In. .... *illus*	250
Wrought Iron, Snake Handle, Ring, 4-Footed, 1800s, 23¼ x 11 In............................. *illus*	63

TRUNK

Trunks of many types were made. The nineteenth-century sea chest was often handmade of unpainted wood. Brass-fitted camphorwood chests were brought back from the Orient. Leather-covered trunks were popular from the late eighteenth to mid-nineteenth centuries. By 1895, trunks were covered with canvas or decorated sheet metal. Embossed metal coverings were used from 1870 to 1910. By 1925, trunks were covered with vulcanized fiber or undecorated metal. Suitcases are listed here.

Campaign, Camphorwood, Brass Bound, Brown, 2 Handles, 1800s, 16 x 35 x 16 In.....*illus*	1220
Campaign, Molded Edge Top, Brass Handles, Hasp & Lock, Bracket Base, 1800s, 18 x 33 x 17 In.	819
Camphorwood, Hinged Lid, Brass Fittings, Iron Handles, 1800s, 20 x 41 In.	688
Camphorwood, Hinged Lid, Brassbound, Deer, Hearts & Flowers, 1800s, 11 x 24 x 12 In.	497
Camphorwood, Hinged Lid, Brassbound, Iron Handles, 1800s, 17 x 37 In.	813
Dome Top, Hinged Lid, Pine, Dovetailed Case, Canted Sides, Iron Hardware, c.1815, 15 x 26 x 13 In.	156
Dome Top, Hinged Lid, Wood, Slatted, Padlock, Embossed, Fitted Tray, 32 x 18 x 21 In.	35
Dome Top, Leather, Geometric Patterns, Iron Binding, Spain, 1600s, 18 x 39 x 20 In.	594
Dome Top, Wood, Iron Straps, Old Green Paint, Marked, Martin Fischer, 1868, 24 x 33 In.	330
Foot Locker, Metal Hinges, Red Cross Stenciling, Wood, Fisher-Price, 1940s, 17 x 30 In...*illus*	300
Louis Vuitton, Bowl Shape Bag, Leather, Brown Paint, 16 x 15 x 7 In.	344
Louis Vuitton, Garment Bag, Canvas, LV Monogram, Hanger, Leather Tag NLD, 49 x 33 In.	780
Louis Vuitton, Garment Bag, Coated Canvas, Monogram, Leather Trim, Folds, 42 x 23 In.	460
Louis Vuitton, Garment Bag, Monogram Canvas, Top Handle, 22 x 15 x 23 In. ....*illus*	450
Louis Vuitton, Steamer, Monogram Print, Iron & Wood Bands, c.1930s, 13 x 39 x 21 In.	5400
Louis Vuitton, Suitcase, Alzer 60, Hard Side, Monograms, Leather Handle, LV Label, 28 x 19 In.	2125
Louis Vuitton, Suitcase, Canvas, Double Zip, 2 Buckles, Handle, 21 x 31 x 10 In..........*illus*	726
Louis Vuitton, Suitcase, Hard Sides, Fabric Straps & Shield, 1950s, 7 x 19 x 24 In. ......*illus*	1310
Louis Vuitton, Suitcase, LV Canvas, Orange Band, Casters, 26 x 29 In.	123
Louis Vuitton, Suitcase, Mesh Window, Flap, Ventilation Holes, Brass Grommet, 13 1/2 x 18 x 10 In.	366
Louis Vuitton, Suitcase, Monogram, Red Stripe, Black Wood Base, 9 1/2 x 20 x 19 1/2 In.*illus*	2400
Louis Vuitton, Suitcase, Monogram, Stratos 60, Leather Trim, 16 3/4 x 23 3/4 x 7 1/2 In.	677
Mark Cross, Train Case, Hinged Lid, Crocodile Leather, Black, 3 Locks, 1950, 8 x 29 x 15 In.. *illus*	781
Pine, Immigrant's, Flowers, Blue Ground, Iron Straps, Dated 1866, 22 x 28 In.............*illus*	932
Pine, Iron Straps, Square Feet, 15 x 30 x 20 In.	244
Steamer, Doll's, Blue, Metal, Brass Plated Corners, Railroad Stickers, 1950s, 9 x 16 x 9 In..*illus*	30
Steamer, Dome Top, Hinged Lid, Metal Edge, Wood Band, Gilt Lock, 33 x 36 1/2 x 22 In.*illus*	748
Steamer, Goyard, Cloth On Wood, Leather Edges, Metal Mounts, Label, Paris, 1800s, 40 x 22 In.	2775
Storage, Gilt Medallion Details, Red, Chinese, 12 1/2 x 30 1/2 x 21 In.	123
Storage, Hinged Lid, Carved Flowers, Brass Corners, Footed, Anna Hansdater, 1607, 17 x 22 x 15 In.	1037
Suitcase, Beech Plywood, Leather Handle, Enameled Steel, c.1935, 18 x 25 x 9 In.	219
Travel, Hinged Lid, Aluminum, Fabric Lined, Latch, England, 10 x 32 x 17 In., Pair	240
Wood, Painted, 3 Panels, Red Ground, Flowering Vases, Continental, 1878, 19 x 43 x 22 In.	720
Wood, R.H. Doolan, Van Tassell Terr., Cheyenne, Wyo., U.S.A., 1918, 36 x 20 x 12 1/2 In.	188

TUTHILL

Tuthill Cut Glass Company of Middletown, New York, worked from 1902 to 1923. Of special interest are the finely cut pieces of stemware and tableware.

Bowl, Rex, Signed, 3 x 8 In.	660
Ferner, Honeycomb & Engraved Primrose, 3-Footed, Signed, 3 1/2 x 7 In.	150

TYPEWRITER

Typewriter collectors divide typewriters into two main classifications: the index machine, which has a pointer and a dial for letter selection, and the keyboard machine, most commonly seen today. The first successful typewriter was made by Sholes and Glidden in 1874.

IBM, Service Selectric II, Correcting, Tan, Black Case, 7 x 20 x 15 In.	37

Trivet, Silver Plate, Rococo Style, Tapering Legs, Christofle, 3 1/2 x 13 In.
$250

Turner Auctions + Appraisals

Trivet, Wrought Iron, Snake Handle, Ring, 4-Footed, 1800s, 23 1/4 x 11 In.
$63

Pook & Pook

TIP

Mildew in your old trunk? New cure— special volcanic rocks. They attract and absorb odors.

Trunk, Campaign, Camphorwood, Brass Bound, Brown, 2 Handles, 1800s, 16 x 35 x 16 In.
$1,220

Rafael Osona Nantucket Auctions

Trunk, Foot Locker, Metal Hinges, Red Cross Stenciling, Wood, Fisher-Price, 1940s, 17 x 30 In.
$300

T

Morphy Auctions

Trunk, Louis Vuitton, Garment Bag, Monogram Canvas, Top Handle, 22 x 15 x 23 In.
$450

Leland Little Auctions

Trunk, Louis Vuitton, Suitcase, Canvas, Double Zip, 2 Buckles, Handle, 21 x 31 x 10 In.
$726

Ahlers & Ogletree Auction Gallery

Trunk, Louis Vuitton, Suitcase, Hard Sides, Fabric Straps & Shield, 1950s, 7 x 19 x 24 In.
$1,310

Charleston Estate Auctions

Trunk, Louis Vuitton, Suitcase, Monogram, Red Stripe, Black Wood Base, 9 ½ x 20 x 19 ½ In.
$2,400

Michaan's Auctions

Trunk, Mark Cross, Train Case, Hinged Lid, Crocodile Leather, Black, 3 Locks, 1950, 8 x 29 x 15 In.
$781

Leland Little Auctions

Trunk, Steamer, Doll's, Blue, Metal, Brass Plated Corners, Railroad Stickers, 1950s, 9 x 16 x 9 In.
$30

Garth's Auctioneers & Appraisers

Trunk, Steamer, Dome Top, Hinged Lid, Metal Edge, Wood Band, Gilt Lock, 33 x 36 ½ x 22 In.
$748

Stevens Auction Co.

Trunk, Pine, Immigrant's, Flowers, Blue Ground, Iron Straps, Dated 1866, 22 x 28 In.
$932

Pook & Pook

Privileg, Cella 165, Qwerty Keyboard, White & Black, Suitcase, Germany, 1970s, 3 x 12 x 12 In...	250
Remington, Qwerty Keyboard, Green Ground, Leather Case, 5 x 12 x 13 In.	78
Royal, Industrial, Black, Circular Keys, Gilt Letters, 1950s	225
Smith Premier, Qwerty Keyboard, Black& White, Suitcase, 1930s, 4 x 10 x 11 In.	300
Valentine, Plastic, Steel, Red, Rubber, Ettore Sottsass, Italy, 1969, 4½ x 13½ x 15½ In.*illus*	375

TYPEWRITER RIBBON TIN

Typewriter ribbon tins are now being collected. The lithographed tin containers have been used since the 1870s. Most popular with collectors are tins with pictorial graphics.

Allied, Seagull, Wave, Allied Carbon & Ribbon Mfg. Corp.	18
Madame Butterfly, Geisha, Red, Miller Bryant Pierce, 2⅝ In.	22
Silver Craft, Wreath, Silver, Black, Carter's Ink Co., Boston	15
Type Bar, Smith Corona Co., Black, Red, 2½ In.	10
Vertex, Roytype Ribbon, Royal Typewriter Co., N.Y., 2½ In.	14

UMBRELLA

Umbrella collectors like rain or shine. The first known umbrella was owned by King Louis XIII of France in 1637. The earliest umbrellas were sunshades, not designed to be used in the rain. The umbrella was embellished and redesigned many times. In 1852, the fluted steel rib style was developed and it has remained the most useful style.

Lucite, Black, Red & Silver, Wood Shaft, Silk Fabric, c.1850, 38 x 32 In.	39
Parasol Handle, Silver, Enamel, Hardstone, Marked, G.A.S, Vienna, c.1870, 4¼ In.	1625
Parasol, Bamboo Handle, Battenberg Lace, 26 x 29 In.	31
Parasol, Ivory Handle, Carved, Floral, Lace, Folding, 28 x 15½ In.	274
Parasol, Porcelain Handle, Painted, Couples, Cobalt Blue, Gilt Trim, Bamboo Pole, c.1880, 12 In.	120
Wood Handle, LV Monogram, Louis Vuitton, 36 In.*illus*	594

UNION PORCELAIN WORKS

Union Porcelain Works was originally William Boch & Brothers, located in Greenpoint, New York. Thomas C. Smith bought the company in 1861 and renamed it Union Porcelain Works. The company went through a series of ownership changes and finally closed about 1922. The company made a fine quality white porcelain that was often decorated in clear, bright colors. Don't confuse this company with its competitor, Charles Cartlidge and Company, also in Greenpoint.

Match Striker, Cream Ground, Circling Design, Molded, c.1800	261
Oyster Plate, 6 Wells, Painted, Light Pink, Shells, Gilt Trim, 1800s	580
Oyster Plate, 6 Wells, Shell, White Round, Gold Trim, Seaweed & Urchins, c.1879, 9½ In.	475

UNIVERSITY OF NORTH DAKOTA, *see North Dakota School of Mines category.*

VAL ST. LAMBERT

Val st lambert

Val St. Lambert Cristalleries of Belgium was founded by Messieurs Kemlin and Lelievre in 1825. The company is still in operation. All types of table glassware and decorative glassware have been made. Pieces are often decorated with cut designs.

Bowl, Centerpiece, Gilt, Shaped Stem, Rectangular Base, 1900s, 10 x 13 In.	250
Candlestick, Hexagonal Cup, Faceted Stem, 2 Knops, Hexagonal Foot, 9½ In., Pair	170
Candlestick, Teardrop, Pair, 9¾ x 5 In.	31
Coaster, Bottle, Brussels, Fruits In Center, Engraved Mark, 5¾ In.	24
Fruit Platter, Brussels, Fruits In Center, Sticker, 1⅛ x 13 In.	24
Rose Bowl, Chartreuse Cut To Clear, c.1908, 4¼ x 5 In.	150

Flea Market Tricks

Ever go to a flea market, buy something heavy, but not want to carry it around with you all day? No problem. Ask the dealer to keep it and then pay for it. Take a picture with your phone of both the item and the booth number sign. You will have a way to find the booth when it is time to pick up a purchase. Be sure the dealer's name is on your receipt.

Typewriter, Valentine, Plastic, Steel, Red, Rubber, Ettore Sottsass, Italy, 1969, 4½ x 13½ x 15½ In.
$375

Wright

TIP
Store parasols and umbrellas closed.

Umbrella, Wood Handle, LV Monogram, Louis Vuitton, 36 In.
$594

U
V

Auctions at Showplace, NYC

Van Briggle, Bowl, Gray Matte, Blue, Squat, Triangular Design, Signed, 1906, 3 ½ x 10 ¼ In.

$1,046

California Historical Design

Van Briggle, Vase, Bulbous Shape, Central Flower Head, 2 Bracketing Leaves, c.1930, 6 x 7 In.

$649

Soulis Auctions

Van Briggle, Vase, Climbing Bear, Mottled Persian Rose, Matte Glaze, c.1920, 15 ½ x 5 ½ In.

$2,250

Toomey & Co. Auctioneers

Vase, Full Ship, Etched, Clear, Square Rim, 9 ¼ In.	156
Wine, Hock, Cut To Clear, Blue, Emerald, Light Green, Pink, Purple, Yellow, 7 ⅝ In., 12 Piece	875

VAN BRIGGLE POTTERY

Van Briggle Pottery was started by Artus Van Briggle in Colorado Springs, Colorado, after 1901. Van Briggle had been a decorator at Rookwood Pottery of Cincinnati, Ohio. He died in 1904 and his wife took over managing the pottery. One of the employees, Kenneth Stevenson, took over the company in 1969. He died in 1990 and his wife, Bertha, and son, Craig, ran the pottery. She died in 2010. The pottery closed in 2012.

Bowl, Gray Matte, Blue, Squat, Triangular Design, Signed, 1906, 3 ½ x 10 ¼ In. .... *illus*	1046
Bowl, Tan & Green Matte Glaze, Carved, 1904, 3 ¼ x 5 ½ In.	1125
Lamp, Bedside, Blue Matte Glaze, Leaf, Handle, Round Base, c.1910s, 5 ¾ x 4 ½ x 4 In.	185
Vase, Blue Matte, Turquoise Glaze, Heart Shape Leaf, c.1950s, 6 ¾ x 3 In.	123
Vase, Bud, Triple Gourd, Joined At Bulbs, Brown Glaze, Turquoise Drip, Midcentury, 7 x 6 In.	175
Vase, Bulbous Shape, Central Flower Head, 2 Bracketing Leaves, c.1930, 6 x 7 In. .... *illus*	649
Vase, Climbing Bear, Mottled Persian Rose, Matte Glaze, c.1920, 15 ½ x 5 ½ In. .... *illus*	2250
Vase, Coneflower, Blue To Green Matte Glaze, 1920s, 12 ¼ x 5 ⅝ In.	585
Vase, Green Matte Glaze, Pinecone, Signed, 1905, 3 ¾ x 7 ½ In.	1722
Vase, Silvered Ground, Brown Lines, Rolled Rim, c.1908-11, 7 x 3 ½ In. .... *illus*	1500
Vase, Stylized Flowers, Green Matte Glaze, 1907, 8 x 2 ½ In.	1560

VASELINE GLASS

Vaseline glass is a greenish-yellow glassware resembling petroleum jelly. Pressed glass of the 1870s was often made of vaseline-colored glass. Some vaseline glass is still being made in old and new styles. The glass fluoresces under ultraviolet light. Additional pieces of vaseline glass may also be listed under Pressed Glass in this book.

Bucket, Wood Texture, Top Handle, 2 ¾ x 2 ½ In.	48
Butter, Cover, Daisy & Button, 5 x 7 ½ In.	96
Cake Stand, Daisy & Button, 5 x 9 ½ In. .... *illus*	120
Candlestick, Dolphin, Square 2-Step Base, Petal Socket, 1800s, 10 In., Pair	265
Candlestick, Hollow Stems, Hexagonal Base, Boston & Sandwich, 1800s, 7 ¾ x 4 In., 4 Piece.	527
Candlestick, Swirl & Panel Optic, Urn Shape Socket, Circular Foot, 1910s, 12 In., Pair	508
Vase, Opalescent Drippings, Lobed Base, 7 In.	88

VENETIAN GLASS, see Glass-Venetian category.

VENINI GLASS, see Glass-Venetian category.

Verlys VERLYS

Verlys glass was made in Rouen, France, by the Societe Holophane Français, a company that started in 1920. It was made in Newark, Ohio, from 1935 to 1951. The art glass is either blown or molded. The American glass is signed with a diamond-point-scratched name, but the French pieces are marked with a molded signature. The designs resemble those used by Lalique.

Bowl, Birds & Dragonflies, Frosted, Opalescent, 11 ½ In. .... *illus*	112
Bowl, Fish Design, Clear, Frosted, 2 Fishtail Handles, Marked, 4 ½ x 9 In.	180
Vase, Lance, Dusty Rose, Wide Mouth, Square Base, 8 In. .... *illus*	86

VERNON KILNS

Vernon Kilns was the name used by Vernon Potteries, Ltd. The company, which started in 1912 in Vernon, California, was originally called Poxon China. In

1931 the company was sold and renamed Vernon Kilns. It made dinnerware and figurines. It went out of business in 1953. The molds were bought by Metlox, which continued to make some patterns. Collectors search for the brightly colored dinnerware and the pieces designed by Rockwell Kent, Walt Disney, and Don Blanding. For more prices, go to kovels.com.

Bowl, Serving, Mushroom, Painted, Glazed, Fantasia, Walt Disney, 1940, 12 x 6 x 1 In. *illus*	144
Hawaiian Flower, Platter, 14 In.	110
Homespun, Carafe, Stopper, Handle, 8 ½ In.	6
Monterey, Teapot, Lid, White, Red & Blue Leaves, Footed, 7 ½ x 10 In....................	40

VERRE DE SOIE

Verre de soie glass was first made by Frederick Carder at the Steuben Glass Works from about 1905 to 1930. It is an iridescent glass of soft white or very, very pale green. The name means "glass of silk," and it does resemble silk. Other factories have made verre de soie, and some of the English examples were made of different colors. Verre de soie is an art glass and is not related to the iridescent, pressed, white carnival glass mistakenly called by its name. Related pieces may be found in the Steuben category.

Bottle, Blue Stopper, Signed, F. Carder, Steuben, 3 ¼ x 1 ¾ In.	171
Compote, Flared Rim, Footed, Carder, 5 x 8 ¼ In..	76
Compote, Lid, Red Cintra Pear Finial, Celeste Blue Baluster Stem, White Foot, Steuben, 6¾ x 4½ In.	512

VIENNA, *see Beehive category.*

VIENNA ART

Vienna Art plates are round lithographed metal serving trays produced at the turn of the twentieth century. The designs, copied from Royal Vienna porcelain plates, usually featured a portrait of a woman encircled by a wide, ornate border. Many were used as advertising or promotional items and were produced in Coshocton, Ohio, by J. F. Meeks Tuscarora Advertising Co. and H.D. Beach's Standard Advertising Co. Some are listed in Advertising in this book.

Plate, Young Woman, Profile, Red Cap, Long Brown Hair, Wood Frame, Gilt Gesso, 1905, 14½ In. .	113
Plate, Young Woman, Seated, Flower Crown, Red & Gilt Border, Square Frame, 15 In.	192

VILLEROY & BOCH POTTERY

Villeroy & Boch Pottery of Mettlach was founded in 1836 when two competing potteries merged. Francois Boch and his sons began making pottery in France in 1748. They moved to Mettlach in 1809 and merged with competitor Nicolas Villeroy in 1836. The firm made many types of wares, including the famous Mettlach steins. Collectors can be confused because although Villeroy & Boch made most of its pieces in the city of Mettlach, Germany, the company also had factories in other locations. The dating code impressed on the bottom of most pieces makes it possible to determine the age of the piece. Additional items, including steins and earthenware pieces marked with the famous castle mark or the word *Mettlach*, may be found in the Mettlach category.

Bowl, Garden, Fruit & Pink Flowers, Green Rim, Square, 1998, 8 ½ In., 12 Piece..................	500
Bowl, Scalloped Rim, Black & White Pastoral Scene, Flowers, Yellow Border, 2000s, 2 x 12 In. *illus*	100
Cake Plate, Black & White Pastoral Scene, Flowers, 2000s, 11 In. .... *illus*	63
Charger, Stick Spatter, German Quote, Red Rim, White Ground, c.1910, 15 ½ In. .... *illus*	42
Plate, Bread & Butter, Fruit, Pink Flowers, Square, 1998, 6 ¼ In., 12 Piece	469
Sandwich Tray, Black & White Pastoral Scene, Flowers, 2000s, 13 x 6 In.................... *illus*	100
Terrine, Hand Mold, Wild Boar, Oak Branches Handle, Jean Paul Gourdon, 14 x 30 x 10 In. .	3050
Tureen, Glazed Stoneware, Figural Knob, Handles, c.1920, 9 x 13 x 11 In............................	282

Van Briggle, Vase, Silvered Ground, Brown Lines, Rolled Rim, c.1908-11, 7 x 3 ½ In.
$1,500

Treadway

Vaseline Glass, Cake Stand, Daisy & Button, 5 x 9 ½ In.
$120

Woody Auction

Verlys, Bowl, Birds & Dragonflies, Frosted, Opalescent, 11 ½ In.
$112

White's Auctions

Verlys, Vase, Lance, Dusty Rose, Wide Mouth, Square Base, 8 In.
$86

Apple Tree Auction Center

U
V

VILLEROY & BOCH

Vernon Kilns, Bowl, Serving, Mushroom, Painted, Glazed, Fantasia, Walt Disney, 1940, 12 x 6 x 1 In.
$144

Weiss Auctions

TIP
You can cover up a small chip in an enamel or even a piece of porcelain with a bit of colored nail polish. It comes in almost every color now.

Villeroy & Boch, Bowl, Scalloped Rim, Black & White Pastoral Scene, Flowers, Yellow Border, 2000s, 2 x 12 In.
$100

Lion and Unicorn

Villeroy & Boch, Cake Plate, Black & White Pastoral Scene, Flowers, 2000s, 11 In.
$63

Lion and Unicorn

Villeroy & Boch, Charger, Stick Spatter, German Quote, Red Rim, White Ground, c.1910, 15 ½ In.
$42

Garth's Auctioneers & Appraisers

Villeroy & Boch, Sandwich Tray, Black & White Pastoral Scene, Flowers, 2000s, 13 x 6 In.
$100

Lion and Unicorn

Villeroy & Boch, Vase, Jasperware, Handles, Bulbous, Classical Figures, Round Foot, Late 1800s, 14 In., Pair
$2,375

Hindman

Volkmar, Pitcher, Green Matte Glaze, Raised V Logo, Leon Volkmar, c.1905, 9 x 7 x 6 In.
$125

Toomey & Co. Auctioneers

Volkmar, Vase, Pillow, Barbotine, Man & Woman, Marked, CV, Paper Label, 9 ⅜ x 6 ¾ x 2 ½ In.
$195

Toomey & Co. Auctioneers

TIP
Restoring and reusing old things is the purest form of recycling.

U
V

Vase, Jasperware, Handles, Bulbous, Classical Figures, Round Foot, Late 1800s, 14 In., Pair *illus*	2375
Vase, Modern Designs, Lavender, Black, White, Mid 1900s, 10 ½ x 6 ¾ In.	281

VOLKMAR POTTERY

Volkmar Pottery was made by Charles Volkmar of New York from 1879 to about 1911. He was associated with several firms, including the Volkmar Ceramic Company, Volkmar and Cory, and Charles Volkmar and Son. He was hired by Durant Kilns of Bedford Village, New York, in 1910 to oversee production. Volkmar bought the business and after 1930 only the Volkmar name was used as a mark. Volkmar had been a painter, and his designs often look like oil paintings drawn on pottery.

VOLKMAR
Corona N.Y

Mug, Tankard Shape, Standard Glaze, Mottled Green, Brown, Yellow, Scroll Handle, Marked, 7 ¼ In.	62
Pitcher, Green Matte Glaze, Raised V Logo, Leon Volkmar, c.1905, 9 x 7 x 6 In. *illus*	125
Tile, Scenic, Trees By Stream, Green Tones, Earthenware, Molded V, c.1910, 8 x 8 In.	5000
Vase, Pillow, Barbotine, Man & Woman, Marked, CV, Paper Label, 9 ⅜ x 6 ¾ x 2 ½ In. *illus*	195

VOLKSTEDT

Volkstedt was a soft-paste porcelain factory started in 1760 by Georg Heinrich Macheleid at Volkstedt, Thuringia. Volkstedt-Rudolstadt was a porcelain factory started at Volkstedt-Rudolstadt by Beyer and Bock in 1890. Most pieces seen in shops today are from the later factory.

Figurine, Ballerina, Long Skirt, Multicolor Applied Flowers, Circular Base, 1900s, 9 In.	500
Figurine, Girl, Parrot & Lute, White Lace, Green Back, Feathers In Hair, Gilt Trim, 9 x 8 In. *illus*	407
Figurine, Man & 2 Women, Talking, Standing, Mirror, 1900s, 8 In. *illus*	250
Figurine, Man & Woman, Gilt, Man Has Pot & Spoon, Ens & Eckert, Marked, 6 In., Pair	125
Figurine, Parrots, Multicolor, White Tree Branch, Porzellanfabrik Karl Ens, 1919-45, 11 x 14 In.	625
Figurine, Woman, Yellow Lace Dress, Ermine Cape, Purple Lining, Pink Roses, 1900s, 8 In. *illus*	500
Group, 2 Parrots, Blue, Green, Yellow, On Flowering Branch, Karl Ens, 1919-45, 11 x 14 In. *illus*	625
Group, Dancing Couple, Man, Red Jacket, Woman, Yellow Skirt, Flowers, 1900s, 7 ¾ In.	138
Group, Grandmother's Birthday, Seated Older Woman, Young Couple, 3 Children, 16 x 22 In. *illus*	1652
Group, Woman, Dancer, White Lace Dress, Applied Flowers, Oval Base, Gilt, 1900s, 10 ½ In.	750

WADE

Wade pottery is made by the Wade Group of Potteries started in 1810 near Burslem, England. Several potteries merged to become George Wade & Son, Ltd., early in the twentieth century, and other potteries have been added through the years. The best-known Wade pieces are the small figurines called Whimsies. They were first were made in 1954. Special Whimsies were given away with Red Rose Tea beginning in 1967. The Disney figures are listed in this book in the Disneyana category.

WADE
Figures
c. 1936+

Figurine, Angel Fish, Brown, Tan, Black, 3 ¼ x 4 In.	24
Figurine, Antiques Shop, S. Farthing, Whimsy-On-Why, Set 2, 1981, 1 ½ In. *illus*	10
Figurine, Barley Mow, Whimsey-On-Why, Set 1, No. 8, 1980	45
Figurine, Fox, Seated, Winking, Tan, Cream, Edward Hare Series, c.1997, 4 ½ In.	45
Figurine, Pony, Lying Down, White Glaze, 1950s, 1 ½ In.	7
Pitcher, Woodland Scene, Squirrel, Acorn, Green, 8 In.	70

WAHPETON POTTERY, *see Rosemeade category.*

WALL POCKET

Wall pockets were popular in the 1930s. They were made by many American and European factories. Glass, pottery, porcelain, majolica, chalkware, and metal wall pockets can be found in many fanciful shapes.

Folk Art, Mirrored, Horseshoe, Kissing Cockatoos, Multicolor, 2 Drawers, c.1880, 28 x 16 In. *illus*	3050
Teak, Carved, Half Shells, Engraved, Birds On Trees, Board Shape, Chinese, 1800s, 10 x 6 In., Pair	1220

Volkstedt, Figurine, Girl, Parrot & Lute, White Lace, Green Back, Feathers In Hair, Gilt Trim, 9 x 8 In.
$407

World Auction Gallery

Volkstedt, Figurine, Man & 2 Women, Talking, Standing, Mirror, 1900s, 8 In.
$250

Lion and Unicorn

Volkstedt, Figurine, Woman, Yellow Lace Dress, Ermine Cape, Purple Lining, Pink Roses, 1900s, 8 In.
$500

Lion and Unicorn

This is an edited listing of current prices. Visit **Kovels.com** to check thousands of prices from previous years and sign up for free information on trends, tips, reproductions, marks, and more.

W

Volkstedt, Group, 2 Parrots, Blue, Green, Yellow, On Flowering Branch, Karl Ens, 1919-45, 11 x 14 In.
$625

Lion and Unicorn

Volkstedt, Group, Grandmother's Birthday, Seated Older Woman, Young Couple, 3 Children, 16 x 22 In.
$1,652

Apple Tree Auction Center

TIP
Vintage watches should be cleaned regularly, probably once a year.

Wade, Figurine, Antiques Shop, S. Farthing, Whimsy-On-Why, Set 2, 1981, 1½ In.
$10

Wall Pocket, Folk Art, Mirrored, Horseshoe, Kissing Cockatoos, Multicolor, 2 Drawers, c.1880, 28 x 16 In.
$3,050

Rafael Osona Nantucket Auctions

Watch, Edmond Tompion, Swing Out, Verge Fusee, Silver Case, London, Pocket, c.1810, 2 In.
$286

White's Auctions

Watch, Elgin, 14K Gold, Guilloche Case, Engraved Lid, Roman Numerals, 1¾ x 2¼ In.
$622

Hartzell's Auction Gallery Inc.

Watch, Le Coultre, Lapel, 14K Gold, Hinged Pendant Ring, Enamel, Diamond & Pearl, Woman's
$480

Alderfer Auction Company

Watch, Longines, Open Face, 14K Gold, 21 Jewel, Art Deco, Pocket, 1¾ In.
$351

Thomaston Place Auction Galleries

Watch, Tiffany & Co., Minute Repeater, 18K Yellow Gold, No. 80338, White Enamel, Pocket
$6,958

Fontaine's Auction Gallery

WALLACE NUTTING *photographs are listed under Print, Nutting. His reproduction furniture is listed under Furniture.*

WALT DISNEY, *see Disneyana category.*

WALTER, *see A. Walter category.*

WARWICK

Warwick china was made in Wheeling, West Virginia, in a pottery working from 1887 to 1951. Many pieces were made with hand painted or decal decorations. The most familiar Warwick has a shaded brown background. The name *Warwick* is part of the mark and sometimes the mysterious word *IOGA* is also included.

Bowl, Child's, Animals, Dressed In Clothes, Red Band, Santone, c.1944, 2¼ x 5 In. 18
Pitcher, Hibiscus, Bud, Brown Tones, Molded Handle, 1900s, 7½ x 5 In. 35
Plate, 2 Fish, White, Floral Design, Pale Yellow Border, Gold Trim, 8 In. 48
Vase, Princetown, Crested, Flared Rim, Cream, W.H. Smith, 2⅜ In. 15

WATCH

Watches small enough to fit in a man's pocket were important in Victorian times. It wasn't until World War I that the wristwatch was used. All types of watches are collected: silver, gold, or plated. Watches are listed here by company name or by style. Wristwatches are a separate category in this book.

American Watch Co., Coin Silver Case, Jewel, Stem Set, Roman Numerals, Size 18, c.1909 132
Breguet, Astronomical Quarter, Repeating, 18K Gold, Pierre Benjamin Travernier, No. 2835, 2 In. 175000
Charles Oudin, Lapel, Gold, Off-Center Dial, Roman Numerals, Woman's, c.1830, 1 In. 594
Edmond Tompion, Swing Out, Verge Fusee, Silver Case, London, Pocket, c.1810, 2 In. *illus* 286
Elgin, 14K Gold, Guilloche Case, Engraved Lid, Roman Numerals, 1¾ x 2¼ In. .... *illus* 622
Elgin, Lapel, 14K Gold, White Face, Pink Center, Gold Hands, Woman's 480
Elgin, Presentation, 14K Yellow Gold, G.M. Wheeler, Pocket, 1896, 2¼ In. 2160
John Moncas, 18K Gold, Chain Fusee, Open Face, Roman Numerals, Floral Border, Liverpool, 2 In. . 3000
Le Coultre, Hunting Case, 18K Gold, Minute Repeating, Roman Numerals, GCF Freres, c.1890, 2 In. 6875
Le Coultre, Lapel, 14K Gold, Hinged Pendant Ring, Enamel, Diamond & Pearl, Woman's *illus* 480
Longines, Chronometer, Stainless Steel, Center Seconds, Silvered Dial, Stem Wind, 1945, 2 In.. 1500
Longines, Open Face, 14K Gold, 21 Jewel, Art Deco, Pocket, 1¾ In. .... *illus* 351
Longines, Open Face, Silver, Arabic Numerals, Manual Wind Movement, Pocket, 1½ In..... 163
Omega, Chronograph, Olympic, 18K Gold, Split Second, Arabic Numerals, Leather Case, 2½ In. 8750
Pendant, Silver, Enamel, Blue, 8 Green Leaves Around Dial, Art Deco, Woman's 167
Rolex, 18K White Gold, Datejust, Embossed Dial, Diamonds, Woman's, Box 7020
Theo. B. Starr, Open Face, 14K Gold, Arabic Numerals, Second Hand Dial, Pocket, 1¾ In. . 403
Tiffany & Co., Minute Repeater, 18K Yellow Gold, No. 80338, White Enamel, Pocket.... *illus* 6958
Trenton, Open Face, Gilt, Greek Key Border, Pocket, 2½ x 2 In. 88
Waltham, Gold Filled, 15 Jewel, White Enamel, 2-Dial Face, Pocket, 3 In. 63
Waltham, Hunting Case, 14K Gold, Multicolor, Arabic Numerals, Mahogany Box, 1½ In.... 938
Waltham, Open Face, 14K Gold, Riverside, Red Minute Track, A.M. Watch Co., 2 In. 1500
Waltham, Open Face, GCT, Metal Case, 24-Hour, Black Dial, Master Navigation, 2 In......... 406
Waltham, Open Face, Gold Filled, 21 Jewel, Pocket, c.1915 156
Waltham, Vanguard, Open Face, 23 Jewel, Railroad Dial, Size 16, Plated Chain, c.1953.... *illus* 330

WATERFORD

Waterford type glass resembles the famous glass made from 1783 to 1851 in the Waterford Glass Works in Ireland. It is a clear glass that was often decorated by cutting. Modern glass is being made again in Waterford, Ireland, and is marketed under the name Waterford. Waterford merged with Wedgwood in 1986 to form the Waterford Wedgwood Group. Most Waterford Wedgwood assets were bought by KPS Capital Partners of New York in 2009 and became part of WWRD Holdings. WWRD was bought by Fiskars in 2015 and Waterford is now a brand owned by Fiskars.

Watch, Waltham, Vanguard, Open Face, 23 Jewel, Railroad Dial, Size 16, Plated Chain, c.1953
$330

Main Auction Galleries, Inc.

Waterford, Bucket, Champagne, Millennium, Flared, Footed, 1900s, 10⅝ x 9¾ In.
$212

Fontaine's Auction Gallery

Waterford, Decanter, Ships, Diamond, Ball Shape Stopper, Squat Base, Signed, 10 x 7½ In.
$100

Greenwich Auction

W

Waterford, Paperweight, Flower Head, Yellow, Box, 5 In.
$62

Apple Tree Auction Center

Waterford, Pitcher, Diamond Cut, Country Club, Monogram, 9½ In.
$34

Hartzell's Auction Gallery Inc.

Watt, Rooster, Pitcher, No. 15, 5½ In.
$79

Ruby Lane

Watt Giveaways

Watt bowls were made as "giveaways" in big stores. Some pieces had printed words inside with the name of a company and phrases like "To a Good Cook."

Bowl, Marquise, Diamond, Flared Rim, Purple, Shelton, Box, 8 x 5 In.	62
Bucket, Champagne, Millennium, Flared, Footed, 1900s, 10⅝ x 9¾ In. ....._illus_	212
Chandelier, 10-Light, Drip Pan, Pendant Drops, Cut Glass, 2 Tiers, 1900s, 31 x 24 In.	2000
Compote, Diamond, Glass, Scalloped Rim, Round Base, 6 In.	56
Decanter, Ball Stopper, Diamond, 10½ In.	74
Decanter, Lismore, Cut Glass, Long Neck, Stopper, Late 1900s, 9¼ x 7¼ In.	145
Decanter, Ships, Diamond, Ball Shape Stopper, Squat Base, Signed, 10 x 7½ In. ....._illus_	100
Decanter, Stopper, Diamond, Knopped Neck, Round Base, 10 In.	98
Figurine, Clear, Woman Cradles Her Child In Arms, Etched In Base, 1900s, 7 In.	75
Glass, Rocks, Cut Glass, Acid Etched, 3¼ x 2¾ In., 8 Piece	75
Lamp, Cut Glass, 2 Parts, Diamond, Flared Rim, Domed Base, 1900s, 18¾ x 9½ In., Pair..	305
Paperweight, Flower Head, Yellow, Box, 5 In. ....._illus_	62
Paperweight, Seahorses, Standing, Clear, 7⅜ In., Pair	123
Pitcher, Diamond Cut, Country Club, Monogram, 9½ In. ....._illus_	34

WATT

Watt family members bought the Globe pottery of Crooksville, Ohio, in 1922. They made pottery mixing bowls and tableware of the type made by Globe. In 1935 they changed the production and made the pieces with the freehand decorations that are popular with collectors today. Apple, Starflower, Rooster, Tulip, and Autumn Foliage are the best-known patterns. Pansy, also called Rio Rose, was the earliest pattern. Apple, the most popular pattern, can be dated from the leaves. Originally, the apples had three leaves; after 1958 two leaves were used. The plant closed in 1965. Reproductions of Apple, Dutch Tulip, Rooster, and Tulip have been made. For more prices, go to kovels.com.

Apple, Baker, Lid, 3-Leaf	95
Apple, Bowl, 3-Leaf, 7½ In.	61
Apple, Creamer, 3-Leaf, No. 62, 4½ In.	55
Apple, Ice Bucket, Lid, 3-Leaf, 7 x 7½ In.	105
Apple, Mixing Bowl Set, 2-Leaf, No. 6, No. 7, No. 8, 3 Piece	58
Apple, Mixing Bowl, 3-Leaf, Ribbed, No. 5.	40
Apple, Pitcher, 3-Leaf, No. 17, 9 In.	80
Apple, Pitcher, 3-Leaf, Yellowware, No. 15, 5½ In.	29
Apple, Pitcher, 3-Leaf, Yellowware, No. 62	38
Pansy, Platter, Round, 14½ In.	85
Rooster, Pitcher, No. 15, 5½ In. ....._illus_	79
Starflower, Baker, No. 60, 6 x 2¼ In.	45
Starflower, Bowl, No. 74, Yellow Ground, 5 In.	45
Starflower, Pitcher, 5-Petal, No. 15, 5½ In.	75 to 84
Tear Drop, Casserole, 2½ Qt.	65
Tulip, Pitcher, No. 62, 12 Oz.	39

WAVE CREST

WAVE CREST WARE

Wave Crest glass is an opaque white glassware manufactured by the Pairpoint Manufacturing Company of New Bedford, Massachusetts, and some French factories. It was decorated by the C.F. Monroe Company of Meriden, Connecticut. The glass was painted in pastel colors and decorated with flowers. The name Wave Crest was used starting in 1892.

Ashtray, Pedestal, Scroll Mold, Gray Tones, Blue Flowers, Metal Base & Rim, 4 x 4 In.._illus_	125
Biscuit Jar, Silver Plate Lid, Swirl Mold, Yellow & White, Pink & Blue Flowers, Bail, 8 x 5 In.	120
Bonbon, Yellow Flowers, Pink & White Swirl Mold, Silver Plate Rim & Handle, 2 x 7 In._illus_	70
Dresser Box, Collars & Cuffs, Pink Lettering, Gilt Metal Collar, c.1900, 6 x 7½ In.	185
Dresser Box, Hinged Lid, Cream, Pink Flowers, Puff Mold, Metal Collar, 3¾ x 7 In.	150
Dresser Box, Hinged Lid, Egg Crate Mold, Green, Gilt, Opal Panel, Courting Scene, c.1900, 4 x 7 In.	595
Dresser Box, Hinged Lid, Egg Crate Mold, Flowers, Gilt Collar, Lion's Head Feet, 6½ In. ...._illus_	360

W

Wave Crest, Ashtray, Pedestal, Scroll Mold, Gray Tones, Blue Flowers, Metal Base & Rim, 4 x 4 In.
$125

Woody Auction

Wave Crest, Bonbon, Yellow Flowers, Pink & White Swirl Mold, Silver Plate Rim & Handle, 2 x 7 In.
$70

Woody Auction

Wave Crest, Dresser Box, Hinged Lid, Egg Crate Mold, Flowers, Gilt Collar, Lion's Head Feet, 6 ½ In.
$360

Woody Auction

Wave Crest, Ferner, Seafoam Mold, Cobalt Blue, Pink Flowers, Gilt Metal Feet, 5 x 8 In.
$450

Woody Auction

Wave Crest, Holder, Whiskbroom, Yellow, Flowers, Embossed Scrolls, Gilt Metal Cherub Frame, 8 x 8 In.
$400

Woody Auction

Wave Crest, Humidor, Hinged Lid, Scroll Mold, Pink, White Panels, Blue Flowers, Square, 6 ½ x 5 In.
$210

Woody Auction

Wave Crest, Letter Holder, Egg Crate Mold, Cream, Light Blue Flowers, Beaded Metal Collar, 4 x 5 ¾ In.
$150

Woody Auction

W

TIP

When restoring antiques or houses, take pictures before and after for records of colors used, exact placement of decorative details, and insurance claims.

Weapon, Armor, Full Suit, Etched, Molded, Oak Platform, Victorian, 76 In. $3,600

Morphy Auctions

Weapon, Blackjack, Ropework, Baleen, Twisted Shaft, Weighted Ends, 1800s, 11½ In. $500

Eldred's

Dresser Box, Hinged Lid, Herons Over Water, Multicolor Panels, Flowers, Gilt, 4 x 7 In.	594
Dresser Box, Hinged Lid, Swirl Mold, Pink, Blue Flowers, Metal Collar & Feet, 6¼ x 7 In.	240
Dresser Box, Puff Mold, Cream Tones, Pink & Green Flowers, 3 x 7 In.	60
Ferner, 8-Sided, Yellow To Green Ground, Pink Flowers, Metal Collar, 4½ x 8 In.	108
Ferner, Seafoam Mold, Cobalt Blue, Pink Flowers, Gilt Metal Feet, 5 x 8 In. *illus*	450
Holder, Whiskbroom, Yellow, Flowers, Embossed Scrolls, Gilt Metal Cherub Frame, 8 x 8 In. *illus*	400
Humidor, Hinged Lid, Scroll Mold, Pink, White Panels, Blue Flowers, Square, 6½ x 5 In. *illus*	210
Jewelry Box, Cameo Carved Wave Crest, Sailboat & Trees, 2 x 4 In.	850
Jewelry Box, Hinged Lid, Shell Mold, Pink Flowers, Metal Collar, Banner Mark, 2¾ x 3 In.	84
Jewelry Box, Swirl Mold, Multicolor, Flowers, 3½ x 5½ In.	80
Letter Holder, Egg Crate Mold, Cream, Light Blue Flowers, Beaded Metal Collar, 4 x 5¾ In. *illus*	150
Plaque, Embossed Scroll, Blue Tone, Pink Orchids, Gilt Metal Frame, 10 x 8 In.	650
Plaque, Scrolls, Mold, Scenic Medallion, Cherub, Pink, White, Blue, Gilt Metal Frame, 16 x 12 In.	2500
Powder Jar, Hinged Lid, Pink Flowers, Swirl, Gilt Metal Collar, 5 x 5⅞ In.	71
Sugar Shaker, Pink Dogwood Blossoms, Helmschmeid Swirl, Silvertone Lid, 3 In.	25
Vase, Bottle Shape, Opal, Light Blue To White, Pink Flowers, Gilt Collar & Handles, c.1900, 17 In.	447
Vase, Opal, Pink Flower Panel, Landscape, Gilt Collar, Handles, Banner Mark, c.1900, 12 In.	1012
Tobacco Jar, Lid, Melon Form, Blue Flowers, Leaves, Cream Ground, Swirl, c.1900, 5 In.	155

WEAPON

Weapons listed here include instruments of combat other than guns, knives, rifles, or swords and clothing worn in combat. Firearms made after 1900 are not listed in this book. Knives and Swords are listed in their own categories.

Armor, Full Suit, Etched, Molded, Oak Platform, Victorian, 76 In. *illus*	3600
Blackjack, Ropework, Baleen, Twisted Shaft, Weighted Ends, 1800s, 11½ In. *illus*	500
Breast Plate, Sheet Iron, Medial Raised Band, Flared-Out Base, Folded Edges, 1800s, 14 x 15 In.	72
Cannon, Cast Iron, Black Paint, 2 Wheels, 28 x 62 x 14 In.	633
Crossbow, Stone, Wood, Brass Runner, Cocking Mechanism, British, 37 In.	1200
Gun, Flintlock Pistol, Brass, Wood Handle, Middletown, Conn., 14 In.	1000
Helmet, Iron, Cabasset, Morion Style, Narrow Brim, Spain, Late 1600s, 8 x 8 x 10 In.	875
Pistol, Percussion, Brass Barrel, Shell Carved Stock, Silver Mask Butt Cap, 1800s, 7 In.	861
Rifle, Wheel Lock, 50 Caliber, Octagonal Barrel, Steel Trigger, 1800s, 28 In.	3750
Shield, Indo-Persian Dahl, Convex Dome Shape, Concentric Circles, 4 Brass Prunts, 12 In.	502
Spear, Iron Tail, Carved, Wood, Leather, Africa, 1900s, 51¼ In.	195

WEATHER VANE

Weather vanes were used in seventeenth-century Boston. The direction of the wind was an indication of coming weather, important to the seafaring and farming communities. By the mid-nineteenth century, commercial weather vanes were made of metal. Many were shaped like animals. Ethan Allen, Dexter, and St. Julian are famous horses that were depicted. Today's collectors often consider weather vanes to be examples of folk art, even though they may not have been handmade.

American Eagle, Full Body, Open Wings, Copper, On Ball, 1900s, 50 x 20 In.	210
Arrow, Copper & Gold Leaf, Mounted, Late 1800s, 36½ In. *illus*	406
Arrow, Copper, Patinated, Central Ball, Oak Base, 16 x 34 x 6½ In.	761
Automobile, Driver, Arrow, Zinc, White Ball, Green Paint, Rectangular Base, 32 x 22 In.	250
Beaver, Full Body, Copper, Patina, Ball, Stand & Directionals, 1900s, 56 In.	4375
Car & Driver, Full Body, Cast Iron, Directional, Kretzer No. 131, 8 x 32 In.	502
Cart, Sulky, Driver, Horse, Copper, Base Metal, 27 x 20 In.	384
Codfish, Hollow Body, Pressed Copper, Soldered Joints, Maine, 1800s, 30 x 9 x 2 In.	6435
Cow, Full Body, Standing, Zinc, Patina, Bullet Holes, 15 x 28 x 4 In. *illus*	3900
Cow, Sheet Metal, Directional, Stand, 16½ x 16 In.	106
Directional, Copper & Iron, Letters, Ball, 39 In.	120
Directional, Copper, Letters, Ball, Rectangular Wood Base, 1900s, 31½ In.	277

Weather Vane, Arrow, Copper & Gold Leaf, Mounted,
Late 1800s, 36½ In.
$406

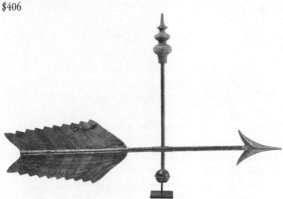

New Haven Auctions

Weather Vane, Cow, Full Body, Standing, Zinc, Patina, Bullet Holes,
15 x 28 x 4 In.
$3,900

Alderfer Auction Company

Weather Vane, Dragon, Hollow Body, Copper, Zinc Head, Arrow, Ball,
Black Metal Base, c.1880, 20 x 27 In.
$9,360

Thomaston Place Auction Galleries

Weather Vane, Eagle, Spread Wings, Gilt, 2 Balls, Arrow, Directionals,
1800s, 59 x 30 x 29 In.
$1,089

Fontaine's Auction Gallery

TIP
*Have your chimney cleaned if you move
into an old house or if you burn wood
regularly. A creosote buildup can cause
an explosion. Nesting animals can cause
fire or smoke.*

Weather Vane, Galleons, 2 Ships, Sails, Arts & Crafts, Copper, Stand,
1800s, 41 x 87 In.
$3,355

CRN Auctions

WEATHER VANE

Weather Vane, Grasshopper, Copper, Molded, Green Glass Inset Eyes, 1900s, 24 1/8 In.
$188

Hindman

> **TIP**
> *Remove the rust from iron by soaking the piece in kerosene for 24 hours, or use any one of several commercial preparations made for the removal of rust. Wash, dry, and coat the piece with a light oil to protect it.*

Weather Vane, Heron, Flying, Gold, Metal Base, 15 1/2 x 19 x 13 In.
$472

Copake Auction

Weather Vane, Horse, Running, Full Body, Copper & Zinc, W & E, Ball Center, 1800s, 28 x 36 x 42 In.
$1,029

Fontaine's Auction Gallery

Weather Vane, Rooster, Copper, Zinc, Gilt, Custom Stand, Square Base, c.1900, 15 x 4 x 11 In.
$1,638

Freeman's

Weather Vane, Topper, Whale, Copper, Attached Fins, Wood Stand, 1900s, 9 3/4 x 26 In.
$313

Eldred's

Dragon, Hollow Body, Copper, Zinc Head, Arrow, Ball, Black Metal Base, c.1880, 20 x 27 In. *illus*	9360
Dragon, Hollow Body, Outstretched Wings, Copper, Metal Base, 17 x 30 In.	1130
Eagle, Perched, Open Wings, Copper, Molded, Gilt, Ball, Early 1900s, 20 x 25 In.	406
Eagle, Spread Wings, Gilt, 2 Balls, Arrow, Directionals, 1800s, 59 x 30 x 29 In. *illus*	1089
Ear Of Corn, Zinc, Cast Iron, Painted, Directional, 4 x 24 In.	1888
Fire Pumper, 2 Horses, Driver, Copper, Gilt, Tubular Steel Frame, Black Stand, 1875-88, 1900s.	3510
Fish, Sheet Metal, Cod Shape, Mounting Pipe, Directional Arrow & Finial, 26 ¼ x 35 ½ In.	644
Fox, Zinc, Painted, Mounted, Brass Hunting Horn, 1800s, 25 ½ x 25 ½ In.	3444
Galleons, 2 Ships, Sails, Arts & Crafts, Copper, Stand, 1800s, 41 x 87 In. *illus*	3355
Gamecock, Flattened Hollow Body, Copper, Soldered Joints, Folk Art, 29 x 32 x 10 In.	4388
Grasshopper, Copper, Molded, Green Glass Inset Eyes, 1900s, 24 ⅛ In. *illus*	188
Heron, Flying, Gold, Metal Base, 15 ½ x 19 x 13 In. *illus*	472
Horse & Sulky, Copper & Brass, Cast Directionals, Shaped Stand, c.1980, 55 x 32 In.	168
Horse, Blackhawk, Running, Copper, Molded, Cushing & White, Waltham, Mass., 19 x 24 In.	3250
Horse, Metal Sheet, Arrow, Cardinal Directions, Stand, 1900s, 27 ½ In.	187
Horse, Running, Full Body, Cast Iron, Gilt, Copper Support, 1900s, 13 In.	657
Horse, Running, Full Body, Copper & Zinc, W & E, Ball Center, 1800s, 28 x 36 x 42 In. *illus*	1029
Horse, Wood, Painted Black, Primitive, On Iron Stand, 40 In.	215
Pig, Flattened Body, Copper, Molded, Zinc Curly Tail, Verdigris, Old Gilt, c.1885, 34 In.	3750
Rooster, Copper, Swell Body, Gilt, On Stand, 1800s, 22 In.	2091
Rooster, Copper, Zinc, Gilt, Custom Stand, Square Base, c.1900, 15 x 4 x 11 In. *illus*	1638
Rooster, Full Body, Cast Iron, Tin Tail, Painted Globe, Wood Base, 39 x 24 x 12 In.	2280
Rooster, Full Body, Copper, Old Gilt & Verdigris Surface, Late 1800s, 31 x 21 In.	625
Rooster, Hollow Body, Copper, Verdigris, Arrow, Directional, Late 1900s, 76 In.	293
Rooster, Standing, Full Body, Copper, Arrow, Gold Paint, 1910s, 34 x 33 In.	660
Rooster, Wrought Iron, On Directional Arrow, Scrolls, Attached To Barn Piece, c.1800, 32 In.	960
Sailboat, Aluminum, Arrow, Directional, 24 x 18 x 14 In.	61
Sailboat, Copper, Tin, American Flag, Early 1900s, 20 x 28 ½ In.	188
Schooner, Copper, Cast Brass Directionals, Mounted, Pipe, 1900s, 29 x 31 x 5 ½ In.	1053
Topper, Whale, Copper, Attached Fins, Wood Stand, 1900s, 9 ¾ x 26 In. *illus*	313

WEBB

Webb glass was made by Thomas Webb & Sons of Ambelcot, England. Many types of art and cameo glass were made by them during the Victorian era. Production ceased by 1991 and the factory was demolished in 1995. Webb Burmese and Webb Peachblow are special colored glasswares of the Victorian era. They are listed at the end of this section. Glassware that is not Burmese or Peachblow is included here.

Webb

Bowl, Cameo Glass, Yellow Ground, Butterfly & Flowers, Signed, 2 x 3 ½ In. *illus*	1700
Bowl, Rock Glass Style, 7 Engraved Flowers, Spiral Flutes, Footed, Round Base, 6 x 9 In.	4800
Bride's Basket, Bowl, Pink, Gold, Silver Holder, Angels, Trumpet, Signed, Victorian, 5 x 10 In.	1840
Vase, Cabinet, Round Rim, Bulbous, Blue, Flower, Cameo, Butterfly Mark, c.1900, 3 In.	241

WEBB BURMESE

Webb Burmese is a shaded Victorian glass made by Thomas Webb & Sons of Stourbridge, England, from 1886. Pieces are shades of pink to yellow.

Dish, Shell Shape, Floral Spray, Butterfly, Queen, 1800s, 2 x 13 x 12 In.	250
Fairy Lamp, Cherry Branch, Clear Clarke Base, Candle Insert, 4 x 4 In. *illus*	250
Vase, Trumpet, Gilt Metal Weighted Base, 6 x 4 In.	275

WEBB PEACHBLOW

Webb Peachblow is a shaded Victorian glass made by Thomas Webb & Sons of Stourbridge, England, from 1885.

Scent Bottle, Falcon Head, Shaded Red To Pink, Gilt, Silver Screw-On Lid, 1885, 7 In. *illus*	5184
Vase, Bulbous Base, Bottleneck, Dragonfly, Leaves, 10 x 4 In.	188
Vase, Butterfly, Flowers, Bulbous Base, Flared Ruffled Rim, 4 ½ x 4 ½ In.	210

Webb, Bowl, Cameo Glass, Yellow Ground, Butterfly & Flowers, Signed, 2 x 3 ½ In.
$1,700

Woody Auction

Webb Burmese, Fairy Lamp, Cherry Branch, Clear Clarke Base, Candle Insert, 4 x 4 In.
$250

Woody Auction

TIP
Small collectibles can be hung as window-shade pulls.

Webb Peachblow, Scent Bottle, Falcon Head, Shaded Red To Pink, Gilt, Silver Screw-On Lid, 1885, 7 In.
$5,184

Bonhams

W

Wedgwood, Bowl, 2 Water Nymphs, Fisherman's Net, Scrolling Waves, c.1882, 10 x 18 x 8 In.
$4,575

Rafael Osona Nantucket Auctions

> **TIP**
> *Figurines are often damaged. Examine the fingers, toes, and other protruding parts for repairs.*

Wedgwood, Bowl, Fairyland Luster, Cobalt Blue, Geese Rim, Daisy Makeig-Jones, Octagonal, c.1920, 3 x 5 In.
$1,170

Thomaston Place Auction Galleries

Wedgwood, Cachepot, Jasperware, Blue, White Classical Figures, Lion Mask & Rings, Footed, 7 x 8 In.
$406

Hindman

Wedgwood, Candlestick, Jasperware, Ceres & Cybele, Blue & White, 1786, 12 ½ In., Pair
$1,000

Nadeau's Auction Gallery

Wedgwood, Cheese Dome, Jasperware, Underplate, Blue, White Figures, Leafy Border, 10 x 6 x 8 In.
$500

Susanin's Auctioneers & Appraisers

Wedgwood, Pitcher, Jasperware, Blue, George Washington & Benjamin Franklin, Oval Vignettes, 7 In.
$469

Charlton Hall Auctions

Wedgwood, Plate, Majolica, Farm Girl Holding Wheelbarrow & Dog, Octagonal, c.1860, 9 x 9 In.
$83

Charleston Estate Auctions

Wedgwood, Vase, Black Basalt, Jasperware, Portland, White Figures, 2 Handles, 8 x 5 ½ In.
$420

Alderfer Auction Company

Wedgwood, Vase, Fairyland Luster, Fantasy Forest, Crossing Bridge, 1900s, 8 ¾ In.
$7,500

Lion and Unicorn

WEDGWOOD

Wedgwood, one of the world's most successful potteries, was founded by Josiah Wedgwood, who was considered a cripple by his brother and was forbidden to work at the family business. The pottery was established in England in 1759. The company used a variety of marks, including Wedgwood, Wedgwood & Bentley, Wedgwood & Sons, and Wedgwood's Stone China. A large variety of wares has been made, including the well-known jasperware, basalt, creamware, and even a limited amount of porcelain. There are two kinds of jasperware. One is made from two colors of clay; the other is made from one color of clay with a color dip to create the contrast in design. In 1986 Wedgwood and Waterford Crystal merged to form the Waterford Wedgwood Group. Most Waterford Wedgwood assets were bought by KPS Capital Partners of New York in 2009 and became part of WWRD Holdings. A small amount of Wedgwood is still made in England at the workshop in Barlaston. Most is made in Asia. Wedgwood has been part of Fiskars Group since 2015. Other Wedgwood pieces may be listed under Flow Blue, Majolica, Tea Leaf Ironstone, or in other porcelain categories.

WEDGWOOD & BENTLEY		**W WEDGWOOD** ENGLAND 1759
Wedgwood & Bentley 1769–1780	Wedgwood 1940	Wedgwood 1998–present

Biscuit Jar, Jasperware, Blue, Silver Mount, Top Rim, Handle, White Relief, 6 ½ In.	125
Bowl, 2 Water Nymphs, Fisherman's Net, Scrolling Waves, c.1882, 10 x 18 x 8 In. .... *illus*	4575
Bowl, Fairyland Luster, Cobalt Blue, Geese Rim, Daisy Makeig-Jones, Octagonal, c.1920, 3 x 5 In. *illus*	1170
Box, Jasperware, Heart Shape, Blue, White Relief Christmas Tree, Holly On Sides, 3 In.	15
Cachepot, Jasperware, Blue, White Classical Figures, Lion Mask & Rings, Footed, 7 x 8 In. *illus*	406
Candlestick, Jasper Dip, Lilac, White Classical Figures, Flower Border, 1875, 7 In., Pair	280
Candlestick, Jasperware, Ceres & Cybele, Blue & White, 1786, 12 ½ In., Pair .... *illus*	1000
Cheese Dome, Jasperware, Underplate, Blue, White Figures, Leafy Border, 10 x 6 x 8 In. .. *illus*	500
Coffeepot, Jasperware, Blue Matte Finish, Cherubs, 1900s, 2 In.	88
Compote, Black, White Neoclassical Scenes, Acanthus Foot, Marked, 7 In.	88
Girandole, 2-Light, Jasperware, Gilt Bronze, Obelisk Shape Prism, 14 x 14 ½ In., Pair	246
Mug, Beatrix Potter, Mama Rabbit, Flopsy, Mopsy, Cottontail & Peter, 1993, 2 ¾ In.	10
Pitcher, Jasperware, Blue Figures, White Matte Ground, 1900s, 5 In.	75
Pitcher, Jasperware, Blue, George Washington & Benjamin Franklin, Oval Vignettes, 7 In. ... *illus*	469
Plaque, Black Basalt, Lord Of The 2 Lands, Egyptian Scene, Giltwood Frame, 1900s, 15 ¼ x 9 In. ..	750
Plaque, Black Basalt, Milton, Profile, Carved Border, Oval, 6 ½ x 5 ½ In.	416
Plaque, Fairyland Luster, Torches, Palace, Daisy Makeig-Jones, Early 1900s, 10 ⅞ x 8 In.	7040
Plaque, Jasperware, Green, Classical Scene, Figural, Frame 5 ¾ x 17 ½ In.	438
Plate, Majolica, Farm Girl Holding Wheelbarrow & Dog, Octagonal, c.1860, 9 x 9 In. .... *illus*	83
Server, Salad, Jasperware, Tricolor, Scrollwork, Lattice, 1800s, 12 ¾ In.	150
Tureen, Lid, Neoclassical, White Glaze, Scroll Handles, Italy, Late 1800s, 6 ¾ x 8 In.	182
Urn, Lid, Jasperware, Light Blue Ground, Figures & Handles, 11 In., Pair	1152
Vase, Black Basalt, Jasperware, Portland, White Figures, 2 Handles, 8 x 5 ½ In. .... *illus*	420
Vase, Fairyland Luster, Fantasy Forest, Crossing Bridge, 1900s, 8 ¾ In. .... *illus*	7500
Vase, Fairyland Luster, Imps On Bridge, Daisy Makeig-Jones, Early 1900s, 8 ⅞ x 6 In.	6765
Vase, Figural, Flowers, Powder Blue, Gilt, Brass, Mounted As Lamp, Late 1800s, 23 In.	60
Vase, Flared Rim, Ram's Head Handles, Queen Victoria Pattern, 1900s, 10 x 8 In.	275
Vase, Jasper Dip, Flared Rim, Black, White Figures, Mirrored Patina Stand, 1800s, 14 In.	813
Vase, Shouldered, Concentric Circles, Gray, Keith Murray, 11 x 8 ¼ In. .... *illus*	875

WELLER

Weller pottery was first made in 1872 in Fultonham, Ohio. The firm moved to Zanesville, Ohio, in 1882. Artwares were introduced in 1893. Hundreds of lines of pottery were produced,

Wedgwood, Vase, Shouldered, Concentric Circles, Gray, Keith Murray, 11 x 8 ¼ In. $875

Palm Beach Modern Auctions

Weller, Baldin, Umbrella Stand, Ivory Color, Embossed Apple Tree, 22 ¼ In. $165

Bunch Auctions

Weller, Coppertone, Vase, Earthenware, Semigloss, c.1930, 27 ½ x 12 ½ In. $2,210

Toomey & Co. Auctioneers

W

TIP
Pet doors should be less than 6 inches across to keep out small children who might then open a regular door for a burglar.

including Louwelsa, Eocean, Dickens Ware, and Sicardo, before the pottery closed in 1948.

LONHUDA

Weller Pottery 1895–1896	Weller Pottery 1895–1918	Weller Pottery 1920s

Weller, Dickens Ware, Vase, Matte Glaze, Tavern, Board Game, Charles B. Upjohn, 1900, 17⅞ x 8 In.

$625

Toomey & Co. Auctioneers

Weller, Eocean, Jardiniere, Jonquils, Pink To Green Ground, Tripod Feet, c.1900, 12½ In.

$120

Garth's Auctioneers & Appraisers

Aurelian, Jardiniere, Pedestal, Twist Shape, Strawberry, Dark Brown, 37 x 14 In.	800
Baldin, Umbrella Stand, Ivory Color, Embossed Apple Tree, 22¼ In. *illus*	165
Bedford Matte, Umbrella Stand, Embossed Poppies, c.1915, 20 x 11 In.	468
Blue Ware, Vase, Classical Maidens, Dancing, Flowers, Cylindrical, Early 1900s, 12 In.	125
Coppertone, Bowl, Frog, Water Lily, Green Paint, 15 x 10 In.	423
Coppertone, Vase, Earthenware, Semigloss, c.1930, 27½ x 12½ In. *illus*	2210
Coppertone, Vase, Mottled Green, Handle, Pouting Lip, Stamp, 28 x 12 In.	1125
Dickens Ware, Stein, Monk, Drinking, Brown To Green Matte, Handle, c.1900, 5½ In., Pair	132
Dickens Ware, Vase, Flowers, Bulbous, 10 x 9 In.	1625
Dickens Ware, Vase, Matte Glaze, Tavern, Board Game, Charles B. Upjohn, 1900, 17⅞ x 8 In. *illus*	625
Eocean, Jardiniere, Jonquils, Pink To Green Ground, Tripod Feet, c.1900, 12½ In. *illus*	120
Etched Matte, Vase, Pouting Lip, Orange, Daisies, 10¼ x 3¼ In. *illus*	344
Figurine, Popeye Dog, Sitting, Head Up, Glazed, 4 x 4 In. *illus*	406
Flemish, Jardiniere, Pedestal, Parrots, Chrysanthemums, Rudolph Lorber, c.1920, 32 In. *illus*	427
Flower Frog, Woman Kneeling, Pale Green Glaze, 6 x 5 In. *illus*	175
Fru Russet, Vase, Figural Frog Climbing Side, Marked, 4 x 3½ In. *illus*	2210
Hudson, Vase, Blue & Cream, Flowers, 10 x 4 In.	225
Hudson, Vase, Incised, Boat, Whale, Earthenware, Dorothy England, c.1930, 5 x 4⅛ In.	500
Hudson, Vase, Water Lily, Lavender, Blue Ground, 2 Handles, Hester Pillsbury, 7¾ In. *illus*	228
Ivory, Jardiniere, Forest, Animals, Signed, c.1920s, 6¼ x 10½ x 7 In.	246
Juneau, Vase, Leaves, Molded Rim, 2 Handles, Mottled Pink Glaze, 1930s, 12 In. *illus*	108
La Moro, Vase, Grapevine, Brown Underglaze, Signed, Martha Gray, c.1915, 15 In.	84
Louwelsa, Jug, Brown, Currants, Handle, Marked, 5 x 4 In.	70
Louwelsa, Vase, Blackberry Vines, Leaves, Shaded Brown, Tapered, Handle, M. Lybarger, 13 In.	135
Louwelsa, Vase, Flowers, Tapered, Cylindrical, Hester Pillsbury, Early 1900s, 12 x 4¼ In.	117
Louwelsa, Vase, Indian Portrait, Dark Brown Glaze, Signed, A. Dunlavy, 12½ In. *illus*	1029
Matte Green, Bowl, Buttress, Squares, Bedford, c.1910s, 7 x 3 In. *illus*	185
Matte Green, Vase, 2 Handles, Flower, Bedford, c.1910, 19¾ x 10¼ In.	2829
Muskota, Jardinere, 2 Girls In Forest, Matte Glaze, Raised Decoration, c.1920, 9 In.	216
Sicardo, Bowl, Monumental, Foot Rim, Marked, 1900s, 7½ In.	1280
Sicardo, Vase, Art Nouveau Style, Elongated Shape, Flowers, Leaves, 1900s, 17 x 5 In. *illus*	1440
Sicardo, Vase, Nasturtium, Earthenware, Luster Glaze, c.1905, 7 x 6 In. *illus*	1125

WEMYSS

Wemyss ware was first made in 1882 by Robert Heron & Son, later called Fife Pottery, in Scotland. Large colorful flowers, hearts, and other symbols were hand painted on figurines, inkstands, jardinieres, candlesticks, buttons, pots, and other items. Fife Pottery closed in 1932. The molds and designs were used by a series of potteries until 1957. In 1985 the Wemyss name and designs were obtained by Griselda Hill. The Wemyss Ware trademark was registered in 1994. Modern Wemyss Ware in old styles is still being made.

Dish, Pink Rose, Green Leaves & Rim, White Ground, Scotland, c.1900, 5 In.	120
Figurine, Pig, Roses, Hand Painted, Marked, 4 x 6 In., Pair *illus*	360
Inkwell, Heart Shape, 2 Lids, Pink & Green, Robert Heron & Son, c.1860, 7 x 7 x 2½ In.	98

Weller, Etched Matte, Vase, Pouting Lip, Orange, Daisies, 10 ¼ x 3 ¼ In.
$344

Palm Beach Modern Auctions

Weller, Figurine, Popeye Dog, Sitting, Head Up, Glazed, 4 x 4 In.
$406

Treadway

Weller, Flower Frog, Woman Kneeling, Pale Green Glaze, 6 x 5 In.
$175

Woody Auction

Weller, Flemish, Jardiniere, Pedestal, Parrots, Chrysanthemums, Rudolph Lorber, c.1920, 32 In
$427

Neal Auction Company

Weller, Fru Russet, Vase, Figural Frog Climbing Side, Marked, 4 x 3 ½ In.
$2,210

Treadway

Weller, Hudson, Vase, Water Lily, Lavender, Blue Ground, 2 Handles, Hester Pillsbury, 7 ¾ In.
$228

Garth's Auctioneers & Appraisers

Weller, Juneau, Vase, Leaves, Molded Rim, 2 Handles, Mottled Pink Glaze, 1930s, 12 In.
$108

Garth's Auctioneers & Appraisers

W

Weller, Louwelsa, Vase, Indian Portrait, Dark Brown Glaze, Signed, A. Dunlavy, 12½ In.
$1,029

Fontaine's Auction Gallery

TIP

Iridescent pottery like Sicardo should be carefully cleaned. Wash in mild detergent and water. Rinse. Dry by buffing vigorously with dry, fluffy towels. Then polish with a silver cloth as if it were made of metal. Buff again with a clean towel.

Weller, Matte Green, Bowl, Buttress, Squares, Bedford, c.1910s, 7 x 3 In.
$185

California Historical Design

W

WESTMORELAND GLASS

Westmoreland glass was made by the Westmoreland Glass Company of Grapeville, Pennsylvania, from 1889 to 1984. The company made clear and colored glass of many varieties, such as milk glass, pressed glass, and slag glass.

Westmoreland Glass
c.1910–c.1929, 1970s

Westmoreland Glass
Late 1940s–1981

Westmoreland Glass
1982–1984

Ashburton, Wine, 5¼ In.	12
Beaded Swirl & Ball, Cruet, 5¼ In.	35
Beaded Swirl, Sugar & Creamer	62
Lily Of The Valley, Milk Glass, Vase, Footed, Scalloped Rim, 7 In.	17
Old Quilt, Milk Glass, Sweetmeat, 4 In.	12
Paneled Grape, Pitcher, Footed, Pint	21

WHEATLEY POTTERY

Wheatley Pottery was founded by Thomas J. Wheatley in Cincinnati, Ohio. He had worked with the founders of the art pottery movement, including M. Louise McLaughlin of the Rookwood Pottery. He started T.J. Wheatley & Co. in 1880. That company was closed by 1884. Thomas Wheatley worked for Weller Pottery in Zanesville, Ohio, from 1897 to 1900. In 1903 he founded Wheatley Pottery Company in Cincinnati. Wheatley Pottery was purchased by the Cambridge Tile Manufacturing Company in 1927. Cambridge Tile closed in 1985.

Lamp, Green Matte Glaze, Flowers, Red, Leaf Base, c.1910, 21¾ x 11½ In.	1722
Tile, Dragon Face, Open Mouth, Green, Wood Frame, 9¾ x 9¾ In.	520
Vase, Green Leathery Glaze, Arts & Crafts, c.1905, 8⅜ x 5 In. *illus*	687
Vase, Slip Decoration, Painted, Black, Flowers, Oval, 1880, 12 x 7½ x 2¾ In. *illus*	1169

WILLETS MANUFACTURING COMPANY

Willets Manufacturing Company of Trenton, New Jersey, began work in 1879. The company made belleek in the late 1880s and 1890s in shapes similar to those used by the Irish Belleek factory. It stopped working about 1912. A variety of marks were used, most including the name *Willets*.

Bowl, Centerpiece, Enamel, Floral, Gilt Rim, Eleanor Stewart, Belleek, c.1910, 8¾ x 3¾ In.	417
Dish, Flowers, Gilt Trim, White Ground, Crimped Rim, Belleek, 1½ x 6 In.	42
Mug, Fruit, Painted, Light & Dark Brown, Glaze, Belleek, 4¼ x 4¾ In.	175
Pitcher, Pomegranate, Flowers & Leaves, Blue Handle & Rim, Belleek, 5¼ x 8 In.	123

WILLOW

Willow pattern has been made in England since 1780. The pattern has been copied by factories in many countries, including Germany, Japan, and the United States. It is still being made. Willow was named for a pattern that pictures a bridge, birds, willow trees, and a Chinese landscape. Most pieces are blue and white. Some made after 1900 are pink and white.

Creamer, Churchill, 3⅝ In.	15
Cup & Saucer, Alfred Meakin, Demitasse, 1930s *illus*	40
Cup, Spode	6
Grandfather Cup, Ridgway, 3¾ x 5¼ In.	38
Gravy Boat, Underplate, England	88

Weller, Sicardo, Vase, Art Nouveau Style, Elongated Shape, Flowers, Leaves, 1900s, 17 x 5 In.
$1,440

Cottone Auctions

TIP
Use coasters under glasses and flower vases on marble-topped tables. Marble can stain easily.

Weller, Sicardo, Vase, Nasturtium, Earthenware, Luster Glaze, c.1905, 7 x 6 In.
$1,125

Toomey & Co. Auctioneers

Wemyss, Figurine, Pig, Roses, Hand Painted, Marked, 4 x 6 In., Pair
$360

Nadeau's Auction Gallery

Wheatley, Vase, Green Leathery Glaze, Arts & Crafts, c.1905, 8⅜ x 5 In.
$687

Toomey & Co. Auctioneers

Wheatley, Vase, Slip Decoration, Painted, Black, Flowers, Oval, 1880, 12 x 7½ x 2¾ In.
$1,169

California Historical Design

Willow, Cup & Saucer, Alfred Meakin, Demitasse, 1930s
$40

Ruby Lane

W

Window, Leaded, Arched, Circle & Diamond Pattern, Blue Sky, Sparrows, Early 1900s, 82 x 71 In.
$1,500

Fontaine's Auction Gallery

Window, Leaded, Arched, Leaves, Vines & Flowers, Frame, Early 1900s, 40 ½ x 34 In.
$5,143

Fontaine's Auction Gallery

Window, Leaded, Geometric, Flowers, Multicolor, Wood Frame, c.1900, 22 x 48 x 1 ⅜ In.
$219

New Haven Auctions

Window, Leaded, Prairie School, Chevrons, Green, Gold, Oak Frame, E.E. Roberts, Illinois, 52 x 8 In.
$1,690

Toomey & Co. Auctioneers

Window, Stained, Blue Iris, Green Leaves, Square, 38 x 38 x 1 In.
$277

Charleston Estate Auctions

Window, Stained, Religious, Christ, Apostles, Eucharist, Continental, Germany, Late 1800s, 23 x 46 In.
$1,560

Alex Cooper Auctioneers

W

Plate, Dinner, Churchill, 10 In.	13
Platter, British Anchor Co., Great Britain, 1920s, 14 In.	145
Salt & Pepper, Wooden Base, Oval, Japan, 3¾ In.	20

WINDOW

Window glass that was stained and beveled was popular for houses during the late nineteenth and early twentieth centuries. Some was set in patterns like leaded glass. The old windows became popular with collectors in the 1970s; today, old and new examples are seen.

Casement, Arts & Crafts, Leaded Glass, Oak Frame, c.1915, 39½ In., Pair	2000
Leaded, Arched, Circle & Diamond Pattern, Blue Sky, Sparrows, Early 1900s, 82 x 71 In.*illus*	1500
Leaded, Arched, Flowered Urn, Scrolling Design, Multicolor, Frame, Early 1900s, 40 x 33 In.	5445
Leaded, Arched, Leaves, Vines & Flowers, Frame, Early 1900s, 40½ x 34 In. *illus*	5143
Leaded, Arched, Multicolor, Theophile Hippolyte Laumonnerie, 1922, 87 x 24 In., Pair	3750
Leaded, Geometric, Flowers, Multicolor, Wood Frame, c.1900, 22 x 48 x 1⅜ In. *illus*	219
Leaded, Prairie School, Chevrons, Green, Gold, Oak Frame, E.E. Roberts, Illinois, 52 x 8 In.*illus*	1690
Leaded, Red Flowers, Green, Yellow, 46½ x 28 In., Pair	460
Leaded, Round, Multicolor, Geometric Design, Flower Center, c.1900, 44½ In.	204
Panel, Leaded, Clear Glass, Accent Yellow Corner Squares, 43 x 10 In., Pair	84
Panel, Stained Glass, Faceted, Clear Oval, Flowers, Scrolls, Wood Frame, 60 x 45 In.	1890
Stained, Blue Iris, Green Leaves, Square, 38 x 38 x 1 In. *illus*	277
Stained, Geometric Design, Multicolor, Caramel Ground, Painted, Frame, 24 x 32 In.	209
Stained, Multicolor, Oval, Wood Frame, 1810s, 30½ x 44 x 7 In.	1500
Stained, Religious Figure, Blue, Red, Green, Metal, Frame, 28 x 35½ In.	212
Stained, Religious, Christ, Apostles, Eucharist, Continental, Germany, Late 1800s, 23 x 46 In. *illus*	1560

WOOD CARVING

Wood carvings and wooden pieces are listed separately in this book. There are also wooden pieces found in other categories, such as Folk Art, Kitchen, and Tool.

4 Birds, On Branch, Continental, 10½ x 23 In.	390
Abstract, Wavy, Circular Base, Signed, Fitzgerald, 2004, 33½ In.	281
African Man, Horsehair, Dried Seeds & Vines, Cloth, Teeth, Late 1900s, 21 x 10 x 14 In.	282
American Eagle, Outstretched Wings, Arrows, Patriotic Shield, Late 1800s, 15 x 6 x 47 In.*illus*	2394
Antelope, Painted, Ceremonial Headdress, Africa, 49¾ In. *illus*	281
Archangel, Raphael, Holding Staff, Cherub, Dog, Tobias, Ball Feet, Continental, 1800s, 26 In.	688
Artist's Figure, Articulated Ball Joints, Screws, Limbs, Joints, Late 1800s, 12¾ In.	531
Baby, Sitting Up, Sleeping, 1900s, 24 In. *illus*	188
Bear, Seated, One Leg Raised, Black Forest, Early 1900s, 12½ In.	484
Bear, Walking, Glass Eyes, Painted, Black Forest, c.1910, 6 x 11 x 4 In. *illus*	540
Bird, Fish Shape, Holes, Signed, Emil Milan, 15 In.	106
Bird, On Branch, Blunt Bill, Brown, Shelf Fungus, Painted, Late 1800s, 12 x 10 In.	323
Bird, Painted, Seated, Mounted, Brown, Half Round Log Base, 1900s, 6½ In.	378
Blackamoor, Standing, Finger On Lips, Multicolor, 1800s, 34 x 14 x 14 In.	761
Boat, Wuramon, Shells Decoration, Asmat, New Guinea, 1900s, 9¾ x 9¼ x 67 In.	1063
Book Stand, Bears On Logs, Sliding, Black Forest, Early 1900s, 6 x 17 x 7 In. *illus*	325
Boy, Curly Hair, Open Arms, Italy, 1850s, 24 x 21 In. *illus*	875
Bracket, Mermaid, Shell Shape Base, Gilt, England, 1800s, 20 x 18 x 12 In., Pair	3438
Bracket, Woman, Winged, Mickey Sabety, Oceanside, 32¾ x 12½ In., Pair	660
Brook Trout, Open Mouth, Signed, Mike Borrett, 2000s, 20 In. *illus*	937
Bull, Walnut, Standing, Pointed Tail, c.1950, 19 In.	188
Bulldog, Standing, Wrinkled Face, c.1920, 7 In. *illus*	188
Bust, Athena, Oak, Walnut Stain, Belle Epoch, 16 x 11 In. *illus*	410
Bust, Woman, Wearing Hat & Makeup, Copper Paint, Art Deco, 15 In.	500
Cardinal, Marked, Capt. Fred Huhs, Hampton Bays, On Rocky Base, 7 x 8 In. *illus*	295
Cat, Lying Down, Painted, Orange, Black Stripes, Signed, Pam Schifferl, 12¼ In. *illus*	428
Centaur, Female, Bare-Breasted, Shooting Arrow, Board Base, 49 x 48 x 29 In.	738

Wood Carving, American Eagle, Outstretched Wings, Arrows, Patriotic Shield, Late 1800s, 15 x 6 x 47 In. $2,394

Freeman's

Wood Carving, Antelope, Painted, Ceremonial Headdress, Africa, 49¾ In. $281

Eldred's

Wood Carving, Baby, Sitting Up, Sleeping, 1900s, 24 In. $188

Hindman

This is an edited listing of current prices. Visit **Kovels.com** to check thousands of prices from previous years and sign up for free information on trends, tips, reproductions, marks, and more.

W

Wood Carving, Bear, Walking, Glass Eyes, Painted, Black Forest, c.1910, 6 x 11 x 4 In.
$540

White's Auctions

Wood Carving, Book Stand, Bears On Logs, Sliding, Black Forest, Early 1900s, 6 x 17 x 7 In.
$325

Soulis Auctions

Wood Carving, Boy, Curly Hair, Open Arms, Italy, 1850s, 24 x 21 In.
$875

Hindman

Wood Carving, Brook Trout, Open Mouth, Signed, Mike Borrett, 2000s, 20 In.
$937

Eldred's

Wood Carving, Bulldog, Standing, Wrinkled Face, c.1920, 7 In.
$188

New Haven Auctions

> **TIP**
> Sculptures should be dusted with a clean, dry paintbrush. Never use water.

Wood Carving, Bust, Athena, Oak, Walnut Stain, Belle Epoch, 16 x 11 In.
$410

Thomaston Place Auction Galleries

Wood Carving, Cardinal, Marked, Capt. Fred Huhs, Hampton Bays, On Rocky Base, 7 x 8 In.
$295

Copake Auction

Wood Carving, Cat, Lying Down, Painted, Orange, Black Stripes, Signed, Pam Schifferl, 12¼ In.
$428

Pook & Pook

Wood Carving, Cherub, Holding Blanket, Wall Hanging, Italy, 1800s, 12 x 5½ x 5 In., Pair
$484

Fontaine's Auction Gallery

Wood Carving, Deer Head, Black Forest, Organic Horns, Medallion Shape Mount, 30 x 20 x 20 In.
$1,024

Rachel Davis Fine Arts

Wood Carving, Eagle, Painted, God Bless America Banner, Liberty Shield, 15 x 33 In.
$438

Eldred's

Wood Carving, Elephant, Ebonized Lacquer, Carrying Ostrich Egg, 13 x 10 In.
$96

Nadeau's Auction Gallery

Wood Carving, Female, Ancestral Figure, Shell, Fiber, Papua, New Guinea, Early 1900s, 52 In.
$250

Charlton Hall Auctions

W

Wood Carving, Goat, Standing, Stacked Stone Ground, Circular Base, Black Forest, Late 1800s, 21 In.

$847

Fontaine's Auction Gallery

Wood Carving, Hunter, Holding Rifle, Dog, Tree Stump Base, Germany, Late 1800s, 22¾ In.

$666

Fontaine's Auction Gallery

Cherub, Holding Blanket, Wall Hanging, Italy, 1800s, 12 x 5½ x 5 In., Pair .... *illus*	484
Chickadee, Painted, Domed Base, Jess Blackstone, New Hampshire, Mid 1900s, 2 In.	1063
Column, Grapevine, Parcel Gilt, Italy, 1800s, 73 x 12 In., Pair	1250
Cornucopia, Slat Basket, Painted, Overflowing, Various Fruits, 1900s, 28 x 85 In.	344
Creche Figure, Female, Holding Vase, Matching Pedestal, Dark Base, India, 1900s, 9 In. ...	150
Deer Head, Black Forest, Organic Horns, Medallion Shape Mount, 30 x 20 x 20 In...... *illus*	1024
Diorama, Horse, Jockey, Carved, Painted, Glass Eyes, John Stormonth, Frame, 1872, 25½ x 21 In...	1512
Dragon Peacock, Open Mouth, Teeth, Tongue Out, Green, 62 x 36 x 12 In.	366
Eagle, Gilt, Red, White, & Blue Shield, Bellamy Style, c.1910, 7¾ x 27 In.	1500
Eagle, Left & Right Facing, 3 Parts, Open Wings, Nails, Braces, 16 x 38 x 6¼ In., Pair.........	1342
Eagle, Painted, God Bless America Banner, Liberty Shield, 15 x 33 In. .... *illus*	438
Eagle, Spread Wings, 1 Foot On Ball, Perched On Rock, Gilt, 2 Dowel Holes, 24 x 11½ In.	488
Eagle, Spread Wings, Clutching Arrows, Liberty Shield, 17 x 43 In.	1750
Eagle, Spread Wings, Crossed Arrows, Pine, White Paint, Bellamy Style, 1800s, 40 x 14 x 4 In. ..	2691
Eagle, Spread Wings, Painted, Multicolor, Wilhelm Schimmel, 7 In.	4182
Eagle, Spread Wings, Standing, Head Turned To Side, On Branch, 1900s, 10 In.	192
Eagle, Stylized, Art Deco, Rectangular Block Base, American School, 5 x 14½ x 1 In...........	125
Elephant, Ebonized Lacquer, Carrying Ostrich Egg, 13 x 10 In.................................... *illus*	96
Elephant, Standing, Trunk Down, On Stand, Rosewood, 1900s, 22 x 24 In.	900
Elk Head, Glass Eyes, Scrollwork, Acorns & Leaves, Black Forest, Late 1800s, 58 x 46 x 30 In..	8470
Female, Ancestral Figure, Shell, Fiber, Papua, New Guinea, Early 1900s, 52 In............. *illus*	250
Female, Standing, Rocky Base, Spiraling Cornucopia, Multicolor, 1950s, 61 In.....................	1080
Finial, Pineapple Shape, Circular Base, c.1865, 21½ x 10 In., Pair....................................	2520
Finial, Turned Top, Square Molded Plinths, Black Paint, 1800s, 10 In.	813
Fisherman, Standing, Hardwood, Pool, Basket, Rope, 1900s, 10¼ In...........................	60
Ganesha, Hindu Deity, Elephant Head, Leaves, Rectangular Base, 49 x 23 x 8 In.	500
Goat, Standing, Stacked Stone Ground, Circular Base, Black Forest, Late 1800s, 21 In. *illus*	847
Handle, Knife, Fevered Sumatran, Seated, Indonesia, 1800s, 3¼ In.	410
Head, Bald Man, Circular Base, Mardonio Magana, 10 x 5½ x 6½ In.	2500
Headdress, African, Painted, Geometric Design, On Black Square Base, 34 In.	156
Horse, Raised Foot, Multicolor, Painted, Italy, Late 1800s, 54 x 52 In.	438
House Bird, Black Alder Wood, Wire Legs, Charles & Ray Eames, Vitra Box, 8 x 11 In..........	460
House Wren, Painted, Shaped Base, Signed, Bob & Bonnie Allen, 3½ In.	151
Hunter, Holding Long Gun, Dog, Dark Brown Patina, Continental, 1800s, 13 x 9 x 4 In.	384
Hunter, Holding Rifle, Dog, Tree Stump Base, Germany, Late 1800s, 22¾ In. .... *illus*	666
Madonna Of Altotting Bavaria, Standing, Holding Child, Painted, 1700s, 28 In....... *illus*	1500
Man, Standing, Pith Helmet, Yellow Jacket, Tie, Round Base, 1900s, 61 x 18 x 12 In.	406
Mask, Beadwork, Cowrie Shell, Painted, Africa, 1900s, 11½ x 14½ In.................................	125
Mask, Face, Closed Eyes, Applied Patina, Jute, Hanging, Punu, Gabon, c.1900s, 11 x 7 x 4 In.	157
Mask, Karanga, Mossi, Figural, Burkina Faso, Africa, 28½ x 8½ x 5 In.	219
Mask, Kifwebe, Bird Face, Closed Eyes, Stand, Songye, Congo, c.1900s, 13 x 8 x 6 In. ....*illus*	1040
Men, 2 Sitting, 3 Climbing Stick Center, Circular Base, 35½ In..........................	813
Mermaid, Painted, Green Necklace, Wall Hanging, 21 x 28 In.	366
Model, Church, Illuminated, Front Drawer, Gilt Finial, c.1900, 30 x 16½ In...............*illus*	960
Model, Stagecoach, Painted, Black, Yellow & Red, Rectangular Base, c.1890, 19 In......*illus*	281
Nude Torso, Rectangular Base, Miguel Estrella, Mexico, 1900s, 28 x 18 x 8 In.	300
Nude, Woman, Standing, Quadrilateral Base, Varnish, c.1960, 61 In.	406
Ornament, Wall, Fruit Garland, Wheat, Leaves, Gilt Accents, 30 x 5 In., Pair.....................	500
Ornament, Wall, Marquetry, Lapis Lazuli, Continental, Late 1800s, 68 In.	406
Panel, Gamebirds & Rabbit, Relief, Walnut, Arched Top, Scrollwork Crest, 1800s, 24 x 18 x 4 In...	936
Panel, Mission, San Juan Capistrano, Signed, Eric Lasch, c.1940s, 12¾ x 18 In.	185
Panel, Oak, Relief Carved Grapevine, Black Forest, Germany, c.1870, 12 x 10½ In..............	180
Panel, Openwork, Honeycomb, Lattice, Chinese, 1900s, 79 x 22½ x 1 In., 3 Piece	469
Panel, Red Lacquer & Gilt, Village Scene, Bridge, River, Chinese, 36 x 84 In.	406
Panel, Relief, Hardwood, Prunus, Pine, Bamboo, Chrysanthemum, 54⅞ In., Pair..............	2806
Pedestal, Animal Motif, Man, Rectangular Base, Scroll Feet, Southeast Asia, 20 x 13 x 17 In..	125
Picture, Indians, Luis Potosi, 47 x 10 In.	111
Plaque, 2nd National Bank, Philadelphia, Tree, Buildings, Round, 30 In.............................	510
Plaque, Angel, Spread Wings, Open Arms, Contemporary, 19½ In.	113

Wood Carving, Madonna Of Altotting Bavaria, Standing, Holding Child, Painted, 1700s, 28 In.
$1,500

Hindman

Wood Carving, Mask, Kifwebe, Bird Face, Closed Eyes, Stand, Songye, Congo, c.1900s, 13 x 8 x 6 In.
$1,040

Wright

Wood Carving, Model, Church, Illuminated, Front Drawer, Gilt Finial, c.1900, 30 x 16½ In.
$960

Neal Auction Company

Wood Carving, Model, Stagecoach, Painted, Black, Yellow & Red, Rectangular Base, c.1890, 19 In.
$281

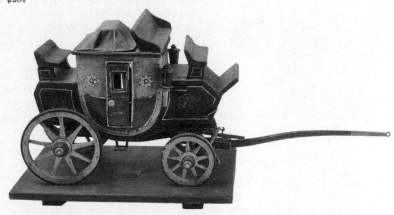

New Haven Auctions

Wood Carving, Plaque, Sperm Whale, Painted, Clark G. Voorhees Jr., 1800s, 17½ In.
$1,500

Eldred's

Wood Carving, Santo, Blue Robe, Gilt, Raised Base, Baroque, Italy, 1600s, 55 x 20 In.
$3,998

Auctions at Showplace, NYC

W

Wood Carving, Seahorse, Rolled Tail, Fin, Gold Paint, 1900s, 18 x 9¼ In. $406

Eldred's

Wood Carving, St. Sebastian, Half Clothed, Tied To Tree, Arm Raised, Italy, 1700s, 52 In. $2,813

Hindman

Plaque, Bird, Black-Bellied Plover, Head, A. Elmer Crowell, c.1925, 5 In.	2625
Plaque, Brook Trout, Multicolor, Steve A. Forestdale, Dated 2008, 9 In.	469
Plaque, Carp, Hardwood, Brown, 39 x 15 x 7 In.	366
Plaque, Cherub, Grapes, Acanthus Leaves, Gilt, Multicolor, 15 x 8 x 4 In.	125
Plaque, Corn, Grapes, Leaves, 1800s, 22 In.	295
Plaque, Eagle, Spread Wings, Arrows On Feet, Federal, P.S. Atkinson, 13 x 36 In.	976
Plaque, Eagle, Spread Wings, Banner, E Pluribus Unum, Bellamy, Early 1900s, 7 x 45 In.	531
Plaque, Eagle, Spread Wings, Grasping Arrows, American Shield, Painted, Late 1800s, 42 x 14 In.	1920
Plaque, Eagle, Spread Wings, Paint, Gilt, Jerome Howes, 1900s, 13 x 42 In.	2125
Plaque, Eagle, Spread Wings, Shield, Flag, Gilt, Painted, Pine, 11 x 30 In.	2223
Plaque, Game, Leaves, Bird & Deer, Black Forest, 1800s, 29 x 17 In.	469
Plaque, Indian, Profile, Man's Face, Feathers In Hair, Embossed U.S.A., c.1910, 10¼ In.	492
Plaque, Oak, The Rogues Conference At The Inn, Seated Figures, Late 1800s, 18 x 11½ In.	250
Plaque, Panel, Warring Figures, Pierced, Relief, Gilt, Chinese, 1900s, 24¾ x 16 In.	480
Plaque, Rabbit, Pheasant, Wolf, Rifle, Bag, Oval, Black Forest, Germany, 1800s, 13 x 10½ In.	688
Plaque, Sperm Whale, Fir & Spruce, Acrylic Paint, Contemporary, Sunny B. Wood, 36 In.	1037
Plaque, Sperm Whale, Hanging, White & Blue Paint, Chain, 41 x 11 In.	250
Plaque, Sperm Whale, Painted, Clark G. Voorhees Jr., 1800s, 17½ In. .... *illus*	1500
Rattlesnake, Glass Eyes, Burn Decorated, Troy Webb, 1900s, 2 x 36 x 12 In.	130
Rooster, Painted, Square Base, Signed, Peter Storm, Dated 1982, 7 In.	113
Rooster, Painted, Standing, Multicolor, Mounded Base, Signed, 14 In.	239
Santo, Blue Robe, Gilt, Raised Base, Baroque, Italy, 1600s, 55 x 20 In. .... *illus*	3998
Santo, Mary & Child, Standing, Halo, Carved, Gilt, Square Base, Continental, 1700s, 13 In.	344
Sea Gull, In Flight, Teak, Metal Stand, c.1970, 17 x 19 x 11 In.	288
Seahorse, Rolled Tail, Fin, Gold Paint, 1900s, 18 x 9¼ In. .... *illus*	406
Shogun, Court Official, Saidai-Jin, Pedestal, Japan, 26 x 29 x 13 In.	1845
Shorebird, Pole Stand, Rectangular Base, Thomas Langan, 31 In.	443
Sign, Earle's Museum, Inscribed, Jim Earle, 6 x 17½ In.	128
St. Sebastian, Half Clothed, Tied To Tree, Arm Raised, Italy, 1700s, 52 In. .... *illus*	2813
Stag's Head, Antlers, Painted, Black Forest, Wall Mount, 27 x 20 x 11 In.	1200
Stag's Head, Wall Mount, Antlers, Glass Eyes, Leaves, Black Forest, 1800s, 45 x 20 In.	3750
Stamp, Coffin, Whaling Logbook, Tropical Wood, Whale Ivory Handle, 1800s, 1¾ In.	5000
Torso, Female, Nude, Circular Slab Base, Folk Art, Late 1800s, 37½ In.	1000
Tree, 7 Birds, Squirrel, 6 Branches, Signed, 19 In.	2394
Whale, Finback, Inset Glass Eyes, Painted, Wick Ahrens, 2006, 33 x 10 In. .... *illus*	8775
Whale, Humpback, Carved, Painted, Roger Mitchell, Kingston, Mass., 38 In. .... *illus*	625
Whale, Humpback, Painted, Black & White, On Stand, Irving Briggs, 14 x 11 x 24 In.	366
Whale, Nantucket, Contemporary, Brown, Signed, Marcus Foley, 61 In.	5625
Whip Hook, Figural, Squirrel, Horn, Amber Glass Eyes, Black Forest, 14½ x 4 In.	563
Woman, Face, Crown, Necklace, Carousel Part, Continental, 1900s, 18 x 14 x 7 In.	594
Woman, Holding Lamb, Painted, Signed, Lou Schifferl, 12 In.	340
Woman, Standing, Flowy Dress, Hardened Expression, 1900s, 13½ In.	84
Woman, Standing, Wearing Red Swimsuit, Painted, Early 1900s, 17¾ In.	156

WOODEN

Wooden wares were used in all parts of the home. Wood was used for many containers and tools. Small wooden pieces are called *treenware* in England, but the term *woodenware* is more common in the United States. Additional pieces may be found in the Advertising, Kitchen, and Tool categories.

Barrel, Flour, Hinged Lid, Stenciled & Grain Painted, Metal Band, 25½ In. .... *illus*	344
Barrel, Hornbeam, Carved, Cylindrical, Late 1800s, 24 In.	1000
Barrel, Oak, Lid, Hoops, Thin Branches, 1800s, 21 x 18 In.	150
Billiard Table, Miniature, Geometric Design, Continental, 1800s, 53 x 73 In.	2500
Book Carrier, Chinoiserie, Scroll Handles, Black Ground, 1800s, 6 x 19½ In.	175
Bowl, Barber, Turned, Cutout, Pierced Hole, Attached Rope, England, 1800s, 3 x 10 In.	4688
Bowl, Finn Juhl, Carved, Teak, Kay Bojesen, Denmark, c.1950, 5 x 11 In.	3438
Bowl, Grolla, Turned Wood, 5 Spouts, Grapevine, Carve, Top, 8½ x 4½ In.	18

Wood Carving, Whale, Finback, Inset Glass Eyes, Painted, Wick Ahrens, 2006, 33 x 10 In.
$8,775

Thomaston Place Auction Galleries

Wood Carving, Whale, Humpback, Carved, Painted, Roger Mitchell, Kingston, Mass., 38 In.
$625

Eldred's

Wooden, Barrel, Flour, Hinged Lid, Stenciled & Grain Painted, Metal Band, 25 ½ In.
$344

Hindman

TIP

Don't use cooking oil to polish furniture, cutting boards, even wooden salad bowls. The oil will eventually become rancid and the wood will have a bad odor and may even contaminate food.

TIP

The average burglar spends 60 seconds breaking into a house. If you can delay him with bars, locks, or other security measures, he may become impatient and leave.

Wooden, Brushpot, Furled Lotus Leaf & Stem, Lotus Buds & Leaves Base, Chinese, 1700s, 7 In.
$188

Eldred's

Wooden, Bucket, Peat, George III, Brassbound, Mahogany, Removable Liner, c.1765, 17 x 14 In.
$2,432

Neal Auction Company

Wooden, Chair, Elephant, Standing, Seat In Open Back, India, 24 x 24 x 32 In.
$288

Merrill's Auctions

Wooden, Container, Removable Lid, Treen, Vinegar Sponge, Mustard Ground, Mid 1800s, 10 x 8 In.
$720

Garth's Auctioneers & Appraisers

W

Wooden, Dish, Leaf Shape, Laminated Birch & Teak, Tapio Wirkkala, Finland, c.1951, 1 x 6 x 4 In.
$6,875

Wright

Wooden, Dog Carrier, Dome Top, Pine, Metal, H.S. Cooley, M.D., Keyport, N.J., c.1900, 32 x 40 x 27 In.
$1,080

Garth's Auctioneers & Appraisers

TIP
Don't store wooden bowls and other pieces on their sides. This can cause them to warp.

Wooden, Firkin, Painted, Green Surface, Swing Handle, 1800s, 11 In.
$554

Pook & Pook

Bowl, Norfolk Pine, Honey Color, Gourd Shape, North Pacific Islands, c.1940, 8 x 9 In.........	2490
Bowl, Oval Shape, Burl, Red Patina, 1700s, 12 ½ x 4 ¾ In............	531
Bowl, Tapered, Cone Shape, Marked, Norfolk Island Pine, 3 x 8 In.	556
Bowl, Treen, Bird's-Eye Maple, Turned, Wide Rim, Oiled, 1800s, 4 x 15 In.	660
Bowl, Treen, Carved Burl, Dry Natural Surface, 1700s, 7 ½ x 18 ½ In.	508
Bowl, Turned, Copper Wrapped Rim, Deep, 1800s, 7 ½ x 17 In.........	369
Bowl, Turned, Thick Rim, Blue Paint, Deep, 1700s, 12 In.	349
Brushpot, Furled Lotus Leaf & Stem, Lotus Buds & Leaves Base, Chinese, 1700s, 7 In.. *illus*	188
Bucket, Hoop & Stave Construction, Red Brown Washed, New England, 1800s, 6 x 12 In.....	750
Bucket, Inlaid, Mahogany, Swing Handle, Metal Liner, Stand, George III, 1700s, 20 x 14 In. .	313
Bucket, Mahogany, Brown, Bail Handle, Fenestrated Sides, 1800s, 13 In.	1250
Bucket, Oak, Brass Bound, Lion's Head & Ring Handles, Late 1800s, 12 x 14 In..........	192
Bucket, Peat, George III, Brassbound, Mahogany, Removable Liner, c.1765, 17 x 14 In. *illus*	2432
Bucket, Peat, Mahogany, Ebonized, Brass Liner, Swing Handle, Victorian, c.1850, 16 ½ x 11 ½ In..	492
Bucket, Picking, Swing Handle, Painted, Gray, 1800s, 11 x 11 In.	344
Bucket, Piggin, Deep, Painted, Scandinavia, 1800s, 24 ½ In........	290
Bucket, Sugar, Lid, Oak, Bentwood, Swing Handle & Bands, Copper Tacks, 1850s	90
Bucket, Treen, Carved, Oval Shape, Painted, 1800s, 9 x 6 x 7 In.	219
Bucket, Wire Bands, Bail Swing Handle, Grain Painted, Marked Eddy's, 1830s, 6 In.	168
Candleholder, 2 Rectangles Joined By Post, Small Depressions Below, 6 x 16 In.................	313
Candleholder, Figural, Angel, Kneeling, Picket, 30 x 15 x 9 In.	1872
Canister, Poplar, Lid, Painted, Sponge Decoration, Pennsylvania, 1800s, 10 In.	800
Canister, Treen, Turned, Brown, Circular Base, 1800s, 6 In.	113
Canister, Treen, Vinegar Sponge, Turned Bulbous Body, Stepped Lid, c.1850, 8 x 5 In..........	700
Canteen, Purse Shape, Carved, Handles, Geometrics, Pennsylvania Dutch, 1700s, 6 x 7 In. .	375
Chair, Elephant, Standing, Seat In Open Back, India, 24 x 24 x 32 In............... *illus*	288
Change Cover, Tavern, Figural, Woman, Pine, c.1850, 9 ⅝ In.	1024
Cigar Case, Mahogany, Carved, Philphlot Decoration, 1800s, 4 ½ x 7 In.	123
Container, Dome Lid, Treen, Yellow Paint, Footed, c.1850, 7 In.	450
Container, Lift Lid, Treen, Brown, Cylindrical, Mid 1800s, 8 x 5 In........	660
Container, Removable Lid, Treen, Vinegar Sponge, Mustard Ground, Mid 1800s, 10 x 8 In.*illus*	720
Dish, Leaf Shape, Laminated Birch & Teak, Tapio Wirkkala, Finland, c.1951, 1 x 6 x 4 In. *illus*	6875
Dog Carrier, Dome Top, Pine, Metal, H.S. Cooley, M.D., Keyport, N.J., c.1900, 32 x 40 x 27 In.. *illus*	1080
Firkin, Canted Sides, Lift-Off Lid, Wire Bail, Iron Bands, 1800s, 13 x 12 In	102
Firkin, Lid, Swing Handle, 4 Bands, 12 In.	86
Firkin, Painted, Green Surface, Swing Handle, 1800s, 11 In......... *illus*	554
Firkin, Pine, Painted, Multicolor, Star On Lid, 1800s, 9 In.........	1353
Firkin, Sugar Bucket, Slats, 4 Finger Bands, Paint, Wire Handle, New England, 1800s, 10 x 10 In...	325
Gavel, Isaac C. Parker, Hanging Judge, Frame, 1896, 10 ½ x 3 ½ x 1 ¾ In............	8288
Hibachi, Cylindrical, Bamboo, Roosters, Metal Lining, Multicolor, Japan, 14 ½ In...............	406
Hibachi, Tin Lined Compartment, Mesh Metal Lid, 11 x 10 x 7 In................ *illus*	384
Humidor, Burl Walnut, Square Shape, Dunhill, 6 x 9 ½ x 9 ½ In.	288
Humidor, Cigar, Dog & Fox, Basket, Rectangular Base, Black Forest, Late 1800s, 6 x 8 x 4 In. ...	344
Hutch, Watch, Carved Bone, Turned Standard, Drawer, Hamilton Watch, c.1870, 9 x 4 x 3 In....	732
Ice Bucket, Handle, Lid, Teak, Stamped, Dansk, Denmark, c.1965, 15 x 7 In. .... *illus*	188
Jar, Lift Lid, Treen, Chalice Shape, Brown, Footed, Mid 1800s, 5 In........	228
Jardiniere, Carved, Gilt, Scroll Finials, Bracket Feet, Neoclassical Style, Octagonal, 31 In..*illus*	1408
Jardiniere, Chinoiserie, Black Ground, Removable Tole Liner, Octagonal, 1800s, 7 x 14 ½ In..	575
Juggler's Pin, Cherry, Turned, Parcel Gilt, Spalding, 3 Lb., 20 In., Pair............	63
Keg, Oval, Oak, Brass Bands, Decal, Coat Of Arms, Bung Plug, Early 1900s, 24 In................	204
Knife Tray, Mahogany, Fan, Sawtooth, Dovetailed, Handle, 1800s, 5 x 11 x 7 In.......... *illus*	277
Knife Tray, Yew Wood, Flat Base, Early 1800s, 5 ½ x 13 In.	164
Mannequin, Clothing Form, Headless, Full Body, Child's Size, 42 In............. *illus*	1200
Obelisk, Orange Paint, Green Hardstone Base, 35 x 5 ¾ In., Pair.........	640
Panel, Remnant, Carved Finials, Orange Lacquer, 1800s, 36 ½ x 20 x 2 In., Pair	360
Propeller, Airplane, Laminated Hardwood, Brass, Steel, S&S Aircraft, Winnipeg, 91 In.	863
Propeller, Airplane, Laminated Oak, Aluminum Edge, Canvas Covered Tip, 96 x 3 In. *illus*	1053
Serving Tray, Mahogany, Oval Shape, Carved Gallery Rim, 2 Brass Handles, 24 x 18 In.	671

Wooden, Hibachi, Tin Lined Compartment, Mesh Metal Lid, 11 x 10 x 7 In.
$384

Roland NY Auctioneers & Appraisers

Wooden, Ice Bucket, Handle, Lid, Teak, Stamped, Dansk, Denmark, c.1965, 15 x 7 In.
$188

Wright

Wooden, Jardiniere, Carved, Gilt, Scroll Finials, Bracket Feet, Neoclassical Style, Octagonal, 31 In.
$1,408

Neal Auction Company

Wooden, Knife Tray, Mahogany, Fan, Sawtooth, Dovetailed, Handle, 1800s, 5 x 11 x 7 In.
$277

Pook & Pook

Wooden, Mannequin, Clothing Form, Headless, Full Body, Child's Size, 42 In.
$1,200

Chupp Auctions & Real Estate, LLC

Wooden, Tray, Round, Rosewood, Silver, Tapio Wirkkala, Kultakeskus Oy, Finland, 1957, ¾ x 10¾ In.
$375

Wright

Wooden, Urn, Cutlery, Georgian Style, Mahogany, Telescoping Lid, Acorn Finial, Early 1900s, 26 In., Pair
$960

Neal Auction Company

Wooden, Propeller, Airplane, Laminated Oak, Aluminum Edge, Canvas Covered Tip, 96 x 3 In.
$1,053

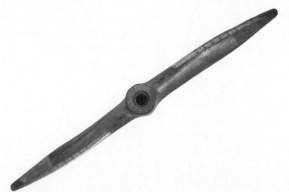

Thomaston Place Auction Galleries

W

Wooden, Watch Hutch, Walnut, Carved, Cutout Block Shape, Mid Atlantic, Folk Art, 1850s, 7 x 5 x 2 In.
$152

Jeffrey S. Evans & Associates

Wooden, Whirligig, Directional, Birdhouse, Painted, Wood & Wire, Victorian, 31 x 16 x 14 In.
$750

Hindman

TIP
Wooden boxes, toys, or decoys should not be kept on the fireplace mantel or nearby floor areas when the fire is burning. The heat dries the wood and the paint. Unprotected wooden items on warm TV sets and stereos may also be damaged.

Serving Tray, Oval, Carved, Flower Bands, 2 Handles, Continental, 1900s, 23½ x 15 In.	212
Sign, Home Is The House That Shelters A Friend, Oak, Iron Chain, c.1910, 22 x 7 In............	678
Sign, Private Property, Gold & Black, c.1885, 10 x 85 x 2¼ In.	726
Tankard, Cylindrical, Painted, Red Ground, Handle, Flowers, Blue, Black, Norway, 1900s, 12 In..	88
Tankard, Lift Lid, Flowers, Painted, Scandinavia, 1800s, 11 In..	378
Tray, Bread Slice Shape, Maple, Plywood, Soinne & Kni Oy, Finland, c.1955, 21 x 16 In., Pair...	260
Tray, Pine, 3-Sided Gallery, White Paint, Hardwood Stand, Late 1800s, 33 x 15 x 18 In.	240
Tray, Round, Rosewood, Silver, Tapio Wirkkala, Kultakeskus Oy, Finland, 1957, ¾ x 10¾ In.. *illus*	375
Trencher, Oblong, Shallow, Reddish Brown Paint, Leather Hanging Tab, 1800s, 4 x 10 x 21 In.....	420
Tub, Oval, Green Paint, Oak Hoop, Brass Ring Hanger, c.1815, 7 x 17 x 11 In........................	720
Tub, Oval, Painted, Yellow & Black, Pierced Heart Handles, 1800s, 6 In.	176
Urn, Cutlery, Georgian Style, Mahogany, Telescoping Lid, Acorn Finial, Early 1900s, 26 In., Pair. *illus*	960
Urn, Lift-Off Lid, Treen, Mahogany, 1800s, 12 x 5½ In.	176
Vase, Treen, Solid Base, Cabinetmaker, Robert Treate Hogg, 7 In....................................	30
Watch Hutch, Walnut, Carved, Cutout Block Shape, Mid Atlantic, Folk Art, 1850s, 7 x 5 x 2 In..... *illus*	152
Whirligig, Directional, Birdhouse, Painted, Wood & Wire, Victorian, 31 x 16 x 14 In. .. *illus*	750

WORCESTER

Worcester porcelains were made in Worcester, England, starting in 1751. The firm went through many name changes and eventually, in 1862, became The Royal Worcester Porcelain Company Ltd. Collectors often refer to Dr. Wall, Barr, Flight, and other names that indicate time periods or artists at the factory. It became part of Royal Worcester Spode Ltd. in 1976. The company was bought by the Portmeirion Group in 2009. Related pieces may be found in the Royal Worcester category.

Beaker, Vicars Island, Lake, Black & Orange Paint, Flight & Barr, 1796, 3¾ In.	1111
Chamberstick, Painted Scene, Shaped Base, Flight & Barr, Early 1800s, 3 In., Pair .... *illus*	1845
Jug, Circular Panel, Cow, Crown, Flowers, Leaves, Abergavenny, 1813, 6 In.	1196
Mug, Blue Ground, Front Panel, Dog Running, Grainger & Co., c.1810, 3½ In.	1281
Plate, Farm, Pig, Sty, Boar On Reverse, Anthemion Border, Chamberlain & Co., 1839, 10½ In..	3075
Vase, Falstaff, Oval Portrait, Blue Ground, Dragon Handle, Thomas Baxter, 1814, 9¾ In.. *illus*	3685

WORLD WAR

World War I and World War II souvenirs are collected today. Be careful not to store anything that includes live ammunition. Your local police will tell you how to dispose of the explosives. See also Sword and Trench Art.

WORLD WAR I

Canteen, Palco, Aluminum, Round, 1915	18
Cigar Box, Who Stands If Freedom Falls?, Battle Scene, Royal Portraits, Silver Plate, 1915 ..	191
Helmet, Adrian, RF Emblem, Metal, Leather Liner, France, 10½ In. .... *illus*	178
Helmet, Brodie, Doughboy, M1917, Army Green Paint, Liner, Steel................................ *illus*	69
Helmet, First Infantry Div., Leather Chin Strap, U.S., 1917	150
Picture, Needlework, 2 Carte De Visite, Allies' Flags, Mahogany Ogee Frame, Britain, 21 x 28 In. .	468
Poster, Fight, Third Liberty Loan, Howard Chandler Christy, Frame, 1917, 39½ x 28 In. .... *illus*	531
Poster, Food Is Ammunition Don't Waste It, Signed, 29 x 21 In..................................... *illus*	325
Poster, In The Name Of Mercy, Casualty, Red Cross Nurse, Albert Herter, 40 x 30 In............	118
Poster, Nurse, Reaching Out, Red Cross Apron & Cap, Solders, Flag, H. Fischer, 20 x 25 In..	220
Poster, Sow The Seeds Of Victory, James Montgomery Flagg, 1918, 32 x 21 In......................	1062
Poster, War Clouds Gather, Manhood Willing But Unarmed, Hazel Roberts, 1916, 25 x 19 In.	455
Stretcher, Gold Medal Folding Camp Furniture, Racine, Wisconsin, c.1917, 80 In........ *illus*	36
Sword, Saber, Patton, Model 1913, World War I, Springfield Armory Mark, 42¾ In.	167
Theodolite, Artillery Director, No. 5, Gun Sight, Brass, Great Britain, 1914, 15 x 7½ x 6 In.	115
Uniform, Tunic, USMC, 1st Marine Aviation Force, P1917, Eagle Buttons, Wool, 16 x 13 In. ....*illus*	523

WORLD WAR II

Artillery Shell, Naval, Dummy, Projectile Head, Brass Neck, Wood Body, Steel Base, 33 x 4 x 4 In.	400
Ashtray, Adolf Hitler, Help, Mouth Wide Open, Painted, Terra-Cotta, 6 x 4 x 4 In.................	1334

Worcester, Chamberstick, Painted Scene, Shaped Base, Flight & Barr, Early 1800s, 3 In., Pair
$1,845

Pook & Pook

Worcester, Vase, Falstaff, Oval Portrait, Blue Ground, Dragon Handle, Thomas Baxter, 1814, 9¾ In.
$3,685

Bonhams

The Military Smokes
Seventy-five percent of tobacco production was provided to the military during World War II.

World War I, Helmet, Adrian, RF Emblem, Metal, Leather Liner, France, 10½ In.
$178

White's Auctions

World War I, Helmet, Brodie, Doughboy, M1917, Army Green Paint, Liner, Steel
$69

Donley Auctions

World War I, Poster, Fight, Third Liberty Loan, Howard Chandler Christy, Frame, 1917, 39½ x 28 In.
$531

Copake Auction

World War I, Poster, Food Is Ammunition Don't Waste It, Signed, 29 x 21 In.
$325

Soulis Auctions

World War I, Stretcher, Gold Medal Folding Camp Furniture, Racine, Wisconsin, c.1917, 80 In.
$36

Jeffrey S. Evans & Associates

TIP
Never move an object that might explode. Call the local police bomb squad. Many accidents are caused by old souvenir hand grenades and firearms.

World War I, Uniform, Tunic, USMC, 1st Marine Aviation Force, P1917, Eagle Buttons, Wool, 16 x 13 In.
$523

Morphy Auctions

World War II, Bell, Ship, U.S. Navy, Nickel Plated, Bronze, Acorn Nut & Clapper, 10½ x 9¾ In.
$761

Thomaston Place Auction Galleries

W

World War II, Cap, Waffen SS Panzer M43, Black Wool, Eagle & Skull Zigzag Machine Stitch, 2 Buttons
$1,260

Morphy Auctions

World War II, Flight Suit, U.S. Army Air Force, L-1 Type
$127

Donley Auctions

World War II, Jacket, Flight, Brown Leather, Patches, USAAF Type A, SSgt. Chester R. Bigelow, 14 x 16 x 6 In.
$5,040

Morphy Auctions

World War II, Life Vest, Rubberized Canvas, Orange, Silver Hardware, U.S. Navy MK-1, 10 x 10 In.
$600

Morphy Auctions

World War II, Poster, America's Answer!, Production, Gloved Hand, Wrench, Jean Carlu, 1942, 29 x 39 In.
$875

Swann Auction Galleries

World War II, Poster, Freedom Of Worship, Buy War Bonds, Canvas, Norman Rockwell, 1943, 60 x 45 In.
$192

Garth's Auctioneers & Appraisers

Bell, Ship, U.S. Navy, Nickel Plated, Bronze, Acorn Nut & Clapper, 10½ x 9¾ In........... *illus* 761
Boots, Winter, Black, Leather, Brown Lace, M1944, U.S., 1943, 12 In. 92
Canteen, U.S., Brown Cloth, Lid Chain, Foley Mfg. Co., 1942.. 69
Cap, Waffen SS Panzer M43, Black Wool, Eagle & Skull Zigzag Machine Stitch, 2 Buttons. *illus* 1260
Cup, British War Relief Society, Barrel Shape, Spode, c.1940, 4½ In., 6 Piece 48
Dagger, German Luftwaffe, Original Scabbard, Straps, Silver Portepee, 16¾ In.................. 480
Dagger, Kriegsmarine, Nickel Plated Blade, Brass Scabbard, Germany, 15 In...................... 1024
Dagger, Luftwaffe, Engraved, Scabbard, Clemen & Jung.. 1265
Flag, Krieg's, Black & White, Red Ground, Germany, c.1935-45, 125 x 75 In......................... 1029
Flight Suit, U.S. Army Air Force, L-1 Type.. *illus* 127
Gorget, 3rd Reich SA/SS, Nickel Plated Brass, Patina, Eagle & Swastika 900
Hat, Overseas, U.S., General, Sterling Silver Star Pin, Marked, Paylud 81
Helmet, M1, Liner, Staff Sergeant Rank, Shell, Chin Strap 196
Helmet, M30, Bucket Cap Style, Metal, Czechoslovakia.. 115
Jacket, Bomber, Air Force, Brown Leather, Zipper 406
Jacket, Flight, Brown Leather, Patches, USAAF Type A, SSgt. Chester R. Bigelow, 14 x 16 x 6 In..... *illus* 5040
Jacket, Special Police, War Service, Oakland, Wool, Women's, c.1942 180
Lamp, Portside, Kriegsmarine, Red Paint, Electric, Germany 92
Life Vest, Rubberized Canvas, Orange, Silver Hardware, U.S. Navy MK-1, 10 x 10 In..... *illus* 600
Model, Submarine, USS Sea Fox, Half Hull, Aluminum, On Teak Plaque, 1944, 37 x 10 x 40 In. 585
Model, USS Missouri, Japanese Surrender, Plexiglas Case, M.F. Gowen, 16½ x 61 x 12½ In.. 322
Overcoat, U.S. Army Officer's, First Lieutenant Bars Pinned, Buttons, Belt, 39S.................. 29
Poster, America's Answer!, Production, Gloved Hand, Wrench, Jean Carlu, 1942, 29 x 39 In.... *illus* 875
Poster, Freedom Of Worship, Buy War Bonds, Canvas, Norman Rockwell, 1943, 60 x 45 In.....*illus* 192
Poster, Keep It Under Your Stetson, Man Holding On Rope, c.1942, 38 x 28 In....................... 1875
Poster, Save Freedom Of Worship, Buy War Bonds, Norman Rockwell, 30 x 21½ In.............. 118
Sword, Officer's, Lutzow, Scabbard, Knot Handle, Eickhorn, Germany................................... 1955
Trade Stimulator, Dummy Bomb, Wood, Steel, Ft. Mifflin, Stahot Heater, 1930s, 31 In., Pair..... *illus* 270

WORLD'S FAIR

World's Fair souvenirs from all of the fairs are collected. The first fair was the Great Exhibition of 1851 in London. Some other important exhibitions and fairs include Philadelphia, 1876 (Centennial); Chicago, 1893 (World's Columbian); Buffalo, 1901 (Pan-American); St. Louis, 1904 (Louisiana Purchase); Portland, 1905 (Lewis & Clark Centennial Exposition); Seattle, 1909 (Alaska-Yukon-Pacific Exposition); San Francisco, 1915 (Panama-Pacific); Paris (International Exposition of Modern Decorative and Industrial Arts), 1925; Philadelphia, 1926 (Sesquicentennial); Chicago, 1933 (Century of Progress); Cleveland, 1936 (Great Lakes); San Francisco, 1939 (Golden Gate International); New York, 1939 (World of Tomorrow); Seattle, 1962 (Century 21); New York, 1964; Montreal, 1967; Knoxville (Energy Turns the World) 1982; New Orleans, 1984; Tsukuba, Japan, 1985; Vancouver, Canada, 1986; Brisbane, Australia, 1988; Seville, Spain, 1992; Genoa, Italy, 1992; Seoul, South Korea, 1993; Lisbon, Portugal, 1998; Hanover, Germany, 2000; Shanghai, China, 2010; and Milan, Italy, 2015. Memorabilia of fairs include directories, pictures, fabrics, ceramics, etc. Memorabilia from other similar celebrations may be listed in the Souvenir category.

Banner, 1893, Chicago, Columbus & Globe, 1492-1892, 35 x 25 In.. 135
Book Press, 1893, Chicago, Cast Iron, Gilt, Highest Award, 17 x 12 x 14 In........................... 381
Box, Hinged Lid, 1851, London, Crystal Palace, Tortoiseshell, Wood Case, 1830s, 2 x 9 x 3 In. 610
Cane, 1939, New York, Pullout Map, Amusement Area, 35 In. 92
Chocolate Pot, 1904, St. Louis, Machinery Building, Transfer, Porcelain, Gilt, Germany, 9 In.. *illus* 72
Game, 1904, St. Louis, Board, Foxy Grandpa, Complete, 16 x 9 In.. 300
Lamp, 1939, New York, Electric, Glass, Saturn, Ring, Conical Base, 11 In.................... *illus* 1265
Letter Holder, 1904, St. Louis, Desktop, Gilt Metal, Cascades & Festival Hall Base, 6 In....... 108
Poster, 1964, New York, Go By Train, Pennsylvania Railroad, Dated 1961, 33 x 21 In...*illus* 266
Toy, 1893, Chicago, Trolley, Horse Drawn, Jackson Park Via Grand Boulevard, Bliss Mfg., c.1895, *illus* 1625

World War II, Trade Stimulator, Dummy Bomb, Wood, Steel, Ft. Mifflin, Stahot Heater, 1930s, 31 In., Pair
$270

Selkirk Auctioneers & Appraisers

World's Fair, Chocolate Pot, 1904, St. Louis, Machinery Building, Transfer, Porcelain, Gilt, Germany, 9 In.
$72

Selkirk Auctioneers & Appraisers

World's Fair, Lamp, 1939, New York, Electric, Glass, Saturn, Ring, Conical Base, 11 In.
$1,265

Blackwell Auctions

W

World's Fair, Poster, 1964, New York, Go By Train, Pennsylvania Railroad, Dated 1961, 33 x 21 In.
$266

Soulis Auctions

WPA, Group, Abraham Lincoln & Family, Ceramic, Multicolor, Grace Luse, Ohio, c.1935, 5 ¾ In.
$187

Toomey & Co. Auctioneers

Wristwatch, Bulova, 18K Yellow Gold, Baton Hands, Silver, Automatic, Waterproof, 7 ¼ In.
$2,280

Michaan's Auctions

Wristwatch, Cartier, Tank Watch, Gold Plated, Roman Numerals, Crocodile Leather Band, 7 ½ In.
$1,688

Leland Little Auctions

World's Fair, Toy, 1893, Chicago, Trolley, Horse Drawn, Jackson Park Via Grand Boulevard, Bliss Mfg., c.1895
$1,625

Hindman

Wristwatch, Hermes, Medor, Gold Plate, Water Resistant, Flip Top Case, Orange Leather Band, 8 In.
$1,140

Abington Auction Gallery

World's Fair, Vase, 1893, Columbian Exposition, Opalescent, Jack-In-The-Pulpit, Flowers, France, 6 In.
$336

Charleston Estate Auctions

Wristwatch, Baume & Mercier, Riviera, Quartz, Stainless & Diamond, 18K Yellow Gold, Woman's, 7 ½ In.
$854

Neal Auction Company

W

Vase, 1893, Columbian Exposition, Opalescent, Jack-In-The-Pulpit, Flowers, France, 6 In. *illus* — 336

Vase, 1904, St. Louis, Dark Green, 2 Handles, Cascade Gardens, Victoria, Carlsbad, Austria, 6 In. — 180

Vase, 1904, St. Louis, Top Hat Shape, Gilt, Palace Of Liberal Arts, Victoria, Carlsbad, Austria, 4 In. . — 48

WPA

WPA is the abbreviation for Works Progress Administration, a program created by executive order in 1935 to provide jobs for millions of unemployed Americans. Artists were hired to create murals, paintings, drawings, and sculptures for public buildings. Pieces are marked *WPA* and may have the artist's name on them.

Banner, Circus Scene, Block Print, Red Border, Barbara Warren, Milwaukee, 32 ½ x 34 In. — 1625

Group, A Christmas Carol, Bob Cratchit, 2 Children, Dog, Ceramic, Edris Eckhardt, 9 In. .... — 484

Group, Abraham Lincoln & Family, Ceramic, Multicolor, Grace Luse, Ohio, c.1935, 5 ¾ In.......*illus* — 187

Model, Trolley, Orange, East & West End Line, Wisconsin, 1930s, 7 x 11 x 3 In. — 450

Poster, Early Is The Watchword!, Cancer Is Curable, Rooster, Silkscreen, c.1937, 14 x 11 In. — 531

Poster, Indian Court, Apache Dancer, Golden Gate Expo, Louis Siegriest, 1939, 36 x 24 In. . — 832

Print, Elizabethan Fashion, Man & Woman, Lithograph, Hand Colored, Plate No. 42, 23 x 18 In.. — 26

Puppet Set, Human Figures, Wood Head & Hands, Fabric Clothing 14 In., 6 Piece .... — 344

WRISTWATCH

Wristwatches came into use during World War I. Wristwatches are listed here by manufacturer or as advertising or character watches. Wristwatches may also be listed in other categories. Pocket watches are listed in the Watch category.

Baume & Mercier, Riviera, Quartz, Stainless & Diamond, 18K Yellow Gold, Woman's, 7 ½ In.. *illus* — 854

Bueche Girod, 18K Yellow Gold, Oval, Tile Dial, Florentine Bracelet, Woman's, 7 x 1 In. ..... — 2500

Bulova, 18K Yellow Gold, Baton Hands, Silver, Automatic, Waterproof, 7 ¼ In.............*illus* — 2280

Cartier, Tank Americaine, Yellow Gold, Cream Dial, Brown Leather Band............................ — 2880

Cartier, Tank Watch, Gold Plated, Roman Numerals, Crocodile Leather Band, 7 ½ In .....*illus* — 1688

Cartier, Vermeil, Quartz, Gold Dial, Black Band, Woman's, 1 ¾ In. .... — 488

Chronograph, Hemipode, Rose Gold Case, Rubber Band, Marc Newson, 45 x 45 In. .... — 18750

Croton, 14K Yellow Gold, Link Band, 7 Rows, Battery Operated, 6 In. .... — 780

Girard-Perrigaux, Ferrari, 18K Rose Gold, Automatic, Crocodile Leather Band, 1 ½ In. .... — 2160

Hermes, Medor, Gold Plate, Water Resistant, Flip Top Case, Orange Leather Band, 8 In....... *illus* — 1140

Longines, 10K Gold, Automatic, Grand Prize, Mystery Dial, Florentine Case, Leather Band, 8 In... — 480

Longines, 14K Gold, Square Dial, Leather Band... — 308

Longines, Admiral, 10K Gold Filled, 5-Star Automatic, Leather Band............................ — 316

Movado, Moonphase, Triple Date, Gold Top Bezel & Crown, Black Leather Band, 1 ¼ In...... — 480

Omega, 18K Yellow Gold, Brown Leather Band, Round, 8 ¼ In.. — 840

Omega, Automatic, Seamaster, Calendar Watch, Stainless Steel, 1 3⁄10 In. .... — 920

Orator, 18K Yellow Gold, Swiss Tank, Automatic, Brown Alligator Leather Band, 8 ½ In...... — 480

Pequignet Moorea, Gilt Hands, Silver Band, Woman's, Wood Box .... — 156

Perry, Platinum, Diamond, 17 Jewel, Swiss, Woman's ....*illus* — 585

Rolex, Oyster Perpetual, Chronometer, Stainless Steel, Leather Band, 1 ½ In. .... — 2750

Rolex, Silver & Goldtone Face, Brown Leather Band, No. 23106, 2317...........................*illus* — 1625

Tiffany & Co., Atlas, Stainless Steel, Chronograph, Blue Dial, Roman Numerals, Quartz, 1 ¾ In. — 1625

Vacheron & Constantin, 18K White Gold, Tonneau Case, Ivory Dial, Leather Band, Geneve, 1 3⁄8 In. — 3125

YELLOWWARE

Yellowware is a heavy earthenware made of a yellowish clay. It varies in color from light yellow to orange-yellow. Many nineteenth- and twentieth-century kitchen bowls and jugs were made of yellowware. It was made in England and in the United States. Another form of pottery that is sometimes classed as yellowware is listed in this book in the Mocha category.

Figurine, Cat, Seated, Oblong Base, Rockingham Glaze, Late 1800s, 11 ¼ In....................... — 813

Figurine, Lion, Walking, Green, Brown, Mottling, England, 1800s, 4 ½ x 7 In.............*illus* — 531

Wristwatch, Perry, Platinum, Diamond, 17 Jewel, Swiss, Woman's
$585

Thomaston Place Auction Galleries

Wristwatch, Rolex, Silver & Goldtone Face, Brown Leather Band, No. 23106, 2317
$1,625

Turner Auctions + Appraisals

Yellowware, Figurine, Lion, Walking, Green, Brown, Mottling, England, 1800s, 4 ½ x 7 In.
$531

Wiederseim Auctions

X Y Z

Yellowware, Mixing Bowl, Blue Seaweed, White Slip Band, Footed Base, 6 x 13 In.
$136

Hartzell's Auction Gallery Inc.

Zsolnay, Vase, Baluster Shape, Pink & Yellow Flowers, 1900s, 16 x 7 x In., Pair
$600

Bruneau & Co. Auctioneers

> **TIP**
> Be careful load-
> ing the dishwasher.
> Metal utensils that
> touch ceramic dishes
> may leave marks on
> the china. Dishes
> can also show black
> marks if rubbed
> against the stainless
> steel sink. The marks
> can be removed with
> a wet sponge and a
> bit of silver polish or
> other mild abrasive.

Flask, Fish Shape, Rockingham Glaze, 1800s, 8¾ In. 281
Mixing Bowl, Blue Seaweed, White Slip Band, Footed Base, 6 x 13 In. .... *illus* 136

LA MORO — ZANESVILLE

Zanesville Art Pottery was founded in 1900 by David Schmidt in Zanesville, Ohio. The firm made faience umbrella stands, jardinieres, and pedestals. The company closed in 1920 and Weller bought the factory. Many pieces are marked with just the words *La Moro.*

Planter, Arts & Crafts, Gray, Dark Green Splashes, Brown & Black Drip Glaze, c.1925, 4 x 5 In. 35
Vase, Ball Shape, Handles, Black, Yellow Drip, 7 x 8 In. 175
Vase, Feather, Shouldered, Tapered, Ring Foot, Burgundy Matte Glaze, 1920s, 8 In. 125

ZSOLNAY

Zsolnay pottery was made in Hungary after 1853 and was characterized by Persian, Art Nouveau, or Hungarian motifs. A series of new Zsolnay figurines with green-gold luster finish is available in many shops today. Early Zsolnay was not marked, but by 1878 the tower trademark was used.

Zsolnay Porcelanmanufaktura
1878

Zsolnay Porcelanmanufaktura
1899–1920

Zsolnay Porcelanmanufaktura
1900+

Figure, 2 Bears Fighting, Brown & White, 9 x 6 x 11 In. 71
Vase, Art Nouveau, Trees, Sang De Boeuf Glaze, Tapered, Stand-Up Rim, 5 Towers Mark, 8 x 3 In. . 750
Vase, Baluster Shape, Pink & Yellow Flowers, 1900s, 16 x 7 x In., Pair .... *illus* 600

INDEX

This index is computer-generated, making it as complete and accurate as possible. References in upper-case type are category listings. Those in lowercase letters refer to additional pages where pieces can be found. There is also an internal cross-referencing system used in the main part of the book, so if you look for a Kewpie doll in the Doll category, you will be told it is in its own category. There is additional information at the end of many paragraphs about where to find prices of pieces similar to yours.

PHOTO CREDITS

We have included the name of the auction house or photographer with each pictured object. This is a list of the addresses of those who have contributed photographs and information for this book. Last year many auction houses merged and names and addresses changed. We put the most recent available information in this list. Every dealer or auction has to buy antiques to have items to sell. Call or email a dealer or auction house if you want to discuss buying or selling. If you need an appraisal or advice, remember that appraising is part of their business and fees may be charged.

Abington Auction Gallery
3263 N. Dixie Hwy.
Fort Lauderdale, FL 33334
abingtonauctions.com
954-900-4869

Ahlers & Ogletree Auction Gallery
700 Miami Cir. N.E., Suite 210
Atlanta, GA 30324
aandoauctions.com
404-869-2478

Alderfer Auction Company
501 Fairgrounds Rd.
Hatfield, PA 19440
alderferauction.com
215-393-3000

Alex Cooper Auctioneers
908 York Rd.
Towson, MD 21204
alexcooper.com
410-828-4838

American Bottle Auctions
915 28th St.
Sacramento, CA 95816
americanbottle.com
800-806-7722

Andrew Jones Auctions
2221 S. Main St.
Los Angeles, CA 90007
andrewjonesauctions.com
213-748-8008

Apple Tree Auction Center
1625 W. Church St.
Newark, OH 43055
appletreeauction.com
704-344-4282

Auctions at Showplace, NYC
40 W. 25th St.
New York, NY 10010
nyshowplace.com
212-633-6063

Bakker Auctions
359 Commercial St.
Provincetown, MA 02657
bakkerproject.com
508-413-9758

Bertoia Auctions
2141 DeMarco Dr.
Vineland, NJ 08360
bertoiaauctions.com
856-692-1881

Bill and Jill Insulators
103 Canterbury Ct.
Carlisle, MA 01741
billandjillinsulators.com
781-999-3048

Blackwell Auctions
5251 110th Ave. N., Suite 118
Clearwater, FL 33760
blackwellauctions.com
727-546-0200

Blanchard's Auction Service LLC
1891 Morley-Potsdam Rd.
Potsdam, NY 13676
blanchardsauctionservice.com
315-265-5070

Bonhams
101 New Bond St.
London W1S 1SR
  United Kingdom
bonhams.com
+44 20 7447 7447

Bruneau & Co. Auctioneers
63 4th Ave.
Cranston, RI 02910
bruneauandco.com
401-533-9980

Brunk Auctions
P.O. Box 2135
Asheville, NC 28802
brunkauctions.com
828-254-6846

Bunch Auctions
1 Hillman Dr.
Chadds Ford, PA 19317
bunchauctions.com
610-558-1800

California Historical Design
1901 Broadway
Alameda, CA 94501
acstickley.com
510-647-3621

Carey Auctions
P.O. Box 500
Youngstown, PA 15696
careyauction.com
814-539-7653

Carlsen Gallery
9931 State Route 32
Freehold, NY 12431
carlsengallery.com
518-634-2466

Charleston Estate Auctions
918 Lansing Dr., Suite E
Mt. Pleasant, SC 29464
charlestonestateauctions.com
843-696-3335

Charlton Hall Auctions
7 Lexington Dr.
West Columbia, SC 29170
charltonhallauctions.com
803-779-5678

Chupp Auctions & Real Estate, LLC
890 S. Van Buren St.
Shipshewana, IN 46565
auctionzip.com/IN-Auctioneers/40698.html
260-768-7616

Clars Auction Gallery
5644 Telegraph Ave.
Oakland, CA 94609
clars.com
510-428-0100

ComicConnect.com

Conestoga Auction Company
A Division of Hess Auction Group
768 Graystone Rd.
Manheim, PA 17545
hessauctiongroup.com
717-664-5238

Copake Auction
266 E. Main St.
Copake, NY 12516
copakeauction.com
518-329-1142

Cordier Auctions
1500 Paxton St.
Harrisburg, PA 17104
cordierauction.com
717-731-8662

Cottone Auctions
120 Court St.
Geneseo, NY 14454
cottoneauctions.com
585-243-1000

Cowan's Auctions
6270 Este Ave.
Cincinnati, OH 45232
cowanauctions.com
513-871-8670

Crescent City Auction Gallery
1330 St. Charles Ave.
New Orleans, LA 70130
crescentcityauctiongallery.com
504-529-5057

CRN Auctions
57 Bay State Rd.
Cambridge, MA 02138
crnauctions.com
617-661-9582

Crocker Farm, Inc.
15900 York Rd.
Sparks, MD 21152
crockerfarm.com
410-472-2016

Donley Auctions
8512 S. Union Rd.
Union, IL 60180
donleyauctions.com
815-923-7000

Doyle
175 E. 87th St
New York, NY 10128
doyle.com
212-427-4141

DuMouchelles
409 E. Jefferson Ave.
Detroit, MI 48226
dumoart.com
313-963-6255

Early American History Auctions
P. O. Box 3507
Rancho Santa Fe, CA 92067
earlyamerican.com
858-759-3290

eBay
ebay.com

Eldred's
P.O. Box 796
1483 Route 6A
East Dennis, MA 02641
eldreds.com
508-385-3116

Etsy
Etsy.com

Fairfield Auction
707 Main St. (Route 25)
Monroe, CT 06468
fairfieldauction.com
203-880-5200

Fontaine's Auction Gallery
1485 W. Housatonic St.
Pittsfield, MA 01201
fontainesauction.com
413-448-8922

Freeman's
1808 Chestnut St.
Philadelphia, PA 19103
freemansauction.com
215-563-9275

Garth's Auctioneers & Appraisers
P.O. Box 758
Columbus, OH 43216
garths.com
740-362-4771

Girard Auction & Land Brokers, Inc.
P.O. Box 358
15 Ohio St.
Wakonda, SD 57073
girardauction.com
605-267-2421

Glass Works Auctions
102 Jefferson St.
East Greenville, PA 18041
glswrk-auction.com
215-679-5849

Goldin Auctions
P.O. Box 358
160 E. Ninth Ave., Suite A
Runnemede, NJ 08078
goldinauctions.com
856-767-8550

Greenwich Auction
83 Harvard Ave.
Stamford, CT 06902
greenwichauction.net
203-355-9335

Guyette & Deeter, Inc.
1210 Talbot St., Unit A
St. Michaels, MD 21663
guyetteanddeeter.com
410-745-0485

Hake's Auctions
P.O. Box 12001
York, PA 17402
hakes.com
717-434-1600

Hannam's Auctioneers
The Old Dairy
Norton Farm
Selborne, Hampshire GU34 3NB
    United Kingdom
hannamsauctioneers.com
+44 1420 511788

Hartzell's Auction Gallery Inc.
521 Richmond Rd.
Bangor, PA 18013
hartzellsauction.com
610-588-5831

Heritage Auctions
P.O. Box 619999
Dallas, TX 75261
ha.com
214-528-3500

Hindman
1338 W. Lake St.
Chicago, IL 60607
hindmanauctions.com
312-280-1212

Hudson Valley Auctions
P.O. Box 432
Cornwall, NY 12518
hudsonvalleyauctions.com
914-213-0425

Hunt & Peck Auctions, LLC
14 E. Luray Shopping Center
Luray, VA 22835
huntandpeckauctions.com
540-742-1239

I.M. Chait Gallery/Auctioneers
1410 S. Olive St.
Los Angeles, CA 90015
chait.com
310-285-0182

Jaremos
6101 Long Prairie Rd., Suite 744-169
Flower Mound, TX 75028
jaremos.com
630-248-7785

Jeffrey S. Evans & Associates
P.O. Box 2638
Harrisonburg, VA 22801
jeffreysevans.com
540-434-3939

John McInnis Auctioneers
76 Main St.
Amesbury, MA 01913
mcinnisauctions.com
978-388-0400

John Moran Auctioneers
145 E. Walnut Ave.
Monrovia, CA 91016
johnmoran.com
626-793-1833

Julien's Auctions
13007 S. Western Ave.
Gardena, CA 90249
juliensauctions.com
310-836-1818

Kaminski Auctions
117 Elliott St.
Beverly, MA 01915
kaminskiauctions.com
978-927-2223

Kodner Galleries, Inc.
45 S. Federal Hwy.
Dania Beach, FL 33004
kodner.com
954-925-2550

Le Shoppe Auction House
Le Shoppe Too
3225 Orchard Lake Rd.
Keego Harbor, MI 48320
leshoppetoo.com
248-481-8884

Ledbetter Folk Art Auction
1001 Springwood Ave.
Gibsonville, NC 27249
ledbetterauctions.com
336-524-1077

Leland Little Auctions
620 Cornerstone Ct.
Hillsborough, NC 27278
lelandlittle.com
919-644-1243

Lion and Unicorn
200 Oakwood Ln., Ste. 200
Hollywood, FL 33020
lionandunicorn.com
954-866-8044

Lyon & Turnbull
33 Broughton Pl.
Edinburgh, EH1 3RR
   United Kingdom
lyonandturnbull.com
+44 131 557 8844

Main Auction Galleries, Inc.
137 W. 4th St.
Cincinnati, OH 45202
mainauctiongalleries.com
513-621-1280

Martin Auction Co.
P.O. Box 2
100 Lick Creek Rd.
Anna, IL 62906
martinauctionco.com
618-833-3589

Matthew Bullock Auctioneers
421 E. Stevenson Rd.
Ottawa, IL 61350
bullockauctioneers.com
815-220-5005

Matthews Auctions, LLC
19186 Nokomis Rd.
Nokomis, IL 62075
matthewsauctions.com
217-563-8880

McMurray Antiques & Auctions
P.O. Box 393
Kirkwood, NY 13795
mcmurrayauctions.com
607-775-5972

Merrill's Auctions
P.O. Box 558
Williston, VT 05495
merrillsauction.com
802-878-2625

Michaan's Auctions
2751 Todd St.
Alameda, CA 94501
michaans.com
800-380-9822

Mid-Hudson Auction Galleries
179 Temple Hill Rd., Suite 100B
New Windsor, NY 12553
midhudsongalleries.com
914-882-7356

Milestone Auctions
38198 Willoughby Pkwy.
Willoughby, OH 44094
milestoneauctions.com
440-527-8060

Morphy Auctions
2000 N. Reading Rd.
Denver, PA 17517
morphyauctions.com
877-968-8880

Nadeau's Auction Gallery
25 Meadow Rd.
Windsor, CT 06095
nadeausauction.com
860-249-2444

Nation's Attic
448 S. Pattie St.
Wichita, KS 67211
nationsattic.com
316-371-1828

Neal Auction Company
4038 Magazine St.
New Orleans, LA 70115
nealauction.com
800-467-5329

Neue Auctions
23533 Mercantile Rd., Suite 119
Beachwood, OH 44122
neueauctions.com
216-245-6707

New Haven Auctions
14 Business Park Dr., Suite 5
Branford, CT 06405
475-234-5120
newhavenauctions.com

Norman C. Heckler & Company
79 Bradford Corner Rd.
Woodstock Valley, CT 06282
hecklerauction.com
860-974-1634

North American Auction Co.
34156 Frontage Rd.
Bozeman, MT 59715
northamericanauctioncompany.com
406-600-4418

Nye & Company
20 Beach St.
Bloomfield, NJ 07003
nyeandcompany.com
973-984-6900

Palm Beach Modern Auctions
417 Bunker Rd.
West Palm Beach, FL 33405
modernauctions.com
561-586-5500

Pasarel Auctions
Khayim Levanon St. 18
Netanya 42631
   Israel
pasarel.com
+972 54-431-5171

Phillips
450 Park Ave.
New York, NY 10022
phillips.com
212-940-1200

Pook & Pook
463 E. Lancaster Ave.
Downingtown, PA 19335
pookandpook.com
610-269-4040

Potter & Potter Auctions
5001 W. Belmont Ave.
Chicago, IL 60641
potterauctions.com
773-472-1442

Quittenbaum Kunstauktionen GmbH
Theresienstrasse 60
80333 Munich
   Germany
quittenbaum.de
+49 89 273702125

Rachel Davis Fine Arts
1301 W. 79th St.
Cleveland, OH 44102
racheldavisfinearts.com
216-939-1190

Rafael Osona Nantucket Auctions
21 Washington St.
Nantucket, MA 02554
rafaelosonaauction.com
508-228-3942

Rago Arts and Auction Center
333 N. Main St.
Lambertville, NJ 08530
ragoarts.com
609-397-9374

Rich Penn Auctions
P.O. Box 1355
Waterloo, IA 50704
richpennauctions.com
319-291-6688

Richard D. Hatch & Associates
913 Upward Rd.
Flat Rock, NC 28731
richardhatchauctions.com
828-696-3440

Richard Opfer Auctioneering, Inc.
1919 Greenspring Dr.
Timonium, MD 21093
forgegallery.com/opferauction
410-252-5035

Ripley Auctions
2764 E. 55th Pl.
Indianapolis, IN 46220
ripleyauctions.com
317-251-5635

Robert Edward Auctions
P.O. Box 430
Chester, NJ 07930
robertedwardauctions.com
908-226-9900

Roland NY Auctioneers & Appraisers
150 School St.
Glen Cove, NY 11542
rolandauctions.com
212-260-2000

Ron Rhoads Auctioneers
20 Bonnie Brae Rd.
Spring City, PA 19475
ronrhoads-auction.com
610-385-4818

Route 32 Auctions
3097 E. State Rd. 32
Crawfordsville, IN 47933
route32auctions.com
765-307-7119

RR Auction
1 State Route 101A, Suite 3
Amherst, NH 03031
rrauction.com
603-732-4280

RSL Auction
P.O. Box 635
Oldwick, NJ 08858
rslauctionco.com
908-823-4049

Ruby Lane
rubylane.com

Sabertooth Auctions
804 Coldwater Rd.
Murray, KY 42071
sabertoothauctions.com
270-227-2730

Seeck Auctions
P.O. Box 377
Mason City, IA 50402
seeckauction.com
641-424-1116

Selkirk Auctioneers & Appraisers
555 Washington Ave., Suite 129
St. Louis, MO 63101
selkirkauctions.com
314-696-9041

Sotheby's
1334 York Ave.
New York, NY 10021
sothebys.com
212-606-7000

Soulis Auctions
P.O. Box 17
Lone Jack, MO 64070
dirksoulisauctions.com
816-697-3830

Stadsauktion Sundsvall
Heffners Alle 43
856 33 Sundsvall
   Sweden
stadsauktionsundsvall.se
+46 60 17 00 40

Stevens Auction Co.
P.O. Box 58
Aberdeen, MS 39730
stevensauction.com
662-369-2200

Stony Ridge Auction
4230 Fremont Pike, Box 389
Lemoyne, OH 43441
stonyridgeauction.com
419-297-9045

Strawser Auction Group
200 N. Main St.
P.O. Box 332
Wolcottville, IN 46795
strawserauctions.com
260-854-2859

Susanin's Auctioneers & Appraisers
900 S. Clinton St.
Chicago, IL 60607
susanins.com
312-832-9800

Swann Auction Galleries
104 E. 25th St.
New York, NY 10010
swanngalleries.com
212-254-4710

Sworders
GES and Sons Limited
Cambridge Rd.
Stansted, Mountfitchet, Essex CM24 8GE
  United Kingdom
sworders.co.uk
+44 1279 817778

Taranova Auctions Inc.
56 Allanhurst Dr.
Etobicoke, ON M9A 4K1
  Canada
taranovaauctions.com
+1 416-731-5163

TavernTrove Auctions
P.O. Box 80191
Raleigh, NC 27623
taverntrove.com
919-807-9147

Thomaston Place Auction Galleries
51 Atlantic Hwy.
Thomaston, ME 04861
thomastonauction.com
207-354-8141

Toomey & Co. Auctioneers
818 North Blvd.
Oak Park, IL 60301
toomeyco.com
708-383-5234

Treadway
2029 Madison Rd.
Cincinnati, OH 45208
treadwaygallery.com
513-321-6742

Treasureseeker Auctions
123 W. Bellevue Dr., Suite 2
Pasadena, CA 91105
treasureseekerauction.com
626-529-5775

Tremont Auctions
615 Boston Post Rd.
Sudbury, MA 01776
tremontauctions.com
617-795-1678

Turner Auctions + Appraisals
461 Littlefield Ave.
South San Francisco, CA 94080
turnerauctionsonline.com
415-964-5250

Ukiyoe Gallery:
Japanese Woodblock Prints
2801 Washington Rd., Suite 107, #268
Augusta, GA 30909
liveauctioneers.com/auctioneer/5952
914-646-9576

Weiss Auctions
74 Merrick Rd.
Lynbrook, NY 11563
weissauctions.com
516-594-0731

White's Auctions
19 Jackson St.
Middleboro, MA 02346
whitesauctions.com
508-947-9281

Wiederseim Associates
1041 W. Bridge St.
Phoenixville, PA 19460
wiederseim.com
610-827-1910

William Smith Auctions
P.O. Box 49
Plainfield, NH 03781
wsmithauction.com
603-675-2549

Woody Auction
P.O. Box 618
317 S. Forrest St.
Douglass, KS 67039
woodyauction.com
316-747-2694

World Auction Gallery
228 E. Meadow Ave.
East Meadow, NY 11554
worldauctiongallery.com
516-307-8180

Wright
1440 W. Hubbard St.
Chicago, IL 60642
wright20.com
312-563-0020

KOVELS

Need ACCURATE and RELIABLE information about antiques & collectibles?

Want the inside scoop on what's hot and what's not? Looking to downsize or settle an estate?

Nationally recognized for their deep knowledge and understanding of the market, Terry Kovel, Kim Kovel, and their team of experts can help you "Identify, Price, Buy, and Sell" — and maybe discover future treasures!

Visit Kovels.com and easily find prices, research marks, delve into identification guides, read the latest news from the antiques and collectibles world, and (last but not least!) enjoy other readers' Q&As.

On Kovels.com you can:

Identify – Use our **exclusive database to identify marks** on pottery, porcelain, silver, and other metals. We guide readers in identifying the age and maker of an item – the first step in determining value. Not sure what you have? **Search our Identification Guides** written in a clear, precise language for the beginner-to-advanced collector. Even universities rely on our data!

Price – Access prices of more than a million antiques and collectibles, ranging from colonial-era furniture to folk art to 20th-century toys, pottery, and furnishings. Read in-depth sales reports to see what's selling now – and why!

How to Buy or Sell – Read **expert advice** on how to get the most for your money, or sell at the best price. Sources include auction houses, clubs, publications, and other experts. Use our **Business Directory** to find auction houses, publications, collectors clubs, and restorers in your area.

News – Get the latest news on collecting trends. Have a collectibles mystery? Search our extensive digital archive of Kovels' articles. Get the current issue of our award-winning publication, *Kovels On Antiques & Collectibles,* as well as **48 years of information-packed articles.**

Collectors Corner – Find hundreds of **readers' questions** with answers by Kovels' experts, many with pictures. Plan your next trip to a popular flea market or show by using the **Calendar of Events.** And take advantage of the collective knowledge of the entire Kovels' community of collectors by posting a question, joining a conversation, or starting a thread of your own in the Kovels.com **Forums.**

JOIN NOW AND SAVE 15% ON ANY ANNUAL MEMBERSHIP USE COUPON CODE

KOVELSGET15

Want weekly antiques and collectibles news delivered to your inbox? Sign up for our free weekly eNewsletter, Kovels Komments, on **KOVELS.COM.**

CELEBRATING OUR 49TH YEAR

Are you a DEALER or COLLECTOR who NEEDS to KNOW what's happening?

Auctions, trends, and the economy impact prices every year. **Some markets are more volatile than others.**

SUBSCRIBE NOW to our award-winning monthly print newsletter, *Kovels On Antiques & Collectibles*.

This is **THE SOURCE** that helps **COLLECTORS and DEALERS** keep up with the fast-changing world of antique, vintage, and collectible treasures.

- Learn about prices at the latest sales, shows, and auctions.

- Spot emerging trends so you can cash in.

- Discover the true value of dozens of collectibles as prices change month to month.

- Find out how to avoid fakes and frauds and learn about fakes being sold right now!

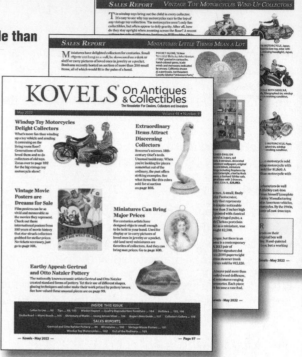

✂ -

Become a more successful collector! Try *Kovels On Antiques & Collectibles* print newsletter for just <u>$27 a year</u> (12 issues), a savings of 40% off the regular price! To subscribe, visit Kovels.com, call, or send this order form to the address below.

Name_____

Street_____

City_____ State_____ Zip_____

Telephone (_____)_____

☐ MasterCard ☐ Visa ☐ AmEx ☐ Discover ☐ Check *(payable to Kovels)*

Name on Card_____

Card No. _____

Signature_____

Email Address_____

KOVELS On Antiques & Collectibles
P.O. Box 292758
Kettering, OH 45429-8758

Or call us at (800) 829-9158 and mention offer **5H22PB55**.

5H22PB55